A GAZETTEER of the STATE of PENNSYLVANIA 1832

Thomas F. Gordon

HERITAGE BOOKS
2025

HERITAGE BOOKS

AN IMPRINT OF HERITAGE BOOKS, INC.

Books, CDs, and more—Worldwide

For our listing of thousands of titles see our website
at
www.HeritageBooks.com

A Facsimile Reprint
Published 2025 by
HERITAGE BOOKS, INC.
Publishing Division
5810 Ruatan Street
Berwyn Heights, MD 20740

Library of Congress Catalog Card Number 74-82526

Originally published by T. Belknap, 1832
Philadelphia

Reprinted in 1975 by Polyanthos, Inc.
New Orleans, Louisiana

— Publisher's Notice —
In reprints such as this, it is often not possible to remove blemishes from the original. We feel the contents of this book warrant its reissue despite these blemishes and hope you will agree and read it with pleasure.

International Standard Book Number
Paperbound: 978-0-7884-2888-3

INTRODUCTION

There can never be too much emphasis placed on the value of old gazeteers in locating and identifying an ancestor or researching an historically important person.

Fortunately for those genealogists working in Pennsylvania, such a tool is available. Thomas F. Gordon, an eminent historian, published a complete gazeteer for the state in 1834. Probably no other person was as qualified for the task as he. Prior to the *Gazeteer of Pennsylvania*, he had published a *History of Pennsylvania from its discovery to 1776*, a *History of New Jersey from its discovery to 1789*, a two volume history of America as well as *The History of ancient Mexico*.

In the same year his *Gazeteer of Pennsylvania* appeared, he published *Gazeteer of New Jersey* and they were followed two years later by *Gazeteer of New York*. Little is known of his background but the caliber and number of his publications speak for the man. His *Gazeteer of New Jersey* has recently been reprinted by Polyanthos to the great benefit of genealogists.

Genealogical research in Pennsylvania, at best, is difficult. Research in land records in particular is most difficult due to the lack of a specific location within a given county. Often the only definite description of land is the name of a road, a mountain or a creek found in the text of a deed but which do not appear on a modern map. This is also true of many villages, towns and settlements which existed in years past but which have now completely disappeared or the names have been changed.

In such instances even the best of current maps are of no use at all and eighteenth and nineteenth century maps are not readily available in most parts of the United States. But in the Gazeteer can be found the names and locations of all the cities, towns, villages, rivers, creeks, mountains, lakes, and hamlets that existed in Pennsylvania in 1832 including Lizard Creek Valley in Northampton County, Racoon Creek in Washington County, Greersburg, now Darlington in Beaver County, Youngwoman's Town in Lycoming County, and

Dible's Gap in Dauphin County. Once found in the Gazeteer, these sites can, in most instances, be correlated to present-day jurisdictions.

Also included are statistical tables for each county listing all townships which existed in 1832 with population schedules and the number of taxables for each township and a map of the state for the same date.

The last portion of the Gazeteer lists all the post offices in the state in 1832 with the name of the postmaster. This section in itself is a most valuable tool for the genealogist.

Long out of print and little known to most researchers, this reprint must certainly prove invaluable to the historian and the geographer as well as to the genealogist.

Mary K. Meyer
Assistant Librarian and Genealogist,
Maryland Historical Society

1975

ADVERTISEMENT.

In offering to the public this first attempt at a Gazetteer of Pennsylvania, the publisher trusts it will be received with the indulgence due to the enterprize. The reflecting reader will justly appreciate the difficulties in procuring minute and *accurate* topographical and statistical information; and will not be surprized if, notwithstanding the efforts of the compiler, by visits to many parts of the state, by personal intercourse with official and intelligent gentlemen of *every county*, and by laborious research among the public records, some inaccuracies should be found in the work. It is due to the compiler, however, to say, that circumstances have prevented him from revising the work in its progress through the press, and, that for errors produced by that cause he is not responsible. In the first edition of such a work error is unavoidable; but the publisher flatters himself, that there is not more in this than in others of like character, and that it will prove useful and satisfactory to the public.

It was supposed, when put to press, that the volume, including a concise historical sketch of the State, would not exceed five hundred pages; but it has swelled considerably beyond that limit, and imposed on the publisher the necessity of omitting the historical sketch, or of giving a meagre and unsatisfactory outline. He has preferred the former, in the hope that at no distant day a second edition will afford him an opportunity of presenting a full historical view of the commonwealth, of supplying any omission, and of correcting any error which may have occurred in the present.

ERRATA.

PART I.

Page 20, line 31, for Morristown read Norristown; line 34, for lowered read covered—page 24 l. 55, for duthy on fereign, read duty on foreign—P. 25 l. 24, for filled up, read fitted up.—P. 27 l. 14 for state, read slate—The matter relating to the climate of the northern division of Pennsylvania has been wholly omitted.—P. 33 l. 28, for Cannaught read Connaught; l. 37, for letters read titles.—P. 38 l. 59, for rapidity read cupidity.—P. 40 l. 45, for Sheet Mountain read Short Mountain.—P. 52 l. 2, for ovaduct read viaduct.—P. 61 l. 15, for mayhew read mayhem.—P. 63 l. 8, for setting mills read slitting mills.

PART II.

Page 2 line 31, for Capons read Capous.—P. 11 l. 29, for source read course.—P. 22 for Muncy read Muncy.—P. 40 l. 37, for visiting read viewing.—P. 43, for Sykens read Lykens.—P. 46 l. 25, for forges read furnaces.—P. 47, lines 50 and 51, for North-Hill read Northkill, and for Bollman's read Bernville. P. 48 l. 41, for Nescopee read Nescopec.—P. 49 l. 24, for Bedfast read Belfast.—P. 51, l. 7, for bond read bound.—P. 62 l. 31, for Coalesville read Coatsville.—P. 65 l. 51, for Wingshocking read Wingohocking.—P. 69 l. 23, for griers read gneiss.—P. 75 l. 16, for letters read lottery.—P. 78 l. 3, for Roxburg read Roseburg.—P. 84, for Johnsontown read Johnstown.—P. 89 l. 37, for Setart's read Letart's.—P. 93 l. 14, for resentatives read representatives; l. 34, for 100 read 1000.—P. 95 and 198, for Morristown read Norristown.—P 119, for Conynham read Conyngham.—Cowdersport, part of the article omitted.—P. 136 l. 9, for commenced read convened.—P. 139 l. 17, for invested read interrupted; l. 34, for fort read port.—P. 142 l. 53, for Raphs read Raphoe.—P. 173, l. 21, for Antictam read Antietam.—P. 207 l. 28, for immediate read intermediate.—P. 211 l. 33, for Broomfield read Bloomfield.—P. 217 and 234, for Mouture's read Monture's.—P. 224 l. 31, for formed read farmed.—P. 247, part of article Liberty township, Adams county, left out.—P. 259 l. 21, for creep out read crop out; l. 45, for Licking read Lick—P. 263 l. 37, for Millsburg read Millersburg.—P. 264 l. 38, for Smethfield read Smethport.—P. 267 l. 19, for Timmermanstown read Zimmermanstown,—P. 276 and 277, for Mr. Hants read Mr. Hauto, and in page 277 and 278 correct same error.—P. 284 l. 31, for 60 read 6.—P. 293 l. 3, for Mexus read Mexico.—P. 313 l. 43, for Hellander's read Hollander's.—P. 345 l. 24, for Dr. Frost read Dr. Troost.—P. 347 l. 37, for sheet read short.—P. 386 l. 24, for Manntawny read Manatawny.—Pp. 452, 485, 489, for Tredypin read Tredyfrin.—P. 490 l. 33, for Messrs. Kerns read Messrs. Keim.—P. 494 l. 9, for case read use.—P. 498 l. 22, for 1668 read 1768.—P. 261, at foot of statistical table, for 23,517 read 13,517.

PART I.

GAZETTEER

OF PENNSYLVANIA.

PENNSYLVANIA.

Pennsylvania* extends from N. Lat. 39° 43′ to N. Lat. 42° 16 ; and from 2° 20′ E. to 3° 36′ W. from Washington City. It is bounded, in common with the state of Delaware, from the Delaware river by a circular line, around New Castle county, to the N. E. limits of Cœcil County, Maryland, - miles 24

Due North to the North E. angle of Maryland, - - - - - -	2
Along the northern limits of Maryland, - - - - - - - -	203
In common with Virginia from from th N. W. angle of Maryland to the S. W. angle of Greene County, - - - - - - - - - -	59
Due North in common with Ohio and Brooke Counties of Virginia, to the Ohio river, - - - - - - - - - - - - - - -	64
Continuing the last noted limit in common with Ohio to lake Erie, -	91
Along the S. E. shore of Lake Erie to the western limit of New-York,	39
Due South along Chatauque county of New-York, to N. Lat. 42°, -	19
Thence due east, in common with New-York to the right bank of Delaware river, - - - . - - - - - - - - - - - - -	230
Down the Delaware to the N. E. angle of the state of Delaware, -	230
Having an entire outline of - - - - - - - - - -	961

The greatest length of Pennsylvania, is due West from Bristol, on the Delaware river, to the eastern border of Ohio county in Virginia, through 356 minutes of longitude along N. Lat. 40° 09′. This distance on that line of latitude, is equal to 315 American statute miles.

The greatest breadth, is 176 miles from the Virginia line, to the extreme Northern angle, on Lake Erie. General breadth, 158 miles.

The area of Pennsylvania has been variously stated, but probably not very accurately determined. In both Morse's and Worcester's Gazetteers, the superficies is given at 46,000 square miles. According to Mr. Darby it includes above 47,000 square miles. Rejecting the fractional excess, and using the curve superficies the state will contain thirty million and eighty thousand statute acres.

Mountains.—The structure and position of its mountains have given to Pennsylvania an aspect peculiar to itself. The Appalachian system in the United States generally extends in a direction from south-west to north-east; but in Pennsylvania the whole system is inflected from that course, and passes the state in a serpentine direction. Towards the south boundary the mountains lie about north north-east, gradually inclining more eastwardly as they penetrate northward; and in the central counties many of the chains lie nearly east and west; but as they extend towards the northern border of the state, they again imperceptiby incline to the north-east and enter New-York and New-Jersey in nearly that direction.

* For much of the matter relating to the general geographical description of the state, we are indebted to the meritorious labours of Mr. Darby.

The influence of the mountains in modifying the general features of the country is very obvious far beyond where the ridges are sufficiently elevated to be classed as parts of the Appalachian system. And it would seem that the mountain system, is commonly too restricted in Pennsylvania, as in the adjacent states.

Without attending to minor claims, the mountains of Pennsylvania, advancing from the south-east to the north-west, are as follows:

Though omitted in most maps, a chain enters the south boundary of York county, and cut by the Susquehannah river, rises in, and traverses Lancaster county between Pecquea and Octarara creeks; and between the sources of the Conestoga and Brandywine; separate sfor a short distance Lancaster and Chester, and is penetrated by the Schuylkill above Pottstown. Rising again and stretching north-east, it forms first the boundary between Montgomery and Berks: thence between Lehigh and Bucks, and, separating Northampton from Bucks, reaches the Delaware. Pursuing a north-east course through New-Jersey, separating Sussex from Huntingdon, Morris and Bergen counties, it enters New-York between the sources of the Wallkill and Passaic rivers; and extending in broken ridges through the southeast part of Orange county, forms the Highlands near West Point, and thence runs north-east to the Green mountain, under which name it enters Canada.

Thus prominent and continuous from the Susquehannah to the north-east, this chain is equally so through Maryland, Virginia and North-Carolina.

North-east from, and nearly parallel to, the South mountain, another very remarkable ridge traverses New-Jersey and Pennsylvania; and similar to the former, the latter is unknown in either of these states by any general name. Its continuation in New-York is designated by that of Shawangunk. Between the Susquehannah and Potomac, it is termed relatively the South Mountain, and in Virginia and the Carolinas, it forms the Blue Ridge; and, entering the north-east part of Georgia, is gradually lost amongst the sources of Chatahooche river.

After Mr. Darby, we have adopted or extended the name Blue Ridge into Pennsylvania. This remarkable chain enters the state on its southern line, and streching north between Adams and Franklin counties, reaches the Southern angle of Cumberland where it turns to northeast, and extending towards the Susquehannah, separates Cumberland from Adams and York Counties. About six miles below Harrisburg, it is pierced or broken down by the Susquehannah river; again rising below the mouth of Swatara, it crosses the southern angle of Dauphin; thence known as the Conewago hills, separates Lebanon from Lancaster county, enters Berks, and reaches the Schuylkill at Reading. Continuing through Berks, Lehigh and Northampton counties, passes Allentown, Bethlehem, and Easton, where it is interupted by the Delaware below the latter town.

Extending through Sussex county, the Blue Ridge enters New-York and is finally teminated in the Shawangunk on the west side of Hudson river, and amongst the branches of the Wallkill.

In one respect, the south-east mountain and Blue Ridge in Pennsylvania and New-Jersey, differ from other sections of the Appalachian system. The two chains, we have noticed, are formed of links more detached than are those more remote from the Atlantic ocean, but otherwise in respect to component matter, range and vegetation, are in every place well marked sections of the general system. The very unequal elevation of their various parts may perhaps be also adduced as a characteristic of the south-east mountain and Blue Ridge. The former does not it is probable, in any part of Pennsylvania or New-Jersey, rise to 1000 feet above the level of the Atlantic ocean; whilst in New-York some of the peaks, particularly Butterhill, have 1000 feet of elevation above tide water; and in Massachusetts and Vermont, it towers to near 3000 feet. If generally taken, the Blue Ridge in Pennsylvania and New.Jersey is more elevated than the south-east mountain, yet no particular part of the mountain rises to an equal elevation with the Highlands on either bank of the Hudson.

The third, and in some respects, the most remarkable chain of Pennsylvania, is the Kittatinny. Known by divers local names, this mountain, in a survey advancing from south-east to north-east, first rises distinctly in Franklin county, and like other chains in the southern margin of the state, ranges a little east of north; but bending more to the north-east extends to the Susquehannah, separating Cumberland and Perry counties. Five miles above Harrisburgh, the Kittatinny is interrupted by the Susquehannah river. Broken, also, by the Swatara, the Schuylkill, the Lehigh and Delaware, it enters New-Jersey, through which it passes into New-York, and forms by its continuation the Catsberg. The general aspect of the Kittatinny is much more continuous than that of any other mountain chain of Pennsylvania. It is, however, very far from being uniform in elevation, varying from 800 to perhaps 1500 feet above tide water.

North-west from Kittatinny, though more elevated, the chains are much less distinctly defined. Between the Kittatinny mountain, and the north branch of the Susquehannah river, the intermediate country is in a great part composed of high, ragged mountains, and narrow, deep, and precipitous valleys. This is the most sterile and least improvable part of Pennsylvania; but it is the region producing the most extensive masses of Anthracite coal known on the globe.

The confusion in the natural arrangement of the Anthracite section of Pennsylvania, is more apparent than real. The Kittatinny mountain and Susquehannah river lie nearly parallel upwards of seventy miles; distant from each other about 35 miles. The intervening space is filled by lateral chains, rising in many places, far above any part of the Kittatinny. Among these, two are worthy of particular notice, and serve pre-eminently to elucidate the very peculiar topography of interior Pennsylvania.

Bedford and Franklin counties are separated by a chain there known as Cove mountain. With a change of name, to Tuscarora mountain, the latter chain separates Franklin from Huntingdon, and Perry from Mifflin, and reaches the Susquehannah nearly opposite the southern extremity of Northumberland county. Rising again below the Mahantango river, and broken into vast links, the chain divides into nearly equal parts the space between the Kittatinny mountains and the main branch of the Susquehannah river. Broad mountain, passed on the road from Easton and Bethlehem to Berwick, is one of the great links of this central chain.

More accurate surveys would, it is supposed, identify Sideling hill, of Bedford county, Jack's mountain, of Huntingdon and Mifflin, and the central chain of Union, Columbia and Luzerne counties. The chain which rises on both banks of the Susquehannah in Luzerne is amongst the most interesting features, not only in the United States, but of the world. Below Sunbury a chain commences or is continued up the Susquehannah along its left shore, which is divided by the river above Danville, and again above Catawissa. From the latter place it stretches north-east through Columbia, and enters Luzerne by the name of Nescopeck mountain, mingles with other chains, and terminates in the southern part of Wayne county. Nearly parallel to the Nescopeck, another chain leaves the Susquehannah above the borough of Northumberland, and traversing Northumberland and Columbia counties, enters Luzerne where it is broken by the Susquhannah, sixteen miles below Wilkesbarre. Skirting the left bank about eight miles, it is again crossed by the river, and continuing its course north-east passes about two miles and a half from, and opposite Wilkesbarre. Preserving this course, it is for the third and last time crossed by the Susquehannah above the mouth of Lackawannock creek, ten miles above Wilkesbarre, and stretching towards the Delaware is lost in Wayne county. Beyond the main of Susquehannah to the north-west, chains lie nearly parallel to those southeast from the river. The construction of the country on both sides of the Susquehannah is nearly the same.

To the eye, the region included between the west branch of Susquehannah and Potomac, bears a strong analogy to that between the west and north branches of Susquehannah, but a minute scrutiny exposes great changes, advancing south-west, towards the borders of Maryland. Soil and vegetation both differ materially. The beech, hemlock, and sugar-maple forests, are succeeded in the valleys by oak, hickory, and elm. Thus far the entire drain of Pennsylvania is into the Atlantic ocean. The chain called "Allegheny" forms, in the southern parts of the state, the dividing ridge between the Atlantic slope and Ohio valley; and has probably from this circumstance received its pre-eminence amongst the mountain chains of Pennsylvania, Maryland, and Virginia. Only about sixty miles of its range in the former state, however, does separate the sources of the streams of the two great natural sections, the Atlantic slope and Ohio valley. The Allegheny chain, leaving Allegheny county in Maryland, separates Bedford and

Somerset counties, and extending in a northerly direction, also separates the north-west part of Bedford, from the south-east part of Cambria county. At the extreme northern angle of Bedford, the mountain turns to the north-east, and is thence drained on both sides by the tributary streams of the Susquehannah. Discharging the waters of the west branch to the north-west, and those of the Juniata and Bald Eagle rivers to the south-east; the Allegheny reaches the west branch of Susquehannah at the mouth of the Bald Eagle river.

Whatever may be the elevation of its summit, the base of the Allegheny chain between Bedford and Somerset, and Cambria countries, constitutes the height of land between the Ohio river and Atlantic tides; and forms also a similar demarcation in Maryland.

As a mountain chain, it yields in grandeur of scenery and in elevation above its base not only to the Broad mountain, but to many other chains of the Appalachian system.

Chesnut Ridge is the next chain west of the Allegheny; the two chains extending nearly parallel, and about twenty miles asunder. Though not of the greatest elevation, this is one of the most extended chains of the system to which it appertains; reaching by various local names over Virginia into Tennessee, and most probably into Alabama. As placed on our maps, it enters Pennsylvania at the north-west angle of Maryland, and ranging a little east of north forms the boundary between Fayette and Somerset; thence between Westmoreland and Somerset, and finally between the north-east angle of Westmoreland and south-west of Cambria county. At the extreme north-east angle of Westmoreland this Ridge reaches the Kiskiminitas river, and as delineated, its termination. So far from being so in nature, this chain preserves its idenity through the state farther north than any other chain of the system.

Laurel Hill is the last chain of the system in Pennsylvania. What has been already observed respecting the height of the chains nearest the Atlantic ocean, may be repeated in relation to the Chesnut Ridge and Laurel Hill; that though not very elevated, they nevertheless exist as well defined mountain chains. The latter is a very extended branch of the system reaching from the northern part of Pennsylvania into Alabama. This chain traverses Virginia by various names; separates Virginia from Kentucky as Cumberland mountain; traverses Tennessee and penetrates Alabama under the latter term; and, interrupted by Tennessee river, it forms the Muscle Shoals, and is imperceptibly merged into the central hills of Alabama. Similar to Chesnut Ridge, Laurel Hill is terminated on our maps near the Kiskiminitas, though in reality, extending to near the south boundary of New-York.

In addition to the great chains we have been surveying, many of minor importance might be noted; but we have deemed a view of the most striking parts sufficient. If engrouped into one view the mountains of Pennsylvania exhibit many very interesting points of observation. The Appalachian system is here upwards of one hundred and fifty miles wide. The particular chains do not average more than three miles, if so much, in breadth.

The Appalachian system is formed, as we have seen, by a number of collateral chains lying nearly parallel. Each chain is again formed by ridges which, interlocking or interrupted by rivers, extend generally in a similar direction with the chain to which they particularly appertain. The chains differ materially from each other in elevation and in continuity. In some, at each side of the system, the hills are of very unequal height above their bases, and above tide water. The South-east mountain and Blue Ridge are prominent examples.

The area covered by the bases of the mountains has been estimated by Mr. D. at 6,750 square miles, or near one-seventh of the superficies of the state.

Rivers.—The State is drained by the Delaware, Susquehannah, Ohio, Potomac, and Genessee Rivers, and the extreme N. W. angle by Lake Erie. The portions of the basins of these rivers which are in the state, are of very unequal extent. Those of the Delaware, Susquehannah, and Ohio, include the greater part of the Commonwealth, and divide it into three sections the Eastern, Middle and Western.

		Sq. Miles.	Acres.
The Delaware	drains	6,710	4,294,400
The Susquehannah	"	21,390	13,685,600
The Genessee	"	150	96,000
The Potomac	"	1,590	1,017,600
The Ohio	"	16,760	10,598,400
Lake Erie	"	380	243,200
		46,980	29,935,200

The range of the rivers of Pennsylvania, is one of the most interesting subjects in all physical geography. It may be assumed as a general principle, that the mountain streams particularly, either flow north-east, or south-west, along the mountain valleys or directly at right angles to that course, through the mountain chains. The conformity of the river courses to the mountains, is in a striking manner obvious in the Delaware and Susquehannah. The Delaware rises by two branches in the western spurs of the Catsbergs. The Cookquago to the north-west and Popachton to the south-east, flow from their sources south-west about fifty miles, draining Delaware county in New York. Reaching within about five miles from the north-east angle of Pennsylvania, the Cookquago turns to south-east and continuing that course five or six miles receives the Popachton. The united streams maintain a south-east course, fifty miles to the mouth of the Nevisink, and northern extremity of New-Jersey. The Delaware here touches the north-west foot of the Kittatinny chain, along which it turns to the south-west thirty-five miles to the mouth of Broadhead's creek, from Pike and Northampton counties. Winding to the south below the entrance of Broadhead's creek, it breaks through the Kittatinny and enters the fine valley between that chain and the Blue Ridge. At the north-west base of the latter, at Easton, the river again forms a mountain pass, and five miles farther down, another through the south-east mountain. At the south-east base of the latter chain the river once more assumes a south-east course after having meandered through the Kittatinny Valley about thirty miles.

At Trenton, thirty-five miles below the south-east mountain, the river passes the primitive ledge, and meets the tide ; and five miles below, near Bristol and Bordentown, again turns to south-west. Passing along or near the primitive rock, it receives near Philadelphia the Schuylkill from the north-west. Forming its last great bend five or six miles below Newcastle, the bay of Delaware opens into the Atlantic ocean in a south-east direction.

The entire length of the Delaware is by comparative courses from the Catsbergs to the Atlantic ocean, three hundred and ten miles, not quite one-half being tide water. Though rolling over numerous rapids, no cataracts interrupt the navigation, which at times of moderately high water, reaches by both constituent branches into New-York. The general course is, with a trifling deviation to the west, south and north, the sources of the Cookquago and Popachton, being very nearly of the same longitude as Cape May. When viewed on a map, the various sections of this river have the appearance of artificial arrangement; the two lower bends strongly prove the geological influence of the mountain system. Though but little elevated above the ordinary surface of the country through which it passes, the great primitive ledge pursues a direction remarkably similar to that of the Appalachian chains. From Bristol to its lowest bend below Newcastle, it flows down the south-east margin of the primitive; separating the sandy shores of New Jersey from the micaceous soil of Pennsylvania and Delaware.

Like the Susquehannah and the Potomac, the Delaware receives nearly all its large tributary streams from the west. Of these, only two, the Lehigh and Schuylkill, are of considerable magnitude.*

* It is proposed to excavate a canal along the valley of this river to the State line. Sixty miles of this work, extending from Bristol to Easton, have been completed by the State.

From the position of their valleys as channels of intercommunication and from the mineral treasures found along their mountain sources, the Schuylkill and Lehigh have become of great importance. The Lehigh rises by various mountain branches in Northampton, Pike, Wayne and Luzerne counties; uniting below Stoddartsville, and forming a small, but precipitous river current, pouring first to the south-west, it gradually turns south and south-east, passes Mauch Chunk village, and winding between mountain masses, finally breaks through the Kittatinny, and continuing to the south-east meets the north-west base of the Blue ridge at Allentown. Here it turns to the north-east along the base of the latter chain, and passing Bethlehem joins the Delaware at Easton. The Lehigh is truly a mountain torrent; there is no other stream of equal length in the United States which presents greater difference of level between the points of source and discharge.

In a comparative course, it is about twenty-five miles from Stoddartsville to Mauch Chunk, and the fall in the intermediate distance 845 feet; ten miles in a direct line below Mauch Chunk, it passes the Kittatinny, and falls 245 feet in that short space. From the Lehigh Water Gap, or passage through the Kittatinny to its junction with the Delaware, it falls 205 feet in a comparative course of thirty-five miles The entire fall from Stoddartsville to Easton, 1210 feet; comparative course seventy miles. From the junction of its constituent branches below Stoddartsville to its extreme source is about fifteen or twenty miles, giving an entire length of near 100 miles. The fall above Stoddartsville, probably amounts to 500 feet; and if so, this rapid river falls upwards of 1700 feet in 100 miles; and what may be considered in a peculiar manner remarkable, no actual cataract worthy of notice exists in all its course. Above the Water Gap, the bed of the Lehigh lies at the base of steep or precipitous mountains, rising in most places from the margin of the stream. The scenery is in a peculiar manner wild, bold, picturesque and romantic. Below the Kittatinny, the features of nature are less grand along the banks; but still follow in a rich succession of strongly contrasted and elegant landscape. The varied character of its shores is preserved to its final egress into its recipient at Easton.

The Lehigh is now rendered navigable by dams and pools and connecting canals, for some distance above Mauch Chunk. This very usefnl and arduous work has been effected by the Lehigh Coal and Navigation Company, under the direction of Messrs. White and Hazard, the superintending engineers. (See Mauch Chunk.)

The Schuylkill rises in and drains about five-eighths of Schuylkill county: formed by two branches, which unite immediately above, and pass through the Kittatinny mountain, seven miles south-east from Orwigsburg. Below the mountain it turns to nearly south, in which direction it continues through the Blue Ridge at Reading, after having received Maiden creek from the north-east, and the Tulpehocken above that town from the north-west. Below the Blue Ridge, the river again winds to south-east, passes the South-east mountain above Pottstown, and receiving the Perkiomen, and some lesser creeks from the north, crosses the primitive ledge above, and joins the Delaware below Philadelphia. Its entire length, by comparative courses, is about one hundred miles, twenty above and eighty below the Kittatinny mountains.

A strong resemblance is perceivable between the Schuylkill and the Lehigh, though the scenery along the former, is less rugged than that which skirts the latter stream.

The Schuylkill is now navigable by canals and locks to Port Carbon. The Union canal company have completed a connection between the Susquehannah and Schuylkill by the Swatara and Tulpehocken valleys.

The Susquehannah enters Pennsylvania by two great branches, the Susquehannah proper, and the Chemung or Tioga. Below their junction at Tioga point, the united streams flow a little south of east, fifteen miles to the foot of the Appalachian system, south of Towanda. Leaving the secondary, and entering on the transition formation, it turns south-east and following that general course fifty miles, breaks through several chains and finally, at the mouth of the Lackawannock, nine miles above Wilkesbarre, enters the Wyoming valley and turns to south-west; continuing the latter course near seventy miles down the mountain valleys to Northumberland and Sunbury, and to the mouth of the West Branch. In the entire distance from Tioga Point to Sunbury, the Susquehannah receives no tributary stream of forty miles direct length ; the Towanda, Wyalusing, Tunkhannock, Lackawannock, Fishing Creek, and some lesser branches, are mere mountain creeks, rapid, but not more than from twenty-five to fifty-five miles in general course.

Including all its higher north-east branches, the Susquehannah is peculiar in the structure of its valleys. Wide bottoms of two and sometimes three stages spread along the convex side of the bends, whilst mountains of more or less elevation rise on both sides of these spreading vales. Exuberant fertility is at a single step, followed by rocky and sterile steeps. The natural timber of the bottoms is in a great measure different from that on the mountains. In the former, sugar-maple, black walnut, elm, beach, and other trees, indicative of a productive soil, abound ; on the slope of the mountains, pine, oak, and chesnut, and above the Lackawannock hemlock, are the prevalent timber trees. As a navigable stream, the Susquehannah is much less interrupted by rapids or dangerous shoals, than from the tortuous course it pursues through an extensive mountain system, could be expected. It is also remarkable, that where the various branches of this river pass the respective chains, rapids seldom, and perpendicular falls no where, exist. The Western branch is in all its extent, a river of Pennsylvania Rising far within the secondary formation, its extreme western source in Indiana co., reaches within less than thirty-five miles of the Allegheny river at Kittanning. Flowing north-east about seventy miles across Clearfield, it receives the Sinnemahoning from the north-west in the south-west angle of Lycoming. Below its junction with the Sinnemahoning it continues north-east fifteen miles, and thence south-east twenty miles to the mouth of Bald Eagle creek, in Centre County. Below the Bald Eagle, the course is a little north of east, thirty-five miles to Pennsborough or Muncy, receiving in the intermediate distance from the north, Pine creek, Lycoming, and Loyalsock. From Pennsborough the course is nearly south, twenty-five miles to the mouth of the North east branch, and thirty-five from thence to that of the Juniata. About eight miles below the entrance of Juniata, the Susquehannah, having again assumed a south-eastern course, passes the Kittatinny mountains ; and ten miles below that chain, the Blue Ridge. Maintaining the latter course sixty miles below the Ridge, this great river is lost in the tides of the Chesapeake bay.*

Juniata, the south-west branch of Susquehannah rises in, and drains the northern part of Bedford county. The sources of this stream are in the eastern slopes of the Allegheny chain, and flowing nearly twenty miles east, it passes Bedford, and breaking through several mountain chains, turns abruptly to a course a little east of north forty miles, and receives the Frankstown branch below and near the borough of Huntingdon, in Huntington county. The general course of Frankstown branch is from north-west to south-east, and below their junction, the united streams follow that course fifteen miles breaking through Jack's mountain. Again inflected to north-east, the Juniata leaves Huntingdon and enters Mifflin county, and pursuing that direction near thirty miles, passes Lewistown, and again winding south and south-east, breaks through Shade mountain into Tuscarora valley. Crossing that valley, in a course of ten miles, it reaches the north-west base of Tuscarora mountain down which it flows ten miles, where, near Millerstown, it pierces the latter in Perry county, over which it flows fifteen miles to the Susquehannah River.

Like other branches of the Susquehannah, the Juniata, is as remarkable for its rapid course as for its exemption from perpendicular falls. Though originating in, and having its entire course amongst craggy mountains, it is navigable at high water to near Bedford.†

The Potomac derives but a small portion of its waters from Pennsylvania. It

* The State Canal follows the bed of the river along the main stem and North branch, 126 miles from Columbia to the dam at Nanticoke falls, and along the west branch about 60 miles from Northumberland to the mouth of the Bald Eagle River.

† The State canal follows the valley of this river to Holidaysburg at the eastern base of the Allegheny mountain, where the rail road portage commences.

has its sources in nearly the highest table land of the Appalachian system. The extreme western fountain, of the north branch, is in the south-east slopes of the Allegheny or Backbone chain, N. Lat. 39° 10′. Flowing north-east along the foot of the Allegheny to the mouth of Savage creek, or thirty-five miles south-east, through Will's mountain, into Cumberland valley, which it crosses about ten miles, it is again turned to north-east twenty miles, and continuing thus, it reaches the town of Cumberland. At the latter place, occurs another abrupt bend through a mountain pass into the South Branch valley. The latter stream is of much greater magnitude than the Potomac proper. Rising by numerous creeks in Pendleton county, Virginia, as far south as north Lat. 28° 20, in general comparative course of one hundred miles, the South branch becomes a fine navigable river. Below the mouth of the South branch, the Potomac gradually reassumes a north-east direction, which it preserves about thirty miles to Hancock's town, where it turns to the south-east, and pierces Sideling hill chain and in a few miles lower down, the Kittatinny, entering the Great Conecocheague valley. From Hancock's town the course of the Potomac is a little south of east, twenty-five miles. Afterwards, the river inclines to south-east by south, twenty-five miles to the north-west base of the Blue Ridge and mouth of Shenandoah. Rising in and draining Augusta county in Virginia, the South branch of Shenandoah rises below N. Lat. 38°. Augmented by innumerable mountain streams, it flows from Augusta over Rockingham and Shenandoah into Frederick county, where, joined by the North branch, and continuing a general course of north-east over Frederick and Jefferson counties, it unites with the Potomac at Harper's ferry, after a comparative course of about one hundred and fifty miles. At their junction, the volume of the Shenandoah yields very little in magnitude to that of the Potomac. The united waters immediately break through the Blue Ridge, and continuing south east about fifty miles, mingle with the Chesapeake tides at Georgetown, within the District of Columbia. The general comparative course of the Potomac above tide water, is by the south branch about two hundred; by the Potomac proper, one hundred and fifty, and by the Shenandoah one hundred and sixty miles.

Like those of the Delaware and Susquehannah, the great confluents of the Potomac, are from the right bank.

Savage river and Will's creek from Allegheny, Conecocheague from Washington, and Monocacy from Frederick county in Maryland, are comparatively trivial, when compared with the branches of Potomac derived from Virginia.

At Cumberland, the Potomac reaches within five, and at Hancock's town within two miles of the south boundary of Pennsylvania.

Leaving the Atlantic slope, we perceive a great river valley stretching from Pocahontas county, Virginia, over western Pennsylvania into New-York. This valley extends nearly due north and south at an angle of about forty-five degrees, to the range of the Appalachian mountains, and reaches from N. Lat. 38° 30′ to N. Lat. 42° 20′. The extremes giving sources to two rivers that of the north to the Allegheny, and that of the south to the Monongahela. These streams flowing directly towards each other meet at Pittsburg very nearly at the middle point of the valley. Their united waters taking the name of Ohio turns to the west, or rather north-west, as far as the entrance of Big Beaver river. With a very partial exception, western Pennsylvania is drained by the Allegheny and Monongahela.

Having its source in Potter county in Pennsylvania, and interlocking with the head branches of the Susquehannah and Genessee, the Allegheny flows north-west about fifty miles into Cataraugus county, New-York. Abruptly turning to south west and preserving that general course one hundred miles, and receiving French creek from the north-east, it thence bends to south-east forty miles, to the mouth of Mahoning. About the middle of the latter course, Clarion river and Red Bank creek, two large branches, enter from the north-east. From Mahoning to Pittsburg, the general course is again south-east about fifty miles.*

Kiskiminitas, a very considerable accessory stream of the Allegheny river,

* The state canal runs along the west bank of the river from opposite the mouth of the Kiskiminitas to Pittsburg, somewhat more than 30 miles.

rises in the mountain valley, between the Allegheny and Chesnut Ridge chains, and flowing north-west, breaks through Chesnut and Laurel Hill, and after a comparative course of seventy-five miles, unites with the Allegheny, near midway between the mouth of Mahoning and Pittsburg. From the mouth of this river, the state canal extends along its valley, and that of the Conemaugh (another name for the same stream) to Johnstown, a distance of about 70 miles.

Mahoning and Red Bank creeks have their sources in Chesnut Ridge, and with each a course of about thirty-five miles, the former north-west, and the latter, south-west, join the Allegheny in Armstrong county. Toby's Creek or Clarion river has interlocking sources with those of Sinnemahoning and the Allegheny river. The Red bank rises in the same region with Clarion river and Sinnemahoning; and Mahoning with Red Bank, and the west branch of Susquehannah.

In point of surface drained, Kiskiminitas is the largest confluent of the Allegheny and it has interlocking sources with those of the west branch of Susquehannah, Juniata, and Youghiogheny.

Allegheny river receives but two considerable tributaries from the right, French, and Conewango creeks. The latter rises in Chatauque county, New-York, by three branches; the Chatauque, Casadauga and Conewango, which unite in New-York, and forming a navigable stream, assume a south course, enter Warren county, Pennsylvania, and fall into the Allegheny, at the town of Warren after a comparative course of forty miles.

French creek has its source in the extreme south-west angle of New-York, and increased by numerous branches from Erie and Crawford counties, Pennsylvania, forms a navigable river at Meadville. Flowing to the south-east from Meadville twenty-five miles, it unites with the Allegheny river at Franklin, in Venango county. The entire comparative course of French creek is about eighty miles. Along this stream the state canal has been excavated 19½ miles towards the mouth.

There is no other feature in the hydrography of the United States more remarkable than the country from which Chatauque and French creeks have their sources. The extreme north-west waters of the former flow from within three, and of the latter, from within five, miles of the margin of Lake Erie.

The Allegheny and its branches are the recipients of the northern part of the great western basin of Pennsylvania, and are but little impeded by falls though their current is rapid.

The Monongahela, formed by two branches, the Monongahela proper and Cheat river, which rise in Pocahontas, Randolph, Harrison, Lewis, Monongahela and Preston counties, of Virginia, and unite two miles within the south boundary of Pennsylvania. The general length above Pennsylvania, about one hundred miles nearly a north course. Preserving the latter direction sixty miles in Pennsylvania, and receiving the Youghiogheny from the south-east, the Monongahela mingles with the Allegheny at Pittsburg and forms the Ohio.

The various branches of the Monongahela which derive their sources from the western chains of the Appalachian system similar to the Potomac, claim a more than ordinary share of attention, as forming the proposed link in a great line of canal improvement. Cheat river flows from the north-western slope of the Allegheny mountain, and draining the eastern part of Randolph county, passes Chesnut Ridge, enters Preston county, and there a navigable stream, continues north, to within five miles of the south boundary of Pennsylvania. Turning to the west it crosses the south line of Pennsylvania and unites with the Monongahela.

Youghiogheny rises in the extreme south-western angle of Maryland, between the sources of Potomac and Cheat rivers. Pursuing a northern course into Pennsylvania, and augmented by Castleman's river, its northern branch, it turns to north-west, and breaking through Chesnut Ridge and Laurel Hill, joins the Monongahela at M'Keesport, eighteen miles above Pittsburg. This is a fine mountain stream which, in all seasons except in periods of long drought, contains more than sufficient water for a supply of the most capacious canal; general comparative course, about one hundred miles; thirty in Maryland, and seventy in Pennsylvania. The Youghiogheny heads with the Cheat branch of Monongahela, with the north branch of Potomac, and by Castleman's river, with Juniata and

Kiskiminitas. At Pittsburg, the Ohio is formed by the confluence of the Allegheny and Monongahela. The former is the principal stream. From Pittsburgh to Beaver river, the Ohio pursues a north-west course twenty-five miles; thence winding to the west twenty miles, in which it leaves Pennsylvania and enters into Ohio. Within the latter state, the Ohio river inflects to a course a little west of south, seventy miles; reaching in that direction, nearly the same latitude with the south boundary of Pennsylvania. The peculiar courses of the Monongahela and Ohio, form one of the most remarkable intermediate peninsulas presented by the topography of the United States. The two streams flow in very nearly opposite directions, the intervening space being from thirty-five to forty miles wide with a mean length of sixty miles. Though hilly, rather than mountainous, this peninsula is elevated to from 600 to 1000 feet in the dividing line of its waters, above the adjacent rivers. A number of creeks, none of which can exceed a comparative course of twenty-five miles, are poured from the interior spine into the respective recipients. The dividing ridge is evidently continued north of Ohio river, broken by that stream a few miles below Pittsburg. The northern extension is continued, inflecting between the western sources of Allegheny, and the eastern sources of Big Beaver river, and is finally lost on the south-eastern shores of Lake Erie; the southern, stretching between the confluents of Ohio and Monongahela rivers, mingles with the Appalachian chains between the sources of the latter and Little Kenhawa. This ridge is the western buttress of the upper basin of Ohio, and affords a very striking example of the real difference between a chain of hills and one of mountains. The ascent by the rivers to the Western ridge of Pennsylvania is so gradual, and the hills scattered in such promiscuous windings, through the sources of the streams, that an ascent of six or seven hundred feet, in a few miles, is imperceptible; on the contrary, the mountain chains extend in regular lines uninfluenced in their direction, by the water courses and are abrupt and steep in their declivities. The mountain seems to have existed previous to the rivers, whilst the hills appear to have been formed by the abrasion of water.

Big Beaver, the first river which enters the Ohio, pours its current from the north, and falls into its recipient, twenty-five miles below the confluence of the Allegheny and Monongahela: Big Beaver is formed by the Mahoning, Shenango, Neshannock and Conequenessing creeks. The Shenango rises in Ashtabula county, of Ohio, and Crawford of Pennsylvania, within twelve miles of the south-east shore of Lake Erie, interlocking sources with those of Grand river, Conneaut, and French creek, and pursuing a nearly south course of Mercer, receives the Conequenessing from the north-east and entering Beaver county, unites with the Mahoning and forms Big Beaver. The Mahoning is, in reality, the main branch; rising in Columbiana, Stark, Trumbull and Portage counties, Ohio; its course is first nearly north, thirty miles to near Warren of Trumbull. Winding to south east, it pursues that course thirty-five miles, entering Pennsylvania in the south-west angle of Mercer and joining the Shenango at N. Lat. 41°, about two miles within Beaver county. Below the junction of the Mahoning and Shenango, Big Beaver flows a little east of south, twenty miles into Ohio river. Conequenessing is the eastern constituent stream of Beaver, draining the peninsula between the Allegheny, Ohio, Big Beaver and Shenango rivers. The State Canal follows this stream to the town of Newcastle 24¾ miles from its mouth.

The valley of Big Beaver is nearly circular and about seventy miles diameter; area 5850 square miles. It is worthy of remark, that the general courses are nearly on a direct north-west line; of the Youghiogheny below the mouth of Castleman's river, Monongahela and Ohio from the mouth of Youghiogheny to that of Big Beaver, and the latter, and Mahoning, to about three miles above Warren. This range of navigable water is from one hundred and eighty to two hundred miles, following the sinuosities of the streams.

The sources of the Mahoning interlock with those of the Tuscarawas branch of Muskingum, and Cuyahoga and Grand river of Lake Erie.

Geology.—The Geologists have divided the State of Pennsylvania, as the United States, into three great sections; the boundaries of which are irregular and very inaccurately defined, viz.: the Primitive, Transition and Secondary. But neither of these divisions, though composed, chiefly, of the rocks which characterize it, is unmixed with the strata, which pertain to some one of the other divisions. The secondary perhaps is the most uniform, The following abstract is drawn from the memoir of Mr. W. Maclure, published in the Transactions of the American Philosophical Society, vol. 1. New Series, 1818. Subsequent and more minute explorations of the land, may have already detected some errors in the views of this gentleman; and more, perhaps, will yet be discovered, but we know of no general description entitled to greater consideration. The observations of Mr. Maclure, he assures us, "are the result of many former excursions in the United States, and the knowledge lately acquired by crossing the dividing line of the principal formations, in twenty-five or thirty different places, from the Hudson to the Flint River; as well as from intelligent men whose situation and experience made the nature of the places near which they lived, familiar to them; nor has the information which could be acquired by specimens where the locality was accurately marked, or the remarks of judicious travellers, been neglected."

The South-eastern portion of the state is classed with the primitive formation; to which classification the small portion of alluvial, overlaying the primitive rock, should not be deemed an exception. "The Northwestern boundary of this formation, is marked by a line running fifteen to twenty miles East of Lake Champlain; twelve miles East of Middlebury, State of Vermont; west of Bennington, twelve to fifteen miles; East of Hudson, along the westward of Stockbridge; twelve miles southeast of Poughkeepsie, skirting the Highlands; it crosses the Hudson River, at Phillipstown, by Sparta, about ten or fifteen miles East of Easton, on the Delaware, and terminates in a point a few miles North of Bethlehem, recovering, fifteen miles west of Trenton On the south side of the river, it passes about the same distance west of Philadelphia, eight miles East of Downingstown, terminates East of York, by Petersberg, crosses the Susquehannah twenty-two miles west of Washington; and joins the Blue Ridge, along the top of which is the dividing line between the primitive, and transition, to Magotty Gap, from thence to four miles East of the lead mines at Austinville, and following a southwestern direction, by the stony and iron mountains, six miles southeast of the warm springs in Buncomb county, in North Carolina, to the eastward of Hightown on the Coresee River; and a little to the westward of the Talapoosee river, it meets the alluvial near to the Alabama, which runs into the bay of Mexico.*

The rocks of this formation are Granite, Gneiss, Mica Slate, Clay Slate, Primitive Limestone, Primitive Trap, Serpentine, Porphyry, Sienite, Topaz Rock, Quartz-Rock, Primitive Flinty Slate, Primitive Gypsum, White Stone. "The strata of these rocks run from a north and south, to a northeast and southwest, direction, and dip generally to the south-east, at an angle of more than 45° from the horizon; the highest elevation is towards the northwestern limits, which gradually descends to the southeast, where it is covered by the alluvials; and the greatest mass, as well as the highest mountains are found towards the northern and southern extremities of the northwestern boundaries." "The outline of the mountain of this formation generally consists of circular, waving, detached masses, with rounded flat tops; or conically waving in small pyramidal tops."

* Mr. Darby, (Geog. Hist. and Statistical repository, No. 2,) giving a sketch of the geology of Pennsylvania, formed, as he says, in part from Maclure's geology, and partly from his own observations, makes a more definite line, for the N. W. boundary of the primitive frontiers. "The line rather indefinitely marked in Nature which limits this primitive tract, crosses the Delaware river near New Hope—extending in a southwesterly direction, through Bucks, Montgomery, and Chester counties, to near Kennet square in the latter. From Kennet square the primitive extends nearly west to the centre of York county, where it again turns to southwest, and finally leaves Pennsylvania, entering Frederick county, in Maryland. A small triangular strip of primitive extends into Pennsylvania, forming the northern part of Bucks county, below the mountain ridge, which separates that county from Lehigh.

Within the limits prescribed to the primitive, there are portions of transition and secondary formations. "A range of the latter extends with some intervals from the Connecticut to the Rappahannock rivers, in width, generally from fifteen to twenty-five miles, bounded on the northeast, at New-Haven by the sea, where it ends to recommence on the south side of Hudson river. From Elizabethtown to Trenton, it touches the alluvial; from a little above Morrisville, on the Delaware, it extends by Morristown to Maytown, on the Susquehannah; thence passing three miles west of York by Hanover; and one mile west of Frederickstown, in Maryland, it is bounded by, or rather appears to cover, a tongue of transition, which occupies a progressively diminishing width, as far south, as the Yadkin river, at Pilot's mount.

"This secondary appears to belong to the oldest red Sand Stone formation; though in some places about Leesburg, Reading, &c., the red sand stone only seems as a cement to a pudding formed transition lime stone, and other transition pebbles, with some quartz pebbles, large beds of green stone trap, and wacke of different kinds, which leaves in many places this sand stone formation, and forms the small hills or long ridges that occur so frequently in it." "The stratification in most places runs from an east and west, to a northeast and southwest course, and dips generally to the northwest, at an angle most frequently under twenty-five degrees from the horizon, covering both the primitive and transition formation at every place where their junction could be examined." "In the red sand stone formation, grey coppper ore has been found near Hartford and Washington, Connecticut; copper pyrites and native copper in New Jersey; copper pyrites, blend and galena, in Pennsylvania on the Perkiomen creek, running nearly south and north, across the east and west direction of the red sand stone; and a small bed from a half to three inches thick of brown or red copper ore is interspersed and follows the circular form of the iron bed at Grubb's mines.*

There is also, within the prescribed limits of the primitive, a bed of transition rock, running nearly southwest from the Delaware to the Yadkin river, dipping generally to the southeast, 25 or more degrees, in width from two to fifteen miles. It runs from the west of Morrisville to the east of Morristown, passes Lancaster, York, Hanover, Frederickstown, Bull run mountain, Milton, foot of Pig River, Marlinsville, and finishes near Mount Pilot on the Yadkin river. Between the Delaware and Rappahannock it is partially lowered by the red sand stone formation, and is in the form of a long ridge, the thick end touching the Delaware, and the sharp end terminating at the Yadkin river."

This vein is called secondary, by Mr. Darby. It is narrow between the Delaware and Schuylkill rivers, but widening southwest from the latter, embraces the central parts of Chester, Lancaster and York counties. It consists of beds of blue, grey, red and white, small grained transition lime stone, alternating with beds of grey wacke, and grey wacke slate, quartzy granular rocks, and a great variety of transition rocks. Much of the limestone is intermixed with grey wacke slate; parts of it contain so great a quantity of small grained sand as to resemble the dolomite, and, in many places, marble of various colours and quantities, some of which is in grained and white, fit for the statuary, occurs.

Granite in large masses is not found in the state. The principal rock is Gneiss, which includes considerable beds, in places, of a very large grained granite, which run and dip as the Gneiss does. In these beds, emeralds, phosphate of lime, tourmaline, garnet, cymophane, octahedral iron ore, graphic granite, &c. are found. These beds are mixed, and alternate occasionally in the same Gneiss, with the primitive limestone, horneblende, and hornblende slate, serpentine, magnetic iron ore and feldspar rocks. In some places the gneiss runs into the mica slate; in others, large nodules of quartz or feldspar, and in others, horneblende takes the place of mica; and probably all the primitive rocks may be found in the gneiss formation. The mineral substances found in the primitive, are garnets in the granite and mica slate, from the size of a pin's head to many inches in diameter; staurotide, andalusite, epidote in vast variety and abundance, tremolite, all the varieties of magnesian rocks, emerald, &c. &c. &c. and it is probable that almost

* Mr. Darby includes this sand stone in the transition formation.

every mineral discovered in similar situations on the ancient continent of Europe will be found on this. The metals in this formation, are various; such as iron in various forms, black lead, native and grey copper ore, molybdena, arsenical pyrites, red oxyde of zinc, gold to the south, manganese, north and south, white ore of cobalt in Connecticut and New-Jersey, &c. &c. These metalic repositories appear in beds, disseminated, or or lying masses. Veins to any great extent have not yet been discovered in this formation.

"The transition formation is limited on the southeast side, by the northwest boundary prescribed to the primitive rocks, and on the northwest by the southeast edge of the great secondary formation, on a line that passes considerably to the westward of the ridge, which divides the eastern and western waters, in Georgia and North Carolina, and part of Virginia; and runs near it in the northern part of that state, and in the state of Pennsylvania and New-Jersey. The line of demarcation runs between the Alabama and Tombigbee rivers to the northwestward of the north fork of the Holstein, till it joins the Allegheny mountains, near the Sulphur Springs, along that dividing ridge to Bedford county, in Pennsylvania, and from thence northeast to Fort Ann, near lake Champlain. The separation of this from the secondary formation, is not so regularly and distinctly traced as in the other formations; many large valleys are found of horizontal secondary limestone, full of shells, whilst the ridges on each side consist of transition rocks. The two formations interlock and are mixed in many places, so as to require much time and attention to reduce them to their regular and proper limits. It is however probable, that to the northwest of the line here described little orn o transitiou, will be found, although to the south of it, partial formations of secondary may occur."

"The transition formation is generally broadest, where the primitive is narrowest, and *vice versa;* and runs from twenty to one hundred miles broad; the stratification bears from a north and south, to a north-east and south-west direction, dipping generally to the north-west, at an angle in most places under 45° from the horizon."—"The outline of the mountains of this formation, is almost a straight line, with few interruptions bounding long parallel ridges of nearly the same height, declining gently towards the side where the stratification dips from the horizon, and more precipitous on the opposite side, where the edge of the stratum breaks out to the day."

"This formation is composed of the following rocks, viz.: a small grained transition limestone of all the shades of color from a white to a dark blue, and in some places intimately mixed with a stratum of greywacke slate, in many places an intermixture of small grained particles, having the appearance of a sand stone with excess of lime cement. This occurs in beds from fifty to five thousand feet in width, alternating with greywacke and greywacke slate. Near the borders of the primitive is found a silicious aggregate, having particles of a light blue color, from the size of a pin's head to an egg, disseminated in some places in a cement of slaty texture, and in others in a quartzose cement; a fine sand stone cemented with quartz in large masses, often of a slaty structure, with small detached scales of mica intervening; a rock not far from the borders of the primitive, partaking both of the porphyry and the greywacke, having both feldspar crystals and rounded pebbles in it, with a cement of a kind of dull chlorite slate in excess; another, though rarer, with pebbles and feldspar crystals in a compact petrosilicious cement; and a great variety of other rocks, which from their composition and situation, cannot be classed but with the transition."

"The limestone, greywacke, and greywacke slate generally occupy the valleys, and the quartzy aggregates the ridges; amongst which is what is called the country burr stone, or mill stone grit; which must not be confounded with another rock, likewise denominated mill stone grit, which is a small grained granite, with much quartz, found in the primitive formation. There are many and extensive caves in the limestone of this formation, where the bones of various animals are found."

"Beds of Coalblende or Anthracite accompanied by alumslate, and black chalk, have been discovered in this formation, in Rhode Island, and in immense quantities on and near the Lehigh, Schuylkill and Susquehannah rivers; and a large body of alumslate, on Jackson's river Virginia, and in several places in Pennsylvania; many considerable veins of the sulphate of barytes cross it in different places. Iron and lead are the principal metals found in this formation; the lead, in the form of Galena, in clusters; the iron, disseminated in pyrites, hematitic and magnetic iron, or in beds; and considerable quantities of the sparry iron ore in beds, and disseminated in the limestone."

The south-east limit of the secondary formation is bounded by the irregular and ill defined border of the transition, from between the Alabama and Tombigbee rivers to Fort Ann, near Lake Champlain. On the north-west side, it follows the shores of the great lakes and loses itself in the alluvial of the great Basin of the Mississippi; occupying a surface east of the Mississippi from two hundred to five hundred miles in breadth, and extending probably on the west side of that river, to the foot of the stony mountains.

Immense beds of secondary limestone, of all the shades from a light blue to a black, interrupted in some places by extensive tracts of sand stone, and other secondary aggregates, appear to constitute the foundation of this formation on which reposes the great and valuable coal formation extending from the head waters of the Ohio in Pennsylvania, with some interruption, all the way to the waters of the Tombigbee, accompanied by the usual attendants, slaty clay, and freestone with vegetable impressions, &c.; but in no instance covered by, or alternating with, any rock, resembling basalt, or indeed any of those called the newest flœtz trap formation."

"Along the south-east boundaries not far from the transition, a rock salt, and gypsum formation has been found." And in western Pennsylvania, salt has been discovered between the Allegheny mountain and the Ohio, in very many places, and may perhaps be obtained in that district at the distance of from 500 to 750 feet from the surface.

Metallic substances, heretofore found in this formation, are ironpyrites, disseminated both in the coal and limestone; iron ores, consisting principally of brown, sparry, and clay iron stone in beds; galena, but whether in beds or veins has not been ascertained."

Large detached masses of granite, are found lying on this formation from Harmony to Erie, and from thence by the Genessee country to Fort Ann; though in many places, no granite of this kind has been found in places nearer than two hundred miles, at the falls of the Mohawk, or perhaps on the north side of the lakes.

The great mineral treasures of Pennsylvania, are coal, iron, and salt; all these are abundant, and with her agriculture will form the principal sources of her future prosperity. The Anthracite coal is found in the transition formation, and with some inconsiderable exceptions in that which is east of the Susquehannah river. Its present known limit on the north, is in the Tunkhannock mountain, on the sources of the Lackawanna river and on the confines of Susquehannah, Wayne and Luzerne counties. It extends thence, along the valley of that stream to the Wyoming valley; thence through the Wyoming valley to the hills near Berwick, on the Susquehannah river, making together a distance of eighty miles. This coal tract is from half a mile to five miles wide, and is estimated at an average width of two miles; throughout the whole of which, coal is found in strata of from five to fifty feet thick. Estimating the average thickness of the stratum of coal at twelve feet, (which is said to be less than the truth) this field contains 1,395,870,000 tons of coal, which with all the appliances which could reasonably be given, could not be exhausted in ten thousand years.*

Another coal field is known to exist, embracing the south-eastern section of Luzerne county, and a portion of the south-western part of Northampton county, and extending thence westward to the Susquehannah river, by Bucks and Catawissa mountains, the probable northern boundary of the field, and along Spring mountain, and the Mahonoy mountains, the probable southern boundary through Schuylkill, Columbia and Northumberland counties, also to the Susquehannah river. This field has not been thoroughly explored, its width may be more than seven miles, and its length from the Lehigh to the Susquehannah rivers more

* View of Judge Scott.

than sixty miles. At Beaver Meadow, north of the Spring mountain in Northampton county, and at many places along the valley of the Mahonoy, coal in great abundance and of excellent quality, in strata of perhaps 50 feet in thickness, has been opened to the day, and efforts are making to bring it from these points to market. (*See articles, Beaver Meadow and Mahonoy Creeks.*)

Another very extensive coal measure, if another it may be called, commences on the right bank of the Lehigh river, at the Mauch Chunk mountain, in Northampton county, (*See Mauch Chunk,*) and extends thence through Schuylkill and Dauphin counties also to the Susquehannah, a distance of not less than 75 miles. This measure is bounded on the south-west by a mountain chain, which we believe bears the name of Mahoning, near the Lehigh, Sharp mountain from its configuration, in Schuylkill county, and from its relative position, Third mountain in Dauphin county. On the north-west its limit may be the Broad mountain, which has a continuous course by that name across, and from the Lehigh river through Schuylkill county, and ends in Lyken's township, Dauphin county, where it is called the Short mountain. The width of this tract is variable, averaging about 6 miles. It embraces the mines of the Nesquihoning, Mauch Chunk, Tamaqua, the Schuylkill, of Pottsgrove and its vicinity of the West Branch of the Schuylkill, of Pine Grove, and Swatara, and of Stoney Creek, Bear Meadow, and other places of Dauphin county. We have said, in conformity with an opinion generally expressed, that the Sharp mountain forms the south-east boundary of the coal region throughout its whole extent. But, this is disproved by the fact, that anthracite has been discovered in all the ridges, in greater or less quantities, north of the Kittitinny mountain, in Dauphin county. The north-western limit of the region generally, is the Susquehannah river, but the coal basin of Luzerne county, runs under that stream, and the coal is seen in the bed of the river, and in the Shawnee mountain on the north-west of the river. And we have been informed that it has been discovered, some miles more to the south-west. Coal has not yet been discovered in Pennsylvania north-east of the Lehigh river; but as it is an unexplored region of the same geological character as the anthracite district, it may yet be discovered in that direction; which is rendered more probable by the known existence of narrow veins of anthracite in the Greywacke eminences of Sullivan and Ulster in the State of New York, connecting the Catskill mountains with the anthracite ranges of Pennsylvania. With the exception of a vein of anthracite, *said* to have been recently discovered in the Delaware water Gap, that mineral is not known to occur, within ten miles of the Kittatinney mountain, or of the Shawangunk, a part of the same chain which presents similar rocks.

The anthracite region is in a great measure covered by mountains running parallel with the Kittatinny, often broad, with table land summits, and rising generally about 1500 feet above the ocean. With the exception of some narrow valleys, this region has little surface inviting cultivation. The summits, by repeated fires have been divested of much timber, leaving thinly scattered, pitch, or yellow pine and white oak, and are generally too stony for tillage, but they may at some future period, afford ranges for cattle and sheep. These mountains, at present, mostly in the state of nature, afford retreats for panthers, wolves, bears, deer, and other animals, resident in the unsettled parts of our country. Between twenty and thirty panthers were killed within three years, by the hunters of Lowrytown, a settlement on the Upper Lehigh, appendant to the Mauch Chunk company.

The beds and veins of anthracite range from northeast to southwest, and may often be traced for a considerable distance by the compass. The veins have the inclination of the adjacent strata of greywacke, with which they often alternate, usually between 20 and 45 degrees. In some places they are horizontal, in others vertical, in others in basins; and the strata of particular mines generally have the form of the upper surface, immediately over them; and are therefore sometimes curved, or irregular, or saddle, or mantle shaped, and sometimes dome shaped. The beds and veins of coal have commonly narrow strata, of dark coloured, fine grained argillaceous slate, for roof and floor; which generally contains sulphuret of iron, and disingerates on exposure to the air. The sulphates of iron and alumine are often observed in this schist, and it frequently presents impressions of plants, and sometimes marine shells. Impure pulverulent coal is generally connected with this slate. The quality of the coal varies in different parts of this region, in purity, density and inflammability. It is in many places injuriously affected by the admixture of slate; in others it has so little coherence, that it cannot be profitably transported. That upon the Lehigh is said to be purer than that in the vicinity of the Schuylkill; but if this be true, the defect is perhaps overbalanced by the superior inflammability of the latter. That in Dauphin County is reported to possess so much inflammable matter, that it has been mistaken for bituminous coal.* All these coal fields are approachable by water, and have given occasion for the improvement of navigation on the Lackaawanna, the Lehigh, Schuylkill, and the north branch of the Susquehannah rivers.

The bituminous coal region of the state, is almost, perhaps wholly, within the secondary formation. If such be the fact, that formation extends, in the southern part of the state, much farther east of the great Allegheny chain, since bituminous coal is found abundantly east of the Raystown branch of the Juniata river in Huntingdon and Bedford counties. West of that mountain, it is found almost every where, from the northern to the southern boundary of the state, and if wanting any where, it is in the northwest corner. It has been traced from Bedford and Tioga counties, to Maryland, and may be found in every hill on the western line from Crawford county Southward. It occurs on the Allegheny mountain, at a considerable elevation, and elsewhere, in nearly a horizontal position, alternating with grey sand stone, which is often micaceous, and bordered by argillaceous schist. The veins are generally shallow, varying from one inch to six feet in thickness. The mean depth is about five feet. The beds most proximate to the eastern market, are Lycoming and Clearfield counties: to reach those of the former was a principal inducement for making the state canal along the west branch of the Susquehannah river, to the mouth of the Bald Eagle creek.

Iron ore occurs in various parts of Pennsylvania, but no great quantity is found, and none, we believe, smelted, in the primitive formation. It is most abundant, and of the best quality, in the extensive calcareous valleys situated between the ridges of the Appalachian mountains, particularly in the counties of Centre, Huntingdon, and Mifflin. It is mostly raised from beds of argillaceous earth, resting on limestone. The best ores of iron in this country exist in or adjacent to calcareous districts. The iron manufactured in the above named counties, under the name of Juniata iron, is distinguished for tenacity, malleability and other valuable qualities. Furnaces and forges, situated on never failing streams, are numerous. Bituminous coal is often used for making pig iron, &c., and a company has in the present year been incorporated by the legislature for manufacturing iron by means of coke. About 50 per cent. of iron in pigs is extracted from the Juniata ore, and it loses one-third in passing from the bloom, to the bar iron. In western Pennsylvania, iron ore is only less abundant than coal, and it is also very extensively manufactured; but soft bar iron, we understand, cannot be made from ores west of the Allegheny mountain. Upon the east of the Susquehannah in the transition region, iron and anthracite coal are rarely found contiguous to each other.

The committee on the manufactures of iron appointed by the Tariff Convention held at New York, October 1831, return for Pennsylvania in 1831, 46 furnaces making 32,156 tons of pig iron, and 5,506 tons of castings. This number of furnaces is too low. The actual number is perhaps not much short of 60, and the quantity of iron produced, full 50,000 tons Each ton in the form of bar iron and castings manufactured, occasions the consumption of agricultural products to the amount of $27 35 cents, and estimating the quantity in bar iron at 40,000 tons, the iron works of Pennsylvania, consume of her agricultural products $1,000,000 annually. Uunder the protection of a high duthy on fereign iron, the price of domestic iron has been greatly reduced; and under assurance of contin-

* The coal of the Susquehannah is readily kindled in grates of the ordinary construction, and by the experiments recorded in the 2d vol. of the Journal of Science, contains double the quantity of hydrogen gas found in the coal of the Schuylkill and Lehigh.

ued protection and increased facilities of transportation, still greater reduction may be expected. In 1828, the average price of American hammered iron in the principal cities east of the Susquehannah, was 105 dollars, and at Pittsburg and Cincinnati, 125 dollars; the average 118 1-2. In 1829, the average was 114 2-3 and in 1830, average 96 2-3.

We have already observed, that rock salt pervaded very extensively, the whole of the great secondary formation. Salt springs are common in various parts of western Pennsylvania. The water is generally weak near the surface, but it is very strong when produced from the depth of from 350 to 700 feet. One spring, containing as much salt as the ordinary waters of Salina, has been discovered by boring, about 20 miles from Montrose, in Susquehannah county, bordering on the State of New York. Salt springs are found on several of the tributaries of the west branch of the Susquehannah as on the Loyalsock in Lycoming county, and on the Sinnemahoning in Clearfield county; on the Clarion river or Toby's Creek, in Armstrong and Venango counties; on the sources of the Conneautte Creek, in Crawford countrv; on the Buffalo and Conequenessing creeks, in Butler county; on the Beaver Creek, in Beaver county, and very frequently, in the southern counties, as far east as Bedford county. But the most productive saline springs of Pennsylvania, are on the banks of the Conemaugh, Kiskiminitas and Allegheny rivers; and upon the last, about 30 miles above Pittsburg.

The following statement relative to the Pennsylvania salt works, is from a communication made for Hazard's Register in January, 1828, by a "Large Proprietor." Since that period, they have increased very considerably in number. There are upon the Kiskiminitas or Conemaugh river, 30 wells filled up with furnaces and pans, and now making salt. These wells produce on an average, 2,000 barrels each, a year, which at five bushels to the barrel, make 300,000 bushels. The capital invested in these works is about 100,000 dollars, including lands. The salt costs about 90 cents per barrel, when packed, and with the interest on the capital employed, 100 cents. It sells at the works, at 2 dollars per barrel. The product of these works may be increased to 3,000 barrels each, with increased profit, inasmuch as the expenses would not increase with the rate of product.

These wells are on the line of the Pennsylvania Canal, and their products will pay about 1400 dollars toll, per annum.

There are, on the Allegheny river, 5 wells, making about 7000 barrels: on the Monongahela, are 3, making 5000; 3 or 4 on the Sewickly, a branch of the Youghhogeny, making 4000, one on Beaver making 1000; and two on Chartier's Creek, producing 2000 barrels. The whole of the salt now produced in western Pennsylvania, is about 80,000 barrels. Ten or twelve new wells now preparing upon the Kiskiminitas will increase the amount to 100,000 barrels annually.

The cost of boring and fitting up a well with furnaces and other apparatus, is from 2,500 to 3,000 dollars. The salt is made by rapid evaporation, and consequently, is in fine chrystals, similar to the Liverpool salt. Solar evaporation requiring a large expenditure for reservoirs, is not adopted. Coal, the only fuel used, is obtained at about 3-4 cents the bushel, the price of mining. It is run out and drawn to the furnaces by rail ways. The furnaces lean against the hills in which are two strata of this fuel 4 or 5 feet thick and inexhaustible.

The wells are from 400 to 500 feet, and sometimes 750 feet deep; tubed with copper, having copper pumps worked by horse power, (some are now worked by steam,) the water rising to the atmospheric or suck pump distance. It is thrown into large troughs, that the earthy particles not held in solution may subside; and is thence passed into a shallow pan of cast iron; after boiling, it is drawn off into vats, where the oxide of iron, some earthy salts with some muriate of soda are precipitated. The clear brine is thence removed to another boiler, in which the salt, in fine chrystals is deposited, and removed to drain. No use is made of the sulphate of soda, of which there is much in the water.

The cost of making salt in bulk, without barrel, &c. is 12 1-2 cents per bushel, and to transport it to Philadelphia by the canals will cost 25 cts. It may, therefore, be profitably sent to the Philadelphia market. The capacity of the country on the Kiskiminitas and Allegheny, to produce salt, is doubtless very great

4

The number of wells continues to increase, and a million or more of bushels may be transported, to the east and west, by means of the Pennsylvania canal. The consumption of this article west of the Allegheny has been estimated at two millions of bushels, beside 100,000 bushels of coarse Turks Island salt, used in salting meats: for which purpose, the *fine* salt of the country is not adapted. The increase of population in the west is 300,000 per annum; and this will require an increase of 230,000 bushels of salt. The capacity to meet the increased demand is unquestionable. The water is strongest at Kenhawa in Virginia and Kiskiminitas. At these places it requires but 60 gallons to make a bushel of salt, whilst at most other places 120 gallons is requisite. By a committee of the tariff convention held at New York, October 26, 1831, the capital then employed in the salt works of Pennsylvania, was estimated at $400,500 and the annual product at 600,000 bushels.

In considering the adaptation of the soils of Pennsylvania for agriculture, the geological divisions furnish the most convenient form of classification. We have seen that the state consists principally of the transition and secondary formations, having a small quantity of primitive, east of the mountains; and from these causes, it contains the greater quantity of good lands in proportion to its surface of any of the Atlanctic states. The primitive does not extend more than 25 miles north-west from the south-east border of the state. The soil is light and indifferent where the Gneiss, granite or serpentine prevails. The limestone may form a tolerable soil, as the country though broken is not hilly, and has nothing that can be called a mountain. On the rivers and smaller streams where the alluvial is formed, the soil is strong and rich, and large bodies of marsh along the Delaware, are remarkable, for their fertility, especially in grasses. The uplands manured with lime, or animal excrement, or treated with gypsum and clover, become highly productive, and the crops frequently equal the product of the richer soil of the west. Eighty bushels of corn and forty bushels of wheat, are sometimes obtained from the acre, but such crops are rare, and the cost of production makes a large portion of their value. Still the vicinity to markets, the excellent roads, the steady price and constant demand for dairy and garden products, and for every species of small crops, make the business of the farmer in this district abundantly profitable, and the inhabitants content. Consequently the emigration from it to the "great west" is inconsiderable.

"The extensive transition formation which succeeds the primitive, occupies nearly seventy miles in breadth to the top of the dividing ridge, between the western and the eastern waters, which forms the summit of the Allegheny mountains.* In this place the transition is wider than in any other part of our range of mountains, and is only interrupted for about twenty or thirty miles between Norristown and Reading by being covered by the oldest red standstone formation, The soil through the whole of this tract when level, is tolerably good; where formed by the alluvial of the rivers, it is generally rich and fertile: but the quartzy and silicious aggregates, which most frequently occupy the mountains, decompose into light sandy soil, though the valleys between the mountains are rich and productive." The vein, south-east of the old red sand stone called by Mr. Maclure transition, and by Mr. Darby, secondary, is narrow between the Delaware and Schuylkill rivers, but widens south-west from the latter, comprehending the central parts of Chester, Lancaster, and York counties. Limestone and marble, of very superior quality, abound in this formation, and consequently, the soil is very productive; of which the great valley of Chester county affords the most delightful and satisfactory testimony. In the primitive, south-east of this valley in Chester county, we are informed that small beds of limestone are found, which add much to the strength of the neighboring soils."

The valley between the Blue Ridge and the Kittatinny mountain, sometimes oalled the Kittatinny valley, and also known as the great limestone valley of Pennsylvania, is from 15 to 20 miles wide inflecting with the mountains.

* If the old red sand stone formation be included in the transition, the latter will exceed 90 miles in width.

It is nearly equally divided between the limestone and slate formations, its whole length. The section within the state is about one hundred and sixty miles in length, and covers an area of near 3000 square miles. The south-east part is formed of transition limestone, the north-west of clay slate. On the Lehigh the limestone and slate touch at a place called the Slates, seven or eight miles above Allentown. Thence the line of separation extends south-west, through Berks county leaving Kutztown on the lime stone, crosses Schuylkill nearly midway between Reading and Hamburg and the Tulpehocken north-east of Womelsdorff, leaving the latter upon the limestone; thence through Lebanon county, leaving the borough of Lebanon upon the limestone and reaching the Swatara near the mouth of the Quitapahilla. From the latter creek to Hummelstown, in Dauphin county, the Swatara forms the boundary, generally. That village and its immediate vicinity is based on limestone, and immediately at the bridge over the Swatara, on the road to Harrisburg, the river leaves the state and pursues the residue of its course to the Susquehannah, over limestone. The division line between limestone and slate, follows a south-west course from Hummelstown to the mouth of Paxton Creek, in the borough of Harrisburg, which rests on the alluvial deposite, partly on the slate, and partly on the limestone.—South-west of this point on the Susquehannah, to the Maryland boundary, the demarcation between the limestone and slate curves with the contiguous mountains, leaving on the former rock in Cumberland county, Carlisle and Shippensburg, and in Franklin county, Chambersburg and Greencastle,—and it quits Pennsylvania nearly with the Conecocheague Creek.

This limestone section is comparatively level, with a very superior soil,—studded with towns and villages, extremely well cultivated, and inhabited by a large population, enjoying in profusion the comforts of life—pursuing with little exception the business of agriculture. As in almost all limestone countries, spring water reaches the surface of the earth at distant points, and in very unequal quantities, leaving intermediate spaces so deficient, as to be distressing to the inhabitants. The slate region is more broken than the limestone, and its soil of inferior quality; but this is in some measure compensated, by the great ease with which it may be cultivated, and when the lime manure on the slate soil shall be extended, it is probable that the product of the slate will equal that of the limestone districts. Water is more equally diffused over the former, than the latter. In respect to forest timber, no striking difference is observable.

The remainder of the transition formation north-west of the Kittatinny mountain, varies considerably in agricultural value, which seems to be determined pretty much by the quantity of limestone, which blends with the soil. East of the north branch of the Susquehannah river, throughout the anthracite region, the whole country may be pronounced sterile, with the exception of the alluvial flats of the Delaware and Susquehannah rivers, and their greater tributaries. West of the Susquehannah river, and north of the Kittatinny mountain, the country would seem to be universally based on limestone; it fills most of the principal valleys, and is believed to underlay the mountains. Wherever it disintegrates into soil, that soil is fertile, but frequently subjected to the inconvenience we have already mentioned, the unequal distribution of water. The mountains, composed of slate and sand stone, are generally barren. There are valleys however, where the limestone does not appear, which are rendered very fertile by the alluvion from the mountains.

The vegetable productions of the transition are very various. Almost every forest tree indigenous to the climate may be found on the mountains, the slopes and valleys of the Susquehannah; and it would be difficult to conceive a species of scenery of which it does not afford an example.

The river navigation of the primitive and transition formations, agreeable to their general character, is obstructed by many rapids and falls; and is liable to the freshets of mountain torrents, breaking through narrow and rocky passages, with all the extremes and inconvenience of too much or too little water.

The secondary formation, extending from a line running on or near the Allegheny mountain, may be stated as generally fertile; for though the soil may be sandy on the hills where the sand stone prevails, it is uniformly rich in the valleys. It loses little of the vegetable mould by washing, owing to its general horizontal position; and the accumulation of such vegetable manure is in proportion to the time the trees have been growing on the soil. That portion of the surface of this district between the Allegheny mountain and the Chesnut Ridge contains all of it that is mountainous; but these mountains partake of the character of the formation in the position of the strata, and character of the soil. In approaching the Allegheny from the eastward, it presents a bold and precipitous front; and from two to five miles will bring the traveller to the summit, whence the descent westward is scarcely perceptible. Much of it might be called table land, for even on the summit, tracts of level and frequently excellent land extend for miles, in which are many fine farms, the soil of which though somewhat cold, repays the labor of cultivation. The Laurel Hill, next west of the Allegheny, is little below the latter in height. It is so steep, rugged, and precipitous that it cannot be cultivated. Its scenery is wild, and aspect very forbidding. The Chesnut ridge is comparatively low, and its appearance less savage, and soil less forbidding. The whole of western Pennsylvania might be characterized as table land; low water-mark at Pittsburg is one hundred and fifty-two feet above Lake Erie, 727 above the Hudson at Albany, and 756 feet above the Atlantic ocean at Cape May. The apices of the highest ranges of hills are about 1200 feet, above tide water level in the Chesapeake. The soil of the mountain valleys is well watered and excellent. Leaving the mountains, the country consists of arable hills, or as it is commonly called, rolling ground. Near the water courses the hills are sometimes too steep for cultivation, although possessing a fine soil, and clothed with a luxuriant growth of timber. This description embraces the greater part of Westmoreland, the western part of Fayette, Washington, Allegheny, Beaver and Indiana. The three first named counties have the finest land; and Washington is placed first in rank. Mercer, Crawford, and Erie, have large bodies of level land of excellent quality; better adapted to grass than grain. Butler, Armstrong, Venango and Warren, have soils so various, that it is difficult to give them a general character. Whilst large bodies might be pronounced almost worthless, and others deemed valuable only for their timber, there are extensive tracts which will not suffer in comparison with any land in Pennsylvania.

The general, nay almost universal fertility of Western Pennsylvania, must of course be ascribed to the constituents of its soil, which is a loam, having in various proportions, limestone, slate, coal, gypsum, salt, and vegetable and animal remains. The coal is often used as manure, and slaty clay, which alternates so often with the limestone, contains carbon, which augments its productive qualities when decomposed into soil.

The soil best adapted to small grain, is that producing abundance of white oak, plentifully mixed with hickory, chestnut, walnut, other species of oaks, ash &c., the white oak predominating—for indian corn, that in which hickory, walnut, cherry, or sugar maple, most abound. Beech, maple, black ash, &c., indicate good grass land; and the various species of oak, except rock oak, are common to such soils. Pine lands are not favorable to any species of grain, but produce grass when favorably situated.

Almost every species of timber abounds on the Allegheny mountain, except white oak. Pine of the several kinds predominates. Poplar, beech, sugar maple, chestnut and birch are next in abundance. Wild cherry abounds in some parts, as also, black, red, and rock oaks, walnut, ash and hickory. Pines, poplars, and chestnuts grow to huge size. In some places, where the soil is rich and humid, it is covered with a vegetation so dense and luxuriant, as to seem almost impenetrable. Chestnut, and red and rock oak are most abundant on the Laurel Hill, and chestnut prevails on the Chestnut ridge, where also poplar, oak, and most trees usually on high grounds abound. Pine, except on the mountains, is rarely seen in western Pennsylvania. Hemlock skirts the borders of some of the streams. Cedar is rarely met with any where.

In the valleys, and along the water courses, hickory, ash, sugar maple, cherry, elm, &c. &c. abound; the majestic sycamore skirts the borders of most of the large streams, and various oaks crown the hills, and black walnut, in many places, indicates a soil of extreme fertility.

In the neighborhood of Lake Erie, beech and sugar maple, fill the forest. The soil is good, but difficult to clear, owing to the long spreading roots of those trees.

On the head waters of the Allegheny and some of its tributaries are immense forests of white pine, from which the country bordering the Ohio is supplied with boards and shingles of the finest quality, at very low prices.

The forest trees generally are of a large size, healthy and luxuriant in appearance, and frequently as thick as they can stand. Fruit trees are abundant, and the soil and climate promotive of their fruitfulness. Grapes in great variety grow spontaneously; some of them of excellent quality, worthy of cultivation, as several successful experiments evince.

Western Pennsylvania partakes of the advantages of river navigation, which belong to the great western secondary formation. The streams are navigable almost to their sources. From the ease with which they navigate the small creeks and streams, almost every farmer may have a landing place near his plantation, and receive at a small expense, the limestone, plaster, or coals, necessary to agriculture and the other arts. Even where a canal is necessary in this formation, the level situation, and nature of the rocks, makes the accomplishment easier than in the other classes.

The state of Pennsylvania," says Mr. Maclure, an experienced and competent judge, "is perhaps the best cultivated, of all the states in the Union; that is, more of the farmers have dropped the ancient practice of wearing out one field, and going to clear away the trees of another, without adopting any system of manuring by plaster, or rotation of crops, so as to keep the lands, once cleared, continually in heart. Most of the Pennsylvania farmers, like the farmers in Europe, make their fields better and richer, in proportion to the time they have been in culture. It is therefore, partly to art and industry, and partly to nature, that we are indebted for the prosperous state of agriculture in this commonwealth."

Climate.—In treating the climate of Pennsylvania, the state might, with propriety, be divided into three districts, under the denominations of Eastern, Western and Northern Pennsylvania. We shall abstract from the memoir of Dr. Benjamin Rush, principally relating to the eastern part of the state, a description of the climate of that section, adding some facts and reflections which our own observations have enabled us to make.

It is supposed that the climate of Pennsylvania has undergone, and is still undergoing, a material change—that thunder and lightning are less frequent—the cold of our winters, and the heat of our summers become less uniform—the springs much colder, and the autumns more temperate—and that generally the winters are less cold, and the summers less hot, than they were some sixty years since. It is possible, but we think doubtful, that the variability of the climate has increased; but the average severity of heat and cold we believe has not been diminished. Alternations of cold and mild winters, and of hot and cool summers, of early and late commencements of frost, of drought, and superabundant rains have been continued, but irregularly from the earliest accounts of the province, to the last winter (1831–2) when rigorous cold weather commenced in November, and the Delaware river was frozen fast on the 7th December. The ice was broken up by an immense freshet in all the streams, about the 20th to the 25th January, and great injuries, estimated at several millions, was done to bridges, canals, farms, and other species of property, upon the western waters. A review of the seasons, from 1681 to the present time, shows no less than 39 years, in which the navigation of the Delaware was obstructed by ice in the month of December. In 1681, December 11, it was frozen over in one night. In 1740, on the 19th December, the navigation was stopped, and the river was closed until the 13th March. In 1790, the river closed on the 8th December, and in 1797, on the 1st of that month. The earliest notice we have seen of the weather on the shores of the Delaware, is in the Journal of De Vries, who left the Texel, on the 12th December, 1630, and arrived in the Delaware at the close of January, or commencement of February, the usual season of our coldest weather, when unimpeded by the season, which he reports as so mild, that his men could work in the open air in their shirt sleeves, he erected on Lewe's Creek, the fortification called "*Fort Osslandt*." In 1780, in the month of January, the mercury stood for several hours at 5° below 0 F., and during the month, except on one night, never rose in the City of Philadelphia, to the freezing point. In 1817, Feb. 7, the water froze in most of the hydrant plugs, and in some of the street mains. In 1827–8, the winter was uncommonly mild, the navigation of the Delaware was altogether unobstructed. The atmosphere was filled with dense fog, during the months of December, January, and February, and during that period, including days on which the sun was apparent for some hours, there were not more than 17 days of clear weather. We gathered flowers from the unprotected garden in Feb., and pasturage was good at that season. The winter of 1778-79 was also uncommonly mild; but there was ice sufficient to obstruct the navigation—on the 22d March, the orchards were in full bloom—and the meadows as green as ordinarily in the month of June. But on the 23d, snow fell two feet deep, which destroyed nearly all the fruits of the year. From these instances of variation which may be easily multiplied, it is apparent, that the climate, ever since it has been known to Europeans, has been, perhaps as changeable as at present, and that seasons alike mild, and others alike severe, have been known to alternate from the earliest to the latest times.* By a table for the month of January, during 20 years, from 1807 to 1827, the mean temperature of the month varied from 42° to 27°, and the mean of the whole period is 39° of Farenheit.

With these remarks we may observe, that there are seldom more than 20 or 30 days in summer or winter, in which the mercury rises above 80° in the former, or falls below 30° in the latter season. Some old people have remarked, that the numbers of extremely cold and warm days in successive summers and winters, bear an exact proportion to each other; and this appears to have been strictly true in some years.

The warmest part of the day in summer, is at 2 o'clock in ordinary, and 3 in the afternoon, in extremely warm weather. From these hours, the heat gradually diminishes till the ensuing morning. The coldest part of the four and twenty hours is at the break of day. There are seldom more than three or four nights in a summer, in which the heat of the air is nearly the same as in the preceding day. After the hottest days, the evenings are generally agreeable, and often delightful. The higher the mercury rises in the day time, the lower it falls the succeeding night. The mercury from 80° generally falls to 66°, while it descends when at 60°, only to 56°. This disproportion between the temperature of the day and night, in summer, is always greatest in the month of August The dews at this time are heavy, in proportion to the coolness of the evening. They are sometimes so considerable as to wet the clothes; and there are instances in which the marsh meadows, and even creeks, which have been dry during the summer, have been supplied with their usual water, from no other sources than the dews which have fallen in this month, or in the first weeks of September. The violent heats of summer seldom continue more than two or three days without intermission. They are generally broken by showers of rain, sometimes accompanied by thunder and lightning, and succeeded by a north west wind, which produces an agreeable and invigorating coolness in the air.

The warmest weather is generally in July; but intensely hot days are often felt in May, June, August and September, and it has happened, that the mean heat of August, has been greater than that of July. The transitions from heat to cold, are often very sudden, and sometimes to very distant degrees. After a day in which the mercury has stood at 86° and even at 90°, it falls in the course of a single night to the 65th and even to the 60th degree; insomuch that fires have been found necessary the ensuing morning especially if the change in the temperature of the air has been accompanied by rain and a south east wind. In a summer month the mercury has been known to fall 20° in an hour and a half. There are few summers in which fires are not agreeable during some part of them. Mr. Rittenhouse informed Dr. Rush, that he had never passed a summer during his residence in the country, without discovering frost, in every month of the year except July.

The weather is equally variable during the greatest part of the winter. The mercury has fallen from 37° to 4½° below 0 in 24 hours. In this season, nature seems to play at cross purposes; heavy falls of snow are often succeeded by a thaw which in a very short time leaves no vestige of the snow. The rivers have

* See Rush's Memoir on the Climate of Pennsylvania, for other instances of severe, mild and variable weather.

been frozen so as to bear horses and carriages of all kinds, and thawed so as to be passable in boats, two or three times in the course of the same winter. Ice is commonly formed gradually, and seldom until the rivers have been chilled by snow. Yet sometimes its production is sudden; and the Delaware has more than once been frozen over in a night, so as to bear the weight of a man.

Frost and ice appear in the neighborhood of Philadelphia, commonly about the latter end of October, or beginning of November. But intense cold is rarely felt until about Christmas. Hence, the vulgar saying, "As the day lengthens, the cold strengthens." The coldest weather is from the middle of January to the 10th of February. As in summer, there are often days in which fires are agreeable, so in winter, they sometimes are incommodious. Vegetation has been observed in all the winter months. Garlic was tasted in butter in January, 1781. The leaves of the willow, the blossom of the peach tree, and the flowers of the dandelion, were all seen in February, 1779, and Dr. Rush says that 60 years since, he saw an apple orchard in full bloom, and small apples on many of the trees in the month of December. A cold day in winter is often the precursor of a moderate evening. The greatest degree of cold recorded in Philadelphia, is 5° below 0, and of heat, 95°. The standard temperature is 52½° which is the temperature of our deepest wells, and the mean heat of common spring water.

The spring in Pennsylvania is generally unpleasant. In March, the weather is stormy, variable, and cold. In April, and sometimes far in May, it is moist and accompanied by a degree of cold which has been called rawness. From the variableness of the spring, vegetation advances with unequal pace in different seasons. The colder the spring, the more favorable it proves to the fruits of the earth. The hopes of the farmer from his fruit trees, in a warm spring, are often blasted by frost in April or May, and sometimes even by snow, at a later period. The colder the winter, the greater the delay in the return of spring. Sometimes the weather during the spring months, is cloudy and damp, attended occasionally with gentle rain, resembling the spray from a cataract of water. This weather seldom continues more than two or three days.

The month of June is the only month in the year, which resembles a spring month in the southern countries in Europe. The weather is then generally temperate, the sky is serene, and the verdure of the country is universal and delightful.

The autumn is the most agreeable season of the year in Pennsylvania. The cool evenings and mornings which generally begin about the first week in September, are succeeded by a moderate temperature of the air during the day. This species of weather continues with an increase of cold scarcely perceptible till the middle of October, when the autumn is closed by rain, which sometimes falls in such quantities as to produce destructive freshets in the rivers and creeks; and sometimes descends in gentle showers, which continue with occasional interruptions by a few fair days, for two or three weeks. These rains are the harbingers of winter, and the Indians have long since taught us that the degrees of cold during the winter, are in proportion to the quantity of rain which falls during the autumn.

From this account of the temperature of the air, it is apparent, that there are seldom more than four months, in which the weather is agreeable without a fire.

In winter, the winds generally come from the north-west in fair, and from the north-east in wet weather. The north-west winds are dry as well as cold. The winds in fair weather in the spring, and in warm weather in the summer, blow from the south-west and from the west north-west. The south-west winds likewise usually bring with them those showers of rain in the spring and summer which refresh the earth. They also moderate the heat, when succeeded by a north-west wind. Now and then showers come from the west and north-west.

The moisture of the air is much greater than formerly, occasioned probably by the exhalations, which in former years fell in the form of snow, now descending in rain. The depth of the snow, is sometimes between two and three feet; in 1829–30 it was near four, but in general it is from six to nine inches. Hail frequently falls with snow in the winter. At intervals of years, heavy showers of hail fall in the spring and summer. They commonly run in veins of thirty or forty miles in length, and from a half mile to two miles in breadth. On such occasions, destruction of grain, grass, and windows, to great value, is not unfrequent. From sudden changes in the air, rain and snow often fall together, forming what is commonly called sleet. In the uncultivated parts of the state, snow sometimes lies on the ground till the first week in April. The backwardness of the spring has been ascribed to the passage of the air over the beds of snow and ice which remain after the winter months have passed, on the north-west grounds and waters of the state, and of the adjacent country.

The dissolution of the ice and snow in the spring is sometimes so sudden, as to swell the creeks and rivers in every part of the state to such a degree, as not only to lay waste the hopes of the husbandman from the produce of his lands, but in some instances to sweep his barns, stables, and even his dwelling into their currents. Of this power of the flood, the years 1784, and 1832, afford memorable examples. The wind, during a general thaw, comes from the south-west or south-east.

The air, when dry, has a peculiar elasticity, which renders the heat and cold less insupportable, than the same degrees of both are in moister countries. It is in those cases only when summer showers are not succeeded by north-west winds, that the heat of the air becomes oppressive, from being combined with moisture. The waters in many parts of the state have diminished considerably. Hence, many mills erected upon large and deep streams of water, now stand idle in dry weather; and many creeks, once navigable in large boats, are now impassable for canoes. This diminution of the waters is ascribable to the removal of the forest, and the consequent siccation of the land.

The average quantity of water which falls yearly is from twenty-four to twenty-six inches, according to the statement of Dr. Rush. But this would seem much too small, since a table of 20 years, from 1810 to 1829 inclusive, 14 of which were kept by P. Legeaux, Esq. at Spring Mills, and six at the Pennsylvania Hospital, gives 35-16 inches and a table for 10 years ending 1827, kept by Dr. Darlington, of West Chester, gives 49-92 inches. In the first table the highest was 43-135 in. in 1814, and the lowest 23-354, in 1819. In the last table, the highest was 54-1 inches in 1824, and the lowest, 39-3 inches in 1822.

The aurora borealis and meteors are sometimes seen in Pennsylvania. Storms and hurricanes recur with the intervals of years. They are most frequent and destructive in autumn, and are attended by rain. Trees are torn up by the roots, and streams are suddenly swelled beyond their beds, and do much injury. Most commonly the wind is from the south-east and south-west.

From these remarks we may justly conclude with regard to Eastern Pennsylvania that there are no two successive years alike—even the successsive seasons and months differ from each other every year. Perhaps there is but one steady trait in the character of our climate, and that is, it is never steady, but uniformly variable.

Western Pennsylvania is subject to like, perhaps to greater, if not more frequent changes than the Eastern portion of the state. It is certainly visited by greater excess of heat and cold. "During the months of July and August, it is not uncommon for the thermometer of Fahrenheit to rise to upwards of 96° in the shade. This high temperature does not endure for many days, nor for many hours of the same day, and only during a southerly wind. The wind veering to the north or north-west, will depress the mercury 10, 20, 30, or 40° in the course of a few hours. During the 27th, 28th, and 29th, January, 1821, the thermometer stood at from 13 to 14° below zero. This was an instance however, of rare and severe cold; yet in almost every winter the mercury sinks below 0, the north and particularly the north-west wind prevailing. From this low point upon change of wind to the southward, the temperature will rise 10, 20, or 30° in the course of a few hours. In the latter end of March, 1828, the thermometer rose for a few days above 60°; in the beginning of April, it was below the freezing point. In winter, the north-west wind, uninterrupted by mountain and unmitigated by the sea, sweeps with unbroken force over the whole country north-west of the Allegheny mountain, bearing the rigour of frost from the immense lake of ice, and wastes of land, buried in snow. In the summer, the south wind from the Gulf of Mexico, following the valley of the Mississippi, blows over land for near two thousand miles, brings an increased degree of heat, which accounts satisfactorily for the high temperature of the summers. The whole of this region is remarkable for its healthiness.

POPULATION.—The population of Pennsylvania has not increased as rapidly, as from her very favorable moral and physical position might have been expected. The causes of her tardy progress in this respect, are most probably the uncertainty of title to western lands, occasioned by the most wretched system pursued by the colonial and state governments in disposing of them, and the difficulty and expense in transporting the products of her mines, forests and soil to profitable markets. Both these impediments to her greatness have in a measure ceased. The land titles in most, perhaps in all the counties, are well assured. An extensive and magnificent system of intercommunication, executed at the expense of the state, will embrace and unite the most important sections of the country; and ramifications, at private cost, of her rail roads and canals, will soon open to every productive district a new and expeditious road to market; and the irresistible attractions of plenty and ease, will rapidly fill up the measure of her population.

The state is divided into 52 Counties, considering Philadelphia City and County as one. And the following table shows, at one view, the periods at which the several counties were organized; the population at the decennial periods; the taxables in 1828, and the assessed value of real estate in the several counties in 1829, so far as we have been able to obtain it.

The elements of the population of Pennsylvania are more various than those of any other portion of the Union. From its first organization, the state has been the asylum of the oppressed of all countries, the permanent elysium of emigrants from the northern states, and the resting place between the present and future life, for the enriched emigrant of the south. The great mass of the present population consists of the descendants of English, Irish, German, Scotch, Dutch, Swedes, French and Italian emigrants. The English language is generally spoken, but there are neighborhoods in which the German is almost exclusively used, and we have heard from native Pennsylvanians as broad a brogue as we have ever heard from the lips of a Cannaught man. If the amalgamation of many nations, like that of many metals, would make a composition, brilliant and useful as Corinthian brass, we might look for it in Pennsylvania. From the date of the charter to Pennsylvania, all religions have found equal protection here, and the state consequently possesses a full portion of the variety of Christian professors. The most numerous denominations however, are Presbyterians, Roman Catholics, German Lutherans, German Calvinists, Methodists, Episcopalians, Baptists, Quakers and Moravians.

The Cities of Pennsylvania are three, Philadelphia, Lancaster and Pittsburg; for a particular account of which we refer to their respective letters. The seats of justice in most of the counties are boroughs, and a great proportion of the other towns of the state are also incorporated, experience having taught that the power of continued action obtained by corporate bodies, is equally effective in promoting the convenience and comfort of the citizens, and in surmounting physical difficulties.

The State, as we have seen, is divided into 52 Counties, which are not only territorial districts, but are incorporate entities, endowed with distinct and important powers of self government, entitled also to special representation in the legislature, in proportion to the number of their respective inhabitants.

Of the population of 1830, there were white males,	665,812	
Females,	644,088	
		1,309,900
Coloured free males,	18,377	
Females,	19,553	
		37,930
Slaves.—Males,	172	
Females,	231	403
		$1,348,233

STATISTICAL TABLE OF THE STATE OF PENNSYLVANIA.

Counties	When establish'd	Area in sq miles	POPULATION BY CENSUS. 1790	1800.	1810.	1820	1830.	Taxable in 1828	Assessed value.	No. of Rep's
Philadelphia City	1682	2	28522	41220	53722	137097	80408	16556	40751787	7
Philadelphia Co.	1682	120	25869	39789	57488		108381	20750		8
Bucks	1682	600	25401	27496	32371	37842	45745	9076	14422514	4
Chester	1682	738	27937	32093	39527	44451	50910	0231	13432000	4
Lancaster	1729	928	36141	43043	53927	68336	76631	14991	23524103	6
York*	1749	900	37747	25643	31938	38759	42859	8526	7051458	3
Cumberland	1750	545	18243	25386	26757	23606	29226	5342	9014941	2
Berks	1752	874	30179	32497	43046	46275	53152	10202	6463328	4
Northampton	1752	1000	24250	30062	38145	31765	39482	7382	6067859	*a* 4
Bedford	1771	1520	13124	12039	15746	20248	24502	4442	1023275	2
Northumberland	1772	457	17161	27796	36327	15424	18133	3581	2150833	1
Westmoreland	1773	1004	16018	22726	26492	30540	38400	6516	3185801	3
Washington	1781	888	23866	28293	36289	40038	42784	8134	4146422	3
Fayette	1783	824	13325	20159	24714	27285	29172	5897	3650606	2
Franklin	1784	756	15655	19638	23173	31892	35037	6095	6668495	2
Montgomery	1784	450	22929	24150	29683	35793	39406	8242	8594922	3
Dauphin	1785	528	18177	22270	31883	21653	25243	4602	4470799	2
Luzerne	1786	1784	4904	12839	18109	20027	27379	4482	1660985	2
Huntingdon	1787	1185	7568	13008	14778	20142	27145	5009	3273396	2
Allegheny	1788	754	10309	15087	25317	34921	50552	10236	8022230	4
Mifflin	1789	826	7562	13609	12132	16618	21690	4199		2
Delaware	1789	177	9483	12809	14734	14810	17323	3633		1
Lycoming	1795	2290		5414	11006	13517	17636	3081	1206205	*c* 2
Somerset	1795	1066		10188	11285	13974	17762	3344	1130308	*b* 2
Greene	1796	600		8605	12544	15554	18028	3141	1081547	1
Wayne	1798	720		2562	4125	4127	7663	1381	1200894	
Adams	1800	528		13172	15152	19370	21378	4192	4740577	2
Centre	1800	1370			10681	13706	18879	3618	2258533	*d* 2
Beaver	1800	646		5776	12168	15340	24183	4208	1609427	2
Butler	"	785		3916	7346	10193	14681	2810	1060761	1
Mercer	"	830		3228	8277	11681	19729	3490	1345175	1
Crawford	"	974		2346	6178	9397	16030	3034	1392970	1
Erie,	"	720		1468	3758	8553	17041	2867	1938301	1
Warren	"	832		230	827	1976	4697	920	466472	} 1
Venango	"	1114		1130	3060	4915	9470	1930	635000	}
Armstrong	"	941		2399	6143	10324	17625	3257	1100785	1
Indiana	1803	770			6214	8882	14252	2732	886080	} 1
Jefferson	1804	1200			161	561	2025	356	509801	}
McKean	"	1442			142	728	1439	307	530080	
Clearfield	"	1425			875	2342	4803	892	682192	
Potter	"	1100			29	186	1265	247	472220	
Tioga	"	1100			1687	4021	8978	1635	691031	
Cambria	"	670			2117	3287	7076	1144	355176	
Bradford	1810	1174				11554	19746	3365	1528722	*e* 2
Susquehannah	1810	800				9960	16787	2594	903375	1
Schuylkill	1811	745				11339	20744	2715	1815263	1
Lehigh	1812	335				18895	22256	4321	4578034	2
Columbia	1813	574				17621	20059	3521	2800000	1
Union	1813	551				18619	20795	3772	2891851	2
Lebanon	1813	288				16988	20557	3563	5185853	1
Pike	1814	772				2894	4843	892	643971	
Perry	1820	540				11342	14261	2980		1
		43822	434373	602365	810163	1049458	1348233	254182		100

a Including Wayne and Pike. *b* Including Cambria. *c* Including Potter and McKean. *d* Including Clearfield. *e* Including Tioga.

The population, taxables and value of the County of Juniata, are included in Mifflin county, of which it formed part.

The apparent diminution in the population of several counties arises from the division of such counties.

The population of the counties as given in the topographical part of the work, was taken from the returns of the Marshals, partly as published in Hazard's Register, and partly from MSS. That given in this table is from the returns as published by Congress. There are many discrepancies arising, we presume, from errors in adding the columns.

The administration of the affairs of the County is confided to three Commissioners, one of whom is elected annually to serve for three years. Their principal charges are, to raise funds for the making of Roads and Bridges, for building and maintaining of houses and prisons for county purposes, for the education of the poor, and in some instances for their support; also, to make contracts for and to superintend the execution of the various matters which fall within their province. The Courts of Quarter Session of the counties, have in most cases a supervisory jurisdiction over the acts of the Commissioners, and unite with them in filling vacancies which occur in the board. The Commissioners elect a County Treasurer annually, who may not serve more than three years out of six. The accounts of the Commissioners and their Treasurer are settled annually by their Auditors, one of whom is elected yearly, to serve three years. Each county testifies its acts by its appropriate seal.

The Counties are subdivided into Cities, (for cities make, we believe, in every case part of the corporate being of the counties in which they are locate ') Boroughs, and Townships, and each subdivision is governed by its peculiar officers. The cities have their Mayors, Mayor's Courts, Select and Common Councils, Commissioners and High Constables. They are divided into wards, which choose annually each its Constable and Assessors of property for taxation, and Inspectors of the elections. The Boroughs have their chief and other Burgesses, Constables, Assessors, Inspectors, Overseers of the poor, &c. The Townships are definite districts of the County, which are formed at the instance of the inhabitants as their convenience may dictate, by the Court of Quarter Session. Each township is a body corporate for many purposes. It elects overseers of the poor, is charged with raising funds for, and maintaining the destit''te; overseers of the roads, whose duty it is to keep in order the highways which do not pertain to other corporations, as turnpikes, &c.; Assessors, Town Clerks, Constables, &c.

Roads.—Pennsylvania merits unquestionably the praise of having constructed the first stone turnpike in the Union, and we think also that of having attempted the first canal over one hundred miles in length. The turnpike road from Lancaster to Philadelphia, 62 miles long, was commenced in the year 1792, and finished in 1794, at the expense of $465,000, by a private company. So early as 1762 it was proposed to connect the waters of Lake Erie and the Ohio with those of the Delaware, by the improvement of the rivers, convenient portages, and intermediate canals. In prosecution of this great conception, Dr. Rittenhouse and others surveyed and levelled a route for a canal between the waters of the Susqvehannah and Schuylkill rivers, by means of the Swatara and Tulpehocken Creeks. But a company was not incorporated for making such a canal until 29th September, 1791. We shall hereafter notice the result of its labors.

Since the year 1792, 220 turnpike companies have been authorized by law. Many of the roads have been executed according to their original conception, others have been curtailed or otherwise modified, and some have been abandoned. Turnpike roads however, extend into every part of the state. None have yielded profitable returns to the stockholders by direct dividends, but every one feels that he has been repaid for his expenditures in the improved value of lands, and the economy of business. The roads, particularly such as lead through a populous country, are constructed of stone, others are of earth, all made upon plans which would not now be approved, but which nevertheless enable the traveller drawn in a coach by four horses to travel from Philadelphia to Pittsburg, a distance of 303 miles, in 60 hours, and on shorter journies at the rate of from 6 to 7 miles the hour. The law prohibits any angle on these roads greater than 5°, and few roads have steeper ascents than 3 3-4 degrees.

The annexed table, from 1792 to the year 1822, compiled by a committee of the State Senate, exhibits an alphabetical list of the turnpike road companies which have received letters patent,—shows the years in which the roads were severally commenced and completed,—the length contemplated by the respective charters, the number of miles completed prior to 1822,—the amount of subscriptions to the capital stock made by individuals, and by the Commonwealth,—the cost of the road per mile, including bridges, &c.,—the subscription price of shares,—the amount of debts of each company.

TURNPIKE ROADS.

When begun.	NAMES OF TURNPIKE ROAD COMPANIES.	Length contemplated.	Ms. completd	Individual subs.	State subscriptions.	Cost per mile.	original price of shares.	Debts of the co.	Finished
		Miles.	Ms.	Dolls.	Dolls.	Dolls.	Dolls.	Dolls.	
1811	Anderson's ferry, Waterford & N. Haven.	13	13	39600	10000	3969	100	10000	1813
*	Armstrong and Indiana	24	0	12500	9000		25		—
1815	Bedford and Stoystown	29	29	40400	104000	6211	50	30339	1818
1820	Bellefonte and Philipsburg	29	20	12500	20000		50	6000	—
1817	Bellmont and Easton	64	64	34200	17500	972	50	12235	1821
1821	Bellmont and Ochquaga	18	0	7000	5000		50		—
1811	Berlin and Hanover	10	10	30700		3200	50	2000	1817
1816	Berks and Dauphin	41	34	63905	29000	3800	50	9600	—
1812	Bethany and Dingman's choice	50	33	20400	8000	904	50	3352	—
1813	Bridgewater and Wilkesbarre	64	36	13500	25000	600	50		—
1804	Bustleton and Smithfield	8	8	80000		10000			—
1821	Butler and Mercer	32	6	8750	19666	655	25		—
1812	Cayuga & Susquehannah (rest in N. Y.)	3	3		6000	1000			1813
1808	Centre	75	75	62000	80000	1200—3500	50	10000	1814
*	Centre and Kishcoquillas	23		15000	20000		50		—
1812	Chambersburg	15	15	51700		3500	100	2715	1815
1815	Chambersburg and Bedford	55	55	113850	167500	6000	50	80000	1820
1803	Cheltenham and Willowgrove	11	11	80800		8000	100		1804
1804	Chestnut-Hill and Springhouse	8	8	70000			100		1805
1813	Clifford and Wilkesbarre	43	12	6950	6500	1200	50		—
1806	Coshocton and Great Bend	50	50	81000		1620	50		1811
1814	Danville	11	11	7000		6 or 700	25	3200	1816
1803	Downingstown, Ephrata & Harrisburg	68	68	116500	60000	3750	100	56500	1819
1805	Easton and Wilkesbarre	60	48	60000	12500	1541	50		1815
1807	Erie and Waterford	14	14	20502	5000	1571	50		1809
1811	Falmouth	6	6	19200		3200			1811
1803	Frankford and Bristol	28	28	205300		10 & 5000	100	3988	1812
1809	Gap and Newport	30	30	91000	20000	3666	50	5500	1819
1801	Germantown and Perkiomen	25	25	285000		11287	100		1804
1811	Gettysburg and Black's tavern	23	5	19200		2880	100		—
1809	Gettysburg and Petersburg	22	22	90400		4200	100	1800	1814
1814	Greensburg and Pittsburg	31	31	62000	89000	6 to 7000	50	27000	1817
1812	Hanover and Carlisle	30	20	70000	10000	4000	100	30000	—
1808	Hanover and Maryland line	7	7	37500		5350	100		1809
1816	Harrisburg, Carlisle, and Chambersburg	41	41				50		—
*	Harrisburg and Millerstown	26		25000	40000				—
1814	Hibernia	18	5	10000		2000	50	2000	—
1815	Huntingdon, Cambria, and Indiana	80	80	55950	171850	3435	50	35009	1821
*	Indiana and Ebensburg	26		14325	12000		25		—
1805	Lancaster, Elizabeth, and Middletown	26	26	67400	10000	4506	100	7500	1812
1801	Lancaster and Susquehannah	10	10	48300		5816	300		1803
*	Lewistown and Huntingdon	32		30550	50000		50		—
1814	Lewistown and Kishcoquillas	6	6	22000		4000			1821
1812	Little Conestogo	21	21	26375	10000	2523	50	16625	1816
1821	Luzerne and Wayne	26		15300			25		—
*	Manchester	3							—
1814	Marietta and Mountjoy	5	5	15000		3233		8000	1815
1818	Mercer and Meadville	29	29	18025	19666	960	25	6704	1821
1815	Middletown and Harrisburg	9	9	21000	14000	5000	50	10000	1818
1809	Milford and Owego	89	67	62250	31000	1300	25	14000	—
*	Mill creek								—
1821	Millerstown and Lewistown	26	5	70000	39500	2000	50		—
1815	Morgantown, Churchtown, & Blue Ball	10	10	10000	9000	3000	50	4233	1818
1818	New Alexandria and Conemaugh	9	9	10925	16100	3789	50	9038	1820
1813	New Holland	15	10	23000	10000	3200	100	1949	—
*	New Milford and Montrose								—
1811	Perkiomen and Reading	29	29	133000	53000	7000	50	56000	1815
1810	Philadelphia, Brandywine & N. London	40	9	33000	15000	3500	50	18000	—
1821	Philadelphia and Great Bend	63		15000	12000		50		—
1792	Philadelphia and Lancaster	62	62	465000		7500			1794
1820	Philipsburg and Susquehannah	19	19	6500	16000	1245	50	2500	1821
*	Pickering creek								—
1820	Pittsburg and Butler	30	20	11500	19000	1020	25		—
1819	Pittsburg and New Alexandria	28	28	22900	48360		50	10234	1821
1818	Pittsburg and Steubenville	28	5	30000	12000	5150	50	600	
1812	Ridge	24	24	90000	25000	7500	50	140000	1816
*	Ridley (law expired)								—
1819	Robstown and Mount Pleasant	21	5	40800	10000	4597	50	600	—
*	Smithfield								—
1818	Somerset and Bedford	33	15	40000	12500	3000	50	6238	—
1817	Somerset and Mount Pleasant	29	17	53050	12500	3568	50		—
1814	Springhouse, Northampton & Bethlehem	42	5	19440	10000	7000	50	15000	—
1816	Stoystown and Greensburg	37	37	71000	112000	6000		32000	1819
*	Strasburg and Fannetsburg	36		30000			50		—
1804	Susquehannah and Lehigh	30	30	22000	10000	1050	100	1111	1806
1818	Susquehannah and Tioga	80	64	48400	30400	880	100		—
1818	Susquehannah and Waterford	126	118	50000	140000	1450	25	9000	—
1809	Susquehannah and York	12	12	33700	5000	4000	100		1810
1819	Washington and Pittsburg	25	10	50000	12000	5000		8000	—
1819	Washington and Williamsport	19	5	10500	10000	2330	50		—
1819	Waynesburg, Greencastle & Mercersburg	42	24	103000	15000	3792	100	500	—
1818	York and Gettysburg	29	29	90000	40000	4000	100	6500	1820
1807	York and Maryland line	18	18	80800		4500	100	2000	1809
1811	York and Conewago canal	11	11	60000		5500	100	8100	1812
1815	United States Road	80	80			8000			1821

We add a table of the title of the acts which have been passed since that report, not having the means of obtaining the information possessed by the Committee of the Senate, to whose labors we are indebted for the preceding table.

LIST

Of the Corporate Titles of all the turnpike road companies, authorizied by the Legislature, in the order in which the acts were passed.

Date of Acts,	Title of Road.	Counties thro' which they pass.
March 30, 1822,	Kemberton and Yellow Springs,	Chester, Butler.
April 2, "	Butler and Franklin,	Venango, Butler.
" "	Butler and Kittaning,	Armstrong.
January 29, 1823	Abington and Waterford,	Luzerne, Susquehannah
March 31, "	Ararat,	Susquehannah, Wayne.
" "	Columbia, Chiques and Marietta,	Lancaster.
Feb. 19, "	Monongahela and Brownsville,	Allegheny.
March 31, "	Susquehannah and Tioga, extended to the Centre turnpike,	Luzerne and Schuylkill.
January 24, 1824	Mount Pleasant,	Wayne.
March 3, 1825,	Huntingdon and Philipsburg,	Huntingdon and Centre.
April 11, 1825,	Greensburg and Robstown,	Westmoreland.
" "	Greensburg and New-Alexandria,	do.
" "	Bellefonte, Aaronsburg and Youngmanstown,	Centre and Union.
" "	Ebensburg and Conemaugh,	Cambria.
" "	Milesburg and Smithport,	Centre, Clearfield, McKean.
April 10, 1826,	Manyunk and Flat Rock,	Philadelphia.
" "	Milesburg and Snow Shoe,	Centre.
" "	Warren and Jefferson Turnpike	Warren and Jefferson.
" "	London and Drake's Ferry,	Franklin, Huntingdon.
" "	Clearfield and Jefferson,	Clearfield, Jefferson.
" "	Roseburg and Mercer,	Armstrong, Butler Venango, Mercer
April 8, 1826,	Potter's Old Fort and Water Street,	Centre, Huntingdon.
April 9, 1827,	Wilksbarrie, Mauch Chunk and Northampton,	Luzerne, Northampton and Lehigh.
April 4, 1827,	Mercer and Vernon,	Mercer Co.
" "	Mercer, Greenville and Kinsman,	do.
April 10, 1826,	Indiana and Pittsburg,	Indiana, Alleghany.
April 13, 1827,	Shippenville and Foxburg,	Venango.
March 27, 1827,	York Haven and Harrisburg Bridge,	York and Cumberland.
January 17, 1828	Lackawaxen,	Wayne.
Feb. 7, 1828,	Pittsburg and Coal Hill,	Allegheny.
Feb. 16, "	Peter's Mountain,	Dauphin.
April 10, "	Columbia, Washington and Port Deposit,	Lancaster.
" "	Monongahela and Coal Hill,	Allegheny.
" "	Dundaff and Tunkhannock,	Luzerne, Susquehannah.
" "	Carbondale and Blakely,	do.
" "	Snow Shoe and Packenville,	Centre and Clearfield.
" "	Willow Grove and Doylestown,	Bucks.
April 12, 1828,	Faulkner's Swamp and Berks County,	Montgomery, Berks.
April 3, 1829,	Wilsonville and Lackawaxen,	Wayne.
April 16, "	Salem and Dyberry,	do.
" "	Athens and Troy,	Bradford.
" "	Spring House and Sumneytown,	Montgomery.
" "	Pittsburg Farmer & Mechanics' turnpike,	Allegheny.
" "	Reading, Reamstown and Ephrata,	Berks, Lebanon, and Lancaster.
" "	Union and Pittsburg,	Fayette, Westmoreland and Allegheny.
April 23, 1829,	Lycoming and Tioga,	Lycoming and Tioga.
January 14, 1830	Pittsburg and Birmingham,	Allegheny.

March 10,	1830	Shippensville and Emlenton,	Venango.
March 20,	"	Milford and Owego, (Lateral road)	Susquehannah, Luzerne.
April 5,	"	Dauphin and Sunbury,	Dauphin and Northam.
"	"	Dillsburg and Berlin,	York and Adams.
April 6,	"	Bedford and Frankstown,	Bedford, Huntingdon.
"	"	Gettysburg and Hagerstown,	Adams.
April 5,	"	Marietta, Bainbridge, Falmouth and Portsmouth,	Lancaster, Dauphin.
April 3,	"	Armagh and Conemaugh,	Indiana.
April 2,	"	Honesdale and Clarksville,	Wayne.
January 17,	1831	Honesdale and Germanville,	do.
January 25,	"	Tunkhannock Bridge and Carbondale,	do.
April 1,	"	Williamsport and South Creek,	Lycoming, Tioga, Bradford.
March 30,	"	Warren and Ridgeway,	Warren, Jefferson.
"	"	Honesdale and Big Eddy,	Wayne.
"	"	Bald Eagle, Nittany and Bellefonte,	Centre.
Feb. 17,	"	Armstrong and Clearfield,	Armstrong, Clearfield.
Feb. 23,	"	Muncey and Monroe,	Lycoming, Bradford.
March 2,	"	Cherry Ridge and Lackawana,	Wayne, Luzerne.
March 14,	"	Dundaff and Henesdale,	Susquehannah, Wayne
March 18,	"	Hummelstown, Middletown & Portsmouth,	Dauphin.
March 25,	"	Bethany and Honesdale,	Wayne.
	1832,	Somerset, Bedford, and Maryland,	———
	"	Susquehannah and Great Bend,	Luzerne.
	"	Berry's Mountain Company,	Dauphin.
	"	Honesdale and Delaware,	Wayne.
	"	Perkiomen Bridge and Sumneytown,	Montgomery.
	"	Pottsville, Minersville, and Carbondale,	Schuylkill, Northumberland.

It is altogether impracticable to state the aggregate length of these roads, or even by estimate to make an approximation to it, inasmuch as neither the route, nor the point of departure, nor the point of termination, is fixed by the act in many cases. It is probable, however, that more than 3000 miles of Road has been authorized to be made, and that between 22 and 24 hundred have been constructed.

Two stone Turnpike roads run from Philadelphia by Pittsburg, one by the southern, the other by the northern route. One continuing road runs from Philadelphia to the town of Erie on the lake, through Sunbury, Bellefonte, Franklin and Meadville. Two roads run northward from Philadelphia, one to the New York State line, in Bradford county, passing through Berwick, and one to the northern part of the state, in Susquehannah county, passing through Bethlehem; and one continued road runs from Pittsburg to Erie, through Butler, Mercer, Meadville, and Waterford.

All these turnpike roads have been undertaken by private companies, many of which have been aided by liberal subscriptions on the part of the state. We may notice here, because of its great importance, the east and west state road leading through the northern tier of counties; much of the expense of this road has been paid by the state. It is passable, but needs much improvement which it will gradually receive, as the country becomes populated.

Rail Roads.—Short and rudely constructed Rail ways, leading from quarries and mines, have been in use in several parts of the state, for about twenty years. The first act passed in America, authorizing a company to make a rail road for public use, was that of 31st March, 1823, granting permission to Mr Stevens and others to make a rail way from Philadelphia to the Susquehannah at Columbia, a distance of 84 1-2 miles. That company did not commence the work, and the state has since nearly completed a like road between these points, which we shall notice more particularly when treating of the great plan of the Commonwealth for internal improvement. Authority has been given to some thirty three companies for making rail roads in various parts of the state. Some of these projects are the result of over excited rapidity, and will probably never be executed; but most of them are based upon the actual improvement of the country and will supply the place of turnpikes, and are required, by the increased demand for the agricultural and mineral products of the Commonwealth.

The following is a table of the titles of the acts authorizing the rail roads at present executed, in progress, or in contemplation.

DATE OF ACT.	TITLE.	COUNTIES.
31 March, 1823.	Philadelphia and Columbia Rail Road,	Philadelphia, Delaware, Chester, Lancaster.
11 April, 1827,	Oxford Rail Road Co. of Chester Co.	Chester.
3 April, 1826,	Susquehannah and Delaware Canal and Rail Road,	Luzerne.
11 March 1826,	Lackawana and Susquehannah Rail Road,	do.
16 April, 1827,	do. do. do.	do.
8 April, 1826, 14 April. 1828,	Danville and Pottsville Rail Road,	Northumberland and Schuylkill.
3 March, 1826,	Of the Union Canal Company,	Schuylkill.
14 April, 1828,	Little Schuylkill Rail Road substituted for Canal,	do.
14 " "	Schuylkill Valley Rail Road, do.	do. do.
14 " "	Sandy and Beaver Canal,	Beaver.
7 Feb. 1828,	Tioga Rail way, substituted for Canal,	Tioga.
7 " "	Mill Creek and Mine Hill,	Schuylkill.
27 Feb. "	Baltimore and Ohio.	
24 March, 1828,	Mine Hill and Schuylkill Haven,	do.
24 " "	State Rail Road, from Philadelphia to Columbia, and across the Allegheny mountain.	
9 April, 1828,	Lycoming Rail Road and Navigation Company.	
12 April, "	Tioga Rail and Road Company.	
14 " "	Orwigsburg Rail Road Company,	Schuylkill.
20 " 1829,	Mount Carbon,	do
22 " 1829,	Lick Run in Lycoming County.	do.
23 " 1829,	Northern Liberties and Penn township,	Philadelphia.
30 Jan. 1830,	Waullenpaupack Improvement Company,	Wayne, Luzerne.
	Lateral of Mill Creek and Mine Hill.	Schuylkill.
16 March, "	Phillipsburg and Juniata,	Huntingdon, Centre.
6 April, "	Tuscarora and Cold Run Tunnel and Rail Road Company.	Schuylkill.
6 " "	Middleport and Pine Creek Rail Road	do.
6 " "	Delaware and Susquehannah.	Pike and Luzerne.
7 " "	Lyken's Valley,	Dauphin.
7 " "	Beaver Rail Road and Coal Company,	Northampton, Lehigh, Schuylkill.
17 Feb. 1831,	Philadelphia, Germantown, and Norristown Rail Road Company.	Philadelphia and Montgomery.
18 " "	Westchester Rail Road Company,	Chester.
30 March, 1831,	Lorberry Creek Rail Road Company,	Schuylkill.
11 " "	Bald Eagle, Nittany Valley Turnpike and Rail Road Company.	Centre.
1 April, "	Fishing Creek Rail Road Company,	Schuylkill.
	Rail Road Company of Philadelphia, and Delaware Company of Southwark,	Philadelphia.
2 " "	Swatara and Good Spring Creek,	Schuylkill.
	Roush Creek,	do.
	Cumberland Valley Rail Road,	Cumberland.
	Rock Cabin and Tangascootack Rail Road,	Centre.
	Beaver Meadow Rail Road Company authorized to extend their Road to the river Lehigh or the Delaware Canal, at or near Easton,	Northampton.
1832.	Philadelphia and Trenton Rail Road Co.	Philad'a, Bucks.
	Franklin Rail Road Company,	Franklin.
	York and Maryland Rail Road Company,	York.
	Leggett's Gap Rail Road Company,	Mifflin.

Norristown, Berks and Lehigh Rail Road Company,	Montgomery, Lehigh, Berks.
Adams County Rail Road Company,	Adams.

The following concise notice of some of the roads undertaken by private companies, is the most our limits will admit.

The Rail Roads created by the mineral wealth of Schuylkill county, are,

	COST.
The Schuylkill valley road, running 10 miles, from Mount Carbon, to Tuscarora,	$55,000
Lateral roads connecting with this, 10 miles,	20,000
Mill Creek Rail Road, 4 miles,	14,000
Laterals, 3 miles,	6,000
West branch Rail from Schuylkill Haven, 15 miles, to the Broad mountain,	150,000
Laterals intersecting do. 5 miles,	10,000
Mount Carbon, extending 9 miles up the two branches of the Norwegian creek,	100,000
Pinegrove Rail Road, extending 5 miles, from the Coal mines to the Swatara feeder, estimated,	30,000
The Little Schuylkill Rail Road, 23 miles in length, commences at Port Clinton, and extends up the Little Schuylkill river, to the mountain, estimated,	250,000

Thus the Coal mines of Schuylkill County, alone, have created 83 miles of Rail Road, and caused the expenditure, or rather the profitable investment of $635,000.

In Northampton county, the Mauch Chunk mines have given being to the rail road leading to the great mine on Mauch Chunk mountain, nine miles in length,

	47,520ft.
Lateral or branch roads,	8,069
Roads and their branches in the mine,	11,437
	67,026

Total length of single tracts, 12,695—1000 miles, cost $38,726=$3,050 the mile. It will be observed that the cost of making the bed of this road, one of the best turnpikes in the country, is not included. And to the road around the head of Mauch Chunk and Nesquihoning mountain, to the mines at Room Run, 28031 ft. or 5 miles and 1631 ft. (For a more particular account of these roads, see the article, "Mauch Chunk.")

The Beaver Meadow mines in the same county, have caused the projection of rail roads, to the Little Schuylkill, to the Lehigh river, along the valley of that river to Northampton, and from thence towards Philadelphia. None of these projects have been further prosecuted than the formation of companies disposed to execute them. Some one, or all of them will be executed, when the public shall be satisfied that coal can be brought by it, or them, profitably to market.

In Luzerne county, similar roads have been projected along the valley of the Lackawana, to bring its coal to the improved navigation of the Susquehannah.

And in Dauphin county, a rail road is being constructed from the coal mines of the Sheet mountain, crossing William's valley at right angles, at the mines to the northern base of Berry's mountain, along which it is continued to its western termination, at the river Susquehannah. Whole length 16 miles. This road will probably be completed in the autumn of 1833.

To these rail roads, made with a view to the coal trade, we may add the following, which have been commenced and in progress, viz: the Philadelphia, Germantown, and Norristown rail road, the whole distance of which is about 16 miles, 5 of which have been completed and are in daily use; the Danville and Pottsville rail road, now called after the late Mr. Stephen Girard. This is one of several projects for connecting the Susquehannah river, with the city of Philadelphia; and public opinion has decided that it is the most practicable one. From the confluence of the north and west branches at Sunbury, the surveyed line will be 44 miles, 174 poles, to the eastern extremity in the Mount Carbon rail road, 2½ miles northward from Pottsville. To which must be added, seven miles connecting the road with Danville. The estimated cost of a single track to Sunbury is $675,000, and with a double tract the further sum of $148,102. The original act authorizing a company to make this road was passed 8th April, 1826; but nothing effectual having been done under it, a supplement was enacted, appointing new commissioners to receive subscriptions, enlarging the permitted amount of capital stock from $300,000 to $1,000,000, and authorizing a branch road to Catawissa; since which some auxiliary acts have been passed. A sufficient portion of the stock for executing the most useful and profitable parts of the road had been subscribed, and the work is progressing with vigour. (*For a further notice of this road, see the article "Pottsville."*) From an inspection of the lists of rail roads and canals, authorized by law, which we give, it will be seen that many projects have been offered to connect the great rivers of the state, the Susquehannah and the Delaware. One of these has been effected, and two others, by the state rail road from Columbia to Philadelphia, and the rail road from Sunbury to Pottsville, are like to be speedily completed. Other projects for connecting these rivers, at higher points, as at Catawissa, Berwick, and Wilkesbarre, must, we think, wait sometime for maturity.

The following table comprizes titles of acts, passed by the legislature, authorizing the incorporation of lock and canal navigation companies.

DATE OF ACTS.	TITLE OF COMPANIES.	COUNTIES.
Sept. 29, 1791,	Schuylkill and Susquehannah Navigation,	Daup. Leb. Berks.
April 10, 1792,	Delaware and Schuylkill do.	Berks, Mont. Phila.
" " 1793,	Conewago canal west side of river,	York.
	Brandywine canal and lock Navigation,	Chester.
Feb. 27, 1798,	Lehigh Navigation (1814, March 22)	Northap., Luzerne.
Feb. 19, 1801,	Chesapeake and Delaware Canal,	Maryland, Delaware.
Feb. 7, 1803,	Conecocheague Navigation,	Franklin.
March 17, 1806,	Conestoga Lock and Dam Navigation,	Lancaster.
April 2. 1811,	Union Canal,	Dauphin, Leb. Berks.
March 20, 1813,	Conewago canal, east side of river.	Dauphin, Lancaster.
March 26, 1814,	Neshaminy Lock Navigation,	Bucks.
March 8, 1815,	Schuylkill Navigation,	Sch. Berks, Mont. Phil.
Feb. 5, 1817,	Lackawana Navigation,	Luzerne.
March 24,	Monongahela Navigation,	Fay. Gree. Alleg. Was. West.
March 20, 1813,	Lehigh Navigation, by White & Co.	Northamp. Luzerne.
March 29, 1819,	Scuylkill West Branch Navigation,	Schuylkill.
	Octorara Navigation,	Lancaster, Chester.
1820,	Conestoga, to be made Navigable by Jas. Hopkins,	Lancaster.
March 27, 1823,	Harrisburg Canal and Lock Navigation,	Dauphin.
April 1, 1823,	Shenango Canal Company,	Crawford.
March 13,	Improvement and Slack Water Navigation,	
April 26, 1825,	Of the Lackawaxen river,	Luzerne,
March 28, 1820,	Canal & lock Navigation of the Brandywine,	Chester, Delaware.
March 3, 1825,	Conestoga Navigation Company,	Lancaster.
April 12,	Codorus Navigation Company,	York.
Feb. 20, 1826,	Lock Navigation on the Little Schuylkill,	Schuylkill Co.
Feb. 9, 1826,	Chesapeake Bay and Ohio River,	Somerset, Fayette, Westmoreland, Alleg.
Feb. 20, "	Tioga Navigation Company,	Tioga.
March 25, "	Susquehannah and Lehigh (Nescopeck,)	Colu. Luz. North'n.
April 7, "	Petapsico and Susquehannah Canal,	York.
April 3, "	Susquehannah and Delaware Canal and Rail Road,	Northampton.
April 5, "	Northumberland Canal and water right Co.	Northumberland.
April 10, "	Sunbury Canal,	do.
April 14, 1827,	Pennsylvania and Ohio Canal Company,	Beaver, Allegheny.
" " "	Shamokin Creek,	Northumberland.
April 16, 1827,	Allegheny and Conewango Canal,	Warren, Venango.
" 14, "	Norwegian Creek Slack water Navigation,	Schuylkill.

April 11, 1827,	Stony Creeck Slack water Navigation,	Dauphin.
March 22, 1827,	Mahanoy Navigation Company,	Northampton.
" 20, "	Schuylkill Valley Navigation,	Schuylkill.
" 22, "	Delaware and Schuylkill lock navigation,	Philadelphia.
April 7, 1830,	Waullunpaupack Improvement Company,	Wayne, Luzerne.
Feb. 23, "	Penn's Creek Navigation,	Union.

We believe of these many projects for improving the internal communication of the state, by navigation, the following, only, have been executed: The Union Canal, the Schuylkill navigation, the Lehigh navigation, the Delaware and Hudson canal, the Chesapeake and Delaware canal, the Conestoga navigation, the Cordorus navigation, and the Conewago canals. We have already described the Lehigh, the Conestoga, and the Codorus navigation, and refer the reader to those articles. We proceed to give a concise description of the others.

On the 29th September, 1791, the legislature incorporated a joint stock company to connect the Susquehannah and Schuylkill rivers by a canal and slack water Navigation; and a second company was incorporated by act of 10th April, 1792, to unite the Delaware and the Schuylkill, by a canal extending from Norristown to Philadelphia, a distance of 17 miles. The Schuykill river from the former place to Reading was to be temporarily improved, and this with the works of the Susquehannah company, to form an uninterrupted water communication with the interior of the state. The place of union, however, was soon afterwards changed on the recommendation of Mr. Weston, an English engineer, and it was resolved to extend the Susquehannah canal to the Delaware, a distance of seventy miles. About 15 miles of the most difficult parts of the two works, comprizing much rock excavation, heavy embankments, extensive deep cuttings, and several locks *of bricks* were nearly completed; when after an expenditure of 440,000 dollars, the works were suspended by reason of the pecuniary embarrassments of the stockholders of the companies. The suspension of these works, and subsequently of the Chesapeake and Delaware canal, discouraged every similar work, which was projected for many years afterwards. Frequent attempts were made in vain even though the state tendered the assistance of 300,000 dollars to resume operations. In the year 1811, the two companies, composed chiefly of the same stockholders, were united under the title of "*The Union Canal Co.*" By the act uniting them, they are specially authorized to extend their canal from Philadelphia to Lake Erie, to make such further extension in any other part of the state as they might deem expedient. A large amount of new stock was indispensable to the success of the company, which they were authorized to create by act of 29th March, 1819, and for payment of interest thereon, the avails of a lottery granted by the last preceding act, were pledged. By act 26th March, 1821, the Commonwealth guaranteed the interest, and granted to the company a monoply of lotteries.

Thus sustained, the managers resumed their operations in 1821. The line of the canal was relocated, the dimensions changed, and it was rendered navigable in 1827, thirty-seven years after the commencement of the work, and sixty-five after the date of the first survey.

The Union Canal is nearly 80 miles in length, from Middletown on the Susquehannah, to a point on the Schuylkill, a short distance below Reading (exclusive of a pool and towing path of 2 miles, 73 chains) on the latter river, and of the navigable feeder from the Swatara, 6½ miles long, and of the pool of the great dam upon that stream, reaching to Pine Grove. Its total length including the branches is about 90 miles. At Middletown it is connected with the Susquehannah river and Pennsylvania canal, and at Reading with the works of Schuylkill navigation company. Its route is nearly parallel with the Tulpehocken and Swatara creeks, and the creek between their head waters runs near the town of Lebanon. The lockage of 519 ft. is overcome by 93 lift, and two guard locks, which are 75 ft. in length, and 8 ft. 6 inches in breadth. Two of the locks which overcome a height of 16 ft. connect the canal with the state works, and were made at the expense of the Commonwealth. The canal is 36 feet wide on the surface, 24 feet at the bottom, and 4 ft. in depth. There are 43 waste weirs, 49 culverts, 135 bridges, 12 small and two large aqueducts, and 12 miles of solid stone wall, to protect the work from the abrasion of the streams.

The canal is divided into three parts or sections, the eastern, the summit, and the western. The eastern is 37 miles, 61 chains in length, to which must be added a towing path and pool of 3 miles, 42 chains. The descent of 311 ft. is effected by 54 lift, and 2 guard locks. The summit is 6 miles, 78 chains in length, to which must be added the navigable feeder dam.

This section being through a limestone district, much deep rock excavation was requisite, and so faithless is the bed which this rock affords that it became necessary to plank it throughout. There is on this section, west of Lebanon, a tunnel excavated through solid rock, 729 feet long, 18 feet wide, and 16 feet high. The summit is supplied by water from the Swatara, conducted to it by the feeder already mentioned, and as the canal is above the level of the feeder, the water is thrown into it by two large water wheels and pumps; and a provision against accidents to these works is made by the erection of two steam engines, one of 120 and the other of 100 horse power. The regular supply of water by this stream in dry seasons proving insufficient, the company resolved on a novel and extraordinary expedient to obtain a *store* of water, which they have successfully effected. A dam has been constructed in the Swatara Gap of the Blue Mountains, through which the Creek passes, near to the northern declivity of the mountain, at which the pass is 430 feet wide. The dam is divided into two parts, and constructed on different principles. That on the west is of brick work, filled in with stone, and backed with earth; that on the east is of stone and earth. The first measures 200 feet across the stream, and 40 feet in perpendicular height. The timbers are 10 by 12 inches square, those at the base of white oak and of the superstructure of white pine, laid at right angles, forming squares of from 6 to 8 feet, from centre to centre, firmly tree nailed, filled with stone and strongly fitted against the mountain which supplies an abutment of solid rock at the west end. The east side of the cribs is supported and confined by an immense stone abutment, laid in hydraulic cement, which rises to the height of 48 feet, 8 feet higher than the cribs, and is intended to protect the embankment of earth and stone from the ice freshets. The open in front of the cribs is of white oak planks. The cribs extend up the stream 110 feet, with a backing of earth extending in the same direction to the distance of 110 feet more, making the base 220 feet up the stream, by 200 feet across the same, covering a surface of 44000 square feet. The second part, an embankment of stone and earth, extends from the stone abutment, above described, to the east side of the gap, 230 feet, and at the base 260 feet up the stream, and 60 feet wide at the water surface. Its eastern extremity is well protected by a natural abutment of solid rock in the mountain. This embankment rises two feet higher than the stone abutment, having an altitude of 50 feet, and covers a surface of 59,000 square feet, which united to the sum of the space covered by the crib work, make 103,800 square feet, for the base of the structure, part of which is natural.

The sluice gates, 12 in number, are of cast Iron, having each a surface of 2 square feet, are connected by pieces of yellow pine timbers, which rise above the surface of the water, and may be raised or lowered by means of screws. The sluice gates and machinery are surrounded by strong frame work to guard the whole from injury by ice freshets and floating timber The sluice house is connected with the western shore by a bridge, raised beyond the utmost height of the water in the reservoir, so that the gates may be regulated with ease and safety at every stage of the water.

The water from the reservoir passes through a substantial stone lock on the east side into the canal. When at its greatest height the lift of the lock is 10 feet, but it diminishes as the water is drawn off, and may be reduced 10 feet without effecting the communication with Pine Grove. When filled, the reservoir forms a lake which covers between 700 and 800 acres, an object of equal beauty and utility.

The western Division is 33 miles, 4 chains in length, to which must be added 60 chains of pool and towing path. The descent of 208½ feet is made by 39 locks.

From Pine Grove the company have constructed a rail way through a gap of the Sharp Mountain to the coal region; and they anticipate that at no distant day the supply of coal from this source will compete with that from the Schuylkill. The company are also of the opinion that the capacity of the canal may readily be made adequate to transmit for some years the commerce of the Susquehannah which is adapted to that mode of conveyance. Boats of 40 tons burthen have passed through their locks, but the boats ordinarily and advantageously navigating the canal do not exceed 25 tons burthen.

The total amount of tonnage for one year, ending 1st November, 1831, was 59,970 tons, yielding $59,137,21.

The works of the *Schuylkill Navigation Company* consist of a series of canals and pools, which extend from Fair Mount, at Philadelphia, to Mill Creek, at Port Carbon, in Schuylkill county, a distance of 110½ miles. The company for executing this important work was incorporated under the Act of 8th March, 1815. and being required by the act to commence operations at each end of the route simultaneously, their labours were nearly useless, until the whole line was made navigable in 1826. The canals extend 63 and the pools 47 miles. The pools upon this and even upon Lehigh river, where the canals are larger, have been forced, by their increase depth, and width to yield greater facililities to the passage of boats, than the canals, and regrets are entertained that dams and pools had not been adopted to the greatest possible extent. Thirty four dams upon the Schuylkill create pools and supply canals for the whole line. A tow path runs sometimes on the left and sometimes on the right bank. The dam at Fair Mount, we have already described (See Philadelphia.) And all the other dams on the river afford sites for water works as at Manyunk, Conshehocken, Norristown, Phœnixville, &c. &c. and yield increasing incomes to the company. The descent in the river is overcome by 29 locks, which is 80 ft. long, and 17 broad. The canals are generally 36 ft. wide, and 3 ft. deep. In some places wider and deeper, and in a few passes for short distances, they are not more than 30 ft. It is said to be the most arduous and expensive enterprize yet achieved by individual efforts in our country. The lockage is nearly equal to that on the New York canal. Much rock excavation, embanking, and the first tunnel attempted in the Union, were executed. Very considerable difficulties, and great expenses were occasioned by the fissure in the limestone rock over which much of the canal has been carried. Indeed, such appeared the probability of the continuance of those difficulties and expenses, that the company have determined to abandon a section of the canal above Reading, and to resort to the rivers. The cost has been about $2,600,000; and the dividend for the year 1832, will be about 9 per cent.

The Delaware and Hudson Canal partly in the State of New York and partly in the State of Pennsylvania, owes its origin to some enterprising proprietors of coal lands in the upper part of the Lackawaxen, river valley, in Luzerne county, who were desirous to find a market for this mineral in New York. It has been made principally by New York capital. It commences at the Hudson River, at the mouth of the Roundout, and thence runs to the Delaware River the distance of 59 miles to Port Lewis. On this section are 60 lift locks, and one guard lock of hammered stone, laid chiefly in hydraulic cement. There is also an aqueduct, over the Neversink River 224 feet in length, upon stone piers and abutments; one over the Ronudout, entirely of stone, upon two arches, one of 60 and the other of 50 feet chord; and ten others of various dimensions, upon stone piers and abutments, over lateral streams; 15 culverts of stone, and 93 bridges, having stone abutments and wing walls.

Port Lewis is less than a mile from Carpenter's point, formed by the junction of the Neversink and Delaware rivers, at which point the States of New York and New Jersey corner on Pennsylvania, and from this town there is a view of the territory, of three States, and of the Delaware River, and of the fertile valley of the Neversink.

From this point the line of the canal is carried up the east side of the Delaware, to a point opposite the mouth of the Lackawaxen River, where a dam has been thrown across the Delaware, by means of which the canal is fed, and boats cross the river. From McCarty's point formed by the junction of the Lackawaxen and the Delaware, it ascends the valley of the former, 25 miles to the forks of the Dyberry, where the canal terminates at the thriving village of Honesdale, Wayne co. On the Delaware section of 22 miles, there are wooden locks, and on the Lackawaxen section of 25 miles, are 37 locks of the same description. These locks are secured by a substantial dry stone wall, and so constructed that the wooden lining can be taken out and replaced, without disturbing the rest of the lock. The whole distance from Roundout to Honesdale is 108 miles; in which there are 103 lift and two guard locks. Honesdale is elevated 1000 feet above the tide water at the Hudson. The canal varies from 32 to 36 feet in width upon the water line, and is 4 feet in depth. The locks are 76 feet in length, between the gates, and 9 feet wide. The boats which ply on the canal carry from 25 to 30 tons.

From Honesdale a rail road leads to Carbondale in Luzerne co. distant 16 miles, overcoming an elevation of 855 feet. This road is constructed of timber, and plated with iron, and upon the elevations and passing over the levels, the coal cars are drawn up and let down by means of five stationary steam engines, and three self-acting or gravitating planes. The cost of this great work exceeds two millions of dollars. In the year 1831 the company delivered at Roundout 41,475 tons coal. The product of their labours for 1832 bids fair to be much greater.

The Chesapeake and Delaware Canal though not in Pennsylvania, is a Pennsylvania work connecting the Estuiaries of the two great Rivers of the State, and enabling her merchants to carry to their proper market a large portion of the produce of the valley of the Susquehannah.*

This work has cost a much larger sum than was anticipated. The estimate of the board of examining engineers being $1,354,364,64, and the actual cost, $2,201,864,03.

Having thus noticed the chief works of internal improvement which have been executed by joint stock companies, it remains for us to give a concise view of the system adopted and pursued by the State herself.

The first legislative effort toward the establishment of a general system of internal improvement, was by the act of 27 March, 1824, authorizing the appointment of three commissioners to explore a route for a canal from Harrisburg to Pittsburg, by the waters of the Juniata and Conemaugh rivers, and by the west branch of the Susquehannah and Sinnemahoning with the waters of the Allegheny—and also the great valley of Chester and Lancaster counties—and a route from a point on the Schuylkill river in the county of Schuylkill, thence by Mahanoy creek, the river Susquehannah, the Moshanon or Clearfield and Black Lick Creeks, the Conemaugh, the Kiskiminitas and Allegheny rivers to Pittsburg. We know not what proceedings were had under this act, but it is apparent, from the next subsequent one, that public opinion not only approved the measure, but encouraged a great extension of it. The preamble to the act of 11th April, 1825, asserts that the establishment of a communication between the eastern *and western waters of this state and the lakes* by means of navigable streams and canals, would advance our Agriculture, Commerce, and Manufactures, would unite in a common interest the great natural divisions of the State, and would in the end be an important source of revenue to the Commonwealth. That the less interests of the State require that this great and important work, should be the property of the Commonwealth, and that the Commonwealth ought to embark in it with that zeal and energy that is best calculated to carry it into effect.—And therefore the act provides for the appointment of five canal commissioners, and directs them to explore and report, upon the following routes,—one from Philadelphia through Chester and Lancaster counties, and thence by the west branch of the Susquehannah, and the waters thereof to the Allegheny and Pittsburg,—also from the Allegheny to Lake Erie;—one other from Philadelphia by the Juniata to Pittsburg, and from thence to Lake Erie; one other from the city of Philadelphia to the northern boundary of the State, towards the Seneca or Cayuga Lakes; one other through Cumberland and Franklin counties to the Potomac river; and one by the Conecocheague or Monocosey and Cenewago to the Susquehannah—and the best route through the

* It was the wish of the author to give a full description of this canal, but the limits of the work will not admit it.

county of Bedford to connect the route of the proposed Chesapeake and Ohio canal with the Juniata route above named.

In August 1825, a convention of the representatives of the friends of internal improvement was holden at Harrisburg. It consisted of 113 members delegated from 46 counties. This respectable body declared "that the improvement of the Commonwealth would be best promoted, and the foundations of her prosperity and happiness most securely established, by opening an entire and complete communication from the Susquehannah to the Allegheny, and Ohio, and from the Allegheny to Lake Erie, by the nearest and best practicable route, and that such a work is indispensably necessary to maintain the character and standing of the State and to preserve her strength and resources!

By the act 25th Feb. 1826, to provide for the commencement of a canal, to be constructed at the expense of the State. to be styled the "*Pennsylvania Canal,*" the canal commissioners were required immediately to locate and contract for making a canal, &c. from the river Swatara, at or near Middletown, to, or near a point on the east side of the river Susquehannah opposite the mouth of the river Juniata; and from Pittsburg to the mouth of the Kiskiminitas—and as soon as they should deem it expedient and practicable to construct a navigable feeder of a canal from French Creek to the summit level at Conneaut Lake, and to survey and locate the route of a canal from thence to Lake Eric. By art of 9 April, 1827, the canal commissioners were required to locate and contract for making a canal up the valley of the Juniata, from the eastern section of the Pennsylvania canal, to a point at or near Lewistown; another up the valley of the Kiskiminitas and Conemaugh, from the western section to a point at or near Blairsville; another up the valley of the Susquehannah, from the eastern section of the Pennsylvania canal to a point at or near the town of Northumberland; also commence operations on the feeder from French creek to the summit level at Conneaut lake, and to contract for so much as might be adapted to either of the routes in contemplation, for connecting the Pennsylvania canal with Lake Eric, and to cause an examination to be made from the mouth of French creek, by way of Waterford, to the bay of Presqueisle, and from Conneaut lake to lake Erie. And in case it should appear after due examination, that a canal could be construced between a point at or near Philadelphia, or at Bristol or any intermediate point between Bristol and the head of tide water, and a point at or near the borough of Easton; then to locate and contract for making a portion of such canal. By this act also, directions were given to ascertain the practicability and cost of an entire navigable communication between the west branch of the Susquehannah and the Allegheny river—and the location and cost of canals, from Northumberland up the north branch of the Susquehannah to the state line—from the western section of the Pennsylvania canal, near the mouth of the Kiskiminitas to a point on lake Erie, by the Allegheny river and French creek, at or near the borough of Erie—from the city of Pittsburg to the said point on lake Eric, by the route of Beaver and Chenango—to survey and estimate the route for a canal, and also a railway, with locomotive or stationary engines from Philadelphia through Chester and Lancaster counties, so as to connect by the nearest and most eligible route with the eastern section of the Pennsylvania canal—to survey, &c. a route down the Brandywine river, to a point north of the Delaware state line, thence across the dividing ridge, between said river and Chester creek, thence down the same to the river Delaware—and for a portage or railway across such ridge—to ascertain the practicability and cost, of connecting the north branch of the Susquehannah and the Lehigh rivers, by means of a canal or railway—to survey the east and west sides of the Susquehannah river to the Maryland line, and report on the practicability of extending the canal to such line—to survey and report on the practicability of a canal along the valley of the Delaware, from Philadelphia or Bristol, &c. to Carpenter's point—to survey and make estimates for a canal through the valleys of the Conedogwinet, Yellow Breeches, and Conecocheague creeks, with a view to the connection of the Susquehannah and Potomac; to view the ground from the west end of the Harrisburg bridge to the borough of Chambersburg, in the county of Franklin, and from the west end of the Columbia bridge, through York and Gettysburg to Chambersburg, for the purpose of constructing a rail-road—to examine the proposed ronte of the Schuylkill and Delaware canal, through the district of Southwark, and report whether it will form a necessary link in the line of the Pennsylvania canal.

By act of 24th March, 1828, the commissioners were requested to locate and contract for making canals—from the commencement of the Pennsylvania canal at the mouth of the Swatara, to Columbia in Lancaster county; from Lewiston to the highest point expedient and practicable for the canal on the Juniata; from a point at or near Northumberland to the Bald Eagle on the west branch; from Northumberland to the New-York state line on the north branch; from a point at or near Taylor's Ferry to Easton; and from Blairsville to the highest point expedient and practicable for a canal on the Conemaugh: to locate but not to contract for, a canal from Easton to Carpenter's Point, where a junction may be made with the Deleware and Hudson canal; to locate a route for a rail road across the Allegheny mountain to connect the Juniata and Conemaugh sections of the Pennsylvania canal, and to contract for the completion thereof. To locate a rail road from the city of Philadelphia through the city of Lancaster to Columbia on the Susquehannah, and from thence to the west end of the borough of York; to survey the valley of the Monongahela from Pittsburg to the Virginia state line; the valley of the Susquehannah from Columbia to the mouth of the Conestoga river, with a view to improve the navigable communication; to make surveys, &c., from Huntingdon through Woodcock valley and Bedford; and by the head waters of the Allegheny to Johnstown in Cambria county, and with a view of connecting these streams by a canal or rail road; to survey, &c., from Lewistown by the Kishcoquillas creek and through the valley of that name to the town of Huntingdon; to survey, &c., from same point on the Schuylkill canal to a point or points on the Susquehannah river between Catawissa and Sunbury, with the view of connecting these points by a rail road; to make further surveys of the valley of the Allegheny from the mouth of the Kiskiminitas to the mouth of the French Creek, with a view to make a canal, or slack water communication for steam or other boats.

By the Act of 23d April, 1829, the Commissioners were required to locate the route of a suitable navigation either by canal, or by canal and slack water between the city of Pittsburg or the mouth of the Kiskiminitas and the borough of Erie; to improve the navigation of the Monongahela river from the city of Pittsburg to the Virginia state line; at such line and in such manner as the Legislature might thereafter direct.

Having thus stated in the most concise manner possible the whole extent of the Pennsylvania system of internal improvement, we proceed to exhibit with the same conciseness the extent of the works which have been effected. We request the reader will travel with us over the several routes, and attend to our remarks and illustrations as we proceed.

Commencing, then, at Carpenter's Point on the Delaware, or rather at Dunning's Ferry, 2½ miles above the point where the river is 415 feet wide. It is proposed here to erect a dam 10 feet high upon a foundation of smooth slate rock, within 15 chains of the Hudson canal, with which the Delaware canal may be readily connected; thence to follow the valley of the river a distance of 70 miles to Easton. This route is attended with much labour and many difficulties. Bluff rocky mountains run close to the shore, rendering expensive embankments in the river necessary; and the bottom land is very undulating, requiring also heavy embankments and frequent and deep excavation. The descent in the whole line is 268½ feet, and the whole expense is estimated at $1,430,669. 17.* No portion of this line has yet been commenced, but the line has been located with the view of a connection with the next described line.

The canal from Easton to Bristol commences in a dam raised 10 feet high at the mouth of Lehigh river; at Easton, thence it follows the valley of the river to

The statement above is from the survey of H. G. Sargent, in 1827. A second survey, by Maj. Douglass, gives the length of 66 6-10th miles, and cost for canal and locks, 9 feet wide, $776,798, 80, and for canal and locks, 11 feet, $885,502. 10.

Morrisville; thence by an inland route to Bristol on the Deleware. The whole distance as reported by the Engineer, is 56 miles, and the lockage or descent 170 feet. Estimate of cost for a canal, 5 feet deep, $686,596. 77. The whole of this line has been excavated, and the distance appears to be 59 3-4 miles.

It would seem that it has been unwisely located and very unfaithfully executed, and that a fatal error has been committed in attempting to supply its whole length from the Lehigh river. Other feeders have since been introduced, viz.: one for conveying into the canal the waters of Durham creek is 1890 feet long and 12 feet wide at the bottom; and another near Lumberville, introducing the waters of Milton creek, is 1509 feet long; and a wing dam has been erected at Well's Falls, with a water wheel to supply the canal with water from the combined locks near New Hope to Bristol. The Canal Commissioners in the report of 21st Dec., 1830, state the amount of expenditure at $1,178,,385. 61; and in their report of 15th Dec., 1831, add, that $97,330. 51 had been expended in repairs, &c. Since that period very large sums have been laid out upon this section, and one boat only laden with coal has passed through its whole length. At Bristol a large and commodious basin has been made for accommodation of the boats, &c., doing business upon the canal.

From Bristol, a line has been surveyed, terminating at Kensington, near Philadelphia. It runs from the former along the turnpike road to the Nashawiny creek, thence crossing the turnpike it passes between the turnpike and river, to the place of termination. The distance is 17½ miles, and the estimated cost for a five foot canal is $200,799,10. No portion of this line has been excavated, and it is not hazarding much to say, will not be, whilst vessels may float from Bristol to Philadelphia in one tide, on the broad bosom of the Delaware.

The communication from Philadelphia westward, by the improvements on the part of the Commonwealth, is by a rail way, which runs through the counties of Philadelphia, Montgomery, Delaware, Chester and Lancaster to Columbia, on the Susquehannah, and there connects with the great central line of canal and portage, leading to Pittsburg. The whole line from the intersection of Vine and Broad streets, pursuing the old canal line, and crossing at Peter's farm, to the end of the canal basin at Columbia, is 81⅗ miles—5 miles only, longer than the present turnpike road. From Vine and Broad streets to the foot of the Schuylkill inclined plain, the distance is two miles and two thirds. The foot of the plain is 47 feet 9 in. above mean high tide, and the railway runs nearly on that level from Philadelphia to that place. The Schuylkill plane is 2714 ft. long, and its elevation from foot to head is 18 ft. The plane at Columbia is 1914 feet in length, and has an elevation from foot to head of 90 ft. The surface in the canal basin at Columbia, is 237½ ft. above mean high tide in the Schulykill at Fair Mount, and 19 ft. 4 inches above low water mark in the Susquehannah. At the heads of the inclined plains at Schuylkill and Columbia, it is intended to station steam engines of from 90 to 50 horse power. The line of location of this railway seems unparallelled for its facilities and advantages. The highest point on the line is at the gap of Mine Ridge, thirty miles east of the basin of Columbia. But by a cut of 31¼ feet, for a short distance this is reduced 560 ft. above mean high tide, to 327¼ above the head of the plane at the Schuylkill, and to 233 feet above that at Columbia. Although the cutting on the location is generally light, except at the gap mentioned, yet the elevation will not on any part of the distance between the head of the place at Schuylkill, and the head of the place at Columbia, a space, of 77 miles exceed 30 ft. to the mile in either direction, being less than one third of a degree. "In practice," say the Canal Commissioners in their report of December, 1830, it will be found that a locomotive engine with 20 tons of lading will travel the whole distance from Columbia to Philadelphia in a day of 10 hours. The rise in the direction of the greatest trade from the head of the place at Columbia to the summit of Mine Gap Ridge, is about 233 ft.; the rest of the distance is nearly level or descending. A good Pennsylvania waggon horse, will, on this railway, convey ten tons a distance of 27 miles per day with ease.

The Schuylkill river at Peters' island, is crossed by a viaduct of stone, 980 feet long, which is also intended to be a road bridge for travellers. Many other extensive viaducts are formed on the route. But we believe the most remerkable are those over the Great and Little Conestoga creeks; the first 1400 feet in length, and 23 in breadth, standing on 10 piers; and the second, on the plan of Mr. Burr's bridges, is 40 feet above the surface of the water, and about 1000 feet in length. The whole line of this road is constructed on the plan of the latest improvements in rail roads, and in the most substantial manner. The commissioners in their report of December 15, 1831, declare their belief that 17 miles of single track, from the Schuylkill westward, and 12 and a half miles from Columbia eastward, will be laid by the first day of May next, and may be extended for the whole line by the 4th day of Dec. next; and that the entire work, which will consist of a double track, can be completed in two years: and they estimate the whole cost at $2,297,120 21, being equal to $28,173 63 per mile.

From Columbia the reader will now betake himself with us to the eastern division of the Pennsylvania canal, which mounts the eastern bank of the Susquehannah from Columbia to a point opposite to Duncan's island, then crosses the Susquehannah by a towing path bridge, and terminates at the outlet lock of the Susquehannah division, at Duncan's island. There is a feeding dam across the river here, 1998 ft. long, 8 1-2 ft. high, with a base of 30 feet, composed of strong timbers cubbed together; running through Lancaster and Dauphin counties, a distance of 42 miles and 85 hundredths of a mile. This portion is divided into two sections. The first, $18\frac{7}{8}$ miles in length, lies between the town of Columbia and the Swatara river. Ten miles of it have been completed, and the remainder is expected to be finished during the year 1832. The prominent works on this part of the line, are an aqueduct over the Swatara, 300 feet long and 18 feet wide, with a road bridge attached to it; two outlet locks of 10 ft. lift each, and 100 by $17\frac{1}{2}$ feet in the chambers, to connect the basin at Columbia with the river Susquehannah; and two lift locks, overcoming a fall of 16 feet.

The remainder of this division, extending from Middletown, where it unites with the Union canal, and where outlet locks connect it with the Susquehannah river, is in length 24 miles, and was the first portion of the state canal put under contract. There are on this portion, 6 lift locks on the main line; 1 lock of 3 feet, leading from the main line to the basin at Middletown, and 2 locks from the basin to the river, having each 9 feet lift. The canal on this division is 28 feet wide at bottom; 40 feet at top water line, and 4 feet deep. The top water line of the basin in which the Pennsylvania and Union canals unite, is 52 1-2 feet above that of the basin at Columbia, and 290 feet above tide. The top water of the large basin at Harrisburg is 312 feet, and the surface line of the pool around Duncan's island 332 feet above tide.

The cost of this division is by estimate for the first portion, - -	$585,501
And actual expenditure for the second, - - -	832,036
	$1,417,537

Being arrived at the west end of the east division of the Pennsylvania canal, we may choose whether to proceed immediately westward by the Juniata, or northward by the Susquehannah. As the latter is the shorter route, we will ask the reader to bear us company upon that.

The Susquehannah division commences at the termination of the eastern division, at the outlet lock on Duncan's island, and runs along the west side of the Susquehannah river, through the counties of Perry, Mifflin and Union, and terminates at the south end of the towing path bridge, at Northumberland. Its length by the towing path, is 39 miles. The country through which it passes is favorable, the bottoms wide and gently sloping to the river; the excavation easy, and material for banks good. The original estimate for constructing this division, was $598,376 32

The actual cost has been - - - - 1,039,256 78

There are eleven locks on the line.

At Northumberland, which we have now reached, we may again choose to proceed westward or northward by the canal. We shall again take the latter. A dam has been constructed across the main stream, below the confluence of the west and north branches, which should, perhaps, have been described in the last division. It is 9 1-2 feet high above the bottom of the river, and 2783 feet long: there is a shute in it, for the passing of rafts, 62 feet wide, and 650 feet long. This dam has been twice built, and each time unfaithfully executed, and has cost near $82,500. It supplies the Susquehannah division.

The north branch division commences at the canal basin, in the town of Northumberland, and runs a northeasterly course along the northern bank of the Susquehannah, through the counties of Northumberland, Columbia and Luzerne, to the entrance of the Wyoming valley. Its length, from the basin at Northumberland to the feeder dam at Nanticoke falls, is 55 miles and a half. The country, like that of the last sections, was generally favorably adapted to canals. The canal has the same width and depth as below. There are on this division, 7 lift and 1 guard locks, constructed of wood, 17 ft. wide, and 90 ft. long in the chambers. The rise from the top water line in the basin at Northumberland, to the surface line of the pool at Nanticoke, is 68$\frac{89}{100}$ ft. The comb of the feeder dam at the latter place, is 8 ft. $\frac{34}{100}$, above four feet water in the canal. The dam carries a pool five miles above it, into Wyoming valley, and within two miles and a half of Wilkesbarre. The original estimate of cost for this division was $407,335 30. But the actual cost, exclusive of repairs, was $1,096,178 34½.

The Wyoming line of the north branch division commences at the Nanticoke dam and extends up the stream 16 miles and 316 perches, to a point near the mouth of the Lackawannock creek, where it is supplied with water by a feeder from the creek, 203½ perches in length. There are 13 miles and 11 perches of canal, and 3 miles and 305 perches of slackwater and towing path. The most important mechanical works here, are, 1 aqueduct and 5 lift locks. The whole lockage is 43 feet. The canal runs on the Wilkesbarre side of the river. A side cut, and an outlet lock into the river at Forty fort, is proposed for the accommodation of the inhabitants on the western side. The Wyoming division, it is contemplated, will be completed in the fall of 1832. Its estimated cost is $220,594 56. When this line shall have been completed, a water communication will have been made to the heart of the coal region of Luzerne county.

We must now descend the stream to the junction of the west branch, to describe the west branch division, which commences at the south end of the towing path bridge, across the western arm of the Susquehannah at Northumberland, and runs along the east side of the stream through the county of Northumberland, to the feeder dam at Muncy hill, a distance of 23 miles and a quarter. The towing path extends along the pool, some distance farther, making the whole length of navigation 24 miles and a half. The country through which this canal runs, was most favorable for the purpose. The river bottoms are very wide, their slopes gradual, the lands generally cleared. The soil sandy loam or gravel, with little rock, and the lockage inconsiderable. There are on this division, six lift locks, and one guard lock, overcoming a rise of 41 ft. The comb of Muncy dam is one foot above the canal level at the guard lock, and 9 feet above low water in the river below the dam. The pool extends above 2 miles. The estimated cost of this division, was - $197,851

Actual cost, - - - - - - - 426,791

It was filled for navigation in November, 1830, but the unusual floods of 1831 undermined the dam. It has since, however, been rebuilt; but the navigation upon the division has been inconsiderable. A small prong extends 200 perches from the main stem of the west branch division, to Lewisburg in Union county. There will be on it, one dam 2½ feet high, across the river, and 2 locks overcoming a lockage of 21 ft. The contract was made for this work for the sum of $22,000; the work to be finished by the 1st day of September 1832.

The Lycoming line of the west branch division commences at the head of the pool of the Muncy dam, and extends thence along the valley of the river 41 miles 68 perches, to the Big island opposite to the mouth of Bald Eagle creek. On this line there are 31 miles and 12 perches canal, and 10 miles 56 perches slackwater and towing path; 7 dams, varying from 4 to 10 feet in height; 4 aqueducts, and 12 guard and lift locks, which overcome a rise of 80 ft. The estimate of the cost of this line, which it is supposed may be completed in December, 1832, is $500,587 54. But to render this line profitable, it must be extended 5 miles further up the river to the coal beds, and a cross cut of 3 miles and 132 perches, must be made between the pool of the dam at the Great island and Bald Eagle creek.

We must now descend the main Susquehannah to Duncan's island, for the purpose of pursuing the route of the Juniata river westward.

From the outlet lock at the end of the eastern division, to the point on Duncan's island, at which the Juniata division commences, the distance is 1 mile and $\frac{53}{100}$. The rise from the surface line of the pool in the Susquehannah, at the outlet, to the top water line at the commencement of the Juniata division, is 20 ft. 9 inches. This portion of the canal forms part of the Susquehannah division.

The Juniata division commences on Duncan's island, in the county of Dauphin, and runs through the counties of Perry, Mifflin and Huntingdon, to a point one fourth of a mile above the town of Huntingdon. Its length by the towing path, is 89 ms. The top water line at the connection of the Juniata and Susquehannah divisions, on Duncan's island, is 352½ ft. above mean high tide at Philadelphia. This is a very difficult and expensive division. The entire course of the Juniata river is through a mountainous country. The mountains are very high, their sides steep and rocky; in some cases extending parallel with the stream; in others, their general range intersects the stream, leaving merely a gap for its passage. The margin between the mountains and the river, is, in many places, very contracted. The banks are generally bold and well adapted for slackwater navigation. The dimensions of the canal are the same as on the other sections. In its course there are 35 lift locks, 3 guard locks, 1 outlet and 4 river locks. The lift locks are 15 by 90 feet in the chambers; the lockage is 251½ feet. The top water line at Huntingdon 604 ft. 3 in. above tide. There are on this division, 4 dams from 8 to 9 feet high; 19 aqueducts; 25 waste weirs, and 60 culverts. The division is completed and in excellent order for navigation. The estimates for constructing this division, were $1,741,508. The first contracts were made in August, 1827. The actual cost, including damages, but excluding repairs, was $2,490,290 13½.

The Frankstown line of the Juniata division extends from a point, one third of a mile above Huntingdon to Hollidaysburg. It is 38 miles 102 perches in length, of which 22 miles and 156 perches will be canal, and 15 miles 266 perches slackwater navigation, made by 14 dams in the river. At Hollidaysburg a basin, 1650 feet long, and 120 feet wide, has been located, where a connection is established with the Allegheny portage road. Two feeders will supply the first level; a dam will be built in the Beaver Dam branch at Hollidaysburg, and the pool of the dam, which is crossed by the rail road, will also answer for a basin. It will be 150 feet in length, and 100 feet wide. The two basins are connected by a short feeder canal, 36 perches long, of the same dimensions as the main canal. Another feeder is taken from the south fork of the Juniata;—it is 3 miles and 48 perches long, and 10 feet wide at the bottom. On this line there are 14 dams, varying from 5 to 27 1-2 feet in height; 6 aqueducts; 6 towing path bridges crossing the river; 8 guard, and 43 lift locks, overcoming a rise of 330 3-4 feet. It is supposed that this line may be completed in October, 1832, and that its cost will be $698,181 56.

The Allegheny portage rail road, commences at the east end of the lower basin at Hollidaysburg, and crosses the Allegheny mountain to the west end of the basin at Johnstown. Its length is 36 miles and 221 perches; but between the head of the basin at Johnstown and the Upper basin at Hollidaysburg, the distance is only 35 miles and 310 perches. The summit of the mountain where the rail road crosses it, is $1398\frac{71}{100}$ feet above the eastern and $1171\frac{58}{100}$ ft. above the western basin; and 2332 feet above the tide water of the Delaware. Connections will be formed between the rail road and canal, by piers and slips, at both ends of each basin. These piers and slips have been set apart for the use of the commonwealth, and will occupy the whole ground (about 100 ft. wide) between the basins and the rail road, for 150 ft. in length at the west end, and 200 ft. at the east end of each basin.

A space of 120 feet wide has been staked out and appropriated to the use of the commonwealth, the entire length of the rail road, upon the supposition that the incalculable trade of the Mississippi basin and the lakes, will require an additional number of tracks over the mountain. The bed of the road is graded 25 ft. wide, for a double set of tracks. There will be five inclined planes on each side of the mountain intended for stationary engines, as soon as the quantity of trade passing over the road shall require so much power. Horse power may be used in the commencement, as the inclination of none of the planes is greater than many portions of our turnpike roads; the greatest angle of inclination with the horizon being only 5 deg. 51 min. and 9 seconds. But in as much as the trade from the west will greatly overbalance that from the east, and the bituminous coal at and near the summit of the mountain, can be used to equalize the preponderance, it is believed that on the east side of the mountain, the rise of the planes may be overcome on the self acting principle; thus making gravity the motive power, thereby dispensing with horses and steam on the five eastern planes. The most important works on the Allegheny portage, are a tunnel about 19 miles west of the crest of the mountain; it is 900 feet long and 16 feet wide: an ovaduct of stone with a single arch of 80 feet span, over the Little Conemaugh; and also one of wood, of two spans of 33 feet each over the Beaver Dam branch of the Juniata. The rail road, when completed with a double set of tracks of stone and iron, with the necessary machinery, is estimated to cost $1,271,718 18. One set of tracks it is supposed will be laid along the whole line by the first of May, 1833; and that the entire work may be completed by the first day of September of that year.

Having thus in the most speedy, agreeable and advantageous manner, surmounted the great Allegheny, and descended to the basin at Johnstown, we embark upon the western division of the Pennsylvania canal. From this point the canal runs through the counties of Cambria, Indiana, Westmoreland, Armstrong, Butler and Allegheny, and terminates in the Monongahela river, at Pittsburg. Whole length, 105 miles. From Johnstown to the Allegheny river it pursues the valley of Conemaugh or Kiskiminitas river, these names being given to parts of the same stream. This, throughout its whole course of 74 miles, is a narrow stream, with high steep banks, well adapted for slackwater navigation. There is upon it 27 miles of slack water, and the canal commissioners have expressed regret that the proportion of such navigation had not been greater. On the 30 miles of canal between Johnstown and Blairsville, the average fall of the river, is upwards of eight feet per mile, requiring equal to one lock per mile. Below Blairsville to the Monongahela, the fall is but 3 feet per mile, requiring 1 lock per two miles and a half.

The canal crosses the Allegheny river above the Kiskiminitas by an aqueduct, and thence follows the western bank of the river about 30 miles nearly to its mouth, where it re-crosses the stream, and by a tunnel through Grant's hill, unites by outlet locks with the Monongahela. Outlet locks also connect it with the Allegheny river on the north side of the town.

The estimated cost of the whole western division, was $1,498,910 10. The actual cost, including repairs, has been $2,873,217. This portion of the Pennsylvania canal is in good order and in daily use.

It is proposed to connect lake Erie with Conneaut lake, in Crawford county; and from that point by separate routes, with the Allegheny river and the Ohio. The first of these routes is nearly completed. The French creek feeder extends 19 1-2 miles; a further extension on the western end of 3 miles, now being made, or actually made, will connect it with the Conneaut lake, and of 160 perches at the north end will connect it with French creek, near Meadville. The Franklin line of this division commences on the Allegheny river, at the mouth of French creek, and extends up the latter stream 22 miles and 88 perches to its intersection with the feeder. On this line there are five miles and 52 perches of canal, and 17 miles and 36 perches of slack water and towing path. The principal works are 11 dams, varying from 7 to 16 feet in height, and 3 guard and 16 lift locks, which overcome a rise of 120 1-2 ft. The estimated cost is $270,681 32. It is supposed that it may be completed by the 15th of November, 1832.

The second route is by the Beaver division, which commences on the Ohio river at the mouth of Big Beaver, and extends up the Beaver and Shenango creeks $24\frac{3}{4}$ miles to the town of New Castle. Of this division there are 8 miles 16 perches of canal, and 16 miles 224 perches of slackwater and towing path. There are on it 7 dams, varying from 7 to 14 feet in height, 2 aqueducts, and 17 guard and lift locks, overcoming a rise of 132 feet. The two outlet locks will each be 25 feet wide, and 120 feet long within the chambers. They are designed to admit the smaller class of steamboats that ply in the Ohio, into the pool of the first dam, to accommodate the trade of the town of Beaver and the villages near it. The estimated cost of this division is $335,317 82. The whole of the line to New Castle, it is supposed will be finished by the 1st day of December, 1832. From New Castle, the work is destined to run northward through Mercer county to Conneaut lake, in Crawford, and thence to lake Erie. It is also contemplated by means of the valley of Mahoning river, to connect this line with the state of Ohio.

The expenses of these stupendous works have been indeed very great, and have in all instances exceeded much the original estimates of their cost. The treasury has been compelled to encounter the loss consequent upon the ignorance and inexperience of legislators and canal commissioners, engineers, and contractors; which, when applied in such extensive scope as these works afforded, could not fail to be heavy

Besides, much loss has been sustained by the elements, the force of which it is not practicable at all times to calculate, nor consequently to provide against. The sum actually expended, by the report of the canal commissioners, 31st Dec. 1831, was twelve millions, one hundred and twenty-six thousand, nine hundred and sixty-one dollars, and fifty-five cents.

Bridges. The numerous bridges of Pennsylvania have given it the name of the "*State of Bridges.*" It is impossible to procure a full descriptive list of their number. Between 60 and 70 companies have been incorporated for building bridges, and above 50 have been constructed by those which have gone into operation, at an expense of $2,750,000. But in many of the counties, very large and expensive bridges have been erected at county charge, costing from 30 to 40, and even 60,000 dollars each. These structures are usually of stone. We shall describe the principal bridges over the Delaware, the Schuylkill, the Susquehannah, the Allegheny, Monongahela, and other rivers, when speaking of the counties in which they are severally located. The following table exhibits the principal ones, including such as have been constructed by the aid of the commonwealth. The wooden bridges of Pennsylvania are unrivalled in number, in magnitude, and in boldness of design. They have been adopted as models in several parts of Europe.

BRIDGE COMPANIES.

Date of Act.	*Title.*	*Counties.*
25th Mar. 1823,	Juniata bridge company,	Huntingdon.
18th Mar. 1826,	Lehigh water gap, in Lehigh and	Northampton.
"	Lehigh at Kantz's ford,	do.
29th Mar. 1827,	Susquehannah, near the north line of the state,	Susquehannah.
17th April, 1827,	" at or near Athens,	Bradford.
27th Mar. "	Lehigh, at Bethlehem,	Lehigh.
5th Mar. 1828,	Juniata, at Mifflin,	Mifflin.
14th April, "	Manyunk—over the river Schuylkill,	Philadelphia.
31st Mar. "	West branch Susquehannah,	Northumberland.
16th Mar. 1830,	Monongahela bridge company at Brownsville,	Fayette.
2d April, "	Conemaugh, at Clark's ferry,	Westmoreland.
6th April, "	Juniata, at Huntingdon,	Huntingdon.
"	West branch of the Susquehannah, at Milton,	Northumberland.
"	Schuylkill, at Norristown,	Montgomery.
17th Jan. 1831,	West branch Susquehannah, at Clearfield,	Clearfield.
14th Mar. "	North east branch Susquehannah, at Towanda,	Bradford.
23d Mar. "	Youghiogheny river, at Robbstown,	Westmoreland.
30th Mar. "	Susquehannah, York Haven,	Lancaster York.
14th Mar. "	Conemaugh, near Saltzberg,	Indiana.
1st April, "	Delaware, at Taylorsville,	Bucks.
"	Lehigh river, above Lizzard creek,	Northampton.
"	McMichael's creek, Stroud t-ship,	do.
"	Loyalhanna,	Westmoreland.

To this table may be added the bridge over the Susquehannah at Danville, to which the legislature has contributed 10,000 dollars; over the Schuylkill at Norristown, 6,000; over French creek at Franklin, 5,000. And the sums expended by the state, in subscription to aid the repairs of the bridge over the Susquehannah at Columbia, and that over the Monongahela at Pittsburg, both destroyed by freshets in 1832.

es for erecting which have received letters patent, showing the rivers and streams over which they pass, the years in which they
gth and width, elevation above the usual level of the water, and whether roofed or not, the number of arches by which suppor
s also the amount of individual and state subscriptions to the capital stock, the subscription price of the shares; and the amou

EAMS.	Length between abut- ments.	Width	Individ- ual sub- scrip- tion.	State subscrip tion.	Or'gnl price of shares	Debts of the co.	Elev'n above levelof water.	No. of arches	Piers com- posed of	Roofed or not.	When made passable	RE
	Feet.	*Feet.*					*Feet.*					
.	1122	38	45,435	40,000	25	9,814	38	6	Dressed stone	Roofed	1819	
nc.	600	20	9,500	15,000	—		40	4	Timber	Roofed	1816	Destroyed by a t
1.	500	20	6,000		25		18	5	Wood	nt roofed	1815	Destroyed by an
rn route.	295	28	10,000	5,000	50	—	35	1		to be r.	Unfin'd.	
	1064	—	160,000		100		28	5	Stone	Roofed	1806	
e.	1050	33	160,000		50		21	6	Stone	Roofed	1814	Cost of bridge n of capital is e
	—	—	—	—	—	—	—	—				
	570	29	50,000		100		45	3	Stone & timber	Roofed	1806	
glass manf.	720	30	11,300		50	1,100	28	5	Stone & wood		Unfin'd.	
lin.	300	30	7,000	3,000	25	—	30	3	Stone	Roofed	1821	Unofficial. No
.	—	—	—	—	—	—	—	—				Project abandon
ap.	—	—	—	—	—	—	—	—			Unfin'd.	Swept away by I
on.	530	32	15,000		50	1,000	22	chains	Stone	nt roofed	1814	
urg.	1500	37	57,450	40,000	25	5,000	—	8	Stone	Roofed	1818	
e.	—	—	—	—	—	—	—	—				Not commenced.
m. bridge.)	550	42	300,000		10		31	3	Stone	Roofed	1805	Cost of this brid pital, $150,000
	—	—	—	—	—	—	—	—				
pper Ferry.	348	35	80,200		50	43,826	35	1	No piers	Roofed	1812	Greatest arch in
s.	316	18	40,000		50	1,650	24	3	Stone	Roofed	1817	Carried away by
k.	187	21	10,150		50		23	1	No piers	Roofed	1810	
's Ford.	—	—	—	—	—	—	—	—				Destroyed by ice
n.	340	28	10.850	3,000	50	not known	18	2	Stone	Roofed	1821	
l's Ferry.	600	—	29,500	20,000	100	6,000	50	2	Stone	Roofed	1817	Destroyed by ice
a.	5690	30	419,400	90,000	100		23	53	Stone	Roofed	1814	Cost of bridge, capital employ
	—	—	—	—	—	—	—	—				
.	—	—	—	—	—	—	—	—				Project abandon
rg.	2876	40	65,000	90,000	20		50	12	Stone	Roofed	1817	This bridge is in by an Island.
	—	—	—	—	—	—	—	—				
nberland.	1825	32	40,000	50,000	25	800	41	8	Stone	Roofed	1814	This bridge the s
Derr'stown.	1120	30	40,000	20,000	50		25	5	Stone	Roofed	1818	
ck.	1256	28	23,000	8,000	100		30	6		Roofed	1818	
arre.	700	28	27,435	13,000	50	12,000	30	4	Stone	Roofed	1819	
at Bend.	600	20	6,500		50		8	9 piers	Timber	nt roofed	1814	
oga Point.	450	28	5,500		50	—	26	4	Stone	nt roofed	1820	
			1629200	382,000		81,190						

SYNOPSIS OF THE CONSTITUTION.

* The present constitution of Penn. was adopted in 1790. By it the political power is distributed into three divisions, the legislative, executive, and judicial.

The *legislative power* is vested in a general assembly, composed of a senate and house of representatives. Members of the first are chosen for four years, in and for districts designated septennially. Their number is fixed by the legislature, at not less than one fourth, nor greater than one third of that of the number of representatives. The *representatives* are chosen annually, and senators, when to be elected, on the second Tuesday of October. Their number cannot be less than 60, nor more than 100. The general assembly meets on the first Tuesday of December annually.

The supreme executive power is vested in a governor, who is elected by a majority of votes triennially, on the first Tuesday of October; he cannot hold his office longer than nine, in any term of twelve years. His salary is four thousand dollars per annum.

The judicial power is vested in a supreme court, in courts of oyer and terminer and general gaol delivery, in a court of common pleas, orphans court, registers court, and a court of quarter sessions of the peace for each county, in justices of the peace, and such other courts as the legislature may from time to time establish. The judges of the supreme court, and the several courts of common pleas, are appointed by the governor, and hold their offices during good behavior.

By the act of 20th April, 1829, the senate consists of thirty-three members, at a ratio of 7,700 taxables to each senator; and the house of representatives of one hundred members, at a ratio of 2,544 taxables to a representative. The wages of the members are three dollars per day, of the clerks $300 per ann., and $4 per day during the session. The state is divided into twenty-five senatorial districts, constituted as follows:—1st. city of Philadelphia, which elects two senators; 2d. county of Philadelphia, two; 3d. Montgomery county, one; 4th. Delaware and Chester, two; 5th. Bucks, one; 6th. Berks and Schuylkill, two; 7th. Lancaster county, two; 8th. Dauphin and Lebanon, one; 9th. Northumberland and Union, one: 10th. Luzerne and Columbia, one; 11th. Bradford, Susquehannah and Tioga, one; 12th. Northampton, Lehigh, Wayne and Pike, two; 13th. Lycoming, Centre, Clearfield, McKean and Potter, one; 14th. York and Adams, two; 15th. Franklin, one; 16th. Cumberland and Perry, one; 17th. Huntingdon, Mifflin, (*Juniata*) and Cambria, one; 18th. Westmoreland, one; 19th. Fayette and Greene, one; 20th. Washington, one; 21st. Allegheny, one; 22d. Somerset and Bedford, one; 23d. Erie, Crawford, and Mercer, one; 24th, Venango, Warren, Armstrong, Indiana and Jefferson, one; and 25th. Beaver and Butler, one.

(For the distribution of the members among the counties, we refer to the table of population, page 34.)

The principal executive officers established by the constitution and the laws, are the governor, the secretary of the commonwealth, state treasurer, auditor general, surveyor general, secretary of the land office, the board of property, the attorney general, the board of canal commissioners, and the commissioners of the internal improvement fund. The subordinate ones are sheriffs, coroners, county commissioners, constables, overseers of the poor, roads, &c.

The militia of the state is organized in 16 divisions, of two brigades each. Every white male citizen between 18 and 45 years, except United States officers, drivers of the mail stage, ferrymen on post roads, post masters, ministers of religion, school masters, pilots, sheriffs, jailors, or judges of courts, must be enrolled. Major generals are elected by the brigadier generals and field officers, and the brigadier generals and all inferior commissioned officers, by the enrolled citizens, every seven years: none but citizens of the United States are eligible. The militia is paraded, and trained in companies on the first Monday, and in battalion on the second Monday in May every year, under penalty of one dollar fine for each day's absence for privates, two dollars for subalterns, three dollars for captains, and five dollars for field officers. Fines to be collected on the warrant of the brigade inspector, by levy on the goods of the delinquent. Volunteers may be separately organized, and elect their own officers; make their own by-laws; appropriate their fines to the use of the com-

* For want of room, the publisher is obliged to substitute a synopsis of the constitution, for a correct and full one, prepared by the author

pany or battalion, and are armed by the state. Volunteers who have served seven years are exempt from duty, except in case of invasion. The discipline of the militia is the same as that prescribed for the army of the United States.

The grand total of the militia of Pennsylvania in 1830, was **178,942**, to wit: 16 generals of division, 32 of brigade and their staffs, and one adjutant general, 207; infantry militia, including officers, **145,894**; volunteer cavalry, 1,891; volunteer artillery, **2,943**; volunteer infantry, **17,372**; and volunteer riflemen, 10,842.

The state had in her arsenals, or in possession of volunteers, 46 pieces of ordnance, 24,863 muskets and rifles, 2,760 tents, &c. &c.

REVENUE.

The revenue of the state is derived from the following sources, and for the year 1831, in the quantities respectively affixed to the several items.

From lands, to wit, amount of purchase money, with interest thereon, - - - -	91,102 68	
Fees on warrants and patents, - - - -	10,567 92	
Office fees, - - - - - -	1,658 58	
		103,329 18
Auctions, viz. auctioneers' commissions, - -	12,100 00	
Auction duties - - -	126,504 85	
		138,604 85
Dividends on stocks belonging to the state, viz. on		
Bank stock, - - - - - -	106,498 50	
Bridge, canal, and turnpike stocks, - -	34,398 12	
		140,896 62
Taxes, viz. On bank dividends, - - -	30,572 98	
On offices, - - - - -	7,464 53	
On writs, - - - - -	18,979 89	
Tavern licenses, - - -	40,146 94	
On dealers in foreign merchandize, - -	51,445 38	
On collateral inheritances, - - -	19,062 81	
On tin and clock pedlars' licences - -	2,029 33	
Hawkers' and pedlars' licences - - -	1,593 60	
		171,295 46
Fees in the office of secretary of state, - -	448 60	
State maps sold, - - - - -	446 26	
Pamphlet laws sold, - - - - -	81 88	
Militia and exempt fines, - - - - -	1,381 41	
Canal tolls, - - - - - -	38,241 20	
		40,599 35
The preceding may be considered permanent sources of revenue, varying only in their products.		594,725 46
The following receipts are accidental:		
Escheats, - - - - - - -	20	
Loans, - - - - - -	2,199,948 54	
Premiums on loans, - - -	103,196 91	
From the commissioners of internal improvement fund,	125,000	
Old debts and miscellaneous, - - - -	11,087 66	
		3,033,978 57

The expenditures for the year 1832, were for

Internal improvements, - - - -	2,335,373 72
Expenses of government, - - - -	195,306 91
Militia expenses, - - - -	20,525 72
Members of courts martial, - - - -	2,343 28
Pensions and gratuities, - - -	22,226 84
Education, - - - -	11,185 13
Interest on loans, - - - -	91,525 00
Internal improvement fund, - -	362,682 40
State maps, - - - - -	329 75
Penitentiary at Philadelphia, - -	3,746 53
Penitentiary near Pittsburg. -	2,624 25

Conveying convicts, - - - - -	1,177 96	
Conveying fugitives, - - - - -	596 06	
Pennsylvania claimants, - - - - -	56 55	
Defence of the state, - - - - -	107 50	
Miscellaneous, - - - - -	9,128 94	
		$3,058,926 54

The state possesses at present a very small portion of unsold lands, which are valuable, except some reserves in the new counties and county towns. A part of the proceeds of sales of her lands, have been invested in the stock of the Pennsylvania Bank, but large sums are still due from purchasers,

Supposed about, - - - -	2,000,000 00	
She possesses bank stock, - - -	2,108,700 00	
Turnpike stock, - - - -	1,911,243 39	
Bridge stock, - - - -	410,000 00	
Canal stock, - - - -	200,000	
		$6,629,943 39

The commonwealth was indebted, Jan. 1831, for

Turnpike appropriations, - - -	112,324 98	
Bridge do. - - - - -	6,000	
River do. - - - - -	18,190 52	
Miscellaneous claims, - - - -	33,614 98	
On loans, - - - -	12,140,000 00	
She has borrowed during the year 1831, -	2,199,948 54	
		$14,509,989 02

This debt must be reduced, however, by so much of the appropriations for turnpikes and bridges, as was paid during the year 1831, amounting perhaps to a sum as large as that charged above to those accounts.

By the act of 25th March, 1831, all ground rents, moneys at interest, and all debts due from solvent debtors, whether by promissory note, except bank notes, penal or single bill, bond, judgment, mortgage and stocks in corporations, (wherein shares have been subscribed in money,) and on which any dividend or profit is received by the holder thereof, and public stocks, except stocks issued by the commonwealth, and all pleasure carriages kept for use, are subjected to a yearly tax of one mill on every dollar of the value thereof; to be assessed in the manner prescribed by the act, and collected as the county rates and levies; and to be paid by the county treasurers into the state treasury. And the sum so raised, is vested in the commissioners of the internal improvement fund, and applied to the payment of interest chargeable on that fund. This act is limited to five years from its date.

By another act of the same date, the commissioners of each county are required, during the continuance of the act, to add yearly to the county rates and levies for the use of the commonwealth, one mill upon the dollar of the adjusted valuation of all the real and personal property, persons, trades, and occupations, now taxable, for the purpose of raising county rates and levies, to be paid into the county treasury; and by the county treasurers into the state treasury; to be vested also in the commissioners of the internal improvement fund, and applied to the payment of interest chargeable to said fund. And such fund is to be charged with the same, and the school fund to be credited therewith, and with the interest at five per cent. annually, until the school fund shall be sufficient to produce an annual interest at that rate, of one hundred thousand dollars; when the proceeds of such fund is to be distributed, and applied to the support of common schools.

Provisions for Education. "*Knowledge is power.*" It is more, it is virtue, and the means of happiness: and so strongly impressed were the framers of the constitution of Pennsylvania with this truth, that they made it the duty of the legislature to provide for the establishment of schools throughout the state, in such manner that the *poor* may be taught gratis. Had the constitution required that a general and uniform provision should be made for the education of the citizens, without discrimination, it would have been wiser and probably more effective. The necessity of such a general provision is but too apparent, since "more than one half the children of the commonwealth, between the ages of 5 and 15 years, have not the benefit of school instruction;—hence a large proportion of our adult population can neither read nor write; and in some places the inhabitants of whole districts are growing up destitute of instruction, unacquainted with their duty as citizens, unfortified by the influence of religion, and left to become fit subjects for that wild spirit of party that has so often shaken to the centre our social relations—or to be the perpetrators of crime, and the miserable inmates of our gaols and penitentiaries."—(*Report of committee of legislature*, 1831.)

From the adoption of the constitution of 1790, until 1809, no legislative provision of a general nature was made. An act was then passed "for the education of the *poor, gratis*." It required a report to be made by the assessors of the townships, wards, and boroughs, to the commissioners of the respective counties, of all children between the ages of five and 12 years, whose parents were unable to provide for their education: and that when the lists had been approved by the commissioners, that such parents should be notified thereof, and be permitted to send their children to the most convenient schools, at the expense of the county. This law has many important defects; the chief of which is, the brand of pauper, which it stamps upon the pupils; the opportunity it afforded for deception in the undue gratification, the cupidity of teachers, and their total irresponsibility. Notwithstanding its defects, however, this act continued in force until it was repealed by that of 29th March, 1824; providing, that every township should elect three "schoolmen," who should superintend the education of the poor children within their townships, and "cause them to be instructed as other children are treated; the expenses of tuition to be paid by the county." But each county might authorise the schoolmen to divide the township into school districts, and to establish schools at the township expense, to which all children belonging to the district might be sent for 3 years, at any time between the ages of 6 and 14 years. This law was applicable to the whole state, with the exception of certain school districts in the city and county of Philadelphia, and city and county of Lancaster. It was repealed in 1826, and the act of 1809 was revived.

By the act of 2d April, 1831, however, the basis of an efficient school fund was laid. The secretary of the commonwealth, the auditor general, and the secretary of the land office were appointed commissioners to receive and manage the school fund, with power to receive and hold for the use thereof, all gifts, grants, and donations that may be made thereto; and all the monies due the commonwealth by the holders of unpatented lands; also all monies secured to the commonwealth by mortgages or liens on land for the purchase money of the same; (this land debt is estimated at two millions of dollars,) as also all fees received in the land office, with the addition of the sum of one mill on the dollar, added to the county rates by the act of 25th March, 1831, are assigned to the common school fund, and held by the commonwealth for the use thereof, at the interest of five per cent. per annum. The interest is directed to be added to the principal as it becomes due, and the whole amount to be holden by the commonwealth, subject to the payment of interest on loans made to the state for internal improvements, until the interest shall amount to one hundred thousand dollars annually, after which the interest is to be distributed annually to the support of common schools, throughout the commonwealth, in such manner as shall hereafter be provided by law.

The committee who reported the bill making this liberal appropriation, anticipate that a few years (four,) will produce the sum requisite for distribution, and that thenceforward the means will be available, for supporting an efficient system of education, that may be enjoyed by every citizen of the commonwealth.

Besides the general provisions for education above noticed, special ones have been enacted for portions of the state. Thus in 1818, the city and county of Philadelphia were erected into a district, called the "first school district" of Pennsylvania, the peculiar organization of which we have described in the article "*Philadelphia*." By the act April 1, 1822, the city and county of Lancaster was erected into the "second school district," with privileges and duties similar to the first. By the act of 11th April, 1827, the same system was established at Harrisburg; and by act of 19th Feb. 1828, at Pittsburg.

Many scholastic institutions of the higher grade, have been long established in the commonwealth. The university of Pennsylvania, one of the most useful and respectable in the union, was first chartered in 1753, and received its present form in 1780. (*See Philadelphia.*) It has real and personal estate valued at $167,059 33, and an annual income of $15,290 39. The Western university was chartered in 1819. Six colleges have also been founded, viz. Dickinson college, at Carlisle, incorporated September 9th, 1783; Franklin college, at Lancaster, March 10, 1787; Washington college, at Washington, 1787; Jefferson college, at Canonsburg, January 15, 1802; Allegheny college, at Meadville, March 25, 1817; Lafayette college, at Easton, March, 1826. This last institution embraces, among other objects, instruction in military tactics, and civil engineering; and Madison college, at Uniontown, incorporated March 7, 1827, to which a department of agriculture is to be attached.

Academies, or high schools, designed for teaching the higher branches of English education, with the classical languages, and rudiments of mathematics, have been established in almost every county in the commonwealth; generally one in every county town, and sometimes in some other considerable towns of the county. Some of these colleges and academies are eminently useful; but most of them are hot bed plants, that require care and protection to make them fruitful. In the thickly populated counties, almost every neighborhood is provided with primary schools, in which reading, writing, and arithmetic, are taught. We refer the reader to the article Philadelphia, for a notice of the "Friends' schools," and other institutions of a literary character in that city. And we may also notice, that by the act of 23d April, 1829, the classical and agricultural school in Susquehannah county was established.

To most of these institutions, the legislature has granted considerable pecuniary aid; to the universities and colleges generally large sums, and to each of the academies two thousand dollars.

Maintenance of the poor. The system for the maintenance of the helpless poor, like most others in the United States, has been copied from that of England. It is avowedly bad, operating as an encouragement to indolence and vice, and is oppressive on the industrious. But no means have yet been proposed, which have tended greatly to its amelioration. By the general law, overseers of the poor are elected in March, annually, in each township, &c., who are empowered, with the concurrence of two justices of the peace, to assess the tax necessary; to contract with any person for a house or lodging, for keeping and employing the poor, and may take the benefit of their work towards their maintenance; to put out as apprentices all such poor children, whose parents are dead or unable to maintain them. Such overseers are bodies politic and corporate in law, and may take devices and bequests not exceeding in yearly value five hundred pounds. Each township or district is required to support only the poor legally settled therein, and has power to remove paupers to their places of settlement, and to prevent the residence of persons likely to become chargeable. A peculiar system exists in the city and part of the county of Philadelphia, for a knowledge of which we refer the reader to the article "Philadelphia." And in most of the southeastern and middle counties, alms houses on large and productive farms have been erected, by which employment is given to such paupers as are able to work, and the cost of maintenance is reduced. In some cases, these poor-house districts consist of one or more townships, but commonly they embrace the whole county. The directors of these institutions generally serve three years, one of whom is elected annually by the people. They draw upon the county treasury, under proper restriction, for the funds they need, and they settle their accounts annually with the county auditors. They are also a body politic in law. No compensation is allowed to the overseers, but the directors of county poor houses are usually paid a salary of forty dollars per annum. Persons refusing to perform a term of service are liable to a heavy fine.

Criminal Jurisprudence, and Penitentiary System. The history of Pennsylvania, even from her first colonization to the present time, displays a continued effort to ameliorate the criminal code, and improve prison discipline, and to render punishment, what philosophy and philanthropy teaches us it should be, at once the terror of evil doers, and the reclaimation of offenders. Our space does not permit us to trace her course in this labor of love, by which she has attained high consideration among the enlightened of both hemispheres, and we must confine ourselves to a concise notice of her last experiment on this interesting subject. The intercommunion of the prisoners of our penitentiaries having been found the greatest barrier to their reform, the idea of separate confinement very naturally suggested itself, to those who devoted themselves to the improvement of the penitentiary system. But solitary confinement without occupation, which was originally proposed, was deemed the severest of all punishments, as an outrage on humanity, which the spirit of the age would not tolerate, that must destroy the health of the prisoner, and result in rendering him an idiot or a madman, according to his peculiar temperament. The plan met with much resistance, notwithstanding which it was adopted by the legislature, and measures taken for its execution, by an act passed 3d March, 1818, authorizing the erection of the Western penitentiary at Pittsburg, and the act of 20th March, 1821, for the building of the Eastern penitentiary, at Philadelphia. The first was completed according to the original plan, in 1828, at an expense of $183,091 87½. But large additional expenditures have been rendered necessary, by modifications in the penal code. Both the Western and Eastern penitentiaries were built on a similar plan of construction, solely with a view to solitary confinement. The latter, however, is the larger, and the more perfectly adapted to its object, and we therefore give a description of it.

The Eastern state penitentiary is situated on one of the most elevated, airy, and healthy sites in the vicinity of Philadelphia. The ground occupied by it, contains about 10 acres. The material with which the edifices are built is gneiss, in large masses; every room is vaulted, and fire proof. The design and execution, impart a grave, severe and awful character to the external aspect. The effect on the imagination of the spectator is peculiarly impressive, solemn and instructive. The architecture is in keeping with the design. The broad masses, the small and well proportioned apertures, the continuity of lines, and the bold simplicity which characterizes the facade, are happily and judiciously combined. This is the only edifice in this country, which conveys an idea of the external appearance of those magnificent and picturesque castles of the middle ages, which contribute so eminently to embellish the scenery of Europe. The front is composed of large blocks of hewn stone; the walls are 12 feet thick at the base, and diminish to the top, where they are 2¾ feet in thickness. A wall of thirty feet in height, above the interior platform, encloses an area 640 feet square; at each angle of the wall is a tower, for the purpose of overlooking the establishment; three other towers are situated near the gate of entrance. The facade or principal front is 670 feet in length, and reposes on a terrace, which, from the inequalities of the ground, varies from three to nine feet in height; the basement or belting course, which is 10 feet high, is scarped, and extends uniformly the whole length. The central building is 200 feet in length, consists of two projecting massive square towers, 50 feet high, crowned by projecting embattled parapets, supported by pointed arches, resting on corbets or brackets. The pointed, munnioned windows in these towers, contribute in a high degree to their picturesque effect. The curtain between the towers is 41 feet high, and is finished with a parapet and embrasures. The pointed windows in it are very lofty and narrow. The great gateway in the centre is a very conspicuous feature; it is 27 feet high, and 15 wide, and is filled by a massive wrought iron portcullis, and double oaken gates, studded with projecting iron rivets, the whole weighing several tons; nevertheless, they can be opened with the greatest facility. On each side of this entrance, (which is the most imposing in the United States,) are enormous solid buttresses, diminishing in offsets, and terminating in pinnacles. A lofty octangular tower, 80 feet high, containing an alarm bell and clock, surmounts this entrance, and forms a picturesque proportional centre. On each side of this main building, (which contains the apartments of the warden, keepers, domestics, &c.) are screen wing walls, which appear to constitute portions of the main edifice; they are pierced with small blank pointed windows, and are surmounted by a parapet; at their extremities are high octangular towers, terminating in parapets, pierced by embrasures. In the centre of the great court is an observatory, whence long corridors, eight in number, radiate; (three only of these corridors, &c., are at present finished.) On each side of these corridors, the cells are situated, each at right angles to them, and communicating with them only by small openings, for the purpose of supplying the prisoner with food, &c., and for the purpose of inspecting his movements without attracting his attention; other apertures, for the admission of cool or heated air, and for the purpose of ventilation, are provided. A novel and ingenious contrivance in each cell, prevents the possibility of conversation, preserves the purity of the atmosphere of the cells, and dispenses with the otherwise unavoidable necessity of leaving the apartment, except when the regulations permit—flues conduct heated air from large cockle stoves to the cells. Light is admitted by a large circular glass in the crown of the arch, which is raking, and the highest part 16 feet 6 inches above the floor, (which is of wood, overlaying a solid foundation of stone.) The walls are plaistered, and neatly whitewashed; the cells are 11 feet 9 inches long, and 7 feet 6 inches wide; at the extremity of the cell, opposite to the apertures for inspection, &c., previously mentioned, is the door-way, containing two doors; one of lattice work or grating, to admit the air and secure the prisoner; the other, composed of planks, to exclude the air, if required; this door leads to a yard (18 feet by 8, the walls of which are $11\frac{1}{2}$ feet in height,) attached to each cell. The number of the latter, erected on the original plan, was only 266, but it may be increased to 818 without resorting to the addition of second stories. The cost of this building when completed will probably exceed an half million of dollars.

After these buildings had been constructed, with a view to solitary confinement only, the opponents of this mode of punishment so far prevailed with the legislature as to obtain a modification of the plan, and to connect manual labor with separate confinement. Much inconvenience occurred in adapting the Western penitentiary to this purpose: the Eastern one from the space connected with the cells readily admitted of the substitution.

By the act of 23d April, 1829, it was provided that criminals, convicted of the following offences, viz., murder in the second degree, man slaughter, high treason, arson, rape, sodomy, burglary, forgery, passing counterfeit money, robbery, kidnapping, mayhew, horse stealing and perjury, should be sentenced to suffer punishment by separate or solitary confinement at labor, in the manner and for the time prescribed by law, in the penitentiary of the district to which the court convicting, belonged—to be kept singly and separately at labor, in the cells or work yards; and be sustained upon wholesome food of coarse quality, and furnished with clothing suited to their situation. And by the act of 28th March, 1831, the inspectors of the Eastern penitentiary are authorized to construct at least four hundred additional cells, and every person convicted in any court in the eastern district, whose punishment was imprisonment at hard labor, &c., for the term of a year or more, to be sentenced to separate confinement at labor, &c., in the Eastern penitentiary for the same period; and that persons thereafter convicted of crimes, subject to imprisonment for less than a year, should undergo their sentence in the county prison.

The respective penitentiaries are governed by a board of inspectors, composed of five taxable citizens, appointed by the supreme court. The inspectors appoint wardens, and inferior officers, and serve for two years. The inspectors receive no compensation—the salaries of the officers are paid by the state, but the expenses of the prisoners by the counties from which they are respectively sent. This system of punishment is emphatically called the system of Pennsylvania, and consists in *solitary confinement at labor, with instruction in labor, in morals and religion.* It is an experiment, in the success of which all good men are interested, and the prospect of a beneficial result is highly flattering, so far as it relates not only to the morals of the prisoner, but to the means of supporting him from the produce of his labor. Solitary confinement has not, as was predicted, been found injurious to the mental or physical health of the prisoner.

When a convict first arrives, he is placed in a cell and left alone, without work, and without any book. His mind can only operate upon itself; generally, but few hours elapse before he petitions for something to do, and for a Bible. No instance has occurred, in which such a petition has been delayed for more than a day or two. If the prisoner have a trade that can be pursued in his cell, he is put to work as a favor; as a reward for good behavior, and as a favor, a Bible is allowed to him. If he have no trade, or one that cannot be pursued in his cell, he is allowed to choose one that can, and he is instructed by one of the overseers, all of whom are master workmen in the trades they respectively superintend and teach. Thus work, and moral and religious instruction, are regarded and received as favors, and are withheld as a punishment.

Commerce and Manufactures. It is not practicable to obtain a correct knowledge of the commerce or manufactures of the state. Almost the whole of the trade of the great state of New York, centres in her metropolis, and the books of her custom houses, upon Manhattan bay, and the lakes, afford a pretty accurate view of her foreign commerce and coasting trade. But Philadelphia is not the port for one half of the state of Pennsylvania. The great valley of the Susquehannah pours a vast portion of its treasures into the city of Baltimore, and the Ohio and Mississippi bear away the whole of the surplus produce of Western Pennsylvania. Hence New Orleans and Baltimore, are nearly as much ports of the state, as Philadelphia itself. The most, therefore, that can be done, towards an exhibition of the commerce of the state, is to shew the imports and exports of the city of Philadelphia, of which, however, the trade of West New Jersey forms a component part. For this purpose we refer to the treasury report of 1830, not having been able to procure in season that of 1831. The tonnage which entered the ports was 77,016, and that which departed was 67,829. Of the number of American vessels and their tonnage, there were entered 72,009 tons, and departed 63,022, giving employment in repeated voyages, to 3,907 seamen, and there were registered in that year 448 seamen. The hospital money received from seamen amounted to $4,111 31.—$2,934 97 were received from registered vessels, contributed by 4082 seamen, and $1,176 34 from enrolled and licensed vessels, contributed by 1173 seamen. During the same period, six vessels, tonnage 791,80, surrendered their registers, and were enrolled and licensed. 7 enrolled and licensed vessels, tonnage 923, took registers,—3 vessels, tonnage 257, had their registers changed in consequence of the alteration in their construction. New registers were issued for 64 vessels, tonnage 13,534 tons. The enrolments and licenses of 78 vessels, tonnage 5,033, were changed in consequence of new owners.

The imports into the state amounted to $8,702,122; the exports to $4,291,793. The whole amount of the exports of the U. S. for 1830, was $73,849,508, and that of the imports, $70,876,920, and the excess therefore of the exports was $2,972,588. Of this excess, Pennsylvania contributed her fair proportion, and consequently exported more than she imported. If we add therefore to her imports, one million for goods from Baltimore and New Orleans, we may safely estimate her exports at ten millions of dollars; one half the amount of the exports of New York. But when it is considered that this amount of exports does not include her flour, her iron, or coal, shipped coastwise, we must estimate the commercial products of the state much higher.

The quantity of flour inspected at Philadelphia in 1831, was 474,076 barrels. We might perhaps double this quantity, for the amount of flour, or equivalent of grain exported, much of which passes to Baltimore and to New Orleans. We have already stated the amount of iron manufactured at about 50,000 tons, a large proportion of which descends the Ohio.

The coal business has already became a very important item in the trade of Pennsylvania, and its increase must, ultimately, pay abundantly the vast amount of money and labor, which have been expended upon it.

There is every reason to believe, that if the means of conveying coal to market will permit, that the demand and supply will increase for many years in the same ratio, until a million of tons per annum will be produced. And this amount is far within the bounds of rational conjecture. That quantity, however, will, at present prices, make a gross annual return of 6⅓ millions, and will employ 10,000 vessels for its transportation.

On the subject of manufactures we may observe, that we have no means to determine the quantity and value of the products of most branches of this kind of industry. The cities of Philadelphia and Pittsburg are eminently distinguished for their manufactures, and there is scarce a thriving town in the state, which has not some extensive and profitable manufactory within it. We give the following, as an approximation to the quantity and value of the manufactured articles, which require legislative protection.

Iron, 50,000, at an average value of 70 dollars the ton, 3,500,000. Salt, 100,000 barrels, at 5 bushels to the barrel, at $2 the barrel, 200,000. *Cotton.*—This article employs 61 mills, with a capital of $3,758,500, and produce for sale, 2,192,865 lbs. of yarn, and 21,332,467 yards of cloth, employing about 30,000 men, women, and children—value of product, $2,681,462. There are several considerable woollen manufactories near Philadelphia and Pittsburg, and many small establishments dispersed throughout the state; but we do not possess any means to ascertain the quantity or value of their product.

Of flint glass, there is one furnace at Philadelphia, with 6 pots; at Pittsburg 4, with 32 pots; at Wellsburg 2, with 12 pots. Four furnaces for hollow green ware at Philadelphia, and one at Williamsport. For the manufacture of cylinder window glass, at Pittsburg 4, at Brownsville 5, at Williamsport 1, at Brimingham 1, New Geneva 1, New Albany 1, Bridgeport 1, Perryopolis 1, Dundaff 1, Wayne co. 1, and perhaps others with whose location we are unacquainted. Of the glass manufactories, we cannot give the quantity or value of product. The window glass and hollow ware, made at, and in the neighborhood of, Pittsburg, is estimated at more than $500,000 per annum.

We may close this short and very imperfect account of the commerce and manufactures of the state, with observing, that her capacity for the production of iron, salt, and glass, is as boundless as her coal fields.—That every species of manufacture, the success of which depends upon an abundant and cheap supply of fuel, must here find the most favorable situation.—That cotton and woollen manufactures, whether propelled by steam or water power, may be as profitably established and conducted either in the eastern or western part of the state, as in any other portion of the Union; the many dams and pools caused by our system of internal improvements, affording a great number of advantageous sites for water works.—That her numerous rolling and setting mills, steel furnaces, scythe and sickle, and edge tool manufactories; her manufactories of ships, steam engines, steamboats, leaden shot, and colors, of oils, of distilled spirits, of malt liquors, of carriages and household furniture, of paper, of books, of tobacco, and of the thousand other fabrics which minister to the necessities and comforts of man, are all conducted with great skill, in an extensive and profitable manner.

PART II.

GAZETTEER

OF PENNSYLVANIA.

Aaronsburg, post town, of Haines t-ship, Centre co. 20 miles E. by the road from Bellefonte, and 40 miles W. by N. from Sunbury, 196 from Washington City, and 88 from Harrisburg, contains some 30 dwellings, several stores and taverns. A turnpike road running through it, intersects that leading from Lewistown to Bellefonte. Aaronsburg is separated from the town of Millheim by Mill Creek.

Abbott's Creek, Luzerne co., rises and has its course in Providence t-ship. and flows N. W. about 7 miles, through the Moosic mountain into the Lackawannock river.

Abbottstown, p-t. Berwick t-ship, Adams co., on the turnpike road leading from York to Gettysburg, 15 miles E. from the latter, 86 N. from W. C., and 32 S. W. from Harrisburg. A turnpike road passes through this town S. to Hanover, and thence into the state of Maryland; Beaver Creek, a tributary of the Conewago, flows N. by it, to that stream, forming part of the boundary line between Adams and York counties. The town contains about 75 dwellings, 3 stores, 3 taverns, and 2 churches.

Abington, v. of Abington t-ship, Montgomery co. (See Morestown.)

Abington, post town, Luzerne county, 15 miles N. E. from Wilksbarre, and by post road 137 miles N. N. E. from Harrisburg. 245 from W. C.

Abington, t-ship, Luzerne county, bounded N. by Nicholson, E. by Greenfield, S. by Providence, S. W. by Falls, and W. by Tunkhannock t-ships. Its timber is principally beech, sugar-maple, ash, red cherry, and hemlock. Tributaries of the Tunkhannock and Lackawannock creeks either head in, or flow through this township, affording many excellent mill sites; and springs of the purest water may be found on almost every hundred acres of land.

The soil is better adapted to grazing than to the growing of grain. When cleared, white clover springs up spontaneously, and grows luxuriantly. Timothy is the principal grass cut for fodder, of which, from one to two tons per acre are produced. A considerable portion of this township is settled, and some parts well cultivated. Wild lands of a good quality are selling here, from three to five dollars per acre. This township produces annually for market, considerable quantities of maple sugar, butter, cheese, (of a good quality,) wool, domestic flannels, and linens, oats, horses, cattle and sheep.

The Philadelphia and Great Bend turnpike road passes nearly through its centre. An act has been passed to authorize the incorporation of a company for making a turnpike from this township, to Montrose; and township roads are opened in every direction. The settlers are principally from New England, and are a hardy, industrious, and thriving people.—School houses are erected in every neighborhood, in which schools are kept during the greater part of the year.

Abington is situated about 25 miles N. E. from Wilkes-Barre, has three post-offices, and contains about 1200 inhabitants. Taxables in 1828, 239. Greatest length and breadth, 7 miles. The lower or southern part of the township is hilly, but the remainder, level and well adapted to agriculture. The soil is a gravelly loam.

The township is drained by the tributaries to the South-eastern branch of the Tunkhannock creek, which crosses it from East to West, in two places; and by Legates creek, which flows Southerly into the Lackawannock. The Capons range of mountains, and the Lackawannock mountain cover its Southern part.

Abington, t-ship, Montgomery co., bounded on the N. E. by Moreland t-ship, S. E. by Philadelphia co., S. W. by Cheltenham t-ship, and N. W. by Springfield and Upper Dublin t-ships. Its form is a parallelogram, whose longest sides are 8, and shortest sides 3 miles; area 15,360 acres. Distance from Philad. 12 ms. Surface rolling, soil, limestone and fertile loam of a good quality, generally well cultivated and productive. Population chiefly Quakers, in 1830, 1524. Taxables, 300. The Cheltenham and Willow Grove turnpike crosses the township centrally, on which are located the post villages of Jenkintown, and Abington, (commonly called Morestown) and Willow Grove. The Quakers have a meeting-house near and east of Jenkintown, known as Abington meeting, and there is a Presbyterian church at Morestown. The Pennepack creek runs through the S. E. angle, and receives a tributary from the neighborhood of Jenkintown.

Abraham's plains, a rich alluvial flat on the N. W. side of the Susquehannah river at the foot of the Shawnese mountains in Kingston and Exeter townships, Luzerne co., distinguished as the battle-field on which was fought the fatal fight between the Americans, and the Indians, British and tories, on the 3d of July, 1778. The village of New Troy now stands on these plains, and they are covered by an industrious, intelligent and thrifty population.

Abraham's creek, a small stream which rises in and flows south through Kingston t-ship, Luzerne co., into the Susquehannah river, near the village of New Troy, at which place some mills are erected upon it.

Adams co. was divided from York co. by act of assembly 22d Jan. 1800, which gave it the following boundary. "Beginning in the line of Cumberland co., where the road from Carlisle to Baltimore leads through Trent's Gap; thence along the said road to Binder's; thence a straight line to Conewago creek, opposite the mouth of Abbott's run; thence along the line of Manheim and Berwick townships westwardly, until it strikes the road leading from Oxford to Hanovertown; and from thence a due south course until it strikes the Maryland line; thence along the Maryland line to the line of Franklin co.; thence along the line of Franklin and Cumberland counties to the place of beginning." It is therefore bounded W. by Franklin, N. by Cumberland, E. by York counties, and south by the state of Maryland. It extends 27 miles in length E. and W., and in breadth N. and S. 24 miles. Area 528 square miles, or 337,920 acres. Its central latitude is 39° 50′ N., long. W. from W. C. 00 10′.

The surface of the county is much

diversified. The south mountain or first great chain of hills west of the sea board, runs along the western and northern boundary, in which are some valuable minerals, particularly iron and copper, if iron pyrites have not been mistaken for the latter.

There are no navigable streams in the county, but many which afford useful mill powers; the principal are the Conewago creek, which flows N. E. to the Susquehannah river, having its source near the south mountain, and receiving the greater proportion of the waters of the county; and Marsh creek, which has its source in the same hills, and flows S. E. to the Monococy river in Maryland; receiving from the co. Rock creek, Willoways and Piney creeks, and some others, draining the southern parts of the county. There are several sulphur springs on Marsh creek, in Hamilton-ban and Liberty t-ships. York sulphur springs, formerly in much repute and frequented by fashionable company, and still worthy of all the patronage they once received, are in Latimore township, on the turnpike road from Carlisle to Baltimore, 16 miles from the former. (See York Springs.) There are 5 notable bridges in the county, three over the Conewago, one over Rock, and another over Marsh creeks.

The S. E. portion of the county consists of the secondary formation, in which limestone of various qualities is found. The northern and western parts are composed of the old red sandstone formation.

The soil is of various qualities, from the worst to the best. The limestone lands generally yield an ample reward to labor. But the agricultural improvement is not equal to that in some other counties. The inhabitants do not readily change their ancient habits, and the benefits of modern science advance slowly among them.

The population is principally composed of the descendants of Germans, and settlers from New Jersey, and amounted, by the census of 1830, to 21,379, and the taxables in 1828, to 4,192. Of the population, there are 10,401 white males, 10,341 white females, 283 free colored males, 309 free colored females; 25 male slaves, 20 females slaves. There were 108 aliens; 14 deaf and dumb, and 8 blind persons.

The prevailing religion of the county is Lutheran, and there are many churches of this denomination here. The theological seminary of that church, under the direction of Professor Schmucker, has been several years established in Gettysburg. There are however some Presbyterians, Roman Catholics, Methodists, Quakers, United Brethren, and a few Seven-day Baptists. There are 30 churches within the county. An academy is also established at Gettysburg, which was incorporated in 1810, and received from the legislature a donation of $2000, on condition that the trustees should extend the benefits of the institution to a certain number of poor children, gratis; and by the act of 31st March, 1812, this sum was appropriated one half to the purchase of a library, and the other to be invested in some fund towards the support of the teacher. A building for the use of the academy has been erected in the town by private liberality.

There are three newspapers in the county, two English and one German, all weekly, and printed at Gettysburg.

The other public buildings of the county consist (excluding churches) of a court-house, county offices, of brick, and prison, of stone, at Gettysburg; and a bank at the same place, with a capital of $125,298.

The principal trade of the county consists in the exchange of its surplus produce of wheat, rye, corn, barley, and oats, and some iron, for the foreign necessaries required by its inhabitants. There are 65 grist, 75 saw mills and ten fulling mills, dispersed through the county, adequate to the wants of the people, but no manufactories of cloth or wool, save 8 or 10 carding machines and fulling mills, which minister to the domestic fabrics of the farmers. A forge has lately been erected at the foot of the mountain in the S. W. part of the county, 8 or 10 miles from Gettysburg, in Hamilton-ban township, called Maria forge, by Messrs. Stevens and Paxson. There is also a furnace, known as Chest Grove, in Huntingdon t-ship.

The business of the county is principally with the city of Baltimore, by two turnpike roads, one from Gettysburg by the way of Petersburg, York co., the other passing across this county from Carlisle to Hanover in York co. and thence into Maryland. A turnpike road runs from York to Gettysburg, and from Gettysburg to Chambersburg, and another to Mummasburg.

The county contains some 14 or 15 towns and villages, of which Gettysburg, borough and county town, is the chief. Among others worthy of notice are Berlin, Abbottstown, Petersburg, Littlestown, Millarstown, Oxford, Hunterstown, &c. (See these titles.)

This county, in conjunction with York county, forms the fourteenth Senatorial District, and sends two members to the Senate; and it sends alone, two members to the House of Representatives.

United with Franklin, Cumberland and Perry, it forms the eleventh Congressional District; and

United with Cumberland and Perry, the 9th Judicial District, over which John Reed, Esq. presides. The Courts are holden at Gettysburg on the 4th Mondays of January, April, August, and November, annually.

Adams County belongs to the Southern District of the Supreme Court, which holds an annual session at Chambersburg on the Monday week next following the end of the second week of the term of the Western District. The Western District term commences on the first Monday of September.

This county contributed towards the Revenue of the State, in 1831,—

In payment for tavern licenses, . .	$683 55
Tax on bank dividends, ...	501 27
Dividends on turnpike stock, . . .	1,200
Tax on writs, ...	71 05
Duties on foreign merchandize . .	499 33
For state maps, ...	57
For pamphlet laws, ...	1 46
For hawkers' and pedlers' licenses,	15 20
	$3,028 86

The valuation of taxable property in this county, as returned by the commissioners in 1829, was, real estate, $4,740,577, and of personal estate, comprehending horses and cattle only, and occupations, $239,306. The rate of levy was 23 cents on the one hundred dollars.

Statistical Table of Adams County.

Townships, &c.	*Greatest. lgth.*	*bth.*	*Area in Acres.*	*Face of the Country.*	*Soil.*	*Population.* 1810.	1820.	1830.	*Taxables.*
Berwick,	7	3	10,240	Level.	Red gravel.	1,799	1,207	1,417	228
Cumberland,	11	4	20,580	do.	do.		1,022	1,010	213
Conewago,	7¼	3½	8,320	do.	Limestone.		839	878	198
Gettysburg,				do.	Slate & r. grav		1,102	1,473	281
Hamilton-ban,	10¾	8¼	31,360	do.	L'stne. & r. gr.		1,053	1,379	282
Hamilton,	6¾	4	10,240	do.	R. grav. & flint		1,075	1,047	215
Huntingdon,	8	3½	17,280	Rolling.	L'stone & gr.	1,014	1,198	1,284	264
Germany,	8	4	14,080	Level.	do.		1,272	1,517	322
Franklin,	12	8½	32,000	do.	Red sand.	788	1,456	1,588	320
Menallen,	15	9½	53,760	do.	do.		1,872	2,063	387
Mountjoy,	5½	5½	14,720	do.	Blue slate.	636	935	991	191
Mountpleasant,	8	7	19,200	do.	Red sand.	531	1,483	1,498	285
Latimore,	7¾	4	14,720	do.	do.	666	856	1,011	179
Liberty,	11	6	19,840	do.	Clay.		1,027	1,097	226
Reading,	8	6	15,360	do.	R. sand & slate		833	1,001	177
Tyrone,	10	4	15,360	do.	R. & slate.	648	840	817	159
Strabane,	9¾	7¼	20,480	do.	Slate.	732	1,300	1,308	265
The census of the remainder of the county for 1810, the townships are not given separately.						7,233		21,379	4192
						15,152	19,370		

Adamsburg, p-t. Westmoreland co. 176 miles W. from Harrisburg, 6 miles W. of Greensburg, on the turnpike road leading from the latter place to Pittsburg, contains 25 houses, 3 taverns, 4 stores, and a steam grist mill.

Adamsburg, Beaver t-ship, Union co. at the foot of Black Oak Ridge, about 12 ms. S. W. of New Berlin, contains 25 dwellings, 1 store, 1 tavern, and a Presbyterian church.

Adams, t-ship. Lycoming co. bounded by Nippenose t-ship, S. by Centre co. E. by Washington t-sp. and W. by Wayne t-ship, centrally distant from Williamsport 10 ms. S. W. Greatest length 9, breadth 7½ miles. Area 32,640 acres. Surface, mountainous; soil, limestone. This township is badly watered, the springs falling through the limestone, sink almost as soon as they appear above the ground. It includes nearly half of Nippenose, or oval limestone valley. Taxable population, 63. Taxable property in 1829—seated lands, $13,751 50. Unseated lands $13,014; personal estate, $2,968. Amount of tax levied, $220.97—rate ¾ of a cent on the dollar.

Adamstown, post town and village, Cocalico t-ship, Lancaster co., on the road from Lancaster to Reading, 20 miles from the former and 10 from the latter, and 46 miles S. E. from Harrisburg, contains some 20 dwellings, stores and taverns.

Adams' creek, Napier t-ship, Bedford co. a tributary of Dunning's creek.

Addamsville, p-o. Berks co. 152 ms. from W. C. and 61 from Harrisburg.

Addison t-ship, Somerset co. bounded N. by Turkeyfoot t-ship, E. by Elklick t-ship, S. by the state of Maryland, and W. by Fayette co. Centrally distant from the town of Somerset 20 miles, greatest length 10 miles, breadth 6 miles. Area 35,000 acres. Surface very hilly. Soil reddish gravel. Taxable population, 234. Taxable property in 1829, real estate $96,075, personal estate $6280. Rate of tax, 5 mills on the dollar. Negro mountain lies on the E. and Youghiogheny r. on the W. boundary. The latter receives from the town-ship, Castleman's r. which runs along the N. boundary augmented by Negro Glade run, Jones run and Rogers run, which rise in the t-ship. The Cumberland or great national road enters the state in this t-ship, and upon it lies the post-town of Petersburg. Winding Ridge and Horse Hill are noted eminences. Coal is found on the E. bank of the Youghiogheny, near the Horse Shoe Bend, and lime at the head of Negro Glade run.

Agnew's Mills, Venango co. so called after the Postmaster, I. Agnew. Distant 248 miles from W. C. and 203 from Harrisburg.

Air, t-ship, Bedford co. bounded N. by Dublin, E. by Franklin co. S. by the state of Maryland, and W. by Belfast, centrally distant from Bedford Borough 25 ms., greatest distance 11, breadth 4½ miles. Area 24,960 acres. Surface mountainous with rich limestone valleys. Pop. in 1830, 1517. Taxables 279. Cove mountain bounds it on the E. and Scrub Ridge on the W. The valley between is drained by Big Cove creek and near the head of the valley is the Borough of McConnelsburg.

Alba, p-o. Bradford co. 241 miles from W. C. 129 from Harrisburg.

Albany, t-ship, Bradford co. bounded N. by Asylum, E. by Luzerne co. S. by Lycoming co. and W. by Monroe. Centrally distant 12 miles S. E. from Towanda. Greatest length 13, breadth 7½ miles. Surface, hilly, soil, gravelly loam. Pop. in 1830, 284, taxables 64. It is drained N. W. by Towanda creek, and S. E. by the W. Branch of the Mahoopeny creek. The p-t. of New Albany is 227 miles N. W. from W. C. and 116 from Harrisburg.

Albany, a t-ship of Berks co. bounded N. E. by the county of Lehigh, N. W. and W. by the Blue mountains, S. W. by Windsor t-ship, and S. by Greenwich t-ship. It is drained by Mill and Pine creek and Stony run, tributaries of Maiden creek, which intersects the t-ship into two unequal parts, running in a S. W. direction. There are mills on each of these streams, and on Pine creek several forges. Besides the hills on its northern boundary, there is a notable one on the South, known by the name of "Round Top." There are 2 Churches near the Lehigh boundary line, one Presbyterian, the other Lutheran, another near Union Furnace. The surface of the country is hilly. Soil, gravelly and poor. Pop. in 1810, 996, in 1820, 1182, 1830, 1129. Taxables, 284.

Aleppo, t-ship, Greene co. the extreme S. W. t-ship of the State, bounded N. by Richhill, E. by Centre and Wayne t-ships, S. and W. by the State of Virginia. Centrally distant from Waynesborough 15 miles. Greatest length 11 miles, breadth 10 miles. Area, 52,480 acres. Surface, very hilly. Soil, fertile loam. Pop. in 1830, 838. Taxables 134. The t-ship is drained N. E. by McCourtneys fork of 10 mile Creek, S. E. by the head waters of Dunkard creek, N. W. by several forks of Wheeling creek, and S. W. by branches of Fish creek.

Alexandria, West, p-t. Donegal t-ship, Washington co. on the national road, near the W. boundary of the t-ship, 15 miles S. W. of Washington borough, 245 from W. C. and 228 from Harrisburg, contains from 40 to 50 dwellings, 3 taverns, and 3 stores, a Presbyterian church. There is a Catholic chapel 3 miles E. from the town.

Alexandria, p-t. and borough, Porter t-ship, Huntingdon co. upon the turnpike road leading from the borough of Huntingdon to Ebensburg, and upon the Frankstown branch of the Juniata r. 155 miles N. W. from W. C. and 97 S. W. from Harrisburg, 8 miles N. W. from the borough, contains 64 dwellings, chiefly brick and frame, 2 houses for worship, 1 school, 8 stores, 11 taverns, 3 smith's shops, 2 tanneries, 1 brewery, 1 distillery and 1apothecary. It was incorporated by act of 11th April 1827.

Alexandria, New, t. of Deny t-ship Westmoreland co. on the right bank of the Leyalhanna r. and on the turnpike road leading to Pittsburg, 10 miles N. E. from Greensburg, 199 miles from W. C. and 171 from Harrisburg. It contains 25 dwellings, 2 taverns and 3 stores.

Allegheny creek, Robeson t-ship, Berks co. a tributary of the Schuylkill r. It is a mill stream and has a furnace on it near the mouth.

Allegheny Mountain Little, forms part of the boundary on the S. between Bedford and Somerset cos. and the W. boundary of Londonderry t-ship of the former county.

Allegheny, t-ship Somerset co. bounded N. by Shade t-ship, E. by Bedford co. S. by Southampton, and W. by Brothers valley and Stoney creek. Centrally distant from Somerset S. E. 15 miles, greatest length 14, breadth 6. Area, 55,200. Surface, very hilly. Soil, Reddish gravel. Taxable population 95—taxable property in 1829, real estate $19,717, personal, including occupations, &c. 2,936, rate of tax, 5 mills on the dollar. The Little Allegheny mountain is on the E. and the great Allegheny on the W. boundary. It is drained on the S. by Wills' creek, and its tributaries, Rush creek and some minor streams; on the E. by the Rays-town branch of the Juniata r. The turnpike road from Bedford to Somerset runs, centrally W. through the t-ship north of which, near the E. boundary, are three salt licks which gave name to a run flowing northward to the river.

Allegheny, t-ship, Huntingdon co. bounded N. E. by Antes t-ship, S. E. by Frankstown t-ship S. W. by Bedford co. and N. W. by Cambria co. Centrally distant W. from the borough of Huntingdon 20 miles. Greatest length 10, breadth 7 miles. Area, 39,040 acres. Surface, mountainous. Soil, red shale, fertile in the valley. Pop. in 1830, 2,058. Taxables 190. It is drained by Beaver Dam creek, which flows S. E. into the Frankstown branch of the Juniata r. The t-ship is chiefly covered by the Allegheny mountain, on which, in the S. E. angle runs the rail road portage near Blair's Gap and post office. Burgoon's Gap is on the W. side of the t-ship. Iron is found on the E. and a furnace has been erected near the beds. Franktown and Hollidaysburg are in the adjoining t-ship on the S. E. There were in this t-ship in 1828, 3 grist mills, 6 saw mills, 5 distilleries, 1 furnace, 1 fulling mill, 1 oil mill, 2 tan yards.

Allegheny, t-ship, Venango co. bounded N. by Warren co. E. and S. by the Allegheny r. W. by Wind Rock and E. Branch t-ships. Centrally distant N. E. from Franklin borough 20 miles. Greatest length 12, breath 6 miles. Area, 39,680 acres; Surface hilly; soil, gravel. Pop. in 1830, 596. Taxables 120. The t-ship is drained by Stewart's and Hickory creeks. The first flowing S. E. and the second S. into the river.

Allegheny Bridge, p-o. of Keating t-ship, McKean co. 288 miles N. W. of W. C. and 215 from Harrisburg.

Allegheny Borough, Ross t-ship, Allegheny co. on the point formed by the Ohio and Allegheny r. opposite to the city of Pittsburg, from which it is separated by the latter river, but connected therewith by a covered bridge, completed in 1819, of six arches resting on piers of dressed stone, and elevated above the level of the water 38 feet, length 1122 ft. breadth 38, cost $95,249, of which the state subscribed $10,000. The ballance was supplied by individuals who form an incorporated company. (For a description of this town see Pittsburg.) The Borough was incorporated 14th April, 1828.

Allegheny, t-ship, Westmoreland co. bounded N. E. by the Kiskiminitas r. S. E. by Washington t-ship, S. W. by Poketos creek which separates it from Plumb t-ship, Allegheny co. and W. and N. W. by the Allegheny r. Centrally distant from Greensburg N. W. 22 miles. Greatest length 12, breadth 11 miles. Area, 43,520 acres. Surface, hilly. Soil, loam, gravel and limestone. Taxable population, 291. Besides the streams above mentioned, the t-ship is drained by Chartier's creek on the W. and by Pine run and some smaller streams on the East.

Allegheny, t-ship, Armstrong co. bounded N. E. by Crooked creek, dividing it from Kittaning and Plumb creek t-ships, S. E. by Indiana co. S. W. by the Kiskiminitas r. which separates it from Westmoreland co. and N. W. by the Allegheny river. Centrally distant S. from Kittaning borough 12 miles. Greatest length 13, breadth 10. Area, 53,760 acres. Surface, hilly. Soil, gravelly loam. Pop. in 1830, 2,966. Taxables 602. It is drained by several small creeks and runs which flow into the great streams that surround it. Several salt springs are found near the Kiskiminitas river, and on Crooked creek, and several salt works are erected on their banks.

Allegheny, t-ship, Cambria co. bounded N. by Susquehannah t-ship, E. by Clearfield t-ship, S. by Somerhill and W. by Cambria. Centrally distant N. E. from Ebensburg 6 miles. Greatest length 10, breadth 6 miles. Area, 32,000 acres. Pop. in 1830, 844. Taxables 200, valuation of taxable property 1829, viz: seated lands $35,899, unseated $7,852, personal estate $7,467. Rate of tax 8½ mills in the dollar. The t-ship is drained N. by Clearfield and Chest creeks.

Allegheny Mountains, sometimes called the Appalachian Mountains. This name is given by some Geographers to the whole of the chain of mountains which traverse the continent between the Ohio river and the lakes, and the sea coast, embracing the South mountains and the Kittatinny range. Of this system, within the State we have already given a general view in the first part of this work. But, the name of Allegheny is specially given to that range of hills which divides the waters of the States through which it passes and directs their course East and West. The Allegheny proper, termed the back bone of the State, enters Somerset county from Maryland between Elk creek and Greenville t-ships, and runs N. E. across the State into Lycoming co. where it appears to be broken into separate masses, and finally to subside in Susquehannah co. In its course, it separates Bedford from Somerset co. and Cambria from Huntingdon co. But only for 60 miles of its course does it separate the sources of the streams of two great natural sections, the Atlantic slope and the Ohio valley. It is penetrated westward, near the southern boundary of the State by the sources of Castleman's river, and eastwardly in Lycoming co. by the west branch of the Susquehannah. Its average height in Pennsylvania may be stated at about 1200 feet above the valleys, with a summit, which for the greater part of its course, can scarcely be said to undulate. In this State, grit or sandstone forms its nucleus. It may be remarked here, that, with few exceptions, in this and the other ranges of Pennsylvania the steep ascent looks to the west, whilst the eastern rises slowly and gradually. Not one acre in ten of this ridge is susceptible of culture, yet in some parts of it there is excellent land, and much of it is said from experiment to be favorable to the culture of the vine.

This superciliary ridge has presented an insurmountable barrier to the continuation of the line of canals in the State; and has compelled the engineers, who had overcome many other chains, to resort to a rail-road portage across its summit. This rail-road extends about 36 ms. from Hollidaysburg on the Juniata river in Huntingdon co. to Johnsontown on the Conemaugh. The name Allegheny is of Indian origin, and is said on some authorities to mean endless; but we observe that others translate it when applied to the river, "Fair Water."

Allegheny River, rises on the W. side of the Allegheny mountains in Lycoming co. Pennsylvania, within a few miles of the head waters of the Sinnemahoning creek, a navigable stream which falls into the Susquehannah river, to which there is a portage of 23 miles. Thence by a northerly course it passes into the State of New-York, and winding to the N. W. about 20 miles, turns gradually to the S. W. and re-enters Pennsylvania; and meandering the same direction 180 miles unites with the Monongahela river at Pittsburg. The lands on each side of this river for 150 miles above Pittsburg, consist of white oak and chestnut ridges, and in many places of poor pitch pine, interspersed with tracts of good land and low meadows. Few rivers, perhaps none, excel the Allegheny in the transparency of its waters. Its mean velocity is about two and a half miles an hour. In its course it receives many large tributary streams, among which are the Kiskiminitas, Mohulbuekitum, Toby's and French creeks. The last is navigable to Waterford in Erie co. from which to lake Erie is but 14 miles. The trade by the Allegheny, with the lakes has heretofore been considerable. Several thousand barrels of salt, have annually passed from the Onandago salt works, and the quantity of boards and timber floated down the stream is immense. The Allegheny joining the Monongahela nearly at right angles, and its current being more rapid, generally marks its course by the transparency of its waters contrasted with the muddiness of the other; and a separation is observable for three miles below their junction. The Allegheny at its mouth is above 500 yards wide. This river and the Ohio, until it empties into the Mississippi, were alike called by the name Allegheny by the Indian tribes who once inhabited their banks, and that name literally translated means "Fair Water." The same sense is conveyed by the word "*Ohio*," the former being in the language of the Delaware, and the latter of the Seneca Indians. The

French name "Belle Riviere" is therefore but a translation.

The facilities which this river presented for connecting the metropolitan cities of the State, and for extending commerce with the northwest portion of the Commonwealth, could not be overlooked; and accordingly the great State canal enters its valley by an aqueduct which crosses the river near the mouth of the Kiskiminitas, and reaches Pittsburg by a course of 30 miles; and an act was passed authorizing the connection of this river with the lakes, by means of French creek and the Conneaut lake. A navigable feeder between the Creek and lake, and connected with the river, has been completed.

But in this age of wonders, the rapid current of this mountain river has been subjected to the dominion of steam. Boats of a peculiar construction, invented by Mr. Thos. Blanchard of Connecticut, of an hundred tons burthen, but of light draught of water have ascended the river to Olean N. Hamilton, in Cataragua county, state of New-York, near the head of the river and 270 miles from its mouth, a point 600 feet above the level of the river at Pittsburg, 1400 feet above the ocean, and 2500 miles distant from it by the course of the river. Regular trips are now made to and from Pittsburg and Franklin, the latter situated at the mouth of French creek in Venango county, 125 miles from the former, in about four days, even at low stages of the river, when rafts pass with difficulty. And it is supposed, that with comparatively small expenditure, this navigation can be perfected at all seasons, when the Ohio is navigable. One of the parties who made the first trip to Olean Point, in May, 1830, thus describes the country along the river.

"The scenery along the Allegheny river affords the greatest variety, and is in many places truly sublime. It would be generally very much like the North river scenery if equally improved and cultivated, more particularly so from Warren up to the Great Valley. There the hills rise higher and the river narrows. Its courses are in all directions, and its mountains in all shapes, dressed at this season of the year in its richest robes. The wild flowers along the shores, the beautiful evergreens and towering pines and hemlocks, interspersed with the lighter maple green, give to the whole scenery an indescribable beauty."

This river for the greater part of its course runs not in a valley like most other rivers, but in a deep bed, far below the general surface of the country, making its way at the foot of precipitous rocky steeps, which form either one shore or the other. There are few places in which the opposite shores are both rocky. One side generally consists of hills covered with oak, and rising from the water's edge, at a slope of one or two hundred feet in 40 perches. In some places a margin of two or three rods wide is low enough to be covered with floods, but these flats are rarely of great extent. The floods on this river rise from 20 to 30 feet above its low water surface. The steep rocky shores change sides frequently, seldom remaining on the same side for a length of two miles in any one place. Rocks of immense size lie at the foot of these steeps, evidently "time fallen," having been dislodged from above by the power of the frost. Some have fallen into deep water,—a single rock of a size sufficient to build a lock is frequently seen,—they are of sandstone and cleave readily in any direction. Of this stone the fine Pittsburg glass is made. It is most commonly taken from the mouth of Clarion river, where it is most free from impurities. Where a stream issues from a chasm in the shore, there is often a shallow place, and a fall in the river of three or four feet. A remarkable character of this river is, that it consists altogether of long sheets of deep still water, separated by short shallows, seldom exceeding 20 or 30 rods in length. Wherever the river washes the steep mountain base, it is, with few exceptions, deep; and the same degree of steepness continues under the water, that is visible above it. A beach, however, is formed by the debris of the mountains, in most places; the pebbly shore on the opposite side is invariably shallow.

These peculiar features of the river render a side cut or canal along its banks very expensive, if not impracticable, whilst they afford extraordinary facilities for improving the navigation by dams and locks. Judge Geddes, who surveyed the rivers in 1826 at the instance of the Canal Commissioners, with a view to the construction of a canal from the mouth of French creek to the Kiskiminitas river, reports the distance at 87 miles, 918 yards, and estimates the cost of a canal at $1,595,393, an average of about $18,380 per mile. Some miles of the route it is supposed would cost near $50,000 each. The fall in the river from the mouth of French creek to the mouth of the Kiskiminitas is 235 feet, something more than $2\frac{1}{2}$ feet to the mile.

About seven and a half miles above Kittanning, argillaceous slate is seen, composing part of the perpendicular shore in the cliffs of which plume alum presents itself.

The mineral wealth of the Allegheny country is important. Salt, iron and coal are obtained in many places on the part which has been surveyed. The salt water is found chiefly below the mouth of the Mahoning creek; and little coal is got above the mouth of the Clarion river; but iron is found every where. Furnaces are in operation at Bear creek, Scrub Grass creek and Sandy creek. The quality of the ore on French creek is deemed suitable for bar iron, and a forge has been erected near Franklin. Of the agricultural products of the country, little can be said, and not a great deal expected.

The river and its branches were declared public highways by acts 21st March, 1789, and 4th March, 1807.

Allegheny county, was taken from Westmoreland and Washington counties by act of 24th Sept. 1788, which provided the following boundary. Beginning at the mouth of Flaherty's run on the South side of the Ohio river, from thence by a straight line to the plantation on which Joseph Scott, Esq. now lives, on Mouture's run, to include the same, from thence by a straight line to the mouth of Miller's run on Chartier's creek, thence by a straight line to the mouth of Perry's mill run, on the east side of the Monongahela river; thence up the said river to the mouth of Becket's run; thence by a straight line to the mouth of Sewickly creek, on Youghiogheny river; thence down the said river to the mouth of Crawford's run; thence by a straight line to the mouth of Brush creek, on Turtle creek; thence up Turtle creek to the main fork thereof; thence by a northerly line, until it strikes Poketos creek; thence down the said creek to the Allegheny river; thence up the Allegheny river to the north boundary of the State; thence along the same to the western line of the State; thence along the same to the river Ohio; and thence up the same to the place of beginning. And by the act 17th Sept. 1789, these boundaries were enlarged by an addition from Washington county, under the following lines, "Beginning at the river Ohio, where the boundary line of the State crosses the said river; from thence in a straight line to White's mill, on Raccoon creek; from thence by a straight line to Armstrong's mill, on Miller's run; and from thence by a straight line to the Monongahela river, opposite the mouth of Perry's run.

These very ample bounds, given 43 years ago, have been greatly curtailed by the establishment of the counties of Beaver, Butler, Armstrong, Venango, Mercer, Crawford, Warren, Erie, and the county of Allegheny is now bounded on the N. by Butler, on the E. and S. E. by Westmoreland, on the S. W. and W. by Washington, and on the N. W. by Beaver counties.

This county has many historical reminiscences connected with it, or rather with Pittsburg, its metropolis, to which we shall append all that we propose to introduce into our work relating to it. (See Pittsburg.)

Allegheny belongs to the great secondary formation which extends westerly from the Allegheny mountain and abounds with bituminous coal. In the hills about Pittsburgh, along the Monongahela and Allegheny rivers, and other parts of the county, this valuable mineral is found near the surface, in strata of from one inch to six feet thick, generally bedded on schistose sandstone, and overlaid with black aluminous slate.

The surface of the country is generally hilly; but the river and creek bottoms, and indeed the sides of most of the hills, are exuberantly fertile.

The country consists principally of arable hills and alternate valleys, or as it is commonly called, rolling ground. Near water courses the hills are frequently too steep for cultivation, though having a fine soil, and clothed with the most luxuriant growth of timber. Such hills having the proper exposure would be well adapted to the culture of the wine vine.

In the valleys and along the water courses, ash, sugar-maple, cherry, elm, &c. abound; the majestic sycamore skirts the borders of most of the larger streams. Leaving the valleys, the different species of oak are found to predominate. Black walnut abounds in some places, and indicates a soil of great fertility. The forest trees generally are of a large size, healthy and luxuriant in appearance. Wood is plenty and cheap. Fruit trees are abundant, and the soil and climate well adapted to their fruitfulness. Grapes in great variety grow spontaneously, some of an excellent quality, well worth cultivation.

The county is well watered. It is divided from S. E. to N. W. by the Monongahela and Ohio rivers; the latter being formed by the union of the Allegheny river with the former, which approaches from the N. E. The Monongahela has a course by and through the county of about 35 ms. along its meanderings, before it meets with the Allegheny, and the latter winds by and through the county about 27 miles, to Pittsburg. It is the clearer, more rapid and stronger stream, and generally displays its character in the purity of its water, for a considerable distance after the union. The Monongahela receives from the county on the east the Youghiogheny river, Turtle creek and nine mile run; and from the west, Peter's creek, Thompson's run and Sawmill run. The Allegheny receives from the north, Bull, Deer and Pine creeks, and several smaller streams; and from the south, Poketos, Plumb, and Sandy creeks, and some lesser branches. The Ohio river receives from the south, Chartier's creek, Mouture's and Flaherty's runs, and from the north Hawser's and Jones' run and Big and Little Sewickly creeks.

The great state canal follows the source of the Allegheny river from the mouth of the Kiskiminitas, about 30 miles, to the Ohio at Alleghany town, opposite to Pittsburg. It communicates also with the Monongahela river by a aqueduct across the river and a tunnel through Grant's hill and outlet locks. This tunnel is solidly arched throughout with sand stone, laid in hammer-dressed range work. (See Pennsylvania canal in Part I, Western division.)

A survey has been made of the valley of the Monongahela river, with a view to a navigation connected with the Ohio and Chesapeake canal, and the river has been reported as admirably adapted to a slack water navigation, by means of dams and locks, but unfitted for a canal. (See Monongahela.) It is probable that at no distant day, the former mode of improvement will be adopted.

A mineral spring has lately been discovered in St. Clair t-ship, west of the Monongahela river, four miles

S. W. from Pittsburg, to which the name of the Pittsburg mineral spring has been given. It issues from the fissures of a rock on the side of a small hill, and discharges about a gallon of water per minute, which is conveyed by a tunnel into a reservoir, from which it is pumped to supply a bath house. The temperature of the spring is nearly the same at all seasons. The specific gravity of the water, when compared with distilled water, is as 1002 to 1000. It contains muriate of soda 2 parts, muriate of magnesia $\frac{1}{2}$, oxide of iron 1, sulphate of lime $\frac{1}{2}$; carbonic acid gas in one quart, 18 inches. And it is recommended by Dr. Mead as beneficial in all cases where chalybeates are given.

A bed of marble, of the species called birds eye, has been discovered about six miles from the city and one and a half mile from the canal. It cuts smoothly, takes a fine polish, and is well adapted for ornamental purposes.

A turnpike road from Blairsville unites with another from Greensburg, in Wilkins' town ship, and proceeds thence to Pittsburg. Two turnpike roads run west from the city, one for a few miles and the other to the state line. A turnpike road also leaves the city and runs north by Woodville to Butler.

There are two very fine bridges at Pittsburg. One across the Allegheny and the other over the Monongahela r. The first is 1122 feet long by 38 feet wide, and 38 feet above the level of the water, consisting of six arches resting on piers of dressed stone and protected by a roof. It was erected by an incorporated company in 1819, at the cost of $95,249, of which the State subscribed 40,000. The second is 1500 feet long and 37 wide, and has 8 arches resting on stone piers—roofed—finished in 1818, by an incorporated company at an expense of $102,450, to which the State also subscribed $40,000. The first connects the borough of Allegheny and the second the borough of Birmingham with the city.

The principal towns are Pittsburg, situated at the head of the Ohio r. at the confluence of the Allegheny and Monongahela rs. lat. 40° 27′ N. lon. 3° 2′ W. from W. C., Bayardstown, Alleghenytown, and Birmingham, which are suburbs of the city, Perrysville, Lawrenceville, Manchester, Middleton, Jefferiestown, Noblesborough, Elizabethtown, McKeesport, Perritsport, Howardsville, Wilkinsburg and East Liberty. (See these titles.)

The Western University is in Pittsburg. In this institution the Pittsburg Academy has been merged. An extensive Presbyterian Theological Seminary has been established at Alleghenytown, and a celebrated boarding school, stands on Braddock's fatal field, a few miles south of the city. Schools for the rudiments of an English education, are in sufficient number for the wants of the people scattered over the county.

Religion is holden in great reverence by the inhabitants of the county, and due provision made by private subscription for the maintenance of the clergymen of the several denominations. Two thirds of the inhabitants are Presbyterians, after whom the Methodists and Baptists are the most numerous.

The exports of the county are the usual agricultural products of the country, wheat, rye, corn, oats, whiskey, and the manufactures of Pittsburg, consisting of the various fabrications of iron, glass, delft-ware, cotton and wool, and last, though not least, of steamboats, and steam engines. (See Pittsburg.)

There are two banks in the county located at Pittsburg, viz: The bank of Pittsburg, and the branch of the bank of the U. S. There are in this city several insurance agencies from the eastern cities.

There are 8 periodical journals published in Pittsburg, viz: The Pittsburg Gazette, semi-weekly, the Pittsburg Statesman, Mercury, Allegheny Democrat, The Manufacturer, The Pittsburg Recorder, (religious,) Sylvester's Journal and the Antimasonic Times.

The county paid to the state treasury the following sums in 1831.

Dividend on Stock in the Allegheny Bridge Company . .	3,200	
Dividend on Stock in the Monongahela Bridge Company . .	2,400	
Dividend on Stock in the Pittsburgh and Steubenville Turnpike	360	
Tax on Bank Dividends—Bank of Pittsburgh	2,211	
Tax on Offices	55	24
Tax on Writs	1,054	53
Tax on Writs in Supreme Court.	261	41
Tavern licenses	3,423	54
Tax on dealers in Foreign Merchandize	682	45
Tin and Clock pedlar's licenses	46	60
Canal tolls	2,646	64
	$16,341	41

Valuation of taxable property in 1829, including real and personal estate, and occupations, $8,022,220.

The population, composed of the descendants of Irish and German settlers, but chiefly the former, by the census of 1830, was 37,964, of whom 18,892 were white males, 18,313 females. Free colored males 399, females 330, male slaves 7, female slaves 23. Included in the foregoing there were 740 aliens, 36 deaf and dumb, and 15 blind. Taxables 7583. This table does not include the city of Pittsburg. That contains 12,542 inhabitants. Taxables 2,653. Making the population of the county 50,504, and the taxables 10,236. (See table annexed.)

Allegheny county forms the 21st Senatorial District, and sends one Senator; and four members to the House of Representatives.

Conjoined with Beaver, Butler, and Armstrong, it forms the 16th Congressional District of the State, and united with Beaver and Butler counties it makes the fifth Judicial District, Charles Shaler Esq. President. The Courts are holden at Pittsburg on the 3d Monday in November, and the 4th Mondays of January, April and August, annually. The county belongs to the western district of the Supreme Court, the session of which is holden annually at Pittsburg on the first Monday in September.

The public buildings in the county consist of the Court-house and county offices, of brick, in the city of Pittsburg; the Western University on Grant's Hill; the United States Arsenal about two miles above the city, on the south side of the Allegheny, enclosing four acres, on which there is a large depot of arms and ordnance; the Theological Seminary in Alleghenytown, and the State Prison also in the same place, to which may be added the water works of the city. (For a more particular description of these buildings see Pittsburg.)

The *West Pennsylvania Lyceum* has been established in this county, with the design of extending the system of education in which manual labor is conducted with the study of the elements of a liberal education.

There is a county temperance society and several auxiliary associations in the t-ship, whose efforts have produced the discontinuance of several distilleries, and have contributed essentially to the decrease of intemperance. The county is however yet subjected to an annual tax of near $20,000, for the support of paupers, who have been rendered chargeable by this vice.

STATISTICAL TABLE OF ALLEGHENY COUNTY.

Townships, &c.	Greatest Lth.	Greatest Bth.	Area in Acres.	Face of Country.	Soil.	Population. 1810	1820	1830	Taxables.
Alleghenytown bor.				Hilly, but almost universally arable.	Loam, composed of the debris of the various strata of clay, sand stone, limestone, &c. &c. Coal in every part of the county.			2801	
Birmingham bor.								520	
Bayardstown bor.								2125	
*Deer t-ship.	13	4½	34,560			674	1075	1642	312
Elizabeth	10½	10½	35,200			2368	2493	2517	571
Fayette	11	8	37,760			2016	2000	2302	536
Findlay	9	6½	17,920					1326	270
Franklin	6	6	11,080					658	112
Indiana	9	7½	32,000			692	1198	1777	356
Jefferson, included in Deer t-ship.								1425	307
Mifflin	12	7	32,000			1953	2221	1162	269
Moon	6½	4½	14,720			1622	2014	1048	221
Ohio	11½	8	17,920			832	1477	1079	221
Pitt	7½	6	13,440			2441	4381	3924	1218
Pine	7	6	26,880			588	795	984	241
Plum	11	7	30,720			1174	1639	1724	356
Ross	7	6	23,040			1327	1979	2196	725
Robinson	6½	6	16,640			899	1392	1371	275
St. Clair	12	8	39,040			3080	4142	4614	965
Versailles	6	5	10,240			883	867	911	233

Allegripus Mountain, Hopewell t-ship, Bedford co. commencing near the S. boundary and extending N. through the greater part of the t-ship, when it is broken by the Raystown branch of the Juniata r. at Stonerstown; thence it continues N. E. through Hopewell, to the main stream of the river near the borough of Huntingdon, being in length about 30 miles.

Allen, t-ship, Northampton co. bounded on the N. by Lehigh and Moore t-ships, on the S. by Hanover and Bethlehem t-ships, on the E. by Upper and lower Nazareth t-ships, and on the W. by the Lehigh r. which separates it from Lehigh co. Its principal towns are Kreidersville, Howartown and Bath. Greatest length, 8 ms., greatest breadth 5¼. Population in 1830, 2106. Taxables, in 1828, 417. (See Statistical Table of Northampton county.) There are 2 churches belonging to the Lutherans in the t-ship,—there are also several mills on the waters of Hockendoque and Calesoque creeks.

Allensville, p-o. Mifflin co. 84 miles S. W. of Harrisburg.

* This includes Jefferson t-ship, whose boundaries we do not know.

Allentown, (See Northampton in Lehigh co.)

Allen, t-ship, Cumberland co. bounded N. by E. Pennsborough, E. by the Susquehannah r., S. by York co. and W. by Monroe t-ship. Centrally distant from Carlisle 12 miles. Greatest length 8, breadth 4 ms. Area, 10,240 acres. Surface, level. Soil, limestone, fertile. Pop. in 1830, 2337. Taxables, 418. The Yellow Breeches creek forms the t-ship and county boundary on the S. Tindler's Spring in the N. W. angle, and Cedar Spring near the N. E. angle are noted fountains. The towns of Cumberland and Lisburn lie on the Yellow Breeches creek. The first at its confluence with the Susquehannah river, opposite to the town of New-Market, 16 miles S. E. from Carlisle. The second is a post-town on the border of Monohan t-ship York co. about 14 miles from Carlisle. Allen p-o. is at Cumberland, 107 miles N. of W. C. and 16 W. of Harrisburg.

Alsace, t-ship, Berks co. on the E. side of the river Schuylkill. Pop. in 1810, 1275, in 1820, 1640, in 1830, 1943. Taxables, 402. Bounded on the N. E. by Ruscombmanor, N. W.

by Meriden creek t-ship, W. by the river Schuylkill, E. by Exeter and Oley t-ships. Area, 21,420 acres. Its surface is mountainous, and the Neversink and Penn's mountains are chiefly remarkable. The valleys are principally lime-stone, well cultivated and highly productive ; the hill sides, which are also generally cultivated, are not so fruitful, but repay well the labor bestowed upon them when manured with lime, which is easily obtainable at a moderate expense. It surrounds the borough of Reading, and is intersected by the Philadelphia and Central turnpikes, and by other great roads which lead northward and eastward. In a secluded and romantic gorge of the Penn mtn. is Kesler's chalybeate spring, at which is a house of public entertainment, much frequented by the inhabitants of Reading ; and a small woollen factory, driven by a rivulet which precipitates itself sparkling and leaping down the ravine. Under the feverish excitement given to manufactures in the late war, a considerable sum of money was expended here in erecting a woollen factory, the principal building of which is the present tavern house. Several small streams have their sources in the hills, of which the principal is Roush's creek, upon which there are several mills. Iron ore is abundant in the Penn mountain, and is transported to the furnaces in this and the neighboring counties. Spies church is in the N. E. angle of the town-ship, and another church about a mile and a half from Reading on the road to Rutztown—both common to the Lutherans and Presbyterians.

Alum bank, p-o. St. Clair's t-ship, Bedford co. 136 ms. N. W. from W. C. 114 from Harrisburg.

Amberson's Valley, Fannet t-ship, Franklin co. between the Blue and Dividing mtns. Amberson's creek flows through it the whole extent of the town-ship into the West Branch of the Conecocheague creek. There is a noted Sulphur Spring here.

Amity, t-ship of Erie co. bounded N. by Venango t-ship and by the State of New-York, E. by Concord, S. by Union and W. by Waterford t-ships. Centrally distant S. E. from Erie 18 ms. Greatest length 7, breadth 5 ms. Area, 22,400 acres. Surface hilly. Soil, gravelly loam, productive in grass and adapted to grazing. Pop. in 1830, 335, taxables 52. The French creek crosses the N. W. angle, and the south branch of that stream rises in the S. E. angle of the town-ship. The post-town of Wattville or Wattsburg is on the north boundary in a fork of French creek.

Amity, t-ship of Berks co. Pop. in 1810, 1090, in 1820, 1279, in 1830, 1378. Taxables, 284. The township is a square of 4 by 4 miles, and contains 10,500 acres—bounded on N. by Oley and Earl t-ship, on the S. by the Schuylkill r., on the E. by Douglas t-ship, and on the W. by Exeter. Manokesy Hill, centrally situated, is a strongly marked feature of its topography. Manatawny creek crosses the northeastern corner, and the Manokesy creek, the S. W. corner of the township in their courses to the Schuylkill r. There are several mills on each. The surface of the country is undulating, and the soil red gravel, well cultivated and productive, worth from 15 to 60 dollars per acre. Towns, Warrensburg and Weavertown. At the latter there is a church of Lutherans and Presbyterians. An English Presbyterian church at Warensburg, one near the Manokesy hill. The Perkiomen turnpike road crosses the township near its southern boundary.

Amity, p-t. Amwell t-ship, Washington co. distant about 10 miles S. of Washington borough, on Bane's fork of 10 mile creek, on the road to Waynesborough, 228 miles S. W. from Harrisburg, contains 25 dwellings, 2 stores, one tavern and a Presbyterian church.

Amwell, t-ship, Washington co. bounded N. by Strabane t-ship, E. by West Bethel, S. by Greene co. and W. by Morris and Canton t-ships. Centrally distant from the borough of

Washington 10 ms. Greatest length 11, breadth 9½ ms. Area, 33,280 acres; surface hilly; soil, loam; coal abundant. Taxable Pop. in 1830, 359. The t-ship is drained by the N. Fork of 10 mile creek, by the Little N. Fork and Bane's Fork of the same creek. The p-t. of Amity lies in the S. W. angles, distant S. from Washington borough about 10 miles.

Andalusia, p-o. Bensalem t-ship, Bucks co. on the turnpike road from Philadelphia to Bristol, 14 ms. from the former, 157 from W. C., 119 from Harrisburg. The mail arrives at this office daily.

Andersonsburg, p-o. Perry co. 40 miles N. of Harrisburg.

Antes, t-ship, Huntingdon co. bounded N. E. by Warrior Mark t-ship, S. E. by Tyrone t-ship, S. W. by Allegheny t-ship, and N. W. by Cambria co. Centrally distant from Huntingdon N. W. 20 miles. Greatest length 10, breadth 8 ms. Area, 49,280 acres; surface, mountain and valley; soil, red shale. Taxable pop. in 1830, 207. The W. branch of the Juniata runs N. through the co. On its E. banks are beds of iron ore. The Brush mountain lies on the E. of the t-ship, and the Allegheny mountain on the West. Antestown is the name given to the p-o. of the t-ship, which is 119 ms. S. W. from Harrisburg. There is a small village in the t-ship called Davidsburg. There were in the t-ship in 1828, 4 grist mills, 8 saw mills, 1 distillery, and one powder mill.

Antelauny or Maiden creek, Lehigh co. rises in Linn t-ship, and running westerly along the Blue mountain, passes into Berks co. and thence into the Schuylkill r. It drives many mills, but it is too small in Lehigh co. to be navigable.

Anthracite, village of Mauch Chunk t-ship, Northampton co. at the coal mine on Mauch Chunk mtn. inhabited by the miners and their families.

Antrim, t-ship, Franklin co. bounded N. by St. Thomas, Hamilton, and Guilford t-ships, S. by the state of Maryland, E. by Washington t-ship, and W. by Montgomery and Peters t-ships. Centrally distant from Chambersburg 11 ms. Breadth 8¼ ms. Area, 38,400 acres; surface, level, rocky; soil, limestone. Pop. in 1830, 3829; taxables 768. It is drained on the W. by the Conecocheague creek and its tributaries, on the E. by a branch of Kettle creek. The Waynesburg, Green Castle and Mercersburg turnpike road runs through it, on which, near the W. boundary, lies the p-t. of Greencastle.

Annville, t-ship, Lebanon co. bounded N. by East Hanover, E. by Lebanon t-ship, S. and W. by Londonderry. Centrally distant from the borough of Lebanon about 6 miles. Greatest length about 10 ms. greatest breadth 7 ms. Area, 21,700 acres; surface pricipally level; soil, limestone and gravel. Pop. in 1830, 2736; taxables 440. The Swatara creek forms the northern boundary; the Quitapahilla crosses the t-ship centrally to the western line; along which it runs to its confluence with the former, receiving from the S. Killinger's run, which has its whole course between this and Londonderry t-ship. On the Quitapahilla there is a forge. Millerstown, a p-t. lies on the turnpike road from Lebanon to Harrisburg, distant 5 ms. W. from the former and 19 ms. E. of the latter. The p-o. called "Annville," is 129 ms. from W. C. and 19 E. of Harrisburg.

Apollacan creek, Choconut t-ship, Susquehannah co. rises in that t-ship, and flows N. W. into the East branch of the Susquehannah r. in the State of New-York. It is a mill stream but unnavigable in this State.

Appollo, p-o. Armstrong co. 219 ms. N. W. of W. C. 188 ms. W. of Harrisburg.

Aquanshicola creek, Northampton co. rises in Ross t-ship, about a mile E. of the Wind Gap, on the N. side of the Blue mtn. and running along its base S. W. by W. falls into the Lehigh r. at its entrance into the Water Gap. It is a rapid stream, drives several mills, but is not navigable for any kind of craft.

Ararat mount, a spur of the Moosic mtn. lying on the borders of Wayne and Susquehannah cos. chiefly in Jackson t-ship of the one, but extending partially into Preston t-ship of the other. It is a hill of considerable elevation, but of gentle and easy access, and is covered with an excellent soil. Its summit commands a wide and delightful view to the west.

Armagh t-ship, Mifflin co. bounded N. by the Path Valley mtn. which divides it from Centre co. E. by Union co. S. by Jack's mtn. and W. by Union t-ship. Centrally distant from Lewistown 12 ms. N. E. Greatest length 22 ms. breadth 6. Area 66,560 acres; surface mountainous, with fine valleys; soil in the valleys, limestone. Taxable pop. 428. The t-ship. is covered with knobs and ridges, and is drained by the Great and Little Kishicoquillas creeks, which unite in a gorge of Jack's mtn. through which runs the turnpike road from Lewistown to Bellefonte. The Kishicoquillas valley extends nearly half through the t-ship. from W. to E.

Armagh, p-t. of Wheatfield t-ship. Indiana co. on the turnpike road from Ebensburg to Pittsburg, 15 ms. S.E. of the borough of Indiana, 175 ms. from W.C. 141 W. from Harrisburg, and 13 ms. E. from Blairsville; contains about 40 dwellings, 4 stores, and 6 taverns.

Armstrong co. was established by act 12th March, 1800, sec. 8, which provides "that so much of the cos. of Allegheny, Lycoming and Westmoreland as are included within the following boundaries, should form a separate co. Beginning on the Allegheny r. at the mouth of the Buffalo creek, the corner of Butler co. thence N. along the line of the said co. of Butler to the N. E. corner of the same, supposed to be at the Allegheny r. and if the N. E. corner of the said co. of Butler shall not strike the Allegheny r. then from the said corner on a line at a right angle from the first line of the co. of Butler, until the said line shall strike the Allegheny r. thence by the western margin of the said r. to the mouth of Toby's creek; thence crossing the r. and up the said creek to the line dividing Wood's and Hamilton's districts, thence S. along the said line, to the present line of Westmoreland co. thence S. 35° W. to the Kiskiminitas r. thence down the said r. to the mouth thereof, on the Allegheny r. thence across the said r. to the W. margin thereof; thence down the said r. to the mouth of Buffalo creek, the corner of Buffalo co. the place of beginning." And until the co. should be organized, it was annexed to Westmoreland co. And it was declared that the st. jus. should be fixed on the Allegheny r. at a place not more than 5 ms. distant from Old Kittanning t.

By act of 6th April, 1802, commissioners were appointed to fix the st. jus. and upon their report, and by act of 4th April, 1804, trustees were appointed to survey 150 acres of land at the place where General Armstrong defeated the Indians, being part of a tract which James and John Armstrong had given to the Governor in trust for the co. and to lay out lots for the public buildings, and to sell the remainder of the tract in town lots, containing not more than two thirds nor less than one fourth of an acre, and to apply the proceeds to the erection of co. buildings.

By the act of 2d March, 1805, the co. was organized for judicial purposes.

The co. is bounded N. by Venango co. from which it is separated by the Allegheny r. and Toby's creek, E. by Jefferson and Indiana cos. S. and S. W. by Westmoreland, and W. by Butler. It is about 35 ms. in length, with a mean breadth of about 20 ms. Area 941 sq. ms. Kittanning, the co. t. is in N. lat. 41°, and long. 2° 30′ W. from W. C.

The surface of the country is much

variegated with hill and valley, in many places broken, and the soil is not less diversified. Large bodies of land are almost worthless; others are valuable chiefly for their timber, but there are extensive tracts which are scarcely inferior to any land in the state.

The timber, according to the soil, is black, red, white and rock oak, chesnut, hickory, ash, walnut, sugar maple, elm, cherry; pine and cedar are not abundant.

This county, like the rest of the country of Pennsylvania, N. W. of the mountains, pertains to the secondary formation and abounds with limestone, coal and salt. The two last are most plentiful in the S. part of the co. particularly along the Kiskiminitas and Allegheny rs. and Crooked creek. Banks of coal are found along Red Bank and Mahoning creeks, 12 feet thick. Alumine is found on the Mahoning near its junction with the Allegheny r. and copperas upon Red Bank creek. Iron ore is every where abundant, and lead ore has been discovered in Kittanning t-ship. on the left bank of the Allegheny r.

The co. is very well watered. The Allegheny r. divides it into two unequal parts, winding from the N. W. angle in an eliptical curve to the S. W. receiving from the E. the following streams, which have their sources in the mts. viz. Clarion r. or Toby's creeks, the N. boundary; Red Bank creek, Mahoning creek, Crooked creek, and the Kiskiminitas r. which forms the S. W. boundary. Cowanshannock, Pine and Piney creeks are considerable, but less important streams. Buffalo creek is the largest on the western side of the r. and it flows S. to unite with it at the town of Freeport, in the S. W. point of the co. The Pa. canal enters the co. about 9 ms. above Warren t. crossing the Kiskiminitas to the N. bank, which it pursues to the Allegheny r. and passing the r. by an aqueduct, runs about $1\frac{1}{2}$ ms. further in the co. quitting it below Freeport.

The turnpike road from Indiana to Kittanning runs N. W. about half way across the co. and thence to Butler; and upon it, near the S. E. boundary, lies the small v. of Middletown. The Mercer and Roseburg turnpike runs nearly parallel with the Clarion r. Freeport, Kittanning, and Lawrenceburg, are towns on the Allegheny; the first and least on the W. and the second on the eastern bank. Hulingsburg, Callensburg, and Roseburg, are in the N. E. part of the co. near to the Clarion r.

The population of the co. about one half of German descent, and from Northampton co. by the census of 1830, was 17,625, of whom 8970 were white males; 8078 white females. Males colored, free, 49; females, 47; slaves none. Of these there were 56 aliens, 9 deaf and dumb, and 10 blind. The taxables in 1828 were 3257.

The principal religious sect is Presbyterian, and the other sects rank in numbers, in the following order: Methodists, Lutherans, and German reformed. There are common schools in the co. adequate to the wants of the people; and there is an academy at Kittanning, where the languages and mathematics are taught. There are two newspapers, viz. "The Armstrong Advertiser," and "Kittanning Gazette," both published in the town of Kittanning.

United with Westmoreland, Cambria, and Indiana, this co. forms the tenth judicial district, over which John Young, Esq. presides. The courts are holden in Kittaning, on the third Mondays of March, June, September and December.

The co. belongs to the western district of the supreme court, the session of which is holden at Pittsburg on the first Monday in September annually.

United with Indiana, Jefferson, Venango and Warren, it forms the 24th senatorial district of the state, and sends one senator, and sends alone one representative to the assembly. Connected with Allegheny, Beaver and

Butler, it forms the sixteenth congressional district.

The public buildings of the co. consist of a court house, offices of brick, and a prison of stone, an academy incorporated in 1821, to which the legislature granted the sum of $2000.

The trade of the co. consists of the usual agricultural staples, and of salt and iron. For the manufacture of the last there are three furnaces. Bear creek furnace, on Bear creek, in the N. W. corner of the co. owned by H. Baldwin, Esq. said to be the largest in the U. S. at which 40 tons of metal have been made per week. Allegheny furnace on the W. side of the Allegheny r. about two miles above Kittanning, making about 14 tons of metal weekly. It belongs to A. McNickle. The third, near the Kiskiminitas r. and the Pa. canal, belongs to J. W. Biddle, and makes about 15 tons weekly. There are no forges in the co. The pigs are sent by the canal to Pittsburg, where they meet with ready sale. There are now 24 salt works in operation in this county, which make at least 65,500 barrels of salt, 5 bushels to the barrel, annually, which sell at the works at $2 12 the barrel. Twenty additional works, it is supposed, will be in operation in August 1832. To obtain a supply of salt water, the earth is commonly perforated to the depth of 400 feet and sometimes of 700 feet. In this penetration, the auger is driven by steam, horse, or hand power, at an expense of $2 per foot, when the depth does not exceed 500 feet; but over that depth, at $3 the foot. The fuel commonly used for evaporation is coal, and in some cases it may be thrown from the beds into the furnace.

The best improved lands sell at from $12 to $20 the acre ; and unimproved from $1 to $6.

The receipts of the co. for co. purposes were, in 1828, $8808; expences $6759, in which were included $9 53 for teaching poor children! and $36 25 for wolf and panther scalps.

The co. paid into the state treasury, in 1831, for tax on writs . . .	182 25
Tavern licenses . .	234 08
	$416 33

STATISTICAL TABLE OF ARMSTRONG COUNTY.

Townships.	Greatest Lth.	Greatest Bth.	Area in Acres.	Face of country.	Population. 1810	1820	1830	Taxables.	Valuation.	Unseated	Pers.
*Allegheny t-ship	13	10	53,760	Hilly.	820	1443	2966	602	122,193	11,382	21,081
Buffalo . . .	13	10	41,000	Gentle hills.	1150	1597	2458	429	107,858	10,375	16,414
Clarion . . .	13½	12	68,480	Do.			2067	340	91,218	11,060	16,536
Kittaning . . .	17½	7	51,200	Hilly.	1197	976	1629	281	75,624	15,626	18,426
Kittaning bor. .					309	318	526	123	38,045	8,015	7,550
Perry	8	7	24,960	Part hilly, rolling.			853	157	41,294	9,460	9,331
Plumb creek . .	12	7½	40,960	Do.		1340	1456	262	71,226	10,253	14,302
Redbank . . .	15	12	81,920	Do.	943	2042	1660	293	57,116	26,180	12,054
Toby	17	8½	46,080	Do.	611	1156	1362	363	86,137	16,351	15,445
Sugar creek . .	12	11½	57,600	Hilly.	1113	1482	1870	344	84,771	6,209	17,311
Wayne	11	7½	46,080	Undulating.			878	153	34,545	19,645	7,147
*Kiskiminitas, taken from Allegheny in 1831				Hilly.	6143	10,324	17,625	3259			

Rate of tax 5 mills on the dollar.

Armstrong creek and valley, Halifax t-ship, Dauphin co. S. of Berry's mtn. about 18 ms. N. of Harrisburg. The creek has a S. W. course of about 12 or 13 ms. and empties into the Susquehannah r. about a mile above the village of Halifax. The valley and creek branch around a spur of Berry's mtn.

Armstrong t-ship, Ind. co. bounded N. E. by Washington t-ship, S. E. by Centre, S. W. by Conemaugh t-ships, and N. W. by Armstrong co. Centrally distant W. from the borough of Ind. 7 ms. Greatest length 6½, breath 6½. Area, 23,120 acres; surface level; soil, clay and gravel. Pop. in 1830, 814; taxables, 161. It is drained by Crooked creek, which flows W. through it.

Asylum, t-ship, Bradford co. bounded N. and N. E. by the Susquehannah r. E. by Luzerne co. S. by Albany t-ship, and W. by Monroe t-ship. Centrally distant S. E. of Towanda about 12 ms. Greatest length 13, breadth 7½ ms. Area, 33,280 acres; surface, hilly; soil, gravelly loam. Pop. in 1830, 529; taxables 91. It is drained by Duvals creek on the N. Sugar creek on the E. a branch of the Big Mahoney on the S. E. and Towanda creek on the S. W. and several less considerable streams. The rapid in the Susquehannah r. known as Wyalussing Falls, is in the E. part of the t-ship. French town lies in the extreme N. E. angle of the t-ship, in a deep bend of the Susquehanah r. There is a p-o. in the t-ship called Asylum, 248 ms. N. W. of W. C. and 137 from Harrisburg.

Aston, t-ship, Delaware co. bounded N. E. by Middleton, S. E. by Chester, S. and S. W. by Upper Chichester and W. by Concord. Central distance W. from Philadelphia 20 ms. Length 4¾, breadth, 2¼. Area, 6400. Chester Creek runs along the eastern boundary and Painter's creek crosses into it near the middle of the t-ship. Log t. and Village Green, are villages within it. Surface, level; soil, fertile loam. Pop. in 1830, 1070; taxables in 1828, 224.

Attleborough, p-t. of Middletown t-ship, Bucks co. on the road leading from Bristol to Easton, where the road from Trenton to Norristown crosses the same, is situated on a piece of high rich table land, 6 ms. from the Delaware r. 1 from Neshamony r. 7 from Bristol, 9 from Trenton, 20 from Philadelphia, 16 from Doylestown and 125 from Harrisburg. It is one of the most beautiful, healthy and pleasant situations in the county, having a commanding view of the surrounding country for 15 or 20 miles. The water is excellent, the air pure, and through the past sickly seasons, this village has been exempt from disease. Within a mile of the town are two chalybeate springs, having the usual qualities of such healthful fountains. The village contains from 80 to 100 dwellings and about 600 inhabitants, —4 places of public worship, viz: 2 Quaker, 1 Methodist, and 1 African; an extensive tannery and currying establishment, 1 tavern, 2 dry goods stores, 1 iron store, 3 apothecaries, 2 able physicians, 2 confectionaries, 2 coach making establishments, at one of which the business has been conducted very extensively in all its branches for many years; 4 wheelwrights or wagon makers, who do a large business; and also, other mechanics, such as smiths, carpenters, joiners, turners, cordwainers, tailors weavers, coopers, painters, &c. &c. and a brick yard, at which a large business is done. Two daily stages pass through the town to Easton, one from Philadelphia and the other from Bristol, both profitable to the proprietors and accommodating to travellers. The country around Attleborough is much improved, the land of the first quality, in a high state of cultivation and very productive.

Athens, t-ship, Bradford co. bound. N. by the state of New-York, E. by Litchfield t-ship, S. by Orwell, Wyalussing, Sheshequin, Ulster and Smithfield t-ships. Centrally distant N. of Towanda 13 ms. Greatest length 14, breadth 6½ ms. Area, 38,400 acres; surface, hilly; soil, gravelly clay. Pop. in 1830, 1253; taxables, 190. The Susquehannah r. enters the t-ship from the N. E. and the Tioga r. from the N. W. The rivers approach each other within a mile near the town of Athens; below that town they diverge, widening the distance between them, to about a mile and a half, but unite about 2 miles above the S. line of the t-ship, forming the Presqu'il of Tioga Point. These rivers receive from the t-ship several considerable creeks. The village of Athens is a p-t. 143 ms. N. W. from Harrisburg, and contains 25 or 30 dwellings, &c. and an academy incorporated on the 22d March,

1813, with a donation of $2,000. Over the Tioga r. there is erected a bridge, completed in 1820, 450 feet long, 28 wide, resting on 4 stone piers, at a cost of $5,500. The town was incorporated 29th March, 1831.

Athens, p-t. Bradford co. (See the preceding article.)

Athens, t-ship, Crawford co. Pop. in 1830, 121.

Auburn, t-ship, Susquehannah co. bounded N. by Rush, E. by Springville t-ships, S. by Braintrim t-ship, Luzerne co. and W. by Wyalussing t-ship, Bradford co. Its greatest length E. and W. is 8 ms.; greatest breadth, N. and S. 6 ms. Area, 30,720 acres. It is watered by Tuscarora creek, Little Meshoppen creek and the west and middle branches of the Great Meshoppen creek, which flow southwardly to the Susquehannah r. Surface, rolling; soil, clay and gravel. Pop. in 1820, 208, in 1830, 516; taxables, by return of 1828, 65.

Augusta, t-ship, Northumberland co. bounded N. and W. by the Susquehannah r. E. by Rush and Shamokin t-ships, and S. by Lower Mahanoy and Little Mahanoy t-ships. Greatest length 10, greatest breadth 8 miles. Area 37,120 acres. Surface diversified; soil, alluvial, red shale and gravel. Pop. in 1830, 2,131. Taxables, 450. The Mahanoy mountain bounds it on the S. and the Shamokin Hills cover the N. E. It is drained by the Great and Little Shamokin creeks, which unite about a mile E. of Sunbury, and flow thence S. W. into the Susquehannah r. The Pottsville and Sunbury turnpike road crosses to the latter town, lying on the Susquehannah r. immediately below the confluence of the N. and W. branches. Sunbury, post and county town, is in this township, and there is also a post office called Augusta.

Aughwick creeks, Great and Little, and *Aughwick valley;* the Little Aughwick rises in Dublin t-ship, Huntingdon co. and flows S. 9 miles into Bedford co. thence N. W. into Springfield t-ship, Huntingdon co. about 5 ms. to the Great Aughwick. It is navigable for canoes to about 7 ms. from its mouth. The Great Aughwick rises in Dublin t-ship, Bedford co. and flows N. W. through the Great Aughwick valley 26 ms. by a comparative course into the Juniata r. about 3 ms. above Hamiltonville. It is navigable for boats, about 18 ms. to the mouth of the Little Aughwick.

Aurora, p-o. Bucks co. 173 ms. from W. C. and 87 from Harrisburg.

Bacharts run, West Penn t-ship, Schuylkill co. a tributary of Lizzard creek, rising in the Blue mountain.

Bainbridge, a p-t. of West Donnegal t-ship, Lancaster co. on the Susquehannah r. about 20 ms. N. W. of the city of Lancaster, 103 N. of W. C. and 18 S. of Harrisburg.

Bairdstown, Derry t-ship, Westmoreland co. on the left bank of the Connemaugh r. and on the turnpike road from Ebensburg to Pittsburg, 17 ms. N. E. of Greensburg, and opposite to Blairsville, contains 25 or 30 dwellings, 2 taverns and a store.

Bakertown, p-o. Allegheny co. 239 ms. N. W. from W. C. 217 W. of Harrisburg.

Bake oven knob, a distinguished eminence of the Blue Ridge in Keidelburg t-ship, Lehigh co.

Bald Eagle, t-ship, Lycoming co. bounded W. and N. by the W. branch of the Susquehannah r. E. by Wayne t-ship, and S. by Centre co. Centrally distant from Williamsport S. W. 25 ms. Greatest length 7, breadth 2 ms. Area, 3840 acres; surface, level; soil, alluvial. Taxable pop. in 1830, 69. The p-o. of the t-ship is distant N. W. 214 ms. from Washington and 107 from Harrisburg. The taxable property in 1829 consisted of seated lands valued at $22,417; personal estate 3,166. Amount of tax levied $191 86; rate of levy $\frac{3}{4}$ of 1 per cent.

Bald Eagle mountain, between the main branch of the Susquehannah and the west branch, separating Northumberland and Columbia counties from

Lycoming co. and extending N. E. into Luzerne co.

Bald Eagle mountain, Pittston t-ship, Luzerne co. E. of Jacob's mtn. and W. of Chestnut hill.

Bald Eagle, t-ship, Centre co. bounded N. E. by Lycoming co. S. E. by Amar t-ship, S. W. by Howard t-ship and N. W. by Lycoming co. Centrally distant N. from Bellefonte 16 ms. Greatest length 25, breadth 7 ms. Area, 68,480 acres; surface, mountainous; soil, valleys limestone, mountains, slate; pop. in 1830, 835; taxables, 153. The Bald Eagle creek flows N. E. through the t-ship along the N. side of the Muney hills into the west branch of the Susquehannah, receiving from the t-ship, along the S. W. line, Beach creek, upon the bank of which, salt has been discovered. The main ridge of the Allegheny fills the interior of the t-ship, from which Tungascootae creek flows N. E. into the river. The town of New Providence is in the N. E. angle of the t-ship, near which is a furnace.

Bald Eagle mountain, Bald Eagle creek and valley; a ridge of the Allegheny takes the name of Bald Eagle mountain, upon the confines of Huntingdon and Centre cos. N. E. of the Juniata r. and running N. E. about 30 ms. to Miles' borough, takes the name of Muny hills, under which it runs the same course about 24 ms. to the west branch of the Susquehannah at Dunnstown. The Bald Eagle creek rises in Centre co. and runs along the N. foot of the ridge, about 50 ms. to the river. It is a large stream and navigable for boats above Milesboro'. Bald Eagle valley, through which the creek flows, is bounded N. W. by the main Allegheny ridge. The valley is about 5 ms. wide, the width varying little in its whole length. The soil is limestone, rich and productive.

Bald Eagle valley, Huntingdon co. (See "Sinking valley.")

Bald Ridge, Lausanne t-ship, Northampton co. a continuation of the Spring mtn. The river Lehigh divides it from the Pohopoko mountain.

Baldwin, p-o. Butler co. 249 ms. from W. C. and 209 from Harrisburg.

Barnetts run, Belfast t-ship, Bedford co. a tributary of the N. branch of the Conoloway creek.

Barre, t-ship, Huntingdon co. bounded N. by Centre co. E. by Mifflin, S. and W. by West t-ship. Centrally distant N. E. from Huntingdon borough 13 ms. Greatest length $12\frac{1}{2}$, breadth $11\frac{1}{2}$ ms. Area, 48,640 acres; surface, mountainous, with fruitful limestone valleys. Pop. in 1830, 1770; taxables in 1828, 367. The t-ship is drained by Standing Stone and Shaver's creeks. Stone mtn. is on the S. E. and Tussey's mtn. on the N. E. boundary. Ennisville p-t. is centrally situated in the t-ship, 170 ms. N. W. of W. C. and 93 S. W. of Harrisburg. The t-ship contained in 1828, 4 grist mills, 18 saw mills, 3 distilleries, 2 fulling mills and 1 tan yard.

Barren hill, p-o. and village of Whitemarsh t-ship, Montgomery co. 7 ms. S. E. of Norristown, 148 N. E. of W. C. and 93 S. E. from Harrisburg, on and between the Chesnut hill and Perkiomen turnpike, and the Ridge turnpike roads, which here approach within the 8th of a mile of each other. There are around the hill, in detached clusters, about 30 dwellings, 4 taverns and 2 stores. The Lutheran church, an old and much noted place of worship, stands on the crown of the hill. This hill, composed of sandstone and sterile yellow loam, once well merited the name it bears, but the judicious use of lime and stable manure is fast changing its surface into rich and luxuriant clover fields.

Barrville, a village of Buckingham t-ship, Bucks co. on the road from Willow Grove to Centreville, about 3 ms. S. E. of Doylestown. It contains some 4 or 5 dwellings.

Barry, t-ship, Schuylkill co. bounded on the N. E. by Schuylkill t-ship, S. by Norwegian t-ship, S. W. by Lower Mahantango t-ship, N. W. by upper Mahantango t-ship, Cumberland and Columbia cos. Its form is very irregular; its greatest length is about 14 ms. and greatest breadth 6 ms. and it contains about 38,000 acres. The several ridges of the Mahanoy and spurs of the Broad mountains cover its surface, but the intervening valleys have a soil of red shale and are tolerably fruitful. In one of these valleys to the S. E. flows Deep creek, in two others the Great and Little Mahanoy creeks, all of which are tributaries of the Susquehannah, whilst the west branch of the Schuylkill, which pours its waters into the Delaware, winds its way through the Broad mountain, and falls at the t-ship line in a beautiful cascade of 50 feet pitch. The turnpike road from Reading to Sunbury and Danville, crosses the t-ship. The Mahanoy and the Broad mtns. abound with anthracite coal. Pop. in 1830, 443; taxables in 1828, 73.

Bart, t-ship, Lancaster co. bounded N. by Strasburg, E. by Sadsbury, S. by Coleraine and Drumore, and W. by Martick. Centrally distant from Lancaster city about 14 ms. S. E. Length 7, breadth 5¾ ms. Area, 19,027 acres. The N. branch of Octarara creek runs S. through the t-ship, upon a tributary of which is a furnace and several mills, and there are also some mills on the main stream. There are altogether 5 grist mills and 3 saw mills in the t-ship. Mine Ridge, a lofty chain of hills, encircles the t-ship on the W. and N. in which copper has been discovered, but the mines are not wrought. There is a p-o. in the t-ship, called Bart, 110 ms. from W. C. and 54 from Harrisburg. Surface, rolling; soil, limestone and clay. Pop. in 1830, 1750; taxables, 329.

Bath, p-t. Northampton co. on the road from Easton to the Lehigh Water Gap, 11 ms. from the former, 200 from W. C. 107 from Harrisburg, contains 20 dwellings, 2 stores, 1 tavern, 2 grist mills, 1 tannery, 120 inhabitants. The Manockissy creek runs through the town.

Beach Grove, p-o. Salem t-ship, Luzerne co. on the river Susquehannah, 18 or 20 miles from Wilkesbarre 5 from Berwick, 203 from W. C. 95 from Harrisburg. The place takes its name from Mr. Nathan Beach, an active and distinguished citizen of the county.

Beach creek, Centre co. rises in Bogg t-ship, and flows N. E. along and through the main ridge of the Allegheny and Howard t-ship, and falls into the Bald Eagle creek, having a course of about 30 ms.

Beallsville, fine p-t. on the U. S. road, Washington co. 8 ms. W. from Brownsville, and 17 E. from Washington, the co. town, on the boundary line between Pike run, and E. Bethlehem t-ships, 218 ms. N. W. from Washington, and 206 ms. S. W. from Harrisburg; contains about 50 dwellings, 5 stores, and 3 taverns.

Bean's cove, a short and fertile valley of Southampton t-ship, Bedford co. between Flint Stone Ridge and Tussey's mtn.

Bear run, Cumberland t-ship, Adam's co. a tributary of Rock creek.

Bear creek, Little Towamensing t-ship, Northampton co. rises on the S. side of the Broad mtn. and flows a S. W. course of about 5 ms. along the foot of the mtn. into the r. Lehigh, about 2 ms. above Lausanne.

Bear t-ship, Venango co. the extreme N. E. of the co. bounded N. by Warren co. E. by Jefferson co. S. by Saratoga t-ship, and W. by Hickory t-ship. Centrally distant, N. E. 32 ms. from the borough of Franklin. Greatest length 7, breadth 6 ms. Area, 26,880 acres; surface hilly. Soil, gravelly loam. The t-ship is not organized, and is almost uninhabited. It is annexed to Teonista t-ship. The Teonista creek crosses the t-ship diagonally from N. E. to S. W. and receives from it Bear, Little, Coon, Ross, and Sughanale creeks.

Bear creek, a fine stream of Luzerne co. rising between the Bald mtn. and Chesnut hill, and flowing S. into the Lehigh above Pompion Falls. For a part of its course it forms the boundary between Covington and Wilkesbarre t-ships.

Beard's mill creek, a tributary of the Wyalussing creek, rises in Bridgewater t-ship, Susquehannah co. and flows into the Susquehannah r. near the W. boundary of the t-ship. It has two branches, mill streams, but not navigable.

Beaver Dam t-ship, Erie co. bounded N. by Harbor creek t-ship, E. by Greenfield and Venango t-ships, S. by Waterford t-ship, and E. by Mill creek, and McKean t-ships. Centrally distant S. E. from Erie borough 7 ms. Greatest length 7, breadth 5½ ms. Area, 24,640 acres; surface, rolling. Soil, gravelly loam. Pop. in 1830, 443; taxables 75. The t-ship is drained W. by Walnut creek, N. W. by Mill creek, and S. by Le Bœuf creek.

Beaver t-ship, Crawford co.; pop. in 1830, 185.

Beaver creek, a tributary of the Conewago, which forms part of the boundary line between York and Adams cos.

Beaver Dam run, Westmoreland co. rises in Salem t-ship, and flows N. through Washington t-ship into the Kiskiminitas r. having a course of about 15 ms.

Beaver lake, Covington t-ship, Luzerne co. a small sheet of water, about 4 ms. W. of the Lehigh r. which discharges itself into that stream by Pond creek.

Beaver creek, Lancaster co. rises in Bart t-ship, and flows N. W. across Martic t-ship, into the Pequa creek. It divides Martic from Strasburg t-ship.

Beaver creek, Little, also a tributary of Pequa creek, rises in Strasburg t-ship, and has a course S. W. about 5 ms.

Beaver creek, Beaver t-ship, Union co. a tributary of Little Mahoniely or Middle creek, flowing through Moser's valley on the N. side of Black Oak Ridge.

Beaver creek, t-ship, Venango co. bounded N. by Elk creek t-ship, E. by Paint creek t-ship, S. and S. E. by Toby's creek, which separates it from Armstrong, and W. by Richland t-ship. Centrally distant S. E. from the borough of Franklin 20 ms. Greatest length 11, breadth 9 ms. Area, 44,800 acres; surface, rolling. Soil, chiefly limestone. Pop. in 1830, 460; taxables, 115. It is drained S. by Beaver creek, Canoe run, and Deer Paint creek, all which empty into Toby's creek, upon which there are several salt springs, and some salt works.

Beavertown, p-t. of Beaver t-ship, Union co. in Moser's valley, 10 ms. S. W. of New Berlin, 169 N. W. from Washington, and 59 from Harrisburg. It contains 15 dwellings, 1 store, and 1 tavern.

Beaver, South, t-ship of Beaver co. bounded N. by Little Beaver t-ship, E. by Chippewa, S. by Ohio t-ships, and W. by the state of Ohio. Centrally distant N. E. from Beaver borough 10 ms. Greatest length 7, breadth 5½ ms. Area, 17,920 acres; surface, hilly. Soil, limestone, and loam of the first quality. Pop. in 1830, 829; taxables, 174. The t-ship is watered by Little Beaver and Brush creeks.

Beaver t-ship, Union co. bounded N. by Jack's mtn. which separates it from Hartley t-ship, E. by Centre t-ship, S. by Shade's mtn. dividing it from Perry t-ship and Mifflin co. and E. by Mifflin co. Centrally distant from New Berlin 13 ms. Greatest length 12, breadth 8 ms. Area, 51,840 acres; surface, diversified. Soil, chiefly limestone. Pop. in 1830, 2280; taxables, 359. Little Mahonielly or Middle creek runs E. through the t-ship, receiving from it Beaver and Swift creeks. Beavertown and Adamsburg lie N. of Black Oak Ridge. The former is a p-t. 169 ms. from W. C. and 59 from Harrisburg.

Beaver, big, t-ship, Beaver co. bounded N. by N. Beaver t-ship, N. E. and E. by Beaver r. S. by Chippewa t-ship, and W. by Little Beaver. Centrally distant N. W. from Beaver borough 12 ms. Greatest length, 7, breadth 5 ms. Area, 17,280 acres; surface, hilly. Soil, loam and limestone of excellent quality. Pop. in 1830, 1243; taxables, 223. The t-ship is drained by a branch of Beaver creek. Salt is found upon the bank of Beaver r.

Beaver p-t. borough, and st. jus. of Beaver co. situated on the Ohio r. about a mile below the confluence of the Beaver r. with that stream, 251 ms. from W. C. and 229 from Harrisburg; contains about 150 dwellings, several stores and taverns, brick court-house, and county offices, stone prison, an academy, 1 Presbyterian and 1 Methodist church. There are two weekly papers printed here, viz. "The Republican," by Andrew Logan, and "The Argus," by William Hurry. The town is seated in a rich alluvial bottom, and within a mile of the route of the state canal, and possesses attractive facilities and prospects of business.

Beaver meadow, Lausanne t-ship, Northampton co. a vast mountain morass, partly reclaimed to agriculture, which has doubtless received its name from the inhabitants which once occupied it. There is upon it at present a solitary house. The tract is bounded S. by Spring, and N. by the Little Spring mtn. and is situated 14 ms. from Mauch Chunk by the Berwick turnpike road, and 1½ ms. W. of the road. This secluded spot has risen into consideration, by the quantity and quality of anthracite coal which it contains. The mine was opened in 1813, by Mr. Beach of Salem, on the Susquehannah r. who sold 550 acres of the tract to Joseph Barnes of Philadelphia, who has since conveyed it to a company, incorporated by an act of assembly passed in April, 1830, and authorized to construct a rail road to intersect any rail road leading to the Schuylkill; and also a rail road to the river Lehigh, terminating above Mauch Chunk, with a capital of $250,000. By a supplement passed April, 1831, the company was authorized to increase the capital stock to $800,000, and to continue the rail road down the valley of the Lehigh to any point on that river or to Easton. The company has been organized, but has not commenced operations. The cost of a rail road by the Lehigh route to Easton, by the report of the engineer, is estimated at $12,636 per mile, and the length of the road at 65 miles; and the cost of transportation is rated at $2 81 per ton at Philadelphia. The length of the rail road communicating with the canal at Mauch Chunk will be 18 miles. The coal of the Beaver meadow is universally regarded as the best quality. The mine is in the side of the hill; there is no roof, or only a thin one; it is worked open to the day, like a quarry, is already fairly disclosed, and there is no apparent impediment to obtaining any quantity desired. Smiths come from a great distance to obtain this coal, because it is so free from sulphur, and in every respect so good.

Beaver creek, Blockley t-ship, Phil. co. rises in and near Hamilton, and flows about 2 ms. to the r. Schuylkill, near the new alms house.

Beaver creek t-ship, Venango co. bounded N. by Elk creek, E. by Paint creek, S. E. and S. by Clarion r. and W. by Richland t-ship. Centrally distant S. E. from Franklin 20 ms. Greatest length, 11, breadth 9 ms. Area, 44,800 acres; surface rolling. Soil, limestone. Taxable pop. in 1830, 115. The r. receives from the t-ship Beaver creek, Dier Paint creek, and Canoe run. The turnpike road to Franklin crosses the N. E. angle. Salt springs are found on the banks of the r. and several salt works are erected.

Beaver county was created by act 12th March, 1800, which provided that those parts of Allegheny and Washington cos. included within the following boundaries, should form the new co. of Beaver, viz. "beginning at the mouth of Big Sewickly creek on the Ohio r. thence up the said creek to the west line of Alexander's district of depreciation lands; thence northerly along the said line, and continuing the same course to the N. line of the first donation district; thence westerly along the said line to the western boundary of the state, thence S. along the said boundary, across the Ohio r. to a point in the said boundary, from which a line to be run at right angles eastwardly, will strike White's mill on Raccoon creek, and from such point along the said E. line to the said mill, leaving the said mill in the county of Beaver; thence on a straight line to the mouth of Big Sewickly creek, the place of beginning." By an act of 28th September, 1791, the governor was instructed to survey 200 acres of land in town lots, near the mouth of Beaver creek, on or near the ground where the old French town stood, and also 1000 acres adjoining, on the upper side thereof, as nearly square as might be, in out lots, not less than five nor more than ten acres each. This was the town of Beaver. And by the 17th section of the act of 1791, 500 acres of the lands reserved by the state near this town were granted for the use of such school or academy as might be thereafter established by law. By the same act, the new county for the purposes of government was annexed to Allegheny co. By the act of 21st Feb. 1803, trustees were appointed for the school lands, with authority to lease them, and erect buildings for a school, and to receive grants or donations therefor. By the act 2d April, 1803, the county was fully organized for judicial and other purposes. It is bounded N. by Mercer co. W. by the state of Ohio, S. by Washington co. and E. by Allegheny and Butler cos. Length N. and S. 34, breadth E. and W. 19 ms. Area, 646 sq. ms. Central lat. 40° 50′ N., long. 3° 20′ W. from W. C.

This county belongs to the secondary geological formation; the strata throughout lying horizontal, and preserving that uniformity which distinguishes the great valley W. of the Allegheny mountains. The mineral deposits here have been very partially explored. Yet iron ore of the various kinds has been found in many parts; and sulphur and alum in various states of combination. Limestone and bituminous coal may be had in every neighborhood. Mineral springs are common, but insufficiently tested. One, however, near Frankford, the S. W. corner of the county, has obtained some celebrity, and is resorted to in the season of drinking the water, it is said with great advantage, by persons laboring under chronic diseases and general debility. Careful analysis has determined that this water contains carbonic acid gas, carbonate of iron and magnesia, muriate of soda, and sulphuretted hydrogen gas. Salt water has been found in several places; and two or more salt works have been erected, wells having been sunk to the depth of 4 or 500 feet.

The county is well watered. The Ohio r. enters it about 14 ms. below Pittsburg, and pursues a northern course for about 12 ms. where receiving Big Beaver creek it turns S. W. and crosses the co. by that course 15 ms. receiving the Big Sewickly and Raccoon creeks. The Big Beaver r. is formed by the union of the Mahoning and Shenango rs. on the line dividing North Beaver from Shenango t-ship. in the N. W. part of the co. whence it flows southerly and centrally about 25 ms. to the Ohio. Little Beaver creek rises in Big Beaver t-ship; and after a devious course, part of which is in the state of Ohio, it flows into the Ohio r. on the state line. The Big Beaver creek receives from the E. the Slippery Rock, and the Conequenessing creeks, which, arriving from the N. E. and S. E. unite in North Sewickly t-ship, and also some less considerable streams.

There is a fine bridge across the Big Beaver, near its mouth, more than 600 feet in length, said to be one of the finest specimens of bridge architecture in the state. There is also a bridge worthy of note, over the Slippery Rock creek, a short distance above its junction with the Conequenessing.

The portion of the county S. of the Ohio, and a district extending 10 ms. N. of that river have generally a hilly surface, interspersed with fine bottoms, and large tracts of level and rolling land, admirably adapted for grain and grazing farms; and particularly for raising sheep. Many thousands of these useful animals may be kept here, the soil and situation being congenial to their nature. The mulberry and the vine grow here luxuriantly, and in many places spontaneously. Fruit trees of the species proper to the climate thrive, especially upon the hill sides. The northern part of the county has generally a level or gently undulating surface, with some high lands, and many fertile vales, adapted to corn, hemp and grass. There is here also a due proportion of upland of the best quality, suitable to the culture of wheat, rye, barley, oats, and all the variety of agricultural purposes. Cultivation is yet one half short of the extent to which it may be carried and the product is double the quantity necessary for the consumption of the inhabitants. The timber is very plentiful, consisting of the several species of oak, ash, sugar maple, walnut, sycaamore, &c. &c.

Thirty-three years ago, two thirds of the county was a wilderness, without a white inhabitant. Most of the first settlers "began the world" with small families, and small capitals; and endured cheerfully the labors and privations incident to new settlements. The comforts, and in some cases the very necessaries of life were brought from a great distance, over almost impassable roads, at exorbitant prices or by a ruinous expenditure of time. Under such circumstances the progress of improvement was for some years inevitably slow; but the primary difficulties having been in a great measure surmounted, it now advances with rapid pace. The forest is subdued, and the surface of the country prepared for tillage, a large portion of the arable land being already cleared; and in some places the destruction of the timber has been excessive.

The capacity of the county for commerce and manufactures is extraordinary. The Allegheny and Monongahela rivers afford means of intercourse with the N. and S. E. for several hundred miles; the S. and the W. are approachable by the Ohio, and its connectives; the state canal connects it with the eastern cities, and the Beaver division, when completed, will give access to the state of Ohio, the Ohio canal and to the lakes. The canal on the Beaver division was commenced in pursuance of the act of 21st March, 1831, requiring the canal commissioners to make a canal or slack-water navigation, to be made from the Ohio r. at the mouth of Big Beaver creek, up that creek, to the town of Newcastle; and appropriating the sum of $100,000 to be expended thereon. The length of this work, which extends a short distance upon the Shenango creek, is 24¾ m.; of which there are 8 ms. 16 perches of canal, and 16 ms. and 224 perches of slack-water and towing path. The contracts on it were let the 20th of July and the 19th of Oct. 1831. There are on it 7 dams, varying from 7 to 14 feet in height, 2 aqueducts and 17 guard and lift locks, overcoming a rise of 132 feet. The 2 outlet locks are 25 feet wide, and 120 feet long within the chambers, and designed to admit the smaller class of steamboats that ply on the Ohio, into the pool of the first dam, for the accommodation of the trade of the town of Beaver, and the flourishing villages on the banks and near the mouth of the creek, and the extensive manufactories propelled by the water taken from the Beaver falls. The cost of this division of the Penn. canal is estimated at $335,317. The commissioners expect to complete it by Dec. 1832. A rail road from Pittsburg through the Beaver valley, to connect with the Ohio canal has been projected.

Within a few years, extensive manufactories have sprung up, in which wool, cotton, iron, rags and wood are manufactured into articles of primary importance. These are chiefly on the Big Beaver, and are driven by the power obtained from the falls, which is very great, and little variable. (See Big Beaver river.) There are here also 7 merchant grist mills, having from 2 to 4 run of stones.

In the year 1830 the business of steam and keel boat building carried on at the mouth of the Big Beaver creek exceeded $50,000.

At Economy (see that title) the manufacture of wool and cotton is extensively prosecuted by steam power, with machinery of the latest improvement, and kept in the best order. The culture and manufacture of silk, has been successfully attempted here; and the result affords the most flattering inducements to similar enterprizes, since Mr. Rapp, the actuary of the Economy society, avers that "adhering to the instructions given in books treating on the culture and manufacture of silk, he found no difficulty in keeping the worms healthy, in unwinding or reeling the silk or weaving it." And thus encouraged, the society have devoted themselves to this employment, have made extensive plantations of the white mulberry and have some millions of spinsters at work. Their silk cloths are remarkable for their firmness and lustre, and are earnestly sought for at prices which amply repay the manufacture. It will be a cause of national regret, should the late commotions in the society impede the progress of this new and interesting branch of industry.

The principal towns are Beaver borough, the county town Economy, Fallstown, Brighton and New Brighton, Sharon, Bridgewater, Mount Jackson, Griersburg, Georgetown, Frankford, and Hookstown.

The county was settled by inhabitants from other parts of Pennsylvania, and from the north of Ireland, and by the census of 1830 the population was 24,206, averaging 37 and a fraction to the square mile. Of these, there were white males 12,232; females 11,833; free black males 81; females 60; aliens 153; deaf and dumb 6; blind 9. In 1800 the population was 5,776, in 1810 12,168, in 1820, 15,340. The people are religious, orderly and thrifty. There are in the county 25 churches; of which 8 are Presbyterian, 6 Seceders, 5 Methodists, 2 Episcopalians, 2 Baptists, 2 Quakers. There are bible, missionary and tract societies, and the system of Sunday schools is generally adopted, in situations that admit of them.

There is one academy at Beaver borough, before noticed, and another at Griersburg, located at the junction of Big Beaver, Little Beaver, South Beaver, and Chippewa townships, which was incorporated in 1806, and received from the State a donation of $600. Common schools are established in every vicinity, sufficient in number to teach the children the rudiments of an English education.

There are two weekly newspapers published in the town of Beaver, viz. "The Republican," and the "Argus."

The price of improved lands on the rich Ohio bottoms, varies from 4 to 30 dollars the acre, and may be stated to average $12. In other parts of the county improved land may be purchased at from 4 to 6 dollars per acre and unimproved lands of excellent quality at 4 dollars.

Beaver county belongs to the 23d senatorial district, including Crawford and Mercer counties, sending 1 member to the senate; and alone it sends 2 members to the house of representatives; united with Allegheny, Butler, and Armstrong counties it forms the 16th congressional district of the state. And connected with Butler and Allegheny, it constitutes the 5th judicial district. Charles Shaler, Esq. President. It forms part of the western district of the supreme court, which holds an annual session at Pittsburg on the first Monday in September.

This county paid to the state treasury in 1831, for tax on writs $200 79;

tavern licenses 600; duties on dealers in foreign mdz. 350; state maps 3 75; total $1,154 54. The taxable real estate returned by the commissioners in 1829 was $1,609,427; in 1814, as adjusted by the committee of ways and means of the house of representatives, the value was 1,667,805.

STATISTICAL TABLE OF BEAVER COUNTY.

Townships, &c.	Greatest		Area in Acres.	Surface of Country.	Soil.	Population.			Taxables.
	Lth.	Bth.				1810	1820	1830	
Griersburg,							146		
Beaver, North,	8	6	23,680	Undulating.	Loam, Lime.	932	1206	1892	343
Beaver, Big,	7	5	17,280	Hilly.	Do.	702	742	1243	223
Beaver, Little,	9	5½	25,600	Rolling.	Do.	1379	1144	1825	336
Beaver, South,	7	5½	17,920	Hilly.	Do.	1351	800	829	174
Beaver Borough,				Level.	Alluvial.	426	605	914	186
Brighton,	6½	6	17,280	Hilly.	Loam, Lime.		738	901	225
Chippewa,	7	5	15,360	Do.	Do.		443	580	100
*Fallstown,				Do.	Do.			386	
Green,	6	5½	23,680	Rolling.	Loam.	1245	1194	1709	284
*Economy,				Hilly.	Do.			1220	356
Hanover,	8	5	24,960	Rolling.	Loam, Lime.	1090	1147	2359	308
Hopewell,	8	6	22,400	Hilly.	Loam.		1035	1492	272
Moon,	7	6½	23,680	Do.	Do.	1035	826	1360	226
Ohio,	7½	5½	19,840	Rolling.	Loam.	1128	1075	1122	201
Shenango,	12½	6	37,120	Do.	Loam, Lime.	679	1098	1907	308
Sewickly, New,				Hilly.	Loam.	878	1367	1902	257
Sewickly, North,	9½	8½	47,360	Rolling.	Loam, Lime.	1323	1774	2475	412
						12,168	15,340	24,206	4208

* Fallstown and Economy t-ships are taken from New Sewickly, and as the precise boundaries are unknown to us, we do not attempt to give their length, breadth, or area. Many t-ships of 1820 were not formed in 1810.

Beaver, or Big Beaver river; Big Beaver is formed by the Mahoning, Shenango, Neshanock and Conequenessing creeks. The Shenango rises in Ashtabula co. of Ohio and Crawford co. Penn. within 12 ms. of the S. E. shore of lake Erie, interlocking sources with those of the Grand rivers, Coneaut and French creeks, and pursuing a nearly S. course, over Mercer, receives the Conequenessing from the N. E. and entering Beaver co. unites with the Mahoning and forms Big Beaver r.

The Mahoning is in reality the main branch, rising in Columbiana, Stark, Trumbull and Portage cos. Ohio; its course is first nearly N. 30 ms. to near Warren, in Trumbull; winding to the S. E. it pursues that course 33 ms. entering Penn. in the S. W. angle of Mercer and joining the Shenango N. lat. 41°, about 2 ms. within Beaver co. Below the junction of the Mahoning and Shenango, Big Beaver flows a little E. of S. 20 ms. into the Ohio r.

The valley of the Big Beaver is nearly circular and about 70 ms. in diameter, area 3850 sq-ms. It is worthy of remark that the general courses are nearly on a direct N. W. line; of the Youghiogheny below the mouth of Castlemans river, Monongahela and Ohio, from the mouth of Youghiogheny to that of Big Beaver; and the latter and Mahoning to about 3 ms. above Warren. This range of navigable water is upwards of 130 ms. direct, and from 180 to 200 ms. following the sinuosities of the streams.

The sources of the Mahoning interlock with those of the Tuscarawas branch of the Muskingum, and of Cayahoga, and Grand rivers of lake Erie.

The falls of this river, which afford

admirable sites for mill works, commence about 5 ms. above its confluence with the Ohio; and consist of a succession of rapids, with a few and comparatively small perpendicular pitches for about $\frac{2}{3}$ of that distance. The valley of the river here, is about half a mile wide, bounded by high and in many places perpendicular hills, and the channel, from 4 to 500 feet, of continued solid rock. At the head of the falls the river takes a S. E. course, which it pursues until turned by a bold and rocky precipice, around which it circles to the S. leaving on the W. shore, a plain of from 20 to 60 feet above the surface of the water.—Checked in its progress to the S. E. it is turned to the S. W. against the western hills, leaving on the eastern shore a margin similar to that above noticed; but again arrested in its course, it gradually resumes the general direction to the S. dividing the valley so as to admit the occupancy of both banks. The courses of the stream offer every facility for its employment, and the level plains present convenient, healthy and agreeable sites for work-shops and dwellings.

The plain on the W. near the head of the falls affords ample space for a manufacturing town. Its aspect is to the S. E. gently inclined to the water's edge. The water may be taken from the river at any desirable point, with a fall of 22 feet, and in any quantity short of the whole volume of the stream. At the S. end of this plain is the village of Brighton, which is rapidly improving. The proprietor, (Mr. Patterson,) an experienced and enterprising manufacturer, is making extensive improvements. The commissioners appointed under an act of congress, after due examination of the prominent sites for water-works in West Pennsylvania, Virginia, Kentucky, Tennessee, Indiana, and Ohio, gave this a decided preference.

Below, and on the opposite side of the river is the village of New Brighton, whose situation is not inferior in any respect to that above described. The borough of Fallstown is on the W. bank, near the termination of the rapids, properly called the falls of Beaver. A little lower down, on the same side, are the villages of Sharon and Bridgewater. Near the mouth of the river, is the Beaver bridge, with its piers and abutments based on solid rock, and which, as a specimen of bridge architecture, is said to be unrivalled in Pennsylvania. At the point is "Stone's Harbor," one of the safest and most commodious on the Ohio r. It is the principal depot for the trade passing up and down the valley of Beaver, and to and from the western reserve, &c. in the state of Ohio.

The whole amount of the fall here is 75 feet. A dam of 8 feet at the head of the falls would give a head and fall of 65 feet. The volume of water during the greater part of the year is so great, that it will probably ever exceed the quantity required for manufacturing purposes. At low water, it is estimated that the power of the stream is sufficient to drive 168 pairs of 5 feet burr stones. By an act of 31st March, 1831, the legislature authorized a canal, or slack-water navigation to be made from the Ohio, at the mouth of Big Beaver, up that stream to the town of Newcastle, consisting of 16 ms. 224 perches of slack water, and 8 ms. and 16 perches of canal, and estimated to cost $335,317 83 cents. 22 ms. and 240 perches have been put under contract.

Beaver creek, usually called Little Beaver, to distinguish it from Big Beaver, is an excellent mill stream of Columbiana co. O.; which after a course of S. E. about 30 ms. falls into the Ohio r. within the borders of Penn. It receives from Beaver co. a considerable branch also called Little Beaver creek, which, rising in Little Beaver t-ship, flows around the t-ship, and falls into the main stream in the State of Ohio.

Beaver Little, t-ship, Beaver co. Pop. 1810, 1379, in 1820, 1144, in 1830, 1825. Bounded N. by N. Beaver, E. by Big Beaver, S. by S. Beaver, and W. by the state of Ohio.

Centrally distant from Beaver borough 14 ms. Greatest length 9, breadth 5½ ms. Area, 25,600 acres; surface, rolling; soil, fertile loam and limestone of the first quality. It is drained by a branch of the Little Beaver creek, which rises in the N. W. angle of the t-ship, and flows across it and along the E. and S. boundary. The p-t. of Griersburg lies on this stream in the S. E. angle of the t-ship, 263 ms. from W. C. and 241 from Harrisburg.

Beaver North, t-ship, Beaver co. Pop. in 1810, 932, in 1820, 1206, in 1830, 1892; taxables, 343. It is bounded N. by Mercer co. E. by Mahoning and Beaver rs. S. by Big and Little Beaver t-ships, and W. by the state of Ohio. Centrally distant from Beaver borough 20 ms. Greatest length 8, breadth 6 ms. Area, 23,680 acres; surface, undulating; soil, loam and limestone of the first quality. Hickory creek flows E. and near the N. line into the Mahoning. On it is the p-t. of Mount Jackson, 22 ms. N. W. of Beaver borough, 275 from W. C. 243 from Harrisburg.

Beaver creek, Dauphin co. rises in the Blue mtn. and flows S. about 9 ms. to the Swatara creek, dividing Lower Paxton t-ship from Hanover. It has some mills upon it near its mouth.

Beaver run, on the N. line of U. Chanceford t-ship, York co. flows N. E. into Fishing creek.

Beaver creek, a tributary of the Conewago, rises and has its course in Warrington t-ship, York co.

Beaver creek, Manheim t-ship, Schuylkill co. a tributary of the W. branch of the Schuylkill r. which flows into it, about a mile above the confluence of the latter with the main stream.

Beaver creek, Brandywine t-ship, Chester co. flows through East Caln t-ship, into the E. branch of the Brandywine r. a short distance above Downingstown. It has several mills upon it.

Beaver gap, a pass in Tussey's mountain, from Hopewell t-ship to Woodbery t-ship, Bedford co. A stream which passes through the gap is called Beaver run.

Beaver run, E. Nantmeal t-ship, Chester co. a mill stream and tributary of French creek.

Bedford co. was taken by act of 9th March, 1771, from Cumberland co. and embraced the country within the following limits. Beginning where the province line crosses the Tuscarora mountain, and running along the summit of that mountain to the gap near the head of the Path valley; thence with a N. line to the Juniata; thence with that river to the mouth of Shaver's creek, thence N. E. to the line of Berks co.; thence along the line N. W. to the W. boundary of the province; thence S. according to the several courses of that boundary to the S. W. corner of the province; and from thence E. with the S. line of the province to the place of beginning. But this very extensive area has been greatly reduced by the successive erections of Westmoreland, Huntingdon and Somerset counties. And it is now bounded N. by Huntingdon and E. by Franklin counties, S. by the state of Maryland, and W. by Somerset and Cambria counties. Greatest length N. and S. about 44 miles; greatest breadth E. and W. about 34 miles; area 1520 square miles.

The surface of the country is very mountainous. The Cove and Tuscarora mountains are on the E.; proceeding thence W. we cross Scrub Hill, Sideling Hill, Town Hill, Clear Ridge, Warrior Ridge, Tussey's mountain, Evitt's or Dunning's mountain, Will's mountain, Buffalo ridge, and the Allegheny mountain. Beside these principal hills there are many not sufficiently important to receive names; consequently the country is much broken and stony, and a great proportion of its soil is ungrateful to the cultivator. But, between these lofty ridges are delightful valleys, in which are large and fertile farms, comfortable houses, healthy and prolific familes, and abundance of the comforts of life. In many of these valleys there is fine limestone land, well cultivated. Those in which is McConnelstown, Friends cove, and

Morrison's cove are particularly rich and fertile. The latter more especially, in the vicinity of Martinsburg, is said to be one of the richest districts in the state. The average price of improved lands of the best quality in the county is $30 per acre. Mountain lands sell at from 25 to 50 cents.

The timber is chiefly white oak, chestnut, hickory, pine and sugar maple.

Rivers, &c. The streams of this county flow in various directions. Yet those on the S. seek the Potomac through the state of Maryland, whilst those from the middle and northern parts of the county, flow into the Juniata r. The principal is the Raystown branch of the Juniata, which, rising at the eastern foot of the great Allegheny mtns. runs E. by the town of Bedford to the centre of the county, whence being turned northward at the Big Bend, by the Cove mtn. it runs N. and N. E. to unite with the Frankstown branch about three miles below the town of Huntingdon. It receives in its course from the S. Buffalo creek, Shaver's creek, Cove creek, Clear creek, and Brush creek; from the N. W. Dunning's and Yellow creeks. The chief tributaries from this county to the Potomac are Will's, Evitt's, Flintstone Town, Sideling Hill, Conoloway's and Licking creeks.

A turnpike road runs W. across the mtns. from Chambersburg in Franklin co. by Bedford, to Somerset borough in Somerset co.

Bedford springs, near the town of Bedford, have become one of the most fashionable and beneficial watering places of the United States. (See article *Bedford Springs.*)

The county of Bedford is wholly of transition formation, and in common with other parts of such formation, abounds with mineral wealth, of which bituminous coal and iron, of the best quality and in various forms, are found almost in every part of the county, but particularly on the waters of the Juniata, and in Morrison's cove.

The county was originally settled by emigrants from other parts of the state, and from the north of Ireland. The Germans and their descendants have however possessed themselves of the best lands. Many of these pertain to Tunker and Menonist sects and are remarkable for the simplicity, sobriety, frugality and thrift of these highly useful christians.

The population of this county was, in 1790, 13,124; in 1800, 12,039; in 1810, 15,746; in 1820, 20,248, and in 1830, 24,557. Of the last number, 12,188 were white males, 11,937 white females; 204 free colored males, 228 free colored females; 1 slave. There were 35 aliens, 13 deaf and dumb, and 8 blind persons. Taxables, in 1828, 4,442. We are indebted to an interesting memoir of Mr. Thomas B. McElwee for the following notice of the population of this county, and for some other particulars we shall give in relation to it. And we avail ourselves of this opportunity to express a wish that every county had as good an annotator. In such cases a Gazetteer of Pennsylvania might be made a mirror of the state.

"Every landholder lives by the sweat of his brow. We have no slaves, nor do we boast of an exemption from that which it would be degradation to be subject to. Such a miserable thing as a slave, and such an arrogant thing as the master of a slave, are unknown to us."

The usual wages of a good hand, when boarding and lodging is provided, is from 5 to 7 dollars a month; if by the day, from 31 to 37½ cts. The cradler has from 75 to 80 cents per day, the reaper and mower from 37½ to 50 cents. The food of the agricultural laborer, or *help* as he is called, is the same as that of his employer. No farmer in the county could get a hireling, if he made any distinction; and the entire family, maids, men and children, wife and master, eat at the same table. The quality of the fare depends on the circumstances of the master; usually it is coffee, wheat bread, and bacon, fresh meat, poultry, or salt fish for breakfast; white bread, bacon, fresh or salt meat, poultry, with abundance of vegetables or pies, and a glass of whiskey for dinner; tea, the same sort of meat and bread for supper; sometimes mush and milk in winter."

"In summer farmers work from sunrise to sunset, allowing an hour or an hour and a half for breakfast, and the same for dinner. In winter they breakfast by candle-light, and join their work at the first dawn of day; they are called to dinner, eat and go to it again." "Such a domestic as an English butler, is unknown; and servants almost as much so. The farmers adopt the admonition given by Martha Trapbois, to Glenvarlock, 'The wise man is his own best assistant,' and are aware that no man is truly independent, who depends on the labor or fidelity of others for his comfort."

So much of this gentleman's picture of rural economy is applicable to every agricultural district in the state, except in the vicinity of cities and large towns, where *gentleman farmers* do not feed with their domestics and laborers. But there are some traits of his pencil which, if not pertaining exclusively to Bedford co. belong to the new settled countries of the N. and W. These we present to the reader, as highly graphic, and he may apply them to most of the western counties of the state.

"When we wish to clear a piece of land, we in the first place stake it off, and provided with a grubbing hoe, take up by the roots every bush or sapling which a stout man can shake in the root, by grasping the stem and bending it backwards and forwards. If the roots give to this action, it is called a *grub*, and must be taken up. Dog-wood, iron-wood and witch-hazle are always classed among grubs whether they shake in the root or not. After the land is grubbed, the brush is picked up in heaps. We then cut down every thing which does not exceed 12 inches across the stump. Such parts of the sapling as are fit for *ground poles* are chopped at the length of 11 feet; such parts as are fit for firewood are left for that purpose, and the top brush is thrown upon the heaps made of the grubs. Next the trees are *deadened* leaving one or two for shade. This process consists in chopping entirely round the tree a *curf* of three or four inches wide. A tree is not well *deadened* unless it be cut to the red; the axe penetrating through the sap, but it is not thought necessary to chip out more than the bark of oak timber. Sugar maple, gum &c. must be chipped out half an inch or an inch. The advantages of *deadening* timber, are immense; labor is saved in chopping down and burning the *stuff* on the ground. Indeed, in this country it is not possible to cut down the timber, unless we live in the vicinity of Bedford, because farmers are not rich enough to pay for it. The dead timber gives us fire wood for years, which obviates the necessity of resorting to the woods. When it falls the roots are taken out with the tree. On the other hand the falling branches incommode us for years; covering our grain every winter and causing a great labor in picking up. The trees fall over the fences and demolish them; sometimes they fall on horses and cattle, killing or maiming them; and not unfrequently men and boys have been killed."

"As soon as the brush will burn, it is fired, and every particle consumed. The fire sometimes *gets away* from the workmen, and great havoc is committed on fences, woods and mountains. After the clearing is burned, the rail timber is chopped and logged off, the rails mauled, fences made, and the tops of the rail timber hauled home for fire wood. If saw logs or building timber are wanted, they are cut down and hauled off. At any time between the 1st of Sept. and middle of Oct. the ground is *scratched*, (rough ploughed) a bushel of wheat to the acre sown broad cast, harrowed in and crossed. New ground is sometimes ploughed twice, but this is so seldom done as scarcely to form an exception, though it is admitted that a second ploughing adds a fourth to the crop."

"Wheat is universally the first crop sown on new land, unless we clear a patch for potatoes. The average crop is from 12 to 20 bushels per acre. The second crop is rye, oats follow, and then corn. This is the usual course. It is then left out for a year or two, and the course begins again, until it will produce nothing.

In eight or ten years the timber begins to fall rapidly. When the ground is pretty well covered with old logs, the farmer goes in to *nigger* off. This is effected by laying the broken limbs and smaller trees across the logs and putting fire to it. Boys or women follow to *chunk up* the fires. In a day or two the logs are niggered off, at the length of 12 or 15 feet; sometimes the entire tree is consumed. When the trees are thus reduced to lengths that can be handled by men, the owner has a log rolling. He *gives the word* to 18 or 20 of his neighbors the day before the frolic, and when they assemble they generally divide the force into two companies. A captain is chosen by acclamation, for each company, and the captains choose their companies, each naming a man alternately. When the whole is formed they set to work, provided with hand spikes, and each company exerts itself to make more log heaps than the other. Nothing is charged for the work, and the only thing exceptionable in these frolics is the immoderate use of whiskey. In general great hilarity prevails; but these meetings, like all others in this county, are sometimes disgraced by dreadful combats between the persons composing them. Bedford co. like most mountainous countries, possesses a large proportion of stout athletic men. Bravery is a predominant feature in their character, and they value themselves in proportion to their strength. Hence arise animosities which are seldom allayed but by battle. They possess one noble quality, however, and that is, forgiveness of injuries. After a fair trial of strength, though each may have been so severely cut and bruised as to be disabled for several days, they will meet in perfect harmony, and no trace of malice or even resentment appears. This, to one who has already looked upon the indignity of a blow as meriting the chastisement of death, seems impossible, but there can be no doubt of their tacit reconciliation.

The general price of clearing land is five dollars per acre, put under fence of six rails, and a ground pole, four feet worm, and ready for the plough. Sometimes it is cleared on the shares, and then if the proprietor finds the grubber in boarding and lodging, finds horses, seed and feed, and puts it in himself, the grubber gets the first crop or half the two first. If the undertaker finds every thing he gets the two first, or the three first crops according as he can make his bargain, and the bargain is usually determined by the quality of the land and the difficulty of clearing. Meadow land is cleared for from four to seven crops."

"In addition to our log rolling frolics, we have frolics to haul out dung, to husk corn, and to raise our buildings.

The first, the dung frolic, is getting out of use, and never ought to have been practiced, because a man can do the labor himself.

The corn husking is done at night. The neighbors meet at dark; the corn has been previously pulled, and hauled in a pile near the crib. The hands join it, the whiskey bottle goes round, the story, the laugh, and the rude song are heard. Three or four hundred bushels are husked by 9 or 10 o'clock—a plentiful supper is provided, and sometimes the frolic ends with a stag dance; that is, men and boys, without females, dance like mad devils, but in good humor, to the time of a neighbor's catgut and horse-hair, not always drawn with the melody and judgment of Gilliaume."

"Our buildings are made of hewn

logs, on an average 24 feet long by 20 wide; sometimes a wall of stone, about a foot above the level of the earth, is raised as a foundation; but in general four large stones are laid at the corners, and the building raised on them. The house is covered sometimes with shingles, sometimes with clap-boards. The advantage of the latter kind of roof is, it requires no lathes or rafters, and no nails, and is put on in much less time. It has been called a poor man's make-shift, and its use can only be justified by the poverty and other circumstances of the country. The ground logs being laid, a saddle shaped Λ on the upper edge, is cut with an axe, at the ends, as long as the logs are thick, then the end logs are raised and a notch cut to fit the saddle. This is the only tie or binder they have; and when the building is raised as many rounds as is intended, the ribs are raised, on which a course of clap boards is laid, butts resting on a butting pole. A press pole is laid upon the clap-boards immediately over the ribs, to keep them from shifting by the wind, and the pole is kept to its birth by stay blocks, resting in the first course against the butting pole and then against each preceding pole. The logs are run upon the building on skids by the help of wooden forks. The most experienced axe-men are placed on the building as corner men; the rest of the company are on the ground to carry the logs and run them up. In this way a building is raised and covered in a day, without a mason, and without a pound of iron. The doors and windows are afterwards cut out as the owner pleases. As the country becomes rich and more densely settled, those hastily constructed buildings give way to more durable and more comfortable ones; but at present there are very few buildings in the country, except on the turnpike, of any other material than logs.

We raise no tobacco in the field. It is occasionally raised in gardens for family use. It will however grow well in our rich lands. A gentleman in the adjoining county of Somerset, where the climate is much colder than it is here, so much so that in some parts of it Indian corn will not ripen, has for a number of years raised from five to ten acres of tobacco annually, and found a profitable market for his crop in Baltimore. It is very certain that the soil and climate of Pennsylvania can produce more tobacco than her population consumes.

We raise no cotton or sugar cane, but we manufacture sugar from the sugar maple (*acer saccharinum*). This tree, which arrives at a size rivalling the largest white oaks, flourishes in our sandy bottoms, spouty drafts, on the sides of our mountains, and the summit of the Allegheny. It is slow of growth, hard to kill, but when once dead, soon rots. The roots are numerous and strong, interlaced on or near the surface of the ground, so that it is impossible to plough near them.

When the sugar season begins, which is generally about the first of March, the sugar maker repairs his camp, if it is out of order. The camp is a small shed made of logs, covered with slabs or clapboards, and open at one side. Immediately before the opening, four wooden forks are planted, on which is placed a strong pole. From this are suspended as many wooden hooks as the sugar boiler has kettles, usually four. Wood is hauled, and it requires a large quantity to boil during a season. The troughs to receive the water are roughly hewn, of cucumber, white or yellow pine, or wild cherry, and contain from one to three gallons. The trees are tapped with a $\frac{3}{4}$ auger, about one inch or an inch and a half deep. In the hole is placed a spile or spout 18 inches long, made of sumach. Two spiles are put in a tree. A good camp will contain 150 or 200 trees. When the troughs are full, the boiler goes round with a sled drawn by horses, on which are placed two barrels to receive the water. Having filled the barrels he returns to camp and fills up the vessels, which consist of his meat vessels, &c. well cleaned. The water which is gathered in should be immediately boiled, because it makes the best sugar. If left to stand a few days it becomes sour and ropy. The kettles are filled as they boil down, until all is boiled in. In order to ascertain when the syrup is fit to stir off, a little of the molasses is taken out in a spoon and dropped into a tin of cold water. If the molasses is thick, it will form a thread in the water, and if this thread will break like glass when struck with a knife, it must be taken off the fire, and is fit to stir off. The kettle is set on the ground and occasionally stirred till it cools and granulates. Great judgment is required, and the most exact attention to take it off at the very moment it is fit. If it is taken off too soon, the sugar will be wet and tough; if it is left on too long it will be burnt or be bitter, and scarcely fit for use. Some boilers try it by taking a few drops of the molasses between the thumb and finger, and if it ropes like glue when it cools, it is said to be in sugar. A tree is calculated to produce, a season, a barrel of water of 30 gallons, and it requires six gallons to make a pound of sugar. This estimate, however, appears too large. I have never known a camp turn out, one tree with another, more than three pounds. In Jamaica it is not unusual for a gallon of raw cane liquor to yield a pound of sugar. It is supposed there can be no doubt of the fact that our trees do not produce as much as formerly. Many of the trees have been injured by fire, but the fatal cause of their deterioration is the auger. When a tree is cut down which has been frequently tapped, there is a black and rotten streak for a foot above and below many of the auger holes. The great miracle is that a single sugar tree is alive in Bedford; but the Almighty Fabricator of the universe has in his infinite wisdom and beneficence bestowed on this precious tree a tenacity of life truly wonderful. Though every year assaulted by the axe, the auger, or by fire, it clings to existence, and yields to its ungrateful possessor a luxury and necessary of life, which, but for it, would command a price which would debar its use from the poor. The average price of maple sugar is from 6 to 10 cents per pound.

A society was formed in Centre county, two or three years ago, with the Hon. Charles Houston at its head, for the purpose of propagating the sugar tree and extracting the water from the roots. Whether they have succeeded in their enterprise, or whether the society has perished amidst political turmoil, I know not. In this county a few partial attempts have been made to plant out the trees found in the woods, and they have succeeded."

There are now in operation in the county three furnaces, Elizabeth, Hanover and Hopewell; at each of which from 25 to 30 tons of pig metal are made weekly, and employment given to more than 100 hands. There are 6 forges, viz. Bedford, Hopewell, Lemnos, Hanover air, and the two Maria forges, which make each about 250 tons of bar iron annually, and employ about 50 hands. Many other iron works are about to be erected. There are also about 70 grist and merchant mills, 80 saw mills, 25 fulling mills, some of which manufacture cloth—about 150 distilleries, 2 nail factories, one or two oil mills, and about 20 carding machines. There is a considerable manufacture of cotton and wool in Providence township, and another in Morris cove.

The following remarks of an inhabitant of Bedford co. on the important subject of education, merit attention, inasmuch as they are applicable to many other parts of the state. "The system of common school education in Pennsylvania is a bad one, and Bedford co. has experienced her full share of the evil. The aid heretofore granted by the legislature to common schools has been cold and reluctant; and it would have been better, perhaps, had it been altogether denied, for then the people might have been roused to the procurement of their own moral aliment. There is not a state in the union where the necessity of public provision for general education is more intensely felt, and yet there is none in which this subject has been more inefficiently treated. Were the rising generation of Germans taught only to speak English, what an immense change it would create in the resources and wealth of the state—what an addition it would give to the happiness of thousands, who now suffer from the lack of knowledge. Here, when we lose sight of the town of Bedford, with but few exceptions, we find hovels for schools, and men who would be retained in no other employment, engaged in forming the plastic minds of our children. And even these miserable receptacles and nurseries of knowledge are so sparingly scattered around us, that perhaps there are not two for every five hundred children in the county."

There is, however, an academy in the town of Bedford, which was incorporated in 1810, and has received from the legislature a donation of two thousand dollars.

The public buildings of the county in Bedford borough, consisting of the court-house, offices and jail, are substantially built. The court-house indeed is said to be uncommonly ornamental, planned after the Tuscan order, and said not to be surpassed by any like buildings in the state. There are also several neat churches here.

The towns are Bedford, Shellsburg, Martinsburg, Woodberry, Stonerstown, Bloody run, Werefordsburg and McConnellstown. For a description of which see their respective titles.

Bedford co. belongs to the 22d senatorial district, including Somerset, which sends one member to the senate; and the county has two members in the house of representatives.

With Franklin and Somerset counties, it forms the sixteenth judicial district, and the courts are held, at the town of Bedford, on the fourth Mondays of January, April, August and November. President, Alexander Thompson, Esq.

The state treasury received from this county, in 1831,

Tax on Writs	251 23
For tavern licenses,	926 67
Dividends on turnpike stock, viz.	
Chambersburg and Bedford,	5,650 62
Bedford and Stoystown,	1,000 00
Duties on dealers in foreign mdz.	237 51
State maps,	9 50
Tin and clock pedlars,	57 00
	$8,132 53

The taxable property by the return of the assessors of 1829 was valued,—real estate, $1,023,275; personal estate, including occupations, $142,892.

STATISTICAL TABLE OF BEDFORD COUNTY.

Townships.	Greatest Lth.	Bth.	Area in acres.	Population. 1810	1820	1830	Taxables.	R. Est.	Pers.	Ms.
Air	11	4 1-2	25,960	1179	1760	1517	279	117,960	8988	5
Bedford bor.				547	789	870	163	78,820	2244	4
Bedford t-ship	15 1-2	4 1-2	32,640	1342	1321	1344	237	78,862	8204	6
Belfast	17	8	64,640	750	1196	1373	274	29,375	8020	6 1-2
Bethel	11 1-2	9 1-2	70,400	1095	1083	1208	140	57,409	8576	5 1-2
Colerain	21	5 3-4	47,360	876	986	1170	200	71,298	7508	4 1-2
Cumberland valley	16	4	34,200	570	683	747	150	23,216	5368	8
Dublin	12 1-2	9 1-2	53,760	820	713	801	160	24,795	4492	8
Greenfield	18	12 1-2	83,200	855	1114	1465	262	63,016	8176	4 1-2
Hopewell	19	14	75,520	1297	1327	1634	326	56,967	8940	6
Londonderry	16 1-2	7 1-2	43,520	486	602	726	135	23,835	5000	6
McConnellsburg bo.						491	92	16,974	1296	9
Napier	16	12 1-2	85,120		1764	2154	434	76,647	11,324	6 1-2
Providence	13	12	80,000	1492	1822	2209	413	76,639	13,568	5 1-2
Southampton	14	12 1-2	93,440	952	1158	1322	270	27,255	9224	6
St. Clair	14	10 1-2	44,800	1847	1748	2134	336	67,119	11872	5 1-2
Woodberry	18 1-2	8 1-2	69,120	1658	2155	3375	582	133,088	20,092	5 1-2
				15,746	20,248	24,536	4,442	1,023,275	142,892	

Bedford, p-t. borough and seat of justice of Bedford co. situated on the great road leading from Phil. to Pittsburg on the Raystown branch of the Juniata r. 200 ms. W. of Phil. and 100 E. of Pittsburg and 126 N. W. from Washington, and 105 W. from Harrisburg. Lat. 40° N. lon. 1° 30′ W. of Washington C. It was formerly called Raystown; from it the stream on which it lies took its name. The site of the t. is uncommonly beautiful and healthy, built on an eminence formed of limestone and silex; it is always clean. Almost enveloped by mountains which pour their limpid streams into the valley, and which are shaded by thick forests, it enjoys delightful summers, never incommoded by heat, but always refreshed by pure and cooling breezes. West of the town is Will's mountain, which is elevated more than 1300 feet and rising to the N. of Bedford it runs a few degrees W. of south. On the E. is Dunning's mountain, running parallel to Will's, and having an altitude of 1100 feet. These mountains are about a mile and a half distant from each other at their bases. The borough contains by the census of 1830, 879 inhabitants, and 163 taxables of whom 417 were white males, 405 white females, 27 black males, 30 black females. The buildings, consisting of 150 dwellings, 8 stores, 8 taverns, &c. are mostly of stone or brick, the streets are spacious and have a business-like appearance. The citizens have adorned the town by several handsome public buildings, among which the Catholic, German, Lutheran, and Reformed, and the new Presbyterian churches, and the court house, are the most remarkable. The last, completed in 1829, surpasses in beauty most buildings of the kind in the state. It is of the Tuscan order, and the rules of architecture are said to have been carefully observed by the native artists engaged in its erection. It is seen to great advantage in approaching the town by the turnpike road from the E. whence its beautiful symmetry, lofty columns and commanding cupola, are all in view.

The borough was incorporated by act of assembly of 13th March, 1795, and again by act of 5th Feb. 1817. The officers are burgesses, assistants, high constable and town clerk.

The summer here especially in the mornings and evenings, is cooler than it is either E. or W. on the same parallel of lat. A large volume of air on the W. of Dunning's mtn. is not heated by the rays of the sun before 10 o'clock in the morning, and a like volume on the E. of Will's mtn. begins to cool two hours before night—hence the heat is never intense, and cool breezes generally prevail. The scenery around Bedford, though picturesque and possessing many charms, is more remarkable for its beauty than its grandeur.

The chief attraction of Bedford is the mineral springs in its vicinity. These rise in a beautiful valley one mile and a half S. of the town, formed by a Spur of Dunning's mtn. and a ridge running parallel with Will's mtn. These hills have an elevation of about 450 feet. Through this valley, which is about a mile and a half in length, runs a copious stream called "Shaver's creek," which flows into the Raystown branch one mile E. of the borough. The hill on the E. of the valley is called Constitution Hill, and at its base arise, within a short distance, the following medicinal and other fountains; viz. Anderson's or the principal medical spring; Fletcher's or the Upper spring; the Limestone spring; the Sweet springs; the Sulphur spring and the Chalybeate spring.

The curative power of these springs is said to have been discovered in the following manner. In the year 1804, a mechanic of Bedford, when fishing for trout in the stream near the principal fountain, was attracted by the beauty and singularity of the waters flowing from the bank, and drank freely of them. They proved purgative and sudorific. He had suffered many years from rheumatic pains, and formidable ulcers in the legs. On the ensuing night he was more free from pain, and slept more tranquil than usual, and this unexpected relief induced him to drink daily of the waters, and to bathe his limbs in the fountain. In a few weeks he was entirely cured. The happy effect which they had on this patient, led others, laboring under various chronic diseases, to the springs. In the summer of 1805 many valetudinarians came in carriages and encamped in the valley, to seek from the munificent hand of nature their lost health. Previous to this time a dense copse of shrubs enveloped the springs and rendered access to them difficult. The inhabitants of Bedford applied themselves to remove these obstacles. Upon digging away the bank, it was found, that about 20 feet from the spot where they first issued, they poured themselves through the fissure of a limestone rock ; which lies nearly parallel with the surface of the mountain, making with the horizon, an angle of 35° ; covered with a mixture of clay and freestone gravel, about three feet deep. The principal spring now issues from this rock, in a copious and perpetual stream, at the height of 25 feet above Shaver's creek, and within nearly the same distance of the margin.

Fletcher's spring is about 15 perches S. of Anderson's, and discharges about six gallons of water per minute ; the sensible qualities of which differ little from those of Anderson's. The analysis of Dr. Church gives for the latter—18½ cubic inches of carbonic acid gas to the quart of water, sulphate of magnesia or epsom salts, 20 grs. sulphate of lime 3.75, muriate of soda 2.50, muriate of lime 0.75, carbonate of iron 1.25, carbonate of lime 2, loss 0.75. Fletcher's gave rather more iron, and common salt, less magnesia, and about the same proportion of other substances. This spring rises 60 feet from the base of the mountain. It once issued 25 feet higher on the hill, than at present. Between its original source and the bottom of the hill, is a large bank manifestly of secondary formation. It would seem that this bank has been raised by deposite from the stream, and that at some remote period a much larger volume of water issued from the mountain at this place ; the channel was partly filled up with the deposition, and that the waters formed a new passage through the the fissures of the limestone rock below. There are many hundred tons of this reliquium, of a greyish color and easily pulverized ; with the stronger acids it effervesces violently, and there is a copious evolution of fixed air.

About 40 perches N. E. of the principal fountain is the rich sulphur spring, which rises in the bed of the creek.

Anderson's spring discharges about 20 gallons of water per minute, the temperature of which is 55° F.

It emits no smell when issuing from the fountain, is perfectly transparent, and its taste is very soft and agreeable to most palates. When exposed in a clear glass vessel a pellucid mineral substance is seen, which after a few days is dissolved and becomes invisible. The water deposits in the tubes which convey it to the baths, a large quantity of oxidized iron. A glass tumbler exposed in the fountain became enveloped with a coat of this oxyde.

These springs are much frequented during the warm months. They have been found salutary in cases of internal worms—in removing incipient consumption of the lungs—or checking a tendency to that disease—in the removal of chronic obstructions and in inflamation of the viscera, particularly of the liver, especially such as follow autumnal fevers and protracted intermittents—and indeed in all cases of deranged excitement of the viscera, consequent on bilious fever, remittent or intermittent, whether in their acute or chronic states—dyspepsia, constipated bowels from torpid liver—incipient dropsies, calculus, diabetes, chronic nephrites, hemorrhoids, rheumatism, cutaneous eruptions and ulcers, in which the system has been brought to sympathize, the obstructions and profluvia which afflict females, &c. &c. Good effects are experienced also in almost all cases of debility, whatever their causes, which not unfrequently baffle the physician, and from year to year teaze the patient. The water, however, is not the only agent in ministering to the diseased. The pure elastic air of the mountain, where there are no miasmatic effluvia,—the elevation of the country which counteracts the morbid effects of the sun—the change of scene and the exercise on rugged roads, and various and cheerful company, all contribte to the amelioration of health. The water in almost all cases operates as a laxative and diuretic—sometimes as an emetic and sudorific. It uniformly strengthens the digestive organs, and stimulates the appetite. When used moderately it stimulates the spirits and animates the countenance; taken in excess it causes languor and stupor, and by rapid depletion, general debility. When prescribed with judgment it is powerful over the two great classes of disease, that of debility, and that of strength.

This region is not less interesting for its geological structure that its sanative effects. To render the springs accessible to visiters, and to obtain ground for a promenade and for bath houses, and other buildings, it became necessary to excavate the base of the hill, the distance of one hundred yards. In the prosecution of this work a section of the rocks, of about 150 feet in length and about 10 feet high, was laid bare. This, and all the northern part of the hill, appears to be composed of limestone, in strata, from two inches to two feet thick, dipping from 40 to 55° S. W. At the northern part of the excavation, is a vein running into the hill in which are several varieties of organic remains, which, lying at the foot of the hill, and lowest in position, may be considered as among the inferior order of such remains, at least as here arranged. At the distance of 25 yards S. in the same section, and immediately opposite the S. end of the bath house, a second stratum, running into the hill, six feet thick, is exposed. This, unlike those above and beneath it, is fetid carbonate of lime, also filled with organic remains. South of this, there are nine strata in which there are no such remnants. About 100 yards S. of Anderson's spring there is an appearance of sandstone, but not in place, which lies over the limestone. Fifty yards further S. from the foot of the hill, sandstone has been taken for buildings, which is soft and pulverulent and contains the impression of a variety of shells, such as the *producti terebratulæ* a species of *Pecten*, &c.

These are the third deposite of organic remains, in the order of position. At a little distance further S. in the road, and upon the surrounding surface, and *still* in the sandstone formation, are abundance of specimens of such remains, of various sizes, from that of a quarter of a dollar to that of the palm of the hand.

From the specimens thus found it appears that as we ascend in the order of formation and position, that the fossils are not only greater in variety, but become more complex and perfect in their structure and organization. Few localities present a more interesting subject for observation and contemplation, than Constitution Hill; no one on visiting its structure and duly weighing the various phonomena will doubt that these deposites of organized substances must have taken place at epochs far distant from each other.

Federal Hill on the opposite side of the valley is nearly of the same dimensions at the base as Constitution Hill. Its geological structure is the same, except that no veins of organic remains are perceptible. The southern slope is overlaid with sand stone, in which are fossil shells, such as are found in the sand stone of the first mountain. Organic remains are however observable in the limestone by the side of the road on the eastern slope, and nearly at the foot of the hill for a quarter of a mile from the springs. At this distance stands a grist mill on Shover's creek, immediately opposite to which and on the West side of the road leading to Bedford, the hill presents a vertical mural precipice of more than a hundred feet, composed like the hill opposite of stratified limestone. At about the height of 30 feet below the summit of this precipice, there is a vein about two feet thick apparently filled with fossils, but its position renders its examination difficult. Specimens have been taken from the lower part of the vein where it was covered with earth. At the foot of the precipice, and by the road-side, may be found many interesting specimens, which have probably rolled from the heights above; but many of them have been broken for the purpose of repairing the road. The rock from the mill to about a quarter of a mile above, runs into perfect slaty limestone.

The road leading to the springs from Bedford has a serpentine course on the eastern slope of Federal hill and on the West side of Shover valley. The buildings for the accommodation of visiters are at the base of Federal hill and consist, in the first place, of two houses each two and a half stories high, and 130 feet in length; these have comfortable rooms for families and individuals. The north building has in front, upon the valley and Constitution Hill, two spacious covered balconies for ladies, which extend the whole length of the house and the southern building has a similar balcony for gentlemen. There is also a drawing room of about 20 by 25 feet, a ball and dining room of 100 feet in length. In the front of this building in the valley below, enclosed within a handsome Chinese railing, there is elevated upon a pedestal of rough masonry a statue of Hygeia, the goddess of health, with a patera in her hand. From the stock passed through the statue there flows a stream of pure water, brought from the main spring, into the bowl. This embelishment, though not of perfect symmetry, adds a pleasing and not uninteresting object to the surrounding scenery.

At the distance of 15 or 20 rods South of the principal buildings, there has been erected, much to the injury of the prospect, a two story frame building, of 140 feet in length. From its spacious balconies, however, the visiters have an agreeable prospect to the north.

The principal access from the several houses of accommodation, to the springs, is by a raised way across the valley to a small bridge over Shover's creek. From the springs zigzag walks are cut upon the western slope of Constitution Hill, to its summit, which, but for the towering forest trees, would afford in all directions, a most interesting and romantic view. The valley opposite Anderson's spring is about 150 yards wide and in its entire length, almost a perfect level, which is beautifully adorned by forest trees of native growth, dotted over its surface.

The bounteous and wonderful supply of water which flows from the springs, the natural beauties of the valley, susceptible of the highest improvement, the lofty bounding hills, and the wide and romantic view from their summits, together with the facility of obtaining all the comforts and luxuries of life, including wild and tame animals and vegetables of every kind, and above all, the high value of the medicinal springs, present a combined attraction scarce surpassed in any country; and this valley might certainly be rendered the most inviting watering place in the United States.

Bedford, t-ship Bedford co. bounded N. by Woodbury, E. by Coleraine, S. by Cumberland valley and W. by Napier and St. Clair t-ships. Greatest length 15½, breadth 4½ ms. Area 32,640 acres; surface, mountain and valley. Soil of the valley, lime-stone. Pop. in 1830, 1344. Taxables, 277. It is bounded E. by Will's, and W. by Dunning's mountain, and watered by the Raystown branch of the Juniata r. which crosses it centrally by the town of Bedford, by Dunning's creek and by Shover's creek or Morris' run on the bank of which are the celebrated Bedford springs. The Philadelphia and Pittsburg turnpike road passes through the t-ship.

Bedminster, t-ship Bucks co. bounded N. by Nockamixin, N. E. by Tinicum, S. E. by Plumstead, S. by New Britain and Hillton, S. W. by Rockhill, and W. by Haycock, t-ships. Greatest length 6 ms. breadth 6 ms. Area 18,451. The Tohickon creek forms its W. N. and N. E. boundary, whilst Deep run, a tributary of that stream, crosses to the east. The N. E. branch of the Perkiomen creek proceeds from the centre of the t-ship toward the S. W. There are three churches in the t-ship, one on the east, another on the West side of Deep run, and a third near the Tohickon creek on the west boundary. The town of Dublin is on the southern boundary on the road to Durham. Surface Rolling; soil red shale, and clay. Pop. in 1830, 1594. Taxables in 1828, 338. Taxable property by the return of assessors 1829, $583,438.

Beelen's Ferry and p-o. on the right bank of the Juniata river, Juniata t-ship, Perry co. distant 8 ms. N. of E. from Bloomfield, 129 from W.C. and 43 from Harrisburg. *Belfast* t-ship, Bedford co. Pop. in 1810, 750, in 1820, 1196, in 1830, 1373. Taxables in 1828, 274. It isbounded N. by Dublin E, by Air, S. by Bethel and W. partly by Bethel, and partly by Providence t-ships. Centrally distant from Bedford borough 20 ms. S. E. Area 64,640 acres; surface mountainous; soil, slate in the mountains, limestone in the valleys. Scrub ridge bounds it on the E. and Sideling hill on the W. It is drained by Licking creek and its tributaries, and by the N. branch of the Great Conoloway creek. The turnpike road to Bedford passes through the north part of the t-ship. Valuation of taxable property 1829, real estate $29,375, personal estate &c. $8020. Rate of assessment 6½ mills on the dollar.

Bellefonte, p-t. borough and st. jus. of Centre co. on the right bank of Spring creek, in Spring t.ship, lat 40° 50′ N. lon. 0° 40 W. from W. C. distant from that city N. W. 192 ms. and from Harrisburg 85 ms. It is situated in a valley of limestone land highly susceptible of cultivation, abounding with excellent timber and inexhaustible quantities of iron ore, of the best quality, easily smelted and yielding 62½ per cent. of metal. Spring creek, which has it source in Penn's valley, about 9 ms. S. of the town, is a large stream of limestone water, which scarcely ever rises, never falls and never *freezes*; it is rapid, has bold banks and is well adapted to propel machinery. It has upon it a great number of furnaces, forges and rolling mills, for the manufacture of bar and sheet iron; grist mills, saw mills, fulling mills, tilt-hammers and oil mills, and affords sites for many more. It discharges itself into the Bald Eagle creek 2½ ms. N. of Bellefonte, piercing the Bald Eagle mtn. The town has some high land around it, but none which is not capable of producing from 25 to 30 bushels of wheat to the acre; and from lands adjacent to the town once denominated *barrens*, that quantity has been frequently obtained. Bituminous stone coal is abundant within 10 miles of the town in the Allegheny mtn. and is employed in the iron works near it, and a turnpike road has been or is about to be made from the town to the mines. The inhabitants count much upon the prosperity of the place when the west branch canal shall be completed, to which they will have access by Spring and Bald Eagle creeks. The town contained in 1810, 203, in 1820, 433, in 1830, 699 inhabitants. There are 120 dwellings, 1 Presbyterian, 1 Methodist, 1 Catholic, 1 United Brethren, churches; an academy, incorporated 8th Jan. 1805, to which the legislature gave sundry lands and the sum of $2000; a masonic lodge, a cotton manufactory, court house, county offices and jail. Bellefonte and its vicinity are said to excel in salubrity almost every part of the United States. The town including Smithfield was incorporated by act of 18th March, 1814.

Belmont, a small village of Mount Pleasant t-ship, Wayne co. near the Moosic mtn. 14 ms. N. W. of the borough of Bethany, and 170 N. E. from Harrisburg. The Oquago and Great Bend turnpike roads cross here.

Belleville, p-t. Mifflin co. in Union t-ship, on the E. side of Stone mtn. 169 ms. N. W. from W. C. and 77 from Harrisburg, contains 15 or 20 dwellings, 2 stores and 3 taverns.

Belleville, a village of Plainfield t-ship, Northampton co. on the road from Easton to the Wind Gap, 9 ms. from Easton, containing 3 dwelings, 1 tavern, 1 store, 1 church, free to every denomination of christians.

Belle Vernon, p-t. of Washington t-ship, Fayette co. in the extreme N. W. part of the t-ship, on the E. bank of the Monongahela r. 18 ms. N. W. of Uniontown, 217 ms. from W. C. and 194 from Harrisburg; contains 35 dwellings, 2 stores, 1 tavern, 1 school, 1 steam boat yard, 1 grist mill and 1 saw mill.

Ben's creek, Somerset co. a tributary of Stoney creek, rising in Jenner t-ship, and flowing N. E. by a course of about 10 ms. to its recipient in the N. E. angle of Conemaugh t-ship.

Bendersburg, Mifflin t-ship, Dauphin co. 28 ms. N. of Harrisburg, on the road leading from Millersburg along the S. side of Syken's valley to the Susquehannah r. contains 10 dwellings, a tavern and store; the Sykens valley rail road passes near the town.

Bensalem, t-ship, Bucks co. bounded N. and N. E. by Middleton, E. by Bristol, S. E. by the Delaware r. W. by Philadelphia co. and N. W. by Southampton. Greatest length, 8 ms. greatest breadth $3\frac{1}{2}$. Area, 11,502 acres. The Neshaminy creek runs on its eastern boundary, over which there are two good bridges, and the Poquessing upon the west. Both streams furnish excellent mill seats, and are improved by hydraulic works of various kinds. The Bristol turnpike road runs across the t-ship. Surface, level; soil, clay, gravel and loam, well cultivated and abundantly productive. Pop. in 1830, 1811; taxables in 1828, 345. There is a p-o. at Andalusia, a small hamlet on the Bristol road, 14 ms. from Philadelphia; value of taxable property in 1829, $561,592.

Bentley's creek, Bradford co. rises in Springfield t-ship, and flows through Ridgeway t-ship, into Tioga r. in the state of New-York, having a course of about 12 ms.

Bentleysville, p-t. of Somerset t-ship, Washington co. on the S. fork of Pigeon creek, 16 ms. S. E. of Washington borough, 222 N. W. of W. C. 202 W. of Harrisburg; contains 20 dwellings, 2 stores, 1 tavern, grist mill and saw mill.

Berks co. was formed from parts of Philadelphia, Lancaster, and Chester cos. by act of assembly passed 11th March 1752. It has since been reduced by the annexation of a part to the county of Northumberland, (21st March, 1772) and by the erection of Schuylkill co. (1st March, 1811) which latter took from Berks the t-ships of Brunswick, Schuylkill, Manheim, Norwegian, Upper and Lower Mahantango, and Pine Grove. This county was settled chiefly by Germans, and their descendants form the great mass of the population, among whom it is in no wise rare to find individuals born in the county, who can neither speak nor comprehend English.

This county lies in the valley formed by the South and the Kittatinny mts. and partakes of the geological formation, which remarkably distinguishes that valley in its whole extent in Penn. of about 160 miles. The southern part of the valley is formed of transition limestone, the northern part of clay slate. These two rocks inflect with the mountains, and touch each other in most places as if joined by art. The line of separation extends

S. W. leaving Kutztown on the limestone and crosses the Schuylkill nearly midway between Reading and Hamburg, and the Tulpehocken, N.E. from Womelsdorff, leaving the latter also on the limestone. Iron ore is found in both formations, but is most abundant and of better quality on the limestone than on the slate.

The county is bounded on the S. W. by Lancaster and Lebanon, on the N. W. by Schuylkill, on the N. E. by Lehigh, and on the S. E. by Montgomery and Chester. Its length E. and W. is 38 ms. and mean breadth 27 ms. Area, 1026 sqare miles. It is traversed by one humble chain of mountains, and is limited, on the N. and the N. W. by the Blue mtn. and on the S. E. by the South mtn.

The physiognomy of the country seems to vary with the basis of the soil. The limestone section is comparatively level, and the soil rich. The slate region is more broken, and the soil inferior. The timber does not present any very striking difference, except that the pine is more commonly found on the latter than the former. In the limestone formation, although the water is abundant, it is unequally diffused. On the slate the distribution is more equal.

The Schuylkill r. divides the county into two almost equal parts, entering it through the Blue mtn. near the boundary line between Upper Berne and Windsor t-ships, it pursues an almost due southerly course to Reading, whence declining eastwardly the river makes its exit from the county at the angle of junction with the counties of Chester and Montgomery. The waters which feed the Schuylkill from the W. are Irish, North Kill, Little North Kill, Tulpehocken, Spring, Cacoosing, Wymissing, Angelica, Allegheny, Hay, and Mill creeks; from the E. Maiden, Dry, Roush, Manokesy, and Manataway creeks. Some of the head waters of the Lehigh r. have their sources in the N. E. part of the county, whilst the N. W. sends forth the Swatara, to meet the Susquehannah r. and to form a medium of intercourse between the Schuylkill and that noble stream. Canals formed by the Schuylkill navigation company follow the banks of the Schuylkill r. along almost its entire course, through the county. The continuity of the canals is broken only by several short dams. The Union canal follows the Tulpehocken and unites with the Schuylkill navigation at Reading.

There are two fine bridges across the Schuylkill at Reading, built of wood on stone piers, and covered with substantial roofs.

Roads intersect the county in all directions, among which are very excellent stone turnpikes, leading from Reading towards Philadelphia, towards Harrisburg, and towards Orwigsburg.

The principal ts. are Reading, Womelsdorff, Hamburg and Kutztown.

The population by the census of 1830 is 53,357, of whom 113 were aliens; 32 deaf and dumb, and 22 blind; 26,606 were white males, 26,174 white females; 298 free colored males; 272 free colored females, and 7 slaves.

Berks, Lehigh, and Northampton, form the 3d Judicial district of Penn. The county courts are holden at Reading on the 1st Mondays in January, April, Aug. and Nov. Prest., Mr. Mallary. Berks is a part of the Lancaster district of the supreme court, by act of March 11th 1809. It is the 8th senatorial district of the state, and sends two members to the senate.

With Schuylkill and Lehigh it forms the 8th congressional district, represented in the 22d Congress by Henry A. Muhlenberg and Henry King.

The public buildings of the county consist of a court house of brick, a small and old building unworthy of the county, occupying the centre of the borough of Reading. A jail, a poorhouse, and house of employment, established under an act of 1824, for the maintenance of the poor of the county, situate on a farm called Angelica, formerly of Gov. Mifflin, of 480 acres of excellent land, 3 ms. S. W. of Reading. The front of the house

100 feet, depth 40 feet, with wings 40 by 30 feet, built of brick of two stories, with elevated basement, cost of farm and buildings, 33,000. Average number of poor in the house 115; there are also a number of poor maintained out of the house. The whole at an average expense, beside the produce of the farm of $4000 per ann. paid by the county commissioners from the public fund, on the order of the directors of the poor. An academy, a large and commodious brick building in the town of Reading, incorporated in 1788, to which the state gave, by the incorporating act, 5000 acres of land, and in 1807, $2000 in money, and in 1817 a further donation of 448 acres, and 81 perches of land. The Greek and Latin languages, and mathematics are taught here in addition to the rudiments of an English education.

Out of the town of Reading, the provisions for education are scanty, and in many places, there are none for teaching the English language, the inhabitants erroneously believing, that a knowledge of science and letters will not increase the magnitude of their crops. German industry, patience and perseverance, are indeed valuable, and agricultural implements, which become more effective in proportion to the general intelligence of the mind that directs them. The prevailing religion of the county is German, Lutheran, and German Presbyterian. These sects dwell together in christian harmony, commonly placing their churches near each other, and not unfrequently worship in the same church. There are in the county 37 churches in which the Lutherans worship.

The staple commodities of Berks county, are wheat, rye, corn, oats, buckwheat, salted provisions, and iron.

Flour, and iron, and wool hats, are the chief manufactures. Grist and merchant mills are numerous in the county, and those on and near the Schuylkill have by the canal ready and speedy access to the markets on the sea board. At the town of Reading the principal manufactories of hats are located, and many thousand dozen are sent annually to the south and west.

The annexed statement by Mr. Daniel McKeim, of the iron manufactures of the county, has much interest and is entitled to much credit. See Table A.

This county paid to the State Treasury in 1831.

For tax on writs,	487,20
Tavern licences (1830)	2226,41
Tax on dealers in for. mdz. (1830),	1107,66
Collateral inheritances,	704,32
Licences to pedlars (1830,)	357,20
	$4882,79

The value of taxable property, by assessment of 1829 was, of real estate $6,463,338, of personal estate including occupation, $852,730. Amt. of tax levied $18,780.

(A.)

STATEMENT OF THE FURNACES, FORGES, LABORERS, &c. employed in Berks County, embracing a period of three years.

Names.	Workmen in 3 years.	Dependents supported.	Horses employed.	Wood consumed: cords	Tons of pigmetal made.	Tons of castings.	Bushels grain consumed.	Bls. of beef and pork.
Reading Fur.	228	1056	198	23,822	3568	95	33,000	150,000
Hopewell,	168	1600	84	15,000	1000	700	21,000	78,500
Joana,	168	1358	80	15,000	1200	500	21,000	78,500
Mount Penn,	220	1050	120	15,000	1700	500	16,890	92,000
Oley,	150	765	75	10,500	1050	360	14,226	46,500
Sally Ann,	150	750	51	10,800	1300	25[illegible]	11,650	36,000
Mary Ann,	153	765	81	12,000	1350	330	12,500	47,000
Windsor,	195	1075	48	11,200	650	750	8600	49,000
Moselm,	18	90	15	4500	643	00	2000	2000
Union,	18	90	15	6000	700	00	2500	15,000
Kernsville,	12	60	12	4500	250	100	3000	3000

FORGES &c. continued.

Names.	Men employed.	Dependents supported.	Horses employed	Cords of wood used.	Grain consumed.	Lbs. of meat used.	Tons of bar iron.	Tons of Blooms
Channing Forge,	99	475	70	9006	9000	98,550	800	
Gibralter,	168	740	60	9000	12,000	175,000	000	
Dowell,	85	425	60	5000	7000	65,000		1900
Sixpenny,	62	310	36	3000	5500	56,000		1000
Birdsborough,	94	470	52	7500	10,500	81,000	750	600
Speedwell,	99	99	54	3450	11,000	86,000	205	
North Kill,	36	160	22	3000	5000	33 000	300	300
Green Tree,	19	82	12	1600	2500	17,000	150	
Moselm 2 Forges,	110	550	60	7500	13,000	102,000	300	
Rockland,	53	265	31	4500	6000	5000	450	750
Union,	61	305	37	3000	5600	25,000		
Spring,	41	205	40	3750	6000	36,000	375	600
Oley,	35	165	61	3600	5000	32,000	300	
New District,	30	146	48	3000	4000	26,000	240	
District 2 Forges,	62	320	64	5300	7000	63,000	480	
Mount Pleasant,	98	453	47	9600	10,000	78,000	720	
Dale,	32	146	19	3100	3500	25,000	240	
Rockland,	18	81	17	2500	2400	16,500	150	
Pine,	90	460	61	8500	10,000	79,000	700	

Thus it seems that during three years, eleven forges have produced 14,411 tons pigs and 3587 tons castings; 24 forges have manufactured 6,160 tons of bar iron and 5,150 tons of bloom. That these forges and furnaces have employed 2,770 laborers, and given bread to 14,516 persons, have maintained 1,630 horses, and consumed 223,622 cords of wood, 281,366 bushels of wheat, rye and corn, and 1,731,550 lbs. of beef and pork. Let the farmer add to these articles of consumption others which have been also necessarily consumed, and then ask himself, does not the protection of manufactures add to his wealth and happiness.

STATISTICAL TABLE OF BERKS COUNTY.

Townships, &c.	Greatest Lth.	Greatest Bth.	Area in Acres.	Face of Country.	Soil.	Population. 1810	1820	1830	Taxables.
Amity,	4	4	10,500	Undulating.	Red gravel.	1090	1279	1378	284
Alsace,	5¾	5¼	21,420	Mostly mts.	Chiefly grav.	1275	1637	1943	402
Albany,	6¼	5	21,000	Hilly.	Gravel.	996	1182	1129	200
Bethel,	8	5	27,000	Diversified.	Do.	924	1294	1482	281
Brecknock,	7	2	9,500	Hilly.	Do.	495	536	866	180
Caenarvon,	5	2½	8,500	Diversified	Lime., Grav.	723	829	861	175
Cumru,	7	7	32,000	pt. lev. pt. h.	Gravel.	2017	2462	2705	497
Colebrookdale,	5	3	9,600	Hilly.	Do.	792	1046	1219	230
Douglass,	5¼	2	7,000	Undulating	Do.	660	709	838	156
Earl,	4½	3¼	9,520	Mount'ous.	Do.	653	934	979	183
East District,	3½	3	6,500	Large hills.	Do.	394	509	562	114
Exeter,	4½	4½	13,500	Undulating	Red Gravel.	1194	1416	1455	291
Greenwich,	6½	4½	19,000	Hilly.	Gravel.	1104	1237	1407	274
Heidleburg,	8	7	37,000	pt. lev. pt. h.	Lime., Grav.	2802	3605	4101	923
Hereford,	5½	4½	15,950	Hilly.	Gravel.	1140	1431	1716	316
Kutz-town,									133
Longswamp,	5	4½	13,500	Hilly.	Mostly grav.	998	1371	1702	297
Lower Bern,	6¾	5½	34,000	Hilly.	Do.	1240	1791	2154	410
Maiden Creek,	4¾	4	13,000	Mostly lev.	Lime., Grav.	918	1192	1350	294
Maxatauny,	5½	4¾	14,960	Do.	Do.	1530	1845	2108	254
Oley,	5	4¼	13,600	Level.	Mostly lime.	1284	1410	1469	290
Pike,	4½	2½	6,500	Large hills.	Gravel.	552	645	752	147
Reading Borough	1¾	1¾	1,850	Level.	Grav., Lime.	3462	4278	5859	1068

STATISTICAL TABLE OF BERKS COUNTY—*Continued.*

Townships, &c.	Greatest Lth.	Greatest Bth.	Area in Acres	Face of Country.	Soil.	Population. 1810	1820	1830	Taxables.
Richmond,	5	4	12,480	Mostly lev.	Grav., Lime.	971	1135	1550	268
Robeson,	$6\frac{1}{4}$	5	21,000	Hilly.	Gravel.	1807	2065	1970	371
Rockland,	5	4	12,000	Large hills.	Do.	1026	1131	1342	257
Ruscomb Manor,	4	4	10,000	Do.	Do.	932	1056	1243	250
Tulpehocken,	11	7	48,000	Diversified	Lime., Grav.	2294	3838	2300	424
Union,	$5\frac{1}{4}$	4	14,000	Large hills.	Gravel.	706	921	1046	191
Upper Bern,	$7\frac{3}{4}$	7	34,000	Hilly.	Do.	1342	2017	2117	406
Windsor,	8	$5\frac{1}{4}$	24,450	Hilly.	Do.			2298	368
U. Tulpehocken,	8	6	30,720	Diversified	Lime., Grav.			1456	268
						36,838	46,251	53,357	10202

Tulpehocken was divided since the census of 1820.

Berlin, p-t. and borough, of Brother's valley t-ship, Somerset co. on the road from Bedford to Uniontown, on the head waters of Stoney creek, about 4 ms. S. of the turnpike road leading from Bedford to Somerset, and about 9 ms. S. E. of the latter; 157 miles from W. C. and 135 from Harrisburg; contains 100 dwellings, a Lutheran and German Reformed church, 5 stores and 2 taverns. Incorporated 27th of Feb. 1821.

Berlinville, or Lehighville, Lehigh t-ship, Northampton co. on the road from Easton to Berwick, 2 miles E. from the Lehigh water gap and one from the river; contains 7 dwellings, 1 store and 2 taverns.

Berlin, East, p-t. Hamilton t-ship, Adams co. on the Conewago creek, 15 miles N. E. of Gettysburg, 14 W. of York, 90 from W. C. and 24 from Harrisburg, contains 80 dwellings, 5 stores, 3 taverns, 1 church, and the necessary handicrafts.

Berlin, t-ship, Wayne co. Pop. in 1830, 175. Taxable property in 1829, seated lands, $14,701; unseated lands, $97,609; personal estate, $2742. In 1828 there were 37 taxables, 4 frame and 19 log houses, 2 saw mills, 5 looms and 1 school.

Bermudian creek rises in Adams co. near the N. boundary, and flows thence S. E. and E. into York co. through Washington t-ship into the Conewago creek, having a course of about 20 miles.

Bermudian, p. o. of Washington t-ship, York co. 96 miles from W. C. and 18 from Harrisburg.

Bern, Lower, t-ship, Berks co. bounded N. by Upper Bern, S. and W. by the Tulpehocken cr. and E. by the Schuylkill river. Greatest length $6\frac{1}{2}$, breadth $5\frac{1}{2}$ miles. Area, 34,000 acres. Surface of country hilly; soil, chiefly gravel. Pop. in 1810, 1240; in 1820, 1791; in 1830, 21,54. Taxables in 1828, 410. Lower Bern is watered by the Schuylkill river, the Tulpehocken creek, and a small tributary of the latter called Plum creek. It is intersected by roads which pass thro' it in all directions. There are two churches in the township, known as Epler's church and Bern church respectively. The town of Bernville is in the extreme N. W. part of the township, about 14 miles from Reading, at which there is a post-office.

Bern, Upper, t-ship of Berks co.; bounded N. by the blue mountain, S. by Lower Bern, E. by the r. Schuylkill, and W. by Upper Tulpehocken. Greatest length $7\frac{1}{2}$ miles, breadth 7 miles. Area 34,000 acres. Surface hilly, soil gravel. Pop. in 1810, 1342; in 1820, 2017; in 1830, 2,117. Taxables in 1828, 406. It is watered by the Schuylkill r. and by a stream which flows into that river near the S. E. corner of the t-ship. North-hill church and Bellman's church are both near its southern boundary line, and are distant from each other about 4 miles; another church is centrally situated, all common to the Lutherans and Presbyterians. The Schuylkill canal runs along a part of the eastern boundary line.

Bernville, a town of Lower Bern t-ship, Berks co. distant about 14 ms. N. W. of Reading. Contains 40 dwelling houses, 1 store, 2 taverns. Pop. 250.

Berry's Mountain, Dauphin co. rises on the E. margin of the Susquehannah r. about 20 ms. N. of Harrisburg, and extends E. about 13 ms. forming the S. boundary of Upper Paxton, Mifflin and Lykens t-ships.

Berrysburg, p-t. of Mifflin t-ship. Dauphin co. on the road leading from Millersburg on the Susquehannah r. through Lyken's valley into Schuylkill co. It is 35 ms. N. of Harrisburg and 149 from W. C.; contains about 20 dwellings, 2 stores and 1 tavern.

Berwick, sometimes called Abbottstown, village, Adams co. about 15 ms. W. of Little York. (See Abbottstown.)

Berwick, p-o. and borough of Briar creek t-ship, Columbia co. on the N. side or right bank of the Susquehannah r. 21 ms. N. E. of Danville, about the same distance S. W. of Wilkesbarre, and about 37 ms. N. W. of Mauch Chunk, 196 ms. from W. C. and 86 from Harrisburg. From this town a turnpike road runs to Lausanne on the Lehigh r. 2 ms. above Mauch Chunk, passing near the Beaver meadows. The road crosses the Susquehannah by a bridge (which connects Berwick with Nescopec village,) commenced in 1814, and completed in 1818, at a cost of $52,435, of which the state subscribed $27,435. It is in length 1256 feet, and 28 feet in width, and rests upon 6 stone piers, and is roofed to protect it from the weather. Another turnpike road runs from Berwick to Tioga. Part of the town extends into Luzerne co. and the bridge is wholly within that county. The Penn. canal runs through the town. There are here about 100 dwellings, 5 stores, 2 taverns and a Methodist church. The route for a canal to connect the Susquehannah at this place, with the Delaware at Easton, has been surveyed. The practical distance from Berwick to Mauch Chunk is reported at $112\frac{1}{2}$; the direct distance 63 ms. The elevation to be overcome 1636 feet, by 20 locks of 5 feet lift, 128 do. of 12 feet, making 148 locks. If inclined planes were adopted from Berwick to Mauch Chunk, and divided into 50 feet lifts, it would require but 33 feet lifts, equal to passing 11 ms. of canal, which, the direct distance being added, 63 ms. gives the practicable distance from Berwick to Mauch Chunk, 74 ms. or 38 ms. less than by the common locks. Hence the distance (by inclined planes) from Berwick via Lehigh, &c. to Philadelphia, would be 221 ms. to New-York by Morris canal, 248 ms. and by the Delaware and Raritan canal 278 ms.

With the use of the common locks, the practical distance between Berwick and Philad. would be 42 ms. less by the Lehigh than by the Union canal, and by inclined planes 80 ms. less; and Berwick would be 20 ms. nearer to Philad. than to Baltimore, by the Susquehannah canal. But if a boat from Berwick be destined to New-York, one half the distance will be saved by the Lehigh route.

Berwick, t-ship, Adams co. bounded N. by Hamilton t-ship, E. by York co. S. by Conewago t-ship, and W. by Mount Pleasant t-ship. Centrally distant E. from Gettysburg 11 ms.; greatest length 7, breadth 3 ms. Area, 10,240 acres; surface, level; soil, red shale. Pop. in 1830, 1417; taxables, 228. The Conewago creek flows along the western boundary, and receives a branch which divides this from Conewago t-ship. Beaver creek, another tributary, flows on the E. and forms part of the boundary between York and Adams cos. Abbottstown lies on the N. E. angle, and Oxford near the W. line both on the turnpike road from York to Gettysburg. Both are post towns.

Bethany, p-t. borough, and st. just.

of Wayne co. on Dyberry creek, lat. N. 41° 37′, lon. E. 1° 42′, 123 ms. from Philadelphia, 36 from Milford, 111 from New-York, 265 from W. C. and 162 from Harrisburg. It is situated on a commanding eminence, declining on every side except the N. and overlooks the adjacent country for a great distance. It contains about 50 dwellings, a court house, and fire proof offices, a Presbyterian church, an academy, incorporated in 1813, and endowed by the State with $1000, with a condition that at least two poor children should be annually taught therein gratis; 3 stores, a printing office, and several artists and mechanics establishments. There is a grist mill near, and some glassworks, employed chiefly upon window glass, of which from 10 to 12,000 boxes are made annually. The Easton and Belmont, and the Bethany and Dingmans choice turnpike roads pass through the town. The borough was incorporated by act of 31st March, 1821. Pop. in 1830, 327; taxables, 65; assessed value of taxable property in 1829, viz. real estate $13,162; personal est. including occupations $9448.

Bethel, t-ship, Lebanon co. bounded N. E. by Schuylkill and Berks cos. S. E. by Jackson t-ship, S. by Lebanon t-ship, and W. by Swatara. Centrally distant from the borough of Lebanon 7 ms. Greatest length 13, breadth 7 ms. Area, 29,400 acres; surface, the N. part mountainous, the southern level; soil, chiefly gravel. Pop. in 1830, 1604; taxables 284. The little Swatara creek passes through the southern part of the t-ship, and receives from it Elizabeth r. and Deep run. In the fork of the former lies Stumpstown, the p-t. near which S. and E. are two churches of the German Presbyterians and Lutherans respectively.

Bethel, t-ship, Berks co. pop. in 1810, 924, in 1820, 1294, in 1830, 1482; taxables 281. Bounded N. by the Blue mtn. which separates it from Schuylkill co. S. and E. by the Little Swatara creek, which divides it from Tulpehocken t-ship, and S. and W. by Lebanon co. Greatest length 8, greatest width 5 ms. Area, 27,000 acres. The great road from Rehrersburg to Jonestown crosses it on the S. that to Pine Grove on the E. that to Sunbury centrally, and the state road on the W. Besides the Little Swatara, Grosskill creek and its branches are the principal streams; on which there are several grist mills. The surface of the country is diversified, the soil gravelly, and not remarkably productive. Millersburg is the only town, it consists of about 30 dwellings, 3 taverns, 1 store, a church, jointly used by the German Presbyterians and Lutherans. There is a p-o. here called Bethel, distant 144 ms. from W. C. and 34 ms. from Harrisburg.

Bethel, t-ship, Bedford co. Pop. 1810, 1095, in 1820, 1083, in 1830, 1208. Bounded N. by Providence, Bedfast and Air t-ships, E. by Franklin co., S. by the state of Maryland, and W. by Southampton t-ship. Centrally distant S. E. from Bedford borough 21 ms. Greatest length 11½, breadth 9½ ms. Surface, mountainous; soil, in the valley, limestone. Cove mtn. is on the E., Raystown Hill on the W. boundary, from which Sideling Hill runs about 6 miles E. It is drained by the Great Conoloway and its tributaries, the North Branch and White Oak run, Pigeon Cove creek, Five Lick run, and by the Little Conoloway creek and Buck run. The p-t. of Werefordsburg lies on the Great Conoloway, near the S. boundary of the t-ship.

Bethel, Mount, Lower, t-ship Northampton co. bounded N. by Hamilton and Stroud t-ships, W. by Plainfield, S. by Forks and the Delaware r. and E. by Upper Mount Bethel. Greatest length 11½ ms. greatest width 8¼ ms. Surface partly hilly and partly level; soil chiefly gravel, with some limestone near the river. It is watered by Richmond, Martin's and Muddy creeks. Population in 1830, 2666; taxables in 1828, 483. Richmond is the chief town. Offset Knob, a spur of the

Blue mtn. is the most prominent feature of the northern part of the t-ship. There is a Lutheran church near Martin's creek, within a mile of the Delaware.

Bethel, t-ship, Delaware co. bounded N. by Concord, E. by Aston and Upper Chichester, S. W. by the state of Delaware. Centrally distant from Phil. 22, and from Chester 7 miles. Greatest length 4½, greatest breadth 3 miles; area, 5000 acres. It is drained by some branches of Naaman's cr. and a tributary of Chester cr. There is a village at the N. E. corner, called Corner Ketch. Surface, level; soil, clay. Pop. in 1830, 367; taxables in 1828, 71.

Bethel, Mount, Upper, township of Northampton co. bounded N. by Stroud and Smithfield t-ships, E. by the river Delaware, S. and W. by Lower Mount Bethel. Greatest length 9 ms. greatest width 5 miles. Surface hilly and rolling; soil, limestone, well cultivated and fruitful. Pop. in 1830, 2241; tabables in 1828, 450. It is watered by Cobus creek, which empties itself into the Delaware; Williamsburg and Buttztown are the only villages. Slate quarries, which produce excellent roofing and ciphering slates, lie near the Delaware, and have been wrought to a considerable extent, under the direction of Col. James M. Porter, the proprietor. The p-o. of the t-ship, called Mount Bethel, is 208 ms. from W. C. and 121 from Harrisburg.

Bethlehem, a town on the north side of the river Lehigh, Northampton co. 12 ms. above Easton, and 51 north of Philadelphia, 184 ms. N. of W. C. and 91 N. E. from Harrisburg, the first and most considerable establishment of the society of United Brethren, commonly called Moravians, in the United States. The situation, on a rising hill, is particularly romantic; a fine mill stream and the Lehigh canal passing through the lower part of the town, affording considerable facilities to business. The number of private dwellings in the year 1831, amounted to 112. The public buildings consisted of a remarkably large church, a boarding school for young ladies, established since the year 1788, a school-house for boys, and two peculiar establishments, in one of which a number of widows find an asylum in their old age, and in the other unmarried women, chiefly likewise of advanced age, board together, under proper regulations and the guardianship of the society. The town contains about 800 inhabitants, is well supplied with water from a copious spring, situated at the foot of the hill, carried up 114 feet perpendicularly to a cistern on its summit, by forcing pumps, in iron pipes, worked by the mill stream, and thence conducted into every street. The same stream furnishes adequate water power for several mill works and other establishments requiring it. There are two large hotels in the town, for the accommodation of travellers and occasional residents, and a third has been recently built close to the canal. Most of the usual mechanical trades are actively carried on, and five or six stores supply the town and vicinity with goods of every description; but there is no manufacturing establishment on a large scale to be met with. The boarding school for young ladies has for more than forty years enjoyed very extensive credit in the United States; it is conducted under the superintendence of the elders of the society. There is a wooden bridge over the river, resting on stone piers, 400 feet in length, in 4 arches. Many erroneous conceptions concerning the peculiarities and regulations of this religious community being still prevalent, a somewhat detailed account of the true state of the case may prove acceptable. It appears that the ancient church of the United Brethren in Moravia having been entirely suppressed, together with all Protestant churches in the Austrian dominions at the conclusion of the thirty years war, descendants of that religious community, who secretly adhered to the religion of their fathers, began to emigrate into

Saxony in the early part of the last century, and were received and protected on his estates in Upper Lusatia, by Count Zinzendorf. They there built the town of Herrnhut, and under his guidance established a community after the model of their ancient ones in Moravia. Numbers of religiously disposed persons, approving of their social regulations, which were intended to promote the practice of vital christianity, joined themselves to this community, and all agreed to lay by their differences upon disputed doctrinal points, taking the Scriptures for their only guide, and making a sincere desire practically to live up to its precepts the only bond of their social union, whilst they felt themselves impelled to exert all their faculties to promote a knowledge of the gospel, particularly among heathen nations. This prompted them, among the rest, to attempt to effect this among the Indians of our continent; which, together with an edict of the Saxon government, promulgated at the instance of Austria, forbidding the reception of further emigrants from Moravia at Herrnhut, caused their patron, Count Zinzendorf, to accept offers of General Oglethorpe to send a colony to the province of Georgia, which was effected in the year 1736. Being there disturbed by the Spanish war, the colonists removed to Pennsylvania about the year 1741, towards the close of which the Count himself arrived in that province, and purchased for them a tract of land on the Lehigh, on which Bethlehem is situated, and began to be built in 1742. The colony was numerously reinforced direct from Europe in that year. The greater part of the colonists being poor, they knew of no other way of effecting their settlement, than by uniting as it were in one single family, all the members of which combined their exertions and labor for the common necessities, and for the discharge of the interest accruing upon the very large sums of money, which had been borrowed upon the credit of some confidential individuals among them, for defraying the expenses of their transportation from Europe and the first establishment of the colony, as well as the purchase of the land upon which they lived, the title to these lands remaining in the individuals who became bond for the loans. A large number being actively employed in the main object of their union, of spreading the knowledge of the gospel among the neighboring Indians and preaching it to their then destitute German countrymen, in various places in Pennsylvania. These persons derived their support, as far as their own industry proved insufficient, and the expenses of their travels, from the same source, and thus by indefatigable exertions the society became gradually enabled to establish its affairs on a firm foundation, while the town of Bethlehem continued to increase by further emigrations, and several other similar establishments were commenced. After this state of things had continued for about thirty years, and its object had been fully answered, the common family connexion was dissolved by universal consent, and the individuals became the owners by purchase of the private houses, &c. and thenceforward carried on the different mechanical trades, which had been established, each upon his own account. A few particular branches of business, were in like manner assumed by a town committee, elected from time to time by the members of the society, and administered for the benefit of the community, in providing by their avails for all common disbursements, such as the maintenance of the ministry, the building and support of the churches, school houses, &c. The lands remained in the possession of the individuals and their devisees, who were answerable for the debts originally contracted or since accumulated, and being let out into a number of farms, form at this day the security for these debts, and their avails are devoted to the discharge of the interest. In every other respect the inhabitants of Bethlehem and the other Moravian establishments, are precisely in the situation of other persons elsewhere, holding their house-lots on leases, under an equitable ground-rent. However, in the towns of Bethlehem, Nazareth, and Litiz, none but members of the society can become owners of such lots, in order to avoid the difficulties which otherwise might ensue, in the maintenance of sundry regulations subsisting among them, for the promotion of morality and good order, as the towns are not incorporated. The community is governed by a set of regulations to which each individual when of age becomes a voluntary subscriber, with the right of withdrawing himself from the society at pleasure, in which case howevhe is required to disposed of his property and to remove from the town, if a householder. The execution of the regulations rests with the elders appointed by the church in general, and with a town committee biennially elected by the male members of full age. Provision is made by voluntary contributions for the indigent. All other contributions towards the social objects, as for instance, the support of the missions, of the aged ministers, &c. are likewise voluntary, exceping only the town expenses for water works, fire engines, and police affairs, which are assessed upon the inhabitants, by a committee elected by them for that purpose. Similar regulations subsist in the other establishments of the Moravians before mentioned.

This society is distinguished by some amiable peculiarities, among which their simplicity of manner and love of music are most remarkable. In the latter almost every member is a performer. In the burial of their dead, they observe ceremonies different from those of the country generally. When a death occurs, part of the choir ascend the steeple where a requiem is played upon the trombones, and the melancholy notes, as they fall on the ear in a calm morning, are peculiarly solemn and impressive. The corpse is exposed in the "corpse house," a small plain stone chamber overhung by weeping willows, for the space of three days; at the expiration of which it is borne to the grave, accompanied by music. The grave yard is divided into plots by avenues, planted with trees; and males, females, adults, children, and strangers have appropriate and separate resting places. Each grave is marked with a small marble slab, about a foot square, on which, according to the regulations of the society, the name, age and place of birth of the deceased, alone are noted. These graves, contrary to the custom of other christians, have the feet to the south.

Bethlehem, East, t-ship. Washington co. pop. in 1810, 1806, in 1820, 2239; taxables in 1830, 535. It is bounded N. by Pike run t-ship, E. by the Monongahela r. S. by 10 mile creek, S. E. by the N. fork of that creek, and W. by West Bethlehem. Centrally distant from the borough of Washington, 18 ms. Greatest length 9, breadth 7 ms. Area, 16,000 acres; surface, hilly; soil, loam, abundance of coal. Besides the streams above named there are several smaller ones, which flow into them. The national road crosses the river by a bridge in the N. E. angle of the t-ship, and forms part of its N. boundary. On this road in the t-ship, are the villages of Kripstown, Centreville, and Bealsville. The latter is a p-t. Fredericktown also a p-t. is on the river below the Great Bend, and Millsborough, a p-t. is on the N. bank of 10 mile creek at its confluence with the river, at which there is a ferry. One of the p-ts. of the t-ship, is called E. Bethlehem, 210 ms. from W. C. and 203 from Harrisburg.

Bethlehem, West, t-ship, Washington co. pop. in 1810, 1849, in 1820, 2187; taxable pop. in 1830, 389. Bounded N. E. by Somerset t-ship, S. E. by E. Bethlehem, S. by Greene co. and W. by Amwell, and N. W. by Strabane t-ships. Centrally distant from the borough of Washington 12 ms. length 10, breadth 7 ms. Area, 30,720 acres; surface, hilly; soil, loam, abundance of coal. The N. fork of 10 mile creek crosses the S.

part of the t-ship, and receives from the W. boundary the Little North fork, whose sources interlock with Ramsey's creek and several other streams. The national road runs N. W. through the t-ship, about 12 ms. S. E. of the borough of Washington. The small village of West Buckingham, at which there is a p-o. is in the t-ship.

Bethlehem, t-ship, Northampton co. bounded northward by Nazareth t-ship, southward by the river Lehigh, eastrd. by Moore t-ship, and wstrd. by Hanover t-ship, and the Manokissy creek. It receives its name from the village of Bethlehem, founded by the Moravian brethren, which is its chieft. Buttztown, a small village on the road to Easton, 3 ms. from Bethlehem, is in this t-ship. It is watered by the Lehigh r. and the Manokissy creek. The latter turns several mills in the t-ship. Its greatest length is $5\frac{1}{2}$ ms. greatest width $4\frac{1}{2}$ ms.; surface, rolling; soil, limestone. Pop. in 1830, 2430; taxables in 1828, 417. The township is generally well cultivated and highly productive. (*See statistical table of Northampton county.*)

Beula, once a small town of Cambria t-ship, Cambria co. about 2 ms. N. W. of Ebensburg. The place is now in ruins, containing but one house.

Big Pond creek, Upper Smithfield t-ship, Pike co. has its principal source in a large pond north of the Milford turnpike road, and flows into the Delaware r. 4 ms. below Shohola creek. It has some mills near its mouth.

Biles' island, in the river Delaware, between Bordentown and Trenton, in Falls t-ship, Bucks co.

Bilo's cross roads, small village at the intersection of the roads leading to Attleborough, and Fallston, about 24 ms. N. E. of Philadelphia and 15 S. E. from Doylestown.

Birchardsville, p-o. Susquehannah co. 280 ms. from W. C. and 172 from Harrisburg.

Birch run, Manallan t-ship, Adams co. a tributary on the Conecocheague creek.

Birdsborough, village of Robeson t-ship, Berks co. on the right bank of the Schuylkill, at the confluence of Hay creek with that stream, and upon the canal; 8 ms. below Reading.

Big creek, Towamensing t-ship, Northampton co. is formed by the junction of Pohopoko and Head's creeks, at the foot of the Pohopoko mtn. from which place rafts descend to its mouth. It flows southwesterly through a cultivated valley, to which it gives name, and falls into Lehigh r. on the E. side about 4 ms. above the Water Gap. It is navigable for rafts about 10 ms.

Big creek valley, Towamensing t-ship, Northampton co. lying along the Big creek, between Kettle mtn. and Fire Line hill. This valley is cultivated, and produces rye, corn, and grass. A road running N. E. from Lehighton to the Wilkesbarre turnpike, passes through it.

Big Creek mountain, in Towamensing t-ship, Northampton co. lying on the Lehigh r. between the Broad mtn. and the Kettle mtn.

Big creek, Schuylkill t-ship, Schuylkill co. rises in Mine Hill, and flows S. to the Schuylkill r. near the new town of Patterson, about 7 ms. from Port Carbon. It is valuable as affording access and drainage to many rich coal mines.

Birmingham, borough and p-t. Huntington co.; pop. 1820, 43. It is on a branch of the Juniata, about 15 ms. from the town of Huntingdon, 163 ms. from W. C. and 105 from Harrisburg; is built on a hill side, contains between 30 and 40 houses, 5 stores, 1 church, 1 school, and 3 taverns. It is a thriving place, and considerable business is done in it. In 1824 it contained but nine houses. It was incorporated as a borough at the session of the legislature, 1827–8. There are several mills in the neighborhood, and a baptist church in the town. A lead mine near the village was worked upwards of twenty years ago; iron abounds here, and iron works are in operation.

Birmingham t-ship, Delaware co. bounded N. & W. by Chester co. N. E. by Thornbury, E. and S. E. by Concord, and S. by the state of Delaware.

Central distance from Philadelphia 22 ms. W., from Chester 11 ms. N. W. Length 3¾ ms. breadth 2¾ ms. Area 4480 acres. Surface hilly; soil, clay and loam. Pop. in 1830, 584; taxables in 1828, 100. The Brandywine r. runs along the western boundary and receives from the t-ship a small creek which crosses it from E. to W. Compas-town lies near the Chads Ford, on the Brandywine r. Painter's cross roads post-office is on the road to the Ford, but on the E. boundary of the t-ship, distant 116 ms. from W. C. and 84 from Harrisburg.

Birmingham, t-ship, Chester co. bounded N. E. by Thornbury, S. E. by Birmingham t-ship, Delaware co. S. W. by Pennsbury and N. W. by East Bradford. Central distance W. of Philadelphia, 23 ms. S. of Westchester 5 ms. Length 2¾, breadth 2½ ms. Area 3,500 acres; surface level; soil, limestone. Pop. in 1830, 377. Taxables 65. The Brandywine river forms the W. boundary of the t-ship, in which lies the "battle-field" where the bones of the slain, and weapons used in the memorable fight of the Brandywine, are still occasionally found. Birmingham church lies in the N. E. angle of the township, and Dilworthtown, a post town, in the S. E. angle.

Birmingham, p-t. and borough, St. Clair t-ship, Allegheny co. on the W. bank of the Monongahela r. about a mile above the city of Pittsburg. Pop. in 1830, 520. There are about an hundred dwellings and several manufactories. (*But see Pittsburg.*) The town was incorporated by act of Assembly, 10th April, 1826.

Black creek, a large tributary of the Nescopeck creek, which rises in Sugarloaf t-ship, Luzerne co. and flows westerly, S. of Buck's mountains, to within 4 ms. of Columbia co., when, turning north, it passes through that mountain, and falls into the Nescopeck at the foot of the Nescopeck mountain. The valley along this creek contains some excellent land, and is pretty densely settled. Little Black creek is a tributary which rises between Buck's mountains and Pismire Hill.

Black creek, Pine Grove t-ship, Schuylkill co., a tributary of the Swatara creek, which rises and has its course between the Second mountain and the Sharp mountain.

Black's Eddy, a rapid of the Delaware river, in Plumstead t-ship, Bucks co. at which is a small village of 6 or 8 dwellings, a tavern, store and post-office. It is 191 ms. N. of Washington, 118 N. E. from Harrisburg.

Black Horse, p-o. Chester co. 129 ms. N. of W. C. and 55 S. E. from Harrisburg, in W. Caln t-ship, on the turnpike road from Philadelphia to Lancaster, about 40 miles from the former and 22 from the latter.

Black Legs, p-o. Indiana co. 202 ms. N. W. from W. C. and 170 W. from Harrisburg.

Black Lick creek, a tributary of the Conemaugh river, rises in Cambria co. and flows S. W. into Indiana co. to its recipient at Blairsville. It is a large stream, having a course of more than 30 ms.; is navigable for boats to Black Lick run, 9 ms. from its mouth, and for canoes to Little Black Lick creek, 17 miles higher.

Black Lick t-ship, Indiana co. bounded N. by Centre t-ship, E. by Wheatfield, S. by the Conemaugh r. and W. by Conemaugh t-ship. Centrally distant S. W. from Indiana borough 10 ms.; greatest length 9½, breadth 8 ms.; area, 32,000 acres; surface, hilly; soil, loam and gravel. Pop. in 1830, 1,850; taxables, 321. Black Lick creek crosses the t-ship to the river, and at their confluence, on the north side of the creek, lies the town of Newport, and on the south the borough of Blairsville, which is a post town.

Blair's Gap, through Dunning's mountain, p-o. of Allegheny t-ship, Huntingdon co., by the post road 120 ms. W. from Harrisburg and 158 from W. C.

Blair's Valley, in the S. part of Montgomery t-ship, Franklin co. E. of Two-Top mountain.

Blairsville, p-t. and borough, Black Lick t-ship, Indiana co. on the Conemaugh r. on the S. side of Black Lick creek, at its confluence with the former stream. The state canal passes through the town, and a turnpike road leads from it W. to Pittsburg, and E. to Ebensburg. Pop. in 1380, 957; taxables, 182. It is 189 miles N. W. from W. C. and 161 W. from Harrisburg, and about 14 ms. S. W. of Indiana borough. In 1827 this thriving village contained 501 inhabitants;—within two years from that time four brick houses of public worship were erected, viz. a Presbyterian and a Methodist meeting-house, an Episcopal church and a Catholic chapel, and preparations were made for building a German Lutheran church. There were in the village in Nov. 1829, 47 brick, 72 frame, 47 log, and 4 stone houses, and several brick buildings under way, and has a fair prospect of steady and rapid increase. There is a newspaper published in the town, called "*The Blairsville Recorder*." The following statement of the number of passengers and vehicles which passed the bridge over the Conemaugh here, in 1829, will give some, though imperfect, idea of the travelling in West Pennsylvania: Foot passengers, 12,527; single horses, 4,372; one-horse wagons, 374; two-horse wagons, 245; four-horse teams, 781; five-horse teams, 1,566; six-horse teams, 1,438; cattle, 497; sheep, 98; swine, 475. In addition to which, the stages crossed 730 times, and there were 325 yearly subscribers who crossed back and forward more or less every day. There are here now, probably, 200 dwellings, 7 taverns and 12 or 15 stores. The town was incorporated by act 25th March, 1825.

Blakely, t-ship Luzerne co. bounded E. by the co. of Wayne; S. E. by Covington, S. W. by Providence, and N. W. by Greenfield. This t-ship was called Blakely from respect to the memory of Capt. Johnston Blakely, who commanded the U. S. sloop of war Wasp, and signalized himself in an engagement with the British sloop Avon. The timber in the northern part is principally beech, maple, hemlock, ash, and cherry; in the southern, pine, oak, hickory, and chestnut. The Lackawannock enters near its N. E. angle and flows through a deep valley of fertile land, of 2nd quality, between the Moosic and Lackawannock mountains, S. W. until it intersects its S. western boundary, a distance of about 15 ms. dividing it into nearly two equal parts. The anthracite coal formation commences near the sources of the Lackawannock, not far from Belmont, and extends through the whole valley of the Lackawannock, cropping out upon the hills and mountains on each side. It is every where exposed in the bottom and banks of the river, and in all the little ravines formed by its tributaries. The coal mines of the Hudson and Delaware canal company were in this t-ship. But in 1830 the new t-ship of Carbondale was formed. The rail-road from the basin at the western termination of the Lackawaxen canal, terminates here; and Carbondale, a village containing several stores, mechanics shops, and 40 well built dwelling houses, and about 250 inhabitants, has grown up upon a spot where, four years since, but a single log cabin was to be found. The company have constructed an excellent artificial road from Carbondale to intersect the Milford and Owego turnpike upon the top of Moosic mountain, at Rix's Gap, a distance of about three miles; the Milford and Owego turnpike, passes through the northern division of this t-ship: the Luzerne and Wayne co. turnpike, passes through its eastern, and the Clifford and Wilkesbarre turnpike, through its western division; and a company has been incorporated for making a turnpike road from Carbondale, along the Lackawannock river, to intersect the Clifford and Wilkesbarre turnpike, a distance of about ten miles, from whence there is an excellent road to Wikesbarre. A considerable portion of this t-ship will admit of cultivation.

Numerous mill sites are furnised by the Lackawannock and its tributaries. It is situated about 23 miles N. E. from Wilkesbarre, has two post offices, and contained a taxable pop. in 1828 of 98. But this number has been greatly increased by the operation of the Delaware and Hudson company, and upon the usual ratio of one taxable for five inhabitants, may be justly estimated at 200.

The surface of the country, is variegated by mountain and valley. The soil is alluvial, slate and gravel. The greatest length of the t-ship is 15 miles, and greatest width 7¾ miles.

Blockley, t-ship Philadelphia co. on the W. side of the river Schuylkill, bounded N. and E. by that river, S. by the same, and by Moyamensing t-ship, W. by Cobb's creek which separates it from Delaware co. and N. W. by Montgomery co. Its greatest length is 5, breadth 4 ms. Area 7,580. Surface, gentle declivities; soil, sandy loam. Pop. in 1330, 3401; taxables in 1828, 742. Beside the streams that bound it, Mill creek which flows centrally S. E. through the t-ship into the river Schuylkill above Grays ferry and Indian run, a tributary of Cobb's creek, are the principal water courses; upon both of which there are several small factories of wool and cotton, and for other purposes. The Chadsford turnpike runs S. W. across the tsp; the Lancaster turnpike and the Pennsylvania rail road, north west. West Philadelphia, at which is a post office, Mantua, Hamilton, Maylandsville and Haddington, are villages of the t-ship. The bank of the river Schuylkill is adorned with many handsome country seats, which overlook the pool made by the dam at Fairmount water works, and which are very advantageously seen from the tow-path along the river. And the seat of the Hamilton family has long been distinguished, with its large mansion, extensive and well-stocked gardens and beautiful grounds. The new and very extensive alms-house and house of employment, for the poor of several districts of the county, is now being erected upon the margin of the river opposite to the arsenal of the United States.

Bloody run, p-t. of Providence t-ship, Bedford co. on the left bank of the Juniata river, 8 ms. E. from Bedford borough, 118 ms. from W. C. and 96 from Harrisburg; contains 20 dwellings, 2 stores, 2 taverns, and a Methodist church of stone.

Bloom, t-ship, Columbia co., bounded N. by Fishing creek t-ship, E. by Brier creek t-ship, S. by the Susquehannah river, which separates it from Cattawissa and Mifflin, and W. by Fishing creek, which separates it from Mount Pleasant and Hemlock; centrally distant from Danville 12½ miles. Greatest lgth. 6¼, bdth. 6¼ ms.; area, 16,640 acres; surface, chiefly level; soil, sandy loam, and limestone. Pop. in 1830, 2,081. Taxables, 414. Knob mountain runs along its northern boundary. Orangeville, Williamsburg and Bloomsburg are villages on Fishing creek; the last is a post town, distant 10 miles N. E. of Danville.

Bloomsburg, p-t. Bloom t-ship, Columbia co. on Fishing creek, about 2 ms. above its confluence with the Susquehannah river and 10 ms. N. E. of Danville, 185 ms. N. W. of W. City, and 75 ms. from Harrisburg. It contains about 100 dwellings, 5 taverns, 5 stores, 1 Presbyterian and 1 Lutheran church.

Bloomfield, p-t. borough and st. jus. of Perry co. in Juniata t-ship, in a valley between the Mahoney and limestone ridges, 36 ms. by post route from Harrisburg, and on the Little Juniata creek. It contains a court house, and public offices of brick, a stone jail, 5 stores, 5 taverns, 1 Presbyterian and 1 Methodist church, a printing office, at which is published the "Perry Forester," a weekly paper. There are also here 2 tailor shops, 1 saddler, 4 cabinet makers, 1 hatter, 1 tinner, 2 blacksmiths, 2 tanners, 2 carpenters, more than half a dozen lawyers, and half as many doctors. The population of the town is about 350. Scarce five years have passed since the site of this town was a clover field, without a building upon it. The town was incorporated into a borough by act of 14th March, 1831.

Bloomfield, t-ship, Crawford co. pop. in 1830, 197.

Bloomfield, post office, Bloomfield t-ship, Crawford co. 313 ms. N. W. from W. C. and 246 from Harrisburg.

Bloomfield, East, also a p-o. of Bloomfield t-ship, Crawford co. 323 ms. from W. C., 262 from Harrisburg.

Blooming Grove creek, a tributary of the Lackawaxen, rises in Palmyra t-ship, Pike co. runs into the Lackawaxen about 3 ms. below the falls. It is a small mill stream but not navigable.

Blossburg, p-o. Tioga co. 235 ms. N. W. of W. C. and 126 of Harrisburg.

Blue Knob, a noted hill of Greenfield t-ship, Bedford co.

Blue Lick creek, Allegheny t-ship, Somerset co. a tributary of Castleman's river.

Bob's creek, Greenfield t-ship, Bedford co. a tributary of Dunning's creek.

Boeuf, Le, (See Le Boeuf.)

Boggs, t-ship, Centre co. bounded N. E. by Howard t-ship, S. E. by Bald Eagle Ridge, which divides it from Spring t-ship, S. W. by Patten t-ship, and N. W. by the W. branch of the Mushanon creek, which separates it from Clearfield and Lycoming cos. Centrally distant from Bellefonte N. W. 12 ms. Greatest length 21, breadth 12 ms. Area, 109,440 acres; surface, mountainous; soil, slate, gravel and limestone. Pop. in 1830, 1311; taxables, 249. The main ridge of the Allegheny fills the centre of the t-ship E. of which, is the Bald Eagle valley, drained by the Bald Eagle creek, upon which at the foot of the Bald Eagle mtn. lies the p-t. of Milesborough, at which there are some valuable iron works. The turnpike road from Bellefonte runs through the town. Beach cr. rises in the t-ship, and flows E. into Bald Eagle. Bituminous coal of good quality is found on the W. of the mtn.

Bolesburg, p-t. Ferguson t-ship, Centre co. on the main branch of Spring creek, and on the E. border of the t-ship, 10 ms. S. E. of Bellefonte, contains about 25 dwellings, a Lutheran church, store and tavern. There is a grist mill, in its vicinity. It is 183 ms. N. W. of W. C. and 82 from Harrisburg.

Bolivar, p-t. of Fairfield t-ship, Westmoreland co. upon the left bank of the Conemaugh r. at the mouth of Tub mill creek 25 ms. N. E. of Greensburg, 189 from W. C. and 166 from Harrisburg, contains 20 dwellings, 2 taverns, and 1 store and a forge.

Bonaghton, small village of Mount Pleasant t-ship, Adams co. on the road leading from Gettysburg to Petersburg about 5 ms. distant from each.

Bottstown, West Manchester t-ship, York co. within a mile west of York, on the Gettysburg t-ship road. It may be considered as the suburb of the borough.

Bow creek, a small marsh stream, part of the boundary line between Philadelphia and Delaware cos. dividing Kingsessing t-ship in the former, from Tinicum t-ship in the latter. Distant from Philadelphia about 8 ms.

Bowman's hill, Upper Makefield t-ship, Bucks co. near the N. line of the t-ship, on the Delaware r. has its name from Dr. Bowman, an early settler, who was buried here at his own request. It has become the common cemetery of the vicinage.

Bowman's mountain, called the Bald mtn. near the western limits of Luzerne co. is a high regular barren ridge whose average altitude may be 1000 feet. It extends from the E. to the W. branch of the Susquehannah r. between which it appears to have no other name than those above mentioned, except that in a small territory, on the head of Fishing creek the inhabitants call it the North mtn. W. of the Susquehannah it forms the main branch of the Allegheny mts.; crossing the E. branch of the Susquehannah at the mouth of the Tunkhannock and Bowman's creeks, and extending N. E. it takes the name of the Tunkhannock mtn. and terminates in the Elk mtn. Susquehannah co.

Bowman's creek and valley, Luzerne

co. The creek rises in Union t-ship, and flows through the valley a N. E. course, of about 20 ms. crossing the t-ships of Lehman, Dallas, Northmoreland, and Eaton, to the Susquehannah r. The valley is from 2 to 3 ms. wide, bounded S. E. by Bowman's mtn. and N. W. by Mahoopenny mtn. The land is generally poor; and the few inhabitants are settled chiefly near the river.

Boyerstown, p-o. Berks co. 159 ms. from W. C. and 68 from Harrisburg.

Bradford, West, t-ship, Chester co. bounded N. by East Caln, E. by East Bradford and Pennsburg, S. by East Marlborough and Newlin, and W. by E. Fallowfield t-ship. Central distance from Philadelphia 33 ms. W. and 11 ms. S. W. of West Chester. Length 6, breadth $4\frac{1}{2}$ ms. Area, 11,150 acres; surface hilly; soil, limestone. Pop. in 1830, 1550. Taxables in 1828, 253. It is drained by two small tributaries of the Brandywine r. The county poor-house is on the line which separates this t-ship from Newlin. The village of Marshalton, which is a p-t. lies on the boundary line between E. and W. Bradford, on the road to W. Chester, near which is a church.

Bradford, small t. of Plumb creek t-ship, Armstrong co. in a fork of Plumb creek, about 12 ms. S. E. of Kittanning, contains some 6 or 8 dwellings.

Branchtown, p-t. Bristol t-ship, Philadelphia co. on the Willow Grove turnpike road, 6 ms. from Philadelphia, 142 from W. C. 104 from Harrisburg, contains 6 or 8 stone dwellings, a store and tavern. It is pleasantly situated.

Bradford, East, t-ship, Chester co. bounded N. by E. Caln t-ship, N. E. by W. Whiteland, E. by W. Goshen and Westown, S. by Birmingham and Pennsburg, and S. W. and W. by W. Bradford. Central distance W. of Philadelphia about 24 ms. S. W. of W. Chester $2\frac{1}{2}$ ms. The Brandywine r. courses the S. W. boundary, and receives from the t-ship, its W. branch, into which Valley creek and other less considerable streams empty. Many mills are erected on these streams. Marshalton, p-t. and village, lies on the boundary between this and W. Bradford. Length 6 ms. breadth $3\frac{1}{2}$ ms. Area, 11,300 acres; surface, hilly; soil, limestone. Pop. in 1830, 1099; taxables, 227.

Bradford, t-ship, Clearfield co. bounded N. and N. W. by the W. branch of the Susquehannah r. E. by Mushanon creek, which divides it from Clearfield co. S. by Cambria co. and W. by Clearfield creek. Pop. in 1830, 631; taxables, 134.

Braddock's Field. "Nine miles above Pittsburg, and immediately on the north bank of the Monongahela river in Mifflin t-ship, Allegheny co. is the celebrated battle ground called "Braddock's field," famed for the destruction of an army intended to capture Fort Du Quesne, (now Pittsburg.) On this spot the imprudent General Braddock fell, and Washington first displayed the military qualities which distinguished him. Here 50 Frenchmen and 250 Indians nearly destroyed the 49th, and 51st regiments of British regulars, though aided by many provincial troops, amounting in the whole to 2,200 men. The battle was fought on the afternoon of the 9th of July, 1765. Sixty-six years have passed away and yet the crumbling bones of men and horses are seen in every field for a mile in circuit. For many years they were shrouded by shadowy woods, but these have yielded to the busy axe, and the plough is annually driven amongst the sculls of the slain. Rich harvests wave over fields fertilized by the blood and bodies of a thousand unburied men.

The retreating survivors carried their wounded general with them, until he died. He was buried 40 miles distant from the battle ground, in the centre of the road his advancing army had cut. To prevent the discovery of his grave, troops, horses, and wagons, were passed over it. Some of his affectionate soldiers so marked the trees near the place where he was laid, that the exact spot might afterwards be discovered. And the travellers attention is even now called to "Braddock's grave."

It was long rumoured that the General was shot by his men. More recently it has been asserted by one who could not be mistaken, that in the course of the battle he ordered the provincial troops to form a column; that they, adhering to the Indian mode of fighting from the shelter of the trees, he, in his vexation rode up to a young man named Fawcett and with his sword rashly cut him down. That Thomas Fawcett, a brother of the deceased, soon learned his fate, and watching his opportunity revenged his brother's death by shooting Braddock through the body; of which wound he died. Thomas Fawcett was lately living near the Laurel Hill."

Bradford, co. was erected by the act of 21st Feb. 1810, which prescribed the following boundaries, and conferred upon it name of Ontario co. It comprehends those parts of the then counties of Luzerne, and Lycoming included within the following lines; beginning at the fortieth mile stone, standing on the N. line of the state, and running S. to a point due E. of the head of Wyalusing falls in the river Susquehannah, thence S. W. to the nearest point of Lycoming co. line, thence in a direct line to the S. E. corner of Tioga co., at the Beaver dam on Towanda creek, thence N. along the E. line of Tioga co. to the eightieth mile stone, standing on the N. line of the state, thence along the said line to the 40th mile stone, the place of beginning. This act further declared that the commissioners therein appointed should fix the place of holding courts of justice, at any place at a distance not exceeding seven miles from the centre of the co. by the act 28 March, 1811. The trustees of the co. were required to establish a point E. of the Slippery Rocks, at the head of the Wyalusing falls, in the river Susquehannah, for the S. E. corner of the county, from thence a line W. to the said rocks, and thence a S. W. course to the nearest point of Lycoming co. as a southern boundary. By the act of 24 March, 1812, the co. was organized for judicial, and other purposes and the name changed to Bradford, and the courts were directed to be holden, until public buildings should be erected, at the house of Wm. Means in the t-ship of Towanda.

The co. is bounded N. by the state of New York, E. by Susquehannah co. S. E. by Luzerne, S. W. by Lycoming, and W. by Tioga co.; greatest length 40 ms. breadth 35 ms. Area 1174 ms. Central lat. N. 41° 45', long. from W. C. E. 0° 30'.

This co. lies in the great western secondary formation, and though it has not been extensively and minutely explored, it is ascertained that there is an abundance of bituminous coal, salt springs and iron ore. The face of the country is hilly and rocky, and the soil varied. On the Susquehannah and other streams, large bodies of first rate alluvial land are found, but extensive tracts of broken and poor land spread between the water courses.

There is no very lofty or regular chain of mountains in this co. but the chains of the Appalachian system, whose continuty is broken and height depressed in Lycoming co. are here scattered as it were into comparatively low hills, whose soil is generally unfruitful.

The principal stream of the co. is Susquehannah r. It enters the co. near the middle of the northern boundary, and flows through it by a devious course in a S. E. direction, and quits it below the Wyalusing falls. It receives from the E. the Wepassening creek, the Wysox, the Rummerfield, and Wyalusing creeks; and from the W. the Tioga r. which unites with it, about five miles below the northern boundary, at Tioga point; Sugar creek and its branches, Towanda creek and its middle and southern branches, Duvals creek and Little Sugar creek, with some other streams less considerable.

The valley of this river has been surveyed with the view to the formation of a canal along it to the New York line, and at a day not far distant the county will be supplied with its imports from the Philadelphia market, which are now principally obtained from the city of New York.

The Susquehannah and Tioga turnpike road commences at Berwick in Colombia co. and passing through Luzerne, enters Bradford in Asylum t-ship, and crosses the co. in a N. W. direction striking the Tioga r. in the state of New York between Bently and South creeks. Another turnpike road, authorized by the state of New York, is designed to connect the Cayuga lake with the Susquehannah r. in this county.

The principal towns are Athens, Towanda, the co. town, and French town. The first situate upon and between the Tioga and Susquehannah rivers, and the others on the right bank of the latter stream. Towanda is 230 ms. N. of W. C. and 128 from Harrisburg.

The population of the county consists chiefly of New England settlers and their descendants. It amounted, by the census of 1820, to 11,554, and by the census of 1830, to 19,615, of whom 9,814 were white males, 9,717 white females, 49 free colored males, 35 free colored females, including 35 aliens.

Bradford belongs to the 11th senatorial district, which includes Susquehannah and Tioga counties, sending one member to the senate, and joined with Bradford and Tioga sends two members to the house of representatives.

United with Union, Northumberland, Columbia, Luzerne, Susquehannah, Lycoming, Potter, and McKean, counties it forms the 9th congressional district, and connected with Susquehannah and Tioga counties it forms the 13th judicial district. The courts are holden at Towanda on the Mondays of December, March, June and September annually. President, Edward Herrick, Esq. The public buildings of the co. consist of a court house, offices, and prison. An academy at Athens was incorporated by the act of 22 March, 1813, by the style of "The trustees of the Athens academy" the building for this institution was erected at indivdual expense, and the legislature granted the sum of $2000, to be invested in some safe fund, the interest of which to be applied to the purposes of the institution, on condition that there should be admitted gratis to the academy any number of poor chidren that may at any time be offered not exceeding four ; not to remain longer than two years, should others apply.

In the year 1831, a geological society was formed by the citizens of this county, of which E. Mason, Esq., was appointed president, and Mr. Millar Fox, secretary. The immediate object of this society is to procure specimens of minerals found in this county, have them analyzed, which, whilst the society is in its infancy, will be done by the society in Philadelphia, and the result sent back, together with specimens found in other places.

There is one newspaper published in the county, called the "Bradford Settler."

The staples of the county are grain, flour, whiskey, fruit, salted provisions, live stock, and lumber, and when they can be transported to market at a saving price, iron and coal may be added to the number. The produce of the county seeks its market by the natural channel of the Susquehannah, but the return supplies chiefly come by the way of New-York, and are purchased in that capital. The completion of the Pennsylvania canal, on the north branch of the Susquehannah, will give this business to Philadelphia.

The county of Bradford paid into the state treasury in the year 1831 :

For tax on writs,	35 00
Tavern licences,	42 28
Duties on dealers of for. mdze.	30 81
Tin and clock pedlers' licenses,	57 00
	$165 09

Taxable property in the county, by assessment of 1829, viz :

Real estate, - -	1,528,722
Personal estate, including occupations, -	187,669
	$1,716,391

Rate of levy, 5 mills on the dollar.

STATISTICAL TABLE OF BRADFORD COUNTY.

Townships, &c.	Greatest Lth.	Greatest Bth.	Area in Acres.	Face of Country.	Soil.	Population. 1820.	Population. 1830.	Taxables.
*Albany,	13	7½	35,420	Generally hilly, except along the margins of the streams.	Gravelly loam on the hills; valleys, alluvial, vegetable.		284	64
Asylum,	13	7½	33,280			471	529	91
Athens,	10	6½	38,400			1108	1253	190
Burlington,	9	4	23,040			560	527	98
Canton,	9¾	8	45,444			569	1175	201
Columbia,	7½	6	28,820			823	1235	198
Franklin,	12½	10	70,400			297	583	103
*Litchfield,							487	89
Monroe,	16½	6½	32,000				988	150
Orwell,	8½	7¾	34,560			713	1190	197
Pike,	10	4	25,600			689	1438	238
Ridgberry,	6	6	23,040			210	560	102
Sheshequin,	6	3¾	9,520				720	124
Smithfield,	7½	6	24,320			695	1126	197
Springfield,	7½	6½	30,720			506	765	160
Troy,	9¾	4½	24,960			536	874	173
Towanda,	7½	5	16,640			1024	978	157
Ulster,	7¼	2¼	7,040			704	405	70
Warren,	6	6	21,760			389	756	133
Wells,	7½	6½	30,720			301	752	130
Windham,	6	5	19,200			350	655	121
Wysox,	12	12	30,080			1083	1351	205
Wyalusing,	10½	10½	50,040			546	753	174
*Tuscarora,							285	
						11,554	19,669	3,365

* Townships marked thus (*) are not laid down on the state map, and as their precise lines are unknown to us, we do not attempt to give their dimensions or areas. Litchfield is taken from Athens; Albany from Asylum; Tuscarora from Wyalusing, and the area given to the latter in the table includes the former.

Braintrim, t-ship, Luzerne co. bounded N. by Bradford and Susquehannah counties; E. and S. E, by Tunkhanna t-ship, S. by the Susquehannah r. which separates it from Windhamp t-ship, and W. by the county of Bradford. The river shore in this township was originally covered with black walnut; from which it is called "Black Walnut Bottom." The hills produce pine, oak and hickory, and will generally admit of culture, and when improved, produce good crops of summer and winter grain. The Tuscarora, and the Big and Little Meshoppen creeks afford excellent mill sites. A woollen factory has been in operation for several years upon the Big Meshoppen, furnishing a market for wool, and manufacturing excellent cloths for the surrounding country. The proprietors, Messrs. Sterling and Parker, deserve great praise for their persevering exertions in this branch of domestic manufacture. A considerable surplus of agricultural products, and large quantities of lumber, are annually produced and floated down the Susquehannah to market. Braintrim is situated about 40 miles N. W. from Wilksbarre. The great post-road from Tunkhannock to Athens passes through it. It has a post-office, called "Braintrim," 264 ms. from W. C., 154 from Harrisburg. The surface is hilly; soil, gravel and alluvion. Taxable pop. in 1828, 116. Greatest length, 11¾ ms.; greatest width, 3¾ miles. Area, 19,840 acres.

Brandywine creek, rises in Chester co. by two branches; the first has its source in E. Nantmeal t-ship, and flows through Uwchlan and E. Caln, by Downingstown and thence into E. Bradford t-ship, where it unites with the W. branch. The latter rises in

Honeybrook t-ship, and runs a S. E. course, watering W. Caln, Brandywine, Sadsbury, E. Caln, E. Fallowfield and Newlin. Each branch is more than 20 ms. in length. The united streams run S. E. into and through the state of Delaware, separating the city of Wilmington from the village of Brandywine, into Christiana creek, which falls into the Delaware, about 35 ms. below Philadelphia. The whole length of the river is about 48 ms. It is bordered by high rocky banks, and is navigable to the mills at Brandywine village, where the water is six or eight feet deep, at the height of the tide. In 4 ms. of its course above Wilmington, it has a fall more than equal to the height of the hill on which Wilmington is built, or of 109 feet; hence the possibility of gaining power sufficient for the employment of 4 times the machinery at present turned by the body of the stream at Brandywine mills, or 58 wheels. In this distance there are many manufactories of wool, cotton, paper, gun-powder, &c. &c. The main stream and its branches throughout their course afford valuable mill seats, which are usefully improved. (See Coalsville, Downingstown.) This river is distinguished in American history for the disastrous battle fought near its banks between the American and British armies, on the 11th Sept. 1777, in consequence of which, Gen. Howe obtained possession of Philadelphia on the 26th of that month. The battle-field is in Birmingham t-ship, Chester co. near Chads ford, where vestiges of the conflict are yet occasionally found.

Brandywine, t-ship, Chester co. bounded N. by W. Nantmeal t-ship and Uwchlan, S. by E. Caln, and W. by W. Caln. Central distance N. W. from Philadelphia 30 ms. from W. Chester 8 ms. Length 6¾ ms.; breadth 4. Area, 15,960 acres; surface, rolling; soil, sandy. Pop. in 1830, 1455; taxables 341. The W. branch of the Brandywine r. runs along the W. boundary and the eastern branch along the eastern boundary, and Beaver creek runs centrally through the t-ship, N. W. and S. E. The northern hills which bound the great Valley are on the southern line. Brandywine Manor p-o. is on the turnpike road between Downingstown and Waynesburg, about 30 ms. W. from Philad. and 63 S. E. from Harrisburg.

Brandywine Manor, p-o. See preceding article.

Brecknock, t-ship, Berks co. bounded N. by Cumree t-ship, N. W. and W. by Robeson t-ship, S. by Caernarvon, and S. and W. by Lancaster co. Greatest length 7, width 2 ms. Area, 9,500 acres; surface, hilly; soil, gravel. Pop. in 1810, 495, in 1820, 536, in 1830, 866; taxables in 1828, 175. It is watered by Big Muddy and Little Muddy creeks, which rise in opposite ends of the township, and unite in Lancaster co. and run to the Conestogo r.

Brecknock, t-ship, Lancaster co. bounded N. E. by Berks co. S. E. by Caernarvon t-ship, S. W. and W. by Earle t-ship, and N. W. by Cocalico. Centrally distant from the city of Lancaster, N. E. 20 ms. Greatest length 7, breadth 5 ms. It is drained by the three branches of Muddy creek, one of which runs on the N. the other on the S. boundary, and the third intersects the t-ship centrally. All of which are mill streams and have mills upon them. Area, 17,306 acres; surface, hilly; soil, red shale. Pop. in 1830, 1048; taxables, 230.

Brickersville, p.o. Lancaster co. 122 ms. from W. C. and 54 from Harrisburg.

Briar creek, t-ship, Columbia co. bounded N. partly by Fishing creek t-ship, and partly by Luzerne co. E. by Luzerne co. S. by the Susquehannah r. which separates it from Mifflin t-ship, and W. by Bloom t-ship. Centrally distant from Danville 18 ms. Greatest length 7½, breadth 6 ms. Area, 26,880 acres; surface, chiefly level; soil, sandy loam, and limestone. Pop. in 1830, 1706; taxables 347. The Susquehannah and Tioga turnpike road crosses the t-ship from Berwick. Shickshinny creek flows through the N. E. point easterly, into the Susquehannah r. and Briar creek southwardly into the same r. Berwick, borough and post town, is at the S. E. angle. Knob mtn. courses the northern boundary.

Bridgewater, a manufacturing village of Brighton t-ship, Beaver co. on the W. side of Beaver r. The village of Sharon is adjacent and both may be considered as one town. There are here a saw mill, salt works, for which coal is found within a few perches; an iron foundry, brewery, several boat yards; a wind mill factory, and other mechanical and manufacturing establishments. "Stone's harbor," is also here, considered as one of the safest and most commodious on the Ohio. It is the principal depot for the trade passing up and down the Beaver valley, and to and from the Western Reserve in the state of Ohio. There is a bridge across the river here, known as the Big Beaver bridge, 600 feet in length, erected at an expense of 22000 dollars, and said to be unrivalled in point of execution. One erected on the same site in 1816 was destroyed by a tornado in Sept. 1821. Bridgewater and Sharon, contain together about 110 dwellings, 4 taverns, 5 stores and 1 Episcopal church.

Bridgewater, t-ship, Susquehannah co. bounded N. by Silver Lake and Lawsville t-ships, E. by New Milford and Brooklyn, S. by Springville t-ship, and W. by Middleton and Rush t-ships. Its greatest length E. and W. is 10 miles, greatest breadth N. and S. $8\frac{1}{2}$ miles; area, 47,360 acres. It is drained on the N. by Snake creek and its tributaries; on the S. by the Great Meshoppen and its middle branch, on the E. by Hopbottom creek, and on the W. by Beard's Mill creek, a tributary of the Wyalusing. There are several lakes in the t-ship, the chief of which are two on the boundary of Springville t-ship, and one near the village of Montrose. Two turnpike roads run through it, the Milford and Owego diagonally from S. E. to N. W. and the Wilkesbarre and Bridgewater centrally N. and S. They intersect each other at Montrose, the county town. The surface of this t-ship is hilly; the soil, loam, sustained by hard pan. Its population in 1830 was 2450; taxables by return of 1828, 381.

Briceland's Cross Roads, p-t. Washington co. on the turnpike road from Pittsburg to Steubenville, on the line between Smith and Hanover t-ships, contains some 6 or 8 dwellings, 2 stores and a tavern; 248 miles from W. C. 228 from Harrisburg.

Bridgepoint, Doylestown township, Bucks co. containing 2 or 3 dwellings, a store, a grist and oil mill, and a very fine stone bridge, erected by the co.

Bridgeport, p-t. and borough of Luzerne t-ship, Fayette co. on the Monongahela r. on the W. side of Dunlap's creek, at its confluence with the former stream. It is a considerable town, containing 737 inhabitants, and 141 taxables. Iron ore is found, and iron works established in its vicinity. It lies 12 miles N. W. of Uniontown, the st. just. of the county. It is connected with Brownsville by a bridge across Dunlap's creek, and is surrounded by a rich and pleasant country, inhabited chiefly by members of the society of Friends. It contains between 135 and 140 dwellings, 7 stores, 3 churches, 2 taverns, 3 schools, 1 steam engine factory, 1 steam boat, a cotton manufactory of 1200 spindles, driven by steam, belonging to General Krebs & Co. a steam saw mill, a saw mill and grist mill driven by water, 1 card manufactory, 1 steam paper mill, 1 glass manufactory, and an air foundry. Few situations proffer greater inducements to the settler. Improved lands may be purchased in the neighborhood at from 20 to 60 dollars the acre. Coal for manufacturing purposes is abundant. The great national road passes the town, and the Monongahela river offers the best high way to market at Pittsburg, and the towns on the Ohio and Mississippi ten months in the year. The town was incorporated into a borough by act of 9th March, 1814.

Bridgeport, small village of Upper Merion t-ship, Montgomery co. on the right bank of the Schuylkill river and canal opposite to Norristown, 1 tavern, 1 store, a factory and 8 dwellings. (*See Norristown.*)

Brighton, t-ship, Beaver co. bounded N. by Chippewa t-ship, E. by Beaver river, S. by the Ohio river and W. by Ohio t-ship. Greatest length 6½, breadth 6 ms. Area, 17,200; surface, hilly; soil, loam and limestone. Pop. in 1830, 901; taxables, 225. The falls of Beaver, distinguished for their mill sites, are included between the N. and S. boundaries of the t-ships.

Upon the Beaver river, within the t-ship, are the villages of Brighton, Fallston, Sharon and Bridgewater, all of which have manufactories of various kinds, and are thriving places. (See the articles relating to these towns.) Beaver, the county town, is also within the t-ship, on the N. bank of the Ohio r.

Brighton, t. on both sides of Big Beaver r. Beaver co. The part on the E. bank of the river is called New Brighton. The towns are connected by a bridge 500 feet in length. Situated near the head of the Beaver falls, this place enjoys very advantageous mill sites. (See Beaver r.) On the W. side of the r. is a cotton factory with 2000 spindles, a grist mill, saw mill, and 2 woollen carding machines; on the E. side, a grist mill, saw mill, sash factory, a wool carding establishment, a chair factory, and other mechanical and manufacturing establishments. The west side, or the old town, contains also 40 dwellings, 1 store, 1 tavern; and the east, or New Town, 50 dwellings, 2 taverns and 2 stores.

Bristol, borough and p-t. Bucks co. on the Delaware r. nearly opposite Burlington, in New Jersey, 20 ms. above Philadelphia, and 12 below Trenton. This town is beautifully seated on the W. bank of the Delaware, and has a fine view of the river above and below it. Its commanding situation and the boldness of its shores, recommended the site to the early attention of the primitive settlers, and some years before 1720, as appears by the recital in the borough charter, a town had been built here, in which there was then a church, a meeting house, a court house, and a prison; and it had then been for a long time the county town. It was incorporated by Sir Wm. Kieth, on the 14th of November, 1720. Bristol has long been a favorite resort of the citizens of Philadelpnia, and its increase of late years, though not very considerable, has been chiefly owing to the impulse given by citizens who have sought a country residence here. The name of the town previous to the charter, was Buckingham, but that of Bristol was given to it in that instrument, most probably on account of the mineral springs which it contains. There are two of these springs; over one of them a bathing house was erected many years since. This is distant from the principal part of the town, about half a mile, in a N. W. direction, in a low piece of ground or meadow, and within a few yards of the head of a pond. It has received the name of Bath. The surface of the water is covered with a dark yellow or ochre colored substance, usually indicative of chalybeate springs. It has been pronounced by distinguished medical men to be serviceable in some complaints, and at one period enjoyed considerable repute. The other spring is at the W. end of the village, and is of similar character to the former. These waters were analyzed, and an account published of them by Dr. Rush, in the year 1773. At present Bristol contains about 200 dwelling houses, a church, a Quaker and Methodist meeting, a masonic lodge, and a bank, 4 taverns, and 6 or 7 stores. Some of the dwellings are very neat and commodious, and the bank, erected as a country residence by Mr. Craig, of Philadelphia, is a tasteful imitation of Grecian architecture. The Delaware canal commences here, and communicates with the Lehigh canal at Easton. A spacious basin has been made, at Bristol, for the reception of boats and produce, and the coal and other trade which will pass this town by means of the canal will probably contribute much to its prosperity. The Bristol and Trenton turnpike road passes through it, on which a daily mail travels, and three steam boats touch here on the way to and from Bordentown and Trenton every day. A small creek branches north of the borough, and insulates it. The projected rail road will run through the town. Bristol may be recommended as a healthful, pleasant and convenient residence for those who have business in the neighboring city of Philadelphia.

Bristol, t-ship, Bucks co. bounded N. and N. E. by Falls t-ship, on the E. and S. E. by the Delaware r. S. W. by Bensalem t-ship, and N. W. by Middleton t-ship. Greatest length 7 ms. breadth 3 ms. Area, 10,374 acres. Central distance from Philadelphia 20 ms. N. E. from Doylestown 20 ms. S. E. Surface, level; soil various, clay, gravel and sandy loam, and generally fertile. Besides the village of Bristol, which is the p-t. there is a small and handsome village called Newport, on the Neshaminy creek, about three and a half ms. N. W. of Bristol, at which there are some excellent mills. Pop. in 1830, 1532.

Bristol, t-ship, Philadelphia co. is bounded N. W. N. and N. E. by Montgomery t-ship, E. by Oxford, S. by the Northern Liberties. Greatest length 5½ ms. breadth 3 ms. Area, 5660 acres; surface, hilly and rocky, with good bottoms. Pop. in 1830, 1425; taxables 347. It is centrally distant about 6 ms. from Philadelphia. The Tacony crk. divides it from Oxford on the E. and receives at the extreme S. E. point Wingshocking creek which has its source in Germantown t-ship, near Mount Airy. Upon the Tacony lies Grub town, at which there is an extensive cotton manufactory, and there is another similar factory on the same stream, about a mile below it. The Willow Grove turnpike runs N. through the t-ship, upon which, 6 ms. from Philadelphia, is Branch town, a p-t. and Miles town lies half a mile beyond it. There are two schools in the t-ship, one near the N. the other near the S. boundary.

Britain, New, t-ship, Bucks co. bounded N. E. by Plumstead, S. E. by Doyleston, S. and S. W. by Montgomery co. and N. W. by Hilltown. Centrally distant from Doylestown 5 ms. W.; from Philadelphia, 25 ms. N. W. Length 6¼, breadth 4½ ms. Area, 12,261 acres; surface, rolling; soil, sandy loam. Pop. in 1830, 1201; taxables in 1828, 270. It is drained by the N. and N. W. branches of the Neshaminy creek, upon which there are several mills. The p-o. of the t-ship, is distant 164 from W. C. and 104 from Harrisburg.

Britain, Little, t-ship, Lancaster co. bounded N. E. by Colerain, S. E. by Chester co. S. by the state of Maryland, S. W. by the Susquehannah r. and N. W. by Drumore t-ship. Centrally distant from the city of Lancaster 20 ms. S. E. Greatest length 10½ ms. breadth 6 ms. Area, 34,457 acres; surface, rolling; soil, clay. Pop. in 1830, 2527; taxables, 394. The Octarara creek and its W. branch flows on the N. E. and S. E boundary, and the Conewingo creek crosses it centrally from N. to S.; near the middle of the t-ship is situated Little Britain church. Little Britain p-o. is near the S. W. boundary, 81 ms. from W. C. and 58 from Harrisburg. There are in this t-ship 2 forges, 5 tanneries, 2 fulling mills, 11 grist mills, 11 saw mills, 3 clover mills and a small woollen factory.

Brockwayville, p-o. Pine t-ship, Jefferson co. 226 ms. N. W. from W. C. and 154 from Harrisburg.

Broadhead's creek, rises in Pike co. and flows an almost due S. course through Stroud t-ship, Northampton co. into Smithfield creek, a short distance

E. of Stroudsburg. It is not not navigable, but is a rapid stream and drives several mills in its course.

Broad mountain, the fourth in range N. of the Kittatinny or Blue mtn. rises in Lykens t-ship, Dauphin co. about 16 ms. E. of the Susquehannah r. where it bears the name of Short mtn. running N. E. into Schuylkill co. it receives the name of Broad mtn. which it bears thence throughout its course in Schuylkill co. and in Northampton, E. of the Lehigh r. but when broken by the Pokono creek, it assumes the name of the Pokono mtn. The second name is given because of the great width of the ridge when compared with the southern ranges. It is remarkable for the quantity of anthracite coal contained within its bowels. Between the Lehigh and Susquehannah rs. many of the richest mines of Schuylkill co. are in this mtn. and the coal is equally abundant at its termination in Lykens valley, Dauphin co. (*See Lykens valley.*)

Broad Top, mtn. extends N. E. from Hopewell t-ship, Bedford co. into Union t-ship, Huntingdon co. It abounds with bituminous coal.

Brockville, p-t. Clearfield co. 222 ms. N. W. of W. C. 149 from Harrisburg.

Broken Straw, t-ship, Warren co. bounded N. by Sugar Grove t-ship, S. E. by the Allegheny r. S. by Deerfield, and W. by Spring creek. Centrally distant west from Warren borough 10 miles; greatest length 8, breadth 8; area, 30,880 acres. Pop. in 1830, 755; taxables in 1828, 163. Broken Straw cr. runs centrally thro' the t-ship into the river, upon which, opposite Young's run, is the p-town of Youngsville, 9 or 10 ms. west of Warren. The p-o. called Irvine's is also in the t-ship, lying on the west side of Irvine's run, which forms part of the eastern boundary. The surface of the t-ship is undulating, except near the river, where it is hilly. The river bottoms are excellent.

Broken Straw cr. rises by Frampton's branch, in the state of N. York, whence it flows by a circuitous course through the E. part of Erie co. into Warren co. seven miles below the town of Warren. The course of the stream in Pennsylvania is about 35 miles, of which 20 are navigable. It receives a small branch from Crawford co. Nine ms. from its mouth it receives the waters of the Little Broken Straw; both streams are excellent for mills.

Broken Straw, Little, creek of Warren co. flows S. through Sugar Grove, North West and Broken Straw t-ships, into the Big Broken Straw creek.

Brookfield, t-ship, Tioga co. formerly part of Delmar, situate S. of Wellsborough. The surface of the country is hilly; soil, loam; well timbered with beech, maple, hemlock and pine; cleared land well adapted to grazing. Pop. in 1830, 332; taxables in 1828, 60.

Brooklin, t-ship, Susquehannah co. bounded N. by New Milford t-ship, E. by Harford and Lennox t-ships, S. by Luzerne co. and W. by Springville t-ship. Centrally distant S. E. from Montrose 8 miles; greatest length 11 miles; breadth 5 miles; area 26,880 acres. Pop. in 1830, 1350; taxables, 187. The t-ship is drained by Martin's creek, which forms its eastern boundary. The Dundaff and Montrose turnpike road crosses it from S. E. to N. W. and the Abington and Waterford turnpike crosses the N. W. angle of the t-ship. There is a post office on the former road, 267 miles from W. C. and 159 from Harrisburg.

Brookville, p-t. and st. jus. of Jefferson co. situated on the Susquehannah and Waterford turnpike road, 44 ms. S. E. from Franklin, 238 N. W. from W. C. and 165 from Harrisburg, and immediately at the head of Red Bank creek, which is formed by the confluence of the three branches of the Sandy lick at this point. Red Bank has commonly sufficient water for steamboats, on the Blanchard plan. At the sale of the town lots in June, 1830, the lots brought from 30 to 300 dollars each. The proceeds of the sale were destined to pay the expense of building the court house. It is supposed that this new town will become the place of deposit for the iron manufactured in the countics of Centre and Clearfield, designed for the Pittsburg market. The first building in the town was put up in August, 1830. There are now here about 40 dwellings, a brick court house and offices, 4 stores and 4 taverns.

Brother's Valley, t-ship, Somerset co. bounded N. by Stoney Creek t-ship, E. by Greenville, Southampton and Allegheny t-ships, S. by Elk lick t-ship, and W. by Milford and Somerset t-ships. Centrally distant from Somerset borough 8 ms. Greatest length 11, breadth 8 miles; area, 55,200 acres; surface, rolling; soil, dark clay. Taxable population in 1830, 378; taxable property in 1829, real estate $183,064; personal $14,244; rate of tax, 5 mills on the dollar. The Allegheny mountain bounds it on the east. Castleman's river flows N. W. along the S. boundary, receiving from the t-ship Buffalo lick, Blue lick and some minor streams; and the branches of Stoney creek penetrate the N. part of the t-ship, near which is the p-t. of Berlin, about 9 ms. S. E. of the borough of Somerset. There is also a p-o. in the S. E. angle of the t-ship.

Brower, p-o. Berks co. 147 miles from W. C. and 66 from Harrisburg.

Brown's Mills, p-t. Mifflin co. 167 ms. N. W. of W. C. 60 from Harrisburg.

Brownsville, p-t and borough of Fayette co. Redstone t-ship, on the right bank of Monongahela river and on the national or Cumberland road from W. C. to Wheeling, 205 ms. from the former, 198 ms. from Harrisburg, 12 from Union, the co. town, N. W. 25 S. E. from the town of Washington, and 35 South from Pittsburg. It was formerly known as Red Stone old fort, and is in a neighborhood composed principally of Friends, and in a rich and highly cultivated country. It is separated from Bridgeport by Dunlap's creek, over which is a convenient bridge. A bridge over the Monongahela is about being erected by a joint stock company, to rest on two abutments and two piers of stone, from 50 to 60 feet high: the length is 630 feet, and the estimated cost $50,000. The town contains 220 dwellings, 5 churches, 22 stores, 5 taverns, 1 mill, 4 schools, 1 steam engine factory, and a steamboat yard, and 1 glass manufactory. Pop. in 1830, 1233; it was incorporated 9 Jany. 1815.

Brown, t-ship, Lycoming co. is bounded N. by Tioga co. E. by Lycoming and Mifflin t-ships, S. and S. W. by Pine creek t-ship, and W. by Dunstable t-ship and by Potter co. Centrally distant N. W. of Williamsport, 25 ms. greatest length 22, breadth 21 ms. Area, 160,000 acres; surface mountainous, soil various. Taxable property in 1829—seated lands $13,476, unseated lands $47,294; tax levied $720 85, rate $\frac{3}{4}$ of one per cent. There is a p-o. named after the t-ship. It is drained by Pine creek and its tributaries. Iron and coal are found in the t-ship, and some iron works have been erected. The country is covered with wood, and uninhabited except sparse settlements along the water courses.

Brownsburg, Upper Makefield t-ship, Bucks co. a small p-t on the bank of the river Delaware, near Bowmans hill, contains 4 or 5 dwellings, 1 store and 2 taverns, distant about 11 ms. from Doylestown, 174 from W. C. and 123 from Harrisburg.

Browns creek, Burlington t-ship, Bradford co. rises in the t-ship, and flows S. E. to Sugar creek.

Brumfieldville, p-t. Berks co. 153 ms. from W. C. and 62 from Harrisburg.

Brunswick, t-ship, Schuylkill co. bounded N. by Schuylkill t-ship, E. by West Penn, S. by Berks co. and W. by Pine grove t-ship. Its form is irregular, its greatest length E. and W. is about 14 ms. breadth about 9 ms. Area, 60,940 acres. Its surface is hilly, and a portion of it is mountainous. The Blue mountain runs along the southern, and the Second mountain along its northern boundary. The intervening space is diversified by many hills, of which the Little mountain, near Orwigsburg, is the most prominent. The soil, is red shale, and white gravel, (but limestone occurs near Orwigsburg,) and with due cultivation is tolerably productive. North of the Blue mountain on the Little Schuylkill there is a bed of fine sand supposed to be highly valuable in the manufacture of glass. The Great and Little Schuylkill unite their waters in the southern part of the t-ship, above the Blue mountain, and receive from it several tributaries, of which Pine creek is the chief. The Little Schuylkill traverses near the whole t-ship, from the north to the south boundary. Orwigsburg, McKeansburg, Port Clinton, and Louisburg are towns within the t-ship. Orwigsburg is the st. jus. and Port Clinton a coal creation, from whence the coal brought by the Little Schuylkill rail road, is shipped on the canal for Philadelphia. Pop. in 1830, exclusive of Orwigsburg, 2298. Taxables 371.

Brush, creek and valley, Providence t-ship, Bedford co. The valley lies between Sideling and Rays hills. The creek rises in two branches, one running N. and the other S. uniting on the E. side of Rays Hill, which having penetrated they flow into Shaver's creek.

Brush creek, Westmoreland co. rises in Hempfield t-ship and flows N. W. by a course of about 17 ms. to Turtle creek.

Brush mountain, Huntingdon co. a forked ridge which rises in the N. W. angle of Frankstown t-ship, one branch running N. and the other N. E. to the Juniata r. enclose the t-ship of Tyrone, separating it from Morris t-ship, on the E., and from Antes t-ship on the W.

Brush run, Mount Pleasant t-ship, Adams co. a tributary of the Conewago cr.

Bryants, p-o. Fayette co. 179 ms. N. W. of W. C. and 178 W. of Harrisburg.

Buckingham, t-ship, Wayne co. bounded N. E. and E. by the Delaware r. S. by Lebanon and Damascus t-ships, W. by Mount Pleasant, and N. W. by Scott t-ship. Its form is very irregular, greatest length 11½ ms. greatest breadth 11½ ms. It is drained chiefly by the Great and Little Equinunk creeks, which have their sources in small ponds or lakes which empty into the Delaware about 10 ms. apart. Stockport, distant from Bethany, the co. t. N. 23 ms. and situated in the northern part of the t-ship, is the p-t. and contains about 200 inhabitants. The surface of the country is hilly, but covered with a heavy growth of beech and sugar maple. The soil is loam and gravel. Pop. in 1830 was only 179, taxables in 1828, 40. Taxable property in 1829, seated lands, $9791, unseated $32,408. Personal estate including occupations, $3289. Rate 4 mills on the dollar. There are in the t-ship, which comprises 39,040 acres, 12 frame, and 12 log houses, 1 grist mill, 3 saw mills, 1 loom, and 2 schools.

Buckingham, t-ship Bucks co. bounded N. and N. W. by Plumstead, E. by Solebury. S. E. by upper Makefield and Wrightstown S. W. by Warwick, and W. by Doylestown t-ships, centrally distant from Philadelphia 25 ms. N. and 4 ms E. from Doylestown. Greatest length 6½ ms. greatest breadth 5 ms. Area 19,490 acres. A fine stream of water rising from many small springs in the *grit* land above the York road, and some larger supplies from the limestone land below, unites its several branches, and running through the S. W. end of Wrightstown, falls into the Neshaminy. The Indian name of this stream was Lahaskeekee, written on our maps "Lackawissa." It is at present known as Randals run, and a southern branch as Roberts run. Two rocky ridges of the same Indian name run parallel with each other, by a N. E. course to the Delaware. The soil of the t-ship is various, loam, clay, and gravel; the surface generally level. It is chiefly inhabited by "Friends," who have a meeting house near the borders of Solebury, Centreville, Barrville, Newark or Halifax. Greenville, and Pineville, are villages of the t-ship. The first is a p-t., called Buckingham, 164 miles from W. C. and 112 from Harrisburg, pop. in 1830, 2193, taxables 467. There is in this t-ship a free school, founded by Amos Austin Hughes, who devised to its use a plantation in the t-ship, with a very considerable sum of money. This institution was incorporated and the inhabitants of the t-ship empowered to appoint trustees, by act of assembly passed 25 Feb. 1813.

Buckingham, West, p-t. of W. Bethel t-ship, Washington co. S. E. of Washington borough 14 ms.

Bucks mountains, a lofty and broken range of hills in Sugar-loaf t-ship, Luzerne co. parallel to, and about 5 ms. S. of the Nescopeck mountains. It is crossed by the Reading and Berwick turnpike road.

Buck run, a tributary of the W. branch of the Brandywine r. which rises near the S. boundary of Sadsbury t-ship, Chester co. and flows S. E. to its recipient in Newlin t-ship, and drives, in its course of about 15 ms., several mills.

Buck tavern, p-t. of Haverford t-ship, Delaware co. on the turnpike road from Philadelphia to Lancaster, 8 ms. from the former, 143 from W. C. and 88 S. E. from Harrisburg. There are several good dwellings here on the extreme verge of the county.

Buckthorn, p-o. Columbia co. 189 ms. from W. C. 79 from Harrisburg.

Bucksville, p-t. Nockamixon t-ship, Bucks co. 15 ms. N. E. of Doylestown, 177 ms. from W. C. and 106 from Harrisburg; contains a tavern, store, and three or four dwellings.

Buck, p-o. Lancaster co. 92 ms. N. of W. C. and 54 S. E. of Harrisburg.

Bucks county is one of the three counties established by William Penn, upon the settlement of the province in 1682. It extended indefinitely northward, and was reduced to its present size by the formation of Northampton co. on 11th March, 1752. The lower and central parts of the county were originally settled by quakers, principally English and Welsh, and the northern part by Germans, who retain with the language of their fathers much of their habits and customs. The county is distinguished in the early history of Pennsylvania for being the residence of the proprietary, who had a spacious and commodious dwelling there, some ruins of which are still visible upon the banks of the Delaware. The manor of Pennsbury, which was appurtenant to this mansion, comprised many acres of excellent soil, which, at this day, is distinguished for its fertility, and forms a considerable portion of Falls township.

The surface of this county is underlaid and divided by three distinct geological formations. The primitive formation, consisting of griers rock, enters the county below New Hope and extends S. W. through it. The width of this formation from the Delaware is imperfectly marked. It is succeeded by a secondary tract in which limestone of an excellent quality is found. Next to this is a broad belt of the old red sandstone, which pertains to the transition formation.

A valuable mine of plumbago, or black lead, has been wrought for some years. It lies in Southampton t-ship, on the top of Edgehill, one and a half mile N. N. E. from Smithfield. in Philadelphia co. It has been excavated to the depth of near 100 feet. The water is raised from it by two pumps, worked by a single horse, to within 30 feet of the surface, where it passes off by a side drain. Within three years by these imperfect means, with the assistance of from three to six hands, 25,000 dollars worth of the mineral has been raised. The plumbago of this mine is said to be the purest known except that of one mine in England. It is barrelled up and sold at from fifteen to forty cents per pound.

Bucks county is bounded on the N. E. and S. E. by the Delaware river, which separates it from the state of

N. Jersey, on the S. W. by Philadelphia and Montgomery counties, and on the N. W. by Lehigh and Northampton. Its greatest length is 37 ms. and mean width 16 ms. Area 600 sq. ms. The surface of the country on the S. is tolerably level, but becomes rolling and even hilly towards the N. and N. W., but it is in general delightfully variegated. Central lat. 40° 20′, lon. 1° 50′ E. of W. C. The soil, like the surface, is much diversified, but it is generally of good quality. That of the limestone basis is the strongest. But there are some excellent alluvial lands on the Delaware,of which Pennsbury manor affords the best sample; and the debris of the red sand stone, when manured with lime, produce admirable crops of wheat and other grain, and exceedingly fine grass.

The county is well but not abundantly watered. Next to the Delaware, which washes the eastern and south-eastern boundary, the Neshaminy is the most considerable stream. This runs nearly centrally through the county, for near half its length, and of its tributaries, some intersect the western boundary in several places, whilst others approach the eastern one. This river, for such it may be justly called, empties into the Delaware, about 3 miles below Bristol. The N. E. branch of the Perkiomen creek rises in this county. Tohickon, a considderable creek, joins the Delaware at the S. E. angle of Tinicum township. There are several other inconsiderable streams, among which, Ingham's spring merits special notice. The principal roads are kept in tolerable repair; but there is only one turnpike, that running from Philadelphia to Morrisville, which passes through the county.

The state canal from Easton to Bristol, passes through the county, and at the latter place communicates with the Delaware by a large and commodious artificial basin.

The chief towns are Bristol, Doylestown, Newton, Hulmeville, Attleboro', Morrisville, Danville, New Hope, Falsington, Springtown, Strawntown, &c. (See these titles respectively.) Near the first is a hamlet called Bath, which once was in considerable repute as a watering place, having some medicinal springs; but although the place has attractions, we believe it is not now much resorted to.

There are several fine bridges in the county, across the Neshaminy river, and particularly over the Delaware, at Morrisville, at New Hope, and at Centreville. The Trenton bridge is 1100 feet long, and 36 wide.

The population according to the census of 1830, is 45,740, of whom 877 were aliens, 14 deaf and dumb, 9 blind, 6 slaves, 22,674 white males, 21,650 white females, 751 free colored males, and 650 free colored females.

The counties of Bucks and Montgomery constitue the 7th judicial district of the state, over which John Fox, Esq. presided in 1831. The county courts are holden at Doylestown on the 4th Monday in April, and 2d Mondays in September, December, and February.

The counties of Bucks, Northampton, Wayne, and Pike form the 8th congressional district, represented in the 22d congress by Peter Ihrie, Jr. and Samuel H. Smith. Bucks alone forms the 5th senatoral district, sending one representave.

The public buildings consist of a court house of stone, in which are also the county offices. It is a neat structure, surmounted with a cupola, and surrounded by an enclosed lot or park, in the most elevated part of the town, from which there is a delightful view of the country particularly on the S. and W. for several miles. A county prison is nearly adjacent to the court house, and a poor house, in Warwick t-ship, about 4 ms. from Doylestown.

The latter is a large and commodious building of stone, capable of accommodating comfortably 200 persons. The site is well chosen for health and beauty, and has annexed to it an extensive farm, highly cultivated. This institution was established by virtue of an act of assembly passed 10th April 1807, at the expense of the county. It is managed by three directors, one of whom is chosen annually and serves for a term of three years. They have also charge of all the paupers of the county, whether resident or not, in the poor house. Their expenditures are paid from a tax levied by the commissioners of the county at the requisition of the directors and disbursed by their order on the county treasurer. The directors may hold in trust &c. lands &c. not exceeding the yearly value of $10,000, and personal estate to any amount—may erect suitable buildings, &c. for the accommodation of the poor—appoint a treasurer annually—may employ and remove at pleasure, stewards, matrons, physicians and surgeons—and may bind out as apprentices, such poor children as come under their notice—and may exercise all other powers vested in the overseers of the poor. The directors are required to account yearly with the county auditors, and to exhibit annually to the court of quarter sessions, a list of the number, ages and sexes of the persons maintained and employed in the house of employment, or supported or assisted by them elsewhere; and of the children by them apprenticed, with the names and occupation of the masters, &c. and submit, when required, to the examination of visitors appointed by the court of quarter sessions, their books and accounts, payments and receipts, and a statement of sales, purchases and bequests, &c. The directors are required to visit the poor-house at least monthly, and are allowed an annual compensation of $40 each. Vacancies in the direction may be supplied by remaining directors.

Besides the general provisions made by law for the education of the inhabitants, the people have in several districts exerted themselves to provide proper means for the education of their children. Thus an "academy and free school of Bucks county," was established at Newtown; "The Falls township free school," in 1807, "The Union academy of Doylestown," in 1808. The Hughosian free school, in Buckingham t-ship, in 1813. To the first of these institutions the Commonwealth granted $4000 on the 16th of March, 1798; to the second the rents of certain lands, together with corporate powers, on the 24th March, 1807; to the third a power to raise $3000 by lottery, in 1805, and the sum of $800 in 1807, upon the condition that poor children, not exceeding three at one time, should be taught gratis, but none to continue longer than one year, and in 1827 this academy was incorporated.

This co. is chiefly agricultural, and its farmers in the southern and central parts, do not yield in skill and wealth to any in the state. An agricultural society is established in the county, and the utility of the institution may be inferred from the steady advance in the improvement of the quality and quantity of cattle and sheep, and the increase of the soil. There are, however, manufactures of various kinds, carried on extensively. Paper and buttons are made at Morrisville; there are extensive cotton and woollen factories at Milford, or Hulmeville, and at New Hope.

The farmer's bank of Bucks county, the only one within the county, was established under the general act of assembly of 21st March, 1814, and was originally located at Hulmeville, but has since been removed to Bristol, where it continues. In 1830 its capital was $60,000, notes in circulation, $76,228; deposits and unclaimed dividends $30,454 44; bills discounted $101,686 99. The New-Hope bridge company carried on banking operations for a few years, but several years since became embarrassed, and have not again, we believe, resumed their operations.

This county paid into the state treasury in 1831

For tax on banks,	$103 06
Tax on writs,	665 67
Tavern licences,	1,062 23

Duties on dealers in foreign mdze. 857 50
Tax on collateral inheritances, 778 93

$3,467 39

The taxable real estate of the county was assessed in 1826 at $12,941,919, in 1829, $14,422,564.

STATISTICAL TABLE OF BUCKS COUNTY.

Townships, &c.	Greatest Lgth.	Greatest Bth.	Area in acres.	Face of country.	Population in 1810.	Population in 1820.	Population in 1830.	Taxables.	Valuation in 1826	Valuation in 1829
Bristol bor.			336	Level.	628	908	1262	202	262,080	291,222
Bristol t-ship,	7	3	10,374	do.	1008	1667	1532	252	479,797	537,578
Bensalem,	8	3 1-2	11,502	do.	1434	1667	1811	345	523,341	561,592
Bedminster,	6	6	18,451	Rolling.	1199	1248	1594	338	553,530	583,438
Buckingham,	6 1-2	5	19,490	do.	1715	1862	2193	467	682,150	733,892
Doylestown,	4 1-2	4	9,603	do.		1430	1781	362	403,326	507,690
Durham,	3 1-2	3	6,337	Hilly.	404	485	750	127	253,480	275,559
Falls,	5 1-2	5 1-2	16,784	Level.	1649	1880	2266	397	889,552	969,604
Haycock,	6 3-4	4	12,139	Hilly.	836	926	1047	221	206,363	236,502
Hilltown,	6 1-4	4	17,187	Rolling.	1335	1501	1669	378	489,829	528,632
Lower Makefield,	5 1-2	5 1-4	11,452	do.	1089	1204	1340	264	498,162	538,339
Upper Makefield,	6 1-4	4 1-2	13,008	do.	1271	1367	1517	314	520,320	577,702
Middletown,	6 1-2	6	12,569	do.	1663	1891	2178	424	628,450	700,000
Milford,	5 3-4	5	15,953	do.	1334	1195	1970	402	413,998	436,474
Morrisville bor.			432	do.	266	391	531	91	80,693	85,693
Newtown,	5	3 1-2	7,268	Level.	982	1060	1344	233	297,988	368,830
New Britain,	6 1-4	4 1-2	12,261	Rolling.	1474	1082	1201	270	367,845	395,752
Northampton,	7 1-2	4 1-2	13,975	do.	1176	1411	1521	311	656,825	708,036
Nockamixon,	7 1-2	4 1-2	16,848	Hilly.	1207	1650	2049	407	286,416	327,875
Plumstead,	6 1-2	4	16,738	do.	1407	1790	1849	402	418,450	463,332
Richland,	5 1-2	4	14,476	Level.	1317	1385	1719	344	398,090	440,270
Rockhill,	7 1-2	5	19,618	Hilly.	1508	1567	2012	424	490,450	538,136
Solebury,	7 3-4	4 1-4	17,312	Rolling.	1659	2092	2961	503	796,352	945,432
Southampton,	4 3-4	2 1-4	8,254	do.	739	907	1228	234	367,303	403,643
Springfield,	10 1-2	4	18,312	do.	1287	1580	2078	429	531,048	635,716
Tinicum,	8 3-4	7	18,497	do.	1017	1249	1643	331	453,176	503,099
Warminster,	4 1-2	2 1-2	6,443	Hilly.	564	695	709	155	309,264	338,462
Warrington,	4	2 1-2	5,397	do.	429	515	512	113	161,910	187,893
Warwick,	5 1-4	3 1-4	10,678	do.	1287	1215	1132	216	333,687	372,829
Wrightstown,	3 1-2	3	5,082	Level.	562	618	660	148	188,034	229,292
			366,746		32,371	37,842	46,059	9,104	12,941,919	14,422,564

Buffalo, t-ship, Butler co. bounded N. by Clearfield t-ship, E. by Armstrong co. S. by Allegheny co. and W. by Middlesex t-ship. Centrally distant from the town of Butler S. E. 11 miles. It forms a square of 8 ms. Area, 40,960 acres; surface, hilly; soil, loam. Pop. 1830, 1012; taxables, 159. It is drained on the N. W. by Thorn creek, a tributary of the Conequenessing, S. E. by Great and Little Buffalo creeks, S. W. by Ball creek, tributaries of the Allegheny r. The timber of this t-ship has been much injured by fire. It contains some glade lands, which are deemed of good quality.

Buffalo, t-ship, Armstrong county, bounded N. by Sugar creek t-ship, E. and S. by the Allegheny river, which separates it from Kittanning and Allegheny t-ships and from Westmoreland county, and W. by Butler co. Centrally distant S. W. from Kittanning borough 6 ms. Greatest length 13 miles, breadth 10; area, 41,000 acres; surface, gentle hills; soil, loam. Pop. in 1830, 2458; taxables 429. It is drained by Glade run on the E. and Buffalo creek on the W. both running S. into the Allegheny r. The p-t. of Freeport is on the river, below the mouth of the Kiskiminitas, and at the mouth of Buffalo creek, in the extreme S. W. corner of the township. The state canal to Pittsburg runs through the town.

Buffalo creek, Armstrong co. rises in Sugar Creek t-ship and flows south through Buffalo t-ship, near the west line of the co. into the Allegheny r. at the town of Freeport. It has a course of about 20 ms.

Buffalo creek, Great and Little, Union co. The former rises on the confines of Centre co. and flows east through Union, into the W. branch of the Susquehannah r. at the town of Lewisburg, receiving in its course Rapid run, Spruce run, and the Little Buffalo crs. the last rising in White Deer t-ship, and running S. to its recipient.

Buffalo mountain, a ridge of the Allegheny, running N. W. across Union co. forming the northern boundary of Buffalo valley.

Buffalo valley, Union co. a fertile and beautiful vale of limestone soil, extending from W. to E. nearly thro' the county. Bounded N. by the Buffalo ridge, and S. by Jack's mountain and the Shamoken ridge, and drained by Buffalo creek.

Buffalo, East, township, Union co. bounded N. by White Deer and Kelly t-ships, E. by the West Branch of the Susquehannah river, S. by Union t-ship, and W. by West Buffalo t-ship. Centrally distant N. of New Berlin 6 miles; greatest length 8, breadth 7 miles; area, 19,200 acres; surface diversified; soil, limestone. Pop. in 1830, 2130; taxables, 548. Buffalo creek runs on the N. and Turtle run on the S. boundary, E. into the river. The p-t. of Lewisburg lies at the confluence of the former with the Susquehannah r. about 8 ms. N. E. of New Berlin, and upon the turnpike road to Bellefonte. Valuation of real estate by the assessment of 1829, $535,642.

Buffalo, p-t. Buffalo t-ship, Washington co. in a fork of Buffalo creek, on the national road 7 ms. S. W. of Washington borough, 244 from W. C. and 225 from Harrisburgh, contains 10 dwellings, 2 taverns and 1 store.

Buffalo creek, Centre and Union cos. falls into the west branch of the Susquehannah, after watering a fertile strip of land called Buffalo valley and flowing 22 ms.

Buffalo creeks, Great and Little, Perry co. The first rises in Liberty valley, Toboyne t-ship, and flows E. through Saville and Juniata townships into the Juniata r. N. of Middle Ridge, having a comparative course of about 24 ms. The second rises in Saville t-ship, and flows parallel with the first south of Middle Ridge, into the river below Newport. Its length is about 10 ms.

Buffalo Ridge, a range of hills extending through the N. part of Londonderry t-ship, and the S. part of Napier t-ship, Bedford co. and forming the W. boundary of Millikin's cove.

Buffalo creek, Washington county, a tributary of the Ohio r. rises by several branches, but principally by two in Buffalo t-ship.

Buffalo, West, t-ship, Union co. Pop. 1810, 1416; 1820, 1430; in 1830, 1404. Taxables 415; bounded N. by White Deer mountain, E. by White Deer, Buffalo, and Union t-ships, S. by Centre and Beaver t-ships, and W. by Hartley t-ships. Centrally distant N. W. from New Berlin, 8 ms. greatest length 15, breadth 6 ms. Area, 50,660 acres; surface much diversified; soil limestone in Buffalo and Dry valleys. Between White Deer mountain, and Nittany mountain lies the narrow valley of White Deer cr. S. of Nittany is also a narrow valley between it and Buffalo mountain. S. of Buffalo is the fertile and beautiful valley of Buffalo. Jack's mountain lies on the S. boundary, and is deemed the highest land in the county. The streams of the t-ship, are White Deer creek, Rapid run, Buffalo creek, and Penn's creek. Mifflinsburg, p-t. lies in Buffalo valley at the foot of a high ridge about 5 ms. N. W. of New Berlin, and on the turnpike road leading to Bellefonte.

Buffalo, New, village of Buffalo t-ship, Perry co. on the west bank of the Susquehannah r. 12 ms. N. E. of Bloomfield, contains about 25 dwellings, 2 stores, 2 taverns, and 1 Presbyterian church. There is a ferry here across the river.

Buffalo, post t-ship, Perry co. bounded N. by Greenwood and Liverpool t-ships, E. and S. by the Susquehannah river which separates it from Dauphin co. and W. by the Juniata river. Centrally distant E. from Bloomfield 11 miles greatest length and breadth 9 ms. Area 23,680 acres; surface hilly; soil slate. Pop. in 1830, 1270; taxables 281. The turnpike road to Lewistown runs along the Juniata. At Montgomery's ferry across the Susquehannah, there is a post office. New Buffalo village is on the Susquehannah about 5 ms. above the entrance of the Juniata, at which there is also a ferry. There are two ferries, one in the north, and the other in the south part of the t-ship, over the Juniata. Buffalo mountain separates it on the N. from Greenwood and Liverpool t-ships, extending about 9 miles between the rivers.

Buffalo mountain, see preceeding article.

Buffalo Lick creek, Brothers Valley t-ship, Somerset co. a tributary of Castleman's river, rises and has its course S. W. within the t-ship.

Buffalo, t-ship, Washington co. Bounded N. by Hopewell, E. by Canton, S. by Morris and Finslay, and W. by Donnegal t-ships. Centrally distant W. from Washington borough 7 ms. greatest length 7, breadt 6½ miles. Area 20,480, acres; surface hilly; soil loam. Coal abundant. It is drained by Buffalo creek and its branches which flow N. W. into the Ohio river. The national road runs S. W. through the t-ship; on it are the post towns of Martinsburg and Claysville, the first, 6 ms. S. W. of Washington borough, and the second about 10 ms. and on the W. line of the t-ship, and the p-t. of Buffalo, between the preceding.

Bull creek, rises in Buffalo and Middlesex t-ships, Butler co. and flows S. E. into Deer t-ship, Allegheny co. and into the Allegheny river.

Bull skin, t-ship, Fayette co. bounded N. and N. W. by Westmoreland co. E. by Salt lick, S. by Connellsville and W. by Tyrone t-ships. Centrally distant from Uniontown 16 ms. greatest length 9, breadth 4½ miles. Area, 24,320 acres; surface hilly; soil limestone and loam. Pop. in 1830, 1231; taxables 251. The Chestnut ridge is on the E. boundary, Jacob's creek on the north; Mount's creek flows S. W. through the t-ship, giving motion to several mills, and having some iron works upon its head waters. Jacob's creek is crossed by a chain bridge, at the N. W. angle.

Bunker Hill, a noted eminence of Swatara t-ship, Lebanon co. south of Jonestown.

Burgettstown, p-t. of Smith t-ship, Washington co. situated centrally in the t-ship 17 ms N. W. from Washington borough, contains about 40 dwellings, several stores and a tavern. It is 246 miles from W. C. and 223 from Harrisburg.

Burlington, small village of East Penn t-ship, Northampton co. on the road from Lehighton to Mauch Chunk, about 2 ms. from each, contains four or five dwellings and a store.

Burlington, t-ship, Bradford co. bounded N. by Springfield and Smithfield t-ships, E. by Towanda, S. by Franklin and W. by Troy t-ships; centrally distant from Towanda borough about 9 miles; greatest length 9, breadth 4 ms. Area 23,040 acres; surface hilly; soil, gravelly loam; pop. in 1830, 527; taxables 98. The Susquehannah and Tioga turnpike road crosses the S. W. angle. The t-ship is drained by Sugar creek, which runs centrally and eastwardly through, receiving from Smithfield t-ship, Brown's and Tom Jack's creeks. Burlington post office is 249 ms. from W. C. and, 138 from Harrisburg.

Burlington, t-ship McKean co. bounded N. by Cooper t-ship, E by Shippen, S. by Clearfield co. and W. by Jefferson co. Centrally distant S. from Smithport, 25 miles; length 13, breadth 8 miles. Area 66,560 acres; surface hilly; soil gravelly; pop. in 1830, 160. It is drained W. by a tributary of Clarion r. and E. by a branch of Rich Valley creek, coal and iron are said to be abundant. The country is almost an uninhabited desert, but is finely timbered and well adapted to grazing.

Bustleton, p-t. of Lower Dublin t-ship, Phila. co. 11 ms. from Phila. on the Bustleton and Smithfield turnpike road, 148 from W. C. and 110 E.

from Harrisburg, contains about 35 dwellings, 2 stores, 2 taverns, an academy, a Baptist church, and a valuable public library. The general election for the inhabitants of the N. E. section of the county is holden here. A stage leaves it daily via Holmesburg for Phila. At the Pennepack creek, about half a mile S. of the town, is a grist mill and manufactory, at which there are some 10 or 12 dwellings. There is a fine bridge over the creek, and the scenery around it is picturesque and beautiful. The academy has received aid from the legislature in various forms; by letters, privileges and by donation of money. The last we believe was a sum of 500 dollars, given in 1813 to repair the injury done to the building by a remarkable storm, by which its roof and belfry were blown away.

Burn's creek, Belfast t-ship, Bedford co. a tributary of the N. branch of the Conoloway creek.

Burnt Cabins, p-t. on the N. E. boundary of Dublin t-ship and of the county, about 30 ms. E. of Bedford borough, 109 from W. C. and 59 from Harrisburg.

Bursenville, or *Bursenton*, p-t. of Springfield t-ship, Bucks co. 20 miles N. E. from Doylestown, 183 N. from W. C. and 100 E. from Harrisburg, contains some half dozen houses, a store and tavern.

Burtztown, Bethlehem t-ship, Northampton co. 8 ms. W. from Easton and 4 from Bethlehem, contains five dwellings, one tavern and one store.

Bushkill, t-ship, Northampton co. bounded N. by Ross t-ship, S. by Upper Nazareth, E. by Plainfield, and W. by Moore t-ship. It contains two small villages, one called Edmonds and the other Jacobsburg ; at the latter there is a furnace. The Bushkill creek traverses the t-ship in a S. W. direction and receives from it several feeders. Pop. in 1830, 1402 ; taxables in 1828, 277. The surface of the country is hilly ; the soil, white gravel, red shale and slate, and parts of it tolerably productive.

Bushkill creek, Northampton co. rises near the Wind Gap, at the foot of the Blue mtn. and running a S. E. by S. course falls into the Delaware at Easton, about 100 perches above the mouth of the Lehigh. It is between 20 and 30 ms. long, is one of the finest mill streams in the state ; is not navigable, but drives one forge, and a number of excellent mills for grinding grain and sawing timber.

Bushkill, p-o. Pike co. 232 ms. N. E. of W. C. 137 from Harrisburg.

Bushkill creek, Pike county, rises in Palmyra t-ship, and by a S. W. course of more than 20 miles flows through Delaware and Middle Smithfield t-ships, to the Delaware r. forming in part the southern boundary of Delaware t-ship. It receives in its course several considerable streams, and gives motion to several mills.

Bushville, p-t. in Delaware t-ship, Pike co. 25 ms. S. E. from Milford, and about 40 ms. from Easton, 239 from W. C. and 144 from Harrisburg. The p-o. is called "Delaware."

Butler county, was taken from Allegheny, by the act of 12th March, 1800, and limited as follows: Beginning at the mouth of Buffalo creek, on the Allegheny r. thence by a line running due W. until it strikes a line of Beaver co. thence N. by the line of said co. to the N. E. corner thereof, thence by a line N. 35°, E. 14 ms. thence by a line running due E. continuing said course to where a line, running due N. from the mouth of Buffalo creek, the place of beginning, will intersect said line ; unless the last mentioned line should first strike the Allegheny r. then and in that case to run down said river along the several courses thereof, until it will intersect said line, thence by said line to the place of beginning. The act also provided that the place for holding the courts of justice for the county should be fixed by the legislature at any place at a disance not greater than four miles from the centre of the county.

By the act of 8th March, 1803, it is further provided, that certain trustees for the county should cause to be surveyed 300 acres of land situate on the N. side of Conequenessing crk. which Samuel and John Cunningham, and Robert Graham granted to the governor for the use of the county, and to lay out a convenient lot of land thereon, not exceeding five acres, whereon the county buildings might be erected, and the remainder into town lots, none of which to contain more than five acres. And the name of Butler was given to the town so to be laid, and the lots were directed to be sold for the use of the county.

The county was organized for judicial and other purposes by the act 2d of April, 1803. It is bounded N. by Venango co. E. by Armstrong co. S. by Allegheny, W. by Beaver and N. W. by Mercer counties. Length 33, breadth 33 ms. area 785 sq-ms.; central lat. N. 40 , 50′, lon. from W. C. 2° 50′ W.

Butler county with the whole country west of the mountains belongs to the secondary formation, and abounds with various minerals. Iron is found in many places in the county, particularly in Bear creek, in the N. E. part of the county, and in Parker, Venango, Slippery Rock, and Conequenessing t-ships; salt also in many places, at the depth of from 300 to 500 ft. and salt works are erected, at or near Harmony and near Butler borough. Bituminous coal abounds in every part, in strata from 2 to 5 feet, which are generally approached with convenience by the margin of the streams. The strata lie universally horizontally and are covered with slate. Lead ore is believed to exist in Connequenessing t-ship, upon the creek about 3 ms. above Harmony. This opinion is derived from Indian tradition, and from the remains of a small furnace near the creek by which it is supposed the natives extracted the ore. Members of Cornplanter's tribe, in crossing the the country, still, it is said, assert their knowledge of the mine, and propose for a liberal compensation to show the place; but as the lands belong to a Philadelphia owner and the inhabitants have little confidence in the promises of the Indians, these offers have not been accepted. A bed or beds of plumbago or black lead have been found in the county, but have not been wrought.

The county was settled principally by emigrants from Western Pennsylvania, from Washington, Fayette, Westmoreland and Allegheny counties, generally of Irish and German descent, and by a few native Irish, Scotch and Germans. The settlements commenced in 1792, under the act of 3d April of that year, providing for the settlement of that portion of the state lying north and west of the Ohio and Allegheny rivers, and Conewango creek. Little progress was, however, made until 1800, when the county was erected and the county town laid out.

The first settlers had many difficulties and privations to encounter, before they could render the riches of their lands available, among which the scarcity of food and the means to procure it, were not the least. The provisions of the act of 1792, gave occasion for much misunderstanding between the land speculators and the actual settlers, and induced a course of litigation which was ruinous to the latter, compelling many to abandon the cherished labors of their lives, and the homes of their hearts, and to seek new and safer asylums, in which a comfortable subsistence could be obtained only by a repetition of their early labors. Those who remained, compounded with the land owner, or abided by the decision of the courts of law.

The most prominent speculators were of two descriptions, one by survey and warrant, the other by mere survey and agreement with the actual settlers, conditioned that the settler should receive for settlement to be made pursuant to the provisions of the above recited act, from one to two hundred acres according to contract. In the construction of these agreements many difficulties arose, productive of protracted law suits, which greatly retarded the settlement of the county. But most of these vexed questions are now at rest, and a quiet title to lands here may be had. We may mention however another source of title to lands in this district of country, upon which not a shadow of doubt has rested. Extensive tracts were laid out in 1785 in lots of 200, 250, 300, and 500 acres, which were given as gratuities to soldiers of the revolution, &c. in the Pennsylvania line. Part of district No. 1, in Muddy creek t-ship, and district No. 2 is wholly in the county. The original grantees, unwilling to assume the labors, and without taste for the pleasures of a peaceful agricultural life, generally sold their rights, and these *donation* tracts, generally of excellent quality, are mostly occupied and improved.

About the year 1800, Delman Basse Muller, a native of Germany, purchased an extensive tract in Nicholson's dist. of depreciation lands, in Butler co. and in Alexandria district, lying partly in Beaver, but his improvements were chiefly in Butler co. In 1803 he sold a considerable portion of this tract in Butler, to George Rapp and his associates, forming the society of the Harmonites. The enterprize, industry and economy of this people soon made the "desert blossom as the rose." They founded the village of Harmony, and other extensive improvements, and their rapid increase in wealth and the comforts of life, together with their singular practices and discipline, rendered them an object of curious speculation, not only for their neighbors, but for inquiring minds in every part of the union. The first houses of their town were built with round logs and covered with straw, but in a season or two these gave place to substantial and convenient brick and framed buildings. (*See Economy.*) The example of this society was a most beneficial stimulant to the industry of the other inhabitants of the county.

In 1814 the society sold their possessions, comprising between 6 and 8 thousand acres of land, nearly one half of which they had cleared, to A. Zuyler, from the eastern part of Pennsylvania, for the sum of $100,000. The purchaser, himself a man of great enterprize, indefatigable industry and a practical farmer, soon sold many lots in the town of Harmony, and a number of the farms to Pennsylvania Germans, who with equal industry and skill in agricultural and mechanical arts, have the advantage of being untrammelled by the wills of others in their domestic, moral, religious or political economy; and though their labors may not be so systematically and so profitably directed, their own and the public happiness is not the less promoted.

In 1796–7, a number of Scotch families from the isle of Lewis, in the northern part of Scotland, settled in Conequenessing t-ship, midway between the towns of Butler and Harmony. Their descendants are numerous and now enjoy peace and plenty, the fruits of the labors of their fathers. They have erected a house of public worship, of brick, called the White Oak Spring meeting, on the Butler and Harmony road, where a large congregation attend public worship. They are of the associate Presbyterian reformed or Unionists.

The people of the county are religiously disposed, but these settlements being sparse, most ministers of the gospel have charge of several congregations, from whom they receive a remuneration, commonly above $300, and never above $500. The Presbyterian, including Unionists, Seceders, and Covenanters, is the most numerous religious sect,—but the Methodists increase rapidly. There are some Baptists in the county, and many Roman Catholics, who are settled chiefly in Buffalo, Clearfield and Donegal town ships. There are in the county, including those of the town of Butler, about 30 churches pertaining to the various denominations of christians.

The inhabitants of this county are obnoxious to the charge commonly made against other portions of Pennsylvania, of being indifferent to education. The price of tuition usually paid for each pupil is from 5 to 6 dollars per annum. For this sum teachers are not scarce, but they are commonly unqualified. Generally the farmers have erected a school in every vicinage, which is open during the winter. In summer few schools are taught, except in the larger towns. There are two newspapers published weekly in the town of Butler, viz. the Western Centinel and Democratic Press, and the Butler Repository.

There are in the county 40 grist mills 48 saw mills, 7 fulling mills, 3 powder mills, and 3 oil mills. Improved lands sell at from 3 to 10 dollars per acre; unimproved from 2 to 4 dollars. There are in the county about 35 stores and 26 taverns. There are several furnaces, and forges; one of each on Slipery Rock creek, 14 ms. N. E. of Butler borough; two furnaces, one on each side of the Western county line, but both deriving their supplies from the county; the one called Bassenheim, propelled by water power, the other, Bear creek, driven by steam. The furnaces are competent to produce three tons of pigs daily. The market for iron as for all other surplus produce of the county, is Pittsburg. Considerable quantities of grain, flour, salt, whiskey, salted provisions, and live stock, are annually sent thither, partly by the Allegheny r. and partly by carriages, &c.

Butler counnty, though long obscured by adverse circumstances, is now in a very thriving condition. The tide of emigration has commenced to flow upon it, and will in a few years most probably cover all the vacant lands for settlement. Many sales were made in the past year, (1831,) to Germans lately from Germany, particularly in Buffalo and Conequenessing t-ships. These emigrants select land which is not heavily timbered, and which here is denominated "*glade*," and has been overrun by fire before or since the settlement of the county. In this choice they display much judgment for such land, though comparatively sterile in appearance, by the want of timber, is when cultivated most productive. In 1831 there were raised on this species of land in Buffalo t-ship, by the Messrs. Walkers, 3200 bushels of patatoes from 5 acres of ground. The best timbered lands of the county, when cleared, will scarce do more. The glades are covered with thick underwood, of pine, oak and white oak, hickory and willow, growing from large stools or stumps, in many cases from three to four feet in diameter; which proves that not many years since very large trees overshadowed the soil.

The face of the country is generally favorably disposed for agriculture, affording due proportions of meadow and arable land, to every farm of moderate size. The former is admirably adapted to timothy; the latter is sufficiently high and rolling for every species of grain, and when properly and seasonably cultivated, remunerates well the labor bestowed upon it. The county has advantages which cannot be too highly appreciated, an abundance of pure water, and a salubrious atmosphere. No instance of fever and ague has been known within it.

A turnpike road passes from Kittanning and another from Pittsburg through the county town. The latter is the great road from Pittsburg to the lakes; another turnpike road is about to be made from Roxburg, Armstrong county, to Mercer through Mariusville and Harrisville.

The timber, varying according to situation, consists of white, black, and other oaks, beech, maple, black ash, sugar maple, cherry, elm, black walnut and sycamore. The forest trees generally are large, healthy and luxuriant, and frequently as thick as they can stand. Fruit trees are abundant in the cultivated tracts; grapes grow profusely and spontaneously, and some attention has lately been paid to their cultivation and amelioration.

The county is well watered; the

Allegheny river touches its N. E. and S. E. boundaries, and receives from it Lowry's, Crawford's, Redick's, and Jones' runs, Bear creek, several branches of Big Buffalo creek, and the Little Buffalo creek. Westward, it is drained by Slippery Rock creek and its several branches, Muddy creek, Conequenessing and Brush creeks, tributaries of the Big Beaver; and by a branch of the Big Sewickly creek, which flows into the Ohio.

This county, like many others in Pennsylvania, has been the residence of the mammoth. In 1819, whilst digging the well at the salt-works, about 1½ mile N. E. of the town of Butler, the grinder of one of these huge animals was found, four feet below the *surface of the rock*, among several fragments of much decayed bones. Its weight was five pounds, length, seven inches. A turnpike road extends from Pittsburg to the town of Butler, a distance of 33 ms. and from Butler to Mercer, in the co. of Mercer, about the same distance.

The principal towns of the county are Butler, Freeport, Woodville, Harmony, Lawrenceburg, Zelionople, Portersville, Centreville, Harrisville, Mariusville, Unionville, &c.

In 1800 the pop. amounted to 3,916, in 1810, to 7,346, in 1820 to 10,193, in 1830 to 14,681; of whom 8,423 were white males; 6,183 white females; 39 free col'd. males, and 46 free col'd. females.

The public buildings of the county are the court house, public offices and prison, and an academy at the town of Butler. The latter was incorporated by the act of 6th Feb. 1811, with six trustees, and empowered to acquire a yearly income not exceeding four thousand dollars. Two thousand dollars were then granted to the institution, upon condition that five poor children should receive annually the benefits of the institution *gratis*; and by the act of 12th March, 1813, a tract of donation land in the county was given to the corporation.

Butler, with Beaver, belongs to the 25th senatorial district, which sends one member to the senate, and the county sends one member to the house of representatives. United with Allegheny, Beaver and Armstrong, it forms the 16th congressional district, sending two members to Congress. Connected with Beaver and Allegheny counties, Beaver makes the 5th judicial district of the state, over which Charles Shaler, Esq. presides. The courts are held in Butler on the second Monday of Nov. and third Mondays of Jan., April and August, annually.

The staples of the county are the ordinary agricultural products, wheat, rye, corn, whiskey, &c. Its manufactures consist of salt and iron; considerable quantities of the former are made, and the production of the latter is increasing. It is generally sent in pigs to Pittsburg, where it finds a profitable and ready market.

This county paid into the public treasury in 1831:

For tax on writs, - - - -	22 67
Tavern licenses, - - - -	256 59
Duties on dealers in for. mdze.	322 83
	$602 09

Valuation of taxable property by assessment of 1829:

Real estate, - - - -	1,060,761
Personal do. - - - -	239,308

Rate of levy 23 cts. on the hundred dolls.

STATISTICAL TABLE OF BUTLER COUNTY.

Townships, &c.	Greatest Lth.	Greatest Bth.	Area in Acres.	Face of Country.	Soil.	Population. 1810	1820	1830	Taxables.
Butler Bor.								580	116
Butler t-ship,	8	8	40,960	Rolling,	Clay, loam,	453	472	768	145
Buffalo,	8	8	40,960	do.	do. lime,	375	582	1012	159
Centre,	8	8	40,960	do.	Clay, loam,	742	972	1322	241
Clearfield,	8	8	40,960	do.	do.	288	515	617	129
Conequenessing,	8	8	40,960	do.	Lime, clay,	1284	977	1944	358
Cranberry,	8	8	40,960	do.	do. gravel,	543	765	1046	200
Donegal,	8	8	40,960	do.	do.	671	960	1085	228
Mercer,	9	5	18,380	do.	do.	588	641	771	172
Middlesex,	8	8	40,960	do.	do.	538	1010	1231	244
Muddy creek,	8	8	40,960	Hilly,	do.	395	868	1317	239
Parker,	10	6	38,400	Rolling,	Gravel,	399	659	945	165
Slippery rock,	13½	6	43,200	do.	Loam, gravel,	658	865	1541	313
Venango,	10	5	32,000	do.	do.	377	353	499	102
						7346	10,193	14,683	2,801

Butler, p-t. borough and seat of justice of Butler co., situated in the N. E. angle of Butler t-ship, in a fork of Conequenessing creek, 270 miles a little north of W. from Phil., 164 from Harrisburg, and about 32 ms. N. E. from Pittsburg; from the latter place there is a turnpike road to Butler, and from Butler another to Mercer, a turnpike road also runs from the town to Kittanning. Pop. of the town in 1830, 580, taxables 116. The town lies in a bend of the Conequenessing creek, and there are mills on each side. On Kearn's branch within a mile of the town, there is a salt spring and salt works. There is an academy, established in 1811, incorporated, and endowed by the Legislature, with $2000 and a tract of land. The building is of stone. The town was incorporated by act of assembly 26 Feb. 1817. The town contains 70 dwellings, a court house, handsome and capacious, with offices attached, built of brick, centrally situated on elevated ground in the public square, commanding a fine view of the surrounding country, a prison of stone, having a yard in the rear with a high stone wall, 2 Presbyterian, a Unionist, Methodist, Roman Catholic, and Episcopalian churches, all of brick, except one, which is of stone. The situation of the town is very agreeable, and much admired by travellers.

Butler, t-ship, Butler co. bounded N. by Centre, E. by Clearfield, S. by Middlesex and W. by Conequenessing t-ships. It is a square of 8 miles; area 40,960 acres; surface rolling; soil, loam; pop. in 1830, 768. Taxables, 145. Butler, the co. town, is in the N. E. angle of the t-ship, from which a turnpike road leads S. W. to Pittsburg, and another N. W. to Mercer. (See Butler bor.) It is drained by the Conequenessing creek and its branches which flow S. W. through the t-ship. Salt springs are found near and N. E. of Butler borough, upon Kearn's branch of the creek.

Buttermilk falls, on the W. branch of the Susquehannah river, between Centre and Clearfield counties, about 5 miles below the town of Karthaus.

Buttermilk falls, Falls t-ship, Luzerne co. near the confluence of the Buttermilk falls creek. The fall is 30 feet, and the frothy appearance assumed by the water has induced the name.

Butztown, p-t. of Upper Bethel t-ship, Northampton co. 16 ms. W. from Easton, 187 N. E. from W. C. and 97 from Harrisburg, contains 5 dwellings, 1 store, 1 tavern, 1 grist mill, 1 saw mill, and 1 distillery.

Byberry, t-ship, Phil. co., lies in the N. E. end of the co. centrally distant from Phil. 14 ms. bounded N. by Southampton, N. E. and E. by Bensalem t-ships, Bucks co. S. by Lower Dublin, S. W. and W. by the Manor of Moreland. Its length is about 5 ms. breadth variable, but at most 3 ms. Area 5,966 acres.

The family of the Waltons, who were among the first settlers, gave it the name of Byberry, in reference to a place of that name where they had dwelt in England.

The face of the country is agreeably diversified, and there are some fine rising grounds, particularly in the upper section of the t-ship. Edge Hill crosses the northern corner, near to which is the source of Poquessing creek. This stream forms the line between the counties of Phil. and Bucks and empties into the Delaware, half a mile below White Sheet bay. The main stream and its western branches water most of the farms in Byberry.

The soil for cultivation is a sandy loam, from 6 to 8 inches deep, lying on a stiff loamy subsoil, from 4 to 6 feet in depth. In the neighborhood of Townsend's mill, where the Poquessing winds between two stony ridges, there is the singular appearance of two natural abutments of rock opposite to each other, as if nature intended to lend her aid in the construction of a bridge over the stream. From the singular correspondence between the opposing faces of these rocks, it is debatable, whether they have been forcibly separated, or the effect have been produced by the attrition of the water.

About three fourths of a mile down the creek near the road to Dunk's ferry, a point 6 or 8 perches in breadth, appears to have once projected from the western bank 12 or 15 perches, into the valley. It is supposed that the creek formerly passed round it; but the current striking directly against the base, undermined it and formed a passage through the hill. The aperture is now 3 or 4 perches in width, and the point of the hill near 20 feet in heighth, and containing about one half acre, stands alone in the valley.

In a rock on Aaron Walton's land is a representation of the print of a man's foot; and a similar impression is visible on a rock near the mouth of Poquessing creek.

The indigenous timber is hickory, black, white, red and Spanish oak, poplar, chestnut, maple, sassafras, beech, dogwood, red cedar, gum, persimmon, wild cherry, and in one place, pine.

There are three grist mills in the t-ship, two saw mills, several retail stores and shops for mechanics, but no factory nor *tavern*. The fabric of corn brooms is sufficiently great to merit notice, and not less than 60,000 are annually sent from this township to market. The inhabitants generally are farmers, and a majority Quakers. There are a few Episcopalians, Baptists and Presbyterians The Friends meeting is near the centre of the t-ship. By its side a log school house was early erected, which was torn down in 1772. The school house was continued in one end of the meeting house until 1789, when a stone building was erected for its accommodation. Since the year 1750 this school has been regularly continued, except one summer, during which the school house was rebuilt. In 1794 John Comly, distinguished as the compiler of an English Grammar, which has reached the 15th edition, commenced giving instruction in this school in the Greek and Latin languages and the higher branches of the mathematics. There is here also a public library, founded in 1794 by some young men of the t-ship. An article of this association prohibits the introduction of all atheistical and deistical books, all novels, plays and romances, and other books supposed to have a tendency to corrupt the morals of mankind. It contains about 800 volumes. There are now in the t-ship four other schools, regularly kept up and reputably conducted.

Byberry was settled soon after the arrival of Wm. Penn, in 1682. The first white inhabitants were Giles Knight and William Ellis. The first inhabitants were Friends. The population of the t-ship, by the census of 1830, amounted to 1018; taxables in 1828, 226.

At the time of the arrival of the Europeans here the country was covered, not with heavy timber, but with saplings and underbrush; and in many places with coarse grass, which grew more than five feet high. Hence it would seem that it was cultivated by the aborigines, who most probably dwelt here in great numbers. Indian darts made of flint, and stone axes and other curious implements of Indian manufacture, have been frequently found. Since the settlement the timber, notwithstanding the industry and increase of the whites, grew in size and in quantity.

Agriculture is in an improved, improving, and thrifty state; the wealth of the inhabitants accumulates, and is apparent in the substantial and comfortable character of their dwellings, out buildings, &c.

There is a p-o. called after the t-ship, distant 115 ms. from Harrisburg, 153 from W. C. and 15 from Phila.

Cacoosing creek, Berks co. a tributary of the Tulpehocken creek, rising in Heidelberg and Cumru t-ships, between which it is the division line for the whole of its course of about 8 ms.

Caernarvon, the extreme southern t-ship and point of Berks co. bounded N. by Robeson t-ship, S. and E. by Chester co., and S. and W. by Lancaster co. Greatest length 5 ms. breadth 2; area, 10,520 acres; surface, level; soil, limestone. Pop. in 1830, 1,440; taxables, 301. The east branch of the Brandywine r. crosses the t-ship near the E. and the W. branch at the west end. On the former the post town of Downingstown is located, and on the latter the post town of Coatsville. The Philadelphia and Lancaster turnpike road passes through both villages. This t-ship lies chiefly in the great valley, is admirably cultivated, and contains some of the finest and most productive farms in the world, and few travellers who pass through it can well avoid the breach of the tenth commandment, or refrain from envying the inhabitants their tranquil life and abundant comforts. Their spacious and neat dwellings of stone, and their capacious and overflowing garners, their fields studded with cattle and whitened with sheep, are substantial witnesses of their happiness.

Caernarvon, t-ship, Lancaster co. bounded N. E. by Berks co., S. by Chester co. and Salisbury t-ship, Lancaster co., W. by Earl t-ship, and N. W. by Brecknock t-ship. Centrally distant from Lancaster city, about 20 ms. Greatest length, 6½ ms., greatest breadth 5, area 14,000 acres. The Conestogo cr. flows through it from E. to W. The Downingstown and Harrisburg turnpike crosses the southern angle, and the Morgantown turnpike, centrally, from E. to W. on which, near the middle of the t-ship, is the post village of Churchtown, 55 ms. from Harrisburg, 20 from Lancaster, and 5 from Morgantown; surface hilly; soil red shale. Pop. 1830, 1629. Taxables 310. This t-ship contains three forges, four distilleries, three tan yards, three grist mills, one saw mill and two hemp mills.

Cairio, p-o. Lancaster co. 128 ms. N. of W. C. and 64 from Harrisburg.

Caladaque, is a small creek which rises in Allen t-ship, Northampton co., and running south-westerly, falls into the Lehigh r. in Lehigh co. about 2 ms. below Hockendoque. It has several mills upon it.

Calhounsville, or *McAllisterville*, p-t., Mifflin co., on the line dividing Greenwood t-ship from Fermanagh, about 15 ms. N. E. from Lewistown. It lies at the foot of a mountain, girded by Cocalimus and Lost creeks, 158 ms. from W. C. and 51 from Harrisburg. It is a small place of some half dozen houses.

Callensburg, p-t. of Toby t-ship, Armstrong co. on the Mercer and Roseburg turnpike road, about 20 ms. N. of Kittanning, contains some half dozen dwellings, the town having been lately laid out. It is 251 miles from W. C. and 191 from Harrisburg.

Callender's creek, Stoney creek t-ship, Somerset co., a tributary of Stoney creek; it receives the waters of Maple Swamp run and Clear run.

Caln, East, t-ship, Chester county, bounded N. by Brandywine and Uwchlan t-ships, E. by West Whiteland, S. by East and West Bradford and by East Fallowfield, W. by West Caln and Sadsbury. Central distance N. W. from Philad. about 33 miles; from West Chester 7 ms. Length 9 miles, breadth 2½, area 8500; surface diversified; soil, limestone and gravel, generally productive. Pop. 1810, 723; in 1820, 829; in 1830, 861. Taxables in 1828, 175. Conestogo cr. rises in and drains this t-ship, and the Conestogo turnpike road crosses it from E. to W. Iron ore is found in the mtn. which fills its N. E. extremity. Morgantown lies upon the turnpike road, at which there is a post office.

Caln, West, t-ship, Chester county, bounded N. by Honeybrooke, E. by Brandywine and East Caln, S. by Sadsbury and W. by Lancaster co. Central distance W. by N. from Philadelphia, 44 ms; from West-Chester 14 ms. N. W.; length, 5½, breadth, 4¼ ms.; area, 16,900 acres; surface, hilly; soil, gravel. Pop. in 1830, 1,490; taxables, 254. The west branch of Brandywine r. flows along the east boundary, on which there is a furnace and a forge, and several mills. West Caln church is in the S. E. end of the t-ship. This is a fruitful and well improved t-ship, but is not comparable to East Caln.

Cambellstown, p-t. of Londonderry t-ship, Lebanon co., on the turnpike road from Euphrata to Harrisburg, distant from the borough of Lebanon 10 ms. S. W., from Harrisburg 15 ms. S. E., and 125 N. W. from W. C. It contains 15 dwellings, 2 stores and 2 taverns.

Cambria, t-ship, Cambria co. bounded N. and N. E. by Susquehannah t-ship, E. by Allegheny, S. E. and S. by Somerhill t-ship, and W. by Jackson t-ship and by Indiana co.; greatest length 15 miles, breadth 15; area 56,640 acres: surface, hilly; soil, clay, gravel and sand. Pop. in 1830, 726; taxable property in 1829, seated lands, $42,179; unseated, $8,736; personal, $12,012. Rate of levy 8½ mills to the $100. Taxables, 200. It is drained W. by Blacklick creek, and S. by the N. branch of the Little Conemaugh. Ebensburgh, the post and county town, is in this t-ship, on the turnpike road from Hollidaysburg to Indiana. The small town of Beula, now in ruins, is about 2 miles S. W. of Ebensburg, on the turnpike road leading to Greensburg, and the village of Munster is in the eastern angle of the t-ship, on the turnpike road leading to Hollidaysburg.

Cambria county, was formed from Somerset and Huntingdon counties, by the act 26th March, 1804, which gave it the following limits: beginning at the Conemaugh river, at the S. E. corner of Indiana co.; thence a straight line to the Canoe place on the W. branch of the Susquehannah, thence E. along the line of Clearfield co. to the S. W. corner of Centre co. on the heads of Mushanon creek; thence S. along the Allegheny mountain to Somerset and Bedford co. lines; thence along the line of Somerset and Bedford counties, seventeen miles, until a due west course from thence will strike the main branch of Paint creek; thence down said creek, the different courses thereof, till it empties into Stoney creek; thence down Stoney creek, the different courses, to the mouth of Mill creek; thence a due west line till it intersects the line of Somerset and Westmoreland counties; thence N. along the same line, to the place of beginning. Thus the co. is bounded N. by Clearfield co., E. by Huntingdon and Bedford, S. by Somerset and W. by Westmoreland and Indiana cos. Length 35, breadth 19 ms., area 670 sq. ms. Central lat. 40° 30′ N. Lon. from W. C. 1° 40′ W.

By the above cited act it was also provided, that the place for holding courts of justice for the co. should be fixed at any place, not at a greater distance than 7 miles from the centre of the co. And by the act 29th March, 1805, the seat of justice was established at Ebensburg, and the trustees of the county were authorized to receive assurances for certain lots and lands for the use of the county, granted by Messrs. John and Stephen Lloyd, to dispose of such lots and erect public buildings, and by the act of 20th Jan. 1807, the county was organized for judicial and other purposes.

Cambria co. lies upon the west border of the great central transition formation of the United States, and upon the east of the still greater secondary formation of N. America, the boundaries of which, in the county, are not very distinctly defined. Coal is abundantly found in various parts of the county, but more particularly in the southern division. And there is iron, as it is said by some, but denied by others, in Clearfield co. The whole county is a mountain, the great Allegheny being on the eastern border, and the Laurel hill on the west. Approaching the former mountain from the eastward, it presents a bold and precipitous front, and from two to five miles brings the traveller to the summit, from whence the descent westward is scarcely perceptible. A portion of the mountain is arable, and some well cultivated farms may be seen upon its top. The Laurel Hill, in the S. W. part of the county, falls but little short of the elevation of the Allegheny, but it is depressed as it proceeds northward. Its scenery is wild, and its aspect dreary and forbidding. The Conemaugh river has broken its way through it in this county. The soil in the valleys is well watered and generally of excellent quality.

Almost every species of timber abounds on the mountains, except the white oak. The various species of pine predominate, but on the Laurel hill, chestnut, red and rock oak are very abundant. Some of the trees grow to a huge size, and where the soil is rich and humid, it is covered with vegetation so dense as to seem absolutely impenetrable. In the valleys and along the water courses, hickory, ash, sugar maple, cherry, elm, &c. &c. grow luxuriantly.

The Conemaugh river rises on the W. side of the Allegheny mtn. near the middle of the eastern boundary, and bears the name of the little Conemaugh. Flowing S. W. it receives the N. branch, which rises near Ebensburg and the S. fork which has its source in a cedar swamp, at the foot of the Allegheny. Thence continuing the same course, it unites at Johnsontown with Stoney creek, a stream as large as itself; thence taking a N. W. course, it breaks through the Laurel hill about 12 ms. N. of the S. W. angle. Stoney creek receives from the county on the E. Paint creek and Solomon's run, and from the W. Mill creek and Bens creek. On the N. the county is drained by the W. branch of the Susquehannah, Chest creek and the head waters of Clearfield creek, and on the W. by Black lick creek, Big and Little. The rail road portage from Hollidaysburg connecting the Juniata with the Conemaugh crosses the mtn. in the S. part of the county, and communicates with the Conemaugh r. at Johnsontown, where a large and commodious basin has been prepared. The turnpike road from Huntingdon to Pittsburg crosses the county by Ebensburg, whence another turnpike road leads to Indiana.

The principal towns are Ebensburg, Johnsontown, Munster and Loretto.

The population of this county is composed of various elements,—of emigrants from N. Jersey, and E. Pennsylvania, from Scotland, Ireland, and in the vicinity of Ebensburg, principally from Wales. It has increased in number rapidly, having more than doubled itself in the last ten years. In 1810, the population amounted to 2117 souls; in 1820, to 3287, and in 1830, to 7096, of whom 3829 were white males, 3205 white females, 26 free colored males, and 36 free colored females. The taxables in 1828 were 1144.

The public buildings consist of a county court house, offices and prison, and an academy. The institution for which the latter was erected was incorporated in 1819, with a donation from the state, of $2000, conditioned that $1000 should be raised for its use by private subscription, and any number of poor children not exceeding 5 should be taught gratis, annually, each for a period of not more than two years.

The exports consist of live stock principally, and of timber, among which the excellent cherry plank and boards are most valuable. A sufficient quanty of maple sugar is made in the county for the wants of the inhabitants.

Improved land sells from 5 to 20 dollars the acre; unimproved from 50 cents to 4 dollars.

In conjunction with Huntingdon and Mifflin, Cambria forms the 17th senatorial district, sending one member to the senate, and in conjunction with Somerset it sends two members to the house of representatives. United with Bedford and Somerset, it forms the 13th congressional district, sending one representative to congress. With Westmoreland, Indiana and Armstrong counties, it makes the 10th judicial district, over which John Young, Esq. presides. And it belongs to the western district of the supreme court.

The county paid into the state treasury in 1831, for

Tax on writs,	$100 00
Tavern licenses,	217 36
Duties on dealers in foreign mdze.	99 50
	$416 86

The value of taxable property in the county, by the assessment of 1829, amounted,

Seated lands to	$222,636
Unseated lands,	132,540
Personal estate,	50,576
	$402,752

STATISTICAL TABLE OF CAMBRIA COUNTY.

Townships, &c.	Greatest Lth.	Greatest Bth	Area in Acres.	Face of country.	Population. 1810.	1820.	1830.	Taxables.	Valuation.
Allegheny t-ship,	10	6	32,000	Level.	610	947	844	200	43,751
*Cambria "	15	15	56,440	Rolling.	868	604	736	200	50,915
Clearfield "				do.			436	76	53,011
Conemaugh "	21	10		do.	639	807	2088	326	76,989
Connemaugh town, or Johnstown,						116	513		
Ebensburg bor.						168	270		
Jackson t-ship,				Rolling.			440	66	40,751
Munster town,						84	107		
Loretto town,						44	71		
Summerhill t-ship,	21	9½		Rolling.		517	852	158	41,284
Susquehannah,				do.			722	118	48,474
					2117	3287	7079	1144	

*Jackson t-ship has been lately taken from Cambria and Somerset t-ships, and Susquehannah and Clearfield from Allegheny, and as we have not the precise boundaries, we do not give the dimensions nor areas of the new or altered town ships.

Cambridge, a small village lying on the line which divides Honeybrooke t-ship, Chester co. from Lancaster co. distant 17 miles N. W. of Westchester.

Canaan, t-ship, Wayne co. bounded N. by Mount Pleasant, S. by Salem, E. by Palmyra and Dyberry t-ships, and W. by Susquehannah and Luzerne cos. Its form is that of an L; its greatest length 12 ms. breadth 8 ms. Lackawannock creek indents its eastern boundary, and branches of the Dyberry and Middle creeks, intersect it in various parts. The Moosic mts. are on the W. boundary. The Belmont and Easton turnpike road crosses it centrally N. and S. and the Milford and Owego S. E. and N. W. Surface, partly mountainous, partly level, covered with dense forests; soil, white gravel and loam; pop. in 1830, 1134; taxables, in 1828, 187. There is a p-o. at Mount Republic, 10 ms. W. of Bethany, and another at Clarksville, 8 ms. S. W. of the county town. Taxable property in 1829, seated lands $67,461, unseated 53,811; personal estate, including occupations $13,189.

Canoe mountain, a ridge of Morris t-ship, Huntingdon co. which has its name from its shape, connected with Brush mtn. Upon its W. side lies Scotch valley, drained by Canoe creek, and on its E. Canoe valley.

Canoe creek and valley. (*See preceding article.*) There is a p-o. here on the turnpike road 168 ms. N. W. from W. C. and 110 S. E. from Harrisburg.

Canonsburg, p-t. Washington co. on the road from Pittsburg to Washington borough, and on Chartiers creek, 18 ms. from the former and 7 from the latter town, in the extreme E. angle of Chartiers t-ship, 236 ms. from W. C. and 219 from Harrisburg. The town contains about 70 dwellings, a Presbyterian church, 5 or 6 stores, and 3 or 4 taverns. It was incorporated into a borough, 22d February, 1802.

Jefferson college was founded at this place by the legislature in 1802. An academy had existed here for many years previously, which formed the nucleus of the present institution. In the year 1806 the legislature granted to it $3000, providing at the same time for the admission of any number of poor children not exceeding four, who may at any time be offered in order to be taught, *gratis*, none to continue longer than two years if others should apply for admission. By an act of 1821 the state made a further grant of $5000. The institution is chiefly indebted to private benefactions and the exertions of its friends for its prosperity. The funds arising from tuition are the principal means of supporting the professors. Four thousand five hundred dollars have been bequeathed to the institution by individuals, to aid in educating poor, but pious young men, for the gospel ministry, and numbers have already experienced the benefit of this bequest. The college possesses a philosophical and chemical apparatus, adequate to a practical illustration of these sciences. The college library contains 1000 volumes, and that of the societies attached to the institution 1600. There are four academic instructers. In 1828, 259 students had graduated, of whom 245 are now living; 120 have been ministers, of whom 111 are living; 29 graduated in 1827. There were, in 1828, 101 under graduates; 43 students professing religion, and 9 indigent students. The branches of learning taught are similar to those in the Department of Arts in the University of Penn. The whole expense incident to the education and support of a student here, does not exceed $125 per ann. The college edifice is of brick, 76 by 45 feet, and will accommodate from 150 to 200 students. Under the charter of this college a medical school was established in 1826, at Philadelphia, which has received a considerable share of public patronage, and promises extensive usefulness. A Lyceum of natural science has lately been established in the college, with a view to collect and preserve the various objects of the natural history, and the Indian antiquities, in which the western states abound. The Alumni of the college, and the friends of natural science generally, are invited to aid the labors of the society.

Canton, post t-ship, Bradford co. bounded N. by Troy, E. by Franklin t-ships, S. by Lycoming co. and W.

by Tioga co. Centrally distant from Towanda, S. W. 20 ms.; greatest length $9\frac{3}{4}$; breadth 8 ms. Area, 85,-444 acres; surface, hilly; soil, gravelly loam. Pop. in 1830, 1175. The Towanda creek, enters the t-ship by the S. W. angle and flows N. E. through it, receiving many tributaries from it. The p-o. here is 249 ms. from W. C. and 138 from Harrisburg.

Canton, t-ship, Washington co. bounded N. by Mount Pleasant, E. by Chartiers, Strabane, and Amwell t-ships, S. by Morris t-ship, W. by Buffalo and Hopewell t-ships; greatest length 10, breadth 5 ms. Area, 20,480 acres; surface, pretty level; soil, loam, coal abundant. The borough of Washington lies partly in the t-ship, through which the national road continues westerly. The t-ship is drained by Chartiers creek and its tributaries, the chief of which is George's creek on the N. E. boundary.

Capous range, a continuation of the Shawnese range of hills, on the E. side of the Susquehannah, stretching thro' Exeter, Pittston, and Providence t-ships, Luzerne co. and forming in part the northern boundary of the Lackawannock valley. They rise in some places 1125 feet above their base, and abound in anthracite coal.

Capous creek, rises in the Capous range of mtns. in Providence t-ship, Luzerne co. and flows S. W. into the Lackawannock r.

Carbondale, t-ship, Luzerne county, was lately taken from Blakely t-ship, and is bounded N. and W. by Greenfield t-ship, E. by Wayne co. S. by Blakely t-ship. It lies in the upper end of the Lackawannock valley, bounded by mountains, and includes the coal mines of the Delaware and Hudson company.

Carbondale, p-v. Carbondale t-ship, Luzerne co. on the Lackawannock creek, at the head of the Lackawannock valley, is one of the sudden creations which have been effected by the coal trade. Distant from W. C. 247 and from Harrisburg 139 miles. The village commenced with the works of the Hudson and Delaware canal and coal company, four years since, and now contains about 40 dwellings, 7 stores, 3 taverns. At its suburb, New Dublin, there are 130 shanties, occupied by the miners.

The coal mine here is one of the most extensive and best of the Lackawannock region, and a large quantity of coal is taken from it annually, and transported to the New York market by the rail road and canal, (for a description of which see "canals of Pennsylvania, in the introduction.") Acts of assembly have passed for constructing a turnpike and rail-road down the Lackawannock valley, and a rail-road to the mouth of the Chenango river, on the Susquehannah, in the state of New York, and also for a canal along the Lackawannock creek to the Susquehannah, above Wilkesbarre, thereby to open a communication from Carbondale to the S. and N. The coal mine here is situated in the front of a hill. The coal has been quarried in a continued line for sixty rods, and presents a front of good coal of twenty feet in thickness, besides several feet more of roof coal, stained and shattered by time and the weather. The miners have lately began to follow the bed, without removing the superincumbent materials, pillars of coal being left to support the weight. About $3\frac{1}{2}$ acres of the bed have been removed. The communication from Hudson's river to Carbondale, the work of the Hudson and Delaware canal company, is by a canal from the Hudson to the Delaware, near Carpenter's Point; thence up the eastern bank of the Delaware to the mouth of the Lackawaxen; thence crossing the Delaware by a pool formed by a dam across that river and up the Lackawaxen to Honesdale, at the Forks of the Dyberry, where it terminates in an artificial basin, a distance of little more than 100 miles, thence by a rail-road across the Lackawannock mountain to Carbondale, 16 ms. The expenditure of the company on their road, canal and mines, exceed two millions of dollars. The coal fields of the company contain about 3,500 acres. From the 20th March, 1831, to the 5th November, there passed over the rail road 54,328 tons of coal. The company have sold lots in their villages of Roundout, (New York,) Honesdale and Carbondale, to the value of $28,951 82, and at Roundout leases have been made producing an annual rent of $1,592.

Carlisle, p-t. borough and seat of justice, of Cumberland co. on the p-r. from Phil. to Pittsburg, 118 miles from the former, and 178 from the latter, and about 16 miles W. of Harrisburg and the Susquehannah r. in the centre of a rich and well watered limestone valley, and standing on rising ground, presents a rich and variegated landscape, of mountains, woods, and cultivated farms. It was founded in 1751 by the proprietaries, who purchased several farms for that purpose. In 1753 it contained 5 log houses, but being a border town, and military post, it throve rapidly. It now contains near 650 houses, and 3708 inhabitants. The principal streets cross each other at right angles, and are neatly paved. A large open space was originally left in the centre, which is in a great part occupied by two stone churches, a market house, and a commodious court house, and fire proof offices. Beside these the public buildings in the town are six other churches, pertaining to the English Presbyterians, Episcopalians, Lutherans, German Presbyterians, Methodists, Scotch Presbyterians, and Roman Catholics. Dickenson college, built of limestone, is situated on an elevated spot, on the west part of the town, erected on the site of an elegant brick edifice, which was burned in 1803. The present building is 150 feet in length, 4 stories high, and surmounted by a beautiful dome, from which there is an extensive view of the valley and the mountains by which it is bounded, and particularly of the north mountain for about 80 miles of its range. This college received its name in memory of the great and important services rendered to his country by John Dickenson, and in commemeration of his liberal donation to the institution. It was established and incorporated by the legislature in 1783, but the funds then requisite were supplied by private munificence. But in 1786 the state gave to it the sum of $500, and 10,000 acres of land, and in 1791, $1500, and in 1795 the further sum of $5000. The building for the accomodation of students having been destroyed by fire, in 1803 the legislature authorized the treasurer of Cumberland co. to pay to the trustees of the college $6000, from the arrearages of state taxes due from the co. by way of loan; and by an act of 1806 this loan was increased to $10,000. The amount received under these two acts, was but $8,400, and in 1819 the debt was remitted by the state. In 1821 a further donation was made by the legislature of $6000, in consideration of a reconveyance to the state of the 10,000 acres of land, previously granted, which had proved a burthen rather than a relief to the institution, and a further sum of $2000 annually for five years, was also granted. After struggling for years, with difficulties, the result of deficiency in the active funds of the institution, the trustees were compelled to suspend its operations in the year 1816; in which prostrate condition it continued until revived by the aid afforded in 1821. Since that period, it has been extensively useful. By the act of 1795 it was stipulated that there should be admitted into the college any number of students, not exceeding 10, who may be offered, to be taught reading, writing, and arithmetic, *gratis*. In 1828 the college had six academical instructers, 22 graduates, and 109 under graduates, and assisted six indigent students. The expenses of a student here for one year, with the exception of his books, candles and clothing, are estimated at $176. A little to the E. of the town there are extensive barracks and other buildings, erected in the revolutionary war, for the accommodation of troops, and preservation of public stores. The town was incorporated by act of assembly 13th April, 1782, by the name of the burgesses, and inhabitants of the borough of Carlisle, with two chief burgesses, five assistants, high constable and town clerk. Fairs are authorized to be holden here on the fourth thursdays of May, and October, annually.

There are some springs and a limestone cave near Carlisle which merit attention. The sulphur springs, about four miles N. of the town, on a branch of the Conedoguinit creek, were formerly much frequented, and there is here a large building for the accommodation of visiters. In the centre of a large field, a mile and a half also N. of the town, is the "Hogshead spring," in a conical excavation nearly 60 feet in circumference having a lime stone wall on one side, and a gentle and regular descent upon the other. Six or eight feet below the summit is an arched opening, through which is a passage declining at an angle of 40°, and 10 feet deep, wide enough to admit a man stooping. At the bottom of this cavity is a pool of delicious water, apparently stagnant, yet sweet, cool, and refreshing; qualities which it always preserves, but there are no visible means by which the basin receives, or discharges it. Setart's spring, about 2 miles S. of the borough, is remarkable for sending forth a volume of water sufficient, at the source, to turn two mills; the stream passes near Carlisle on its way to the Conedoguinit, and drives several other mills in its course.

On the banks of the Conedoguinit, about 1½ miles from the town is the cave. The entrance is by a semicircular archway, seven feet high, in a limestone rock, of 20 feet perpendicular elevation. So true and finished is the curve of this portal, that the spectator is induced to believe it to have been perfected by art; and such opinion is corroborated, by the apparently dressed surface of the interior. The first or antechamber has a length of 90 yards, and is high enough to admit the visiter to stand erect. Three passages branch from it. That on the right is broad and low, and from the moisture of the stones, frequently difficult of access. It leads to a chamber as large as the first; this apartment bears the name of the Devil's dining room. Some persons assert, that there is a narrow and unexplored passage leading from it, which has been sought by others in vain. The centre passage from the antichamber is very narrow, and in direction, similar to a winding stair, and is impassable, after a progress of ten yards, and terminates in a perpendicular excavation. The left hand passage, at the distance of three or four feet from the entrance, turns suddenly to the right, and extends nearly thirty yards, with sufficient breadth and height to permit a small boy to creep along it; but it becomes thenceforth, too strait for further progress. About seven feet from the entrance of this gallery are several small pools of water formed by the drippings of the roof, which have been mistaken for springs.

This cavern is dark and damp, and must be examined by torch light. An opinion prevails in the neighborhood that the Indians formerly made it a deposit for their spoils, and an asylum in seasons of danger, and it may possibly have served as a tomb; but none of the articles usually buried with the Indians have been found here; yet human bones were formerly seen in it.

Carmichaels town, or New Lisbon, Greene co. p-t. 220 miles from W .C. and 210 from Harrisburg, contains about 60 dwellings, 3 stores, and 3 taverns, and about 300 inhabitants. There is an academy here called "Greene academy," incorporated by act of assembly 20 March, 1810, by which $2000 were given to it conditioned that a number of poor children not exceeding six should be taught annually therein.

Carpenter's mills, p-o. Lycoming co.

204 miles N. W. from W. C. and 95 from Harrisburg.

Cascade run, a tributary of Spring creek, which rises in Providence t-ship, and runs S. W. into Pittston t-ship, Luzerne co.

Cascade run, a small stream rising in Exeter t-ship, Luzerne co. and flows S. W. into the river Susquehannah.

Cashes creek, Damascus township, Wayne co. flows by the village of Damascus, into the Delaware river near the Casheton falls.

Cash town, a small village of Franklin t-ship, Adams co. on the turnpike road from Gettysburg to Chambersburg, about 8 miles N. W. of the former, contains 12 dwellings, 1 store and 2 taverns.

Castleman's river, Somerset co. is formed by the union of the Little Youghiogheny river with Cox's creek in Milford t-ship. The Little Youghiogheny and Castleman's rivers may properly be treated as one stream, which, rising in Allegheny co. Md. between Meadow and Negro mtns. flows N. E. about 12 miles into Pennsylvania; and curving through Somerset co. falls into the Great Youghiogheny, 11 ms. N. of the Maryland line, opposite the east foot of Sugar-loaf mtn. The fall in this stream is very great; where intersected by the national road its bed is 1979 feet above the level of the ocean, and from thence to its mouth it falls 1000 feet.

Cattara creek, Rush t-ship, Schuylkill co. a branch of Locust creek, a tributary of the Little Schuylkill r.

Catawissa, p-t. Catawissa t-ship, Columbia co. on the left bank of the Susquehannah r. about10 miles above Danville, 182 ms. from W. C. and 72 ms. from Harrisburg; contains about 100 dwellings, 1 Methodist, 1 Lutheran and 1 Quaker meeting-house, 2 taverns and 4 stores. A project is entertained by the inhabitants of this town and its vicinity of connecting the Susquehannah r. here with the Schuylkill by a rail road uniting with that already made along the valley of the Little Schuylkill. An act was passed 13th March, 1816, authorizing a company to be incorporated for building a bridge across the Lehigh river, opposite or near the town, but the work has never been commenced.

Catawissa, t-ship, Columbia co. bounded N. by the Susquehannah r. E. by Mifflin t-ship, S. and S. E. by Schuylkill co. W. and S. W. by Northumberland co.; centrally distant S. E. of Danville 10 miles; greatest length 13¼, breadth, 11 ms.; area, 67,200 acres; surface, hilly; soil, clay and gravel; pop. in 1830, 3130; taxables, 561. The Catawissa mtn. runs through the N. part of the t-ship, and the Little mountain through the southern; between which lies the broad valley of Roaring creek. One branch of that stream girds the S. sides of Little mountain, and flowing round its W. end, divides this t-ship from Northumberland co. Another branch of the creek flows through the valley, and unites with the first about 3 miles above its junction with the Susquehannah. Iron ore abounds in this t-ship, and there are 2 furnaces and 2 forges in it. The post town of Cattawissa is on the Susquehannah r. about 10 ms. above Danville.

Cattawissa mountain; (see Cattawissa t-ship, Columbia co.)

Cecil, t-ship, Washington co. bounded N. by Robeson t-ship, E. by Allegheny co. S. by Chartiers creek, which divides it from Peters and Strabane t-ships, and W. by Chartiers and Mount Pleasant t-ships; centrally distant from Washington, N.E. 10 miles; greatest length 9, breadth 4½ miles; area, 24,960 acres; surface, partly level, partly hilly; soil, loam; coal, abundant. Miller's branch of Chartiers creek passes S. E. through the middle of the t-ship, upon which there are 5 or 6 mills. There is a Presbyterian church in the t-ship.

Cedar creek, Lehigh co. rises from one large spring in Macungy t-ship, and turns a large flour mill about six perches below the fountain; and after a course of 3 miles, falls into the Little Lehigh. The volume of this singular stream appears invariable, in wet or dry weather; it never freezes, and the grass, which grows to the water's edge, looks green at all seasons, and is always uncovered, the water dissolving the snow of winter as it falls. Some distance N. W. from the fountain of Cedar spring, is a stream which, after a course of 3 miles, sinks into the earth. It is conjectured that this stream forms the Cedar creek fountain.

Cedar creek, p-o. Lamar t-ship, 208 miles from W. C. and 101 from Harrisburg.

Centre county, was formed from Mifflin, Northumberland, Lycoming, and Huntingdon, by act 13th Feb. 1800, which gave it the following boundaries: beginning opposite the mouth of Quinn's run, on the W. branch of the Susquehannah; thence a straight line to the mout of Fishing creek, where it empties into the Bald Eagle creek; thence to the N. E. corner of Miles, late Haines, t-ship, including Nittany valley; thence by the N. E. boundary of the said t-ship, to the summit of Tussey's mtn., thence by the summit of said mountain, by the lines of Haines t-ship in Northumberland co., Potter t-ship in Mifflin co. and Franklin t-ship in Huntingdon co. to a point 3 ms. S. W. of the present line between Mifflin and Huntingdon counties; thence by a direct line to the head of the S. W. branch of Bald Eagle creek; thence, a direct line to the head waters of Mushanon; thence down the same to the Susquehannah, and down the Susquehanah to the place of beginning. The county was at the same time fully organized. It is now bounded on the N. by Lycoming co. on the E. by Union, S. E. by Mifflin, S. by Huntingdon, and W. by Clearfield counties. Length 58, breadth 36 miles; area, 1370 square ms. Central lat. 41° N.; long. from W. C. 0° 20′ E.

By the same act, the trustees therein named were authorized to take assurances for the payment of money and grants of land, stipulated for by James Dunlop and James Harris, and such others as might be offered to them, in trust to dispose thereof, one moiety in some productive fund for the support of an academy or public school in the county, and with other monies to be raised in the county, to erect public buildings for the county in the town of Bellefonte.

Centre county lies wholly within the Appalachian system of mountains, and it belongs wholly to the great central transition formation. The soil partakes of all the shades of quality, from the most productive river alluvion, to the most sterile mountain summits; from the exuberant limestone to the unyielding silicious rock. There is here as great a portion of mineral wealth as is to be found in any portion of equal extent in the United States. Iron of the best quality is found in all parts of the county, and coal on the Allegheny mountain. Almost every variety of indigenous forest tree may be found on the mountains, the slopes and the valleys. And the scenery of the country is varied, often beautiful, sometimes sublime, and always picturesque. The editor of the Bellefonte Patriot, in speaking of his county, has given us the following spirited passage. "We will close our remarks with one word for our county in general; most emphatically called *Centre county;* and as it is the heart of the state by geographical position, so it is the head by local advantages. We except none, unless Huntingdon and Mifflin. True, we have mountains, but we have plains, and our mountains are as valuable as valleys. First, they preserve health; we have no fevers, nor chills; but many births and few deaths; second, our mountains abound with fine timber of every kind and quality; and third, with mineral wealth; and fourth, when fruit is destroyed by frost on our valleys, it is preserved on our mountains. In short, for fertility of soil, mineral resources, manufacturing advantages, and every thing which can contribute to man's comfort and happiness, it is scarce equalled, certainly not surpassed, by any county in the state. It is none of your whortleberry, cranberry, or hemlock counties, calculated for the nurture of wolves, bears and panthers, and not for the residence of man; but a county abounding with advantages, which have not yet been duly estimated, but which undoubtedly will be, when the *West Branch canal* is constructed, and the American protecting system goes into vigorous operation."

The following mountain ridges and vales occur in crossing this county from the east. Path valley mtn. is on the E. boundary; next and scarce separated from it, is Tussey's mtn.; west of this is George's and Penn's valleys, bounded W. by the Brush mtn.; in the N. E. part of the last valley rises the Short mtn. Beyond Brush mtn. is Brush valley, bounded by a ridge of the Nittany mtn.; between this and the two other ridges of the same name, lie Pheasant and Little Pheasant valleys, and Sugar valley; west of the longest Nittany Ridge, is the Great Nittany valley, which extends to Bellefonte. West of this valley is a long ridge, which, S. E. of Spring creek, bears the name of Bald Eagle ridge, and N. W. of the creek, that of Muncy hill. It extends through the whole county and from Little Juniata r. to the W. branch of the Susquehannah, a distance of about 55 ms. The Bald Eagle valley runs between this ridge and the chain of the great Allegheny mtn. and is drained by the Bald Eagle creek which flows N. E. through its whole length into the W. branch of the Susquehannah, at the Great Island opposite to Dunnstown. The western portion of the county is covered by spurs from the Allegheny, and is bounded by the Mushanon creek and the W. branch of the Susquehannah.

The county is not well watered; the streams are numerous, but in the limestone valleys E. of the Bald Eagle ridge and Muncey hill most of them have very short courses, sinking into the earth, through the crevices of the rocks, and in many places it is difficult to obtain water for domestic purposes. Wells have been sunk 200 ft. through the rock without success. Spruce creek is the only stream which issues from the county on the south. Spring creek and Cedar creek break through the ridge into Bald Eagle creek, which receives from the Allegheny mtn. Marsh creek, and Beach creek, and some smaller streams. That mountain sends westward to the Mushanon, the Little Mushanon, Cold stream, and other but less creeks. The Bald Eagle is navigable for boats for about 20 ms. from its mouth and above Milesborough.

A turnpike road from Lewistown in Mifflin co. to Bellefonte, runs N. W. through the co. and another from the last place runs N. westward to Franklin, &c. Another turnpike road has lately been commenced from Milesborough to Smithsport, by which coal may be brought for the iron works at Milesborough, Bellefonte, &c. from the West of the Allegheny. Another turnpike road passes through Aaronsburg towards the Susquehannah r.

The principal towns of the county are Bellefonte, Walkersville, Pattensville, Milesborough, Earlysburg, Millheim, Aaronsburg, Rabersburg, New Providence, Hublersville, &c.

The population is composed chiefly of Germans and Irish and their descendants, and amounted in 1800 to 5000 souls, in 1810, to 10,681, in 1820, 13,796, in 1830 to 18,735; of these there were 9495 white males, 18,973 white females, 152 free colored males, 110 free colored females, 5 slaves. Of aliens there were 35, deaf and dumb 6, blind 2. Taxables in 1028, 3618.

The public buildings of the county consist of the court house, county offices, and prison; a building for an academy, which was incorporated by the act of 8th January, 1805, and in which was vested the property above mentioned, given to the trustees of the county for its use. And by act of 9th January, 1805, the legislature granted to the institution the sum of $2000, to be applied in the erection of a building, on condition that poor children not exceeding six in number, at one time, should be taught, gratis, but none to continue longer than two years; also 5 Presbyterian, 5 German, Lutheran, and Reformed, 4 Methodist, 1 Baptist, 1 Episcopalian, 1 Catholic churches, and 1 Quaker meeting.

Connected with Clearfield, Lycoming, McKean and Potter counties, Centre forms the 13th senatorial district, sending one member to the senate, and with Union and Clearfield, sends two members to the house of resentatives. Connected with Huntingdon, Mifflin, and Clearfield, it forms the 12th congressional district. United with Huntingdon and Mifflin counties, it forms the 4th judicial district. President, Thomas Burnside. The courts are holden at Bellefonte on the 4th Mondays of January, April, August, and November, annually.

The export trade of the county consists of wheat, about 200,000 bushels, clover seed, about 600 bushels, whiskey, 1500 barrels, and iron from 9000 to 10,000 tons.

There are many manufactories of iron in the county, and they continue to increase. The following are the principal: *Tussey furnace*, situated about 14 ms. from Bellefonte, competent to the manufacture of 100 tons of pig metal annually; now or late the property of Messrs. Stewart and Lyon. *Centre furnace*, 9 ms. from Bellefonte, directly opposite the end of the Nittany mtn. capable of making 1500 tons annually; the property now or late of Messrs. Miles & Green. *Spring furnace*, about 4 ms. from Bellefonte, on Spring creek, will manufacture 1000 tons per annum. The property of General Benner. *Logan furnace*, 3 ms. from Bellefonte, on Logan's branch of Spring creek, capable of making 1200 tons annually. It is the property of Messrs. Valentine and Thomas. *Eagle furnace* about 5 ms. from Bellefonte, in Bald Eagle valley, capable of making 1200 tons annually, belonging to R. Curtin, Esq. *Mount Hecla furnace*, 7 ms. from Bellefonte, in Logan's gap of Nittany mtn. will make 1200 tons; the property of Judge McKinney. *Washington furnace*, 15 ms. from Bellefonte on Fishing creek, capable of making 1200 tons of pig metal annually. *Howard furnace*, in a gap of Muncy hill, upon Lick run.

Phillipsburg forge, 15 ms. from Bellefonte, on the waters of Big Mushanon, makes about 200 tons bar iron annually. The enterprizing owners, Messrs. Hardman, Phillips & Co. have also a manufactory for making wood screws, which are in every way superior to those imported. They are made with great facility and in great quantities. To the screw manufactory is attached a cupola. *Rock forges*, 4 or 5 ms. from Bellefonte, capable of making about 600 tons of bar iron annually. To this establishment belongs a *rolling mill* for rolling boiler, nail, slit and sheet iron, and a nail manufactory, the whole the property of Gen. Benner. *Bellefonte forge*, situate a half mile from Bellefonte, on Logan's branch of Spring creek, a new forge on the same stream a short distance above the preceding one—a rolling mill for rolling bar iron from the bloom, the whole capable of manufacturing of bar, bolt, boiler, nail and slit iron, annually 800 tons. *Milesborough forge*, situate one mile and a half from Bellefont, in the gap of Muncy mtn. on the waters of Spring creek, capable of making 400 tons annually. Connected with it, there are a rolling mill for rolling boiler, sheet, nail and slit iron, and a nail factory; they are the property of Gen. Miles & Co. *Eagle forge*, 5 ms. from Bellefonte, on Bald Eagle creek, is capable of making 400 tons of bar iron annually. It is the property of R. Curtin. *Washington forge*, at the furnace of the same name, will make 300 tons annually; the property of Mr. Henderson. *Harvey's forge*, on Fishing creek about 20ms. from Bellefonte, capable of making 400 tons of bar iron annually. These works employ about 600 workmen, and maintain near 4000 persons.

There is a woollen manufactory at

Boalsburg, one at Milesburg, and two in Spring t-ship, and a cotton manufactory at Bellefonte. The usual mode of transportation is by the Bald Eagle creek, and the W. branch of the Susquehannah, and when the canal along the latter shall be extended to the mouth of the creek, the iron maufactures of this county will greatly increase, because it will then be enabled to compete with any in the state. The enterprizing manufacturers of the county are prepared to put the navigation of the Bald Eagle creek into the best order, when the canal shall have been completed. Much iron, however, is sent to the west for the supply of the towns on the Ohio.

There are Bible and Temperance societies in the county, and Sunday Schools, wherever the population is numerous enough to admit of their establishment.

Improved lands sell at from 15 to 30 dollars the acre.

STATISTICAL TABLE OF CENTRE COUNTY.

Townships, &c.	Greatest Lgth.	Greatest Bth.	Area in acres.	Face of country.	soil.	Population in 1810.	Population in 1820.	Population in 1830.	Taxables.
Bald Eagle,	25	7	68,480	Mount.	Valleys, limestone; mount., slate.	1146	685	835	153
Boggs,	21	12	109,440	do.			847	1311	249
Ferguson,	14	11	46,080	do.		1066	1189	1755	287
*Gregg,				do.				1564	306
Hains,	21	6	61,440	do.		1791	2350	1850	396
Howard,	21	10	78,720	do.		761	105	1291	237
Half Moon,	17	15	60,800	do.		561	713	994	172
Logan,	16	6	36,480	do.			431	603	101
Lamar,	11	5 1-2	26,880	do.			858	1567	306
Miles,	25	7	64,460	do.		1069	1188	1054	223
Potter,	11	10	53,760	do.		1584	1810	1872	372
Rush,	19	8	56,960	do.			173	410	81
Patton,	25	8	71,680	do.		297	483	577	106
Spring,	10	7	36,480	Div'fied.		1550	887	1307	284
Walker,	10	6 1-2	28,160	do.		553	694	1076	224
Bellefonte borough,						303	433	699	121
						10,681	13,796	18,765	3,618

* Gregg t-ship has been lately taken from Haines and Potter, but not having its precise boundaries we are unable to give the dimensions and area, and we give Haines and Potter as they stood before the change.

Centre, t-ship, Greene co. bounded N. by Morris, E. by Franklin, S. by Wayne, and W. by Aleppo and Richhill t-ships. Centrally distant from Waynesburg 5 ms.; greatest length 9; breadth 7 ms.; area 26,800 acres; surface, hilly; soil, loam. Pop. in 1830, 1,020; taxables 185. The t-ship is drained by several forks of Ten Mile creek and the main stream, on which is the post town of Clinton, 5 ms. W. from Waynesburg.

Centre, t-ship, Butler co. bounded N. by Slippery Rock and Parker t-ships, E. by Donegal t-ship, S. by Butler t-ship, and W. by Muddy Creek t-ship. Centrally distant from Butler borogh 7 ms. N. W. The t-ship forms a square of 8 ms.; area 40,960 acres; surface hilly; soil, gravelly loam. Pop. in 1830, 1322; taxables 241. The t-ship is drained on the S. by several branches of the Conequenessing creek, and on the W. by branches of Muddy and Slippery Rock creeks. The turnpike road from Butler to Mercer runs N. W. through it.

Centre, a village on the bank of the Delaware r. in Solebury t-ship, Bucks co. about 34 ms. N. E. of Phila. and 10 from Doylestown, and 4 from New Hope. There is a bridge over the r. at this place, resting upon 7 stone piers, beside the abutments; a substantial structure, protected from the weather by a roof, but not profitable to the joint stock company which erected it. The village contains 6 houses, a tavern and store.

Centre, t-ship, Indiana co. bounded N. by Washington t-ship, N. E. by Greene, S. E. by Wheatfield, S. W. by Blacklick, and N. W. by Armstrong t-ships. Centrally distant from Indiana borough S. 5 miles; greatest length 10, breadth 8 ms. Area, 46,720 acres; surface, hilly; soil, loam, clay. Population in 1830, 1237; taxables 282. The t-ship is drained by Yellow creek, which, uniting with Twolick creek, flows S. to Blacklick creek. The borough of Indiana is partly in this t-ship.

Centre, t-ship, Union co. bounded N. by West Buffalo and Union t-ships, E. by Penn and Washington t-ships, S. by Perry t-ship, and W. by Beaver t-ship. Centrally distant from New Berlin S. W. 5 miles; greatest length 8, breadth 8 miles; area 30,080 acres; surface diversified; soil, partly limestone. Pop. in 1830, 1952; taxables, 221. Jack's mountain is on the N. and Shade mountain on the S. boundary; Penn's creek flows on the N. E. and the Little Mahonialy, or Middle creek, through the middle of the t-ship. Middleburg, a p-t. is on the latter, and the village of Centreville on the former stream. Valuation of taxable property by the census of 1829, $252,280.

Centre Square, p-o. Whitepaine t-ship, Montgomery co. 153 ms. N. E. from W. C., and 106 E. of Harrisburg, and 4 ms. E. from Morristown. There are here 2 dwellings, a tanyard, a tavern and store.

Centreville, a p-t. of Wayne co. in Mount Pleasant t-ship, 12 ms. N. W. from Bethany, containing about 20 dwellings, 2 stores, 2 taverns, and a Presbyterian church. The p-o. is called Mount Pleasant, 269 ms. from W. C., and 170 from Harrisburg.

Centreville, a small village in Providence t-ship, Luzerne co. on the Lackawannock river.

Centreville, a village, Buckingham t-ship, Bucks co. receives its names from its position in the t-ship. It is the converging point of 5 public roads, and contains 6 or 8 dwellings.

Centreville, village of Slippery Rock t-ship, Butler co. 14 ms. W. of Butler, on the Butler and Mercer turnpike road, contains about 50 dwellings, 5 stores and 4 taverns. Chief part of the buildings are of brick. It is only a few years since this town was founded.

Centreville, E. Bethlehem t-ship, Washington co. on the national road, 18 ms. S. E. of the borough of Washington, contains 40 dwellings, 4 stores, 2 taverns, and an Episcopalian church.

Centreville, p-o. Crawford co. Oil Creek t-ship, 307 ms. N. W. from W. C. and 240 from Harrisburg.

Centreville, p-t. Centre t-ship, Union co. at the foot of Jack's mtn. on the right bank of Penn creek, about 4 ms. S. W. of New Berlin, contains from 15 to 20 dwellings, a Lutheran church, 2 stores and 2 taverns.

Centreville, village of Schuylkill co. on the E. branch of the Norwegian rail-road, in the coal fields of the N. American coal company, about 4 ms. from Pottsville. (See Pottsville, for description of rail-road.) The following description of the mine at this place is from the pen of the spirited editor of the Miner's Journal, at Pottsville.

"This drift was among the first that was opened, and worked upon the true scientific principles of the water level, and it now extends about fifteen hundred feet under ground. The coal is brought out in ton wagons, propelled by a horse, and there is likewise a ginn, which answers the purpose of a ventilator. The first sensations on entering the place, reconcilable only with Virgil's 'facilis decensus Averni,' are not at all pleasant. The waggish warnings of the workmen, who take a peculiar degree of pleasure in directing visitors to hold down their heads, keep their fingers from the side of the wagon, &c. excite a cold sensation of fear; but when the conductor's light is placed against the solid slate which is the boundary between the externals and infernals, agitation begins to give way to surprise. On the left is the interminable vein of coal, descending at its regular angular dip of forty-five degrees, into the very centre of Symmesonian existence, and there, for aught we know, worked for the benefit of unknown Cyclops. To the right, prop after prop in regular rows supports those portions of the slate where the coal has been excavated, and which must present no unapt resemblance of ancient Herculaneum or Pompeii, now, when the ingenuity of man is making a signal conquest over the most terrific of nature's phenomena. After we are seated in the coal wagon, which is the vehicle for the conveyance of the passengers into the mine, the horse is started, and we proceed in the most impenetrable darkness, rendered more gloomy by the single light which the conductor carries in his hand. After proceeding thus some hundred feet, and at intervals gaining a peep of day-light, from the air shafts on the right, we turn a slight bend, and the whole arcana of this interior world is developed to the astonished visiter. We cannot readily imagine a more awfully grand sight, or a feeling of more terrific grandeur, than when first the numerous lights burst upon us through the darkness. Fancy immediately revels in the youthful remembrance of fierce and august genii, at their dark and midnight incantations, —of the famous grotto into which Peter Wilkins was trepanned, of the perilous adventures of Sinbab the Sailor, and all those " Bible truth stories" of children, in which we are delighted, and which even now carry their inestimable charm with them. When we have arrived at the breast on which the workmen are engaged, we leave the wagons and take footing to the right, up the ascent of the slate. Here we can perceive the method by which the coal is most readily excavated, as immense fragments are successively broken off, and tumbled down to the conveyances by which they are drawn from the mine. We follow this path to the right, through a forest of props, and at last the blessing of daylight is again presented to us, and gratefully indeed does it present itself. The visiter is then hoisted from the pit by the ginn, and once again stands on *terra firma.*"

Ceres, t-ship, McKean co. bounded N. by the state of New-York, E. by Keating t-ship, S. by Ogden t-ship and W. by Warren co. Centrally distant from Smithport, N. W. 16 ms.; greatest length 18, breadth 14 ms.; area 160,280 acres; surface rolling; soil, gravel and loam. It is drained N. by Tunwangwant creek, and W. by Willow, Sugar, and Kenjua creeks. Pop. in 1830, 252. A road crosses it westward to Kenjua, in Warren co. and another northerly into the state of N. York.

Cerestown, p-t. of Keating t-ship, McKean co. on a tributary of the Allegheny r. near the N. York line, 16 ms. N. E. of Smithport, 307 ms. N. W. from W. C. and 198 from Harrrisburg, contains a mill and some 4 or 5 dwellings.

Chambersburg, p-t. borough and st. jus. of Franklin co. is one of the most flourishing inland towns in the state. It is pleasantly situated at the confluence of the Falling Spring and Conecocheague creeks, 143 ms. W. of Philadelphia, 77 N. W. of Baltimore, 90 N. W. of W. C. and 48 S. W. of Harrisburg. The site of its location was selected a century since, for its advantages of water power and soil, by Col. Benjamin Chambers, for his residence and settlement, in a wilderness, through which, at that time, roamed the red men and the animals of the forest. He erected a dwelling and the first mills in the county, and surrounded them by a fort, which sheltered from the incursions of the savages, his family and others who were induced to settle in his neighborhood. The town of Chambersburg was laid out in 1764; but increased little until after the peace of 1783, and the erection of Franklin co. in 1784, since which, it has continued steadily to improve. It forms a t-ship which has the name of Franklin. It contains at present about 500 dwellings, generally of brick or stone, substantially, and many of them tastefully, built. The population in 1830 was 2794. Its public buildings are a brick court-house, and county offices, prison, 8 churches, an academy of brick, 3 stories high, capable of accommodating many students, to which the state has given $2000; a neat banking house, for the accommodation of the "Chambersburg Bank," which is successfully conducted, with a capital of $247,228; and a masonic hall, a handsome structure. It contains many stores, mechanics' and manufacturing establishments, and houses of public entertainment. There are three weekly newspapers published here, two in the English and one in the German language. The inhabitants are industrious, moral and religious, and not deficient in enterprise. The water power now gives motion to 2 flour mills, having each three pairs of stones; 2 fulling mills, a paper mill, a cotton and woollen manufactory, an oil mill, several carding machines and a manufactory of edge tools, carried on to a very great extent, and making articles of superior quality, at a price lower than similar ones can be imported; and in 1831 a large paper mill, for the fabrication of straw paper, was erected. The water power in, and within five miles of, the borough, is adequate to propel an hundred pairs of stones, and furnishes facilities for manufacturing purposes, not surpassed in any part of the state; surrounded by a healthy, fertile, and highly cultivated country. It has the advantage of a turnpike road by the way of Harrisburg to Philadelphia, another by the way of York, and like roads to Baltimore and Pittsburg. A rail road from Harrisburgh to Chambersburg is contemplated; a survey and report has been made thereon, in 1829, by which it appears that the length of the line is nearly 56 miles, and the estimate of cost $7,673 33 per mile. A like report has been made on a road proposed through Gettysburg to York; but the engineer (Wm. R. Hopkins) deems that no advantage which can be derived from the road will justify the expense of its construction.

Chanceford, Lower, p-t-ship, York co. bounded N. and N. W. by Upper Chanceford, E. by the Susquehannah r. S. by Peach Bottom and Fawn t-ships, and W. by Hopewell; centrally distant from the borough of York 20 ms.; area, 25,600 acres; surface, broken and uneven; soil, gravel and poor; pop. in 1830, 1051; taxables, 216; taxable property in 1830, real estate $105,430; personal 8370; occupations 13,715; total $162,905; rate 25 cts. in the $100. Muddy creek flows along the S. W. and S. boundary to the Susquehannah river, receiving from the t-ship Tom's creek and Orson's run. McCall's ferry crosses the Susquehannah about the middle of the eastern line. The post office, called after the t-ship, is 90 ms. from W. C. and 49 from Harrisburg.

Chanceford, Upper, t-ship, York co. bounded N. by Windsor, N. E. by the Susquehannah r. S. E. by L. Chanceford and S. W. by Hopewell t-ships; centrally distant from the borough of York 15 ms. S. E.; greatest length and greatest breadth 9 miles; area 28,800 acres; surface, broken and hilly; soil, gravelly and poor; pop. in 1830, 1,177; taxables, 270; taxable property in 1829, real estate $136,841; personal, 12,349; occupations 13,715; total, $162,905; rate, 25 cents in the 100 dollars. Muddy creek flows on the S. W. and Beaver run on the N. E. and Otter run crosses the t-ship diagonally from N. W. to S. E. The post office, called after the t-ship, is 94 ms. from W. C. and 40 from Harrisburg.

Chapman, t-ship, Lycoming county, bounded N. by Potter co. E. by Dunstable t-ship, S. by Centre co. and W. by Clearfield and McKean counties; centrally distant from Williamsport 45 miles; greatest length 30, breadth 22 miles; area 189,240 acres; surface mountainous; soil various. It is drained by the W. branch of the Susquehannah r. which flows along the S. boundary and through the S. E. angle of the t-ship; by the Sinnemahoning and the east branch of that stream; by Kettle creek, and by many other minor streams which run into the river from the north. The country is a wilderness, which has scarcely been explored, and has a few settlements sparsely strewed along the river and other principal streams. Taxable property in the t-ship in 1829, seated lands $17,550; unseated, 79,765; personal estate $2350; rate of levy $\frac{3}{4}$ of one per cent.

Chapman's run, Covington t-ship, Luzerne co., a tributary of Spring brook, which rises near, and flows in a course of about five miles along the "*Chestnut hill.*"

Chapman's lake, Greenfield t-ship, Luzerne co. is a sheet of water of an elliptical form, about a mile long and half a mile wide, within 2 miles of the S. E. boundary of the t-ship and near the W. side of the road from Wilkes-barre to Dundaff.

Chapman, t-ship, Union co. bounded N. by Penn t-ship, E. by the Susquehannah r. S. by Mifflin co. and W. by Washington and Perry t-ships; centrally distant S. E. of New Berlin 12 ms.; greatest length 10½, breadth 4 miles; area 17,920 acres; surface hilly; soil, gravel and alluvion; pop. in 1830, 1094; taxables 221. The W. Mahantango creek runs along the S. boundary to the river, receiving the E. branch from the west boundary. McKees' falls in the river are in this township.

Chartiers creek, a large stream of Washington and Allegheny counties, rises in Morris t-ship, of the former, and flows a N. N. E. course of 35 or 40 miles into the Ohio r. 5 miles above Pittsburg. It receives Little Chartiers creek from Washington co. about 3 miles below Canonsburgh. From this point it is navigable at high water for boats going down stream.

Chartiers, t-ship, Washington co. bounded N. E. by Cecil, S. E. by Strabane, S. W. by Canton, and N. W. by Mount Pleasant t-ships; centrally distant N. of the borough of Washington 6 miles; greatest length 7½, breadth 7 ms.; area 15,360 acres; surface, hilly; soil, loam; coal, abundant. Chartiers creek flows on the S. boundary, receiving from the t-ship the north branch. The post town of Canonsburg lies in the fork of Chartier's creek and W. Brush run, about 7 ms. N. E. of Washington borough.

Charleston, p-t. Manor t-ship, Lancaster co. on the Susquehannah river, E. side, about 9 miles W. by S. from the city of Lancaster.

Charleston, village of Charleston t-ship, Chester co. contains 8 or 10 dwellings, a manufactory of hemp and flaxen stuffs, 1 store and 1 tavern, situated 11 miles N. E. of West Chester.

Charleston, t-ship Tioga co. centrally situated 4 or 5 miles W. of Wells borough. It forms an oblong of 8½ miles, by 4, and contains 15,760 acres. It is drained by a branch of Crooked creek, and a small tributary of Tioga river; surface level, better adapted to grass than grain. Pop. in 1830, 479. Taxables in 1828, 86.

Charleston, village, on the road from Sumany town, to Quakertown, Milford t-ship, Bucks co. about 35 miles N. W. of Phil. and 16 of Doylestown. Near it is a church, pertaining to the Lutherans, and German reformed.

Charleston, t-ship, Chester co. bounded N. E. by the river Schuylkill which separates it from Montgomery co. S. W. by Tredyfin t-ship, S. by that and by E. and W. Whiteland, and W. by Pikeland t-ships; central distance from Phil. about 22 miles N. W. and from West Chester about 10 miles N. E. French creek passes through the N. E. and valley creek through the S. E. angle of the t-ship; on the former near its confluence with the Schuylkill, is an extensive rolling mill, and cut nail manufactory, and on the latter a forge. Pickering creek drains the t-ship, centrally, and flows also into the river; Charleston church is situated near the N. W. boundary, greatest length, 8½, breadth about 4½ miles; arear, 12,950 acres; surface hilly; soil, sandy loam. Pop. in 1830, 832; taxables 178. There is a post office at the Valley Forge, and another at French mills.

Chatham, p-t. and village of Chester co. on the road from Wilmington to Lancaster, 34 miles S. W. of Phil. and 13 miles S. of West Chester, 100 from W. C. and 66 S. E. from Harrisburg.

Chatham, t-ship, Tioga co. in the S. W. part of the co. watered by Elk creek and its tributaries. It is yet thinly settled. Surface, rolling; soil, loam, well timbered with oak, beech, maple, and some pine. The cleared country better adapted to the production of grass than grain.

Cheat river, rises in the state of Virginia, in Randolph co. and after running a northwardly course, falls into Monongahela river, in Pennsylvania, about 4 miles N. of the southern boundary of the state, and on the line between Greene and Fayette cos. It is about 200 yds. wide at the junction with the Monongahela.

Cheltenham, t-ship, Montgomery co. bounded N. E. by Abington, S. E. and S. W. by Phil. co. W. and N. W. by Springfield t-ship. Its form is oblong, having 7 miles on the longer, and 1½ on the shorter sides; area about 6720 acres, surface gently undulating; soil, loam and gravel, generally well cultivated, and tolerably productive. The Frankford creek, is the only stream of the t-ship, on which there are several flour mills, saw mills, tilt hammers, and a rolling mill. The Cheltenham and Willow Grove turnpike crosses the t-ship, upon which lies Shoemaker town, 8 miles from the city of Phil. where there are a valuable grist mill, and several dwellings. Pop. 1830, 934; taxables in 1828, 213.

Cherry Tree, t-ship, Venango co. bounded N. by Crawford t-ship, E. by E. Branch t-ship, S. by Wind Rock t-ship, and W. by Plumb t-ship; centrally distant N. E. from Franklin borough 17 miles; greatest length 7, breadth 6 miles; area 18,560 acres; surface, rolling; soil, loam; pop. in 1830, 392; taxables 90; the p-o. in this t-ship is 293 miles N. W. from W. C. and 226 from Harrisburg.

Cherry, t-ship, Lycoming co. bounded N. by Bradford co. E. by Luzerne co. S. by Penn. t-ship, and W. by Shrewsbury t-ship. Its greatest length, and breadth, is 12 miles; area about 73,600 acres; surface mountainous; soil, sand, gravel, and slate. It is watered by the Big and Little Loyalsock creeks. The p-o. of the t-ship is called Cherry, distant 221 miles from W. C. and 110 N. W. from Harrisburg. Taxable property in 1829, seated lands $5893, unsettled 52,249 33, personal est. 2239, rate of levy ¾ of one per cent.

Cherry creek, Northampton co. rises at the foot of the Blue mountain, on the N. side near the Wind Gap, and running E. N. E. along the foot of the mountain, falls into the Delaware at its entrance into the Water Gap. It is a rapid stream, not navigable, but has several mills upon it.

Cherryville, a p-t. of Northampton co. situate on the main road from Easton to Berwick, about three miles S. E. of Berlinville, in Lehigh t-ship. It contains 2 dwellings, 1 tavern, and 1 store. It is 190 miles N. from W. C. and 97 from Harrisburg N. E.

Cherry ridge, p-o., Dyberry t-ship, Wayne co. 6 miles S. of Bethany, 264 miles N. W. from W. C. and 165 from Harrisburg.

Chesnut Hill, t-ship, Northampton co. bounded N. W. by Tobyhanna, N. E. by Pokono, E. by Hamilton, S. by Ross and W. by Towamensing. The surface of the country is partly hilly and partly level; the soil, gravel. The greatest length of t-ship is 9 ms.; greatest breadth 8 ms.; area 36,480 acres. It is watered by Head's creek, a confluent of Big creek. There is 1 Lutheran church in the t-ship. Two of the highest hills are known, respectively, by the names of Chesnut Hill and Prospect Hill. Pop. in 1830, 940; taxables in 1828, 215.

Chesnut Hill, a lofty spur of the Wyoming mountain, running E. into Covington t-ship, Luzerne co.

Chesnut Hill, p-t. of Germantown t-ship, Phila. co. on the Germantown and Perkiomen turnpike road, 9 ms. N. W. of Phila. city. There are some 80 dwellings here, and 3 taverns, 2 stores, 2 schools. It is however difficult to say where the village begins or ends, so thickly is the neighborhood settled. It is a fine, high, healthy spot, much resorted to in the summer season, by the citizens of Phila.; several stages going to and returning therefrom twice a day. The Chesnut Hill and Spring-house turnpike road commences here. The population of the town may be about 500 souls.

Chesnut creek, a tributary of Spring brook, which has its source and course in Covington t-ship, Luzerne co. Its length is about 4 miles.

Chesnut Level, p-o. Lancaster co. 89 ms. N. of W. C. 51 S. of Harrisburg.

Chesnut Ridge, a mountain range of Napier t-ship, Bedford co. lying between the Raystown branch of the Juniata and the W. branch of Dunning's creek. The ridge, indeed, extends from Maryland through the cos. of Fayette, Westmoreland and Indiana.

Chest, t-ship, Clearfield co. bounded N. by Pike, E. by Beccaria t-ship, S. by Cambria co. W. by Indiana co. This t-ship was taken from Beccaria, and is watered by the W. branch of the Susquehannah r. and by Chest cr. Pop. in 1830, 494. The surface of the country is hilly and broken; soil, loam.

Chester county, was one of the three counties established by the proprietary, at the settlement of the province, in 1682. It extended indefinitely westward, and was reduced to its present dimensions by the successive formation of the counties of Lancaster and Berks. It was settled by the friends and companions of William Penn, and has been peopled by the English, German, Welch, and Irish Presbyterians. The Germans in the north, where their descendants predominate, and their language is still spoken in some t-ships—the Welch along the Great Valley—the Irish in the southwest—and the English indiscriminately throughout the country. One third of the population is supposed to belong to to the Society of Friends. This co. gave birth to Dr. Allison, Hugh Williamson, Thomas Mc Kean, and Anthony Wayne, all distinguished in American history.

The northern part of the county is of old red sand-stone The middle of transition, in which there are veins of limestone, and the southern, of primitive rocks, chiefly gneiss or mica slate, in some places scarce distinguishable from granite, and which also have small beds of lime stone.

Chester co. presents to the mineralogist a rich field for investigation. Her limestone, serpentine and gneiss, the predominant rocks, contain inexhaustible beds of interesting minerals, and the many quarries in operation greatly facilitate the means of procuring them. These circumstances, with the polite attention manifested to strangers by the inhabitants, and the admirable hospitality which characterizes them, furnish strong inducements to the mineralogist to visit the county.

The science of mineralogy, in its most interesting and useful department, is making rapid advancement in this section of the country. Almost all classes of society take an interest in its promotion, particularly the farmers, and the continuation of their zeal cannot fail to produce valuable results. Already several valuable minerals have been found in abundance. Magnesite and ferruginous oxide of Chrome have been extensively and advantageously worked for Epsom salts, and Chrome yellow. These articles were a few years since, received exclusively from England, but are now made from these materials, of a quality equal to the foreign, and at a less price; and have entirely excluded the foreign article from the market. Among the townships of Chester, East Marlborough, London Grove, Newlin, Pennsbury, Kennet, New Garden, West Marlborough, West Bradford, West Goshen, and West town, Penn, Londonderry, Upper and Lower Oxford, E. and W. Fallowfield, New London, and East and West Nottingham, have been more or less explored.

The townships not yet examined, lie in the S. W. part of the county, and as they contain abundant beds of limestone, and ridges of serpentine, there are doubtless many interesting minerals. For a notice of such townships as have been examined, the reader is referred to several valuable articles written by Mr. G. W. Carpenter, and published in the estimable journal of Mr. Silliman.

The county is bounded by the state of Maryland S. W., Berks, N. W., Montgomery N. E., and Delaware co. and Delaware state S. E. Its length is about 38 ms. mean width 29, area 738 sq. ms. Central lat. 40° N. long. E. W. C. 1° ?0′. The surface of the county is very diversified; the wstrn. part is hilly, even mountainous; the northern part is also hilly; that of the south is of a more level character. Octarara creek, North East river, and Elk river, rise in the S. W. part of the co. and flowing southwardly into Maryland, fall into the Chesapeake bay, and the centre of the county is drained by the Brandywine, Chester, Ridley, and some smaller creeks, which run to the Delaware river. The Schuylkill borders the county on the N. E. The whole district is remarkably well watered. The soil is as various as the face of the country. The valleys are generally very rich, and the Great Valley running S. W. from the river Schuylkill, is perhaps not exceeded in fertility of soil and profitable cultivation, by any spot of equal extent in the U. States. Limestone abounds in many parts of the county. Mr. C. Miner computes that from 5 to 800,000 bushels are annually used as manure, and with the extension of the use of this manure, beneficial cultivation, also extends, and even the hill sides become highly productive. The county is famous for its wheat, barley and oats, butter, mutton and beef, of all which it sells great quantities.

Roads, generally kept in as good order as the face of the country will admit, traverse the county in all directons. The great western stone turnpike from Philadelphia passes through the Great Valley, and a turnpike road from Wilmington to Lancaster, crosses the S. W. part of the county, and another from Warren to Morgantown, the N. W.

The Pennsylvania rail road to Columbia also passes through the valley, and a lateral branch, about nine miles in length, commencing near the eastern entrance of the Great Valley, and ending at West Chester, is now under contract, and is constructed by a company incorporated in 1831, with a capital of one hundred thousand dolls. The spirit with which this enterprise has been prosecuted, is highly honorable to the inhabitants of the county, and especially to the intelligent citizens of the thriving borough of West Chester. It was resolved at a town meeting (the creative organ of the public will and public weal,) on the 10th December, 1830, that it was expedient to make this branch; on the 22d March following, an act of incorporation having been obtained in the intermediate time, the whole stock necessary to complete the undertaking was subscribed; and on the 26th May, the contracts for its execution were entered into.

The Schuylkill canal passes through the N. eastern part of the co. near French creek, and affords valuable sites for such manufactories as are adapted to water power.

The bridges of the county are numerous, generally of stone, and built in the most substantial manner.

The chief towns are West Chester, Downingstown, Coatsville, Cochranville, Phenixville, &c. (See these titles respectively.)

The Yellow springs, in Pikeland t-ship, 30 ms. N. W. from Phila. is a noted watering place, surrounded by beautiful scenery, and is growing yearly in repute. (See title "Yellow springs.") A chalybeate spring, whose tonic virtues are much praised, is found near Coatsville.

The population, by the census of 1830, was 50,908, of whom 269 were aliens; 15 deaf and dumb; 30 blind;

and 5 slaves. The increase since 1820, is 6457; white males, 24,132; females, 23,779; free colored males, 1615; females, 1377.

The counties of Chester and Delaware form the 15th judicial district of the state. The county courts are holden at West Chester, on the 2d Mondays after the 3d Mondays in January, April, July and October. President, Isaac Darlington, Esq.

Jointly with Lancaster and Delaware it forms the 4th congressional district, which, in the 22d congress, is represented by Joshua Evans, William Keister, and David Potts, Jr.

The public buildings of the co. consist of a court house of stone, with a wooden cupola, two academies, a jail, and a poor house. The latter was erected at the expense of the co. on a tract of land in West Bradford t-ship, in 1799, pursuant to an act of the legislature passed 27th Feb. 1798. It is governed by three directors, one of whom is chosen at the general election, annually, whose term of service is three years, and is maintained, when necessary, by a tax especially levied by the county commissioners on the requisition of the directors. The directors are allowed a compensation of forty dollars per annum, with additional compensation for attending suits. The disbursements are paid by the county treasurer, on orders drawn by the directors. The institution is under the immediate direction of a steward and matron, whose joint salaries do not exceed $400 per annum. The number of paupers is between 3 and 400, who are maintained at an average expense of 52 cents each per week, or $27 12 per annum.

Among the inhabitants of the county, there is a decided literary and scientific taste displayed in the provisions for education and in the atheneum and cabinet of natural sciences at W. Chester. At this place also there is an academy, which in 1817 received from the state treasury a gratuity of $1000. Many schools are found throughout the county, supported wholly at private expense. Among which the Friends' boarding school, for pupils of both sexes, established in West-town t-ship, and the school for girls at Kimberton, are most noted. The "Chester academy" established by act of the legislature, 30th March 1811, is located, in East Whiteland t-ship, on the Lancaster turnpike road. The building for its use is neat and commodious. It received a donation from the state of $2000, conditioned that $1000 should be raised for its use by private subscription.

Although distinguished as an agricultural district, Chester county has considerable claims to attention on account of its manufactures. Its rich beds of iron ore, give employment to one furnace, one foundry, five forges, three bloom mills, two rolling mills, and several tilt hammers. There is a cotton manufactory on the canal, above Phenixville. A very extensive nail manufactory, and rolling mill at the latter place. A cotton factory and large gun manufactory at the valley forge. A manfactory of hemp and flaxen stuffs at the village of Charleston, a woollen manufactory at Clintonville; at or near Coatesville, there are 3 paper mills, 2 cotton factories, a rolling mill, and nail factory, and there are other manufactories of various kinds throughout the county.

Chester county bank, located in the borough of West Chester, was established under the act of the legislature 21st March, 1814; capital paid in, 90,000 dollars; deposits and unpaid dividends, by report of the auditor general 5th January, 1831, $204,192 01. The par value of shares is $50 each. The stock is much prized and is rarely in the market. These facts bear conclusive testimony of the prudent and successful manner in which this institution is conducted.

The county paid to the state treasury for tax on bank dividends, $2,520; writs, $749,22; tavern licenses, $1209,61; duties on dealers in foreign mdze. $1444,51; collateral inheritances, $298,90; pamphlet laws, $10,00; tin and clock pedlar's licenses, $85,50; total, $6,317 74.

STATISTICAL TABLE OF CHESTER COUNTY.

Townships, &c.	Greatest Lgth.	Greatest Bth.	Area in Acres.	Population. 1810.	Population. 1820.	Population. 1830.	Taxables.	Value. Rl. Es.	Value. Pers.E.	Occupants.
Bradford, West,	6	4 1-2	11,150	1219	1739	1550	253	414,317	14,517	17,315
Bradford, East,	6	3 1-2	11,300	1003	1217	1099	227	439,565	14,633	19,109
Birmingham,	2 3-4	2 1-2	3,500	290	323	277	65	132,780	3,630	1,200
Brandywine,	6 3-4	4	15,960	1257	1431	1455	341	358,616	15,076	26,405
Caln, East,	9	2	10,520	974	1162	1440	301	447,284	10,129	44,035
Caln, West,	5 1-2	4 1-4	16,900	1008	1182	1490	254	272,018	6,469	17,015
Charlestown,	8 1-2	4 1-2	12,950	1580	2069	832	178	266,243	7,798	3,305
Coventry,	7 1-2	6	22,300	1608	1977	2131	394	462,264	27,200	3,670
Eastown,	3	2 1-2	4,650	587	618	646	137	187,652	7,739	1,220
Fallowfield, East,	6 1-2	4	9,970	990	857	1156	253	253,798	7,731	8,300
Fallowfield, West,	9 3-4	5	18,700	1157	864	1621	348	290,960	11,363	7,525
Goshen, East, *a*,	4	3	7,350	1273	735	752	173	266,313	11,002	14,310
Goshen, West, *b*,	4	2 1-2	5,600		757	799	156	326,171	10,712	14,310
Honeybrooke,	5 1-2	5 1-4	15,600	1073	1322	1636	352	381,629	9,867	18,291
Kennett,	4 3-4	4 1-4	9,630	947	1032	1145	231	386,428	16,175	4,880
London Grove,	6	4	12,433	983	1097	1150	269	391,167	14,780	34,233
London Britain,	3 1-4	2 1-2	4,800	404	425	518	110	143,274	5,191	2,320
Oxford, Upper,	6 1-4	5	17,200	700	710	900	222	182,734	8,714	3,800
Oxford, Lower,	7 1-2	4	13,950	769	914	1020	224	154,835	6,615	
Marlborough, East,	4 3-4	3 3-4	10,680	1046	993	1252	230	334,361	11,675	3,355
Marlborough, West,	4 3-4	4	9,762	917	852	1101	265	423,534	13,273	19,780
Newlin,	4 1-2	2 1-2	7,100	780	914	794	161	264,438	9,780	2,758
New Garden,	7 1-2	3	11,200	1038	1199	1309	265	415,539	15,941	9,930
New London,	6 1-4	5 1-4	13,860	1018	1198	1591	279	254,938	11,840	26,000
Nottingham, East,	6 1-2	5	19,360	1409	1486	1788	316	200,419	10,958	13,775
Nottingham, West,	5 1-4	3 3-4	9,480	642	474	562	106	57,634	3,681	3,050
Londonderry, *a*,	5	3 1-2	7,200	1164	581	605	132	110,234	5,058	1,085
Penn, *b*,	3 3-4	2 1-2	6,100		481	605	109	137,320	7,000	2,925
Nantmeal, East,	7 1-2	5 1-4	16,600	1544	1873	2029	348	541,552	13,200	1,980
Nantmeal, West,	8	5 1-2	19,400	1188	1443	1498	327	356,770	20,623	25,534
Pikeland,	8 1-2	2 3-4	10,116	1001	1221	1403	282	289,456	11,478	14,055
Pennsbury,	7 1-2	3 1-4	9,880	728	795	856	163	365,845	12,203	3,250
Sadsbury,	8 3-4	3 1-4	16,620	1192	1539	1875	347	451,887	17,500	42,650
Schuylkill,	4 1-2	2 1-2				1434	332	315,757	7,007	2,105
Tredyffrin,	4 1-4	4 1-4	8,950	1258	1449	1582	319	518,804	14,951	200
Thornbury,	4 1-4	1 1-4	2,240	200	202	183	42	113,517	3,032	2,700
Uwchlan,	7	3 3-4	13,000	1178	1198	1423	273	382,557	14,887	9,760
Vincent,	9 1-2	5	23,500	1680	1918	2147	411	462,918	15,663	5,455
Whiteland, East,	4	2 1-2	6,530	779	818	994	197	318,554	11,648	9,900
Whiteland, West,	4	3 1-2	8,100	636	773	850	150	306,926	12,981	8,895
Willistown,	5 1-2	3 1-4	11,800	1175	1306	1411	317	514,450	19,965	4,025
West-Town,	5 3-4	1 1-2	5,550	790	755	741	136	279,182	7,598	9,625
West Chester, bor.	1 1-2	1 1-4	1,120	471	552	1258	236	253,358	5,863	67,780
			472,551	39,596	44,451	50,908	10,231	13,432,000	437,144	236,508

a, Townships divided. *b*, Townships formed since 1810.

Chester, t-ship, Delaware co. bounded N. E. by Providence and Ridley, S. E. by the r. Delaware, S. W. by Upper and Lower Chichester, and N. W. by Middleton. Centrally distance S. W. of Phila. 16 ms.; greatest length 3¼ ms.; greatest breadth 3 ms.; area 4,800 acres; surface level; soil alluvial, generally well cultivated, & highly productive. Pop. in 1830, exclusive of the borough, 1072; taxables in 1828, 317. The borough of Chester, a t-ship and st. jus. of the co. lies on the r. in this t-ship. The great road from Phila. to Wilmington passes through it. Chester creek traverses it diagonally, and Ridley creek forms its eastern boundary. On the latter there are many mills.

Chester, p-t. borough and st. of jus. of Delaware co. 121 ms. N. of W. C. & 96 S. E. of Harrisburg, on the r. Delaware, 15 ms. S. W. of Phila. This is the most ancient t. of Pa. There were several dwellings and a Quaker meeting here, before the grant to Wm. Penn of 1681. It was then known as "*Upland*," but the name of Chester was substituted by the Proprietary at, and before granting the borough charter, on the 31st Oct. 1701. The first adventurers under Penn landed here on the 11th Dec. 1682, and were compelled to remain the winter, the r. having been frozen over on the night of their arrival. On the 4th Dec. 1682, the first provincial assembly was holden here, memorable for having enacted, in a session of three days, seventy laws, comprising an efficient code for the government of a political society. There are still standing in this ancient town, some old houses, among which is the church. Perhaps few places in the country have improved less. There is a water power near it, but it is not great, and the business of the surrounding country lies in Philad. It may contain at present, about 130 dwellings, chiefly of stone and brick. A substantial and neat court house of stone, surmounted by a cupola with a bell, stone offices and a prison, 5 taverns, 4 stores, an atheneum, the Delaware co. bank, a church and Quaker meeting house. A manufactory of straw paper has been lately established near the town. For the accommodation of the trade of the Delaware, there are some piers sunk in the r. opposite the town, which have lately been repaired by the U. S. Pop. in 1830, 848. There are here 6 practising attorneys, and 2 physicians.

Chester creek, rises in West Whiteland t-ship, Chester co. and by a S. eastly course of 17 ms., flows into the Delaware at the borough of Chester. It is navigable for a short distance only, above that town, but is a fine mill stream and has many mills upon it.

Chester, New, a small village of Strabane t-ship, Adams co. in the N. E. angle of the t-ship, on the road from Gettysburg to Berlin, 9 ms. N. E. from the former and 7 ms. S. W. from the latter, contains about 20 dwellings, 1 store and 2 taverns.

Chester Springs, p-o. Chester co. 127 ms. from W. C. and 69 from Harrisburg. (See Yellow Springs.)

Cheyney's Shops, p-t. Delaware co. 121 ms. from W. C. and 81 ms. from Harrisburg.

Chichester, Upper, t-ship, Delaware co. bounded N. and W. by Bethel, N. E. by Aston, E. by Chester and S. by Lower Chichester. It is watered by Hook cr. and a branch of Naamans cr. Central distance from Phila. 19 ms. from Chester 4 ms. Greatest length 3, breadth $2\frac{3}{4}$. Area, 3840 acres; surface, level; soil, loam. Pop. in 1830, 431; taxables in 1828, 102. Upper Chichester church is situated near the southern boundary.

Chichester, Lower, t-ship, Delaware co. bounded N. by Upper Chichester, E. by Chester, S. E. by the river Delaware, S. W. by Delaware state. Central distance from Philadelphia 20 ms. S. W. from Chester borough 5 ms. It is watered by Hook creek, a branch of Naamans creek, and some other small streams. Upper and Lower Chichester are noted for fine apple orchards and the quantity and quality of the cider which they produce. Surface, level; soil, loam. Pop. in 1830, 465; taxables, in 1828, 91.

Chilisquaque, t-ship, Northumberland co. bounded N. by Turbut, E. by Columbia co. S. by Point t-ship, and W. by the W. branch of the Susquehannah r. Centrally distant 8 ms. N. of Sunbury. Greatest length $5\frac{1}{4}$ ms. breadth $5\frac{1}{4}$ ms. Area, 14,720 acres; surface diversified; soil, limestone, and rich. Pop. in 1830, 1035; taxables 279. Chilisquaque creek, which gives name to the t-ship, passes through it from N. E. to S. W. into the Susquehannah r. On or near the creek lie two villages, one called Pottsgrove, a post town, and the other bearing the ill omened name of Sodom. There is a p-o. we believe, at the latter also; 174 ms. from W. C. and 64 from Harrisburg.

Chilisquaque creek, rises in the Muncy Hills, on the border of Lycoming and Columbia cos. and flows S. and S. W. through the latter and through Northumberland co. into the Susquehannah, on the N. side of Mentour's ridge, having a course of 2 or 3 and 20 miles.

Chippewa, t-ship, Beaver co. bounded N. by Big Beaver, E. by Beaver r. S. by Brighton, and W. by South Beaver. Centrally distant from Beaver borough N. W. 7 ms. Greatest length 7, breadth 5 ms. Area, 15,300 acres. Surface, hilly; soil, loam on the hills, limestone in places. Pop. in 1830, 580; taxables 100.

Chiques, Great and Little creeks, both

have their sources in the Conewago hills, Lebanon co. about 7 ms. apart, and flowing S. W. through Lancaster co. to the Susquehannah, unite their waters about 2 ms. above their confluence with that river. They are fine streams and give motion to many mills in their course.

Choconut, t-ship, Susquehannah co. bounded N. by the state of New York, E. by Silver lake t-ship, S. by Middleton t-ship, and W. by Bradford co. Its length E. and W. is 8 ms. breadth N. and S. 6 ms. It is drained by the Choconut and Apollacan creeks, which flow northerly into the Susquehannah, in the state of New York. The former is fed by a small lake, at the southern part of the t-ship; both are mill streams, and turn several mills in their course. The Milford and Owego turnpike runs across the S. W. angle, on which is the village of Friendsville, at its intersection of the southern boundary. The surface is hilly; soil, gravel and clay. There is a p-o. at Friendsville, and another in the t-ship, called Choconut, the latter distant 285 ms. from W. C. and 177 from Harrisburg.

Choconut creek, Choconut t-ship, Susquehannah co. flows northerly through a hilly country into the state of N. Y. and falls into the Susquehannah r. a short distance below Chenango Point. It is a mill stream, improved by many water works, but is not navigable.

Choke creek, Covington t-ship, Luzerne co. flows about 5 ms. S. E. into the Lehigh r. near the Great falls. It is a mill stream but not navigable.

Chrystal lakes, Upper and Lower. The former lies on the boundary line between Luzerne and Susquehannah cos. in Greenfield and Clifford t-ships, in the angle formed by the Milford and Owego turnpike road, and the road from Willkesbarre to Dundaff. The latter lies within a mile S. E. and altogether in Greenfield t-ship. The waters of the first flow into the Lackawannock r. and of the second into the Elkwood branch of the Tunkhannock creek.

Churchtown, p-t. Lancaster co. 129 ms. N. from W. C. and 54 S. E. from Harrisburg, on the Lancaster & Reading turnpike road, 21 ms. N. E. from the former, and in Caernarvon t-ship, contains some 8 or 10 dwellings, store and tavern.

Churchville, small village of Bucks co. on the line dividing Northampton and Southampton t-ships, 11 ms. S. E. from Doylestown, contains a church and 4 or 5 dwellings.

Clarksburg, p-t. of Pymatuning t-ship, Mercer co. at the confluence of the Pymatuning and Shenango creeks, 10 ms. N. E. of Mercer borough, contains about a dozen dwellings, a store, tavern, and mill.

Clark's creek, Dauphin co. rises in Rush t-ship, and flows S. W. between the Third and Peter's mtn. through Middle Paxton t-ship, in the river Susquehannah, turning several mills in a course of about 25 ms.

Clark's ferry and post office, Rye t-ship, Perry co. upon the Susquehannah r. below the confluence of the Juniata r. with that stream, and above the town of Petersburg, about 43 ms. N. W. from Harrisburg, 137 from W. C. and 10 ms. E. of Bloomfield.

Clark's Knob, a spur of the Blue mtn. which runs into Fannet t-ship, Franklin co. and forms part of the E. boundary of Amberson's valley.

Clarksville, a p-t. of Wayne co. situated 8 ms. S. W. from Bethany, in Canaan t-ship, near Rix's gap. Contains 10 or 12 dwellings, 2 taverns, and 2 stores.

Clarksville, p-t. of Morgan t-ship, Greene co. at the fork of 10 mile creek, 2 ms. from its confluence with the Monongahela r and 10 ms. N. E. of Waynesborough, 217 ms. N. W. of W. C. and 210 S. W. from Harrisburg. The town is beautifully situated and contains about 40 dwellings, several stores and taverns.

Clarion river, or *Great Toby's creek*, rises in Sergeant t-ship, McKean co. and flows a S. W. course through Jefferson co. thence forming the boundary between Armstrong and Venango counties, it flows into the Allegheny

r. at Foxburg. It has a course of about 70 ms. S. W., is navigable for boats 55 ms. and for canoes about 10 ms. further. Vast quantities of lumber are sent to market annually by this stream to Pittsburg and the towns on the Ohio.

Clarion, t-ship, Armstrong county, bounded N. by Clarion r. which separates it from Venango co. E. by Jefferson co., S. by Red Bank t-ship, and W. by Toby t-ship; centrally distant N. E. from Kittanning borough 26 miles; greatest length 13½, breadth 12 miles; area 68,480 acres; surface, gentle hills; soil, loam; pop. in 1830, 2067; taxables 340. It is drained by Laurel run, Mill, Piney and Licking creeks, which flow N. W. into Clarion r. The post towns of Roseburg and Hulinsburg lie in the N. parts of the t-ship; the latter on the N. bank of Piney creek. The former is known by the name of Clarion.

Claysville, p-t. Washington co. on the line between Buffalo and Donnegal t-ships, on the national road, 10 ms. W. of Washington borough and 20 E. from Wheeling, 239 ms. from W. C., 222 from Harrisburg; contains 60 dwellings, 3 or 4 stores, as many taverns and a Presbyterian church.

Clearfield, co., was taken from Lycyming by act of 26th March, 1804, which gave it the following limits: "Beginning where the line dividing Cannon's and Broadhead's district, strikes the W. branch of the Susquehannah; thence N. along the said district line until a due west course from thence will strike the S. E. corner of McKean co. thence W. along the sthrn. boundary of McKean co. to the line of Jefferson co., thence S. W. along the line of Jefferson co. to where Hunter's district line crosses Sandy Lick creek; thence S. along the district line to the Canoe place on the Susquehannah r. thence an easterly course to the S. W. corner of Centre co., on the heads of Mushanon creek, thence down the Mushanon creek, the several courses thereof, to its mouth; thence down the W. branch of the Susquehannah r. to the place of beginning." It was provided also by the act, that whenever such county, according to the ratio of apportionment of representation, shall be entitled to a separate representation, provision should be made for its full organization. And by the act of 1st April, 1823, a line was directed to be traced "from the mouth of the Second run, emptying into the west branch of the Susquehannah from the north side below Buttermilk falls at the true bearing of north, 35° W. until it intersects the present county line, and so much as may be cut off from Lycoming co. by the line so run, shall be added to Clearfield county."

By the act 14th March, 1805, the powers of the commissioners of Centre co. were extended over Clearfield; but by the act of 23d Jan. 1812, the citizens of the co. were authorized to elect their own commissioners; and by the act of 4th April, 1805, commissioners were appointed to fix the county town, which was established on lands of Abraham Witmer, and a town was there laid out, to which the name of "*Clearfield*" has been given. The county was finally and fully organized by the act of 29th Jan. 1822, which provided for the judicial administration thereof. It is bounded N. by McKean co., N. E. by Lycoming, S. E. by Centre, S. by Cambria, W. by Indiana and N. W. by Jefferson; length 45, breadth 32 miles; area 1425 square miles; central lat. 41° 4′ N., lon. 1° 30′ W. from W. C.

This county belongs to the great secondary formation which forms the valley between the Allegheny and the Stoney mountains, and abounds with coal, salt, iron, and other valuable minerals. Its surface is broken, hilly, nay mountainous; but the mountains, though having a general inclination N. E. and S. W. do not form regular chains or ridges, but are broken and turned in all directions. Upon our map names are given to very few of these hills. Elk mountain, in the N. W. part of the county, is the most continuous and most prominent. The soils are as various as the surface. The limestone and alluvial lands of the valleys are excellent. The scenery almost everywhere is delightful, and the climate very healthy. The timber is of all the varieties indigenous to the country; the hills and the vales affording the proper sustenance for those respectively adapted to them.

The county is extremely well watered. The west branch of the Susquehannah, which rises in Cambria co. crosses this county diagonally from the S. W. to the N. E. and receives in its course from the south, Chest creek, Clearfield and Little Clearfield creeks, and the Mushanon creek, which separates it from Centre county; from the north it receives Anderson's and Little Mushanon creeks, and many small runs. The river is navigable for canoes to the remote S. W. corner of the county; and the creeks we have named are also navigable. The N. part of the county is drained by the Bennet's branch of the Sinnemahoning, which flows E. to the Susquehannah, receiving the Driftwood branch and other streams from the north. Westerly, flow the waters of Toby's creek, Sandy Lick and Mahoning creeks, tributaries of the Allegheny river.

The turnpike road from Bellefonte to Franklin, runs N. W. through the county, passing by Philipsburg and Curwinville, and about four miles S. of Clearfield. The Milesburg and Smithport road also pursues a similar direction; Clearfield and Jefferson a westerly, and Clearfield and Armstrong a south-westerly course.

The towns are Clearfield, Curwinville and Karthaus; Phillipsburg lies on the Mushanon creek near the eastern boundary, but in Centre county.

This county is yet thinly settled, but it grows in population rapidly. In 1810, it had 875 inhabitants; in 1820, 2342; in 1830, 4803, of whom 2485 were white males, 2265 females; 28 free colored males, 25 free colored females. Included in the foregoing were 24 aliens, 6 deaf and dumb and 3 blind. The taxables in 1828 were 892.

The public buildings of the county consist of the court-house, prison, and county offices, and a building for an academy, which was incorporated in 1827, and received from the state a donation of $2000, one moiety to be paid toward the erection of the building, the other moiety to be vested as a permanent fund; conditioned that $1000 should be raised for the institution by private subscription.

The exports of the county, by way of the Susquehannah, consist of about 5000 bushels of wheat, some other grain, some flour and pork, from 5 to 800,000 feet of lumber, about 6000 tons of bituminous coal, and 600 tons of iron. The coal business is yet in the hands of the farmers and mechanics, who devote the winter and spring to mining it and boating it to market. Of the producers of grain and provisions, of the manufacturers of flour, lumber and iron, and of the miners of coal, many are their own carriers, and rely upon the spring freshets for conveying their merchandize to market, the returns for which are indispensable to meet their engagements at home. The Clearfield coal is said to be of excellent quality, and in the yet imperfect state of the trade may be profitably sold at Middletown, at 15 cts. the bushel; at this price it may compete in the Philadelphia market with the Richmond coal, which frequently sells at 20 to 25 cts. by the cargo.

United with Lycoming, Centre, Mc Kean and Potter counties, Clearfield forms the 13th senatorial district, sending one member to the senate, and in conjunction with Centre county it sends two members to the house of representatives; and with Huntingdon, Mifflin and Centre counties, it forms the 12th congressional district, sending one member to congress. Connected with Huntingdon and Centre, it forms the 4th judicial district, Thomas Burnside, Esq., president. The court is holden at Clearfield on the 3d Mondays of October, December and March, and on the first Monday of July, annually.

The taxable property of the county by assessment of 1829, was rated, the seated lands at $432,192; unseated $250,000, and personal estate, including occupations, at $32,946. The rate of levy was 5 mills on the dollar.

This county paid into the state treasury in 1831:

For tavern licenses, $100 00
Duties on dealers in for. mdze. 70 02

$170 02

STATISTICAL TABLE OF CLEARFIELD COUNTY.

Names of t-ships.	Population. 1820.	1830.	Taxables. 1828.
Brady		431	50
Bradford	572	631	134
Beccaria	236	434	82
Chest		494	74
Covington	90	250	47
Decatur		319	58
Fox		437	75
Gibson	235	405	71
Lawrence	447	683	135
Pike	702	819	166
	2342	4803	892

Clearfield, t-ship, Butler co. bounded N. by Donegal t-ship, E. by Armstrong co. S. by Buffalo t-ship, and W. by Butler t-ship. Centrally distant from the town of Butler S. E. 6 miles. It forms a square of 8 miles; area 40,960; surface rolling; soil in the bottoms, loam and sand, on the upland gravel, and clay; pop. in 1830, 617; taxables 129. It is drained E. by branches of Buffalo creek, and W. by branches of the Conequenessing. There are salt springs on the E. boundary. The wood of the t-ship, has been much injured by fire, but the land is now becoming heavily timbered.

Clearfield, p-t. and borough, and seat of justice of Clearfield co. on the right bank of the W. branch of the Susquehannah river, N. lat. 41° 1′ W. long. from W. C. 1° 28′, distant N. W. from Harrisburg 129 miles, contains a court house, county offices, prison, some 30 or 40 dwellings, stores, and taverns. An academy was established here and incorporated, and endowed with the sum of $2000 by the act of assembly 12th Feb. 1827.

Clearfield, Ridge, p-o. Pike t-ship, Clearfield co. and on the W. branch of the Susquehannah river, 14 miles S. of Clearfield borough, and about 5 from Curwinville, and 125 miles from Harrisburg.

Clearfield creeks, Big and Little, Clearfield co. the first rises on the confines of Cambria, and Centre, counties, and runs a N. course of about 18 ms. to the W. branch of the Susquehannah river, separating Beccaria from Bradford t-ships; it receives the second from the S. W. about 6 miles below its mouth.

Clearfield, t-ship, Cambria co. bounded N. by Clearfield co. S. by Allegheny t-ship, E. by Huntingdon co. and W. by Susquehannah t-ship; surface rolling; soil, clay, sand and gravel; pop. in 1830, 436; taxables, 76. Valuation of taxable property in 1829, seated lands &c. $23,144, unseated $30,867, personal $1976; rate of levy 8½ mills on the dollar.

Clear Ridge, Bedford co. a mountain range, a continuation of the Ragged mountain, rises about the middle of Southampton t-ship, and extends N. through Providence t-ship, to the Raystown branch of the Juniata.

Clear creek, Providence t-ship, Bedford co. rises in the E. of Tussey's mountain, and penetrating Warrior Ridge, flows into, and along the valley formed by that Ridge, and Clear Ridge, into the Raystown branch of the Juniata river.

Clermontville, p-o. McKean co. 272 miles N. W. from W. C. and 201 from Harrisburg.

Clifford, t-ship, Susquehannah co. bounded N. by Gibson t-ship, E. by Wayne co. S. by Luzerne co. and W. by Lennox t-ship. Its length E. and W. is 8 miles, breadth N. and S. 5 ms. area 25,600 acres. It is drained by the Lackawannock creek, which forks here into two branches, and by the Elkwood branch of the Tunkhannock;

Upper Chrystal lake lies on its Southern boundary near the village of Dundaff, and the Montrose turnpike road, which passes diagonally through the t-ship. The Moosick mountain skirts its eastern boundary, and the Elk mountain the extreme knob of Tunkhannock mountain rises on the northern boundary, and forms the eastern termination of the main Allegheny mountain in Pennsylvania. The surface is hilly generally; soil clay, and gravel, and loam, with a subsoil of hard pan; pop. in 1830, 866; taxables in 1828, 157.

Clinton, t. of Centre t-ship, Greene co. situated on Ten Mile creek, 8 ms. W. of Waynesburg.

Clinton, t-ship, Lycoming co. bounded N. E. and S. E. by the W. branch of the Susquehannah river, S. W. by Washington t-ship, and W. by Nippenose t-ship. Centrally distant from Williamsport S. E. 6 miles; greatest length 13, breadth $4\frac{1}{2}$ miles; area, 16,000 acres; surface, hilly. This t-ship has a front of about 20 miles on the river, and for about 8 miles does not exceed 2 in depth; the remainder is a semi-ellipsis formed by the Muncy bend of the river. It is not abundantly watered, the streams being few, short and inconsiderable. Valuation of taxable property in 1829, seated lands $54,050; personal est. $5458; rate of levy $\frac{3}{4}$ of one per cent.

Clinton, p-o. Allegheny co. 246 ms. from W. C. and 224 from Harrisburg.

Clintonville, Chester co. about 12 ms. N. E. of West Chester, and 14 from Phila. contains 6 or 8 dwellings, a woollen manufactory, 1 store and 1 tavern. The vicinity is remarkable for its beautiful limestone.

Clover creek, Woodbury t-ship, Huntingdon co. rises in the confines of Bedford co. and flows N. W. along the W. side of Tussey's mtn. into the Raystown branch of the Juniata.

Coal Castle, a hamlet in Norwegian t-ship, Schuylkill co. on the W. branch of the Schuylkill r. and on the rail-road, at the foot of the Broad mountain. It contains about a dozen houses, inhabited by miners.

Coan creek, a tributary of the Swatara creek, which rises in Lower Mahantango t-ship, and passes through the "Gold Mine Gap" of the Sharp mtn. and thence through Pine Grove t-ship, about 4 ms. to its recipient.

Coatesville, p-t. and village in the Great Valley, upon the turnpike and rail-road between Phila. and Columbia, 36 ms. distant from either, 114 from W. C. and 60 from Harrisburg, and on the line dividing East Caln and Sadsbury t-ships, and on the E. side of the W. branch of the Brandywine river. On this stream, within a few ms. of the town, are three large paper mills, two cotton factories, a rolling mill and nail factory, and other hydraulic establishments. About a half mile from the town is a chalybeate spring, of whose medicinal virtues favorable reports have been made. The town is thrifty, contains various mechanics, and a newspaper is published here called "The Coatesville Examiner."

Cobb's creek, Delaware co. rises in Haverford t-ship, and flows a sinuous course of about 10 ms. and for about half of that distance forming the boundary line between Phila. and Delaware cos. It is a smart brook, with considerable fall, and has many mills upon it. It unites with the Darby creek, a short distance below the village of Darby, and thence flows into the river Delaware.

Cobus creek, Northampton co. rises in Upper Mount Bethel t-ship, about 3 ms. below the Water Gap. It it not navigable. It flows E. by a course of about 7 ms. into the Delaware r.

Cocalico, t-ship, Lancaster county, bounded N. E. by Berks co. S. E. by Brecknock and Earl t-ships, S. W. by Elizabeth, and N. W. by Lebanon co. Central distance from the city of Lancaster N. E. 24 ms.; greatest length 12 ms. greatest breadth 9; area, 40,960 acres; surface, hilly; soil, red shale and loam. Pop. in 1830, 4902; taxables 973. The Conewago hills fill the greatest portion of the t-ship, and it is drained by the Cocalico creek, and Swamp creek its tributary. Trout creek, also a tributary, is on the line between this and Elizabeth t-ship. The Downingstown, Euphrata and Harrisburg turnpike road crosses the S. W. portion of the t-ship, on which, at the intersection of the road from Reading to Lancaster, the town of Euphrata is located. Reamstown and Adamstown also lie on the same road, at each of which there is a p-o.

Cocalico creek, rises in Heidelburg t-ship, Berks co. and flows south west through Cocalico t-ship, Lancaster co. to which it gives name, and between Earl and Warwick t-ships into the Conestogo r. receiving in its course Swamp, Trout, Middle and Harmer creeks. It has a course of more than 20 miles, is a fine stream and turns many mills.

Cocalimus creek, rises in Greenwood t-ship, Mifflin co. and flows S. E. into Greenwood t-sp. Perry co. and thence into the Juniata r. below Millarstown, having a course of about 15 ms.

Cochranville, p-t. and village, West Fallowfield t-ship, Chester co. on the turnpike road from Wilmington to Lancaster, 27 ms. W. from Phila. and 16 S. W. of West Chester, 102 from W. C. and 59 from Harrisburg, contains some half dozen dwellings, a store and tavern.

Codorus, t-ship, York co. bounded N. by Manchester, E. by York and Shrewsbury, S. by Maryland, W. by Manheim and Heidelburg, and N. W. by Paradise t-ship. Centrally distant S. W. from the borough of York 10 miles; greatest length 13, breadth 6½ miles; area 35,200 acres; surface, rolling; soil, gravelly and indifferent. Pop. in 1830, 2331; taxables 505; taxable property in 1829, real estate $354,622; personal $26,355; occupations, &c. $34,375; rate, 25 cents in the $100. The t-ship is nearly encircled by the W. and S. branches of the Codorus creek, which unite on the extreme N. E. point, and receive several streams in their course. Jefferson, the p-t. lies near the middle of the S. W. boundary. There are 2 churches, one in the N. and the other in the S. part of the t-ship. The p-o. called after the t-ship, is 89 ms. from W. C. and 38 from Harrisburg.

Codorus, large creek of York co. whose branches drain the whole of the S. W. portion of the co. The west, south and east branches unite on the N. E. boundary of Codorus t-ship, and the main stream flows thence N. E. through the borough of York, with a course of about 15 ms. to the Susquehannah r. forming the line between Manchester and Hellam t-ships. This creek is very rapid and subject to great freshets, which have at times done great injury to the improvements along the banks. A slack-water navigation has lately been made upon it from the borough to the river, a distance of 11 ms. of which 8 consist of artificial pools and 3 of canal. There are nine locks, and the work is said to be executed in the most approved and substantial manner. There are mills at almost every mile upon the main stream and its chief tributaries.

Coffee run, p-o. Huntingdon co. 141 ms. N. W. of W. C. 89 S. W. of Harrisburg.

Coffee creek, p-o. Warren co. 336 ms. N. W. from W. C. and 266 from Harrisburg.

Cohocksink creek, Philadelphia co. rises in Penn t-ship, a little E. of the 3 mile stone on the Ridge road, and flows a S. E. course into the Delaware river below the Kensington bridge over the stream. It is in part the boundary of the incorporated and unincorporated Northern Liberties, and is in part the motive power of the extensive cotton manufactory, known as the globe mill.

Colebrookdale, t-ship, Berks county, bounded on the N. E. by Hereford t-ship, S. E. by Montgomery co. N. W. by District, Pike and Earl t-ships, S. W. by Earl and Douglas; greatest length 5, breadth 3 miles; area 9,600 acres; surface, hilly; soil, loam and gravel, good quality, generally productive; value, from 30 to 60 dollars per acre. Pop. 1810, 792; in 1820, 1046; 1830, 1219; taxables in 1828, 230. The head waters of the Iron Stone creek and of Swamp creek rise in this t-ship. There is a church nearly centrally situated, common to the Presbyterians and Lutherans, near which is a p-o. bearing the name of the t-ship, 163 ms. from W. C. and 72 from Harrisburg. A mine of black lead has been discovered, and a bed of iron ore, said to be of good quality.

Colerain forge, Franklin township, Huntingdon co. 163 ms. N. W. from W. C. and 102 S. W. from Harrisburg.

Colerain, t-ship, Lancaster county, bounded N. by Sadsbury, E. by Upper and Lower Oxford, S. by Little Britain, and W. by Drumore. Centrally distant from the city of Lancaster 17 ms. S. E. Its form is nearly that of an equilateral triangle, the length of whose sides is about 7 miles; area, 47,360 acres. The main branch of the Octarara creek bounds it on the E. and the west branch of that stream on the W.; surface, rolling; soil, gravel and clay. Pop. in 1830, 1202; taxables 209. There are two forges on the N. branch, near its junction with the W. and there are two grist mills and three saw mills in the t-ship. The p-o. called after the t-ship, is 104 ms. N. of W. C. and 61 from Harrisburg.

Colerain, t-ship, Bedford co. bounded N. by Woodberry, E. by Hopewell, Providence and Southampton, S. by Southampton, and W. by Bedford and Cumberland valley; greatest length 21 ms. breadth $4\frac{3}{4}$; area, 47,360 acres; surface, level; soil, limestone. Pop. in 1830, 1170; taxables 200. Tussey's mtn. lies on the E. Evitt's and Dunning's mtn. on the W. The Raystown branch of the Juniata flows eastwardly through the t-ship and receives from the S. Cove creek, and from the N. Tussey's run; the former drains Friend's Cove valley, and the latter Snake Spring valley. The Bedford turnpike road runs near the bank of the river.

Collinsville, p-t. Allegheny t-ship, Huntingdon co. contains 3 or 4 dwellings, a tavern and store. Allegheny furnace is near the town.

Colt's Station, village, centrally situated in Greenfield t-ship, Erie co. 11 ms. E. of Erie, and 287 N. W. from Harrisburg.

Columbia, Columbus. (*See New Columbus, &c.*)

Columbus, t-ship, Warren co. bounded N. by the state of New York, E. by Sugar Grove t-ship, S. by Spring creek t-ship, and W. by Erie co. Centrally distant from the borough of Warren, N. W. 20 ms.; length 12, breadth 8 ms; area, 45,440 acres; surface, undulating; soil, loam and alluvion. Pop. in 1830, 552; taxables in 1828, 98. The Big Broken Straw creek runs through the t-ship, southwardly, near the west boundary, and the Little Broken Straw near the E. boundary. The soil is of good quality, heavily timbered, and where cleared productive.

Columbia, Glass Manufactory, on the right bank of the Delaware river, in Upper Smithfield t-ship, 12 ms. above Milford. A bridge is thrown across the Delaware here, by a company incorporated, under an act of assembly 19th March, 1816. It is 720 feet long, 30 feet wide, and cost twelve thousand four hundred dollars.

Columbia, p-t. and borough of W. Hempfield t-ship, Lancaster co. 11 ms. S. W. from the city of Lancaster, 75 ms. W. from Philadelphia, 28 ms. S. E. from Harrisburg, and 99 N. from W. C. on the E. bank of the Susquehannah r. and on the southern turnpike road from Philadelphia to Pittsburg. This place was settled in 1726 or 7, by Robert Barber, Samuel Blunston, and John Wright, Quakers, from Chester co. the descendants of whom still reside in the vicinity. In and near the town many Irish and Germans afterwards established themselves. The town was incorporated by act of 25th Feb. 1814. Much of the trade of the Susquehannah river centered here, and in future it will necessarily engross a greater portion, since the state canal on the Susquehannah commences here, and also the rail road connecting that river with the Delaware at Philadelphia. A fine bridge was erected over the river here in 1814, by an incorporated joint stock company, in which the state took stock to the amount of $90,000 dollars. The bridge was 5690 feet long and 30 feet wide, and consisted of 53 arches elevated 23 feet above the ordinary level of the water, and cost $231,771. The whole capital of the company was $419,400; the balance is employed in banking, the company having banking privileges by their charter. This structure was greatly injured by the freshet of February, 1832, in which the ice of the river was piled even upon the roof of the bridge, and nearly one half of the structure was swept away by the flood. It is now about to be rebuilt, to which purpose the state has liberally contributed.

The public buildings of the town consist of a town hall, of brick, two stories high, built in 1828, in which is a town clock, market house in rear of town hall, Friends' meeting house, Roman Catholic chapel, Presbyterian church, Methodist Episcopal church, German church, and 2 houses of worship for colored people. There are a post office, bank, library, and beneficial associations, 6 day schools, 2 fire companies, 2 volunteer companies, and a weekly newspaper, called "The Spy."

There are here 7 or 8 large warehouses on the banks of the river, for the reception of country produce. Excellent spring water is introduced through all the principal streets, by iron pipes, from the reservoir situated at the head of the town. This reservoir is supplied by pipes from two springs about a mile distant. Within the borough are mineral springs which are said to possess valuable medical qualities. A daily line of stages runs through the town, between Baltimore and Philadelphia, and another from the borough to Harrisburg. It contained by the census of 1830, 2046 inhabitants, and about 400 houses.

Columbia, t-ship, Bradford co. bounded N. by Wells, E. by Springfield, S. by Troy, t-ships, and W. by Tioga co. Centrally distant from Towanda 20 ms. N. W.; greatest lenght $7\frac{1}{2}$, breadth 6 ms.; area, 28,800 acres; surface, hilly; soil, loam. Pop. in 1830, 1235; taxables, 198. The t-ship is drained S. E. by the main branch of Sugar creek. Columbia Cross roads p-o. centrally situated in the t-ship, is 254 ms. N. W. of W. C. and 148 from Harrisburg.

Columbus, New, p-t. of Huntingdon t-ship, Luzerne co. on the turnpike road from Berwick to Tioga, 206 ms. N. W. of W. C. and 92 from Harrisburg.

Columbia, p-t. of Fallowfield t-ship, Washington co. on the W. bank of the Monongahela r. 16 ms. E. of the borough of Washington.

Columbia county, was taken from Northumberland at the same time with Union, 22d March, 1813. The inhabitants were authorized to exercise the usual county powers, and to enjoy county privileges from the 1st Monday in September, 1813. By the act of 22d January, 1816, part of the town ships, Chilisquaque and Turbit, in Northumberland county, were annexed to Columbia; and by act of 3d March, 1818 part of Columbia county was annexed to Schuylkill county. This county is now bounded N. by Lycoming, E. by Luzerne, S. E. by Schuylkill and S. W. and W. by Northumberland; length 25, breadth 23 ms. Area, 574 sq.ms.; central lat. 41° N. long. from W. C. 0° 30′ E.

Columbia county is spread over the Appalachian system, & pertains to the great transition formation of the northern continent, and like most parts of that formation in Pennsylvania it abounds with mineral wealth. The anthracite fields extend from Schuylkill and Luzerne counties into the town ships on the E. of the Susquehannah, and iron ore of excellent quality is found in all parts of the county. The surface of the county is very unequal and much diversified by mountain, hill, and valley, and the alluvial bottoms of the Susquehannah r. Viewing the county from E. to W. we observe Little mtn. Roaring creek and Catawissa valleys, Bucks mtn. Middle Hill, Long mtn. and Catawissa mtn. and the Susquehannah r. · Crossing the river we have in the northern part of the county, Knob mtn. North mtn. a continuance of Bowman's, the Bald mtn. and the Muncy hills; and in the southern part of the county are Limestone, Mahoney and other ridges.

The Susquehannah river divides the county into two unequal parts, and receives from it the Catawissa and Roaring creeks, and from the west, Fishing creek and Mahoning creek. The Chilisquaque creek which drains the western part of the county, flows S. W. into the W. branch of the Susquehannah. The state canal follows the N. branch of the r. through its course in the county. There is a bridge across the river at Berwick. (*See Berwick.*)

The principal towns are Danville, Catawissa, Mifflinsburg and Berwick, on the margin of the river, Bloomsburg, Jerseytown, Washington, Williamsburg, Orangeville and Espytown. The only turnpike roads in the county are that known as the Susquehannah and Tioga, which commencing at Berwick, runs through an eastern angle of the county, and that along the W. bank of the river from Northumberland to Danville.

The population of the county consists chiefly of Germans and their descendants. In 1820 it amounted to 17,621, and in 1830, 20,049, of whom 10,287 were white males, 9,644 white females,, 53 free colored males, 45 free colored females, 237 aliens, 8 deaf and dumb, and 6 blind.

The public buildings of the county are the court house, county offices, of brick, prison, of stone, and an academy. The institution for which the latter was built, was incorporated by the legislature in 1818, and is located at Danville. Twenty-two places of worship, of which 5 pertain to Presbyterians, 7 to the Lutheran and German reformed societies, and 10 to Methodists. There are established in the county, Bible and Missionary societies and Sunday schools, where circumstances permit. Luzerne and Columbia form the 10th senatorial district, sending one member to the senate, and Columbia of itself sends one member to the house of representatives. Connected with Union, Northumberland, Luzerne, Susquehannah, Bradford, Lycoming, Potter, and McKean, it forms the 9th congressional district, returning three members to congress. United with Northumberland, Lycoming and Union, it forms the 8th judicial district; Seth Chapman, Esq. president. The courts are holden at Danville on the first Mondays of January, April, August, and November, annually. This county belongs to the middle district of the supreme court, a session of which is holden annually at Sunbury, in the month of June.

The exports of the county are estimated at 120,000 bushels of wheat, 4,000 bushels clover seed, 3,000 barrels of whiskey, 300 tons of pork, and a small amount of lumber, some live stock, and some iron castings.

There are in the County 33 grist-mills, 60 saw-mills, 4 fulling-mills, and 2 oil-mills, 2 furnaces and 2 forges in Catawissa t-ship, and 2 iron foundries, one at Danville, and the other near Berwick, at which very neat castings are made. The rail-road from Pottsville to Danville now being made, will give increased facilities to the trade of this county, and will render Danville, the county town, the depot for much of the produce which descends the river. There are 3 newspapers published in the county, viz.: the Danville Intelligencer, Columbia County Register, and the Berwick Gazette. Improved lands are sold at from 20 to 40 dollars the acre, and unimproved from 25 cents to 8 dollars.

The value of taxable property by the assessment of 1829, amounted to $2,800,000; the amount of tax raised on personal estate, $700, and the rate of levy on both was 25 cents in the hundred dollars.

This county paid to the state treasury in 1831 for tax or writs, $22,331

in 1831 for tax or writs,	$22,331
Tavern licenses,	57,144
Duties on dealers in foreign merchandise,	30,031
State maps,	3,395
Collateral inheritances,	633
Tin and clock pedlars licenses,	10,071
Total,	$130,634

STATISTICAL TABLE OF COLUMBIA COUNTY.

Townships, &c.	Greatest Lth.	Greatest Bth.	Area in Acres.	Face of Country.	Soil.	Population. 1820.	Population. 1830.	Taxables.
Greenwood,	11	8	30,720	Part chiefly hilly, part level.	Clay, loam.	1078	1110	208
Madison,	8	5	16,000	Do.	Do.	1330	1554	248
Hemlock,	9½	6	29,440	Do.	Do.	1464	1681	303
Bloom,	6¼	6¼	16,640	Chiefly level.	Loam, lime.	1626	2081	414
Briar creek,	7½	6	26,880	Do.	Do.	1719	1706	347
Liberty,	8	4½	18,560	Chiefly level.	Clay.	1146	1111	230
Sugarloaf,	9½	8	36,480	Hilly.	Sand, gravel.	505	678	127
Mount Pleasant,	6	4½	12,880	Do.	Do.	673	715	134
Mifflin,	9	9	37,120	Do.	Do.	1492	1791	335
Limestone,	10	6	18,560	Level.	Limestone.	426	540	100
Derry,	11	5½	17,920	Do.	Clay, lime.	1662	1688	347
Catawissa,	13¼	11	67,200	Hilly.	Clay, gravel.	2520	3130	561
Mahoning,	7	4	13,440	Mountainous.	Do.	1478	1796	358
Fishing Creek,	7¾	5½	19,200	Do.	Do.	502	568	102
						17,621	20,049	3521

Compasstown, a small hamlet of Birmingham t-ship, Delaware co. on the Brandywine r. near Chads ford, 12 ms. N. W. of Chester.

Concord, t-ship, Delaware county, bounded N. by Thornbury, E. by Aston, S. by Bethel and W. by Birmingham; centrally distant from Philad. 20 ms. W.; greatest lgth. 4¾, brdth. 3 miles; area, about 8000 acres; surface, hilly; soil, loam. Pop. in 1830, 1002; taxables in 1828, 203. It is watered by Painter's creek, a branch of Chester creek, a mill stream studded with mills. A Quaker meeting-house and an Episcopal church stand within two miles of each other, on opposite sides of the road, leading to Chads ford on the Brandywine river. There is a post office near the former.

Concord meeting-house, p-o. Concord t-ship, Delaware co. 122 ms. from W. C. 82 from Harrisburg.

Concord, p-v. Path valley, Fannet t-ship, Franklin co. upon the Tuscarora creek, 120 ms. from W. C. 54 from Harrisburg.

Concord, t-ship, Erie co. bounded N. by New-York, E. by Warren co. S. by Wayne t-ship, and W. by Amity t-ship; greatest length 7, breadth 5 miles; area, 22,400 acres. Pop. in 1830, 225; taxables, 45; surface, hilly; soil, gravelly loam, adapted to grazing; drained W. by a tributary of the S. branch of French creek, and E. by Frampton's branch of Broken Straw creek.

Conedogwinit creek, rises in Franklin co. and flows thence by a N. E. course between the north and south mountains into, and through Cumberland co. passing about 1 mile N. of Carlisle, and falls into the Susquehannah 2 ms. above Harrisburg, having a comparative course of near 50 miles, but as it is very serpentine it is much longer, following the meanders of the stream.

Conecocheague creek, Franklin co. rises by two branches, one heading on the boundary between Perry and Franklin counties, and between the North and Tuscarora mtns. and the other near Chambersburg, interlocking with the sources of the Conedogwinit: the two branches flowing to the south, unite between Greencastle and Mercersburg, and entering Maryland, fall into the Potomac at Williamsport. This stream from Chambersburg to its mouth, almost everywhere separates the limestone and slate ranges.

Conecocheague hill, Tobyne t-ship, Perry co., the range next S. of the Tuscarora mtn. It runs about 18 miles.

Conemaugh, t-ship, Somerset co. bounded N. and N. E. by Cambria co. E. by Shade t-ship, S. by Jenner t-ship and W. by Westmoreland co.; centrally distant N. of Somerset borough about 17 miles; greatest length 9 miles, breadth 4; area 16,360 acres; surface, hilly; soil, light clay. Pop. in 1830, 767; taxables, 130; taxable property in 1829, real estate, $56,496; personal, including occupations, 5848; rate of tax 5 mills on the dollar. The post office is called after the t-ship, and is 165 ms. N. W. from W. C. and 143 from Harrisburg. Stoney creek bounds it on the E. and N. E. and receives from the t-ship at the N. E. angle, Ben's creek. Mary Ann forge lies on Stoney creek, in the S. E. angle of the t-ship, opposite to the mouth of Shade creek, and near it is a post office. Bituminous coal is found on Oldman's run, a tributary of Stoney creek.

Conemaugh, t-ship, Indiana county, bounded N. E. by Armstrong t-ship, E. by Black Lick t-ship, S. and S. W. by the Conemaugh river, and W. by Armstrong co.; centrally distant 13 miles S. W. of Indiana borough; greatest length 10, breadth 9 miles; area 23,680 acres; surface, hilly; soil, rich loam. Pop. in 1830, 2104; taxables, 473. It is drained by Blacklegs creek and some smaller streams. Salt springs are found on the bank of the river near Saltzburg, a post town of the t-ship, where extensive and very productive salt works are erected.

Conemaugh river, is formed by the union of the Little Conemaugh creek, with Stoney creek, in Conemaugh t-ship, Cambria co. at the village of Johnstown. The river runs N. W. under this name, about 50 miles, forming the boundary between Westmoreland and Indiana counties, when it receives below Saltzburg, the Loyalhanna river. Thence it assumes the name of the Kiskiminitas river, and flows about 26 miles still N. W. into the Allegheny river, about 24 miles above Pittsburgh. This stream forms an important link in the chain of canals in Pennsylvania. The rail-road portage across the Allegheny mountain ends at Johnstown, at the head of the Conemaugh, and the canal is resumed, and continues along this and the Kiskiminitas and Allegheny rivers to Pittsburg.

Conemaugh, Little, creek, rises in Cambria co. by two forks, and unites as above stated, with Stoney creek at Johnstown. (See Stoney creek).

Conemaugh, t-ship, Cambria co., bounded N. by Summerhill t-ship, E. by the Allegheny mountain, which separates it from Bedford co., W. by the Laurel hill, which divides it from Westmoreland co. and S. by Somerset co.; centrally distant S. W. from Ebensburg 15 miles; greatest length 21, breadth, 15 miles; surface, hilly; soil, clay and limestone. Pop. in 1830, 2088; taxables 326; taxable property in 1829, seated lands, &c. $5888, unseated, $18,101. Little Conemaugh from the N. E. and Stoney creek from the S. E. unite in the west part of the t-ship, at Johnstown, to form the Conemaugh river. The great rail road portage across the Allegheny mountain ends here, and the transportation by water is resumed; the canal following the north bank of the Conemaugh river.

Conemaugh, t., Conemaugh t-ship, Cambria co. (See Johnstown).

Conestoga, t-ship, Lancaster co. bounded N. by Lancaster t-ship, N. E. by Lampiter, S. E. by Martick, S. W. by the Susquehannah river, W. by Manor; centrally distant from Lancaster 5 miles S.; greatest length 7, breadth, $4\frac{3}{4}$ miles; area, 17,920 acres; surface, rolling; soil, clay and gravel, of excellent quality, and well cultivated. Pop. in 1830, 2120; taxables, 436. The Conestoga creek flows along the W. boundary, and the Pequa creek along the E. Upon both there are several mills. Willow Street is a hamlet near the N. W. boundary, and Safe Harbor another at the confluence of the Conestoga creek with the Susquehannah. The post office, called after the township, is 107 miles from W. C. and 43 from Harrisburg.

Conestoga river, Lancaster co., has its sources in Caernarvon t-ship, and flowing westerly, receives the Cocalico creek at the junction of Warwick, Earl, Laycock and Manheim t-ships; thence flowing south-westerly it passes the city of Lancaster and falls into the Susquehannah about 10 miles below Columbia. It is a beautiful and powerful stream, and drains one of the best cultivated and most productive tracts in the United States. A slack water navigation has been made from Reigart's landing, within the bounds of the city of Lancaster, to Safe Harbor on the Susquehannah, a distance of 18 miles, by nine dams and locks; the pools varying in length from one to three miles, and preserving a breadth of from 250 to 350 feet, with a depth in the channel of never less than four feet, forming beautiful sheets of water. The towing path is on the left bank of the river. The locks are 100 feet by 22, sufficiently large for arks or boats 90 feet in length, and for rafts of timber, or boards of the same size. The lifts vary from 7 to 9 feet. This valuable work has been executed at an expense of about $4000 per mile, by a private company, who have obtained at each dam a water power highly valuable to themselves and to the city and vicinity of Lancaster. When the navigation of the Susquehannah below the mouth of the Conestoga shall be improved, that city will have many of the advantages of a port. The canal serves at present to transport many articles of commerce to and from the river Susquehannah in vessels of from 60 to 100 tons burden. There is a fine stone bridge over this stream on the Lancaster turnpike road, built by Mr. Whitmor, at his private expense, under authority obtained from the state, for which he was remunerated by the tolls.

Conestoga creek, Little, Lancaster co. rises in Warwick t-ship, and flows sthwrdly by a serpentine course of about 15 ms. into the Conestoga river at the foot of Turkey hill, receiving in its course several streams, among which the west branch is the most considerable. It is a fine stream and has many mills upon it.

Conequenessing creek, rises by two branches in the N. E. and S. E. parts of Butler co. which uniting in Butler t-ship, form the main E. branch of Big Beaver river, into which it flows by a W. and N. W. course, through Butler and Beaver counties, joining its recipient, in North Sewickly t-ship, of the latter co. Its whole length by comparative courses may be about 40 miles. Its principal tributaries from the S. are Brush creek, Break Neck creek, and Glade run; from the north, Little Conequenessing, Yellow, and Slippery Rock creeks.

Conequenessing, t-ship, Butler co. bounded N. by Muddy Creek t-ship, E. by Butler t-ship, S. by Cranberry and W. by Beaver co. centrally distant W. from Butler borough 10 miles. The t-ship is 8 miles square; area 40,960 acres; surface rolling; soil loam, clay, and gravel; pop. in 1830, 1944; taxables 358. It is watered by the Conequenessing, and Little Conequenessing, Break Neck, and Yellow creeks. The p-t. of Harmony, lies in the W. part of the t-ship, on the S. bank of the Conequenessing creek, and within a mile of it, lower down the stream, is the village Zelienople. Harmony was built by the association of the Harmonites, now settled at Economy, in Beaver co. Portersville, another p-t., and Prospect, a village, are also within the t-ship. There are extensive bottoms, upon the Conequenessing cr. whose soil is of rich loam, and sand, easily tilled, and produces abundantly, wheat, and corn. The following statistical account of this t-ship, is a model for a statistical table which we should like to possess of every t-ship, in the state. Taxable value $191,755. The pop. consists of 115 native Germans, 849 German descendants; 454 native Irish, 454 Irish descendants; 25 native Scotch; 140 Scotch descendants; English natives 23, English descendants 129; descendants of Low Dutch 19, of Swedes 8, Welsh 17. Professors of religion 643, viz. Lutherans 197, Menonists 99, Presbyterians 91, Associate Reformed 90, German Reformed 77, Covenanters 25, Seceders 18, Methodists 18, Baptists 10, Catholics 10, Quakers 7. Such as are 16 years old and upwards, who have not made profession of religion, 300, number of families destitute of Bibles, 31, persons of 15 years old and upwards who cannot read, 60; number of gallons whiskey consumed in 1831, 3044, distilled 7850, number of coal banks known, 60, schools during winter 9, churches and meeting houses, 7.

Conewago, t-ship, York co. bounded N. by Newberry, S. E. by Manchester, S. W. by Dover, and W. by Warrington t-ships; centrally distant from the borough of York, about 7 miles, N. W. greatest length $7\frac{1}{2}$, breadth 6 miles; area, 16,000 acres; surface hilly; soil red shale, of good quality. Pop. in 1830, 1094; taxables 231; taxable property, real estate, $162,472; personal estate 9165, occupations 14,100, rate 25 cts. on the $100. The Conewago Hills cross it on the N. W. The Great Conewago creek flows along the N. boundary and the Little Conewago creek on the E. uniting in the N. E. Strimestown, a small hamlet, lies near the N. line.

Conewago, t-ship, Adams co. bounded on the N. by Berwick t-ship, E. by York co. S. by Germany t-ship, and W. by Mount Joy t-ship; centrally distant from Gettysburg S. E. 10 miles; greatest length $7\frac{3}{4}$, breadth $3\frac{1}{2}$ miles; area 8,320 acres; surface level; soil, limestone. Pop. in 1830, 878; taxables 198. The Conewago creek crosses the t-ship, and flows northwardly along its W. boundary, receiving Plumb creek from it.

Conewago hills, a prominent chain which rises in York co. through which it runs to the Susquehannah and thence about 35 miles N. E. on the boundary line between Lancaster and Dauphin and Lebanon counties. This is a portion of the chain known as the South mountain.

Conewago creek, one stream thus called rises in Lebanon co. and flows S. W. along the N. base of the Conewago hills to the Susquehannah r. at the village of Falmouth, forming the boundary between Lancaster and Dauphin counties, having a course of more than 20 miles.

Conewago creek, a much larger stream than the preceding, which rises in the S. E. angle of Adams co. thence running N. and N. E. enters York co. on the line between Paradise and Washington t-ships, and thence by a meandering course to the Susquehannah river, into which it flows, about 5 miles below that town. It receives the Little Conewago creek, which rises and has its whole course in York co.

Conewango, t-ship, Warren co. bounded N. by Pine Grove t-ship, E. by Elk t-ship, S. by the Allegheny r. and W. by Broken Straw t-ship. Length 7, breadth $6\frac{1}{2}$ miles; area 20,480 acres; surface somewhat hilly along the river, but undulating two or three miles from it; soil on the river bottoms deep alluvion, and fertile loam in the interior; pop. in 1830, 837; taxables in 1828, 210. The Conewago creek runs N. and S. through it, and divides it into two unequal portions. At its confluence with the river, lies the borough, post and county town of Warren. Jackson's run is a tributary of the creek.

Conewango, p-o. Warren co. 320 miles N. W. of W. C. and 266 from Harrisburg.

Conewango creek, flows into Warren co. from the state of New York 12 miles N. of, and empties into, the Allegheny river. This is a large and navigable stream. From Russell's mills (five miles) to the New York state line, it is a deep sluggish stream and and will admit of steamboat navigation at all times, when not frozen, and possesses the same character for 30 miles above. From Russell's mills to Warren, 7 miles, it is more rapid, the fall being 60 feet. But loaded keel boats &c. ascend in a good state of the water without difficulty. There are four double, and two single saw mills, upon these rapids.

Conewanta creek, Harmony t-ship, Susquehannah co. rises in Jackson t-ship and flows through the former into the Susquehannah river, at the easternmost point of the great bend around the Oquago mountain. It is a mill stream, rapid and unnavigable.

Conewingo creek, rises in Lancaster co. and flows S. E. through Little Britain t-ship, and the state of Maryland, into the Susquehannah river. It is a mill stream with a course of about 12 miles.

Coney creek, Donegal t-ship, Lancaster co. a small stream which flows from the Conewago hills by a course of about 6 miles into the river Susquehannah. It has several mills on it.

Conneaut, t-ship, Crawford co. so named from the lake which is near it. Centrally distant about 12 ms. W. of Meadville; surface, rolling; soil, gravelly. Pop. in 1830, 547. The state canal will pass through this t-ship.

Conneaut lake, Sadsbury township, Crawford co. a beautiful sheet of water, having an area of 4 ms. by 2, abounding with fish. It forms a link in the water communication between the Allegheny r. and lake Erie.

Conneautte, t-ship, Erie co. bounded N. by McKean t-ship, E. by Waterford and Le Boeuf t-ships, S. by Crawford co. and W. by Elk Creek t-ship. Centrally distant S. from Erie borough 15 miles; greatest length and breadth 7; area, 31,360 acres; surface, hilly; soil, gravel and loam. Pop. in 1830, 743; taxables, 132. Conneautte lake, from which the t-ship has its name, lies a little S. E. of the centre of the t-ship. The Conneautte creek, which rises near the N. line of the t-ship, in McKean t-ship, flows S. E. into the lake, and issuing from it on the S. flows thence about 6 ms. into French cr. in Crawford co. Another creek also rising in McKean t-ship flows S. E. through this t-ship, and unites with Conneautte cr. below the S. boundary.

Conneautte lake and creek. (See preceding article.)

Conneaut, town, is a small town of Crawford co. upon the S. side of Conneaut lake, on the road leading to Meadville, 8 ms. N. W. containing some 10 or 15 dwellings, a store and tavern.

Conneautville, p-t. of Beaver t-ship, Crawford co. on Conneaut creek, 14 ms. N. W. of Meadville, 313 from W. C. and 252 from Harrisburg; contains several dwellings, a store, tavern and mill. The proposed canal to Erie will pass near the town.

Conneaut, t-ship, Erie co. bounded N. by Springfield t-ship, E. by Elk Creek t-ship, S. by Crawford co. and W. by the state of Ohio. Centrally distant from the borough of Erie S. W. 23 miles; greatest length $8\frac{1}{2}$, breadth 6 miles; area 32,640 acres; surface, hilly; soil, gravel and loam. Pop. in 1830, 1324; taxables, 214. The t-ship takes its name from the Conneaut creek, which, rising near Harminsville, runs N. to the vicinity of Lexington, a village of this t-ship, and thence W. and N. through the state of Ohio, to lake Erie. The proposed route of the state canal is along this creek, and by Lexington to Erie borough. Lexington, which lies near the N. line of the t-ship, is the p-t.

Connellsville, t-ship, and borough, Fayette co. bounded N. by Tyrone and Bullskin t-ship, E. by Salt Lick, S. by Wharton and W. by Dunbar t-ships. Centrally distant from Uniontown N. E. 12 ms. greatest length 6 ms. breadth 4 miles; area, 8960 acres; surface hilly; soil, limestone, and loam; coal abundant; pop. in 1830, 1205; taxables 220. The Chestnut Ridge covers the E. part, and the Youghiogheny river flows on the S. and W. boundary. On this river lies the town of Connellsville, 12 miles N. E. from Union 31 W. of Somerset, and 45 S. E. from Pittsburg. The t-ship is drained by the river and by Mount's creek, which flows into it a short distance above the town. The town was incorporated into a borough by act 1st March, 1806, and contains from 100 to 120 dwellings, 2 churches, 3 schools, 9 stores, 5 taverns, 2 grist mills and 1 saw mill, driven by water and one air foundry.

Conoloway creek, *Great and Little*. The first rises in Bethel t-ship, Bedford co. in the Raystown hills, and flows S. E. into the Potomac r. passing the t. of Werefordsburg. It receives from Bethel t-ship Five Lick run, Pigeon Cove creek, and the North Branch, which flows S. from Belfast t-ship. The Little Conoloway rises in Sideling Hill, near the S. boundary of the state, in which it has but a short portion of its course, and flows into the same recipient.

Conshehoken. a newly created village of Plymouth t-ship, Montgomery co. on the left bank of the Schuylkill r. on the canal formed by the Schuylkill navigation co. 12 ms. from Phila. and 4 from Norristown. The water power acquired by the dam has caused the birth of this new manufacturing t. It now contains 6 dwellings, 1 store, 1 tavern, a rolling mill and a grist mill, with the most favorable prospects of rapid increase.

Conynham, a village and p-t. of Sugarloaf t-ship, Luzerne co. situate on the Nescopeck valley, upon the turnpike road leading to Berwick, 12 ms. from the latter place, 18 from Lausanne, on the Lehigh r. and about 20 ms. by the road from Wilkesbarre, 206 ms. N. from W. C. and 96 from Harrisburg. It is built upon one sheet at the foot of the Buck mtn. and upon the Little Nescopeck creek. It contains about 50 dwellings, several stores and taverns.

Cook's island, in the N. branch of the Susquehannah r. opposite Lodge's run and about 3 ms. above Northumberland borough.

Cookstown, Washington t-ship, Fayette co. at the confluence of Cook's run with the Monongahela r. 16 ms. N. W. of Uniontown, 214 from W. C. and 191 S. W. from Harrisburg, contains about 115 dwellings, 2 churches, 3 schools, 5 stores, 2 taverns, 1 steamboat yard, and 600 inhabitants.

Coolbaugh's post office, Wayne co. 228 ms. N. E. from W. C. 133 from Harrisburg.

Cool Spring, town, Mercer county, bounded N. by Sandy creek, E. by Sandy Lake t-ship, S. by Springfield t-ship, and W. by Delaware t-ship. Centrally distant N. E. from Mercer borough 6 ms. The t-ship is an oblong of 8 by 6 ms. area 30,720 acres; surface, level; soil, limestone. It is drained S. by Cool Spring creek and Otter creek, branches of the Neshanock. The turnpike road from Mercer to Meadville runs N. through the t-ship. Pop. in 1830, 1099; taxables 178; taxable property in 1829, real est. $70,219; personal $14,904; rate of tax 5 mills on the dollar.

Cooper, town, McKean co. bounded N. by Sergeant t-ship, E. by Shippen, S. by Burlington t-ship, W. by Jefferson co. Centrally distant from Smithport 16 ms; greatest length 13, breadth 8 ms.; area 66,560 acres; surface, hilly; soil, gravel and loam.

Cooperstown, a small village of Plumb t-ship, Venango co. 10 ms. N. of the borough of Franklin, contains some 4 or 5 dwellings, a store, tavern and mill.

Coply creek, Lehigh county, rises in

North White Hall t-ship, and running S. easterly falls into the Lehigh river, about 5 miles above the borough of Northampton. It turns several mills, but is unnavigable and fails much in dry seasons.

Corkin's creek, a considerable mill stream of Damascus t-ship, Wayne co. which flows into the Delaware r. about 4 ms. below Casherton falls.

Corner Ketch, a small hamlet in the N. angle of Bethel t-ship, Delaware co. on the road from Chester to Chad's ford, about 7 ms. N. W. of the former, contains 4 dwellings, a smith shop and a store.

Coventry, t-ship, Chester co. bounded N. E. by Montgomery co. S. E. by Vincent t-ship, S. W. by East Nantmeal t-ship, and N. W. by Berks co. Central distance N. W. from Phil. 30 miles; from West Chester N. 15 miles; length 7½, breadth 6 miles; area, 22,300 acres; surface hilly; soil, sandy loam. Pop. in 1830, 2131; taxables 394, in 1828. French creek crosses the S. W. angle, and Pigeon creek flows centrally through the t-ship to the river Schuylkill, which courses the eastern boundary. On all these there are mills; Pughtown, the post town, lies in the extremity of the S. W. angle. There are not less than 5 churches, four of which are in the opposite angles of a quadrangle, and the 5th at the intersection of the diagonal lines. The Schuylkill canal runs along the E. line of the t-ship.

Covington, p-t. and borough of Covington t-ship, Tioga co. on the right bank of Tioga river, and on the E. and W. state road, contains about 30 dwellings. It was incorporated into a borough by act 21st March 1831. It is 241 miles from W. C. 135 from Harrisburg.

Covington, t-ship, Clearfield co. bounded N. by Gibson t-ship, E. by Lycoming and Centre counties, S. by the W. branch of the Susquehannah river which separates it from Bradford t-ship, and W. from Lawrence t-ship. Centrally distant from Clearfield borough N. E. 16 miles; greatest length 15, breadth 13 miles; surface hilly; soil, slate, loam and gravel. Pop. in 1830, 250; taxables 47. It is drained by Philipin or Deer run, Sandy run, Little Mushanon creek, and other streams which flow S. E. into the Susquehannah river. The post town of Karthaus is in the E. part of the t-ship, on the river, at which there are some iron works.

Covington, t-ship, Tioga co. bounded N. by Tioga and Jackson t-ships, E. by Sullivan t-ship, S. by Lycoming co. and W. by land now or formerly Delmar t-ship. Centrally distant S. W. of Wellsborough 15 miles. It forms an oblong of 22 by 8 miles, comprising 112,640 acres. The Tioga river enters the t-ship from Sullivan on the E. and flows N. centrally through it for about two thirds of its length, receiving several tributaries on either hand. The surface is somewhat hilly and rugged, particularly along the river; the soil is gravel, loam and clay, well timbered, and much lumber is sent to market by the river. Coal, and iron ore abound. There is a small village in the t-ship, on the E. and W. state road, and on the right bank of the river, called Covington four corners, near which is a post office, 13 miles E. of Wellsborough, 241 from W. C. and 135 from Harrisburg. Pop. in 1830, 361; taxables 67.

Covington, t-ship, Luzerne co. (so named in honor of Brigadier Gen. Covington, of the army of the United States, who fell in the battle of Williamsburg, in U. C. during the late war,) is bounded E. by Wayne co. S. E. and S. by the Lehigh river, S. W. by Wilkesbarre t-ship, and N. W. by Pittston, Providence and Blakely t-ships. Its greatest length is about 23 miles, greatest breadth about 9 miles; area 105,600 acres.

There is a thriving settlement in its northern division, upon the lands of Henry W. Drinker, Esq. The experiment of keeping sheep upon the wild and uncultivated mountains and highlands, in this and Wilkesbarre t-ships, during the spring and summer months, has been tried for several successive years. The result has proved most favorable. The Philadelphia and Great Bend turnpike, passes through its northern division, and the Easton, and Wilkesbarre turnpike and a great stage road, through its southern. Stoddartsville, at the great falls of the Lehigh, was a few years since a very flourishing village. It has felt the pressure of the times and is now going to decay. This is the extreme point to which the Lehigh coal and Navigation company are authorized to extend their improvements in the navigation of that river. The contemplated canal or rail road from the mouth of the Lackawannock, to the water Gap upon the Dalaware, must pass through this t-ship. Its streams afford abundant and never failing mill power, and its forest the choicest of timber. The pop. of the t-ship, in 1830, was about 550, taxables in 1828, 106.

Covington, New, p-o. Luzerne co. 241 miles from W. C. and 144 from Harrisburg.

Cove mountain, Rye t-ship, Perry co. This mountain forms an irregular semi-ellipsis on the Susquehannah river.

Cove mountain, a part of the chain of the Blue mountain separating the S. W. boundary of Franklin co. from Bedford, part of the chain S. of the Tuscarora mountain.

Cove creek, Big, rises in Dublin t-ship, Bedford co. and flows S. by McConnellstown, W. of Cove mountain about 12 miles to Licking creek.

Cove creek, Little, in Franklin co. rises on the E. side of Cove mountain, and flows S. through Warren t-ship, to Licking creek.

Cove creek, Coleraine t-ship, Bedford co. runs N. through Friends Cove valley into the Raystown branch of the Juniata river. It is a rapid mill stream.

Cowanshannock creek, Armstrong co. rises on the W. border of Indiana co. and flows W. and N. W. through Wayne and Kittanning t-ships into the Allegheny river, about 3 ms. above the town of Kittanning.

Cowdersport, p-t. and co. t. of Potter co. on the fork of the Allegheny r. a few miles from its source. The town plot consists of 90 acres, two thirds of which are in town lots, and two public squares in the town, one for the county buildings and the other for an academy, together with 150 acres of land contiguous to the town, for the use of such academy, they conveyed to the trustees of the county of Potter, and John Keating made a further donation of 500 dollars in money, also for the use of such academy, in consideration whereof, the seat of justice was established by the legislature at this spot. The county not having been yet organized for judicial purposes, the public buildings have not been yet erected in the town, but some four or five years since, legislative provision was made for felling the timber on the public square and other lots. The town now contains some 8 or 10 dwellings, store and tavern. Authority has been obtained for making a turnpike road from Jersey Shore borough, in Lycoming co. to Cowdersport. The town is distant 283 ms. N. W. from W. C. and 174 from Harrisburg.

Cox's creek, Somerset co. rises in Somerset t-ship, and flows by the borough of Somerset, through Milford t-ship to Castleman's river.

Coxtown, a small village, Berks co. containing about 20 houses, 1 tavern and 1 store. Distant from Reading, about 12 miles.

Cox'stown, small village of Susquehannah t-ship, Dauphin co. on the turnpike road 4 ms. N. of Harrisburg, contains some half dozen houses and 2 taverns.

Cox'sville, small hamlet of Buck's co. on the line between Northampton and Warwick t-ships, 7 ms. S. E. of Doylestown; contains 3 or 4 dwellings.

Coylesville, p-t. Butler co. 226 ms. N. W. of W. C. and 194 W. of Harrisburg.

Craig's Meadow, p-o. Northampton

co. 223 ms. N. E. from W. C. and 97 from Harrisburg.

Cranberry run, Sugarloaf t-ship, Luzerne co., a tributary of Black cr., flowing from the S. W. which enters the latter at the foot of Green mtn. and at the head of canoe navigation.

Cranberry, t-ship, Butler co. bounded N. by Conequenessing t-ship, E. by Middlesex, S. by Allegheny co. and W. by Beaver co. Centrally distant distant S. W. from Butler borough, 13 ms. It forms a square of 8 miles; area, 40,960 acres; surface, hilly, or rolling; soil, loam and clay. Pop. in 1830, 1046; taxables, 200. It is watered chiefly by Glade run, Breakneck and Brush creeks. Post office of the t-ship is 244 miles N. W. from W. C. and 213 from Harrisburg. It takes its name from an extensive cranberry swamp.

Cranberry, t-ship, Venango county, bounded N. and W. by the river Allegheny, E. by Pine Grove t-ship, S. by Rockland t-ship; centrally distant E. from Franklin borough, 7 ms.; greatest length 15½ ms.; breadth 8 ms.; area, 33,280 acres; surface, level; soil, gravel. The turnpike road from Bellefonte to Franklin runs N. W. through it. The t-ship is attached to French creek t-ship.

Crawford county, was taken from Allegheny co. by act 12th March, 1800; and by the same act the seat of justice was located at Meadville, on condition that the inhabitants and proprietors of that place and its vicinity should subscribe, and secure the payment of four thousand dollars to the trustees of the county, either in specie or land, at a reasonable valuation, within four months from the passage of the act, for the use of a seminary of learning within the county, and in case of default the trustees were authorized to fix the seat of justice at any place within four miles of Meadville. And by the act of 5th March, 1804, the commissioners were directed to erect the court-house and public offices of the county, upon the public square of the town of Meadville. Crawford county is now bounded on the N. by Erie co., on the E. by Warren and Venango counties, on the S. by Mercer and Venango, and on the W. by the state of Ohio; length 41, breadth 24 miles; area, 974 square miles; central lat. 41° 40′ N.; lon. from W. C. 3° west. It lies wholly in the great western secondary formation, and contains the minerals usually pertaining to it. Iron ore has been found in various parts of the county; salt licks and salt springs in the N. W., and indications of coal are seen in the south; a bituminous oil issues from several sources on Oil creek, known in commerce as Seneca oil; it colours the waters and emits a strong odor, even at the mouth of the creek. The oil is burned in lamps, and used in various ways; but is particularly valued for its bituminous qualities. The inhabitants make excavations in the low and marshy grounds, which are immediately filled with water, covered with oil, which they skim off. Considerable quantities are annually sent to the eastern markets.

The surface of the country is undulating, and the soil generally of a good quality, and there is little or none worthless in the county. It is however better adapted to grazing than grain farms, yet there is an ample portion suited to the latter purpose. It is well watered and timbered, and is particularly favorable to health. The principal stream is French creek, which flows S. and S. E. by the town of Meadville, and unites with the Allegheny river at the town of Franklin, in Venango co. It is a beautiful stream, and navigable for large boats and rafts the greater part of the year. The great system of artificial navigation in Pennsylvania embraces this stream. The canal along it commences at the Allegheny river, at the mouth of the creek, and extends up it 22 miles and 88 perches, to its intersection with the feeder. On this line there are 5 miles and 52 perches of canal and 17 ms. and 36 perches slack water and towing path. The principal works are 11 dams, varying from

7 to 16 ft. in height, and 3 guard and 16 lift locks, which overcome an elevation of 120½ feet. This work is partly executed, and the remainder under contract. Its cost, when completed, is estimated at $270,681. And the canal commissioners report that it may be completed by the middle of Nov. 1832. The French creek feeder commences near Bemis' mill, on the east side of the creek, 2 ms. N. of Meadville, passes through the town and crosses the creek 6 ms. below, and falls into the valley of Conneaut creek, which it pursues to the Conneaut lake. Its length is 19½ ms. It is proposed to connect this creek by means of Conneaut lake and Conneaut creek, with lake Erie. There are two creeks which bear the name of Conneaut; one running S. E. to French creek, the other N. W. to lake Erie. Beside these waters there are in the county, E. of French creek, Oil creek, which runs S. to the Allegheny; Muddy creek, Woodcock creek, Big and Little Sugar creeks, and the Cussawago on the west, tributaries of French creek. The Shenango creek flows along the W. boundary, and drains by one of its branches the extensive Pymatuning swamp. There are also three lakes in the county; the Conneaut, near the summit of the Pennsylvania canal, the Oil Creek and the Sugar Creek lakes. The first is a beautiful sheet of water, about five ms. by two, abounding with fine fish; the others are smaller but equally pleasant. One turnpike road running S. connects Meadville with Mercer, another S. E. leads to the town of Franklin, and a third proceeds N. by Waterford to Erie. The towns are Meadville, Centreville, Conneaut town, Harmonsville, Conniotville and Pottersville. The population of the county, drawn from various sources, amounted in 1800, to 2346; in 1810 to 6176; in 1820, to 9397; and 1830, to 16,005, of whom 8336 were white males, 7634 white females; 21 free col'd males, 14 free col'd. females. There were but 35 aliens in the county, 1 deaf and dumb and 1 blind.

The exports of the county are the usual agricultural products; and being chiefly a grazing country, cattle and horses. Its principal market is Pittsburg, whence is drawn the chief supply of imports. There are about 30 stores, which pay license, and a sufficient number of taverns. The manufactures are strictly domestic, and supply three fourths of the consumption of the county. In 1829, there were 32 grist mills, 65 saw mills, 8 fulling mills, 2 paper mills, 2 oil mills, 5 carding machines, 41 distilleries, and a few asheries. 145,831 lbs. of maple sugar, 177,360 lbs. black salts and potash, and 48,754 galls. whiskey were manufactured. There were 51,522 acres of cleared land, 12,169 of meadow; 2970 horses, 18,081 cattle and 18,999 sheep. These articles, with the exception of sugar, salts and whiskey, have greatly increased since that period. Col. Magaw, the patentee of straw paper, has an extensive manufactory of that cheap and valuable article, at Meadville. The public buildings of the county consist of the court house, a very handsome structure of brick and cut stone, surmounted by a cupola, the county offices and prison, several neat churches, an academy, Bently hall, pertaining to Allegheny college, and the state arsenal. (For a particular description of these, see the article *Meadville.*)

There are in the county about 28 churches for divine worship, for the various denominations of christians, and about 62 schools.

The several societies established in the county, for benevolent and other useful purposes, are a Bible society, the Sabbath School Union, extended generally through the county, and having about 63 schools. A colonization society, auxiliary to the American colonization society. An internal improvement society, an agricultural society, and an emigration society.

The care taken for the academy

was co-existent with the county. It was incorporated by the act 31st March, 1807, and several other acts have been passed for the benefit of the institution; among others, the act of 1811, granting it the sum of $1000. It is well supplied with a competent principal and other respectable teachers. The languages and the various branches of an English education, including Mathematics, Natural Philosophy, Chemistry, &c. and Drawing. There are also other respectable schools. The library of the college is uncommonly extensive and valuable, having been enriched by the bequests of the Rev. Wm. Bently and Judge Winthrop, and by the donation of Isaiah Thomas, Esq. all of Mass. It contains more than 8000 volumes, valued at more than 12,000 dollars. The bench and the bar, and the medical men of the county, are respectable for their virtues and talents.

Crawford belongs to the 23d senatorial district, sending one member to the senate. It sends also one member to the house of representatives. Joined with Erie, Mercer, Warren and Venango, it forms the 18th congressional district, represented in the 22d congress by John Banks. Connected with Venango, Mercer and Erie, it forms the 6th judicial district. President, Henry Shippen, Esq. The courts are holden at Meadville on the 4th Mondays of November, February, May and August. The county belongs to the western district of the supreme court, which holds its session at Pittsburg, on the first Monday in September annually.

The co. paid into the state treasury in 1831, for tax on writs,	$140,00
Tavern licenses,	158,84
Duties on dealers in foreign merchandise,	210,70
Total,	$519,54

Taxable property in 1829, seated lands, 969,204; unseated, $438,766; personal including occupations, $171,-049; rate 5 mills in the dollar; am'nt of tax levied, $7,S20,09½.

The following notice of a curious mound in the county, is taken from the N. Y. Jour. of Commerce, 1830. "On an extensive plain near Oil creek, there is a vast mound of stones, containing many hundred thousand cart loads. This pyramid has stood through so many ages that it is now covered with soil, and from its top rises a noble pine tree, the roots of which running down the sides, fasten themselves in the earth below. The stones are many of them so large, that two men can scarce move them; and are unlike any in the neighborhod; nor are there quarries near, from which so large a quantity could be taken. The stones were, perhaps, collected from the surface, and the mound one of the many that have been raised by the ancient race which preceded the *Indians*, whom the Europeans have known. These monuments are numerous further north and E. and in the S. and W. are far greater, more artificial and imposing."

The intelligent correspondent of the Crawford Messenger, to whom we are indebted for much of the matter of this article, observes, that the county "possesses all the conveniences and comforts of living, that are enjoyed east of the mountains. It is a healthy pleasant country to live in; and capable of producing an abundance of all the productions common to the eastern part of the state; and when the canal from Lake Erie to Philadelphia shall have been completed, they can be placed in the market of that city, at a rate much more profitable to those that produce them, than like products east of the mountains can be so placed—and for the plainest of all reasons, that the lands producing them, can be procured at one fifth the expense of lands of equal quality east of the mountains. Very good unimproved lands may be purchased here at two dollars to four dollars per acre, depending in a great measure, *at present*, on their particular situations—and well improved farms at from 5 dollars to 8 dollars per acre. This country is peculiarly adapted to raising of stock. The numerous droves of fine horses and cattle taken out of it every season, is the best evidence of its fitness for stock; and there is no mode of farming so easy and profitable as that of raising stock, more particularly in a country like this, where grass is produced so abundantly. This section of the state must, at no distant day, become a great *stock country*. Emigration to it, is rapidly increasing.

The following table shows the names and numbers of the t-ships, in this county. Within the last two years there has been an alteration in the form and bounds of most of them, and as we have not their boundaries, we are unable to give their area, &c.

STATISTICAL TABLE OF CRAWFORD COUNTY.

Townships, &c.	Population. 1810	1820	1830	Taxables.
Bor. of Meadville,	457	649	1076	228
Meadville t-ship,	786	1311	1026	338
Randolph,			561	108
Wayne,	502	663	250	177
Oil Creek,	340	495	484	
Troy,			146	
Athens,			121	
Rome,			365	
Sparta,			304	
Richmond,			252	
Bloomfield,	114	214	197	109
Rockdale,	401	776	225	274
Woodcock,			1150	
Venango,	434	630	886	178
Cussawago,	384	642	544	186
Spring,			690	
Beaver,	236	419	185	189
Conneaut,	285	562	547	162
Hayfield,			644	
Vernon,			797	
Sadsbury,	540	789	902	254
North Shenango,	727	952	952	296
South Shenango,			662	
Fallowfield,	551	742	686	222
Greenwood,			876	
Fairfield,	421	553	632	142
Sommerhill,			845	
	6178	9397	16,005	3034

Crook's island, in the N. branch of the Susquehannah r. below the mouth of Gravel run, and about six miles above Northumberland.

Crooked creek, a tributary of the Allegheny r. rises in Green t-ship, Indiana county, and flows W. and N. W. through Armstrong co. into its recipient, 6 miles above Kittanning borough.

Crooked creek, Tioga county, rises near Wellsborough, and flows N. E. into the Tioga river, in Tioga t-ship. It gives name to a p-office, distant 262 miles N. W. from W. C. and 156 from Harrisburg.

Cross Creek, t-ship, Washington co. bounded N. by Hanover, N. E. by Smith, E. by Mount Pleasant, S. by Hopewell t-ships, and W. by the state of Virginia. Centrally distant from the borough of Washington N. W. 15 miles; greatest length 9, breadth 8 miles; area 32,000 acres; surface undulating; soil, loam; coal abundant. Population in 1830, 2147; taxables, 438. Cross creek, which gives name to the t-ship, rises on the borders of Hopewell and Mount Pleasant t-ships, and runs along the S. boundary N. W. to the Ohio river. Harman's creek, on the N. boundary, pursues the same course to the same recipient. The p-town of Eldersville, lies in the N. part of the t-ship.

Cross Creek village, p-o. Washington co. 245 miles from W. C. and 227 from Harrisburg.

Crowner's run, Heidelberg t-ship, Lehigh county, rises about the centre of the t-ship, and flows southwardly, to the Jordan creek, with which it unites, on the line between Lowhill and North Whitehall t-ships.

Crum creek, rises in Willistown t.ship, Chester county, and flows by a S. W. course of about 18 miles, through Delaware county, into the River Delaware. There are many mills on the stream, and it is noted for the abundance of building and curb-stone transported from it, to the city of Philadelphia. There is also some fine sand stone upon it used for whet stones.

Culbertson's, p-o. Mercer county, 283 miles N. W. of W. C. and 265 from Harrisburg, so called after Joseph Culbertson, the Post-master.

Cumberland county. Upon the representation of the inhabitants of the western part of Lancaster co. of the great hardships they laid under, by being at so great a distance from the borough of Lancaster, where the courts of justice were held and the public offices kept; and how hard and difficult it was for the sober and quiet part of the inhabitants of that part of the county to secure themselves against thefts and abuses, frequently committed amongst them by idle and dissolute persons, who resorted to the remote parts of the province, and by reason of the great distance from the court or prison, frequently found means to make their escape. It was provided by the assembly on the 27th January, 1750, for remedy of such inconveniences, and for the relief of such inhabitants, That, all and singular the lands, lying within the province of Pa. to the westward of Susquehannah, and northward and westward of the co. of York, be erected into a co. to be called Cumberland; bounded northward and westward with the line of the province, eastward partly with the r. Susquehannah, and partly with the said co. of York; and southward in part by the said co. of York, and part by the line dividing the said province from that of Maryland. By the same act the new county was authorized to send two representatives to the assembly.

These ample limits were reduced, 1st, by the erection of the co. of Bedford, March 9, 1771; 2d, of Northumberland, March 21, 1772; of Franklin, September 9, 1784; and finally by the erection of Mifflin co. September 19, 1789, and by Perry co. March 22d, 1820. This co. is now bounded N. by Perry co. E. by the Susquehannah r. which separates it from Dauphin, S. by York and Adams cos. and W. by Franklin co. Length 34, breadth 16 ms. area 545 ms. Central lat. 40° 10 N. long. from W. C. 0° 15′ W.

Cumberland lies altogether in the valley between the South, or as Mr. Darby terms it, the *Blue Ridge* and the Kittatinny or Blue mtn. and belongs, in part at least, to the great central transition formation of the state, and partakes of the singular structure which distinguishes this valley in its whole course; the eastern moiety being composed of limestone, and the western of aluminous slate. The surface of the country seems determined by the nature of its base. The limestone section is comparatively level, and the soil vastly superior to that of the slate. Water, too, is much more equally distributed on the latter than on the former formation; but no striking difference is observed in regard to the timber. The iron ore of the co. is chiefly, if not wholly, in the limestone formation. The mtn. chains which bound the co. on the N. W. and S. E. extend laterally their spurs towards each other. The intervening valley is drained by considerable crs.; the Yellow Breeches on the S. E. and the Conedogwinit on the N. W. The first rises in the S. angle of the county, and receives in its course Mountain creek from the E. and several small streams on either side, and forming in part the boundary between this and York co. flows into the Susquehannah r. at the town of New Market. The second has its source in the mountains of Franklin co. and flows N. E. thro' this county into the river at the village of Fairview, near and above Harrisburg, receiving from the mountain very many rivulets, and some streams from the plain, the principal of which are Green Spring, Big Spring and Letart Spring creeks. The last turns two mills immediately at its source, and Big Spring has its banks studded with mills. There are several other remarkable springs, such as the sulphur spring at the foot of the Blue mountain, Boiling spring near the base of the South mountain, and Carlisle springs about 4 ms. N. of Carlisle borough. (See Carlisle.)

The turnpike road from Harrisburg to Chambersburg crosses the co. S. W. by the borough of Carlisle; and another road directed towards Baltimore runs from that borough S. E. by Petersburg and Abbottstown, in Adams co. and by Hanover in York co. to the state line.

There is a limestone cave on the bank of the Conedogwinit creek, about half a mile N. of Carlisle, which is of considerable extent and an object of curiosity, a description of which, and of the Hogshead spring, also in the vicinity of that borough, will be found in the article, Carlisle.

The population of the co. is composed chiefly of the descendants of the Germans and Irish, who were the first settlers. It amounted in 1800 to 25,386, in 1810, when greatly reduced by the formation of other counties, to 26,757; in 1820, after the subtraction of the co. of Perry, to 23,606; and in 1830, to 29,227, of whom 14,228 were white males, 14,047 white females, 482 free colored males, 463 females, and 7 slaves. There were also included in the foregoing 13 aliens, 23 deaf and dumb, and 4 blind.

The public buildings of the county consist of the court house, public offices and prison, all plain buildings, Dickenson college (for which see Carlisle), a number of neat and commodious churches in the borough and in various parts of the county, the United States barracks, and the poor house.

The last was established pursuant to an act of 24th March, 1808, and located by commissioners elected by the inhabitants of the county. It is governed by three directors, who serve for three years, one of whom is elected annually. They are incorporated and have power to hold lands, &c. not exceeding the yearly value of $5000, to erect the necessary buildings for the employment and maintenance of the poor, &c. &c. The house is supported by tax levied by the county commissioners at the instance of the directors. The directors are allowed $20 per annum, to defray the expenses incident to their office. There are two newspapers printed in the county.

The surplus produce of the county consists of wheat, rye, oats, flour, whiskey, peach and apple brandy, live stock and salted provisions. The manufactures are chiefly of a strict domestic character, except iron. About 250,000 barrels of flour are sent to market annually. Considerable quantities of iron are made, which with other subjects of trade, have usually found a market by the turnpike road, or by the Susquehannah river to Baltimore. The Union canal and the Columbia rail road, will give the inhabitants a better market at Philadelphia. There are two furnaces in Southampton, a furnace and forge in Dickenson, a furnace at New Cumberland, furnace and forge in South Middleton, one at Lisburn, Allen t-ship, not in operation, and another forge in Allen. Heister & Co. are erecting an extensive rolling-mill in East Pennsboro. There are in the county 62 grist, 55 saw, 8 oil, 11 fulling and 9 clover mills. There is also a very extensive woollen manufactory, chiefly employed on carpets and cassinetts, on Mountain creek, in South Middletown t-ship. Cumberland sends two members to the house of representatives; connected with Adams, Franklin and Perry, it forms the 11th congressional district, sending two members to the house of representatives; united with Perry and Adams it forms the 9th judicial district, President, John Reed, Esq. The courts are holden at Carlisle on the 2d Mondays of January, April, August and November. The county belongs to the southern district of the supreme court, which holds an annual session at Chambersburg, on the Monday week, next following the end of the second week, of the term of the western district. The term of the western district commences on the first Monday in September. There are about 25 churches in the county, Bible and missionary societies, several tract societies and Sunday school associations.

This co. paid into the treasury in 1831,

for tax on bank dividends,	$967,61
Tax on writs,	375,44
Tavern licenses,	864,65

Duties on dealers in foreign merchandise, 682,58
Tin and clock pedlars licenses, 114,00
Hawkers and pedlars licenses, 15,20
Total, $2,819,48

STATISTICAL TABLE OF CUMBERLAND COUNTY.

Townships.	Greatest Lgth.	Greatest Bth.	Area in Acres.	Face of country.	Population. 1810.	Population. 1820.	Population. 1830.	Taxables.	Valuation.
Allen,	8	4	10,240	Level.	1837	2995	2337	410	935,187
Borough of Carlisle,				Do.	2491	2908	3708	467	693,142
Dickenson,	10 1-2	10 1-2	51,240	Part hilly, level.	1749	2007	2523	413	1172,112
*East Pennsborough,	7	6	21,740	Do.	2365	3513	2196	412	995,103
Frankford,	8	5 3-4	25,600	Hilly.	807	1274	1282	257	252,935
Hopewell,	7 1-4	4	14,080	Do.	769	820	952	152	145,578
Mifflin,	14	7	33,280	Do.	1289	1461	1431	261	300,949
Monroe,	6 1-2	5	16,640	Level.			1555	317	567,422
Newton,	11 1-2	5	32,000	Do.	1312	1144	1349	365	482,598
North Middleton,	9	7	26,880	Hilly and level.	2351	1514	1932	306	584,100
*Silver Spring,	7	5	22,400	Do.			1792	477	839,318
*Southampton,	6	5	17,040	Hilly.	709	1088	1484	256	501,424
*Shippensburg,			12,800	Level.	1159	1700	1800	333	199,448
South Middleton,	10	6 1-2	25,600	Hilly and level.		1500	2072	355	568,400
West Pennsborough,	10 1-2	4	17,340	Level.	1264	1553	1733	375	712,148
Newville bor.							530		65,077
Mechanicsburg,							654		
Shippensburg bor.						1247	1608		
						23,606	29,218	5342	9,014,941†

* Township altered.
† This sum includes the valuation of personal property. The rate of levy varies in the several t-ships from 1 1-4 to 2 3-4 mills on the dollar.

Cumberland valley, t-ship, Bedford co. bounded N. by Bedford t-ship, E. by Coleraine and Southampton, S. by the state of Maryland, and W. by Londonderry t-ship; centrally distant S. W. from Bedford borough 15 miles; greatest length 16 miles, breadth, 4; area, 34,200 acres; surface level; soil, limestone. Population in 1830, 747; taxables, 150. Evit's mountain lies on the E. and Will's mountain on the West. Evit's creek runs S. through the whole extent of the t-ship.

Cumberland, t-ship, Greene co. bounded N. and E. by the Monongahela river, which separates it from Fayette county, S. by Greene and Monongahela t-ships, W. by Franklin and N. W. by Morgan t-ships. Centrally distant E. from Waynesburg 11 miles; greatest length, 10 miles; greatest breadth, $6\frac{1}{2}$; area, 23,680 acres; surface level; soil, loam.

Population in 1830, 1,896; taxables, 357. The t-ship is drained chiefly by Muddy creek, which rises in, and flows through it to the Monongahela r. On the creek is the p-t. of Lisburn, 12 miles E. of Waynesburg.

Cumberland, t-ship, Adams county, bounded N. by Menallen t-ship, E. by Strabane and Mount Joy, S. by the state of Maryland, W. by Liberty, and Hamiltonban, and N. W. by Franklin t-ships; greatest length 11, breadth 4 miles; area 20,580 acres; surface, level; soil, red gravel.

Population in 1830, 1010; taxables 213. Rock creek bounds it on the E. and Marsh creek on the W. and unite a short distance below the state line, on the south. The former receives Bear run, and the latter, Willoughby run, from the t-ship. Gettysburg, p-town, borough, and seat of justice, lies in the E. part of the t-ship, between Willoughby run, and Rock creek.

Cumberland, *New*, p-t. and borough, of Allen t-ship, Cumberland county, at the confluence of the Yellow Breeches creek with the Susquehannah river, and opposite the town of New Market, 3 miles S. W. of Harrisburg, and 16 miles E. of Carlisle, and 113 N. of W. C. contains from 30 to 40 dwellings, two stores, and a tavern. It was incorporated by act of 21st March, 1831.

Cumru, t-ship, Berks co. bounded

E. by the Schuylkill river, S. E. by Robeson t-ship, S. W. by Brecknock t-ship and Lancaster county, N. W. by Heidelberg t-ship, and N. by the Tulpehocken creek. Length 7, breadth 7 miles ; area 32,000 acres ; surface partly level, partly hilly ; soil, limestone and gravel, of excellent qualtiy, and generally very productive in grain and grass. Population in 1810, 2,017 ; in 1820, 2,462 ; in 1830, 2,705 ; taxables in 1828, 497. Besides the Tulpehocken and Schuylkill rivers, this t-ship is watered by the Wymissing, Angelica and Flying run creeks. Welsh mountain and Flying hill, are distinguished hills. The village of *Sinking Spring*, which receives its name from a spring which after flowing a few rods from its source, returns to the earth. The village is about 4 miles from Reading, on the Harrisburg turnpike, contains 12 dwellings, 2 taverns, 2 stores; a church here is common to the Lutherans and Presbyterians, as is also Allegheny church, at the extreme southern end of the t-ship. The poor house of the county is also in this t-ship, about 3 miles from Reading, upon Angelica Farm, formerly the property of Governor Mifflin.

Curwinville, p-t. Pike t-ship, Clearfield county, on the W. branch of the Susquehannah river, about 6 miles S. W. of Clearfield borough and 132 miles W. of Harrisburg.

Cussawago, t-ship, Crawford co. Population in 1830, 544.

Daggett's mills, p-o. Tioga county, distant, 277 miles N. W. from W. C. and 159 from Harrisburg.

Dale, p-o. Berks co. 164 miles from W. C. and 71 from Harrisburg.

Dallas, t-ship, Luzerne county, bounded N. E. by North Moreland, S. E. by Kingston and Plymouth, and S. W. by Lehman t-ships. It was thus named in honor of Alexander I. Dallas. Its surface is uneven and in part mountainous. Soil, gravel, loam and slate. Population in 1830, 650 ; taxables in 1828, 120. Harvey's lake, a beautiful sheet of water surrounded with romantic scenery and stored with fine trout, perch, and sunfish, lies in this t-ship, and is the resort of many parties of pleasure, during the summer months. The outlet of this lake, Bowman's creek and other streams, furnish excellent mill power. The t-ship is centrally distant 8 miles from Wilkesbarre N. W., and the p-o. bearing the name of the t-ship, is 214 miles N. W. from W. C. and 104 from Harrisburg. Lehman t-ship was taken from it in 1829.

Dalmatia, p-t. Lower Mahanoy t-ship, Northumberland co. (*See Georgetown.*)

Damascus, p-t. of Wayne county, in the t-ship of Damascus, near the Delaware river, 16 miles N. E. from Bethany, 290 miles N. of W. C. and 191 from Harrisburg, containing about a dozen dwellings, a Baptist church, a tavern and a store. A substantial bridge crosses the river here, 550 ft. in length.

Damascus, t-ship, Wayne county, bounded N. by Buckingham t-ship, N. E. and E. by the Delaware river, S. by Dyberry t-ship and by Pike co. and W. by Dyberry and Lebanon t-ships ; greatest length, 12 miles ; greatest breadth, 10 miles. The Coshecton and Great Bend turnpike passes from the Delaware river, opposite to the Newberry turnpike of New-York, through the t-ship, in a N. W. course. Damascus, a p-t. is on this road near the river, and the Coshecton Falls ; distant 16 miles N. E. of Bethany. Surface, hilly ; soil, gravel and loam. Pop. in 1830, 613 ; taxables in 1828, 128 ; taxable property in 1829, seated lands, 39,407 ; unseated lands, 59,924 ; personal estate including occupations, 8698.

Danville, or Danboro, p-t. Plumstead t-ship, Bucks co. at the intersection of the roads from Doylestown and the Delaware river, about 4 miles N. of the former, 165 miles N. of W. C. and 118 E. of Harrisburg. It contains 12 dwellings, 1 tavern, and a store.

Danville, p-t. and seat of justice of Columbia co. on the right bank of the Susquehannah river, 25 miles above

Northumberland, 175 miles from W. C. 65 from Harrisburg; N. lat. 40° 57′, long. W. C. 1° 36′ west. A turnpike road from Pottsville, leads to this town, and a company has been incorporated, and stock to the amount of half a million of dollars has been subscribed, for connecting the Susquehannah and Schuylkill rivers, by means of a rail road on this route. The town contains about 130 dwellings, 7 stores, seven taverns, one Episcopalian and one Presbyterian church, an academy incorporated by act of 23d March, 1818. There is a bridge across the Susquehannah river here.

Darby, Upper, t-ship, Delaware co. bounded N. by Haverford t-ship, E. by Phil. co. S. by Darby t-ship, and W. by Ridley t-ship. Central distance from Phil. about 8 miles; length 5, breadth 3 miles; area 7680 acres, surface hilly; soil, loam. Pop. in 1830, 1325; taxables in 1828, 239. Darby creek flows through the middle of the t-ship, and Cobb's creek forms its eastern boundary, and receives a considerable tributary from it. These streams have many mills upon them, and on the first is an extensive cotton manufactory.

Darby, t-ship, Delaware co. bounded N. by Upper Darby, E. by Phil. co. S. by Tinicum t-ship, and W. by Ridley. Central distance W. from Phil. 8 miles; length 4, breadth 2¾ miles; area 5120 acres; surface level; soil, clay and loam; pop. in 1830, 1085; taxables in 1828, 233. It is watered by Darby and Cobb's creeks which unite on the eastern boundary. Both are mill streams fully employed. Darby village, and Horntown, are villages of the t-ship.

Darby, p-t. and village of Darby t-ship, Delaware co. on the E. side of Darby creek, 7 miles S. W. of Phil. on the main road to Chester. It is pleasantly located in the vale of Darby creek, contains 30 or 40 dwellings, 2 stores, 2 taverns, a grist mill, and fulling mill, and a Quaker meeting-house. It is 129 miles from W. C. and 103 S. E. from Harrisburg.

Darlingsville, p-o. of Pike co. named after the post master, Samuel Darling, 261 miles N. E. of W. C. and 169 from Harrisburg.

Dartmouth, p-o. Tioga co. distant 254 miles from W. C. 148 from Harrisburg.

Dauphin co. was separated from Lancaster by act of 4th March, 1785, which gave it the following limits; 'beginning on the W. side of the Susquehannah river opposite the mouth of Conewago creek; thence up the middle of the said creek to Moor's mill; and from thence to the head of said cr. and from thence by a direct line to the S. E. corner of Heidelberg t-ship, where it strikes the Berks co. line; thence N. W. by the line of Berks co. to Mahantango creek; thence along the same by the line of Northumberland co. and crossing the river Susquehannah, to the line of Cumberland co. thence down the Susquehannah on the W. side thereof by the line of Cumberland co. and that part of the line of York co. to the place of beginning, on the W. side of the river Susquehannah." The co. was reduced to its present limits by the act of 16th Feb. 1813, which erected Lebanon co. from Dauphin and Lancaster. The seat of justice for the co. was fixed at Harrisburg by the act of 5th April, 1793.

Dauphin co. is now bounded N. by Northumberland co. N. E. by Lebanon, and Lancaster on the S. E. and by the Susquehannah river on the W. or rather by the western bank of that river, the whole stream being within Dauphin co. The course of the river through the county is 48 miles. Its length is 33, and mean width 16 miles; area 528 square miles; central lat. 40° 25′ N. long. 0° 15′ E. of W. C. Its name was given in honor of the son of Louis XVI of France.

For much of the following description of the county we are indebted to Mr. Roberts, its respectable and intelligent prothonotary.

The county belongs to the great central transition formation of the state, commencing on the S. by the

South mountain, known here as the Conewago Hills, and extending deep into the Appalachian system of mountains. Its surface varies much in form and fertility. One fourth may be estimated as mountainous, and altogether unfit for cultivation; one fourth hills and woodland which may be subjected to the plough, but is not yet improved, and the remainder as in tillage, varying in quality from the arid slate to the productive limestone, and more prolific river bottom. Traversing the county northward we cross in succession, the Conewago hills, the Blue mtn. the Second, Third and Peters mountains, between Peters mountain and Berry's mountain, are several minor ranges, less continuous, and between Berry's and the Mahantango mountains are some ridges of like character. The valleys lying between the mountains north and west of the Blue mountain, are of red slate, alternating and blending occasionally with red sandstone, and are favorable to the growth of grain, clover, and fruit trees. From the foot of the Blue mountain, east and south to Harrisburg, off of the river bottom, limestone is found alternating with blue and other slate, partaking more of the argillaceous character, and the soil is fertile. At Harrisburg where the great Cumberland valley crosses the river, limestone of a more decided character commences, and continues through the county east, in the range of the valley to the Lebanon county line, and S. E. until it is lost beneath the Conewago hills. The whole limestone range here, as well as elsewhere, is most fertile and richly rewards the labors of the agriculturist. From Harrisburg N. E. and between the valley just described and the Blue mountains argillaceous slate, occasionally interrupted by a friable brown sand stone, predominates. The soil here is thin and sterile, but is susceptible of great improvement by the use of lime. Between the limestone valley and the Susquehannah, and south and east of the Swatara, bordering on Lancaster co. the Conewago hills present a character altogether different from the other ranges of hills in the county. Here red sand stone and slate are overlaid and intermingled with masses of globular and angular rock having the appearance of primary formation. The soil in this section of the county is thin and unfavorable to the production of grain, but well suited to every variety of fruit, adapted to the climate. The t-ships next the river have a portion of river bottom, composed of sand, vegetable mould and boulders or loose fragments of rock rounded and smoothed by attrition. This alluvion overlays unformable strata of rock, which is washed by the river and exhibited in its bed and banks. This land is generally preferred to limestone, yielding more certain, and quite as abundant crops.

The mountains commencing with the Blue mountain extend across the whole upper part of the county to the Northumberland county line, in longitudinal ranges, elevated from 600 to 900 feet above the surface of the Susquehannah, which generally cuts them to the base at right angles. The valleys, as has already been said, which separate the mountains, are composed of red slate and red sand stone, but the geological character changes as soon as we ascend the mountains, where we find pudding stone, grey wacke, and a yellow and sometimes white conglomerated sand stone, bearing impressions of animal remains of the Moluscous order, and sometimes of Ammonites. In the red sand stone and slate of the valleys, and the limestone and slate of the country on the S. E. of the mountains, no appearances of organic remains have been discovered. The limestone from Harrisburg, east, through Hummelstown, is of the kind denominated sparry, from the crystallized carbonate of lime which fills compactly and cements the transverse, and sometimes the longitudinal fissures of the rock. The line of bearing of the whole rock formation of the county is parallel to the mountains, running west of south and east of north, at an angle of from 60 to 75 degrees. The dip is east, varying from an angle of thirty degrees, to almost a perpendicular. Off the mountains the angle is seldom more than 45°, but on the mountains the rock is so nearly perpendicular, that it is sometimes difficult to determine its inclination.

Anthracite coal has been found in all the mountains north of the Blue mountain, in greater or less proportions. Owing to its distance from the river, very little has yet been mined. Veins have been opened on the Third mountain, which separates Stoney cr. from Clark's valley, in Middle Paxton t-ship, and on the Short and Bear mtns. dividing Lyken's from Williams' valley, in Lykens t-ship. At the latter place several strata have been opened of the thickness of seven or eight feet. The coal is of good quality, and appears to possess in some degree the qualities of the bituminous. It is lighter than the anthracite of Mauch Chunk, Pottsville and Wilksbarre, ignites more easily, and emits, when burning, greater flame, but throws off less sulphureous gas than the bituminous. It makes an exceedingly pleasant and agreeable fire for the grate, and will be valuable for all manufacturing purposes. A rail road is now being made from the mines to the river. (See Lyken's valley.) The coal is overlaid with a light stratum of shale, bearing, as is usual, impressions of vegetable remains, and both are contained between strata of conglomerate quartzose rock, similar to that common to the mass of the mountain.

The streams of the co. are the Swatara, which, rising in the mtns. of Schuylkill co., traverses Lebanon co. and the lower part of Dauphin, to unite with the Susquehannah at Middletown. It receives from Dauphin on the north, Bow run, Manady creek and Beaver's creek, and from the south, Spring creek and Mine run. Paxton creek, rising in the Blue mountain, and flowing W. and S. W., in the rear of Harrisburg, empties into the river two miles below the town. Another "Spring creek," also falls into the river near the mouth of the Paxton. North of the Blue mountain, Fishing creek flows between it and the Second mountain; Stoney creek between the Second and Third mountain; Clark's creek, between the Third and Peters' mountain; Powell's and Armstrong's creeks, between Peters' and Berry's mountain; and the Big and Little Wiconisco creeks between Berry's and the Mahantango mountains. All these mountain streams rush westwardly to the Susquehannah river.

There are three turnpike roads leading from Harrisburg to Philadelphia; one by the way of Reading, Berks co., one by way of Euphrata and Downingstown, in Lancaster and Chester counties, and one through the city of Lancaster. There are two turnpikes from Harrisburg to Pittsburg; one by the southern route through Carlisle, Chambersburg, Bedford, &c., the other by the northern route up the Juniata, through Mifflin, Lewistown, Huntingdon, &c. crossing the Allegheny mountain at Blair's gap. There is also a turnpike road from Harrisburg to Baltimore, through Middletown and York, excepting five miles, between Middletown and the river at Conewago falls. An act has been passed by the legislature, with an appropriation of $18,000, for making a turnpike road from York Haven on the west side of the river to the end of the bridge opposite Harrisburg, a distance of 14 miles, which, when completed, will form a continuous line of turnpike roads from Harrisburg through York and Baltimore to Washington City. The Pennsylvania canal enters Dauphin co. by an aqueduct over the Juniata river at the head of Duncan's island, about a mile and a half above the junction of the Juniata with the Susquehannah, and sixteen miles from Harrisburg. It is thence constructed along the western side of the island to its lower end, where it enters the Susquehannah. The boats pass the latter river by means of a dam and tow bridge. Thence the canal is continued to Middletown, 9 ms. below Harrisburg, where it meets the Union canal, which follows the Swatara, 20 miles through the county to this point. From Middletown the state canal is now being made to Columbia.

Two bridges cross the Susquehannah in this county; one at Duncan's island, mentioned above, used for ordinary travelling as well as for a tow bridge, erected by the state; and the other at Harrisburg, built by a company, in which the state is a stockholder, to the amount of $90,000 dollars. Both are of wood, resting on stone piers and roofed. The first is of lattice work, on a horizontal line; the latter is built with arches, upon which the passage way & superstructure rest, 50 ft. above the surface of the river at low water.

Dauphin county was first settled by emigrants, principally from Ireland and Germany, whose descendants compose the great majority of its population. By the census of 1810, the population was 31,883; in 1820, after the county of Lebanon had been taken from it, 21,663, and in 1830, 25,303, of whom 12,287 were white males, 12,085 white females; 469 free col'd. males, 444 col'd. females; 18 slaves. There were 386 aliens, 5 deaf and dumb, and 6 blind.

The prevailing religious sects are German Reformed, German Lutheran, Methodist and English Presbyterians.

There are 3 forges for the manufacture of bar iron, 2 furnaces for iron castings, 58 grist mills, 42 saw mills, 8 carding and fulling mills, 6 oil mills, 5 clover mills, 3 woollen factories and 1 paper mill in the county.

The exports of the county consist of wheat, flour, whiskey, live stock and salted provisions, which seek a market by the Susquehannah river at Baltimore, and by the Union canal at Philadelphia. There are two banks in the county, both in Harrisburg, one a branch of the Pennsylvania Bank, and the other the Harrisburg Bank, with a capital of $158,525. A favorable view will be entertained of the commerce of the county, from the fact, that in the month of November, 1830, more than 130 wagons were several times counted in Harrisburg at once, loaded with produce for that market.

Dauphin, connected with Lebanon, forms the eighth senatorial district, sending one member to the senate, and Dauphin alone sends two members to the house of representatives; and so connected, it forms also the 6th congressional district. United with Schuylkill and Lebanon, it forms the 13th Judicial district, Calvin Blythe, president. It belongs to the Lancaster district of the supreme court.

The public buildings in the county consist of the state capitol and public offices, spacious and ornamental structures, (for a particular description of which, see "*Harrisburg*,") a small state arsenal upon the public square, court-house and county offices, of brick, and prison, of stone; the Harrisburg academy, which has received from the legislature at sundry times 2000 dollars in money, and the donation of a lot of ground, a Lancasterian school and a poor house, a masonic lodge and several churches. The number of children taught in the Lancasterian school averages about 300, at an expense to the county of 7 dollars for each pupil. The county relieves, on an average, about 325 paupers per annum, at at expense of $7,850, besides the product of the farm pertaining. The county levy for 1829, was, for all purposes, $20,000. There are 8 printing offices at Harrisburg, six of which issue newspapers, four semi-weekly, during the session of the legislature, and the remainder weekly. Of the weekly papers two are German.

Dauphin county paid to the state treasury in 1831:

For tax on writs,	437	27
Duties on deal'rs in for. mdze.	1600	32
State maps,	19	51
Tin and clock pedlars' licenses,	85	00
Collateral inheritances,	134	38
Hawkers' & pedlars' licenses,	131	10
Bridge stock dividends,	6750	00
Tax on bank dividends,	1014	66
	$10,172	24

STATISTICAL TABLE OF DAUPHIN COUNTY.

Townships.	Lgth.	Bth.	Area.	Surface.	Population. 1810.	1820.	1830.	Taxa. 1828.	Valua. 1832.
Lykens,	10	7	31,500	Mount. Valleys.	1116	1356	1636	283	$277,570
Mifflin,	7	5	24,400	Do.		1195	1570	251	129,658
Upper Paxton,	6	6	15,000	Do.	1116	1444	1617	294	201,504
Halifax,	11	5	18,000	Do.	1364	2062	1772	434	209,019
Jackson,	19	6	40,000	Mountainous.			830	165	128,478
Rush,	20	3	25,600	Do.			58	8	14,358
Middle Paxton,	10	5	18,600	Do.	707	973	1241	286	239,681
Susquehannah,	6	5	15,300	Undulating.	3287	4166	5737	1031	1,129,721
Lower Paxton,	7	4	18,000	Do.	1180	1283	1371	286	323,513
Hanover,	10	7	36,000	Do.	461	2618	2543	493	400,368
Swatara,	9	5	15,800	Do.	2291	2355	2771	521	827,314
Derry,	8	7	18,000	Hilly.	2481	2704	2273	392	645,403
Londonderry,	7	6	17,500	Do.	800	1100	1822	323	401,029
					14,803	21,246	25,303	4602	

Dauphin, p-t. formerly called Port Lyon, of Middle Paxton t-s. Dauphin county, on the turnpike road from Harrisburg to Millerstown on the Susquehannah, 8 miles from the former, and on the left bank of the Susquehannah at the confluence of Stoney creek with the river, and 119 miles from W. C. contains about a dozen dwellings, 2 stores and a tavern. On the S. side of the creek is an extensive tannery, carried on by Eldridge & Brich, of Philadelphia.

Davidsburg, village of Antes t-ship, Huntingdon county, W. of the Brush mountain and the left bank of the Little Juniata river, about 20 miles N. W. of Huntingdon borough, contains 5 or 6 houses, store, tavern and tan-yard.

Davisville, p-t. of Southampton t-ship, Bucks co. 10 miles S. of Doylestown, 169 N. from W. C. and 118 E. from Harrisburg, contains 3 or 4 dwellings.

Decatur t-ship, Mifflin co. bounded N. by Armagh t-ship, E. by Union county, S. by Greenwood t-ship, and W. by Derry t-ship, centrally distant N. E. from Lewistown 14 miles; greatest length 13, breadth 9 miles; area, 55,680 acres; surface mountainous; soil, slate and gravel. Jack's mountain is on the N. and Shade's mountain on the S. boundaries, and Limestone and Black Oak ridges are in the interval. Jack's creek has its source in the N. E. confines of the t-ship, and flows S. W. about 20 miles into the Juniata river, about one mile below Lewistown.

Decatur, t-ship, Clearfield county. Population in 1330, 434; taxables, 82.

Deer, t-ship, Allegheny county, bounded N. by Butler county, E. by the Allegheny river which divides it from Westmoreland, S. by Indiana t-ship, and W. by Pine t-ship. Centrally distant N. E. from Pittsburg 16 miles; greatest length 13, breadth $4\frac{1}{2}$ miles; area, 34,560 acres; surface hilly, coal abundant; soil, loam. Population in 1830, 1,642; taxables, 312. It is drained by Bull and Deer creeks, which flow S. to the river. The turnpike road from Pittsburg to Butler, runs through the t-ship, near the west line.

Deerfield, t-ship, Tioga co. bounded N. by the state of New York, E. by Elkland, S. by land now or formerly of Delmar t-ship, and W. by Westfield. Centrally distant, N. W. from Wellsborough 13 miles. It forms an oblong of 11 miles by $4\frac{1}{2}$, containing about 34,000 acres. It is drained on the N. E. by Cowanesque creek, and on the S. E. by Marsh creek, a tributary of Crooked creek; surface hilly; soil, gravelly loam. Population in 1830, 320; taxables in 1828, 71.

Deerfield t-ship, Warren co. bounded N. by Spring creek and Broken Straw t-ships, E. by the Allegheny river, which separates it from Limestone t-ship, S. by Venango county, and W. by South West t-ship. Centrally distant from Warren S. W. 20

miles; greatest length 12, breadth 9 miles; area, 40,320 acres; surface somewhat hilly, and soil alluvial along the river bottoms; gravelly loam in the interior, well wooded. The p-o. of the t-ship is named after it, and is distant 309 miles N. W. of W. C. and 242 from Harrisburg.

Deep creek and valley, Lower Mahantango t-ship, Schuylkill county, S. of the Mahantango mountain. The creek flows into Long Pine creek.

Deep run, a tribuary of Tohickon creek, Bucks county, rising in Hilton t-ship, and flowing eastwardly about 7 miles through Bedminster t-ship, falls into its recipient about 5 miles from its mouth.

Deep run, a tributary of the Little Swatara creek, which has its source and course in Bethel t-ship, Lebanon county.

Deer Lick creek, Rush t-ship, Susquehannah county, a tributary of the Wyalusing creek, which rises and has its course in that t-ship, and flows N. into the main stream between Lake creek and the middle branch.

Deer Creek, Deer t-ship, Allegheny county, rises with many branches in the N. part of the t-ship, and flows S. through this and Indiana t-ship, into the Allegheny river.

Delaware county, was separated from Chester co. by act 26th Sept. 1789, by which the following boundaries were prescribed to it: "Beginning in the middle of Brandywine r. where the same crosses the circular line of Newcastle co. thence up the middle of the r. to the line dividing the lands of Elizabeth Chads and Caleb Brinton, at or near Chads' ford; and from thence on a line as nearly straight as may be, so as not to split or divide plantations, to the great road leading from Goshen to Chester, where the Westown line intersects said road; and from thence along the lines of Edgemont, Newtown and Radnor, so as to include those t-ships, to the line of Montgomery county, and along the same and Philadelphia co. line to the river Delaware, and down the same to the circular line aforesaid, and along the same to the place of beginning." By the same act the st. jus. was established at the borough of Chester.

The co. is bounded N. and N. E. by Montgomery co. E. by Philadelphia co. S. E. by the river Delaware, S. by the state of Delaware, and S. W. and W. by Chester co. Central lat. N. 39° 55′, long. 1° 33′ E. from W. C. Length 16, breadth 11 miles; area 177 sq. ms.

This co. with the exception of a narrow margin of alluvion along the Delaware, pertains to the primitive formation, and its constituent rock is gneiss in every variety of cohesion. This furnishes an abundance of excellent building stone, and the quarries of Crum and Ridley creeks are famed for the quantity and quality of curb and building stone which they send to Philadelphia. The soil formed by the decomposition of this rock, vivified by lime and stable manure, under the care of its industrious, enterprising and skilful inhabitants, is scarce surpassed in fertility by any in the state. The alluvion which borders the primitive region is reclaimed from the waters by mounds or dykes, *banking*, and affords a large quantity of excellent meadow and pasturage, upon which innumerable cattle, brought from the west and south, are fattened for the Philadelphia market.

A mine of copper ore has been opened on Chester creek, about a mile above the town of Chester. The ore *is said* to contain 53 per cent of copper, 48 ounces of silver in every 100 lbs. and one grain of gold in each ounce of the ore. The sulphuret of molybdena is found here, also in quantities.

The surface of the country above the alluvion is rolling, and becomes somewhat hilly towards the west.

This co. was the first settled of the province. It was the early and favorite habitation of the Swedes, and Upland, the present borough of Chester, was already a village when Penn came to take possession of his province, in October, 1682. His pioneers sent out in the preceding year landed at this place on the 11th December, and the Delaware having frozen over that night, they were hospitably entertained during the winter by its inhabitants. At that period the Quakers had a congregation and a meeting house here. On the 4th December, 1782, the Proprietary commenced an assembly of the Freemen, who, in three days, passed 65 laws, comprehending the chief subjects of legislative attention in a society without commerce or foreign connections, affording an instance of unanimity and prompt legislation never equalled except in a despotic monarchy.

The streams of this co. are, Cobb's creek, upon its eastern boundary; Darby creek, Crum and Ridley creeks, Chester creek, Hook creek, Mukinipates and the Brandywine, which touches its western boundary. These streams all flow into the Delaware, and are navigable through the alluvion, from a half to nine ms. in extent, but in the greater distances having very serpentine courses. A canal about a mile in length, with two locks, has been made by George G. Leiper, Esq. from the tide water of the Ridley creek to his extensive quarries. The enterprise is creditable to the proprietor, and the execution of the work to the artists employed in it.

Authority was granted in 1812 for constructing a turnpike, which was designed as a link in the great southern road, but the stockholders, after paving it for 8 or 10 miles, found the undertaking unprofitable and have not completed it. It is almost the only instance in which an attempt of this kind in the vicinity of Philadelphia has not succeeded. A company was incorporated in 1831, for making a railroad to Chester, but the work has not been commenced; and it is now proposed to obtain authority from the legislatures of Pennsylvania and Delaware to connect the line with that now made from New Castle to French town.

The agricultural population of this county consists chiefly of the descendants of the first settlers, Swedes, English, Welsh and Irish, and no inconsiderable portion of it is connected with the religious sect of Quakers, but the Baptists, Episcopalians and Presbyterians, have churches in the co. The county is certainly thrifty, and the population of no part of the state enjoys more fully the comforts of life; but the increase of its inhabitants was slow, until the impulse given by the establishment of manufactories. In 1800 the population amounted to 12,809; in 1810 to 14,734; and in 1820 to 14,810, increasing in ten years 76 persons only; but in 1830 the number amounted to 17,361, making an increase of 2551. Of this number 8142 were white males, 7958 females, 705 free colored males, 554 females and 2 slaves. There were 386 aliens, 5 deaf and dumb, and 6 blind.

The public buildings in the county consist of a lazaretto, in Tinicum t-ship, where there are erected two large buildings for hospitals, and also dwelling houses for the physician, steward, &c. &c. and commodious stores, for the reception of cargoes when it is found necessary to unlade vessels. All these buildings are of brick, and are neat and commodious. At Chester are the court house, public offices and prison, a Quaker meeting house, an ancient church; and a bank with a capital of $77,510; a poor house and house of employment, established on a farm, governed by three directors, one of whom is elected annually, and maintained by a tax levied by the co. commissioners, at the instance and upon the estimate of the directors. There are 9 Quaker meeting houses in the co. 1 Baptist, 1 Presbyterian and 4 Methodist churches, and schools sufficient for teaching the rudiments of English education.

There are also 2 newspapers printed at the borough of Chester, viz. the Upland Union, and the Weekly Visitor.

The exports of the co. consist of wheat, corn, rye, oats, flour and other great agricultural products; and also of large quantities of horned cattle, sheep, fowls, and esculent vegetables, for the Philadelphia market, and also a vast amount of stone, for building and for curbing the streets. The co. claims, too, high consideration for its manufactures, which are found upon almost every stream. Some idea may be formed of the business and capabilities of this co. by the statistical account from a report of a committee of the co. appointed to ascertain the facts, in 1828; some important additions have since been made. There are 38 flour mills, 16 of which grind 203,600 bushels of grain per annum; 53 saw mills, 16 of which cut 1,717,000 ft. of lumber per annum; 14 woollen factories, employing 228 hands; 12 cotton manufactories make 704,300 lbs. of yarn per annum, value $232,445; employ 415 hands, wages $51,380, 5 rolling and slitting mills, which roll 700 tons sheet iron per ann. value $105,000, employ 30 hands, wages $7,200; 11 paper mills, manufacture 31,296 reams of paper per annum, value $114,712, employ 215 hands, wages $29,120; 2 powder mills manufacture 11,900 quarter casks per annum, value $47,600, employ 40 hands, wages $12,000; 1 nail factory manufactures 150 tons of nails per annum, value $20,000, employs 8 hands, wages $2,400; 4 tilt, blade and edge tool manufactories, 2 of which manufacture per annum 2,000 axes, 200 cleavers, 1200 dozen shovels, 200 dozen scythes, and 500 drawing knives; 1 power loom factory weaves 30,000 yds. per week, value $3000, employs 120 hands, wages per week $500, looms 200; 2 oil mills manufacture 7,000 gallons linseed oil; 1 machine factory, 5 snuff-mills, 2 plaister or gypsum mills, 3 clover mills, 3 bark mills, and 1 mill for sawing stone. There are also 42 mill seats on the principal streams, which are unimproved; making in the whole 158 mills and factories in operation, and 42 mill seats unimproved in a district not exceeding 12 miles square, in the five kinds of manufactories which have returned the number, viz. paper, woollen, cotton, powder and edge tools, employing 1,038 hands.

R

Delaware, Chester and Lancaster cos. form the 4th congressional district, sending three representatives to Congress, and now represented in the 22d congress by Joshua Evans, William Heister and David Potts, Jr. United with Chester it forms the 4th senatorial district of the state, sending two members to the senate, and alone it sends one member to the house of representatives. Connected with Chester it forms the 15th judicial district—Isaac Darlington, president. The courts are holden at Chester on the 2d Mondays after the 3d Mondays in Jan. April, July and October. The county belongs to the eastern district of the supreme court, which holds 2 sessions annually, at Philadelphia, on the 2d Monday in March and 2d Monday in December.

Delaware paid into the treasury of the state in the year 1831, for

Tax on writs,	$124,78
Tavern licenses,	400,14
Duties on Dealers in foreign merchandize,	422,53
On collateral inheritances,	544,85
	$1,492,30

STATISTICAL TABLE OF DELAWARE COUNTY.

Townships.	Greatest Lgth.	Greatest Bth.	Area in Acres.	Face of Country.	Soil.	Population. 1810.	Population. 1820.	Population. 1830.	Taxables.
Aston,	4 3-4	2 1-4	6400	Level.	Clay.	765		1070	224
Bethel,	4 1-2	3	5000	Level.	Clay.	299	394	367	71
Birmingham,	3 3-4	2 3-4	4480	Hilly.	Clay.	586	515	584	100
Chester borough,				Level.	Clay.		657	848	
Chester,	3 1-4	3	4800	Level.	Clay.	1056	1295	1672	317
Concord,	4 3-4	3	8000	Hilly.	Loam.	1061	1032	1002	203
Chichester, Upper,	3	2 3-4	3840	Level.	Loam.	417	413	431	102
Chichester, Lower,	2 1-4	1 3-4	2560	Level.	Clay.	511	502	465	91
Darby,	4	2 3-4	5120	Level.	Clay.	1085	692	1085	233
Edgemont,	4	2 3-4	5700	Hilly,	Loam.	611	640	758	170
Upper Providence,	4	2 1-4	3840	Level.	Loam.	561	736	748	160
Nether Providence,	4	2	5000	Level.	Clay.	594	566	747	158
Marple,	4	4	6400	Hilly.	Loam.	649	700	793	171
Springfield,	3 1-4	2 1-4	3840	Level.	Clay.	541	600	700	144
Newtown,	4	4	6400	Hilly.	Loam.	601		667	141
Middletown,	4 1-2	4 1-2	7680	Level.	Clay.	948	994	1188	228
Tinicum,	3 1-2	1 1-4	2000	Level.	Alluvial.	249	182	166	30
Upper Darby,	5	3	7680	Hilly.	Loam.	966	1004	1325	239
Ridley,	4	3 1-4	6400	Level.	Clay.	991	893	1058	279
Haverford,	3 3-4	3 1-2	7680	Hilly.	Loam.	754	750	980	191
Thornbury,	4 3-4	2 1-2	6000	Hilly.	Loam.	564	537	610	124
Radnor,	3 1-2	3 1-4	7680	Hilly.	Loam.	925	1059	1097	257

Delaware River, and Bay. This river, called by the Indians *Poutaxas*, *Marisqueton*, *Makeriskitton*, *Makerisk-kiskon*, *Lenape wihittuck*, (stream of the Lenape,) by the Dutch *Zuydt*, or South River, *Nassau* River, and by the Swedes, *New Swedeland stream*, one of the most considerable of N. America, rises by two principal branches in the state of New York, the northernmost of which, called the Mohawk's or Cookquago branch, issues from Lake Utsayemthe, lat. 42° 45′, takes a S. W. course and turning S. E. crosses the Penns. line, in lat. 42°, and about 7 miles from thence receives the Popachton branch from the N. E. The latter rises in the Katskill mountain. Thence the river runs southwardly, until it touches the N. W. corner of New Jersey, in lat. 41° 24′. It has a very crooked course above and below the Blue mountains; the country is very mountainous through which it passes, until it leaves the Water Gap.

The Delaware Water Gap is one of the greatest natural curiosities of the state. It would seem from the quantity of alluvial lands above the mountain, that at some remote period a dam of great height here obstructed its progress. If it had been as high, or half as high as the mountain, it would have raised the water so that it might have run into the North River. It probably had an elevation of 150 or 200 feet, forming a lake of more than 50 miles in length, covering the Meenesink settlements. This height must have formed cataracts similar, the quantity of water excepted, to that of Niagara. It has been conjectured, that this this dam was engulphed by some great convulsion of the earth, and the following reasons have been assigned for this opinion. The distance through the mountain is about two miles, within which the river has an average width of half a mile, and the water is as still as a mill pond, so that a raft will be driven by the impulse of the wind up or down; and the boatmen report that 98 years ago, they could not find bottom with their longest lines. Had the mountain been worn by abrasion, such a gulf would not have existed, and the bottom of the river here would have consisted of the same material which forms the side of the pass; but the bottom is of alluvial mud, and the nucleus of the mountain is of a hard granite, peculiar to the place. It is also well known that alluvial particles which float in the swift current, subside in the pools; and it has been noted by an accurate observer, that the river is always much more muddy (or rily as the phrase is,) above, than below the gap. Hence a large proportion of the alluvion carried down the stream must have been deposited in this gulph. Supposing the dam to have sunk 1000 years ago, and two feet of earth per annum, to have been thus deposited, 2000 feet must thus have been heaped upon the original dam, supposed to have been 150 or 200 feet high.

The "Gap" is 30 miles above Easton, and 80 from Philadelphia. It may be most conveniently approached by Dutotsburg, on the N. side of the mountain where good accommodations may be obtained, and from whence by an agreeable morning's walk the visiter may ascend to the summit of the mountain, and enjoy one of the finest and most extended prospects in Pennsylvania.

At Easton, the Delaware receives the Lehigh river, which rises in Wayne, Luzerne and Northampton counties. From the S. Mountain below Easton to the tide water at Trenton, the river has a S. W. course of about 60 miles, in which there are 25 noted rapids, with an aggregate fall of 165 feet. But the navigation has been improved, and is safe at the ordinary height of the water. From Trenton to Philadelphia the distance is about 35 miles; and to Bristol, 15 miles. From Easton to Bristol the Delaware division of the state canal has been completed, and is now navigable, affording by its connection with the Lehigh canal, a most desirable and advantageous communication with the Lehigh coal mines, and the valley of the Lehigh river. At Philadelphia, the river is divided into two channels by Petty's Island and Smith's Island. The western channel near the centre of the city is 900 feet wide, with a mean depth of 305 feet, and from the island to N. Jersey 2100 feet, with a mean depth of 9 feet; the whole area equal to 46,350 feet—affording a commodious and safe harbor, to which ships of the line may ascend. About 7 miles below Philadelphia, the Schuylkill river flows into the Delaware. Chester, Marcus Hook, New Castle, and the new city of Delaware are the only towns below Philadelphia on the river. At the last, is the outlet of the Chesapeake and Delaware canal, which unites the two bays by an artificial water course of 14 miles in length, through which vessels usually employed in the Bay trade, pass. Opposite Delaware city is Delaware fort, a large fortress, which commands the passage of the river.

Here the Bay may be said to commence, 45 miles from the city of Philadelphia, and extends 70 miles to the ocean, with a width varying from 3 to 30 miles, occupying an area of 630,000 acres. Its navigation is dangerous and difficult, being invested by many shoals, which often prove destructive to vessels. It opens into the Atlantic ocean N. W. and S. E. between cape Henlopen on the right, and cape May on the left, which are about 20 miles apart. The bay and river are navigable from the sea, to the great or lower falls at Trenton, 155 miles. A 74 gun ship may go to Philadelphia, 120 miles. The distance across the land, by a S. E. course through New Jersey to the sea coast, is but 60 miles. Sloops go to Trenton falls, and boats of 8 or 10 tons burthen 100 miles higher up, and Indian canoes, 150 miles.

The bay of Delaware below fort Penn, offers no safe harborage, nor is there S. of New York for several hundred miles, any place where a vessel during the rudest season of the year, when approach to the coast is most dangerous, may seek protection against the elements. The losses which have arisen from this cause, have induced the national government to commence the erection of an artificial port, or breakwater, at the entrance of the bay. The law for this purpose was passed in 1828–9, and the work is in steady progression, and will speedily be completed. The anchorage ground, or roadstead, is formed by a cove in the southern shore, directly W. of the cape and the seaward end, on an extensive shoal called the *Shears*; the tail of which makes out from the shore about 5 miles up the bay, near Broadkill creek, from whence it extends eastward, and terminates at a point, about two miles to the northward of the shore at the cape. The breakwater consists of an insolated dyke or wall of stone, the transversal section of which is a trapezium, the base resting on the bottom, whilst the summit line forms the top of the work. The other sides represent the inner and outer slopes of the work, that to the seaward being much greater than the other. The inward slope is 45°, the top is horizontal, 22 feet in breadth, and raised $5\frac{1}{2}$ feet above the highest spring tide; the outward or sea slope is 39 feet in altitude, upon a base of $105\frac{3}{4}$ feet; both these dimensions being measured in relation to a horizontal plane passing by a point 27 feet below the lowest spring tide. The base bears to the altitude nearly the same ratio, as similar lines in the profiles of the Cherbourg and Plymouth breakwaters. The opening or entrance from the ocean is 650 yards in width, between the N. part of the cape and the E. end of the breakwater. At this entrance the harbor will be accessible during all winds coming from the sea. The dyke is formed in a straight line from E. S. E. to W. N. W.; 1200 yards is the length of this portion of the work, which is properly the *breakwater*. At the distance of 350 yards from the upper or western end of the breakwater, (which space forms the upper entrance,) a similar dyke of 500 yards in length, is projected in a direct line W. by S. $\frac{1}{2}$ S. forming an angle of 146° 15′ with the breakwater. This part of the work is more particularly designed as an *icebreaker*.

The whole length of the two dykes, now partly constructed, will be 1700 yards. They will contain, when finished, 900,000 cubic yards of stone, composed of pieces of basaltick rock and granite, weighing from a quarter of a ton to three tons and upwards. The depth of water at low tide is from four to six fathoms throughout the harbor, which will be formed by these works and the cove of the southern shore, and which is calculated to afford a perfect shelter over a water surface of 7 tenths of a square mile.

The are five bridges erected over the river Delaware. One at Morrisville and Trenton; (*See Morrisville,*) one at New Hope; (*See New Hope,*) one at a place about 4 miles above New Hope, called Centreville; one at Easton, and one at the Columbia glass manufactory. Authority has also been given to erect a bridge over the river at Philadelphia, and another at Taylorsville, above Centreville. The Delaware and Hudson canal crosses the river, by means of a dam constructed below the mouth of the Lackawaxen.

Delaware, t-ship, Pike co. bounded N. by Lackawaxen and upper Smithfield t-ships, E. and S. E. by the Delaware river, S. by middle Smithfield t-ship, and W. by Palmyra t-ship; greatest length $14\frac{3}{4}$, greatest breadth 14 miles. It is watered by Dingmans creek, Bushkill creek, and its tributaries, which run N. and S. through it, and by several minor streams. The surface is broken and uneven; soil gravelly loam. There is a post town at Dingmans ferry, on the Delaware, about 40 miles above Easton, and 10 below Milford, at which there is an academy, established and incorporated under act of 4th March, 1813, and aided by a donation from the state of $1000.

Delaware run, Turbut t-ship, Northumberland co. a small tributary of the Susquehannah river.

Delaware, t-ship, Mercer co. bounded N. by Salem, E. by Cool Spring, S. by Lackawannock and W. by Pymatuning t-ships. Centrally distant N. W. from Mercer borough, 7 miles. It forms an oblong of 8 by 6 miles; area 30,720 acres; surface somewhat hilly; soil, clay, and loam. Taxable property in 1829, real estate $67,546; personal $9,166; rate 4 mills on the dollar. The Shenango creek enters the t-ship, in the N. W. angle, and making what is termed the big bend, flows out of it westerly, south of the centre of the W. line, receiving from the t-ship, Lackawannock creek, which enters it at S. E.

Delaware, p-o. Pike co. (see Bushville.)

Delmar, t-ship, Tioga co. formerly occupied nearly the whole of the south west quarter of the co. but has been subdivided of late into several t-ships. The whole of this section of the co. is watered by Pine creek, and its branches, the main stream rising in the centre of Potter co. flows E. S. E. and S. W. into the west branch of the Susquehannah, above Jersey Shore borough, in Lycoming co. and is navigable from W. of the Potter co. line. The country is hilly; soil, gravel, heavily timbered with oak, beech, hemlock, and white pine. Much lumber is sent to market by Pine creek and the Susquehannah river. It is estimated that five millions of feet were floated down these streams in the spring of 1832. Pop. of the t-ship in 1830, 622; taxables 135.

Derry, t-ship, Dauphin co. bounded N. by the Swatara creek which separates it from Hanover, E. by Londonderry t-ship, S. by Lancaster, and W. by the Swatara creek. Centrally distant from Harrisburg S. E. 12 miles; greatest length 8, greatest breadth 7 miles; area 18,000 acres; surface diversified; soil, limestone and slate. Pop. in 1830, 2273; taxables 392, valuation 1832, $645,403.

Derry, t-ship, Columbia co. bounded N. by Lycoming co. E. by Madison t-ship, S. by Mahoning and W. by Limestone t-ship. Centrally distant N. of Danville 10 miles; greatest length 11, breadth 5½ miles; area, 17,920 acres; surface level; soil clay and limestone. Pop. in 1830, 1688; taxables 347. The S. boundary follows the Mahoney ridge. The Chilisquaque creek flows S. through the t-ship, near the W. boundary, and after passing the p-v. of Washington, turns S. W. into Limestone t-ship. It receives several small streams from the right and left; post office is 187 miles from W. C. and 77 from Harrisburg.

Derry, t-ship, Westmoreland co. bounded N. and N. E. by the Conemaugh r. S. E. by Chestnut ridge, and S. W. and W. by Loyalhanna river. Centrally distant N. E. from Greensburg 14 miles; greatest length 18, breadth 12½ miles; area 74,880 acres; surface, hilly; soil, loam, gravel and limestone. In addition to the rivers, the t-ship is watered by Stoney run, and McGee's run. Port Johnson is in the N. angle of the t-ship, at the confluence of the Conemaugh and Loyalhanna rivers, below and nearly opposite to Saltzburg. Salt is abundantly found here on both sides of the Conemaugh r. New Alexandria, a post town, lies on the Loyalhanna river above the mouth of Crabtree creek, and on the turnpike road leading from Ebensburg to Greensburg, and New Derry, also a post town north of Mc Gee's run.

Derry, t-ship, Mifflin co. bounded N. E. by Decatur and Fermanagh t-ships, S. E. by Milford t-ship, S. W. by Wayne t-ship, and N. W. by Jacks mountain, which seperates it from Union and Armagh t-ship; greatest length 12, breadth 8 miles; area 34,560 acres. Lewistown, the county town, lies on the river Juniata, at the foot of Limestone ridge; north of which, and S. of Jack's mountain, is Ferguson's valley. The Kishcoquilla creek flows S. through the t-ship, into the river at Lewistown, and Jack's creek S. W. uniting with the river, about a mile below the town. The turnpike road from Duncans island to Huntingdon, runs W. through the town, and the turnpike road to Bellefonte, runs N. from it.

Derry, New, p-t. of Derry t-ship, Westmoreland co. 14 miles N. E. of Greensburg, 188 from W. C. and 166 from Harrisburg, contains 12 houses, 2 stores and 2 taverns.

Dial Knob, a noted eminence of the Capous range of mountains, lying on the boundary line between Exter and Pittstown t-ships, Luzerne co. near the Suspuehannah river. It is 1125 feet high, and is in the centre of the Luzerne coal region, about 10 miles in a direct line N. E. of Wilkesbarre.

Diamonds mills, village of Greene t-ship, Indianna co. at the confluence of Buck run, with Two Lick creek, 10 miles N. E. of Indiana borough, contains 4 or 5 dwellings, 1 store, and a mill.

Dible's Gap, a pass in the Mahantango mountain, Upper Paxton t-ship, Dauphin co. about 27 miles in a direct line N. of Harrisburg.

Dickenson, t-ship, Cumberland co. bounded N. by West Pennsborough, E. by South Middleton t-ships, S. by Adams co. and W. by Newton t-ship. Centrally distant S. W. from Carlisle 10 miles; greatest length, and breadth 10½ miles; area 51,240 acres; surface partly hilly; soil limestone. Pop. in 1830, 2523; taxables 413. It is drained by the Yellow Breeches creek, which flows eastwardly through the middle of the t-ship, and by its tributary, Mountain creek; upon the former, there is a furnace near the centre of its course, and another called Pine Grove on the latter, near the S. boundary. Iron is abundant in the South mountain, and that near Pine Grove is of extraordinary purity. The post office, called after the t-ship, is 108 miles N. of W. C. and 36 W. of Harrisburg.

Dick's Hill, a noted eminence of Rye t-ship, Perry co. extending about 7 miles W. from Juniata river, in the N. part of the township.

Dillsburg, or *Dillstown*, p-t. Carroll t-ship, York co. 20 miles N. W. of the borough of York, 98 from W. C. and 12 from Harrisburg.

Dilworthtown, p-t. of Birmingham t-ship, Chester co. 23 miles W. of Philadelphia, and 5 S. of West Chester, 118 miles from W. C. and 79 from Harrisburg, contains 15 or 20 dwellings, &c.

Dill's ferry, over the river Delaware in Upper Mount Bethel t-ship, Northampton co. about 18 miles above Easton, 210 N. E. from W. C. 123 from Harrisburg. There is a post office here. The town of Columbus in N. Jersey is on the opposite bank.

Dimmockville, p-o. of Susquehannah co. 274 miles from W. C. and 175 from Harrisburg.

Dingman's Ferry, p-t. of Delaware t-ship, Pike co. 28 miles above the Delaware Water Gap, and 8 below Milford, 244 N. E. of W. C. and 149 from Harrisburg. There is a ferry over the Delaware from this place. An academy was established here and incorporated by act of 4th March, 1813, to which the state gave $1000.

District, *East*, t-ship, Berks co., bounded N. by Longswamp, S. by Cole Crockdale, E. by Hereford, S. E. by Pike, and N. E. by Rockland. Greatest length 4½, breadth 3½ miles; area, 6,500 acres; surface, large hills; soil, gravel, and very indifferent, average value when improved, about $20 per acre. Pop. in 1830, 562; taxables, 1828, 114. Pine creek, a confluent of the Manatawny, rises in this t-ship, on which there is a furnace.

Dividing mountain, a ridge of the Allegheny, about 10 miles in length, in Fannet t-ship, Franklin co. which runs N. E. and S. W. and separates Path valley from Amberson's valley.

Doe run, a tributary of Buck run, which divides East Fallowfield from Londonderry t-ship, Chester co. It is a small stream with several mills upon it, having a course of about 8 miles.

Doe run, p-o. Chester co. 107 miles from W. C. and 64 from Harrisburg.

Dolinton, p-t. of Upper Wakefield t-ship, Bucks co., situated at the intersection of the Newtown and Falsington roads, and near the S. township. Distant from Phila. about 25 ms. N. E.; from Doylestown, 13 ms. S. E.; 171 ms. from W. C. and 133 from Harrisburg. Contains a tavern, 7 or 8 dwellings, and a church.

Donegal, t-ship, Washington co., bounded N. by Hopewell, E. by Buffalo, S. by Findlay t-ships, and W. by the state of Virginia; centrally distant from Washington bor. 12 miles; greatest length 8, breadth 6½ miles; area, 25,600 acres; surface, very hilly; soil, loam; coal, abundant. Pop. in 1830, 2093; taxables, 470. The t-ship is drained N. W. by the Dutch fork of Buffalo creek, Bush run and Castleman's run. The national road runs S. W. through it, upon which lie Clay'sville on the E. and West Alexandria on the W. boundary; both post towns.

Donegal, t-ship, Westmoreland co. bounded N. E. by Ligonier t-ship, S. E. by Laurel Hill, which divides it from Somerset co. S. W. by Fayette co. and N. W. by Chesnut ridge, which separates it from Mt. Pleasant and Unity t-ships; centrally distant from Greensburg 16 miles; greatest length 11, breadth 10½ miles; area, 60,160 acres; surface, hills and valley; soil, limestone and loam. Pop. in 1830, 2052; taxables, 337. It is drained on the E. by Four-mile run, Two-mile run, and Loyalhanna creek, and on the W. by the head waters of Jacob's and Indian creeks; upon both of which there are iron works. Hopewell furnace is on the latter. The turnpike road from Somerset to Washington runs N. W. through the t-ship. The post office, named after the township, is 183 ms. N. W. of W. C. and 161 from Harrisburg.

Donegal, t-ship, Butler co., bounded N. by Packer t-ship, E. by Armstrong co. S. by Clearfield t-ship, and W. by Centre t-ship. It forms a square of 8 miles; centrally distant from Butler borough 9 ms. N. E.; area, 40,960 acres; surface, rolling, hilly; soil, loam, clay, sand, gravel. Pop. 1830, 1085; taxables, 228. It is drained, N.E. by Bear creek, S. E. by a branch of Buffalo, and W. by tributaries of the Conequenessing creek. Iron ore and stone coal of excellent quality are found here, and invite to the manufacture of iron.

Donegal, t-ship, Lancaster co., bounded N. by Mount Joy t-ship, E. by Raphs t-ship, S. and S. W. by the Susquehannah r. and N. W. by Dauphin co.; centrally distant N. W. from Lancaster, 17 ms.; length 11, breadth 6½ ms.; area, 33,891 acres. Pop. in 1830, 6058; taxables, 1132. This t-ship has been divided into E. and W. Donegal, but we have not the line of division. East Donegal contains 13 distilleries, 2 tan yards, 4 grist mills, 1 saw mill and 2 breweries. West Donegal, 8 distilleries, 1 fulling mill and 4 grist mills. The t-ship is bounded E. by Little Chiques creek, Share's run and Coney creek. The turnpike road from Lancaster to Harrisburg, runs on the N. line, on which are the villages of Mt. Joy, Richland, Springville and Elizabethtown; the first and last are post towns. Marietta, Bainbridge and Falmouth, are on the river, all of which are post towns; and Maytown, 2 miles from the river, also a post town.

Douglass, t-ship, Berks co. bounded N. by Colebrookdale, E. by the river Schuylkill, S. by Montgomery co., W. by Amity and Earl t-ships; greatest length 5¼, width 2 miles; area, 7000 acres; surface, undulating; soil, gravel, not remarkably fertile. Pop. in 1810, 660; in 1820, 1046; in 1830, 1210; taxables, 230. The Philadelphia and Reading turnpike road crosses the township near its southern boundary. There is a forge on the Manatawny creek, called Pine forge, and a post office called Douglassville, 147 miles N. from W. C. and 64 E. from Harrisburg.

Douglass, t-ship, Montgomery co. bounded N. E. by Upper Hanover, S. E. by New Hanover, S. W. by Douglass t-ship, Berks co., W. by Colebrookdale, and N. W. by Hereford t-ships, in the latter co. The surface is hilly, and soil red shale. The form of the t-ship is a parallelogram of 7½ miles by 2; area, 10,240 acres. The west branch of the Perkiomen and Swamp creek run across, on each of which there is a mill. Pop. in 1830, 941; taxables in 1828, 205.

Douglass' Mills, p-t. Perry t-ship, 129 ms. from W. C., 42 N. W. from Harrisburg.

Dover, t-ship, York co., bounded N. E. by Conewago, S. E. by W. Manchester, S. by Paradise, W. by Washington, and N. W. by Warrington t-ships; centrally distant from the borough of York 8 miles; greatest length $8\frac{1}{2}$ miles, breadth 7 ms.; area, 23,040 acres; surface, hilly; soil, red shale of good quality. Pop. in 1830, 1874. The Great Conewago creek follows the W. and N. W. boundary, and the Little Conewago the S. W. Salmon creek is a tributary of the former, and Fox run of the latter. The Conewago hills cross it from S. W. to N. E. Dover, a post town, and Weigelstown, lie on the road from York borough to Ross Town, the former distant from the borough N. W. 7 miles, and the latter about 5 miles. Taxable property in 1829, real estate, 304,431; personal, 18,380; occupations, 37,640; total, $360,451; rate, 25 cts. on the $100.

Dover, p-t. York co. (see preceding article) distant from W. C. 94 miles, and 12 from Harrisburg.

Downing's Town, a p-t. and village of East Caln t-ship, Chester co. on the turnpike road from Philadelphia to Lancaster, 33 ms. W. of N. from the former, and about the same distance from the latter. It is situated in the great valley, surrounded with rich and fertile farms, and contains many noble and spacious houses of stone, and perhaps no place in the state affords a more satisfactory impression of rural wealth and contentment than this village and its vicinity. It comprehends 40 dwellings, several stores, 2 taverns, 1 or more grist mills, a woollen factory, and a Quaker meeting house. The East Branch of the Brandywine river passes through the town.

Doylestown, t-ship, Bucks co. bounded N. by Plumstead, E. by Buckingham, S. E. by Warwick, S. by Warrington, and W. by New Britain t-ships. Centrally distant from Phila. 25 miles; greatest length $4\frac{1}{2}$, greatest breadth 4 miles; area, 9603 acres. The surface of the t-ship is rolling; soil, gravelly loam, well cultivated and productive. The Neshaminy crosses the southern portion of the t-ship, and receives from it Pine run, and another mill stream which rises N. E. of Doylestown. The main road from Phila. to Easton passes through the t-ship, on which are the towns of Bridgeport, at the confluence of the last mentioned stream with the Neshaminy (and here also is a noble stone bridge, of several arches, built at co. expense,) Houghville, at which there is a woollen manufactory, and Doylestown, a p-t. and st. jus. Pop. in 1830, 1781; taxables in 1828, 362.

Doylestown, p-t. and st. jus. Bucks co. 26 ms. N. of Phila. in Doylestown t-ship. This town is situated upon a high hill, and has a commanding view of a delightful and fertile country which surrounds it, and is not less remarkable for salubrity than for the beauty of its location. The public buildings consist of a neat and commodious stone court house, in which are the co. offices, and of a capacious stone prison. There are in the town about 100 dwellings, 5 stores, 6 taverns. Two daily stages pass through it to Easton. A branch of the Neshaminy creek passes near to and east of the town. There is here a Presbyterian church, an academy, which is incorporated and has received several donations from the state, an academy of natural sciences, an agricultural society, and four weekly newspapers, viz. The Bucks County Intelligencer, The Bucks County Republican, The Doylestown Democrat, and the Doylestown Express; the last is a German paper.

Drake, or Dreek creek, a small stream of Northampton co. running N. of Pine hill. It is a rapid stream, and has a course of 6 or 8 ms. to the Lehigh r. into which it flows about 2 ms. below the Rock Eddy falls.

Drinker's run, a small tributary of the Lehigh r. which rises in and has a course of 5 ms. in Covington t-ship, Luzerne co.

Dromore, t-ship, Lancaster county, bounded N. by Barts, N. E. by Coleraine, S. E. by Little Britain, S. W.

by the Susquehannah r. and N. W. by Martick t-ship. Centrally distant from the city of Lancaster 15 ms. S. E.; greatest length 10 miles, greatest breadth 6; area, 29,391 acres; surface, rolling; soil, clay. Pop. in 1830, 1629; taxables 310. The W. branch of the Octarara cr. forms the N. E. boundary, and Muddy creek makes part of the N. W. line. Conewingo creek crosses it from N. W. to S. E. and upon this stream there is a forge, and Fishing and Fairfield creeks flow from it into the Susquehannah river. Fairfield is a small village near the S. W. boundary; and the p-o. centrally situated in the t-ship, is called Mount Pleasant. There are in the t-ship 1 furnace, 1 distillery, 1 tanyard, 1 fulling mill, 3 grist mills, 5 saw mills, 2 oil mills, 1 carding machine, 2 tilt hammers, 1 rolling mill.

Drumheller's Mill creek, rises in Luzerne co. and flows S. W. thro' Lausanne t-ship, Northampton co. into Quakak cr. a tributary of the Lehigh r. It is a mill stream, but not navigable.

Dry ridge, a mountain range of Napier t-ship, Bedford co. between the Raystown branch of the Juniata river and Buffalo creek.

Dry run, p-o. Franklin co. 113 ms. N. W. from W. C. and 63 S. W. from Harrisburg.

Dublin, Lower, t-ship, Philadelphia co. bounded N. E. by the t-ship of Moreland and by Bucks co., S. E. by the r. Delaware, S. W. by the t-ship of Oxford, and N. W. by Montgomery co. Centrally distant from Phila. 10 ms.; greatest length 5, breadth 3 ms.; area 9500 acres; surface, gentle declivities; soil, sandy loam, and generally well cultivated. Pop. in 1830, 2705. The Pennypack creek flows centrally through it by a comparative and S. E. course of 5 ms. giving motion to 4 grist mills, 1 slitting mill, 1 tilt and blade mill, 1 cotton manufactory, 3 saw mills, 1 woollen factory, and 1 calico printing factory, very extensively conducted, belonging to S. Comly, near to Holmesburg. It receives a considerable branch from the t-ship, called Saw Mill run, on which there is also a woollen factory. The creek is navigable to Lewis' mills, 2 ms. from its mouth. Lewis' grist mill is one of the oldest in the state, having been erected in 1697. Holmesburg and Bustleton are villages and post towns. The "Fox Chase" and "Sandy Hill" are hamlets of the t-ship. There are two academies, "Lower Dublin" and "Bustleton," both of which have received aid by lotteries granted by the state. There are also several other schools in the township. There are 3 Baptist meeting houses, the Pennypack meeting, 1 at Bustleton, and 1 at Holmesburg. The first is venerable for its age, and has been served by the most distinguished preachers of that sect. There is also a Methodist and an Episcopal church, the former at Holmesburg, and the latter, called "All Saints," on the Bristol road, about 10½ ms. from the city. The poor house, for the incorporated district of Oxford and Lower Dublin, is situated on the Pennypack cr. near Holmesburg. Two turnpike roads cross the t-ship, the Bristol and the Smithfield roads.

Dublin, Upper, t-ship, Montgomery co. bounded on the N. E. by Horsham and Moreland, on the S. E. by Abington, on the S. by Springfield, on the S. W. by Whitemarsh, and on the N. W. by Guinedd t-ship. It is drained by several tributaries of the Wissahiccon creek; greatest length 3½, breadth 3 ms.; area 6720 acres; surface, rolling; soil, limestone and loam. Pop. in 1830, 1292; taxables, 293. The p-o. called after the t-ship, is 153 ms. from W. C. and 167 from Harrisburg.

Dublin, a p-t. and small village on the line between Hilltown and Bedminster t-ship, Bucks co. about 7 ms. N. W. of Doylestown, 166 from W. C. 97 from Harrisburg, contains 6 or 8 dwellings.

Dublin, t-ship, Bedford co. bounded N. by Huntingdon co. E. by Franklin co. S. by Air and Belfast t-ships, and W. by Hopewell t-ship. Centrally distant E. from Bedford 25 ms.; greatest length 12½, breadth 9½ ms; area 53,760 acres; surface, level valley; soil, limestone. Pop. in 1830, 801; taxables, 160. The Tuscarora mtn. is on the E. boundary, and Sideling hill on the W. Scrub ridge runs into it from the S. and Shade mtn. from the N. Sidney Knob, a noted hill, is a spur of the Tuscarora.

It is drained on the S. by the head waters of Licking creek, on the N. by Little Augwick creek and Wooden Bridge creek. There is a small hamlet on the E. boundary, called the Burnt Cabins, at which there is a p-o.

Dublin, t-ship, Huntingdon county, bounded N. by Tell township, E. by Franklin co. S. by Bedford co. and W. by Springfield t-ship. Centrally distant S. E. from Huntingdon borough 21 ms.; greatest length 8½, breadth 5 ms.; area 25,350 acres; surface, mountainous; soil, clay. Pop. in 1830, 666; taxables, 153. It is drained on the N. W. by Shade cr. on the S. by Little Augwick creek. Augwick valley occupies the middle of the t-ship, running N. E. and S. W. The Tuscarora mtn. lies on the E. and Shade mtn. on the W. boundaries. This t-ship contained, in 1828, 1 grist mill, 6 saw mills, 2 distilleries, 1 fulling mill, 1 oil mill, 1 tanyard.

Dunbar, t-ship, Fayette co. bounded N. by Tyrone t-sp, E. by Youghiogheny r. which separates it from Connellsville t-ship, S. by Wharton and Union t-ships, and W. by Franklin. Centrally distant N. E. from Union 8 ms.; greatest length 10, breadth 6 ms.; area 23,600 acres; surface, rolling; soil, loam and limestone. Pop. in 1830, 1722; taxables, 377. Laurel hill is on the S. E. boundary, whence proceeds Dunbar run, which flows N. W. and enters the r. at the p-t. of New Haven, opposite to Connellsville, giving motion to a forge, some mills and factories. East Liberty, another p-t. lies on the r. in the N. W. corner of the t-ship.

Duncansville, Allegheny township, Huntingdon co. 2 ms. E. of Blair's gap, and about 25 ms. N. W. of Huntingdon borough, contains 10 dwellings, 3 taverns, 1 store, 2 smith shops, and a brewery.

Duncan's island, a large island, at and above the confluence of the Susquehannah and Juniata rs. formed by the branching of those streams. The eastern section of the Pennsylvania canal connects here with the Juniata division by a dam, and a bridge and tow path across the Susquehannah r. a short canal through the island and an aqueduct over the Juniata r.

Dundaff, a p-t. and borough in the S. E. angle of Clifford t-ship, Susquehannah co. near Upper Chrystal lake, and on the road from Bethany to Montrose, 20 ms. N. W. of the former and 22 S. E. from the latter. It contains 1 Presbyterian church, and 1 banking house, formerly the property of a bank now extinct, 35 dwellings, 3 stores, 3 taverns. An extensive manufactory of window glass was established here in 1831, which in the close of the year manufactured 350 boxes of 8 by 10 glass per week. The town was incorporated 5th March, 1828, and an academy established thereat, incorporated by act 16th Feb. 1830.

Dunk's ferry, over the Delaware r. Bensalem t-ship, Bucks co. 16 miles above Philadelphia and 4 below Bristol.

Dunkville, small village of 6 or 8 dwellings, on the turnpike road between Phila. and Bristol, 18 ms. from the former and 4 from the latter.

Dunkard, t-ship, Greene co. bounded N. by Greene and Monongahela t-ships, E. by Monongahela and Cheat rs. S. by the state of Virginia, and W. by Whitely t-ship. Centrally distant from Waynesburg S. E. 15 miles; greatest length 10, breadth 6 miles; area 22,400 acres; surface, rolling; soil, loam. Pop. in 1830, 1336; taxables, 235. Dunkard creek runs N. E. through the t-ship, and receives from it several small streams. Cheat r. and the Monongahela flow into the E. part of the t-ship from Virginia, and unite on the E. boundary, about 3 ms. N. of the state line.

Dunkard creek, a considerable stream which rises by many branches in Aleppo t-ship, Greene co. and flows along the S. boundary of the state, sometimes deviating into Virginia, the whole length of Greene co. to the Monongahela on its eastern boundary. It receives many tributaries from the N. and S. in its course of more than 30 ms.

Dunlap's creek, Fayette co. rises in German t-ship and flows N. to the Monongahela r. forming the boundary between Red Stone and Luzerne t-ships. Brownsville lies on the E. and Bridgeport on the W. bank of the creek, at its confluence with the r.

Dunning's mountain, is a continuation of Evitt's mountain from the vicinity of the town of Bedford. It runs N. E. about 7 ms. thence turning to the N. W. it continues that course about 5 ms. and thence N. 15 ms. to the Frankstown branch of the Juniata river.

Dunstable, t-ship, Lycoming county, bounded N. and N. E. by Brown t-ship, E. by Pine Creek t-ship, S.E. and S. by the W. branch of the Susquehannah r. and W. by Chapman t-ship. Centrally distant W. about 30 miles from Williamsport; greatest length 30, breadth 15 ms.; area, 92,800 acres; surface, mountainous; soil, various, chiefly limestone and slate. (See Lycoming co.) Pop. in 1830, about 500; taxables 100; valuation of taxable property in 1829, seated lands $28,454; unseated $8570; personal est. $4303; rate of levy $\frac{3}{4}$ of 1 per cent. Beside the river, the principal stream is Lick run. But there are many other smaller streams in the t-ship. The country is almost a desert, but has lately grown into notice by the discovery and working of some coal mines on Lick run and other parts of the t-ship. The course of the r. here is from E. to W. finding its way *among* the mtns. and not breaking down and *crossing* the chains. The mtns. range from S. W. to N. E.; on their N. sides they are precipitous, rising so abruptly from the waters edge as scarce to afford space for a road, though between Lick run and Queen's run (3 ms. below Lick run), some 40 acres of interval or cotton land is found, presenting a favorable site for a town in regard to the coal operations of the two streams. On the N. of the r. the mountains have an elevation apparently of from 600 to 1000 feet; on the opposite side they are lower and less steep. Leaving the r. the traveller forsakes the habitation of man, nor, for many a weary mile, can a trace of his hand be found, unless, perchance, in the occasional marks of the surveyor, or the lair of the hunter; all seems interminable wilderness. There is not even an "*opening*" to be seen to offend the eye or sicken the heart of the most confirmed "*Leather Stocking.*" But the region is not devoid of inhabitants. Here may be seen every variety of the indigenous serpent, from the garter to the rattle snake; and the wolf and the bear, the elk and the deer, prowling and bounding in these wilds. Improvement and population are confined to the narrow strips of land occurring on the borders of the r. and its larger tributaries. A string of settlements, some of them creditable to the owners, extend, with frequent interruption however, from the mtns. to the head of the river. Dunnstown, p-t. lies on the S. E. angle of the t-ship, upon the left bank of the r. about 25 ms. from Williamsport, 219 from W. C. and 112 from Harrisburg. It contains about 20 dwellings, a store and tavern.

Dunnstown, Dunstable t-ship, Lycoming co. (see preceding article.)

Durham, t-ship, Bucks co. bounded N. by Lehigh co. E. by the river Delaware; S. by Nockamixen t-ship, and W. by Springfield. Centrally distant N. E. from Doylestown 20 miles; and 12 ms. S. of Easton; greatest length $3\frac{1}{2}$ miles, greatest breadth 3 miles; area 6337 acres. Cook's or Durham creek passes centrally through the t-ship, upon which there is a p-o. and furnace, and a small village of 6 or 7 houses, with a mill, store, and tavern. Surface hilly; soil, clay. Pop. 1830, 750; taxables in 1828, 127. In this t ship there is a singular limestone cave, which merits notice. It is vulgarly called the Devil's Hole, and is situate about 50 miles from Philadelphia, in the angle of confluence of Durham creek and the Delaware. The entrance is about 100 yards W. of the latter, and 200 from the point of confluence. The height of the eminence enclosing the cavity is about 200 feet above the circumjacent land. From the pathway of the entrance, to the top of the rock above, the height is above 40 feet. Three or four persons may enter abreast, but not more, as the portal is obstructed by a ledge of rocks. The cave is divided into three great apartments, communicating with each other, by steep and rugged passages. After a descent of about 30 feet the first apartment is seen in its greatest extent, of which it is difficult to form a correct estimate, by reason of the irregularity in the walls and roof. Some idea of the dimensions of these chambers may be formed by the following measurements.

	Lth.	Bth.	Ht.
First apartment, average,	90 ft.	33,	20,
Second do. do. .	96,	40,	20,
Third do. do. . .	93,	16,	17,

Length of whole cave to the water's edge at the bottom. . . . . 279, feet.
Breadth of the water, . . 20, feet.

The temperature of the air in this vault is from 54 to 62, the latter being that of the outer apartment. Some part of the vault is covered with a white crust somewhat crystallized; probably a petrefaction of the calcareous matter which exudes through the rock. It is easily severed with a hammer and in some places by the finger. Over other parts of the arch there are incrustations of a dark color, which have the appearance of moss, but is as hard as the rock, and over it the water continually trickles.

By supposition the descent in a right line forms an angle of 40° with the horizon.

At the bottom is a bason of excellent water, 20 feet in width, bounded by a wall, through which a conduit runs further into the earth, and communicates with the creek and river. The surface of the water in the pool rises and falls with that in the latter, and a freshet in the river, nearly fills the lower chamber. At the partition between the first, and second apartments, there is a lateral branch of the cave extending 32 feet in length eastwardly, and sufficiently wide, to permit the passage of two persons. From this there are two smaller branches, one running 22 feet north, the other 14 S., wide enough only to admit a single person.

Durham creek, rises in springfield t-ship, Bucks co. and by a N. E. course of 10 miles flows through Durham t-ship, into the Delaware, near the cave called the Devil's Hole. It is a fine stream and turns several mills in its course.

Dutotsburg, a village and p-t. of Northampton co. situated on the river Delaware at its entrance into the water gap, about 22 miles from Easton, and at the foot of the Blue mountain on the N. side in Smithfield t-ship. It contains 8 dwellings and 1 tavern. It is 215 miles N. E. from W. C. and 128 from Harrisburg.

Duval creek, Asylum t-ship, Bradford co. rises in the t-ship, and flows N. E. along the N. W. boundary into the Susquehannah river.

Dyberry, t-ship, Wayne co. bounded N. by Mount Pleasant and Lebanon t-ships, E. by Damascus t-ship and Pike co., S. by Palmyra and Canaan t-ships, and W. by Canaan. It is shaped like an L. Greatest length, E. and W. 14 ms.; greatest breadth N. and S. 10 miles. It is drained by the Lackawaxen and Dyberry creeks and their tributaries. The Milford and Owego, and the Bethany and Dingman's Choice turnpike roads pass through the t-ship. There are in this t-ship 7 stores, 9 taverns, 3 grist mills,

13 saw mills, 1 fulling mill, 1 carding machine, 36 looms, and 9 schools. Surface, hilly; soil, gravel and loam. Pop. in 1830, 1078; taxables in 1828, 232; taxable property in 1829, seated lands, $78,825; unseated, 44,509; personal estate, including occupations, 14,648.

Dyberry creek, a main branch of the Lackawaxen river, rises in Mt. Pleasant t-ship, Wayne co. and flows south-easterly through Lebanon and Dyberry t-ships, and near Bethany to Honesdale, where it unites with the Lackawaxen. Its valley is deep, no where exceeding half a mile in breadth, and has rich allŭvial flats. It is navigable for ābout 4 miles above its mouth. (See Honesdale.)

Dyerstown, a small hamlet on the road to Easton, from Doylestown, about 2 miles from the latter, in Plumstead t-ship, Bucks co.

Earl, t-ship, Berks co. bounded N. by Pike, S. by Amity and Douglass, E. by Douglass and Colebrookdale, and W. by Oley. Greatest length, $4\frac{1}{2}$, brdth. $3\frac{1}{4}$ ms.; area, 9,520 acres; soil, gravel; surface, very hilly; the South mountain passing through it. Pop. in 1810, 653; in 1820, 934; in 1830, 979; taxables in 1828, 183. Manatawny creek passes through its S. W. corner, on which there is a forge, called Spring forge.

Earl, t-ship, Lancaster co. bounded N. by Cocalico and Brecknock, E. by Caernarvon, S. by Salisbury and Leacock, and W. by Manheim and Warwick t-ships; centrally distant from the city of Lancaster 13 miles N. W.; Length about 12 ms; average breadth about 8 miles; area, 48,936 acres; surface, rolling; soil, red shale and gravel. Pop. in 1830, 5344; taxables, 989. It is drained by the Conestoga creek, which receives here from Brecknock t-ship, Muddy creek. The Dowingstown and Harrisburg turnpike road crosses it from S. E. to N. W. and the Lancaster and Morgantown turnpike from S. W. to N. E. On the former is situated Swope Town and Hinckletown, on the latter New Holland. Hanstown lies in the northern part of the t-ship. There is a post office on the Harrisburg t-ship, near the Blue Ball tavern, called Earle, and one at New Holland, and a third at Hinkletown. There is also a forge on the Conestoga creek, near the eastern boundary, and there are 8 distilleries, 1 fulling mill and 4 grist mills in the t-ship.

Earleysburg, p-t. of Potter t-ship, Centre co. near the turnpike road leading from Lewistown to Bellefonte in Penn's valley, about 8 miles S. E. of the latter town.

East Branch, t-ship, Venango co. bounded N. by Crawford and Warren t-ships, E. by Allegheny t-ship, S. by Windrock t-ship, and W. by Oil creek, which separates it from Cherry Tree t-ship; centrally distant N. E. from Franklin borough 16 miles; greatest length, 7 miles, breadth 6 miles; area, 19,200 acres; surface, rolling; soil, gravel and loam. Population, very scanty. The township is not organized, and is annexed to Cherry Tree t-ship. There is a bituminous oil spring in the N. part of the t-ship, upon Oil creek.

East Liberty, p-t. of Dunbar t-ship, Fayette co., on the south bank of the Youghiogheny river, in the N. W. angle of the t-ship, 11 miles N. E. of Uniontown, distant 201 ms. N. W. of W. C. and 178 S. W. from Harrisburgh.

East Liberty, t. of Pitt t-ship, Allegheny co. 6 ms. E. of Pittsburg, on the turnpike road, and near the head of Higley's run; contains about 70 dwellings, 3 or 4 stores, as many taverns, and a Presbyterian church.

Easton, a p-t. and bor. Northampton co., is the seat of justice, and the largest town in the county; distant, 190 ms. N. E. from W. C. and 101 from Harrisburg, 56 N. from Philadelphia, and 73 S. W. from New-York. It is situated at the confluence of the rivers Delaware and Lehigh, and extends from the mouth of the latter, along the former, nearly a half mile, to the Bushkill creek, so that the town is bounded on three sides by water. It is built on ground which ascends in an angle of 5 deg. above the horizon, extending directly west from the Delaware. It contains five streets, running east and west, and three north and south, which have paved walks upon their sides. In the centre of the town is a public square, surrounding the court-house. The other public buildings are, five churches, Presbyterian, Episcopalian, 2 German Lutheran, &c. and an academy, in which the languages are taught. By act of assembly 9th March, 1826, a college was established, under the title of "La Fayette College." But we are ignorant of the progress made in confirming the institution. The buildings are chiefly of stone or brick, and two stories high. The number of dwellings are about 600, besides shops and other out houses, one third of which are of brick. Easton was incorporated into a borough on the 23d of Sept. 1789, and now forms a township. There is an elegant bridge, of wood, of three arches, covered, 600 feet long and 24 feet wide, over the Delaware, which cost $80,000. Across the Lehigh, a chain bridge, suspended on four chains, hanging in two loops and two half loops, having two pass ways for teams, and a foot-walk between, guarded by hand railings. Its length is 423 feet, width 25 feet. There are also two other bridges over the Bushkill. There are two daily lines of stages which run between this town and Philadelphia, and also stages from it to every part the country. There are here 5 fire engines, 3 hose carriages with 2300 ft. hose; 2 volunteer companies and 1 troop of horse; 7 physicians, 13 lawyers, &c. &c. The country adjacent to the town is bold, broken, and romantic. The soil is highly productive, and being well cultivated, gives a most pleasing aspect to the vicinity of Easton. Farm houses, orchards, fields and meadows, are commingled along the bottoms of the river and the slopes of the hills. Bushkill creek, one of the finest mill streams of the United States, passes the Chestnut ridge within the borough, and by a winding and precipitous course affords many valuable mill seats. There are within the boundaries of the town 3 oil mills, 6 grist mills, 2 saw mills, 2 distilleries, 3 tanneries, 1 brewery, 1 wholesale grocery and liquor store, 33 retail stores, 3 drug and medicine stores, four printing presses, which issue 5 weekly papers, with a full proportion of other stores, shops, and mechanical professions, necessary to the comforts of a rich and thriving population; a library, formed in 1811, containing about 3000 volumes, and an interesting cabinet of minerals, &c.; 2 banks, one a branch of that of Pennsylvania, the other, the Easton Bank, erected under the act of assembly of 1814, with a capital of $400,000. The trade of the town is very considerable, particularly in the article of flour, which constitutes the principal staple of the county. Pop. in 1810, 1657; in 1820, 2370; in 1830, 3529; taxables in 1828, 660. The town is supplied with water, conveyed in iron pipes from a spring about a mile from the borough.

Easton, South, a village lately laid out by the Lehigh navigation company, on the S. bank of the Lehigh river, and opposite to Easton. There are already several good houses put up in this town, and many more will doubtless be immediately erected, since the advantages derivable from the water created by the Lehigh canal, are here very great, and offer attractions of no ordinary character to the capitalist and the manufacturer.

Eastown, t-ship, Chester co. bounded N. and N. W. by Tredyffrin, S. W. by Radnor, S. by Newtown, and W. by Willistown t-ships. Centrally distant from Philadelphia 16 miles; length, 3 miles; breadth, $2\frac{1}{2}$; area, 4,650 acres; surface, gentle declivities; soil, sandy loam. Population in 1830, 648. Taxables in 1828, 137. Darby creek crosses the t-ship, from W. to E. diagonally.

Eaton, t-ship, Luzerne county, (so

named in honor of Gen. William Eaton, a native of Massachusetts, and the hero of Derne, in Barbary,) is bounded N. N. E. and E. by the Susquehannah river, which separates it from Tunkhannock and Falls, S. by Northmoreland, and N. W. by Windham. It is generally hilly, and some part of it mountainous; the Allegheny hills covering almost its whole suface. Bowman's ridge terminates in this t-ship, on the Susquehannah river, in a high eminence called the "Knob," whose altitude is 1150 feet above the river. A good portion of it may be cultivated. It produces some agricultural products, and considerable lumber for market. The great stage route from Wilkesbarre to Montrose, passes through it. It is situated about 25 miles N. of Wilkesbarre, has a p-office, called after the t-ship, distant from W. C. 251 miles, and 143 from Harrisburg. Bowman's creek flows through it in a N. E. course, and unites with the river on the N. side of the Knob, turning several mills on its way. A ferry is established over the river, above the mouth of the creek. The t-ship is irregular in form. Its greatest length E. and W. is 10 miles; breadth N. and S. about 6 miles; area, 25,600 acres. Population in 1830, about 600. Taxables in 1828, 110.

East Penn, t-ship, Northampton co. bounded N. by Mauch Chunk t-ship, S. by Lehigh county, E. by the Lehigh river, and W. by Schuylkill co. Its greatest length is 8 miles; breadth, 6½ miles. The surface of the country is mountainous; the soil, gravel and red shale. Population in 1830, 807. Taxable in 1828, 222. Burlington and Lehighton are villages within this t-ship. The latter is a thriving and beautifully situated place, near which is a church, and the Mahoning creek, on which is a furnace. Lizzard creek also passes through the t-ship, to the Lehigh river, over which is an excellent bridge. The Lehigh water gap and Kunckle's gap, through the Blue mountains, are on the southern part of the t-ship. The chief product of the t-ship is rye. There is a p-office here called after the t-ship, distant 191 miles from W. C. and 91 from Harrisburg.

Ebensburgh, a borough, p-t. and st. of jus. of Cambria county, 70 miles E. from Pittsburg, and 2 miles N. E. from Beula, N. lat. 40° 31,' long 1° 41' W. from W. C. Popula. in 1830, 270. It is situated on the Allegheny mountain, and commands a grand and extensive view of the surrounding country. There is a considerable body of fine timbered land in the neighborhood. The population of the town and the adjacent country is composed chiefly of industrious, moral and thriving people from Wales, and Ireland. It contains between 30 and 40 houses, 3 meeting-houses; 1 Baptist, 1 Congrega. 1 Catholic, 6 taverns, 7 stores, and a p-o. The turnpike road from Hollidaysburg to Indiana runs through the town, and another turnpike road runs from it to Pittsburg .A handsome brick academy was built here by an appropriation of $2,000, by the state, in 1819. A new court-house has lately been erected, of brick, and county offices. Formerly, the courts were held for years, in the second story of an old ricketty wooden building, the lower story being occupied as the jail. A ludicrous story is told of a mountain suitor who, being obstreperous in his drink, was committed for contempt of court, to this prison. This punishment induced a fit of devotion, attended by an unconquerable desire for Psalm-singing, in the gratification of which, he purchased the aid of a fellow prisoner. Their joint performance overpowered even the loudest tones of the advocate who was addressing the jury, and compelled the court to adjourn until the term of committal of the prisoner had expired. The town was incorporated by act 15th Jan. 1825.

Economy, a p-town and German settlement of the Harmonites, on the Ohio river, 18 miles below Pittsburg, in Ohio t-ship, Beaver co. 241 miles

N. W. of W. C. 219 from Harrisburg. This settlement has been made by Mr. George Rapp and his followers, who constitute the society of the Harmonites, who emigrated to this country from Swabia, on account, as they assert, of persecution for their religious opinions. Mr. Rapp arrived in the U. S. in 1803 or 4, a year in advance of his followers, and purchased a tract of land in Butler co. which the association settled and improved, building a town to which they gave the name of Harmony. They planted a vineyard, built mills, reared sheep, and established a large cloth manufactory, which they made profitable. But having the cultivation of the grape much at heart, but which not thriving as they wished, and believing the climate not adapted to their merino sheep, they sold their property in Butler co. and removed to the state of Indiana near the Wabash. Here they cleared a large body of land, built a beautiful village, a cotton and woollen manufactory, a brew-house, a distillery and steam-mill. But the climate proving unhealthy, they resolved to return to Pennsylvania. Pursuant to this resolution they bought many acres of land around their present residence, to which they removed in 1825.

Their town consists of more than 150 houses, chiefly of frame, neatly constructed on broad rectangular streets, 2 parallel to the river, and 4 crossing them. Among these are, an elegant church, a large woollen and cotton factory of brick, a store, tavern, a large steam-mill, also of brick, a brewery, distillery, tan-yard, and various work-shops. They have also a large and commodious house, 120 feet by 5, arched underneath, in which they have a concert hall, a museum of natural curiosities, a collection of minerals, a mathematical and drawing-school, and a library. They have also a steamboat plying on the Ohio. The thriving condition of this association will be understood when we observe, that according to the report of Mr. Frederick Rapp, it purchased for its *own consumption* in the year 1829, $88,946 45 value of commodities from the surrounding country. To his detailed statement Mr. Rapp adds, "that all articles and merchandise purchased to sell again, as well as any produce of our farming and manufacturing departments, are not included.

It is generally understood that the great cohesive principle of this association is, its religious tenets and discipline, with which we are unacquainted. The labor of the community and its product are common property. Mr. George Rapp is the priest and patriarch, who has the supervision and control of the temporal and spiritual concerns of the community. Candidates are admitted after a probation of six or nine months, during which they are instructed in the principles and regulations of the society. They have formed at different times two constitutions; one at the Wabash and the other at Economy, whose provisions are very similar; but the last are more favorable to such as wish to withdraw from the association. It contains in substance the following conditions: 1. Persons holding property, uniting with the society, put it into the common stock; and may, when quitting the community, withdraw the principal, without interest.

2. Adjuncts without property, leaving the society, without permission, or due notice, receive neither dividend nor compensation for their services.

3. Those who withdraw after proper notice, or with the approbation of the society, receive such an outfit, as the society in its discretion may grant.

The Duke of Saxe Weimar, who two or three years since visited this community says, "The ware house was shown to us, where the articles made here for sale or use are preserved; and I admired the excellence of all. The articles for the use of the society are kept by themselves, as the members have no private possessions, and every thing is in common; so must they in relation to all their personal wants, be supplied from the common stock. The clothing and food they make use of, is of the best quality. Of the latter, flour, salt meat, and all long keeping articles, are served out monthly; fresh meat, on the contrary, and whatsoever spoils readily, is distributed whenever it is killed, according to the size of the family, &c. As every house has a garden, each family raises its own vegetables, and some poultry; and each family has its own bake oven. For such things as are not raised in Economy, there is a store provided; from which the members, with the knowledge of the directors, may purchase what is necessary, and the people of the vicinity, may also do the same."

"Mr. Rapp, finally conducted us into the factory again, and said, that the girls had especially requested this visit, that I might hear them sing. When their work is done, they collect in one of the factory rooms, to the number of 60 or 70, to sing spiritual and other songs. They have a peculiar hymn book, containing hymns from the Wurtemburg psalm book, and others written by the Elder Rapp. A chair was placed for the old patriarch, who sat amidst the girls, and they commenced a hymn in a very delightful manner. It was naturally symphonious and very well arranged. The girls sang four pieces, at first sacred, but afterwards, by Mr. Rapp's desire, of a gay character; with real emotion did I witness this interesting scene."

"All the workmen, and especially the females, have very healthy complexions, and moved me deeply with the warm hearted friendliness with which they saluted the elder Rapp. I was also much gratified to see vessels containing fresh sweet smelling flowers, standing on all the machines. The neatness which universally reigns here, is in every respect worthy of praise."

"The elder Rapp is a large man, 70 years old, (now 73 or 4,) whose powers, age seems not to have diminished. His hair is grey, but his blue eyes, overshadowed by strong brows, are full of life and vigor. His system is somewhat similar to Owen's community of goods, and all members of the society work together for the common interest, by which the welfare of each individual is secured. But to the assurance of temporal prosperity, the tie of religion is superadded, which was entirely wanting in Owen's community; and results declare that Rapp's system is the better."

"It is most striking and wonderful that so plain a man as Mr. Rapp should so successfully bring, and keep together a society of 800 persons, who in a manner, honor him as a prophet, and that he should have power even to suspend the intercourse of the sexes. He found the society becoming too numerous, and induced the members to live with their wives as with sisters. Sexual intercourse is still discouraged yet marriages constantly occur, and children are born every year, for whom a school is provided."

"The members of the community manifest the very highest degree of veneration for the elder Rapp, whom they address and treat as a father. Mr. Frederick Rapp is a large good looking personage, above 40 years of age, possesses profound mercantile knowledge, and is the temporal, as his father is the spiritual, chief of the community. All business passes through his hands, and he represents the society, which, notwithstanding the change in the name of the residence, is still called the Harmony Society, in their dealings with the world."

Since the above was written, a portion of the society, weary of the restraint upon the sexual intercourse, as it is said, have withdrawn from Harmony, and under the auspices of Count Leon, are preparing to establish themselves elsewhere. The secession had at first the appearance of hostility, which might have proved vexatious and injurious to both parties, but their differences were amicably settled, and Mr. Rapp and his adherents remain at Economy in peace, but we know not whether they have new modelled their discipline.

Eddy's creek, a tributary of Spring Brook, rises in Covington t-ship, Luzerne co. throngh which it flows in a S. W. direction about 5 miles.

Edgement, t-ship, Delaware co. bounded N. E. by Newtown, S. E. by Upper Providence, S. by Middleton, W. by Thornbury and N. W. by Chester co. Central distance from Phil. about 21 miles; from Chester 9 miles N. W. Length 4, breadth 2½ miles; area 5700 acres; surface hilly; soil loam. Pop. in 1830, 758; taxables in 1828, 170. Ridley cr. passes sthrdly through the S. E. angle of the t-ship. There is a post office in the t-ship, distant 123 miles from W. C. and 83 S. E. from Harrisburg.

Edinburg, village of Mahoning t-ship, Mercer co. on the road leading from New Castle to New Bedford, and on the left bank of the Shenango cr. 14 miles S. W. of Mercer borough, contains 12 dwellings, 2 stores, 1 tavern and a grist mill.

Edmonds, a small village in Bushkill t-ship, Northampton co. on the road to Smith's Gap, about 9 ms. from Easton, contains 4 houses, and 1 store.

Edsallville, p-o. Bradford co. 262 ms. N. W. of W. C. & 156 from Harrisburg.

Eldersville, p-t. of Cross Creek t-ship, Washington co. about 16 miles N. W. of Washington borough, 250 from W. C. and 227 from Harrisburg, contains 3 or 4 houses.

Elderton, formerly called Middleton, p-t. of Plumb creek t-ship, Armstrong co. on the turnpike road from Indiana to Kittanning, 16 ms from the latter, 202 from W. C. and 170 from Harrisburg, contains about 30 dwellings, 2 stores, and 2 taverns.

Eldredville, p-o. Lycoming co. 223 miles N. W. from W. C. and 112 from Harrisburg.

Elizabeth, t-ship, Allegheny county, bounded N. E. and E. by the Youghiogheny r. which separates it from Westmoreland co. S. by Westmoreland co. W. and N. W. by Monongahela r. The two rs. unite at the extreme N. point of the t-ship. Centrally distant from Pittsburg S. 14 miles. Greatest length 10½, breadth 10½ ms. area 35,200 acres; surface hilly; soil, loam; coal abundant. Pop. in 1830, 2517; taxables 571. The are many short and inconsiderable streams which flow into the rivers E. and W. At the confluence of the chief of these with the Monongahela lies the p-t. of Elizabethtown, 14 ms S. of Pittsburg. This is, however, a town on paper only. The p-o. here is 240 ms. from W. C. and 216 from Harrisburg.

Elizabethtown, Elizabeth t-ship, Allegheny co. (See preceding article.)

Elizabeth, t-ship, Lancaster county, bounded N. by Lebanon co. S. E. by Cocalico t-ship, S. W. by Warwick. Central distance from Lancaster N. 13 ms. Greatest length 7 ms.; greatest breadth 6½; area, 24,521 acres; surface hilly; soil, red shale and gravel. Pop. in 1830, 1928; taxables 370. This t-ship is extremely well watered. Trout creek runs along its eastern boundary; Middle creek and its tributary, Seglock creek, traverse it centrally, and Hammer creek forms in part the W. line. Hopewell forges are on this last stream, near the north boundary, at which there is a p-o. and Elizabeth furnace is on Seglock creek. The Downingstown and Harrisburg turnpike road passes diagonally thro' the t-ship from S. E. to N. W. upon which, about the middle of the t-ship, is situated Elizabeth church. The t-ship contains also 3 distilleries, 1 tanyard, 2 fulling mills, 10 grist mills, 7 saw mills, 1 hemp and 1 oil mill. Brickersville is the p-t.

Elizabeth Town and Borough, a p-t. in Mount Joy t-ship, Lancaster co. on the turnpike road from Lancaster city to Harrisburg, about 18 ms. from each, and in the forks of Coney creek, 110 ms. from W. C. contains some 30 or 40 dwellings, 2 or 3 taverns, and 2 stores. It was incorporated 13th April, 1827.

Elizabeth river, a tributary of the Little Swatara creek, so called, in Bethel t-ship, Lebanon co. in the fork of which lies Stumpstown.

Elk creek, Chester co. rises in Londonderry t-ship, and flows in a segment of a circle, forming the W. boundary of that and of the t-ships of Penn and New London, whence it flows through the state of Maryland into the Susquehannah r. turning many mills in its course.

Elk Lick, t-ship, Somerset co. bounded N. by Milford and Brother's Valley t-ships, E. by Greenville t-ship, S. by the state of Maryland, and W. by Addison and Turkey Foot t-ships. Centrally distant S. of Somerset borough 15 ms. Greatest length 10, breadth 8 ms.; area 52,000 acres; surface, gentle declivities; soil, dark clay. Pop. in 1830, 1531; taxables 241; taxable property in 1829, real estate $85,716; personal $10,216; rate of tax 5 mills on the dollar. The p-o. is called after the t-ship. The Allegheny mtn. is on the E. and the Negro mtn. on the W. boundary. The Little Youghiogheny flows N. E. through and along the N. boundary, receiving from it Elk Lick creek, which gives name to the t-ship. The p-t. of Salisbury lies in the S. E. angle, between Little Meadow and Big Piney runs.

Elk Lick creek. (See preceding article.)

Elk Creek, t-ship, Venango county, bounded N. by Pine Grove t-ship, E. by Farmington and Paint Creek t-ships, S. by Beaver Creek t-ship, and W. by Richland. Centrally distant S. E. from Franklin borough 17 ms. Greatest length 12, breadth 5 miles; area, 32,000 acres; surface, level; soil, loam. Pop. in 1830, 572; taxables 115. The turnpike road from Clearfield to Franklin runs through the S. W. angle of the t-ship. The t-ship is drained by Six Mile run, which flows W. nearly the length of the t-ship; and on the S. by the Beaver, Canoe and Dyer Paint creeks.

Elk Creek, t-ship, Erie co. bounded N. by Fairview, E. by McKean and *Conneautte* t-ships, S. by Crawford co. and W. by *Conneaut* t-ship. Centrally distant S. W. from Erie 16 miles. Length 8, breadth 7 ms.; area 35,840 acres; surface, hilly; soil, gravelly loam. Pop. in 1830, 562; taxables 92. It is drained S. by the Cussawago creek, N. by a branch of Elk cr. and W. by a tributary of the Conneaut. Salt springs are found on the banks of the last stream. There is a p-o. in the t-ship, which bears its name.

Elk creek, Erie co. rises on the E. line of McKean t-ship, and flows by a W. and N. W. course of about 20 ms. through McKean, Fairview and Springfield t-ships, into Lake Erie, about 16 ms. S. W. of Erie borough, receiving several tributaries in its course.

Elk, t-ship, Warren co. bounded N. by the state of New York, E. and S. by the Allegheny r. and W. by the Conewango cr. the former dividing it on the E. from McKean co. and the latter from Pine Grove t-ship. Centrally distant from the town of Warren 8 ms. The t-ship, we believe, is yet unorganized. It contains some excellent lands on the creek and river bottoms, among which is the tract held by Cornplanter and his followers, the scanty remnant of the Aborigines of Pennsylvania. (See article Warren county.)

Elkland, t-ship, Lycoming county, bounded N. by Bradford co. E. by Shrewsbury t-ship, S. by Muncy and Loyalsock t-ship, W. by Lycoming t-ship, and N. W. by Tioga co. Centrally distant N. E. from Williamsport 25 ms. Greatest length 21, breadth 17 ms.; area, 131,200 acres; surface mountainous; soil, various. Taxables in 1830, 92; valuation of taxable property in 1829, seated lands $12,792, unseated lands $57,728, personal est. $2862. The principal stream of the t-ship is Loyalsock creek, which rises on the confines of Bradford co. and flows S. W. into the W. branch of the Susquehannah, several miles below Williamsport. It receives a portion of its waters from Elk lake, near the N. boundary of the co. The t-ship is very sparsely inhabited, having a few settlements in the flats on the margin of the principal streams.

Elkland, t-ship, Tioga co. bounded

N. by the state of New York, E. by Lawrence and Tioga t-ships, S. by what is now or was formerly Delmar t-ship, and W. by Deerfield t-ship. Its length and breadth is about 11 miles, and contents about 65,000 acres; surface, hilly; soil, gravel, loam and clay, heavily timbered. Pop. in 1830, 606; taxables, 116. Cowanesque cr. flows eastwardly through it, near the northern boundary, and Crooked creek near the S. and along the N. E. boundary into the Tioga r. There is a p-o. bearing the name of the t-ship, distant from W. C. 273 ms. and 167 from Harrisburg.

Ellerslie, p-o. Susquehannah county, 287 ms. N. W. from W. C. and 179 from Harrisburg.

Elliotsburg, p-o. Perry co. 121 ms. N. W. of W. C. and 34 from Harrisburg.

Emaus, p-t. of Lehigh co. It is a Moravian village situate at the foot of the South mountain, in the t-ship of Salisbury, built on one street, and is distant about 5 ms. S. S. W. from Northampton, 183 N. from W. C. and 90 N. E. from Harrisburg. The land on which this town is erected and that of the immediate vicinity was bequeathed by two members of the society for the maintenance of a clergyman, and the promotion of missions. The town contains about 20 houses, and 1 store.

Embreeville, p-o. Chester co. 106 ms. N. of W. C. 73 S. E. of Harrisburg.

Emporium, p-o. Lycoming co. Shippen t-ship, 25 miles S. W. of Smethport, 293 from W. C. and 186 from Harrisburg. There are two or three families here, some salt springs and salt works, on the Drift wood branch of the Sinnemahoning creek.

Ennisville, p-t. Barre t-ship, Huntingdon co. on Standingstone creek, contains four dwellings, a store, and tavern; it is distant 170 miles N. W. from W. C. and 93 S. W. from Harrisburg.

Ephrata, p-t. of Cocalico t-ship, Lancaster co. at the intersection of the Reading Road with the Downingstown and Harrisburg turnpike, 60 ms. N. W. of Phil. 13 N. E. from Lancaster, 125 from W. C. and 38 from Harrisburg. Contains from 15 to 20 dwellings, 2 taverns, a store and paper mill. New Ephrata is a smaller village of 6 or 8 houses, about a mile further west on the turnpike road. These settlements were made by the singular religious sect called Tunkers, Dunkers or Dumplers, of which the following is a concise history. The word "Tunker," of which the other names are corruptions, means baptism by immersion. With the Quakers and Menonists, this sect refused to swear or bear arms. The fraternity traced its origin from the baptism of John, and admitted no other confession of faith than the New Testament. They administered the Eucharist at night in imitation of our Saviour, washing at the same time each others feet agreeably to his example & command. They worshiped on the first day of the week and kept the Jewish Sabbath, wore long beards, and dressed in plain and coarse garments of ancient fashion. This sect rose in Germany in 1705, and consisted chiefly of Calvinists, who by their outward sanctity obtained the name of Pietists, and induced upon them no inconsiderable share of persecution. Under the guidance of Alexander Mack, a miller of Schrieshiem, a society originally of 8 persons was formed, which soon after increasing, and becoming impatient of the reproof of their neighbors, removed to Creyfield in the duchy of Cleves, whence a company of 8 or 10, directed by Mack, who devoted the whole of his property to their service, removed to Pennsylvania in 1719 and settled at Germantown. The church here grew rapidly, receiving members from the banks of the Wissahickon and from Lancaster co. and soon after established a community under one Peter Beeker, who was chosen *official baptiser* in that county. At the head of this association, Conrad Beissel, under the name of Friedsam Gottrecht, *anglice*, *Peacable God-right*, had sufficient art to place himself. By his influence the observance of the seventh day of the week was adopted in 1728, when his disciples separated from the other Tunkers, and were rebaptised by him. Becoming more ascetic he adopted the life of a recluse, and retired to a solitary cottage, which had been erected by a hermit called Emilech. He was drawn from his solitude by strife in his community, which having appeased, the unmarried brethren built themselves a humble dwelling near to to his. Additional huts were put up by new converts, several females joined the sisterhood, who had a dwelling apart for themselves. But the sisters it would seem, took little delight in their state of single blessedness, and two only, (aged and ill favoured ones, we may suppose) continued steadfast in renunciation of marriages.

The zealots gave to their new habitations the names of *Zohar*, *Hebron*, *Massa*, and *Cades*, and that of *Kedar*, to the house in which they celebrated love feasts. This building was soon after transformed into a "sister convent," and another house of worship was erected, and in 1738, a dwelling for the brethren. This last was called Zion, and the whole settlement, Ephrata. Thus a solitary life was changed for a conventical one. Zion became a "*Kloster*," was put under monastic rule, and the brethren adopted the habit of the Capuchins. One Onesimus was appointed Prior, and Beissel assumed the name of "*Father*." But these mutations, and the presumption of Beissel, offended several members, who withdrew from the society.

The property of the society consisted of about 250 acres of land. Its labor and profits were in common. Marriage and sexual intercourse were forbidden; but members disposed to matrimony were suffered to withdraw, taking with them their proportion of the common stock. The sexes dwelt apart, lived on vegetables solely, slept on wooden benches, with billets of wood for pillows, and attended worship four times in the twenty-four hours. This life macerated their bodies, and rendered their complexions pale and bloodless. The dress of the males consisted of a shirt, trowsers and vest, with a long white gown and cowl, of wool in winter, and linen in summer. That of the females, differed only in the substitution of petticoats for trowsers; they covered their faces with their cowls, when going into public. In walking, all used a solemn steady pace, keeping straight forward, with their eyes fixed upon the ground; not turning to give an answer when asked a question. Thus accoutred, with sandals on their feet, forty or fifty followed each other in Indian file, in occasional visits to their friends at Germantown. On the death of Beissel, his authority devolved on one Millar, who, wanting the vigorous mind of his predecessor, was unable to preserve the society from rapid decay. All engrossing as religious fanaticism usually is, and attractive as it sometimes proves by its singularities, nature and reason have proved too strong for it in this case, and the Tunker sect has been almost extinguished in the unequal conflict. Ephrata still exists, but the peculiarities of its inhabitants are no more. They marrry and are given in marriage, eat, drink, and dress like their neighbors; but they are still remarkable for the purity of their lives, the simplicity of their manners, and the fervor of their devotion. Their religious principles are not fully known, but they deny the doctrine of original sin, and the eternity of punishment, and believe that the day of judgment will be one of light and instruction, by which the human race will be restored to happiness. Contention with arms or at law, they deem unchristian.

Equinunk creek, *Great*, a considerable tributary of the Delaware river, has its principal sources in Scott and Mount Pleasant t-ships, Wayne co. and flows through Buckingham to the river, about 5 miles below Stockport.

Equinunk, *Little*, a creek of Buckingham t-ship, Wayne co. which rises in a small lake in Damascus t-ship, and runs N. E. to the Delaware.

Erie county. The province of Pennsylvania, as granted to William Penn, included but about five miles of the shores of Lake Erie, upon the extreme west. But the intelligent men who after the revolution had charge of the interests of the state, foreseeing the many advantages she might derive from an extensive frontupon this inland sea, obtained from the U. S. the grant of the triangular tract on the lake, now belonging to the state, for the consideration of $151,640 25, which were paid in continental certificates of various descriptions. The deed of confirmation from the U. S. is dated March 3d, 1792. Prior to that date, the state had purchased and paid for the Indian right to the soil. The tract contained 202,187 acres, and is now included with other lands in Erie county, and was formerly comprehended within the bounds of Allegheny county. From the latter it was separated by act 12th March, 1800, and the place for holding the courts of justice was fixed at the town of Erie; but this, with Crawford, Mercer, Venango and Warren, formed one county under the name of Crawford, for all county purposes, for several years. By the act 2d April, 1803, Erie county was fully organized for judicial and other purposes. The county is bounded N. partly by lake Erie, and partly by the state of New York, E. by that state and by Warren co. Penn. S. by Crawford co. and W. by the state of Ohio. Length 36, breadth 20 miles; area, 720 square miles; central lat. 42° N., long. from W. C. 3° west.

Geologically considered, the county pertains to the great western secondary formation, and most probably contains the minerals usually found in it. Salt springs have been discovered in various places, but no salt works have yet been erected, nor have any coal mines been explored. An immense mine of bog ore of excellent quality is said to exist in the county, near the line of the canal, from Elk creek to Erie, and from which the ore is taken to the state of Ohio. The surface of the country is undulating, its soil sandy loam, clay, gravel, and tolerably productive, but better adapted for grass than grain farms. The dividing ridge which crosses the county from S. W. to N. E. marks a striking distinction in the county on each side. The southern portion produces excellent grass in great abundance, but is not fertile in grain; the northern, sloping to the lake, is considered well adapted to wheat.

The principal streams of the county, flowing to the lake on the E. of the town of Erie, are Four Mile, Six Mile, Twelve Mile,Sixteen Mile and Twenty Mile creeks; west of the town, Walnut creek, Trout run, Elk creek, Crooked and Raccoon creeks. Conneaut creek rises in Crawford co. near Conneaut lake, and flows N. to near Lexington in this county, thence W. into the state of Ohio, and thence N. E. through that state to the lake. The Pennsylvania canal is designed to follow the valley of this stream. French creek enters the county from the E. and flows S. W. through it into Crawford, receiving Le Boeuf creek, which has its source in Le Boeuf lake, near the town of Waterford. Conneautte lake in Conneautte t-ship, near the S. line of the co. sends forth Conneautte creek. Beside these, there are several less considerable streams in the co. Lake Pleasant in the S. W. angle of Venango t-ship, supplies a small tributary to French creek. The towns are Erie, Waterford, Burgettstown, Colt's Station, Wattsville, Union Mills, Lexington, Fairview, &c. A turnpike road runs from Erie by Waterford, Meadville and Mercer, to Pittsburg, a distance of 136 miles, and the country is intersected in all directions by tolerably good county roads.

The population of the county is chiefly composed of settlers from the lower part of Penn. and from the New England states. The latter predominates. It amounted in 1800, to 1,468; in 1810, to 3,758; in 1820, to 8,553; nnd 1830, 16,906. Of this number,

8,776 were white males, 8,018 females; 62 colored males, and 50 females. There were 33 aliens, 11 deaf and dumb, and 3 blind.

The export trade of the county consists of the usual agricultural products, wheat, rye, salted provisions, and cattle. The assessors in 1827, reported the number of horses in the county at 2,883; neat cattle, 25,844; sheep, 25,936.

The trade carried on by the lake is now extensive, and grows rapidly. The number of American vessels amounted in 1831, to 69; of which 10 were steam boats, and the whole tonnage was 5,024 tons. The Brittish vessels at the same period were 17, but their tonnage is not known. A considerable proportion of the business which employs these vessels, centres in the town of Erie, and a much larger proportion it is presumed will be obtained, when the Pennsylvania canal shall be completed. The possession of this trade, comprising that of the parts of New-York, Pennsylvania, Ohio, Michigan, Huron, Indiana and Illinois, which border on the lake, is an honorable and interesting subject of contest between the states of Pennsylvania and New York.

In regard to the greater facility of transportation by the proposed Pennsylvania canal, the intelligent editor of the "*Erie Observer*" remarks, 14th May, 1831, "It has often been urged in the legislature and the newspapers of this county, when discussing the propriety of extending the Pennsylvania canal to Erie harbor, as originally projected, that natural localities, habit, and the superior facilities of the New York canal, secured the immense trade of the country bordering upon lake Erie and the upper lakes to the city of New York; and that the attempts to divert it into any other channel, would be vain and useless. In answer to these objections we will waive every other argument, and rest upon the peculiar character of the entrance to the New York canal, as containing in itself, absolute proof that a change of markets would immediately take place, were our proposed canal completed. The breaking up of the ice in the lake is always preceded by powerful westerly winds. These force the vast bodies of ice which have accumulated in the whole lake during the winter, into Buffalo bay, where it remains until dissolved by the sun, or forced from the shore by strong easterly gales, which rarely occur on this lake. Thus Buffalo harbor, the mouth of the great New York canal, is almost always barred up with ice, from five to six weeks after the rest of the lake is in fine navigable condition."

"The first vessel cleared from this port the present season (1831) for the islands, on the 20th March. She might have left sooner, as the ice passed down some days before. After that time, vessels continued to sail between Erie and Detroit, without interruption from the ice. Buffalo harbor, during all this time, was not approachable within 15 miles, for the reason above mentioned, until the 8th inst. when a steam boat succeeded in forcing her way out. Here then we have a period of 49 days of good navigation to all other ports on the lake, except the important ports which form the entrance to the New York and Welland canals, during which, the mercantile community in this extensive region, have been compelled to delay their heavy shipments of produce for an eastern market, a space of time sufficient for them to have returned from Philadelphia, and quietly settled their summer arrangements. Nor is this all. For the same difficulty attends the merchant trading with New York, late in the fall as early in the spring. This is occasioned by the freezing of the canal, from three to six weeks before we have any appearance of ice in the small streams here, or *before a canal would freeze between here and Pittsburg*. A glance at the map will plainly shew the cause of this difference."

"When it is considered that remittances are principally made from the west in produce ; that the winter is the season in which this is mainly collected, and the great importance it is to the merchant to be early in market, both on account of saving interest on his investments, and to be prepared as soon as possible for his spring and summer business, it cannot be doubted that the difficulties in getting to New York *would turn the entire trade of these great inland seas to Philadelphia*, were the first contemplated Pennsylvania canal from the Delaware to lake Erie completed."

The correctness of the preceding statement in relation to the effects of the frost, is fully supported by a statement furnished by the collector, in the same paper of July 31, showing the exact time when the navigation commenced between Buffalo and Erie, during the last 29 years ; from which it is obvious that the merchant west of Buffalo cannot calculate upon setting off with his produce before the 15th of May, which is indeed the time usually fixed upon by them. A canal from Erie to Phila. would always be open by the first of April, and oftentimes earlier ; and the navigation between Erie and the ports above is never obstructed by ice after that time.

The public buildings of the co. consist of the U. S. forts at Erie and the buildings at the navy yard, the court house, county offices and prison, an academy at the town of Erie, and another at the town of Waterford. The academy at Waterford was incorporated in 1811, and was endowed by the legislat. with 500 acres of land near, and 15 inlots in, the town of Waterford, and in 1816 with 8 other inlots ; and by an act of 24th Feb. 1820, the trustees of the academy were authorized to sell the 500 acres, at a price not less than $10 per acre, and required to vest the proceeds in some productive fund, and apply the interest thereof to the compensation of the teachers of the academy. The Erie academy was incorporated in 1817, and was also endowed by the state with 500 acres of land joining the town of Erie, and 15 inlots in that town ; also with $2000, proceeds of sale of lots in Erie, and in 1821 by other lots in the town.

The prevailing religious sects are, Episcopalians, German Lutherans, Methodists, Presbyterian and Roman Catholic societies. There is an auxiliary Bible society, tract societies, temperance societies, and Sunday school unions, in the co. Two newspapers, the Erie Gazette, and the Erie Observer, are printed weekly in the borough of Erie.

Erie, Crawford, Mercer, Warren and Venango, form the 18th congressional district, sending one member to congress, and represented in the 22d congress by John Banks. This county, with Crawford and Mercer, belongs to the 23d senatorial district, sending one member to the senate, and alone it sends one member to the house of representatives. United with Venango, Mercer and Crawford counties, it forms the 6th judicial district ; president, Henry Shippen, Esq. The courts are holden at Erie on the first Mondays of April, August, November and February. The county belongs to the western district of the supreme court, which holds an annual session at Pittsburg on the first Monday of September. This county paid into the state treasury in 1831, $1054 85. The value of taxable property in 1829 was, real estate, $1,938,301 ; personal estate, including occupations, $284,557. Rate of levy, 26 cents on the $100.

STATISTICAL TABLE OF ERIE COUNTY.

Townships, &c.	Greatest Lth.	Bth.	Area in Acres	Population. 1820	1830.	Taxables.
Amity,	7	5	22,400		385	52
Beaver Dam,	7	5½	24,640	142	443	75
Conneaut,	8½	6	32,640	631	1324	214
Conneautte,	7	7	31,360	438	743	132
Concord,	7	5	22,400	53	225	45
Elk Creek,	8	7	35,840	288	562	92
Fairview,	8	7	23,040	536	1529	255
Greenfield,	6	5½	19,200	281	664	79
Harbor Creek,	8	5½	23,860	555	1104	170
Le Boeuf,	8	5	25,600	505	554	122
McKean,	7½	7	32,280	440	984	138
Mill Creek,	7½	7	24,960	1017	1783	311
North East,	7	5½	19,200	1068	1706	310
Springfield,	8	6	24,320	895	1520	281
Union,	7	5	22,400	200	235	44
Wayne,	7	5	22,400		197	44
Waterford,	7	5	22,400	579	1006	186
Venango,	6	5½	21,120	290	683	108
Bor. of Erie,				635	1329	209
				8553	16,906	2867

Erie, p-t., bor., st. jus. and port of entry of Erie co. Mill Creek t-ship, situate on the shore of Lake Erie, lat. 42° 7′ N., lon. W. 3° from W. C. and 333 ms. N. W. from that place, and 272 from Harrisburg, and 80 miles S. S. W. from Buffalo. This is the Presque isle of the French, but stands on the main land, opposite to the peninsula, from which its name was derived. The best part of the village lies in one street from the harbor, on the road to Waterford. But the ground plan of the town extends three miles along the lake by one mile in breadth. It contains about 250 dwellings, and by the census of 1830, 1451 inhabitants, of whom 250 are taxables. The public buildings are, a court-house, offices and prison, an academy, 1 Presbyterian, 1 Associate Reformed and 1 Episcopalian church. The academy was incorporated 25th March, 1817, and received a donation of lands from the state. The town was incorporated in 1805. "The spirit of speculation," says the Erie Observer, "which has wrought such wonders along the line of the Erie canal, has never visited this borough. The soil is owned by its occupants, and no part of it is covered with foreign mortgages, no extensive business is done on fictitious capital. Our water power is equal to our present wants, and when the canal shall enter lake Erie, it may be increased if desired." The town is situated on a bluff, affording a prospect of the bay and the peninsula which forms it, and of the lake beyond. The basin is a fine one; but the entrance to it has been much obstructed by a sand bar, which the exertions of the general and state governments have in a considerable degree removed, and steam vessels now cross it without difficulty. The peninsula was, within a few years, a sand bank, but is at present covered by young timber. This was, during the late war, an important military and naval station; since which, the town has not much increased; but it is supposed that the improvement of the harbor will contribute to its extension. A little to the right of the town, on a high bank overlooking the bay, are the remains of the old French fort, overgrown with weeds and thistles, but still distinct in the outlines. Half a mile beyond it (passing a ravine) is the block house, erected during the late war for the protection of the navy yard, on the opposite side of the bay. At this place Perry's fleet was built, with incredible despatch, scarce seventy days having elapsed from the time the workmen commenced cutting the timber from the forest, when the squadron was ready for action. The young and intrepid victor of Erie is still gratefully remembered here. At a public dinner given to him and his officers before the battle, he declared that he would return a conqueror, or in his shroud. His victory retrieved the disaster of Detroit, finished the war in this quarter and restored tranquillity to the bleeding frontier. The prize vessels now lie sunk in the harbor, near the navy yard. The largest vessel is partly above the water and in a decayed state. Near her, is the brig Niagara, in the cabin of which, the gallant commodore wrote his famous despatch, "*We have met the enemy and they are ours.*" The old garrison of Gen. Wayne, in which he died on his return from the Indian wars, still exists, but in a ruinous state. The general was buried, at his own request, under the flag-staff of the fort. A rude paling and a rough stone long marked his grave; but his remains have been removed by his relatives.

A turnpike road extends from Erie, by Waterford to Pittsburg, 136 miles. The town has a communication with New-York by means of the lake and the New-York canals; with Ohio by the lake and the canal of that state; and will communicate with Philadelphia by the Pennsylvania canal. From its very advantageous position it would seem destined to become a city of much importance. Large beds of the sulphate of alumina, compounded with the sulphate of iron, have been found near the town, from which, it is said, the alum of commerce may be made. Since the construction of the piers at the entrance of the harbor, by which a deep and safe channel has been formed, the water of the lake has been gradually wearing away the neck of the peninsula at the head of the basin, and has formed a channel 7½ ft. in depth, through which schooners and steamboats have passed, and which is expected to become deep enough to admit the largest vessels on the lakes. Six miles is gained to vessels up and down and touching at this port, by this passage.

Erwinna, p-t. on the r. Delaware, 37 ms. N. of Phila. in Bucks co. about 15 ms. from Doylestown, 186 from W. C. 122 from Harrisburg.

Espytown, p-t. Columbia co. 188 ms. N. W. of W. C. and 78 from Harrisburg, on the W. bank of the Susquehannah r. on the road from Danville to Berwick, 12 ms. from the former, contains 20 dwellings, 2 stores, 1 tavern.

Ettinger's tavern, p-o. Pokono t-ship, Northampton co.; there are here 2 dwellings, a grist and saw mill.

Eulalia, t-ship, Potter co. embraces a considerable part of the co. is very thinly inhabited, containing about 300 souls, a considerable portion of whom are almost in the hunter state, and dependent upon the wild animals of the forest for subsistence. The t-ship is drained by the E. branch of the Sinnemahoning and its tributaries. Its surface is hilly; soil, vegetable mould and gravelly loam. Taxables in 1828, 59.

Evansburg, p-t. and village of Lower Providence t-ship, Montgomery co. on the Germantown and Perkiomen turnpike road, 7 ms. from Norristown and 24 from Phila. It contains some 15 dwellings, 2 stores, 2 taverns, a mill and a school house.

Evansburg, p-t. of Crawford co. 305 ms. N. W. from W. C. and 250 from Harrisburg.

Evansburg, Butler co. Cranberry t-ship, on the old Franklin road, 23 ms. from Pittsburg, 4 E. of Harmony, and 12 E. of Butler. Breakneck cr. runs immediately S. of it. This town was laid out in Oct. 1831. There are consequently but few houses in it.

Evit's creek, Cumberland Valley t-ship, runs S. the whole extent of the t-ship into the state of Maryland.

Evit's mountain, Bedford co. rises in Maryland, N. of the Potomac, and runs into Bedford co. to the Raystown branch of the Juniata r. dividing Cumberland Valley and Bedford t-ships from Southampton and Coleraine t-ships. Its length in the state is about 18 ms.

Exeter, t-ship, Berks co. bounded N. and E. by Oley, S. by Union and Robeson, S. E. by Cumru, E. and N. by Alsace. Greatest length 4½, by 4½ in breadth; surface, undulating, and on the N. W. hilly; soil, red gravel, not very productive. Pop. in 1810, 1194; in 1820, 1416, in 1830, 1455; taxables 291. The Manokesy creek crosses the N. E. corner of the t-ship, and Roush creek enters it on the N. W. and passes through the t-ship by a southern course to the Schuylkill. The Neversink mtn. and other elevated hills, mark the western boundary. The Perkiomen and Reading turnpike runs a N. W. course through it for about 6 miles. It has a church, common to Presbyterians and Lutherans. Exetertown, a small village, lies on the turnpike road, 8 miles from Reading and near the eastern boundary line; it contains about half a dozen houses, 1 tavern and 1 store.

Exeter, t-ship, Luzerne co. bounded N. by the Susquehannah r. and falls, E. and S. E. by Providence and Pittston t-ships, S. W. by Kingston, and N. W. by Northmoreland.—Greatest length N. and S. 10½, greatest breadth N. E. and S. W. 9 miles. Its form is very irregular; area 25,600 acres; its timber consists of pine, oak, hickory, and chestnut. Its surface is very uneven; part of its soil is excellent, and most of it may be cultivated. The southern angle of this township includes part of Abraham's Plains, the celebrated battle ground of the 3d July, 1778, where the military force of the valley, under the command of colonels Butler and Denison, were drawn into an ambuscade, and literally cut to pieces by the Indians and Tories, under the command of the British colonel, Butler, and the Indian chief, Brandt. Near the battle ground stood a fort called Wintermoot's, after a notorious, blood-thirsty and ferocious tory of that name, who claimed the adjacent land. The battle ground is within a mile of the northern extremity of the valley, and about 10 ms. by the road N. E. from Wilkesbarre. Subscriptions have recently been solicited throughout the valley, for the purpose of erecting a monument to the memory of those who fell in that disastrous battle. The object is praiseworthy, and it is hoped will not fail of being accomplished. The great stage road and turnpike from Wilkesbarre to Montrose passes through Exeter and over the battle ground. Beside the Susquehannah r. which laves its northern, eastern and southern boundary, it is drained by Sutton's creek, which flows from Dallas and Northmoreland t-ships N. E. into the r. by Gardner's creek and Cascade run, and by several less considerable streams. The Shawney range of mtns. passes through it, and covers a large portion of its surface. Anthracite coal is found on the east side of the mtns. Dial Knob, a distinguished eminence on the E. side of the river, is 1125 feet high. Exeter p-o. is situated on the turnpike road about a mile N. of Sutton's creek, distant 237 miles from W. C. and 129 from Harrisburg. Pop. in 1830, 767; taxables in 1828, 144.

Factoryville, p-o. Luzerne county, Braintrim t-ship, 250 ms. from W. C. and 142 from Harrisburg.

Fairdale, p-t. of Rush t-ship, Susquehannah co. upon Lake creek, 8 ms. S. W. of Montrose, 273 from W. C. and 162 from Harrisburg, contains 3 or 4 dwellings and a mill.

Fairfield, t-ship, Lycoming co. bounded N. by Elkland t-ship, E. by Muncy t-ship, S. by the river Susquehannah, and W. by Hepburn t-ship; centrally distant N. E. from Williamsport 9 ms. greatest length and breadth 7 miles; area 27,520 acres; surface mountainous, valleys and river bottom. Pop. in 1830, 600; taxables 135. Carpenter's run flows on the E. and Loyalsock creek on the W. boundary; each receives tributaries from the t-ship, from which also, some other but smaller streams flow into the river. There is a post office at Carpenter's mills. Valuation of taxable property in 1829, seated lands, &c., $59,651, unseated lands, 3553; personal property 5914, rate of tax $\frac{3}{4}$ of one per cent.

Fairfield, a village of Hamilton-ban t-ship, Adams co. about 10 miles S. W. of Gettysburg, contains 40 dwellings, 2 stores, 2 taverns, and 2 churches.

Fairfield, a small hamlet, of Drumore t-ship, Lancaster co. near the S. E. boundary, and at the head of a creek of the same name, which flows into the Susquehannah river.

Fairfield, p-t. Hamilton-ban township, Adams co. in a fork of Middle creek, about 8 miles S. W. of Gettysburg, distant 84 miles from W. C. and 42 from Harrisburg.

Fairfield, West, p-t. of Fairfield t-ship, Westmoreland co. 23 miles E. of Greensburg 184 from W. C. and 161 from Harrisburg, contains 7 dwellings, 2 taverns, 1 store.

Fairfield, t-ship Westmoreland co. bounded N. E. by the Conemaugh r. S. E. by Laurel Hill, S. W. by Ligonier t-ship, and N. W. by Chestnut Ridge. Centrally distant E. from Greensburg 22 miles; greatest length 12, breadth 10 miles; area 55,680 acres; surface chiefly valley; soil, limestone and loam. Pop. in 1830, 2422. The post town of Bolivar, and the village of Lockport on the river, in the N. E. angle of the t-ship, and the village of West Fairfield, is centrally situated in the t-ship. The streams which flow from the t-ship into the river are Gavode run, Hendick's run, Tubmill creek, and Roaring run, each of which have a course of about 10 or 12 miles.

Fairmont, p-o. Lancaster co. 117 ms. from W. C. and 43 from Harrisburg.

Fairview, t-ship, Erie co. bounded N. by lake Eric, E. by mill cr. and McKean t-ships, S. by Elk Cr. t-ship, and W. by Springfield. Centrally distant from the bor. of Erie S. W. 11 ms. greatest length 8, breadth 7 ms. area 23,040 acres; surface hilly; soil gravelly loam. Pop. in 1830, 1529; taxables 255. Walnut cr. crosses the N. E. angle of the t-ship, and Elk cr. flows thro' the S. part. The post town of Fairview lies on Lake Erie, at the mouth of Walnut creek, about 9 miles S. W. of the borough of Erie, 349 from W. C. and 279 from Harrisburg.

Fairview, a small village of Manor t-ship, Lancaster co. on the Susquehannah river, about 9 miles W. of the city of Lancaster.

Fairview, t-ship, York co. bounded N. and N. E. by the co. of Cumberland, E. by the Susquehannah river, S. by Newberry and Warrington t-ships, and E. by Menohan t-ship. Centrally distant N. W. from the borough of York 17 miles; greatest length 9, breadth 7 miles; area 18,500 acres; surface partly hilly; soil part limestone, part gravel. Pop. 1830, 1885; taxables 369; taxable property 1829, real estate, $261,267, personal 14,025 occupations &c. 27,333, total 302,625, rate, 25 cts. in the $100. The Yellow Breeches creek courses it on the N. W. and N., Fishing and Newberry creek drain it on the S. E. The post town of New Market lies at the confluence of the first creek, with the Susquehannah, opposite to Cumberland town, three miles below which is Simpson's ferry, across the river.

Fairview, town, East Pennsborough t-ship, Cumberland co. at the confluence of the Conedogwinit creek with the Susquehannah, 2 miles above Harrisburg, and 14 N. E. from Carlisle, contains 6 or 7 dwellings.

Fairview, small village of Butler co. contains some half dozen dwellings, a tavern and a store.

Fallowfield, t-ship, Washington co. bounded N. by Nottingham t-ship and the Monongahela river, E. by that river which separates it from Westmoreland co., S. by Pike run t-ship, and W. by Somerset. Centrally distant from Washington borough E. 17 miles; greatest length and breadth 7 miles; area 22,400 acres; surface very hilly; soil, loam; coal abundant. Pop. in 1830, 2142; taxables 383. The t-ship is drained on the N. by Pigeon, and on the S. by Maple creek. The town of Columbia lies on, and in, a deep bend of the river, distant 21 miles from Washington. Williamsport, also a post town, is likewise on the river, at the junction of the N. line of the t-ship with the stream, and on the N. bank of Pigeon creek.

Fallowfield, t-ship Crawford co. surface hilly; soil, gravelly. Pop. in 1830, 686; taxables in 1828, 222.

Fallowfield, East, t-ship, Chester co. bounded N. by East Caln and Sadsbury, E. by West Bradford and Newlin, and W. by West Fallowfield t-ship. Central distance from Phil. W. 35 miles, from West Chester 13 miles; area 9970 acres; surface hilly; soil, gravel and slate. Pop. in 1830, 1126; taxables 253. This t-ship lies S. of the great valley. The W. branch of the river Brandywine passes through it, and Buck run, a mill stream or tributary, courses the W. and S. W. boundary. There are four churches in the t-ship.

Fallowfield West, t-ship, Chester co. bounded N. by Sadsbury, E. by East Fallowfield, S. by Londonderry and Upper Oxford, and W. by Lancaster co. Central distance W. of Phil. 37 miles; from West Chester S. W. 7 miles; greatest length 9¾ miles; greatest breadth 5 miles; surface gentle declivity; area 18,700 acres; soil loam and slate. Pop. in 1830, 1621; taxables in 1828, 348. Buck run is on the E. boundary, Doe run forms one part, and Pusey's creek another part of the southern boundary, and Octara creek separates it from Lancaster co. Cochranville, the post town, lies on the Wilmington and Lancaster turnpike road.

Falls, t-ship, Luzerne co. bounded N. W. by Tunkhannock, N. E. by Abington; S. E. by Providence and Exeter t-ships, and S. W. by the Susquehannah river. This t-ship derives its name from a beautiful cascade in Buttermilk Falls creek. Its timber is white and yellow pine, oak, hickory, chesnut, and some beech, maple and hemlock. Its surface is very uneven, part of it mountainous; but a considerable portion of its soil produces good crops of grain and grass. It furnishes a considerable quantity of lumber annually for market. It is situated about 18 miles N. of Wilkesbarre, and the p-o. called after the t-ship, is 242 miles from W. C. and 134 from Harrisburg. Buttermilk Falls creek rises in Abington t-ship, and by a course of about 9 miles due west, crosses Falls t-ship to the Susquehannah river, receiving a considerable increase of volume from a stream issuing from Breeches pond, near the N. line of the t-ship. The pond has its name from the likeness of its form to a pair of breeches. The creek pours its waters over a precipitous rock 30 feet high, and the color of the water produced by agitation, gives it its name. At the Falls there are some valuable mills. Gardner's creek flows a S. W. course through the t-ship, and enters the Susquehannah in Exeter t-ship. It also receives an accession of water from a small lake. Falls t-ship is nearly square in form, extending about 7 miles on its several sides. Area, 35,840 acres. Pop. in 1830, 739; taxables in 1828, 134.

Falls, t-ship, Bucks county, bounded N. by Lower Makefield, E. and S. by the river Delaware, and W. by Bristol and Middleton t-ships. Centrally distant 25 ms. N. E. of Philadelphia; greatest length and breadth 5½ miles; area, 16,784 acres. It has its name from the falls of the river Delaware, opposite to Trenton. Surface, rolling; soil, loam and sand. Pop. in 1830, 2266; taxables in 1828, 397. The turnpike road from Bristol to Trenton passes diagonally through the t-ship. Scott's creek and Penn's creek have their course southwardly through it. Tullytown, Falsington, Morrisville and Tyburn, are villages within it. There is a p-o. at Morrisville. In this t-ship is Pennsbury manor, a tract of land originally of 8431 acres, of excellent quality, selected by William Penn, for his own residence. On this the proprietary built a large mansion, and occasionally resided, when in his province. It was torn down just before the revolution, and all that remains of Penn's improvement, is a frame house originally built for his brewery. A noble bridge, erected by an Incorporated company, and suspended from arches, crosses the river Delaware, opposite from Morrisville to Trenton.

Falls creek, or run, a tributary of the Lehigh river, which rises and has its course in Covington t-ship, Luzerne county, and enters the river below its first principal falls.

Falls run, Sugar Loaf t-ship, Luzerne co. rises in Columbia co. and falls into Black creek, between Middle Hill and Bucks mountain.

Falling Spring cascade, Exeter t-ship, Luzerne co. is a beautiful waterfall at high water. It is formed by a small stream which falls down the Lackawannock mountain into the Susquehannah river. The fall is about 50 feet perpendicular, over a rocky ledge.

Falsington, village, Falls t-ship, Bucks county, on the road from Morrisville to Hulmeville, 17 miles S. E. of Doylestown. Several roads from various parts of the county centre here. There are here about 20 dwellings, 2 stores, 1 tavern, and 120 inhabitants.

Fallston, borough and post-town, on the W. bank of Big Beaver river, in Brighton t-ship, Beaver co. near the lower end of the rapids, known as the Falls of Beaver. It is a compact, well built village, with a population of 500 souls. It has a water power of 85 cubic feet per second, with a head and fall of 15 feet, equal to one twelfth of the whole water power of the river at low water. There are established here, 2 scythe factories, 1 grist, 1 saw mill, 1 paper mill, a wire factory, a woollen factory, a wool carding establishment, 2 cotton factories, an oil mill, a wool carding machine factory, and other manufacturing branches. There are about 120 dwellings, 5 stores, 2 taverns and a Quaker meeting-house; incorporated by act 19th March, 1829.

Falmouth, post-town of Donnegal t-ship, Lancaster county, on the Susquehannah river, opposite to York Haven, and at the confluence of the Conewaga creek with the river, 22 miles N. W. from the city of Lancaster, 98 from W. C. and 15 from Harrisburg, contains about 20 dwellings, &c.

Fannet, t-ship, Franklin co. bounded N. E. by Perry co. S. E. by Lurgan t-ship and Letterkenny t-ship, S. W. by Metal t-ship, and N. W. by Huntingdon co. Centrally distant N. from Chambersburg 16 miles; greatest length 13, breadth 7½ ms.; area, 38,400 acres; surface, mountainous; soil, partly limestone, partly slate. Pop. in 1830, 2112; taxables, 285. The Tuscarora mountain is on the western line, on the east of which is Path valley, through which flows the Tuscarora creek. Near the head of the valley is the small town of Concord. Dividing ridge separates this from Amberson's valley, which is bounded E. by the Blue mountain.

Fannetsburg, p-t. of Metal t-ship, Franklin co. on the road from Strasburg to Bedford, 12 miles in a direct line N. W. from Chambersburg, in Path valley, and on the W. branch of Conecocheague creek, 105 ms. N. W. of W. C. and 55 S. W. of Harrisburg. The valley is between 2 and 3 miles wide, bounded on the east by the North mountain, and W. by the Blue mountain. The town contains about 20 dwellings, &c.

Fannington, t-ship, Venango co. bounded N. by Teonista and Saratoga t-ships, E. by Toby's Creek t-ship, S. by Paint Creek t-ship, W. by Elk Creek and Pine Grove t-ships. Centrally distant E. from Franklin bor. 25 miles; greatest length 8, breadth 5 miles; area, 25,600 acres; surface, level; soil, gravel and loam. Population very sparse. It is drained S. W. by Dier Paint creek, and N. W. by Raccoon creek. It is not organized, but is attached to Pine Creek t-ship.

Fawn, post t-ship, York co. bounded N. E. by Lower Chanceford, E. by Peach Bottom t-ships, S. by the state of Maryland and W. and N. W. by Hopewell t-ship; centrally distant S. E. from the borough of York, 20 ms.; greatest length 6 miles; area, 17,920 acres; surface, hilly, or rather undulating; soil, gravel and poor. Pop. in 1830, 785; taxables, 174; taxable property, 1829, real estate, $87,775; personal, 9010; occupations, &c. 9985; total, $106,770. Muddy creek follows the N. E. boundary, and receives the S. W. branch which divides the t-ship from Hopewell. The post office of the t-ship is called "*Fawn Grove*," distant from W. C. 81 miles, and from Harrisburg 52.

Fayette, t-ship, Allegheny co. bounded N. by Moon t-ship, N. E. by Robinson t-ship, S. E. by Chartiers creek, which divides it from St. Clair, and W. by Washington co. Centrally distant from Pittsburg S. W. 11 miles; greatest length 11, breadth 8 miles; area, 37,760 acres; surface, hilly; soil, loam; coal, abundant. Pop. in 1830, 2302; taxables, 536. Mouture's run is on the N. boundary, and upon it, in the N. E. angle, lies the post town, Jeffriestown, 12 miles W. of Pittsburg and 2 miles N. of the turnpike road leading to Steubenville. Chartiers creek is on the S. and receives several considerable branches from the t-ship, on one of which, near the middle of the township, is the post town of Noblesboro', distant S. W. from Pittsburg 10 miles.

Fayetteville, p-t. of Green t-ship, Franklin co. on the turnpike road from Gettysburg to Chambersburg, 18 ms. from the former and 9 from the latter, 77 from W. C. and 59 from Harrisburg.

Fayette co., is bounded N. by Westmoreland co., E. by Somerset co., S. by Maryland and Virginia, W. by Greene and Washington counties. Central lat. 39° 55′ N.; lon. from W. C. 2° 33′ W. Length 30, breadth 27 ms.; area, 824 square miles. The county lies partly in the central transition and partly in the secondary formation. Its surface, from the centre E. is mountainous, and every where hilly. Laurel Hill is on the E. boundary, and Chestnut ridge crosses the county centrally from S. W. to N. E. Coal and iron abound in every part of the county, and salt springs occur frequently in the south and west, upon some of which salt works are erected. There are also sulphur springs east and west of the Chestnut ridge. The soil is various; that of the east part, on the mountains, of slate and gravel; in the western part it consists of loam, composed of the debris of sand stone, slate and limestone; in some of the t-ships extensive veins of limestone are found near the surface, but in others it lies deep. Cheat river runs a few ms. on the S. W. boundary, until it unites with the Monongahela. The latter r. forms the western boundary of the county, and receives from it George, Brown, Dunlap, Redstone and Cook's creeks, and many less considerable streams. The Youghiogheny river enters the state E. of Laurel Hill, and forms for some 12 or 15 miles the boundary between Somerset and Fayette counties; breaking westward through this ridge, and flowing round Sugarloaf mountain, it crosses the county diagonally towards the N. W., cutting in its course the Chestnut ridge also. This river, which is very rapid and precipitous in its course, forms a link in the proposed Chesapeake and Ohio canal, receives from the E. side of the county, Indian, Mount, and Jacob's creeks, and from the W. many, but not very considerable streams. In the rapids called the Ohiopile falls, the river descends 60 feet in the space of a mile. The S. part of the county between Chestnut and Laurel ridge is drained by the Big and Little Sandy creeks, which unite in the state of Virginia and flow into the Cheat river.

The national turnpike road enters the county at Smythfield, crossing the Youghiogheny river at that place, passes through the village of Monroe and the borough of Uniontown, and traverses the Monongahela r. at Brownsville, by means of a substantial bridge. (*See Brownsville.*) By the side of this road, on the bank of a small run, is the grave of *Braddock the Proud*, whose self conceit and obstinacy caused not only his own death, but a much greater evil, in the loss of a gallant army, and the exposure of the western frontier to the mercies of a savage foe. The towns and villages of this county are numerous. Ascending the Youghiogheny river, we have on its western bank Perryopolis, East Liberty, New Haven, and opposite to it, Connellsville and Smithfield. Descending the Monongahela, we have New Geneva, Bridgeport, Brownsville, Cookstown and Belvernon; beside which there are the towns of Woodbridge, Hayden, Smithfield, Germantown, McCleland, New Salem, Meritstown, Middletown, &c. The public buildings of the county consist of the court house, offices and prison; many churches, in every part of the county, a masonic hall, and bank at Brownsville, with a capital of $107,033. The Presbyterian and Methodist are the most prevailing religious sects; the first has six and the latter five churches. The Baptists have four; Baptist Christians 2, Seceders from the Baptists 2; Episcopalians 3, German Reformed 2. There are, an auxiliary Bible society, tract societies, temperance societies and Sunday school unions. Abundant provision is made in the county for communicating to the children of the inhabitants the rudiments of an English education. And by an act of 4th Feb. 1808, an academy was established and incorporated at Uniontown, and endowed by the legislature with the sum of $2000, and by an act of 1828–9, this institution was merged in Madison college, established by the Pittsburg conference of the Methodist Episcopal church. Here the classics and the higher branches of science and literature are taught.

The state of agriculture is in a very respectable condition; large quantities of grain are raised, and much wheat manufactured into flour, and sent to Baltimore and Washington by the national turnpike road, and to New Orleans by the Monongahela and Ohio rivers. There are in the county 75 grist mills, 30 saw mills, 21 fulling mills, 2 blast furnaces and 1 forge in Dunbar t-ship, 2 furnaces in Bullskin t-ship, 3 furnaces and 1 forge in George t-ship, 2 furnaces in Salt Lick t-ship, 1 furnace & 1 forge in Springhill t-ship, 2 furnaces and 1 forge in Union t-ship. There are several woollen manufactories in the county, an extensive cotton manufactory at Brownsville, belonging to General Kreps & Co. and several glass works actively and profitably conducted.

The best land S. W. of the Laurel Hill and Youghiogheny river, sells from 20 to 60 dollars per acre; in the latter case the tracts are small, with good buildings, and the lands in a high state of cultivation; the remainder of this section is worth from 12 to 30 dollars per acre. The great body E. of Laurel Hill, unimproved, is worth from 50 cts. to 5 dollars; improved, from 4 to 12 dollars per acre. The population of the co. is composed chiefly of settlers from Virginia, and of Penn. Germans and their descendants. It is enterprizing, industrious, and frugal, and consequently thrifty and happy. In 1800, it amounted to 20,159; in 1810 to 24,714; in 1820 to 27,285, and in 1830, to 29,237.

Fayette and Greene counties form the 19th Senatorial district sending one senator to the assembly, and alone Fayette sends two members to the house of representatives. These two counties also form the 14th congressional district, and send one representative to congress. Conjoined with Greene and Washington, it composes the 14th judicial district of the state. The courts are holden at Uniontown, on the 1st Mondays of March, June, Sept. and Dec. Fayette belongs to the western district of the supreme court, which sits at Pittsburg on the 1st Monday in Sept. annually.

The real estate of the co. by the assessment of 1829, was valued at $3,650,606, personal $283,139; occupations $636,113; rate of levy, 26 cts. on the $100.

STATISTICAL TABLE OF FAYETTE COUNTY.

Townships, &c.	Greatest Lth.	Greatest Bth.	Area in Acres	Face of Country.	Soil.	Population. 1810	Population. 1820	Population. 1830	Taxables.
Bridgeport t.						280	624	737	141
Brownsville t.						698	976	1233	220
Connellsville,	6	4	8960	partly roll'g	lime & coal,	498	600	1205	220
Bullskin,	9	4½	24320	rolling, mtn.	limestone,	1439	1484	1231	251
Dunbar,	10	6	23680	rolling,	do.	2066	1895	1722	217
Franklin,	10	7	21120	hilly,	loam,	1623	1749	1464	338
George,	11	9	28800	level,	loam & lime,	2086	2031	2416	455
German,	7	6½	20480	rolling,	limestone,	2079	2379	2395	463
Henry Clay,	10½	10	38720	mtnous,	gravel,			804	151
Luzerne,	8	7	16000	level,	limestone,	1538	1610	1625	314
Menallen,	8	6	14080	rolling,	lime & grav'l	1228	1376	1083	261
Redstone,	7	6	16640	do.	do.	1224	1207	1209	241
Saltlick,	20	14	81280	mtnous,	gravel,	994	1172	1499	262
Springhill,	8½	6½	23680	level,	limestone,	1837	2086	1934	457
Tyrone,	12	4	21760	hilly,	do.	989	1058	1139	235
Union borough,						999	1058	1341	273
Union t-ship,	9	8½	33920	level,	limestone,	1821	1947	2475	467
Washington,	8	7	32000	rolling,	do.	2160	2749	2926	551
Wharton,	21	9	76800	mtnous.,	gravel,	922	1206	809	196
New Geneva t.						233			
						24714	27285	29237	5874

Ferguson, t-ship, Centre co. bounded N. by Spring t-ship, E. by Potter t-ship, S. by Huntingdon co. and W. by Half Moon and Patton t-ships. Centrally distant S. from Bellefonte 11 ms.; greatest length 14, breadth 11 ms.; area, 46,080 acres; surface, mountainous; soil, in the valleys limestone. Pop. in 1830, 1755; taxables 287. Tussey's mtn. is on the south boundary. The t-ship is drained N. by Spring cr. and its branches. Iron abounds in it, and iron works are erected at Centre Spring and at Pattonsville. Bolesburg, Pattonsville, and Whitehall, are villages of the t-ship.

Fermanagh, t-ship, Juniata county, bounded N. by Decatur t-ship, E. by Greenwood t-ship, S. by the Tuscarora mtn. and W. by the Juniata r. Centrally distant E. from Lewistown 11 miles; greatest length about 12 ms. breadth 10; area, 53,120 acres; surface, mountainous; soil, limestone and slate. Pop. in 1830, 1432; taxables 409. The t-ship is drained principally by Lost creek and its several branches. Mifflin, Mexico and Thompsontown, are post towns in the S. part of the t-ship, on the turnpike road from Lewistown, on the state canal, and on the Juniata r.

Findlayville, p-t. of Peters t-ship, Washington co. upon the turnpike road from Washington to Pittsburg, 12 ms. N. E. of the former, 220 N. W. from W. C. and 229 S. W. from Harrisburg.

Findlay, t-ship, Allegheny county, bounded N. E. by Moon t-ship, S. E. and S. by Fayette t-ship, S. W. by Washington co. and N. W. by Butler co. Centrally distant N. W. from Pittsburg 15 miles; greatest length 9, breadth 6½ miles; area, 17,920 acres; surface, hilly; soil, loam. Pop. in 1830, 1326. It is drained N. by some branches of Raccoon creek, and on the S. by Mouture's run.

Findlay, West, t-ship, Washington co. bounded N. by Donegal t-ship, E. by East Findlay t-ship, S. by Greene co. and W. by the state of Va. Centrally distant S. W. of Washington borough 14 ms. Greatest length 8½, breadth 5 miles; area 24,320 acres; surface, very hilly; soil, loam. Pop. in 1830, 1218; taxables 406. It is drained chiefly by Templeton's and Robinson's forks of Wheeling cr.

Findlay, East, t-ship of Washington co. bounded N. by Buffalo t-ship, E. by Morris, S. by the state of Virginia, and W. by West Findlay t-ship. Centrally distant from Washington borough S. W. 10 miles; length 9½ ms. breadth 6; area, 24,320 acres; surface, very hilly; soil, loam. Pop. in 1830, 1219. It is drained by branches of Wheeling creek.

Fishing creek, Lancaster co. rises in Drumore t-ship, and flows southerly into the r. Susquehannah, turning in its course several mills.

Fishing creek, Dauphin co. rises in Hanover t-ship, above Smith's gap in the Blue mtn. and flows S. W. between that mtn. and the Second mtn. about 8 ms. into the Susquehannah r. turning a mill near its mouth.

Fishing creek, a large stream which has its source in Lycoming county, whence it receives many tributaries, and forcing its way through the Bald mountain, in Sugarloaf t-ship, Columbia co. it flows S. through the latter co. into the Susquehannah r. about 3 ms. above Catawissa, its volume having been much increased by the waters of Huntingdon cr. from Luzerne co. by Little Fishing cr. from Columbia co. and by several other streams.

Fishing Creek, t-ship, Columbia co. bounded N. by Sugarloaf t-ship, E. by Luzerne co. S. by Briar Creek and Bloom t-ships, and W. by Mount Pleasant and Greenwood. Centrally distant N. E. from Danville 17 miles. Greatest length 7¾, breadth 5½ miles; area 19,200 acres; surface, mountainous; soil, clay and gravel. Pop. in 1830, 568; taxables, 102. Fishing creek flows S. through the t-ship, receiving from Huntingdon creek and from Greenwood t-ship Green creek. The p-o. is 199 ms. N. W. from W. C. and 89 from Harrisburg.

Fishing creek, York co. rises in

Fairview t-ship, and flows S. E. thro' Newberry into the Susquehannah r. about 3 ms. above the Conewago falls, having a course of 9 or 10 miles, and turning several mills in its way.

Fishing creek, York co. Windsor t-ship, rises in the t-ship and flows E. into the Susquehannah, about 7 ms.

Fishing creek, York county, Peach Bottom t-ship, a tributary of Muddy creek.

Fishing creek, Rye t-ship, Perry co. rises E. of the Cove mtn. and flows along its southern side into the Susquehannah r.

Flint Stone ridge, a mtn. range in the S. part of Southampton t-ship, Bedford co. on the W. side of Bean's cove.

Flourtown, village of Springfield t-ship, Montgomery co. on the Spring-house turnpike road, 8 ms. S. E. of Norristown, contains above 20 dwellings, a German Reformed church, 5 taverns and 2 stores. It is about 12 ms. from Phila.

Foglesville, p-t. of Macungy t-ship, Lehigh co. at the junction of the Allentown and Millerstown roads, distant 9 ms. S. W. from Allentown, 170 N. E. from W. C. 76 from Harrisburg, contains some half dozen dwellings, a tavern, store, &c.

Forks, t-ship, Northampton co. near the confluence of the Delaware and Lehigh rs. Bounded N. by Plainfield and Lower Mount Bethel t-ships, S. by the Lehigh r. and borough of Easton, E. by the borough and Delaware r., W. by Upper and Lower Nazareth and Bethlehem t-ships. Length $6\frac{1}{4}$, breadth 6 ms.; surface level; soil, limestone, well cultivated and productive. Pop. in 1830, 1989; taxables 389. Drained by Bushkill creek and several of its tributaries, and is traversed by many roads leading to Easton.

Fountain Inn, p-o. Chester co.

Foxtown, p-t. of Richland t-ship, Venango co. at the confluence of the Clarion and Allegheny rs. 20 ms. S. E. of Franklin borough, 203 from Harrisburg, and 243 from W. C. contains 4 or 5 houses, store and tavern.

Fox Chase, village of Lower Dublin t-ship, Phila. co. pleasantly situated in the W. angle of the t-ship, on the Oxford road, about 8 ms. from the city, contains some 15 or 20 dwellings, a store and tavern.

Fox run, Dover t-ship, York co. a small tributary of the Little Conewago creek.

Foxtown, Stroud t-ship, Northampton co. on the road from Stroudsburg to Dutotsburg, contains 8 dwellings.

Fox, t-ship, Clearfield co. bounded N. by McKean co. E. by Gibson and Lawrence t-ships, S. by Pike t-ship and W. by Jefferson co. Centrally distant from the town of Clearfield 17 ms.; greatest length 18 ms.; breadth 16; surface, hilly; soil, gravelly loam. Pop. in 1830, 437; taxables 75. It is drained N. E. by Bennet's branch of the Sinnemahoning r. and S. E. by Kersey's and Toby's creeks. Elk mtn. extends nearly across the t-ship from S. W. to N. E. There is a p-o. at Kersey's mill, in the N. W. angle of the t-ship, and another bearing the name of the t-ship.

Franconia, t-ship, Montgomery co. bounded N. E. by Bucks co. S. E. by Hatfield t-ship, S. W. by Lower Salford, and N. W. by Upper Salford. Greatest length 3 miles, greatest breadth 3 miles; area, 5440 acres. The N. E. branch of the Perkiomen creek, Indian creek, Great Pike creek, and Skippack creek, drain the t-ship. Surface, level; soil, red shale. Central distance from Norristown, about 14 miles, N. from Philadelphia 30 miles. Population in 1830, 998; taxables in 1828, 190. There is a p-o. here called after the t-ship, 171 miles from W. C. and 106 from Harrisburg.

Frankford, borough and p-t. of Oxford t-ship, Philadelphia county, on the turnpike road to Bristol, 4 miles from the city of Philadelphia, 141 from W. C. and 103 from Harrisburg. It contains about 300 dwellings, and by the census of 1830, 1637 inhabitants. There are within the borough 5 taverns, 8 or 10 stores of various kinds, and a due proportion of the mechanical professions. There is much business done in and around this town. Upon the Tacony creek which skirts it on the W. and S. are several valuable grist and saw mills, and an extensive calico printing works, established by Samuel Comly. The road to Frankford from the city is excellent, the country around it is well cultivated, and it is much resorted to in the summer season. There are two stages which ply twice a day between it and the city, and a third which passes through it daily, from Holmesburg. The mail stage for New York runs daily through it, and in the winter season when the Delaware is obstructed by ice; several stages run through it to New York. There is a Lutheran church and a Quaker meeting, and we think other places of worship. The borough was incorporated by act 7th March, 1800.

Frankford, t-ship, Cumberland co. bounded N. and W. by Mifflin t-ship, E. by Perry co. and N. by Middleton t-ship, and S. by W. Pennsborough. Centrally distant N. W. from Carlisle, 9 miles; greatest length and breadth, 5¾ miles; area, 25,600 acres; surface hilly; soil, slate. Population in 1830, 1282; taxables, 257. The Conedogwinit creek courses the southern boundary, receiving from the t-ship several small tributaries. The N. part of the t-ship is covered with spurs of the Blue mountain. McClure's Gap, is on the E. boundary. There is a sulphur spring centrally situated, in the t-ship.

Frankford, a small village and p-t. of Hanover t-ship, Beaver co. near the S. boundary, about 22 miles S. W. of Beaver borough, contains between 30 and 40 dwellings, 3 stores, and 2 taverns. It is 254 miles N. W. from W. C. 231 W. of Harrisburg.

Franklin, t-ship, Adams co. bounded N. and E. by Menallen, S. E. by Cumberland, S. by Hamiltonban t-sps. and W. by Franklin co. Centrally distant N. W. from Gettysburg 8 ms.; greatest length 12, breadth 8½ miles; area, 32,000 acres; surface level; soil, red shale. Population in 1830, 1588; taxables 320. It is drained by the N. and S. branches of Marsh cr. on the S. E. the Conewago on the N. E. and a branch of the Conecocheague on the W. which rises near the Green Ridge. The turnpike road from Gettysburg to Chambersburg runs through the t-ship, and another turnpike leads from the former place to Mummasburg, within the t-ship.

Franklin, t-ship, Bradford county, bounded N. by Troy and Burlington t-ships, E. by Moore, S. by Lycoming co. and W. by Canton. Centrally distant from Towanda, about 12 miles. Greatest length 12¾, breadth 10 miles; area, 70,400 acres; surface hilly; soil, gravelly loam. Population in 1830, 583; taxables 103. The main branch of the Towanda creek crosses the upper part of the t-ship from E. to W. and the middle branch of that creek rises in the t-ship, and flows through it diagonally from S. W. to N. E. Both receive considerable accessions in their course through it. Franklindale p-o. is 248 miles N. W. from W. C. and 137 from Harrisburg.

Franklin, post t-ship, York county, bounded N. E. by Monohan t-ship, S. E. by Washington t-ship, S. W. by Adams co. and N. W. by Cumberland co. Centrally distant from the borough of York N. W. about 20 miles; greatest length 5, breadth 4 miles; area, 10,240 acres; surface, rolling; soil, loam and gravel. Pop. in 1830, 1003; taxables, 224. Taxable property in 1829, and real estate, $153,261; personal, 8639; occupations, 22,770; total, 184,670; rate, 25 cts. in the 100 dollars. It is drained chiefly by a branch of the Bermudian creek. The post-town of Franklin lies in the E. angle, 17 miles N. W. from York, 100 miles from W. C. and 14 from Harrisburg.

Franklin, t-ship, Greene co. bounded N. E. by Morgan t-ship, E. by Jefferson, S. E. by Whitely, S. by Wayne, W. by Centre, and N. W. by Morris. Greatest length 9, breadth

7 miles; area, 30,720 acres; surface, rolling; soil, loam; population 2347; taxables, 401. The t-ship is drained by Ten Mile creek and its tributaries. The borough of Waynesburg, the co. town, is centrally situated in it, through which a turnpike road from Union town, Fayette co. to the state line passes.

Franklin, t-ship, Fayette co. bounded N. E. by Tyrone, E. by Dunbar, S. by Union and Manallen, W. by Redstone and Washington t-ships. Centrally distant N. from Union, 9 miles; greatest length 10, breadth 7 miles; area, 21,120 acres; surface hilly; soil, loam. Pop. in 1830, 1464; taxables, 338. The Youghiogheny river flows along the N. boundary, and Redstone creek upon the S. and S. W. Both receive small tributaries from the t-ship.

Franklin county was taken by act of assembly, 9th Sept. 1784, from the southern part of Cumberland co. designated by the name of the Conecocheauge settlement, so called from its principal stream, the Conecocheauge creek. It is bounded northward by the counties of Perry and Cumberland, W. by the county of Bedford and part of Huntingdon, E. by the county of Adams, and S. by the state of Maryland. Its greatest extent E. and W. is 34, and N. and S. 38 miles; area, 734 square miles, or 469,760 acres. Central lat. 39° 55′ N. long. from W. C. 0° 40′ W.

This county belongs to the great central transition formation, and lies in the Kittatinny valley, commonly known as the great limestone valley of the state. It is bounded on the E. by the South mountain, which has a course here nearly N. and S. with an elevation above the level of the middle of the valley, from 6 to 900 feet. On the W. it is limited by a higher and more rugged range of mountains, whose general direction is N. E. The Western Tuscarora or Cove mountain, rises about 1700 feet above the valley. The chief mineral discovered, is iron ore, of which there is great abundance, of excellent quality. In the western mountains, for many miles along the Path valley, continuous beds of this ore have been developed, of great depth and easily accessible. At a short distance W. of the South mountain and running parallel with it, from one end of the county to the other, is a vein of superior pipe and honey comb ore, showing itself at intervals in the limestone strata, and generally in nests, as is usual with this species of ore. In appearance this ore is not distinguishable from that of the Juniata, and the iron made from it is not inferior. In both these mineral regions, fuel and water power for the manufacture of iron are abundant, and under the stimulus applied by the American system, a great extension of the iron business here may be immediately expected. A tradition from the first white settlers near the South mountain reports, that the Indians obtained lead from these hills, but no exertions yet made for its discovery have been successful. White marble is seen in various parts of the county, and from the extent and variety of the limestone districts, considerable variety of that valuable and beautiful stone is supposed to exist. The limestone on the surface is of a blue color, and solid texture, lying in strata of various depths, inclined generally about 45 degrees from the horizon, dipping commonly to the S. E. It is intersected by perpendicular fissures. It contains marine fossils in great variety, the largest and finest specimens of the *cornu* ammonis found in the United States, are to be obtained from the quarries near Chambersburg. This stone affords at once a valuable material for building and fencing, and inexhaustible sources of manure.

The valley between the mountains, affords much diversity of aspect and soil. The greater part is limestone land of good quality, well watered by springs, fertile, and in high state of cultivation. Its quantity is estimated at about 180,000 acres; and it is generally divided into farms of from 100 to 300 acres each, nine tenths of which are cultivated by their owners, with the aid of their families. The general character of this land is undulating, very little of it being so hilly or broken, that it may not be subjected to the plough. The Conecocheague creek separates the lime and slate formations. The latter, narrow at the Maryland line, widens towards the N. and embraces a considerable portion of the N. W. section of the county, and is supposed to amount in the whole, to 160,000 acres. Though not so fertile and productive as the limestone land, and deemed of inferior quality, yet as it is cultivated with less labor and expense, and abounds in streams which create great quantities of natural meadow, producing large quantities of grass and hay for stock, those who cultivate it with care and skill are little behind their limestone land neighbors, in the means of comfortable and independent subsistence. Between the South mountain and the line at which the limestone appears at the surface, running parallel to the mountain, two miles in width through the county, is a belt, called "*Pine Lands*," which for fertility and certainty of product is not surpassed by any land in the county. Its area is estimated at 20,000 acres, and its surface is loam composed of sand and clay, among which many *boulders* are visible. This soil has a depth from ten to eighteen inches, and rests on a bed of red and yellow clay, underlaid at a great depth by the limestone rock.

The mountainous districts comprise about 110,000 acres. The South mtn. is covered by an almost unbroken forest, shading a soil too sandy and sterile for grain or grass, but favorable to the growth of forest trees, and of the peach, plumb and cherry trees, and of the vine. The ridges on the west have greater diversity of surface and soil. Their sides are frequently rugged and broken, but between them are valleys of various extent and soil. The Path valley situated here, is a very interesting portion of the county. Its general direction is N. E. and it possesses the same variety of soil, water and cultivation, with the rest of the county. It has, however, a more picturesque aspect. The mountain heights fringed with verdure, almost overhang the well cultivated and laughing farms below. This, with a continuous but smaller valley, called Amberson's, is divided into 2 t-ships, which contain about 700 taxable inhabitants.

The principal streams of the county have their sources in the mountains not far from their summits, whence they flow towards the middle of the valley, and nearly all unite in forming the Conecocheague creek, a large stream which empties into the Potomac at Williamsport, in Maryland. The Antictam creek rises in the South mountain and parts contiguous, and flows southward also into Maryland. The Conedogwinit creek springs from the North mountain, and runs northward for several miles, whilst West Conecocheague on the W. of the intervening mountain, has an opposite though nearly a parallel course. These main trunks and their tributary branches, intersect the country in all directions, and furnish a supply of water not only for agricultural, but for manufacturing purposes, to a great extent. This power now gives motion to about 80 stone and brick mills, for the manufacture of flour; 100 saw mills, 20 fulling mills, 5 furnaces, 7 woollen factories for spinning and weaving, and some manufactories of iron. (See Chambersburg.) Whilst the mills now erected are sufficient to manufacture double the quantity of grain grown in the county, little more than one half the water power of the streams, is yet applied to useful purposes.

The staple agricultural products of the county, are the common ones of the state, wheat, rye, corn and oats. To the growth of barley, hemp, and flax, there is an extensive fertile soil, peculiarly adapted, yet neither is cultivated in quantities proportionate to the interest of the cultivator, and the demand of the community. For the cultivation of hemp there is every inducement which a fertile soil can afford, with every advantage for water-rotting. From one hundred and fifty to two hundred thousand barrels of flour, are annually sent to the market of Baltimore, whence the county receives its chief supplies.

The grasses mostly cultivated are clover, timothy, and herds-grass. The last, introduced some years since, has been carried by the wings of the wind to almost every part of the co. and is supplanting in many places, the indigenous sour grasses of the wet soils. The orchard grass lately and partially introduced, has flourished so as to encourage its cultivation. Some of the citizens have given much attention to the growth of the white mulberry, and the feeding of the silk worm. On one farm near Green Castle, there are many thousand plants fit for transplanting, and are offered for sale on reasonable terms. The soil and climate invite to the cultivation of silk, and we trust that the inhabitants will awake to the sense of the value and profit of this article of trade.

The prevailing forest trees are the white, black, red, swamp and chestnut oak, chestnut, poplar, elm, black and white walnut, hickory, acacia or locust, ash, maple, sycamore, red, white and pitch pine. The red cedar, black mulberry, and sassafras, are found in small quantities in many parts of the county; the chestnut only on or near the mountains; the pine and chestnut oak, also principally in the mountains, and rarely in the limestone soil. The sugar maple first discovers itself in the mountains on the west. So great is the variety of forest trees common to the soil of this part of the state, that on a small surface not exceeding one acre, may be found of native growth ten or fifteen kinds.

Much has been done in this county for promoting facile intercourse, by the construction of roads and bridges. There are more than 400 miles of public roads, of which 63 are stone turnpikes. These have been made at an expense to the inhabitants of more than $230,000. There are 23 large stone bridges erected by the county, t-ship, and turnpike companies.

There are 40 churches in which religious instruction is regularly dispensed, and christian ordinances piously observed. There are auxiliary, Bible, and colonization and tract societies, and Sunday School Unions in the county. Four newspapers are printed in the county, viz: The Franklin Repository, Franklin Republican, Franklin Telegraph, and Anti-Masonic Gazette. One of them is in the German language.

A great portion of the dwellings of the inhabitants are of stone and brick; in the limestone sections nearly all the barns and stables for cattle are of that material. The value of taxable property by the assessment of 1829, was $6,668,495. This assessment is about 25 per cent below the amounts the owners would be willing to accept. The assessed value of real estate in the county in 1814, amounted to $11,500,980, and the difference is that of the values of the currency at the two periods. The prices of lands varying with their qualities and situations is from 5 to 50 dollars per acre.

The population of the county is composed chiefly of Irish and Dutch settlers, and their descendants. It amounted in 1800, to 20,151; in 1810, to 23,173; in 1820, to 31,909, and in 1830, to 35,103. The taxables in 1828, to 6095.

For an account of the public buildings of the county, we refer the reader to the article "*Chambersburg*," observing here, that there is a competent number of schools to teach the children of the county the rudiments of an English education, and that a county alms-house and house of employment, has been established some years. The average number of paupers is about 70, who are maintained each at the annual expense of about $37, beside the aid derived from the farm, which contains 160 acres of good land.

The chief towns of the county are Chambersburg, the seat of justice, Greencastle, Waynesburg, Mercersburg, St. Thomas, Louden, Fannetsburg, Roxbury, Strasburg, Greenvillage and Fayetteville. For a description of Chambersburg we refer to that article. The towns of Greencastle, Waynesburg, and Mercersburg are considerable for their size, each having a number of neat and substantial stone and brick houses, edifices for public worship, many stores and public houses, and surrounded by a country admirable for its beauty and fertility, and for the comfortable improvements of its independent proprietors. The other villages are in a very thriving state.

Franklin county forms the 15th senatorial district; sends one member to the senate, and two to the house of representatives. Conjoined with Adams, Cumberland and Perry, it composes the 11th congressional district, which sends two members to congress; united with Bedford and Somerset counties, it makes the 16th judicial district, over which Alexander Thompson, Esq. presides. The courts are holden at Chambersburg on the 2d Mondays of January, April, August and November. It belongs to the southern district of the supreme court, which holds its session at Chambersburg, in September annually.

This county paid into the state treasury in the year 1831, for dividends on turnpike stock, $5650,00

Tax on bank dividends,	1186,00
Tax on writs,	536,52
Tavern licenses,	2244,48
Duties on de'lrs in for. mdze.	224,09
State maps,	23,75
Pamphlet laws,	1,43
Tin and clock pedlars licenses,	117,00
Hawkers and pedlars licenses,	65,20
Total,	$12,045 47

STATISTICAL TABLE OF FRANKLIN COUNTY.

Townships, &c.	Greatest Lth.	Greatest Bth	Area in Acres	Face of country.	Soil.	Population. 1810	1820	1830	Taxables.
Antrim,	9	8¼	38400	level, rocky	limestone,	2864	4120	3829	768
Fannet,	13	7½	38400	mtnous.,	part, slate,	1398	1747	2112	285
Franklin,						1781	2405	2794	487
Greene,	13	6	32640	level,	lime., slate,	1497	2010	2554	465
Guilford,	14	7	33920	do.	limestone,	1961	2439	2873	528
Hamilton,	9½	7¾	21760	hilly,	slate,	1263	1688	1461	251
Letterkenny,	12	10½	40400	level,	chiefly slate,	1549	1820	1965	382
Lurgan,	9	7¼	19200	do.	do.	874	1523	1252	224
Metal,	15	5	23680	mtnous.,	lime & shale,	1236	1294	1296	248
Montgomery,	11	8	46080	level,	limestone,	2693	3398	3509	595
Peters,	12	8	30720	do.	chiefly do.,	1762	2776	2268	410
Southampton,	11¾	5	21760	do.	do.	1060	1348	1655	266
Warren,	11	5	23040	hilly,	slate & shale	436	527	572	107
Washington,	11	8½	49920	rolling,	limestone,	2709	4797	5184	751
St. Thomas	11½	7	25600	do.	chiefly slate,		2405	1778	328
						23083	31892	35103	6095

Franklin, t-ship, Huntingdon co. bounded N. by Centre co. E. by Tussey's mountain which separates it from West t-ship, S. by Morris and Tyrone t-ships, and W. by Warriormark. Centrally distant from Huntingdon t-ship N. W. 12 miles. Greatest length 8 miles, breadth 6½; area, 22,400 acres; surface, mountainous; soil, limestone. Population in 1830, 1200; taxables, 220. The W. branch of the Little Juniata river, flows along the S. boundary, and receives from the t-ship Warrior's run and Spruce creek, between which is Coleraine Forge post-office. On both streams there are iron works; Huntingdon furnace on the former, and Coleraine forge and others, on the latter. There were in the t-ship in 1828, 4 grist mills, 7 saw mills, 1 fulling mill, 2 furnaces and 4 forges.

Franklin, t-ship, Lycoming county, bounded N. by Penn town-ship, E. by Luzerne co. S. by Columbia co. and W. by Moreland t-ship. Centrally distant E. from Williamsport 30 miles. Greatest length 18, breadth 9 miles; area, 46,080 acres; surface mountainous; soil various, chiefly slate and gravel. Population in 1830, 400; taxables, 74. Value of taxable property in 1829, seated lands, &c. $19,721. Personal estate, 2229. Rate of tax 75 cts. in the hundred dollars. It is drained by the Little Muncy cr. on the S. W. and Fishing cr. on the S. E. Bald mountain passes centrally through the t-ship, from W. to E.

Franklin, p-t. borough, and st. of just. of Venango county, on the right bank of French creek, at its junction with the Allegheny river. Lat. 41° 22′ N. Long. 2° 50′ W. from W. C. Distant by p-r. from that place 279 miles, and 212 miles from Harrisburg, and 70 miles from Pittsburg. The town was laid out by the commissioners appointed under the act of 18th April, 1795, in about 700 lots. It contains above 400 inhabitants, and is rapidly improving, particularly since the introduction of steamboats on the Allegheny. It contains a stone court house and jail, an Episcopalian church of brick, and a Presbyterian church of frame. A mail stage runs through it three times a week, and six mails arrive weekly, on horseback. The Susquehannah and Waterford turnpike road passes by the town. There are here 13 stores, 6 taverns, 1 grist mill, an academy to which the legislature gave $2000 in the year 1813, and also two forges. There is a bridge across French creek 200 feet long. There is a good steamboat navigation on the river, for four or five months in the year, by boats of the Blanchard construction, of 60 or 100 tons burthen. From the mouth of French creek, 43 miles of the Penn. canal designed to connect lake Erie with the Allegheny river are finished, and under contract. The town was incorporated 14th April, 1828.

Franklin, t-ship, Allegheny county, bounded N. by the co. of Butler, E. by Pine t-ship, S. by Ohio t-ship, and W. by the co. of Beaver. Greatest length 6, breadth 6 ms; area, 14,080 acres; surface hilly; soil, loam; coal abundant. Pop. in 1830, 1326; taxables, 270. It is drained by the E. branch of the Big Sewickly creek, upon which there are several mills.

Franklin, t-ship, Westmoreland co. bounded N. by Allegheny t-ship, N. E. by Washington, E. by Salem, S. by North Huntingdon, and W. by Allegheny co. Centrally distant N. W. of Greensburg 12 miles; greatest length, 11½; breadth, 8 miles; area, 32,000 acres; surface, hilly; soil, limestone and loam. It is drained on the N. W. by the Poketos creek, and on the S. W. by Turtle creek. The turnpike road from Ebensburg to Pittsburg, passes centrally through the t-ship, and upon it, near the W. line in a fork of Turtle creek, are the small towns of Murraysville and Nolensville.

Franklin, or Rocktown, a small village of 8 or 10 houses, and a tavern, on the turnpike road between Middletown and Lancaster, in Londonderry t-ship, Lancaster co. 12 miles from Harrisburg.

Frankstown, t-ship, Huntingdon co. bounded N. E. by Tyrone and Morris t-ship, S. E. by Dock mountain, which separates it from Woodberry t-ship, S. W. by Bedford co. and N. W. by Allegheny and Antes t-ships. Centrally distant S. W. from Huntingdon borough 19 miles. Greatest length 13, breadth 8 miles; area, 51,200 acres; surface, mountain and valley; soil, limestone in the valleys. The Frankstown branch of the Juniata river enters the t-ship on the S. through the Frankstown Gap of Dunning's mountain, and flowing along Lock mountain through the t-ship by Frankstown, passes out at the N. E. angle; it receives Beaver Dam creek above Frankstown, upon which lies the town of Hollidaysburg. The town of Newry lies on Poplar run, a small branch of the river. Brush mountain fills the N. angle of the t-ship. On the Beaver Dam creek, W. of Hollidaysburg, commences the rail road portage across the Allegheny mountain, to Johnstown. There were in this t-ship in 1828, 9 grist mills, 6 saw mills, 15 distilleries, 1 fulling mill, and 3 tanyards.

Frankstown, Branch of the Juniata river. (See Juniata River.)

Frankstown, post-town of Huntingdon county in Frankstown t-ship, on the Frankstown branch of the Juniata river, 20 miles nearly W. from Huntingdon borough, and on the turnpike road from that place to Ebensburg, and about two miles E. of Hollidaysburg, contains 30 dwellings, 3 taverns, 8 stores, a tannery, a brewery, and a school house.

Frazer, p-t. Chester county, 128 miles from W. C. 74 from Harrisburg.

Frederick, t-ship, Montgomery co. bounded N. E. by the Perkiomen cr. which separates it from Upper Salford and Marlborough, S. by Perkiomen and Skippack, S. W. by Limerick, N. W. by New Hanover, and N. by Upper Hanover. Greatest length, 7 miles; greatest breadth, 6 miles; area, 13,440 acres. It is drained by the Perkiomen and Swamp creek, a tributary. Surface, rolling; soil, red shale. Pop. in 1830, 1047; taxables in 1828, 208. Central distance from Norristown, about 15 miles, from Philadelphia, 30 miles.

Fredericktown, p-t. E. Bethlehem t-ship, on the W. bank of the Monongahela river, two miles N. of the mouth of Ten Mile creek, 8 above Brownsville, and 18 miles S. W. of Washington borough, 206 miles from Harrisburg, and 213 N. W. from W. C. contains 40 or 50 dwellings, 2 stores, and 3 or 4 taverns.

Freeburg, p-t. Washington t-ship, Union co. on a branch of Middle cr. 8 miles S. E. of New Berlin, 157 ms. N. W. from W. C. and 47 from Harrisburg, contains about 40 dwellings, 3 stores, and 2 taverns.

Freedensburg, p-t. Wayne t-ship, Schuylkill co. about 10 miles W. of Orwigsburg, 157 N. W. from W. C. and 47 from Harrisburg, contains about 40 dwellings, 3 stores, and 2 taverns.

Freemansburg, a small village and post-town in Bethlehem t-ship, on the road from the Wind gap to Philadelphia, 8 miles from Easton, 187 from W. C. and 97 from Harrisburg, containing 4 dwellings, 1 tavern, 1 store. A bridge crosses the Lehigh here, having 2 arches. A dam in the river Lehigh is near this town, and the canal runs in front of it, between the town and river.

French creek, Chester co. rises in Union t-ship, Berks county, and flows thence through E. Nantmeal, Coventry, Vincent, Pikeland and Charleston t-ships, Chester co. into the river Schuylkill. It is a fine mill stream. Phœnixville is at its mouth. (See Phœnixville.)

French's mills, p-o. Bradford co. 268 miles N. W. from Washington, and 162 from Harrisburg.

French town, Asylum t-ship, Bradford co. in a deep bend of the Susquehannah river, 7 miles S. E. of Towanda.

French creek, t-ship, Mercer county, bounded N. by Crawford co. E. by Venango co. S. by Sandy Lake t-ship, and W. by Sandy Creek t-ship. Centrally distant from the borough of Mercer N. E. 16 miles. Greatest length $8\frac{1}{2}$, breadth $6\frac{1}{2}$ miles; area, 35,520 acres. French cr. crosses the N. E. angle of the t-ship, and receives from it Deer and Mill creek; and Sandy cr. crosses the S. W. angle. Surface of the t-ship is level; soil, clay and loam, and not of good quality. Population in 1830, 457; taxables 78; taxable property in 1829, real estate, $58,085; personal, 1494; rate of tax, 4 mills on the dollar.

French Creek, t-ship, Venango co. bounded N. by French creek, E. by the Allegheny river, S. by that river and Sandy Creek t-ship, and W. by Mercer co. Greatest length 29, breadth 7 miles; area 28,800 acres; surface hilly; soil, gravel. Pop. in 1830, 1055; taxables 237. The borough of Franklin is in this t-ship, at the confluence of the French creek with the Allegheny river. Sandy creek flows along the S. boundary into that river.

French creek, a large stream of north western Penn. rises in Chatauque co. New York and pursuing a comparative course of 15 miles S. W. enters Pennsylvania, in Erie co. and thence continuing the same course, about 35 miles, to Meadville, in Crawford co. it there receives the Cussawago from the N. W.; thence running S. E. 25 ms. it unites with the Allegheny river at the borough of Franklin in Venango co. It is navigable as high as the mouth of Le Boeuf creek 5 ms. S. from Waterford. The French creek feeder intended to feed the contemplated canal from the Allegheny river to Erie, commences at Bemus' mills, on the E. side of the creek, about 2 miles N. of Meadville, passes through the town, and to about 6 miles below it, where it crosses the creek, and falls into the valley of the outlet of Conneaut lake, which it pursues to the summit level near the lake with which it communicates. The length of the feeder is 19½ miles; it is nearly completed. The estimated cost, is $250,000.

Freeport, p-t. of Buffalo t-ship, Armstrong co. at the confluence of the Buffalo creek with the Allegheny r. 14 ms. below Kittanning borough, and two miles below the mouth of the Kiskiminitas river, 225 miles from W. C. and 179 from Harrisburg. The state canal passes through the town, crossing the creek by an aqueduct; and an office for the collection of tolls is established here. The first tolls taken were in June, 1829. The town contains about 50 dwellings, 5 or 6 stores, 4 taverns and 1 church.

Freystown, village of Spring Garden t-ship, York co. within two miles E. of York, on the turnpike road from Wrightsville. It may be deemed a suburb of the town of York.

Friendsville, p-t. and village, Middletown t-ship, Susquehannah co. situate at the intersection of the turnpike road from Montrose to Owego with the N. line of the t-ship. It contains 6 dwellings, 1 store, and tavern. Distant 10 miles from Montrose N. W., and 283 from W. C. 175 from Harrisburg.

Friend's Cove valley, Colerain t-ship, Bedford co. bounded by Tussey's mountain on the E., Evits mountain on the W., and the Raystown branch of the Juniata on the N. It is drained by Cove creek, a mill stream.

Fruitstown, a small hamlet of Derry t-ship, Columbia co. on a branch of the Chilisquaque creek, 12 miles N. of Danville.

Fruithill, p-t. Clearfield co. 188 miles N. W. from W. C., and 130 from Harrisburg.

Frysburg, a small village and p-t. of Upper Saucon t-ship, Lehigh co. on the turnpike road from the Springhouse tavern to Bethlehem, 178 ms. N. frow W. C., and 92 N. E. from Harrisburg. It contains 10 or 15 dwellings, a store, tavern and Lutheran church.

Furnace creek, a tributary of the Quitapahilla creek, Lebanon co. rises on the N. side of the Conewango hills in Lebanon t-ship, and flows N. W. to its recipient about 8 miles. There is a bed of iron ore near its source, and Cornwall furnace, which gives name to the creek.

Gainsburg, town of Londonderry t-ship, on the turnpike road betwcen Middletown and Lancaster, contains 8 or 10 dwellings, a store and tavern.

Gallows run, a small tributary of the Delaware, on the boundary line between Nockamixon and Durham t-ships, Bucks co.

Gamble's, p-o. Allegheny co. 210 miles N. W. from W. C. and 188 W. of Harrisburg.

Gap tavern, p-o. at the E. foot of the Mine Ridge, Sadsbury t-ship, Lancaster co. on the Lancaster and Newport turnpike road, 16 miles E. of Lancaster, 125 N. of W. C. and 51 S. E. of Harrisburg.

Gardner's creek, rises in Abington t-ship, Luzerne co. and flows S. W. through Falls and Exeter t-ships, into the river Susquehannah. It is a mill stream but not navigable.

Gay's port, a small village of Frankstown t-ship, Huntingdon co. on a branch of the Juniata river, between Hollidaysburg and Frankstown; its foundation was laid in 1829, and it now contains several dwellings.

Gebhert's, p-o. of Somerset co. 154 ms. N. W. from W. C. and 132 from Harrisburg.

Georgetown, p-t. Greene t-ship, Beaver co. on the N. side of Mill creek, on the S. side of the Ohio river, 12 miles S. W. of Beaver borough.

Georgetown, p-t. of Sandy Creek t-ship, Mercer co. on the turnpike road leading from the borough of Mercer to Meadville, 15 ms. N. of the former, and about the same distance from the latter, 263 ms. from W. C. and 241 from Harrisburg, contains 35 dwellings, 3 stores, and 3 taverns.

Georgeville, village of Mahoning t-ship, Indiana co. on the road from Indiana borough to Jefferson co. 15 ms. N. from the borough, contains 4 or 5 dwellings, 2 stores, 1 tavern.

Georgetown, or *Dalmatia*, Lower Mahanoy t-ship, Northumberland co. p-t. on the Susquehannah river, centrally situate in the t-ship, 146 ms. from W. C. and 36 from Harrisburg, contains 75 dwellings, 4 taverns and 2 stores.

George, t-ship, Fayette co. bounded N. E. by Union, S. E. by Wharton, S. W. by Springhill, and N. W. by German t-ships. Centrally distant S. W. from Uniontown 7 miles; greatest length 11, breadth 9 miles; area 28,800 acres; surface, level; soil, loam and limestone. Pop. in 1830, 2416. Laurel hill is on the E. boundary. The t-ship is drained by George's creek and its branches, York's run and Middle and South Forks. There are many beds of iron, and several forges in the t-ship. Smithfield, Hayden and Woodbridge, are towns lying in the southern part of the t-ship; the first is a post town.

George creek, Fayette co. rises by four branches in George t-ship, and flows S. W. through Springhill t-ship, into Cheat river, S. of the town of N. Geneva.

Germantown, t-ship, Phila. county, is bounded N. E. partly by Montgomery co. and partly by Bristol t-ship, E. by Bristol, S. by Penn, S. W. by Roxborough t-ships, and N. W. by Montgomery co. Length 5½ ms. breadth 2, area 7040 acres; centrally distant from Phila. 8 ms. Surface hilly; soil, loam and alluvial bottoms. Pop. in 1830, 4642; taxables in 1828, 1032. It is drained on the N. W. by the main stream of the Wissahickon, which receives from the t-ship Creisham cr. and another small branch; and the Wingohocking cr., rising at the foot of Mount Airy, runs S. W. into the Tacony cr., in Bristol t-ship. The Germantown turnpike road, continued by the Perkiomen turnpike road, runs centrally through the t-ship, its whole length. And a rail-road from Phila. to Norristown, is now being constructed, which will pass through Germantown. The whole of the turnpike road, from the brow of Logan's hill to the upper end of Chestnut hill, a distance of five miles, may be considered the street of a continuous village, with substantial, comfortable dwellings, mostly of stone or brick, occupied as the homes of men who have retired to enjoy the competency gained by a life of industry, or of thrifty mechanics and manufacturers, who find in the neighboring city a ready market for the product of their labors, or as snug and agreeable country seats of the citizens. There must be from seven to eight hundred houses in this *lengthy* village, many stores, and all the species of business which a large and rich population requires and produces. Churches belonging to several denominations of Christians, viz. Tunkers, Menonists, Lutherans, German and English Presbyterians, Methodists, Episcopalians, &c. &c. Schools, for the accommodation of not only the local population, but also for pupils from the city and elsewhere, among which, the Germantown academy and Mount Airy academy are most distinguished. The first was founded in 1784, and in 1821 received a donation from the state of $2000. The present principals of the institution, Messrs. Classin and Jenks, are much esteemed. Annexed to it is a seminary for young ladies. Mount Airy college, as it is sometimes called, is a large and commodious building, beautifully situated, at which the exercises are conducted on the plan of the military school of Capt. Partridge, and pupils are adequately prepared for the military academy at West Point.

Germantown is among the first settlements of the province after the purchase of Wm. Penn. The conveyance from the proprietary to Francis Daniel Pastorius, is dated the 12th of the 8th month, 1683, and the survey made by the surveyor general, 2d of 3d month, 1684, comprised 5700 acres of land, the original price of which was one shilling per acre. The original purchasers were of Frankfort and Crefelt, in Germany; the first settlers chiefly from Cresheim, which name was given to their settlement. The Germantown *town* lots were located and surveyed in 1687, and distributed by lot, in 1689. The town was in that year incorporated as a borough by Wm. Penn, then in England. F. D. Pastorius, *civilian*, was chosen first bailiff, and Jacob Tellner, Dirk Isaacs op den Graff, and Herman op den Graff, burghers and town magistrates, who, together with eight yeomen, formed a general court, which sat once a month. It made laws and levied taxes. There is no principle in modern policy, if modern it be, more beneficial than the division of a great community into many small and subordinate ones, which, having an integral existence, and adequate power to supply local regulations and means for their enforcement, are enabled speedily and effectually to promote the happiness of the individual members. But this early incorporation of Germantown, was greatly in anticipation of the proper period for such an event; for the town lost its charter in 1704 by non-user, there not being a sufficient number of persons willing to serve in the general court. We believe that an application for its re-incorporation, has been made to the legislature at its present session (1832).

Germantown is much frequented by the citizens of Phila. on pleasure and business, and several commodious stages run to and from it at convenient hours of the day. This intercourse will become more frequent when the rail-road shall have been completed, and the rapidity of conveyance shall have, in effect, so diminished the distance between the two places, that a man of business shall find little inconvenience in residing at Germantown, and attending to his affairs in the city, when he can pass as soon from his dwelling in the former place to his store in the latter, as he now does from one of the western or northern streets to the south and eastern ones.

German, t-ship, Fayette co., bounded N. by Luzerne and Red Stone, E. by Menallen and George, S. by Springhill t-ships, and W. by the Monongahela r., which separates it from Greene co. Centrally distant W. from Uniontown, 8 ms.; greatest length 7, breadth 6½ ms.; area, 20,480 acres; surface rolling; soil, limestone and loam. Pop. in 1830, 2395; taxables, 463. It is drained by Brown's run, Middle run, and some smaller streams which flow westerly into the river, and by Dunlap's cr., which runs on the E. boundary. M'Cleland's town is centrally situated on the road leading from Union to Waynesburg, 7 miles W.

of the former, and Germantown, about 3 miles S. W. of M'Clcland town, in the S. W. angle of the t-ship. The latter is the p-t.

Germantown, German t-ship, Fayette co. (see preceding article), contains about 60 dwellings, 1 church, 2 schools, 4 stores and 2 taverns.

Germany, t-ship, Adams co., bounded N. by Mount Pleasant and Conewago t-ships, E. by York co., S. by the state of Md., and W. by Mount Joy t-ship. Centrally distant S. E. from Gettysburg, 10 ms.; greatest l'th 8, breadth 4 ms.; area 14,080 acres; surface level; soil, limestone and gravel. Pop. in 1830, 1517; taxables 322. Wilalloways cr. forms the W. boundary. Piney cr. drains it centrally on the S. and the head waters of the Conewago on the N. The turnpike r. from Gettysburg to the Md. line, passes through the middle of the t-ship, on which lies the p-t of Petersburg, 10 ms. S. E. of Gettysburg.

Germany, village, Shade t-ship, Somerset co., on Conover's branch of Shade's cr., 5 ms. W. of the Allegheny mtn, and about 6 ms. N. of the turnpike road, leading from Bedford to Greensburg.

Gettysburg, p-t. borough and st. jus. of Adams co., Cumberland t-ship, 28 ms. S. W. of the borough of York, and 35 from Harrisburg, is a pleasant town, containing, by the census of 1830, 1473 inhabitants, who are principally engaged in mechanical pursuits; and about 250 dwellings. The town stands on an elevated piece of ground, where the Philad. and Baltimore roads meet in their course to Pittsburg, distant 114 miles from the one and 52 from the other; and is surrounded by a fertile and well cultivated country. By its location, it enjoys no inconsiderable share of the advantages resulting from the intercourse between those cities and the west. At the session of the legislature in 1828, a subscription for $20,000 worth of the stock of a company for making a turnpike road from Gettysburg to Hagerstown, in Md. was authorized, but the balance of the necessary sum not having been subscribed by individuals, the work has not been commenced. The construction of this road would connect Phila. and Wheeling by a continuous turnpike. Gettysburg was laid out a few years before the organization of the co., by Mr. James Gettys, deceased, and is at present inferior to few towns in the state, of the same size. The theological seminary of the Lutheran church was located here two or three years ago, and is at present under the superintendence of Prof. Shmacker. There is also an academy, incorporated by act March, 1810, to which the legislature made a donation of $2000, conditioned that a number of poor children, not exceeding four, should be annually taught therein.

The public buildings consist of a court house and county offices, a prison, a building for the academy, a bank and four churches, two pertaining to the Presbyterians, one to the Methodists, and one to the German Lutherans; all these buildings except the prison are of brick. There are nine stores and nine taverns. The town is supplied with good water by means of pipes leading from a spring within its limits. There are 3 newspapers published here weekly, one of which is in the German language. This place is noted for the manufacture of carriages of every description. It is contemplated to form a rail-road from the town to intersect the Baltimore and Ohio raid-road. The distance of the line does not exceed 8 miles 297 perches, over a surface said to be peculiarly favorable.

Gibson, t-ship, Susquehannah co. bounded N. by Jackson t-ship, E. by Wayne co. S. by Clifford t-ship, and W. by Harford and Lennox t-ships. Its greatest length E. and W. is 8 ms. breadth 7½. It is watered by the Tunkhannock and Lackawannock creeks, whose branches penetrate it from W. to E. respectively. The Philadelphia and Great Bend turnpike crosses it diagonally. It has a post office, called Gibson, situated in the N. W. angle.

Its surface is hilly ; soil, clay and gravel. Pop. in 1830, 1081 ; taxables in 1828, 196. The post office is 283 miles from W. C. and 184 from Harrisburg.

Gibson, t-ship, Clearfield co. bounded N. by McKean and Lycoming counties, E. by Lycoming co. S. by Lawrence and Covington t-ships, and W. by Fox t-ship. Centrally distant N. E. from the town of Clearfield 22 miles; greatest length 20, breadth 10 miles; surface, mountainous; soil, gravelly loam. Pop. in 1830, 405 ; taxables, 71. Bennet's branch of the Sinnemahoning creek runs N. E. through the t-ship, and receives from it on the N. the Driftwood branch, and on the S. Stegner's and Shmitmyer's run. Salt springs are found on the Sinnemahoning creek, near the E. boundary, and several salt licks in the western part of the t-ship.

Gilmoreville, p-t. Butler co. 244 ms. N. W. of W. C. and 212 from Harrisburg.

Glade run, a tributary of the Allegheny r. rising in Sugar Creek t-ship, and flowing S. E. through Buffalo t-ship, falls into its recipient 8 or 9 ms. below Kittanning. The stream gives name to the post office of Buffalo t-ship, and is 214 ms. from W. C. and 181 from Harrisburg.

Glass creek, Upper, Smithfield t-ship, Pike co. a small tributary of the Delaware r. having its whole course within the t-ship.

Gold Mine gap, an opening in the Sharp mountain, between Lower Mahantango and Pine Grove t-ships, and near the S. W. line of Schuylkill co. Through this gap the Coan creek flows southward into the Swatara river.

Goshen, East, t-ship, Chester co., bounded N. by East and West Whiteland, E. by Willistown, S. by Westtown, and W. by West Goshen t-ships; central distance about 18 miles W. of Phila. and 4 ms. E. of West Chester ; greatest length 4 miles, breadth 3 ; area, 7350 acres ; surface, mostly level; soil, sandy loam, well cultivated and productive. Ridley and Chester creeks pass S. E. through the t-ship, each turning several mills. East Goshen meeting-house is situated on the Phila. road, east of the centre of the t-ship. Pop. in 1830, 752 ; taxables in 1828, 173. The post office here, called Goshenville, is 119 ms. N. of W. C. and 79 S. E. from Harrisburg.

Goshen, West, t-ship, Chester co. bounded N. by West Whiteland, E. by East Goshen, S. by West town t-ship, and W. by East Bradford t-ship ; central distance from Phila. W. 21 ms. ; length 4 miles, breadth $2\frac{1}{2}$; area, 5600 acres ; surface, gentle declivity , soil, sandy loam, well cultivated and productive. Pop. in 1830, 799 ; taxables in 1828, 156. Two branches of Chester creek flow through the t-ship southerly, and a tributary of the east branch of the Brandywine proceeds from it westerly. West Chester, p-t., bor. and seat jus. of the county, is near the western boundary of the t-ship.

Grapeville, t. Hempfield township, Westmoreland co. on the turnpike road leading from Greensburg to Pittsburg, about 4 ms. W. of the former; contains 15 dwellings, 2 taverns and 1 store.

Gratztown, p-t. of Lyken's t-ship, Dauphin co. 151 ms. N. of W. C. and 38 from Harrisburg, on the road leading from Millerstown to Schuylkill co., contains from 30 to 40 dwellings, 3 stores and 4 taverns.

Gravel run, Northumberland co. a tributary of the Susquehannah river, which for part of its course forms the boundary between Rush and Augusta t-ships, and has its source in the former.

Graysville, or *Graysport*, Morris t-ship, Huntingdon co. opposite the mouth of Spruce run, 169 ms. N. W. from W. C. and 96 from Harrisburg; contains about 7 dwellings and 1 store.

Gray's Settlement, p-t. Erie co. 327 ms. N. W. from W C. and 266 from Harrisburg.

Great Bend, t-ship, Susquehannah co. bounded N. by the state of New-York, E. by Harmony t-ship, S. by New Milford t-ship, and W. by Lawsville. It forms a square of 6 miles on each side, and contains 23,040 acres. It is watered by the Susquehannah r. which, forming a great bend around the Oquago mountain, gives name to the t-ship and to a village within it, and is the recipient of several small streams, among which, Salt Lick and Mitchell's creeks are the most considerable. Oquago mountain covers the greater portion of the northern part of the t-ship. The Great Bend turnpike passes northerly and centrally through it. The surface is hilly: soil, clay and gravel. Pop. in 1830, 797; taxables in 1828, 114.

Great Bend, p-t. and village, Susquehannah co. is situated in Great Bend t-ship, at the junction of Salt Lick creek with the Susquehannah river, about 8 miles below the entrance of the latter into the state, upon an extensive flat, which is surrounded on all sides by high hills. From this place a turnpike road is made to Coshocton on the Delaware, which is intersected by others from different parts of the country. The village is built on both sides of the river, over which a bridge of timber, 600 feet in length and 20 in width, was built in 1814, upon nine piers, by individual subscription, at an expense of $6500. The town is irregularly built; contains 35 dwellings, several stores and taverns, about 200 inhabitants; 2 churches, Baptist and Presbyterian, and a seminary for young ladies. It is 13 miles E. of Montrose.

Great Salt Works, p-o. Indiana co. Conemaugh t-ship, 207 ms. N. W. from W. C., and 175 W. from Harrisburg.

Greene county, is bounded N. by the co. of Washington, E. by the river Monongahela, on which it has a front of about 25 miles, S. and W. by the state of Virginia. It has in length E. and W. 32 ms. and in breadth N. and S. 19 ms. and contains 597 sq. miles. Central lat. 39° 50′ N. long. 3° 15′ W. from W. C.

Belonging to the great secondary formation of the state, this co. has a due proportion of the three minerals, coal, iron and salt, which abound in Western Pennsylvania. Bituminous coal is found almost every where in the hills, in inexhaustible quantities, and in many instances along water courses, within one, two, or three feet of the surface. Big Whitely creek has for its bed a stratum of coal, in some places for miles, which, during the summer months when the water is low, is taken for the supply of the surrounding country. The labor of digging and transporting it constitutes the whole cost. It is said that there are extensive beds of iron ore on Dunkard and Ten Mile creeks. There were formerly a forge and furnace in operation on the latter stream, but they have been long idle and are falling to decay. Salt licks are known on Dunkard's creek, near the S. E. corner of the co. but there are no salt works erected.

The surface of the co. is greatly diversified by hill and valley, and the soil varies from the richest river bottoms to the poorest gravelly ridges. The co. is very well watered; the principal streams are Dunkard, Big Whitely, Little Whitely, Muddy and Ten Mile creeks, all of which flow eastward into the Monongahela river. Wheeling and Fish creeks rise by several branches and flow westward to the Ohio; their sources are not distant from each other. The valleys of these streams are among the most delightful of Pennsylvania, rich, and where the axe has not yet done its work, covered with every variety of timber indigenous to the west, of the largest growth. The intervening ridges, running E. and W. are also overshadowed by luxuriant forest trees. The northern sides of the hills have a deep, rich soil, adapted to corn and grass, and the south, though generally less fertile, produce wheat and rye abundantly. The western part of the co. is at present deemed too hilly for agriculture, but may one day be profitable to the herdsman and vine-dresser. Even now few counties of the same extent and population send to market larger quantities of stock of every description, and the breeding of horses, cattle, sheep and swine, is deemed the most advantageous mode of employing lands, and immense droves are sent annually into the eastern part of this state and into Maryland. Large quantities of flour and whiskey are also taken by the Monongahela river to Pittsburg, and thence to New Orleans. This river affords a facile and safe navigation for more than ⅔ of the year.

There are no turnpike roads in the co. but good state and county roads traverse it in every direction; and all the streams which cannot be safely forded are crossed by substantial bridges.

The co. was originally settled by emigrants from Maryland and Virginia whilst yet possessed by the aboriginal inhabitants; but the efforts of the intruders to establish permanent homes were wavering, and were frequently defeated by the natives previous to the arrival of the Crawfords, the Minors, the Swans, the Corblys and some other equally daring and enterprising pioneers. During the first seven years the emigrants were frequently assailed, in their persons and property, by the Indians, and their courage in repelling the savage foe and their patience in enduring the privations caused by his depredations, now afford many a tale for the winter evening fire-sides of their descendants. The co. is now settled by persons from all parts of the U. S. and some from Germany, Ireland, England and Scotland. The population amounted in 1800 to 8605, in 1810 to 12,544, in 1820 to 15,554, and in 1830 to 18,028; of whom 8884 were white males, 8823 white females, 157 free black males, 154 free black females, and 1 slave; of the whole there were 28 aliens, 5 deaf and dumb and 16 blind. Taxables in 1828, 3141. This population is divided into all the variety of religious sects known in the United States; but the Methodist is the most numerous. The clergy are supported here, as elsewhere, by the contributions of their respective flocks, which are said to be not only ample but liberal. There are county tract, Bible and missionary societies; and there are two Masonic lodges within the co. Schools, wherein are taught the rudiments of an English education, are established in every vicinage; and the indigent are taught at the expense of the county, under the provision made by the laws of the commonwealth. There is an academy at Carmichaelstown, which was incorporated in 1810 and received from the state a donation of $2000; and another institution called the Franklin school, also incorporated, in Franklin t-ship.

There is in the county one woollen factory, on a large scale, on Ten Mile creek. But its operations have not hitherto been commensurate with its capacity; but having lately fallen into the hands of an Englishman of skill and enterprise, it is supposed that its business will be much extended.

The county contains about 40 grist mills, as many saw mills, 20 fulling mills, 6 oil mills, seated chiefly on Dunkard, Big and Little Whitely, Ten Mile, Wheeling and Fish creeks, all of which are strong and steady streams.

The public buildings of the county consist of a commodious court house and offices, of brick; a county prison, of stone; the churches pertaining to the various religious sects, and the academy and school already mentioned. There is one newspaper published at the seat of justice, Waynesburg, called the Waynesburg Messenger.

The towns are Waynesburg, centrally situated, Clarksville, Newport, New Lisbon, commonly called Carmichaelstown, Jefferson, Greensburg, heretofore a place of business, near to which is an extensive glass manufactory, Maple town, Mount Morris, Morrisville and Clinton.

Greene, united with Fayette county, forms the 19th senatorial district of the state, sending 1 member to the senate, and alone it sends 1 member to the house of representatives. Conjoined with Fayette, also, it composes the 14th congressional district, sending

1 member to congress. Greene, Fayette and Washington constitute the 14th judicial district, over which Thomas H. Baird presides. The courts are holden at Waynesburg, on the third Mondays of March, June, September and December. The co. belongs to the W. district of the supreme court.

Greene co. contributed to the state treasury in 1831,

For tax on writs,	$220,00
Tavern licenses,	158,54
Duties on dealers in for'n mdz.	239,55
	$618,09

The value of taxable property in the co. by assessment of 1829, was, real estate $1,081,547, personal estate $122,100, rate of tax 30 cts. on the $100.

STATISTICAL TABLE OF GREENE COUNTY.

Townships.	Greatest Lth.	Greatest Bth.	Area in Acres.	Population. 1820	Population. 1830	Taxables
Aleppo,	11	10	52480	570	838	134
Cumberland,	10	6½	23680	1731	1896	357
Centre,	9	7	26880	795	1020	185
Dunkard,	10	6	22400	1472	1336	235
*Franklin,	9	7	30720	1591	2347	401
Green,	8	5½	28800	1801	752	142
Jefferson,	10	3	14080	1158	1292	232
Morgan,	10½	6	23680	1622	1723	290
Morris,	9	6	23040	1259	1575	266
Monongahela,	7	3	10440		1250	223
Rich Hill,	8½	8	35840	687	994	151
Wayne,	11	10	34560	848	1130	187
Whitely,	10	7	38400	1722	1875	329
				15554	18028	3141

*Including the borough of Waynesburg.

Greensburg, p-t. of Monongahela t-ship, Greene co. on the Monongahela r. opposite to New Geneva, 18 ms. S. E. of Waynesburg, 217 ms. N. W. from W. C. and 199 from Harrisburg. There are extensive glass works here, established by the munificence of Mr. Albert Gallatin, for a German company, who, having grown rich, have transferred the works to some young men, who conduct them profitably. The town contains about 100 dwellings, 4 stores, 1 tavern, and about 500 inhabitants.

Greensburg, pt. borough and st. jus. of Somerset co. centrally situated in Hempfield t-ship, 170 ms. from Harrisburg, 31 from Pittsburg, and 192 from W. C. It was erected into a borough by act of assembly 9th Feb. 1799; and contains about 150 dwellings, 3 churches, 1 Episcopalian, 1 Lutheran, 1 Presbyterian; 1 steam mill, 7 taverns, 3 of which are large and well kept. There is an academy here, which was incorporated by act 7th March, 1810, by which it also received a donation, conditioned that a number of poor children should be taught gratis.

Green creek, Huntington t-ship, Luzerne co., has its source and course chiefly within the t-ship, and empties into Huntington cr., in Columbia co. It affords excellent mill power.

Green Valley, p-o., Warren co. 331 ms. N. W. of W. C. and 258 from Harrisburg.

Green creek, Columbia co., rises in Greenwood t-ship, and flows S. E. into Fishing cr., forming in part of its course the boundary between Mount Pleasant and Fishing Creek t-ships.

Green mountain, a spur of the Mahanoy range, in the N. E. angle of Schuylkill co., which divides the head waters of the Catawissa cr.

Green ridge, a prominent range of hills on the N. W. part of Hamilton-Ban t-ship, Adams co. It runs N. W. about 10 ms.

Green Castle, borough, Antrim t-ship, Franklin co., on the turnpike r. from Mercersburg to Waynesboro'; 77 ms. N. W. from W. C. and 59 S. W. from Harrisburg, contains about 200 dwellings, chiefly of stone; five churches, 5 schools, 1 mill, 6 stores, as many taverns, and a small woollen manufactory; and about 1200 inhabitants. There are here a colonization society and a tract society, and Sunday schools. The town is surrounded by a rich limestone country, well cultivated and highly productive. A tributary of the E. branch of the Conecocheague cr. runs westerly through the town. It was incorporated by act 25th March, 1805.

Greene, t-ship, Greene co., bounded N. by Cumberland t-ship, E. by Monongahela, S. by Dunkard, and W. by Whitely and Franklin t-ships.

Centrally distant S. E. from Waynesburg 11 miles. Greatest length 8, breadth 5½ ms. Area 28,800 acres. Surface rolling, soil loam. Pop. in 1830, 752 ; taxables 142. It is drained by Whitely cr.

Greene, t-ship, Beaver co., bounded N. by the Ohio r., E. by Moore and Hopewell t-ships, S. by Hanover t-ship, and W. by the state of Va. Centrally distant from Beaver borough S. W. 12 ms. Greatest length 6, breadth 5½ ms. Area 23,680 acres ; surface rolling ; soil loam. Pop. in 1830, 1709 ; taxables 284. The t-ship is drained on the N. W. by Mill cr., on the E. side of which, on the Ohio r., lies the p-t. Georgetown, 12 ms. S. W. of Beaver borough. Hookstown is near the centre of the t-ship.

Greene, t-ship, Indiana co. bounded N. by Mahoning t-ship, E. by Cambria co., S. by Centre and Wheatfield t-ships, and W. by Washington t-ship. Centrally distant from Indiana borough N. E. 10 ms. ; greatest l'th. 12, breadth 11 ms. ; area 77,440 acres ; surface hilly, soil clay. Pop. in 1830, 1130 ; taxables 200. It is drained S. by Two Lick cr. and the N. branch of Yellow cr., and N. E. by Cushcushion cr. Diamond's mills, a small village, lies on Two Lick cr.

Greene, t-ship, Franklin co., bounded N. E. by Southampton, E. by Adams co., S. by Guilford and Hamilton t-ships, and W. by Letterkenny t-ship. Greatest length 13, breadth 6 ms. ; area 32,640 acres ; surface level ; soil, limestone and slate. Pop. in 1830, 2554. It is drained chiefly by the E. branch of the Conecocheague cr. The turnpike roads from Carlisle and from Gettysburg to Chambersburg pass through it. There is a p-o. on the latter road near the E. boundary, and one on the former at Greenville, 5 ms. N. E. of Chambersburg. 95 ms. N. W. from W. C. and 43 S. E. from Harrisburg. The South mountain lies on the E. of the t-ship, in the ravines of which are two remarkable sinking springs.

Greenfield, p-t., Pike run t-ship. Washington co., at the confluence of Pike run with the Monongahela r. upon the N. side of the run, about 20 ms. S. E. of Washington borough, contains some 10 or 12 houses, a store and tavern.

Greenfield, a small village of Schuylkill t-ship, Schuylkill co., situated about 7 ms. N. E. of Orwigsburg, on the road from McKeansburg to Catawissa, in the forks of Cold run. It contains 8 or 10 dwellings, store, tavern, and a grist-mill.

Greenfield, t-ship, Bedford co. bounded N. and N. E. by Huntingdon co. E. by Woodberry t-ship, S. by St. Clair and W. by Cambria co. Centrally distant N. from Bedford borough about 23 ms. Greatest length 18, breadth 12½ miles ; area 83,200 acres ; surface hilly ; soil, clay and loam. Pop. in 1830, 1405 ; taxables 262. It is bounded on the W. by the Allegheny mtn., on the E. by Dunning's mtn., and on the N. E. by several spurs of the Allegheny, and knobs and spurs of the same range cover a considerable portion of the interior. It is drained S. by Bob's cr. and other tributaries of Dunning's cr. and N. by the Frankstown S. W. branch of the Juniata, and by Poplar run.

Greenfield, t-ship, Luzerne co., bounded on the N. by Susquehannah co. ; E. and S. E. by Blakely ; S. by Providence ; and W. by Abington and Nicholson t-ships. Its timber is beech, maple, ash, red cherry and hemlock. Its soil is generally excellent, better adapted to grazing than the growing of grain. The flourishing village of Dundaff, in Susquehannah co., is located near its northern boundary, and the village of Carbondale is springing up as by magic, near its eastern border. The settlers are generally from New England, hardy, industrious, and intelligent. Their prospects are very flattering ; and every circumstance conspires to invite settlers. Indeed no portion of Northern Pennsylvania presents stronger inducements and more favorable prospects to the N. England emigrants than Greenfield, and the neighboring t-ships of Abington, Blakeley, and Nicholson.

It is situated about 30 miles N. E. from Wilkesbarre. Its greatest length N. and S. is about 12 ms., greatest breadth E. and W. $8\frac{1}{2}$ ms. It is drained northward by the tributaries of Elkwood brook; centrally by the sources of the S. branch of the Tunkhannock cr. and southwardly by branches of the Lackawannock r. Pop. in 1830, 1310; taxables in 1828, 193.

Greenfield, t-ship, Erie co., bounded N. by North East t-ship, E. by the state of N. Y., S. by Venango t-ship, and W. by Beaver Dam and Harbor Creek t-ships. Centrally distant from Erie borough E. 11 ms.; length 6, breadth $5\frac{1}{2}$ ms.; area 19,200 acres. It is drained S. by the N. branch of French cr. The p-o., bearing the name of the t-ship, is centrally situate, at Colt's Station.

Greenville, small village and p-t., Buckingham t-ship, Bucks co., on the road from Centreville to New Hope, about 5 ms. from Doylestown, contains a tavern and 3 or 4 dwellings.

Greenville, t-ship, Somerset co., bounded N. E. and E. by Southampton t-ship, S. by the state of Md., W. by Elk Lick t-ship, and N. W. by Brother's Valley t-ship. Centrally distant S. E. from Somerset borough 17 ms.; length 7, breadth 6 ms.; area 19,200 acres; surface very hilly; soil reddish gravel. Pop. in 1830, 545; taxables, 107; taxable property in 1829, real estate $15,924, personal, $2,984; rate of tax 5 mills on the dollar. The Allegheny mtn. is on the W. boundary, and a spur of that mtn. running to the Savage mtn., bounds it on the E. It is drained by Flaugherty's run, which flows N. W. to the Little Youghiogheny r.

Greenville, p-t. of West Salem t-ship, Mercer co., on the W. bank of the Shenango cr., near the E. line of the t-ship, 14 ms. N. W. of the borough of Mercer, 281 ms. from W. C., and 244 from Harrisburg, contains about 50 dwellings, a Presbyterian, Seceder, and Methodist church, 3 taverns and 4 stores. The country around it is rich, and the town thriving rapidly. It is expected by the inhabitants that the Beaver division of the canal will be continued through the town to Erie.

Greenville, p-o., Luzerne co., 251 ms. N. W. from W. C., and 141 from Harrisburg.

Greenville, p-t., Greene t-ship, Franklin co., on the road from Carlisle to Chambersburg, 5 ms. N. E. of the former.

Greenwich, t-ship, Berks county, 8 miles E. of Hamburg, and 18 miles N. E. of Reading. Bounded N. by Albany t-ship, E. by Lehigh co. S. E. by Maxatauny t-ship, S. by Richmond, and W. by Windsor. Greatest length $6\frac{1}{2}$, breath $4\frac{1}{2}$ miles; area, 13,500 acres; surface hilly; soil, gravel. Population in 1830, 1407; taxables in 1828, 274. Maiden cr. passes through the N. W. corner of the t-ship, and forms the boundary line between it and Windsor. Sacony creek, a branch of Meriden cr. flows with a devious course of five miles along its S. boundary, receiving in its course Mill creek and other small tributaries. None of these streams are navigable, but all afford excellent sites for mills, which are generally improved. Round Top hill, 20 miles from Reading, on the N. boundary of the t-ship, is a conspicuous feature of its topography. There is a church near the main Reading road called Dunkels.

Greenwood, t-ship, Mifflin co. bounded N. by Shade mountain and West Mahantango creek, which separate it from Union county, E. by the Susquehannah river, S. by Turkey ridge which divides it from Perry co. and W. by Fermanagh t-ship. Centrally distant from Lewiston E. 21 miles; greatest length 17, breadth 10 miles; area, 72,320 acres. It is drained S. by Cocalimus creek which flows into the Juniata river, and E. by W. Mahantango which runs into the Susquehannah. Turkey valley runs along the S. boundary on the N. of Turkey ridge. Ridgeville, p-t. lies in the N. part of the t-ship, on the Mahantango creek, embosomed by mountains, and Calhounsville, p-t. is on the W. line.

Greenwood, town-ship, Crawford co. Pop. in 1830, 876.

Greenwood, t-ship, Columbia county, bounded N. W. by Lycoming co. E. by Sugar Loaf and Fishing creek, S. by Mount Pleasant, and S. W. by Madison t-ships. Centrally distant N. E. from Danville 15 miles; length 11, breadth 8 miles; area, 30,720 acres. Pop. in 1830, 1110; taxables, 208. The t-ship is drained by the tributaries of Fishing creek. It has a post-office called "Greenwood," distant 205 ms. N. W. from W. C. and 96 from Harrisburg.

Greenwood, t-ship, Perry county, bounded N. by Mifflin co. E. by Liverpool t-ship, S. by Buffalo t-ship, and W. by the Juniata river. Centrally distant 10 miles N. E. of Bloomfield; length 6¼, breadth 5 miles; area, 17,040 acres. Population 1830, 967; taxables, 189.

Greersburg, or Darlington, p-t. and borough in the S. W. angle of Little Beaver t-ship, on a branch of the Little Beaver creek, Beaver co. 11 ms. N. W. from Beaver borough. There is an academy established here by act 24th Feb. 1806, to which the legislature granted the sum of $600. The town contains about 60 dwellings, 4 stores, 3 taverns, and 1 Presbyterian church. It was incorporated by act of 28th March, 1820, and its name was changed to Darlington, by act of 6th April, 1830.

Gregg, t-ship, Centre county, bounded N. by Hains and Miles t-ships, E. by Mifflin co. S. by Potter t-ship, and W. by Miles. Surface mountainous, with rich limestone valleys; the hills slate. Population in 1830, 1564; taxables, 306. It is watered by Sinking creek, one of the largest streams in the county.

Grimville, p-o. Berks co. 156 ms. N. from W. C. and 67 E. from Harrisburg.

Grubtown, Bristol t-ship, Phila. co. on the Tacony creek, about 8 miles from Philadelphia. There is an extensive cotton manufactory here, with the necessary buildings for the accommodation of the proprietary and workmen.

Gulph mills, p-o. Upper Merion t-ship, Montgomery co. (See Merion, Upper,) distant 146 miles from W. C. and 90 from Harrisburg.

Gunner's run, a small stream which rises in Penn t-ship, Philadelphia co. near Nice town, and receiving two or three small tributaries, empties into the Delaware at the upper end of the district of Kensington, immediately below the glass works.

Guthriesville, p-o. Chester co. 126 miles N. of W. C. and 66 S. E. of Harrisburg.

Guy's mills, p-o. Crawford co. 307 N. W. from W. C. and 246 from Harrisburg.

Guinea town, a small hamlet of Haverford t-ship, Delaware co. on the Haverford road, and near the Lancaster turnpike road and Buck tavern, 10 miles from Philadelphia W.

Guilford, t-ship, Franklin county, bounded N. E. by Greene t-ship, E. by Adams co. S. by Washington and Antrim t-ships, and W. by Hamilton t-ship. Centrally distant from Chambersburg S. E. 6 miles. Greatest length 14, breadth 7 miles; area, 33,920 acres; surface, level; soil, lime and slate. Population in 1830, 2873; taxables, 528. The E. branch of the Conecocheague creek forms the W. boundary of the t-ship, and receives from it Falling spring, a mill stream, and some other less considerable supplies. The turnpike road from Gettysburg to Chambersburg passes through it.

Guilford, p-o. York county, 78 ms. from W. C. and 44 from Harrisburg.

Gwynedd, t-ship, Montgomery co. bounded on the N. E. by Hatfield, Montgomery and Horsham, S. E. by Upper Dublin, S. W. by Whitpaine and Worcester, and N. W. by Towamensing t-ships, Greatest length 8, breadth 3 miles; area 15,360 acres; distance from Phila. 20 miles, from Norristown 8 miles. The Wissahickon creek flows S. E. through the t-ship, and the Towamensing crosses its N. E. angle; both are mill streams, and the former turns several mills in the t-ship. Gwynedd church is centrally situated. The Spring House tavern, and Bethlehem turnpike road runs through the S. E. angle. The surface is rolling; soil, sandy loam. Pop. in 1830, 1402; taxables in 1828, 286. The p-o. named after the t-ship, is 157 miles from W. C. and 96 from Harrisburg.

Haddington, village of Blockley t-ship, Phila. co. on the Haverford road about 4 miles W. of Phila. contains about 50 dwellings, two taverns, two stores, an academy, several mechanical trades, and a small woollen manufactory at the foot of the hill upon Indian run, upon which there are also several other small factories, above and below the town.

Hains t-ship, Centre co. bounded W. and N. by Miles t-ship, E. and S. E. by Union co. S. W. by Gregg t-ship. Centrally distant E. from Bellefonte 19 miles; greatest length 21, breadth 6 miles; surface mountainous; soil, limestone in the valleys. Pop. in 1830, 1850; taxables 306. Path valley mountain is on the S. E., Brush mountain on the N. W. and in the interval are Tussey's mountain, and Short mountain, and Penn's valley. The t-ship is drained by two creeks, which flowing W. some miles are lost in limestone fissures. Millheim and Aaronsburg, lying in the valley, and separated by Elk creek, are post towns of the t-ship.

Half Moon, t-ship, Centre co. bounded N. E. by Patton t-ship, S. E. by Ferguson t-ship, S. by Huntingdon co. and S. W. by Rush t-ship. Centrally distant S. W. fron Bellefonte 18 ms. greatest length 17, breadth 15 miles; area 60,800 acres; surface mountainous; soil, limestone in the valleys. Pop. in 1830, 994; taxables 172. It is drained N. E. by the Bald Eagle creek, and S. E. by Half Moon run, which flows into Spruce creek. The main ridge of the Allegheny mountain is on the W. boundary, E. of which is Bald Eagle valley bounded E. by Bald Eagle ridge. The p-o. in the t-ship is 178 miles from W. C. and 101 from Harrisburg.

Halifax, t-ship, Dauphin co. bounded N. by Upper Paxton and Mifflin t-ships, E. by Jackson t-ship, S. by Middle Paxton & W. by the Susquehannah r. centrally distant N. of Harrisburg 9 miles; greatest length 11, breadth 5 miles; area 18,000 acres; surface, hilly on the N. E. and S.; soil, red shale. Pop. in 1830, 1772; taxables 444. Peters mtn. bounds it on the S., and between it & Berry's mtn. there is another considerable ridge dividing Armstrong's & Powell's valleys, which are drained by Armstrong's and Powell's creeks respectively. At the foot of Berry's mtn., Montgomery's Ferry crosses the Susquehannah. And on that river, about the middle of its course along the t-ship, lies the post town of Halifax.

Halifax, p-t. of Halifax t-ship, Dauphin co. on the E. bank of the Susquehannah river, distant in a direct line N. from Harrisburg, 17 ms. 131 from W. C. Armstrong creek flows on the E. of the village, near which it drives a mill, and empties into the river about a mile above it. The town contains from 70 to 80 dwellings, a church, 4 stores and 5 taverns.

Hallam, t-ship, York co. bounded N. E. by the Susquehannah river, S. by Windsor t-ship, W. by Spring Garden, and N. W. by East Manchester. Greatest length 5, breadth 5 miles; area 18,560 acres; surface level; soil, limestone, good quality. Pop. in 1830, 1876; taxables 348. The Codorus creek forms the N. W. boundary and Grist creek flows E. to the Susquehannah, through the t-ship. The turnpike road from Columbia to York passes westwardly through it; Wrightsville a thriving village and post town, lies on the Susquehannah river opposite to Columbia, with which it is connected by a covered bridge of 5690 feet in length. (*See Columbia.*) Taxable property in 1829, real estate $348,279, personal, 13,660 ; occupations 33,410 total $395,349. Rate 25 cts. in the $100.

Hamburg, p-t. Windsor t-ship, Berks co. near the Schuylkill water gap of the Blue mountain, on the turnpike road from Reading to Pottsville, 16 miles N. of the former, 156 from W. C., and 56 E. from Harrisburg contains from 60 to 80 dwellings, a church common to the Lutheran and German Presbyterians, 5 stores, and 5 taverns, 1 grist mill, and about 500 inhabitants. The Schuylkill canal runs near the town. There is a bridge over the river here; and a furnace at Kern's mill about a mile from the town. The country about it is tolarably well cultivated and productive.

Hamilton, t-ship, Northampton co. bounded N. by Pokono, S. by Lower Mt. Bethel and Plainfield, E. by Stroud, and W. by Chestnut hill and Ross t-ships. Greatest length 6¼, width 6¼ miles; surface, partly hilly, or rather mountainous, and partly level; soil, gravel. Pop. in 1830, 1428; taxables 275. It is drained by Mc Michaels, Pokono and Cherry creeks which flow easterly through it to the Delaware.

Hamilton-ban, t-ship, Adams co. bounded N. by Franklin, E. by Cumberland, S. by Liberty t-ships, and W. by Franklin co. Centrally distant from Gettysburg 7 miles; greatest length 10¾ miles, breadth 4 miles; area 31,360 acres; surface level; soil, limestone and red gravel. Pop. in 1830, 1379. The N. boundary follows the S. branch of Marsh creek, and the main stream of that creek forms the east line; Middle creek, Muddy run Tom's creek flow S. from the t-ship. Green ridge on the N. W. and Jack's mountain on the S. W. are prominent hills. Iron and copper are found in the latter; near the E. boundary there are some sulphur springs. Fairfield, a small village, lies in a fork of Middle creek near the S. line.

Hamilton, t-ship, Adams co. bounded N. by Reading, E. by Beaver run, which separates it from Paradise t-ship, York co. S. by Berwick t-ship, and W. by Mount Pleasant. Centrally distant N. E. from Gettysburg 12 miles, length 6¾, breadth 4 miles; area 10,240 acres; surface level; soil, red gravel and flint. Pop. in 1830, 1047; taxables 215. The Conewago creek flows round the W. and N. boundary receiving Beaver run on the E. The post town of Oxford is on the turnpike road from York to Gettysburg which divides this from Berwick t-ship, on the south. The turnpike road from Carlisle to the Maryland line passes southwardly through the t-ship. Berlin, another post town, is in the N. E. angle on the banks of Conewago creek.

Hamilton, t-ship, Franklin co. bounded N. E. and N. W. by Letterkenny and Greene t-ships, S. E. by Guilford, S. by Antrim, and W. by St. Thomas t-ships. Greatest length 9½ miles, breadth 7¾; area 21,760 acres; surface hilly; soil, lime and slate. Pop. in 1830, 1461; taxables 251. It is drained on the E. by the main branch of the Conococheague creek and on the W. by Back creek, a tributary of the former. The turnpike road from Chambersburg to Bedford passes centrally through the t-ship.

Hamiltonville, or *Newtown Hamilton*, p-t. of Wayne t-ship, Mifflin co., upon the W. bank of the Juniata r., and upon the state canal, at the S. end of the Juniata valley, 21 ms. S. W. of Lewistown, and 10 ms. from Waynesburg. The *town* until the spring of 1828, contained only four huts, since that time, owing to the impulse given by the construction of the state canal, which passes through the town, many improvements have been made. There are now here some 20 houses, several stores and public houses.

Hamilton, village, of Blockley t-ship, Phila. co., laid upon the Hamilton estate, consists of several streets running E. and W., and crossed by others at right angles. There may be from 50 to 70 dwellings; a church, school house, several stores and taverns, and some pleasant country seats. The centre of the village is somewhat more than a mile from the permanent bridge over the Schuylkill.

Hamlinton, p-o., Wayne co., named after the postmaster, Oliver Hamlin, 241 ms. N. of W. C. and 150 N. E. from Harrisburg.

Hammer creek, Lancaster co., flows from the Conewago hills, through Elizabeth t-ship, into the Cocalico cr. It gives motion to Hopewell furnace and forges.

Hammer creek, York co., rises in the state of Md., and runs N. through Manheim t-ship, Pa., to the line of Heidelberg t-ship, thence by a course of about 4 ms. N E. it unites with the W. branch of the Codorus cr. It is a mill stream.

Hamor's Store, p-t., Delaware co., 129 ms. from W. C., 93 S. E. from Harrisburg.

Hampton, p-t., of Reading t-ship, Adams co. on the turnpike r. leading from Carlisle to Baltimore, about 14 ms. N. E. of Gettysburg, 90 from W. C. and 28 S. W. of Harrisburg, contains 30 dwellings, 2 stores and 3 taverns, and about 180 inhabitants.

Hanna's town, p-o., Hempfield t-ship, Westmoreland co., 3 ms. N. E. of Greensburg, and near Crab-tree creek.

Hannahstown, a small village of Buffalo t-ship, Butler co. on the Freeport road, 8 ms. from Butler, contains half a dozen houses, 1 store and 1 tavern.

Hanover, t-ship, Northampton co., bounded N. by Allen t-ship, S. W. by Bethlehem, and S. and E. by Lehigh co. Greatest length 2½ ms., greatest width 2 ms. ; surface level ; soil, limestone. Pop. in 1830, 348 ; taxables in 1828, 65. It is drained by the Manokissy cr. which runs along its S. E. boundary.

Hanover, t-ship, Lehigh co., the only t-ship of that co. on the E. side of the Lehigh r. It is bounded N. by Allen t-ship, E. by Hanover and Bethlehem, and S. by Lehigh t-ships, all of Northampton co., and on the W. by the Lehigh r. The Calesoque cr. flows into the Lehigh, which runs also along the S. boundary, through its N. W. angle. The form of the t-ship is irregular. Its greatest length N. and S. is about 5 ms., breadth E. and W. 4 ms ; area 9600 acres ; surface level ; soil, limestone of excellent quality, well cultivated, and abundantly productive. Upon the line dividing it from Hanover t-ship, Northampton co., is a Lutheran church. Its central distance from the borough of Nothampton, is about four miles N. E. The Allentown chain bridge over the Lehigh, connects it with the town. Pop. in 1830, 1102 ; taxables in 1828, 212 ; taxable property, 1829, real estate, $239,468, personal, 8,760 ; rate of levy 13 cts. on the hundred dollars. Assessed value of lands per acre, 1st quality, $35, 2nd quality, $25, 3rd quality, $18.

Hanover, New, t-ship, Montgomery co., bounded N. by Upper Hanover t-ship, E. by Frederick, S. E. by Limerick, S. W. by Pottsgrove, and W. by Douglass. Greatest length 8 ms., greatest breadth 4½ ; area about 13,000 acres. The W. branch of the Perkiomen cr. passes through the N. W. angle of the t-ship, and Swamp cr. centrally. The surface of the country is hilly, it being partly within the first great chain of hills which runs through the state. The population is German, and have two churches upon opposite sides of a branch of Swamp cr., one of which is called the Swamp church, near which there is a p-o. The soil is loam and red shale ; tolerably productive. Pop. in 1830, 1344 ; taxables in 1828, 323. A mine, said to contain gold, was formerly wrought in this t-ship, and recent attempts have been made to work it, and some specimens of the ore have been exhibited at Pottstown in the past year (1831). The p-o., called after the t-ship, is 150 ms. from W. C. and 75 from Harrisburg.

Hanover, Upper, t-ship, Montgomery co., bounded N. E. by Lehigh and Bucks cos., S. E. by Marlborough and Limerick, S. by New Hanover and Douglass, and W. by Berks co. Its greatest length is 6 ms., mean breadth 5. The central distance from Phila. 35 ms. N. W., and 22 N. W. of Norristown. It is watered by the main stream and W. branch of the Perkiomen cr. The surface is very hilly; soil, red shale. Pop. in 1830, 1300; taxables in 1828, 258. New Goshenhoppen is a p-t. and small village centrally situated in the forks of the Perkiomen cr., 20 ms. N. of Norristown, 173 from W. C. and 84 from Harrisburg.

Hanover, East, t-ship, Lebanon co., bounded N. and W. by Dauphin co. E. by Swatara t-ship, S. by Annville and Londonderry t-ships. Centrally distant from the borough of Lebanon about 11 miles. Greatest length 11, breadth 6½ ms.; area 30,700 acres; surface gentle declivities in the S.; the Blue mountain and the Second mountain cross the N. part; soil, chiefly gravel. Pop. in 1830, 2498; taxables 404. The Swatara cr. follows the E. and S. boundaries, and receives from the t-ship Reed's run, Indian and Raccoon crs. It has a p-o. called "East Hanover," 131 ms. from W. C. and 21 E. from Harrisburg.

Hanover, t-ship, Beaver co., bounded N. by Greene t-ship, E. by Hopewell, S. by Washington co., and W. by the state of Va. Centrally distant from Beaver borough about 18 ms. Greatest length 8, breadth 5 ms.; area 24,960 acres; surface rolling; soil, loam and limestone. Pop. in 1830, 2359; taxables 308. It is drained E. by Big and Little Travis crs., tributaries of Raccoon cr. The village of Frankford is centrally situated near the S. boundary.

Hanover, t-ship, Luzerne co., bounded N. E. by Wilkesbarre, E. and S. E. by the Lehigh r. and Northampton co., S. W. by Sugarloaf and Newport t-ships, and N. W. by the Susquehannah r. That portion of this township which lies in the Wyoming valley is thickly settled, and the land is of an excellent quality and well cultivated. The mountainous part is covered with timber, consisting of white and yellow pine, oak, hickory, and chestnut; some portion of which, may be cultivated.

Anthracite coal is found every where in this t-ship, from the river to near the summit of the mtn., a distance of 2 or 3 ms. The argillaceous iron stone abounds in the mtn. and it is believed of sufficient richness to justify its being worked upon an extensive scale. In the western division are the E. branch of the Nanticoke and Solomon's crs., which are pretty good mill streams. In the latter, about mid-way up the mtn, and 2 ms. from Wilkesbarre, in what is called Solomon's Gap, is a beautiful cascade, which has long been visited as a great natural curiosity. Its wild romantic aspect, and the delightful natural scenery around it, have within a few years been considerably injured by the erection of a very superior merchant mill immediately below the falls, by Gen. Wm. Ross, of Wilkesbarre, who is the proprietor of this valuable water power. But the lovers of nature are still highly gratified with a visit to this romantic spot.

In its eastern division are Pine, Wright's, Terrapin Pond, and Sandy crs., which empty into the Lehigh, and the sources of the Nescopeck and the Big and Little Wapwallopen, which flow into the Susquehannah. The Nescopeck and Wright's mill cr. have become important streams in the proposed connection of the Susquehannah with the Lehigh, the former as the channel of the canal, and the latter as a feeder.

Penobscot Knob, 1050 feet above the river, the highest peak of the mtn. in this t-ship, affords an extensive and sublime prospect. The great stage route from Wilkesbarre to Harrisburg passes through the town. Nanticoke falls are near its western angle. The form of the t-ship is irregular. Its greatest length is about 14 ms., greatest breadth 7; area 56,320 acres. Pop. in 1830, 1173; taxables in 1828, 173.

Hanover, t-ship, Washington co., bounded N. by Beaver co., E. by

Robinson and Smith t-ships, S. by Cross cr. t-ship, and W. by the state of Va. Centrally distant N. W. from W. borough 22 ms. Greatest length $8\frac{1}{2}$, breadth $7\frac{1}{2}$ ms.; area 23,040 acres. surface hilly; soil, loam; coal abundant. Pop. in 1830, 1573; taxables 247. The turnpike road from Pittsburg to Steubenville on the Ohio, runs westerly through the t-ship, and upon it is the p-t. of Briceland's cross roads, on the E. boundary. Herman's and Indian crs. flowing to the Ohio r., drain the t-ship westward.

Hanover, village, Hanover t-ship, Lehigh co. contains 12 houses and about 80 inhabitants. There is here one tavern and store. It is situated on the road from Allentown to Bethlehem, about two miles from the former, on the county line between Lehigh and Northampton.

Hanover, West, t-ship, Dauphin co. bounded N. by the Second mountain, E. by Lebanon co. S. by the Swatara river, which separates it from Derry t-ship and W. by Lower Paxton t-ship. Greatest length 10, breadth 7 miles; area, 36,000 acres; surface, undulating; soil, argillaceous slate and sand stone. Pop. in 1830, 2543; taxables, 493; valuation in 1832, $400,368. Beaver creek runs along the W. boundary, Manady creek and Bow run flow through it, all S. to the Swatara. The post office, having the name of the t-ship, is 126 ms. N. W. from W. C. and 15 ms. S. E. of Harrisburg.

Hanover, p-t. and bor. Heidelberg t-ship, York co. lies in the western part of the t-ship, 17 ms. S. E. of the borough of York, 80 ms. from W. C. and 27 from Harrisburg. Three turnpike roads proceed from this borough, one to Berlin, one to Petersburg and Carlisle, and a third into Maryland, towards Baltimore. It contains about 200 dwellings, several stores and taverns. It was incorporated by act 4th March, 1814.

Hanstown, a hamlet in the north part of Earl t-ship, Lancaster co. about 14 ms. N. E. from the city of Lancaster.

Harewood, p-o. Susquehannah co. 282 ms. from W. C. 174 from Harrisburg.

Harford, t-ship, Susquehannah co. bounded N. by New Milford t-ship, E. by Gibson, S. by Lennox and W. by Brooklyn; greatest length $6\frac{1}{2}$ miles, mean width, $5\frac{1}{2}$ miles; area, 22,880 acres. It is drained by Martin's, Partner's and Van Winkle's creeks, all branches of the Tunkhannock, and good mill streams. The first is fed by a small lake near the N. W. angle of the t-ship. The Milford and Owego turnpike crosses the S. W. angle diagonally, and the Wilkesbarre and Great Bend turnpike runs from south to north. A post office is located at the village of Harford, near which there are two churches.

Harford, village and p-t. Harford t-ship, Susquehannah co. It is built on one street, and contains 8 or 10 dwellings, 2 stores, 1 tavern; there are 2 churches near the town. It is 13 ms. S. E. of Montrose, 264 from W. C. and 156 from Harrisburg.

Harlandsburg, p-t. of Slippery cr. t-ship, Mercer co. in the S. E. angle of the t-ship, upon the N. bank of the cr. 14 ms. a little E. of S. from Mercer bor. 260 N. W. from W. C. and 228 from Harrisburg, contains 20 dwellings, 2 taverns and 3 stores.

Harbor Creek, t-ship, Erie co. bounded N. by lake Erie, E. by North East and Greenfield t-ships, S. by Beaver Dam t-ship, and W. by Mill Creek and McKean t-ships. Centrally distant N. E. from Erie borough 6 ms.; greatest length 8, breadth $5\frac{1}{2}$ ms.; area, 23,860 acres. It is drained by several small streams which flow into the lake. It has a post office bearing the name of the t-ship.

Harmonsburg, p-t. of Sadsbury t-ship, Crawford co. N. of Conneaut lake, on the Conneaut creek and road leading to Meadville, distant 10 ms. N. W. from the latter place, 305 ms. from W. C. and 244 from Harrisburg.

Harmony, p-t. of Conequenessing t-ship, Butler co. on the S. bank of the Conequenessing creek, 14 ms. S. W. by W. of the borough of Butler, and

12 ms. N. E. by E. of the borough of Beaver, Beaver co. 249 ms. N. W. from W. C. and 218 from Harrisburg. This town was founded by the society of Harmonites in 1804, who afterward removed to the Wabash, and subsequently to Economy, on the Ohio river, in Beaver co. (For an account of this association see *Economy.*) It originally consisted of log houses, but now contains from 35 to 40 brick and frame buildings, 2 mills, a small town hall, 2 or 3 stores and a tavern. At the departure of the Harmonites, their property here was purchased by Mr. Zuyler, from Eastern Penn. who has introduced many German settlers into the town and neighboring farms, who have well filled the void which the removal of the Harmonites created.

Harmony, t-ship, Susquehannah co. bounded N. by the state of New-York, E. by Wayne co. S. by Jackson t-ship and W. by Great Bend t-ship; length, 8 ms. breadth 6; area, 30,720 acres. The Susquehannah r. flows into the t-ship from the state of New York, southward along the eastern side of the Oquago mountain, and turning west around that mountain into Great Bend t-ship. Several streams flow through Harmony into the river, the chief of which are Starucca and Conewanta creeks. The Oquago mountain fills the whole of the N. W. angle. The remainder of t-ship is hilly; the soil is gravel and clay. Pop. in 1830, 341; taxables in 1828, 53.

Harmony, village and p-t. of the above t-ship, is situated on the Oquago turnpike road, and the eastern bank of the Susquehannah r. within 2 miles of the state line, and about 18 miles due N. E. of Montrose. It contains 6 or 7 dwellings, 1 store and 1 tavern.

Harrisburg, p-t., bor., st. jus. of Dauphin co. and capital of the state, is situated on the E. bank of the Susquehannah r. 97 miles from Philadelphia and 35 from Lancaster, 110 from W. C., 200 from Pittsburg; lat. 40° 16′ N.; lon. 0° 5′ 30″ E. from W. C. The eastern part of the site of the town is a gently swelling hill or high bank between the river and Paxton cr.; and along the vale of the latter runs the state canal. The lower part lies on the level plain above the mouth of the creek. The town has 5 streets parallel with each other and with the river, and 6 others which intersect these at right angles. In the centre of the town there is a large hollow square cut by crossing streets, and surrounded by buildings; in the centre of this stands the market house. The town, including M'Claysburg, which, though not in the borough bounds, is separated from it by an alley only, has 636 buildings, comprehending dwellings and work shops, of which 201 are of brick, 431 frame and 4 of stone. The public buildings erected by the town and county, are a large court house, (with offices attached) built of brick, two stories high, surmounted by a cupola and bell. This house was for many years occupied by the state legislature; a stone jail, having in the rear a spacious yard enclosed by a high stone wall. A large county school house, of brick, two stories high, with a cupola, in which the pupils are taught after the Lancasterian method. This was erected by virtue of an act of assembly, by which provision was made for the gratuitous education of the poor. The whole number of pupils in this institution in 1829, was 278, of whom 94 were pay students; the remainder were educated at the public expense, at the cost of $6 84 for each student. Of churches, there are 9, viz. Lutheran, 1, Presbyterian 1, German Reformed 1, Episcopalian 1, Roman Catholic 1, Methodist 1, Unitarian 1, Baptist 1, and African 1. Several of these are neat structures; the Catholic church is the most remarkable for architectural beauty. There is also a masonic lodge, a large and handsome building. There are 8 printing offices, seven of which issue journals, of which 4 are published semi-weekly during the session of the legislature, and weekly during the recess, viz. the Pennsylvania Reporter, the Pennsylvania Intelligencer, Harrisburg Chronicle, and The Statesman; and three weekly, viz. The Republican, Die Amerikanische Bauer, and Die Morganroethe.

The town contains 2 banks, 1 a branch of the bank of Penn. and the other the "Harrisburg bank," chartered 9th May, 1814, with an authorized capital of $600,000, of which 168,300 only have been paid it.

The commercial prospects of this borough are very flattering. By means of the state canal it may participate largely in the trade of the great tract of country drained by the Susquehannah r. and its tributaries.

Over the Susquehannah, in front of the town, is erected a fine wooden bridge, roofed, and supported by stone piers, in two parts, separated by an island; completed in 1817, by the architect Mr. Burr, under the direction of an incorporated company. Its length is 2876 feet, width 40 feet, elevation 50 feet; cost 155,000 dollars, of which the state subscried 90,000.

The capitol, or state house, is a magnificent structure, standing on the highest part of the town. From its cupola may be seen one of the finest landscapes of the state, embracing a wide extent of cultivated country, swelling hills, the meanders of the river, and the adjacent mountains. The building fronts the river to the west, which is seen through State street, a handsome avenue 60 feet wide. The pile consists of the main building, or state house, and two wings for the public offices, designed to be connected together by low ornamented walls, with gateways. The centre building is set back of the wings, so far that the inner columns of the porticos of the parts are in range, thus affording an uninterrupted view through them all. The ground slopes in front, and the main entrance is from State street, by plain and massive gates and a flight of steps. There is another entrance by a similar gateway on the south. The lot is surrounded by a low brick wall, surmounted by wooded palisades.

The main building is 180 feet front, 80 feet deep, 2 stories high. The lower story contains the vestibule and stair case, the chambers of the senate and house of representatives, and several small apartments for the accommodation of the members of assembly and its officers. The 2d story is appropriated for an *executive chamber*, where the governor transacts business and receives the visitors, committee rooms, 4 in number, of large dimensions, and 2 rooms appropriated to the state library, now consisting of about 4000 volumes.

The main entrance is by a circular portico, the whole height of the building, sustained by 6 Ionic columns of red sandstone, painted white, 4 feet in diameter, and 36 feet high; the portico receding 37 feet to a circular wall. The floor of the portico on which the columns rest is 4 feet 6 inches high from the ground, and is attained by 5 steps of sand stone, and paved with massive flags of the same material. From the floor to the top of the cornice the distance is 46 feet, and the whole height of the front 50 ft. 6 in. From the top of the cornice to the top of the dome is 57 ft. 6 in. making the whole height 108 ft. The front on either side of the portico is divided into 3 equal parts, 1 of which is given to the corner, projecting with 1 window, which lights the transcribers' apartment at one end, and a retiring room of the senate chamber at the other. The remaining parts contain 3 windows, which give light to the senate and representative chambers. Under the porticos are 4 windows on the first floor, 2 of which communicate with the senate and representative chambers respectively, and the others with small apartments appropriated to the sergeants at arms. The ends are divided into 4 equal parts; one is given to each corner, projecting with 1 window, the remaining two contain 3 windows, the central one of which is Venetian. The divisions and lights of the second story correspond with those of the first. The rotundo above the roof is composed of 16 columns, 22 inches in diameter and 17 feet high, and is 48 feet in diameter outside of the columns. There is a space of 3 feet between the columns and wall. The diameter of the inside is thirty-four ft. The dome is 40 feet in diameter. It contains 8 windows, 3 ft. 6 in. wide and 9 ft. 6 in. high, and 8 niches of like dimensions. Four of the latter are partly covered with the faces of the clock, and the remainder are designed for the reception of statues.

From the great portico we advance to the vestibule by large folding doors in the external wall. The vestibule is elliptical, having on its longest axis 40 ft. and on its shorter 34 ft. There are 8 doors opening into it in each story, 2 of which in the first communicate with the senate and representative chambers respectively, and a 3d, more properly an arch way, leads to a double flight of stairs, which, mounting half the height of the story, unite and conduct to the second floor. On this floor the staircase again divides and ascends into the roof and rotundo. The vestibule is partly floored over, leaving a circular opening surrounded with a railing, through which from below may be seen the openings of the several landings, the vaulted ceiling, and through that the interior of the rotundo, with its fluted roof.

The senate chamber, on the left of the entrance, is 75 ft. by 57 ft. in the clear, and 21 ft. high. The hall of the representatives has the same length and height, and 68 feet in breadth. The senate chamber is arranged for the accommodation of 36 members, to each of whom is allotted a space of 3 ft. 6 inches. Their desks are 2 ft. wide and the platform or benches on which they rest slightly raised one above another, and 5 ft. 9 inches wide. There is a space of 5 ft. between the members' seats and gallery. The latter will contain several hundred persons. The chair of the speaker, centrally placed in the length of the room, is supported on an ornamented *dais*, with a columnar and neatly carved back. Behind the chair is an open space lighted by the Venetian window, from which doors lead to closets on either hand, used as offices by the clerk. There are also the retiring rooms for the members.

The hall of representatives is disposed after the same manner; but being designed for the accommodation of 108 members the retiring rooms are wanting. Each member has a space of 2 ft. 9 inches, a desk 1 foot 9 incs. resting on a platform four feet six inches.

The wings, much smaller in every way than the main building, are however in keeping with it, and have porticos of similar form, and when connected by the wall yet to be built, will have a fine effect in the plan. At present they have an isolated appearance.

The whole pile is simple and plain in its exterior and in its internal distribution, but having a bold and distinct contour it is grand and imposing.

Harrisburg was founded in 1785, by Mr. John Harris, who inherited the ground on which it stands from his father; we are indebted chiefly to a memoir of Mr. Samuel Breek, for the following interesting anecdote of the elder Mr. Harris. He was a Yorkshire man born in humble life, who emigrated to America soon after the first arrival of Wm. Penn, bringing with him the whole of his property, 16 guineas. His first employment here was in clearing away the wood, and in grubbing the streets of Philadelphia. "Being an enterprizing man, he soon became an active pioneer, and with the fruits of his industry, commencing a trade with the Indians, penetrated by degrees to the westward, until he reached the Susquehannah, on the left bank of which r. he built himself a cabin, and sat down permanently at the very spot where the town of Harrisburg now stands. His first purchase of land was a tract of 500 acres, bought of Edward Shippen for £190. The deed bears date the 19th December, 1733. He opened a profitable commerce with his red neighbors, who were numerous about the Paxton creek, and had several villages in the vicinity, along the Susquehannah shore." "It happened one day that a number of his Indian customers, who had been drinking freely, called for an additional supply of rum. On Mr. Harris' refusing to gratify them, they dragged him from his hut, and bound him to a mulberry tree, at the foot of which he now lies buried. They declared their intention to burn him alive, and bade him prepare for instant death. Dry wood was gathered, and fire held in readiness to kindle it. The yells of the exasperated savages echoed along the shore, while with demoniac gestures they danced around their victim. In vain he supplicated for mercy, and offered every thing in exchange for life. The fire was brought to the pile, and about being applied, when a band of friendly Indians burst from the forest and set him at liberty. His liberators were conducted by his negro slave Hercules, who on the first demonstration of violence, had fled to a neighboring Indian village for succour. Mr. Harris gratefully emancipated the slave to whose presence of mind and active zeal he was indebted for life, and the descendants of Hercules inhabit the town, now built around the spot where he so nobly acquired his fredom. Mr. Harris, in order to perpetuate the remembrance of this deliverance among his descendants, directed that after his death his body should be deposited at the foot of the Mulberry tree. The trunk of that tree is still standing, which flourished in full vigor when Wm. Penn first landed on the shores of the Delaware.

Harrisburg was incorporated by act of assembly passed 1st Feb. 1808, under the style of the Chief Burgess, Assistant Burgess and Town Council of the Borough of Harrisburg," with the usual corporate powers.

The population by the census of 1830, exclusive of McClaysburg, was 4307. McClaysburg in 1830, had 219 inhabitants, making the population of the *town* 4526.

A plan has recently been proposed of using the water of the Susquehannah river, (by means of a race or aqueduct, commencing at McAlisters, 6 miles above the town,) for supplying the borough with water for domestic and hydraulic purposes. A power, it is supposed, may be thus gained sufficient to drive 30 pairs of 5 feet stones. Several stages for the E. and W. parts of the state, one S. to Baltimore and Washington, and northward, leave Harrisburg daily.

Harrison, t-ship, Potter co. contains about 500 inhabitants, and by the return of 1828, 104 taxables.

Harrison's Valley, p-o. Potter co. 294 miles from W. C. 188 from Harrisburg N. W.

Harrisville, small p-t. of Mercer t-ship, Butler co. near the W. boundary, 20 miles N. W. of Butler borough, on the old Pittsburg and Franklin road, on an extensive prairie. It contains 8 or 10 dwellings, 2 stores and 2 taverns, all of wood, except one house, which is of brick. The turnpike from Mercer to Roseburg runs through it.

Hartley, t-ship, Union co. bounded N. by Nittany mountain, E. by West Buffalo t-ship, S. by Beaver t-ship, and W. by Centre co. Centrally distant from New Berlin, N. W. 11 ms. greatest length 18 miles, breadth 10; area 38,000 acres; surface, mountainous; soil, chiefly limestone in the valleys. Pop. in 1830, 2085; taxables 329. It is drained E. by Rapid run, Buffalo creek and Penn's creek. Several ridges of the Allegheny mountains terminate in the t-ship. The post-town of Hartleyton is near the E. boundary.

Hartleyton, p-t. Hartley t-ship, Union co. about 8 miles a little N. of W. from New Berlin, 71 from Harrisburg and 179 from W. C. contains 30 dwellings, 3 stores, 3 taverns and a Lutheran church.

Hartsville, commonly called Hart's cross roads, a post town on the line between Warminster and Warwick t-ships, Bucks co. 18 miles N. of Phila. and 6 miles S. E. of Doylestown, 156 miles N. E. of W. C. and 113 E. from Harrisburg, contains 10 or 12 houses, a store and tavern.

Hart's Cross Roads, p-t. Crawford co. 305 miles N. W. from W. C. and 247 from Harrisburg.

Hartzellstown, small village in Lower Nazareth t-ship, Northampton co. containing 4 dwellings, 1 store and 1 tavern.

Harvey's creek, Luzerne co. Two branches of this stream rise at the foot of Bowman's mountain about a mile asunder, and flow parallel with each other about 7 miles S. E. uniting near the N. W. boundary of Plymouth t-ship, thence by a course deflecting W. of about 5 miles the joint stream flows into the Susquehannah opposite Nanticoke falls. The eastern branch forms the outlet of Harvey's lake, a large and beautiful sheet of water stocked with trout and other fish. The creek furnishes excellent mill seats, and drives one mill near its mouth.

Harvey's lake, a beautiful sheet of water, in Dallas t-ship, Luzerne co. situate near the S. W. border. It is about 2½ miles long by 1 mile wide, is surrounded by delightful romantic senery, and is a favorite resort of the disciples of Isaac Walton, who find much sport in angling for trout, perch and sunfish, with which the lake abounds.

Harvyville, p-t. Luzerne co. 204 miles N. W. from W. C. and 94 from Harrisburg.

Harvey's p-o. Greene co. 241 miles N. W. of W. C. and 284 S. W. from Harrisburg.

Hatborough, p-t. and village, Moreland t-ship, Montgomery co. on the road to New Hope, 17 miles N. from Phila. and 16 miles N. E. from Norristown, 152 miles from W. C. and 114 from Harrisburg. It is a very pleasant village situated in a fertile and well cultivated district, and consists of about 40 dwellings, chiefly of stone, 2 taverns, 2 stores. The Pennypack creek flows near the town, on which there is erected a grist mill. An academy, incorporated in 1812, is established, and is called the Loller Academy, after Robert Loller, from whom it received a considerable endowment. There is also a public library.

Hat tavern, p-o. Lancaster co. 122 miles from W. C. and 48 from Harrisburg.

Hatfield, t-ship, Montgomery co. bounded N. E. by Bucks co. S. E. by Montgomery t-ship, S. W. by Lower Salford, Towamensing and Gwynedd, N. W. by Franconia t-ships. Greatest length 5 miles, greatest breadth 4 miles; area, 12,800 acres; centrally distant from Philadelphia 24 miles N. N. W., from Norristown 12 miles N. The Neshaminy creek passes through the S. E. angle, and a branch of the Towamensing drains it on the W. The Spring House and Bethlehem turnpike road crosses the S. E. angle and runs along the E. boundary, on which lies the small town of Lexington. Surface, rolling; soil, sandy loam. Population in 1830, 835; taxables in 1828, 211.

Haverford, t-ship, Delaware co. bounded N. and N. E. by Montgomery co. S. E. by Upper Darby t-ship, W. by Marple, and N. W. by Radnor. Central distance from Philadelphia 8 miles; length 3¾, breadth 3½ miles; area, 7680 acres; surface, hilly; soil, sandy loam, well cultivated and productive. Population in 1830, 980; taxables in 1828, 191. Darby creek follows the western line, and Cobb's creek runs within the t-ship, near to the eastern line. There is a post-office in the t-ship, distant 135 miles from W. C. and 98 S. E. from Harrisburg.

Hay creek, Robeson t-ship, Berks co. a tributary of the Schuylkill river. It drives several mills and a forge, which is located near its source.

Haycock, t-ship, Bucks co. bounded N. by Springfield, E. by Nockamixon, S. by Bedminster and Rockhill, and W. by Richland. Centrally distant 12 miles from Doylestown; greatest length 6¼ miles, greatest breadth 4 miles; area, 12,139 acres; surface hilly; soil, gravel. The Tohickon creek runs along the whole of its S. boundary, and receives from the t-ship a considerable stream, which traverses it from N. E. to S. W. Haycock run, which forms the eastern boundary, is also a tributary of the Tohickon. Haycock hill, is an eminence which runs along the Run, almost across the t-ship from N. to S. and its form gives name to the t-ship. Strawhntown is a p-t. and village on the road from Montgomery square to Bethlehem. Population of the t-ship in 1830, 1047. Taxables in 1828, 221.

Hayden, village of George t-ship, Fayette co. on the middle fork of George creek, 8 miles S. W. of the town of Union, contains about 25 dwellings, 1 school, 1 store, 1 tavern, 1 grist mill and 1 saw mill.

Hayfield, t-ship, Crawford county. Population in 1830, 644.

Head's creek, Northampton co. rises in Chestnut Hill t-ship, and by a S. W. course flows into the "Big creek" in Towamensing t-ship.

Hecktown, small village of Lower Nazareth t-ship, Northampton county, on the road from Bethlehem to the "Wind Gap" 7 miles from Easton, 9 from Bethlehem, contains about 12 dwellings, 1 store, 1 tavern, and a Lutheran church called the "Dryland church."

Heidelberg, t-ship, Lebanon co. bounded N. by Jackson t-ship, E. by Berks co. S. by Lancaster co. and W. by Lebanon t-ship. Central distance from Lebanon about 9 miles; greatest length 11, breadth 8 miles; area, 35,800 acres; surface chiefly level; soil mostly limestone. Pop. 1830, 2,822; taxables, 457; valuation of taxable property in 1829, real estate, $356,229; personal estate, 21,522; rate of tax, 13 cts in the $100; assessed value of lands, first quality $18; second quality $14; third quality $8, per acre. The town-ship is drained on the N. E. by Mill creek, a tributary of the Tulpehocken, and on the S. W. by Hammer creek, a branch of the Conestoga river. Both are mill streams. In the forks of the former lies Heidelberg church. Shefferstown, the post-town, is about 8 miles S. E. of the borough of Lebanon.

Heidelberg, t-ship, York co. bounded N. by Paradise, E. by Codorus, S. by Manheim t-ships, W. and N. W. by Adams co. Centrally distant S. W. from York, about 15 miles; greatest length 6½, breadth 6 miles; area, 11,120 acres; surface level; soil, limestone, of good quality. Pop. in 1830, 1523; taxables, 286; taxable property, 1829, real estate, $441,116; personal, $16,545; occupations, $28,-050; total, $485,711; rate, 25 cts. in the $100. Codorus creek runs along the E. line receiving Hammer creek, which partly bounds the t-ship on the S. E. and another creek from the centre of the t-ship, which unites with it on the N. E. The borough of Hanover lies on the W. from which proceed 3 turnpike roads, one running N. to Berlin, in Adams co. another N. W. to Carlisle, and a third S. E. to Baltimore.

Heidelberg, t-ship, Lehigh county, bounded N. and E. by Northampton co. S. E. by North Whitehall t-ship, S. by Low Hill t-ship, and W. by Linn t-ship. Its figure is irregular, the greatest length about 8 miles, and greatest width about the same. Area, 30,080 acres. It is centrally distant from Northampton 14 miles; is drained by Trout creek and Jordan creek, and its tributary, Crowner's run, and by the Lehigh river, which forms part of its eastern boundary. Its surface is very hilly, the Blue ridge crossing the N. part. The soil is white gravel, and produces excellent rye and fruits. The Lehigh Water gap, through which the river passes the mountain, is at the extreme N. E. point of the t-ship. (See Lehigh Water gap.) Bake Oven knob is a distinguished eminence at the N. W. corner. It is centrally distant about 14 miles N. W. from Northampton, and Seegersville, a small village and post-town of the t-ship, lies about 17 miles N. W. from that borough. Pop. in 1830, 2208; taxables in 1828, 510. There are in the t-ship 8 grist mills, 7 saw-mills, a furnace, 2 gun and rifle manufactories, 3 stores, 5 taverns, 1 Lutheran church and 4 schools.

Heidlersburg, p-t., Tyrone t-ship, Adams co., on the road leading westward from Berlin, 9 ms. N. E. from Gettysburg; 81 ms. from W. C. and 24 S. E. from Harrisburg.

Heidelberg, t-ship, Berks co., bounded N. W. and N. E. by the Tulpehocken cr., S. E. by the Cacoosing cr., and S. W. by Lancaster county. Greatest length 8, width 7 ms.; area 37,000 acres; surface, part level, part hilly; soil, limestone and gravel, generally of excellent quality and highly productive of grain and grass. Pop. in 1830, 4101; taxables, 923. This t-ship is chiefly watered by the Tulpehocken cr. and its tributaries, Spring and Cacoosing crs. The Reading and Harrisburg turnpike runs through it diagonally, near ten miles, and the road to Sunbury nearly parallel for the like distance. The p-t. of Womelsdorf is on the turnpike, 14 ms. from Reading, and Newmanstown, on the Shafferstown road, is intersected by the Lancaster co. line. There is a Moravian church and "Hains church," one at Womelsdorff, and one at Newmanstown, all common to the Lutherans and Presbyterians.

Hell Kitchen mountain, Sugarloaf t-ship, Luzerne co., commences at the head of Nescopeck valley, and extending N. E. terminates near the Lehigh. This is a very high, rocky and barren ridge, having no timber on its top, where fern and small bushes only find support.

Hellen, p-t., Clearfield co., 221 ms. N. W. from W. C., 149 miles from Harrisburg.

Hellerstown, p-t., Northampton co., Lower Saucon t-ship, on the S. side of Saucon cr. and about 4 ms. S. E. of Bethlehem, contains 15 dwellings, 2 stores, 3 taverns and 1 grist mill. It is 183 ms. from W. C., and 93 from Harrisburg.

Hemlock, t-ship, Columbia co. bounded N. by Madison, E. by Mt. Pleasant and Bloom t-ships, S. by the Susquehannah r., and W. by Mahoning t-ship. Centrally distant from Danville 6 ms.; greatest length 9½, breadth 6 ms.; area, 29,440 acres; surface diversified; soil, loam and clay. Pop. in 1830, 1681; taxables, 303. Mahoning cr. crosses the N. W. angle. Little and Great Fishing crs. are on the E. line; the latter receives from the t-ship Hemlock cr. The state canal follows the Susquehannah along the S. boundary.

Hemlock creek (see preceding article).

Hempfield, East, t-ship, Lancaster co. bounded N. by Warwick t-ship, E. by Manheim, S. by Manor, W. by W. Hempfield, and N. W. by Raphoe t-ships. Centrally distant from the city of Lancaster about 5 ms.; length 5½ ms., breadth 5 ms., area, 14,145 acres; surface, partly hilly, partly level. Pop. in 1830, 2072; taxables, 394. The Little Conestoga cr. divides it from Manheim. The Columbia turnpike r. runs along the S. boundary, and the Marietta and Harrisburg turnpike rs. cross it diagonally. The town of Petersburg lies in the N. E. angle, about 5 ms. N. W. of the city of Lancaster, and the p-t. of E. Hempfield is on the Marietta road, 3 ms. W. of Lancaster city, 115 N. from W. C. and 33 from Harrisburg. The t-ship contains 14 distilleries, 1 tanyard, 3 grist mills, 1 saw, 1 hemp, and 1 oil mill.

Hempfield, West, t-ship, Lancaster co., bounded N. by Raphoe t-ship, S. by Manor, E. by E. Hempfield t-ships, and W. by the Susquehannah r. Centrally distant W. from Lancaster 8 miles; greatest length 8, greatest breadth 5 miles; area 13,880 acres; surface, hilly; soil limestone. Pop. in 1830, 3898; taxables, 705. Great Chiques cr. flows along the northern boundary, and Strickler's cr. near the southern. The Lancaster and Columbia and the Marietta turnpike roads run through it from east to west; on the former, near the east line, is situated the small p-t. of Mount Pleasant.

The borough of Columbia lies on the Susquehannah r. in the t-ship.

Hempfield, t-ship, Westmoreland co. bounded N. by Salem, E. by Unity and Mount Pleasant, S. by East Huntingdon, and W. by North Huntingdon t-ships. Greatest length 12, breadth 11 ms. ; area 56,320 acres ; surface hilly ; soil, loam and gravel. Pop. in 1830, 4565 ; taxables, 701. It is drained by Brush cr. and by the Big and Little Sewickly creeks. The turnpike r. from Somerset to Pittsburg, passes W. through the t-ship, on which lie Greensburg, the co. town, Grapeville and Adamsburg. Hanna's Town is 3 ms. N. E. of Greensburg, near Crabtree cr., and the small village of Randolph is about 3 ms. E. of Greensburg.

Henlock's creek, Union t-ship, Luzerne co., is fed by 3 ponds, 2 in the above named t-ship, called the North and South pond, and the 3d in Lehman t-ship, called Three Cornered pond. The cr. empties into the Susquehannah r., on the boundary line between Plymouth and Union t-ships.

Henderson, p-o., Mercer co., so called from Robert Henderson, the post-master, distant N. W. from W. C. 280 ms. and 223 from Harrisburg.

Henderson, t-ship, Huntingdon co., bounded N. by West t-ship, E. and S. E. by Mifflin co., S. W. and W. by the Juniata r., which separates it from Union and Porter t-ships. Greatest length 12, breadth 9 miles ; area, 42,880 acres. In 1828, there were in the t-ship, 3 grist mills, 9 saw mills, 7 distilleries, 1 fulling mill, 1 oil mill, 1 brewery, 4 tan yards, and 1 carding machine.

Henry Clay, t-ship, Fayette co., lately taken from Wharton t-ship, is bounded N. by Wharton and Salt Lick t-ships, E. by Somerset co., S. by the state of Maryland, and W. by Wharton t-ship. Area 38,720 acres ; surface mountainous ; soil gravelly. Pop. in 1830, 804 ; taxables, 151. The Youghiogheny r. bounds it W. and N. and receives Hall's run, Oswalt's run, Gabriel's run. Ohiopile falls, in the river, are in the extreme N. point of the t-ship. Sugarloaf mtn. stretches from the river S. to the state line. Between its N. foot and the river are some salt works. The national road crosses the t-ship from S. E. to N. W.

Henry's lake, Covington t-ship, Luzerne co., the source of Roaring brook or Gully creek, situated near and on the E. side of the turnpike r. leading to Dundaff.

Henry'sburg, Centre co., a small village, which was incorporated by act of assembly, 30th Nov. 1829, for the purpose of enabling the citizens to levy a tax on real estate within its limits, to keep in repair the pipes which supply the town with water. It contains about 20 dwellings, &c.

Hepburn, t-ship, Lycoming county, bounded N. and N. E. by Elkland t-ship, S. E. by Fairfield, S. by Loyalsock, W. by Lycoming, and N. W. by Jackson t-ships. Centrally distant N. from Williamsport 9 miles; greatest length and breadth 14 ms. ; area, 87,680 acres ; surface hilly, mountainous ; soil, slate and gravel. Plunket's creek forms the E., the Loyalsock the S. E., and Lycoming the W. and N. W. boundaries. There is a p-office, called Lycoming creek. Pop. in 1830, about 1060 ; taxables 1828, 201.

Hereford, t-ship, Berks co., bounded on the N. E. by Lehigh co., on the S. E. by Montgomery co., on the S. W. by Colebrookdale and District t-ships, and on the N. W. by District and Longswamp townships. Length $5\frac{1}{2}$, breadth $4\frac{1}{2}$ ms. ; area 15,950 acres ; surface hilly. Pop. in 1830, 1716 ; taxables, in 1828, 316. Shoub's mtn., on the N. E. boundary, is a striking feature of the landscape. It is watered by the main and west branches of the Perkiomen creek. There are two churches in the t-ship, pertaining to Presbyterians and Lutherans, one Roman Catholic, and one pertaining to the Shwinckfelders. Four forges. There is a p-o. at Hoof's inn, which has the name of the t-ship.

Herrick, t-ship, Susquehannah co., bounded N. by Jackson t-ship, E. by

Wayne co., S. by Clifford t-ship, and W. by Gibson t-ship. Centrally distant from Montrose borough, S. E. 20 miles; greatest length 6, breadth $3\frac{1}{2}$ miles; area, 19,560 acres; surface hilly. Elk mtn., a low part of the Allegheny, is on the S. W. angle. Soil, gravel and clay. Pop. in 1830, 468; taxables, 88. The township is watered by the head waters of the Lackawannock r. The Philadelphia and Great Bend turnpike road runs N. W. through it.

Herriotsville, p-o., Allegheny co., 233 miles from W. C. and 211 from Harrisburg.

Hettricks, p-o., York co., 83 ms. N. W. from W. C. and 44 S. W. from Harrisburg.

Hickory, t-ship, Venango co., bounded N. by Warren co., E. by Bear t-ship, S. by Teonista t-ship, and W. by the Allegheny river, which separates it from Allegheny t-ship. Centrally distant N. E. from Franklin borough, 26 miles; greatest length 7, breadth $6\frac{1}{2}$ miles; area 24,320 acres; surface rolling; soil, gravel and loam. The t-ship is very thinly inhabited, and is annexed to Teonista.

Hickory, p-o., Washington co., 239 ms. from W. C. and 222 from Harrisburg.

Hickorytown, Plymouth t-ship, Montgomery co., on the Perkiomen turnpike road, 3 miles S. E. of Norristown, contains 8 dwellings, 2 taverns, and 1 store.

High Spire, p-t. of Swatara t-ship, Dauphin co., on the turnpike r. leading from Middletown to Harrisburg, 3 miles from the former and 6 from the latter, and 105 miles from W. C., contains about a dozen houses, 2 taverns and a store.

Hillegass, p-o. Montgomery co., named after the postmaster, George Hillegass, distant 170 miles from W. C. and 77 from Harrisburg.

Hillsboro', p-t. W. Bethlehem t-ship, Washington co. on the national road, midway between Washington bor. and Brownsville, 11 ms. from each. It is built on a single street, contains from 20 to 30 dwellings, 4 stores and 4 taverns, and 160 inhabitants. It is elevated 1750 ft. above tide water, 917 above the Monongahela at Brownsville, and 1002 feet above the Ohio at Wheeling. It is distant from W. C. 217 miles, and from Harrisburg 210.

Hillsgrove, p-o. Lycoming co. 211 ms. N. W. from W. C. and 100 from Harrisburg.

Hillville, p-o. Mercer co. distant from W. C. 279 ms. and from Harrisburg 247 ms.

Hilltown, t-ship, Bucks co. bounded N. E. by Bedminster, S. E. by New Britain, S. W. by Montgomery co. and N. W. by Rockhill t-ship. Greatest length $6\frac{1}{4}$, breadth 4 ms.; area 17,187 acres. It is drained by some small branches of the Neshaminy creek; a small village called Dublin lies on the dividing line between it and Bedminster, at which there is a p-o. Pop. in 1830, 1669; taxables in 1828, 378. There is a p-o. in the t-ship, called "Hilltown," 168 ms. from W. C. 97 from Harrisburg.

Hinckletown, p-t. Earle t-ship, Lancaster co. on the turnpike road leading from Waynesburg to Harrisburg, on the right bank of the Conestoga cr. about 13 ms. N. E. from the city of Lancaster, 128 from W. C. and 43 from Harrisburg, contains 8 or 10 dwellings.

Hockendoque creek, Northampton co. rises at the foot of the Blue mtn. on the S. side, near what is called Smith's gap, and running S. westerly, passing Kernsville and Kreidersville, falls into the Lehigh about 10 ms. below the Water gap. It has a number of excellent flour mills upon it, but is too small for navigation.

Hogestown, p-o. Cumberland co. 113 ms. N. of W. C. and 9 W. of Harrisburg, contains 10 or 12 dwellings, 1 store and 1 tavern; it is on the turnpike road leading from Harrisburg to Carlisle.

Hog island, in the river Delaware, 10 ms. below the city of Phila. a considerable and rich isle, from which the water is embanked, and which is fertile and productive of grass.

Holester's creek, a mill stream of Damascus t-ship, Wayne co. flowing into the Delaware r. in the N. E. part of the t-ship.

Hole creek, Swatara t-ship, Lebanon co. a tributary of the Swatara, which flows southerly along the S. side of the Blue mtn.

Holland, New, village on the W. side of the Susquehannah river, in East Manchester t-ship, 8 ms. N. E. of the borough of York.

Hollidaysburg, p-t. Frankstown t-ship, Huntingdon co. upon Beaver Dam cr. and upon the turnpike road leading from Huntingdon borough to Ebensburg, about 23 ms. W. from the former; 174 miles N. W. from W. C. and 116 S. W. from Harrisburg, contains 30 houses, 4 taverns, 4 stores, 2 smith shops. From the basin near this t. the rail road portage runs across the Allegheny mtn. connecting the E. and W. sections of the Penn. canal, and terminates at Johnstown.

Holmesburg, p-t. and village of Lower Dublin t-ship, Phila. co. about 9 ms. from the city on the Bristol road, 145 N. E. from W. C. and 167 from Harrisburg, contains about 70 houses, 2 taverns and 4 stores. Pennypack cr. which passes it, is navigable for sloops to Lewis' mill, in its immediate vicinity. The dwelling houses and other buildings of Holmesburg are finished neatly, and the streets and footways are kept in good order. The old mill, formerly belonging to the Lewis' family, was built in 1697; it is a substantial stone building, and must have been considered a great establishment when the oldest settlement of Penn. counted but 16 years. Near it stands a commodious cotton factory, of five or six stories, erected 12 or 15 years ago, and in the same neighborhood are two saw mills. Old Andrew Butler, who died 30 years ago, used to relate that he assisted in building the bridge on the post road over Pennypack, in the year of the hard winter, 1740. In point of style it is much inferior to bridges of modern construction; but the firmness and durable character of the workmanship are remarkable. When the turnpike was run over the bridge, the managers thought it best to let it stand as it was, not being certain, it was said, that a new one as substantial could be erected in its place. Holmesburg was laid out as a town by John Holmes, Esq. about thirty years ago. Previous to that time the Washington tavern, and a blacksmith shop at the foot of the hill, were the only buildings close to the post road. In the vicinity of the town northward, along the Pennypack creek, are several manufacturing establishments.—That for printing cottons is particularly worthy of notice.

Home, Rush t-ship, Schuylkill co. laid out a year or two since by the Messrs. Duncan, of Phila. in the Locust Valley, above the gap at the intersection of the Catawissa and Berwick roads. It is said to possess advantages not common in this part of the country; to be surrounded by good farm land, in densely settled country, having abundance of limestone in the neighborhood. We believe few houses have yet been erected here.

Honesdale, a borough and p-t. of Wayne co. situated in the Lackawaxen valley, at the confluence of the Dyberry and Lackawaxen creeks, 3 ms. and a half S. E. of Bethany, 268 N. of W. C. and 165 from Harrisburg. Four years ago the site of this village was occupied by woods; but since the inception of the Lackawaxen canal and rail road, both of which terminate at this place, a thrifty town has sprung up, in which there are about one hundred dwelling houses, several stores and taverns, and the office of the Delaware and Hudson canal company. From Honesdale a rail road, made by that company, extends up the valley of the west branch of Lackawaxen; and crossing the river near the mouth of Vanorba brook, continues in a western direction through Canaan t-ship, and across the Moosic mtn. at Rix's gap to Carbondale, being 16 miles in length, overcoming an elevation and descent of 1812 feet, by 8 inclined planes, at the head of each of which is a stationary steam engine, to effect the ascent and descent of the wagons. The town was incorporated by act of 28th Jan. 1831.

Honeybrook, t-ship, Chester county, bounded N. by Lancaster and Berks cos. E. by West Nantmeal t-ship, S. by West Caln and Brandywine t-ships, and W. by Lancaster co. Central distance from Phila. 38 ms. N. W. and from West Chester 16. Greatest length 5½, breadth 4½ miles; area, 15,600 acres; surface, gentle declivity; soil, sandy loam. Pop. in 1830, 1636; taxables, 352. It is watered by the sources of the east and west branches of the Brandywine r. The Welsh mtn. runs along the northern boundary; Waynesburg, a p-t. lies near the centre of the t-ship, on the Dunningstown, Ephrata and Harrisburg turnpike road, and Cambridge near the middle and on the W. boundary line.

Hookstown, a small village and p-t. centrally situated in Greene t-ship, Beaver co. upon a branch of Mill cr. about 13 ms. S. W. of Beaver bor. 258 N. W. from W. C. and 241 from Harrisburg, contains 40 dwellings, 2 stores and 2 taverns.

Hoosack's creek, a tributary of Spring brook, which rises and has a course of about 4 ms. in Covington t-ship, Luzerne co.

Hopbottom creek, Susquehannah co. rises in Bridgewater t-ship, and flows S. E. into Martin's creek, Lennox t-ship. It is a mill stream but not navigable.

Hopewell, t-ship, York co. bounded N. by York and Windsor t-ships, E. by Chanceford and Fawn t-ships, S. by the state of Maryland, and W. by Shrewsbury t-ship. Centrally distant S. E. from the borough of York 14 ms. greatest length 10, breadth 8½ miles; area 34,560 acres; surface, undulating; soil, loam of good quality. Pop. in 1830, 1941; taxables 370; taxable property in 1829, real estate $255,400 personal, 18,862; occupations 20,820; total, $295,082; rate 25 cts. on the $100. Mechanicsburg, a p-t. lies on the western boundary upon the head waters of Deer creek, which flows into Maryland.

Hopewell, t-ship Cumberland co. bounded N. by Franklin and Perry counties, E. by Mifflin and Newton t-ships, S. by Southampton t-ship, and W. by Franklin co. Centrally distant W. from Carlisle about 21 miles; greatest length 7¼, breadth 4 miles; area 14,080 acres; surface, hilly; soil, slate. Pop. in 1830, 952; taxables 152.

Hopewell, t-ship, Bedford co. bounded N. E. by Huntingdon co. E. by Dublin t-ship, S. by Providence, and W. by Coleraine and Woodberry t-ships. Centrally distant N. E. from Bedford borough 15 miles; greatest length 19, breadth 14 miles; area 75,520 acres; surface mountainous; soil, in the valleys, limestone. Pop. in 1830, 1634; taxables 135. It is drained chiefly by the Raystown branch of the Juniata, which receives from the t-ship Well's creek, flowing through Well's valley, Riper's run, Yellow creek, Six Mile creek, and some smaller streams. Bituminous coal and iron are found in almost every part of the t-ship. Stonerstown, a p-t. lies on the river near the N. E. boundary 19 miles N. E. of the town of Bedford. Another p-o. in the t-ship, is called "Hopewell."

Hopewell, t-ship, Washington co. bounded N. by Cross creek and Mount Pleasant t-ships, E. by Canton, S. by Buffalo and Donegal t-ships, and W. by Virginia. Centrally distant N. W. from Washington borough 12 miles; greatest length 10, breadth 7 miles; area 27,520 acres; surface hilly; soil, loam. Pop. in 1830, 1897; taxables 431. Buffalo creek and Brushy run follow the S., and Cross creek the N. boundary. The post town of West Middleton is on the road leading from Washington to Wellsburg, 11 miles N. W. of the former.

Hopewell, t-ship, Beaver co. bounded N. by Moon t-ship, E. by Ohio r., S. by Allegheny co. and W. by Hanover t-ship. Centrally distant S. from Beaver borough, 10 miles; greatest length 8, breadth 6 miles; area 22,400 acres; surface hilly; soil, loam. Pop. in 1830, 1492; taxables 272. It is drained by Raccoon creek, which flows N. into the Ohio river.

Hopewell, t-ship. Huntingdon co. bounded N. E. by Porter t-ship, S. E. by Union t-ship, S. W. by Bedford co. and N. W. by Woodberry t-ship. Centrally distant from Huntingdon borough S. W. 13 miles; greatest length 17, breadth 8 miles; area, 47,360 acres; surface, mountainous; soil, in the valleys, limestone. Pop. in 1830, about 1150; taxables, 220. In 1828 there were in the t-ship, 4 grist mills, 3 saw mills, 7 distilleries, 2 oil mills and 1 hemp mill.

Hopewell cotton works, p-o. Chester co. 94 miles N. of W. C. and 68 from Harrisburg.

Horman's creek, Washington co. rises in Smith t-ship, and flows between Hanover and Cross Creek t-ship, S.W. and N. W. to the Ohio river; by a course of about 12 miles.

Horntown, a small hamlet of Darby t-ship, Delaware co. 8 miles S. of Phila. and about the same distance from Chester, contains 4 or 5 dwellings.

Horreltown, Union t-ship, Mifflin co. lies in the Kishicoquillas valley, contains 25 or 30 houses, 2 taverns and 2 stores.

Horsham, t-ship, Montgomery co. bounded N. E. by Bucks co. S. E. by Moreland t-ship, S. W. by Upper Dublin and Gwynedd, and N. W. by Montgomery t-ships. Greatest length 6, breadth 3 miles; area 11,040 acres; Central distance N. of Phila. 20 miles, from Norristown 11 ms. It is watered by the W. branch of the Neshaminy and by the Pennypack creeks. Horsham Quaker meeting house lies in its S. E. angle, and the post town of Horsham square about the centre of the t-ship. Soveral excellent roads pass through it. Its surface is level; soil, chiefly limestone. Pop. chiefly Quakers, in 1830, 1086; taxables in 1828, 267.

Horsham square, p-t. and village of Horsham t-ship, Montgomery co. about 20 miles N. of Phila. 14 from Norristown. It contains 4 dwellings, 1 store, a Quaker meeting house and a library.

Horse valley, Franklin co. in the North, or Blue mountain, extending N. E. from St. Thomas into Letterkenny t-ship.

Horse valley, Toboyne t-ship, Perry co. between the Tuscarora mtn. and the Conecocheague ridge.

Houghville, a small, but pleasant village of Doylestown t-ship, Bucks co. about a mile S. of the town of Doylestown, contains some 6 or 8 dwellings, a store, a tavern and a grist mill.

Howardsville, p-t. Wilkins t-ship, Allegheny co. on the turnpike road leading from Greensburg to Pittsburg, 10 miles S. E. from the latter.

Howard, t-ship, Centre co. bounded N. E. by Bald Eagle t-ship, S. E. by the Muncy hills, which separate it from Walker t-ship, S. W. by Bogg t-ship, and N. W. by the west branch of the Susquehannah river. Centrally distant N. W. from Bellefonte 14 ms.; greatest length 21, breadth 10 miles; area 78,720 acres; surface mountainous; soil, in the valleys, limestone. Pop. in 1830 1291; taxables 237. The main ridge of the Allegheny mtn. runs through the t-ship, E. of which and between it and Muncy hills, is Bald Eagle valley, drained by Bald Eagle creek, which receives Marsh and Beach creeks, from the mountain on the west. The post office of the t-ship, is 202 miles from W. C. and 95 from Harrisburg.

Howertown, a village in Allen t-ship, Northampton co. on the road from Bethlehem to Mauch Chunk. Contains 5 houses, 1 tavern.

Hublersville, Walker t-ship, Centre co. a small village of some half dozen houses, on the road leading from Bellefonte to New Providence, 8 miles E. of the former.

Huckleberry, village of Unity t-ship, Westmoreland co. on the turnpike road from Bedford to Greensburg, 6 miles E. of the latter, contains 6 or 7 dwellings, and 1 tavern.

Hughesville, p-t. Muncy Creek t-ship, Lycoming co. upon Little Muncy cr. about 14 or 15 miles E. of Williamsport, 5 miles N. E. of Muncy bor. 196 from W. C. and 85 from Harrisburg, contains about 30 dwellings, 2 taverns, 1 store and 2 mills. This town is fast rising into importance, and its trade rapidly increasing.

Hulingsburg, post-town, Clarion t-ship, Armstrong co. upon the N. bank of Piney creek, a tributary of Clarion river, 25 miles N. E. of Kittanning borough, 242 from W. C. and 185 from Harrisburg, contains some four or five dwellings, store and tavern.

Hulmeville, formerly called Milford, a post-town and village, Middletown t-ship, Bucks co. on the Neshaminy creek, and at the intersection of the Attleborough and Falsington roads. It is a pleasant town of 30 or 40 dwellings, a grist mill, saw mill, and woollen factory, extensively conducted. There are 2 stores and a tavern. The Farmer's Bank of Bucks co. was formerly located here, but is now removed to Bristol. The town is named after the late Mr. John Hulme, a member of the society of Friends, its founder. The country around it is fertile, and well cultivated. It is 20 miles N. E. of Philadelphia, and 16 miles S. E. of Doylestown, 161 miles from W. C. 123 from Harrisburg.

Hummelstown, post-town of Derry t-ship, Dauphin co. 9 miles E. of Harrisburg, 119 N. of W. C. on the turnpike road leading to Reading, seated in a fertile limestone region, surrounded by a wealthy and industrious German population. It contains about 150 dwellings, a Lutheran church, 4 stores, and 5 taverns.

Humphreysville, post-town, Chester co. 108 miles N. of W. C. and 65 S. E. from Harrisburg.

Hunterstown, post-town of Strabane t-ship, Adams co. centrally situate in the t-ship, on the road from Gettysburg to Berlin, 6 miles from the former, contains 20 dwellings, 2 stores and 2 taverns, and has a Lutheran church near it.

Huntsville, p-o. Luzerne co. 220 miles N. W. from W. C. and 110 from Harrisburg.

Huntingdon, t-ship, Luzerne co. bounded N. E. by Union and Salem, S. E. by Salem t-ships, S. W. and W. by Columbia co. and N. W. by Lycoming co. It is a populous and thriving t-ship. It has 3 post-offices, and contains 1572 inhabitants by the census of 1830, and by the returns of 1828, 260 taxables. The Susquehannah and Tioga turnpike road passes longitudinally through the t-ship. The village of New Columbus is situated on this road near the W. line of the t-ship. North mountain, a western continuation of Bowman's range, passes through its northern part, and Knob mountain forms the southern boundary. The immediate surface is rolling and adapted to agriculture.

Huntingdon creek, is formed by the union of some half dozen streams which flow from Bowman's mountains, Luzerne county, into Huntingdon t-ship. Their united volume turns westerly, and joins Fishing creek in Sugarloaf t-ship, Columbia co. receiving before quitting Huntingdon the waters of Green creek. It drives several mills in the latter t-ship.

Huntingdon, post-town and village, Moreland t-ship, Montgomery co. on the road by the Fox chase to Southampton, in Bucks co. 14 miles N. of Philadelphia, and 15 miles E. of Norristown.

Huntingdon, t-ship, Adams county, bounded N. by Cumberland co. E. by Latimore t-ship, S. E. by Reading, S. and W. by Tyrone. Centrally distant N. E. of Gettysburg 12 miles ; greatest length 8, breadth 3½ miles; area, 17,280 acres; surface rolling; soil, limestone and gravel. Population in 1830, 1284 ; taxables, 264. Bermudian creek forms part of the W. boundary, and crosses the t-ship eastwardly. The post-town of Petersburg is situated on the turnpike road from Carlisle to Hanover, which separates this from Latimore t-ship. The small village of Middleton lies in the N. W. angle of the t-ship. There are two churches on the W. boundary, about 5 miles distant from each other.

Huntingdon, p-t. borough, and st. of just. of Huntingdon co. on the W. side of the Frankstown branch of the Juniata, 45 ms. N. E. from Bedford, and 90 miles W. from Harrisburg, contains about 200 dwellings, a brick court house, a new stone jail, Catholic, Episcopalian, Presbyterian, Methodist and Seceder churches, an academy, 3 printing offices, each printing a weekly journal, viz: the Republican Advocate, The Huntington Gazette, and the Huntingdon Courier; 16 stores, 12 taverns, 4 blacksmith's shops, 2 tanneries, 1 grist and 1 saw mill, 2 distilleries and 1 apothecary. A turnpike road and state canal pass through the town. An academy was incorporated here by act 19th March, 1816. The town is a place of considerable and growing business, and the advantages of communication it possesses with the E. and W. parts of the state, by means of the canal, must add greatly and rapidly to its prosperity.

Huntingdon, North, t-ship, of Westmoreland co. bounded N. by Franklin t-ship, E. by Hempfield, S. by Big Sewickly creek which separates it from S. Huntingdon, S. W. by the Youghiogheny r. and W. by Allegheny co. Centrally distant W. from Greensburg 11 miles; greatest length 11, breadth 8 miles; area, 40,320 acres; surface hilly; soil, loam and limestone. Pop. in 1830, 3170. The streams of the t-ship are Brush creek which flows N. W. to Turtle creek, Long run, Little and Big Sewickly creeks, tributaries of the Youghiogheny river. The turnpike road from Greensburg to Pittsburg runs N. W. through the t-ship, upon which lies the post-town of Stewartsville, in the N. W. angle of the t-ship.

Huntingdon, South, t-ship of Westmoreland co. bounded N. by Big Sewickly creek, E. by E. Huntingdon, S. by Jacob's creek and W. by the Youghiogheny river. Centrally distant from Greensburg 12 ms.; greatest length 12, breadth 8 miles; area, 23,680 acres; surface hilly; soil, loam and gravel. Pop. in 1830, 2294; taxables 385. The turnpike road from Somerset to Washington, runs N. W. through the t-ship. Upon which and on the bank of the Youghiogheny river is the post-town of Robstown. The post-town of Port Royal lies also on that river, about 5 miles above Robstown. A ferry crosses the river about midway between the towns. The proposed route of the Ohio and Potomac canal is along the E. bank of the river in this t-ship.

Huntingdon, East, t-ship of Westmoreland co. bounded N. by Hempfield t-ship, E. by Mount Pleasant t-ship, S. by Jacob's creek, and W. by South Huntingdon t-ship. Centrally distant S. W. from Greensburg 10 miles; greatest length 8, breadth 6 miles; area, 23,640 acres; surface hilly; soil, limestone, loam. Pop. in 1830, 1516; taxables, 299. The turnpike road from Somerset to Washington runs W. through the t-ship. The post-town of Mount Pleasant lies on the E. boundary.

Huntingdon county, was taken from Bedford co. by act 20th Sept. 1787. By the act of 26th March, 1804, part of Huntingdon county was taken to form a part of Cambria. It is bounded S. W. by Bedford co. N. W. by Cambria, N. by Centre, E. by Mifflin and Juniata, and S. E. by Franklin. Length 48 miles, mean breadth 30; area, 1185 sq. ms. or 758,400 acres, of which more than 200,000 acres are first rate land, about 550,000 are well settled and improved, and the remainder is mountainous and covered with timber. Central lat. 40° 31′ N. long. from W. C. 1° 12′ W.

Huntingdon county is wholly within the transition region of the state, and in one of the most mountainous parts. The soil partakes of all the shades of quality, from the prolific limestone, to the barren decomposition of the conglomerate. The most important minerals yet discovered are iron, lead, bituminous coal, salt and alum. Iron is abundantly found every where through the county. The Muncy ridge, a dry barren chain of hills of several miles in breadth, but of inconsiderable elevation, which commences in the N. W. part of Bedford county, and runs parallel with the Allegheny mountain through Huntingdon and Centre counties, is the great depository of this valuable material in that part of the country, from whence nearly all the furnaces are supplied. The ore is rich and abundant, and may be procured in almost any part of these barrens. There are many kinds, the best of which is the "*pipe ore*," commonly lying deep, and frequently under a stratum of limestone. "*Rock ore*" when free from sand is much esteemed; and the "*needle ore*" though not highly valued, is a singular production of nature, assuming the most fanciful shapes. Many pieces have the finest possible polish, and a jet black color, and when broken, appear to have been composed of innumerable needles, all lying in the same direction, the points extremely sharp and the butts blunt, they having formed the polished surface of the lump; when the lumps are broken, the needles may be easily separated with the finger. The lumps are integral and unconnected with each other, and the polish of their surface and the arrangement of their particles, is among the mysteries of nature.

Ore in this region is found in almost every possible situation, as well as in great variety of kinds. It is sometimes scattered on the surface in large quantities, where frequently none can be found below it. Sometimes immediately beneath the soil it is discovered in abundance, and of good quality. The miners term this species "*top ore*." It is generally in small black fragments, of great specific gravity, and the veins by an inclined dip reach a considerable depth. "*Nest ore*" another variety somewhat similar to "*top ore*," is also commonly found near the surface. It is thus called, because it lays in nests or bunches, imbedded in clay. These nests are of every size, from a few inches in circuit, to masses of hundreds of tons. "*Rock ore*," so denominated from being in solid blocks, frequently requiring the aid of gunpowder to break them, is found generally at greater depth. In fact there is no depth yet explored, in the section of which we speak, at which it has not been found. It is more abundant than any other, is of excellent quality, though sometimes difficult and dangerous to raise. It is generally black, though sometimes of a chocolate color. The pipe ore, however, is considered the best. It generally lies deep, and is readily met with in large quantities. Its fanciful forms all indicate it to be a deposite. It resembles icicles more than any thing esle; long spears hanging from the larger masses, sometimes so small, that they may be broken off with the fingers.

Coal is most commonly found in the S. W. part of the county; salt in the northern; lead, centrally and particularly in Tyrone t-ship; marble of various colors and qualities in several t-ships. Several curious caves have been discovered in the limestone sections of the county, in which are stalactites and other petrifactions. One of the most singular of these caverns is in Sinking valley, Tyrone t-ship, for a description of which, see article "*Sinking valley*." There are many mineral springs throughout the county, of great efficacy in certain diseases.

The county is abundantly watered by the Juniata river, and the streams which discharge themselves into the Frankstown and Raystown branches, and into the Little Juniata, Aughwick and Tuscarora creeks. The Frankstown branch rises in the Allegheny mountain and flows through the centre of the county, from west to east. The Raystown branch, after passing thro' a part of Bedford county, runs N. E. uniting with the first about 4 miles below the borough of Huntingdon, where the river is about 120 yards broad, and properly assumes the name of Juniata. Aughwick creek, receiving many tributary streams, flows also N. E. to the river, 16 miles below the borough. The Little Juniata, with its volume increased by the Little Bald Eagle and Spruce creeks, passing from N. W. to S. E. blends with the Frankstown branch, about 7 miles from Huntingdon. The state canal enters the county above Aughwick falls, and follows the windings of the river, for about 50 miles, to Hollidaysburg, where it terminates in a capacious basin; from which the rail-road across the Allegheny mountain commences.

The county is divided into 19 t-ships, and contains a number of flourishing towns and villages, among which are Huntingdon, Alexandria, Williamsburg, Shirleysburg, Petersburg, Frankstown, Hollidaysburg, Newry, Birmingham, McConnelsburg, and Smithfield, &c. &c.

The northern turnpike road to Pittsburg enters the county through Jack's mountain, and keeping the direction of the river, but not following its valley, passes through Huntingdon borough, and the towns of Petersburg, Alexandria, Frankstown, and Hollidaysburg.

The trade of the county, formerly by the Juniata river, and now by the river and canal, is very considerable, in iron, grain, flour, whiskey and lumber. The markets at Harrisburg, Middletown, York-Haven, Marietta and Columbia, intervening depots between the Juniata, and Philadelphia and Baltimore, afford great facilities to the western trader, and the canals and rail-roads now being made, will give new stimulus to the industry of the farmer, manufacturer and merchant. The first will find a ready sale at his own door, for his produce, and articles hitherto deemed of little value for export, such as butter, eggs, beef, pork, poultry, hops, fruit, and cider, which will have a comparative value with his wheat, flour, neat cattle, and swine. The iron manufactures, however, have given to him of late an excellent home market, where most articles of produce bear nearly as great a price as at Philadelphia, whilst the iron which the farmer bought in 1815, at $140 per ton at the works, is now sold at 85 to 90, and is of far better quality than was formerly made.

There are in the county eight furnaces, viz. Huntingdon furnace, belonging to Messrs. Gloninger, Anshultz & Co., in Warrior's Mark township, manufactures about 1500 tons of pigs per annum; Pennsylvania furnace, owned by Messrs. Stewart and Lyon, 20 miles N. of Huntingdon, near the Centre county line, makes 1500 tons pigs, and 50 tons castings; Springfield furnace, pertaining to D. & S. Roger, in Morrison's cove, produces 1400 tons pig metal; and Rebecca furnace, also in the same cove, the property of Peter Shœnberger, makes 1200 tons; Ætna furnace, belonging to Henry S. Spang, situated 14 miles from Huntingdon, west, in Cause valley, yields 1600 tons of pigs; Union furnace, now owned by the Huntingdon Bank; and Bald Eagle furnace, also the property of Messrs. Gloninger, Anshultz & Co. These furnaces altogether make about 8000 tons of iron annually, which are sent to the eastern and western markets. There are 11 forges, belonging chiefly to the owners of the furnaces, which make about 3000 tons of bar iron annually. The Tyrone forges, No. 1 and 2, with a rolling and slitting mill and nail factory, belonging to Messrs. Gloninger, Anshultz & Co., form a very extensive establishment. The mill rolls about 150 tons, 75 of which are cut into nails, at the works, 50 tons are slit into rods, and sent to the west, and about 25 tons are sold in the adjoining counties.

The hands employed at these works

and their dependents, consume annually 101,852 bushels of wheat, 182,742 bushels of corn and rye, 36,141 bush. oats, 32,240 bush. potatoes, 2,745 tons hay, 781,000 pounds of pork and 396,750 lbs. of beef; the quantity of whiskey not estimated. There are exported about 20,000 bbls. flour, and 4000 bbls. distilled spirits; formerly considerable quantities of lumber were sent to the Susquehannah, but this branch of trade has ceased to be profitable.

There are in the whole county, 62 grist mills; 84 distilleries; 24 tan yards; 8 furnaces; 10 forges; 1 paper mill; 1 mill for cleaning clover seed; 120 saw mills; 11 fulling mills; 5 oil mills; 3 powder mills; 5 carding machines for wool; 2 breweries; 1 hemp mill; 1 slitting and rolling mill, and one hemp factory.

There are in the county 23 churches, of the several religious denominations, of which the Presbyterians have the greatest number. The inhabitants are morally and religiously disposed, have established a Bible and tract societies, and instituted Sunday schools where they could be conveniently established. Schools for teaching the rudiments of an English education are established throughout the county, especially in the towns and villages; and there is an academy at the borough of Huntingdon, which was incorporated by an act of 19th of March, 1816, granting a donation to the institution of $2000. "A public school of the county of Huntingdon," located in the borough, was incorporated by an act of 19th of Feb. 1790; the second section of which speaks of "lands therein granted," but no grant whatever is made, either in the printed statute or in the original act, in the office of the secretary of the commonwealth. The Huntingdon bank, in the town of Huntingdon, incorporated in 1814, is in operation, we believe, for winding up its affairs, only.

There are 3 newspapers published weekly in the borough of Huntingdon, viz. the Republican Advocate, Huntingdon Gazette, and Huntingdon Courier.

Huntingdon, Mifflin, and Cambria counties, form the 17th senatorial district, and send one member to the senate, and Huntingdon alone sends two members to the house of representatives. Huntingdon, Mifflin, Centre and Clearfield, make the 12th congressional district, sending one member to the house of representatives. Huntingdon, Mifflin and Centre counties constitute the 4th judicial district. Thomas Burnside, Esq. president. The courts are holden at Huntingdon borough on the 2d Mondays of January, April, August and November.

The population of the county, composed in a great measure of the descendants of Irish and German emigrants, was in 1790, 7562; in 1800, 13,008; in 1810, 14,778; in 1820, 20,142, and in 1830, 27,159, of whom 14,404 were white males; 12,429 white females; 180 free black males; 134 free black females, 5 male and 7 female slaves, four of the latter being above 100 years old. There were 1169 aliens, 21 deaf and dumb, and 5 blind.

The value of taxable property, by assessment of 1829, was, real estate, $3,273,396; personal, $225,219; amount of tax raised, $7000. The market price of improved lands in limestone valleys, is about $30 the acre, unimproved about $6 the acre.

The county paid into the state treasury in 1831,

For tax on bank dividends,	$358 65
on writs,	302 24
Tavern licenses,	1097 19
Duty on dealers in foreign merchandize,	1324 58
Collateral inheritances,	70 42
	$3153 08

STATISTICAL TABLE OF HUNTINGTON COUNTY.

Townships, &c.	Greatest Lth.	Greatest Bth.	Area in Acres	Face of the country.	Soil.	Population. 1810	Population. 1820	Population. 1830	Tax-abl's
Allegheny,	10	7	39040	hilly, mount'ous,	red shale,	1159	773		90
Antes,	$10\frac{1}{2}$	8	49280	hill and valley,	do.		757		07
Barre,	$12\frac{1}{2}$	$11\frac{1}{2}$	48640	valleys,	lime. & red shale,	1053	1387	1770	367
Dublin,	$8\frac{1}{2}$	5	25350	hilly,	clay,	970	632	666	153
Franklin,	8	$6\frac{1}{2}$	22400	valley, mt'nous,	limestone,	571	870		220
Frankstown,	13	8	51200	do.	red shale,	1114	1641		387
Hopewell,	17	8	35840	do.	lime, gravel,	805	1047		220
Henderson,	16	9	42880	do.	clay,	1698	1021		430
-Huntingdon, *town*,						676	848		
Morris,	11	6	27520	mount., valley,	limestone,	533	802		190
Porter,	16	9	17920	do.	alluvial,		1132		220
-Alexandria, *town*,						156	280		
Shirley,	10	10	62080	do.	clay,	862	1374		292
Springfield,	11	10	52480	hilly,	do.	751	900	1221	231
Tell,	$11\frac{1}{2}$	5	28800	mountainous,	limestone,		686	824	171
Tyrone,	10	7	24320	do. valley,	do.	753	813		214
Union,	18	9	86400	do.	gravel,	706	1078	1370	266
Warriormark,	13	6	20480	do.	limestone,	672	852		284
West Township,	12	6	32000	do.	do.	998	1432		328
-Petersburg, *town*,						194	188		
Woodberry,	21	10	55680	valley,	do.		1107	1765	495
Walker,	7	6	22400	do.	do.				145
Population of balance of county, - - - - -								21308	
						14778	15554	27159	5009

The return of the census of the marshal for 1830, is in the above imperfect form. The population of the townships is given only in the cases marked in the table.

Ickesburg, p-t. Saville t-ship, Perry co. in a fork of a tributary of Great Buffalo creek, about 9 ms. N. W. of Broomfield, 126 N. W. from W. C. and 39 from Harrisburg, contains about 20 dwellings, 2 stores, 1 tavern. A Presbyterian church is near it.

Indian creek, Northampton county, a branch of the Hockendocque, with which it unites near Kreider'sville.

Indian run, a small tributary of the Schuylkill river, in Manheim t-ship, Schuylkill county, which flows N. E. along the S. side of the Sharp mtn. There is another stream of this name, which runs into the Schuylkill, from Mine hill, in Schuylkill t-ship.

Indian creek, Montgomery co. rises in Franconia t-ship, and flows S. W. into the N. E. branch of the Perkiomen r. It has a course of about 6 ms.

Indian Town, a small hamlet, centrally situated in W. Nantmeal t-ship, Chester co.

Indian creek, East Hanover t-ship, Lebanon co. rises at the foot of the Second mtn. and penetrates the Blue mtn. flowing S. into the Swatara cr. turning several mills in its course.

Indian creek, a considerable tributary of the Youghiogheny river, rising in Westmoreland co. and flowing S. W. through Salt Lick t-ship, Fayette co. having a comparative course of about 15 ms.

Indian run, Blockley t-ship, Phila. co. a tributary of Cobb's creek. It has a course of 3 or 4 ms. and gives motion to several mills and small factories.

Indiana, t-ship, Allegheny county, bounded N. by Deer t-ship, E., S. E. and S. by the Allegheny r. and W. by Ross and Pine t-ships. Centrally distant N. E. from Pittsburg 10 miles. Greatest length 9, breadth $7\frac{1}{2}$ miles; area, 32,000 acres; surface, hilly; soil, loam. Pop. in 1830, 1777; taxables 356. Its chief streams are Long run, Deer creek, Squaw run and Pine creek.

Indiana county, was established provisionally by the act of 30th March, 1803, and is bounded N. by Jefferson co. E. by Clearfield and Cambria cos. S. and S. W. by Westmoreland co. and N. W. by Armstrong co. Greatest length 33, breadth 23 miles; area,

770 sq. ms. Central lat. 40° 42′ N. long. from W. C. 2° 5′ W.

Lying in the great western secondary geological formation, the county has the surface common to the greater portion of Penn. The hill table land, originally level, is cut in every direction by the streams which traverse it, and by the ravines made by occasional and temporary floods, and its general character is therefore hilly. Coal and salt are abundant. The former is found in every part of the co. commonly in shallow veins, from 1 to 3½ feet thick. The latter, as yet explored, lies chiefly in the southern part, along or near the Conemaugh river, where many salt works are erected, which have in most cases the benefit of coal for fuel near the mouth of the wells. Iron ore has been found in Mahoning t-ship, in the northern part of the co. and probably in other places, but no iron works have yet been erected.

The soil of the country is loam, varied by commixture with sand, gravel and clay; with these, vegetable mould is blended in the valleys, in various proportions, producing in many places exuberant fertility.

The co. is drained on the N. E. by the head waters of the W. branch of the Susquehannah river; on the S. by Black Lick creek and its numerous branches, flowing into the Conemaugh at Blairsville; on the W. by Blacklegs creek, also a tributary of that r. and by Crooked, Plumb, and the Big and Little Mahoning creeks, which, traversing Armstrong co. empty into the Allegheny r. The Mahoning and the Conemaugh, we believe, are the only streams that are navigable within the county. The turnpike road from Ebensburg to Kittanning crosses the co. from E. to W. running through the borough of Indiana.

The co. was originally settled by Irish and German emigrants, and is now possessed by their descendants, the majority of whom are from the former source. The pop. in 1810 was 6214, in 1820, 8882, and in 1830, 14,250, of whom 7197 were white males, 6947 white females, 41 free black males, 56 free black females, and 6 male and 4 female slaves. There were 222 aliens, 12 deaf and dumb, and 2 blind.

That the inhabitants are religiously and morally disposed, may be satisfactorily inferred from the fact that there is a church in the co. for every 650 souls. The regular association of Presbyterians has 10, the Seceders 5, Methodists 2, Lutherans 2, Episcopalians 1, Catholics 1. A Baptist society at Indiana, having no church, convene in a school house. There are a county Bible and missionary society; and Sunday schools in neighborhoods whose population is sufficiently dense to admit of their convenient establishment. Adequate provision, however, has not yet been made for education. But an academy has been established at the borough of Indiana, which was incorporated in 1814 by an act which granted the sum of $2000 for its use. Classical and mathematical instruction is given here. There are four newspapers published weekly, viz. the Indiana Enquirer, and Free Press, at Indiana borough, and the Blairsville Record, and Conemaugh Republican, at Blairsville.

The county possesses 22 grist mills, 30 saw mills, 14 fulling mills, a woollen manufactory, in Centre t-ship, and and another in Wheatfield t-ship, both engaged in the manufacture of cloth and kersinettes; and a foundry in Blairsville for casting stoves, &c.

The chief exports are horses, neat cattle, sheep, swine and salt. The manufacture of salt, with the facilities afforded by the coal beds, and the transportation by the river, is generally a profitable business, and is fast increasing.

The assessed value of taxable property was, in 1829, real estate $886,080, personal $89,168, rate of levy ⅓ of a cent on every dollar.

The county contributed to the funds of the state, 1831, for tax on writs, $280; tavern licenses, $328,13; duties on dealers in foreign mdz. $586,29; state maps, $4,75; collateral inheritances $14,75; hawkers' and pedlars' licenses, $15,20; total, $1229,12.

Indiana, Venango, Warren, Armstrong and Jefferson cos. constitute the 24th senatorial district of the state, sending one member to the senate. Indiana and Jefferson united send one member to the house of representatives.

Indiana, Westmoreland and Jefferson, form the 17th congressional district, sending one member to congress. Indiana, Westmoreland, Cambria and Armstrong make the 10th judicial district, over which John Young, Esq. presides. The courts are holden at Indiana on the 2d Mondays of March, June, September, and December. This co. belongs to the western district of the supreme court, which holds a session at Pittsburg, on the first Monday in September annually.

The chief towns of the county are Indiana borough, Armagh, Blairsville, Newport, Saltzburg, Strongtown, Nicholsburg, Georgeville, Smicksburg, Diamond's Mills, &c.

STATISTICAL TABLE OF INDIANA COUNTY.

Townships, &c.	Greatest Lth.	Greatest Bth.	Area in Acres	Population. 1820	Population. 1830.	Taxables.
Wheatfield,	13	10½	78,720	2020	2961	551
Armstrong,	7½	7½	23,120	587	814	161
Blairsville bor.,					957	182
Blacklick t-ship,	9½	8	32,000	1303	1850	321
Centre,	10	8	46,720	937	1237	282
Conemaugh,	8	5½	23,680	1555	2104	473
Greene,	12	11	77,440		1130	200
Mahoning,	20	12½	133,120	1106	1640	297
Indiana bor.,				317	433	
Washington,	11	10	48,000	1057	957	265
Young,	8	5	18,560			
				8882	14251	2732

Indiana, p-t. borough and st. jus. Indiana co. lat. 40° 38′ N., long. 2° 8 W. from W. C. distant about 157 miles W. of Harrisburg, 26 miles S. E. from Kittanning, and 35 N. E. from Greensburg. It lies on the line between Washington and Centre t-ships, and contains about 60 dwellings, a court house of brick, a prison of stone, commonly untentanted, 8 stores, 5 taverns, 1 Lutheran, 1 Presbyterian, and 1 Seceder church. An academy of stone, 60 by 25, in which the languages, and mathematics are taught, incorporated 28th March, 1816, and to which the state gave $2000. The turnpike road from Ebensburg to Kittanning runs through the town. The town was laid out on a tract of 250 acres of land, granted for that purpose by George Clymer, in 1805.

Independence, p-o. Warren co. 248 miles from W. C. and 231 from Harrisburg.

Ingham, p-o. Susquehannah co. distant 269 miles from W. C. and 156 from Harrisburg.

Intercourse, village of Leacock t-ship, Lancaster co. 3 miles N. of the Phila. turnpike, and 12 E. of Lancaster city, 120 from W. C., and 46 from Harrisburg, contains 8 or 10 dwellings, &c.

Irish creek, a tributary of the Schuylkill river, rising in Upper Bern t-ship, Berks co. through which it flows 5 or 6 miles and joins the Schuylkill, a short distance below the S. E. corner of the t-ship.

Iron Stone creek, Berks co. rises in Colebrook t-ship, and flowing S. W. in nearly a straight course of about 6 miles, falls into the Manatawny in Douglas t-ship. It turns several valuable mills in its course.

Irwin, t-ship, Venango co. bounded N. by Sandy Creek t-ship, S. by Mercer t-ship, Butler co., E. by Scrub grass t-ship, and W. by Mercer co. Centrally distant S. W. from Franklin borough 12 miles. It forms a square of about 7 miles, and is drained on the N. E. by Scrub Grass cr. Area, 31,360 acres; surface, level; soil, loam.

Irvine, post-office of Broken Straw t-ship, at the confluence of Irvine's run with the Broken Straw creek, 7 miles W. of Warren, and 322 from W. C. and 247 from Harrisburg.

Island run, a small stream flowing from Bowman's mtn. in North Moreland t-ship, Luzerne co. along the N. t-ship line into the Susquehannah r.

Israel's mills post-office, Chester county.

Ivy mills, p-o. Delaware co. 122 ms. from W. C. and 83 from Harrisburg.

Jack's mountain, on the S. W. boundary of Hamilton-ban t-ship, Adams county. Copper and iron are found in it, if iron pyrites have not been mistaken for the former.

Jack's mountain, a ridge of the Allegheny range, rises in Springfield t-ship, Huntingdon co. and extends 70 miles, through Centre, Mifflin, and Union counties, to Penn's creek, near New Berlin.

Jack's creek, rises at the foot of Jack's mountain on the confines of Decatur t-ship, Mifflin co. and flows S. W. about 20 miles to the Juniata river, about one mile below Lewiston, receiving in its course Bell's run and Meadow run.

Jackstown, post-town of Henderson t-ship, Huntingdon co. 10 miles S. E. of Huntingdon borough, 137 miles N. of W. C. and 79 S. W. from Harrisburg, contains about 10 dwellings and a store. The acqueduct of the Pennsylvania canal crosses the river here.

Jackson Hall, p-o. of Franklin co. 90 miles N. W. of W. C. and 59 S. E. from Harrisburg.

Jackson, t-ship, Cambria co. bounded N. and E. by Cambria t-ship, S. and E. by Somerhill t-ship, and W. by Indiana county. Surface rolling; soil, clay, loam and limestone; coal abundant. Pop. in 1830, 440; taxables, 66; value of real estate assessed, 40,751 dollars.

Jackson, t-ship, Susquehannah co. bounded N. by Harmony t-ship, E. by Wayne county, S. by Gibson and Harford t-ships, and W. by New Milford t-ship. Greatest length E. and W. 8 miles, breadth N. and S. 6½; area, 32,000 acres. It is drained by the Lackawannock creek, by the Tunkhannock, and by the Vanwinkle branch of the latter creek. Mount Ararat, a spur of the Moosic mount, lies on the E. side of the t-ship, is covered with a good soil, and is easy of access. The Belmont and Oquago turnpike road, enters it at the S. E. angle, and crosses it northwardly, and the Philadelphia and Great Bend turnpike crosses its S. W. angle. There is a post-office in the t-ship, called Jackson, 185 miles from Harrisburg. Surface hilly; soil, clay and gravel. Pop. in 1830, 641; taxables in 1828, 101.

Jacksonville, p-t. Lynn t-ship, Lehigh co. 18 miles from Northampton, and 74 N. E. by E. from Harrisburg.

Jackson, t-ship, Lycoming co. taken from Lycoming t-ship, is bounded N. by Tioga co. E. by Elkland and Hepburn t-ships, S. by Lycoming t-ship, and W. by Mifflin and Brown t-ships. Centrally distant N. W. of Williamsport 14 miles; greatest length 14, breadth 12 miles; area, 70,400 acres. Pop. in 1830, about 430; taxables, 80; surface mountainous; soil, limestone. Lycoming creek forms the E. boundary, and receives from the t-ship Trout Spring, Trout and Hogland's runs. On Trout run there is a post-office, so called, distant 210 miles from W. C. and 101 from Harrisburg. Valuation of taxable property in 1829, seated lands, &c. $8997, unseated $36,218; personal estate, 3453; rate of levy, 75 cts. in the hundred dollars.

Jackson, t-ship, Tioga co. bounded N. by the state of New York, E. by Bradford co. S. by Sullivan and Covington t-ships, and W. by Tioga and Lawrence t-ships. It is the extreme N. E. t-ship of the state. Length 11, breadth 8 ms; area, 44,800 acres. Centrally distant from Wellsborough, 20 miles. Drained on the N. E. by Seely's ereek, and S. W. by Mill cr. There is iron ore on the latter. The surface of the t-ship is hilly; soil, gravel and loam.

Jackson, t-ship, Lebanon co. bounded N. E. by Berks co. S. by Heidelberg, and W. by Lebanon and Bethel t-ships. Centrally distant E. from the borough of Lebanon, about 7 miles; greatest length 7½, breadth 6¾ miles; area, 14,640 acres; surface, level; soil, limestone. Pop. in 1830, 2120; taxables, 405. The Tulpehocken cr. and Union canal cross it from W. to E. nearly parallel with the Reading and Harrisburg turnpike roads. On the latter about the centre of the t-ship lies the post-town of Myerstown. The Swatara creek crosses the N. angle of the t-ship.

Jackson, t-ship, Dauphin co. bounded N. by Paxton, Mifflin, and Lykens t-ships, S. by Rush, E. by Schuylkill co. and W. by Halifax t-ship. Greatest length 19 miles, breadth 6; area, 40,000 acres; surface, mountainous; soil, sandy loam in the valleys, gravel on the hills. Pop. in 1830, 830; taxables in 1828, 165; value of real estate in 1832, $128,478. This t-ship has Peter's mountain on the S. and Berry's mountain on the N. with some broken intervening ridges and valleys. Powell's valley, drained by Powell's creek, and Armstrong's valley, watered by Armstrong's creek, are the chief. Anthracite has been found in the intervening ridges.

Jacksonville, North Huntingdon t-ship, Westmoreland county, on the turnpike road from Greensburg to Pittsburg, 11 miles W. of the former, contains 12 dwellings, 1 tavern, and 2 stores.

Jacobsburg, post-town, Bushkill t-ship, Northampton co. on the road from Nazareth to the Wind gap, 11 miles from Easton, contains 1 store, 1 tavern, 5 dwellings, 1 furnace and grist mill belonging to Matthew S. Henry. It is 197 miles distant from W. C. and 104 from Harrisburg.

Jacob's mountain, Pittston t-ship, Luzerne co. a continuation of the Wyoming mountains along the valley of the Lackawannock, connecting the chain with the Moosick mountain. It rises 960 feet from its base. A branch of Spring brook passes through a gap in this mountain, called Spring gap.

Jacob's creek, a tributary of the Youghiogheny river, rises in Donegal and Mount Pleasant t-ships, Westmoreland co. and flowing S. W. and W. forms in part, the boundary between that county and Fayette.

Jacobsburg, village of Miles t-ship, Brush valley, Centre co. about 13 ms. N. E. of Bellefonte.

Jamieson's Cross Roads, small village of Warwick t-ship, Bucks co. near the centre of the t-ship, 5 miles S. E. of Doylestown, contains 6 dwellings, a tavern, and a store.

Jarrett'stown, Upper Dublin t-ship, Montgomery co. 10 miles eastward from Norristown, contains 5 or 6 dwellings, and a Quaker meeting.

Jarrett's bridge, Lehigh t-ship, Northampton co. over the Lehigh r. was erected by Henry Jarrett, by legislative permission, with authority to collect toll.

Jefferson county, was provisionally erected by act of 26th March, 1804, and is bounded N. by McKean and Warren, E. by McKean and Clearfield, S. by Indiana, and W. by Armstrong and Venango counties. Greatest length 46 miles, mean breadth 26; area, 1200 square miles. Central lat. 41° 15′ N. long. 2° W. from W. C.

Like the rest of N. Western Pennsylvania, the country is hilly, and iron and coal are in abundance; the latter, is in every part of the county. The soil in the valleys is in many places highly fertile, but the great body of the county cannot be rated above second quality. It is abundantly watered, having on the S. Mahoning creek. On the W. Little Sandy Lick creek, and Big Sandy Lick creek, whose branches stretch across the county. Clarion river, or Toby's creek, with its many and large ramifications, intersects the northern half of the co. in every direction.

The state road from Kittanning to Hamilton, in the state of New York, runs diagonally across the county from S. W. to N. E. and the turnpike road from Phillipsburg to Franklin, traverses it from S. E. to N. W. passing through the town of Brookville; and a company has lately been incorporated for making a turnpike road from Ridgeway through Warren county, to the state line of New York, in the direction of Jamestown.

There are 3 small villages in the county, including the st. of just. viz.

Brookville, Punxatawny, and Ridgeway. At the first, which was commenced in August, 1830, there are about 40 dwellings, 4 taverns, and 4 stores; at Punxatawny 10 or 15 dwellings, 2 taverns, and 1 store, and at Ridgeway, some half dozen dwellings, &c. Port Barnet, Centre, Cooper, and Jefferson, are marked on the map as towns. There is a tavern at the first. The others are mere names.

There are 2 or 3 grist mills only, but more than four times as many saw mills, and the export of the county is lumber solely, unless venison hams be included. Two million of feet of white pine boards, &c. were cut in 1830, and rafted down the Big Mahoning, Red Bank, or Salt Lick creek, and Clarion river, to the Allegheny r. and thence to Pittsburg and other towns on the Ohio.

The population is composed of Germans, some English and some settlers from New York, and consisted by the census of 1830, of 2025. That there is room for great increase is obvious, when we observe that this population might be comfortably supported on 2000 acres, whilst 766,000 acres are unsettled. There are several sects of Christians in these wilds, chiefly Presbyterians, Seceders and Methodists. But there is not a church in the county.

Venango, Warren, Armstrong, Indiana and Jefferson, form the 24th senatorial district of the state, sending one member to the senate. Indiana and Jefferson, united, send one member to the house of representatives. Jefferson belongs to the 4th Judicial district, and to the western district of the supreme court, and connected with Westmoreland and Indiana, constitutes the 17th congressional district.

This county paid into the state treasury in 1831 for,

Tax on writs $35; for tavern licenses $33,44; for duties on dealers in foreign mdz. $31,69; total $10,013; value of taxable property in 1829, real est. $509,801; of pers. est. $14,777; rate of levy $7\frac{1}{2}$ mills on the dollar.

Unimproved lands are offered for sale in this county at from 150, to 200 cts. per acre.

STATISTICAL TABLE OF JEFFERSON CO.

Townships, &c.	Greatest Lth.	Greatest Bth.	Area in Acres.	Population. 1820	Population. 1830	Taxables.
Perry,	11	9	49,280	205	2025	86
Pine creek,	15	12	85,760	356	in the	49
Rose,	39	12	289,520		whole	115
Ridgeway,	23	17	262,040		co.	26
Young,	9	9	51,840			70

The population has not been classed by t-ships in 1830

We cannot vouch for the correctness of the boundaries and the contents of the t-ships of this co. They are very thinly inhabited, and in many parts little explored, and the information we obtained from residents is not very satisfactory; Perry and Pine creek, were the only t-ships in 1820.

Jefferson, p-t. Codorus t-ship, York co. near the W. boundary and a branch of Codorus creek, 12 miles S. W. of the borough of York.

Jefferson, t-ship, Greene co. bounded N. by 10 Mile creek, E. by the Monongahela river, S. by Cumberland t-ship, and W. by Franklin t-ship. Centrally distant E. from Waynesburg 8 miles; greatest length 10; breadth 3 miles; area 14,080 acres; surface, rolling; soil, loam. Pop. in 1830, 1292; taxables 232. The post town of Jefferson is situated on the creek, about 4 miles from its mouth, 215 N. W. from W. C., and 214 S. W. from Harrisburg.

Jefferson, p-t. & bor, Jefferson t-ship, Greene co. (*See preceding article*). The town is surrounded by beautiful scenery, and contains about 100 dwellings, and 500 inhabitants, 5 stores and 3 taverns. It was incorporated by act 14th April, 1827, and includes what was formerly known as the town of Hamilton.

Jefferson, t-ship, Allegheny co. lately taken from Deer t-ship. Pop. in 1830, 1425; taxables 307.

Jeffersonville, p-t. Norristown t-ship, Montgomery co. on the turnpike road from Norristown to Reading, 3 miles N. of the former, 145 from W. C. and 87 from Harrisburg, contains some 6 or 8 dwellings, 1 tavern, and a store.

Jeffriestown, Fayette t-ship, Allegheny co. on Mouture's run, about 2 miles N. of the turnpike road leading to Steubenville, 12 miles W. of Pittsburg. A small collection of houses.

Jenkintown, a post-town and village of Montgomery county, on the Cheltenham and Willow Grove turnpike road, 10 miles from the city of Philadelphia, and about 15 miles from Norristown, 146 from W. C. and 108 from Harrisburg. It is pleasantly situated in an agreeable and fertile country, and contains about 30 dwellings, 2 stores, 2 taverns. The Abington Quaker meeting is at a short distance from the village. The country around is well cultivated and productive; the limestone range of the county lies a mile or two west of the town.

Jennerville, post-village, centrally situated in Penn t-ship, Chester county, 36 miles S. W. from Philadelphia, and 16 miles from West Chester, 96 miles N. of W. C. and 65 from Harrisburg, contains 4 or 5 dwellings, a tavern, and store.

Jenner, t-ship, Somerset county, bounded N. by Conemaugh t-ship, E. by Shade and Quemahoning, S. by Somerset t-ship, and W. by Westmoreland co. Centrally distant N. W. of Somerset borough 12 miles; greatest length 10, breadth 8 miles; area, 48,800 acres; surface, rolling; soil, reddish clay. Pop. in 1830, 1167; taxables, 208; taxable property in 1829, real estate, $74,238; personal, including occupations, $6200; rate of tax, 5 mills on the dollar. Bituminous coal is found in several parts of the t-ship, and iron ore on Beaver Dam run. The turnpike road from Bedford to Greensburg, runs through it, on which lies the p-t. of Jennerville, in the fork of Beaver Dam run, about 10 miles N. of Somerset borough. It contains 10 or 12 houses, store and tavern.

Jennerville, (see preceding article.)

Jersey town, post-town, Madison t-ship, Columbia co. near the middle of the southern boundary, 7 miles N. E. of Danville, 198 from W. C. and 89 from Harrisburg, contains 2 taverns and 1 store, and an Episcopal church, and between 20 and 30 dwellings.

Jersey shore, borough and p-t. of Mifflin t-ship, Lycoming co. on the left bank of W. branch of Susquehannah r. about 15 miles W. of Williamsport. It contains between 5 and 600 inhabitants and 102 taxables, and about 100 dwellings, 6 stores, 5 taverns, and a Methodist church. It is 211 miles N. W. from W. C. and 102 from Harrisburg. It was incorporated by act of assembly 15th March, 1826.

Johnstown, or Conemaugh town, a post-town in the S. W. angle of Cambria county, 40 miles N. W. from Bedford, and 60 E. from Pittsburg, 7 miles from the base of the Allegheny mountain, 160 from W. C. and 138 from Harrisburg, at the junction of Stoney creek and the Little Conemaugh. The village contains above 500 inhabitants, and about 60 dwelling-houses, 7 taverns, 6 stores, 1 mill, and a forge. A basin for the western division of the Pennsylvania canal, in the heart of the town, has occasioned a rapid rise in the value of property here. The town is regularly laid out, on a plot of upwards of 200 acres of ground, completely surrounded by mountains. The water advantages are very considerable, affording a direct communication with Pittsburg, by the canal. The great rail road portage from Hollidaysburg across the Allegheny mountain, terminates here.

Jonestown, a post-town of Swatara t-ship, Lebanon county, near the confluence of the Great and Little Swatara creek, about 7 miles N. W. of the borough of Lebanon, 136 miles from W. C. and 26 from Harrisburg, contains about 100 dwellings, and 1 Presbyterian, 1 Lutheran, and 1 German Reformed church, several stores and taverns.

Jordan creek, Lehigh county, rises at the foot of the Blue mountain in Heidelberg t-ship, and running a very crooked course to the S. E. falls into the Little Lehigh, about 100 perches from its mouth. This stream, with its branches, turns several mills, but it is not navigable. The quantity of its waters depends much upon the season.

Junction, post-office, Buffalo t-ship, Perry co. 127 miles N. W. of W. C. and 17 from Harrisburg.

Juniata river, one of the main tributaries of the Susquehannah river, rises by two principal branches distinguished as the Raystown and Frankstown branches. The Raystown branch rises at the E. foot of the Allegheny mountain, in Somerset and Bedford counties, and flows N. E. and E. about 20 miles to the borough of Bedford, formerly called Raystown, whence the stream had its name, thence still easterly in a direct line about 12 miles, to a place called the Harbor, in Providence t-ship, Bedford co. where it makes a great bend of several miles, and runs N. W. and N. through Hopewell t-ship, Bedford co. and Hopewell and Porter t-ships, Huntingdon co. by a comparative course of more than 40 miles, to unite with the other branch, about 4 miles below the borough of Huntingdon. The Frankstown branch, though shorter and of less volume than the other, derives great importance from being the medium of canal intercourse with the western country. It rises also in Bedford co. near the S. E. corner of Greenfield t-ship, and flows along the W. side of Dunning's mountain N. about 12 miles, to the Frankstown gap, through which it passes to the county of Huntingdon; thence by a N. E. course to Frankstown, 2 miles above which it is navigable; thence by the same course 25 miles in a meandering line by Williamsburg and Alexandria to Petersburg; at the last point it turns S. E. and runs that course by the town of Huntingdon, and about 3 or 4 miles below that town unites with the Raystown branch. The united stream pursues a S. E. course about 14 miles, when it is turned by Owing's hill and the Blue ridge, again to the N. E. 25 miles by Lewistown, winding its way through a defile known as the long narrows formed by the Shade, the Tuscarora and the Narrow mountains, and deflected to the S. E. Pursuing that course about 10 miles by Mifflin town, it is again turned by the Tuscarora mountain, and following its base N. E. about 10 miles, it finds a passage between that and Turkey mountain, and for the last time turns S. E. by Millerstown and Newport some 15 miles, and unites with the Susquehannah river at Duncan's island, 15 miles above Harrisburg. The Raystown branch is the larger and longer stream, and is remarkable for its crooked course, particularly in the vicinity of Harbor mountain. The state canal follows the river, and as we have already said, the Frankstown branch to the foot of the Allegheny mountain, near Hollidaysburg, where the portage commences.

Juniata county, was separated from Mifflin county, by act of 2d March, 1831, and is bounded N. W. and N. by Mifflin, E. by the Susquehannah river, S. E. by Perry county, S. W. by Franklin, and W. by Huntingdon counties. Central lat. 40° 30′ N., long. 0° 30′ W. of W. C. The mean length of the county is about 40 miles, and mean breadth 9; area, 360 sq. ms.

The county belongs to the great central transition formation of the state. Its surface is traversed N. E. and S. W. by several mountain chains. On the southern boundary is the Tuscarora mountain, which, being broken by the Juniata river, assumes on the E. the name of Turkey ridge, and runs to the Susquehannah river. North of this mountain, and W. of the river Juniata, lies Tuscarora valley, bounded northward by Shade mountain, and containing within its bosom a broken chain of hills. Through this valley the Tuscarora creek flows by a devious course of more than 25 miles to the Juniata river, 2 ms. below Mifflintown. It receives several considerable tributaries from the valley, on which are several mills. This valley has about 5 miles in width north of the Shade mountain; a small and narrow valley intervenes between it and Black Log mountain, the northern boundary. The streams here separated by hills flow in opposite directions. Black Log creek S. W., and Licking creek N. E.; the former emptying into the Great Aughwick creek, and the latter into the Tuscarora creek.

Here as in other parts of this region, the basis rock formation seems to be limestone, upon which mountains of slate are superimposed; the valleys in which the limestone is generally at or near the surface, are fertile, and commonly well cultivated, whilst the mountains are broken, frequently precipitous, and generally sterile, yet often covered thickly with oak, chestnut, ash, beech, pine, and maple trees. The portion of the county lying E. of the Juniata river corresponds in character with that already described, having the same continuous chains and like broken ridges. The mountains, however, are compressed more closely, the valleys are narrower, and have a less comparative population. The principal streams here are Lost creek, Cocalimus creek, and the West Mahantango.

The main turnpike road to Pittsburg, by the northern route, follows the valley of the Juniata river from the Susquehannah through the county, passing through the villages of Thompsontown, Mexico and Mifflintown. The state canal pursues the same course, and both have more than 20 miles of length within the county.

The towns of the county are Mifflintown, Mexico, Thompsontown, Calhounsville, or McAlister's town, Ridgeville, Tammanytown, Waterford, and Waterloo.

Like most counties west of the Susquehannah, this was originally settled by Irish and German pioneers, and is now held by their descendants. The population of the t-ships formerly of Mifflin county, which now constitute Juniata county, was, in 1810, 6396, in 1820, 8559, and in 1830, 7672; taxables in 1828, 1804. The prevailing religious sect is Presbyterian. There are 8 or 9 churches in the county, including all denominations; Bible, and tract, and temperance societies have been established, and Sunday schools are held in every vicinage. Common schools are founded and pretty well supported, and the expenditure under the acts of assembly, by the county of Mifflin, before its division, for the education of the indigent, was about $1400 per annum. There is one newspaper, published weekly at Mifflintown.

Although in Mifflin county, when undivided, the manufacture of iron was entitled to much consideration in an account of the business of the county, we believe this is not the case in relation to Juniata county. There is probably iron in abundance in the district, but there are no iron works. The chief exports from Juniata are wheat, flour and whiskey, and the annual quantity of the first has been estimated at 350,000 bushels. The agriculture of the county is said, by its inhabitants, to be in a very thriving and improving condition. The average price of improved lands may be stated at from $25 to $30 an acre. The unimproved lands are chiefly mountainous and little worth.

By the act which created the county, it was annexed to the 12th congressional district, theretofore composed of Huntingdon, Mifflin, Centre and Clearfield counties, which sends one member to congress. It was also given to the 12th judicial district, embracing the counties of Huntingdon, Mifflin and Centre, and the courts are directed to be holden on the first Mondays in February, May, September and December annually, to continue one week at each term if necessary; and it forms a part of the middle district of the supreme court.

Juniata, Mifflin, Huntingdon, and Cambria counties form the 17th senatorial district, sending one member to the senate, and Mifflin and Juniata, united, send two members to the house of representatives.

STATISTICAL TABLE OF JUNIATA COUNTY.

Townships,	Greatest Lth	Greatest Bth	Area in Acres.	Population. 1820	Population. 1830	Tax ab's
Fermanagh,	12	10	53,120	2529	1432	409
Greenwood,	17	10	72,320	1800	2068	520
Milford,	10	6½	37,120	1554	1537	293
Turbett,	19	3	29,560	1165	1134	242
Lack,	14	10	64,000	1511	674	145
Tuscarora,					827	195
				8559	7672	1804

NOTE.—In the separation of Juniata county in 1831, the foregoing townships fell within the new county, with part of Wayne and Derry townships, which are not here given. Lack township, at the first period given above, included Tuscarora.

Juniata, t-ship, Perry co. bounded N. by the Tuscarora mtn. E. by the Juniata river, S. by Mahanoy ridge, and W. by Saville t-ship. Greatest length 10½, breadth 8½ miles; area, 48,660 acres; surface mountainous, consisting of alternate hills and valleys. S. of the Tuscarora is Raccoon creek and valley; S. of Raccoon ridge is Buffalo creek and valley; S. of Middle ridge Little Buffalo creek and valley, and between Limestone ridge and Mahanoy is another valley, in which, near the western boundary, lies Bloomfield, the county town. These ridges and streams run N. E. into the Juniata r. Soil, gravel and slate, limestone in the valleys. Pop. in 1830, 2201; taxables, 407. There is a p-o. at Bloomfield, and another at Beelen's ferry, on the Juniata r. The small village of Newport lies on the same r. at the E. end of Middle ridge, between the mouths of the Great and Little Buffalo creeks. This t-ship has been lately divided by the erection of Centre, but we know not its bounds; it includes the town of Bloomfield.

Juniata, p-o. of Perry co. 131 ms. N. W. of W. C. and 44 from Harrisburg.

Juniata creek, Little, Rye t-ship, Perry co. rises by two branches N. of the Mahanoy ridge, and flows S. E. into the Susquehannah r. at the town of Petersburg.

Juniata Crossings, p-o. of Bedford co. 112 ms. from Washington city, and 90 from Harrisburg.

Juniata Falls, p-o. Juniata county, 130 ms. N. W. from W. C. and 20 from Harrisburg.

Karthaus, p-t. Covington t-ship, Clearfield co. on the left bank of the W. branch of the Susquehannah r. 18 ms. N. E. of the town of Clearfield, 219 from Washington, and 112 from Harrisburg. There are coal, iron, and iron works near the town, and salt springs not far distant.

Kaskawillian creek, Schuylkill t-ship, Schuylkill co. rises in Mine hill, and flows southwardly into the Schuylkill r. near Middleport, about 6 miles from Port Carbon. This stream is important, as affording access and drainage to several good coal mines.

Kaules' creek, a small stream, tributary to the Little Schuylkill r. Schuylkill co. about 6 ms. above Port Clinton.

Keating, t-ship, McKean co. bounded N. by the state of New York, E. by Potter co., S. by Walker and Sergeant t-ships, and W. by Ceres t-ship. Smethport, the co. town, lies in this t-ship, at the confluence of Stanton cr. with Potatoe cr. Port Allegheny and Ceres are also settlements of the t-ship; the former in the S. E. and the latter in the N. E. angle of the t-ship. The t-ship is about 23 ms. long by 14 wide, and contains about 206,180 acres. Its surface is hilly and broken, with extensive and rich alluvial bottoms. The Allegheny river flows through it, by a northerly course, and receives from the t-ship Potatoe cr. a very considerable stream, almost equal to itself. The pop. of the t-ship in 1830 was 493, of whom nearly one half may be residents of Smethport.

Keener's mills, p-o. Adams co.

Kellerstown, a small village of Hamilton t-ship, Northampton co. on the N. and S. turnpike road, 23 ms. from Easton, containing 2 dwellings, 1 tavern, 1 store and a grist mill.

Kelly, t-ship, Union co. bounded N. by White Deer t-ship, E. by the W. branch of the Susquehannah r., S. and W. by Buffalo t-ship. Centrally distant N. from New Berlin 9 ms.; greatest length 6, breadth 4 ms.; area 12,160 acres; surface undulating; soil, limestone. Pop. in 1830, 739; taxables 129; value of taxable property in 1829, $185,743. It is drained by Buffalo creek on the south boundary, which receives from the t-ship Little Buffalo creek and Spruce run.

Kenjua, t-ship, Warren co. bounded N. by the Allegheny r. E. by Mc Kean co. S. by Jefferson co. and W. by Teonista t-ship. Centrally distant S. E. from Warren borough 11 miles; length 19, breadth $7\frac{1}{2}$ miles; area 71, 690 acres; surface variegated, rolling and hilly; soil, gravel, alluvion on the river and creek bottoms. Pop. in 1830, including Elk, 364; taxables in 1828, 64. The Teonista cr. flows southward through the greater part of the t-ship, receiving several considerable branches from it. The p-t. of Kenjua lies in the N. E. angle, near the confluence of Kenjua cr. with the Allegheny r. 10 ms. a little N. of E. from Warren bor. 327 from W. C. and 230 from Harrisburg. It contains a few dwellings, a store and tavern.

Kenjua creek, rises by several branches in McKean co. and flows N. W. 15 or 20 miles into the Allegheny r. in Warren co.

Kennedy's warm spring, Tyrone t-ship, Perry co. on the bank of Sherman's creek, in a romantic and healthy situation, about 11 ms. N. of Carlisle, 22 W. of Harrisburg, 8 from Sterrett's, and 4 from Wager's gap, in the North mtn. and 4 from Landisburg. This spring was long known and frequented by the people of the neighborhood, for its medicinal properties, and in the year 1831 suitable buildings were erected for the accommodation of strangers, whether seeking health or amusement. The water is specially recommended in cases of running sores, cutaneous eruptions, and general debility. It is a gentle purgative and powerful diuretic. The spring rises at the foot of Quaker hill, and emits about 90 galls. of water per minute. Its temperature is that of creek or river water in the summer season. The "fishing and fowling" here, are named as inducements to persons fond of rural sports to make the place a visit.

Kennett, t-ship, Chester co. bounded N. E. and E. by Pennsbury t-ship, S. by the state of Delaware, W. by New Garden, and N. by East Marlborough t-ships. Centrally distant S. W. from Phila. about 28 miles, and from West Chester about 10; length $4\frac{3}{4}$, breadth $4\frac{1}{4}$ miles; area 9630 acres. Surface hilly; soil, limestone. Pop. in 1830, 1145; taxables in 1828, 231. It is drained by Red Clay cr. Kennet Square, the p-t. lies in the N. W. angle of the t-ship. The t-ship is well cultivated and abundantly productive. The assessed value of lands in 1829, was $386,428; of personal property, $16,173, and of occupations, $4880.

Kennett Square, p-t. of Kennett t-ship, Chester co. about 30 ms. S. W. of Phila. and 10 S. W. of West Chester, 103 ms. N. of W. C., 71 S. E. of Harrisburg, contains 15 dwellings, 2 taverns, 1 store and a Quaker meeting house.

Kensington, District of, in the county of Phila. The name of Kensington has long been borne by a suburb of the city of Phila. N. E. of Phila. along the r. Delaware, at which were located the chief ship yards of the city, and where dwelt the greater portion of the fishermen dependant upon the Phila. market. This suburb, with a considerable district annexed, was separated from the t-ship of the Northern Liberties, and incorporated by act of 6th March, 1820, which provides, "That the inhabitants of that part of the Northern Liberties, in the county of Phila. beginning at the mouth of the Cohocksink cr. and the line of the incorporated district of the N. Liberties, thence along the river Delaware to the S. line of the land late Gibson's; thence along the same line to Gunner's creek, and across the same to the S. line of land, late of Isaac Norris, deceased, and now of J. P. Norris; thence along the same line, the several courses thereof, across the Frankford road to the Germantown road; thence down the eastwardly side of the said road to the middle of Sixth street continued; thence along the middle of the same to the line of the incorporated district of the Northern Liberties, and thence along the line of the same to the place of beginning, be a body politic, by the name and title of the 'Commissioners and inhabitants of the Kensington district of the Northern Liberties.'" The district is governed by 15 commissioners, 5 of whom are elected annually, to serve 3 years. It is improving rapidly, and contains many and various manufacturing establishments of cotton, woollen, iron and glass, besides the many mechanics & artisans, dependant upon ship-building. T. W. Dyott has 4 glass furnaces in constant blast, at which vast quantities of white and black ware are made, and the Union glass company manufactures much flint glass, plain and cut, of good quality. The pop. of this district amounted, in 1830, to 13,326, and the taxables, in 1828, to 2757. There is a p-o. in the district, distant 137 ms. from W. C. 99 from Harrisburg, and near 2 from Phila.

Kernsville, a small village and p-o. in Moore t-ship, Northampton co. on the main road from Easton to the Lehigh Water gap, two miles from Cherryville, and on the line between Lehigh and Moore t-ships. It contains 3 dwellings, a tannery, a grist mill and store. It is 195 miles N. E. of W. C., and 102 E. of Harrisburg.

Kersey's, p-o. in the N. W. corner of the co. 236 miles N. W. from Washington, and 154 from Harrisburg.

Kettle creek, Towamensing t-ship, Northampton co. rising between the Big Creek mountain and the Kettle mountain, which after a course of 5 or 6 miles falls into the Lehigh r. a short distance above Mauch Chunk.

Kettle mountain, Towamensing t-ship, Northampton co. on the E. side of the Lehigh, between Fire Line Hill, and the Big Creek mountain. It is a continuation of the Mahoning mtn. opposite Mauch Chunk.

Killinger's run, Lebanon co. forming part of the line between Annville and Londonderry t-ships, flows N. about 6 miles to the Quitapahilla creek.

Kimberton, p-t. and village, Pikeland t-ship, Chester co. 25 miles N. W. from Phila., and 10 miles N. E. of West Chester, 130 from W. C. and 76 from Harrisburg, on the road leading from the Schuylkill river to the Yellow Springs, contains some 4 or 5 dwellings, a store and boarding school.

Kimblesville, p-o. Chester co. 97 miles N. from W. C., and 72 from Harrisburg.

Kingley's, p-o. Crawford co. 313 ms. N. W. from W. C. and 247 from Harrisburg.

Kingston, t-ship, Luzerne county, bounded N. E. by Exeter, S. E. by the Susquehannah river, S. W. by Plymouth and Dallas t-ships. This t-ship has a large portion of first rate timber. The Shawnese mountain extends across the eastern half of the t-ship, and though its altitude is in some places 850 feet above the river, it is of gentle declivity, and its soil is good and produces abundantly. The t-ship yields annually large surplus quantities of wheat, rye, Indian corn, pork and whiskey, which are either floated down the Susquehannah, or transported by wagons across the mountains to the Easton market. It contains two villages, Kingston, formerly called Wyoming, quite upon the southern boundary, and New Troy, near its northern; each of which, has a post office, and contains several stores and mechanics' shops. Kingston village is at present most flourishing. School houses are erected in every neighborhood, in which schools are kept up the greater part of the year. They are partly supported by the annual income from lands, which were originally appropriated to that purpose by the Connecticut settlers.

Anthracite coal abounds in this t-ship, and it is not known that it has been found further to the north, on the west side of the Susquehannah river. Abraham's and Toby's creeks are pretty good mill streams.

In this t-ship are to be seen some remains of an ancient fortification, similar to those found upon the north and western waters. They bear the impress of an advanced knowledge in the art of war. Here also are the remains of Forty-fort, to which Col. Denison, with a feeble remnant of his corps, retired after the battle of the 3d July, 1778. It was from this fort that the Colonel was compelled to negociate for the safety of the aged and infirm, and for the widows and orphans which that disastrous battle had made. It was here that articles of capitulation were agreed upon, and the pledge of safety given by Butler, the British commander, which was nefariously violated.

The great stage route from Wilkesbarre to Montrose passes through this t-ship. It has three post offices and contains 1548 inhabitants, by the census of 1830, and 259 taxables by the return of 1828. Its greatest length is somewhat over 5 miles, and greatest breadth about 4½ miles; area 14,080 acres.

Kingston, formerly called Wyoming, a post town and village of Kingston t-ship, Luzerne co. on the Susquehannah river one mile from, and directly opposite to Wilkesbarre, 223 miles from W. C., and 115 from Harrisburg. The towns are in full view from each other, the river intervening, and the former, like the latter, standing on an elevated alluvial plain; Kingston is on the southern boundary of the t-ship, & is insulated by Troy creek. It is in a most flourishing condition, and contains 50 dwellings, several stores, and taverns, and several mechanics' shops and a church. (*See Kingston t-ship.*) Pop. about 300.

Kingstown, a small village of E. Pennsborough t-ship, Cumberland co. on the turnpike road from Harrisburg to Carlisle, about 6 miles N. E. of the latter.

Kingsessing, t-ship, Philadelphia co. is bounded N. by Blockley t-ship, E. by the Schuylkill river, and S. E. by the Delaware river, W. by Cobb's and Darby creeks, and S. W. by Bow cr. Greatest length 5, breadth 2½ miles; centrally distant S. W. from Philadelphia 7 miles; area, 6,800 acres; surface, mostly level; soil, chiefly alluvial. The ditches and marsh creeks in the lower part of the t-ship, divide it into islands, the chief of which are State island, formerly called Province island, having been purchased by the provincial government for a lazaretto and quarantine ground, and Carpenter's island. In the river Delaware, making part of the t-ship, are Hog, Mud, and Little Mud islands. The first is now rich and fertile embanked meadow, and the second is the site of Fort Mifflin, noted in American history for its obstinate and protracted defence against the British forces in the year 1777. On the marshes of Kingsessing and Passyunk is fed much of the excellent beef for which the market of Philadelphia is famed. Upon the bank of the river Schuylkill about a mile below Grey's ferry is the beautiful and valuable garden and nursery, originally established by the celebrated naturalist Bartram, and now carefully and judiciously cultivated by Col. Carr, who intermarried with his family. Pop. in 1830, 1068; taxables in 1828, 241. There is a post-office having the name of the t-ship, on the Darby road, at the Sorrel Horse tavern, 5 miles from the city, 132 from W. C. and 102 from Harrisburg.

Kirkbridesville ferry, on the bank of the Delaware river, opposite to Trenton, 31 miles from Philadelphia, 20 miles S. E. from Doylestown. There is a tavern here, but that is the only building immediately at the place, save sheds and stable.

Kirks mills, p-o. of Little Britain t-ship, Lancaster co. on Raccoon's run, 25 miles S. E. of Lancaster, 85 from W. C. and 63 from Harrisburg.

Kishcoquillas creeks, Big and Little. The first rises in Armagh t-ship, Mifflin co. by several branches, which uniting near the centre of the t-ship, flow S. W. along the N. foot of Jack's mountain. The latter rises in Union t-ship, and flows N. E. along the same side of the mountain, to meet the first in a ravine, through which the blended streams flow S. through Derry t-ship, to the Juniata river at Lewistown. They are rapid mountain streams, admirably adapted to mill works, and have some mills upon them.

Kishcoquillas valley, extends from the middle of Henderson t-ship, Huntingdon co. N. E. through Union t-ship, Mifflin co. into Armagh t-ship. It is in length about 26 miles. It is drained by the Great and Little Kishcoquillas creeks. Bounded E. by Jack's mountain, by the Stoney and Path mountains.

Kiskiminitas river. (See Conemaugh river.)

Kiskiminitas, t-ship, Armstrong co. taken from Allegheny t-ship in 1831, is bounded N. E. by Plumb Creek t-ship, S. E. by Indiana county, and S. W. by the Conemaugh river, and N. W. by Allegheny t-ship. Centrally distant S. E. of Kittanning 15 miles; greatest length 8½, breadth 7 miles; area, 22,720 acres. The town of Warren lies on the river, and the post-office bearing the name of the t-ship, is 210 miles N. W. from W. C. and 188 from Harrisburg. There are several valuable salt works upon the river, at which large quantities of salt are made and sent to the western towns by the state canal, which follows the river in part through the t-ship.

Kittatinny mountains. This range passes through Sussex county, N. J. crosses Delaware river at the Delaware Water gap, into Northampton county, Penn., and continuing S. W. crosses Susquehannah river 5 miles above Harrisburg, separates Perry from Cumberland, and Franklin from Huntingdon and Bedford counties, and runs into Maryland, W. from Conecocheague creek; crosses Potomac river, between Back creek and Shenandoah rivers. It is finally merged amongst the other mountain ridges of Virginia. It must be deemed the first chain on the E. of the Appalachian system of mountains. (*See part I.*)

Kittatinny valley, between the Kittatinny range and Blue ridge. In Penn. it varies from 8 to 15 miles in width, and is uniformly composed of a limestone base towards the Blue ridge, and of clay slate on the side of Kittatinny mountain. The line of separation between those two rock formations crosses Delaware river about 20 miles above Easton; the Lehigh at the slates about 5 miles above Allentown; the Schuylkill above the mouth of Maiden creek; the Susquehannah in the borough of Harrisburg, and the Potomac near the mouth of the Conecocheague. In Virginia the line of division nearly corresponds with Opequan creek, between Jefferson and Berkley counties. It is a common but erroneous opinion that the whole of this valley is based on limestone; that rock is, however, found chiefly on the S. E. side, whilst on the N. W. the slate predominates. Yet veins of limestone occasionally alternate. The whole of the lands of this valley may be deemed fertile. The limestone is most exuberant, but is somewhat uncertain and requires laborious cultivation, whilst the slate, lighter and more easily formed, produces abundantly, if judiciously fed with stable manure and lime.

Kittanning, t-ship and borough, Armstrong co. The t-ship is bounded N. by the Mahoning creek, E. by Wayne and Plumb Creek t-ships, S. by Crooked Creek, and W. by the Allegheny river. Greatest length 17½ miles, breadth 7; area, 51,200 acres; surface hilly; soil, gravelly and fertile loam. Pop. in 1830, 1629; taxables, 281. The turnpike road from Indiana to Kittanning passes N. W. through it. The borough of Kittanning and co. town lies on the E. bank of the Allegheny river, lat. 40° 30′ N. 40 miles N. E. of Pittsburg, and about 155 miles a little N. of W. from Harrisburg. Its population in 1830, amounted to 526 souls; taxables, 123. It contains 90 dwellings, 10 stores, 5 taverns, 3 tanneries, 3 smiths and other mechanics, 7 lawyers and 3 physicians. The Presbyterians have one church here 50 feet square, and the German Reformed and Lutherans have together one, which is 52 by 35 feet. There is a court house and public offices of brick, a prison of stone. Abundance of excellent coal is dug in the town, and delivered to consumers at less than $1 per ton. Provisions are abundant and cheap. Flour may be had at $3 per barrel, beef at 3 cts. per lb. pork 3 cts. venison hams at 1½ cts. fowls 6¼ cts. each, butter 6 to 8 cts. per lb. and eggs at 6 cts. per dozen; add to which a rich, pleasant and healthy country. There is an academy here, to which the state has given $2000, and there is also a public library. The academy was incorporated April 2d, 1821, and the town also by an act of assembly of the same date.

This town bears the name, and is built upon the site of an old Indian village which was burned on the morning of the 8th of August, 1757, by Col. afterward Gen. John Armstrong. With a force of 300 men he approached the place by the river, about 100 perches below the town, at 3 o'clock in the morning, near a cornfield in which a number of the enemy were lodged, out of their cabins, on account of the heat of the weather. As soon as the dawn of day made the town visible, the troops attacked it through the field, killing several of the foe. Capt. Jacobs, their principal chief, sounded the war whoop, and defended his house bravely through loop-holes in the logs, and his Indians generally refused quarter which was offered to them, declaring that they were men and would not be prisoners. Colonel Armstrong, who had received a musket ball in the shoulder, ordered their cabins to be set on fire. Quarter was again tendered and again refused, and one of the savages avowed his contempt of death, solaced as it would be, by the slaughter of many of the assailants. The notes of the death song rose high and loud, and were heard above the crackling and roaring of the flames. At length some of the Indians, among whom were Capt. Jacobs and his family, burst from their houses and attempted to cross the river, but were instantly shot down. The inhabitants of the town had been abundantly supplied by the French with arms and amunition, which were stored in their huts; the former being loaded were discharged in quick succession as the fire came to them, and the latter exploded from time to time, throwing portions of the wigwams and the bodies of the inhabitants high into the air. A party of the natives appeared on the opposite side of the river, and having fired on the troops without effect, crossed the stream below the town, for the purpose, it would seem, of collecting some horses to carry off their wounded. Near 40 Indians were destroyed in this attack, and 11 English prisoners released, and the enterprise, well timed and successfully executed, prevented an inroad which had been planned by the French and Indians, and so intimidated the latter, who had never before been attacked in their towns, that many retired beyond Fort Duquesne. Colonel Armstrong and his officers received the thanks of the corporation of Philadelphia, and a medal was stricken commemorative of their success.

Klingerstown, on the S. E. border of Upper Mahanoy t-ship, Northumberland co. 17 miles S. E. from Sunbury, near the point of junction of Schuylkill, Northumberland and Dauphin counties, and between Mahantango and Long Pine creeks, contains some 10 or 12 dwellings.

Klinesville, p-o. Berks co. 152 miles from W. C., and 63 from Harrisburg.

Knoxville, p-t. Tioga co. distant 282 miles from W. C. and 176 from Harrisburg. It has its name from the post master, Cotton Knox.

Koening's creek, a small tributary of the Little Schuylkill river, which flows into it, about 9 miles above port Clinton. On this stream, is a forge belonging to the estate of the late Mr. Egy.

Kreidersville, p-t. of Northampton co. on the main road from Bethlehem to Berwick, about 10 miles from Bethlehem, in Allen t-ship. It contains 3 houses and one store, one tavern and a grist mill, turned by the Hockendocque creek; a church is situated within a short distance of the town belonging to Lutherans. It is distant 194 miles from W. C. and 101 from Harrisburg.

Kripstown, East Bethel t-ship, Washington co. on the Monongahela river opposite to Bridge point and on the national road, 23 miles S. E. of Washington borough.

Kunkles gap, in the Blue mountain about midway of the southern boundary of East Penn t-ship, in Northampton co. through which a road passes from Lehighton to Allentown.

Kutztown, p-t. and borough of Maxatawny t-ship, Berks co. on the road leading from Reading to Allentown, 17 miles from each, 160 miles from W. C., and 69 from Harrisburg, upon a branch of Maiden creek. It contains about 120 dwellings, several stores and taverns, and a church pertaining to the Lutherans and German Reformed. It was incorporated by act of assembly 1st March, 1815.

Kulpsville, p-o. Montgomery co. named after the post master, Charles C. Kulp, distant 162 miles from W. C. and 91 from Harrisburg.

Kylersville, p-o. Clearfield co. 194 miles N. W. of W. C. and 122 from Harrisburg.

Lack, t-ship, Juniata co. bounded N. E. by Milford and Turbett t-ships, S. E. by Perry co. S. W. by Huntingdon co. and N. W. by Wayne t-ship, Mifflin co. Length 14 miles, breadth 10 miles; area 64,000 acres; surface mountainous with spacious valleys, in which is a fertile limestone soil. The hills are composed principally of slate. The pop. in 1830 was 674; taxables in 1828, 145. The t-ship was divided since 1820, and Tuscarora taken from it. The Tuscarora mountain prior to that time bounded it on the S. E., and N. of it lie Shade and Log mountains. The streams were Licking, Black Log, and Tuscarora creeks.

Lackawannock, r. has its principal sources in Scott and Mt. Pleasant t-ships, Wayne co. and in Gibson t-ship, Susquehannah co. and flows southwardly along the west side of the Moosic mountain, entering Luzerne co. above Rix's gap, thence deflecting westwardly it pursues a S. W. course of more than 20 miles to the Susquehannah river, into which it empties N. of the village of Pittston, receiving in its course from the east Roaring brook, Abbots creek, and Spring brook, and from the W. Chrystal lake, creek, Legate's and Capous creek, and from both sides other streams less considerable. Its whole length is about 30 miles. It is a rapid and strong stream, and drives many mills in its course. The abundance of anthracite coal on both sides of this r. throughout its course, renders it an object of great interest, not only to the inhabitants of the Lackawannock valley, but to the state at large, and even to the inhabitants of New York, who have already penetrated the valley, by means of the Hudson and Delaware canal and rail road. An act has been passed (1828, 1829,) for incorporating a company, to improve the navigation of the Lackawannock by a canal. The distance from Carbondale, the seat of the coal operations of the Hudson and Delaware company, to the Susquehannah at the mouth of the Lackawannock, is 23 miles, and the extension of the north branch canal sixteen miles, would then make available one of the finest coal regions on earth, now almost worthless. An act has also been obtained for the incorporation of a company for making a rail road, from the Lackawannock coal mines to the mouth of the Shenango river, on the Susquehannah in the state of New York. (*See Carbondale.*)

The valley of the Lackawannock extends from the mouth of the river up the same about 30 miles. The soil is of the second quality, the surface uneven, forming no level plains of any considerable extent; next to the Wyoming valley it is the most populous part of the county of Luzerne. (*See coal formation of Pennsylvania in the introduction, and Carbondale.*)

Lackawannock, t-ship, Mercer co. bounded N. by Delaware t-ship, E. by Springfield t-ship, S. by Neshannock, and W. by Shenango t-ships. Centrally distant S. W. from Mercer bor. 6 miles; greatest length 8, breadth 6 miles; area 30,720 acres; surface hilly; soil, loam. Pop. in 1830, 1163; taxables, 215; taxable property in 1829, real estate $85,170; personal, $11,601; rate of tax, 4 mills in the dollar. The t-ship is drained northward by Lackawannock creek, which rising from a small lake flows N. and N. W. about 6 miles to the Shenango creek.

Lackawaxen creek, or *river*, rises in Mount Pleasant t-ship, Wayne co., and flows through a deep valley, which no where exceeds a half mile in width, and is covered with an alluvial and fertile soil. It unites the greater part of the waters of that county, receiving from it the Dyberry and Middle crs., and the Waullenpaupack on the county line. After its union with these streams, the Lackawaxen justly assumes the rank of a river. The head of the raft navigation is about a mile above the confluence with the Dyberry, but the latter stream is navigable 4 miles above the junction. The tributary streams below the Waullenpaupack are few and inconsiderable. The distance from the highest navigable point of the Dyberry to the mouth of the Lackawaxen is 27 miles, and thence to Philadelphia 170 miles. The river abounds in fish, among which are trout, catfish, perch, and eels. At the mouth of this river, a dam has been erected across the Delaware for supplying the Hudson and Delaware canal with water, and enabling boats to cross the river. From McCarty's point, which is formed by the junction of the Lackawaxen with the Delaware, the Delaware and Hudson canal follows up the valley of the Lackawaxen river to the forks of the Dyberry, where it terminates, and where the rail-road commences, leading to the Lackawanna coal mines, 16 miles distant. At the forks of the Dyberry, the thriving village of Honesdale has sprung up. (See "Lackawanna coal mines," Carbondale.)

Lackawaxen, t-ship, Pike co., bounded N. E. by the Delaware river, on the E. by Upper Smithfield, S. by Delaware t-ships, W. by Palmyra t-ship, and N. W. by Wayne co. Its greatest length is about 21 miles, and greatest breadth about 13 miles. It is watered by the Delaware river, the Lackawaxen, Mt. Hope, Blooming Grove and Shohola creeks. The Milford and Owego, and the Bethany turnpike roads pass in a northwesterly direction.

Lake creek, Susquehannah county, a tributary of the Wyalusing creek, which flows from two small lakes, in and on the boundary line between Bridgewater and Springfield t-ships, and unites with the main stream in Rush t-ship. It affords fine mill-seats but is not navigable.

Lackawannock, t-ship, Mercer co., bounded N. by Delaware t-ship, E. by Springfield, S. by Neshannock, and W. by Shenango t-ships. Centrally distant S. W. from Mercer borough, 6 miles; length 8, breadth 6 miles; area, 30,720 acres; surface somewhat hilly; soil, clay and loam. Pop. in 1830, 1163; taxables in 1828, 215. Value of taxable property, $85,170. The t-ship is drained S. by the Little Neshannock creek, upon which, near the southern boundary, lies the small village and post town of New Wilmington.

Lackawissa, hill, (Indian name, Lahaskeekee,) two rocky ridges which run parallel with each other from the centre of Buckingham t-ship, Bucks co., and which, uniting, cross Solebury t-ship, to the Delaware.

Lairdsville, p-o., Lycoming co., 203 ms. N. W. of W. C. and 92 from Harrisburg, named after the postmaster, John Laird.

Lamar, t-ship, Centre co., bounded N. by Lycoming co., E. by Logan t-ship, S. W. by Walker, and N. W. by Bald Eagle t-ship. Centrally distant from Bellefonte N. E. 16 miles; greatest length 11, breadth $5\frac{1}{2}$ miles; area, 26,880 acres; surface, mtnous; soil in the valleys, limestone. Pop. in 1830, 1567; taxables, 306. Muncy hills are on the N. W., and Nittany mountain on the S. E. In the interval lies Nittany valley, drained by Big Fishing creek. The Washington iron works are on a branch of this stream, near the S. W. boundary of the t-ship. Cedar creek flows N. E. along the east side of Muncy hills, through which it winds its way into Bald Eagle creek.

Lampeter, t-ship, Lancaster county, bounded N. E. by Leacock t-ship, S. E. by Strasburg, S. W. by Conestoga, and N. W. by Lancaster t-ship, Lancaster city and Manheim t-ship. Length $7\frac{1}{2}$, breadth $7\frac{1}{2}$ ms.; area, 24,228 acres; surface rolling; soil, limestone. Pop. in 1830, 3174; taxables, 609. The Pecquea creek flows on its S. E. and the Conestoga river on its N. W. boundary; Mill creek, a tributary of the latter, crosses it diagonally. The Phila. and Lancaster turnpike, and the state rail-road pass through it from E. to W. There is a p-o. at Lampeter Square, a hamlet, distant about 5 miles S. E. of Lancaster city, 114 from W. C., and 40 from Harrisburg. There are in the t-ship 11 distilleries, 3 tanneries, 12 grist mills, and 4 saw mills.

Lampeter Square, a p-t. of Lampeter t-ship, Lancaster co., about 5 ms. S. E. of Lancaster city, contains about 10 or 12 dwellings, 2 taverns and a store.

Lancaster, co., was the fourth county established in the province of Pennsylvania, being the next after Philadelphia, Bucks and Chester, which were the primitive ones, and were simultaneously created; and at present is bounded N. W. by Dauphin and Lebanon counties, N. E. by Berks, E. by Chester, S. by Cecil co., state of Md., and S. W. by the Susquehannah river. Length 33 ms., breadth 28 area 928 ms.; central lat. 40° 3′ N., long. 0° 40′ E. from W. C.

It is, perhaps, the wealthiest county of the state, in natural advantages, having a fine navigable river, which washes its western shore for more than 40 miles, a great diversity of surface and soil, abundantly watered by mill streams; many and excellent roads, the principal of which are paved with stone; a large city, and many fine towns and villages, and a population alike enterprising, patient and industrious, and consequently all powerful in compelling the earth to yield her most precious fruits. The great geological feature of the county is its division between the secondary and transition formations; a broad vein of secondary limestone, underlaying the southern half, whilst a nearly equal belt of transition red sandstone covers the northern. The former affords abundant supplies for building and manure, and superior marble for architectural ornament. This portion of the country also produces large quantities of the oxide of chrome, or chromate of iron, and abundance of magnesite, from which Messrs. McKim & Co. of Baltimore, have taken several hundred tons per annum, and from which they manufacture 1,500,000 lbs. of sulphate of magnesia (epsom salts), annually, supplying the country with these two articles, at a price far less than they can be imported. Iron ore is also abundant in this region, and is found in the hills on the northern boundary. Anthracite coal is said to have been discovered near Reamstown, but neither in quality nor quantity worthy of attention.

Three ranges of hills run through the county from S. E. to N. W., the southernmost chiefly in Martick, Bart and Sadsbury t-ships, includes Mine Ridge, and is notable for iron and copper ore, and other valuable minerals. The copper mines, we believe, are not at present wrought. The second range, more broken and less continuous, and of small elevation, commences at and about Columbia, and includes the Ephrata ridge ; and the third, the highest and most connected, is the Conewago or South mountain.

Crossing the county from E. to W., S. of the parallel of Lancaster, we have Octorara cr., which separates it from Chester, the N. and W. branches of that stream, the Conewingo cr., Fishing creek, Muddy cieek, Tucquean creek, the Pecquea, which runs S. W. over the county, receiving Beaver creek, and Little Beaver creek, and many smaller streams. The Conestoga creek, which, rising in Chester co., flows by a western course into Warwick t-ship, and thence S. W. by the city of Lancaster to the Susquehannah river, being the recipient of many excellent streams which increase its waters from either hand, the chief of which are the East Branch, Cocalico, Trout, Middle and Hammer creeks, and the Little Conestoga creeks ; a slack water navigation has been made on the Conestoga creek. (See that title.) The Great and Little Chiques and the Conewago creek, which separates Lancaster from Dauphin county. All these streams afford advantageous mill sites, and are generally and usefully improved. The state canal follows the Susquehannah on the western border from Columbia northward.

The Philadelphia and Lancaster turnpike road, is notable as the first made in the United States. Its length is 62 ms. ; it was commenced in the year 1792, and finished in 1794, at an expense of $465,000. Other turnpikes have been connected with it, extending from Trenton, on the Delaware, to Steubenville, on the Ohio, a continuous line of 343 miles. From the city of Lancaster this road is continued wesward through the county, about 11 miles to the Susquehannah river at Columbia, which it crosses by a bridge of more than 5000 feet in length. Another turnpike road leads from Lancaster city N. W. to Harrisburg, from which are laterals connecting with the thriving towns of Marietta and Falmouth, on the Susquehannah river. Another turnpike road, commencing at Downingstown, Chester county, traverses the N. E. part of this county for 25 miles, passing through the town of Ephrata, to Harrisburg. The Lancaster and Reading turnpike road proceeds N. E. from the city of Lancaster, through the county, 25 miles ; and the Lancaster and Wilmington turnpike road, entering the county through Mine Hill gap, unites with the Philadelphia road, at Slaymaker's tavern, about 14 miles E. from the city of Lancaster. Country roads, kept in very good order, are made in every direction. The Pennsylvania rail-road from Philadelphia to Columbia, runs through the county nearly due E. and W., and through the business part of the city of Lancaster. Upon this road, in this county, are some extraordinary bridges, for a description of which see the first part of this work. Good bridges, almost universally of stone, have been made over the principal streams where crossed by the great roads ; generally at the expense of the county, or of the turnpike companies ; but in some cases by companies specially incorporated for the purpose, and by individuals authorized by the state. Those most worthy of note are over the Susquehannah river and the Conestoga creek, (for which see Columbia, McCall's ferry, Marietta, Conestoga, and the titles of other streams of the county.)

The chief towns of the county are Lancaster city, the boroughs of Columbia, Marietta, Washington and Strasburg, Falmouth, Bainbridge, Maytown, Elizabethtown, Mount Joy, Manheim, Petersburg, Neffsville, New Market, Fairview, Millerstown, Soudersburg, Paradise, Intercourse, New Holland, Churchtown, Swopetown, Hinckletown, Ephrata, Litiz, Reamstown and Adamstown, &c. &c., for notice of which, see their titles respectively.

We have been unable to obtain an estimate of the value of the exports of this county that can be relied upon ; it equals, certainly, if it does not sur-poss, that of the natural production of any county in the state. These exports consist of grain of every description, common to the country, vast quantities of flour and whiskey, iron in pigs and other castings; in blooms and bars, in sheets, hoops, and rods, and in nails. There are in the county 7 furnaces, 14 forges, 183 distilleries, 45 tan yards, 32 fulling mills, 164 grist mills, 8 hemp mills, 87 saw mills, 9 breweries, 5 oil mills, 5 clover mills, 3 cotton manufactories, one at Humeville, near Lancaster, one in Salisbury, and one in Sadsbury t-ship; 3 potteries, 6 carding engines, 3 paper mills, 1 snuff mill, 7 tilt hammers, and 6 rolling mills, and one or more nail factories. In 1824, there were 333 taverns, and 165 stores, which have increased in number with the improvements of the country since that period.

Much attention has of late been given to the cultivation of the grape, and among the most approved sorts is an indigene taken from an island of the Susquehannah, and called the "Susquehannah grape."

In 1790, the number of the inhabitants of the county amounted to 36,145; in 1800, to 43,043; in 1810, to 53,927; in 1820, to 68,336; and in 1830 to 76,558, of whom 37,632 were white males; 36,372 white females; 1273 free black males; 1215 free black females; 27 male, and 29 female slaves. There were 401 aliens; 35 deaf and dumb, of whom 32 were whites, and 19 blind.

The inhabitants of the county, though not remarkable for enthusiasm, have a decent and proper regard for religion, and are divided, as every where else, in the United States, into various denominations, among which the Lutheran, and German Reformed, are the most numerous. There are many churches pertaining to the Menonists, and some to the Omish, and an establishment of Moravians at Litiz (see Litiz), bearing the impression of the love of order and utility cherished by that sect. The Presbyterians and Methodists have also several churches, and the Quakers have meeting-houses in the S. E. part of the county, and at Columbia and elsewhere. There are, altogether, between 60 and 70 places of public worship in the county.

The provision for education falls far short of what the wealth, and consequent leisure of the inhabitants, should have produced. The "Franklin college," founded here in 1787, has never been adequately encouraged; and although the corporation possesses large and commodious buildings, the institution has no professors, and its halls are empty. Inherent defects of the charter are assigned as the cause of this atrophy; but surely, the power of the legislature was competent to remove the evil, had the people invoked its aid. This indifference to the important subject of education is peculiarly striking, when compared with the warm interest relating to it in the west, and when the abundant wealth of the one section is contrasted with the moderate means of the other. With the exception of this sickly "*college*," we believe Lancaster county was destitute of a public seminary until 1823, when a spirit more favorable to letters seems to have been awakened, and in its first efforts it established an academy at Strasburg, which was incorporated in that year. Since that time (in 1827), another academy was incorporated in Lancaster city, and endowed by the legislature with the sum of $3000. There is also in that city, a seminary on the plan of mutual instruction, where 500 children are taught, and private seminaries, in number equal to the wants of the inhabitants. The number of newspapers printed in the county would authorize the opinion that the inhabitants are generally instructed; in Lancaster, alone, there are 12 newspapers published, 8 in the English, and 4 in the German language, and there are several published in the villages of the county. There are in the city two public libraries, one called "Juliana library," so named after the foundress, Juliana, the daughter of Wm.

Penn ; and there is a county agricultural society, founded in the winter of 1827, '8. An almshouse and house of employment was established on a fine farm on the Phila. turnpike road, a short distance E. of Lancaster, pursuant to an act of 27th February, 1798.

Some interesting remains of intelligent and of brute animals have been found in the county. About 1810, Mr. Joel Lightner, of Soudersburg, discovered some large fossil bones in his quarry, probably of the mastodon or mammoth, buried nine or ten feet below the surface in a hard bed of clay, limestone and calcareous spar ; and a large grinder was, some years previous to that time, picked up near a spring, two miles from this quarry.

In excavating the Pennsylvania canal in 1829, near Bainbridge, the laborers discovered several articles formerly possessed by the aboriginal inhabitants, such as a stone tobacco pipe, neatly formed, a rude tomahawk, a small brass basin, two keys, a small globular bell, and some broken pieces of Indian pottery; but the most interesting object, thus developed, was the skull bone of an Indian, differing materially in shape, from that of the Indians of the present day. The skull is remarkably large, of an oval figure and unusually thin. The frontal bone recedes from the root of the nose and superciliary ridges, and rather lies on the top of the head, than overhangs the forehead. The cranium presenting an appearance more like the skull of a dog than that of a human being. The Choctaw tribe of Indians once had the practice of flattenning their heads in this way, by binding metallic plates on the foreheads of their male children. A chief having this singular head, visited Philadelphia in 1796. Tribes now inhabiting the Missouri at this day have a like habit. The Incas or Kings of Peru, and those related to them by certain degrees of consanguinity, claimed in their domains an exclusive privilege to have their heads thus moddeled. The skull above described, is supposed to have belonged to a male, of about 45 or 50 years of age. This artificial conformation is not known to impair the mind in the slightest degree.

Lancaster, Chester and Delaware counties, form the 4th congressional district, sending three members to congress. Lancaster alone constitutes the 7th senatorial district, sending two members to the state senate, and it has six members in the house of representatives. Lancaster and York counties constitute the 2nd judicial district of the state, over which Walter Franklin, Esq. presides. The courts are holden, in the city of Lancaster, on the 3d Mondays of Jany., April, August and Nov. Besides the ordinary county courts, there is a court called the "district court for the city and county of Lancaster," created by act 27th March, 1820, having jurisdiction in civil cases, where the sum in controversy exceeds $300 ; and the mayor's court of the city of Lancaster, having jurisdiction of criminal matters, within the city. The county belongs to the Lancaster districtof the supreme court, which holds a session, at the city of Lancaster, on the 3d Monday in May, annually.

By the assessment of 1832, the value of real and personal estate, subject to taxation by the acts regulating county rates and levies, in the county, is rated at $24,698,131, upon which the sum of $25,370 65 cts., has been levied for state purposes, and $38,055 98 cts., for county uses. The value of promissory notes, bonds, judgments, mortgages, stocks in corporations, public stock, pleasure carriages, &c., made taxable by the act of 25th March, 1831, is $4,005,841 ; and the tax levied, is $4,005 83 cts.

The marketable value of lands within the county, may be rated at about $80 per acre, of the first quality, and from that down to $15, according to quality and situation, and improvements, where the value of the estate depends chiefly upon lands. But where buildings make a considerable portion of the value, the price of lands rises per acre in proportion to the diminution of quantity.

Lancaster co. paid into the state treasury in 1831, for

Dividends on turnpike stock, 550
Do. Columbia bridge stock, 2,250
Tax on bank dividends, . 1,904 40
Tax on offices, . . . 2,909 46
Tax on writs, ... 703 26
Tavern licenses, . . . 3,202 16
Duties on dealers in foreign mdz., ... 1,044 22
Collateral inheritances, . . 257 57
Pamphlet laws, ... 6 18
Militia and exempt fines, . . 60
Tin and clock pedlars' licenses, ... 285
Hawkers' & pedlars' licenses, 229 90

$13,402 15

STATISTICAL TABLE OF LANCASTER COUNTY.

Townships, &c.	Greatest Lth.	Greatest Bth	Area in Acres	Soil.	Population. 1810	Population. 1820	Population. 1830	Taxables.	Valuation.
Lancaster city,			2560		5405	6633	7704	1720	1532387
Brecknock,	7	5	17306	red shale,	890	1062	1048	230	195201
Bart,	7	5¾	19027	limes.,& clay,	1099	1423	1750	329	279895
Cocalico,	12	9	41044	red shale,	4024	4590	4902	972	1343724
Colerain,	7	7	19497	clay & gravel,	834	1088	1202	209	141647
Caernarvon,	6½	5	15437	red shale,	1084	1412	1629	310	461585
Conestoga,	7	4¾	19601	limestone,	1506	1805	2120	436	785458
*E. & W. Donegal,	11	6½		limestone &c.	3516	3986	6058	1132	1736823
Dromore,	10	6	29391	clay,	1295	1500	1609	333	294845
Earl,	12	8	43986	red shale &c.,	4218	5559	5344	989	2296864
Elizabeth,	7	6½	24521	red shale &c.,	677	1028	1928	370	809804
West Hempfield,	8	5	13880	limestone,	3431	3389	3898	705	1139629
East Hempfield,	5½	5	14145	do.			2072	396	886924
Little Britain,	10½	6	34457	clay,	1700	2169	2527	394	366700
Lancaster t-ship,	3	2½	4045	limestone,	592	730	585	104	327261
Lampeter,	7½	7½	24238	do.	2501	3278	3174	609	1684145
Leacock,	10½	5	25072	limes.,& clay,	2410	2882	3315	625	1550045
Manheim,	7	5	16666	do.	1282	1600	1861	280	1048896
Mount Joy,	9	7½	17733	do.	1551	1835	2106	384	643077
Manor,	8	8	25400	limestone,	2642	3303	3158	835	1708077
Martick,	10	6	31542	limes.,& clay,	1623	1701	2156	414	435515
Raphoe,	11	6¾	26367	do.	2814	3216	3430	690	1064254
Sadsbury,	5½	5	12111	do.	843	1117	1230	235	250016
Salisbury,	8	6	26624	limestone,	1841	2484	3205	604	1233275
Strasburg,	11½	6	25000	do.	2710	3483	4036	843	1515284
Warwick,	10½	9	37012	limes.,& clay,	3439	3777	3848	735	958800
Columbia bor.,			280				2046		
Washington bor.,							607		
					53927	68336	76558	14991	24698131

*Donegal has been lately divided into East, and West. • Before the division the t-ship contained 33,891 acres.

Lancaster, t-ship, Lancaster county, bounded N. by Manheim t-ship and the city of Lancaster, S. E. by Lampeter t-ship, and W. by Manor t-ship. Greatest length 3½, breadth 2½ miles. The Conestoga creek flows in a very serpentine course along its S. E. boundary. Surface hilly ; soil, limestone. Pop. in 1830, 585 ; taxables, 104. The t-ship contains 4 distilleries, 1 fulling mill, 4 grist mills, and a cotton factory at Humeville, on the Conestoga creek.

Lancaster city, the st. of justice of Lancaster co. 62 ms. W. from Phila. and 36 S. E. from the borough of Harrisburg. Long. from W. C. 40′ E., lat. 40° 3′ N. This is the largest inland town of Penn. and has long been distinguished for its thrift and wealth. It is situated in the heart of a rich, populous and well cultivated country, of whose trade it is the chief depot. For the convenience of intercourse between this city and Phila. the first turnpike road of the state was commenced in 1792, and finished in 1794. The commercial prospects of the city of Lancaster have been highly improved by the slack water navigation lately made on the Conestoga creek, which connects the city with the Susquehannah river and the Chesapeake bay, and the state rail road from Columbia to Phila. which passes through it. The streets of the city, which intersect each other at right angles, are chiefly paved and curbed. The ancient buildings are principally 1 story high, in the old German mode, but the modern dwellings are lofty, substantially and commodiously built, and some of them equal in convenience and beauty to any in the state. This city was for many years the seat of government of the commonwealth, which was removed thence to Harrisburg in 1812. The pop. is chiefly German and the descendants of Germans, and amounted in 1830 to 7704; the taxables to 1720. The public buildings consist of a brick court house, at the intersection of King and Queen streets, the two principal streets; a jail, and many places of public worship. The dwellings may amount to 1100.

The town plot contains a square of two miles, comprehending 2500 acres, which is indented by the Conestoga r. upon the east. It was originally laid out in 1728, by James Hamilton, Esq. of Phila. at the request, it is said, of the proprietaries, but certainly with a design on the part of the founder to increase his estate. There was then on its site a single log house. Few lots were sold in fee, the chief part being let on ground rent, on terms so easy as to invite many poor settlers, which caused the town at an early period to become too large for the surrounding country. It was incorporated as a borough by governor George Thomas, by charter dated first May, 1742. In 1754 it contained 500 houses, & above 2000 inhabitants, and was then noted for its manufacture of saddles and guns. But it was said that at that period there was not a single good house in it. The first German Lutheran church, and school house, were built in 1734. The borough charter was confirmed by act of assembly of 19th June, 1777. It was incorporated as a city by an act 20th March, 1818, by the style of the "mayor, aldermen and citizens of Lancaster." It has a select and common council, a recorder and aldermen, who with the mayor (elected by the councils) form the mayor's court. Lancaster is noted in the provincial history of Penn. as having been the scene of an inhuman massacre of unoffending Indians, by some inhabitants of Paxton and Donegal t-ships. These had been rendered furious by the Indian butcheries on the borders, and in the blindness of their rage did not discriminate between the peaceable Indian and the warring savage. On the 14th Dec. 1764, 30 men, well mounted and armed, surrounded the wigwams of a remnant of a tribe of the Six Nations, on the Conestoga manor, and barbarously murdered some women and children, and a few old men, and amongst the latter the chief, Shaheas, who had ever been distinguished by his friendship for the whites. The majority of the villagers, who were abroad at the time of the attack, were placed for protection in the prison at Lancaster. But on the 27th of the same month, a party of 50 men, with faces blackened, from the same t-ships, suddenly entered the town, galloped to the workhouse, which having forced, they surrounded with a guard, and murdered, uninterruptedly, the Indians there, 14 in number. Having effected their purpose they retired undiscovered, nor could the efforts of the government, though strenuously exerted, bring the murderers to justice.

Franklin college was established here by act of assembly, 1787, for the instruction of youth in the German, English, Latin, Greek, and other learned languages; in theology and in the useful arts, science and literature; and was designed particularly for the improvement of the German population. By the incorporating act 10,000 acres of land, within the boundaries of the present counties of Lycoming, Tioga, Bradford and Venango, were granted to the trustees; and by an act of 1788 some lots in the city of Lancaster were vested in them, and soon after the incorporation a sum of money was raised for its use by private subscription. It continued in operation about two years, when the trustees were unable to proceed. Since that time occasionally a Greek and Latin, and sometimes only an English grammar school, has been kept in the buildings belonging to the institution. The Lancaster county academy was incorporated by act of assembly 14th April, 1827, and the sum of $3000 was granted to the institution.

The city contains 2 Lutheran, 1 German Reformed, 1 Episcopalian, 1 Catholic, 1 United Brethren, 1 Presbyterian, 1 Methodist, 1 African, 1 Quaker, and 1 Independent Methodist churches; a seminary on the mutual instruction system, in which 500 children are taught; many private schools, 2 libraries, a reading room, museum, several religious and charitable societies, 8 presses publishing English, and 4 German papers, 17 distilleries, 4 tan yards, six breweries and two potteries.

By the slack water navigation lately made on the Conestoga r. the city of Lancaster has attained the dignity of a port, and produce is embarked there for Phila. via the Susquehannah river and the Chesapeake and Delaware canal. (*For an account of the navigation, see Conestoga creek.*)

Landisburg, p-t. Tyrone township, Perry co. on the N. bank of Sherman's creek, at the confluence of Mouture's run with that stream, 8 miles S. W. of Bloomfield, 117 N. W. from W. C. and 30 from Harrisburg. The poor house of the co. is about 1 mile N. of it. The town contains about 50 dwellings, 1 Presbyterian church, 4 stores and 3 taverns, and between 3 and 400 inhabitants.

Lanesboro', p-o. Susquehannah co. 295 ms. from W. C. and 187 from Harrisburg.

Laurel run, Northampton county, rises in Luzerne county, and pursuing a S. E. course through Lausanne t-ship, falls into the Lehigh river about 7 miles below Sandy creek. It is very rapid, has many falls but no mills, the country through which it has its course being a wilderness.

Laurel run, Wilkesbarre t-ship, Luzerne county, a tributary of Mill cr. into which it enters, a short distance above its junction with the Susquehannah.

Laughlin town, post-town of Ligonier t-ship, Westmoreland co. on the turnpike road leading from Somerset to Greensburg, 21 miles S. E. from the latter, 170 N. W. from W. C. and 148 from Harrisburg, contains about 40 dwellings, 4 taverns, and 3 stores.

Laurel Hill, the high ridge next W. of the Allegheny mountain, forming the boundary between Fayette and Westmoreland counties, and Somerset and Cambria counties. It extends from near the S. boundary of the state for more than 50 miles N. E. (See part 1, mountains of Penn.)

Laurel Hill creek, Somerset co. rises in Somerset t-ship, and flows S. W. parallel with the Laurel hill about 23 miles to the Youghiogheny river, receiving many tributaries in its way.

Laurel Hill, post-office, Somerset county, 162 miles from W. C. and 140 from Harrisburg.

Laurel Hill cave, George t-ship, Fayette county, is on the top of the Laurel Hill mountain, 9 miles S. E. from Uniontown, 3 E. of Fairfield furnace, and half a mile N. E. of Delany's farm. The cave is thus described by a gentleman (Mr. John A. Paxton) who explored it in the year 1816. "The entrance is by a mouth 3 feet by 4, to a passage about 20 feet wide, descending on an inclination of 50 deg. for 50 feet, by a N. W.

course, to a point at which it forks into two avenues of more contracted dimensions, both leading by a considerable descent, into the first chamber. This is about 24 feet in diameter, with a roof of rock 20 feet high. A large descending passage leads from this room, the same course with a very high roof, and is about 12 feet wide for some distance, when it becomes more contracted and opens into the second chamber, which is 100 by 50 feet. A large mass of rocks, which have fallen from the roof, lie on the floor. The roof is low, and at the end of the passage is a spring of excellent water. In this room, the person charged with our tinder box, unfortunately let it fall, and by this accident we lost nearly all of our tinder. A strait, uneven and inclining avenue, conducted us to the narrows, a passage $2\frac{1}{2}$ feet high, and about 50 feet broad, leading horizontally between rocks, with a small descent, for about 150 feet, to a perpendicular precipice. Through this passage we dragged ourselves on our bellies, and the buttons of my coat were torn off by the rocks above. This passage appears to have been formed by the sinking of the nether rock, its support being washed away by the water. The precipice is 22 feet high. I descended it by a rope, but my companions found their way down by aid of projecting rocks. We were now in a very uneven rocky passage, which ascended about 20 deg. for about 234 feet; but as we could find no outlet from it, we returned to the precipice, and discovered another passage to the right, which had a great descent, was very rocky and uneven, and so contracted for about 80 feet, that it was with the greatest difficulty we made our way through it. This led to a second almost perpendicular descent of 30 feet, down which we got with much labor and some risk, into a large avenue or Little Mill Stream Hall, (as I called it,) about 25 feet wide, with a very high roof and sandy floor, with a stream of water running through it, sufficient to turn a grist mill. On the sides of the stream were some large rocks which had fallen from the roof. The avenue is 600 feet long, descending to where the water is lost, through a small aperture in the rock. Returning, we discovered a passage, leading horizontally from the right side of the avenue, the entrance to which is elevated 8 feet above the floor. This was comparatively a pleasant way. The roof, sides and floor were smooth, and we could walk upright. It is about 120 feet long, and communicates with the last and largest chamber, or Great Mill Stream Hall, which is about 30 feet wide, from 30 to 80 high, and 1200 feet long, with a stream sufficient to drive a mill running its whole length. From the source of the stream, where there is a considerable collection of white spar formed by the dropping water, the chamber has a descent of about 30°, to the point where the stream disembogues itself through the wall of rocks. Before we reached this point the avenue became so narrow, that Mr. G. and myself were obliged to creep on our hands and knees through the water, for about 50 feet. Here, in the sand, we found the name of "Crain" written. This was a mortifying discovery, as we had supposed that we were the first who had penetrated so far in this direction. We wrote our names likewise, in the sand, and then rejoined our party. In our way through this great avenue, we had to climb over or creep under a thousand craggy rocks that lay scattered on the floor, and which had fallen from the sides and roof. I have every reason to believe, that none but ourselves had visited the source of the stream and head of the avenue, as we found no signs of human invention, within many hundred feet of the spot. In every other part of the cave the sides were covered with names and marks, made with coal; and if other persons had penetrated thus far, they would certainly have left some token of their perseverance. We were now at the end of our expedition, and as we had plenty of candles left, and had marked with chalk an arrow on the rocks at every turn, we were confident of being able to retrace our steps to the entrance. Returning, we measured with a line the extreme distance we had been, and found it 3600 feet; but we must have travelled altogether, above 2 miles."

Latimore, t-ship, Adams co., bounded N. by Cumberland co., E. by York co., S. by Reading t-ship, and W. by Huntingdon. Centrally distant from Gettysburg N. E. 15 ms.; greatest length, 7¾, breadth, 4 ms.; area, 14,720 acres; surface, level; soil, red shale. Pop. in 1830, 1011; taxables, 179. Bermudian creek crosses the t-ship, from W. to E., and receives from it Latimore creek; Muddy run, also a tributary of the Bermudian, courses the S. boundary. The Carlisle and Hanover turnpike road runs along the E. line, on which, centrally situated, is the p-t. of Petersburg. York sulphur springs lie about 2 ms. S. of the town, near the intersection of the turnpike road with the Bermudian creek.

Latimore creek, (see the preceding article).

Lausanne, t-ship, Northampton co., bounded N. W. by Luzerne co., S. W. by Schuylkill co., S. by Mauch Chunk t-ship, and W. by the Lehigh river. Greatest length 15 ms., width 8½ ms.; surface, very mountainous; soil, gravelly and barren. Pop. in 1830, 508; taxables, in 1828, 165. It is watered by the Lehigh river, and Laurel run. Lowry town, a village of some 30 cabins, planted in the forest, by the Lehigh coal company, is the only town in the t-ship; and as its existence depended on the *lumber* business of that company, the town will probably decay, with the suspension of that business, which will be consequent on the use of canal boats instead of arks, in the transportation of coal. This t-ship embraces the Broad mountain, the Spring mountain, and the Little Spring mountain, all of which probably abound in coal. The very distinguished coal formation of the "Beaver Meadows" lies between the Spring mountains; near which passes the Berwick turnpike road. (*See Beaver Meadows.*)

Lausanne, p-t., of Mauch Chunk t-ship, Northampton co., on the right bank of the river Lehigh, 2 ms. above Mauch Chunk village, 208 from W. C., and 108 from Harrisburg, contains some half dozen dwellings, a store and tavern. The Berwick turnpike road commences here.

Lawall, or *Centreville*, a small village of Bethlehem t-ship, Northampton co., on the main road from Easton to Bethlehem, containing two houses, and one tavern.

Lawrence, t-ship, Tioga co., bounded N. by the state of New York, E. by Jackson t-ship, S. by Tioga and Elkland t-ships, and W. by Elkland. Centrally distant N. E. from Wellsborough 20 ms. It forms an oblong of 8 by 4 ms., divided into nearly two equal parts by the Tioga river, which flows N. through it, receiving tributaries from either hand. Its area is 20,480 acres; surface hilly, rugged and broken along the streams; soil, gravel and clay. Pop. in 1830, 900; taxables, in 1828, 140. The p-office, having the name of the t-ship, is distant from W. C. 261 ms., and from Harrisburg 155, at the borough of Lawrenceville, about 25 ms. N. of Wellsborough. Lawrenceville was incorporated by act 21st of March, 1831.

Lawrenceville, p-t., Tioga co. (see preceding article).

Lawrence, t-ship, Clearfield county, bounded N. by Gibson t-ship, E. by Covington t-ship, S. E. by Bradford t-ship, and S. by Beccaria township. Greatest length 22, breadth 9 miles; surface hilly; soil, gravelly loam. Pop. in 1830, 683; taxables, 135, The W. branch of the Susquehannah crosses the t-ship from the S. W. and receives from the S. the Clearfield and Little Clearfield creeks, and from the N. several streams. Clearfield borough is on the right bank of the river, in the neighborhood of which are extensive beds of coal. The town is about 3 miles N. of the turnpike road running to Franklin, in Venango county.

Lawrenceburg, p-t., Perry t-ship, Armstrong co., on the W. bank of the Allegheny r., and near the E. line of Butler co., about 20 ms. N. W. from Kittanning, and N. E. from Butler borough, 241 ms. from W. C. and 201 from Harrisburg, contains 20 dwellings, 3 stores, 3 taverns, and 1 church common to every denomination of Christians.

Lawrenceville, Pitt t-ship, Allegheny co., on the Allegheny river, about 3 ms. above Pittsburg. At this place is an arsenal, and U. S. military depot.

Lawsville, t-ship, Susquehannah co. bounded N. by the state of N. York, E. by Great Bend and New Milford t-ships, S. by N. Milford and Bridgewater, and W. by Silverlake t-ships. Greatest length N. and S. 8 miles, breadth E. and W. 6 ; area, 30,720 acres. It is watered by Snake creek, whose ramifications extend over the t-ship, in all directions. There is a p-o., called Lawsville, in the S. E. angle of the t-ship, and another, called Lawsville Centre, distant from Harrisburg 171 ms. Surface hilly ; soil, clay and gravel. Pop. in 1830, 873 ; taxables, in 1828, 129. There is a salt spring near the centre of the t-ship, on the bank of the main branch of Snake creek.

Leacock, t-ship, Lancaster county, bounded N. by Earl t-ship, E. by Salisbury, S. by Strasburg and Lampeter, and W. by Manheim. Centrally distant E. from Lancaster about 8 ms. ; greatest length 8½, breadth 5 miles ; area 25,072 acres ; surface, level ; soil, limestone and clay. Pop. in 1830, 3315 ; taxables, 625. Pecquea creek forms the S. E. boundary, and the Conestoga river the W. ; Mill creek crosses it centrally and diagonally. The Philadelphia and Lancaster turnpike road touches the southern angle, and the Lancaster and Morgantown turnpike road crosses it in the N. W., on which, about 9 ms. from Lancaster, is the Leacock p-o., 116 ms. from W. C. and 42 from Harrisburg. The village of *Intercourse* lies on an intermediate road, about 12 ms. E. of Lancaster, and is a post town.

Lebanon county, was formed from parts of Lancaster and Dauphin cos., by act of assembly passed 16th of Feb. 1813, and is bounded on the S. E. by Lancaster co., on the S. W. and N. W. by Dauphin, and on the N. E. by Berks and Schuylkill. Length 17, breadth 17 ms. ; area, 288 sq. miles. Central lat. 40° 25′ N., long. 0° 30′ E. from W. C.

This is one of the finest counties of the state ; and pertains to the great transition formation, lying chiefly between the South mountain and the Kittatinny range and in the great limestone valley. The limestone formation extends from the southern boundary over more than half its surface, and is separated from the slate in most places by the Quitapahilla and Tulpehocken creeks. The southern hills have great abundance of iron ore. The surface of the county is much diversified in its northern and southern parts, but the central parts are level or rolling, and the soil, whether of limestone or slate, generally well cultivated and productive.

The principal streams are the Great and Little Swatara, which flow westerly to the Susquehannah, and the Tulpehocken, which by an easterly course seeks the Schuylkill. On the south, the Conewago, Great and Little Chiques, Hammer and Seglock creeks have their sources in the hills. The valleys of the Swatara, Quitapahilla and Tulpehocken, have supplied a channel for the Union canal, which crosses the county from west to east, and is fed by these streams, and by a reservoir formed on the former in a gap of the Kittatinny mountain. The feeder from this reservoir is navigable, and gives commodious access to the anthracite coal of the Sharp mountain, in Pine Grove t-ship, Schuylkill co. The canal passing through the town of Lebanon, gives it every advantage of commercial communication with the east and the west.

The county is traversed in every direction by good roads. The turnpike from Reading to Harrisburg runs westerly through it, and the turnpike from Ephrata to Harrisburg crosses the S. W. angle.

The chief towns are Lebanon, Miller'stown, Palmyra, Campbell'stown, Sheaffer'stown, Myer'stown, Jonestown.

In East Hanover t-ship, between the First and Second mountain, is a noted cold spring, a famous watering place, much resorted to in the hot weather of the summer, for pleasure and health. Mr. Samuel Winter has erected a large and commodious house of entertainment here, which is 100 feet in length.

The population of the county is almost wholly German, and consisted in 1820, seven years after its erection, of 16,988 souls, and in 1830, of 20,546, of whom 10,377 were white males ; 10,079 white females ; 47 free black males ; 38 free black females ; 1 male and 4 female slaves. There were in the county, 132 aliens, 21 deaf and dumb, and 9 blind.

The public buildings of the county consist of a large and neat brick court house and offices, in Lebanon borough ; a stone prison, surrounded on three sides with a stone wall, 16 feet high ; an alms house and house of employment now being erected on a farm of 170 acres of excellent limestone land, cost $70 per acre, 1½ ms. E. of the borough of Lebanon, on the S. side of the Reading turnpike, and on the head of the Quitapahilla creek. This building is 114 feet long by 40 wide, and of brick ; there is also on the farm a large 2 story brick dwelling, which will be the hospital. The farm was purchased pursuant to an act of 16th of April, 1830. An academy, incorporated in 1816, to which the state made a donation of $2000 ; 17 churches in different parts of the county, 7 of which pertain to the Lutherans, 2 to Methodists, 1 to Catholics, 1 to the Menonists, and the remainder are in common to the Lutherans and German Reformed.

There are county Bible and tract societies ; a library at Lebanon, and 3 journals published weekly at Lebanon, viz. the Morning Star, Pennsylvania Observer, and Lebanon Democrat. By acts of 11th of April, 1827, and 1st of April, 1831, authority was given to establish a bank at Lebanon borough, with a capital not exceeding $200,000.

The manufactures of the county are chiefly of a domestic character, except those of iron, and two woollen factories. B. D. Coleman has two furnaces, one in Londonderry t-ship, called Colebrook, and another in Lebanon t-ship, Cornwall. Jacob B. Wydeman has one forge, and Samuel Light another. Gen. Harrison has a woollen factory on Indian creek, in East Hanover t-ship ; Mr. Light has also a woollen factory, and John Long a fulling mill. The county contains more than 20 grist mills, most of which are stone, and many large and competent to the manufacture of great quantities of flour. The chief exports are wheat flour, rye, and corn and clover seed. Of the last, more than 2000 bushels per annum have been exported. The produce of the county is generally carried to the large and commodious storehouses on the canal at Lebanon, and is thence sent to the city of Philadelphia. The agricultural skill of the county has all that German industry and perseverance can give it, and we know no higher encomium for it.

If the enjoyments of the inhabitants of this county be not very refined, they are simple and stable. It would be difficult, perhaps impossible, to find in any part of the world, a greater portion of comfort more equally diffused and more permanently assured.

The value of limestone lands is from $70 to $75 the acre, and where a farm has the advantage of a mill seat, it is worth from $150 to $175 the acre. The slate lands of good quality bring from $30 to $35 the acre, and the poor lands of Hanover and Swatara townships, sell from $15 to $20 the acre.

The estimated value of real estate in the county, by the census of 1829, was $5,185,853.

The county paid into the state treasury, in 1831, for tax on writs,	$136 86
Tavern licenses,	571 44
Duties on dealers in foreign merchandize,	305 94
" on collateral inheritances,	307 04
Hawkers and pedlars' licenses,	30 40
	$1351 68

Lebanon and Dauphin counties form the 6th congressional district, sending one member to congress; they make also the 8th senatorial district, sending one member to the senate; Lebanon, Dauphin and Schuylkill compose the 12th judicial district, over which Calvin Blythe, Esq. presides. The courts are holden at the borough of Lebanon, on the 1st Mondays after the commencement of the courts in Schuylkill, which are holden on the last Mondays of March, July, October and December. This county belongs to the Lancaster district of the supreme court, which holds an annual session at Lancaster on the 3d Monday in May.

STATISTICAL TABLE OF LEBANON CO.

Townships.	Greatest Lth.	Greatest Bth.	Area in Acres.	Population in 1820.	Population in 1830.	Taxabl's.
Londonderry,	10	6	25,600	1,629	1,874	298
Annville,	10	7	21,700	2,322	2,736	441
Jackson,	$7\frac{1}{2}$	$6\frac{3}{4}$	14,640	1,748	2,120	405
Lebanon,	11	$7\frac{1}{2}$	44,700	4,496	3,556	628
East Hanover,	11	$6\frac{1}{2}$	30,700	1,871	2,498	404
Heidelberg,	11	8	35,800	2,384	2,822	457
Bethel,	12	5	17,920	2,538	1,604	284
Swatara,	10	$3\frac{1}{2}$	15,360		1,510	281
Lebanon boro'					1,826	365
				16,988	20,546	3563

Lebanon, t-ship, Wayne county, bounded N. by Buckingham, E. by Damascus, S. by Dyberry, and W. by Mount Pleasant t-ships. Its greatest length is about $6\frac{1}{2}$ miles, and breadth about 6 miles. It is drained by small tributaries of Dyberry creek. Surface, hilly; soil, gravelly loam. The Coshocton and Great Bend turnpike road crosses it centrally from E. to W. Pop. in 1830, 285; taxables, 58; taxable property in 1829, seated lands, $26,226; unseated, $47,296; personal estate, including occupations, 3770.

Lebanon, t-ship, Lebanon county, bounded N. by Swatara and Bethel t-ships, E. by Jackson and Heidelberg t-ships, S. by Lancaster county, and W. by Londonderry and Annville t-ships. Greatest length 11, greatest breadth 7 miles; area, 44,700 acres; surface, level; soil, limestone, chiefly. Pop. in 1830, 3556; taxables, 628. The Quitapahilla creek rises centrally in the t-ship, and flows E. by the borough of Lebanon, receiving Furnace and Meadow creeks. The Union canal, and the Reading and Harrisburg t-pike cross the t-ship, from E. to W. and pass by the borough. Iron ore is found in the Conewago hills, in the S. part of the t-ship, and Cornwall furnace is established, at the head of Furnace creek.

Lebanon, borough and post-town, Lebanon t-ship, Lebanon co. on the turnpike road from Harrisburg to Reading, 25 miles E. of the former, and 28 miles W. of the latter, 134 miles from W. C. It is the st. of jus. of the county. It is regularly laid out, and the dwellings are chiefly of brick or stone. Pop. in 1830, 1826; taxables, 365. The Union canal passes through the town. There are in the borough 303 dwellings, 12 taverns, 9 stores, 1 grist mill and 1 clover mill, 5 churches, viz: 1 Lutheran, of stone with a large steeple, 1 German reformed, also of stone with a steeple, a Catholic chapel of brick, a Methodist meeting of brick, and a Menonist meeting house, a library, large brick court house and offices, a large stone prison, surrounded by a wall 16 feet high, 4 large store houses on the canal, 3 breweries. The inhabitants are nearly all of German descent, and it is commonly said by them, when at work on their farms and outlots, that the *citizens* are not at home. There are 3 weekly newspapers printed here, viz: Lebanon Morning Star, Penn. Observer, and Lebanon County Democrat. The town was incorporated 20th Feb. 1821. (See Lebanon co.)

Le Bœuf, t-ship, Erie co. bounded N. by Waterford t-ship, E. by Union t-ship, S. by Crawford co. and W. by Conneautte t-ship. Centrally distant S. E. from Erie borough 17 miles; greatest length 8, breadth 5 miles; area, 25,600 acres; surface, hilly; soil, gravelly loam. Pop. in 1830, 554; taxables, 122. French creek enters the t-ship by the N. E. angle, and passes through it by a very devious course into Crawford county, receiving from the t-ship Le Bœuf cr. The turnpike road from Meadville to Waterford, runs N. through it.

Lectler town, a village of Adams county, containing 80 dwellings, 2 stores, 3 taverns and 2 churches.

Leechburg, a new and increasing town on the Kiskiminitas river, and on the State canal at Dam No. 1, contains 30 dwellings, 3 taverns, 3 stores, and a post-office. It is about 13 miles S. of Kittanning, 227 from W. C. and 196 from Harrisburg. The town is named after Mr. Leech.

Leesburg, post-town of Lancaster county, 118 miles from W. C. and 44 from Harrisburg, 9 or 10 miles S. E. of Lancaster, contains 8 or 10 dwellings, 1 store, and 1 tavern.

Legates creek, Luzerne county, rises in Abington and Greenfield t-ships, and flows through a ravine between the Capous and Lackawannock mountain into the Lackawannock river. It is a rapid stream, and drives a mill near its junction with the river.

Lehigh creek, Little, rises in Berks county, and running a S. E. course, receives the waters of the Cedar creek and Jordan, and falls into the Lehigh river at the borough of Northampton. It is a beautiful stream, and has a number of flour mills upon it; but it is navigable only about a half mile from its mouth.

Lehigh river. This beautiful, romantic, rapid and much noted stream, rises in Wayne, Pike, and Luzerne counties, but its various confluents unite near Stoddartsville, on the N. W. border of Northampton county, and the stream being augmented by many mountain creeks, flows by comparative courses 25 miles, to the mouth of Wright's Mill creek. Thence turning nearly S. by a very serpentine course, but in a direct line of 20 miles, it passes Mauch Chunk to Lehighton. Here it deflects to S. E. and pursues that direction 25 miles to Allentown or Northampton. At Allentown, it turns at nearly a right angle towards the South mountain, and assuming a N. E. course along the foot of the mountain, flows past Bethlehem, and reaches the Delaware at Easton, 25 ms. below Allentown. Its entire comparative course is 85 miles. From near its extreme source to Trout creek, it separates Pike and Luzerne counties. From Trout creek to Rock Eddy falls, it divides Northumberland from Luzerne. Below those falls to its passage through the Kittatinny mountain, its course is within Northampton county. Between the mountain and the mouth of Hockendocque creek, it forms the boundary of Lehigh county, from Hockendocque to Bethlehem it flows through Lehigh county, and from Bethlehem to Easton again, its course is through Northampton.

The Lehigh is truly a mountain torrent, which rushes through scenes of exquisite beauty and sublimity, not surpassed by any in the United States. The fall of the river is from Stoddartsville to the mouth of the Nesquehoning creek, about 2 miles above Lausanne and 3 above the village of Mauch Chunk, 845 feet; from Nesquehoning to the Lehigh Water gap, 260; from the gap to Easton, 205. From Easton to tide water, in the Delaware river at Trenton, the stream falls about an hundred feet. The Lehigh at Stoddartsville is therefore elevated 1410 feet above the level of the ocean.

In its natural state, the Lehigh was navigable for boats carrying 15 tons as far as Lausanne, at the foot of the Broad mountain, where a rocky rapid just above the Turnhole, called ***Hatchel-tooth*** falls, impeded the ascending navigation. When the river was low, which is generally the case in August and September, boats with loading could not ascend further than the borough of Northampton, where the river receives considerable accessions from the Jordan and Little Lehigh creeks. From the confluence of the Lehigh with the Delaware, the distance to the landing, at the head of navigation, is by the river about 45 miles. Above Lausanne the country along the river is so mountainous, as to be entirely uninhabitable. These hills extend as far up as the mouth of Bear creek in Luzerne county, and rise so steeply and so abruptly from the bank of the river, that they are in many places inaccessible, overhanging the river in perpendicular ledges, and forming many picturesque and romantic scenes. This part of the country is so rude, wild and barren, that it repels all efforts at settlement; and from the Great Falls at Stoddartsville to Lausanne, a distance of about 30 ms. there was not even one house erected in 1817, the country being a complete wilderness. The river is almost one continued rapid through this whole distance, and so obstructed by rocks, that no attempt had then been made to descend the river with any kind of boat, raft or craft, except in one or two instances by a skiff or canoe.

The navigation of this river has been wonderfully improved, principally by the exertions of those enterprising and ingenious gentlemen, Messrs. Josiah White and Erskine Hazard, who on the 20th March, 1818, obtained from the legislature an act authorizing them to commence their operations. They pursued the labors assiduously for 4 years, in improving the navigation of the river, and developing the riches of the coal mines at Mauch Chunk, and were finally incorporated with others into a body politic, under the title of the Lehigh coal and navigation company, on the 13th Feb. 1822. The privileges bestowed by the charter were more ample and dangerous than the legislature perceived at the time; but more caution has attended subsequent legislation on the subject.

The company commenced operations by completing a descending navigation, only for the purpose of bringing their coal and lumber to market, which was the chief object they had in view. This they effected after the following manner:—Thirteen dams and sluices were built, of a peculiar and novel form, and the obstacles in the bed of the river were removed. The dams served a double purpose, creating pools of navigable water and reservoirs, at certain fixed periods; when the boats, or rather arks, were in attendance at the respective dams, the sluices permitted them to pass with great rapidity; but they consumed a vast quantity of water, and were only adapted to a descending body. Below the dam and sluices the sudden influx of water created an artificial freshet, which increased the depth and rapidity of the r. . On the Delaware r. as far as Trenton, the natural channel was used; below Trenton to Phila. a steamboat was employed to tow the arks, in gangs of 18 or 20 together. The planks of which the arks are built are sold in the city.

After the expenditure of large sums of money, the company resolved to change their plan, and to make a lock navigation, on which steamboats might be employed. Accordingly a lock was built, measuring 135 ft. in length, and 30 in breadth, communicating with a canal 5 feet deep, and lined throughout its whole length, near a mile, with stone. But as this plan proved also very expensive, and the state had about this time commenced the Delaware canal, from Easton to Bristol, another change became expedient. Locks of a different size were adopted, and canals made where they would be cheaper than dams, pools, and tow paths. The latter were extended 10, and the former 35¾ miles. The canals are 45 feet wide at the water line, and 5 feet deep. The locks are 100 feet long, and 22 feet broad, through which it is intended to pass the boats (which are 106 inches wide) in pairs. The locks on the state canal adjoining are 90 by 11 ft.

The amount expended by the company, in improvements of every description, will be detailed in the article Mauch Chunk. That village was built by them, at the mouth of a creek of the same name. The water power of the stream is employed in giving motion to various ingenious machines, invented chiefly by Messrs. White and Hazard.

Various efforts have been made to connect the Lehigh with the Susquehannah, by means of Bear creek, near Wilkesbarre, or by means of Nescopeck or Catawissa creeks, tributaries to the Susquehannah. But as a sufficient supply of water cannot be procured without resorting to machinery, a communication by rail road is now contemplated, and will doubtless be adopted. Since the year 1762, 63 different routes for connecting the Delaware and Susquehannah rivers have been examined and surveyed. One of these routes is in New York, near the state line; 32 were in Delaware and Maryland, and the remainder of course in Penn.

Lehigh Water Gap, the name given to the pass of the r. Lehigh through the Blue mtn. This place possesses much of interest and beauty, among the many beautiful and picturesque scenes along the margin of the Lehigh r. The mtn. is cleft from top to bottom, and rises on either hand apparently 1000 ft. presenting a promontory of rocks and forest. The right bank is most precipitous, and the steep rocks are called "the pulpit rocks." On the left a narrow space of river bottom gives room for the canal, for a road, and a small village called the Lehigh Water Gap. There are some 8 or 10 dwellings here, a p-o. a tavern, a store, a mill, and a kiln for making hydraulic lime, the stone for which is taken from the mtn. There is a dam here across the r. which creates a placid pool in the mtn. gorge; and a bridge below it. (*See Lehigh t-ship.*) The village is about 30 ms. from Easton, 195 from W. C. and 92 from Harrisburg.

Lehigh county, was separated from Northampton by act of assembly passed 6th March, 1812. It is bounded S. E. by Bucks, S. W. by Montgomery and Berks, N. W. by Schuylkill and Northampton, and N.E. by Northampton. Length 28, and width 15 miles; area 389 miles, or 248,960 acres. Central lat. 40° 38′, long. 1° 25′ E. The surface of this county is highly picturesque and varied. Except the 3 south eastern t-ships, Upper Milford, and Upper and Lower Saucon, the residue of the co. lies in the valley between South mtn. and the Blue or Kittatinny mtn. The valley section is nearly equally divided between the limestone and the clay slate formation. The soil, particularly on the limestone tracts, is excellent. The whole co. with but partial exceptions, is well adapted to the culture of grain, grass and fruits, though in many places the surface is excessively broken. The r. Lehigh forms the N. E. boundary between this co. and the co. of Northampton, from the Water gap of the Blue mtn. to the N. line of Hanover t-ship, thence entering the co. it forms the W. and S. boundaries of that t-ship, and by a N. E. course re-enters Northampton. The chief tributaries from the co. to the river are Trout cr. Antelauny, Coplay, Jordan, Cedar, Saucon, and the Little Lehigh creeks. A branch of the Perkiomen rises in this co. among the spurs of the South mtn. The canal of the Lehigh navigation and coal company follows the course of the Lehigh river along and through this co.

A very fine chain bridge is thrown across the Lehigh r. at the town of

Northampton. It consists of 2 loops and 2 half loops, and is suspended by 4 chains. It is 230 ft. long and 30 ft. wide. There are also excellent stone bridges over the Lehigh and the Jordan creeks, near that borough. There is also a bridge at the Water gap, and at other places over the r. Lehigh within the co.

There is a remarkable limestone cave in North Whitehall t-ship, within 2 or 3 ms. of Allentown, on the bank of the Jordan creek, near which is a spring equally remarkable, called the Cavern spring.

The principal towns are Allentown, or Northampton, Segersville, New Tripoli, Trexlerstown, Emaus, Millerstown, Frysburg, &c.

The pop. of the co. is chiefly German. By the census of 1830 it contained 22,266 inhabitants, of whom 11,186 were males, 10,988 females, white; 45 males, 45 females, colored; 68 aliens; 22 deaf and dumb, 3 blind, 1 slave. In 1820 there were 18,895. This co. forms part of the eastern district of the supreme court, which is held in Phila. on the 2d Monday in March and 2d Monday in Dec. and together with Northampton and Berks composes the 3d judicial district of co. courts. The courts are held in Lehigh on the Mondays succeeding the second weeks of the courts of Northampton co. Lehigh and Northampton form the 12th senatorial district, which sends two senators to the state legislature; Lehigh sends two members to the house of representatives; with Berks and Schuylkill it forms the 7th congressional district of the state, represented in the 22d congress by Henry A. Muhlenberg and Henry King.

The public buildings consist of a court house and offices, built of hewn limestone, a spacious prison of like material, and an academy in Northampton, the county town. There are 12 churches in the co. beside three in the borough.

The prevailing religion is Lutheran, Presbyterian and Moravian.

By act 18th March, 1814, the Allentown academy, in the borough of Northampton, was incorporated, and the sum of $2000 granted to it, one half toward the erection of a building, and for the purchase of books and instruments, and the remainder to be vested in aid of other revenues, to compensate teachers, upon condition that a number of poor children shall be admitted into the academy gratis, for a term, each, not exceeding 2 years, in case of other applicants. There is also a sufficient number of schools in every t-ship for the instruction of the children in the rudiments of an English education, there being about 40 in the co. and a public library at Northampton.

There is a bank at Northampton, or Allentown, called the Northampton Bank, with a capital of $123,365, incorporated under the act of March 21st, 1814. By report of the auditor general to the legislature, 5th Jan. 1831, the deposits and dividends unclaimed amounted to $47,055,01; notes and bills discounted $120,701, 80; securities, bonds and mortgages, $182,019,17; stocks and bills of exchange, $20,997,66; specie $40,385, 04; notes of other banks, $30,884,21; real estate, $20,000; notes in circulation, $238,539; dividend 14 per cent.

There is a furnace and forge, belonging to Mr. Balyeth, and a furnace and two forges belonging to Mr. Heinbagh, which are extensively and profitably wrought. There are also 46 grist mills, 28 saw mills, 5 fulling mills, 6 clover mills, 2 oil mills, 33 stores and 40 taverns in the co. The chief business of the co. is agriculture, and the manufacture of flour, and its exports consist of wheat, rye, corn, and flour in barrels, and salt provisions, the greater part of which finds its way to market by the Lehigh r. In the fall of the year and in the early part of the winter the farmers from time to time make up loads of "*marketing*," which they take to Phila. They thus dispose of large quantities of butter, fowls, eggs, cheese, hams, and frequently of their veal and mutton.

Agriculture is generally skilfully prosecuted, and is daily improving. The best lands are rarely in the market, and will readily bring from 60 to $75 per acre; lands of second quality from 30 to $50, and inferior from 15 to $30 per acre. The assessed value of lands subject to taxation, in 1829, was $4,578,034; of personal estate, $85,188; rate of levy 13 cts. in every hundred dollars.

The co. paid into the state treasury, in 1831, for

Tax on bank dividends,	$525,17
Tax on writs,	150,25
Tavern licenses,	735,29
Tax on dealers in foreign mdz.	425,73
Collateral inheritances,	274,62
Hawkers' and pedlars' licenses,	69,35
	$2,180,41

STATISTICAL TABLE OF LEHIGH COUNTY.

Townships, &c.	Greatest Lth.	Greatest Bth.	Area in Acres.	Population. 1820	Population. 1830.	Taxables.
Hanover,	5	4	9,600	866	1102	212
Heidelberg,	8	8	30,080	1900	2208	410
Lowhill,	$4\frac{1}{2}$	3	7,040	703	808	143
Linn,	8	8	33,920	1664	1747	363
Macungee,	8	$5\frac{3}{4}$	29,440	2802	3323	655
*Northampton,				1132	213	40
N. Whitehall,	8	7	21,120	1807	2008	375
Salisbury,	$7\frac{1}{2}$	4	15,360	1165	1342	253
S. Whitehall,	7	6	18,560	1623	1952	331
Upper Milford,	6	$5\frac{1}{2}$	22,400	2416	2829	569
Upper Saucon,	$5\frac{1}{2}$	5	15,360	1642	1905	388
Weissenberg,	$6\frac{1}{2}$	$5\frac{1}{2}$	21,120	1175	1285	260
Northampton b.					1544	322
				18895	22,266	4321

* Including the borough.

Lehigh, t-ship, Northampton county, bounded N. by Towamensing t-ship, S. by Allen t-ship and the Lehigh river, which separates it from Lehigh co., E. by Moore t-ship, and W. by the Lehigh river. Greatest length $6\frac{1}{4}$ ms., greatest width $5\frac{1}{2}$; surface, partly hilly, partly level; soil, gravel and limestone. Pop. in 1830, 1659; taxables, in 1828, 333. The Blue mountain forms the northern boundary, and is broken at the W. corner of the t-ship, by the river, entering the Lehigh Water Gap, and is also broken towards the eastern line by the Little Gap, thro' which a road leads to Berlinville. At the Gap, is a small village, a tavern and store, and a mill for preparing the hydraulic cement, made of limestone, found at this spot. A mill, a short distance below, has been stopped by the damming of the river at this place. A very good toll bridge is erected over the river here. The other villages of the t-ship are Berlinville, now called Lehighville, and Cherryville. It is watered principally by the Lehigh river and Indian creek, a tributary of the Hockendocque.

Lehighton, a post town, Northampton co., on the W. bank of the Lehigh river, about half a mile above the mouth of Mahoning creek. It is 36 miles W. N. W. from Easton, and 4 ms. S. E. from Mauch Chunk, 192 from W. C., and 85 from Harrisburg. Near this town stood the old Moravian settlement of Gnadenhutten, on the N. bank of the Mahoning, about 100 perches from its mouth, where the old church is still standing. Here a treaty was held in July, 1752, between the Moravian brethren and the Shawnese Indians. Nearly opposite Lehighton, on the E. side of the river, stood old *Fort Allen*. Here is a wooden bridge across the Lehigh, 214 feet long and 25 feet wide. The ground plot of the town is laid out upon an elevated piece of table land; the lots are large, affording an extensive garden and yard to each dwelling. The view from the town, though not extensive, is beautiful. It commands a prospect of the river and canal, the valley in which the town of Weissport is located, the Blue mountain in the distance, and a nearer view of the Mahoning mtn. and Lehigh hills. Within half a mile of the village, there has been discovered a mineral spring, the waters of which have proved beneficial in many cases of disease and debility. The valley extending from Lehighton up the Mahoning contains some fine arable land. The town contains some 12 or 15 houses, a store and 2 taverns.

Lehman, t-ship, Luzerne county, bounded N. E. by Windham and Northmoreland, S. E. by Plymouth, S.

W. by Union, and N. W. by Lycoming co. This t-ship was organized in November, 1829; its name was intended as a tribute of respect to the late Dr. Wm. Lehman, of the city of Phila., for many years a member of the house of representatives, chairman of the committee of internal improvement and inland navigation, and a distinguished and active friend and advocate of the great system of canal and rail-road improvement adopted in Pennsylvania. He died at Harrisburg, during the session of the legislature of 1828–9, whilst attending to his official duties. His fellow members of the house of representatives, decreed him a monumental stone, to be erected at the public expense.

This t-ship is very uneven; the great range of the Allegheny passes through its northwestern angle, yet much of it may be cultivated. The timber is pine, oak, hickory and chestnut, with some beech, maple and hemlock. It contains several small lakes, one of which, at the head of the western tributary of Harvey's creek, is here called Lehman's lake; and the tributary itself, of which the lake is the source, called Lehman's creek. Harvey's, Bowman's and Mahoopeny crs. flow through it, and afford numerous mill sites. It has a p-o., and contains 231 inhabitants, and 45 taxables.

Leiperville, a p-t. of Ridley t-ship, Delaware co., on the great southern road, about 12 ms. S. of Phila., 2 ms. N. of Chester borough, 123 ms. from W. C., and 97 from Harrisburg, on Ridley cr., contains about 20 dwellings, a church, a tannery and saw mill, store and tavern. The Leiper canal extends from the river Delaware through the town to the stone quarries on Ridley creek, a distance of about 2 miles.

Lenox, t-ship, Susquehannah county, bounded N. by Harford t-ship, E. by Gibson and Clifford t-ships, S. by Luzerne co., and W. by Martin's creek, a branch of the Tunkhannock. Its western boundary is irregular. Mean length 8, breadth 6 ms.; area 30,207 acres. It is watered by the Tunkhannock creek, and by Martin's and Elkwood branches of that stream. The Tunkhannock mtn. crosses the S. boundary. The Wilkesbarre and Great Bend, and the Montrose turnpikes intersect each other in the N. E. angle of the t-ship. There is a p-o. in the t-ship, called Lenox, 150 ms. N. of Harrisburg. Surface, hilly; soil, clay and gravel. Pop. in 1830, 540; taxables, in 1828, 74.

LeRay'sville, p-t., Pike t-ship, Bradford co., 257 ms. N. W. of W. C., and 146 from Harrisburg. There is an academy here, which was incorporated by act of assembly, 14th of Jan. 1830.

Letart spring, S. Middleton t-ship, Cumberland co., a large fountain, which, at its source, gives motion to several mills; the stream from it flows N. by Carlisle into the Conedogwinit creek.

Letterkenny, t-ship, Franklin co. bounded N. E. by Lurgan and Southampton, S. E. by Greene, S. W. by Hamilton and St. Thomas, and N. W. by Metal and Fannet t-ships. Centrally distant from Chambersburg 7 miles; greatest length 12, breadth 10½ miles; area 40,400 acres; surface, level; soil chiefly slate. Pop. in 1830, 1965; taxables 382. It is drained on the W., N. and N. E. by the Conedogwinit creek, which receives on the E. several tributaries, and on the S. by Raccoon r. a branch of Buck cr. The Blue mountain covers the W. part of the t-ship, in which lies Horse valley. On the E. side of the mountain is the post town of Strasburg, 10 miles N. W. of Chambersburg.

Lewisburg, a small village of 10 or 12 dwellings, on the right bank of the Allegheny river, about 18 miles N. W. of Kittanning. There is here a store and tavern, and a large furnace in operation, late of Henry Baldwin, Esq. Lawrenceburg post office is 2 miles above on the river.

Lewisport, Manheim t-ship, Schuylkill co. upon the canal and near the Sunbury turnpike road, between 4

Liberty, post t-ship, Adams co. bounded N. by Hamilton-ban, E. by and 5 miles N. W. of Orwigsburg. It contains about a dozen houses and 2 taverns.

Lewisberry, p-t. of Newberry t-ship, York co. on the road leading from York Haven to Carlisle, 9 miles N. W. of the former, 107 from W. C. and 10 from Harrisburg.

Lewistown, p-t. borough and st. jus. of Mifflin co. on the N. side of the Juniata river, and Kishcoquillas creek, 55 miles N. W. of Harrisburg and 162 from Phila., and 154 miles E. from Pittsburg; lat. 40° 37′ N.; long. 0° 34′ W. from W. C. The state canal runs through this town, and its citizens appropriately celebrated the opening of the navigation upon it on the 5th Nov. 1829. The town increases rapidly, and has made great advances, since the adoption by the state of its great system of canal navigation. The turnpike road from Duncans island to Huntingdon, runs W. through it, and the turnpike to Bellefonte, in Centre co. proceeds N. from it. A copious mineral spring rises on the farm of J. Milliken, Esq., adjoining the town.

The town consists of 3 streets, crossed by 4 or 5 others at right angles, and has about 300 dwellings, many of them of brick. The court house and public offices, large and commodious of brick, stand in an open square near the centre of the town. There are here 3 churches, several schools, and an academy.

Lewisburg, p-t. Buffalo t-ship, Union co. on the S. side of Buffalo cr. at its confluence with the W. branch of the Susquehannah river, 8 miles N. E. of New Berlin, 172 from Washington, and 63 from Harrisburg, and 7 miles above Northumberland. The progress of this town was long impeded by a litigated title to its lots, but that having been settled, it now advances rapidly. It contains about 200 dwellings, many of which are brick, a grist, and saw mill, 2 churches, 2 or 3 school houses, 3 large commodious store houses on the river bank, 12 stores, and 2 extensive tanneries. This is the customary market for the products of Brush, Penn, and Buffalo valleys. The bridge across the river here is a permanent and beautiful structure, and leads directly from the end of main street to the Northumberland shore. It was finished in 1818, is 1120 feet long, 30 feet wide, and cost $60,000, of which the state subscribed $20,000. The cross cut or water communication from the town to the W. branch canal, is effected by means of a dam in the river not exceeding two and a half feet, a canal half a mile long, and a lock connecting it with the main canal. A turnpike road commences at the Lewisburg bridge, and leading through Mifflinsburg and Hartleyton, intersects the Bellefonte and Lewisburg turnpike.

Lexington, p-t. and small village of Hatfield t-ship, Montgomery co. on the line between that co and Bucks, 24 miles from Phila. and 14 from Norristown, contains 8 or 10 dwellings &c.

Lexington, p-t. Erie co. in the N. E. angle of Conneaut t-ship, about a mile from Conneaut creek, 326 from W. C. and 265 from Harrisburg.

Lexington, village of Milford t-ship, Somerset co. 15 miles W. of Somerset, contains 10 or 12 houses, store and tavern.

Liberty, t-ship, Columbia co. bounded N. by Limestone t-ship, E. by Mahoning, S. & W. by Northumberland co. Centrally distant from Danville about 7 miles; greatest length 8, breadth 4½ miles; area 18,560 acres; surface, chiefly level; soil, clay. Pop. in 1830, 1111; taxables, 230. Mahanoy ridge runs from the middle of the t-ship through the N. E. angle, and Mouture's ridge along the S. boundary. Chilisquaque creek and one of its tributaries drain it on the W. and a branch of the Mahoning creek, on the E. Moorsburg the p-t. lies near the S. point of the Mahanoy ridge, about 7 ms. by the road N. W. of Danville.

Cumberland t-ship, S. by the state of Maryland, and W. by Franklin co. Centrally distant from Gettysburg, 8 ms.; length 11, breadth 6 ms. area 19, 840 acres; surface, level; soil, clay. Pop. in 1830, 1097; taxables, 226. It is drained on the N. & W. by Marsh cr. & on the S. by Middle and Tom's cr. The turnpike road from Waynesburg to Emmetsburg passes thro' the S. W. part of the t-ship, winding round Jack's mountain.

Liberty valley, Toboyne t-ship, Perry co. between the Tuscarora mountains and Conecocheague hill.

Liberty, East, p-t. Pitt t-ship, Allegheny co. on the turnpike leading to Pittsburg, about 6 miles east of that city.

Liberty Pole, p-o. of Northumberland co. 172 miles N. of W. C., and 62 from Harrisburg.

Liberty, t-ship, Tioga co. formerly, we believe, a part of Delmar t-ship, surface, hilly; soil, gravel and clay. Pop. in 1830, 974; taxables in 1828, 165. The p-o. of the t-ship, called by the same name, is distant from W. C. 225 miles, and from Harrisburg 116.

Licking creek, Bedford co. rises in Dublin t-ship, and flows S. and S. E. along Scrub ridge into the state of Maryland, and thence into the Potomac river, receiving from the mountains several considerable streams.

Licking creek, Little, Montgomery t-ship, Franklin co. a tributary of the W. branch of Conecocheague creek.

Licking creek, p-t. Belfast t-ship, Bedford co. on the turnpike road from McConnellstown to Bedford, & upon Licking creek about 6 miles W. from McConnellstown, 99 from W. C., and 76 from Harrisburg, contains 6 dwellings, 1 store, 2 taverns and a mill.

Ligonier, t-ship, Westmoreland co. bounded N. E. by Fairfield t-ship, S. E. by the Laurel Hill, S. W. by Donegal t-ship, and N. W. by Chestnut ridge. Centrally distant S. E. of Greensburg 17 miles; greatest length 10½, breadth 8 miles; area, 51,200 acres; surface, valley; soil, limestone and loam. Pop. in 1830, 1916; taxables 372. It is drained N. by Loyalhanna creek, which receives from the t-ship on the W. 4 Mile run, 2 Mile run, and from the E. Mill creek and some smaller streams. There is coal and several iron works in the t-ship. The turnpike road from Somerset to Greensburg runs N. W. through the ship, and on it are the post-towns of Laughlin and Ligonier; the latter 18, and the former 21 miles from Greensburg.

Ligonier, post-town of the preceding t-ship, 174 miles N. W. of W. C. and 151 from Harrisburg, contains about 30 dwellings, a Presbyterian and a Methodist church, 4 taverns and 3 stores.

Limerick, t-ship, Montgomery co. bounded N. E. by Frederick, S. E. by Perkiomen and Upper Providence, S. W. by the river Schuylkill, W. by Pottsgrove, and N. W. by New Hanover. Greatest length 8 ms. breadth 5 miles; area, 22,400 acres. The Perkiomen and Reading turnpike road, passes centrally through the t-ship. Pop. chiefly German, in 1830, 1743; taxables, in 1828, 267. The post-office, called after the t-ship, is distant from W. C. 150 miles, and from Harrisburg 91 miles.

Limestone, unorganized t-ship, Warren county, bounded N. and E. by Teonista, S. by Venango co. and W. by the Allegheny river. Centrally distant S. W. from Warren borough 11 miles. The surface is rolling except near the river where it is hilly. The river bottoms are rich and easily cultivated. The inhabitants are yet few. Pop. in 1830, 267; taxables, 55.

Limestone, post-office, Armstrong county, 241 miles N. W. from W. C. and 182 from Harrisburg.

Limestone run, a small tributary of the Susquehannah which rises in Columbia county, and flows W. into the Susquehannah, through the borough of Milton. It has a course of about 9 miles.

Limestone, t-ship, Columbia county,

bounded N. E. by Derry t-ship, S. by Liberty t-ship, and W. by Northumberland co. Centrally distant from Danville N. W. about 10 miles; greatest length 10, width 6 miles; area, 18,560 acres; surface, level; soil, limestone. Pop. in 1830, 540; taxables, 100. Limestone ridge penetrates the t-ship, through the S. W. angle, and runs nearly across it. Chilisquaque creek, flows through the t-ship, on the S. W. and Limestone run issues from it on the W.

Limestone ridge, a chain of mountains of Perry co. rising on the E. border of Toboyne t-ship, and extending 20 miles N. E. to the Juniata river. It forms the boundary between Saville and Tyrone t-ships.

Limestone ridge, Mifflin county, rises in Wayne t-ship, and runs N. E. through Derry and Decatur t-ships, to the confines of Union county, having a length of about 32 miles.

Linn, t-ship, Lehigh county, bounded N. by Northampton county, E. by Heidelberg t-ship, S. by Weissenberg, S. W. by Berks county, and N. W. by Schuylkill county. Its greatest length is 8 miles, greatest breadth 8, wedge shaped. It is drained by Maiden creek, which rises here and flows into the Schuylkill, through Berks co. and by Linn run, which seeks the Lehigh. Their sources almost mingle. The Blue mountain crosses the N. part of the t-ship, and below the mountain the country is rolling, and its soil gravelly. Jacksonville and Linnville are post-offices; the one in the S. the other in the N. of the t-ship, distant each about 17 miles from Northampton. New Tripoli, about 15 ms. N. W. from Northampton, is a village of this t-ship. A church is located in a fork of Maiden creek, and another on the S. W. boundary, but in Berks county. Pop. in 1830, 1747; taxables in 1828, 363; value of taxable property in 1829, real estate $430,377; personal, $18,745; rate of assessment 13 cts. in the $100. There are in the t-ship 5 grist mills, 1 saw and 1 fulling mill, 5 stores, 4 taverns, 3 Lutheran and German Reformed churches, and 5 schools.

Linnville, post-town, Linn t-ship, Lehigh county, about 17 miles N. W. of Allentown.

Linn run, a tributary of the Jordan creek which rises in Linn t-ship, near its S. W. boundary, and flows N. E. to the main stream in Lowhill t-ship.

Lionville, post-office, Chester co. 126 miles from W. C. and 72 from Harrisburg.

Linglestown, post-town, Lower Paxton t-ship, Dauphin county, a small village S. of the Blue mountain, 7 miles from Harrisburg, delightfully situated on a high healthy site, on the road leading from Jonestown, in Lebanon county, to the Susquehannah, contains 20 dwellings, a Lutheran church, 2 stores and a tavern.

Line mountain, Northumberland co. a remarkable straight range of hills which extend from the Susquehannah river, about 17 miles, to the E. boundary of the county. Mahanoy creek runs on the N. side and passes through the mountain, and receives the Schwaber creek from its S. side.

Line Lexington, post-town, on the line dividing Bucks from Montgomery county, and partly in Hilltown and New Britain t-ships of the former, and Hatfield t-ship of the latter. The village contains some 10 or 12 houses, is distant about 7 miles N. W. of Doylestown, 168 from W. C. and 96 from Harrisburg.

Line mills, post-office, Crawford co. 311 miles N. W. from W. C. and 250 from Harrisburg.

Lisbon, village of Cumberland t-ship, Greene county, situated on Muddy creek, about 3 miles W. of the Monongahela river, and 12 miles E. of Waynesburg.

Lisburn, post-town, Cumberland co. Allen t-ship, on the Yellow Breeches creek, 14 miles S. E. of Carlisle, 110 miles from W. C. and 13 from Harrisburg.

Litchfield, t-ship, Bradford county, bounded N. by the state of New York,

E. by the t-ship of Windham, S. by Orwel and Wysox t-ships, and W. by Athens. It is drained by some branches of the Wepassening creek. Pop. in 1830, 487. Surface, hilly; soil, gravelly loam. There is a post-office here bearing the name of the t-ship.

Little mountain, Columbia co. rises on the S. W. boundary of Catawissa t-ship, and runs in a semicircular form through that t-ship into Mifflin t-ship, being in length about 14 miles.

Litiz or Leditz, post-town and settlement of the Moravian brethren, in Warwick t-ship, Lancaster county, 8 miles due N. of Lancaster, 117 from W. C. and 43 from Harrisburg, founded in 1757, and now contains more than 70 dwellings, a very handsome church with steeple and bell, several stores and taverns. It possesses that quietness and neatness which characterise the sect by which it is inhabited. A boarding school has long been established here for young ladies, second in reputation only to that of Bethlehem.

Liverpool, post-town of East Manchester t-ship, on the York and Conewago turnpike road, 7 miles N. of the borough of York, and 4 miles S. of York Haven.

Liverpool, t-ship, Perry co. bounded N. by Turkey ridge, which separates it from Mifflin co., E. by the river Susquehannah, S. by Buffalo t-ship, and W. by Greenwood. Centrally distant from Bloomfield 15 miles; greatest length 6½, breadth 5 miles; area, 17,040 acres; surface, hilly, valleys; soil, gravel and slate on the hills, limestone in the valleys. Pop. in 1830, 1104; taxables, 252. The t-ship is drained by several small streams which rise in the hills, on the N. and W. and flow into the river, entering at the town of Liverpool, on the W. bank, where there are extensive iron works. The town has a post-office, and is about 16 miles N. E. of Bloomfield, and about 30 above Harrisburg, 139 miles N. W. from W. C. The town contains about 80 dwellings, 3 or 4 stores, and 3 taverns.

Ploutz and Wild Cat valley, extend across the t-ship to the river.

Livermore, post-office of Westmoreland county, 196 miles N W. of W. C. and 168 S. W. from Harrisburg.

Lizard creek, Northampton county, rises at the foot of the Blue mountain, on the N. side, and following along its base eastwardly, falls into the Lehigh river about a mile above the Water gap. The creek gives name to a cultivated valley through which it flows. It is too rapid and shallow for navigation of any kind. By act of assembly of 1st April, 1831, a bridge is authorized to be erected over the river Lehigh above the mouth of this creek.

Lizard Creek valley, E. Penn t-ship, Northampton co. (*See preceding article.*)

Loag, post-office, Chester co. 136 miles N. from W. C. and 36 S. E. from Harrisburg.

Lock mountain, on the E. boundary of Frankstown t-ship, Huntingdon co. receives its name from its resemblance to the bolt of a lock. It extends N. E. about 14 miles, touching at either extremity the Frankstown branch of the Juniata river.

Lockport, village on the Conemaugh river, and on the Pennsylvania canal, taking its name from the locks near which it is located; distant about 24 miles N. E. from Greensburg, and 2 or 3 miles above the town of Bolivar, contains 15 or 20 dwellings, 2 taverns and 1 store.

Locust mountain, or *Mine hill*, Schuylkill co. lies between the Tuscarora and the Broad mountain. It abounds in coal, and is penetrated in various places by the lateral branches of the Schuylkill valley rail road.

Locust creek, rises in the Broad mountain and flows through a valley, to which it gives name, eastwardly into the Little Schuylkill river. It is a rapid stream, on which there are several mills, but is not navigable.

Locust valley, Schuylkill co. is a depression of the Broad mountain, thro' which flows Locust creek and Newfield creek, tributaries to the Little Schuylkill river.

Logan, t-ship, Centre co. bounded N. and E. by Lycoming co. S. E., S. and S. W. by Miles t-ship, and N. W. by Lamar t-ship. Centrally distant from Bellefonte N. E. 20 miles; greatest length 16 miles, breadth 6 miles; area 36,480 acres; surface, mountainous; soil of the valleys, limestone. There are three ridges in the t-ship, called Nittany. Between the easternmost ones, lies Sugar valley, drained by Big Fishing creek, which after running S. W. through the valley, for about 12 miles, is lost in the fissures of limestone rock. Logan post office is 199 miles from W. C. and 92 from Harrisburg.

Loganville, p-o. York co. 79 miles from W. C. and 31 from Harrisburg.

Logtown, a small hamlet, Aston t-ship, Delaware co. in the N. W. angle of the t-ship, 8 ms. N. W. of Chester borough, containing 3 or 4 dwellings.

London Britain, the extreme S. E. t-ship of Chester co. bounded N. & W. by New London t-ship, S. by the states of Maryland and Delaware, and E. by the latter state, and by New Garden t-ship, Chester co. Central distance from Phila. S. W. 35 miles; length 3¼, breadth 2½ miles; area 4800 acres; surface, gentle declivity; soil, sandy loam. Pop. in 1830, 518; taxables in 1828, 110. White Clay creek passes through, and turns some mills in the t-ship.

London Grove, t-ship, Chester co. bounded N. by West Marlborough, and E. by East Marlborough and New Garden, S. by New London t-ship, and W. by Penn. and Londonderry t-ships. Central distance from Phila. about 34 miles S. W.; length 6 miles, breadth 4; area, 12,433 acres; surface, rolling; soil, limestone and loam. Pop. in 1830, 1150; taxables in 1828, 132. It is drained by White Clay creek, and its central and eastern branches. The Wilmington and Lancaster turnpike road, crosses it diagonally, on which lies Chatham, a p-t. N. of the centre of the t-ship. Another post office is established in the N. W. angle of the t-ship, on the same road, called London Grove post office, distant 97 miles N. from W. C., and 68 from Harrisburg.

Londonderry, t-ship, Chester co. bounded N. by Lower Fallowfield, S. by Penn., E. by West Marlborough and London Grove, and W. by Upper Oxford t-ships. Central distance from Phila. S. W. 35 miles, and from West Chester 14 miles; length 5 miles, breadth 3½ miles; area, 7200 acres; surface, level; soil, sandy loam. Pop. in 1830, 605; taxables 132. It is drained by Doe run, a tributary of the W. branch of the Brandywine, and by the sources of Elk and White Clay creeks. The Wilmington and Lancaster turnpike road crosses it diagonally. There are two churches in the t-ship.

London, New, t-ship, Chester co. bounded N. by Penn. and London Grove t-ships, E. by New Garden and London Britain, S. by the state of Maryland, and W. by East Nottingham t-ships. Central distance from Phila. 36 miles S. W., and from West Chester 18 miles; length 6¼, breadth 5¼ miles; area 13,860 acres; surface, gentle declivity; soil, sandy loam. Pop. in 1830, 1591; taxables 279. Elk creek bounds it on the west, and White Clay creek flows E. through it. There are two churches and one forge in the t-ship, and the post town and village of New London cross roads lies in the N. W. angle.

Londonderry, t-ship, Lebanon co. bounded N. by East Hanover, N. E. by Annville, E. by Lebanon t-ships, S. by Lancaster co., and W. by Dauphin co. Centrally distant S. W. from the borough of Lebanon 8 miles; greatest length 10, breadth 6 miles; area 25,600 acres. The N. and S. parts of the t-ship, are somewhat hilly, the middle level; soil, partly limestone, partly gravel. Pop. in 1830, 1874; taxables 298. The Swatara creek runs on the N. boundary, & receives the Quitapahilla. From the S. E. Klingers run, a tributary of the latter, flows northwardly into it. The Conewago creek flows westwardly through the t-ship, N. of the Conewago hills, on which is Colebrook furnace. The Downingstown, Ephrata and Harrisburg turnpike, and the Reading and Harrisburg turnpike cross it. On the first is the post village of Cambellstown, & and on the second the p. v. of Palmyra.

Londonderry, t-ship, Dauphin co. bounded N. by Hanover t-ship, E. by Lebanon co., S. by Lancaster co. and W. by Derry t-ship. Centrally distant from Harrisburg 14 miles; greatest length 9, breadth 3½ miles; area, 15,500 acres; surface, somewhat hilly; soil, limestone and gravel. Pop. in 1830, 1822; taxables, 323. The Swatara courses the N. boundary and receives from the t-ship Spring cr. on which there are several mills & a forge & a branch of the Conewago cr. drains it on the S. The Harrisburg and Ephrata turnpike, and the Harrisburg and Reading turnpike roads cross it from E. to W. There is a Lutheran church, pretty centrally situated near the E. boundary line.

Londonderry, t-ship, Bedford co. bounded N. by Napier t-ship, E. by Cumberland valley, S. by the state of Maryland and W. by Somerset co. Centrally distant from Bedford bor. S. W. 16 miles; greatest length 16½, breadth 7½ miles; area, 43,520 acres; surface, mountainous; soil, slate. Pop. in 1830, 726; taxables, 135. Will's mountain lies on the E., and Little Allegheny mountain on the W. The intervening valley is drained by Will's creek, the N. branch of which rises at its N. end and flows S. to the main creek, which runs to the Potomac, in the state of Maryland, at the town of Cumberland. Milliken's cove, formed by Buffalo ridge and Will's mountain, is partly in this t-ship, and partly in Napier.

London, New, cross roads, p-t. Chester co. New London t-ship, at the intersection of the roads from Newport and Kennet's square, 37 miles S. W. from Phila. 18 from West Chester, 93 from W. C. and 68 from Harrisburg, contains 9 or 10 dwellings, an academy, a Presbyterian church, 2 stores, 2 taverns, &c.

Long Pond creek, Tobyhanna t-ship, Northampton co. a tributary of the Tobyhanna creek. It takes its name from the small lake or pond in which it has its source.

Long run, Manheim t-ship, Schuylkill co. a tributary of the Schuylkill r. which flows into it on the W. side, opposite to the t. of Schuylkill Haven.

Longswamp, post t-ship, Berks co. bounded N. E. by Lehigh co., S. E. by Hereford t-ship, S. by District, S. W. by Rockland, and N. W. by Maxatawny t-ships. Extreme length 5, breadth 4½ ms.; area, 13,500 acres; surface hilly; soil, limestone and gravel, pretty well cultivated. Pop. in 1810, 998; in 1820, 1371; in 1830, 1702. Taxables in 1828, 297. The p-o. having the name of the t-ship, is 162 ms. from W. C. and 71 from Harrisburg. The t-ship is watered principally by the sources of the Little Lehigh r. and by a creek which rises in the t-ship, and flowing about 4 ms. is lost in a limestone fissure. Mertztown is situated near its northern corner, and contains about a dozen houses, 1 tavern and store, and a church common to the Presbyterians and Lutherans. Trexler's furnace is near the southern boundary.

Long Pine creek and valley, Lower Mahantango t-ship, Schuylkill county, runs westerly between the ridges of Mahantango and the Broad mtns. It rises in Barry t-ship, and by a devious course of about 20 ms. unites with the Mahantango cr. at Klingerstown, and at the point of junction of Northumberland, Dauphin and Schuylkill cos.

Long mountain, Mifflin t-ship, Columbia co. rises near the W. border of the t-ship, and extends N. E. into Luzerne co. to Nescopeck cr. Length about 10 ms.

Loon lake, a small sheet of water on the line dividing Nescopeck and Newport t-ships, Luzerne co. which sends forth a tributary to Little Wapwallopen cr.

Lorretta, p-t. of Allegheny t-ship,

Cambria co. on the Allegheny mtn. about 6 ms. N. E. of Ebensburg, and 3 N. of Munster, 184 N. W. from W. C. and 137 from Harrisburg, contains 15 dwellings, 1 store, 1 tavern, and about 80 inhabitants.

Lost creek, Fermanagh t-ship, Mifflin co. rises in the t-ship by several branches, and flows into the Juniata r. about 2 ms. above the t. of Mifflin.

Lottsville, p-t. of Warren co. Sugar Grove t-ship, on the right bank of the Little Broken Straw creek, 18 ms. N. W. of Warren borough, 332 from W. C. and 259 from Harrisburg, contains several dwellings, some mills, a store and tavern. It is named after the founder, Hewit Lott.

Lowhill, t-ship, Lehigh co. bounded N. by Heidelberg, E. by North Whitehall, S. by Macungy, W. by Weissenberg t-ships. Greatest length 4½ miles, greatest breadth 3; area, 7040 acres. It shape is that of an obtuse wedge. It is watered by Linn, Willow, and Crowner's runs, and by the Jordan creek, into which they empty. A Lutheran church is situated in the S. W. angle, near the t-ship line. The centre of the t-ship is about 10 miles from Allen, N. of W.; surface hilly; soil, white gravel. Pop. in 1830, 808, taxables in 1828, 143; value of taxable property in 1829, real est. $135,132; personal est. $7,350; rate of levy 13 cts. on the $100. There is a p-o. called after the t-ship, distant N. E. from W. C. 182 ms. and 82 from Harrisburg. The t-ship contains 5 grist mills, 3 saw mills, 2 oil mills, 2 clover mills, 3 stores, 5 taverns and 3 schools.

Lowrytown, Northampton co. Lausanne t-ship, at the head of the improved descending navigation of the Lehigh, 15 ms. above Mauch Chunk, in the centre of immense forests of pine timber. Here the Lehigh coal and navigation company have 4 saw mills, a grist mill, a store, and a number of houses for the accommodation of persons engaged in getting lumber for their coal boats and other works. It generally contained about 250 inhabitants; in 1831 the number was reduced to about 180, and the lumber business of the company having been diminished by the change in the mode of transportation of their coal, the improvement at this place will probably be in a great measure abandoned. A road has been opened through this place from the Berwick and Lehigh turnpike to Wilkesbarre, by which the distance from Mauch Chunk to Wilkesbarre is reduced to 32 ms.

Loyalsock, t-ship, Lycoming county, bounded N. by Hepburn t-ship, E. by Fairfield t-ship, S. by the W. branch of the Susquehannah r. and W. by Lycoming creek, which separates it from Lycoming township. Greatest length 6, breadth from 2 to 4 miles; area, about 12,000 acres; surface, mountainous; soil, various. Pop. in 1830, about 600; taxables, 108; valuation of taxable property in 1829, seated lands, &c. $46,193; personal est. $5059; rate of levy, 75 cents in the 100 dollars. Besides the streams above mentioned, the t-ship has Loyalsock creek on the E. boundary, and some small runs which flow to the rivers. Williamsport, the co. town, lies on the r.

Loyalsock creek, Lycoming co. rises on the S. border of Bradford, and W. of Luzerne co. heading with the Towanda and Mahoopeny creeks, and flows S. W. between Muncy and Lycoming t-ships into the W. branch of the Susquehannah, about 4 ms. below Williamsport, having a comparative course of about 35 miles.

Louisburg, a small village of Schuylkill t-ship, Schuylkill co. on the road from McKeansburg to Catawissa, about 8 ms. N. W. of Orwigsburg. It contains 6 or 8 dwellings, a store and a tavern.

Loyalhanna river, Westmoreland co. rises on the W. side of Laurel hill, and flows N. W. through Ligonier t-ship, and thence, forming the boundary between Derry, Unity and Salem t-ships, into the Conemaugh r. about a mile below the town of Saltzburg, having a comparative course of 30 ms. It is a considerable stream, and from its junction with the Conemaugh the latter assumes the name of Kiskiminitas.

Louden, p-t. Peters t-ship, Franklin co. on the road from Chambersburg to McConnelstown, 12 miles from the former and 5 from the latter, and on the W. branch of the Conecocheague creek, near the foot of Cove mtn. 102 ms. N. W. from W. C. and 63 S. W. from Harrisburg, contains about 60 dwellings, 1 church, 3 stores, 5 taverns and a furnace. It lies in a rich limestone valley, bounded by mountains from 1000 to 1200 feet high. We believe it is on the site of old fort Louden.

Lurgan, t-ship, Franklin co. bounded N. E. by Perry and Cumberland counties, S. E. by Southampton t-ship, S. W. by Letterkenny and N. W. by Fannet t-ships. Centrally distant N. from Chambersburg, 13 miles. Greatest length 9, breadth $7\frac{1}{4}$ miles; area, 19,200 acres; surface, level valley; soil, chiefly slate. Pop. in 1830, 1252; taxables, 224. The N. and S. branch of the Conedogwinit creek unite in the N. mountain, and flow through McAllister gap, along the S. W. and S. E. lines of the t-ship, receiving a tributary from the same mountain, which runs along the N. E. boundary, giving to the t-ship an irregular diamond shape, and making it almost an island. In the S. W. angle and at the E. foot of the mountain, lies the post-town of Roxbury. Bituminous coal is found in the mountain.

Luthersburg, post-town, Clearfield county, 212 miles N. W. of W. C. and 146 from Harrisburg.

Lumberville, a post-town on the river Delaware, in Solebury t-ship, Bucks county, near the northern line, and below Bull's island, about 33 ms. N. E. from Philadelphia, and 8 from Doylestown, 175 miles N. of Washington, and 124 E. from Harrisburg, contains 12 or 14 houses, a tavern, 2 stores, and a grist mill. It is a considerable market for lumber.

Luzerne county, was taken from Northumberland, by act 25th Sept. 1786, and was thus named in compliment to the Chevalier de la Luzerne, then French minister near the United States, and is bounded N. by Susquehannah and part of Bradford counties, E. by Wayne and Pike counties, S. E. by Northampton, and S. by Schuylkill counties, and W. by Columbia, Lycoming, and Bradford counties. Its greatest length N. and S. is 52, and breadth E. and W. 42 miles; area, 1430 sq. ms. or 917,200 acres. Central lat. 41° 15′ N. Long. 1° E. from W. C.

The county pertains wholly to the great central formation of the state. The soil is so various in its quality, as to be not easily reducible to any general character. The valleys are commonly rich arable land, yet differing much in their fertility, and the mountains invariably sterile, and unsusceptible of cultivation. The surface is very mountainous, and the ridges run parallel to each other, from S. W. to N. E. like all the Atlantic chains of the continent. The intervening valleys, which vary much in width, are finely improved.

The principal mountains are the Wyoming, on each side of the Susquehannah river, forming the valley of Wyoming; that on the E. is called Bullocks, that on the W. Shawney range; the first is 1000 feet, and the second 850 feet high, and the distance between their summits, by the road opposite to Wilkesbarre is six, and by an air line $5\frac{1}{2}$ miles. At Wilkesbarre the level plain extends on the W. side about a mile and a quarter from the river, and on the E. a half mile. Here the town is built. The Nescopeck mountain, on the N. side of Nescopeck creek, is parallel to nearly as high as the Wyoming. Its range is regular and unbroken, and its summit nearly destitute of timber. It extends from the Susquehannah to the Lehigh river. The Buck mountain, running parallel to the Nescopeck about 5 ms. S. E. of the latter, is a broken ridge which loses its name at both ends of the Nescopeck valley. Hell Kitchen mountain commences at the head of Nescopeck valley, and extending northeastwardly, terminates near the Lehigh. This is a very high, rocky and barren ridge, having no timber on its top, where fern and small bushes only find support. Down the N. side of this mountain, falls Hell Kitchen creek, a small branch of the Nescopeck. Lackawannock mountain is a continuation of the Shawnese range of Wyoming mountains. This, near the Susquehannah, is very high and steep, but becomes lower as it extends northeasterly. It terminates in Susquehannah county, where it is called the Moosic mountain, and a part of it Mount Ararat. Bowman's mountain, called the Bald mountain, near the western limits of the county, is a high, regular barren range, whose average height may be 800 feet, extending from the E. to the W. branch of the Susquehannah, between which, it appears to have no other name than those mentioned, except, that in a small territory on the head of Fishing creek, the inhabitants call it the North mountain. Westward of the waters of the W. branch of the Susquehannah, it forms the main ridge of the Allegheny mountains. It crosses the E. branch of the Susquehannah, at the mouths of Tunhannock and Bowman's creeks, and extending north eastwardly, is called Tunkhannock mountain, and terminates in Susquehannah co. where it is called the Elk mountain. Mahoopeny mountain is a spur only of Bowman's mountain, and terminates at the mouth of Mahoopeny cr. Sugarloaf mountain is a high conical pyramid rising from the centre of Nescopeck valley. It is not connected with any other mountain, and forms a very singular appearance. Its name is derived from its form, and the mountain has given name to a t-ship. The character of these last mentioned hills is much the same; they are thinly covered with timber, generally steep, and in many places very rocky. The Wyoming, the Lackawannock, and the Buck mountains, produce anthracite coal of an excellent quality. It forms an important article of export from Luzerne county, and was taken down the Susquehannah in arks, and now in boats. This coal was first burnt here in grates, in the year 1808, and is now in very general use. The valleys of Luzerne are, the valley of Wyoming, lying on both sides of the Susquehannah river, about 20 miles long and 5 broad. The Susquehannah enters it as its N. E. extremity, through a precipitous gap in the Shawnese mountain, which appears to have been made by the river itself, and flows in a serpentine course through the plains of Wyoming, leaving the valley by a gap similar to that at which it enters, forming what is called Nanticoke falls. In this valley stand the towns of Wilkesbarre and Kingston, opposite to each other, on different sides of the river. This is the most populous valley in the county. (*See "Wyoming valley."*)

Lackawannock valley extends from the mouth of the Lackawannock cr. up the stream about 30 miles. The soil is of second quality, and the land uneven. It ranks in population next to the valley of Wyoming.

Nescopeck valley lies on both sides of Nescopeck creek, and between Nescopeck and Buck mountains. It is about 20 miles long and 5 wide, and does not extend to the river. In population it is next to the Lackawannock valley, and the soil is somewhat better. Bowman's valley, lying on Bowman's creek, between Bowman's and Mahoopeny mountains, is not very populous, and the land is generally poor. It is about 2 miles wide, and 15 long. The principal population is near the river. Tunkhannock valley is very crooked and irregular, about a mile wide, lessening in some places to half a mile, and about 35 miles long. It is most of it cultivated, and is populous considering its small width. Mahoopenny valley, on Mahoopenny creek, is very narrow, and thinly populated. It extends irregularly about

20 miles from the river. The Susquehannah river and its tributary streams, the chief of which are the Mahoopenny, Tunkhannock, Bowman's, Lackawannock, Wapwallopen, and Nescopeck creeks, water nine tenths of Luzerne county. This river is navigable for boats carrying about 20 tons, at all seasons of the year, when not obstructed by ice, which is generally the case, from about Christmas until the middle of March. The N. E. branch of the Susquehannah is much less obstructed by rocks and shoals, than the main river below Northumberland. The boatmen are getting into the use of sails, and in a number of instances, boats loaded with 20 tons, ascend the Wyoming falls, by the force of wind only. The only rapids in the Susquehannah within the limits of Luzerne, which are considered of sufficient importance to be called falls, are the Wyoming falls, and Nanticoke falls. The former is about a mile and a half above Wilkesbarre, is never considered dangerous, and has at all times sufficient water in the channel for the purpose of boat navigation. The latter is at the gap where the river passes out of the valley, and as the water here runs very swiftly into the side of an eddy, rafts of lumber were sometimes broken by the sudden whirl.

All the streams of Luzerne are rapid, and furnish excellent sites for all kinds of machinery. (See the articles relating to the several t-ships, for a particular description of the streams.)

It is estimated that about one twelfth part of the county is cultivated, and that not more than one third is adapted to cultivation, unless the conversion to sheep pastures be so considered. The rough and rocky mountains would feed large flocks. About one third of the arable land is best suited for grazing, the remainder for grain.

The only minerals which have hitherto been discovered in the county, in sufficient quantities to merit notice, are iron and anthracite coal. Two forges have been erected for the manufacture of iron; one on the Lackawannock, the other on Nanticoke creek.

The chief natural curiosities of the county are the water falls, or cascades, of which Solomon's, Wapwallopen, Buttermilk, Hell Kitchen, and Falling spring, are most notable. (See these titles.) In the valley of Wyoming are the remains of ancient fortifications, which may be called artificial curiosities. Of these, 3 are said to be discernible; one, situated in Kingston t-ship, on the W. bank of Toby's creek, upon the flat, about half a mile from the river, is of an oval form, having its longest diameter from the N. E. to the S. W. measuring 272 feet, and from the S. E. to the N. W. measuring 237 feet. There appeared to have been a gateway at the S. W. (*See "Wyoming valley."*)

The timber has long been cut away, and the ground cultivated, but the trees lately felled from the rampart or parapet, were as large as any of the adjoining forest, and one large oak in particular, counted 700 years. There were also old logs found upon these mounds, indicating, that a growth of timber had preceded that which was then standing. The Indians have no tradition concerning the origin of these fortifications, and their history is altogether conjectural. The population of Luzerne consists of a mixed people, from various countries. Northward from Wilkesbarre, the inhabitants are principally from the eastern states, and the descendants of New England men. Southward of that town they are chiefly Germans and the descendants of Germans, with a mixture of Irish and Scotch descendants. It is, however, not common to find amongst them any who cannot speak the English language. In 1790, the number of inhabitants was 4904; in 1800, 12,839; in 1810, 18,109; in 1820, 20,027; and in 1830, 27,304.

No portion of the state recalls more interesting historical recollections, than Luzerne county. Its beautiful and rich valleys have been the favorite resort of the aborigines, for which they have contended among themselves, and with the white man. It was early and duly appreciated by the Connecticut settlers, who moistened the soil with their blood in maintenance of their possessions, though founded on a mistaken title. It has been the seat of the only civil war, which stains the annals of our colonial history, and has displayed as much heroism as any portion of the commonwealth, and suffered more than any other, in support of the revolution. Such brief notices of these subjects as the nature of our work permits, will be found in the introductory chapter, and under the title "*Wyoming valley.*"

The principal towns are Wilkesbarre, Kingston, Tunkhannock, Pittston, Carbondale and Conyngham, &c. for a particular description of which, see these titles

Beside the country roads, which the conveniences of vicinages have required, there are several important turnpike roads through the county. The Berwick and Lausanne road crosses the S. W.. angle. The Wilkesbarre and Northampton penetrates on the S. E. and the Great Bend and the Montrose roads run northerly through it.

The Milford and Owego road crosses the N. E. angle through Blakely and Greenfield t-ships ; affording the shortest and most expeditious stage route from the city of New York to the western part of that state. The Wilkesbarre and Clifford road is completed from the Coshocton and Great Bend turnpike, in Susquehannah co., to Blakely, upon the Lackawannock ; from which there is a good road to Wilkesbarre. This road runs thro' Dundaff, in Susquehannah, and Greenfield and Blakely, in Luzerne counties. A tri-weekly stage is established upon it. The Luzerne and Wayne turnpike passes through Providence and Blakely t-ships, intersecting the Phila. and Great Bend, the Easton and Belmont, and the Milford and Owego turnpikes. The Carbondale road, formed by the Delaware and Hudson company, extends from Carbondale to the last mentioned road, at Rix's gap. The Abington and Waterford road commences in Abington t-ship, and runs through Nicholson and Tunkhannock t-ships. The Wilkesbarre and Bridgewater road traverses Kingston, Exeter, North Moreland, Eaton and Tunkhannock t-ships. On this road a tri-weekly stage runs from Phila. to Buffalo, and a daily stage from W. C. to Sackett's Harbor. Travellers for health or pleasure could not select a more favorable route for a summer's excursion, and, though delighted with the wildly romantic and picturesque prospects which every where present themselves, they would not fail to linger in the yet more delightful valley of Wyoming, viewing its natural beauties and surveying its mineral treasures. The Berwick and Newport road passes through Huntington t-ship ; upon this and on the Berwick and Easton road, tri-weekly stages are also established.

Legislative acts have been passed for the incorporation of other companies to make artificial roads in the county ; the most important of which are, from Wilkesbarre through Solomon's gap, to Lowrytown, on the Lehigh, a distance of little more than 20 miles ; and from Carbondale down the Lackawannock, about 10 miles ; and from Carbondale to Tunkhannock bridge. Like authority has also been given for excavating a canal, from the Susquehannah river, at the mouth of the Nescopeck, up the valley of that stream, thence across the summit of the mountain, down Wright's creek to the Lehigh, a distance of 37 ms. The distance by this route and the North Branch canal, from Wilkesbarre to the mouth of Wright's creek, is about 65 miles ; and also for the incorporation of a company to make a canal or rail-road from the Water gap of the Delaware to the mouth of the Lackawannock creek, at the head of the Wyoming valley. The distance is about 50 ms. It is proposed by this chain of communication to connect the Delaware and North branch divisions of the Pennsylvania canal, and the line between the Hudson and Susquehannah, by means of the Orange and Sussex canal. The design of these projects is to penetrate the Wyoming coal region; but it can scarce be expected that they will be completed whilst a full supply of anthracite can be obtained from sources nearer to market and yielding it at a cheaper rate. Authority has also been given for improving the communication by Lackawannock valley, either by damming the Lackawannock river, by making a canal, or by a rail-road; thus to open a way for the Lackawannock coal, to market by the Susquehannah, and to give the mines in the S. W. part of the valley the advantage of the improvements of the Hudson and Delaware navigation and coal company. The distance from Carbondale to the Susquehannah at the mouth of the Lackawannock is about 23 ms. An act of assembly has authorized the incorporation of a company to make a rail-road from the Carbondale mines to the mouth of the Chenango river on the Susquehannah.

The improvement for transportation of coal, &c. of the Hudson and Delaware company, is by canal from the Hudson to the Delaware near Carpenter's point; thence up the eastern bank of the Delaware, to the mouth of the Lackawaxen, where it passes the Delaware by a pool, formed by a dam in the river; thence up the Lackawaxen to Honesdale, at the forks of the Dyberry; where it terminates in an artificial basin, having completed a distance of a little more than 100 miles; thence a rail-road surmounts the Lackawannock mountain to Carbondale, distant 16 miles. Most of the foregoing canal and rail-road improvements have been projected by capitalists of New-York, and their compleion is more to be desired than expected. But no work is so interesting to the county as the state canal, on the north branch of the Susquehannah. This has been successfully made to the Nanticoke falls, where a dam has been erected; but its extension seems necessary, at least 16 miles further, that by reaching the centre of the coal region, at the head of the Wyoming valley, its full benefit may be obtained by the inhabitants for transportation, and by the state in receipt of tolls. The distance from the Nanticoke dam by the river to the state line, is 106 ms. The Chemung canal, from Seneca lake to Newtown, is now in progress. Newtown is within 14 miles of the boundary, and the interval is an alluvial level. When the north branch canal shall be connected with the Seneca lake, the richest and fairest portion of the state of New York will pour its agricultural and mineral products into the lap of Pennsylvania, which the latter will repay with her iron and coal.

Luzerne, with Union, Northumberland, Columbia, Susquehannah, Bradford, Lycoming, Potter and McKean, form the 9th congressional district, sending three members to congress. United with Columbia county, it constitutes the 10th senatorial district, sending one member to the senate; and alone, it sends two members to the house of representatives; connected with Pike and Wayne it makes the 11th judicial district, over which David Scott, Esq. presides. The courts are holden at Wilkesbarre, on the first Mondays of January, April, August, and November.

The public buildings of the county consist of a court house, county offices, and prison, an academy, and a bank, all in Wilkesbarre (the academy has a large class, and enjoys a high reputation), and several, but not many churches throughout the county. Considerable attention is given by the inhabitants to education, and in some of the t-ships provision has been made in lands, to obtain a fund for the use of schools.

The taxable property of the county, by the assessment of 1829, was valued, viz. real estate, exclusive of unseated lands, $1,119,670; unseated lands, valued at $1 the acre, $351,380 ; unseated lands, purchased at treasury sales, for taxes, valued at $189,935, at $1 per acre. Personal estate, $268,632. The rate of levy is now, and has been for years, one half cent in the dollar.

The county paid into the public treasury, in the year 1831, for

Dividend on bridge stock, at Wilkesbarre,	$350 00
Do. on turnpike stock,	312 50
Tax on bank dividends,	73 25
Tax on writs,	423 89
Tavern licenses,	597 31
Duties on dealers in foreign merchandize,	581 63
Tin and clock pedlars' licenses,	137 60
Hawkers' and pedlars' licenses,	38 95
	$2515 13

The county probably exports, annually, 220,000 bushels of wheat, 1300 barrels of pork, 750 barrels of whiskey, and from 5 to 6000 tons of anthracite coal.

STATISTICAL TABLE OF LUZERNE COUNTY.

Townships.	Greatest L'th.	Greatest B'th.	Area in Acres.	Face of the Country.	Soil.	Population. 1820.	Population. 1830.	Taxables.
Abington,	7	7	22,400	part hil. part lev'l	clay, loam,	1012		239
*Braintrim,	11¾	3¾	19,840	mountainous,	gravel, alluvial,	525		116
†Blakely,	15	7¾		do.	do. do.	450		98
Covington,	23	9	105,600	do.	gravel, slate,	372		106
†Dallas,				mount. hilly,	do. do.	455		120
Eaton,	10	6	25,600	hilly,	do. do.	478		110
*Exeter,	10½	4	25,600	do.	slate, alluvion,	820	767	144
Falls,	7	7	35,840	do.	do. do.		739	134
Greenfield,	12	8½	44,800	rolling,	loam,	712	1310	193
*Hanover,	14	7	56,320	diversified,	loam, alluvion,	879	1173	173
*Huntingdon,	12	5	26,880	mtnous, rolling,	do. do.	1274	1572	260
Kingston,	5	4½	14,080	hills & riv. bott'm	grvl. & sl'te, allu.	1288	1548	259
Nicholson,	8	6	33,920	hilly,	gravel, slate,	543	906	186
*Newport,	10	6	36,480	do.	do. do.	764	849	159
Nescopeck,	10	9	29,440	hills & riv. bott'm	do. do. & alluv.	1004	983	194
*Northmoreland,	13	6	33,480	mountainous,	do. do. do.	644	785	144
*Pittstown,	10	9	48,000	mtnous, hills,	gravel, slate,	825	1017	179
*Plymouth,	9	5	23,040	do., river bottom,	do. do. alluv.	912	1798	197
*Providence,	10	6	35,840	mts., valleys,	gravel, alluvion,	861	976	155
*Salem,	7	6	19,200	mountainous,	do. slate,	787	920	158
Sugarloaf,	23	8	85,760	do.	do. do.	1112	1486	287
Union,	19	8	80,000	mtnous, river bot.	slate, alluvion,	686	1075	151
*Wilkesbarre, & b.	14	6	35,200	mtn. valley,	do. do.	1602	2233	355
Windham,	13	11	67,200	mountainous,	slate,	889	1094	182
Tunkhannock,	11	9	51,200	hilly,	do. and alluvion,	1132	1039	183
†Lehman,				do.			231	
†Carbondale, erected since the census ; included in Blakely township,								
						20027	27304	

NOTE.—The return of the marshal for 1830 does not specify any of the townships in this table before Exeter, but he gives the whole population as we have given it. The total may be correct, but the numbers in the omitted townships are wanting to complete it.

The townships marked thus (*) are the "*certified townships* ;" those with this mark (†) having been newly created or altered, we do not give their areas.

Luzerne, t-ship, Fayette co., bounded N. and W. by the Monongahela river, E. by Red Stone t-ship, and S. by German t-ship. Centrally distant 12 ms. N. W. of Uniontown. Length 8, breadth 7 ms ; area, 16,000 acres ; surface level ; soil, limestone. Pop. in 1830, 1625 ; taxables, 314. This t-ship lies in the Great Bend of the Monongahela river. Bridgeport, the p-t. lies at the confluence of Dunlap's creek with the river opposite to Brown'sville, with which it is connected by a wooden bridge over the creek, about midway of the eastern boundary. Iron is found near Bridgeport, and a furnace is erected near the town.

Lycoming county, was erected from part of Northumberland co. by act of 13th April, 1795; and is bounded N. by Potter, Tioga and Bradford cos., E. by Luzerne co., S. by Columbia, Northumberland, Union and Centre cos., S. W. by Clearfield co. and N. W. by McKean county. Central lat. 41° 15′, long. 0° 30′ W. from W. C. Greatest length 92, breadth 25 miles; area, 2290 sq. ms.

This co. lies partly in the great central transition formation, and partly in the great western secondary formation, but chiefly in the latter. The surface is very mountainous, and the chains, preserving the general S. W. and N. E. direction, are more broken and irregular than they are further to the S. The mass of the mtns. is composed of sand stone, generally fine grained and friable when taken from the bed, but hardening when exposed to the air, slaty in structure, and often abounding in scales of mica—a graywacke slate; the mica appears to increase with the depth of the stone from the surface. This sand stone passes into a pudding stone, or conglomerate rock, a coarser grained graywacke, consisting of rounded quartz pebbles, plentifully embedded in argillaceous paste, and has a general resemblance to the pudding stone of the anthracite ranges, though more loosely aggregated and the pebbles of less size.

In the coal measures of this county, (and the whole of it W. of the main ridge of the Allegheny, abounds in coal and also in iron) a dark colored slate is found in the mtns. rarely seen at the surface, unless in some peculiar situation, by reason that its rapid disintegration breaks it down into soil in a very brief space. This slate usually, but not invariably, forms the roof and floor of the coal strata; that of the roof abounds in vegetable impressions, of ferns, reeds, &c. &c. many of which are singularly large and distinct, but difficult to obtain, or secure on account of the soft and earthy character of the rocks. The strata of the mountain is reported to lie commonly, but not uniformly, in the following order; sand stone, indurated clay, clay slate, coal, and pudding stone, presenting a close correspondence with the series composing all known fields of bituminous coal. An argillaceous iron ore, as is usual elsewhere, is here in close association with the coal. All these strata are based on limestone, which is supposed to pass under the mtns. and to underlie the coal formation. This limestone is of a bluish cast and of a compact structure. We have no account of organic remains having been found in it. It is said to creep out in some few places in the range, and is doubtless the "*carboniferous*" or mtn. limestone of the English geologists; the great foundation rock of the British coal measures.

Traversing this co. from E. to W. and N. of the Susquehannah r. we cross on the E. boundary the main ridge of the Allegheny, W. of which are other ridges of the same mtn. with intervening vallies, through which flow Muncy, Loyalsock, Lycoming, Pine, Kettle, and the main stream of the Sinnemahoning creeks. The west branch of the Susquehannah r. enters the S. W. angle of the co. about three miles below Buttermilk falls, and forms for about 15 miles the boundary line between this and Centre co. and receives the above creeks, in an order reversed from that which we have named, and many smaller, yet considerable streams. Of the latter we may mention Cook's and Young Woman's creeks; Licking run, growing into note from its coal mines; Lorry and Queenshohoque creeks, Carpenter's run, &c. The course of the r. here is E. and W. and it explores its way around the base of the mtns. not crossing and breaking down the chains, as is the case especially with the main r. after the junction of the two branches. On the S. of the r. the Muncy and

Nittany hills continue from Centre co. through which the r. turns to the S. and S. W. The Nittany mountain, on the S. border of the co. assumes the name of the White Deer mtn. In the Muncy range is found a very extraordinary limestone valley, called Nippenose, having an oval form; the longer axis being E. and W. about 10 miles, and the shorter N. and S. 5 miles. Several streams have their sources in the mountains around the vale, and two penetrate them from the south; but all seek subterraneous passages, and do not rise again to day in the valley, unless they congregate in Nippenose creek, which flows N. E. from the valley into the river. The chief tributaries to the river from this part of the co. are the Bald Eagle cr. McElhatten's run, Hagerman's run, Black Hole creek, and White Deer Hole creek. E. of the river, and between the Muncy and the Main ridge of the Allegheny, flows the Little Muncy creek, which empties into the r. about 2 ms. N. W. of Muncytown. White pine, hemlock, oak and chestnut is the prevailing timber, the quantity of which seems inexhaustible.

The pop. of the co. is principally seated along the valleys of the r. and principal streams. Leaving them there is scarce a trace of the hand of man to be discerned, unless in the occasional marks of the surveyor, or lair of the hunter. The panther, the wolf and the bear, the rattle snake, the elk and the deer yet hold undisputed possession of the wilds. Along the Susquehannah a string of settlements, some of which are valuable, extends to the head of the r. The coal fields of this co. being perhaps the most accessible portion of the bituminous region, will add much, at no distant day, to the wealth and population of the co. The principal mines yet opened, lie on Lick and Queen's run, and a place called Tanguscootack, about 7 miles S. W. from Lick run, and 5 distant from the river, and on Lycoming and Pine crs. The coal explored, lies in veins from 4 to 6 feet thick, about 450 feet above the base of the mountain: veins are known to exist above this level; and it is supposed, for very satisfactory reasons, that other veins lie beneath it. There are some large ponds or small lakes in the eastern part of the co., of which Elk lake, near the northern boundary, Lewis' and Hunter's lakes, and Beaver Dam pond, are the most considerable.

To reach this coal region, the state canal has been directed along the valley of the river, and is completed to the Muncy dam, and in progress to the mouth of Bald Eagle cr.

The roads of the co. generally follow the streams, but in some instances cross the summits of the hills. The Susquehannah and Tioga turnpike road runs through the N. E. angle of the co., and authority was given by the act of 1 April, 1831, for making an artificial road from the borough of Williamsport, by Spalding's, South, and Troy crs. to the New York state line, and also for a turnpike road, from the borough of Muncy, through Hillsgrove and Eldredville, in Lycoming co. to intersect the Berwick and Newton turnpike road, at or near Towanda cr. in Monroe t-ship, Bradford co., by act of 23d Feb. 1831. A rail-road and navigation company was authorized by act 9th April, 1828, for reaching the coal mines in Jackson t-ship; and we understand a company has been formed for that purpose.

The chief towns of the county are Williamsport, the seat of justice, Muncy bor. formerly called Pennsborough, Newberry, Jersey Shore bor. Dunnstown, &c. &c.

The population of the county consists of Irish and Germans, and the descendants of these races, and of settlers from other counties in Pa. It amounted in 1810, to 11,006, in 1820, to 13,517, and in 1830, to 17,637; taxables in 1828, 3111. The chief religious sects are Presbyterians, Methodists, German Lutherans, Episcopalians, and Quakers; the latter inhabit principally the t-ships of Muncy, Muncy Creek, Hepburn and Fairfield. A county Bible society has been established, and Sunday schools in every neighborhood adapted to such institutions.

The most important manufacture of the co. is that of iron. There is a furnace on Pine cr. belonging to Kirk, Kelton, & Co.; 2 forges on Lycoming cr. owned respectively by Mr. Hepburn and Mr. McKenny; one forge on Lorry cr. pertaining to Messrs. Slonecker and Co. There is a manufacture of woollens on Muncy cr. owned by Mr. Rodgers, and one on Chatham's run, belonging to Mr. Rich. There are about 50 mills of every kind in the co. The exports of the co. are iron, wheat, lumber, bituminous coal, flour, whiskey, and salted provisions. The wheat may amount to 120,000 bushels, whiskey from 10 to 1200 barrels, pork 130 tons, coal 3000 tons. Of the quantity of lumber, we have no means of making an estimate.

The provisions for education are not remarkable. Schools are established in all the towns and densely populated vicinages; and an academy was incorporated at Williamsport, in 1811, to which the state gave the sum of $2000. There are, however, 3 newspapers published weekly in the co., viz: the Lycoming Gazette, Lycoming Chronicle, and the Muncy Telegraph.

Limestone bottom lands of the best quality, sell from 30 to 50 dollars the acre; inferior improved lands at about 14 dollars the acre, and unimproved good lands at from 2 to 4 dollars the acre. The assessed value of taxable property in 1829, was, seated land, $789,148; unseated, $417,057; personal estate, &c. $145,250. The unseated lands are valued at 50 cts. the acre. The rate of levy was $\frac{3}{4}$ of a cent in the dollar.

The public buildings of the co. consist of the court-house, a fine large structure, and county offices, of brick, a large prison of stone, the academy, and about 15 houses for public worship, distributed throughout the co.

The co. paid into the state treasury in 1831, for tax on writs, $283 77; tavern licenses, $502 45; duties on dealers in foreign mdz. $250 49; state maps, $36 75; hawkers' and pedlars' licenses, $15 20; total, $1088 66.

Lycoming, Centre, Clearfield, McKean, and Potter counties, constitute the 13th senatorial district of the state, sending one member to the senate; Lycoming alone sends two members to the house of representatives. Connected with Union and Northumberland, Columbia, Luzerne, Susquehannah, Bradford, Potter and McKean counties, it forms the 9th congressional district, sending three members to congress. United with Columbia, Union, and Northumberland, it makes the 8th judicial district, over which Seth Chapman, Esq. presides. The co. belongs to the middle district of the supreme court, which holds an annual session at Sunbury, on the Wednesday following the second week of the term of the Lancaster district. The session of the Lancaster district commences on the third Monday in May.

STATISTICAL TABLE OF LYCOMING CO.

Townships, &c.	Greatest Lth.	Greatest Bth.	Area in Acres.	Pop. in 1820	Taxables.
Adams,	9	7½	32640		63
Bald Eagle,	7	2	3840	281	69
Brown,	20	20	160000	322	55
Chapman,	30	21	189240	355	51
Cherry,	12	12	73600		80
Clinton,	13	4½	16000		136
Dunstable,	30	15	92800	474	100
Elkland,	21	17	131200	343	92
Fairfield,	7	7	27520		135
Franklin,	18	8	46080		74
Hepburn,	14	14	87680		201
Jersey Shore bo.					102
Jackson t-ship,	14	12	70400		80
Loyalsock,	5	4	12000	1425	108
Lycoming,	8	7	24320	1201	254
Muncy creek,	10	8	17920	1255	179
Mifflin,	17	9	51840	1038	152
Muncy,	12	8	17040	1564	192
Bor. of Muncy,					108
Moreland t-ship,	8	6	21120	1276	110
Nippenose,	9	4	14080	418	66
Pine Creek,	16	5	23680	428	89
Penn,	24	5	42980		88
Shrewsbury,	29	13	64000	379	71
Williamsport bo.				624	153
Washington,	14	10	55200	1743	240
Wayne,	11	8½	39680	382	63
				23,517	3111

The population in 1830 is not classed in t-ships. The whole of the county contained 17,637.

Lycoming, t-ship, Lycoming co.

bounded N. by Tioga co., E. by Elkland and Loyalsock t-ships, S. by the W. branch of the Susquehannah river, and W. by Mifflin and Brown t-ships. Centrally distant N. W. from Williamsport 7 miles; greatest length 8, breadth 7 miles. Area 24,320 acres; surface, mountainous and river bottom; soil, various, limestone in valleys. Pop. in 1830, about 1300; taxables 254; valuation of taxable property in 1829, seated lands &c. 63,287; unseated lands, 9,437; personal tax 10,601. It is drained chiefly by Lycoming creek, which runs upon the E. boundary, upon which lies the post town of Newbury, at the confluence of the creek with the river.

Lycoming creek, Lycoming co. rises in the S. part of Tioga co. heading with the Towanda creek, and flows S. W. by a comparative course of about 35 miles into the W. branch of the Susquehannah river, about 2 miles W. of Williamsport.

Lycoming creek, p-o. Lycoming co. 201 miles N. W. from W. C. and 92 from Harrisburg.

Lyken's, t-ship, Dauphin co. bounded N. by Columbia co., E. by Schuylkill co., S. by Halifax t-ship, and W. by Mifflin t-ship. Centrally distant from Harrisburg 26 ms.; length 10 ms. breadth —; area 31,500 acres; surface, mountainous; soil, red shale. Pop. in 1830, 1636; taxables, 283. The northern, eastern and southern, boundaries are covered with mts. Williams or Lyken's valley lies between Berry's and the Short mountain, through which the Wiconisco creek passes, receiving Little creek from the N. The Mahantango creek forms the northern boundary.

The Short mountain is a continuation of the Broad mountain, and its abrupt termination in Lyken's valley, 11 miles from the Susquehannah, appears to be the western termination of the numerous veins of coal that are distinctly traced from Mauch Chunk, by Pottsville, to the brink of the precipitous descent in which the mountain is lost in Lyken's valley.

The mountain as it extends westward gradually narrows, preserving for many miles an elevation of about 850 feet above the valleys between which it rises. Several veins of coal have been opened upon the S. & N. side, and 1 which has recently been opened in Bear gap, about 800 feet below the summit of the ridge, yields about 5 feet diameter of pure coal, and can be worked about 300 feet perpendicularly to where the coal breaks into day upon the S. side of the mountain promising an unbroken body of that depth and diameter, for many miles in length.

This singular deposit, which is perhaps one of the greatest in the world, and which promises from the peculiarity of situation, a facility of mining not elsewhere met with in our state deserves a particular description.

The mountain at its termination is one solid unbroken mass, about a mile across, widening gradually upon the top into a perfectly level plain about a mile and a half in diameter. All at once this plain sinks in the centre, longitudinally with the mountain, forming a deep swampy valley in its bosom, which extends N. E. 5 or 6 miles, into which numerous springs flow, the accumulated waters of which produce a considerable stream, bursting through the southern side of the mountain, out of what is called Bear gap, or Bear Hole gap, into Williams' valley, cutting its passage down to the base of the mountain.

This is the only pass by which Bear valley can be entered, and in this pass all the coal seams are found, on both sides, showing evidently that the convulsion, or the bursting of the lake, confined in the interior of the mountain, which formed the gap, crossed the line of the seams and severed them in two.

This pass is from fifty to sixty yards wide, the number of veins already explored on the south side of the south division of the mountain are five, varying in breadth, the smallest four feet of pure coal, and are found about fifty yards apart, dipping about 45° N. and run with the mountain range from N. E. to S. W. There are evidences of nine veins on the south side of this mountain, one or two upon the summit, and four upon the north side, all crossing the gap at right angles. One of these veins upon the apex of the ridge, lately examined, measured 14 feet pure coal, and how much more could not be ascertained, as the slate upon one side was not reached. On the northern division of the mountain several veins have been struck, but no mining commenced, except to ascertain the fact that it also contains abundance of coal.

In the first instance the principal mining operations will be carried on in the gap, where the coal is easy of access, and little tunnelling can be required, and where preparations are now making to lay the rail road. The great advantages of this position will be at once perceived, by observing that in the gorge of this gap, 28 veins can be opened, with separate gangs of miners on each vein, working over each others heads from the base to the summit, on both sides of the gap, running out their laden carts as speedily as filled, upon the rail road, and despatching them at once by steam or horse power, without any other handling of the coal, to the Susquehannah at Millsburg. At the same time other bodies of workmen may be employed at suitable intervals, tunnelling into the same veins, as far as the rail road can be conveniently reached, which will be at least for seven or eight miles along the mountain, until it is found expedient to extend the line still farther east.

It is upon this region that the counties of Dauphin, Cumberland, Lancaster, York and Adams, in Pennsylvania, and the cities of Baltimore, Washington, and Alexandria, and the towns upon the Chesapeake, must principally depend for their supplies of fuel; in the first place, because the distance of carriage is nearly one hundred miles shorter than from the Wilkesbarre mines; in the second, the coal is infinitely superior for family use, for cupola furnaces, and smith's forges, to any other anthracite that has yet reached the market; can be afforded at a cheaper rate; and if a company should be formed, with a sufficient capital to prosecute the business on an extensive and economical plan, a supply to any extent, for home consumption or exportation, could be furnished in a very short time.

The surveys for the rail road have been completed, and the work of grading, we understand, commenced in Bear gap, from which it proceeds in a western direction, 5 miles along the base of the mountain, and from its termination, 11 miles, to Millersburg, at the landing on the Susquehannah, in all 16 miles; with a graduated descent of less than 20 feet to the mile.

McClelandstown, German t-ship, Fayette co. centrally situated on the road leading from Uniontown to Waynesburg, about 7 miles W. of the former, 209 N. W. from W. C. and 200 S. W. from Harrisburg, contains between 40 and 50 dwellings, 1 church, 2 schools, 4 stores, and 3 taverns.

McConnellstown, Air t-ship, Bedford co. post-town and borough, on the turnpike road leading from Chambersburg to Bedford, 19 miles W. of the former and 28 E. of the latter, 93 from W. C. and 70 from Harrisburg. A turnpike road leads from the town to Waynesburg, in Franklin county, and thence into Maryland. Pop. in 1830, 491; taxables in 1828, 92. The borough is pleasantly situated in a valley formed by Cove mtn. and Scrub ridge, and through it flows Big Cove creek, a fine mill stream. The town contains more than 100 dwellings, 5 or 6 stores, the same number of taverns, and 2 Presbyterian churches. It was incorporated 26th March, 1814.

McConnellsburg, Porter town-ship, Huntingdon county, upon Vineyard creek, at the foot of Warrior ridge, about 5 miles S. W. of the borough of Huntingdon, contains 15 dwellings, 3 taverns, 1 store, 1 tan-yard.

McDowell's mills, post-office, Clearfield county, 188 mills, N. W. from W. C. and 78 from Harrisburg.

McEwen'sville, post-office, called after Alexander McEwen, the post-master, 180 miles from W. C. and 70 from Harrisburg.

McKean county, was separated from Lycoming, by the act of 26th March, 1804, and is bounded N. by Cattaraugus and Allegheny counties, in the state of N. Y., E. by Potter county, S. E. by Lycoming county, S. W. by Jefferson, and W. by Warren counties. Length 42, breadth 35 miles; area, 1442 acres; central lat. 41° 45′ N. long. from W. C. 1° 35′ W. The county was organized for judicial purposes, by act 27th March, 1824, and Potter county was provisionally annexed to it.

Lying in the great secondary formation of the West, the county partakes of those characteristics in surface and strata, which mark the western part of the state. It is every where hilly along the streams, but no where mountainous, and abounds with coal, iron and salt. The first is found in every t-ship, and works have been erected for manufacturing salt, at the small village of Emporium, on a branch of the Sinnemahoning creek.

The county is drained northward by the Allegheny river, which, rising in Potter county, N. and E. of Coudersport, flows westerly into this county, and thence northerly into the state of New York. It receives a very considerable branch, called Potatoe creek, about 10 miles S. of the state line, below which the united stream is 100 yards in width. The river is navigable for boats to Coudersport. The Tunuangwant creek also flows N. from the county, and unites with the river in the state of New York, about 15 miles below Hamilton village or Olean Point. The river re-enters the county on the N. W. and flows for about 10 miles along the western boundary, receiving from it Willow, Sugar, and Kenjua creeks. On the S. W. the county is watered by several branches of the Teonista creek, and on the S. E. by the Driftwood branch of the Sinnemahoning.

Authority was given by act 11th April, 1825, for making a turnpike road from Milesburg, in Centre co. to Smethport, in the county of McKean. A part of this road, commencing at Milesburg, has, we believe, been completed. The only places that can claim the slightest pretensions to be considered as towns, are Smethport, Emporium and Ceres; neither of the two last contain 6 houses.

The co. contains 922,880 acres, and 1438 inhabitants, about 6410 acres to an inhabitant. It is consequently little else than an uninhabited wilderness. In 1810 there were within the bounds of the county 142; in 1820, 728. Of the 1438 inhabitants in 1830, 764 were white males, 674 white females. There were among these, 2 deaf and dumb, and 2 blind, but not an alien nor a slave in the county.

From a county thus populated, and the inhabitants scattered abroad on the soil, little provision can be expected for moral wants. There is not a church in the county; yet an academy, endowed as we have above mentioned, and with the further sum of 2000 by the state, was incorporated in the town of Smethfield, by act 19th Jan. 1829. There are in this town also a very substantial and commodious brick court house and offices, a stone prison, &c. There is also a newspaper published in the town.

The country even in its natural condition yielding good pasturage, there are considerable quantities of live stock exported, but few other commodities save lumber, which seeks the western market at Pittsburg and the towns on the Ohio, by the Allegheny river, and the eastern by the Sinnemahoning creek, and the West Branch of the Susquehannah.

The average quality of the lands, is second rate; on the margin of the water courses, they are flats of excellent quality, having a rich, alluvial soil. When improved, these sell from 6 to 12 dollars the acre, and unimproved lands may be had for one or two dollars the acre. By the assessment of 1829, the seated lands were valued at $39,340, unseated $490,740; personal estate at $32,707 25. The rate of levy was 5 mills on the dollar.

The county paid into the state treasury in 1831, for tax on writs $85; for duties on dealers in foreign merchandize, $17 26; total, $102 26.

United with Union, Northumberland, Columbia, Luzerne, Susquehannah, Bradford, Lycoming and Potter, McKean forms the 9th congressional district, sending 3 members to congress. Combined with Lycoming, Centre, Clearfield and Potter, it forms the 13th senatorial district, sending 1 member to the senate; and connected with Lycoming, it sends two members to the house of representatives. The county is annexed to the 13th judicial district, and the courts are holden quarterly at Smethport, on the first Mondays after the courts in the county of Tioga.

STATISTFICAL TABLE OF McKEAN CO.

Townships,	Greatest Lth.	Greatest Bth.	Area in Acres.	Population. 1810	Population. 1820	Population. 1830
Burlington,	13	8	66,560			160
Ceres,	18	14	160,280	142	425	252
Cooper,	13	8	66,560			
Ogden,	18	10	115,800			131
Sergeant,	13	9½	57,200		192	230
Shippen,	15	9	85,760		111	110
Walker,	9½	9	54,720			
Keating,	23	14	206,180			493
Liberty,						62
				142	728	1438

McKean, t-ship, Erie co., bounded N. by Mill Creek t-ship, E. by Waterford and Beaver Dam t-ships, S. by Conneautte t-ship, and W. by Elk Creek and Fairview t-ships. Centrally distant S. from the borough of Erie 9 ms. Greatest length 7½, by 7 ms. in breadth; area, 33,280 acres; surface hilly; soil, gravelly loam. Pop. in 1830, 984; taxables, 138. It is drained N. W. by Walnut creek and its branches, and W. by Elk creek. The turnpike road from Waterford to Erie, crosses the N. W. angle of the t-ship.

McKean's old stand, p-o., Westmoreland co., 199 miles N. W. from W. C., and 177 S. W. from Harrisburg.

McKeansburg, p-t., Brunswick t-ship, Schuylkill co., about 4 ms. N. E. of Orwigsburg, 167 N. W. of W. C., and 64 from Harrisburg, contains about 30 dwellings, 2 stores and 3 taverns.

McKeesport, p-t., of Versailles t-ship, Allegheny co., at the confluence of the Youghiogheny river with the Monongahela, about 16 miles by the river above Pittsburg, 212 miles from W. C., and 189 from Harrisburg, contains about 40 dwellings, several stores and taverns, and a Presbyterian church.

McKees, Half Falls, p-o., Chapman t-ship, Union co., on the W. bank of the Susquehannah river, 17 miles S. E. of New Berlin, 148 N. W. from W. C., and 38 from Harrisburg.

McCreary's Ferry, over the Susquehannah river, in Martic t-ship, Lancaster co., near the confluence of Pecquea creek with that river.

Macungy, t-ship, Lehigh co., bounded N. E. by South Whitehall, and Salsberg t-ships, S. E. by Upper Milford t-ship, S. W. by Berks co., N. W. by Weissenberg t-ship. It is oblong in form; greatest length about 8, greatest width about 5¾ miles; area, 29,440 acres. It is watered by the Jordan and Little Lehigh creeks; and traversed in all directions by country roads. There are three towns, Millerstown, Trexler'stown and Fogle'sville, all on the main road which passes centrally N. W. through the t-ship; all are post-towns. There are two churches in the t-ship, each on a branch of the Little Lehigh creek. The surface of the country is level; the soil, limestone. It is densely populated, by a German race, amounting in 1830 to 3323, of whom 655 are taxables. It is carefully cultivated and abundantly productive. Taxable property, in 1818, real estate, $858,733; personal estate, $36,310; rate of levy, 13 cts.

in the $100. Assessed value of lands, 1st quality, $35, 2d quality, $25, 3d quality, $18 per acre. There are in the t-ship, 7 grist mills and 4 saw mills.

McMichael's creek, Northampton co., rises in Pokono t-ship, and after a devious course of about 12 miles, falls into Smithfield creek, at Stroudsburg. It is a rapid and crooked stream, and turns several mills in its course.

McSherry'stown, Conewago t-ship, Adams co., on the road leading from Hanover, in York co., from which it is distant about 3 ms. W., and from Gettysburg 11 ms. E., contains 20 dwellings, 1 store, and 1 tavern.

McWilliamstown, p-o., Chester co., 112 miles from W. C. and 63 S. E. from Harrisburg.

McVeytown, p-t., of Mifflin co., 150 miles from W. C., and 66 from Harrisburg.

Madison, t-ship, Columbia co., bounded N. by Lycoming co., N. E. by Greenwood t-ship, S. by Hemlock, and W. by Derry t-ships. Centrally distant N. from Danville 10 miles. Greatest length 8, breadth 5 miles; area, 16,000 acres; surface chiefly hilly, but partly level; soil, loam and clay. Pop. in 1830, 1454; taxables, 248. Muncy hills cover the north boundary. Little Fishing creek flows through the S. E. angle, and Mahoning creek through the S. W. There are two post-offices in the t-ship, one at the village of Whitehall, another at Jersey Town.

Madison, p-o., Somerset co., 200 miles N. W. of W. C., and 178 S. W. from Harrisburg.

Madisonburg, village, of Centre co., incorporated by act of assembly, 3d of April, 1830, for the purpose of enabling the citizens to levy a tax on real estate, to keep in repair the pipes which supply the town with water.

Mahanoy, Little, t-ship of Northumberland co., bounded N. by Augusta and Shamokin t-ships, S. E. by Upper Mahanoy, and S. W. by Lower Mahanoy t-ships. Centrally distant from Sunbury, 10 ms. Greatest length 16, greatest breadth 5 ms.; area, 33,280 acres; surface mountainous; soil, gravel and slate. Pop. in 1830, 563; taxables, 105. The Mahanoy mtn. runs along the N. W., and the Line mtn. along the S. boundary. The Mahanoy creek flows through a valley N. of the latter, and the Little Mahanoy creek through a valley of the former, uniting in the S. W. part of the t-ship. There is a vast abundance of anthracite coal here of the best quality, extending several miles along the valley of the Mahanoy cr., through this and into Shamokin t-ship.

Mahanoy, Upper, t-ship, Northumberland co., bounded N. by the Line mtn., S. E. by Schuylkill co., S. by Dauphin co., and S. W. by Lower Mahanoy t-ship. Centrally distant from Sunbury about 13 ms. Greatest length 15 ms.; greatest breadth 6¼ ms.; area, 32,640 acres; surface, mountainous; soil, gravel. Pop. in 1830, 1742; taxables, 307. The Line mtn. is on the N. bound. on the S. side of which flows Schwaben cr., westwardly to the Susquehannah river. The Mahantango hills cover the t-ship S. of the valley of that stream. Klingerstown lies on the S. W. boundary, and the p-t. of Mahanoy lies in a fork of Schwaben creek, near the W. boundary.

Mahanoy, Lower, t-ship, Northumberland co., bounded N. by Augusta, and Little Mahanoy t-ship, E. by Upper Mahanoy, S. by Dauphin co., and W. by the Susquehannah river. Centrally distant from Sunbury S. 14 miles. Greatest length 10, breadth 8 ms.; area, 23,640 acres. Surface diversified. Soil, limestone, gravel. Pop. in 1830, 1738; taxables, 307. The Line mtn. is on the N., along which Schwaben creek flows to the Susquehannah. The Mahantango cr. courses the southern boundary to the same river. Georgetown, or Dalmatia, a p-t., is centrally situated on the Susquehannah river.

Mahanoy, p-t., of Upper Mahanoy t-ship, Northumberland co., 10 ms. S. of Sunbury, 155 N. of W. C., and

45 from Harrisburg, contains 5 or 6 dwellings, store and tavern.

Mahanoy creeks, Great and Little, The former rises in Bush t-ship, in the northern part of Schuylkill co., and flows W. S. W. along the S. side of the Mahanoy ridge, about 50 miles, and falls into the Susquehannah river, 11 miles below Sunbury. About one half its course towards its mouth is in Northumberland county.

There are two streams which bear the name of the Little Mahanoy; one in Schuylkill co., which has its source in Schuylkill t-ship, and is separated from the Great Mahanoy by a spur of the Mahanoy mountains; and the other rises in Little Mahanoy township, Northumberland co., and joins the Great Mahanoy about 7 ms. from its mouth. The Great Mahanoy is navigable for boats for several miles from its mouth.

Mahanoy mountains, a long and wide range of hills, which extend from the Susquehannah river about 8 miles below Sunbury, in a N. E. direction, through the southern part of Northumberland and Columbia counties, and the northern part of Schuylkill county, into Luzerne co. Anthracite coal has been found abundantly in this range, particularly on Mahanoy creek, which flows on the S. side of the ridge.

Mahantango, Lower, t-ship, Schuylkill co., bounded N. E. by Barry and Norwegian t-ships, S. by Pine Grove t-ship, S. W. by Lebanon co., and N. W. by Upper Mahantango t-ship. The Manhatango mountain extends along its northern boundary, and divides it from Upper Mahantango; the Broad mountain crosses it from S. W. to N. E., and the Sharp mountain runs on and near the southern line. Its valleys, however, and hill sides are tolerably fertile, having a soil of red shale, which repays the labor expended upon it. Its shape is irregular; greatest length 11½, breadth 11½ miles; area 84,480 acres. Long Pine cr. crosses the t-ship from east to west, and Deep cr., a considerable portion of it, in the same direction, and the Swatara drains it on the S. Pop. in 1830, 1234; taxables, in 1828, 225. Anthracite coal is found in the t-ship, in Deep cr. valley.

Mahantango, Upper, t-ship, Schuylkill co., bounded N. by Northumberland co., E. by Barry, S. by Barry and Mahantango, and W. by Dauphin co. It is a long and narrow strip of land, in length about 16½ ms., with a mean breadth of 3½ ms; area, about 37,400 acres; its surface is a congregation of hills; the Mahanoy mtn., running along the northern boundary, and the Mahantango mtn. its southern. Two branches of the Mahantango creek flow westwardly through it. The soil is red shale and white gravel, and sterile. Timmerman's Town is near the northern, and within six miles of the eastern boundary; 25 ms. N. W. of Orwigsburg. Pop. of t-ship in 1830, 1150; taxables, in 1828, 191.

Mahantango creek, rises in Upper Mahantango, t-ship, Schuylkill county, and flows W. S. W., about 25 miles, into the Susquehannah river, about 25 miles above Harrisburg. For about 12 miles above its mouth, it forms the boundary between Northumberland and Dauphin counties.

Mahantango mountain, rises on the Susquehannah river, about 25 miles above Harrisburg, and thence by a N. E. course of 30 miles, blends with the Mahanoy mountain.

Mahantango, West, creek, rises on the confines of Union and Mifflin cos., and runs S. W. about 12 miles into the Susquehannah river, forming in part the boundary line between the two counties.

Mahoning creek, Northampton co., rises at the foot of the mountain of that name, and running eastwardly through a cultivated valley, to which it gives name, falls into the Lehigh, just below the village of Lehighton, and nearly opposite old fort Allen. Rafts descend this creek about 4 miles, above which distance, are several mills.

Mahoning creek, of Armstrong co.,

rises on the E. border of Jefferson co., through which it flows into Indiana and Armstrong cos., and unites with the Allegheny river about 10 miles above Kittanning. It is a large and rapid stream, and has a course of about 40 miles.

Mahoning hill, East Penn t-ship, Northampton co., a continuation of the Tamaqua mtn., forming the northern boundary of Lizard Creek valley, ending at the Lehigh river, near Lehighton.

Mahoning mountain, running from the Lehigh river, S. W. into Schuylkill county. It is, we believe, the second mountain, to which this local name is here given.

Mahoning valley, Northampton co., lies along the Mahoning cr., between the Mahoning mtn. and Mahoning hill. There are some very good lands in this valley, remarkable for abundant crops of rye.

Mahoning, t-ship, Columbia county, bounded N. by Derry, E. by Hemlock t-ships, S. by the Susquehannah river, and W. by Liberty. Greatest length 7, breadth 4 ms.; area, 13,440 acres; surface, diversified; soil, clay and gravel. Pop. in 1830, 1796; taxables, 358. Mahoning creek, rising in Madison t-ship, flows S. through this t-ship to the Susquehannah river, by Danville, a borough and county town.

Mahoning creek. (See preceding article.)

Mahoning river, or large creek, rises in Columbiana, Stark, Portage and Trumbull counties, Ohio, and enters Pennsylvania at the S. W. angle of Mahoning t-ship, and Mercer co., and joins the Shenango, to form the Big Beaver river.

Mahoning, t-ship, Mercer co., bounded N. by Shenango, E. by Neshannock t-ships, S. by Beaver co., and W. by the state of Ohio. Centrally distant S. W. from the borough of Mercer, 16 miles. Greatest length 8, breadth 6 ms; area, 30,720 acres; surface, level; soil, clay and loam. Pop. in 1830, 656; taxables, 399. Taxable property in 1829, real estate, $144,807; personal, $21,495; rate of levy, 4 mills on the dollar. The Mahoning river, from the state of Ohio, enters the S. W. angle, and flows into Beaver co., and the Shenango cr. enters the t-ship in the N. and flows also into Beaver co., into the Mahoning. The p-t. of New Bedford lies in the N. W. angle of the t-ship.

Mahoning, t-ship, Indiana co., bounded N. by Jefferson co., E. by Clearfield county, S. by Washington and Greene t-ships, and W. by Armstrong co. Centrally distant N. from the borough of Indiana 16 ms. Greatest length 20, breadth 12½ ms.; area, 133,120 acres; surface, hilly; soil, clay. Pop. in 1830, 1640; taxables, 297. It is drained W. by the Little Mahoning creek, which rises in the township, and flows N. W., having a course of about 22 miles, to its recipient, the Great Mahoning, in the N. W. angle of the t-ship. In the fork below their junction, lies the p-t. of Nicholsburg, 18 ms. N. W. of Indiana borough. The p-o. of the t-ship is called Mahoning. It is 206 ms. N. W. of W. C. and 174 from Harrisburg. Iron ore is found on the Little Mahoning, near the centre of the t-ship.

Mahonoy ridge, Columbia co., rises in Liberty t-ship, and runs N. E. about 7 miles, bounding on the N. the t-ship. of Mahoning.

Mahonoy ridge, Perry co., rises in Tyrone t-ship, and runs N. E. 14 ms. to the Juniata river, dividing Juniata t-ship from Rye t-ship.

Mahoniely, Little, or Middle creek, Union co., rises by several branches in Beaver t-ship, and flows E. and S. E. through the county, about 26 ms. into the Susquehannah river, forming the chief drain of Moser's valley.

Mahoopeny mountain; there are 3 hills in Windham t-ship, Luzerne co. which bear this name. The Mahoopeny mountain proper, a spur of Bowman's mountain which terminates at the confluence of Mahoopeny creek with the Ohio; Big Mahoopeny and

Little Mahoopeny mountains, are parallel ridges perpendicular to the first, and divided from each other by the W. branch of the Mahoopeny creek.

Mahoopeny creek ; there are also 3 streams in Windham t-ship, Luzerne co., which bear this name. The Mahoopeny proper, rises in some ponds or small lakes of Lycoming co. and its sources interlock with those of the Loyalsock creek. It flows N. E. through Union, Dallas, and Windham t-ships to the Susquehannah river, which it enters at the termination of the Mahoopeny mountain. The W. branch of the Mahoopeny flows from Bradford and Lycoming counties easterly into the Mahoopeny creek, about the centre of Windham t-ship. The Little Mahoopeny has its source and course along the N. side of the Little Mahoopeny mountain, and joins the river above the great Mahoopeny creek.

Mahoopeny valley, lies on Mahoopeny creek, in Windham t-ship, Luzerne co. is very narrow and thinly populated, & extends irregularly about 20 miles from the Susquehannah r.

Maiden creek, a large branch of the Schuylkill river, rising in the N. W. angle of Lehigh co. in Linn t-ship, flows with a south westerly inclination through Albany, Greenwich, Windsor, Richmond and Maiden Creek t-ships, Berks co., and after a course of more than 20 miles falls into the Schuylkill 6 miles above Reading. Its main tributaries, are Pine creek, Mill cr. Stoney run, Sacony creek, Moselem creek, upon all of which mills are erected.

Maiden Creek, t-ship, Berks county, bounded N. E. by Richmond, S. E. by Ruscomb Manor, S. by Alsace t-ship, S. W. by the river Schuylkill, and N. W. by Windsor t-ships; length $4\frac{3}{4}$, breadth 4 ms.; area 13,000 acres; surface, level; soil, limestone and gravel, and very productive. Pop. in 1810, 918; in 1820, 1192; in 1830, 1350; taxables, 294. It is watered by the Schuylkill and its great tributary Maiden creek, the latter of which crosses it diagonally from its extreme northern point, to near its remotest southern bounds. There is a Quaker meeting house near the centre of the t-ship, and a Lutheran and Presbyterian church, near the N. W. boundary, about 9 miles from Reading. The turnpike road to Sunbury, runs between 4 and 5 miles through the t-ship, and crosses Maiden creek, over a neat wooden, covered bridge, of one arch. The post office, having the name of the t-ship, is 151 miles from W. C., and 60 from Harrisburg.

Mainsburg, p-o. Tioga co. called after the post master, John Main, distant, 250 miles N. W. from W. C. and 144 from Harrisburg.

Makefield, Upper, Bucks co. bounded N. by Solebury t-ship, E. by the river Delaware, S. by Lower Makefield, S. W. by Newtown, W. by Wrightstown, and N. W. by Buckingham t-ships. Centrally distant from Phila. 25 miles; greatest length $6\frac{1}{4}$, breadth $4\frac{1}{2}$ miles. Pidcocks creek runs along its N. boundary into the Delaware, and two other streams traverse it to the same recipient. There is a post office in the t-ship called Makefield. Dolinton, a small village, lies at the intersection of the roads from Newtown and Falsington. Bowman's Hill on the Delaware is a noted eminence, named after Dr. Bowman, an early settler, who sought its shades for contemplation, and who was buried here at his own request; suface, rolling; soil, clay and sandy loam. Pop. in 1830, 1517; taxables in 1828, 314.

Makefield, Lower, t-ship, Bucks co. bounded N. by Upper Makefield, E. by the river Delaware, S. by Falls t-ship, W. by Middleton & Newtown t-ships. Centrally distant from Phila. about 24 miles N. E.; from Doylestown 15 miles E.; greatest length $5\frac{1}{2}$ miles, by $4\frac{1}{2}$ miles in width. Yardleyville and Bilo's cross roads are villages of the t-ship. The Delaware canal runs along the east boundary; surface, rolling; soil, clay and sandy loam. Pop. in 1830, 1340; taxables in 1828, 264.

Manallen, N. W. t-ship, of Adams co. bounded N. by Cumberland co. E. by Tyrone t-ship, S. E. by Strabane, S. by Franklin t-ships, and W. by Franklin co. Centrally distant N. W. from Gettysburg 11 ms.; greatest length 15, breadth 9½ miles; area 53, 760 acres; surface level; soil, red shale. Pop. in 1830, 2063; taxables, 387. It is drained on the S. by the Conewago creek, E. by Opossum cr. a tributary of that stream, N. by Mountain creek, a branch of the Yellow Breeches, and W. by Birch run, a source of the Concocheague cr.

Manallen, t-ship, Fayette co. bounded N. E. by Franklin, S. E. by Union, S. W. by German, and N. W. by Redstone t-ships. Centrally distant from Uniontown, 4 miles; greatest length 8 miles, breadth 6 miles; area 14,080 acres; surface, rolling; soil, limestone and gravel. Pop. in 1830, 1083; taxables, 261. Redstone cr. follows the N. boundary, and a branch of that stream the E., Dunlap's cr. the S., and branches of those creeks nearly meet on the W. The p-t. of New Salem lies on Dunlap's creek, on the road from Uniontown to Merritt's town, about 7 miles W. from the former, and Middleton lies in a bend of Redstone creek, about 5 miles N. of Uniontown. The national road passes centrally N. W. through the t-ship.

Manchester, *East*, post t-ship, of York co. bounded N. by Newberry, N. E. by the Susquehannah river, S. E. by Hellam, S. W. by West Manchester, and N. W. by Conewago t-ship. Centrally distant from the borough of York 4 miles; greatest length 8½, breadth 5 miles; area, 20,480 acres; surface level; soil, limestone and fruitful. Pop. in 1830, 2212; taxables, 505; taxable property 1829, real estate, $439,003; personal 19,300; occupations &c., 37,595; total, $545, 898; rate of taxation, 25 cts. in the $100. The Conewago creek bounds it on the N. W., and the Codorus on the S. E. The York and Conewago turnpike road passes northerly through the t-ship, upon which is situated the post town of Liverpool, about 7 miles N. of the borough of York. The small village of New Holland lies on the Susquehannah river. The p-o. is called Manchester, and is 93 miles from W. C., and 18 from Harrisburg.

Manchester, *West*, t-ship, York co. bounded N. E. by East Manchester, S. E. by Spring Garden, S. by Codorus, W. by Paradise, and N. W. by Dover t-ships; greatest length 7, breadth 6¼ miles; area 12,800 acres; surface level; soil, limestone, and of good quality. Pop. in 1830, 1269; taxables, 255; taxable property, 1829, real estate $470,103; personal, 14, 340; occupations, 24,670; total $509, 113; rate 25 cts. in the $100. The Conewago creek bounds it on the N. W. and the Codorus on the S. and E. The borough of York lies on both sides of the last creek and partly in this t-ship, and Bottstown may be considered as its eastern suburb.

Manchester, northern t-ship, Wayne co. newly erected; surface, hilly; soil, gravelly loam, covered with white pine, hemlock and beech timber. It contained by the census of 1830, 183 inhabitants, and 1828, 42 taxables; 4 frame, and 17 log houses, 1 store, 1 tavern, 1 grist mill and 1 saw mill. By the assessment of 1829, the seated lands were valued at $11,988; and the unseated, at $48,167; and personal property including occupations at $1932.

Manheim, t-ship, Schuylkill co. bounded on the N. and N. W. by Norwegian t-ship, on the E. by Brunswick t-ship, on the S. by Berks co. and on the S. W. by Pine Grove t-ship; its form is irregular. Its greatest length is about 9 miles, and greatest breadth, about 8½ miles; area, 43, 520 acres. The Sharp mountain runs along the N. boundary, the Blue mountain along the S., and the Second mountain crosses the interval. The Schuylkill river winds through the N. E. portion, and receives in its course the west branch of Indian run, Panther creek, Beaver creek, Long run, Warner's creek, Bear creek and some streams less considerable. Lewis-port, Schuylkill-Haven & Freidensburg, are villages of the t-ship. There is a Lutheran church erected in its S. W. angle. As the surface is mountaintainous, so is the soil, of white gravel, sterile. The pop. in 1830 was 2160; taxables in 1828, 315.

Manheim, t-ship, Lancaster co. bounded N. by Warwick, S. by Lancaster t-ship & city, N. E. by Leacock, S. E. by Lampeter, and W. by Hempfield; length 7, breadth 5 miles; area 16,666 acres; surface rolling; soil, limestone and clay. Pop. in 1830, 1861; taxables, 280. The Great Conestoga river flows on the eastern, and the Little Conestoga on the south western boundary. Moravia creek crosses the N. E. angle. Neffsville, post town, lies 4½ miles due N. of Lancaster city on the road from Lancaster to Litiz. The t-ship contains 9 distilleries, 1 tannery, 4 grist mills, 3 saw mills, 1 hemp mill and 1 oil mill.

Manheim, p-t. and village, Raphoe t-ship, Lancaster co. on the great Chiques creek, 10 miles N. W. of the city of Lancaster, 119 from W. C. and 39 from Harrisburg, contains about 60 dwellings, several stores and taverns.

Manheim, t-ship, York co. bounded N. E. by Codorus, S. by the state of Maryland, W. by Adams co. and N. W. by Heidelberg t-ship. Centrally distant S. W. from the borough of York 16 miles; greatest length 10½, breadth 6¾ miles; area 2816 acres; surface undulating; soil, loam, of good quality. Pop. in 1830, 1278; taxables 302; taxable property in 1829, real estate $231,679; personal 14,908; occupations 17,605; total, $264,192; rate, 25 cts. in the $100. It is drained N. by Hammer creek and a branch of the Codorus. The Hanover and Maryland line turnpike road runs S. through the W. part of the t-ship.

Manookisy creek, Northampton co. rises in Moore t-ship, and running southwardly falls into the Lehigh river at Bethlehem. This is a beautiful stream, flowing through a delightful country, and has a number of excellent mills upon it. But it is not navigable.

Manokesy creek, rises in Alsace and Oley t-ships, Berks co. and by a S. easterly course through the t-ships of Exeter and Amity, joins the Schuylkill, about 12 miles below Reading. It is not navigable, but drives some 10 or 12 mills in its course.

Manokesy hill, an oblong, low and isolated mountain, centrally situated in Amity t-ship, Berks co. about 2 miles from Reading.

Manor hill, p-o. Huntingdon co. 163 miles N. W. of W. C. and 105 S. E. of Harrisburg.

Mansfield, village of Donegal t-ship, Westmoreland co. 16 miles E. of Greensburg, contains 12 houses, 1 tavern and 1 store.

Mansfield, p-o. Tioga co., 246 miles N. W. from W. C., 140 from Harrisburg.

Manor, t-ship, Lancaster co. bounded N. by East and West Hempfield t-ships, E. by Lancaster and Conestoga t-ships, W. and S. W. by the Susquehannah river; centrally distant from the city of Lancaster 6 miles S. W.; greatest length and greatest breadth, about 8 miles. The Conestoga river forms the S. E. boundary, receiving from the t-ship, the Little Conestoga, and its W. branch. Millerstown lies in the E. part of the t-ship, between the Little and Great Conestoga streams, and Fairview, Charlestown, Washington and Newmarket, upon the Susquehannah river. The first four are post towns; there is a post office in the t-ship called Manor, 102 miles from W. C., and 81 from Harrisburg. Turkey hill, a high bluff upon the river, runs several miles on the S. boundary; area, 25,400 acres; surface, partly hilly, partly rolling; soil, limestone. Pop. in 1830, 3158; taxables 835. The t-ship contains 30 distilleries, 15 grist mills, 4 saw mills and a woollen factory.

Mantua, pleasant village of Blockley t-ship, Phila. co. on the road from the upper ferry bridge to to the Lancaster turnpike, on the upper bank of the river, contains some 40 or 50 neat dwellings, a store and Episcopalian church, a boarding school for boys &c. There are several neat country seats here. It is distant about 2½ miles from the centre of the city.

Mattsville, p-t. Richland t-ship, Bucks co. 17 miles N. of Doylestown, 175 from W. C. and 89 from Harrisburg, consists of some 4 or 5 houses, a store and tavern.

Manyunk, p-t. and manufacturing village of Boxborough t-ship, Phila. co. upon the left bank of the r. Schuylkill and on the Flat Rock canal, a link of the Schuylkill chain connecting the Flat Rock pool with that of Fair Mount, 7 ms. from Phila., 143 from W. C. and 98 from Harrisburg. This village has been created by the water power derived from the canal. The first mill was erected here by Capt. John Towers, in 1819. The fall of the water is upon an average of 22 ft. from the surface of the canal to the bottom of the tail race; and the several mills are entitled to the water in the order rented; and the last rented stops first in case of deficiency. The whole are subject to the navigation through the locks. The mode of computing the water rent is by the square inch of aperture. There are now, 1832, 14 mills established here, which employ a force estimated at 332 horse power.

The valley of the Schuylkill here, closely bounded on the W. by high and rugged hills, expands on the E. into a flat bottom, varying in width from 200 to 1000 feet, with a length not exceeding 2 miles; at the head of this plain is Flat Rock dam, which derives its name from a mass of flat rocks below it. A canal running parallel with the river connects this dam with the pool made by the Fair Mount dam. The town contains above 400 dwellings, many of which are very handsome and commodious. The lower and level bank of the r. proving too narrow for the numerous dwellings, streets have been dug in the sides of the hill, and some of the best houses have been built upon the hill top, which is apparently not less than 150 or 200 feet above the bed of the r. Below the dam and at a high bluff of the shores, a bridge of one arch, called Flat Rock bridge, spans the river. A bridge near the centre of the town was erected by Capt. Towers several years since; but that, having been carried away by the stream, another near its site is being erected, by a company incorporated in 1831. A turnpike, also constructed by an incorporated company, leads from the town to the ridge road, a distance of something over a mile. The cost of this work was $17,000. There are in the town 1 Catholic, 1 German Reformed, 2 Methodist and 1 Episcopalian churches, 8 large and well assorted stores, beside many smaller ones; 4 taverns, a large brass and iron foundry, and every species of mechanical operation requisite for an active and thrifty population. Manyunk is the Indian name of the r. Schuylkill.

Mapletown, Monongahela township, Greene co. on Whitely creek, about 15 ms. S. E. from Waynesburg, and 3 from the Monongahela r. is a small hamlet of 6 or 8 dwellings.

Maple Grove, p-t. Armstrong co. 231 ms. from W. C. and 199 from Harrisburg.

Marcus Hook, p-t. of Lower Chichester t-ship, Delaware co. situated on the r. Delaware, about 20 ms. S. from Phila. and 5 from Chester, 116 ms. N. from W. C. and 95 S. E. from Harrisburg, contains about 30 dwellings, 1 Baptist and 1 Episcopalian church, 2 taverns and 3 stores. It is a pleasant village, surrounded by apple orchards, and its cider is in high repute. Some piers have been erected, opposite the town, for the accommodation of shipping.

Marietta, p-t. and borough, East Donegal t-ship, Lancaster co. on the left bank of the Susquehannah, above the mouth of Little Chiques creek, 14 ms. W. of the city of Lancaster, 102 from W. C. and 25 from Harrisburg. The two villages of Waterford and New Haven were included in the act of 6th March, 1812, incorporating the town. A turnpike road runs from Lancaster to the town, and another from the town N. to the Harrisburg turnpike, at Mount Joy. The state canal from Columbia to Middletown passes near it. The town contains more than 100 dwellings, several stores and taverns, and a church. An act passed 9th Feb. 1814, authorizing the incorporation of a company to erect a bridge over the Susquehannah r. opposite to this town; but the project has never been commenced. This is now a thriving place, and very favorably situated for partaking of the advantages resulting from the great internal improvements of the state.

Marlborough, t-ship, Montgomery co., bounded N. E. by Bucks co., S. E. by Upper Salford, S. and S. W. by Frederick, and N. W. by Upper Hanover t-ships. Greatest length 5, greatest width 2¼ ms. The Perkiomen cr. runs along the S. W. boundary, and Swamp cr. along the S. E. division. Centrally distant from Norristown 18 ms. Sumany Town, at which there is a p-o., lies on the line which divides this t-ship from Upper Salford. Surface, rolling; soil, red shale. Iron ore is found in the t-ship. Pop. in 1830, 911; taxables in 1828, 171.

Marlborough, East, t-ship, Chester co., bounded N. by Newlin and W. Bradford, N. E. by Pennsbury, and S. E. by Kennett, S. by New Garden, and W. by London Grove and West Marlborough t-ships. Central distance from Philadelphia 28 ms. S. W., and from West Chester 8 ms. Length 4¾ by 3¾ ms. in breadth; area, 10,680 acres. Pop. in 1830, 1252; taxables, in 1828, 230. Surface, gentle declivity; soil, sandy loam. Pocopsen creek, a tributary of the Brandywine, flows E. through the N. section of the t-ship, and Red Clay creek rises in and crosses the S. W. angle. Unionville, p-t., and village, is centrally situated at the intersection of the roads leading to Kennett's Square and Chad's Ford.

Marlborough, West, t-ship, of Chester co., bounded N. by East Fallowfield, E. by Newlin and East Marlborough, S. by New Garden and London Grove, and W. by Londonderry, and West Fallowfield t-ships. The east branch of Clay creek drains it on the S., and a tributary of the west branch of the Brandywine on the N. Central distance S. W. from Philadelphia 33 ms., and from West Chester 11 miles. Length 4¾, breadth 4 ms.; area, 9762 acres; surface, gentle declivity; soil, sandy loam. Pop. in 1830, 1101; taxables, in 1828, 265.

Margaretta, furnace, p-o., Windsor t-ship, York co., 97 ms. from W. C. and 35 from Harrisburg.

Marple, t-ship, Delaware county, bounded N. by Radnor, E. by Haverford, S. by Springfield, and W. by Upper Providence. Centrally distant from Philadelphia 12 miles W., from Chester, 7 N. Length 4, breadth 4 ms.; area, 6400 acres; surface, hilly; soil, loam. Pop. in 1830, 793; taxables, 171. Darby creek courses the eastern, and Crane creek the western boundary; both are mill streams, and have many mills upon them.

Martic, t-ship, Lancaster co., bounded N. E. by Strasburg t-ship, E. by Bart, and S. E. by Dromore, S. W. by the Susquehannah river, and N. W. by Conestoga t-ship. Centrally distant 10 ms. S. of the city of Lancaster. Greatest length 10, greatest breadth 6 ms.; area 31,542 acres; surface, hilly; soil, limestone and clay. Pop. in 1830, 2156; taxables, 414. Beaver creek bounds it N. E., Muddy creek S. E., and Pecquea creek, N. W., all mill streams; upon the latter is a forge. Martic hills cover a great portion of the t-ship. McCreary's ferry, over the Susquehannah, is below the confluence of Pecquea creek with that stream. There is a post office at Marticville, a small hamlet of 8 or 10 dwellings, 100 ms. from W. C., and 46 from Harrisburg.

Martin's creek, Northampton co., rises at the foot of the Blue mountain, and running a southwesterly course falls into the Delaware, about 26 ms. above Easton. It is not navigable, but affords several excellent mill seats. There is a post office, called after the creek, distant 198 ms. from W. C., and 111 from Harrisburg.

Martin's creek, Susquehannah co., rises in New Milford t-ship, and by a S. W. course falls into the Tunkhannock creek, in Luzerne county. It forms the whole western boundary of Lennox, and partly of Harford t-ships, Susquehannah county, receiving in its course Hopbottom creek and other streams.

Martinsburg, Buffalo t-ship, Washington co., on the national road, about 6 ms. W. of Washington borough. It is a town in name only, there being but a single house, a tavern, here.

Masontown, p-o., Fayette co., 222 ms. N. W. from W. C., 204 S. W. from Harrisburg.

Martinsburg, p-t., Woodberry t-ship, Bedford co., in the N. part of the t-ship, on the head waters of the Frankstown branch of the Juniata river, 22 ms. N. of the borough of Bedford, 134 from W. C., and 112 from Harrisburg, contains 3 stores, 3 taverns, and about 50 dwellings. It is situated in a beautiful limestone valley, called Morrison's cove, bounded on the E. by Tussey's, and on the W. by Dunning's mountain. The valley abounds with iron ore, contains a furnace and 3 forges, and many mills.

Marsh creek, Adams co., rises in Menallen t-ship, and flows S. into the state of Maryland, forming the boundary between Cumberland t-ship and Hamilton-ban and Liberty t-ships. Its course within the state is about 15 ms.

Marshall's creek, Northampton co., rises in Pike co., and flowing S. W. unites its waters with those of Smithfield creek, directly at the mouth of the latter. It is not navigable, but affords several fine mill seats.

Marshalton, a post town and village of Chester co., West Bradford t-ship, 27 miles W. of Philadelphia, and 4 ms. S. W. of West Chester, 117 ms. N. from W. C., and 74 S. E. from Harrisburg, contains some half dozen houses.

Marsh, p-t., Chester co., 136 ms. N. of W. C., and 61 S. E. of Harrisburg.

Mauch Chunk. Under this title, it is proposed to give an account of the famous coal mountain, and the magnificent improvements of which it has been the cause. The name of this mountain is of Indian origin, and in the language of the Lenni Lenappi, (Delawares,) is said to signify *Bear mountain*. It forms a very distinguished portion of the coal formation of the state, and we are told that we owe our knowledge of its mineral treasures to sheer accident ; that a hunter discovered the coal bed, while in search of game, beneath the roots of an uptorn pine. The following account of this important event is given by the venerable Dr. Thomas C. James, of Philadelphia, who, in the year 1804, in company with Anthony Morris, Esq., during an excursion to some lands on the Lehigh, their joint property, visited the mountain.

"In the course of our pilgrimage, we reached the summit of the Mauch Chunk mountain, the present site of the mine or rather quarry of anthracite coal. At that time there were only to be seen three or four small pits, which had much the appearance of the commencement of rude wells, into one of which, our guide (*Philip Ginter*), descended with great ease, and threw up some pieces of coal for our examination. After which, whilst we lingered on the spot, contemplating the wildness of the scene, honest Philip amused us with the following narrative of the original discovery of this most valuable of minerals, now promising, from its general diffusion, so much of wealth and comfort to a great portion of Pennsylvania.

"He said, when he first took up his

residence in that district of country, he built for himself a rough cabin in the forest, and supported his family by the proceeds of his rifle ; being literally a hunter of the backwoods. The game he shot, including bear and deer, he carried to the nearest store, and exchanged for other necessaries of life. But at the particular time to which he then alluded, he was without a supply of food for his family ; and after being out all day with his gun in quest of it, he was returning, towards evening, over the Mauch Chunk mountain, entirely unsuccessful and dispirited ; a drizzling rain beginning to fall, and night approaching, he bent his course homeward, considering himself one of the most *forsaken* of human beings. As he trod slowly over the ground, his foot stumbled against something which, by the stroke, was driven before him ; observing it to be black, to distinguish which there was just light enough remaining, he took it up, and as he had often listened to the traditions of the country of the existence of coal in the vicinity, it occurred to him, that this might be a portion of that " *stone coal*," of which he had heard. He accordingly carefully took it with him to his cabin, and the next day carried it to Col. Jacob Weiss, residing at what was then known by the name of Fort Allen. The colonel, who was alive to the subject, brought the specimen with him to Philadelphia, and submitted it to the inspection of John Nicholson and Michael Hillegas, Esqrs., and of Charles Cist, an intelligent printer, who ascertained its nature and qualities, and authorized the colonel to satisfy Ginter for his discovery, upon his pointing out the precise spot, where he found the coal. This was done by acceding to Ginter's proposal, of getting through the forms of the patent-office the title for a small tract of land, which he supposed had never been taken up, comprising the mill-seat, on which he afterwards built the mill which afforded us the lodging of the preceding night, and which he afterwards was unhappily deprived of by the claim of a prior survey.

" Hillegas, Cist, Weiss, and others immediately after, (about the beginning of the year 1792,) formed the " Lehigh coal mine company," but without a charter of incorporation, and took up 8 or 10,000 acres of unlocated land, including the Mauch Chunk mountain."

The mine now wrought was opened by this company ; but the difficulties of transporting the coal to market were then insurmountable, and their enterprize was abandoned. " The mine remained in a neglected state, used only by the smiths and others of the immediate vicinity, until the year 1806, when Wm. Turnbull, Esq. caused an ark to be constructed at Lausanne, which brought to the city two or three hundred bushels. A portion was sold to the manager of the water works, for the use of the Centre square steam engine. Upon trial here, it was deemed rather an extinguisher than an aliment of fire, was rejected as worthless, and was broken up and spread on the walks of the surrounding garden, in the place of gravel.

The legislature, early aware of the importance of the navigation of the Lehigh, passed an act for its improvement in 1771, and others in 1791, 1794, 1798, 1810, 1814 and 1816. Under one of these a company associated, and after expending more than 20,000 dollars in clearing out channels, relinquished their design of perfecting the navigation of the river.

In the meanwhile the coal mine company, desirous to render their property available, granted leases to several individuals successively ; the last for a term of ten years with the privilege of cutting timber from their lands, for floating the coal to market, was made to Messrs. Cist, Miner & Robinson, upon condition that they should send to Philadelphia 10,000 bushels of coal per annum, for the benefit of the lessees. These gentlemen loaded several arks with coal, only three of which reached the city, and they abandoned the business at the close of the war in 1815.

During the war, Virginia coal became very scarce, and Messrs. White & Erskine Hazard, then engaged in the manufacture of iron wire at the falls of the Schuylkill, having learned that Mr. J. Malin had succeeded in the use of Lehigh coal at his rolling mill, procured a cart load of it, which cost them a dollar per bushel. This quantity was entirely wasted, without getting up the requisite heat. Another cart load was, however, obtained, and a whole night was spent in endeavoring to make a fire in the furnace, when the hands shut the furnace door, and departed from the mill in despair. Fortunately, one of them who had left his jacket in the mill returning for it in about half an hour, observed the door of the furnace to be red hot, and upon opening it, was surprised to find the interior at a glowing white heat. The other hands were summoned, and four separate parcels of iron were heated by the same fire, and rolled, before renewal. The furnace was then replenished, and as *letting the fire alone* had succeeded so well, that method was tried again with a like result.

Thenceforth Messrs. White and Hazard continued the use of anthracite coal, which they procured from Schuylkill county, in wagons, and occasionally in flats by freshets, and also from the Lehigh, in one of Messrs. Miner & Co's. arks. Thus instructed in the invaluable properties of anthracite, Messrs. White & Hazard having disposed of their works on the Schuylkill to the city of Philadelphia, turned their attention to the mines on the Lehigh, with the resolution of creating adequate means for transporting their wealth to market.

In January, 1818, they jointly with Mr. Hants obtained the control of the lands of the Lehigh coal mine company. In the succeeding March, the legislature granted to these gentlemen, ample power for improving the navigation of the river Lehigh, and vested in them, their heirs and assigns, the absolute and exclusive use of the waters of the river, not incompatible with the navigation, and the right to levy tolls upon boats, rafts, &c. *descending* the river, and also upon ascending it, in case a slack water navigation should be made, upon condition, 1st, That they made a descending navigation within six years from the mouth of the Nesquihoning creek to the Delaware, and from the Great falls to the Nesquihoning within twenty years. 2. That in case the legislature deemed such navigation insufficient, the grantees should convert the same into a complete slack water navigation, erecting one lock or other devices overcoming at least 6 feet fall, yearly, until the whole should be completed. 3. That in case of abuse of the privileges granted, or neglect to complete the slack water navigation, within twenty years after requisition made, that the state might resume the grant. 4. That the state might, after the expiration of thirty-six years from the date of the grant, purchase the rights of the grantees to the navigation. And 5th. That upon such purchase, or resumption in case of forfeiture, that the state should fulfil all the obligations enjoined by this act, upon the grantees.

For the purpose of obtaining funds to carry this act into effect, and to conduct the mining operations advantageously, Messrs. White, Hants, and Hazard, formed with others, two associations in July, 1818; the one, denominated "the Lehigh navigation company," for whose use, they granted to trustees, by deed dated 10th August, 1818, all the right vested in them by the above mentioned act, to the benefits of the river Lehigh, reserving to themselves certain residuary profits and exclusive privileges in the management of the company; the other, denominated "The Lehigh coal company," for whose use they also conveyed to trustees, certain estates in sundry tracts of coal lands, reserving also to themselves certain residuary profits, and exclusive privileges in the management of such company.

The navigation company commenced the improvement of the Lehigh in Aug., 1818. In 1820, coal was sent to Phila. by an artificial navigation, and sold at $8 50 per ton, delivered at the door of the purchasers.

The following plan was adopted, to render the passage of the river more facile. The obstacles in the bed of the river were removed, and 13 dams, with sluices of various heights, were constructed of pine logs, at an average expense of three thousand dollars each. The gates of the sluices, of a peculiar construction, were invented by Mr. White, (to whom the company are indebted for many ingenious improvements) and merit particular notice. The gates in the sluice or lock were attached to the flooring by hinges, and rose by the force of water admitted from a floom, constructed parallel with the lock, and when suspended, forming a section of the dam. When the floom was closed, the water beneath the gates passed off, and they fell by their own weight, and the pressure of the fluid from the dams. The dam served a double purpose, forming pools of navigable water, and reservoirs. At fixed periods the arks were passed with great rapidity through the sluices; and the sudden efflux of water gave additional depth and velocity to the stream below. These sluices, admirably adapted to the original plan, have proved inefficient for canal navigation, and have been in a great measure, and perhaps altogether, abandoned. From Easton, the arks pursued the natural channel of the river to Trenton, whence a steamboat towed them to the city in gangs of 18 or 20 together. The arks emptied of their freight were broken up and sold, at a considerable loss to the company. These arks were rectangular barges, 16 ft. wide by 20 ft. in length, connected by iron hinges, so that they accommodated themselves to the motion of the waves.

During this amelioration of the navigation, the coal company erected mills for grinding grain and sawing lumber, and the buildings necessary for sheltering their work people. A large quantity of coal was uncovered at the mine, by removing from its surface a gravelly loam, from a few inches to 4 feet in depth, and disintegrated slate from 2 to 4 feet. This process has been continued, until the excavation has a superficial area of 10 acres, and a depth ,varying from 30 to 70 ft. A road was made to the summit of the mountain, distant from the r. 9 miles, which was soon after paved with stone, or turnpiked in the best manner, upon which 7 tons of coal were conveyed with ease, on 2 wagons drawn by 4 horses.

In 1820 the two companies were amalgamated under the title of "*The Lehigh coal and navigation company*;" and Messrs. White and Hazard, having in the interim acquired the interest of Mr. Hants, they obtained for themselves in the union, the privileges which had been reserved in the original organization of the separate companies.

By an act of assembly passed 13th Feb., 1832, the Lehigh coal and navigation company was incorporated, and the property of the prior associations, and the privileges created by the act of 1818, were invested in them. Their capital stock was limited to $1,000,000, divided into shares of $50 each; and of this capital, their former property formed part. They were empowered to commence a slack water navigation upon the Lehigh, within a year from the date of the act. To this company Messrs. W. and H. became parties, as simple stockholders merely.

To facilitate the ascent of the r., the company resolved on a lock navigation, on which steam boats might be employed. Accordingly a lock was built in —— 182 ., at Mauch Chunk, measuring 135 ft. in length, and 30 in with, and the canal, of more than a mile in length, annexed to it, was excavated five feet deep, and its banks lined with stone. But as this mode was very expensive, and the state had commenced the Delaware canal from Easton to Bristol, a change in the plan became expedient. And in 1827, the company having increased their funds by the sale of ten thousand shares, the balance of their capital, determined on making a canal navigation, which should correspond with the Delaware canal. This great work extending from Easton to Mauch Chunk, a distance of 46¾ ms., consisting of 10 ms. of pools, and 36¾ of canals, was commenced in the summer of 1827, and was in condition to authorize the company to exact toll thereon in July, 1829. The canal is 5 ft. deep, 45 ft. wide at bottom, and 60 ft. at top; the banks are firm, and lined chiefly with stone; the locks are 22 ft. wide, and 100 feet long, and are adapted to pass boats, suited to the Delaware canal, in pairs. The ascent of 364 ft., is overcome by 54 locks and 9 dams. "The whole of the river improvement, from its commencement, as a descending navigation to its final completion, as above, including the amount paid to White & Hazard for their property, rights and privileges, and the extinguishment of Hants's claims, cost about $1,558,000. The toll houses erected along the canal, are of the most substantial and comfortable kind; and in the completion of this noble work, in the language of the acting manager, "there has been no money expended for ornament, though no money has been spared to render it sound and permanent."

Having thus noticed the operations of this enterprising company in improving the navigation of the Lehigh from Easton to Mauch Chunk, we proceed to consider their labors more immediately connected with the raising and shipment of the coal.

Mauch Chunk mountain rises precipitately from the Lehigh river, where it is also the head of the Nesquihoning mountain, which at a short distance from the river diverges from Mauch Chunk proper, towards the N. W. The Mauch Chunk extends S. W. about 13 ms., to the Little Schuylkill r., which divides it from the Tuscarora mtns. Panther creek separates it on the north from the radiating hill of Nesquihoning, and the Mauch Chunk creek divides it from the Mahoning on the south. The vallies through which these creeks run, are deep and narrow. Explorations have been made in various parts of this mountain, and coal has been discovered through its whole extent.

"The geological structure of this coal formation is extremely simple. The upper rock is commonly a sand stone, or a fragmentary aggregate, of which the parts are more or less coarse or fine in different situations. In this region there is much pudding stone, or conglomerate, and much that would be called graywacke, by most geologists. In these aggregates the parts are of every size, from large pebbles to sand. The pebbles are chiefly quartz; and even in the firmest rocks are round, and appear to have been worn by attrition. The cement is silicious, and the masses frequently possess great firmness, resembling the mill-stone grit, and sand-stones of the English coal measures. Beneath this rock there is usually some variety of argillaceous slate, which commonly, though not universally, forms the roof of the coal; sometimes the sand-stone is directly in contact with the coals, the slate being omitted. The slate also forms the floor.

The great mine, as has already been observed, is at the summit of the mountain. The coal is uncovered, and fairly laid open to view, and lies in stupendous masses, which are worked in the open air, as in a stone quarry. The excavation is in an angular area, and entered at different points by roads cut through the coal, in some places quite down to the lowest level. The greatest ascertained thickness of the coal is fifty-four feet; in one place, it is supposed to be one hundred; but is commonly from twelve to thirty-five feet. Several banks of these dimensions are exposed, interrupted only by thin seams of slate, running parallel with the strata. The latter are inclined generally at angles, from five to fifteen degrees, and follow with great regularity the external form of the mountain. In some places they are saddle shaped; in some positions they and the attendant strata are wonderfully contorted and broken; and in one place, both are vertical, yet at a short distance return to the general arrangement. It is impossible to avoid the impression that some great force has disturbed the original formation, by elevating or depressing the strata."

"The entrances to the mine are numbered. At No. 3, is a perpendicular section through all the strata, down to the flooring of slate; and the graywacke, the slate and the coal, are all raised on edge. The strata are in some places vertical, in others, curved or waving, and they are broken in two at the upper part, and bent in opposite directions."

Professor Silliman asks, "Has subterranean fire produced these extraordinary locations? It would seem," he adds, "to favor this view, that the graywacke has, in some places, contiguous to the coal, the appearance of having been baked; it appears indurated, is harsh and dry, and is inflated with vesicles, as if gas, produced and rarified by heat, was struggling to escape." This is a tempting opportunity to indulge in speculation on the origin of coal measures generally. But, the limits of our volume impel us to forbearance. Yet we will avail ourselves of the occasion to say, that we adopt the general opinion, that coal is a vegetable deposit, composed of masses of timber, collected by powerful currents of water; and, that we now behold new coal-beds forming in many of the western waters, where miles of *rafts* are formed, sunken to unknown depths, and covered with strata of earth variously composed. How far these immense aggregates of vegetation may, in the course of time, become causes of subterranean fires, we will not attempt to conjecture. But, that extraneous volcanic force may give new forms to the regions in which they lie, we deem probable, and that at some future—perhaps very remote period, these beds of timber, converted into coal, and their intermediate and incumbent strata of earth turned into rock, may be upraised and broken into the various forms which distinguish the authracite country of Pennsylvania. Such a process we conceive would be but a repetition of that, which contributed to the formation of the Mauch Chunk mountain.

"There are rail roads leading through the mine, for the purpose of conveying the coal to the main road; and others on which the refuse coal, rocks, and rubbish, are made to descend in cars, by gravity, to different points, at which such materials are discharged down the side of the mountain. These rail ways are continued over the valleys, and the rubbish thrown from them has already formed about a dozen artificial hills, shaped like a steep roof, and terminating almost abruptly in a descent of hundreds of feet. The cars are guided, each by one man, who at a proper place, knocks open one end, and discharges the load. In some instances cars have run off from the end of the rail way, and the guides have been thrown down the mountain; but, falling among loose rubbish, such accidents have not proved fatal.

Besides the incombustible refuse, there is small and inferior coal enough here, to supply the fuel for a large city for years. It is not now sufficiently valuable for transportation. Small coal is used successfully at Mauch Chunk and elsewhere in burning lime, and at some future day may be advantageously employed in other manufactures.

Two mines have been recently opened within a mile of the large one; they are portions of the same great mass, and present an inexhaustible supply of fuel.

Notwithstanding this great abundance of coal upon the summit, hopes of procuring it from a part of the mountain nearer to navigation, have induced the "company" to excavate a tunnel two hundred feet below the precipitous ridge, and within two and a half miles of Mauch Chunk. This great enterprize was commenced on the 1st March, 1824, before the construction of the rail way to the "great mine," under the impression that the coal strata here *dipped* to the south. This supposition proved erroneous, and the company for that and other reasons suspended their labors. The tunnel is 16 feet wide, 8 feet high, and penetrates the mountain through hard pudding stone, 790 feet. Three thousand seven hundred and forty-five $\frac{5}{27}$ cubic yards of stone have been removed, at an expense of $26,812, or $7 16 per cubic yard, or $33 94 the lineal foot. The following statement of the particulars of cost, may prove useful to persons disposed to a similar undertaking. The work was suspended on the 9th June, 1827.

23,129¾ days labor, including 2, and sometimes 4 smiths, making and dressing tools, . .	18,667 19
Tools and materials for them,	3,785 86
521 kegs of powder,	1,831 00
Candles and oil for light,	812 71
Lumber (for air-pipes and other fixtures), hauling tools and materials, and supplies for hands,	508 54
268 days, one horse blowing wind, ...	160 80
Superintendance, . .	680 00
	$26,812 00

Shafts were sunk 80 feet in the table land at the base of the narrow rocky ridge; and good coal was found after penetrating seven feet of earth and slate. Coal has been struck in the horizontal tunnel, and though it is not deemed expedient to work it, the expenditure has not been in vain. The tunnel will serve to drain, and give access to the great coal bed above it.

When the company became satisfied of the present inexpediency of making further progress with the tunnel, they resolved to lay a rail way from Mauch Chunk to the great mine, which they commenced under the direction of the indefatigable Mr. White, their manager, on the 8th of January, 1827, and finished so as to pass the first load of coal down the whole line, in three months and 26 days.

"The rail road commences at the Lehigh r., and ascends at the rate of 1 foot in 3½ of the slant; the whole ascent to the top of the promontory is 215 feet, and the slant 700. The loaded wagons descend this inclined plane to the river. At the top of the hill is a building containing the machinery, by which their descent is governed; the most important part of which is a large cylinder, revolving horizontally, and serving to wind the rope attached to the cars. The latter are rolled by hand on a circular platform, which, revolving horizontally upon a perpendicular axis, brings the wagon upon a line with the inclined plane upon which they are launched. The rapidity of their progress is in a measure checked, by the weight of an ascending empty waggon, which being fastened at the other end of the rope, and moving on a parallel rail way on the same plane, necessarily mounts as rapidly as the empty one descends; and when it arrives at the top, it is transferred to the upper rail way by means of the circular platform. But this partial counterpoise is insufficient to moderate properly the speed of the descending car. This object is effectually gained by an iron band which clasps the drum, and which compressed by a lever controls its motion. Accidents have been rare in this descent, but the cars have sometimes deviated, or broken loose, and one man has been killed. They are now guarded against by a very simple, yet ingenious contrivance. The rail way is double, until the most rapid part of the descent is passed; when both ways curve and unite in one. Should a wagon break loose, its momentum will be so great as to prevent its following the curve, and as soon as it reaches this spot, it is thrown out, overturned and lodged on a clay bank, formed for this purpose below. Farther down a bulwark is constructed, overarching the rail way, to intercept the loose coal as it flies from the wagon. When the car arrives at the foot of the inclined plane, it pitches into a downward curve in the rail way, and a projecting bar which secures the lower end of the car, which for this purpose is hung on a horizontal axis, knocks it open, and the coal slides down a steep wooden funnel, into the boat or ark, which receding from the shore by the impulse thus given to it, occasions the coal to spread evenly over its bottom.

The length of the main rail road, from Mauch Chunk to the west end of the coal mine, is 9 miles, or	47,520 ft.
Length of branch roads to the mine, . .	8,069
Roads and their branches in the mine, . .	11,437
Total length of single tracks— $12\frac{695}{1000}$ miles =	67,026

The cost of the road was $38,726 = $3050 per mile.

Cost of the reservoir brake shute and fixtures, $9,500.

Whole cost, . . $48,226

The saving made by this mode of transportation, over that on a stone turnpike road of the best construction on a portage of nine miles is $64\frac{3}{4}$ cents per ton, which after deducting the interest on the cost of the improvement, produced a saving in the remainder of the season after its completion, of more than $15,000, and the road in less than three years use has overpaid its cost. The actual cost of transportation on this road, is thus stated by Mr. White in his report of 1st Jany. 1829, exclusive of tolls or repairs.

Mules and horses cost	$1\frac{1}{3}$	cts. per ton per m.
Hands	$1\frac{1}{3}$	do.
Repairing wagons	$\frac{2}{3}$	do.
Oil	$\frac{1}{5}$	do.
	$3\frac{53}{100}$	cts. per ton per m.

full load one way, and the whole cost divided into the distance one way only. The wear and tear of the road is estimated upon three years use at 1 cent per ton, per mile, making the whole cost of transportation, interest excluded, $4\frac{53}{100}$ per mile. He estimates the cost of transportation by canal in boats of 40 tons burthen at one cent per ton per mile; full load one way, and returning empty.

The rail way is of timber, about 20 feet long, 4 inches by 5, and set in cross pieces made of cloven trees placed $3\frac{1}{2}$ feet distance from each other, and secured by wedges. The rail is shod on the upper and inner edge with a flat bar of iron $2\frac{1}{4}$ inches wide, $\frac{5}{8}$ of an inch thick. These being bedded on the turnpike road for the greater part of the way are very firm and durable; this excellent stone road gave the company great facility in making the rail way, and enabled them to complete it in the very short time employed about it. The height surmounted by the rail road above the inclined plain is 767 feet in $8\frac{1}{4}$ miles equal to about 1° of acclivity in the mile. There are two places for turning out, made as usual by a curved rail road, lying against the main one, and forming an irregular segment of a circle resting upon its cord. If carriages meet on the road, the lighter must return to the place of turning out, or be removed from the rail way track. This sometimes happens with the pleasure cars.

Upon this road the coal is conveyed from the mine to Mauch Chunk village, in cars set on four cast iron wheels about $2\frac{1}{2}$ feet in diameter, each containing one ton and a half of coal. Fourteen of these are connected together by iron bars, admiting a slight degree of motion between two contiguous cars, and are conducted by a single man on one of them, who regulates their movements by a very simple contrivance. A perpendicular lever causes a piece of wood to press against the circumference of each wheel on the same side of the car, acting both ways from the central point between them, so that by increasing the pressure, the friction retards or stops the motion, and as all the levers are connected by a rope, they are made to act in concert. The observer is much interested in beholding the successive groups of wagons moving rapidly in procession without apparent cause. They are heard at a considerable distance as they come thundering along with their dark burdens, and give an impression of irresistable energy. At a suitable distance follows another train, and thus from 300 to 340 tons a day are discharged into the boats. At first the cars descended at the rate of 15 or 20 miles an hour; but the speed was reduced, as it injured the machines and by agitating and wearing the coal involved the driver in a cloud of black dust. The empty cars are drawn back by mules, 8 to a gang of 14 wagons; 28 mules draw up 42 coal, and 7 mule wagons; and the arrangement is so made, that the ascending parties, shall arrive in due season, at the proper places for turning out. This is the case with the pleasure cars, and the line of stages which pass by this route through Tamaque and by the Schuylkill valley rail road to Pottsville.

The mules ride down the rail way. They are furnished with provender, placed in proper mangers; 4 of them being enclosed in one pen, mounted on wheels; and 7 of these cars are connected into one group, so that 28 mules constitute the party which, with their heads directed down the mountain and apparently surveying its fine landscapes, move rapidly along the inclined plane, with a ludicrous gravity, which when seen for the first time proves too much for the severest muscles.

The mules readily perform their duty of drawing up the empty cars, but having experienced the comfort of riding down, they seem to regard it as a right, and very reluctantly descend any other way. The speed first adopted in travelling the rail way injured the health of the mules and horses employed on it, but the moderate rate of 6 or 7 miles the hour, at present used, does not affect them.

The pleasure of the traveller on returning in the pleasure car is mingled with a sense of danger. The 8 miles from the summit are frequently run, in 30 minutes, and some parts of the road are passed over at a still greater speed, nor is the danger apparent only. The axles of the coal cars have been broken, and like accidents may occur to those of the pleasure carriages. In one instance at least a carriage has been thrown from the road and the passengers hurt, but fortunately not very severely. Due care however is taken by the proprietors to keep the pleasure cars in good repair, and to entrust them to careful guides, who cheerfully conform to the wishes of the passengers, relative to the rate of progress.

With the exhaustless mines of the Mauch Chunk, and the admirable means of transporting their product, the company might have reposed in full confidence of an ultimate and speedy and profitable return for their great expenditure. But their vigilant *prevoyant* and energetic acting manager, has found means to take a bond of fate, and to hasten this result by the discovery and development of new mines upon the adjacent Nesquihoning mountain, 4 miles nearer to the landing of Mauch Chunk, and extremely facile of operation. In a defile of the mountain, through which passes a sparkling and bounding rivulet, called "*Room run*," a name soon to be as famous as "*Maunch Chunk*," some 20 veins of coal have been explored, varying in thickness from 5 to 50 feet, making an aggregate of more than 300 feet, nearly 5 times the thickness of the *great mine*. This coalfield is supposed to be a continuation of that of Mauch Chunk, from which it is distant between 4 and 5 miles. Some of these veins have been traced three and a half miles along the mountain. All of them are accessible above the water level; some of them have great facilities for drainage, and are provided with most desirable roofs and floors of slate, which render them susceptible of cheap excavation. This is especially the case of a 28 feet vein, into which three openings at different elevations have been made, whence coal of the first quality and highest lustre has been taken. Other veins approach so near the surface of the mountain, particularly the vein of 50 feet, that it may be best wrought by uncovering, after the manner of the *great mine*. And this labor has accordingly been commenced. It has been observed that the most solid, homogeneous and perfect masses of coal have been found under the thick strata of slate, with a sharp *dip*, and that soft and pliable coal is to be expected beneath an earthy and porous covering. The cause of this difference would seem to be, that in the first case the atmospheric water is excluded from the coal, and is carried away by the upper surface of the slate strata, whilst in the second, it percolates, and softens the coal, dividing it into small particles, which adhere feebly to each other.

Professor Silliman describes a peculiar formation of the great bed of 50 feet, and its contiguous strata. They rise in form of a half ellipse, placed on end with the curve uppermost; the form of the mountain of which they are part. "There is here, he observes, the most striking appearance, that these strata have been raised by force from beneath; and it is difficult to avoid the conviction that they were also broken at the top; for at the upper end of the stratum of coal there is a huge rock, 20 feet in two of its dimensions, and five or six feet in the other, which has been broken off from the roof rock, a greywacke of which it is part, and fallen in; and the coal seems then to have closed all around and shut it in on all sides, except, that in one place on the right hand a little below the top, the rupture is continued to the surface, and that place was then filled and concealed by the loose rubbish and soil, as was also the rock above." These circumstances, he conceives, confirm strongly the truth of the supposition, that an upheaving force, exerted with great energy, has bent, dislocated and broken the strata.

This vein is broken by the ravine, & worn down by the stream which passes thro' it, but reappears on the opposite side where it sssumes a form more curious and extraordinary. The strata as in the corresponding part radiate from the surface, and the interior upper angle, so far as it has been uncovered, is filled with sand stone arranged in reversed concentric arches, laid so regularly as to have the appearance of having been placed by art. The writer saw three of these arches, and the abuting parts of a fourth; the remainder of the last was covered by earth. The stones of the respective arches increase their dimensions with the size of the arch. The form of these arches would seem to militate against the hypothesis of an eccentric force, unless we presume, what is probably true, that the gravitation of the strata in opposite angles of about 45°, produced this result.

To avail themselves in the best manner, of these new treasures, the company have made a rail way, of 5 miles and 1631 feet, of which the following is a correct outline.

Branch from wharfto section 1 commencing 14.23 feet above the top of Mauch Chunk dam,					14.23
1200	feet	section1,	and branch—ascent,	11.90	26.13
1260	do.	do.	2, incl. self act. plane,	120.13	146.26
9912	do.	do.	3, ascent,	97.29	243.55
11348	do.	do.	4, ascent,	96.50	340.05
1260	do.	do.	5, incl. self act. plane,	120.15	460.20
891	do.	do.	6, ascent,	54.82	515.02
1160	do.	do.	7, ascent,	11.15	526.17
750	do.	do.	8, as far as excavated,	21	547.17
250		to 50 feet in ascent, to 6 feet above water,		15.33	56.250

28031 feet, 5 miles and 1631 feet in length.

Total elevation above the bed of the Lehigh at Mauch Chunk 570 feet. The curve of the road is on a radius of 1600 feet.

This road follows the curve of the mountain along the Lehigh for about two miles, and then still winding with the mountain, turns easterly and runs parallel with the Nesquihoning creek to the ravine of the mountain made by Room run which it ascends. It would be difficult perhaps to conceive a method of making a road more substantially than has been adopted on this. The rails are about 20 feet long, 7 inches deep and 5 in width. They are supported on massive blocks of stone, placed in line 4 feet apart, and imbedded firmly in smaller stone, and are secured to these blocks by iron clamps on each side of the rail, about 6 inches wide, but at right angles, and nailed to the rail and to the block by means of four holes drilled in each stone, and plugged with wood. The iron bars are $2\frac{1}{2}$ in. wide, $\frac{5}{8}$ thick. The whole of the road from the coal mines to the landing is descending. On the self acting plane the descending wagon will bring up an empty one. The intermediate road is graduated from 10 to 12 inches descent, in 100 feet, this being considered the lowest grade on which a loaded wagon will descend by gravity, and therefore the most favorable one, that can be devised, when the freight as in this case is all one way.

Doubts have been expressed as to the continuance of the supply of coal from this region. On this subject we will let Mr. White speak, observing that the sceptical may at any time by personal inspection have a full confirmation of his statements. In his official report to the company of 1st Jany. 1830, he says, " in addition to the extensive examinations which took place previous to my last report, explorations have been made which prove we can uncover and quarry our coal in *a continuous opening*, about two miles in extent east and west, having our present quarries about the centre. We have uncovered coal at the summit of the mountain, 320 feet north and south, across the strata of coal, which is of a quality similar to that in the great quarry ; so that we have, beyond all doubts, enough coal that can be quarried without mining, to last more than one generation, even supposing that our shipments exceeded one million of tons a year, and that without extending our quarries more than one mile from the summit. And when our successors have done quarrying they may follow the veins under ground eastward to the river about 7 miles more, and five miles in a western direction."

In his report of the 31st December, 1830, Mr. White adds, my conviction is, that our great coal mine, or quarry, will prove to be a vein of coal about 60 feet thick between the top and bottom slate, and that its extent will bear out my last annual report. Since that report I have examined our coal field in, and about Room run, where that stream breaks across the coal formation, and have had the good fortune to lay open a series of veins of unparalleled extent, of the following dimensions viz., 28, 5, 5, 10, 19, 39, 5, 12, 15, 15, 50, 20, 11, and 6 feet, making the whole number of veins opened 14, and the whole thickness, measured at right angles with the veins 240 feet. Other veins have since been explored. The width of the coal basin at this place north and south exceeds half a mile; and the bearing of the strata lengthwise is south 88° west. If we allow 60 cubic feet of these veins to make a ton of coal in the market, after leaving enough for piers, waste, &c. they will give four tons of coal to each superficial square foot, (counting the whole as one vein,) or 10,560 tons for each foot lengthwise of the coal basin, and consequently 55,756,800 tons for each mile; and allowing our demand to be one million of tons each year from these mines, one mile would last more than 55 years. The part of the coal basin belonging to the company, extends 10 or 12 miles.

We must not omit to notice here a very important and ingenious invention of Mr. White, for the purpose of raising burdens, in which, more than one of our operative classes, will take a deep interest. We allude to the propellers, for which he has taken a patent.

That this machine is very effective,

is made apparent by the following minute of one day's work, done by it at the Mauch Chunk mines. In $10\frac{3}{4}$ hours, 3 horses drove the machinery, and raised 204 wagons, loaded $1\frac{1}{2}$ tons each, up a plane of 35 feet rise, and 210 feet in length. As the propellers require no more attention in passing a wagon, than a piece of common rail road, and there being no gudgeons or machinery to grease except the driving part, the expense of going up hills is reduced to a mere trifle; being confined pretty much to that of the driving power.

As farther exemplifying the facility of labor possessed by the company, we incorporate the following note of one day's work at Mauch Chunk. "Three hundred and forty tons of coal quarried at the mines loaded and brought on the rail road nine miles, unloaded from the wagons, down the chute and loaded into boats. The boats for this coal *all built* the same day. Forty hundred feet of lumber sawed in one day and night."

The other great improvements made by the Lehigh navigation and coal company, are the villages which they have created, and are creating. These are Mauch Chunk, Lowrytown, Anthracite, Nesquihoning and South Easton. A description of the two first will be given here. The others are noticed under their respective titles.

Mauch Chunk village, is situated on the western bank of the Lehigh, in a deep and romantic ravine, between rocky mountains that rise in some parts precipitously to 800 or 1000 feet above the stream. Space was procured for dwellings, by breaking down the adjacent rocks and by filling a part of the ravine of the Mauch Chunk creek. This stream has been used to drive a tilt hammer, two furnaces and a grist mill. The company have erected, and are proprietors of 120 dwellings here, of which, all except "Whitehall," the residence of the acting manager and two or three occupied by the chief clerk, and other superior agents, are of the plainest character, designed solely for protection against the inclemency of the seasons. The hotel, admirably kept by Mr. Kimball, is a large and commodious building of stone, having adjacent another, built for lodging rooms. There are also here a large and very well furnished store conducted by the company, three saw mills, each with two saws, sundry workshops, and lime kiln. The company have from motives of policy heretofore excluded from their premises all persons not immediately under their control. By this means they have been enabled to enforce a stricter practice of morality than could otherwise be obtained, under the penalty of dismissal from a very desirable service, and the ejectment of tenants, at will, from their dwellings.

Tippling houses and the retail of ardent spirits, are prohibited. Drunkards are not suffered to remain. Abuse or neglect of his family, and cruelty to cattle, are grounds of dismissal of any person. There is no regular place of worship; the school house has been appropriated to that purpose, where clergymen of every denomination are invited to preach; and dissipation is prohibited on the Sabbath. By a small annual contribution from each laborer and the heads of families in the village a physician is procured who attends the sick without further compensation.

The completion of the canals and of the rail roads and landings, having enabled the company to ascertain what parts of their property may be sold without interfering with the extension of their coal business; they now offer to the enterprize of the public, lots in the towns of Nesquihoning and Mauch Chunk. They propose an addition to the latter town, to be called E. Mauch Chunk, located on the company's land in what is commonly known by the name of the "Lehigh Kettle," on the east side of the Lehigh, and about one fourth of a mile above Mauch Chunk; at the head of the great navigation of 140 ton boats; and at the foot of the contemplated mountain navigation from Susquehanhannah for boats of 70 tons, and directly opposite to the landing of the company for the coal from the Room run mines. It is the nearest ground to those landings, suitable for an extensive settlement, and has a favorable surface for this purpose, to the extent of half a mile in width by a mile in length. On the upper corner of the plot the river Lehigh may be used with a fall of 20 feet for manufacturing purposes, and the sterility and roughness of the country on the Upper Lehigh will preserve the volume of the river forever undiminished. This spot is four miles from Nesquihoning, 32 from Berwick, 44 from Catawissa, about 38 from Wilkesbarre, and 46 by the canal from Easton.

Mr. White speaks thus of the advantages of this position : "when it is recollected that 1,000,000 tons of coal will employ 1000 workmen in the various business connected with it, and that these with the families will require the aid of professional men, merchants and mechanics of all descriptions, it will not be deemed extravagant to say, that the location and advantages of East Mauch Chunk are such as must insure its speedily becoming one of the largest inland towns in the state, and that it will furnish a nursery from which the coal business may derive as many hands as may be required."

Mauch Chunk village and dependencies contained on the 1st Jany. 1831, 1316 inhabitants, viz. 199 male, 275 female adults, 318 boarders, 73 male children over 10 years, females 64, males under 10, 82, females 74; native children 231. Besides which there were at the pine forest 180 inhabitants.

The hamlet of coal of *Anthracite* or *Coalville*, is upon the summit of the mountain at the "great mine," and contains about 40 houses, a hotel, a neat and comfortable establishment, at which Mr. Ray, the keeper, hospitably entertains his visitors, a school house, and a residence for the superintendants. There are ordinarily here about 250 inhabitants, principally miners.

Before we quit this article it will be proper to take a concise and rapid view of the possessions and advantages of the Lehigh navigation and coal company. They have 13,000 acres of land, extending across the Lehigh, and occupying, with the exception of a small tract in and about Lausanne, the whole of the t-ship, and another tract of 3000 acres about 15 miles from Mauch Chunk upon the Lehigh, abounding in valuable timber, in the pine forest, where they have built Lowry town. They have inexhaustible supplies of the best coal, approachable in the most advantageous manner, and for the transportaion of which, to the great markets of Philadelphia and New York, they have the best and most direct means, their own rail ways and canal, the Delaware canal from Easton to Philadelphia, the Delaware river, and the Morris and Trenton canals to New York. They have at and near Mauch Chunk four villages, containing together about 200 houses and a population of more than 1500 souls. They have on the line of their canal many valuable portions of land, which they have acquired in settling the claims for damages accruing to individuals by their excavations, &c., together with many highly valuable mill sites, with the unrestricted use of the surplus water of the Lehigh after the supply of the canal. They have a large town plot and very valuable mill sites, on the dam on the Lehigh, just above its confluence with the Delaware, where all the advantages of water power, cheap fuel, abundant and valuable iron ore, excellent and cheap building materials, a plentiful and cheap supply of provisions, a healthy and picturesque country, and a near and populous town, are combined with the very important requisite of ready access to the best markets.

All these sources and means of prosperity are now, or soon will be, available to the company, but there are others in prospect which are not less important to the productiveness of their canal, and to the business of their towns. The product of the Beaver Meadow coal mines, which are situated about 11 miles N. W. of Mauch Chunk, near the Berwick turnpike, will probably seek this outlet, as will also the still more important communication with the Susquehannah by the Lehigh r. and Nescopeck creeks, or by the Lehigh, and a series of inclined planes across the country between Mauch Chunk and Berwick, on the Susquehannah r. By the former mode of connection, the distance between Phila. and Berwick, will be 42 miles less, than by the Union canal, and between Berwick and New York, it will be one half less than by the latter canal. By the adoption of planes a further reduction of 38 miles may be made. By the canal, which we understand has been recommended as the only practical one connecting the Susquehannah and Delaware rivers north of Blue mountain, the company very properly anticipate that the trade of the north branch of the Susquehannah and a fair proportion of the west branch will be made tributary to them.

The Lehigh canal unconnected with the Susquehannah is a very important part of the company's possessions, and the tolls receivable upon it will be an important portion of their income; and perhaps the company may find, that it will be more advantageous to them, to throw open the coal trade as they have done their town plots, to public enterprize; contenting themselves with a coal rent, a toll on their roads and canal, and the profits on the increased value of their territorial possessions. In favor of such a course the following remarks may merit consideration. It is impossible now for any company, or companies, to monopolize the coal trade; competition will reduce the profits to the minimum on the cost of getting it to market. That cost will be less, the present facilities of transportation continued, where the business is conducted by individuals. The cost of transportation by the Lehigh routes will be less than by any other. In the hands therefore of individuals, the Lehigh coal may be brought to market cheaper than any other, & in such case, as the quality is unexceptionable and the supply adequate to any demand, the great consumption of the Union would be fed chiefly from this source. Enterprizing individuals assured of a certain business and moderate profits, would by their exertions extend the use of coal, applying it to new objects, and their congregation near the mines would introduce a large population, manufactories of various kinds, and all the arts indispensable to a thriving and increasing people. Under such circumstances the income of the company would become abundant from rent of coal mines, toll on roads and canal, sales of town lots and water sites, &c. &c. But whilst the coal business is in the hands of the company alone, the inducements to settle their lands do not appear very attractive.

Mauch Chunk creek, receives its name from the mountain at whose foot it rises, and along which it runs into the Lehigh r. on the W. side, about a mile and a half below the Nesquihoning. It is a very rapid, though not a large stream. But its great fall renders it very efficient as a mill stream, and it serves to turn several mills employed by the Lehigh navigation and coal company at their village. (*See Mauch Chunk mountain, &c.*)

Mauch Chunk, t-ship, Northampton co. bounded N. by Lausanne and Towamensing t-ships, E. and S. E. by Towamensing, S. by East Penn, and W. by Schuylkill co. The larger portion of this t-ship belongs to the Lehigh navigation and coal company. It is about 12 ms. in length and something over 2 in breadth, and comprises about 13,000 acres. It includes parts of the Mahoning, Mauch Chunk, Nesquihoning and Broad mtns. on the W. side of the Lehigh, and parts of the Broad mtn., Big Creek mountain, and

Kettle mtn. on the E. side of that r. There are 4 villages in the township, Mauch Chunk, Anthracite or Coalville, Lausanne and Nesquihoning; the latter erected on the Nesquihoning cr. within a half mile of the newly discovered coal mines on Room run, and $4\frac{1}{2}$ ms. by a rail-way from the coal landing at Mauch Chunk, was commenced in April, 1831, and in Sept. in that year contained 21 houses and a store. It is drained by Beaver cr. Mauch Chunk cr. Room run, Nesquihoning and Kettle crs. The surface of the t-ship is covered with mountains, the soil gravel. Pop. in 1830, 1348. Taxables in 1828, 262.

Maxatawny, t-ship, Berks co. bounded N. E. by Lehigh co., S. E. by Longswamp t-ship, W. by Rockland, and N. W. by Greenwich. Greatest length $5\frac{1}{2}$, greatest breadth $4\frac{3}{4}$ miles; area 14,960 acres; surface generally level; soil, limestone and gravel, and highly productive. Pop. in 1810, 1530, in 1820, 1845, in 1830, 2108; taxables in 1828, 290. The t-ship is intersected by roads in various directions. Sacony creek, a tributary of Maiden creek, passes north westerly through it, turning several mills in its course; and a branch of the same cr. runs S. W. for about 3 miles in the t-ship. Upon both streams there are several mills. Between the forks of the main branch of the creek is situated a church, common to the Presbyterians and Lutherans, and another at Kutztown. Kutztown, distant 17 ms. from Reading, is in this t-ship. It comprises about 100 dwellings, 3 stores, 6 taverns, and a Lutheran church. Maxatawny p-o. is 165 ms. from W. C. and 74 miles from Harrisburg.

Maytown, p-t. of W. Donegal t-ship, Lancaster co. about 15 ms. W. of the city of Lancaster, 104 from W. C. and 23 from Harrisburg, and about 3 ms. from the r. Susquehannah, contains some 25 or 30 dwellings, stores and taverns.

Meadow run, a small tributary of the Quitapahilla cr. which rises in Lebanon t-ship, Lebanon co. and flows N. to its recipient.

Meadowville, p-o. of Lebanon co. 131 ms. from W. C. and 21 from Harrisburg.

Meadville, t-ship, Crawford co. surrounds the town of Meadville, and contained, in 1830, independent of the borough, a population of 1026 souls.

Meadville, p-t. and st. of justice of Crawford co. is situated on the left bank of French cr. near the northern margin of a rich and handsome valley, through which that stream meanders; about 87 ms. from the town of Erie, on lake Erie, 24 from Franklin, on the Allegheny, and 90 N. of Pittsburg, 297 N. W. from W. C. and 236 from Harrisburg. The town plot gradually rises from the water to its centre, where is a handsome public square of about 5 acres. Immediately fronting the square on the E. is the court house, which, in point of beauty, convenience and workmanship, is said not to be surpassed by any in the state. The plan was gratuitously furnished by the distinguished architect, Mr. Strickland, of Phila. Its walls are of brick and cut stone, and it is adorned by a handsome cupola. On the rising ground, a short distance E. of the court house, is the Presbyterian church, a good and convenient building; its walls are of brick, and it has a spire and well-toned bell. Immediately fronting the public square, on the W. and near to the N. W. corner, stands the Episcopal church, a very tasteful, neat and convenient building, of the Gothic order, with a tower, and contains a neat and well-toned organ; its walls are of brick, painted in imitation of free stone. A short distance W. of the public square is the academy, a large, handsome and convenient building of brick, with a neat cupola and bell. Near the northern border of the town is the state arsenal, a spacious, neat and convenient brick building; and a short distance N. of it, on a commanding eminence overlooking the town and the valley, stands Bently hall, the edifice of Allegheny college. Its walls are of brick and cut stone, in the Ionic order. It consists of a main building, 60 feet front by 44 deep, and 3 stories high, and 2 wings of 30 ft. front each, and 2 stories high, with a basement story under the whole, and has also a handsome cupola. This building would justly be considered an ornament in any city in the Union. The Methodist society have a neat and spacious church; and on the N. border of the town Col. Magaw, well known as the patentee of straw paper, has fitted up a large and convenient frame building for the manufacture of that cheap and valuable article.

Allegheny college was founded by a number of public spirited gentlemen of Meadville, in the year 1815, and was incorporated by the legislature in 1817. $2000 were granted to the institution by the incoporating act, and a further sum of $5000, payable in equal annual instalments. The name of Bentley hall was given to the building, in commemoration of a munificent bequest, made to the institution by the late Rev. Wm. Bentley, D. D., of Salem, Massachusetts. The library of the college embraces the private library of that gentleman, estimated at more than 3000 vols., and a number of English books, presented by Isaiah Thomas, Esq. of Worcester, Mass., to whose liberality the institution is indebted for a pair of fine globes. A noble and splendid addition was made to this valuable collection by the bequest of the late Judge Winthrop, also of Massachusetts, of nearly the whole of his private library, valued, by a low estimate, at $6,500. In rare and valuable works, the library of Judge Winthrop was probably not surpassed, by any one of similar extent in the Union.

In the year 1829, the trustees of the college, deeply impressed with the excellence of the system of education adopted by Capt. Alden Partridge at his academy, at Middletown in Conn., made arrangements with a gentleman from that academy, to establish a similar institution in the college. The course of instruction given by this system is full and thorough, embracing the following branches of literature and science:

Pennmanship, Arithmetic, Geography, English Grammar, Composition, Rhetoric, Logic, Metaphysics, History, Mathematics, theoretical and practical, Latin, Greek, Hebrew, French, Spanish, Natural and Political Law, Moral Philosophy, Political Economy, Natural Philosophy, Civil Engineering, Topography, Chemistry, Mineralogy. These comprise the branches usually included in a full course of collegiate studies, and the cadets who shall have gone through this course, and sustained the requisite examination, will receive a diploma from the college.

As the military organization is the peculiar trait in this system, those institutions in which it has been adopted, are distinguished as military, and an erroneous impression has thus been obtained in regard to their character; it being supposed that their principal object is the training of youth in the art of war. But such is not the fact; for, although a knowledge of the means of defending the country in the field as in the cabinet be essential, still the more immediate and principal benefit of this system, is found in the order, discipline, energy and promptitude, which is thus introduced into our seminaries of learning, together with the manly and noble exercise to which every student is subject, tending to form a sound mind in a sound body.

The situation of the t. of Meadville on the French creek feeder, which has the dimensions of, and is intended to supply the contemplated canal from the Allegheny r. to Erie, gives it important advantages for trade, which will necessarily contribute to the rapid extension of the place. The town contains, by the census of 1830, white males, 553; colored do. 9. White females, 531; colored do. 7, making together, 1100. It was incorporated by act 29th March, 1823.

Means' run, tributary of the Conedogwinit creek, which flows N. along the boundary line between Cumberland and Franklin counties, through Shippensburg to its recepient.

Mechanicsburg, p-t. and thriving village on the S. W. border of Hopewell t-ship, York co., and on the head waters of Deer creek, which flows into Maryland; distant 15 ms. S. E. from the borough of York.

Mechanicsburg, borough and p-t. of of E. Pennsborough t-ship, Cumberland co., near the S. boundary, about 9 miles E. of Carlisle, containing about 100 dwellings, and 554 inhabitants, and one church. It is 105 miles N. W. of W. C., and 11 ms. W. of Harrisburg. It was incorporated 12th April, 1828.

Mechanicsville, p-o., Bucks co., 165 miles from W. C., and 112 from Harrisburg.

Mercer, co. is bounded N. by Crawford co., E. by Venango, S. E. by Butler, S. by Beaver, and W. by the state of O. Length 32, breadth 26 ms. Area 830 sq. ms., or 531,200 acres. Central lat. 41° 15′ N., long. W. from W. C. 3° 15′.

The geological structure of the county belongs to the secondary formation; the horizontal strata of which have been cut by the streams to a considerable depth in various directions, and the plain has thus been converted into a rolling surface, and in many places assumes a hilly character. Bituminous coal is found in abundance in every t-ship in the county; we have not learned whether its usual concomitants, iron and salt, in this region, attend it. Copperas is found in great quantities near the t. of Mercer. The southern part of the county is well adapted to grain; its central and northern parts are better suited to grazing, and the inhabitants claim, that it is the best county in the state for pasturage. The soil is loam, variously compounded of clay, gravel, and sand, and covered with a rich vegetable mould, which in the valleys is often very deep, particularly on the borders of the larger streams.

The county is abundantly watered. The Shenango creek or r. enters the N. W. angle of this, from Crawford co., and is navigable through the whole county. Its course is very crooked, and its waters are augmented by Crooked creek, and by the Little Shenango; the Lackawannock and the Shenango creeks from the E., and the Pymatuning from the W. The Mahoning r. into which the Shenango empties, flows from the state of Ohio, eastwardly, across the S. W. angle of Shenango t-ship, and of this county. The Neshannock rises on the southern confines of Salem and Sandy Creek t-ship, and flowing S. and S. West through the county, unites with the Shenango near, but S. of, the southern line of the co., passing within a mile and a half W. of the borough of Mercer. On the N. E. the co. is drained by Deer creek, and Sandy creek, the latter of which is also the drain of Sandy lake. Slippery Rock creek rises in Sandy Lake t-ship, and runs S. to the Butler co. line, and thence S. W. into Beaver co.

The t-pike road, from Pittsburg by Butler and Mercer to Erie, runs through the county. Another t-pike road has lately been made, or is now making from Roseburg in the co. of Armstrong, to the co. of Mercer. The Beaver division of the Pennsylvania canal, is now under contract from the Ohio r. to the town of New Castle, on the southern line of this county, and in the fork of the Shenango and Neshannock creeks, and the whole line is expected to be completed for public use, by the 1st day of Dec. next. It is in contemplation to extend this canal through Mercer co., to unite with the line connecting the Allegheny r. with lake Erie.

The chief towns of this county are Mercer, Newcastle, Harlandsburg, Edinburg, Bedford, New Wilmington, Clarksburg, Greenville, &c. &c.

The co. was originally settled by persons from other parts of Pennsylvania, but of late years, many Irish, English, and German settlers have established themselves here. The pop. in 1800, was 3228; in 1810, 8277; in 1820, 11,681; and in 1830, 19,733. Of the last number, 9896 were white males; 9628 white females; 99 free colored males; 102 free colored females, and 3 male and 3 female slaves. Of this number also there were 271 aliens, 11 deaf and dumb, and 17 blind.

There is a county Bible society established, and Sunday schools are encouraged in neighborhoods that are densely settled. There are in the county 12 churches, of which 6 pertain to the Presbyterians, 3 to Seceders, 1 to Methodists, and 2 to Unionists.

Country schools are located, where needed, pretty generally through the county, and are numerously attended, especially in the winter season; and an academy was established in the borough of Mercer, and incorporated in 1811; the incorporating act appropriated for the use of the institution the sum of $2000. Two newspapers are published in the co. (*See Mercer borough.*)

The exports of the county are flour, grain, whiskey, and live stock. Of the latter, especially sheep, large quantities are reared; and wool, unless an alteration in the tariff should render it worthless, must soon become an important marketable commodity.

The average price of improved lands is $8 the acre, of unimproved of good quality, $2 the acre. The value of the real estate, by the assessment of 1829, was $1,345,175.

The county paid into the state treasury, in 1831, for

Tax on writs, . . .	227,73
Tavern licenses, . .	158,84
Duty on dealers in foreign merchandize, . .	733,63
	$1120 20

Public buildings of the county consist of a court house and county offices, of brick, a prison, of stone; the academy and the churches we have heretofore mentioned.

Mercer, Erie, Crawford, Warren and Venango counties form the 18th congressional district, sending one member to congress. Mercer, Erie, and Crawford, make the 23d senatorial district, sending one member to the senate; and Crawford and Mercer united, elect one member to the house of representatives. Mercer, Venango, Crawford and Erie, constitute the 6th judicial district, over which Henry Shippen, Esq. presides. The courts are holden at the town of Mercer, on the 3d Monday of February, May August, and November.

STATISTICAL TABLE OF MERCER COUNTY.

Townships, &c.	Greatest Lth.	Greatest Bth.	Area in Acres.	Population. 1820	Population. 1830.	Taxables.
Cool Spring,	8	6	30720	596	1099	178
Delaware,	8	6	30720	424	941	169
French Creek,	8½	6½	35520	277	457	78
Lackawannock	8	6	30720	602	1163	215
Mercer,				506	656	129
Mahoning,	8	6	30720	1647	2369	399
Neshannock,	8	6	30720	1828	1703	316
Pymatuning,	8	6	30720	671	1297	203
Salem,	8	6	30720	700	1117	194
Salem, West,	8	6	30720	1040	1850	340
Sandy Lake,	8	6	30720	427	741	143
Shenango,	8	6	30720	1091	1455	294
Slippery Rock,	9½	8	32200	1027	1523	258
Sandy Creek,	8	6	30720	520	1048	165
Wolf Creek,	10½	6	35000	815	1244	229
Springfield,	8	6	30720	598	1068	180
				11681	10731	3490

Mercersburg, p-t. of Montgomery t-ship, Franklin co. upon the turnpike road from Greencastle to McConnelstown, 10 miles W. from the former, 17 S. W. from Chambersburg, 83 N. W. from W. C. 71 S. W. from Harrisburg. Contains about 140 dwellings, 4 churches viz., 1 Presbyterian, 1 German Reformed, 1 Seceder and 1 Methodist, 6 stores and 4 taverns. The surrounding country is limestone and well cultivated, and consequently productive. About 3 miles N. of the town there is a sulphur spring, whose medicinal qualities are recommended.

Mercer, t-ship, Butler co. bounded N. by Venango co., E. by Venango t-ship, S. by Slippery Rock t-ship, W. by Mercer co. Centrally distant N. from Butler borough 19 miles; greatest length 9, breadth 5 miles; area, 18,380 acres; surface, part rolling part hilly; soil, loam, clay. Pop in 1830, 771; taxables 172. It is drained by the N. branch of Slippery Rock creek, and by Wolf creek, a tributary of that stream. Harrisville, post-town, lies near the W. boundary.

Mercer, borough p-t. and st. jus. of Mercer co. situated in the N. W. angle of Springfield t-ship, near the Neshannock creek, 57 miles a little W. of N. from Pittsburg, and about 190 miles N. W. of Harrisburg in lat. 41° 13′ N. lon. 3° 13′ W. of W.C. taxables 129; taxable property 1829, real estate $66,875; personal, $5825; rate of tax 3½ mills on the dollar. The town contains 120 dwellings, 1 Presbyterian, 1 Union, 1 Methodist and 1 Seceder church; 6 taverns, among which is Hackney's hotel, a large and commodious brick building. In the neighborhood of this town is an extensive manufactory of copperas, established by J. Wright Esq. the quality of which is said to be excellent, and the quantity made, adequate to the supply of the country north of the Ohio. There is an academy in the town, incorporated by act of 30th March, 1811, by which $2000 were given to it, on condition that a number of poor children, not exceeding 5, should be annually taught therein gratis. Two weekly papers, viz. the Mercer Luminary, and Western Republican, are printed here. A daily stage from Pittsburg to Erie, and another 3 times a week from Pittsburg, via Hamony, and one twice a week from Franklin to Warren in Ohio arrive in the town. The town was incorporated by act of assembly 28th March, 1814.

Mercersburg, p-t. and borough, Montgomery t-ship, Franklin co. on a branch of Conecocheague creek, 15 miles S. W. of Chambersburg, 71 from Harrisburg, and 83 N. W. from W. C. A turnpike road runs from Waynesburg through Greenecastle to this town, and thence to McConnelsburg and Bedford. The town contains 140 dwellings, 6 stores, 4 taverns, 1 Presbyterian, 1 Lutheran and German Reformed, 1 Seceder, 1 Methodist church. The town was incorporated by act of assembly 26 Feb. 1831.

Merion, Upper, t-ship, Montgomery co. bounded on the N. W., N. and N. E. by the river Schuylkill, on the S. E. by Lower Merion t-ship, and on the S. and S.W. by Chester co. Its form is very irregular, somewhat in shape of a bow bent; its greatest length is 9, width 5 miles; area 10,880 acres. The Valley cr. runs along the western boundary to the Schuylkill river and drives sundry water works and the valley forge. The Gulph creek is near its east line, on which are some valuable grist mills. There is a post office near the mills, called "Gulph Mills," and another more centrally situated called Reaseville, the former about 3 ms. S. E. and the latter about 3½ miles S. W. from Norristown. Merion church is 2 miles distant from Norristown. Surface, rolling; soil, limestone. Pop. in 1830, 1618; taxables in 1828, 360. It is stated as a singlar circumstance that there are now in this t-ship only *three* taverns, being the same which existed there 100 years ago, each 3 miles from the other, on three points of a triangle to wit, the "*Swedes ford*," the "*Bird in Hand*," and the "*King of Prussia*." The post office, called after the t-ship, is 139 miles from W. C. and 87 from Harrisburg.

Merion, Lower, t-ship, Montgomery co. bounded N. by Upper Mercer, Plymouth and Whitemarsh t-ships, E. and S. by Phila. co., and W. by Delaware co.; greatest length 8½ miles, greatest breadth 5 miles. Central distance from Phila. 10 miles, from Norristown 7 miles. There are three churches in this t-ship. It is watered by the Schuylkill river, Mill creek and a branch of Cobb's creek, all of which are mill streams and well employed. The Phila. and Lancaster turnpike road passes through its S. W. angle. Surface of the country is rolling; soil, rich loam. Pop. in 1830, 2524; taxables in 1828, 522. The post office, called after the t-ship, is distant from

Washington, 150 miles, and 93 from Harrisburg.

Merrit's town, p-t. Luzerne t-ship, Fayette co. on Dunlap's creek, about midway of the E. boundary of the t-ship, 10 miles N. W. of Uniontown, and about 4 miles S. of Bridgeport, 209 miles N. W. from W. C., 194 S. W. from Harrisburg; contains 35 dwellings, 1 church, 1 school, 2 stores, 1 tavern, 1 grist mill and 1 saw mill.

Mertztown, Longswamp t-ship, Berks co. (*See Longswamp*.)

Meshoppen creek, Susquehannah co. rises in the t-ship of Bridgewater, and flows southwardly through Springville t-ship, in that county, and Tunkhannock and Braintrim t-ships, Luzerne co. into the Susquehannah river. It is a fine mill stream, but a fall near its mouth renders it unnavigable for more than half a mile from the river, above which there is a course of rapids which must perpetually bar the ascent of boats. It has three large branches; the middle branch rises also in Bridgewater and flows parallel with the main stream, which it joins above the falls. The west branch rises in Rush t-ship, and mingles with the middle one in Braintrim, and the Little Meshoppen which also has its source in Rush, blends with the Great, a short distance above its confluence with the Susquehannah.

Metal, t-ship, Franklin co. bounded N. E. by Fannet, S. E. by Letterkenny and Hamilton, S. by Peters t-ships, and W. by Bedford and Huntingdon counties. Centrally distant from Chambersburg N. W. 12 miles; greatest length 15, breadth 5 miles; area, 23,680 acres; surface, mountainous; soil, limestone and red shale. Pop. in 1830, 1296; taxables, 248. This t-ship is almost covered with mountains. The Blue mountain is on the E. and the Tuscarora on the W.; between them lies the Path valley, which in the widest part does not exceed three miles. Through this valley flows, by the post town of Fannetsburg, the W. branch of the Conecocheague creek. In the S. part of the t-ship, are beds of iron ore, near which is a furnace.

Mexus, p-t. of Fermanagh t-ship, Mifflin co. on the left bank of the Juniata river, on the state canal and on the turnpike road leading from Lewiston E. about 16 miles from that town, 147 from W. C., and 40 from Harrisburg, contains between 40 and 50 dwellings, 3 or 4 taverns and 2 stores.

Michler's tavern, p-o. on the road from Nazareth to the Wind gap, about 11 miles from Easton. There are here 6 or 8 houses, a furnace belonging to Mr. Henry, a grist mill, and store.

Middle brook, a small stream of Covington t-ship, Luzerne co. which flows into the Lehigh river, between the mouths of Trout and Choke creeks.

Middle creek, Elizabeth t-ship, Lancaster county, rises in the Conewago hills, and runs southwardly through the t-ship, into the Cocalico creek, receiving in its course Seglock creek.

Middle creek, Adams co. rises in Hamilton-ban t-ship, and flows S. E. through Liberty t-ship, into the state of Maryland.

Middle creek, Somerset co. rises in Somerset t-ship, and flows S. through Milford t-ship, into Castleman's river.

Middleburg, post-town of Centre t-ship, Union co. on the left bank of the Mahoniely or Middle creek, about 6 miles S. W. of New Berlin, 162 N. W. from W. C. and 52 from Harrisburg, contains 50 dwellings, 5 stores, 4 taverns, and 1 Lutheran church.

Middleburg, t-ship, Tioga county, formerly part of the t-ship of Delmar. Surface, hilly; soil, loam. Pop. about 375; taxables, 67.

Middleport, a post-town and village, Schuylkill county, on the Schuylkill valley rail road, about 6 miles from Port Carbon, 182 from W. C. and 74 from Harrisburg. The state road from Pottsville to Mauch Chunk, runs parallel with the rail road through the town, and both are intersected by the state road from Orwigsburg to Berwick. The Middleport and Pine cr. rail road, is to intersect the valley rail road, also in the town. These, with the surrounding collieries, are the sources to which Middleport must look for its future advancement. The town contains about 20 houses, 2 taverns and 2 stores, and is inhabited principally by persons connected with the mines.

Middleburg, post-town, Centre t-ship, Union county.

Middletown, t-ship, Susquehannah county, bounded N. by Choconut t-ship, E. by Silverlake and Bridgewater t-ships, S. by Rush t-ship, and W. by Bradford county. It is drained by the Wyalusing creek, and the Middle and North branches of that stream. Length E. and W. 9 miles, breadth 6 miles; area, 34,560 acres. The turnpike road from Montrose to Owego crosses the N. E. angle of the t-ship, and at the intersection of the N. boundary is a small village called Friendsville, at which there is a post-office. Surface, hilly; soil, gravel and clay. Pop. in 1830, 683; taxables in 1828, 114.

Middletown, t-ship, Bucks county, bounded N. by Newtown, E. by Lower Makefield and falls, S. by Bristol and Bensalem t-ships, W. by Northampton co. Centrally distant from Philadelphia 20 miles; greatest length 6½ miles, greatest breadth 6 miles; area, 12,569 acres; surface, rolling; soil, clay. Pop. in 1830, 2178; taxables in 1828, 424. The Neshaminy creek forms a part of its western boundary, and a branch of it, which rises near Newtown, passes through the t-ship, and Bristol creek has its source within it. Its towns are Hulmeville, Attleborough and Oxford. The two former are post-towns. There is a Quaker meeting at Attleborough.

Middletown, t-ship, Delaware county, bounded N. W. by Upper and Nether Providence, S. by Chester, S. W. by Aston, N. W. by Thornbury and Edgemont. Central distance from Philadelphia 20 miles W., from Chester 6 miles N. W. Length 4½, breadth 4½ miles; area, 7680 acres; surface, level; soil, clay and loam. Pop. in 1830, 1188; taxables in 1828, 228. Chester creek courses the western boundary, and Ridley creek the eastern. Wrangle Town is centrally situated in the t-ship.

Middleton, a small village of Huntingdon t-ship, Adams co. in the N. W. angle of the t-ship, 14 miles N. E. of Gettysburg.

Middleton, North, t-ship of Cumberland co. bounded N. by Perry co. E. by East Pennsborough, S. by South Middleton, and W. by West Pennsborough and Frankford t-ships. Greatest length 9, breadth 7 miles; area, 26,880 acres; surface, part hilly, part level; soil, limestone and slate. Pop. in 1830, 1932. The Conedogwinit creek passes centrally through the t-ship, and receives several tributaries from it, among which is Letart creek, flowing near Carlisle, and that borough is one half within the t-ship. Carlisle Springs lie N. of the borough, about 3 miles. The turnpike road from Carlisle to Harrisburg, runs through the S. E. angle of the t-ship. The Blue mountains bound it on the N. through which are Starret's and Long's gaps.

Middleton, South, t-ship, Cumberland co. bounded N. by North Middleton, E. by Monroe, S. by York and Adams counties, and W. by Dickenson. Greatest length 10, breadth 6½ miles; area, 25,600 acres; surface, partly hilly, partly level; soil, limestone. Pop. in 1830, 2072; taxables, 355. The Yellow Breeches creek flows E. through the t-ship, receiving Mountain creek. On the latter, are some iron works. Letart Spring is near the N. boundary, which, at its very source, gives motion to 2 mills. Boiling Spring is on the E. boundary. One half of the borough of Carlisle is in this t-ship. The South mountains cover a considerable portion of the southern part.

Middletown, village of Manallen t-ship, Fayette co. in a bend of Red Stone creek, about 5 miles N. of Uniontown.

Middleton, West, post-town and borough of Hopewell t-ship, Washington co. on the road leading from Washington borough to Wellsburg, on the Ohio river, 11 miles N. W. of the former, 243 from W. C. and 225 from Harrisburg, contains 40 or 50 dwellings, 3 taverns, and 1 store; was incorporated 27th March, 1823.

Middleton, town of Moon t-ship, Allegheny co. on the W. bank of the Ohio river, 10 miles below Pittsburg, and opposite to Neville island, contains about 12 houses, store and tavern.

Middletown, Plumb Creek t-ship, Armstrong co. on the turnpike road leading from the borough of Indiana to Kittanning, about 12 miles from each.

Middletown, Upper, post-town, Fayette county, 206 miles N. W. from W. C. and 183 from Harrisburg.

Middletown, post-town and borough of Swatara t-ship, Dauphin county, 9 miles by the turnpike road S. E. of Harrisburg, and 102 from W. C. near the junction of the Susquehannah and Swatara rivers, at which the Penn. and Union canals unite. It was incorporated into a borough in 1829, and contains, including Portsmouth, immediately at the confluence of the streams, not within the borough limits, 190 dwellings, 2 churches, beside other buildings. There are here 12 taverns, and 7 stores. During the spring freshets in the Susquehannah, there is a large trade here in grain, flour, lumber, iron and coal, brought by the canal and river, and transhipped by the Union canal to Philadelphia. The town was incorporated 19th Feb. 1828.

Middlesex, t-ship, Butler county, bounded N. by Butler t-ship, E. by Buffalo, S. by Allegheny county, and W. by Cranberry t-ship. Centrally distant S. W. of Butler borough 9 miles. It forms a square of 8 miles. Area, 40,960 acres; surface, hilly; soil, loam. Pop. in 1830, 1231; taxables, 244. It is drained by Thorn creek and Glade run, branches of the Conequenessing creek. The turnpike road from Pittsburg to Butler, runs N. E. through the t-ship, and on it, centrally situated, is the post-town of Woodville, 8 miles S. W. of Butler borough, in a fork of Glade run, 20 miles N. E. of Pittsburg.

Middlesex, town of Middleton t-ship, Cumberland county, on the road from Harrisburg to Carlisle, and on the Conedogwinit creek, at the confluence of Letart's creek with that stream, 3 miles from the former, and 5 miles from the latter borough, contains 8 or 10 dwellings, a tavern and mill.

Mifflin county, was formed by virtue of the act 19th September, 1789, from parts of Cumberland and Northumberland counties, and is bounded N. by Centre, E. by Union, S. by Juniata, and S. W. and W. by Huntingdon counties. Length 39 miles, breadth 15 miles. Its form is very irregular, and it may contain about 361 sq. ms. Central lat. 40° 35′ N. long. 1° W. from W. C.

This county is near the centre of the great transition formation of the state. It is surrounded by mountains, and traversed by several ranges of lofty hills. Crossing it from the S. we have Black Log mountain and Blue ridge, N. of which flows Juniata river, through Juniata valley, bounded northward by Limestone ridge, Jack's mountain, Stoney mountain, and Path Valley mountain. The whole of this mountainous region is underlaid with limestone, which, being near and on the surface in the valleys, renders them highly fertile. Iron ore abounds in many parts of the county, but more particularly in Union, Derry, and Wayne t-ships. Its quality is that well known and highly appreciated, as Juniata iron. In the limestone valleys there are some caves, such as are common in limestone countries. That in Wayne t-ship, called Haniwal's cave, is, we believe, the most extensive, having a depth of more than 100 rods. Considerable quantities of saltpetre have been obtained from it at sundry times.

The Juniata river enters this county from Huntingdon county, through Jack's mountain, below Drake's ferry, and forms the S. W. boundary for 7 or 8 miles, pursuing a S. E. course, then doubling by a narrow turn of 2 or 3 miles, it runs a N. E. course by Hamiltonville, Waynesborough, and Lewistown, to the Long Narrows, through which it flows into Juniata co. Its whole course through the county is about 35 miles in length. It receives from the county the Kishcoquillas and Jack's creeks, and several inconsiderable streams. The Pennsylvania canal follows the river through the co. keeping the right bank, for about 5 miles below Jack's mountain, thence crossing by an aqueduct to the left, near to Hamiltonville, it preserves that margin, giving to Waynesburg and Lewistown the advantages of its navigation.

The great western turnpike road, by the northern route, also follows the valley of the Juniata, and passing the towns of Lewis and Waynesburg, runs through the gap, at Jack's mountain. Another turnpike road leads from Lewistown to Bellefonte in Centre co. by which much of the iron of the latter county is conveyed to the Juniata river.

The towns of the county are Lewistown, Waynesburg, Hamiltonville, Belleville, Calhounsville, and McCollester'stown, &c. &c.

The whole population amounted in 1800, to 7000; in 1810, to 12,132; in 1820, to 16,618, and in 1830, exclusive of Juniata county, to 14,323. The taxables in 1828, were 2395.

There are in the county 9 churches, of which the Presbyterians have 5 or 6, the Methodists 2, and Episcopalians 1. There are a county Bible association, several tract societies, Sunday schools in such vicinages as admit of them, and a temperance society in each t-ship. Common schools are established where needed, and usually well attended. An academy was incorporated at Lewistown in 1815, and endowed with the sum of $2000 by the state, and the expense of educating the poor under the laws of the commonwealth, amounts to $1400 annually. There are 2 newspapers published weekly at Lewistown, viz.: the Mifflin Eagle and Juniata Gazette.

The manufactures of the county, with the exception of flour and iron, claim little consideration. There are 3 furnaces and 1 forge. The principal exports are wheat flour, whiskey and iron. The quantity of wheat sent to market, has been estimated at 400,000 bushels, and that of iron at about 2500 tons. The state of agriculture is respectable and daily improving. The average price of improved lands of the best quality, in Armagh and Union t-ships more especially, is about 40 dollars the acre; in other parts of the county from 25 to 30 dollars the acre. There are no unimproved lands save the mountains, and they are of little worth.

The public buildings consist of the court house and county offices, built of brick, a prison of stone, an academy of brick, and the churches we have already mentioned.

Mifflin, Juniata, Huntingdon, Centre and Clearfield counties, form the 12th congressional district, sending 1 member to congress; Mifflin, Juniata, Huntingdon and Cambria counties, the 17th senatorial district, sending 1 member to senate; Mifflin and Juniata together, elect 2 members to the house of representatives. Mifflin, Juniata, Huntingdon and Centre, make the 4th judicial district, over which Thomas Burnside, Esq. presides. The courts are holden at Lewistown, on the third Mondays of January, April, August and November, annually.

This county paid into the state treasury in the year 1831, for tax on writs, - - - -	$319,15
Tavern licenses, - -	649,05
Duties on dealers in for. mdze.	434,93
Collateral inheritances, -	100,87
Tin & clock pedlars' licenses,	28,50
	$1532,50

STATISTICAL TABLE OF MIFFLIN CO.

Townships &c.	Greatest Lth.	Greatest Bth.	Area in Acres.	Pop. in 1820	Pop. in 1830	Taxables.
B. of Lewist'n,				733	1479	292
Derry t-ship,	12	8	34,560	1551	2720	367
Armagh,	22	6	66,560	1613	2132	428
Union,	13	6	28,800	1391	1757	343
Wayne,	15	8½	45,440	2096	3691	429
Decatur,	13	9	55,680	635	765	135
Walker,					1379	401
				8019	14323	2395

Mifflin, t-ship, Dauphin co., bounded N. by Northumberland co., E. by Lyken's t-ship, S. by Halifax, and W. by Upper Paxton t-ship. Centrally distant, N. E. from Harrisburg about 23 miles. Greatest length 6½, breadth 5 miles. Area 24,400 acres. Surface mountainous on the N. and S. Soil, red shale. Population in 1830, 1570. Taxables, 251. Mahantango mtn. forms the N., and Berry's mtn. the S. boundary. Through the latter is a pass called Richard's gap, and on the N. of the mtn. flows Wiconisco creek. A Lutheran ch. is centrally situated in the t-ship.

Mifflin, t-ship, Columbia co., bounded N. by the Susquehannah r., E. by Luzerne co., S. E. by Schuylkill co., and W. by Cattawissa t-ship. Centrally distant from Danville, 17 miles S. E. Greatest length 9, breadth 9. Area, 37,120 acres. Surface hilly. Soil, sand, gravel, and alluvion. Pop. in 1830, 1791. Taxables, 335. Long mtn. rises near the middle of the t-ship, and runs N. E. about 10 ms., to Nescopeck creek, in Luzerne co., and Bucks mtn. also runs from this t-ship into the same co., by a S. W. course. The chief stream of the t-ship is Cattawissa creek, which crosses its S. E. angle. Mifflinsburg, on the Susquehannah r. is the p-t.

Mifflinsburg, p-t., Mifflin t-ship, Columbia co., on the left bank Susquehanna r., 17 ms. above Danville, and 34 below Wilkesbarre, 190 from W. C., and 80 from Harrisburg; contains 15 dwellings, 2 stores, 2 taverns, 1 Methodist and 1 Lutheran church.

Miffln, t-ship, Cumberland co., bounded N. by Perry co., E. by that co. and by Frankford t-ship, Cumberland co., S. by Newton t-ship, and W. by Hopewell. Centrally distant from Carlisle, 17 ms. N. W. Greatest length 14, breadth 7 miles; area 33,280 acres; surface hilly; soil slate. Pop. in 1830, 1431. Taxables 261. The Conedogwinit creek bounds it on the S., and the Blue mts. on the N.

Mifflin, t-ship, Allegheny co., bounded on the N. E. and S. E. by the Monongahela r., on the S. W. by Washington co., and on the N. W. by St. Clair t-ship. Centrally distant from Pittsburg S., 8 ms. Greatest length 12, breadth 7 miles. Area, 32,000 acres. Surface hilly. Soil loam. Pop. in 1830, 1162. Taxables, 269. The chief streams are Thompson's run, Street's run, and Peters cr., all of which flow into the Monongahela r.

Mifflin, p-t., Fermanagh t-ship, the seat of Justice of Juniata co., on the E. side of the Juniata r., on the state canal, and on the t-pike road leading to Lewiston, about twelve miles below that town; 150 from W. C., and 43 from Harrisburg. Contains about 100 dwellings, several stores and taverns, and a Methodist church.

Mifflinsburg, p-t. and borough, W. Buffalo t-ship, Union co., on the S. side of Buffalo creek in Buffalo valley, about 5 miles N. W. of New Berlin, 173 from W. C., and 65 from Harrisburg. Contains about 80 dwellings, 500 inhabitants, 5 stores, 5 taverns, 2 handsome churches, one pertaining to the Lutherans the other to the Methodists; an academy incorporated by act of assembly 14th April, 1827; and the town was also incorporated by another act of the same date.

Mifflin, t-ship, Lycoming co., bounded N. and N. W. by Brown t-ship, E. by Jackson and Lycoming t-ships, S. by the W. branch of the Susquehannah r., and S. W. by Pine creek, which separates it from Pine Creek t-ship. Centrally distant, N. W. from Williamsport, 23 miles. Greatest length 17, breadth 9 miles. Area 17,040 acres. Surface mountainous; soil, lime and gravel. Beside Pine creek, the t-ship is principally drained by Larry creek. Jersy Shore borough lies on the left bank of the r.

Pop. in 1830, about 800. Taxables 152. Taxable property, valuation, seated lands, &c. $48,100; unseated 13,104; personal estate, 6266; rate of levy $\frac{3}{4}$ of 1 per cent.

Milesboro', p-t., of Boggs t-ship, Centre co., upon both sides of the Bald Eagle creek, and upon the t-pike road leading from Bellefonte to Phillipsburg, 2 miles W. from the former, from which it is separated by the Bald Eagle mountain, through a gap of which the road and Spring creek run. The Bald Eagle creek is navigable for boats a short distance above the town and Spring creek to Bellefonte. There are between 30 and 40 dwellings here, a forge, rolling mill, a nail and woollen manufactory, all of which do much business. They are the property of Gen. Miles & Co. The p-o. is 194 miles from W. C., and 87 from Harrisburg.

Milestown, Bristol t-ship, Philadelphia co., on the Cheltenham and Willowgrove t-pike road, $6\frac{1}{2}$ miles from Philadelphia, pleasantly situated on a gentle hill, contains about 25 or 30 dwellings, 2 stores and 1 tavern.

Mill creek, Schuylkill co., rises in the Broad mountain, and flows through Schuylkill and Norwegian t-ship, into the river Schuylkill, by a S. W. and S. E. course of about 10 miles. This stream passes through a rich coal field, and has consequently lately grown into great importance. Port Carbon lies at its junction with the Schuylkill, and a rail road of about 4 ms. extends along the stream, communicating by laterals, with the coal mines.

Mill Creek, t-ship, Erie co., bounded N. by lake Erie, E. by Harbor cr. and Beaver Dam t-ships, S. by M'Kean t-ship, and W. by Fairview t-ship. Greatest length $7\frac{1}{2}$, breadth $7\frac{1}{2}$ miles. Area 24,960 acres. Surface, hilly. Soil, gravelly loam. Pop. in 1830, the borough of Erie exclusive, 1783, taxables, 311. Mill creek, from which the t-ship has its name, flows N. through it, by fort Erie to the lake. Walnut creek runs E. and W. along the southern boundary. The peninsula of Presqu' isle extends about 6 ms. into the lake, forming a capacious harbor (*See Erie*) upon the E. side of which is a light house. The t-pike road from Waterford to Erie, runs N. through the t-ship.

Mill creek, Blockley t-ship, Philadelphia co., rises on the verge of Montgomery co., and flows in a S. W. direction nearly five miles, into the river Schuylkill, a few rods above Grey's ferry. It turns several mills and small factories, and at Maylandsville, a saw mill, snuff mill, &c. &c.

Mill creek, rises in Upper Smithfield t-ship, Pike co., and flows southerly through Smithfield t-ship., Northampton co., into the Delaware. It turns a mill near its mouth, but is not navigable.

Mill creek, Luzerne co., rises in the Bald mtns., Pittston t-ship, and flows N. westerly into Wilkesbarre t-ship, where it empties into the Susquehannah, receiving near the river Laurel run.

Mill creek, a small tributary of the Schuylkill r., which rises and has its course in Lower Merion t-ship, Montgomery co., and falls into the river above Flat rock dam. It is a good mill stream, and has several mills upon it.

Mill creek, Lancaster co., a tributary of the Conestoga r., rises in Earl t-ship, and flows S. W. through Leacock and Lampeter t-ships, into its recipient, turning several mills in its course of about 18 miles.

Millikin's cove, a valley of Bedford co., extending from the N. part of Londonderry t-ship, into the S. part of Napier t-ship, bounded on the E. by Will's mountain, on the W. by Buffalo ridge, and on the N. by the Raystown branch of the Juniata. It is drained by the Buffalo creek.

Millsboro', p-t., E. Bethlehem t-ship, Washington co., on the N. bank of Ten Mile creek, at its confluence with the Monongahela r., 20 miles S. E. of Washington borough.

Miles, t-ship, Centre co., bounded N. by Logan t-ship and by Lycoming co., E. by Union co., S. E. by Hains t-ship, S. W. by Potter t-ship, and N. W. by Walker and Logan t-ships. Centrally distant N. E. from Bellefonte 19 miles. Greatest length 25, breadth 7 miles. Area, 64,460 acres. Surface, mountainous. Soil, limestone in the valleys. Population in 1830, 1054. Taxables, 223. Brush mtn. is on the E., and the Nittany hills on the W. Between them lies Brush valley, extending the whole length of the t-ship. Pheasant and Little Pheasant valleys lie in the Nittany hills, in the S. W. part of the t-ship. Rabersburg, and Jacobsburg, the former a p-t., are in Brush valley.

Milford, post-town, and st. of jus. Pike county, Upper Smithfield t-ship, on the Delaware river, 55 miles from Easton, 115 from Philadelphia, and 157 N. E. from Harrisburg. Lat. 41° 18′ N. long. from W. C. 2° 12′ E. Pop. in 1830, 510, of whom 28 were blacks. An academy was established and incorporated in 1827, with a donation from the state of $2000. Milford lies on an elevated bank of the river, and commands an extensive view of part of the state of New Jersey and state of New York, including many miles of the river, and highly cultivated flats upon its border. There is a fine bridge across the river, on a leading turnpike road passing through the village, on which runs a daily line of stages from New York to Buffalo.

Milford, Upper, t-ship, Lehigh co. bounded N. E. by Salisberg and Upper Saucon t-ships, S. E. by Bucks co. S. W. by Montgomery and Berks counties, and N. W. by Macungy t-ship. It is in form almost square, the longest sides being about 6 miles, and the shortest about 5½ miles. The main road from Sumanytown in Montgomery county to Northampton, passes centrally through it. The N. branch of the Perkiomen creek rises here, which runs to the Schuylkill river, and here is also Upper Saucon creek, which flows into the Lehigh and about 3 ms. below Bethlehem has its source. The surface is diversified, but generally hilly, the South mountain crossing it on the N. and sending forth spurs which reach its southern boundary. The soil is gravel and red shale, tolerably well cultivated and productive. Iron ore abounds on the mountain. There are 2 churches, separated by the Millerstown road, appertaining, respectively, to the Lutherans and German Presbyterians. Pop. of the t-ship in 1830, 2829; taxables in 1828, 569; valuation of real estate in 1829, $492,806; personal, $34,980. Millerstown, a post-town of Macungy t-ship, at the N. foot of the South mountain, is on the N. W. border of the t-ship; and Emaus, another post-town of Salisberg t-ship, lies on its N. E. boundary. There are in the t-ship 5 grist mills, 3 saw mills, 1 oil mill, 1 clover mill, 1 furnace, 4 stores, and 5 taverns, and 4 schools.

Milford, New, t-ship, Susquehannah county, bounded N. by Great Bend and Lawsville t-ships, E. by Jackson, S. by Harford, and W. by Bridgewater. Greatest length E. and W. 7½ miles, breadth N. and S. 6½ miles. It is drained by Mitchell's and Salt Lick creeks, which flow northward to the Susquehannah, and by Martin's, Partner's and Vanwinkles creeks, which run southward to the same river. The Great Bend turnpike road passes through the N. E. section of the t-ship, on which there is a post town called after the t-ship, 290 miles from W. C. and 183 from Harrisburg, containing 20 dwellings, 3 stores, 2 taverns, an Episcopal church. Surface, hilly; soil, clay and gravel. Pop. in 1830, 1000; taxables in 1828, 153.

Milford, N. W. t-ship of Bucks co. bounded N. by Springfield, E. by Richland and Rockhill, S. and S. W. by Montgomery co. and N. W. by Lehigh county. Centrally distant about 36 miles N. W. of Philadelphia, and 18 miles N. W. of Doylestown. Length 5¾, breadth 5 miles; area, 15,923 acres; surface, rolling, gravel and clay soil. Pop. in 1830, 1970; taxables in 1828, 402. Swamp cr. a tributary of the Perkiomen, passes northwardly through the town-ship. Charleston, at which there is a church and post-office, is the only village in the t-ship.

Milford, t-ship, Somerset co. bounded N. by Somerset t-ship, E. by Brother's valley, S. by Turkeyfoot t-ship, and W. by Fayette co. Centrally distant S. W. from Somerset borough, 7 miles; greatest length 16, breadth 7 ms. area, 59,600 acres; surface, level; soil, light clay. Pop. in 1830, 1749; taxables, 340; taxable property in 1829, real estate, 91,236; personal, occupations included, $10,740; rate of tax, 5 mills on the dollar. Laurel hill is on the W. boundary. The t-ship is drained S. by Castleman's r. which receives from it Middle, Scrub Glade and Cox's creeks, and by Laurel Hill creek. On the latter is a furnace near the town of Milford, and iron is found abundantly on Carey's run, a tributary of this stream, and coal on the bank of Castleman's river. The town of Milford lies in the N. part of the t-ship, near Laurel Hill creek, 7 miles S. W. from the borough of Somerset. There is also a post-office centrally situated near Scrub Glade creek.

Milford, town of Milford town-ship, Somerset county, (see preceding article,) contains 3 or 4 dwellings only.

Milford, t-ship, Juniata co. bounded N. W. by Derry t-ship, N. E. by Fermanagh t-ship, on the S. E. by the Tuscarora creek, and on the S. W. by Lack and Wayne t-ships. Centrally distant S. E. of Lewiston, 6 miles; greatest length 10 miles, breadth 6½ miles; area, 37,120 acres; surface, mountainous; soil, limestone in valleys, slate on hills. Pop. in 1830, 1538; taxables, 293. Shade mountain fills the N. part of the t-ship, on the E. of which flows Licking creek, and another range of hills run parallel with Tuscarora creek.

Mill hall, post-office, Centre co. 215 miles N. W. of W. C. and 108 from Harrisburgh.

Milheim, p-o., p-t., Centre county, in Hains t-ship, Penn's valley, separated from Aaronsburg by Elk creek, about 25 miles E. of Bellefonte, 193 from W. C. and 86 from Harrisburg. It contains some 25 dwellings, store, and tavern. The Aaronsburg turnpike road runs through the town. It lies in Penn's valley, E. of the Brush mountain.

Millerstown, or Millersville, post-town, Lehigh county, at the foot of the South mountain, on a small branch of the Little Lehigh, in the t-ship of Macungy, about 9 miles S. W. of Northampton.

Millerstown, Manor t-ship, Lancaster co. a post-town between the Great and Little Conestoga creeks, 4 miles S. W. of the city of Lancaster, 109 from W. C. and 38 from Harrisburg, contains about 60 dwellings, stores and taverns, &c.

Millerstown, Annville t-ship, Lebanon county, on the turnpike road leading from Lebanon borough to Harrisburg, 5 miles west of the former, and about 20 miles N. E. of the latter. The Quitapahilla creek passes near the town, on which there are some mills, and about a mile N. of the town is a Lutheran church. The town contains 120 dwellings, 3 stores and 4 taverns.

Millerstown, post-town, Greenwood t-ship, Perry co. on the Juniata river, opposite the mouth of Raccoon creek, 10 miles N. E. of Bloomfield, and 29 miles above Harrisburg, 136 from W. C. and 29 from Harrisburg, contains above 80 dwellings, 5 stores and 3 taverns—1 Presbyterian church.

Millersburg, town of Berks co. in Bethel t-ship, 24 miles from Reading, on the Sunbury road. It consists of 10 or 15 dwellings, 1 store, 2 taverns, and a church. Miller's grist mill is situated on the Little Swatara creek, within a mile of the town.

Miller's creek, a tributary of the Lackawannock river, rises and has its course in Pittston t-ship, Luzerne co. It joins the river about 4 miles from its mouth.

Millersburg, post-town of Upper

Paxton t-ship, Dauphin co. on the E. bank of the Susquehannah river, at the confluence of the Wiconisco cr. with that stream, about 23 miles N. of Harrisburg, on the road leading to Sunbury. It stands on an elevated spot, a short distance from the river. The rail road now being made from the coal mines in Lyken's valley to the river, will pass near the town. It contains from 60 to 70 buildings, a Lutheran church, 3 stores and 3 taverns.

Millsborough, post-office, Washington county, 214 miles N. W. from W. C. and 207 S. W. from Harrisburg.

Milton, post-town and borough, Turbut t-ship, Northumberland co. on the E. bank of the West Branch of the Susquehannah river, 14 miles N. of Sunbury, built on both sides of Limestone run, 66 miles N. of Harrisburg. Its population in 1830, consisted of 1274, of whom 1259 were white, and 15 colored—aliens 6. There are here above 200 dwellings, 15 stores, 12 taverns, 3 churches belonging 1 to the Presbyterian, 1 to the Seceders, & 1 to the German Reformed. There is an academy here, and a Lancasterian school. A bridge crosses the river, to Union county. The town was incorporated by act 26th Feb. 1816.

Milton, a small village of Solebury t-ship, Bucks co. on the road from Doylestown to Lumberville, about 7 miles E. of the former, contains 6 or 8 dwellings, a tavern, store and grist-mill.

Milton, small village of Solebury t-ship, Bucks county, about 30 miles N. E. from Philadelphia, on the road to Lumberville.

Milltown, post-town, Bradford co. 256 miles N. W. from Washington, 146 from Harrisburg.

Millville, post-office, Columbia co. 202 miles from W. C. and 93 from Harrisburg.

Minersville, post-town and borough, Norwegian t-ship, Schuylkill county, beautifully situated in the valley of the West Branch of the Schuylkill river, upon the West Branch rail road, 7½ miles from Schuylkill Haven, 179 ms. from W. C. 71 from Harrisburg. The principal street is called Sunbury, on which are all the stores and public buildings. It is the old Sunbury road, communicating with the rich valleys in the direction of the Susquehannah. The town contains about 80 dwellings, 6 taverns, 8 stores, 6 blacksmith's shops, 1 saddlery and 1 bakery, 2 tailors' shops, and 2 butchers, 2 saw mills. The population is estimated at 500 souls. The town is surrounded by mines and coal hills, abounding in anthracite of a good quality. It was incorporated by act 1st April, 1831.

Mingo creek, a small tributary of the Schuylkill river, of Upper Providence t-ship, Montgomery county.

Mingo, and Little Mingo creeks, Nottingham t-ship, Washington co. rise within the t-ship, and flow E. to the Monongahela river.

Mitchell's creek, Great Bend t-ship, Susquehannah county, rises in New Milford t-ship, and flows northerly to the Susquehannah river, about 4 miles E. of the Great Bend village.

Monecony island, in the Susquehannah river, opposite to the village of New Troy, and about 5 miles in a direct line from Wilkesbarre.

Monohan, t-ship, York co., bounded N. by Cumberland co., E. by Fariview t-ship, S. by Warrington, and W. by Franklin. Centrally distant from the borough of York, 18 miles; greatest length, 7½, breadth, 4 miles; area, 13,440 acres; surface, undulating; soil, part limestone, part gravel. Pop. in 1830, 1219; taxables, 148; taxable property in 1829, real estate, $174,711; personal, 11,052; occupations, 29,766; total, 215,529; rate 25 cts. in the $100.

Monongahela, t-ship, Greene co. bounded N. by Cumberland, E. by Monongahela river, which separates it from Fayette co. S. by Dunkard t-ship, and W. by Greene t-ship. Centrally distant S. E. from Waynesburg, 14 miles; greatest length 7, breadth 3 miles; area, 10,440 acres; surface, rolling; soil, loam. Pop. in 1830, 1250; taxables, 223. The t-ship is drained by Whitely creek, which enters it about the middle of the W. line and runs N. E. through it to the river. Mapletown lies upon the creek, and Greensburg, a post-town, on the river; the first about 15, and the second 18 miles S. E. of Waynesburg.

Monongahela, r., rises in Randolph co., Va., interlocking with the sources of the great Kenhawa, at N. lat. 38° 30′. Its course is nearly N., 80 ms., to where it receives the west branch, from Lewis and Harrison counties. Below their junction, the united stream flows N. E. 30 ms., to the S. boundary of Pa., which it passes, and 2 miles lower, receives from the S. E. Cheat r., little if any inferior in volume or length, to the Monongahela itself. Cheat r. rises in Randolph co., and flowing through that and Monongahela counties, enters Pa., and unites with the main stream as before noticed. The sources of the Monongahela and Cheat are in the western spurs of the Appalachian mts. Below the mouth of Cheat, the Monongahela flows nearly N., 50 ms., to its junction with the Youghiogheny. The latter rises in the Appalachian mts., in Allegheny co., Md., interlocking with the sources of the N. branch of the Potomac, flows N. into Pa., passing through Fayette and Westmoreland, and entering Allegheny co., unites with the Monongahela at McKeesport, after a comparative course of about 100 ms. Twelve ms. below its junction with the Youghiogheny, the Monongahela unites with the Allegheny, and forms the Ohio at Pittsburg. The entire length of the Monongahela r., by comparative courses, is about 170 ms.; but following the meanders of the streams, either along the main or Cheat branch, the length exceeds 200 miles.

The country drained by this river is in some parts mountainous, and in all hilly.

For down stream navigation, the Monongahela at high water is passable with large boats, as high as the mouth of the W. branch; and by lighter vessels much higher. Cheat r. is navigable into Randolph co., about 30 ms., by a comparative course above its mouth, and the Youghiogheny to the Ohiopile falls, in Fayette co., 60 ms. above its junction with the Monongahela.

A survey of this river has been made under the direction of the canal commissioners, with the view of improving its navigation. The engineer has reported that a canal cannot be made along its valley, at a reasonable expense, principally because of the slippery nature of its banks, the height of the flats or bottoms from the bed of the r., and of the inequality of such flats, which will render much excavation necessary; but, he at the same time reports, the river admirably adapted to the making of a slack water navigation, by a succession of pools and locks; the heights of the bank being unusually favorable for the elevation of water by dams.

Monroe, p-t., Bradford co., bounded N. by Towanda t-ship and the Susquehannah r., E. by Asylum t-ship, S. by Lycoming co., and W. by Franklin co. Centrally distant, S. of Towanda 8 ms.; greatest length 16½ miles, breadth 6½; area, 32,000 acres; surface, hilly; soil, gravelly loam. Pop. in 1830, 988; taxables, 150. The Susquehannah and Tioga t-pike road runs northerly 9 miles through the t-ship, following the valley of the S. branch of the Towanda cr. The p-o. here, called Monroeton, is 237 ms. N. W. of W. C., and 126 from Harrisburg.

Monroe, t-ship, Cumberland co., bounded N. by E. Pennsboro', E. by Allen, S. by York co., and W. by Middleton t-ship. Centrally distant S. E. from Carlisle, 7 ms.; greatest length 6½, breadth 5 ms.; area, 16,640 acres; surface, level; soil, limestone. Pop. in 1830, 1555; taxables, 317. The Yellow Breeches creek flows into, and partly bounds the t-ship on the S., and on the W. boundary gives motion to some iron works. The road from Cumberland-town on the Susquehannah to Carlisle, is on the N. line.

Monroe, p-t., Bucks co., 195 miles from W. C., 113 from Harrisburg.; 18 ms. N. E. of Doylestown, in Durham t-ship, on the bank of the Delaware, contains some 6 or 8 dwellings, store and tavern.

Moon, t-ship, Allegheny co., bounded N. E. by the Ohio r., S. E. by Robinson and Fayette t-ship., S. W. by Findlay, and N. W. by Beaver co. Centrally distant from Pittsburg N. W. 12 ms.; length 6½, breadth 4½ miles; area. 14,720 acres; surface, hilly; soil, loam. Pop. in 1830, 1048; taxables, 221. It is drained on the N., by Raveden's run and Flaugherty's run, and S. by Mouture's run. The p-t. of Middleton lies on the Ohio r., in the S. E. angle of the t-ship, opposite to Neville island, about 10 ms. from Pittsburg.

Moon, t-ship, Beaver co., bounded N. & E. by the r. Ohio, S. by Hopewell t-ship, and E. by Green t-ship. Centrally distant S. from Beaver borough 6 ms.; greatest length 7 ms., breadth 6½; area, 23,680 acres; surface, hilly; soil, loam. Pop. in 1830, 1360; taxables 226. It is drained by Raccoon creek, which passes north through it into the r. Ohio.

Moore, t-ship, Northampton county, bounded N. by Ross, and Towamensing, S. by Allen and Upper Nazareth, E. by Bushkill, and W. by Lehigh t-ships. Length, 4½ miles, breadth 4½; surface, rolling; soil, gravel. Pretty well cultivated, and tolerably fertile. It is watered by sources of the Hockendocque, and Manokissy creeks. Between forks of the former, near the S. W. angle of the t-ship, the small village of Kernesville is situated. The Blue mtn. forms the N. boundary, in in which is an opening denominated Smith's gap.

Moorsburg, p-t. of Liberty t-ship, Columbia co., at the foot of the Mahanoy ridge, 7 ms. by the road N. W. of Danville, 181 ms. from W. C., and 71 from Harrisburg. Contains 20 dwellings, 1 store, 2 taverns, 1 Presbyterian church.

Montgomery, co., originally formed a part of Philadelphia co., from which it was separated by act of assembly of 10th Sept. 1784, and is bounded N. by Lehigh, N. E. by Bucks, S. E. by Phila. and Delaware counties, S. W. by Chester, and N. W. by Berks cos. Length 33, breadth 16 ms; area 425 square ms. Central Lat. 40° 15′; lon. 1° 40′ E. from W. C.

The form of the co. is that of a broken or notched parallelogram. There are no mountains, but there are some bold and striking hills on the N. & W., and the face of the country is agreeably diversified by hill and dale. The soil is generally of good quality, particularly along the valley of the Schuylkill, and in the t-ships of Abington, Upper Dublin, Springfield, Whitemarsh, Plymouth and Upper Merion, in which the limestone prevails. The ordinary timber is black and white oak, walnut, hickory and chestnut. The state of agriculture in the greater part of the co., is equal to that in any part of the U States.

The Schuylkill r. forms the eastern boundary between this co. and Chester, from its extreme western angle to the boundary of Upper Merion t-ship, thence by a meandering course it forms the boundary of Lower Providence, Norriton, Plymouth, and Whitemarsh on the E., and Upper and Lower Merion on the W., and enters Phila. co. at the N. W. angle of Roxbury t-ship. The Schuylkill navigation co. have dammed the r. in not less than 7 places in this co., and have constructed 5 short canals, all of which afford advantageous mill seats. At Norristown, the water power thus obtained, is employed in various extensive manufactories (*see Norristown*); and the foundation of a new and extensive town called *Conshohocken*, has been laid at the dam in Plymouth t-ship. The Manatawney crosses the N. W. angle of the co., and joins the Schuylkill at Pottsgrove. The Perkiomen after receiving several tributaries from Berks, Lehigh, and Bucks counties, crosses this co. from its N. eastern angle in a S W. direction, and after a junction with the Skippack creek, whose sources are altogether within this co., pours its waters into the Schuylkill at the boundary line between Upper and Lower Providence. The Wissihickon also rises in Montgomery and seeks that river through Roxborough. The Pennypack rises in Horsham, and the Tacony in Cheltenham t-ship, and flow into the Delaware, five miles distant from each other. The W. and Lexington branches of the Neshaminy also rise in Montgomery and Hatfield t-ships, of this co. Upon all these creeks and upon their tributary streams, there are many mills erected, for grinding grain and sawing timber, and manufacturing purposes, so that, being only a few miles apart, they contribute greatly to the convenience of the inhabitants.

Besides the common roads, which are numerous, there are 6 stone t-pike roads which traverse this co. 1. The Germantown and Perkiomen road, made pursuant to an act of assembly passed 12th Feb., 1801, crosses the S. E. line of Whitemarsh t-ship, and passes through the t-ships of Plymouth, Norriton, Worcester, Perkiomen, Upper and Lower Providence, to a noble stone bridge across the Perkiomen cr., distant 22 miles from Philadelphia. 2. The Cheltenham & Willow Grove road, commences at Sunville in Philadelphia co., and passes through Miles town, Shoemaker town, Jenkintown, Abington, and ends at Willow Grove, was made by virtue of an act passed 24th March, 1803. 3. The Chesnut hill and Spring house road, formed pursuant to an act of 5th March, 1804, runs through Whitemarsh, and Upper Dublin, to the Spring house tavern in Gwinedd, and is continued thence to Bethlehem, through Montgomery and Hatfield t-ships, by a separate company, incorporated pursuant to an act, passed 4th April, 1805. 5. The Perkiomen and Reading road, made under the acts of 20th March, 1810, 13th Feb. 1811, and 31st March, 1812, passes through Pottsgrove. To this road the state has subscribed $53,000. 6. The Ridge turnpike road commences at Philada., passes through Norristown to the Perkiomen bridge, was made pursuant to act 30th March, 1811; and in this also the state is a stockholder to the amount of $25,000.

A company for the formation of a rail road from Philadelphia, through Germantown to Norristown, a distance of $19\frac{1}{8}$ miles, has been formed, the stock subscribed, and the work is in progress. So advantageous is this road deemed, that though only 8000 shares were to be subscribed for, subscriptions were made for 13,202. The sources of profit looked to, are the products brought to Norristown by the Schuylkill canal, and more particularly by rail roads contemplated, to the coal yards of Schuylkill and Northampton counties, the manufactures of Norristown, the marble, lime and lime stone, and iron of Plymouth and Whitemarsh townships, and the pleasure excursions of the citizens. A company has been incorporated to make a t-pike from the Spring house to Sumanytown; and another from the Perkiomen bridge to the same. The latter, it is believed, will be completed. Authority has also been given to incorporate a company for making a rail road from Norristown to the Lehigh r.

There are several fine bridges in this co.; 1 at Norristown, 1 at Perkiomen, 1 at Pottstown; and it is asserted by the inhabitants of the co., that with the exception of Phila. co., none in the state has erected so many, and such excellent bridges. The Perkiomen bridge cost $60,000; that at Norristown, $31,199 90; that at Pottstown, $1400.

The principal towns are Norristown, the seat of justice, Pottsgrove, both lying on the main road to Reading, Jenkintown, Willow Grove, and Hatboro', on the road to Doylestown, &c. &c. Pop. by census in 1790,

22,929; in 1800, 24,150; in 1810, 29,683; in 1820, 37,569; in 1830, 39,406, of whom 771 were colored; 338 aliens; 26 deaf and dumb; and 16 blind; 1 slave. Well informed gentlemen of the co. say, that the census of 1830 has been very carelessly and inaccurately taken, and that the population is at least 44,000. This seems probable, inasmuch as the capital of 29,683 of 1810, gave in 1820, an increase of 7886, whilst the capital of 37,569 of 1820, is made to give in 1830, 1837 increase only. This cannot be true in a county from which emigration is inconsiderable.

Montgomery co. belongs to the E. district of the supreme court, and with Bucks forms the 7th judicial district of county courts. The county courts are held at Norristown on the 3d Monday in Jan., April, Aug., and Nov. President, 1831, John Fox, Esq. This co. forms the 3d senatorial district of the state, and sends one senator. It also forms the 5th congressional district, and is represented in the 22d congress by Joel K. Mann.

The public buildings consist of a very neat and convenient court house, 70 by 40 ft., 2 stories high, with cupola and bell, and appurtenant offices, and a large and commodious prison, 100 ft. by 36, 3 stories high, with a wing 100 by 50 ft., all built of stone; and a poor house and house of employment, likewise of stone.

The latter, is erected on a farm of about 200 acres, situated in Upper Providence t-ship, on the E. bank of the Schuylkill r. The house will accommodate 200 paupers. It was established pursuant to the acts of assembly of 10th March, 1806; 26 Jan., 1807, and 22d Dec., 1810, at the expense of the co., and is under the direction of three directors, one of whom is elected annually, and serves for a term of 3 years. They are empowered to take in trust real estate to the value of $10,000 per ann., and personal estate to any amount;—to provide for the maintenance of the poor &c.—to erect necessary buildings, appoint stewards, matrons, physicians, &c.—to bind out poor children apprentices, and are required annually to render an account of their receipts and expenditures, to the county auditors, and to return to the court of quarter sessions, a descriptive list of the persons assisted by them, and of children apprenticed, with the names of the masters and their occupations; and to exhibit, when required, to the inspection of visitors appointed by such court, their books, and a statement of moneys receivable and payable, and of sales, purchases, &c. The directors are also required to meet at the house of employment, at least once a month, and may receive $40 per ann. for their services. Vacancies are supplied until the next general election by the remaining directors. Funds are raised by tax levied by county commissioners on requisition of directors, and disbursed by county treasurer, by their order. The average number of poor supported in the house is about 100. On the 1st Jan., 1832, there were 110; viz. 53 white male adults, 22 female adults, 15 male children; blacks, 9 males, 9 females, children, 6 males.

The religious sect of Presbyterians, including the German Reformed, is the most numerous in the co.; there are English Presbyterian churches, 4; German Reformed, 7; Lutherans, 8; Episcopalians, 4; Menonists, 5; Baptists, 2; Quakers, 6. There is a co. Bible society, and several benevolent and beneficial societies in the county. The soil of this co. being generally of a good quality, and much of it super excellent, the state of its agriculture is highly flourishing, and its products in grain, fruits, meadow grasses, esculent vegetables, whiskey, beef, pork, butter, are abundant, and of the best quality; and its very large surplusage finds a ready market in the city of Philadelphia.

The county is also distinguished for its manufactories, as will appear by the following statistical table, carefully compiled by the Hon. J. B. S.

of Norristown, to whom we are also indebted for much of the information contained in this sketch of the county. McCready's spinning mill contains between 5,000 and 6,000 spindles, and Mr. Jamieson's weaving mill, 142 power looms. To the facts of the table, we must add, that each of the marble mills mentioned therein, is competent to saw about 1,000 superficial feet of marble per week; and that in the t-ship of Cheltenham there is a spade and shovel manufactory, at which 14,500 dozen of spades and shovels, &c. are made per annum. It gives steady employment to 40 hands; consumes 100 tons of iron and 250 tons of coal. Near this factory, upon the same stream, (the Tacony creek,) there is a manufactory of chocolate, at which 30 tons of that article are made yearly.

For year 1832.	No. merchant mills.	No. grist mills.	No. saw mills.	Marble or stone mills.	Paper mills.	Oil mills.	Clover mills.	Powder mills.	Rolling mills.	Slitting mills.	Tilt mills.	Cotton factories.	Woollen factories.	Fulling mills.	Tanneries.	No. acres in each t-ship.	Average value per acre in each t-ship.	Whole value of land in t-ship and borough.	No. Horses.	No. cattle.
Norristown, (bor.)	4	1	2	1		1						2			1	520	$500	260,000	70	80
Pottstown, (bor.)	1	1	1											1	1	268	300	80,400	58	64
Abington,	1	3	1										1		1	9,820	40	392,840	348	558
Cheltenham,	2	4	1						1	1	2	1		1		5,433	35	190,155	213	410
Douglass,		5	4		1	2	1									9,442	25	236,050	205	456
Franconia,		3	2												2	9,184	25	229,600	243	714
Frederick,		3	6			6	1	1			1			1	1	10,989	20	219,780	215	478
Gwynedd,		2	3													11,893	30	356,790	307	776
Hatfield,																7,087	20	141,740	168	439
Horsham,		3	3													10,778	40	431,120	259	521
Limerick,															1	14,234	25	355,850	323	690
Lower Merion,		2	2		9							2	2		1	14,558	40	583,320	419	1167
Lower Providence,		4	2												1	9,143	30	274,290	251	627
Lower Salford,		2	1												1	8,344	30	250,320	210	579
Marlborough,		2	2			11		9						1	1	7,382	15	110,730	159	328
Montgomery,		1	1												1	6,874	25	171,850	183	372
Moreland,	1	9	4		1										2	11,315	40	452,600	396	681
New Hanover,		3	7			1									2	12,895	20	257,900	248	585
Norriton,		4	1									1		1	1	9,359	40	374,360	242	548
Perkiomen,		4	4				4							1	1	11,163	30	334,890	310	835
Plymouth,		1	1	1												5,656	50	282,800	274	463
Pottsgrove,	1	2	3			1									1	11,692	25	292,300	234	447
Springfield,		2														4,163	45	187,335	140	303
Towamensing,		3	2													5,946	25	148,650	176	428
Upper Dublin,		6	1				1							1	1	8,560	40	342,400	295	508
Upper Hanover,		7	7			3								1	2	13,713	20	274,260	322	713
Upper Merion,		5	3	1								3				10,354	45	465,930	216	478
Upper Providence,	1	3	3				1								2	13,048	30	391,440	351	803
Upper Salford,		6	5			5		1						3	1	10,672	25	266,800	239	531
Whitemarsh,	6	1	1		4											8,967	50	448,350	449	662
Whitpaine,		3	3												1	7,765	30	232,950	252	583
Worcester,		4					2								1	9,861	30	295,830	285	690
	17	99	76	3	15	30	10	11	1	1	3	9	3	11	27	291,079		$9,332,630	8,060	17,517

Beside the general provisions for education, there are, in this county, two public academies. The Norristown academy was incorporated by act of assembly, 29th March, 1804, to which, in 1805, the legislature granted the sum of $2,000. Loller academy, at the village of Hatborough, was incorporated by an act passed 7th February, 1812, and the estate granted to Nathaniel B. Borleau, in trust by the will of Robert Loller, was vested therein; and by act of 30th March, 1812, a certain school house and lot of ground in Moreland t-ship, was directed to be sold, and the proceeds to be appropriated, the one half to this academy, and the other for the erection of a school house on land of Isaac Pickering. Poor children are educated under the provisions of the several acts of assembly, at the expense of the co. About 800 are thus instructed annually at the cost of $3,477 53.

There are five public libraries in the co., one at Norristown, at Pottstown, at Horsham, at Whitpaine, and at Hatboro', that at the latter place is said to comprise many valuable books. There is a "cabinet of natural sciences" at Norristown, established chiefly by the exertions of P. A. Browne, Esq. of Philadelphia, and employed principally in geological and mineralogical researches. The foundation of a cabinet has been laid, and perseverance on the part of the members cannot fail to render the institution useful to themselves, and profitable to the county. Sunday schools have been established in several parts of the county; and there are four English and one German newspapers printed weekly, viz. "The Norristown Register and Sentinel," (commenced in 1803.) "The Norristown Herald," "The Norristown Free Press," all published at Norristown. "The American Star," printed at Pottstown, and "Der Bauern Freund," or "The Farmer's Friend," (German) published at Sumanytown.

Among the public institutions of the county, may be mentioned, for their beneficial effects, several societies for the apprehension of horse thieves, whose exertions in bringing offenders to condign punishment have much diminished the offence.

STATISTICAL TABLE OF MONTGOMERY COUNTY.

Townships, &c.	Greatest Lth.	Greatest Bth.	Area in Acres.	Population. 1810.	Population. 1820.	Population. 1830.	Taxables.
Abington,	7	3	13,440	1236	1453	1524	300
Cheltenham,	7	1½	6,720	783	956	934	213
Douglas,	7½	2	10,240	687	750	941	205
Franconia,	3	3	5,440	656	848	998	190
Frederick,	7	6	13,440	828	927	1047	208
Gwynedd,	8	3	15,360	1078	1221	1402	286
Hatfield,	5	4	12,800	652	756	835	211
Horsham,	6	3	11,040	938	1081	1086	267
Limerick,	8	5	22,400	1282	1577	1743	315
Lower Merion,	8½	5	14,234	1835	2256	2524	522
Lower Providence,	8	5¼	9,143	904	1146	1193	237
Lower Salford,	5½	5	16,000	558	731	830	167
Marlborough,	5	2¼	7,382	672	839	952	197
Montgomery,	5	3	9,000	580	751	911	171
Moreland,	8	3	15,360	1692	1890	2044	388
New Hanover,	8	4½	13,000	1065	1320	1344	323
Norriton,	7	4½	8,960	1336	1098	1139	245
Perkiomen,	5	4	12,800	902	1146	1278	252
Plymouth,	4	3	6,720	895	928	1091	228
Pottsgrove,	5½	5	11,692	1571	1882	1302	252
Pottstown bor.						676	141
Norristown bor.					827	1089	231
Springfield,	6	2	4,163	550	639	668	166
Towamensing,	3½	3	5,720	488	571	669	163
Upper Hanover,	5	4	12,800	925	1273	1300	258
Upper Dublin,	3½	3	6,720	1050	1259	1292	293
Upper Merion,	9	5	10,880	1156	1285	1618	360
Upper Providence,	8½	6	13,048	1395	1670	1682	326
Upper Salford,	8	5	10,672	836	1008	1108	250
Whitemarsh,	6	2	12,680	1328	1601	1924	379
Whitpaine,	4½	3	8,640	955	1126	1137	249
Worcester,	4¾	4½	9,861	868	977	1135	249
				29,703	35,793	39,406	8242

The average value of lands is stated at about $30 per acre. The market price varies from $5 to $500 the acre, according to situation, quality, and other circumstances. The unimproved or woodland, commonly commands higher prices than arable lands in the same neighborhood. The averages of the several t-ships may vary from $25 to $65 the acre.

By the assessment of 1832, the taxable real estate of the county was valued at $9,332,630 personal estate, in 1829, at $391,060. Usual rate of taxation 20 cents in the $100.

This county paid into the state treasury, in the year 1832, for

Dividends on bridge stock at Pottstown,	240
Tax on bank dividends,	640 03
Tax on offices,	253 79
Tax on writs,	442 57
Tavern licenses,	1,100
Tax on collateral inheritances,	333 42
Pamphlet laws,	6 65
	$3,016 46

It was our intention to insert here, at the instance of the gentleman who furnished it, a list of the post offices in the county, but our limits will not admit. We intend to have a table of all the offices in the state.

Montgomery, t-ship, Montgomery co. bounded N. E. by Bucks co., S. E. by Horsham t-ship, S.W. by Gwynedd t-ship, and N. W. by Hatfield t-ship; greatest length 5, breadth 3 miles; area, about 9000 acres. It is drained by the Wisahickon and the W. branch of Neshaminy creek; the former flows S. to the Schuylkill, and the latter S. E. to the Delaware. The Spring house and Bethlehem turnpike road crosses the t-ship diagonally, on which there is a small v. called Montgomery square; atwhich there is a post office. Centrally situated at the distance of 20 miles N. of Phila. and 11 miles N. E. of Norristown, 160 from W. C., and 100 from Harrisburg; surface, level; soil, red shale and loam. Pop. in 1830, 911; taxables in 1828, 171.

Montgomery square, a small village and p-t. in Montgomery t-ship, Montgomery co. 10 miles E. of Norristown and 20 miles N. of Phila. It contains 4 dwellings, 1 store, 2 taverns and a boarding school for boys, in which the classics are taught.

Montgomery's ferry, over the Susquehannah river from Buffalo t-ship, Perry co. to Halifax t-ship, Dauphin co. There is a post office in the former co. 136 miles N. W. from W. C. and 26 from Harrisburg.

Montgomery, t-ship, Franklin co. bounded N. by Peters, E. by Antrim t-ships, S. by the state of Maryland, and W. by Warren t-ship. Centrally distant S. W. from Chambersburg, 16 miles; greatest length 11, breadth 8 miles; area, 46,080 acres; surface, level; soil, limestone, chiefly. Pop. in 1830, 3509; taxables 595. The W. and S. W. part of the t-ship, is mountainous. The W. branch of the Conecocheague cr. flows diagonally through it from N. W. to S. E. and receives on the N. boundary a small stream from Cove mtn., on which, lies the p-t. of Mercersburg, and receives from the centre of the t-ship, Little Licking cr. The Waynesburg & Mercersburg turnpike r. runs near the N. line. Blair's valley is in the S. W.

Montgomeryville, Montgomery t-ship, Montgomery co. 10 miles E. from Norristown,contains 10 dwellings 2 taverns, 2 stores, and a Baptist church.

Montmorency, p-o. Ridgeway t-ship, Jefferson co. some 25 or 30 miles N. E. of Brookville, 242 from W. C. and 171 from Harrisburg.

Montrose, village, post and county town, of Susquehannah co. It is situated about the centre of Bridgewater t-ship; lat. 41° 48′ north, long. 1° 4′ E. of W. C., 271 miles N. W. of that place and 163 from Harrisburg, upon high ground, whence flow the Wyalusing and the Meshoppen creeks, the one westerly and the other southwardly to the Susquehannah river; and other crs. which run to the same r. on the N. E. From its elevated site it commands a fine view of the adjacent country. The town was commenced in 1811, and it now contains from 80 to 100 dwellings, 10 stores, 4 taverns and several mechanics' shops, with a population of 450 souls. The court house is a neat wooden structure. There are one Presbyterian, 1 Baptist, and 1 Episcopalian church. The Silver Lake bank was established in 1816. The name was given to the village in compliment to Dr. Robert H. Rose, who was a principal donor for the establishment of the st. jus. here. It was incorporated into a borough on the 29th March, 1824. The Susquehannah academy was established here under an act of assembly of 19th March, 1816, which gave to it $2000 on condition that a number of poor children not exceeding five should be taught, gratis, each for a term not exceeding two years.

Montour's ridge, a mountain range which extends across Northumberland co. and forms in part the boundary between it and Columbia co. extending about 12 miles from the west to the N. branch of the Susquehannah river, distant due N. from the borough of Northumberland, about 4 miles.

Montour's run, a tributary of Sherman's creek, Perry co. which rises in Limestone ridge on the N. of Tyrone t-ship, and flows S. to its recipient at Landisburg.

Montour's run, a tributary of the Ohio river, which rises on the line between Washington and Allegheny counties, and flows a S. E. and N. E. course, forming the boundary between Findlay and Fayette, Moon and Robinson t-ships. Its length is about 14 miles; Jeffriestown is on its S. bank in Fayette t-ship.

Moosick mountain, lies on the head of the Lackawannock creek, on the boundary of Wayne, Luzerne and Susquehannah counties. Its southern extremity is in Luzerne co. whence it extends in a N. E. direction across the W. line of Wayne co. in Canaan t-ship, and subsides in Mount Pleasant t-ship. Its height is about 600 feet from its base, and 1910 feet above the level of the ocean. Its ascent is gentle particularly from the western side, and the soil is excellent. Rix's gap affords a convenient passage for the Milford and Owego turnpike road. The length of the m. is about 16 ms.

Moravia creek, Lancaster co. rises in Warwick, t-ship, near Litiz, and flows S. E. about 6 miles, into the Conestoga creek, turning several mills in its course.

Moreland, t-ship, Lycoming co. bounded N. by Penn t-ship, E. by Franklin, S. by Columbia co. and W. by Muncy Creek t-ship. Centrally distant from Williamsport S. E. 20 miles; greatest length 8, breadth 6 ms. area 21,120 acres; surface, hilly; soil, gravel. Pop. in 1830, 600; taxables 110. Value of taxable property, 1829, real estate, $15,906; personal estate, 4140; rate of tax $\frac{3}{4}$ of one per cent. It is drained by the Little Muncy creek. The t-ship abounds with white pine timber of good quality which now finds a ready market at the mills.

Morestown, Abington t-ship, Montgomery co. marked on the map as Abington, on the Willowgrove and Cheltenham t-pike, two miles N. E. of Jenkintown, 14 miles from Phila., and 15 from Norristown. Contains 10 or 12 dwellings, a tannery, a tavern, 2 stores, a Presbyterian church and a boarding school for boys, in which the rudiments of classical learning are taught.

Moreland, t-ship, Montgomery co. bounded on the N. E. by Bucks co. on the S. E. by Phila. co. on the S. W. by Abington, and on the N. W. by Upper Dublin and Horsham t-ships; length 8 miles, breadth, 3; area, 15,360 acres; distant from Norristown 14 miles N. E., from Phila. 16 miles N. The Pennypack creek crosses it diagonally from N. E. to S. E., receiving many tributaries in its course. Hatboro', Willowgrove and Huntingdon, are villages of this t-ship, at each of which, there is a post office.

At Hatborough there is an academy, incorporated by the legislature, at which the higher branches of education are taught. Surface, rolling; soil, fertile loam. Pop. in 1830, 2044; taxables in 1828, 388. This t-ship takes its name from Wm. Moore, one of the first settlers of Pennsylvania, and an early judge of the province. He received the grant of a manor from Wm. Penn, part of which is included in the t-ship. It is said that he exercised here manorial rights, but this is not probable, as no evidence exists of manor courts having been any where established in Pennsylvania. The manor contained 10,000 acres, 3000 of which fell into Phila. co. on the erection of Montgomery co. the remainder into this t-ship.

Moreland, t-ship, Phila. co. part of the manor of Moreland, said to have been granted to Wm. Moore, an early and distinguished settler, and at one time, chief justice of the province. It is bounded N. E. and E. by Byberry t-ship, S. by Lower Dublin t-ship, and W. by Montgomery co. It is centrally distant from Phila. N. E. 13 miles; greatest length 5, breadth 2 miles; area, 3750 acres; surface, generally level; soil, sandy loam, tolerably well cultivated. Pop. in 1830, four hundred & eighteen. It is much the least populous district of the co. The only stream in it is a small and nameless branch of the Pennypack creek. The village of Smithfield is on the N. line and partly in Byberry t-ship, 14 miles from Phila. by the turnpike road, which runs centrally N. E. through the t-ship. (*See Moreland t-ship, Montgomery co.*)

Morgantown, a p-t. of Berks co. Caernarvon t-ship, on the Conestoga turnpike road 13 miles from Reading. There are here 40 dwellings, 2 taverns, 2 stores. Pop. about 250. There is also a church, appertaining to the German Presbyterians. It is distant 133 miles N. of W. C., and 58 E. from Harrisburg.

Morgan, t-ship, Greene co. bounded N. and N. E. by the north fork of Ten Mile creek, which separates it from Washington co. E. & S. E. by 10 Mile cr. which separates it from Jefferson t-ship, south west by Franklin t-ship, and W. by Morris; centrally distant N. E. from Waynesburg 6 miles; greatest length $10\frac{1}{2}$, breadth, 6 miles; area 23,680 acres; surface, hilly; soil, loam. Pop. in 1830, 1723; taxables, 290. It is drained by Ten Mile creek and Ruff's creek, its tributary, which rising in Morris t-ship, flows E. into its recipient. Clarksville, the post town, lies in the fork of Ten Mile creek, 10 miles N. E. of Waynesburg.

Morris, t-ship, Greene co. bounded N. by Washington co., E. by Morgan t-ship, S. by Franklin and Centre t-ships, and W by Rich hill. Centrally distant N. W. from Waynesburg 8 miles; greatest length 9 miles, breadth 6; area 23,040 acres; surface, rolling; soil, loam. Pop. in 1830, 1575; taxables, 266. The t-ship is drained by Bates, Brown's and Bushy forks of Ten Mile creek.

Morris, t-ship, Washington co. bounded N. by Buffalo and Canton t-ships, E. by Amwell, S. by Greene co. and W. by Findlay t-ship. Centrally distant from Washington borough 8 ms. S. W.; greatest length 9, breadth 7 miles; area 28,800 acres; surface, hilly; soil, loam; coal abundant. Pop. in 1830, 2048; taxables, 383. It is drained by the north fork of 10 Mile creek and its branches. Sparta post office is centrally situated in the t-ship.

Morris cove, p-o. Bedford co. 132 miles from W. C. and 110 from Harrisburg.

Morrisville, p-t. and borough on the banks of the Delaware river, 30 ms. by land, N. E. of Phila. by the Bristol and Trenton turnpike road, and directly opposite to Trenton. An excellent mill power is obtained here from the Delaware, and a saw mill, grist mill, paper mill, & button manufactory, are driven by it. The town contains about 100 dwellings, 1 store, 2 taverns. There is a beautiful bridge across the Delaware here, suspended from 5 arches, supported on piers. It is 1100 feet long, and 36 feet wide. The borough contains 432 acres, 531 inhabitants and 91 taxables. Distance from Doylestown 20 ms. S. E.

Morris, t-ship, Huntingdon co. bounded N. by Franklin, E. by Porter t-ships, S. and S. E. by Woodberry, S. W. by Frankstown, and N. W. by Tyrone t-ships. Centrally distant N. W. from Huntingdon borough, 11 miles; Tussey's mountain is on the E. boundary, on the W. foot of which, flows the Frankstown branch of the Juniata river, through Canoe valley, which is bounded W. by the Canoe mountain; Brush mountain is on the W. line, between which, and the Canoe mountain, is Scotch valley, drained by Canoe creek. The turnpike road from Huntingdon to Ebensburg, runs S. W. through the t-ship, on which, centrally situated, is Yellow Springs post office, and Waterstreet and Graysville post offices are also in the t-ship. Iron abounds in the t-ship and there are several iron works upon the river. Greatest length of the t-ship, 11, breadth 6 miles; area, 27,520 acres; surface, mountains and valleys; soil in the valleys, limestone. Pop. in 1830, about 1000; taxables, 190. There were in the t-ship in 1828, 3 grist mills, 5 saw mills, 2 distilleries, 2 furnaces, 1 forge.

Morris, t-ship, Tioga co., surface, hilly; soil, gravel and clay. Pop. in 1830, less than 100; taxables in 1828 12.

Morrisville, p-t. of Richhill t-ship, on the S. fork of Wheeling creek, 17 ms. N. W. of Waynesburg, 225 N. W. from W. C., & 239 S. W. from Harrisburg. Contains some 10 or 12 houses store and tavern.

Morrison's cove, between Tussey's mountain on the E. and Dunnings and Lock mountains on the W., runs from the N. part of Woodberry t-ship, Bedford co. through Woodberry t-ship, Huntingdon co. to the Frankstown branch of the Juniata river. It is drained N. E. by Piney and Cove cr.

Mount Jackson, p-t. of North Beaver t-ship, Beaver co. upon Hickory cr. 22 miles N. W. of the borough of Beaver, and about 3 miles W. of the Mahoning river, 275 miles N. W. of W. C. and 243 from Harrisburg, contains 50 dwellings, 3 stores, 2 taverns. There are several mills on the creek near above and below the town.

Mount Airy, p-o. Berks co. 152 ms. N. of W. C. and 61 from Harrisburg.

Mountville, p-o. Lancaster co. 103 miles from W. C., 32 from Harrisburg.

Mount Lewis, p-t. Lycoming co., 212 miles N. W. from W. C. and 101 from Harrisburg.

Mount Morris, p-t. Whitely t-ship, Greene co. upon the south boundary of the t-ship, and of the state, and on the south side of Dunkard's cr. 14 miles S. E. from Waynesburg, 225 N. W. from W. C. and 239 from Harrisburg, a small village.

Mount's creek, Fayette co., rises in Bullskin t-ship, and flows S. W. thro' Connellsville, into the Youghiogheny r., having a course of about 10 ms.

Mount Pleasant, t-ship, Washington co., bounded N. E. by Cecil t-ship, S. E. by Chartier's, S. by Canton and Hopewell, W. by Cross Creek t-ships, and N. W. by Smith. Centrally distant from the borough of Washington N. W. 10 miles; greatest length 7, breadth 4½ miles; area, 28,800 acres; surface, hilly; soil, loam, and coal abundant. Pop. in 1830, 1327. Taxables, 278. It is drained N. by Raccoon cr., S. & E. by Chartier's creek and branches of that stream, and W. by the middle fork of Cross cr. The p-t. of Mount Pleasant is situated near the middle of the t-ship, from which roads to all parts of the t-ship radiate. The town contains 30 or 40 dwellings.

Mount Pleasant, t-ship, Westmoreland co., bounded N. by Unity t-ship, E. by Chestnut ridge and Donegal t-ship, S. by Fayette co., W. by E. Huntingdon and Hempfield t-ships. Centrally distant S. E. from Greensburg, 9 ms. Greatest length 7½, breadth 7 miles; area, 19,200 acres;

surface, gentle hills; soil, loam and gravel. Pop. in 1830, 2381. Taxables, 433. It is drained on the N. by the Big Sewickly creek, and on the S. by Jacob's creek. The t-pike road from Somerset to Washington, crosses the S. W. angle, and upon it near the W. line, lies the p-t. and borough of Mount Pleasant, about 10 miles S. of Greensburg, 194 N. W. from W. C., and 172 S. W. from Harrisburg; contains about 150 dwellings, 3 taverns, 7 stores, 1 Baptist and 1 Methodist church. It was incorporated 7th Feb., 1828.

Mount Pleasant, village, in the S. E. angle of Beccaria t-ship, Clearfield co., on the waters of Clearfield creek, 18 ms. S. of the borough of Clearfield.

Mount Pleasant, t-ship, Columbia co., bounded N. by Greenwood, E. by Fishing creek and Bloom t-ship, S. by Bloom, and W. by Hemlock t-ships. Centrally distant from Danville, 11 ms. Greatest length 6, breadth 4½ miles; area, 12,800 acres; surface, diversified; soil, sand and gravel. Pop. in 1830, 715; taxables, 134. Green creek and Fishing creek course it on the E. & S. E., and Little Fishing creek on the W.

Mount Pleasant, t-ship, Adams co., bounded N. by Reading, E. by Hamilton, Berwick and Conewago t-ships, S. by Germany and Mount Joy, and W. by Strabane. Centrally distant E. from Gettysburg 17 ms.; greatest length 8, breadth 7 miles; area, 19,200 acres; surface, level; soil, red shale. Pop. in 1830, 1498; taxables, 285. A main branch of the Conewago creek flows along the E. boundary. Plum run, and White run, tributaries of Rock creek, flow S. on the west boundary, and Swift and Bush run N. to the Conewago. Bonaghton lies on a country road leading from Gettysburg to Petersburg, about five ms. from each.

Mount Vernon, p-o., Chester co., 104 ms. N. of W. C., and 64 S. E. from Harrisburg.

Mount Joy, t-ship, Lancaster co., bounded N. by Lebanon and Dauphin counties, on the S. by E. & W. Donegal, on the E. by Raphoe, & on the W. by E. Donegal. Centrally distant from Lancaster city 16 ms.; greatest length about 9 ms., greatest breadth 7½; surface, rolling; soil, limestone, red shale and gravel. Pop. in 1830, 2106; taxables, 384. Little Chiques creek bounds it on the E., and Conewago creek on the N. W. The Conewago hills run along the N. boundary. The Lancaster and Harrisburg t-pike divides it from E. and W. Donegal, on which are the villages of Mount Joy, Richland, Springfield and Elizabethtown. The first and the last are post-towns.

Mount Joy, a p-t. of Mount Joy t-ship, Lancaster co., on the t-pike road from Lancaster city to Harrisburg, about 12 ms. N. W. of the former, 24 from the latter, and 117 from W. C., contains 15 or 20 dwellings, 2 taverns and 1 store.

Mount Joy, t-ship, Adams co., bounded N. by Mount Pleasant, E. by Germany t-ships, S. by the state of Maryland, and W. by Cumberland t-ship. Centrally distant from Gettysburg 6 miles; greatest length and breadth, 5½ ms.; area, 14,720 acres; surface, level; soil, red shale. Pop. in 1830, 991; taxables, 191. Rock creek follows the W., and Wilalloways creek the E. boundary. Gettysburg and Petersburg t-pike road crosses it in a S. E. direction.

Mount Pleasant, t-ship, Wayne co., bounded N. by Scott, E. by Buckingham and Lebanon, S. by Dyberry t-ships, and W. by Susquehannah co. Its form is that of a parallelogram, of which the longer side is about 10 ms., and the shorter 6 ms. The Lackawaxen, Dyberry, and Great Equinunk creeks have their sources in this township. The Moosick mountain extends along its western boundary. The Coshocton and Great Bend, and the Bethany and Dingman's choice t-pikes pass through it, uniting at Centreville, a growing village. Belmont, is another village of this t-ship. The Mount Pleasant p-o is at Centreville,

269 ms. N. of W. C., and 170 from Harrisburg. Taxable property in 1829, seated lands, $82,342 ; unseated 41,131 ; personal estate, including occupations, 16,050. In 1830 the t-ship contained 1258 inhabitants ; 227 taxables ; 124 frame, 51 log dwellings ; 4 stores, 5 taverns, 2 grist mills, 5 saw mills, 33 looms and 6 schools.

Mount Pleasant, p-o., centrally situated in Dromore t-ship, Lancaster county.

Mount Pleasant, p-t., W. Hempfield t-ship, Lancaster co., on the road from Lancaster to Columbia, about 7 miles from the former.

Mount Pleasant mills, p-o., in Perry t-ship, Union co., 10 miles S. of New Berlin, 42 N. W. of Harrisburg, and 152 from W. C.

Mount Republic, p-t., of Canaan t-ship, Wayne co., 10 miles N. W. from Bethany, 269 from W. C., and 164 from Harrisburg.

Moyamensing, t-ship, Philadelphia co., bounded N. by the city of Philadelphia, E. by Southwark and the r. Delaware, S. by the river Delaware, and W. by the Schuylkill. Length 3 ms., breadth 2 ; area, 2560 acres ; surface, level ; soil, alluvial. Pop. in 1830, 6822 ; taxables in 1828, 1766. The N. E. part of the t-ship is densely built, and the houses erected of late years, are generally of brick, and are commodious ; some of them remarkably neat and comfortable, and three stories high ; but a vast proportion of the dwellings are two story, and many of them of wood. A part of the t-ship is in gardens, and the remainder is chiefly meadow land, drained by Hellander's creek and its branches, and many ditches ; and defended from the overflow of the Delaware by dykes along its bank. The t-ship was incorporated by act of 24th March, 1812, and is governed by 9 commissioners, 3 of whom are elected annually, to serve 3 years. It has a poor house, exclusively for the use of the t-ship. Gloucester point, a place much resorted to for recreation, is on the Delaware in this t-ship. A ferry across the Delaware is established here.

Mud island, in the Delaware r., about 8 miles below Philadelphia. Upon this island fort Mifflin is erected, notable in the annals of the revolutionary war, for the protracted defence made by the provincial against the British forces.

Muddy run, Northampton co., a small stream of 6 or 8 ms. in length, which rises between the Pohopoko mtn. and the Tobyhanna creek, and flowing through the Pine Swamp, falls into the Lehigh r. on the E. side. There are several mills upon it, & being very rapid, others may be erected.

Muddy creek, a tributary of the Conestoga r., formed by 3 branches, all of which have their sources in or near Brecknock t-ship, Berks co. There are several mills on the main stream and its branches.

Muddy creek, a small stream on the N. W. line of Dromore t-ship, Lancaster co. ; has a course of about 7 ms. to the Susquehannah r.

Muddy run, Turbut t-ship, Northumberland co., a small tributary of the Susquehannah r.

Muddy creek, York co., rises on the borders of Hopewell and Windsor t-ships, and flows S. E. to the Susquehannah r., dividing the t-ships of Hopewell, Fawn and Peach Bottom from Windsor, and Upper and Lower Chanceford. Its length is about 20 ms.

Muddy run, Hamilton-ban t-ship, Adams co., a branch of Middle creek. There is another stream in this co., so called, which rises in Huntington t-ship, and flows N. E. to the Bermudian creek, forming the boundary between Latimore and Reading t-ships.

Muddy creek, Cumberland t-ship, Greene co., a tributary of the Monongahela r., rising and having its source in the t-ship. The p-t. of Lisbon is on this stream, about 4 ms. from its mouth.

Muddy creek, t-ship, Butler co., bounded N. by Slippery Rock t-ship, E. by Centre, S. by Conequenessing t-ship, and W. by Beaver co. Centrally distant N. W. of Butler borough 12 ms. It forms a square of 8 ms.; area, 40,960 acres; surface, rolling; soil, loam. Pop. in 1830, 1317; taxables, 239. It is watered principally by Muddy creek, a tributary of Slippery Rock creek, which, rising by several branches in Centre t-ship, flows N. W. through this t-ship into Beaver co., having a course of about 15 ms. There are extensive tracts of meadow land on Muddy creek, and this t-ship will one day be remarkable for its pasture and grazing farms. The upland is good.

Mummasburg, Franklin t-ship, Adams co., 5 ms. N. W. of Gettysburg, on Little Marsh creek. A turnpike road runs from Gettysburg to the village, which contains from 15 to 20 dwellings, 1 store and 1 tavern.

Muncy, borough and p-t., formerly called Pennsborough, is situated in Muncy Creek t-ship, Lycoming co., about a mile from the Susquehannah r., and a like distance from Muncy creek. The t. contains about 100 dwellings, 7 stores, 5 taverns, 1 Methodist church, and 1 church common to Episcopalians and Presbyterians, and 500 inhabitants. Within 5 ms. of the borough there are 7 grist mills, and 3 woollen and cotton factories, and 5 distilleries, which consume at least 25,000 bushels of grain per annum. The p-o. at Muncy, is distant N. W. from W. C. 190 ms., and 80 from Harrisburg. The town was originally incorporated by the name of Pennsborough, 15th March, 1826; but was again incorporated, and its name and limits changed by act 19th Jan., 1827.

Muncy, t-ship, Lycoming co., bounded north by Elkland t-ship, east by Shrewsbury and Penn t-ships, S. by Muncy Creek t-ship and the W. branch of the Susquehannah r., which divides it from Washington t-ship, and W. by Fairfield t-ship. Centrally distant N. E. from Williamsport 13 ms. Greatest length 7, breadth 5 miles; area, 17,040 acres; surface, mountainous; soil, various. Pop. in 1830, 1000; taxables, 192; valuation of taxable property in 1829, seated lands, &c. 40,548; unseated, 5232; personal estate, 8580; rate of levy ¾ of one per ct. The Muncy creek runs on the E., and Loyalsock on the W. boundary.

Muncy Creek, t-ship, Lycoming co., bounded N. by Muncy t-ship, N. E. by Penn t-ship, E. by Moreland t-ship, S. by Columbia and Northumberland t-ships, and W. by the west branch of the Susquehannah r. Centrally distant S. E. from Williamsport 13 miles; greatest length 10 ms., breadth 8; area, 17,920 acres; surface, hilly; soil, clay. Pop. in 1830, about 800; taxables, 179; valuation of taxable property in 1829, seated lands, &c. $63,461; personal estate, 7502. The Big Muncy creek enters the t-ship from the N. E., and the Little Muncy creek from the S. W., and uniting near the middle of the t-ship, flow N. W. into the river, N. of Pennsborough. The Muncy hills lie in the S. of the t-ship.

Muncy creek, Lycoming co., rises on the confines of Shrewsberry and Penn t-ships, and flows S. W., forming in part the boundary between those t-ships, into and through Muncy Creek t-ship, to the W. branch of the Susquehannah r., N. of the town of Pennsborough, receiving from the S. E. Little Muncy creek; the greater stream has a course of about 30 ms.; and the less one, of about 16 ms., both are excellent mill streams.

Munster, p-t. of Allegheny t-ship, Cambria co., upon the turnpike road leading W. from Ebensburg, 5 miles E. of that town, 183 from Washington, and 130 from Harrisburg; contains about 20 houses, 2 stores, and 4 taverns, and 120 inhabitants.

Murraysville, p-t. of Franklin t-ship, Westmoreland co., on the turnpike road from Ebensburg to Pittsburgh, 12 ms. N.W. of Greensburg, 214 from W. C., and 186 from Harrisburg; contains 15 dwellings, a Seceders ch., 1 tavern, 2 stores, a grist mill and woollen factory.

Murrinsville, p-t. of Butler co., 251 miles from W. C., and 211 from Harrisburg, on the Butler and Franklin state road, where it is crossed by the Roxbury and Mercer turnpike; distant 18 ms. from Butler; contains some 6 or 8 dwellings, a tavern and a store.

Mushanon creek, rises and runs N. on the boundary line between Centre and Clearfield counties, by a course of about 35 miles to the W. branch of the Susquehannah r. It is a large navigable stream, flowing through a country rich in coal and iron.

Myerstown, p-t., Jackson t-ship, Lebanon co., on the Reading and Harrisburg t-pike road, about 7 miles E. of the borough of Lebanon, 141 N. W. from W. C., and 31 E. from Harrisburg; contains 120 dwellings, 1 Luth. church, 4 stores and 4 taverns.

Nanticoke creek, Hanover t-ship, Luzerne co., is formed of 3 branches which rise in the Wyoming mountains, about 3 ms. asunder; 2 of them in Newport t-ship, which uniting with the third in Hanover, flow into the Susquehannah r. at the foot of the Nanticoke mtn. They penetrate the coal formation, and may prove valuable auxiliaries hereafter in the transportation of that mineral. There is a forge on the Nanticoke creek, which has long been in operation, supplied with iron from the vicinity.

Nanticoke mountain, Luzerne co., rises at the S. W. end of the Wyoming valley, and runs a N. easterly course parallel to, and near the margin of, the Susquehannah r., through Nescopeck and Newport t-ships, ending in a high bluff of 800 ft., at the junction of the Nanticoke creek with the river. Anthracite coal is found upon it in abundance.

Nanticoke falls, in the Susquehannah r. at the northern extremity of Newport t-ship, Luzerne co., formed by the mtn. A dam is erected here for feeding the North Branch canal, which supplies an immense quantity of surplus water, and affords a most advantageous site for manufactories especially of iron; coal and iron ore being found in abundance in the neighborhood, and the rich valley of Wyoming producing full supplies of necessary provisions. It is situated about 8 ms. from Wilkesbarre.

Nanticoke, p-o., Luzerne co., 223 ms. N. W. from W. C., 107 from Harrisburg.

Nantmeal, East, t-ship, Chester co. bounded N. E. by Coventry, S. E. by Vincent, S. by Uwchlan, S. W. by West Nantmeal, and N. W. by Berks county. Centrally distant from Philadelphia 33 miles N. W., and from West Chester, 15 miles; length 7½, breadth 5½; area, 16,600 acres; surface, hilly; soil, gravelly. Pop. in 1830, 2029; taxables in 1828, 348. The North and South Branches of French creek cross the t-ship, and the main stream receives from it Beaver run and Rock run, which courses the E. boundary. The turnpike road from the Warren tavern to Morgantown, in Berks county, traverses the t-ship. Iron ore is found in the northern section, and there are 2 forges, 1 on the North, the other on the South branches of French creek. There are also 2 churches, 1 in the N. and the other in the S. part of the t-ship. There is also a post-office in it called "East Nantmeal," 140 miles from W. C. and 68 from Harrisburg.

Nantmeal, West, t-ship, Chester co. bounded N. by Berks county, E. by East Nantmeal and Uwchlan, S. by Brandywine, and W. by Honeybrook. The East branch of the Brandywine river, runs in a meandering course through it, receiving Indian creek, on which there is a furnace called Springton, and French creek crosses its northern section. The turnpike road to Morgantown passes through the N. E. angle. Indian town, a small hamlet, is centrally situated 34 miles N. W. of Philadelphia, and 13 miles from West Chester. Greatest length of t-ship 8 miles, breadth 5½ miles; area, 19,400 acres; surface, gentle declivities; soil, loam and gravel. Pop. in 1830, 1498; taxables in 1828,

327. The post-office is 132 miles N. from W. C. and 66 S. E. from Harrisburg.

Napier, town-ship, Bedford county, bounded N. E. by St. Clair, E. by Bedford t-ship, S. by Londonderry t-ship, and W. by Somerset county. Centrally distant W. from the town of Bedford, 9 miles; greatest length 19, breadth 12½ miles; area, 85,120 acres; surface, mountainous; soil, clay and loam. Pop. in 1830, 2154; taxables, 434. It is drained E. by the Raystown branch of the Juniata river, which receives from the t-ship the Shawnee branch and Buffalo creek, on the N. E. by the W. branch of Dunning's creek, and by Adam's cr. a tributary of that stream. The turnpike road from Bedford to Greensburg, passes W. through the t-ship, on which is centrally situated the post-town of Shellsburg, and the turnpike road to Somerset, runs S. W. through the t-ship.

Nazareth, post-town, Northampton county, a Moravian town, situated in Upper Nazareth t-ship, on the head of a small branch of the Bushkill creek. It is built principally on two streets, forming a right angle to the S. and W. Its public buildings are a church, and a seminary for boys. Here, all the Moravian male children are educated, and generally a number of boys from abroad. The ground on which the town is built descends to the S. and the houses are generally of stone, one story high; they are built close, and the streets are paved, on each side a footway. This is in magnitude the he third town in Northampton co. and the oldest settlement N. of the South mountain, in the state; the brethren having all first settled here in 1742, and afterwards removed to the river, where they built Bethlehem. Nazareth is 10 miles N. E. by N. from Bethlehem, 8 W. by N. from Easton, 53 N. of Philadelphia, 194 from Washington, and 101 N. E. from Harrisburg. Pop. in 1830, 408; scholars in boy's school, 71; females in sister's house, 35.

Nazareth, Lower, a t-ship of Northampton county, bounded N. by Upper Nazareth, S. by Bethlehem, E. by Forks, W. by Allen t-ships. Surface, level; soil limestone, and very productive, being carefully cultivated; greatest length 4¾ miles, width 3 miles. Pop. in 1830, 1204; taxables, 223. Hectown and Hartzells, are small villages of this t-ship. It is drained by the Manookisy creek.

Nazareth, Upper, t-ship of Northampton county, bounded N. by Moore and Bushkill, S. by Lower Nazareth, E. by Forks, and W. by Allen t-ships. Surface, rolling; soil, gravel and slate, well cultivated and productive; greatest length 4¾ miles, greatest width 2½ miles. Pop. in 1830, 942; taxables in 1828, 164. The village of Nazareth is in this t-ship. It is watered by 2 branches of the Manookisy cr.

Neel's Hole run, Peach Bottom t-ship, York co. a tributary of Muddy creek.

Neffsville, Manheim t-ship, Lancaster county, a post-town four and a half miles due N. of Lancaster city, 113 miles from W. C. and 39 from Harrisburg, contains 10 or 15 dwellings, and a tavern.

Nelson, post-office, Tioga county, distant from W. C. 268 miles N. W. and from Harrisburg, 162.

Nescopeck, t-ship, Luzerne county, bounded N. E. by Newport, S. E. by Sugarloaf t-ships, W. by Columbia county, and N. W. by the Susquehannah river. It has some very good river bottom, but its surface is generally uneven. Big and Little Wapwallopen and the Nescopeck creeks flow through it. Lee's mountain skirts the river on the western boundary. The Nescopeck range runs along the southern line. Nescopeck village, handsomely situated on the bank of the river, has a post-office and several well built houses, distant 196 miles from W. C. and 86 from Harrisburg. A bridge is thrown across the Susquehannah at this place, connecting it with Berwick, a thriving village upon the W. bank of the river. The Berwick and Easton turnpike road and great stage route, passes through this t-ship. Pop. 983; taxables by the return of 1828, 194. The form of the t-ship is very irregular. Its greatest length from E. to W. is 10 miles, and breadth from N. to S. about 9 miles; area, 29,440 acres.

Nescopeck creek, rises in Hanover t-ship, Luzerne county, and thence by a W. and N. W. course of more than 30 miles, flows into the Susquehannah river at Nescopeck village, receiving Little Nescopeck creek and other tributaries by the way. In the vast canal improvement of the state, this creek has become of great importance, as a means of connecting the Delaware and the Lehigh with the Susquehannah.

Nescopeck mountain, Luzerne co. on the N. side of the Nescopeck creek, is a range about 850 feet high, parallel to the Wyoming mountain. It forms a regular and almost unbroken ridge of about 20 miles, nearly destitute of timber on its summit, and extends from the Susquehannah nearly to the Lehigh, forming the southern boundary of Nescopeck, Newport, and Hanover t-ships.

Nescopeck valley, lies on both sides of Nescopeck creek, and between Nescopeck and Buck's mountain in Sugarloaf t-ship, Luzerne county. It is about 20 miles long and 5 wide, and does not extend to the river Susquehannah. In population it ranks next to the Lackawannock valley, and the soil is of a better quality.

Nescopeck, post-town and village, at the confluence of the Nescopeck creek with the Susquehannah river, contains about 20 dwellings, several stores and taverns. The Berwick turnpike road crosses the river here upon a bridge 1256 feet in length, and 28 in width, roofed, finished in the year 1818, at the cost of 31,000 dollars The bridge is the property of an incorporated company in which the state is a stockholder to the amount of $8000. It is proposed to connect the Susquehannah river here with the Delaware by means of a canal along the Nescopeck creek and valley, and by the Lehigh canal.

Nesquihoning creek, a tributary of the Lehigh river which rises in Schuylkill county, and flows S. E. through a valley lying between the Nesquihoning mountain and the Broad mountain, and empties into the river about 4 miles above Mauch Chunk. It is a considerable stream, well adapted to mill purposes, but is not navigable.

Nesquihoning mountain, in Mauch Chunk t-ship, Northampton county, heads with the Mauch Chunk mountain on the Lehigh river, but radiates, and is divided from it by Panther cr. (*See Mauch Chunk.*)

Nesquihoning village, Mauch Chunk t-ship, Northampton county, situated at the foot of the Nesquihoning mountain, upon the Nesquihoning creek. This is one of the creations of the coal region, and was laid out in the spring of 1831, by the Lehigh navigation and coal company, and contains already above 20 houses, a store and tavern. It is 3400 feet from the heart of the coal region, on Room run, 40 miles from the town of Catawissa, on the Susquehannah river, and 30 miles from Berwick, and will form one of the nearest markets for those places. As only one summit intervenes between it and Catawissa, it lies on a favorable route for a rail road between Catawissa or Northumberland, and the waters of the Delaware. The Lehigh navigation and coal company offer lots for sale in this village. It may contain at present, about 120 souls.

Neshaminy river, rises in Hilltown t-ship, in Bucks county, and flows into and through Hatfield and Montgomery t-ships, Montgomery co. into New Britain t-ship, Bucks co. and thence through the latter county by a meandering but generally S. W. course of about 35 miles to the river Delaware, about 3 miles below Bristol. There are over it many fine wooden and stone bridges. The bridge nearest to its mouth on the road to New York, is a draw bridge—is private property, erected by Messrs. Bessonet and Johnson, whose heirs or assigns levy tolls by virtue of act of assembly 6th Sept. 1785. The Neshaminy as far as Bansley's ford, was declared a public highway by act of 9th March, 1771.

Neshannock, t-ship, Mercer county, bounded N. by Lackawannock, E. by Slippery Rock t-ship, S. by Beaver co. and W. by Mahoning. Centrally distant S. W. from Mercer borough 12 miles; greatest length 8, breadth 6 miles; area, 30,720 acres; surface, level; soil, clay and loam. Pop. in 1830, 1703; taxables, 316; taxable property in 1829, real estate, $66,-875; personal, 12,191; rate, 5 mills in the dollar. The Shenango creek crosses the S. W. angle of the t-ship, and receives from it the Neshannock creek, which flows through it from the N. E. Upon the S. boundary, and at the confluence of these streams, lies the post-town of New Castle, 21 miles S. W. of Mercer borough. The Beaver division of the state canal reaches to this town.

Neshannock creek, Mercer. co. rises chiefly in Cool Spring t-ship, and flows S. W. through Springfield and Neshannock t-ships, into the Shenango cr. Its length by comparative courses is about 30 miles.

Newark, or Halifax, or Mechanicsville, a village of Buckingham t-ship, Bucks county, on the road from Centreville to Durham ferry, 4 miles N. E. of Doylestown. It contains some 4 or 5 dwellings, &c.

New Berlin, post-town and seat of justice of Union county, on the left bank of Penn's creek, 11 miles W. from Sunbury, and about 60 miles N. W. from Harrisburg, and 168 from W. C. contains about 70 dwellings, 7 stores, 5 taverns, a very handsome court house and offices of brick, with a cupola; the court house and offices present a front of 180 feet; a prison of stone and 2 handsome churches, 1 Lutheran and German Presbyterian, and the other Methodist. Penn's cr. is navigable for arks and rafts above 50 miles, and yields an abundant water power. There are now 5 valuable grist mills upon it, within 2 miles of New Berlin. A little enterprize and capital now about to be given to it, will make the town the depot of the trade of the rich and fertile valleys of Buffalo, Musser's and Middle creek in this county, and of Penn's and Brush valleys in Centre county. Vast quantities of wheat are now manufactured here.

New Bedford, p-t. in the N. W. angle of Mahoning t-ship, Mercer co. 15 miles S. W. of the borough of Mercer, 279 miles from W. C., and 237 from Harrisburg. Contains 25 dwellings, 2 stores, 1 tavern and a Presbyterian church.

Newberry, t-ship, York co. bounded N. W. and N. by Fairview, E. by the Susquehannah river, S. by Manchester and Conewago, and W. by Warrington t-ship. Centrally distant N. from the borough of York 12 miles; greatest length $10\frac{1}{2}$, breadth 7 miles; area 23,040 acres; surface, undulating; soil, limestone and gravel. Pop. in 1830, 1833; taxables, 385; taxable property in 1829, real estate, $190,097; personal, 13,791; occupations, 32,770; total $236,658. The Conewago creek forms the S. boundary, Stoney run and Beaver creek, the W. Fishing creek flows through the N. E. angle. York-Haven, Newbury and Lewisberry are post towns of the t-ship. The first lies on the Susquehanna river, west side, below the Conewago falls; the second and third, on the road leading from York-Haven to Carlisle, distant from the former 5 and 9 miles respectively.

Newberry, p-t. York co., Newberry t-ship, on the road leading from York-Haven to Carlisle, 5 miles N. W. from the former, 102 miles from W. C. and 14 from Harrisburg.

New Britain, (*See Britain, New.*)

Newburg, p-t. Cumberland co., Hopewell t-ship, 27 ms. W. of Carlisle, 109 N. of Washington, and 37 W. of Harrisburg. Contains 8 or 10 dwellings, store and tavern.

Newbury, p-t. Lycoming t-ship, at the confluence of Lycoming creek with the W. branch of the Susquehannah river, 3 miles above Williamsport, 198 from W. C. and 89 from Harrisburg. Contains about 30 dwellings, a large Presbyterian church, of stone, 2 stores and 3 taverns.

New Castle, a p-t. of Norwegian t-ship, Schuylkill co. situated about 4 miles N. W. of Pottsville, on the Centre turnpike road, in a narrow valley of Mine hill. It is a coal creation, of the last 2 or 3 years, and contains from 80 to 100 houses, some of which are substantially built of stone. The number of inhabitants exceeds 400.

New Castle, p-t. and borough of Neshannock t-ship, Mercer co., on the S. line of the t-ship, in the fork formed by the confluence of the Shenango and Neshannock creeks, 16 miles S. W. of Mercer borough, 264 N. W. from W. C., and 232 from Harrisburg. Contains about 80 dwellings, 5 stores and 3 taverns. The Beaver section of the state canal is authorized to be made to this town. The town was incorporated 25th March, 1825.

New Columbia, p-t. Union co. in the S. E. angle of White Deer t-ship, upon the W. bank of the west branch of the Susquehannah r. above and nearly opposite to the town of Milton in Northumberland co. and 12 miles N. E. of New Berlin, 177 from W. C. and 68 from Harrisburg. Contains about 30 dwellings, 2 stores, and 2 taverns.

Newfield creek, Rush t-ship, Schuylkill county, a tributary of the Little Schuylkill river.

New Garden, t-ship, Chester county bounded N. by London Grove and E. Marlborough, E. by Kennet t-ships, S. by the state of Delaware, W. by London Britain, New London and London Grove t-ships. Central distance from Phila. S. W. 32 ms., from West Chester 12 miles; length 7½, breadth 3 miles; area, 11,200 acres; surface, level; soil, limestone. Pop. in 1830, 1309; taxables 265. Red Clay creek drains it on the E. and the E. branch of White Clay creek runs along its western boundary. The turnpike road from Wilmington to Lancaster crosses it, on which near the S. E. angle is New Garden post office, and near the centre of the t-ship, New Garden church. The post office is 99 miles N. from W. C. and 68 S. E. from Harrisburg.

New Geneva, p-t. of Springfield t-ship, Fayette co., at the confluence of George creek with the Monongahela r., distant 12 miles S. W. from Uniontown, 217 N. W. from W. C. and 199 from Harrisburg. Contains about 60 dwellings, 1 church, 2 schools, 4 stores, 2 taverns, 1 grist mill and 1 saw mill.

New Germantown, p.t. of Toboyne t-ship, Perry co. about 20 miles W. from Bloomfield, 128 from W. C. and 46 from Harrisburg. Contains about 20 dwellings, 120 inhabitants, 2 stores and 1 tavern. There are two German churches in the vicinity.

New Goshenhoppen, p-t. and v. of Upper Hanover t-ship, Montgomery co. centrally situated in the forks of Perkiomen cr., 37 ms. N. W. of Phila. and about 21 N. W. of Norristown.

New Haven, town of Dunbar t-ship, Fayette co., on the W. bank of the Youghiogheny river, 12 ms. N. E. of Uniontown and directly opposite to Connellsville borough. Contains 50 dwellings, 1 church, 2 schools, 4 stores, 3 taverns, a grist mill, saw mill, paper mill and woollen factory, all driven by water, and an air furnace.

New Holland, p-v. of Earl t-ship, Lancaster co., on the turnpike road from Lancaster to Morgantown, distant by the road, 13 ms. from the former, and about the same distance from the latter; 121 miles from W. C., and 39 from Harrisburg. Contains about 25 dwellings, tavern, store and church.

New Holland. (*See Holland, New.*)

New Hope, p-t. and village, Solebury t-ship, Bucks co., on the river Delaware, opposite to Lambertsville

New Jersey; about 34 miles N. E. of Phila. and 11 ms. E. of Doylestown: 170 ms. from Washington, 119 from Harrisburg. It contains about 30 dwellings, several stores, 2 taverns, grist mill, saw mill, paper mill, several factories of cotton and wool.

There is a fine bridge over the river here supported on nine piers: length between abutments 1050 feet, width 33 ft. Individual subscription, $160,000. The piers are of stone and the bridge is roofed, erected in 1814. A portion of the capital is, or was employed in banking, a privilege singularly granted to this bridge company by their charter.

New Jerusalem, p-o. Berks co., 156 miles from W. C., and 65 from Harrisburg.

Newlin, t-ship, Chester co. bounded N. E. by Bradford, S. E. by East Marlborough, S. W. by West Marlborough, and N. W. by East Fallowfield. Centrally distant from Phila. S. W. about 28 miles; from West Chester 8 miles; length $4\frac{1}{2}$, breadth $2\frac{1}{2}$ miles; area 7100 acres; surface, hilly; soil, limestone. Pop. in 1830, 794; taxables in 1828, 161. The W. branch of the Brandywine creek crosses the t-ship from E. to W. and turns several mills within it.

New London. (*See London, New.*)

Newmanstown, p-t. Berks co., Heidelberg t-ship, on the road from Womelsdorff to Shafferstown, and on the boundary line between Lebanon and Berks cos., about 2 miles from Womelsdorff, and 15 from Reading. Contains about 40 dwellings, two taverns and 1 store, and 250 inhabitants, and a church common to the Lutherans and German Reformed.

New Market, p-t. Fairview t-ship, York co., at the confluence of the Yellow Breeches creek with the Susquehannah river; 20 miles N. W. of the borough of York, and about 4 ms. S. W. of Harrisburg.

New Market, town of Upper Mount Bethel t-ship, Northampton co., on the road from Easton to the Delaware Water gap, 17 ms. from the former. Contains 2 dwellings, 1 tavern and 1 store.

New Market, small village on the Susquehannah river, Manor t-ship, Lancaster co.

Newport, t-ship, Luzerne co. bounded N. E. by Hanover, S. E. by Sugarloaf, S. W. by Nescopeck, and N. W. by the Susquehannah r. Anthracite coal is found here in abundance. It contains bog iron ore, which has been worked to a considerable extent, at a forge upon the Nanticoke, which has been long in operation.

Nanticoke falls, where a feeder has been built for the N. Branch canal, is at the extreme N. angle of this t-ship. The immense amount of surplus water which this dam will furnish, and which may be applied to hydraulic purposes, its location at the outlet of the extensive valley of Wyoming, the coal and iron ore in its vicinity, with the facilities of canal transportation are calculated to invite capitalists, and at no very distant day, to produce in its immediate neighborhood a populous and busy manufacturing village. It is situated about 8 ms. from Wilkesbarre; has a p-o. and contains 849 inhabitants; and by the return of 1828, 159 taxables.

Newport, a village on the Neshaminy creek, Bristol t-ship, Bucks co. 18 ms. N. E. from Phil. and 3 ms. N. W. Bristol. It is at the head of tide navigation on the creek, where there are excellent grist and saw mills, and an excellent bridge of wood on stone piers. Number of dwellings from 12 to 15; a store and tavern.

Newport, a p-v. on the W. bank of the Juniata r. in Juniata t-ship, Perry co. above the mouth of the Little Buffalo creek, about 6 ms. N. E. of Bloomfield, 127 from W. C., and 41 from Harrisburg. There is a ferry here across the river. The town contains about 20 dwellings, 3 stores, and 1 tavern. Being directly on the bank of the canal, it has become a considerable depot for the produce of the co.

Newport, t. Blacklick t-ship, Ind.

co., on the N. side of Blacklick creek at its confluence with the Conemaugh r. opposite to Blairsville, and about 14 ms. S. W. of the borough of Ind. The state canal crosses the river on the S. side of the town. The town contains about 6 dwellings.

New Providence, p-o. of Bald Eagle t-ship, on the N.W. side of the Muncy mtn., and on the Bald Eagle creek, 20 ms. N. E. Bellefonte.

New Providence, p-o. Lancaster co. 129 ms. from W. C. and 63 from Harrisburg.

Newry, p-t. Frankstown t-ship, Huntingdon co. on Poplar run, a tributary of the Frankstown branch of the Juniata r. about 24 ms. W. of Huntingdon borough, 150 N. W. from W. C., and 122 from Harrisburg; contains 45 dwellings, 1 German Reformed church, 1 Catholic chapel, 1 school, 3 stores, 1 tavern, and 1 distillery.

Newtown, t-ship, Delaware co., bounded N. E. by Radnor, S. E. by Marple, S. by Upper Providence, S.W. by, Edgemont, and N. W. by Chester co. Greatest length 4 ms.; breadth 4 ms. Cental distance from Philadelphia N. W. 14 miles, from Chester 9 miles N.; area, 6400; surface, hilly; soil, loam. Pop. in 1830, 667; taxables, 141. Newtown Square is a small village in this township at which there is a church. Crum creek courses the W. boundary and Darby creek crosses the N. E. angle.

Newtown, t-ship, Bucks co., bounded N. by Upper Makefield, E. by Lower Makefield, S. by Middletown, W. and S.W. by Northampton, and N. W. by Wrightstown t-ship. Central distance from Philadelphia 20 ms. N. E.; from Doylestown 12 S. E. Length 5 miles, breadth 3½; area, 7,268 acres; surface, level; soil, rich clay loam, well cultivated and productive. Pop. in 1830, 1344; taxables, 233 in 1828. Newtown creek, a branch of the Neshaminy, crosses the township diagonally and drives several mills in its course. Upon this stream the borough of Newtown, formerly the st. jus., is seated, at a point whence roads diverge to every part of the county.

Newtown, p-t. and borough, Newtown t-ship, Bucks co., formerly the st. jus. of the co. (see preceding article,) 12 miles S. of Doylestown, 167 N. of Washington and 129 S. E. of Harrisburg. It contains about an hundred houses, 2 stores, 3 taverns, a Quaker's meeting-house and a Presbyterian church. It is at present particularly famed for the number and excellence of the carriages made in the place.

Newton, t-ship, Cumberland co., bounded N. by Mifflin t-ship, E. by W. Pennsborough and Dickenson t-ships, S. by Adams co. and W. by Southampton t-ship. Centrally distant W. from Carlisle 16 miles; greatest length 11½; breadth 5 miles; area 32,000 acres; surface, level; soil, limestone. Pop. in 1830, 1349; taxables, 365. The Yellow Breeches creek rises in a small lake called Big Pond on the W. boundary at the N. foot of the South mountains, and flows E. through the t-ship, receiving an accession of waters from a fountain on the E. border called the "Three Springs." Stoughstown is on the turnpike road leading from Carlisle to Chambersburg, 14 miles W. from the latter, near which is a large spring, from which a fine mill stream issues. Newville, a borough town, lies on this stream in the N. E. angle of the t-ship, 13 miles west from Carlisle.

Newtown Square, p-t. and village of Newtown t-ship, Delaware co. 12 ms. N. W. from Chester, 131 from W. C. and 94 S. E. from Harrisburg, consisted of 4 or 5 dwellings, a store and tavern and a church.

Newtown, p-t, of Whitely t-ship, Green co., 8 miles S. E. of Waynesburg, 249 miles N. W. of W. C. and 231 S. W. from Harrisburg, on Whiteley creek. It is a village of some 8 or 12 houses.

Newville, p-t. and small village on the line of Warrington and Warwick t-ships, Bucks co. There is a store, a tavern, and 6 or 8 houses. It is about five miles S. W. of Doylestown.

Newville, p-t and borough, Newton t-ship, Cumberland co., upon Big Spring creek, 14 miles W. of Carlisle. It contains about 100 dwellings and several mills and 530 inhabitants, 6 stores, 3 taverns, one Presbyterian, and one Seceder church. Distant 12 miles W. of Carlisle and 30 miles from Harrisburg, and 115 N. from Washington. The town was incorporated by act 26th Feb. 1817.

New Salem, p-t. of Manallen t-ship, Fayette co., on Dunlap's creek, about 7 miles W. of Uniontown, 207 miles N. W. of W. C. and 179 S. W. from Harrisburg, contains 30 dwelling, one church, 2 stores and 2 taverns.

New Wilmington, p-t. of Lackawannock t-ship, Mercer co. upon Little Neshannock creek, 8 miles S. W. of Mercer borough, 274 from W. C. and 242 from Harrisburg, contains 15 dwellings, 2 stores, 1 tavern and a grist mill.

Neversink mountains, Bucks co. 2 prominent hills, near the town of Reading, about which the Schuylkill river makes a remarkable bend of nearly three miles. There is a road across the first of these hills along the side next the river, which approaches fearfully close to its precipitous declivity.

Nevill's island, an island several miles in length in the Ohio river, seven miles below Pittsburg.

Nicetown, Philadelphia co., partly in Penn and partly in Northern Liberty t-ships, upon the Germantown road, four and a half miles from Philadelphia, contains about 40 dwellings, 2 stores and 2 taverns. The country immediately around it, is pleasant, several country seats are in sight from it, and the Germantown rail road runs on the brow of the valley at the northern extremity.

Nicholsburg, p-t. Mahoning t-ship, Indiana co., in the W. fork formed by the junction of the Little Mahoning with the main creek, 18 miles N. W. of Indiana borough, contains 6 or 8 dwellings, store and tavern and mill.

Nicholson, t-ship, Luzerne co. (so named, from John Nicholson, Esq. formerly treasurer of Pennsylvania, who early formed a settlement in the neighborhood,) bounded N. by Susquehannah co., E. by Greenfield, S. by Abington, and W. Tunkhannock t-ships. The Philadelphia and Great Bend turnpike passes through it from north to south, dividing it into nearly two equal parts. Tunckhannock mountain extends across its northern part. It is situated about 35 miles N. from Wilkesbarre; has a post office called after the t-ship, 254 miles from W. C. and 146 from Harrisburg, and contains, by the census of 1830, 906 inhabitants, and by the returns of 1828, 186 taxables. Its greatest length E. and W. is about 8 miles; breadth N. and S. about 6 miles.

Nippenose, or Oval Limestone valley, lies in about equal portions in Wayne and Nippenose t-ships, Lycoming co. The length of its greatest axis is about 10 and of its lesser 5 miles. It is surrounded by high mountains the springs from which, lose themselves in the fissures of the valley. (See Lycoming co.)

Nippenose, t-ship, Lycoming co., bounded N. by the W. branch of the Susquehannah river, E. by Washington t-ship, S. by Adams t-ship, and W. by Wayne t-ship. Centrally distant S. W. from Williamsport 8 miles; length, 9; breadth, 4 miles; area, 14,080 acres; surface, hilly; soil, limestone. Pop. in 1830, about 350; taxables, 66; valuation of taxable property in 1829, seated lands, &c. $30,159, unseated 5,944. Personal est. 2,862, rate of levy $\frac{3}{4}$ of one per cent. Nippenose creek forms the western boundary and is the outlet of Nippenose valley, receiving the many streams which hide themselves in the lime sinks of the valley. The post office of the t-ship bears its name and is 213 miles N. W. of W. C. and 104 from Harrisburg.

Nittany mountains, ridges of the Allegheny which rise in Centre co., and run N. E. into Union and Lycoming counties.

Nittany valley, Walker and Lamar t-ships, Centre co., between Muncy ridge on the N. W. and Nittany mountain on the S. E., is about 12 or 15 miles long. Its greatest width about 5 miles. It is watered by Big and Little Fishing creeks, and by Cedar creek.

Nittany, p-o. Centre co., 208 miles from W. C. and 101 from Harrisburg.

Noblesboro', p-t. of Fayette t-ship, Allegheny co., centrally situated in the t-ship on a branch of Chartier's creek, 10 ms. S. W. of Pittsburg, 234 from W. C., 212 from Harrisburg; contains about 20 dwellings, 1 store and tavern.

Nockamixon, t-ship, Bucks co., bounded N. by Durham t-ship, E. by the r. Delaware, S. by Tinicum t-ship, W. by Haycock t-ship, and N. W. by Springfield t-ship. Centrally distant from Philadelphia 40 ms., and from Doylestown 14 N.; greatest length 7½ miles, breadth 4½; area, 16,848 acres; surface, hilly; soil, gravelly. Pop. in 1830, 2049; taxables in 1828, 407. The shore of the Delaware for several ms. in this t-ship, is formed of high and perpendicular rocks of red sandstone, along which the river has many ripples. Below these rocks are some extensive swamps. There is a p-o. at Ottsville on the line between this and Tinicum t-ship. Gallows run flows into the Delaware on the north boundary line.

Nolandsville, village, of Franklin t-ship, Westmoreland co., 10 ms. N. W. of Greensburg; contains 12 houses, tavern and store.

Norriton, t-ship, Montgomery co., bounded N. by Worcester t-ship, N. E. by Whitpaine, S. E. by Plymouth, S. by the r. Schuylkill, and W. by Lower Providence t-ships. Greatest length 7 ms., greatest breadth 4½; area, 8960 acres. The *manor* which included this t-ship, was sold in 1704 by Wm. Penn the younger, to Wm. Trent, the founder of Trenton, and Isaac Norris, from whom the t-ship has its name, for £850. It is drained by 3 small streams which flow into the Schuylkill. The ridge, and the Germantown and Perkiomen t-pike roads, run nearly parallel with each other through the t-ship. Norristown, a borough, post and county town, is beautifully seated on the r. Schuylkill, and distinguished for its manufactures, the water power for which is derived from the dam made here by the Schuylkill navigation company. (*See Norristown.*) Surface of the country is level; soil, red shale, fertile and well cultivated. Pop., independent of the borough, in 1830, 1139; taxables in 1828, 245.

Norristown, p-t. and borough, Norriton t-ship, and seat of justice of Montgomery co., situated on the river Schuylkill and on the ridge t-pike road, 16 miles N. W. of the city of Philadelphia, 166 from W. C., and 80 S. E. from Harrisburg. It has its name from Isaac Norris, a distinguished friend of Wm. Penn, and an early settler and popular statesman and judge of the province, and joint owner with Wm. Trent, of the township of Norriton. It was incorporated into a borough by act 31st March, 1812, and has a burgess, town council, and high constable elected annually. Its area is about 1 sq. mile; within which there are now (May, 1832) 1300 inhabitants. In 1830, there were by the census 1116. The public buildings here, consist of a court house 70 by 40 ft. two stories high, with a cupola and bell; a house for the county offices, 50 by 36 ft.; a jail, whose S. front is 100 ft. by 36, W. front 100 ft. by 50, all of stone, 2 stories high and rough cast. An academy 40 by 30 ft., 2 stories high, of brick; a banking house; an Episcopal church, 50 ft. front by 80 deep, of stone, in the Gothic style; Presbyterian church of stone 60 by 30 ft., and two engine houses of stone; a library, containing about 1100 volumes. There are here also, a literary society, a cabinet of natural history, two daily primary schools, 2 Sunday schools, 3 weekly newspapers, 8 hotels and taverns, 9 stores, 151 dwellings, 1 brewery, one bottling cellar, 2 oyster houses, 1 hay scales, 2 fire engines, 1 mill for sawing marble, having 174 saws, and capable of sawing 1000 superficial feet per week, 2 mills for sawing timber, 4 merchant grist mills, 1 oil mill, 1 livery stable, 2 lumber yards, 1 coal yard, 1 brick yard, 1 lime kiln, 6 justices of the peace, 11 attornies at law, 1 scrivener, 5 physicians, 2 druggists, 2 butchers, 2 bakers, 8 confectioners, 3 printers, 1 book binder, 2 clock and watch makers, 1 cabinet maker, 1 chair maker, 1 sign painter, 1 hatter, 4 tailors, 2 milliners and mantua makers, 1 tallow chandler, 1 tanner, 1 currier, 3 boot and shoe makers, 1 saddle and harness maker, 5 master carpenters, 2 stone cutters, 1 master mason, 1 brick layer, 1 mill wright, 1 coach maker, 1 wheel wright, 3 blacksmiths, 1 tin manufacturer, 2 coopers, 1 carpet weaver, 1 tobacconist. There are here also, 1 cotton mill belonging to Mr. B. McCready, 150 ft. by 48, 5 stories high, of stone, and roofed with slate, containing near 7000 spindles; another cotton mill belonging to Mr. Friedly, 47 by 38 ft., 2 stories high, of stone, containg 900 spindles; a weaving factory, conducted by Mr. Jamieson, 110 ft. by 45, in part 3 stories high, capable of containing 216 power looms, and having now 143 looms in operation, making 30,000 yards of cotton cloth per week. The bridge across the Schuylkill is 800 ft. long, and with the abutments, 1050 ft. It has 3 arches of wood resting on stone piers, cost $31,199 90, erected by a joint stock company, in which the county has an interest of $10,000, and the state 6000. The streets of the town have lately been levelled and graded, and much of them paved with brick or flags. Thirteen stages pass through the town daily, with from 50 to 100 passengers. The site of the town is pleasant and healthy, and the water power obtained here by the dam of the Schuylkill navigation company and its vicinity to Philadelphia, and communication therewith by the canal, and by the rail road now being made, will make it an extensive manufacturing town. The dam across the Schuylkill is about 110 feet long, and 900 ft. between the abutments, the width of the water fall.

Northampton county. This county was established by act of assembly of March 11th, 1752; and is bounded by the Delaware r. on the E., Bucks co. on the S. E., Lehigh co. on the S., Schuylkill co. on the S. W., Luzerne co. on the N. W., and Pike co. on the N. Its greatest length from N. to S. is 40 ms., and its greatest breadth from E. to W. is 50 ms. It contains 874 sq. miles or 559,360 acres. Full $\frac{9}{10}$ of the population are German, and they merit the high character given to that people, for sobriety, industry, frugality and thrift.

This county is one of the most interesting in the state, by reason of its agricultural improvements, its mineral wealth, particularly iron and the great coal formations of Mauch Chunk and Beaver Meadow, (*see these articles,*) and the admirable canal of the Lehigh navigation and coal company.

Northampton is one of the most diversified counties, not only of Pennsylvania, but of the U. S. It is traversed from N. E. to S. W. by the Kittatinny mtns., or as they are locally called in the county, the Blue Ridge. This chain divides it into 2 very unequal sections; that S. E. of the Kittatinny lies in the form of a triangle, the base along the mtns., and the perpendicular on Lehigh co., and contains nearly 400 sq. ms. The surface, though generally hilly, is as generally arable. The very remarkable slate and lime formation which extends so distinctively from the Delaware to the Susquehannah, in the Kittatinny valley, is peculiarly striking in the lower part of Northampton. The limestone tract skirts the S. mtn, and the argilaceous slate the Kittatinny, each extending from its respective base about half way across the valley. Though both are highly productive in grain, fruits and pasturage, the limestone soil is stronger than the slate; and the features of nature bolder on the former, than on the latter formation.

The townships of Lower Saucon and Williams, are separated from the other parts of the county by the Lehigh, and are traversed by a ridge passing by Bethlehem, and interrupted by the Delaware 2 ms. below Easton. From many of the highest eminences of this range, the highly cultivated section we have noticed, spreads before the eye like a vast garden, terminated by the distant Kittatinny mtns.

That section of the county N. W. of the Kittatinny mountain is remarkably broken into mountainous ridges; of which the Kittatinny is the only one that passes through the county in a direct line. Those in the N. W. are scattered, disunited, and lie rather in groups, than extend to collateral ridges. All, however, have a general N. E. and S. W. arrangement, and leave intervening valleys of more or less width and fertility, as in other parts of Pennsylvania, the Northampton ridges receive special names in different places. The principal ones are, beside the S. mtn. or Lehigh hills and Kittatinny, the Pokono or Second mtn., Mauch Chunk, Nesquihoning, Broad mtn., the Pohopoko, Spring mtn., and Mahoning mtn. The soil in the valleys N. of the Blue mtn., even where arable, is much inferior to that upon the S. Indeed, the mtn. is the division line between 2 climates, and the temperature of the seasons is not less different than the soil. Vegetation is about two weeks later on the N. than on the S. side.

The general character of the soil below the mountain, is gravel, loam and schist, intermixed with sand in many places. It is warm and productive, particularly in grain; produces excellent fruit, and when plaster is used, very good clover. Above the mountain, the soil is principally a mixture of gravel and clay, and above the Pokono mtn., partakes so much of the latter, as to be cold and unproductive. The timber is chiefly pine and hemlock, and is generally small; but the forests on the Upper Lehigh, and particularly the Great swamp produce large and excellent trees. The country is almost a wilderness, uninhabited except along the road to Wilkesbarre, and there sparsely. Below the mtn., the natural timber is principally oak, mingled with hickory and chestnut. There is here, however, but a small portion of the natural forest remaining, cultivation having felled all that impeded its progress. About $\frac{1}{4}$ of the co. is cultivated; about a third of it is susceptible of cultivation. Three fourths of that which is subject to the plough are admirably adapted to grain, particularly rye and wheat.

We may safely assume the general elevation of the cultivated part of Northampton co. in the Kittatinny valley, at 250 to 300 feet, and of the section above the mountain, at 500 to 600 feet.

The rivers of Northampton co. are the Delaware, the Lehigh, and their branches.

The Delaware, which forms the eastern boundary of the co., has a very crooked course, following its windings about 25 miles through a very mountainous country, until it leaves the Water gap. Its banks continue hilly below the mtn. to Welles' falls, S. of the village of New Hope, in Bucks co.

The creeks of the county, below the Kittatinny, advancing S. W. from the Delaware Water gap, are, Crosby's, Richmond, Martin's, Muddy, Bushkill, Manookisy, Caladaque & Hockendocque; the three latter fall into the Lehigh, the residue into the Delaware. Above the Kittatinny, the Delaware receives immediately above the Water gap, Broadhead's creek, partly from Pike and partly from Northampton. The mountain section of the county, however, is more particularly drained by the confluents of the Lehigh; these are from the left, Tobyhanna, Dreck, Muddy, Big creek, and Aquanshicola; from the right, Quacake,

Nesquihoning, Mahoning and Lizard creeks.

The Lehigh is emphatically the r. of Northampton co., having therein most of its sources and the greater part of its course. A detailed description of it, and of the improvements connected with it, will be found under the articles *Lehigh river*, and *Mauch Chunk*, in this work.

The canal of the Schuylkill navigation and coal company, accompanies the Lehigh from Mauch Chunk in its course through the county of Northampton to Easton, where it communicates with the Delaware, and with the state canal. (*For a particular description of it, see that part of the "Introduction which treats of the canals of Pennsylvania"* and "*Mauch Chunk.*")

The chief towns and villages of Northampton co. are Easton, Bethlehem, Nazareth, Mauch Chunk, Anthracite, Weisport, Lowrytown, Richmond, Williamsburg, Dutotsburg, Stroudsburg, Lehighton, Berlinville, Cherryville, Kreidersville, Kernsville, Kellerstown. (*For a particular description of these, see their several titles.*)

A main turnpike road leaves Philadelphia, passes through Philadelphia, Montgomery, Bucks and part of Lehigh counties, enters Northampton in the t-ship of Lower Saucon, and crosses the Lehigh at Bethlehem, where it branches into two routes. One turns N. W. up the Lehigh, passes Kreidersville, and through the Lehigh Water gap, by Lehighton, Mauch Chunk and Lausanne, continues to the banks of the Susquehannah, at Nescopeck. From Bethlehem, the other or northern branch proceeds towards Easton, but breaks into numerous country roads, one of which leads to Nazareth and to the Delaware Wind gap. Here it is divided into two branches; one of which runs N. W. to Wilkesbarre, and the other N. into Pike co. The lower Philadelphia road reaches Easton, between the foregoing and Delaware r. From Easton another road leads up the Delaware to the Water gap. Besides these, numerous cross roads chequer the lower part of the county, and render communication easy and convenient. A *rail road* of 9 miles in length, runs from the village of Mauch Chunk to the coal mine on Mauch Chunk mtn., and another rail road of little more than 5 miles in length, communicates with the mines lately opened by the Lehigh coal company, on the N. of the Nesquihoning mtn.

Good bridges are found in this co., over most of the streams where the convenience of the public has required them. The most notable are those erected over the Delaware at Easton; over the Lehigh at that place and Bethlehem, Lehighton, and Mauch Chunk.

The several *gaps* of which we have spoken are certainly objects of curiosity. The Delaware Water gap is a crooked passage, forming a right angle in the mtn. which appears as if cleft in twain for the egress of the river, and forms perpendicular cliffs of rocks which rise 1200 feet from the river, so near the brink, that the road is cut in the hill. The Lehigh Water gap is a similar passage, but has not such large rocks, nor is it so steep as the preceding.

Moor's cascade is a perpendicular fall of Moor's run, of two separate pitches of about 40 feet each. The first falls into a basin, and the second upon broken rocks, the whole being in a deep glen whose sides rise about an hundred feet. Immediately below is the *turn hole*, a deep eddy in the river Lehigh, bounded by a rocky and perpendicular cliff, 150 ft. high.

The county is not distinguished for manufacturing enterprize. Its distance from market, and the sparseness of its population, afford satisfactory reasons for its backwardness in this particular. With the improved means of transportation produced by the Lehigh and Delaware canals, it is probable that the wealth and attention of its citizens will be more turned into this channel. The ordinary handicrafts prosper, and much flax and wool are converted into clothing of a rude but durable texture, by the hands of the farmers' wives and daughters. Flour, whiskey, lumber, coal and iron, are the great stables of the county. Large quantities of flour are annually sent to Philadelphia by the Delaware, and much will hereafter reach New-York by the Morris canal, which connects with the Delaware in the state of New Jersey opposite to Easton. There are beds of valuable iron ore in various parts of the county, particularly in the t-ships south of the Lehigh; and there are here one furnace and 3 forges in profitable operation.

The German population of the state has been reproached with being indifferent to the progress of letters, and perhaps the inhabitants of this county are not exempt from the charge. Yet, with the aid of the state, an academy and a college, called La Fayette, have been established at Easton, and another at Stroudsburg; and the Moravian institutions have been long distinguished for their attention to the rudiments of education, and their schools at Bethlehem and Nazareth, have had justly much reputation. A library of some 1500 volumes is established at Easton, where many gentlemen display a due regard for science.

The population of this county was in 1810, 38,145; in 1820, 31,765; and by the census of 1830, amounts to 39,267. The apparent diminution of 1820, arises from the abstraction of the townships which form Lehigh county, in 1812. The taxables in 1828 were 7382. Assessed value of real estate $6,360,982. Of the population there were males, 21,418; females, 18,657; colored persons, 192; aliens, 568; deaf and humb, 20; blind, 10; and 1 male slave. The price of land varies of course according to quality and vicinity to market, and ranges from $5 to 100 the acre. The latter price is demanded for some well improved farms in the limestone formation along the Lehigh river.

Judiciary. Northampton forms a part of the eastern district of the supreme court; and together with Berks and Lehigh, constitutes the 3d judicial district. The courts are held at Easton on the 3d Mondays of January, April, August, and November, annually.

Senatorial district. Northampton and Lehigh form the 12th senatorial district of the state, which sends two members to the senate. The county, joined with Wayne and Pike, has four representatives in the assembly. With Bucks, Wayne and Pike, it forms the 8th congressional district, and sends 3 representatives to congress.

There are two banks in the county, located at the town of Easton. (*See Easton.*)

STATISTICAL TABLE OF NORTHAMPTON COUNTY.

Townships, &c.	Greatest Lth.	Greatest Bth.	Population. 1820	Population. 1830	Taxables.
Allen,	8	5 1-4	1847	2106	417
Bethlehem,	5 1-2	4 1-2	1860	2430	425
Bushkill,	7	4	1262	1402	277
Chestnut Hill,	9	8	1026	940	215
East Penn,	8	6 1-2	1082	807	222
Easton Boro',			2370	3529	660
Forks,	6 1-4	6	1659	1989	389
Hanover,	2 1-2	2	358	348	65
Hamilton,	6 1-4	6 1-4	1320	1428	275
Lehigh,	6 1-4	5 1-2	1550	1659	333
Lausanne,	15	8 1-2	220	508	165
L'er Nazareth,	4 3-4	3	1084	1204	223
Lower Saucon,	6 1-2	4 1-2	2208	2508	446
L'er Mt. Bethel,	11 1-2	8 1-4	2472	2666	483
Moore,	4 1-2	4 1-2	1645	1853	398
Plainfield,	9 1-2	2	1127	1285	233
Pokono,	12	7	389	568	94
Ross,	9 1-2	6	873	838	149
Stroud,	8	5 1-2	1143	1631	275
Smithfield,	8 1-2	7 1-2	961	1080	194
Towamensing,	24	10	874	1171	238
Up. Mt. Bethel,	9	5	2182	2241	450
Up. Nazareth,	4 3-4	2 1-2	663	942	164
Tobyhanna,	16	13		279	50
Mauch Chunk,	13	2		1348	262
Williams,	6	3	1590	2707	339
			31,765	39,267	

Northampton, formerly called Allentown, in Lehigh county, situated at the junction of the Jordan and Little Lehigh creeks, about half a mile from the Lehigh river. It is 6 miles S. S. W. from Bethlehem, 18 S. W. from Easton, and 55 N. N. W. from Philadelphia, 178 N. E. from W. C. and 85 E. of Harrisburg. The town is on high ground, and commands a fine view of the surrounding country. It was laid out before the erection of

Northampton county, by William Allen, Esq. provincial chief justice, from whom it received its name. A great portion of the town plot, and many farms about it, still belong to his heirs. Except Nazareth, it is the oldest town above the South mountain, and E. of the Schuylkill river. Its form is square, its streets are at right angles, and it is ornamented by a public square near the centre. It contains a large court house and public offices, of hewn limestone, a spacious prison of the same materials, 3 churches, 1 for Lutherans, 1 for German Presbyterians, and 1 for English Presbyterians, an academy incorporated 18th March, 1814, to which the state gave $2000, and about 260 dwelling houses, besides shops and other out houses, and 2 merchant grist mills. The population in 1830, was 1544; taxables in 1828, 322. A bank called the Northampton bank was established here in 1814. Capital, $123,365. (See article Lehigh co.) Northampton was incorporated as a borough by act March 18th, 1811.

On the main road to Bethlehem and in view of the town, is a chain bridge over the Lehigh, 230 feet long, and 30 feet wide. There are also excellent stone bridges over the Little Lehigh, and the Jordan. The chain bridge over the Lehigh had once a double path, and was an imposing structure, but it was once impaired by fire, and since by the works of the Lehigh canal company; a large stone driven against it in blasting the rocks at the dam of this place, broke one of the chains, and threw a portion of the bridge into the water. It has been repaired, however, and it is strong enough, but it has a ruinous appearance. It is the property of a company.

Northampton, t-ship, Bucks county, bounded N. by Wrightstown, E. by Newtown, S. and S. E. by Middleton, S. W. by Southampton and Warminster, and W. by Warwick t-ships. Centrally distant from Philadelphia, 20 miles N.; from Doylestown, 10 miles S. E. Length 7½, breadth 4½ miles; area, 13,975 acres. The Neshaminy creek forms the N., E. and part of the S. boundary, and receives from the t-ship several small streams. Tinkertown, a small hamlet, is on the line which divides it from Warwick t-ship. Northampton meeting is near the line of Southampton t-ship. Surface, level; soil, rich loam. Pop. in 1830, 1521; taxables, 1828, 311; assessed value of lands, $656,825.

Northampton, Lehigh co. a small t-ship, which surrounds the borough of Northampton. Surface, level; soil, limestone. Pop. in 1830, 213; taxables, 40.

North East, t-ship, Erie county, bounded N. by lake Erie, E. by the state of New York, S. by Greenfield, and W. by Beaver Dam and Harbor Creek t-ships. Centrally distant N. E. from Erie borough, 10 miles; greatest length 7, breadth 5½ miles; area, 19,200. It is drained northward by Sixteen and Twenty Mile crs. and other streams. Burget'stown, a post-town, lies on the road from Erie to Portland, 14 miles N. E. from the former, and 287 miles from Harrisburg.

Northern Liberties. Upon the survey of the plot of the city of Philadelphia in 1682 or 1683, two tracts of land were annexed to it under the designation of "Liberties;" the one W. of the river Schuylkill, and the other north of Vine street. These Liberties were apportioned among the purchasers of lands from the proprietary, at the ratio of 10 acres in the western, and 8 in the northern, for every 500 acres of country land sold. Under the designation of "The Northern Liberties," were included for many years, all the lands contained in the tract N. of the city, S. and E. of Oxford, Bristol, Germantown and Roxborough t-ships. By the incorporation of the city portion of the t-ship, and the erection of Penn t-ship, and the incorporation of Kensington district, the *t-ship* of the Northern Liberties is now bounded N. by the Frankford or Tacony creek which separates it from Oxford t-ship, thence by a line which strikes the Germantown road at the forks, a mile above Nicetown, E. and S. E. by the river Delaware and Kensington district, S. by the incorporated Northern Liberties, and W. by Penn t-ship. This district is, in many places, as thickly settled as a town, and contains the villages of Ballstown, Bridesburg, Richmond, Sunville and Nicetown. It is about $4\frac{1}{2}$ miles long, by 3 miles wide. Its surface is generally level, its soil clay and loam, and generally in a high state of cultivation, and in many parts, employed in extensive horticulture. The Cohocksink creek is on its S. and Tacony on the N. boundary. Gunner's run flows across the t-ship to the Delaware, midway between them. The population by the census of 1830, was 2453.

Northern Liberties, Incorporated. This district was taken from the foregoing, by act 28th March, 1803, by which it was erected into a separate corporation, which provided, That the inhabitants of that part of the Northern Liberties, lying between the W. side of Sixth street and the river Delaware, and between Vine street and Cohocksink creek, be, &c. a corporation and body politic, to be governed by 15 commissioners. Several supplements were enacted to this law, to enlarge or modify the powers of the corporation, all of which with others, were embraced in a consolidated act of 16th March, 1819, which changed the boundary from the W. side, to the *middle* of Sixth street. The District is a suburb of the city, and contains half the area of the city. It is for the greater part closely built, and is paved, watched, and lighted as the city. It is supplied with Schuylkill water by means of the city water works, and grows more rapidly than the city proper. It contained in 1830, about 5500 dwellings, and 28,923 inhabitants.

Northern Liberties, a suburb of the city of Pittsburg. (See Pittsburg.)

Northmoreland, t-ship, Luzerne co. bounded N. by Eaton and the Susquehannah river, E. by Exeter, S. by Dallas and Lehman, and W. by Windham. Its surface is very uneven, indeed mountainous; yet it contains a considerable quantity of land, which will admit of culture. It has 3 post-offices. The Allegheny mountains, including Bowman's ridge, almost cover it. It is drained by Bowman's cr. and its tributaries, which pass centrally through it, by Island run in the N. E. angle, and a branch of Sudon's creek, which rises in a small lake in the S. E. It is wedge shape. Greatest length about 13 miles, greatest width about 6 miles; area, 33,480 acres. Pop. in 1830, 785; taxables in 1828, 144. The post-office named after the t-ship, is distant from W. C. 242 miles, and 134 from Harrisburg.

Northumberland, post-town of Northumberland county, at the confluence of the E. and W. branches of the Susquehannah river, about 54 miles by the road above Harrisburg, and 164 from W. C. A bridge across the E. or N. branch, connects the town with Sunbury, (see Sunbury,) and another over the W. branch, leads to Union co. The Shamokin dam across the river here, is $9\frac{1}{2}$ feet high above the bottom of the river, and 2783 feet long. The chute through it for the passage of boats and rafts, is 64 feet wide, and 650 feet long. This dam has been twice built, and its permanency is still doubtful. The town contains about 150 dwellings, 12 or 13 stores, 10 taverns, and a full proportion of mechanics. Three churches, 1 Presbyterian, 1 Methodist, and 1 German Reformed, an academy incorporated in 1804 and endowed by the legislature with $2000, a market house and town house of brick, a bank with a capital of $200,000, incorporated 1st April, 1831. As at this point the trade of the North and West Branches of the Susquehannah unite, Northumberland has every prospect upon the completion of the state canals, of becoming a place of great business.

The town was incorporated 14th April, 1828.

Northumberland county, was formed from Berks and Bedford counties, by act 21st March, 1772, and is now bounded N. by Lycoming, E. by Columbia, S. E. by Schuylkill, S. by Dauphin, and W. by the main Susquehannah river, and the West branch of that stream which separates it from Union county. Its greatest length is 35 miles, breadth 13; area, 457 sq. ms. Central lat. 40° 52′ N. long. 0° 12′ E. from Washington.

The county lies within the great central transition formation of the state, and like every other portion of that region, is covered with mountains. The portion on the S. E. side of the North branch of the Susquehannah, abounds with anthracite coal, especially the Mahanoy mountain and valley. There are beds of iron ore in Shamokin t-ship, near which a furnace and forge are employed in the manufacture of iron. Contrary to the usual course of the Appalachian ridges, the mountains here run E. and W. and advancing from S. to N. we cross Line mountain, Little Mahanoy, Mahanoy, and Shamokin, below the junction of the two great branches of the Susquehannah river, above their confluence Montour's mountain and the Limestone ridge. The county is washed by the main Susquehannah 20 miles below, and by the West branch 20 miles above Sunbury and Northumberland, and by the N. E. branch 10 miles on both shores, between Danville and Sunbury. It has a river line of 60 miles. Beside these rivers, it is watered by several large creeks, the principal of which are the Mahantango, Mahanoy, and Shamokin, entering the Susquehannah below Sunbury; and Chilisquaque, Limestone and Warrior creeks which flow to the West branch. Having thus much river bottom, it possesses, notwithstanding its mountainous aspect, a large proportion of good, and a considerable quantity of first rate soil. The country N. of the East branch of the river, including the t-ships of Point, Chilisquaque and Turbut, appears to be underlaid with transition limestone, which has, in some places, been raised into the hills. Limestone is said also to exist in Lower Mahanoy t-ship, although every other portion of the county S. of the East branch, is composed of red sand stone, pudding stone, lesser conglomerates, slate, &c. and the soil of the debris of these rocks. The anthracite coal fields of the Mahanoy, are very extensive, stretching through the valley of the Great Mahanoy creek in Shamokin and Little Mahanoy t-ship, and into Schuylkill county, a distance not yet fully explored, but may probably be traced to the Buck mountains of Luzerne, and the Spring mountain and Beaver meadow coal measures of Northampton county, a distance not less than 50 miles. The western termination of the artery is in and near the forks of the Little and Big Mahanoy creeks, 8 miles E. of the Susquehannah river, to which the descent is easy and unimpeded. The near vicinity to the river, the ready and cheap means of transportation offered by the large creek, together with the excellent quality of the coal, give this region a decided advantage over those N. or S. of it. A company has been incorporated for improving the navigation of the Mahanoy.

A turnpike road from Reading, through Pottsville, in Schuylkill co. enters this county across the Mahanoy mountain, and radiates in the centre of Shamokin t-ship, one branch leading to Sunbury, and the other to Danville. The main branch of the road is called the Centre turnpike. A rail road, following in a great measure the route of the turnpike, is now being made from Pottsville to Danville, with a lateral to Northumberland. This road has received the name of the "Girard rail road," in honor of the memory of the late Stephen Girard, Esq. This road will arrest the down trade of both branches of the Susquehannah; of the North branch at Danville and Northumberland, and of the West branch at the latter town. The iron of Centre co. the bituminous coal of Clearfield and Lycoming, the lumber of Potter, Tioga, Bradford and Susquehannah, and the agricultural products of central and northern Pennsylvania, will find a market at Philadelphia by this route.

Northumberland county was settled originally by English emigrants, who were soon supplanted by the more hardy, more laborious and more patient Germans, whose descendants now possess the country. The population of the county after all its reductions, was in 1820, 15,424; in 1830, 18,168, of whom 9267 were white males, 8806 white females, 59 free black males, 46 free black females.

The Presbyterian is the most numerous religious sect, but there are also Lutherans, German Reformed, Methodists, Baptists, Quakers and Unitarians, who together have about 30 churches. There is a county bible society, missionary and tract societies, and Sunday school associations in most parts of the county. Sufficient schools for teaching the rudiments of an English education have been established, and they are kept open during the year. There is an academy at Northumberland, to which the state gave the sum of $2000 in 1808, by the act incorporating it. There are 4 newspapers published weekly in the county; the "Gazetteer" and the "Canal Boat," (German) at Sunbury, "The State's Advocate" and "Miltonian" at Milton.

The state of agriculture is in a good and improving condition, and under the stimulus afforded by the North and West branches of the Pennsylvania canal, now in successful operation, must rapidly increase. The average price of lands of the first quality in the county, is $30 per acre; of second quality, $20; third quality, $10, and 4th quality, from 4 to 5 dollars per acre.

The chief towns are Northumberland, Milton, Pottsgrove and Watsonburg, on the N. side of the East branch of the river, and Sunbury, the county town, Snyderstown, Coal borough, Mahanoy, Georgetown or Dalmatia, on the S. of that stream.

There are several fine bridges in the county; one across the N. E. branch of the Susquehannah, between Northumberland borough and Sunbury, another at Danville, another from Northumberland across the West branch, and a fourth, over the same river, at Milton. (For particulars, see those titles respectively.)

Northumberland, with Union, Columbia, Luzerne, Susquehannah, Bradford, Lycoming, Potter and McKean, form the 9th congressional district, sending 3 members to Congress. Northumberland and Union make the 9th senatorial district, sending 1 member to the senate; alone, the county sends one member to the house of representatives; united with Columbia, Union and Lycoming, it constitutes the 8th judicial district, over which Seth Chapman, Esq. presides. The courts are holden at Sunbury, on the third Mondays in January, April, Aug. and November, annually. The county belongs to the middle district of the supreme court, which holds an annual session at Sunbury, on the Wednesday following the second week of the term of the Lancaster district.

The taxable property of the county by the assessment of 1829, amounted, real estate, to $2,150,833; personal estate, $29,016; rate of levy 30 cts. in the $100.

The county paid into the state treasury in the year 1831, for dividends on bridge stock,	$1,500 00
Tax on writs,	271 25
Tavern licenses,	623 00
Duties on dealers in for. mdz.	360 86
State maps,	9 50
Collateral inheritances,	78 46
Hawker's & pedlar's licenses,	15 20
	$2857 67

STATISTICAL TABLE OF NORTHUMBERLAND COUNTY.

Townships &c.	Greatest Lth.	Greatest Bth.	Area in Acres.	Pop. in 1820	Pop. in 1830	taxables.
B. of Sunbury,				861	1057	293
Augusta,	10	8	37,120	2075	2131	450
Shamokin,	16	10	56,960	1820	1909	362
Rush,	6½	5¼	14,720	1192	1078	245
Turbut,	11	9	46,720	2752	3388	636
B. of Milton,				1016	1281	272
Chillisquaque,	5¼	5¼	14,720	1035	1199	279
Point,	11½	4	17,040	1373	987	327
Little Mahanoy	16	5	33,280	447	563	105
U. Mahanoy,	15	6½	32,640	1639	1742	307
L. Mahanoy,	10	8	23,640	1214	1738	307
B. of Northumberland.					1095	
				15424	18168	3583

North Wales, small village of Gwynnedd t-ship, Montgomery co., containing a Quaker meeting house, a tavern, three dwellings and a post office. Distant 8 miles E. of Norristown.

Norwegian, t-ship, Schuylkill co., bounded N. E. by Schuylkill t-ship, S. E. by Manheim and Wayne, S. W. by Lower Mahantango, and N. W. by Barry t-ships. It has the form of a wedge; mean length, 10 miles; mean width, 5 miles; area, about 32,000 acres. This t-ship, though covered with mountains and hills and containing little arable land of good quality, is one of the most important not only of the county but of the state, and has been a principal scene of the wondrous improvements of which Pottsville is the centre. The Sharp mountain, the southern boundary of the anthracite coal formation of Pennsylvania forms its south line, and the north is marked by the Broad mountain. The main Schuylkill river enters it from the N. E. and receives Mill creek, and two branches of the Norwegian creek; the West Branch, and the West-West Branch of the Schuylkill enter it from the N. and W. all of which give ready access to the veins of coal, by the facilities which their vallies afford for the construction of railways and penetration of the hills. The main river has two dams with canals in the t-ship; the first forms the basin at Mt. Carbon and Pottsville, and the other the basin at Port Carbon. A rail road follows the main stream from the latter place to its source, another is on Mill creek, which extends about four miles, and a third on the two branches of the Norwegian; the latter is known as the Mt. Carbon rail road. On the West and West-West branches, a fourth rail road penetrates the Broad mountain. The towns are Pottsville, which is a borough, including Mt. Carbon, Port Carbon, St. Clairsville, Minersville, Carbondale, Coal Castle and Newcastle. Its population, including the town of Pottsville, was 6343 by the census of 1830, and the taxables, 1068.

Norwich, p-t. McKean co. (*See Sergeant t-ship.*)

Nottingham, East, t-ship of Chester co., bounded N. by Lower Oxford, E. by New London, S. by the state of Maryland, and W. by West Nottingham. Central distance S. W. of Philadelphia 40 miles; from West Chester 20 miles; length, 6½; breadth, 5 miles; area, 19,360 acres; surface, gentle declivity; soil, sandy loam. Pop. in 1830, 1788; taxables in 1828, 316. Elk creek forms the east boundary, and Little Elk creek crosses the t-ship centrally, and N. E. creek separates this from West Nottingham. The post town of Oxford lies on the northern boundary line.

Nottingham, West, t-ship, Chester co. bounded N. by Lower Oxford, N. E. and E. by East Nottingham, S. by the state of Maryland and W. by the Octarara creek, which separates it from the county of Lancaster. Central distance from Philadelphia S. W. about 45 miles; from West Chester about 27 miles. Length 5¾, breadth 3¾, area, 9,480 acres; surface, level; soil, slate and loam. Pop. in 1830, 562; taxables in 1828, 106. N. E. creek divides this from East Nottingham.

Nottingham, t-ship, Washington co., bounded N. by Peters t-ship and by Allegheny co., E. by the Monongahela river, S. by Fallowfield and Somerset t-ships, and W. by Strabane t-ship. Centrally distant E. from Washington borough, 13 miles; greatest length 9; breadth 5½; area, 19,200 acres ; surface, hilly ; soil, loam ; coal abundant. Pop. in 1830, 2118 ; taxables, 348. It is drained on the north boundary by Peter's creek, and on the S. by Mingo and Little Mingo creeks. The turnpike road from Somerset to Washington crosses the Monongahela river, and runs on the south line of the t-ship. On the S. side of this road in the fork of the river and Pigeon creek, is the post town of Williamsport.

Oakland mills, post office, Mifflin co., 148 ms. from W. C. and 41 from Harrisburg.

Octarara creek, a tributary of the Susquehannah river which has its sources in Sadsbury t-ship, in Lancaster and Chester counties respectively. It crosses Cecil co., Maryland, and falls into the Susquehannah, about 10 miles above Havre de Grace. A tributary of the west branch, called the north branch, drains the t-ship of Bart, Lancaster co.

Ogden, t-ship, McKean co., bounded N. by Ceres t-ship, E. by Sergeant and Cooper t-ships, S. by Jefferson co. and W. by Warren co. Centrally distant S. W. from Smethport, 18 ms. ; length, 18 ; breadth, ten miles ; area, 115,800 acres ; surface, high levels ; soil, gravelly, loam and slate. Pop. in 1830, 131. It is drained N. W. by Kenjua, and W. by branches of the Teonista, and S. E. by Furnace and Iron creeks. The country is an almost uninhabited wilderness, but is said to be well adapted to grazing.

Ohio, t-ship, Allegheny co., bounded N. by Butler co., E. by Pine and Ross t-ships, S. W. by the Ohio river, and N. W. by Beaver co. Centrally distant from Pittsburg N. W. 11 miles ; greatest length, 11½ ; breadth, 8 miles ; area 17,920 acres ; surface, hilly ; soil, loam and alluvion. Pop. in 1830, 1079 ; taxables, 221. The chief drains of the t-ship are the Big and Little Sewickly creeks, Jones' and Hawser's runs, all which flow W. to the river.

Ohio, t-ship, Beaver co., bounded N. by South Beaver, E. by Brighton, S. by the Ohio river and W. by the state of Ohio. Centrally distant S. W. of Beaver borough, 10 miles; greatest length, 7½ ; breadth, 5½ miles ; area, 19,840 acres ; surface, rolling ; soil, loam and rich alluvion. Pop. in 1830, 1122 ; takables, 201. The Little Beaver creek flows into the Ohio at the S. W. angle of the t-ship.

Ohioville, p-t. Ohio t-ship, on the road leading from Beaver borough to Dawson's ferry, over the Ohio river. Distant from Beaver, about 15 miles S. W. ; 262 miles N. W. from W. C. and 240 W. from Harrisburg ; contains 30 dwellings, 2 taverns and 2 stores.

Oil Creek, Swatara t-ship, Lebanon co., a tributary of the Great Swatara creek.

Oil Creek, t-ship, Venango county, bounded N. by Plumb and Cherry Tree t-ships, E. by Oil creek, S. by the Allegheny river, and W. by Sugar creek. Centrally distant from Franklin borough N. E. 6 miles ; greatest length, 10 ; breadth, 8 miles ; area, 40,960 acres ; surface, rolling ; soil, gravel and loam. Pop. scanty and the t-ship is annexed to Sugar Creek t-ship.

Oil Creek, t-ship, Crawford county, bounded N. by Bloomfield t-ship, E. by Warren co., S. by Venango co., and W. by Randolph t-ship. Centrally distant 20 miles from Meadville. Pop. in 1830, 484. It is drained by Oil creek and its branches. The post office of the t-ship is 297 miles N. W. from W. C. and 230 from Harrisburg.

Old Fort, post office, Centre co., 182 miles N. W. of W. C. and 75 from Harrisburg.

Oley, t-ship, Berks co., bounded N. Rockland, N. E. by Pike, E. by Earl, S. by Amity, S. W. by Exeter, W. by Alsace, N.W. by Ruscomb manor t-ships ; length, 5 ; breadth, 4¼ miles ; area, 13,600 acres ; surface, level ; soil principally limestone, highly cultivated. Value, average from 40 to 60 dollars per acre. Pop. in 1810, 1284 ; in 1820, 1410 ; in 1830, 1469 ; taxables in 1828, 290 ; watered by the sources of the Manatawny and Manookisy creeks ; contains many mills and one furnace and two forges ; two churches near together, one belonging to German Presbyterians and the other to the Lutherans. There is a post office at Oley furnace, 153 miles from Washington and 62 E. of Harrisburg.

Oley creek, Sugar Loaf t-ship, Luzerne co , a tributary of the Nescopeck creek, which flows between Yager's and Hell Kitchen mountain.

Oley valley, Sugar Loaf t-ship, Luzerne co., on Oley creek, between Yager's and Hell Kitchen mountains. The lands of this valley are of good second quality.

Opossum creek, a tributary of the Conewango creek, rises in Manallen t-ship, Adams co., and flows S. near the E. boundary line into its recipient, having a course of about 8 miles.

Oquago mountain, lies on the northern line of the state and partly in the county of Susquehannah, and in the Great Bend, formed by the Susquehannah, and extends ten miles along the boundary line.

Orangeville, Bloom t-ship, Columbia co., on Fishing creek, 5 miles N. of Bloomsburg, and 15 N. W. of Danville, 191 from Washington city, and 81 from Harrisburg ; contains from 35 to 40 dwellings, 2 stores and 2 taverns.

Orson's run, Lower Chanceford t-ship, York co. a tributary of Muddy creek.

Orwell, post-township, Bradford co. 187 miles N. of Harrisburg, by the post-road along the Susquehannah river, and centrally distant from Towanda N. E. 10 miles. Bounded N. by Windham and Warren t-ships, S. by Wysox and Wyalusing, E. by Pike and W. by Wysox t-ships. Greatest length $8\frac{1}{2}$, breadth $7\frac{3}{4}$ miles ; area, 34,560 acres ; surface, hilly ; soil, gravelly loam. Pop. in 1830, 1190 ; taxables, 197. The Wysox creek flows S. through the t-ship, and receives from it several tributaries. The post-office, called after the t-ship, is 252 miles N. W. from W. C. and 141 from Harrisburg.

Orwigsburg, post-town, borough, and st. of just. of Schuylkill county, stands on a rising ground near a small creek which flows into the Schuylkill river, 7 miles above the Schuylkill Water gap, 10 miles S. E. of. Pottsville, and 26 N. W. from Reading, 167 from W. C. and 59 N. E. from Harrisburg. The Reading and Sunbury turnpike passes through it. The vale in which it lies is surrounded by lofty and beautiful hills, which admit of cultivation to the very tops, and the neighboring country, though broken, is well cultivated and fruitful. The town consists of about 150 houses, many of which are 3 story and of brick, convenient and handsome. The court house and public offices are of brick ; the former, a large substantial building, surmounted by a cupola, and the academy is also a spacious building with a similar ornament. This institution was incorporated in 1813, and received from the state $2000. A spacious Lutheran church has just been erected, of stone. There are here 8 or 10 good stores, half as many taverns, and many mechanic shops. The population of the town was in 1820, 600 ; in 1830, 773 ; taxables in 1828, 139. A large bed of iron ore has lately been discovered near the borough, but its quality is not approved. The town was incorporated by act 12th March, 1813, under two burgesses and assistants.

Otter run, Upper Chanceford t-ship, York co. a mill stream which rises in the t-ship, and flows S. E. about 7 miles into the Susquehannah river.

Ottsville, post-town, Nockamixon t-ship, Bucks county, on the line between that t-ship and Tinicum, on the road to Durham ferry, about 37 miles N. from Philadelphia, and 11 from Doylestown, 174 N. from W. C. 119 N. E. from Harrisburg, contains 6 houses, 1 store and tavern.

Owl creek, West Penn t-ship, Schuylkill county, flows between the Mahoning and Mauch Chunk mountain, into the Little Schuylkill.

Oxford, t-ship, Philadelphia county, bounded N. E. by Lower Dublin t-ship, S. E. by the Delaware, S. and W. by Frankford or Tacony creek and N.

W. by Montgomery county. Greatest length 4, breadth 3 miles; area, 7680 acres; surface, gentle declivities; soil, sandy loam. Pop. including the borough of Frankford, in 1830, 3159; taxables, 751. The Little Tacony creek rises in the N. part of the t-ship, and flows by a very devious course into the Great Tacony, below the borough of Frankford. Upon the latter creek there are several mills in the t-ship, viz.: a saw mill, grist mill, and extensive calico printing works above the borough, and a grist mill and saw mill below it. At the borough, there are 2 fine stone bridges over the creek. The U. S. arsenal lies N. of the creek, at its confluence with the river. The Sissinocksink creek runs by a course of 3 miles into the Delaware, above Frankford creek. The Bristol turnpike runs N. W. through the t-ship. Upon it lies the borough of Frankford, 4 miles from Philadelphia. Upon the Tacony creek also, is the asylum for insane persons, established by the Society of Friends. There is a post-office at Frankford.

Oxford, a village on the road from Attleborough to Falsington, and on the line dividing the t-ships of Middletown and Falls, Bucks county.

Oxford, Upper, t-ship, Chester co. bounded N. by West Fallowfield, E. by Londonderry and Penn, S. by Lower Oxford, and W. by Lancaster co. Central distance from Philadelphia about 41 miles S. W., and from West Chester about 19 miles. Length $6\frac{1}{4}$ miles, breadth 5 miles; area, 17,200 acs.; surface, gentle declivity; soil, sandy loam. Pop. in 1830, 900; taxables, 222. It is drained by tributaries of the Octarara and Elk creeks, upon which there are some mills.

Oxford, Lower, t-ship, Chester co. bounded N. by Upper Oxford, E. by Penn, S. by East and West Nottingham, and W. by Lancaster county. Central distance from Philadelphia 41 miles S. W., from West Chester, 20 miles. Length $7\frac{1}{2}$, breadth 4 miles; area, 13,950 acres; surface, gentle declivity; soil, loam. Pop. in 1830, 1020; taxables, 224. The t-ship is watered by the confluents of the Octarara and Elk creeks. Oxford, post-town and village, lies on the line dividing this from E. Nottingham t-ship.

Oxford, post-town and village, Chester county, on the line dividing Lower Oxford t-ship from East Nottingham, about 41 miles S. W. from Philadelphia, and 21 miles from West Chester, 92 miles from W. C. and 66 from Harrisburg, contains 15 dwellings, 2 taverns, 2 stores, and a Presbyterian church.

Oxford, New, post-town of Berwick t-ship, Adams co. on the turnpike road from York to Gettysburg, 10 ms. N. E. of the latter, 87 N. from W. C. and 36 S. W. from Harrisburg, contains about 40 dwellings, 2 stores, 2 taverns, and 1 church.

Paint Creek, t-ship, Venango co. bounded N. by Farmington t-ship, E. by Toby's Creek t-ship, S. E. and S. by Clarion river or Toby's Creek, and W. by Beaver and Elk Creek t-ships. It is drained chiefly by Little Toby's creek. Centrally distant S. E. from Franklin borough, 25 miles; greatest length 7, breadth $5\frac{1}{2}$ miles. It contains about 19,200 acres; surface, rolling; soil, gravel and loam. The t-ship is not organized, but is annexed to Elk Creek t-ship.

Painter's cross roads, post-office, Birmingham t-ship, Delaware county, 116 miles from W. C. and 84 from Harrisburg.

Painter's creek, a tributary of Chester creek, Delaware county, rises in Thornbury t-ship, and flows S. E. through Concord and Aston t-ships, into Chester creek. It is a mill stream, and has several mills upon it, in a course of about 6 miles.

Palmyra, t-ship, Pike co. bounded N. W. by Wayne county, N. E. by Lackawaxen t-ship, E. by Delaware t-ship, S. by Middle Smithfield t-ship, and W. by Luzerne co. Lackawaxen creek, where the Belmont turnpike crosses it, above the falls, and Wilsonville, on the Milford and Owego turnpike, and Waullenpaupack creek above the falls, are the only towns in the t-ship. The surface is hilly and broken, covered with pine, hemlock and beech timber. The soil is gravelly loam. High Nob is a noted hill on the eastern boundary, near the junction of this t-ship with Lackawaxen and Delaware t-ships. The figure of the t-ship is very irregular, and is much contracted at its N. E. and S. W. extremities. Its greatest length is about 27 miles, and greatest breadth about 20 miles. Pop. in 1830, about 500; taxables in 1828, 90; taxable property in 1829, seated lands, $32,-632; unseated, $29,466; personal, including occupations, $6438.

Palmyra, t-ship, Wayne county, bounded N. by Dyberry t-ship, E. by Lehigh county and Waullenpaupack creek, which bounds it also on the S., and W. by Canaan and Salem t-ships. The Lackawaxen creek passes through it from W. to E. and the Milford and Owego turnpike road, crosses it diagonally to the N. W. Surface, hilly; soil, loam and gravel, well timbered. Pop. in 1830, 404; taxables in 1828, 76. It contains between 50 and 60 dwellings, 2 or 3 stores, 1 tavern, 1 grist mill, 8 saw mills, 18 looms, 4 schools.

Palmyra, post-town, Londonderry t-ship, Lebanon county, on the turnpike road from Lebanon to Harrisburg, about 10 miles from the former, and 14 from the latter, near the line dividing Lebanon from Dauphin county, 124 miles from W. C. contains 25 dwellings, 3 stores and 3 taverns.

Panther creek, Rush t-ship, Schuylkill county, rises in a valley between Mauch Chunk and Nesquihoning mts., and flows westerly to the Little Schuylkill river.

Panther creek, Manheim town-ship, Schuylkill county, a small tributary of the West branch of the Schuylkill river, into which it flows, about 6 miles W. of Orwigsburg.

Paoli, tavern and post-office, on the Philadelphia and Lancaster turnpike road, 16 miles from the former, 133 N. E. from W. C. and 177 S. E. from Harrisburg, in Tredypin t-ship, Chester county. This tavern bears the representation of the Corsican general and patriot, Paoli, whose name on account of its vicinity to this place, has been given to the battle field on which Gen. Wayne, with 1500 men, was defeated, on the night of the 20th Sept. by a very superior British force, under the command of Maj. Gen. Grey. It is said that the assailants were directed to give no quarter, and it is unquestionable that many of the Americans were massacred with ruthless barbarity, after resistance on their part had ceased, and that the cry for quarter was unheeded. The loss of the Americans was 150 men. Upon this field, 2 miles S. W. from the Paoli tavern, in Willistown t-ship, the members of the Chester and Delaware co. battalions of volunteers, some years since, erected a neat marble monument, in memory of the brave men who, on this occasion, fell in defence of their country, and these grateful soldiers have since purchased the tract of land on which the monument is built, and have appropriated it for a parade ground, forever to be used by all such volunteer corps as may think proper to assemble thereon.

Paradise, post-village, Strasburg t-ship, Lancaster county, on the Philadelphia and Lancaster turnpike road, about 10 miles E. of the city of Lancaster, and 52 miles W. of the city of Philadelphia, 118 from W. C. and 44 from Harrisburg, contains from 10 to 12 dwellings, 2 taverns, 1 store.

Paradise, t-ship, York co. bounded N. by Dover t-ship, N. E. and E. by West Manchester, S. E. by Codorus, S. by Heidelberg t-ships, W. by Adams co. and N. W. by Washington t-ship. Central distance from York borough about 10 miles. Length 8, breadth 8 miles; area, 28,800 acres; surface, level; soil, limestone and loam. Pop. in 1830, 1805; taxables, 406; taxable property in 1829, real estate, $505,019; personal, $13,142; occupations, &c. $32,365; total, $550,-

526; rate, 25 cts. in the $100. The Codorus creek, on which there is a forge, is on the S. E. line, and the Conewago creek on the N. W. Beaver creek on the W. Paradise run rises in the t-ship, and flows N. E. into the Little Conewago creek. The York and Gettysburg turnpike road, runs westerly through the t-ship.

Parker, t-ship, Butler co. bounded N. by Venango t-ship, E. by Armstrong t-ship, S. by Centre and Donegal t-ships, and W. by Slippery Rock t-ship. Centrally distant N. E. of Butler borough, 14 miles; greatest length 10, breadth 6 miles; area, 38,400 acres; surface, hilly; soil, loam, sand, clay and gravel. Pop. in 1830, 945; taxables, 165. It is drained on the W. by the N. and S. branches of Slippery Rock creek, and on the E. by Bear creek. On the latter are beds of iron ore, and a furnace is erected near its confluence with the Allegheny river. The post-town of Lawrenceburg lies on the N. E. but in Armstrong county.

Parkersville, post-office, 109 miles from W. C. and 81 from Harrisburg.

Partner's creek, Susquehannah co. rises in New Milford t-ship, and flows southward into Harford, where it unites with Vanwinkle's branch of the Tunkhannock creek. It is a mill stream, but not navigable.

Passyunk, t-ship, Philadelphia co. bounded N. by the river Schuylkill and by the city of Philadelphia, E. by Moyamensing t-ship, S. by the river Delaware, and W. by the river Schuylkill. Length 3¾ miles, breadth 3 miles; area. 5110 acres; surface level; soil, alluvion and loam. Pop. in 1830, 1441; taxables in 1828, 262. This district is covered with gardens and meadows, and is protected from the tides of the Delaware, by dykes along its bank. League island, in the Delaware river, pertains to the t-ship. The bank of the river Schuylkill in the t-ship, is, for parts of its course, high and steep, and affords a pleasant drive along it, and there are on it several public houses for the accommodation of those taking recreation. 2T

Path valley, Franklin co. partly in Metal, and partly in Fannet t-ships. Bounded W. by the Tuscarora mountain, and E. by Dividing mountain, which separates it from Amberson's valley. The Tuscarora creek flows northerly, and the Conecocheague S. through it, and the village of Concord lies at its head. In August, 1829, the remains of a mammoth were discovered in this valley, on the West Conecocheague creek, by Gen. Samuel Dunn. In widening his mill race, one of the workmen discovered a perfect tooth, about 70 feet below the ground. A part was broken, before its nature was known, but the remainder was taken up perfect. The length of the tooth (tusk) was about 7 feet, and its circumference about 14 inches at the root, about which a portion of the jaw bone was found. The tusk weighed 70 lbs. Other bones were discovered at the same time, but they crumbled to pieces on exposure to the air. The enamel on the tusk was firm, and resisted the pick, and the inner part was softened, but retained a beautiful whiteness.

Pattonsville, town of Ferguson t-ship, Centre co. near the head of the Slab Cabin branch of Spring creek, 15 miles S. of Bellefonte. There are some iron works here.

Patton, t-ship, Centre co. bounded W. and N. by Clearfield co. N. E. by Bogg's t-ship, S. E. by Ferguson t-ship, and S. W. by Half Moon and Rush t-ships. Centrally distant from Bellefonte S. W. 14 miles. Greatest length 25, breadth 8 miles; area, 71,680 acres; surface, mountainous; soil in the valleys, limestone. Pop. in 1830, 577. The main ridge of the Allegheny runs through the t-ship N. E., E. of which is Bald Eagle valley, drained by the Bald Eagle creek. The W. part of the t-ship is drained by the Little Mushanon creek. The turnpike road from Bellefonte to Phillipsburg, runs S. W. thro' the t-ship.

Patterson, a small village in Schuylkill county, on the Schuylkill valley rail road, about 7 miles from Port Carbon, at the confluence of Big cr.

with the Schuylkill. It was laid out by Messrs. Patterson, Swift and Porter, and contains about a dozen houses, 2 taverns, and 2 stores. Mine hill, abounding with excellent anthracite coal, approaches the town, and must furnish the means of its future prosperity.

Paxton creek, Dauphin county, rises in Lower Paxton t-ship, whence it receives several branches, and flows W. into the centre of Susquehannah t-ship, thence running S. it passes the borough of Harrisburg, into Swatara t-ship, and unites with the Susquehannah about 2 miles below the borough. It turns some mills before it enters the first alluvial flat.

Paxton, Lower, t-ship, Dauphin co. bounded N. by Middle Paxton, E. by Hanover, S. by Swatara, and W. by Susquehannah t-ships. Centrally distant N. E. from Harrisburg 6 miles; greatest length, 7 miles; breadth, 4 miles; area, 18,000 acres; surface, gentle declivities; soil, gravel. Pop. in 1330, 1371; taxables, 286. Beaver creek, a tributary of the Swatara, flows along the E. boundary, and Paxton creek, which has several branches in the t-ship, passes centrally through the W. boundary. The Blue mountain covers the north line, south of which lies the village of Linglestown.

Paxton, Upper, t-ship, Dauphin co., bounded on the north by Northumberland co., E. by Mifflin t-ship, S. by Halifax t-ship, and W. by the river Susquehannah. Centrally distant from Harrisburg N. 22 milles; greatest length, about 6 miles, and breadth about 6; area, 15,000 acres; surface, partly mountainous, partly gentle declivities; soil, red shale. Pop. in 1830, 1636; taxables, 294. The Mahantango creek flows through the northern part of the t-ship, and the Great and Little Wiconisco creek through the southern, the two latter uniting at the village of Millersburg on the margin of the Susquehannah river. Berry's mountain crosses the south and the Mahantango the north part of the t-ship. In the latter there is an opening known as Dibler's gap. There are two churches centrally situated, on the road leading N.E. from Millersburg.

Paxton, Middle, t-ship, Dauphin co., bounded N. by Halifax, E. by Rush and Hanover, S. by Lower Paxton and Susquehannah, and W. by the Susquehannah river. Centrally distant from Harrisburg N. E. 9 miles; greatest length 10; breadth 5 miles; area, 18,600 acres; surface, very mountainous; soil, gravelly. Pop. in 1830, 1262; taxables, 286. The Blue mountain bounds it on the south, and Petre mountain on the north, between which are the Second and Third mountains. The bluff of the Second mountain, on the Susquehannah river, is 900 feet high. Upon the north side of the Third mountain excellent anthracite coal has been discovered, and the mines are now being wrought. The valleys are drained by Fishing creek, Stoney creek, and Clark's creek. The only church in the t-ship is near Port Lyon on the river. The Lewistown turnpike road, follows the margin of the Susquehannah through the t-ship.

Peach Bottom, post t-ship, York co., bounded N. by Lower Chanceford, E. by the Susquehannah creek, S. by the state of Maryland, and W. by Fawn t-ship. Centrally distant from the borough of York S. E. 26 miles; greatest length, 9; breadth, 5 miles; area, 23,120 acres; surface, level; soil, gravel, slate and poor. Pop. in 1830, 898; taxables, 204. Taxable property in 1829, real estate $91,629; personal 8,860; occupations, &c. 10,880; total $111,369. Rate, 25 cts. in the $100. Muddy creek forms the north boundary and receives from the t-ship Neels Hole run, Fishing creek and other small streams. The post office is at Peach Bottom ferry, on the Susquehannah river, 80 miles N. W. from W. C. and 60 from Harrisburg.

Penn Township, Philadelphia county, bounded north by Germantown t-ship, E. by the Northern Liberties, S. by Spring Garden and W. by the river Schuylkill, which divides it from Blockly, and N. W. by Roxborough t-ship ; length, 4 ; breadth, 3 miles ; area, 7,680 acres ; surface, mostly level ; soil, clay and loam, well cultivated and productive. There are some beautiful knolls and eminences in the north part of the t-ship and along the Schuylkill river, crowned with pleasant country seats. It is drained on the north west by Falls run, which flows into the river Schuylkill at the falls, and gives motion to a small cotton manufactory there ; on the E. and S. E. flow Gunner's run and Cohocksink creek into the Delaware. The Ridge turnpike road runs N. W. through the t-ship, and the Pennsylvania rail road, following the old bed of the Union canal, traverses the Schuylkill at Peter's island, by a bridge now being erected. Parts of Sunville and Nicetown, and the hamlets of Islington and Falls are in the t-ship. There is a post office at Sunville and one at the Falls. Here is also the site of Girard college, for the foundation of which the late Stephen Girard bequeathed the sum of two million of dollars. The population of the t-ship in 1830 was 2507.

Penn, East, (See East Penn.)

Penn, West, t-ship, Schuylkill county, bounded N. by the Tuscarora and Mauch Chunk mountain, E. by Northampton co., S. E. by Lehigh co., and S. W. by Brunswick t-ship. Its mean length is about 10 ms. ; mean breadth 7 miles ; area, about 44,800 acres. The little Schuylkill river drains it on the N. W., Mahoning creek centrally, and Lizard creek and its branches on the south ; the two latter flow eastwardly to the Lehigh. Its surface is very hilly ; its soil gravelly and sterile. But the coal hills of Tuscarora and Mauch Chunk give it a high value. There is in the township a Lutheran church, situated in the northernmost forks of Lizard creek. Population in 1830, 1379 ; taxables in 1828, 262. There is a post office here called after the township, 179 miles from W. C. and 76 from Harrisburg.

Pennsville, a post town and village, Wrightstown t-ship, Bucks county, on the road to New Hope, 25 miles N. of Philadelphia, and 8 miles S. E. of Doylestown, 162 miles from W. C., 116 from Harrisburg ; contains 10 or 12 dwelling houses, store and tavern.

Penn, t-ship, Chester co., bounded N. by Londonderry, E. by London Grove, S. by New London, and W. by Upper and Lower Oxford. Central distance S. W. from Philadelphia 36 miles, from West Chester 16 miles; legth, $3\frac{3}{4}$; breadth, $2\frac{1}{2}$ miles ; area, 6100 acres ; surface, level ; soil, sandy, loam. Pop. in 1830, 605 ; taxables in 1828, 109. It is drained by small tributaries of Elk and White Clay creeks. Jennerville, post town and village, is centrally situated on cross roads.

Pennsbury, t-ship, Chester county, bounded N. and N. E. by E. Bradford, E. by Birmingham t-ship, and by Delaware co., S. by the state of Delaware, W. by Kennet and East Marlborough, and N. W. by West Bradford t-ships. Central distance from Philadelphia 23 miles S. W., from W. Chester 6 miles S. E. ; length, $7\frac{1}{2}$ miles ; breadth, $3\frac{1}{4}$ miles ; area, 9,880 acres; surface, gentle declivities ; soil, limestone. Pop. in 1830, 856 ; taxables, 163. The Brandywine r. courses the whole of the eastern boundary, across which is Chads ford ; Pocopsen creek, and other small tributaries flow from the t-ship into it.

Pennsborough, or Muncy borough, post town of Muncy Creek t-ship, on the left bank of the W. branch of the Susquehannah river, about 14 miles below Williamsport. The town was incorporated by act 15th March, 1826. (*See Muncy town.*)

Penn's valley, Centre co., in Potter and Hains t-ships, bounded N. W. by Brush mountain, and S. E. by the Path Valley mountain ; in length, about 20 miles ; in width, from 2 to 4 miles ; consists of a rich limestone soil, well cultivated and abundantly productive.

Penn Line, post office, Crawford co., 318 miles N. W. of W. C., and 257 from Harrisburg.

Pennsborough, East, p-t., Cumberland co., bounded N. by Perry co., E. by the Susquehannah river, S. by Monroe and Allen t-ships, and W. by N. Middleton t-ship. Centrally distant N. E. from Carlisle, 10 miles; greatest length, 12; breadth, 7 miles; area, 21,740 acres; surface, level; soil, limestone and slate. Pop. in 1830, 2,196; taxables, 412. The Conedogwinit creek flows in a very serpentine course eastwardly, through the t-ship into the Susquehannah, receiving several small streams by the way. At its mouth is the post town of Fairview. Wormleysburg lies on the Susquehannah, two miles below the mouth of the creek, and opposite to Harrisburg. Kingstown is on the turnpike road leading from Harrisburg to Carlisle, six miles E. of the latter. Mechanicsburg is in the south part of the t-ship. The Blue mountain bounds the t-ship on the north. There is also a post office on the turnpike road, at a place called Hoguestown.

Pennsborough, West, t-ship, Cumberland co., bounded N. by the Conedogwinit creek, which separates it from Frankford, E. by North Middleton, S. by Dickenson, and W. by Newton t-ship. Centrally distant W. from Carlisle, 8 miles; greatest length, 10½; breadth, 4 miles; area, 17,040 acres; surface, level; soil, limestone. Pop. in 1830, 1733; taxables, 375. The turnpike road from Carlisle to Chambersburg passes along the S. boundary. The post town of Springfield is on the west, and Smoketown near the east line.

Penn, t-ship, Union co., bounded N by Union t-ship, E. by the Susquehannah river, S. by Middle creek, and W. by Centre t-ship. Centrally distant S.E. from New Berlin, 6 ms.; greatest length, 7; breadth, 7 miles; area, 24,320 acres; surface, diversified. Pop. in 1830, 2034; taxables, 429. Penn's creek flows S. E. through the t-ship, to the river Susquehannah, at Selin's grove.

Penn's creek, rises in the S. E. part of Centre co., and flows E. through Centre and Union counties, by New Berlin, and falls into the Susquehannah river, at Selin's grove, after a comparative course of more than 50 miles, for the great part of which it is navigable for rafts and arks. New Berlin, 12 miles from its mouth, is the natural depot of the descending trade of this stream.

Penn, t-ship, Lycoming co., bounded north by Shrewsbury t-ship, E. by Luzerne co., S. by Franklin and Moreland t-ships, and W. by Muncy and Muncy Creek t-ships. Centrally distant N. E. from Williamsport, 28 ms.; greatest length, 24; breadth, 5 miles; area, 42,980 acres; surface, mountainous; soil, various. Pop. in 1830, 500; taxables, 88. Muncy creek follows its northern and eastern boundary. Value of taxable property, 1829, seated lands, &c.. $15,843; unseated lands, 2266; personal estate, 2665; rate of levy ¾ of one per cent. This t-ship abounds in excellent white pine timber.

Pennypack creek, rises in Horsham t-ship, near Horsham square, Montgomery co., and flows S. W. through Moreland and Abington t-ship, into and through Lower Dublin t-ship to the river Delaware, about 10 miles above Philadelphia. It has a course of abomt 25 ms., following its sinuosities. It is a steady and copious mill stream.

Penobscot knob, a lofty eminence of the Wyoming mtns., 1050 ft. high, situated in Hanover t-ship, Luzerne co.

Perrysville, village of Mifflin co., consists of about 15 dwellings, 1 tavern, and 2 or 3 stores.

Pecquea creek, a fine mill stream of Lancaster co., has its source in Salisbury t-ship, Lancaster co., and in W. Caln t-ship, Chester co., and flows S. W. about 30 ms. into the Susquehannah r., dividing Leacock and Lampeter t-ships from Strasburg, and Conestoga from Martick t-ship. It turns many mills.

Pecquea, p-o, Lancaster co., 126 ms. from W. C., and 62 from Harrisburg.

Perkiomen river, rises at the foot of the S. mtn. in Upper Milford t-ship, Lehigh co., and by a south course of about 30 ms. through Montgomery co., falls into the r. Schuylkill above Pawling's ford, 6 ms. above Norristown. It receives from Berks co. the W. branch, which joins it it in Upper Hanover t-ship, Montgomery, co. and from Bucks co., the N. E. branch which unites its waters in Perkiomen t-ship. Further S. the Skippack cr. adds its volume in Lower Providence t-ship. Other considerable streams beside those named are tributary to this r. The main and confluent streams afford excellent mill sites, which are improved by numerous mills. Upon the banks of this creek, 13 miles from Norristown, is a mine of copper.

Perkiomen, t-ship, Montgomery co., bounded N. by Upper Salford, N. E. by Lower Salford, S. E. by Worcester, S. by Lower and Upper Providence, S. W. by Limerick, and N. W. by Frederick t-ships. Greatest length 5 ms., breadth 4 miles; area, 12,800 acres. Perkiomen and Skippack creeks run through, and give name to the t-ship; the first, entering the N. E., and the second the S. E. angle. There is a p-o. called Shippack, in the t-ship. Central distance fromP hiladelphia, 25 ms.; from Norristown, 8 ms.; surface, hilly; soil, red shale, well cultivated and productive in wheat and grass. Pop. in 1830, 1278; taxables in 1828, 252.

Perkiomen bridge, p-o. (*See Providence, Upper t-ship, Montgomery co.*)

Perritsport, p-t., Versailles t-ship, Allegheny co., at the confluence of Turtle creek with the Monongahela r., 9 ms. S. E. from Pittsburg.

Perry, co., was taken from Cumberland co., and is bounded N. by Juniata co., E. by the Susquehannah r., S. by Cumberland co., and W. by Franklin co. Length 38, breadth 14 ms.; area, 539 sq. ms.; central lat. 40° 23′ N., long. 20′ W. from W. C.

The county lies wholly within the central transition formation of the state. Its south and north boundaries are strongly marked; the first, by the Blue or Kittatinny mtn., and the second, by the Tuscarora mtn. and Turkey ridge; the intermediate space is covered by minor chains, which, though having the same general N. E. and S. W. direction, are much broken and somewhat deflected. Traversing the co. northward from the Blue mtn., we have Bower's mtn., Pisgah hill, Quaker hills and Dick's hill, which seem parts of the same range. Cove mtn. forms a semi ellipsis, which is cut diagonally by the Susquehannah r., upon which the ends rest, being about 6 ms. distant from each other; next rise, Mahanoy, and Limestone ridges, Middle ridge divided from Buffalo mtn. by the Juniata river, and Raccoon ridge. These are in the eastern part of the county; in the western, Conecocheague hill is divided from the Tuscarora mtn. by Horse and Liberty valleys. The whole of this country, like every other portion of the county west of the Kittatinny, and east of the main ridge of the Allegheny, is based on transition lime stone, which approaches the surface in all the valleys, unless where covered by the diluvion of the broken mtns. Most of the valleys of this co. are remarkably fertile. Iron ore is found in various parts of the co. in large quantities, and of excellent quality; and a bed of bituminous coal 6 ft. thick, *is said* to have been discovered on the estate of Thomas Gallagher, Esq., ¾ of a mile above Montgomery's ferry, and 3 miles below Liverpool, on the Susquehannah r. If this be true, it is the bed of bituminous coal nearest to the eastern market, and is indeed invaluable.

The Juniata r. enters the county through Tussey's mtn., and flows through it by a S. easterly course of about 14 ms., to the Susquehannah r. at Clark's ferry, and Duncan's island. The Pa. canal is continued across the Susquehannah here by a pool and towing path, and divides on Duncan's island; one branch crosses by an aqueduct over the Juniata; thence it mounts that river by the right bank to the N. E. end of Juniata t-ship 15 ms., where crossing the r. by a rope ferry, it runs 3 or 4 ms. on the left bank. Another branch ascends the right bank of the main Susquehannah, through the N. E. end of the county, distant 18 ms. The Raccoon creek, between Tussey's mtn. and Raccoon ridge, drains Raccoon valley. Buffalo creek, heading in Liberty valley, flows through Buffalo valley; the Little Buffalo creek runs S. of the middle ridge, all emptying into the Juniata r. Sherman's creek rises by several branches on the confines of this and Franklin co., and flows by an easterly course through the county into the Susquehannah r., at the town of Petersburg, about 2 miles below the mouth of the Juniata r. Fishing cr., a short stream of about 8 miles in length, runs between the cove and Blue mtn. into the same recipient. The Harrisburg and Millerstown turnpike runs from the mouth of the Juniata r. on the left bank to the Juniata county line. The country roads are generally very good.

There is a warm medicinal spring on the bank of Shermans cr., in a romantic and healthy situation about 11 miles N. of Carlisle, 22 W. of Harrisburg, 8 from Sterret's, and four from Wagner's gap in the North or Blue mtn., and four from Landisburg. The waters used in bathing are beneficial in cutaneous disorders, and taken inwardly, operate gently as a purgative, and powerfully as a diuretic. It rises at the foot of Quaker hill, and emits about 90 gals. the minute. Its temperature is nearly that of creek or river water in the summer season. Mr. John Hipple has erected a commodious house here for the entertainment of visitors.

The county was originally settled by German, Irish, English, and Scotch emigrants, and is now holden by their descendants; the greater part, however, are of German origin. The pop. in 1820, was 11,342; and 1830, 14,257, of whom 7173 were white males, 7070 white females, 60 free black males, 60 free black females, 4 slaves. Of these also, 66 were aliens, 10 deaf and dumb, and 1 blind.

The Presbyterian, including the German Reformed, is the most numerous Religious sect. The Lutheran, Methodist, Moravian, Menonist and Roman Catholics, may be ranked in the preceding order, all of whom have an aggregate of 25 churches in the county. Sunday schools are established in every vicinity, whose population is sufficiently dense to admit of them. Country schools, in which may be obtained the simple rudiments of an English education, are located in every t-ship, and are very well attended during the winter season. There are two newspapers published weekly, The Perry Forester, at Bloomfield, and the Liverpool Mercury, at Liverpool. A poor house has also been established in the county, under the provisions of an act of assembly.

There are several small woollen manufactories scattered over the co., but the chief manufacture, is of iron. Juniata furnace, in Centre t-ship, belonging to Capt. Wm. Power, is successfully conducted, as is also Oak Grove furnace, belonging to Mr. John Hay, and Jacob F. Pleis, employed chiefly in casting stove plates. Duncannon forge, lately erected by Messrs. Stephen Duncan and John D. Mahan, at the mouth of Sherman's creek, in Wheatfield t-ship, is an extensive establishment, having every facility of obtaining metal and of transportation, which can be given by the Susquehannah r. and the state canal. The meritorious proprietors of this forge have also built a toll bridge across the creek, by virtue of an act of assembly. The forge of Messrs. Lindley and Speek is on the same stream, 3 miles from its mouth, and is also a large establishment.

The exports of the co. are wheat, unmanufactured and in flour, iron, clover seed, whiskey and live stock. These find a market at Philadelphia, by the Union canal, and the Delaware and Chesapeake canal, and at Baltimore by the river.

The chief towns are Bloomfield, the seat of justice; Germantown, Landisburg, Ickesburg, New Port, Petersburg, Liverpool, &c. &c.

Perry, Adams, Franklin and Cumberland counties, form the 11th congressional district, sending 2 members to congress. Cumberland and Perry make the 16th senatorial district, sending one member to the senate. Perry alone elects one member to the house of representatives; Perry, Cumberland and Adams, constitute the 9th Judicial district, over which John Reed, Esq , presides. The courts are holden in Perry, on the first Mondays in January, April, August and November. The county is annexed to the southern district of the supreme court, which hold an annual session at Chambersburg, on the Monday week next following the end of the second week of the term of the Western district.

This county paid into the state treasury in 2831, for tax on writs, . . .	198 85
Tavern licenses, . .	511 07
Duties on dealers in foreign merchandize, . .	286 38
Collateral inheritances,	23 16
Tin, and clock pedlars licenses, ...	28 50
	$1047 96

STATISTICAL TABLE OF PERRY COUNTY.

Townships &c.	Greatest Lth.	Greatest Bth.	Area in acres.	Pop. in 1820	Pop. in 1830
Buffalo,	9	9	23,680	875	1270
Greenwood,	6 1-4	5	17,040	1660	967
Juniata,	10 1-2	8 1-2	48,660	1748	2201
Liverpool,	6 1-2	5	17,040		1104
Rye,	13	10	58,880	1704	843
Saville,	8 1-2	7 1-2	38,400	1154	1319
Toboyne,	16 1-2	10 1-2	84,480	1965	2310
Tyrone,	9	8	42,880	2236	2758
Wheatfield, included in one of the preceding t-ships.					1485
				11,342	14,257

Perryopolis, p-town of Washington t-ship, Fayette co., on the Youghiogheny r., N. of Washington run, and 14 ms. N. of Uniontown, 209 ms. N. W. of W. C., and 186 S. W. from Harrisburg; contains from 70 to 80 dwellings, 1 church, 2 schools, 3 stores, 2 taverns, and 1 glass manufactory.

Perrysville, p-t., Ross t-ship, Allegheny co., near the N. line of the t-ship, about 8 ms. N. of Pittsburg, 230 from W. C., and 208 from Harrisburg; contains 9 or 10 houses, store and tavern.

Perry, p-o., Venango co., 301 ms. N. W. of W. C., and 234 from Harrisburg.

Perry, t-ship, Armstrong co., bounded N. by the Allegheny and Clarion rivers, E. by Toby t-ship, S. by Sugar Creek t-ship, and W. by Butler co. Centrally distant from the borough of Kittanning 19 ms.; greatest length 8, breadth 7 miles. Pop. in 1830, 853; taxables, 157. The Allegheny river flows into the co. and t-ship from the N. W. On Bear creek are considerable beds of iron ore, and a furnace is established on its bank within a mile of the river. Clarion river unites with the Allegheny, about 3 ms. below the N. W. point of the t-ship. The p-town of Lawrenceburg is on the W. side of the Allegheny r., 20 ms. N. W. of Kittanning, and about the same distance from Butler.

Perry, t-ship, Union co., bounded N. by Beaver and Centre t-ships, on the E. by Washington and Chapman t-ships, on the S. and W. by Mifflin co. Centrally distant from New Berlin S. 11 ms; greatest length 8 ms., breadth 7; area 32,000 acrs.; surface, mountainous; soil, loam and gravel. Pop. in 1830, 1050; taxables, 200. Mount Pleasant p-o. is in the N. E. part of the t-ship, which is drained by the E. & W. branches of the Mahantango creek.

Perry, t-ship, Jefferson co., bounded N. by Rose t-ship, E. by Young, S. by Indiana, and W. by Armstrong counties. Centrally distant S. from Brookville, 16 ms.; greatest length 11, breadth 9 miles; area, 49,280 acres; surface, rolling; soil, gravel & loam. Little Sandy Lick creek flows on the N. boundary, and the Mahoning creek runs through the S. E. angle, Pop. in 1830, about 500; taxables, 86. Punxatawny we believe is the nearest p-o.

Petersburg, town of East Hempfield t-ship, Lancaster county, about 5 ms. N. W. of the city of Lancaster.

Petersburg, post-town, Adams co. on the line dividing Huntingdon from Latimore t-ships, and on the turnpike road leading from Carlisle to the Maryland line, 13 miles S. of Carlisle, and about the same distance N. E. of Gettysburg, 77 N. of W. C. and 20 S. W. of Harrisburg, contains 2 stores, 3 taverns, 1 church and 1 academy. Two miles S. of this town is the York sulphur spring.

Petersburg, post-town, Adams co. Germany t-ship, on the turnpike road leading from Gettysburg to the Maryland line, 10 miles S. E. from the former.

Petersburg, post-town of Rye t-ship, Perry co. on the W. bank of the Susquehannah river, above the mouth of Sherman's creek, 8 miles S. E. of Bloomfield, and 15 miles N. W. of Harrisburg, contains from 35 to 40 dwellings, 3 stores, and 1 tavern. There are 1 Presbyterian and 1 Methodist church near the town.

Peter's mountain, a high mountain which rises on the E. margin of the Susquehannah river, about 12 miles N. W. of Harrisburg, and extends about 28 miles N. E. across the county of Dauphin, forming the N. boundary of Middle Paxton and Rush t-ships.

Peter's mountain, post-office, Dauphin county, 125 miles from W. C. and 15 N. of Harrisburg.

Peters, t-ship, Franklin co. bounded N. by Metal and St. Thomas' t-ships, E. by St. Thomas and Antrim t-ships, S. by Montgomery t-ship, and W. by Bedford co. Centrally distant S. W. from Chambersburg, 12 miles; greatest length 12, breadth 8 miles; area, 30,720 acres; surface, level; soil, limestone. Pop. in 1830, 2268; taxables, 410. It is drained by the West branch of the Conecocheague creek, which runs S. through the middle of the t-ship. The turnpike roads from Chambersburg to Bedford, and from Mercersburg to Bedford, run through it. On the former, is the post-town of Loudon, near which, on the creek, are some iron works, and near the S. boundary of the t-ship, a noted sulphur spring. A very interesting cave has lately been discovered in this t-ship, which, if properly examined and described, might rival in story the much celebrated one of Antipa. ros.

Petersburg, a post-town of Addison t-ship, Somerset co. on the Cumberland or national road, 22 miles S. W. of Somerset borough, contains 20 dwellings, 2 taverns, and 2 stores.

Peters, t-ship, Washington county, bounded N. by Allegheny county, S. E. and S. by Nottingham t-ship, S. W. by Strabane, and N. W. by Cecil. Centrally distant N. E. from Washington borough, 11 miles; greatest length 9, breadth 4 miles; area, 15,360 acres; surface, hilly; soil, loam. Pop. in 1830, 1196; taxables, 259. It is drained on the W. and N. W. by Chartier's creek, and on the S. E. by Peter's creek, which interlocks with a branch of Little Chartier's creek. The post-town of Findlaysville, is in this t-ship.

Petersburg, post-town of West t-ship, Huntingdon county, on the N. side of the Frankstown branch of the Juniata river, about 6 miles above Huntingdon, at the mouth of Shaver's creek, contains about 30 dwellings, 4 stores, 6 taverns, 2 country schools. Juniata forge, whose iron has contributed essentially to establish the high character of the Juniata iron, is in this town. The town was erected into a borough by act 7th April, 1830.

Pheasant, and Little Pheasant valleys, Miles t-ship, Centre co. are mountain vales, lying between the Nittany hills, in the western part of the t-ship,

Philadelphia county, was one of the 3 counties erected immediately after the establishment of the provincial government, in 1682. It was then limited, as now, on the N. E. by Bucks county, and on the S. E. by Chester, which included the present county of Delaware, but it extended indefinitely towards the N. W. Its extension in that quarter was first curtailed by the formation of Berks co. on the 11th March, 1752, and subsequently, of Montgomery, 10th Sept. 1784. It is now bounded on the N. E. by Montgomery and Bucks, on the S. E. by the river Delaware, on the S. W. by Delaware county, and on the N. W. by Montgomery. Its greatest length is 18, breadth 7 miles; area, 120 square miles, or 77,000 acres. Central lat. 39° 56′ 54″. Long. 1° 51′ E. from W. C.

The whole of the county is of primitive geological formation, and its constituent rock, gneiss, in great variety of combination, occasionally mingled with small portions of other rocks, as hornblende, serpentine, slate, &c.; for a minute description of which, and of the interesting minerals found in this vicinity, we refer the reader to the geological survey of Dr. Frost, and to the notices of Messrs. Lea, Say, Vanuxen, &c. An alluvial margin extends along the Delaware river, above and from the Poquessing creek, having an average width of a mile, to the Taconey or Frankford creek. The shore is generally gravelly, high and bold, except at the mouths of the crs. and is handsomely adorned by country seats and farm houses, scarce a gun shot distance from each other. The interval, between the mouth of Taconey creek and the village of Richmond, was originally a marsh, which has been reclaimed by banking, and now affords rich pasture and farm lands, but the buildings of the owners are remote from the tide. From Richmond, to the navy yard in Southwark, the shore is again bold, but from the navy yard to the *embouchure* of Darby creek, the S. boundary, and westward to the great Baltimore post-road, the country was a marsh, over which the waters of the Delaware, Schuylkill and Darby creek, commingled. It is now, however, well banked, well drained meadow, yielding abundant pasturage for thousands of cattle, destined to the Philadelphia market.

The soil of the county varies much in fertility. That which is not alluvial, may be generally characterized as a loam, depending generally but not always, upon the character of the rocky base, but more universally upon the constituents of the sub-soil. It is mixed with sand, gravel and clay, and in places these adjuncts respectively predominate. Aggregately, the soil cannot be deemed fertile, and its natural power of production is soon exhausted, but in most places it repays the money and labor expended in manure, which is obtained in abundance from the stables, streets and *pondrettes* of Philadelphia, and from the lime quarries of Montgomery and Chester counties.

The Delaware river washes the eastern border of the county for about 23 miles, receiving from the N. boundary Poquessing creek, and about 2 miles S. of it the Pennypack creek; three ms. S. of that, the small stream of Sissimocksink; then Frankford creek, Gunner's Run, between Balltown and Kensington; Cohocksink cr. through the Northern Liberties; Hollander's creek S. of the city and N. of Gloucester Point, and finally on the S. border Bow creek, an outlet of Darby creek. The Schuylkill river enters the county at the N. W. angle, and for the distance of $4\frac{1}{2}$ miles forms the boundary line between Philadelphia and Montgomery counties; thence by a meandering and southeasterly course of about 11 miles, bounded by steep, rocky and picturesque shores, crowned with country seats and noble farm houses, it flows by the great manufacturing village of Manyunk, and thence by the city of Philadelphia into the river Delaware, about 5 miles, in a direct line below the city. There are 2 artificial dams across this river which cause beautiful cascades, and add much to the beauty of its scenery, but this effect is merely incidental to the noble and useful purposes for which they were designed. They supply the short canals of the Schuylkill navigation company with water, and the first at Fairmount drives the simple but effective machinery of the city water works, whilst the second gives motion to the mills at Manyunk. Over the Schuylkill river within the county there are now 5 bridges; a floating and drawbridge below the city, the *permanent bridge* at High street, the Upper bridge, near Fairmount, a very neat and handsome structure resting on stone piers at the Falls, and the Flat Rock bridge, above Manyunk and below the Flat Rock dam. The *permanent bridge* was the first great structure of the kind, in America. It was built by a company incorporated in 1798, who commenced it in 1801, and rendered it passable in 1805. The nominal capital of the company was $150,000, but the actual cost of the work was $300,000. Its length is 550 feet, and that of the abutments and wing walls, 750 feet; breadth, 42 feet. It consists of three wooden arches, supported by stone piers with two abutments, and wing walls. The westernmost pier is sunk in a depth of water unexampled in hydraulic architecture, in any part of the world; the top of the rock on which it stands being 41 feet 9 inches below the common tides. The coffer dam for this pier, the plan of which was furnished by Wm. Weston, Esq. of Gainsborough, Eng. had 800,000 feet of timber, (board measure) employed *in* and *about* it. With the exception of the assistance rendered at the commencement of the work by Mr. Weston, who was then about to return to England, and of Mr. Palmer, the whole of this great labor was performed by the mechanics of Philadelphia, under the direction of a committee of the board of managers. And it is to be remarked, certainly not with a view of discrediting science, but as exemplifying the benefits of determined resolution and perseverance, that neither the workmen nor directors had any pretension to *science* in hydraulic architecture, nor had they *experience* in such labors, with the exception of Mr. Timothy Palmer, of Newbury-port, Mass. who designed and erected the superstructure. The masonry is on a plan which, at that time, was uncommon, if not new. The walls of the abutments and wings are perpendicular, without buttresses, and supported by interior offsets. These have been found competent to support the pressure of the filling, without *battening or contreforts.* The abutments are 18 feet thick. The wing walls 9 feet at the foundation, retiring by offsets, till at the parapets they are only 18 inches. The eastern abutment and wing walls are founded on rock, the western are built on piles. In the western pier there are upwards of 7500 tons of masonry. Many of the stones in both piers weigh from 3 to 12 tons. Massive chains are stretched in various positions across the piers, and are worked in with the masonry, the exterior of which is clamped and finished in the most substantial manner.

The wooden superstructure combines the principle of ringposts and braces with that of a stone arch. Half of each post, with the brace between them, form the vousseur of an arch, and lines through the middle of each post, would describe the radii or joints. The platform for travelling, rises only 8 feet from a horizontal line, and the top or cap pieces, are parallel to this. The middle section has the most pressure, owing to the weight of transportation being thrown nearer it, than towards the sides, to which the foot-way prevents its approach. These ways are 5 feet in width, elevated above the carriage ways, and are neatly protected by posts and chains. The span of the small arches is 150 feet, and of the middle arch 194 feet. Height from the surface of the river, 31 feet. It is believed that this bridge in all its parts, will not suffer by comparison, with one so composed, in any part of the world.

The bridge at Fairmount has one arch only, whose chord is 348 feet 6 inches, exceeding that of any other bridge, of ancient or modern times. The one over the Rhine erected in 1754, by Ulrich Grubenhamn of Teaffen, at Schaffhausen, in Switzerland, which was 390 feet in span, having been destroyed by the French, in 1799. This was built by Mr. Lewis Wernwagg, a German millright.

Two additional bridges over the Schuylkill, are now being erected; one by the state at Peter's island, for for the accommodation of the Columbia rail road, and the other at Manyunk by an incorporated company.

There is no creek, scarce any rivulet, crossing a public road in the county, over which there is not a stone bridge erected at the expense of the county, or of some turnpike company. Many of these have cost large sums of money, but they are too common to justify particular description. We may add, however, that authority was given several years ago, for building a bridge over the Delaware, but no effort has yet been made after the failure of the first, to commence this work of doubtful expediency.

All the great roads leading from the city, have been turnpiked, viz.: the road through Frankford and Holmesburg, to Bristol; the road through Milestown to the Willowgrove, through Sunville and Nicetown to Chestnut hill, and thence by the way of Perkiomen bridge to Reading; the road by the falls of Schuylkill to Norristown and Reading; and the road from Philadelphia to Lancaster; to these may be added the Sheet road from Frankford through Bustleton to Smithfield, the Manyunk road, and the road leading to Chads ford. All these are paved with broken stone, and make an aggregate distance of fifty miles within the county. A company has been incorporated for making a rail road from the city to Norristown, of which a single tract of 6 miles, to Germantown, has been completed. A company has also been incorporated, for making a similar rail road from the city of Philadelphia to Morrisville, opposite to the city of Trenton. The Columbia rail road now being made by the state, runs N. W. along the ditch of the old Union canal, crossing the Schuylkill at Peter's island, about 6 miles through the county. The country roads during the summer months are generally in good order; but in the winter season, by reason of the soft nature of the soil, are frequently almost impassable.

The county includes for county purposes, the city proper with all its suburbs, comprehending the incorporated districts of the Northern Liberties, Kensington, Spring Garden, Southwark and Moyamensing. For the space of 2 miles N. of the city and between the two rivers, the extension of the city is almost unbroken. The great turnpike roads for 8 miles further, are the streets of thickly settled villages, parts of which have names, whilst others are innominate. Adopting the ordinary parlance, we may mention in this part of the county, Frankford, Holmesburg, Bustleton, Smithfield, The Foxchase, Sunville, Nicetown, Millerstown, Germantown, Chestnut hill, Roxborough, Manyunk, &c. &c. as villages of the county. West of the Schuylkill are Mantua, West Philadelphia and Hamiltonville, Haddington, Powellton, &c. &c.

The whole county including the city, had by the census of 1830, 188,961 inhabitants, which were distributed thus,

	White Males.	White females.	Free color'd males.
City.	33,031	37,619	4025
Dist.	38,047	39,677	2191
Rest of the co.	12,458	12,513	576
	83,536	89,809	6792

	Free col'd females.	Male slaves.	Female slaves.
City.	5771	3	9
Dist.	2476	0	2
Rest of the co.	556	1	6
	8803	4	17

Grand Total, 188,961

In the city and county there were 4179 aliens, and including those in the asylum, there were deaf and dumb under 14 years of age, 44

Between 14 and 25 years, 66

Above 25 years, 14

Total, 124

In the city and county there were 54 blind persons.

These 188,961 inhabitants are divided into many religious sects, embracing almost every species of Christians. We have no means of determining the number of each religious persuasion, save by the number of churches belonging to each. The Roman Catholics have 6 including their cathedral church, and 1 now being erected at Manyunk. The Protestant Episcopalians have 9 churches in Philadelphia and the Liberties, 1 at Mantua, 1 at Germantown, 1 at Hamiltonville, 1 in Penn t-ship, 1 in Oxford, and 1 in Lower Dublin t-ship. The Presbyterians have 19 churches within the city and Liberties; 1 at Frankford and 1 at Germantown, 1 Scotch Presbyterian, 1 Covenanter's. The Baptists have 6 houses of worship in the city and Liberties; 3 in Lower Dublin, 1 in Blockley t-ship. The Methodists have 10 in the city and suburbs; 1 in Germantown, 1 at Holmesburg. The Friends or Quakers have 8 meeting houses in the city and Liberties; 1 at Germantown, 1 at Frankford, and 1 at Byberry. The Free Quakers have 1 place of worship in the city. The German Lutherans have 6 places of worship in the city, and 1 at Germantown. The German Reformed have 2 in the city. The Dutch Reformed 3 in the Liberties. The Universalists 2 in the city and Liberties. The Swedenborgians have 1 in Southwark. The Swedish Lutheran 1 in Southwark, the oldest place of worship in Philadelphia, and of very peculiar architecture. The Mount Zion Christians have 1 in Moyamensing. The Menonists have 1 church in the Northern Liberties, and 1 at Germantown. "*The Bible Christians*" have 1 also in the Liberties. The Mariner's church in the city, was established for the instruction of seamen. The Unitarians have 1 church, the Jews 2 synagogues. The African Episcopalians have 1, the Presbyterians 2, Baptists 2, Methodists 5 in the city and Liberties. Besides the places of worship above enumerated, there are 4 buildings erected by the Evangelical society, in different parts of the suburbs, and public worship is holden at the Walnut street prison, at the Arch street prison, at the Alms house, Orphan's asylum, Widow's asyulum, and the Magdalen asylum.

The number of institutions for the promotion of religion and morality in the city and county is very great; we give here, however, only those which are most prominent. The Philadelphia Bible society and auxiliaries; the Episcopal Missionary society; the Evangelical society for promoting Christianity among the poor in the suburbs of Philadelphia; the Baptist Missionary society; the Board of Missions of the general assembly of the Presbyterian church; the Philadelphia Missionary society, auxiliary to the United Foreign missionary society; the Young Men's Missionary society; the Female Missionary society; the Missionary society of the Methodist Episcopal church; the Common Prayer Book society; the Episcopal society for the advancement of Christianity in Pennsylvania; the Episcopal Female Tract society; the Religious Tract society; the Mosheim society; the Female society for educating the heathen; the Education society for preparing young men for the ministry; the Philadelphia Auxiliary Colonization society; the Pennsylvania Peace society; Pennsylvania Temperance society; Young Men's Temperance society; the Pennsylvania society for the promotion of public schools, the Phila. Auxiliary Soc. for ameliorating the condition of the Jews, &c. &c.

The institutions of an eleemosynary character, are not excelled, perhaps not equalled by those of any city of the same extent in the world. In this particular Philadelphia has admirably illustrated its name. At the head of these praise worthy associations stands the Pennsylvania hospital. It was founded in 1750, chiefly by the exertions of Benjamin Franklin and Dr. Thomas Bond. The house and its appurtenances occupy the entire square of ground between 8th and 9th, Spruce and Pine streets. It consists of a square central building, united by wings, in the form of the letter L, having 80 feet on the shorter, and 110 ft. on the longer legs. On a line of the eastern wing, and on the north side, is a lock hospital, three stories in height, neatly built and capable of containing fifty patients. The patients of the hospital are paupers, and pay patients; the former average about 100, of whom about one third may be insane. The number of maniacs will average about 110, whose treatment is remarkable for its mildness and humanity. In the central building is a very commodious lying-in ward for married women. The library contains more than 7000 volumes, many of which are rare and costly. The hospital affords an admirable practical school of medicine, and has thereby contributed greatly to the incsease and reputation of the Philadelphia medical college. The institution is governed by 12 managers, elected annually, who choose eight physicians and surgeons. In case of recent accidents, the patient is admitted without preliminary order or question with regard to remuneration. The funds of the institution arise from the interest of its capital stock, say $11,500

Profits on the exhibition of a painting by Benj. West, representing Christ healing the sick, (a donation by that celebrated artist,)	500
And from board of pay patients, about	22,000
From students' tickets, and medical fund, and contributions,	3000
	37,000

In 1830, there were admitted 1343 patients, of whom 782 were paupers, and 561 pay patients.

The area in front of this building, is adorned by a colossal statue of Wm. Penn, in bronze.

The city hospital, erected by the board of health, for patients in the yellow fever and other epidemics, is a large building in the north west part of the city.

There are three dispensaries, established for the purpose of rendering gratuitous medical assistance to the poor at their own houses. These are maintained by private contributions and donations from the humane. The Philadelphia or central dispensary, was established in 1786, and is now located in a neat and commodious building, erected for the purpose, in 1801. It extends relief to more than 4000 patients annually, at the small expense of about $2400. The northern dispensary in the Northern Liberties, was established in 1816. It relieves from 7 to 800 patients annually, at an expense little exceeding $400. The southern dispensary, also established in 1816, gives relief to about 1500 patients annually at the cost of about 600 dollars.

For the relief of the poor of the county, there are several institutions, independent of each other. The principal of these is the incorporation of "the guardians for the relief and employment of the poor of the city of Philadelphia, the district of Southwark, and the townships of the Northern Liberties and Penn," which possesses an alms house and house of employment. This corporation is under the government of 12 managers, elected by the several districts.

The average number of paupers sustained in the alms house during the year ending May 28, 1831, was	1,116
Cost, 87 2-10 cts. each per week	$50,610 04
And the sum expended for the relief of out door paupers, was about	$30,000
The whole expenditure for this year, was	$116,359 09

A tax for the maintenance of the poor is levied at the instance of the managers, by a board of directors of the poor, specially elected for that purpose, who are empowered to raise the necessary sum by a rate of levy not exceeding that of 50 cents upon the

$100, at assessed value of real and personal estate. Passyunk, Blockley, Bristol, Moreland and Byberry t-ships support their poor under the provisions of the general poor laws. Moyamensing, Germantown separately, and Lower Dublin and Oxford united, have their respective poor houses, and special systems. The amount assessed on the incorporated portion of the city and county for the year 1832, is $139, 871,70.

By a late law, (1828) a new alms house is now being erected for the city of Philadelphia, and upon a tract of land of near 200 acres, on the west side of Schuylkill river, the estimated cost of which, with the buildings immediately necessary, exceeds half a million of dollars. Appurtenant to the present alms house, but located in Southwark, is an asylum for poor children, at which the health and morals of the inmates are carefully regarded. At the alms house there is an infirmary, and clinical lectures are delivered to the medical class during the winter, by the professors of the medical school. Two graduates and four medical students reside in the house, and four surgeons and four physicians, and two accoucheurs are attached to the institution. Resident students pay an initiation fee of two hundred dollars, and are boarded and lodged in the house for one year. Medical students pay $10 for a ticket to attend the practice of the infirmary, and have the use of the library, containing near 3000 volumes. The poor maintained in the house who are able to work, are employed in various mechanical labors, and a portion of the expenses of the institution are defrayed by the profits of their work. The great cost of the farm and new buildings has been incurred in the hope that the enormous annual and growing burden of supporting the poor may be thereby diminished.

The Friends' alms-house, situated in the city, is a building forming a hollow square, and consists of a number of small rooms opening to a lot of ground appropriated to the cultivation of herbs. The inmates, without being altogether deprived of the feeling of independence, have a comfortable refuge for their declining years.

The orphan asylum was instituted by a society of ladies, in 1814, to provide for the support and education of children deprived of their parents. From 3d March, 1815, to 1st January. 1830, 232 orphans had been received, and 105 apprenticed. There are from 90 to 100 in the house, who are supported at an expense of about $4,000 per ann. The munificent legacies of the late Frederick Rohne, Esq. confirmed the prosperity and utility of this institution.

The St. Joseph's orphan asylum was instituted in 1807, for the education and support of children of Catholic parents. Twenty three orphans have received support and education from the institution since its establishment; about 30 are at present in the asylum under the care of sisters of charity, who receive no compensation for their services. The institution is supported by donations and annual subscriptions.

The asylum for indigent widows and single women, instituted in 1817, provides a house and respectable maintenance for females in reduced circumstances. It is supported in the same manner as the orphan asylum.

The Pennsylvania institution for the deaf and dumb, incorporated Feb. 8, 1821, is supported by annual contributions from the citizens and liberal appropriations by the state. The system of education adopted here, is that of Abbe de l'Epee and Sicard. The asylum, a fine building with a front and columns of granite, consists of a centre edifice, 50 feet front, by 63 in depth; with wings of two stories each, 25 feet in width, extending at right angles with the centre 92 feet; is located at the corner of Broad and Pine streets. Beside the culture bestowed on the intellectual and moral faculties of the pupils, they are taught some useful trade by which they may support themselves in life, and their labor in the institution produces for it a small pecuniary profit. The average number of pupils during the last few years, has been about 75, and the annual expenditure between ten and eleven thousand dollars.

Christ church hospital was founded for the relief of aged females of the Episcopal church, by Dr. John Kearsley, formerly an eminent physician of Philadelphia. Subsequent bequests and contributions have augmented the funds of this charity, which possesses a large and commodious building in Cherry street, between 3d and 4th streets.

The asylum for lunatics, located near Frankford, about 5 miles from the city, was founded in 1814, chiefly by funds furnished by members of the society of Friends, belonging to the yearly meeting held at Philadelphia. The buildings and farm have cost about $55,000. The former are admirably adapted for the purpose for which they were designed ; and the administration of the institution combines all that humanity and prudence can produce, to cure or solace the unfortunate objects of its care. A physician visits the house daily, and consulting physicians attend from Philadelphia when necessary. The house is under the direction of of twenty managers, a committee of whom visit it weekly.

The provident society was established in 1824, with the view of enabling persons in indigent circumstances to support themselves, by their own industry.

The female society, for the relief and employment of the poor, was instituted in the year 1793, and affords employment to industrious females. The female hospitable society, a similar institution, was founded in 1809.

The saving fund society was incorporated on the 25th February, 1819. It may receive deposits to an amount not exceeding $600,000 ; but not a larger sum than 500 dollars in one year from one person. The institution is managed by twenty five directors, and has been extensively useful.

The saving fuel society is similar in its objects to the last named association. It enables the poor, by the payment of a small sum of money weekly, in the summer and autumn, to obtain fuel at a moderate cost in the winter.

To these institutions we may add the soup societies, for supplying the poor with nourishing soup during the winter. The humane society, for resuscitating persons whose animation may be suspended by drowning, &c. The Magdalen society, for reclaiming debauched women. The Roman Catholic society, for the relief of destitute orphans, and the very many benevolent societies, established by the respective artisans, by the captains of vessels and mariners, by citizens and others for the support and aid of foreigners, as the St. George, St. Andrews, the German society and others, and even by the people of color.

The Philadelphia society, for alleviating the miseries of public prisons, organized in 1787, has the merit of having directed the attention of the authorities of the state to the improvement of the criminal code, and of having moved the public to found the house of refuge. The Pennsylvania society, for the abolition of slavery, the relief of free negroes unlawfully held in bondage, and for improving the condition of the African race, was formed in 1724. The chief end of its institution, the abolition of slavery in Pennsylvania, having been accomplished, the society is employed in improving the condition of the blacks, by supporting elementary schools, in which colored children are gratuitously instructed, and in vindicating the rights of free negroes when fraudulently claimed as slaves.

There are some 40 Masonic lodges in the city and county, under the direction of the Grand Lodge of Pennsylvania, which has a very large hall on Chesnut, above 7th street. A society of similar scope and aim, called odd fellows, consisting also of many lodges, have a large hall in South 5th street below Walnut street.

The "Franklin fund," may also be numbered among the charities of Philadelphia, Dr. Franklin having bequeathed 1000 pounds sterling to the corporation of the city, for the purpose of lending in small sums, "to such unmarried artificers under the age of 25 years, as have served an apprenticeship in the city, and faithfully fulfilled the duties required in their indentures," no one loan to be more than 60,nor less than 15 pounds. The interest is at 5 per cent. The donor calculated that at the end of one hundred years, his gift would increase to 131,000 pounds sterling, of which he recommended that £100,000 should be applied to public purposes, and the balance be left to accumulate for another century, when he supposed it would amount to four millions of pounds sterling, or seventeen millions of dollars, which is then to be divided between the inhabitants of Philad. and the government of the state. Mr. John Scott, in 1816, bequeathed the sum of $3000 to the corporation, to be applied after the same manner. It has not been found practicable to keep in constant employment the sums thus bequeathed, and the capital has not increased as rapidly as the donors anticipated.

The Franklin fund, on the 1st Jan. 1830, amounted to $22,062. Mr. Scott bequeathed to the city the further sum of $4000, to the intent that the interest should be expended in premiums, to be distributed among ingenious men and women who make useful inventions; but no such premium to exceed 20 dollars, and that therewith shall be given a copper medal with this inscription, "TO THE MOST DESERVING."

There is a fund for supplying the necessitous poor with fuel, the capital of which by sundry donations amounts to $1932 28. A fund for the relief of persons in the city hospital, during the existence of the yellow fever, was created by a legacy of £1000, given for the purpose by John Bleakly, Esq. by his will dated 19th April, 1802. The funds for supplying the poor with bread, arises from moneys bequeathed by Messrs. Carter and Pelly, respectively.

But one of the greatest benefactors of the city charities was Mr. John Keble, who bequeathed the residue of his estate to the Episcopal ministers of Philadelphia, to be distributed to pious and charitable purposes, according to their judgment.

But no institution in the city claims greater attention and praise, than the *house of refuge*, established for the reformation of juvenile offenders, whose lamentable fate was formerly incarceration among the greatest adepts of crime, and who were thus educated by society, that they might perpetually prey upon it. The institution was founded by the benevolence of the citizens, who subscribed the sum of $8104,41 towards it; but it has received from the commonwealth, and from the county of Philadelphia, the encouragement and protection necessary to make it extensively and permanently useful. Very large buildings of stone, judiciously adapted to the purposes of the institution, were completed in November, 1828, when the house was opened. As the law authorises the reception of all idle and deserted males, not only of the vicinity, but of any part of the state, under the age of twenty one, and of females under eighteen, the number of inmates has increased with a rapidity which will shortly imperiously require an extension of the means for their support. Two hundred and seventy nine inhabitants can be lodged, educated and employed, viz. 196 boys, and 83 girls. During the year 1830, 52 were apprenticed. The annual expense of maintenance for the institution, is about $1200. The following description of the employment of a single day will afford a correct view of the administration of this charity.

The bell rings at a quarter before 5 o'clock in the morning. At 5, the dormitories are opened, and the boys after washing and combing, assemble in the hall for morning worship ; after which they attend school until seven o'clock, when they breakfast. At half past seven they go to work, at which they continue until twelve, the hour of dinner. After dinner they receive a lesson or a lecture on some useful moral or scientific subject, until one o'clock. From one until five, when they go to supper, they are engaged at their respective employments. If their work be done within the allotted time, half an hour is allowed for recreation. School begins at half past five, at which they remain until a quarter before eight, when, after evening prayers, they retire to rest, and the dormitories are safely locked. With slight variations the occupations and duties of the females are similar.

The managers thus conclude their report of 1831 : "The government of the house is designed to be of a parental character, kind, yet firm ; cautious in the provision of all that can contribute to a substantial and lasting advantage, and yet denying all indulgencies which would merely foment unnecessary desires ; scrupulously just in the distribution of well earned rewards, the system exacts no less anxious and unfailing an infliction of merited punishments. With these principles to guide them, and the countenance and encouragement of a liberal community for their reward, the managers hope to persevere in the good work which they have begun, and with the blessing of divine providence it cannot fail to prosper."

Institutions connected with Literature, Science, and the Arts.—The regard which the Philadelphians have for these objects, has elevated the minds of her citizens generally, and has given to her mechanics a consideration, which men of that class seldom attain elsewhere. Much of this is justly ascribed to the city library. We are indebted for this noble institution to the creative genius of Franklin, at whose suggestion, in 1731, a number of his friends united in one their several collections of books ; and as the members were allowed to take the books they wished to study, to their own homes, the plan soon became popular, and several similar associations were formed, which were amalgamated with the first company. The instrument of association, signed by 38 members, is dated July 1, 1731, and the company was incorporated 25th March, 1742, under the name of the "*Library company of Philadelphia.*" In 1790, the present neat and ornamental edifice was erected on the east side of Fifth street, opposite the state house square. Over the front door is placed a marble statue of Franklin, executed in Italy, and presented by William Bingham, Esq. In 1803, an accession of valuable works, amounting to 2500 volumes, was obtained under the bequest of the Rev. Mr. Preston, rector of Chevening in Kent, England ; and a further valuable addition in 1828, by the bequest of Wm. Mc Kensie, Esq. The number of books now exceeds 24,000, exclusive of the Loganian collection which is in a separate room of the building ; the number of members is above eight hundred. The price of a share is forty dollars and an annual payment, formerly of $2, but now of $4. All persons are permitted to read books at the library without charge.

The Loganian library is a rich collection of ancient and classical works, chiefly in the Greek and Latin languages, made by the celebrated James Logan, and some of his descendants, and was bequeathed to the public, together with the income from certain real estates, for its gradual increase. The amount of the fund is now about 10,000 dollars. The number of vols. 11,000.

The *Atheneum*, established in 1814, and incorporated the ensuing year, contains a valuable collection of books of reference in most departments of literature and science, with the periodical journals of Europe and America, maps, plates, &c. The institution occupies two rooms of the philosophical hall, opposite the city library, one of which contains the library, amounting to near 6000 volumes; and the second is supplied with more than 70 newspapers of the United States, four English, and two French, besides papers occasionally from other parts of the world. The rooms are open daily, (Sundays excepted,) from 8 o'clock A. M. to 10 P. M. The contributors are stockholders, who pay a principal of twenty five dollars, and four dollars annually, or subscribers who pay eight dollars annually. The number of stockholders is about four hundred; subscribers, ninety. The sum of $10,000 was lately bequeathed to the institution by Wm. Lehman, Esq. for the purpose of erecting a suitable building; and Samuel Breek, Esq. has made it a donation of 863 books. Strangers are admitted to the use of the rooms on the introduction of a stockholder or subscriber. More than a thousand thus visit it annually.

The Friends' library, kept in a room of their meeting house at the corner of Arch and 4th street, contains about three thousand volumes, principally on theological subjects. Books may be obtained from it by any respectable applicant every Saturday afternoon.

The "apprentices' library," incorporated 2d of April, 1821, is designed, by the loan of well chosen books to the apprentices of the city and county, to cultivate their minds and improve their hearts. Its success is most encouraging; and the desire of information displayed by a large number of intelligent boys who regularly apply for books, gives the most favorable augury of the future character of the mechanics and tradesmen of Philadelphia. The number of books is about 6000,—and the number of readers about 900. The members pay an annual contribution of two dollars.

The mercantile library, instituted in 1822, consists of about 4000 volumes, principally on commerce, commercial law, the arts, sciences, &c. The members pay on admission, ten dollars, and two dollars annually afterwards.

The Southwark library and reading room, was commenced in 1822, and contains about 6000 volumes. The library and reading room company of the Northern Liberties, was established in 1830. In each of these institutions about 20 newspapers, European and American, besides magazines and reviews, are regularly received.

The Law library, established in 1802 by the members of the bar, is kept in the county court house for the use of the members whilst in the courts; contains about 1400 volumes, the greater portion of which, is composed of the ancient and modern reports of adjudged cases.

The American Philosophical society gives honor at once to the city of Philadelphia, and the U. S. It was founded in 1743, principally by the exertions of Dr. Franklin; in 1766, another institution of a like nature was formed, called "the American society for promoting useful knowledge." The two were united in 1769, under the title of "the American Philosophical society, held at Philadelphia, for promoting useful knowledge." The society has been from time to time aided by the legislature; and it erected in 1785 a large and commodious building, on a part of the state house square, granted for that purpose by the state. The society has a most valuable library of about 6000 vols.; an interesting collection of objects of natural history, principally of minerals and fossil remains. It has published 10 vols. of philosophical transactions, and by a committee specially raised for the subject, three volumes relating to the history of the aborigines of our country.

In 1786, John Hyacinth de Magellan, of London, presented the society with funds for the establishment of an annual premium, to be awarded by the society, to the author of the best discovery or most useful invention relating to navigation, astronomy, or natural philosophy, mere natural history only excepted. The premium consists of an oval plate of standard gold, with suitable devices engraved upon it. The funds having produced an annual surplus, the society offer extra premiums of a gold medal, value not less than $20, nor more than $45, or that sum in money, to the author of the most useful invention, improvement, discovery or communication in any department of science, or of the useful arts.

The academy of natural sciences, founded in 1812, and incorporated in 1817, has contributed much to the stock of general science, and acquired a high and well merited reputation. It has a library of about 5000 vols., comprising the largest collection of works on natural history in the U. S., a large herbarium, and museum of shells, fossils, mineral and geological specimens, birds, quardrupeds, &c. Much of the riches of the cabinet has flowed from the munificence of Wm. McClure, Esq., its president.

The society publishes an account of its labors, under the title of the "Journal of the Academy of Natural Sciences." It has purchased, and occupies the building formerly used by the Swedenborgians for a church. Strangers are admitted at all their meetings save that for business.

The Phila. museum was commenced in 1784, by Charles Wilson Peal, and has been the parent of several similar institutions in the union. Its proprietors are now incorporated, and it is established in rooms formed expressly for its use in the arcade. It contains a large and admirable collection of quadrupeds, birds, reptiles, fish, insects, shells, minerals, fossils, among which is the wonderful mammoth; many miscellaneous articles of works of art, implements, dresses, arms, antiquities &c., from every part of the globe; original portraits, 200 in number, of the officers and diplomatic characters of the revolution, painted by C. W. Peale; many portraits of the professors of the national institute of France, painted by Rembrandt Peale, and many other valuable paintings. Popular lectures are sometimes given here upon subjects of natural science.

The Pennsylvania academy of fine arts was founded in the year 1805, by the voluntary association and contributions of a number of the citizens of Philadelphia, and was chartered by the legislature in March, 1806. This institution at once supplies a refined and rational recreation for the public, improves the general taste, and provides a school for the instruction of American genius in the fine arts of statuary, painting, architecture and engraving. It contains a large and very meritorious collection of models in all these arts; many of them by the most famed European artists.

The college of physicians was instituted in 1787, for the advancement of medical science. It is composed of fellows resident within the city and district, and associates who do not dwell within the prescribed limits.

The Philadelphia medical society, incorporated in 1792, also for the promotion of medical science, consists of honorary and junior members; the former, being such as have obtained a degree in medicine, or have become eminent in the practice of physic; the latter, of students of medicine, or practising physicians, who have not received the degree of doctor in medicine. The society has a fine library.

The Philadelphia college of pharmacy, incorporated in 1822, is composed of druggists and apothecaries; a school of pharmacy has been established with three professorships under the direction of the college.

The Kappa Lambda society; a branch of this association was established here a few years since, by the late Dr. Brown of Alabama. Its main objects, are the promotion of social intercourse and harmony among the members of the profession—the establishment of a code of medical ethics, and generally to advance the character and standing of the medical profession. About seventy of the physicians of the city belong to the society. The North American Medical and Surgical Journal is published under the auspices of this society and its several branches.

The "Franklin Institute," an association worthy of all praise, which is doing much to enlighten with the rays of science, the artists and manufacturers of the country, was incorporated on the 30th March, 1804. Its members consist of manufacturers, artists and mechanics, and persons friendly to the mechanic arts. The object of the institute is pretty fully stated in their charter, to be "the promotion and encouragement of manufactures, and the mechanic and useful arts, by the establishment of popular lectures on the sciences connected with them; by the formation of a cabinet of models and minerals, and a library; by offering premiums on all subjects deemed worthy of encouragement; by examining all new inventions submitted to them, and by such other means as they may judge expedient." Each member pays $3 annually; but the payment of $25 constitutes a member for life, with exemption from further contribution. Two thirds of the managers must be manufacturers or mechanics. Annual exhibitions of domestic manufactures are made by the institute, which continue for several days, and have never failed to attract crowds of visitors. A monthly journal has been established by the society, and lectures are regularly delivered on architecture, practical mechanics and other branches.

The Philadelphia society for promoting agriculture, was instituted in 1785. It holds stated meetings at its rooms in the philosophical hall, where it has a cabinet and library. It for sometime published many communications in the newspapers; but of late years, its labors have been communicated in octavo vols., five of which have already been published. It has been highly serviceable in the promotion of agriculture and improving the breed of cattle.

The musical fund society was incorporated in 1823, with the design of relieving distressed musicians and their families, and the cultivation of the art of music. Its hall will accommodate 1000 persons. The society includes 50 professors of the first eminence, and 300 amateur members.

Literary Journals. Four are published quarterly, viz. American Quarterly Review, American Journal of the Medical Sciences, the N. American Medical and Surgical Journal, the Biblical Repository and Theological Review.—Seven monthly, viz. the Protestant Episcopalian and the Ch. Register, the Museum of Foreign Literature and Science, the Lady's Book, the Casket, American Sunday School Magazine, the Christian Advocate & the Reformer. There are also several weekly journals of less note.

There are at present printed in Philadelphia, 7 daily newspapers, four morning and three evening. The American Daily Advertiser, the United States Gazette, the American Sentinel, and the Pa. Inquirer, (morning). The Phil. Gazette, the National Gazette, the Daily Chronicle, (evening). At each of the offices of these papers, except those of the American Daily Advertiser, and the Daily Chronicle, there are published weekly, semiweekly, or tri-weekly papers, containing the principal articles in the daily newspapers, without the advertisements. The Philadelphia price current is published twice a week; the Saturday Evening Post, Saturday Evening Bulletin, Mechanic's Free Press, Columbian Star, Philadelphian, Pennsylvania Register, the Friend, Philadelphia Recorder, Album, Phila. Souvenir, weekly. The Ariel is issued semi-monthly, and the Advocate of Peace and Independent Balance, occasionally.

Institutions for education. The most important of these is the University of Pennsylvania, which occupied, until lately, the building erected by the state, with the view of presenting it to General Washington. He having declined to accept it, it was purchased by the trustees of the university, in

1798; and was torn down in 1829, and two more appropriate edifices have been erected for scholastic purposes upon the site. This institution originated in an academy and charity school, in 1750, which was chartered and endowed with lands and money from the proprietaries in 1753. In 1779 the legislature gave it a new charter erecting it into a university, placing it under the direction of a new board of trustees, and made liberal provision for its support. The first provost of the college was at the same time removed, and the Rev. Dr. John Ewing was appointed. These proceedings were dissatisfactory to the friends of the old college, and upon their frequent petitions, the legislature in 1789 re-established the college. But the inconvenience of two similar institutions in the same city being soon felt, they were finally united in 1791, under the title of "the university of Pennsylvania."

The university has a department of arts in which there are at present 4 professorships; one of moral philosophy, one of mathematics, one of natural philosophy and chemistry, and one of the languages. There are 3 classes, the senior, the junior, and the sophomore. A department of medicine, whose school, the most ancient in the U. S., is not surpassed in usefulness and reputation by any in the world. The first lectures were delivered here in 1765, by Dr. John Morgan, on the theory and practice of medicine. In the following year, Dr. Wm. Shippen delivered lectures on anatomy, surgery and midwifery. The students are now annually between 4 and 500. A foundation of six gratuitous studentships has been established. The anatomical museum, founded by the late Dr. Casper Wistar, is extensive and valuable. There is a department of law, and also of natural science, but their chairs are unfilled.

The Jefferson medical school was instituted in Philadelphia in 1825, under the charter of Jefferson college, at Canonsburg, Washington co., and was empowered by the legislature to confer the usual degrees in medicine. It possesses a commodious house, built expressly for its use, has been tolerably supported, and has a high and growing reputation. A liberal benefice foundation in the college, bestows annually a gratuitous course of lectures on 10 students. Its anatomical cabinet is also valuable. From 100 to 150 students attend the lectures here annually.

The law academy was established in 1821, under the auspices of an incorporated society, composed of judges and members of the bar, denominated "the society for the promotion of legal knowledge, and forensic eloquence." The academy has about 50 students, besides honorary members. Forensic exercises are held once a week, under the direction of the provost and vice provosts. It is contemplated at some future day, to erect chairs of the various branches of jurisprudence, and to annex the institution to the university of Pennsylvania.

The academy of the Protestant Episcopal church in the city of Philadelphia, was incorporated and endowed 29th March, 1787. Its funds have been increased by a liberal bequest of Andrew Doz, and of the late Mr. John Keble. The funds of this institution are exclusively devoted to procure for youth gratuitous education.

The Friends' school was the first institution incorporated for promoting literature in Pennsylvania. The charter was granted by Wm. Penn, in 1697, to "the overseers of the schools." This body consists of 15 persons, who have under their care 14 schools, in different parts of Philadelphia. In the school house on Fourth, below Chestnut st., the Latin, Greek, and Hebrew languages, Mathematics and Philosophy are taught. Lectures on Botany, Mineralogy, and various branches of science are delivered here. It has an observatory, with some valuable astronomical and philosophical instruments, and a library, containing some rare works.

Public schools for the instruction of the poor, have been established on the most beneficial footing. Various attempts had been made by the legislature to give effect to the 7th article of the constitution, which directs "that the legislature shall, as soon as conveniently may be, provide by law, for the establishment of schools throughout the state, in such manner that the poor may be taught gratis," but unfortunately, they proved inefficient, until the enactment of the law of 3d March, 1818, and its supplements. These erect the city and county of Philadelphia into a district, denominated "the first school district of the state of Pennsylvania." The district is divided into sections, of which the city of Philadelphia is the first; the Northern Liberties and Kensington, the second; Southwark and Moyamensing, the third; and Penn t-ship the fourth. Over these a peculiar system is established. A number of directors is annually appointed for each section respectively, by the corporation of the district in which it is located, who receive no compensation, but are exempted from serving as jurors, abitrators, overseers of the poor, or managers of the alms house, and, except in time of war, from militia duty. From these directors, "the controllers of the public schools for the city and county of Philadelphia," are elected; and that board at present consists of 9 members. It is their duty to determine the number of schools in each section; to prescribe suitable forms of instruction; to superintend such schools, to fix the expense of conducting them, and to draw on the county treasurer therefor. Their proceedings are annually published, and their accounts examined and settled by the auditors of the county. The several boards of directors, are required to establish the schools determined by the controllers, to appoint teachers, to provide all things necessary for conducting the schools, and to have the particular care and management of the same, in their respective stations. The Lancasterian system of education, or that of mutual instruction in its most improved form, is prescribed by law for these schools; and a model school on this system has been established. Indigent children, boys between the ages of 6 and 14, and girls between the ages of 5 and 13, approved by the controllers or directors, as the case may be, are admitted into the schools, where are taught reading, writing, arithmetic, and the geography of the U. States; and the girls are instructed in sewing and knitting. Ten schools have been established in the city and district, at which 4657 pupils were educated during the year ending Feb. 1831, at an expense, including fuel and books, of $18,150 28, and during the same period, $5374 43 were expended for school furniture and real estate, for further accommodation of the schools.

The residue of the county, comprising the country districts, is divided into 4 sections, and classed as follows; the t-ships of Oxford, Lower Dublin, Byberry and Moreland, make the 5th section; the t-ships of Germantown, Bristol and Roxborough, the 6th; the t-ships of Blockley and Kingsessing, the 7th; and Passyunk, the 8th. In these sections, during the last mentioned period, 714 pupils were at school, at an expense of $8576 04. The average expense of educating each pupil in the city and county is stated at $4 per annum.

The system allotted in the latter sections differs from that in the former. Directors are chosen for the several sections, by the court of quarter sessions; under whose direction the children are sent to suitable private schools. The funds are provided by the controllers, as in the former sections; and provision is made by the law for the erection of a section or sections, for the purpose of establishing one or more schools upon the same terms and under the same regulations prescribed for the first four sections. And the power to erect a new section is given to the court of quarter sessions, to be exercised upon the petition of twenty respectable taxable citizens, resident within the bounds of the proposed section.

To these schools, the Sunday schools rank next in importance. It has been ascertained that there are within the city and Liberties, beside those in other parts of the county, 125 Sunday schools, at which 14,581 scholars are taught by 1429 teachers. "The Sunday and adult school union," was established in this city in 1816. This institution is not confined to any sect or district, but extends to the remotest parts of our country. Sixteen years only have elapsed since the formation of this institution, and the number of pupils belonging to the several schools connected with it, is estimated at 400,000, and the number of teachers at 60,000, and that of the schools at 6600, extending through every state and territory. This institution prints and circulates works which the directors deem adapted to promote piety and morality, many of which are written expressly for the society. Its affairs and funds are under the direction of a board, consisting of a president, vice presidents, a corresponding secretary, recording secretary, treasurer, and 36 managers, 24 of whom must reside in the city of Philadelphia or its vicinity. The receipts of the society for the year ending March, 1832, were $118,181 19. The expenditures, $117,703 31.

The Philadelphia society for the support of charity schools, originated in the voluntary meetings of a few young men, in the year 1799, for the instruction of indigent boys in the evenings. When the labors of these philanthropists became known, many others joined with them; and in 1801, they became strong enough to resolve to open a day school, at an expense of 600 or 800 dollars per annum. Arrangements were making to open in the autumn, when a singular circumstance placed the institution upon a solid and permanent foundation. Mr. Christopher Ludwig, an old and respectable German citizen, died in the month of June of that year, leaving the residue of his estate, estimated at $12,000, to the first association of persons who should be incorporated for the purpose of teaching gratis, the poor of all denominations, in the city & districts of Southwark and the Northern Liberties, without respect to the country or religion of their parents or friends. When the will was published, several associations were attempted, but all gave way except this, and that of the trustees of the university, who forming themselves into a society, applied for a charter. A like application was made by the Philadelphia society, which then formed a more perfect constitution, and assumed their present name. The governor (McKean) signed both charters at the same time; and as the act of incorporation was not completed until the charter was enrolled, it became all important to the applicants to reach Lancaster first, where the office for enrollment was then held. The trustees hired an express rider, but Mr. Joseph Bennett Eves, the president of the society, became himself its messenger. Both left Philadelphia at 12 o'clock on the 7th September, 1801. Mr. E. reached Lancaster in 7 hours, (66 ms.); the express gave in, after proceeding part of the way. The charter of the society is dated 8th Sept., 1801, and the society has received the legacy. Their school is in Walnut st., near 6th. Since the commencement of the establishment, near 9000 scholars have been admitted to its benefits; and it educates annually, an average number of 400, half of which are girls. Its capital stock and real estate amount to about $36,000, producing besides the use of the schools, a nett sum of 1900 per annum.

The Adelphi school, supported exclusively by the society of Friends, is situated in Cherry street, and is designed solely for the education of colored boys.

The free schools for the education of negro children, were founded by Dr.

Bray and his associates of England. There are a boys and girls school.

"The Pennsylvania society for the promotion of public schools," was established in 1828, and has already spread much information throughout the state; having furnished a number of teachers for schools on the plan of mutual instruction.

There are besides these we have mentioned, very many other, but more limited associations, for education; among which we may name the Aimwell school society, established in 1796, for the free instruction of female children, by members of the society of Friends. The Philadelphia Union society, instituted in 1804, for similar purposes, by ladies, members of the Presbyterian church. The free schools of the United Episcopal churches, and of the German Lutherans and Calvinists. There is also a free school annexed to the university of Pennsylvania.

Many lectures are given on the sciences and the arts, by eminent professors; and the private academies and seminaries in which the Classics and Mathematics are taught, are very numerous, not only in the city, but in the villages of the county. In Frankford, Lower Dublin, Bustleton, and Germantown, there are academies incorporated by the state.

The following table shows the number of banks in the city and county, and their respective capitals.

NAMES.	LOCATION.	CAPITAL.
Bank of U. States,	City of Philadel.	$35,000,000
Bank N. America,	do.	1,000,000
Bank of Penn.	do.	2,500,000
Bank of Phila.	do.	2,000,000
Farm. & Mech. B.	do.	1,250,000
Commer. Bank,	do.	1,000,000
Mechanics Bank,a	do.	1,000,000
Schuylkill Bank,a	do.	1,000,000
Girard Bank,	do.	4,000,000
Girard Bank,b	do.	1,500,000
Bank of N. Liber.	North. Liberties.	200,000
Bk of Penn tsp.a	Penn Township.	250,000
Bank of S'hwark,	Southwark.	250,000
Kensington Bk,a	Kensington.	250,000
West. Bk Phila b	City.	
Man. & Mec. Bkb	North. Liberties.	
MoyamensingB. b	Moyamensing tsp.	
Germantown,	Germantown.	129,500

The bank of the U. States employs, we believe, about seven millions of its capital in Philadelphia. The bank owned by the late Mr. Girard, is winding up its affairs, and the institution authorized under the name of Girard's Bank, and those marked b, have not yet gone into operation, (May, 1832.) Those marked a, have had about half their authorized capitals paid in.

There are 9 Marine Insurance companies in Phila. some of which also insure against fire, viz.: Insurance Company of North America, incorporated 1794. Capital, $600,000; insures against fire. Of Pennsylvania, incorporated 1794. Capital, $500,000. Union. Capital, $300,000. Phœnix, incorporated 1804. Capital, $480,000. Delaware, incorporated 1804. Philadelphia, incorporated 1804. Capital, $400,000. U. States, incorporated 1810. Capital, $200,000. Marine, incorporated 1809. Capital, $300,000. Atlantic, incorporated 1825. Capital, $300,000.

There are six companies incorporated for the insurance of property against fire only. 1. *The Philadelphia Contributionship*, established in 1752. All persons insuring with the society, are members during the continuance of their interests, that is, whilst the premium for insurance is in deposit. This is commonly known as the "*Hand in Hand*" company, from the device on their badge. The deposit is subject to an apportionment of loss. The profit is derived from interest on the capital, which consists of the aggregate amount of deposits. 2. The *Mutual Insurance Company*, formed in 1784, in consequence of the refusal of the former association to insure houses before which trees were planted. With that exception, it is constituted like the preceding one. The profits of both companies accumulate, and are not divided. 3. The *American Fire Insurance Company* incorporated in 1810, with a capital of $500,000. 4. *Fire Association of Philadelphia*, incorporated in 1820, composed of the members of several of the engine and hose companies.

We believe this company had originally, no other capital than the credit of its members. The directors are personally liable for losses arising from insurance, when they amount to more than the capital stock. The accumulations of the company are now, we understand, alone, sufficient gurantee for its engagements. 5. Pennsylvania Fire Insurance company, incorporated with a perpetual charter in 1825. Capital authorized, $400,000. It makes insurance either permanent, or limited. 6. Franklin Fire Insurance company, incorporated in 1829, with perpetual charter and authority to increase its capital to $400,000.

The Pennsylvania company for insurance on lives and granting annuities, was incorporated in 1812, with a perpetual charter and a capital of half a million of dollars. It makes all kinds of contracts in which the contingencies of life are involved.

The *commercial institutions* of Philadelphia under the state polity are, the wardens of the port, appointed by the governor, consisting of one master warden and six assistants, who are empowered to grant licenses to pilots to make rules for their government, and to decide differences between them and the owners and masters of vessels; to direct the mooring of ships and the manner in which they shall lie, load or unload at the wharves. An appeal lies from their decision to the court of common pleas, provided it be made in six days. The *several inspections of produce* intended for exportation, viz. beef and pork, flour, shad, herrings, butter and lard, flaxseed, shingles, lumber, ground black oak bark, and domestic distilled spirits. The *chamber of commerce* consists of an association of merchants formed in the year 1801, with the design of aiding the trade of the city, by giving effect to such rules and regulations as may from time to time be established with respect to commerce, and the adjustment of mercantile differences between each other. *The Exchange* has heretofore been holden in a plain, but spacious building in Second street, N. and near to Walnut street. But at present a building is being erected upon a very appropriate site near the Girard bank, in style, dimensions and accommodations, more accordant with the wealth of the mercantile community, and the taste of the citizens of Philadelphia. It is the enterprize of a joint stock company, to which the late Mr. Stephen Girard was a very liberal subscriber.

In speaking of the public institutions of Philadelphia we must not overlook those, established to guard against fires. So effectual are these, that the destruction of a building by this element rarely occurs. This immunity from danger arises from the prohibition now co-extensive with the city bounds to erect wooden buildings, and to the ample supply of water, and the ingenious and abundant means of applying it to the extinguishment of fires. Twenty-seven fire engines and 16 hose companies have been established, principally by the youthful and enterprizing inhabitants of the city and Liberties, whose gratuitous services, distinguished for promptitude, perseverance and intrepidity, cannot be equalled by hired laborers. The hose is a leather pipe of about $2\frac{1}{2}$ inches in diameter, through which the Schuylkill water from the hydrants is conveyed to the fire, or to the engines employed in its distribution. Of this, each hose company has about a thousand feet, divided into sections of about 50 feet each, connected by brazen swivel screws. And generally, the engine companies have a small quantity of hose. For the introduction of this excellent invention, the city is indebted to Robert Vaux and Reuben Haines, Esqrs.

The city councils usually appropriate $5000 to be distributed among the fire companies within the city limits.

The transition from a description of the hose companies to the water works, is from effect to cause. *The water works of Philadelphia*, at once the source of safety from fire, of health, and of many pure pleasures, are the laudable boast of her citizens. The practicability of watering the city from the Schuylkill river or from the Wissahickon creek, had long been known to the inhabitants, and did not escape the sagacity of Franklin, who bequeathed his accumulative legacy already noticed, for that purpose. The first attempt was made in 1797, after a plan proposed by Mr. Latrobe, consisting of a reservoir on the E. bank of the Schuylkill, from which water was thrown by a steam engine into a tunnel, through which it flowed to a second engine house, to be again raised by a second steam engine into a reservoir, from which it was distributed by pipes through the city. This work was accomplished in despite of many difficulties in January, 1801. Ten years experience, however, demonstrated this mode to be insufficient to yield a steady and adequate supply of water, and the city councils sought other means to obtain it. Recourse to the Wissahickon, then proposed, was abandoned, because of the magnitude of the cost, estimated at $359,718; and it was resolved to increase the number of the engines on the Schuylkill, at a point above the city, and to throw the water into a reservoir 105 feet above the level of the tide. This plan too, notwithstanding the enormous expense of its completion and support, was soon discovered to be inadequate. A fortunate suggestion, probably caused by the water works at Bethlehem, induced councils to resolve on the erection of a dam and water wheels at Fair Mount. The interfering rights of the Schuylkill navigation company were obtained, on condition that the city would make the locks and canal on the W. side of the river, and the rights of the proprietors of the water power at the falls, 4 miles distant, were purchased for $150,000. On the 19th April, 1819, the work was commenced by Mr. Ariel Cooley, who contracted to make the dam, the locks and canal, the head arches to the race, and the excavation of the race from a solid rock, for $150,000. This contract has been successfully completed. The dam, built with great judgment and in the most permanent manner, runs in a diagonal manner up stream, and when nearly over, runs the rest of the distance at a right angle towards the shore, so as to join the head pier of the guard lock on the western side, by which means a large overfall was created, and the rise above the dam by occasional freshets much abated. The whole length of the overfall is 1204 feet, the mound dam 270 feet, and the head arches 104 feet, making the whole extent of the dam, including the western pier, about 1600 feet, and backing the water up the river about 6 miles. The water power thus created, is calculated to raise into the reservoirs by 8 wheels and pumps, 12 millions of gallons per diem. The lowest estimate of the quantity of water afforded by the river in the dry season, is 440 millions of gallons per 24 hours, and it is found by experience, that 30 gallons on the wheel, will raise 1 into the reservoir. Hence it is obvious that there is a large surplus power, which might be employed in manufactures, but which the city wisely retains for future occasions.

The head pier, guard locks, two lift locks and canal, are constructed in the most substantial manner on the W. side of the river. On the E. the whole shore was of solid rock, which has been excavated to the width of 140 feet, to form the race and site of the mill houses, running parallel with the river. The length of the race is 419 feet, the greatest depth of excavation 60 feet, and the least 16 feet. The gunpowder used, alone, cost the contractor above 12,000 dollars. At the upper part of the excavation are the head arches, 3 in number, extending from the E. end of the mound dam to the rock of the bank.

On the W. of the excavation are erected the mill houses, forming the W. side of the race. The S. end, like the E. side of the race, is of solid rock. The race is about 90 feet wide; the water passage through the arches is 68 feet in width and 6 feet deep, the depth to which the race is excavated below the dam; consequently, the area of the passage gives a continued stream of 408 square feet of water. These arches are on the N. of the race, and the mill buildings being on the W. the water passes from the race to the wheels, and is discharged thence into the river below the dam. The gate of the centre arch is upon the principle of the lock gate, and admits boats into the race; at the S. end of the mill buildings there is a waste gate 8 feet wide, by which (the upper gates being shut,) the water can be drawn off to the bottom of the race.

The mill buildings are of stone, 238 feet long, and 56 wide. The lower section is divided into 12 apartments, 4 of which are intended for 8 double forcing pumps, the others for the fore-bays and water wheels. These chambers are arched with brick, and warmed by stoves; so that in the most inclement season no ice is formed within them. A gallery extends along the building from which the wheels may all be seen at a view. The centre part of the buildings is 190 by 25 feet, with circular doors to the pump chambers, and a range of circular windows over the archways of the wheel rooms. On a line with the cornice of the central part, is the base course of 2 pavillions, with Doric porticoes, which terminate the W. front. One of these is used for the office of the committee, and the other is the residence of an old and faithful servant of the corporation, who has the general care of the property at Fair Mount. On the E. front, immediately over the pumps and forebay rooms, is a terrace 253 feet long and 26 feet wide, paved with brick, and railed, forming a handsome walk along the race and leading by steps at the end to the top of the head arches, mound dam and pier.

There are now 4 wheels at work, and a fifth being constructed. Three of the wheels are of wood, with shafts of iron weighing 5 tons each. The fourth is altogether of cast iron, and weighs about 22 tons. These wheels are competent to throw into the reservoirs full 6,000,000 gallons in the 24 hours. The pumps made by Messrs. Rush & Muhlenburg, under the direction of Mr. F. Graff, are placed horizontally, and worked by a crank on the water wheel, attached to a pitman connected with the piston, at the end of the slides. They are fed under a natural head of water from the fore-bays of the water wheels, and are calculated for a 6 feet stroke; but hitherto it has been found more profitable to work with not more than 5 feet. They are double forcing pumps, and are connected, each of them, to an iron main of 16 inches in diameter, which is carried along the bottom of the race to the rock at the foot of Fair Mount, and thence up the bank into the reservoir. At the end of the pipe is a stop cock which may be closed when necessary. The shortest of these mains is 284 feet long.

There are 4 reservoirs; No. 1 contains 3,917,659 gallons; No. 2, 3,296,434; No. 3, 2,707,295; and No. 4, 10,000,000 of gallons. Total, 19,921,388 gallons, equal to a supply for ten days consumption, in the summer season. These reservoirs are 102 feet above low tide, and 56 feet above the highest ground in the city. From them the water is conveyed in iron mains and iron and wood pipes, into the city and Liberties.

Wooden pipes were originally used for conducting the water, but being subject to bursting and speedy decay, they have long since been abandoned. Iron pipes have been extended through sections of the city where the wooden pipes were decayed and elsewhere, which, added to the iron pipes laid in the districts adjoining the city, exceed 60 miles. The water was introduced into Spring Garden, April 26, 1826, into Southwark June 1, and into the Northern Liberties June 6th, of the same year. The iron pipes, first imported from Europe, are now made in the U. States as well, and as cheaply as abroad.

Whilst the steam engine was in use for raising water, the cost of raising 1,600,000 gallons per day, the extent that could be gained was $30,858 per annum. Two men are sufficient to attend the present works, 12 hours alternately, whose wages, with the expense for fuel, light and tallow, amount to $4 per diem, $1400 per annum. Add to this sum the interest at 5 per cent on the cost of the works, and the difference will be that saved on 1,600,000 gallons of water. But the present works give 6,000,000 of gallons, and the addition of 4 wheels, will increase the quantity to 12,000,000, and the expense only to $10 the day.

The whole cost to the city when first finished, of the works at Fair Mount, is as follows, viz.:

water power at the falls,	$150,000
Damages for overflowing by the dam, erection of dam, locks, head arches, race and piers,	187,182
Three pumps,	11,000
Mill houses, mills, and other works connected with them,	71,250
Iron raising mains,	4,480
New reservoir,	8,600
	$432,512
The entire amount expended by the city for the introduction of the Schuylkill water, will be seen by adding cost of the first works on Centre square,	690,402 81
Do. of second steam works including reservoir,	320,669 84
Total,	$1,443,585 36

Other, but not great sums, are to be added for additional wheels and reservoirs, and the formation of the neat garden at the western foot of Fair-Mount, &c. &c. The income from water rents is about 70,000 dollars per annum, and will increase yearly, for an indefinite period, and will furnish large means for the extinction of the debt, which the water works have created.

Over the central entrance to the mill is a statue of the river god, bound in chains, and verily the genius of the stream thus subject, is a most useful slave. Proteus himself could not have effected more changes, nor the slave of the Lamp have administered more serviceably to his master.

The scenery of Fair Mount, is rich in natural and artificial beauty, and so attractive has it become to citizens and strangers, that several stages find constant employment in transporting visiters to and from it during the whole year, save in the winter months.

Public Buildings, Gardens, &c. The buildings generally of Philadelphia are remarkable for simplicity and neatness of style, and durability of construction. For the latter, the vicinity of the city furnishes abundant material, in stone, marble, lime and clay of the best kind. But in the modern public buildings, these qualities have much grandeur. Christ's church, one of the oldest of the city, merits attention as well for the beauty of its architecture as the height of its steeple, which is 190 feet, and possesses a fine chime of bells. St. Stephen's, 102 ft. long, is an interesting specimen of Gothic architecture. On the western front are 2 octangular towers, 86 feet high, which are to be raised still higher. The pulpit and chancel are highly finished, and the *coup de œil* on entering the church is highly impressive. The windows are embellished with cherubim in stained glass. St. John's, a new Catholic church, is also after the Gothic order, and has excited much admiration. St. Andrew's, an Episcopalian church, has a front copied from the portico of the temple of Bacchus, at *Teos*. The interior is of the same style of architecture, and is highly decorated. A foundation for a spire is laid at the west end of the building. The first Presbyterian church, opposite to Washington square, is a Grecian edifice modelled from the Ionic temple on the river Ilyssus, at Athens. It is of brick, stuccoed in imitation of marble. The roof is surmounted by a cupola with a bell. The fifth Presbyterian church is a neat, brick building, with a well proportioned steeple 165 feet high. Some other churches in the city and Liberties merit attention, among which St. John's and the second Universalist church in the Northern Liberties may be mentioned.

The *old court house* built in 1709, in Second street, has been, and should be preserved, as a perpetual means of contrasting the progress of the wealth and taste of the city with its condition in these respects, soon after its foundation. It was once the focus of business of every kind, the seat of justice, the chapel of itinerant preachers, and the mart of the auctioneer, and is now the head quarters of the nightly watch.

The state house now called Independence Hall, was completed 1735, in a chaste and ornamental style, which has been in several instances defaced, by the *repairs* and substitutions of ignorant agents of the corporation. A just taste now seeks to restore its pristine form. The original steeple was taken down, being decayed, about the close of the revolutionary war. A new one has lately been built, as like the former as could be made from the reminiscences of the citizens, with an illuminated dial plate to the clock, by which the hours of the night may be told. The public offices and halls of the courts are on the E. and W. sides, and cover the whole N. front, exceeding 400 feet in length, of the state house square. If this group of buildings had uniformity of style, they would indeed be an admirable ornament of the city, to which the delightful arcade of Linden trees before them, is a beautiful and grateful addition. From the steps of the Centre hall, these United States were first declared free, sovereign and independent.

The university and medical college halls, are admirable for the beautiful simplicity and appropriate character of their construction. They have each 85 feet front and 112 feet depth, and are separated by an open area of similar dimensions, laid out in grass plats and walks. The whole is enclosed by a low marble wall, and iron railing. The material of the buildings is brick, stuccoed in imitation of gneiss.

The new alms house now being erected, will when completed, consist of 4 buildings, each 500 feet front, 3 stories high, including the basement, of regular ashlar masonry, so placed as to enclose a rectangular yard. A Tuscan portico will front the Schuylkill, having 6 columns, 5 feet in diameter at the base, and 30 feet high. When finished, this will be the palace of the poor. The arcade, on the N. side of Chestnut street, W. of Sixth street, is 100 feet front and 150 feet deep, to Carpenter street. Two avenues run through it, upon both sides of which the stores open, and those of the second story have a gallery before them. The whole is covered by sky lights. The third story is supported by arches, and is divided into 3 large rooms and 2 saloons, all occupied by the Philadelphia museum. Both fronts are of marble. It is the property of a joint stock company. Although this structure is certainly handsome and commodious, this species of *Bazaar* does not seem to accord with Philadelphia taste, and we fear the stock is not profitable to the holders.

The markets of Philadelphia are too celebrated to be passed over. The butcher's meat, poultry, butter, vegetables and fruits in the appropriate seasons, are most admirable in quality and quantity, and in the order and cleanliness of their exhibition. The High street market houses extend from the Delaware river to Eighth street, in length near 4000 feet. On market days, the wagons and cars of the country folks, converted into temporary stalls, reach westward on either side of the way, an almost equal distance. And a similar array of vehicles is frequently seen more than a mile in length, upon Second street. Besides this great market, there are 5 others in the city and Liberties, and additional ones have become indispensable to the convenience of the citizens.

Bank Edifices.—Banking house of the bank of the United States. This building is a copy, by Mr. William Strickland, of the Parthenon at Athens, so far as was consistent with its designated purpose,dispensing with the flanking columns and decorations. The ascent to the porticoes,is by a flight of six steps, to a terrace extending in front of the building and sixteen feet on each flank. On this platform, 87 feet front, and 161 feet deep, including the porticoes, the building is erected. In front, steps of marble lead to the basement, projecting 10 ft. 6 in. upon which rise eight Doric columns,4 ft. 6 inches in diameter, and 27 feet high; supporting a plain entablature and a pediment, the vertical angle of which is 153°. The door of entrance opens into a large vestibule with circular ends, opening into office rooms, and a lobby leading to the banking room. The vestibule ceiling is a prolonged pannelled dome, divided into three compartments by bands enriched with guilloches, springing from a projecting impost, containing a sunken frette. The pavement is tessellated with American and Italian marble throughout. The banking room occupies the centre of the building, and is 48 feet wide by 81 feet E. and W., and is lighted from either end. Two rows of fluted marble columns, of the Greek Ionic order, 22 inches in diameter, with full entablature and blocking course, are placed, each ten feet distant from the side walls. On these the great central and lateral arches of the roof are supported. The first is semi-cylindrical; is 28 ft. in diameter, 81 in length, and sub-divided into seven compartments, richly ornamented. The ceiling is 35 feet from the floor to the crown of the arch, and is executed with great precision and effect. An Isthmian wreath, carved from an entire block of Pennsylvania white marble, surrounds the clock face, which occupies the space of the first pannel over the entablature in the centre, the design of which is copied from the reverse of an antique gem, found at Corinth and described by Stewart, in his work on the antiquities of Athens. The clerks' desks are placed within the intercolumniations; the tellers counters, composed of marble, forming pannelled pedestals, across each end of the banking room, commencing at the first column at each end of the walls.

The stockholders' room is a parallelogram of 28 by 50 ft., lighted from the portico of the south front, with a rich ceiling and otherwise ornamented. The committee rooms from the stockholders, open right and left, flanked by two flights of marble stairs, leading to the apartments of the upper story. A private staircase from the banking room leads to the directors', engravers' and copper plate printers' rooms, which are lighted from the roof.

Bank of Pennsylvania. The banking house of this company, from a design of the late Mr. Latrobe, is like the bank of the United States, a pure specimen of Grecian architecture. It is copied from the temple of the muses on the Ilyssus, near Athens, with two Ionic porticos of six columns each, supporting entablatures and pedaments. The whole building, 125 ft. by 51, is of white Pennsylvania marble. The banking room is circular, surmounted by a dome covered with marble, and lighted by a lantern in the centre. The stockholders' room opens on the western portico, and looks into a small neat garden, surrounded by a low brick wall and iron palisades.

The banking house of the bank of Philadelphia is also from a design of Mr. Latrobe. It is in the Gothic style, and covered with stucco imitating marble. The building has its admirers; but does not receive the general approbation of the citizens.

The banking house of the late Stephen Girard, Esq. was built by the first bank of the United States, and is a beautiful structure with a marble front, and a portico with 6 marble columns of the Corinthian order.

The banking house of Penn township is a plain, neat and massive structure, stuccoed in imitation of granite.

There are several establishments pertaining to the general government, located within the city and county of Philadelphia, which claim a short description. The custom house, after a design from Strickland, is a neat and commodious building, with large stores appurtenant to it. The front of the basement story is of marble, the remainder of the exterior of brick. A niche in the front has a statue, personating commerce, executed by Rush. The mint is a superb building, of the Ionic order, erected under the direction of Strickland, in Chesnut near Broad street, having two fronts of 122 feet, divided into porticoes, 62 feet long, and wings of 30 feet each. The porticos consist each of six marble columns, 3 feet in diameter and 25 feet high. The mass of the building is of brick, faced with thick marble ashlar, and contains every accommodation for officers, workmen and machinery, which the institution can desire. It is at once a beautiful ornament of the city, and honorable to the liberality of the general government. The Schuylkill arsenal is on the east bank of that river, below the city. The buildings, consisting of four large store houses, at right angles with each other, and a dwelling for the commanding officer, and a powder magazine, were erected in 1800. It is a depot of clothing, camp equipage and quarter masters' stores. The Delaware arsenal is in the angle formed by the confluence of the Frankford creek with the Delaware river, and is one of the handsomest military stations in the U. S. It comprises six large stone buildings forming a square, with work shops, &c. It is a principal depot for small arms, nitre, flints, &c. The powder magazine is very commodious, and may contain 500,000 lbs. of powder. The marine asylum, a noble and magnificent structure, created by the funds of American seamen, is on the east side of the Schuylkill river, in the vicinity of the arsenal, and is beautifully situated, having a commanding view of the river and the surrounding country. The building is faced with marble; is 386 feet long, consisting of an Ionic portico of 90 feet, sppported by 8 columns, and wings, each 148 feet. In front and rear of the wings, run covered verandas, supported by cast iron columns. The chapel is 50 feet square and 40 in height to the lantern. This is one of the largest and most beautiful buildings in the vicinity of the city. The navy yard is on the Delaware river, at the south end of Swanson st., in the District of Southwark, surrounded on three sides by a high brick wall, enclosing about 20 acres of ground. It contains a mould loft for modelling ships of war; a blacksmith's shop, in which all the iron work is made for the public ships, built on this station; an hospital; marine barracks spacious enough to contain 150 men, with quarters for the officers, and a handsome dwelling for the commander of marines. The sheers for fixing masts are 120 ft. high, and said to be the most complete in the U. S. There are a large three decker, and a frigate on the stocks here, each covered by a frame building.

Theatres. There are three theatres in the city and one in the Northern Liberties. Those in the city are large, commodious piles, and very ornamental in their appearance. The Chesnut and Arch street theatres were built after the plans and under the direction of Mr. Strickland. The Walnut street theatre has been lately remodelled by Mr. Haviland. The Washington theatre in the Northern Liberties, is a frame building, originally erected in 1828, for an equestrian company; and has lately been fitted up for dramatic performances.

Public squares and gardens. The

wide streets and public squares laid out by William Penn, show a wise regard for the health and pleasure of his city. To his foresight she is indebted for five public squares, which contribute now and will hereafter contribute, more essentially to the enjoyments of the citizens. Penn square, at the intersection of Broad and Market streets; Washington square, on Walnut and Sixth; and Franklin square, on Sassafras and Sixth, are much improved, and the two last are delightful promenades; to which we must add Independence square, formerly the state house lot; all which are much frequented by citizens of every age and rank, and yield a most healthful recreation to the children. Logan square is in the N.W., and Rittenhouse, in the S. W. sections of the city; but these are yet unimproved.

The are several "*botanical gardens*," as they are termed, in the city and Liberties, in which are green houses stocked with exotics, grounds neatly laid out, and large and various collections of fruits and flowers. That founded by the distinguished naturalist Bartram, on the W. bank of the Schuylkill; that of the Messrs. Landreth in Passyunk; that planted by Mr. Mc Mahon, in Penn township, McArans, the labyrinth garden, and *Sans souci*, in the city, in which hotels are established, are the most noted.

Prisons. There are three prisons in the city and co. The first and co. prison, is still and has long been used as a penitentiary. It covers a lot of 400 feet on Sixth, and 200 ft. on Walnut and Prune streets. But measures having been taken for the erection of a new county prison in the township of Passyunk, the present will shortly be removed, and will give a site for private buildings unequalled for beauty in the city. The second, known as the Arch street prison, was built by the state, in the year 1807; was since purchased by the county of Philadelphia, and is now used as a debtor's apartment, and for the confinement of prisoners awaiting trial. The unceasing efforts of Pennsylvania to render the inflictions of punishment for offences against society, not only a terror to evil doers, but also the means of reclaiming the offenders, have caused the erection, at a very great expense, of the W. and E. penitentiaries. These are described particularly in the preceding part of the work. The latter is in Spring Garden district, upon a high and healthy site near the Schuylkill.

As a manufacturing city, Philadelphia (of course including the county) claims the first rank in the Union. In wood, iron, ship building, cotton, woollen, glass, earthern and stone ware, steam engines, and a thousand other handicrafts, she is equally distinguished. The curiosity of the stranger may be excited by the shot tower, for the manufacture of leaden shot, of Mr. Sparks, in Southwark, of a circular form, 30 feet in diameter at the base, and 15 at the summit, and 142 high; and that of Mr. Beck in the city, near the Schuylkill, square in form, with sides of 33 feet at the base, and 22 at the apex, having an elevation of 166 feet. The porcelain factory of Mr. Tucker, in which China is fabricated with the excellence and taste of the best French ware. The very extensive and admirable floor cloth and carpet manufactory of Mr. McCauley, at Bush Hill; and the several glass factories.

In 1830, there were in Philadelphia and its vicinity, 104 warping mills at work, sufficient to employ about 4500 weavers; dyers over 200; spoolers 3000; bobbin winders 2000; whose wages would amount to $1,470,040. Their operations consume 114,400 lbs. indigo per ann., and 1820 barrels of flour for sizing; make 81,000 yds. per day, or $24,300,000 per ann. at 16 cts. per yard, equal to $3,888,000.

The city and county of Philadelphia is divided into three congressional districts, each sending a member to congress. The city alone forms the first senatorial district, and sends two members to senate, and seven members to the house of representatives. The county alone constitutes the second senatorial district, sending also two members to the senate, and eight members to the house of representatives. The city and county compose the first judicial district of the state. President, Edward King, Esq. The courts are holden in the city on the 1st Mondays of March and June, 3d of September, and 1st of December. The supreme court for the eastern district, holds in Philadelphia 2 terms annually, commencing respectively on the 2nd Mondays in March and Dec. In the other four supreme court districts, the power of the court is limited to a revision of the proceedings of other courts, amd to the hearing of appeals in certain specific cases. In the city and county of Philadelphia, that court has original jurisdiction when the matter in controversy exceeds $500 ; and all issues of fact are tried by a jury, before a single judge, at Nisi Prius ; and the judges also hold annually a court of oyer and terminer, for the trial of felonies not cognizable by the court of quarter sessions. The district court for the city and county of Philadelphia, was originally established in 1810, and has been continued from time to time by several acts of the legislature, the last of which was passed in March, 1832. It is composed of three judges ; has four terms, commencing respectively on the 1st Mondays in March, June, September, and December ; and original jurisdiction in cases where the matter in controversy exceeds $100 dollars, but no criminal or appellate jurisdiction. The mayor's court for the city, has like jurisdiction of criminal cases arising within the city, as the sessions has for the co. It is holden by the mayor, recorder, and three aldermen ; has 4 sessions annually, viz., in March, June, Sept., and Dec. The several courts of the U. S. for the eastern district of Pa., are holden in the city of Phila. The district court, holden alone by the judge of the district, has four stated terms annually, viz., on the 3d Mondays of February, May, August, and Nov. ; and special sessions weekly, on Fridays, when business requires. Judge, Joseph Hopkinson, Esq. The circuit court, composed of the district judge and one of the judges of the supreme court, holds two terms annually, on the 11th of April and Oct., has original and appellate jurisdiction.

The city and co. of Philadelphia, paid into the state treasury in the year 1831,

Bank dividends, including div. on Schuylkill navigation,	$125,636 97
Tax on offices, viz. prothonotary of district court,	1,943 34
Do. of common pleas,	1,458 58
Deputy attorney general,	109 50
Under this head should be included the sums paid by the register & recorder, of which no return appears in the auditor's report in 1831 ; these amounted together to the sum of	4,483 11
Tax on writs,	4,439 46
Auction duties,	126,504 85
Auction commissions,	12,100 00
Tavern licenses,	9,708 71
Duties on dealers in foreign merchandize,	24,219 86
State maps,	80 75
Tax on collateral inheritances,	14,334 84
Pamphlet laws,	30 98
Militia and exempt fines,	587 40
Tin and clock pedlars' licenses,	171 00
Hawkers' and pedlars' licenses,	815 90
	$326,625 25

STATISTICAL TABLE OF PHILADELPHIA COUNTY.

Townships, &c.	Greatest Lth.	Greatest Bth.	Population. 1820,	Population. 1830,	Taxables.
City,	2	1	63,802	80,477	16,542
N. Liberties, built part,	1 1-2	1 1-4	19,678	28,923	5,566
Southwark,	1 1-4	1 1-4	14,713	20,746	3,067
Blockley,	4	5	2,655	3,401	742
Bristol,	5 1-2	3	1,257	1,425	347
Byberry,	5	2 1-2	876	1,018	226
Dublin, Lower,	5	3	2,640	2,705	589
Germantown,	5 1-2	2	4,311	4,642	1,032
Kingsessing,	5	2 1-2	1,188	1,068	241
Moyamensing,	3	2	3,963	6,822	1,766
Moreland,	5	2	443	418	103
N. Liberties, out part,	3	4 1-2	1,810	2,453	464
Oxford, including bor. of Frankf'd,	3	4	2,720	3,139	751
Passyunk,	3 3-4	3	1,638	1,441	262
Penn t-ship, including Spring Garden,	4	3	6,598	13,648	2,205
Roxborough,	5	2	1,682	3,334	642
Kensington,				13,326	2,757
			137,974	488,961	37,281

Philadelphia city. We have in the preceding article, given the greater portion of interesting matter which pertains to this head; but shall note here some historical points, and give a concise view of the municipal government. The city stands on a high and level piece of alluvial ground, between the Delaware and Schuylkill rivers. The spot, chosen with great judgment, was designated to Penn by his commissioners, Crispin Bezar and Allen, soon after his arrival in the province; and the plot, nearly in its present form, was surveyed at the close of the year 1682, by the first surveyor general of the province, Thomas Holme. The ground selected was claimed by three Swedes, named Swenson, who relinquished it for a smaller tract at a short distance. These Swedes have given their name to a street of Southwark. The name of the city is derived from a city of Asia Minor, and is compounded of two Greek words,—*Philos*, friend, and *Adelphos*, brother. We are told by Proud that the Indian name of the place was *Coaquenaku*, which is rendered by Heckewelder, *the grove of the tall pines*. It is in lat. 39° 56′ 54″ N., and long. 75° 8′ 45″ W. from Greenwich, 120 ms. distant from the Atlantic Ocean by the course of the river, and about 55 ms. from it, in a direct line S. E. The fronts on the two rivers give it important commercial advantages; the excellent harbor on the Delaware, the level surface of the ground, good clay for bricks, inexhaustible stone quarries in the vicinity, and the salubrity of the atmosphere, render its site in every respect desirable. The city plot surveyed, is two ms. from river to river, and extends on the margin of each one, making the circumference six miles. The street are from 50 to 113 feet in width, running parallel to, and at right angles with each other. Within the original limits it consists of 9 streets, running E. and W. from the Delaware to the Schuylkill, and 25 running N. and S. from Vine to Cedar street. The carriage ways are mostly paved with boulders taken from the r. and its banks, and the foot ways with brick. The latter are separated from the former, and defended by curb stones firmly set. The houses are remarkable for their neatness, commodiousness, and uniformity, and the streets for their spaciousness and cleanliness. In good houses, white marble has been long much used for steps, sills, water table and facia, and latterly, is frequently employed for facing the whole fronts of public buildings, and the fronts of the basement stories of private ones. The Delaware, opposite the city, is near a mile in width, and is navigable for vessels of the largest class. The Schuylkill is about 500 ft. wide at Market street, and is navigable for vessels of 300 tons to the permanent bridge. Authority has been given to connect the two rivers by a canal to cross the peninsula about a mile below the city; but the stock has not yet been taken; the project not being deemed readily practicable, nor probably profitable. But a rail road has been authorized (and the stock subscribed) from river to river, north of the city, which will doubtless be immediately completed.

Since the improvement of the Schuylkill by canals, &c., and the establishment of the coal trade, the western part of the city has rapidly improved; large and commodious stores and wharves, and numerous dwellings have been built; several of the principal streets have been paved, and improvements of various kinds are in progress; and the completion of the Columbia rail road, will give new and powerful impulse to improvements in this part of the city.

The city was originally chartered by the proprietary in 1801, but the provisions of the act of incorporation not being sufficiently popular, it was abrogated at the revolution, and the city continued under a provisional government from the year 1777 to the year 1789, when it received a charter from the commonwealth, for which another was substituted in 1796, under which it is at present governed.

The municipal government of the city is vested in a mayor, recorder, 15 aldermen, and a select and common council. The recorder and aldermen are appointed by the governor, and hold their offices during good behavior. Prior to April, 1826, the councils were obliged to elect the mayor annually from the aldermen; but by an act then passed, they were authorized to select him from the body of the people. He annually appoints the city commissioners, solicitor, high constables, corders of wood, &c., and receives an annual compensation of $2000, besides perquisites of office, supposed to amount to $1000 more.

The members of the councils are chosen at the yearly general elections. Those of the select council serve three years, and those of the common council one. They receive no compensation, sit in separate chambers, and must concur in all legislative acts.

The councils, by committees raised from their own bodies, manage the water works, and superintend generally the paving of the city.

The mayor, recorder and aldermen, or any four of them, constitute the mayor's court, of which we have already spoken.

In an account of the city of Philadelphia, a conspicuous place is due to the benefaction of the late Stephen Girard. This gentleman, a native of Bordeaux, who commenced life as a pennyless sailor, had amassed, many years before his death, several millions of dollars, which he continued actively to employ, until his decease, in commerce and in banking.

He devoted himself and his funds with a clear and sound judgment, to the improvement of the city, by the erection of fine houses in various parts, and by liberal subscriptions and donations in aid of every feasible project of public utility; considering himself, it would seem, as a mere steward, or trustee of his immense property, for the use of the city. He died Dec. 28th, 1831, at the age of 84 years, having bequeathed much the greater portion of his estate, supposed to exceed in value $6,000,000, to his adopted and favorite city. He directed that $2,000,000 of his personal estate should be applied to the erection and support of a college, to be erected on a tract of land in Penn t-ship, containing 40 acres, which he purchased for that purpose; the main and out buildings to be sufficiently spacious for the residence and accommodation of at least 300 scholars, and the requisite teachers and other persons necessary in such an institution. And he further directed, that as many poor white male orphans, between the ages of 6 and 10 years, as the income of the balance of said sum, unexpended in the buildings, shall be adequate to maintain, shall be introduced into the college as soon as possible, and from time to time as there may be vacancies, or as increased ability from income may warrant, others to be introduced; priority of admission to be given in the order of application, and preference to orphans born in the city of Philadelphia.

He further bequeathed the sum of $500,000, that the income thereof should be expended to lay out, regulate, light, and pave a passage or street on the E. part of the city of Philadelphia, fronting the river Delaware, not less than 21 feet wide, and to be called Delaware avenue, extending from Cedar st. along the E. part of Water st. squares and the W. side of the logs, which form the heads of the docks or thereabouts. And to pull down and remove all wooden buildings, as well those made of wood and other combustible materials, as those called brick paned or framed buildings filled in with bricks, that are erected within the limits of the city, and to prohibit the erection of any such building within the city limits, at any future time. And after these objects shall have been attained, that the income of the said capital fund should be applied as the citizens should think fit, from time to time, to the further improvement of the Delaware front of the city. Mr. Girard by his will was also a liberal benefactor to the principal public charities of the city.

The amount of real estate, as valued at the triennial assessment of the present year (1832), is $25,818,144. But this sum certainly does not exceed half its true value, and perhaps is not a great deal more than a third. The expenditures of the city, including interest on its debt, appropriation to the sinking fund, and paving, lighting, watching, and cleansing, amount in the same year, to $305,259 39.

The means for payment of this charge, are rents of real estate, market rts., and contingent receipts from city estates,	$36,446 00
Balance of former taxes,	1,957 57
Balance of water rents,	17,512 08
Taxes levied for 1832,	220,000 00
Surplus water rent for 1832,	29,343 74
	$305,259 39
By reason of the water works, and other great expenses, the city has contracted a debt at 6 per ct., of	$540,100 00
And another at 5 per ct., of	1,425,500 00
	$1,965,600 00

For the redemption of this debt, she has established a sinking fund, towards which she appropriates annually the sum of $16,000 from the water rents, and from the tax fund, $8000, making $24,000, and the incidental profits such as premiums on loans &c., and the annual interest on the capital of the sinking fund. From these sources that fund was increased during the year ending 1st March, 1832, $45,740 17, and then amounted to $330,031 56.

This fund, with the increase of the water rents, (now amounting to 70,000 dollars per annum) it is calculated will extinguish the present debt, as fast as it shall become payable. With the assistance of the Girard fund, and the income of the city, it is also expected that the taxes, now grown onerous, may be speedily reduced.

The reader will find a view of the commerce of Philadelphia in the preceding part of the work, which treats of the general commerce of the state.

Phœnixville, p-t. of Schuylkill t-ship, Chester county, at the confluence of French creek, with the Schuylkill r., about 14 miles N. E. of West Chester, 132 from W. C., and 77 S. E. from Harrisburg, contains about 700 inhabitants, and above 80 dwellings. A very extensive rolling mill and nail factory, originally established by Mr. Thompson, and now belonging to Messrs. Reeves & Whitaker, in which is a steam engine of 100 horse power, made in the city of Pittsburg. Another large rolling mill and nail manufactory belonging to the Messrs. Coates. These two factories produce above 2000 tons of nails per ann.; they receive their iron *down* the Schuylkill canal, chiefly from Berks co. A cotton factory, belonging to Messrs. Smith & Garrigues, having above 2000 spindles, and 50 looms; the machinery of which combines the latest improvements, and is of the best quality. 2 stores and 2 taverns. A canal, which has received the name of the Chester co. canal, excavated by Mr. George Thompson, under an agreement with the Schuylkill navigation company, and communicating with the Providence dam, has supplied abundance of mill power for this town, not only for the works now erected, but for many others; and the proprietors offer mill seats for sale upon reasonable terms. The country around this place is delightful, healthy and rich, provisions abundant and cheap.

Philipsborough, town of New Sewickly t-ship, Beaver co., on the left bank of the Beaver creek, opposite to the town of Bridgewater, to which a fine bridge crosses the river. The town is about 2 miles from Beaver borough; contains about 60 dwellings, 1 store, 1 tavern. The chief business carried on here, is the building of steamboats.

Philipsville, p-o., Erie co., 345 miles N. W. of W. C., and 284 from Harrisburg.

Philipsburg, p-t., of Rush t-ship, Centre co., on the Mushannon creek, which separates it from Clearfield co., and upon the turnpike road leading from Bellefonte to Franklin, 27 miles by the road from the former, 186 ms. N. W. of W. C., 114 from Harrisburg, and about 20 ms. from the confluence of the creek with the west branch of the Susquehannah. This is a handsome village, containing about 50 dwellings, an Episcopal ch., 3 taverns, several stores, a steam grist mill, a forge, wire and screw factory, all of which are carried on extensively. The screws are said to be superior in quality, and cheaper than those imported. The dwelling of Mr. Phillips, on the border of the town, is large and neat. The Mushannon cr. is navigable to the river.

Pigeon creek, Coventry t-ship, Chester co., a tributary of the Schuylkill river; a fine stream, on which there are many mills.

Pigeon hills, Paradise t-ship, York co., extend from Adams co. through the S. W. angle of this t-ship, and nearly to its E. boundary. They give name to a post office, 90 miles from W. C., and 32 from Harrisburg.

Pigeon creek, Washington co., rises by two branches in Somerset t-ship, and flows N. E. through Fallowfield t-ship, to the Monongahela river, at Williamsport. Its length is about 15 miles.

Pickering creek, rises in Uwchlan t-ship, Chester co., and flows through Pikeland and Charleston t-ships into the river Schuylkill, by a course of about 10 miles, turning many mills.

Pike county, was erected by virtue of the act of 26th March, 1814, from Wayne co., and is bounded N. E., E. and S. E. by the river Delaware, which separates it from New Jersey; N. W. by Wayne co., W. by Luzerne and S. by Northampton. The greatest length of the county is 31 miles, and breadth 25 miles; area, 772 sq. miles; lat. 41° 20′ N. long. 1° 50′ E. from W. C. The surface of the county is hilly, or rather mountainous; the soil rocky and generally barren, but covered in many places with fine pine, hemlock, maple and beach timber. From its forests the inhabitants derive their chief support. The county lies wholly in the transition formation, chiefly of the *debris* of the conglomorate, pudding stone and slate rocks. There are, however, extensive alluvial flats along the margin of the Delaware river, that are very fertile, thickly settled, and well cultivated.

The Delaware river bounds the co. on one side, and the Lehigh partly on the other as we have already seen. Blooming Grove creek joins it about midway of its course. The Lackawaxen river, formed by the confluence of the Waullenpaupack creek and Middle creek crosses the county on the north, forming the base of a triangle, of which the Delaware and the line of Luzerne county forms the other sides, and empties into the Delaware. Along its banks for its whole length runs the canal of the Hudson and Delaware canal company. Shoholy, Big Pond, Glass Creek, Saw Kill, Ramy's Kill, Dingman's creek, Little Bush Kill, Bushkill creeks, are all tributaries of the Delaware, which have their sources and course in this county. Trout, Tobyhanna, Broadhead's, Marshall's and Mill creeks, which flow through Northampton county, have their head waters in Pike. There are mills on all these streams; but few of them are navigable.

The principal towns are Milford, the county town, Maria, Bushville, Dingman's Ferry.

The population of the county by the census of 1830, is 4,843, of which there were white males 2,449; white females 2,295; colored males 55; females 43; slaves 1; aliens 54; taxables 1828, 892.

Pike forms part of the eastern district of the supreme court; and together with Luzerne and Wayne, forms the 11th district of the county courts, which are held on the third Mondays of January, April, August and November, annually, at Milford. Connected with Northampton, Lehigh and Wayne, it forms the 12th senatorial district, sending two members to the senate; and in union with Northampton, Wayne and Pike, it sends four members to the house of representatives. Bucks, Northampton, Wayne and Pike, form the 8th Congressional district of the state, represented in the 22d congress by Peter Ihrie, Jr. and Samuel A. Smith.

The lumber business forms the chief employment of the inhabitants, who find a steady and profitable market for all they can prepare, at Philadelphia and at the towns and villages above it on the banks of the Delaware. There are, however, on the Delaware, 8 or 10 miles above Milford, some extensive glass works.

There are few churches in the co., perhaps none except at Milford. But there are two academies, one at Dingman's Ferry, on the Delaware, and the other at the town of Milford. To the latter, incorporated in 1827, the legislature gave $2000; and to the former we believe one thousand.

By the assessment of 1829, the seated lands of the county were valued at $283,516; unseated at $360,455; and the personal estate and occupations at $39,516. The rate of tax was 5 mills on the dollar.

This county paid into the state treasury, in 1831, for

Tax on writs,	50
Tavern licenses,	284 24
Duties on dealers in foreign merchandize,	119 58
Hawkers' & pedlars' licenses	45 60
	$499 42

Pikeland, t-ship, Chester co., bounded N. E. by the river Schuylkill, S. E. by Charlestown t-ship, S. by West Whiteland t-ship, W. by Uwchlan and N. W. by Vincent t-ships. Central distance from Philadelphia about 24 miles N. W.; from West Chester 9 miles north; length, 8½ ms.; breadth 3¼; area, 10,116 acres; surface, gentle declivity; soil, sandy loam. Pop. in 1830, 1403; taxables, 282. Stoney creek, French creek, and Pickering creek, cross it in their course S. E. to the Schuylkill; the two latter turning several mills. Kimberton and the Yellow Springs are post towns of the township. There are two places of public worship.

Pike Run, t-ship, Washington co., bounded N. by Fallowfield, E. by the Monongahela river, S. and S. W. by E. Bethlehem, and N. W. by Somerset t-ship. Centrally distant from Washington borough 18 miles S. E.; greatest length, 10; breadth, 4½ ms.; area, 16,640 acres; surface, hilly; soil, loam. Pop. in 1830, 2081; taxables, 357. Pike run and Little Pike run, rise and have their whole course in the t-ship, flowing E. to the Monongahela river. At their confluence with that stream lies the post town of of Greenfield, on the north side of the run. Centreville and Bealsville post towns are on the national road, which separates this from E. Bethlehem t-ship.

Pike, t-ship, Clearfield co., bounded N. by Fox t-ship, E. by Lawrence, S. by Beccaria, and W. by Indiana and Jefferson co. Centrally distant from the borough of Clearfield W. 11 ms.; greatest length, 16; breadth, 16 ms.; area, 25,600 acres; surface hilly; soil, gravelly loam. Pop. in 1830, 819; taxables, 166. The W. branch of the Susquehannah crosses the S. E. angle of the t-ship, and receives Anderson's creek, which passes by Curwinville and several smaller streams. On the W. the township is drained by the head waters of the Mahoning creek. The Grampian Hill is a noted eminence in a fork of Anderson's creek. The turnpike running to Franklin in Venango co., passes N. W. through the t-ship, on which, near the E. boundary, is the post town of Curwinville, upon the left bank of the river. Iron is found in the E. part of the t-ship, and some lime stone in the northwest.

Pike, t-ship, Berks co., bounded N. and E. by District, S. E. by Colebrookdale, S. W. by Earl, W. by Oley, N. and W. by Rockland; greatest length, 4½ miles by 2½ in breadth; area, 6500 acres; surface, large hills; soil, gravel, poor and indifferently cultivated; valued from 15 to 25 dollars per acre when improved. Pop. in 1810, 552; in 1820, 645; in 1830, 752; taxables, 147. It is watered by the sources of the Manatawny. There are several mills upon these streams, and one forge, called Potts' forge. One church, common to Lutherans and Presbyterians.

Pike, post township, Bradford co., bounded N. by Warren t-ship, E. by Susquehannah co., S. by Wyalusing, and W. by the last named t-ship and by Orwell. Centrally distant from Towanda about 14 miles; greatest length, 10 miles; breadth, 4½; area, 25,600 acres; surface, hilly; soil, gravelly loam. Pop. in 1830, 1438; taxables, 238. The Wyalusing creek flows southwardly through the t-ship, receiving several tributaries from it. The post office is 260 miles N. W. from W. C., and 149 from Harrisburg.

Pimple hill, a small mountain in Tobyhanna t-ship, Northampton co., about two miles north of the Pokono mountain, on the turnpike road from Easton to Wilkesbarre.

Pine creek, Berks co., a confluent of the Manatawny creek, rising in District township, and flowing through Pike and Oley. There are upon it, one furnace, one forge, and several grist mills.

Pine hill, a mountain of Towamensing t-ship, Northampton co., two or three miles north of the Pokono mountain. Its western base is washed by the river Lehigh.

Pine creek, Brunswick township, Schuylkill co., rises in the t-ship and flows S. W. into the Schuylkill river, about six ms. below Schuylkill Haven.

Pineville, a village of Buckingham t-ship, Bucks co., on the road from Newtown to Centreville, and near the line of Wrightstown t-ship, distant 7 miles S. E. of Doylestown. It contains 6 or 8 dwellings.

Pine run, Bucks county, a tributary of the Neshaminy creek, rises in Plumstead t-ship, and flows through Doylestown, and falls into the north branch of the Neshaminy, in New Britain t-ship.

Piney creek, Adams co., rises in Germany t-ship, and flows S. into the state of Maryland.

Pine, township, Allegheny county, bounded N. by Butler co., E. by Deer and Indiana t-ship, S. by Ross t-ship, and W. by Ohio t-ship. Centrally distant N. from Pittsburg, 11 miles; greatest length, 7 miles; breadth, 6; area, 26,880 acres; surface hilly; soil, loam. Pop. in 1830, 984; taxables, 241. It is drained by Pine creek, which gives name to the t-ship, and which, receiving many branches from it, flows S. through Ross and Indiana t-ships, into the Allegheny river.

Pine creek, Allegheny co. (See preceding article.

Piney creek, Woodberry township, Huntingdon co., rises in the t-ship and flows N. E. about 11 miles into the Raystown branch of the Juniata river, about one mile above Williamsburg.

Pine Creek, t-ship, Lycoming co., bounded N. and N. E. by Brown township, E. by Mifflin t-ship, S. by the W. branch of the Susquehannah river, and W. by Dunstable t-ship. Centrally distant from Williamsport N. W. 23 ms.; greatest length, 16; breadth, 5 miles; area, 23,680 acres; surface, mountainous; soil, part limestone, but chiefly gravel. Pop. in 1830, about 500; taxables, 89; value of taxable property, 1829, seated lands, &c. $29,610; unseated, 2,266; personal estate, 3,628; rate of levy, ¾ of one per cent. Pine creek, from which the t-ship has its name, rises on the confines of Tioga co., and flows southeast through Brown t-ship, and along part of the E. boundary of this t-ship into the Susquehannah river, having a comparative course of about 35 ms.

Pine Creek, t-ship, Jefferson county, bounded N. by Ridgeway, east by Clearfield, S. by Young, and W. by Rose t-ships. Centrally distant east from Brookville, 12 miles; greatest length, 12; breadth, 12; area, 85,760 acres; surface, rolling; soil, gravelly loam, abounding with pine timber. It is drained chiefly by the south branch of the Sandy Lick creek, which flows westerly. It contains about 250 inhabitants. Brookville, post and county town, is the nearest post town. Distant 165 miles from Harrisburg.

Pine Grove, t-ship, Venango county, bounded north by the Allegheny r. and Teonista t-ship, E. by Farmington, S. by Elk Creek t-ship, and W. by Rockland. Centrally distant E. from Franklin borough, 16 miles; greatest length, 11; breadth, 8 miles; area, 41,220 acres; surface, rolling; soil, rich loam. Pop. in 1830, 205; taxables, 71. It is drained by Hemlock creek on the N. W. and Six Mile run on the S. W.

Pine creek, a large tributary of the west branch of the Susquehannah river, which, rising in Potter co. several miles E. of Coudersport, flows E. 25 miles into Tioga co., thence S. about 15 miles into Lycoming, and through that county S. W. about 13 or 14 ms. and S. E. about 16 miles, into the river 5 or 6 miles above the borough of Jersey Shore. The creek is navigable above the line of Potter county, a distance from its mouth of near 60 miles. Vast quantities of lumber pass down it annually to the market. Not less than 5 millions of feet are supposed to have been sent from Tioga county, by this route in the spring of 1832. One house sent to market about one million of feet.

Pine Creek, post office, Tioga co., distant 265 miles N. W. of W. C., and 159 from Harrisburg.

Pine Grove, t-ship, Schuylkill co., is bounded on the north by Lower Mahantango, E. by Wayne t-ship, S. by Berks co., and W. by Dauphin and Lebanon counties; greatest length, 13; greatest breadth, 9 miles, as the township was formerly bounded, before the formation of Wayne, when its area was about 40,280 acres. The surface of this t-ship is very mountainous. It is drained by the Swatara creek, whose brances traverse it in every direction. Along the main stream of the Swatara, which flows on the north side of the Blue mountain, runs the navigable "feeder" of the Union canal, including the "great dam" or artificial lake, made by the Union canal company, in a narrow part of the gorge of the mountain through which the creek passes. This great work extends across the pass, abutted by solid rocks, 430 feet, and the water which it arrests covers between 7 and 800 acres. A towing path is constructed along the margin to the head of the pond, a distance of six miles, from which place the canal has been continued four miles to the village of Pine Grove, where basins have been made to facilitate the coal trade. From thence a rail road runs along the valley of the Swatara creek about three miles and a half into the coal region. The township contained in 1830, 1609 inhabitants. The taxables in 1828, were 217. There is a forge in the township, near the village, known as "Pine Grove forge," and three churches.

Pine Grove, post town and borough, Pine Grove t-ship, Schuylkill county, situated on the Swatara creek, at the termination of the feeder of the Union canal. The town has several streets and between 80 and 90 dwellings, four large and commodious hotels, six or seven stores, and two mills. Basins have been made here for the canal boats, and a rail road leads to the coal mines, on the N. of the Sharp mountain. This place will doubtless participate largely in the coal trade. Its population now consists of about five hundred souls. It is distant 18 miles west of Orwigsburg, 151 north from W. C., and 41 east of Harrisburg.

Pine Grove, village, Warren co., situated on the W. bank of the Conewango creek, seven miles above Warren, at the head of the rapids. It is compactly built, containing fifteen dwelling houses, a store, three taverns, and several mechanics' shops. Russell's mills are situtated at this place.

Pine Grove mills, post office, Centre county, 177 N. W. of W. C., and 88 of Harrisburg.

Pine Grove, t-ship, Warren county, bounded N. by the state of New York, E. by Elk t-ship. S. by the Conewango t-ship, and W. by Sugar Grove t-ship. Centrally distant N. from Warren borough 8 miles; length 9½; breadth 7½; area, 33,260 acres; surface, undulating; soil, loam. Pop. in 1830, 652; taxables 1828, 134. The Conewango creek flowing south divides the t-ship into two unequal parts; and receives from the t-ship several small streams, the chief of which is Pine creek from the east. On the right bank, in the t-ship, centrally situated, is the small town of Russellville, or Pine Grove.

Pineville, hamlet of Bucks co., on the line between Buckingham and Wrightstown t-ships, 7 miles a little south of E. from Doylestown. Contains four or five dwellings.

Pisgah hill, a mountain in the south part of Tyrone t-ship, Perry co., on the border of Sherman's creek.

Pismire hill, Sugar Loaf t-ship, Luzerne co., south of the Buck mountains, and between Sandy and Black creeks.

Pitch-Pine run, Tobyhanna t-ship, Northampton co., a tributary of the Pohopoko creek, rising north of Pimple hill and Wilkesbarre turnpike. It is a mill stream, but not navigable.

Pitt, t-ship, Allegheny co., bounded north by the Allegheny river, east by Wilkins t-ship, S. and W. by the Monongahela river; greatest length, 7½; breadth, 6 miles; area, 13,440 acres; surface, hilly; soil, loam. Pop. in 1830, 3924; taxables, 1218, exclusive of the city of Pittsburg, which lies at the confluence of the rs. at the N.W. point of the t-ship. The streams of the township other than the rivers are few and inconsiderable in volume. The township abounds in coal. The great turnpike road runs through it to Pittsburg, on which, six miles east of the city, is the post town of East Liberty. The post town of Lawrenceville lies on the Allegheny river, 4 ms. above Pittsburg.

Pittsburg, city, Allegheny co., is situated in 40° 32′ N. lat., 3° 2″ W. long. from W. C., at the confluence of the Allegheny and Monongahela rivers; 201 ms. N. W. from W. C., 300 ms. W. of Philadelphia, 196 from Harrisburg, 120 S. of Lake Erie, 1100 by land and 2000 by water above N. Orleans. The Monongahela here runs a due N. course, and receives the Allegheny from the E., or perhaps it might be said with more propriety, that the Allegheny receives the Monongahela, the former being the greater stream. The city stands on a level alluvial bottom of small extent; for immediately back of it, and at a distance of not more than half a mile from the point rises Grant's hill, high and almost precipitous, and is the great secondary bank, which spreads itself so as to leave along the Allegheny river, a strip of land of one third or one fourth of a mile wide, of great fertility, and along the Monongahela, a still narrower belt. The hill was named after the unfortunate major Grant, who was defeated here by the French and Indians, in 1758. This spot claims notice politically and commercially from the year 1754, when the French erected a fort here, to which they gave the name of Du Quesne, from the marquis of that name, then governor general of Canada. Its value as a military position had been marked in the preceding year by Gen. Washington, when on a mission from Gov. Denwiddie of Virginia to ascertain the views of the French in this quarter. The fort was captured by the British 1758, and received the name of fort Pitt, in honor of the earl of Chatham.

The city was founded in 1765, but was not regularly surveyed until 1784. On the 22d April of that year, Tench Francis, Esq., who was the attorney of the proprietaries, one of whose manors included the site, instructed Geo. Potts, Esq., to lay out the town, and to divide the rest of the manor into proper lots and farms, and to set a value thereon, that they might be offered for immediate sale. The survey was completed in May or June following, and confirmed by the attorney on the 30th Sept., 1784. For some years it increased slowly; containing in 1786, about 100 houses, erected chiefly on the 3d bank, but of late years it has extended rapidly along the margin of the rivers, and is encroaching upon Grant's hill, houses being built on its sides and summit. It was erected into a borough by an act of assembly, passed 5th March, 1804, and was incorporated as a city by an act of 18th March, 1816.

It is not possible to do justice to this article, without embracing in our views the neighboring towns and hamlets, which form the suburbs of this city. On the W. side of the Monongahela, and about a mile above Pittsburgh, lies the flourishing borough of Birmingham; and immediately opposite to the city, under the high and jutting hill, called coal hill, is a street of manufacturing establishments, which may be considered as an extension of Birmingham, and which is connected with Pittsburg, by a fine roofed bridge, built in 1818, 1500 ft. in length, and 37 in width, having 8 arches supported by stone piers, by a joint stock company, to which the state subscribed $40,000, at an expense of 102,450. In the opposite direction, and north of the Allegheny river, stands the boro' of Allegheny town, on a beautiful plain of great extent, also connected with Pittsburg by a roofed bridge, erected in 1819; in length 1122 ft., breadth 38 ft., and 38 feet above the water, resting on 6 piers of dressed stone,—by a joint stock company, to which the state also subscribed $40,000, at the cost of $95,249. Above Allegheny town about a mile, and on the same side of the river, is the town of Manchester. The Northern Liberties of Pittsburg and Bayardstown, are on the city side of the river, and are closer suburbs.

In 1810 the population of the city of Pittsburgh was about 5000, in 1820, 7248, and the census of 1830 gives to the city proper, 12,542; to Pitt t-ship, in which it lies, 3924; to the borough of Allegheny town, 2801; and to the borough of Birmingham, 520; Bayardstown borough, 2125. During part of the period between 1817 and 1824, this city suffered much from the general stagnation of business, and extensive bankruptcy which prevailed. But since the latter year its prosperity has been wonderful, and bids fair to continue.

The commercial importance of Pittsburg is very great, and the additional facilities of transportation which modern improvements have created, seems to assure an enormous and indefinite increase of business here. By the canal on the Allegheny and Conemaugh rivers, it penetrates central Pennsylvania W. of the Appalachian system, and by the rail road across the mountains and the canal of the Juniata, it reaches to the Susquehannah and the richest counties of the state E. of the mountains, and thence to the sea board. By the Monongahela r. and by the Ohio and Potomac canal, it is connected with the S. part of the state; and with Maryland and Virginia and the seat of the federal government. By the Ohio r. it carries on an active trade with the western states and New Orleans, and by the proposed canals N. and N. W., it may attain a large share of the business of New York, of the state of Ohio, and the N. W. country generally.

There is one bank established at Pittsburg by the state, with a capital of $346,155, and a branch of the bank of the U. S. Insurance against water and fire is commonly made by agents of eastern companies.

The manufactures of this city have already given it much celebrity, both abroad and at home. They first excited attention about the year 1810, and have since, though occasionally depressed by the changes in the general business of the country, continued to grow into their present importance. The vast quantities of coal in the surrounding hills, and the great supplies of iron obtained from the region W. of, and particularly along the mountains, rendered now more accessible by the state canals and the admirable position of the city for commercial enterprize, have made it a vast assemblage of manufacturing establishments, which day and night roll up immense volumes of smoke, darkening the very heavens, and discoloring every object, the houses and their inhabitants. Here are many and extensive forges, rolling and slitting mills, and foundries, supplied with the bars and blooms of Centre, Mifflin, and Huntingdon counties, in the very centre of the state, and from the counties more west. Here are cast ploughs, mill machinery, stoves, cannon and cannon balls; here is constructed a vast number of steamboats with their engines, and employment is given to several thousand artisans, in iron and wood, connected with this great manufacture. Here are 6 or 8 extensive glass manufactories, whose products have been admired in every part of the union, but particularly in the towns S. and W. and N. of Pittsburg. Here are many and extensive cotton and woollen manufactories, paper mills, saw and grist mills, distilleries, &c. &c., all set in motion by steam, raised at the cheapest rate, by coal which costs little more than the price of digging and a short cartage. Between 5 and 6000 wagons arrive here annually from the east, loaded with merchandize for the west; whilst the quantity of flour, whiskey, lumber, and salt, &c. &c., which is brought by the road, the canals and the rivers, for exportation by the Ohio, is immense. It is calculated that thirty millions of feet of plank descend the Allegheny alone, from the pine forests on the sources of that river. The products of the manufactories of Pittsburg certainly much exceed the annual value of $2,000,000.

Within the last two or three years, steamboats have been constructed to ply upon the Allegheny & Monongahela rivers, and during the season of the year when the waters are full, a regular communication, we believe, is maintained with the towns on the former river, as high as Warren. The state canal, which follows the right bank of the Allegheny river, from the mouth of the Kiskiminitas, crosses the river by an aqueduct, at Allegheny town, and by a tunnel through Grant's hill, and communicates by an outlet lock, with the Monongahela river.

Turnpike roads from N., S., E., & W., communicate between the city and the adjacent country. The town is supplied with water by means of steam engines, and the fluid is distributed from an elevated reservoir, thro' the streets by iron pipes. The councils have authorized a company to light the streets, &c. by gas.

The Pittsburg academy was established in 1787, and 5000 acres of land were granted by the state in aid of the institution. It continued to thrive until 1819, when more extensive means of education being required, the legislature incorporated, by act of 18th Feb., 1819, the "Western University of Pennsylvania," to be located at, or near Allegheny town, and authorized the trustees of the academy to convey to the university all their estate, real and personal, and at the same time granted to the latter 40 acres of vacant lands belonging to the commonwealth, bounded by, or adjoining the outlots of Allegheny town. But some difficulty as to title has prevented this grant from being wholly operative. Since that period, in 1826, the legislature has given to the university from the state treasury, $9600. By aid of these donations, and the liberality of individuals, the trustees have been enable to erect on Grant's hill, on the Monongahela side of the town, suitable buildings for the institution. The university is under the direction of the Rev. Dr. Bruce, as president. It has 4 academical instructers, and about 50 students.

The city and its vicinity are well provided with schools, and there is a noted boarding school for young ladies a few miles from Pittsburg, on Braddock's fatal field. There are several political, commercial, and religious papers published in Pittsburg. But a taste for literature is not much diffused, nor very active.

Religious institutions. There are in Pittsburg proper, exclusive of the suburbs, 1 Baptist, 2 Presbyterian, 2 Methodist, 1 Episcopal, and 2 Roman Catholic churches, including the large cathedral on Grant's hill; 1 Covenanter's, 1 Seceder's, 1 German Reformed, 1 Unitarian, 1 Associate Reformed, 1 Lutheran, and 1 African, beside 2 Protestant churches lately erected, making in all, 16 places of public worship. The cathedral, according to the proposed design, when completely finished, will be an ornament not only to the city, but to the U. S.

The "Western Theological Seminary," established by Presbyterians, is located at Allegheny town. The edifice for the institution is beautifully situated on an insulated knoll, about 100 ft. above the level of the river. The main building is 4 stories high, and the wings 3. It is in length 100 ft., and contains 100 rooms, destined each for a single student. There are also commodious rooms for a library, which, by donations from Scotland and from individuals in this country, is already respectable. There were about 30 students here in 1832.

Bible, missionary, and tract societies are duly established, and the institution of a temperance society has had very beneficial effects.

A mineral spring has lately been discovered on the farm of John S. Scully, Esq., in St. Clair t-ship, 4 miles S. W. of the city, to which the name of the Pittsburg mineral spring has been given. It issues from the fissure of a rock, on the side of a small hill, and discharges about a gallon of water per minute, which is conveyed through a tunnel into a reservoir, from which it is pumped to supply the bath house. The water in the spring, when undisturbed for a few hours, is covered with a thin white pellicle, which after some time, assumes an iridescent appearance. It then falls to the bottom and is renewed if the water is not disturbed, as may be more particularly observed every morning.

When the water is first taken from the spring, its appearance in a glass is perfectly clear, its taste is lively and rather pungent, with a peculiar ferruginous flavor, and an odor which has some resemblance to the scourings of a gun barrel, and which is easily recognized as arising from an impregnation of sulphuretted hydrogen gas. If the water be suffered to remain for some hours in a glass, it loses in some degree, its transparency, as well as its lively and pungent taste; numerous air bubles are extracted from it, and a light deposit takes place on the inside of the glass. Vessels which are constantly used, become lined with an ochrey incrustation, which is with difficulty removed, and the bottoms and sides of the well, as well as the substance over which the water flows, have a sediment of the same nature. The temperature of the spring is nearly the same at all seasons of the year. In August, when the temperature was at 85 in the air, that of the water was only 54. Its specific gravity, when compared with distilled water, is as 1002 to 1000. Dr. Mead reports, after due examination, this water to contain muriate of soda, 2 parts; muriate of magnesia, ½; oxide of iron, 1; and sulphate of lime ½; carbonic acid gas in 1 quart, 18 cubic inches; and he recommends it for all purposes in which chalybeates are generally given.

A bed of marble, of the species called bird's eye, has been discovered about 6 ms. from the city, and 1½ from the canal; it cuts smoothly, takes a fine polish, and is well adapted for ornamental purposes.

The corporate powers of the city are vested in a select council of 9 members, three of whom are elected annually, and serve 3 years; a common council of fifteen members elected yearly; a recorder, and 12 aldermen appointed by the governor, and holding their offices during good behavior; a mayor elected annually by the select and common councils, from among the aldermen, and a mayor's court composed of the mayor, recorder, and aldermen, or any four of them.

The coal around the city lies in strata of from 6 inches to 10 or more feet in depth, and is found in the hills which overlook the town, at the height of 300 ft. above the bed of the rivers.

Pittston, t-ship, Luzerne co., bounded N. by Exeter and Providence, N. E. by Providence, S. E. by Covington, S. W. by Wilkesbarre t-ships, and W. and N. W. by the Susquehannah, which separates it from Kingston and Exeter.

It has 3 p-offices, and contains 1017 inhabitants, and by the returns of 1828, 179 taxables. Its greatest length is 10 miles, greatest width 9 miles; area, 48,000 acres. Its form is not regular. The village of Pittston is a p-town.

Pittston, a p-t., at the junction of the Lackawannock and Susquehannah rivers, 9 ms. N. E. of Wilkesbarre, in Pittston t-ship, Luzerne co. It contains some 20 dwellings, a store and a tavern, and a church. It is distant from W. C. 23 ms., and from Harrisburg 124. There is another p-o. at Pittston ferry, about a mile from the village.

Plainfield, t-ship, Northampton co., bounded N. by Hamiltón, S. by Forks, E. by Lower Mount Bethel, W. by Bushkill t-ships. Greatest length, 9½ ms., greatest breadth, 2 ms. It is drained by the east branch of the Bushkill creek. Surface, level, except the northern part, which is crossed by the Blue mtn.; soil, gravel. Pop. in 1830, 1285; taxables in 1828, 233. The northern turnpike from Easton, passes through the t-ship.

Plank Cabin valley, Union t-ship, Huntingdon co., in the S. part of the t-ship, and on the N. of Broad Top mtn.

Plainsville, p-o., Exeter t-ship, Luzerne co., 227 ms. N. W. from W. C., and 119 from Harrisburg.

Pleasant Unity, p-t. of Unity t-ship, Westmoreland co., on the S. side of the Big Sewickly creek, 8 miles S. W. of the borough of Greensburg, 189 N. W. from W. C., and 167 S. W. from Harrisburg; contains 20 houses, 3 stores, and 1 tavern.

Pleasant hill, p-o., in Delaware co., 125 ms. from W. C., and 86 from Harrisburg.

Pleasant valley, p-t. of Springfield t-ship, Bucks co., 17 ms. N. of Doylestown, 179 from W. C., and 109 from Harrisburg, consisting of a store, tavern, a few dwellings, and a German church.

Pleasantville, p-o., Montgomery t.ship, Montgomery co., 172 ms. N. E. of W. C., and 99 E. of Harrisburg.

Plumb, t-ship, Venango co., bounded N. and N. W. by Crawford co., E. by Cherry Tree t-ship, S. and S. E. by Oil Creek t-ship, and S. W. by Sugar Creek t-ship. Centrally distant N. of Franklin borough 10 ms. Greatest length 9 ms., breadth 8 ms.; area, 32,000 acres; surface, hilly; soil, rich loam. Pop. in 1830, 430; taxables, 71. French creek flows southward through the t-ship, receiving several tributaries from it, upon one of which, is the small hamlet called Cooperstown, containing some 4 or 5 dwellings, store, and tavern.

Plumb run, Adams co., a tributary of Rock creek, on the line between Strabane and Mount Pleasant t-ships. There is another stream in the same county, called Plumb creek, which rises and has its course in Conewago t-ship, and is a tributary of the Conewago creek.

Plumb Creek, t-ship, Armstrong co., bounded N. by Wayne t-ship, E. by

Indiana co., S. by Crooked creek which separates it from Allegheny t-ship, and W. by Kittanning t-ship. Centrally distant S. W. from the borough of Kittanning 11 ms.; greatest length, 11; breadth, 7½ miles; area, 40,960 acres; surface hilly, rolling; soil, loam, composed of limestone, sand, clay, &c. Pop. in 1830, 1456; taxables, 262. Plumb creek, which gives name to the t-ship, rises in Indiana co., and flows S. W. about 15 miles to Crooked creek. The turnpike road from Indiana to Kittanning runs N.W. through the t-ship, and on it, within two miles of the E. boundary, lies the post town of Middletown.

Plumstead, t-ship, Bucks co., bounded N. by Tinicum, E. by the Delaware, S. E. by Solebury, S. by Buckingham, S. W. by Doylestown and New Britain, and N. W. by Bedminster t-ships. Central distance from Philadelphia N. 30 ms.; from Doylestown 6 miles; greatest length, 6½; breadth, 4 miles; area, 16,738 acres; surface, hilly; soil, sandy loam. Pop. in 1830, 1849; taxables, 402. It is watered by Tohickon creek, Slut's run, the north branch of the Neshaminy creek, and Pine run. The villages of Danville and Dyerstown lie in the southern angle, and within two miles of the former, is a church. A post office is established near the centre of the N. W. boundary line.

Plumb, t-ship, Allegheny co., bounded N. by the Allegheny river, E. and S. E. by Westmoreland co., S. by Versailles t-ship, and W. by Wilkins t-ship. Centrally distant E. from Pittsburg 14 miles; greatest length, 11; breadth, 7 miles; area, 30,720 acres; surface, hilly; soil, loam. Pop. in 1830, 1724; taxables, 356. Pokono creek is on the N. E., Plumb creek on the N. W., Turtle creek on the S. E. and S., and Thompson's run on the S. W. The turnpike road to Pittsburg runs W. through the t-ship.

Plumb creek. (See preceding article.)

Plymouth, t-ship, Luzerne county, bounded N. E. by Kingston and Dallas t-ships, S. E. by the Susquehannah which separates it from Wilkesbarre, Hanover and Newport, S. W. by Union, and N. W. by Lehman and Dallas. That part of Plymouth which lies in the valley of Wyoming, consists mainly of the richest alluvial soil. A great part of its surface is mountainous; but its mountains are generally of gentle acclivity, and will admit of cultivation. The Plymouth coal mines have been worked to a greater extent, and with more judgement and skill than any other in the valley. It has two post offices, and contains 1798 inhabitants, and by the return of 1828, 197 taxables. The Shawnese range of mountains pass through it from east to west, having an altitude in some parts of 860 feet above the river. The township is drained by Harvey's and Toby's creeks. Nanticoke falls in the Susquehannah, are near the western boundary. Kingston is partly in the township, and Shawney and Plymouth are villages on the banks of the river, about its centre. It is irregularly shaped, its greatest length being nine miles, and greatest breadth five miles.

Plymouth, village and post town, Plymouth t-ship, Luzerne co., pleasantly situated on the bank of the Susquehannah river, about four miles S. W. of Wilkesbarre.

Plymouth, t-ship, Montgomery co., bounded N. by Whitpaine, E. by Whitemarsh, S. by the river Schuylkill and W. by Norriton t-ships; greatest length, 4 ms.; greatest breadth 3 miles; area, 6,720 acres. Central distance from Philadelphia 14 miles; surface, rolling; soil, limestone. The township is famed for the quantity and excellent quality of its lime, and for its marble, with which it supplies the surrounding country and the Philadelphia market. It is principally inhabited by Quakers, who have a meeting house near its eastern boundary, between the Ridge and Germantown turnpikes, which run through the t-ships, around which a little village, containing ten or twelve houses, two stores, and a boarding school for females, has been constructed. Pop. in 1830, 1091 ; taxables in 1828, 228.

Pohopoko mountain. (See Pokono mountain.)

Pohopoko creek, rises in Tobyhanna t-ship, Northampton co., and flows southerly to a junction with Head's creek, in Towamensing t-ship, where the united streams form the "*Big creek.*"

Pocopson creek, a tributary of the Brandywine river, rises in Newlin t-ship, Chester co., and flows easterly five miles to its recipient. It has several mills upon it.

Point, t-ship, Northumberland co., bounded N. partly by Chilisquaque t-ship, and partly by Columbia county, which also bounds it on the east, S. by the north branch, and W. by the west branch of the Susquehannah river. Centrally distant N. of Sunbury about five miles; greatest length, 11½ ms.; breadth, 4 miles ; area, 1,704 acres ; surface, very hilly ; soil, alluvial and gravel. Pop. in 1830, 987 ; taxables, 327. Montour's ridge fills a greater part of the t-ship. Lodge's run crosses it centrally into the west branch. The borough of Northumberland lies in the forks of the Susquehannah, and is the post town.

Point Pleasant, post town of Tinicum t-ship, Bucks co., on the river Delaware and on the lower road to Easton, about 14 miles N. E. from Doylestown, 177 from Washington, and 126 from Harrisburg ; contains eight or ten houses, store and tavern.

Poketos creek, rises in Washington t-ship, Westmoreland co., and flows N. W. about nine miles to the Allegheny river, forming the N. E. boundary of Plumb t-ship, which it divides from Westmoreland.

Pokono, township, Northampton co. bounded northeast by Pike co., S. E. by Hamilton and Stroud t-ships, S.W. by Chesnut Hill, and N. W. by Tobyhanna t-ships. It has its name from the Pokono mountain, which extends centrally across it. Greatest length, 12 miles ; greatest width, 7 ms. ; surface, mountainous ; soil, gravel and barren. Pop. in 1830, 564 ; taxables in 1828, 94. It is drained by the west branch of Broadhead's creek and by Sullivan's, Pokono and McMichael's creeks. The post office of the t-ship called Mount Pokono is 221 miles N. E. from W. C., and 122 from Harrisburg.

Pokono mountain, is the second in range and parallel to the Blue mountain, and distant from it from 7 to 10 miles. It is more broken and irregular than the Blue mtn., and bears several local names. Near the Lehigh river it is called Pohopoko, west of the river for several miles the Mahoning, and in another part on both sides of the Lehigh it is without a name. It crosses and gives name to a township in Northampton county.

Pokono creek, rises in the Pokono mountain, and flows easterly through several townships, and by Stroudsburg to the Delaware, a short distance above Dutotsburg, and turns many mills in its course.

Pond creek, a stream of Covington t-ship, Luzerne co., which rises north west of, and flows through Beaver lake, by a course of about 4 miles, into the Lehigh river.

Port Carbon, Norwegian t-ship, Schuylkill county, a post town and village, which has been created by the coal trade. It was laid out in the spring of 1829, and has been enlarged by additions made by Messrs. Lawton, Rhoads, Swift, Pott, Patterson and McCoombs. At that period there was a single house on the site, completely surrounded with woods. At the time of taking the census in 1830, it contained about one hundred dwelling houses, 912 inhabitants, several stores and taverns. In the syncope which followed the extreme excitement in the coal region, many of the houses are at present, 1832, without tenants ; some of them unfinished, and falling to decay. But the site has many advantages for a town and as the shipping port for a large and rich coal region, must have considerable business. It lies at the confluence of Mill creek with the Schuylkill river, and upon the head of the navigation of the latter. The pool here gives great facilities for lading places, which are connected with the coal mines on both sides of the river, by rail ways; the chief of which are, the Mill creek road, and the Schuylkill valley road. The former extends up Mill creek about 4 miles, and has cost about 4000 dollars. It has connected with it about three miles of lateral roads which cost about $2000 per mile. The latter terminates at Tuscarora, a distance of 10 ms. There are 15 lateral roads which intersect it, making together about 10 miles more. The main branch cost 55,000 dollars, and the laterals are estimated at about 20,000 dollars. Among the buildings at Port Carbon, the seat of Mr. Lawton, and the warehouse of Messrs. Wetherill and Swift, are worthy of attention. A daily stage passes from Pottsville through Port Carbon, by the way of the Schuylkill valley rail road, by Tamaqua to Mauch Chunk. Nineteen miles of this route are by rail roads. (See Schuylkill valley and rail road.) The town is ten miles by the road N. E. of Orwigsburg; 177 from W. C., and 69 from Harrisburg.

Port Clinton, a post town laid out in 1829, in Brunswick t-ship, Schuylkill co., at the confluence of the Little Schuylkill with the main stream, above the Water gap in the Blue mountain. The Little Scuylkill rail road extends from this place along the river N. E. about 23 miles into the coal fields of the Tuscarora and Mauch Chunk mountain, and the Schuylkill canal runs thro' the town. Its increase and prosperity depend on the progress of the coal trade in this quarter. The country around it is mountainous and sterile. The town is 7 miles S. E. from Orwigsburg, 160 N. from W. C., and 60 E. from Harrisburg.

Port Lyon, now called Dauphin, a village on the Susquehannah river, at the mouth of Stoney creek, in Middle Paxton t-ship, Dauphin co., about 8 miles N. of Harrisburg, contains 12 dwellings, 2 stores, a tavern and post office. (See Dauphin.)

Port Johnson, a small town in the north angle of Derry t-ship, at the confluence of the Conemaugh and Loyalhanna rs., nearly opposite to Saltzburg, and 16 miles N. E. of Greensburg. Salt springs are found on both sides of the Conemaugh river.

Port Royal, post village of South Huntingdon t-ship, Westmoreland co., on the right bank of the Youghiogheny river, 16 miles S. W. of Greensburg; contains 3 or 4 dwellings and a store.

Porter, t-ship, Huntingdon county, bounded N. E. by West t-ship, E. by Henderson t-ship, S. E. by Union t-ship, S. W. by Hopewell, W. by Woodbury, and N. W. by Morris t-ships. Centrally distant west from Huntingdon borough 5 miles; greatest length 16, breadth 9 miles; area, 17,920 acres; surface, mountainous; soil, alluvial in valleys. Pop. in 1830, 1132; taxables, 220. The Raystown branch of the Juniata river flows between Terrace mountain and Allegripus ridge, in the south west part of the t-ship; and the Frankstown branch through the north, and on the east line, uniting about three miles below the town of Smithfield, which lies on the west bank of the latter, opposite to Huntingdon; from which a turnpike road leading to Frankstown runs N. W. over Warrior ridge by the town of Alexandria. McConnelsburg lies at the S. W. foot of that ridge, and Hartslog valley runs N. between that ridge and Tussey's mountain, on the west boundary of the t-ship. Vineyard creek flows N. E. between Warrior and Allegripus ridges. There were in the t-ship in 1828, 1 grist mill, 3 saw mills, 6 distilleries, 1 tanyard and 1 carding machine.

Portersville, post town, Butler county, 252 miles from W. C., and 220 from Harrisburg, in Muddy Creek t-ship; contains 8 or 10 dwellings, 1 tavern and 1 store.

Potter county was formerly part of Lycoming, and was separated from it by act of assembly of 26th March, 1804. It is yet unorganized for judicial purposes. The act which separated it from Lycoming re-annexed it to that county for judicial and elective purposes. But the act of 27th March, 1824, which organized McKean county for judicial purposes, annexed Potter to that county, to which it is now appurtenant.

The county lies within the great western geological formation, and has the same surface, soil and minerals which characterize Western Pennsylvania. It consists of high and extensive table land, deeply indentated by the channels of the waters, which, rising near the centre of the county, flow from it in all directions. The Allegheny has its source here and flows N. W. through McKean county into New York. The primary springs of the Tioga river send forth their streams also into New York, whilst the Genesee river, supplied by Rose lake, drains the intermediate space, and pursues its course northward to lake Ontario. Pine creek, Kettle creek, the Sinnemahoning and the Drift wood branches of the west branch of the Susquehannah river flow southward. But the first creek flows eastward from this into Tioga co. The country is yet almost a desert, there being scarce an inhabitant for every six hundred acres of its area. The population is much scattered, and depends still in some measure for subsistence on the game of the forest; so much, indeed, that in 1828 the citizens petitioned the legislature to prohibit by law all persons except actual residents, or the holders of lands, houses or tenements, in the county, from killing deer therein,—a request which, on sound and general principles, was refused. The soil is universally loam, mingled, in the valleys of the rivers, with much vegetable mould. And the timber, consisting of oak, walnut, sugar maple, beach, white pine, &c. is abundant and large. Coal and iron are found in many places.

The population amounted in 1810 to 29 souls only; in 1820, to 186, and in 1830, to 1265. The returns do not apportion this sum among the several t-ships. Taxables in 1828, 247. The value of taxable property was estimated by the assessment of 1829, seated lands at $40,289; unseated lands at $431,931; and personal property including occupations at $4,397.

Coudersport, the county town, and the only town of the county, does not contain more than a dozen dwellings of every description. So little indeed is the county known or visited, that its very representatives in the assembly have scarce traversed it. It forms a part of the 9th congressional district, composed of the counties of Union, Northumberland, Columbia, Luzerne, Susquehannah, Bradford, Lycoming, Potter and McKean. With Lycoming, Centre, Clearfield and Mc Kean it constitutes the 13th senatorial district, sending one member to the senate; and with Lycoming and Mc Kean it sends two members to the house of representatives. McKean and Potter counties for judicial purposes, form but one county, and by the act of 27th March, 1824, they are annexed to the 13th judicial district, of which Susquehannah, Bradford and Tioga counties form the remaining part. The courts are directed to be holden on the Mondays next following the week in which the courts are held in the county of Tioga.

Authority has been given for making a turnpike road across the county from Centre county, and through the t. of Coudersport. The county is divided into five t-ships, viz. Eulalia, Wharton, Harrison, Sweden, and Roulet.

This county paid into the state treasury, in the year 1831, for tavern licenses $9 50, and for duties on dealers in foreign mdze. $19.

Potter, t-ship, Centre co., bounded N. by Miles t-ship, N. E. by Hains t-ship, S. E. by Juniata co., S. W. by Ferguson t-ship, and N. W. by Spring t-ship. Centrally distant S. E. from Bellefonte 10 miles; greatest length 11, breadth 10 miles; area, 53,760 acres; surface, mountainous; soil in the valleys, limestone. Pop. in 1830, 1872; taxables, 372. The turnpike road from Lewistown to Bellefonte runs northwest through the t-ship, upon which is a post office at Potter's mills, in George's valley, and another in Penn's valley, near Earleysburg; distant from W. C. 178 miles, and from Harrisburg 71.

Potts Grove, post village of Chilisquaqe t-ship, Northumberland co., near the Chilisquaque creek, 8 miles N.W. of Sunbury, 174 from W. C., and 67 from Harrisburg; contains some 12 or 15 dwellings, store and tavern.

Potts Grove, t-ship, Montgomery county, bounded N. E. by Douglass and New Hanover t-ships, S. E. by Limerick, south by the river Schuylkill, W. and N. W. by Berks county. Greatest length 5½ miles, main breadth 4 miles; area, 11,692 acres. It is watered by the Manntawny creek, which flows through its south west angle by Sprogel's run and other small streams. Potts Grove village and post town lies on the Reading turnpike road, and near to the Schuylkill river, 36 miles from Philadelphia, besides which there is a small village in the t-ship, called Glasgow. Surface, hilly; soil, red shale. Pop. in 1830, 1302; taxables in 1828, 252.

Potts Grove or Pottstown, borough and p-town, Potts Grove t-ship, Montgomery county, on the Reading turnpike road and near the river Schuylkill, 37 miles north west of Philadelphia, and 20 from Norristown, 163 N. E. from W. C., and 68 E. from Harrisburg. This village is beautifully situated, principally on one broad street. The houses are of stone, brick and frame, and surrounded by gardens. The Manatawny creek at the west end of the town drives some excellent flour mills, and the Schuylkill canal affords the means of obtaining grain in abundance, and of transporting the flour to market. There are in the town between 80 and 100 dwellings, 1 mill, 4 stores, 4 taverns and 2 churches. Pop. in 1830, 676; taxables in 1828, 141. The t. was incorporated by act of assembly of 6th Feb. 1815.

Pottsville, post town and borough, Norwegian t-ship, Schuylkill county. This very handsome town has become famous by the extraordinary rapidity of its growth, and the great extent of speculation connected with it and its vicinity. In 1824, the site of the town had but 5 houses erected upon it. In 1828 the number had increased to 75, and in June 1831, it was 535, of which there were 62 brick, 68 stone, and 405 frame; seventy stores, of various kinds. The public buildings consist of an Episcopal church, a meeting house, and a banking house for the "Miners' bank." The front of the latter is constructed of cast iron. There are several commodious taverns, and two very large and convenient hotels; the one erected by Mr. Seilzinger, and the other by Col. Shoemaker. And at Mount Carbon, which is a suburb and the port of the town, there 20 or 30 dwellings, several large and convenient warehouses. A large and elegant hotel, and range of stores, three stories high. Many of the buildings are very costly, and most of them neat. The town was incorporated by act of 19th February, 1828.

The town of Pottsville, embracing Mount Carbon, which has been principally improved by Mr. J. White, and Morrisville, an intervening cluster of buildings, commences in a gorge of the Sharp mountain, through which the Schuylkill river finds its way. The central turnpike road which ran along the west side of the pass, furnished a ready paved street; but sites for dwellings on a part of the road could be obtained only by digging into and levelling the mountain, or by walling on the precipitous bank of the river. Above Mount Carbon, the ravine widens and gives a more commodious space for building between the Western hill and the Norwegian creek, which empties here into the Schuylkill river; and the hill itself sinks so as to admit streets to be laid out and buildings to be erected upon it. Between the forks of the streams is a flat of land which rises gently from water for a short distance, but soon attains a bolder swell. Upon the Norwegian creek a considerable street is lined with buildings, but on the Schuylkill side, the buildings are more scattered, and the streets undefined.

At Mount Carbon there is a dam thrown across the river, by which a very convenient pool is obtained for lading the boats that ply on the canal. Above the dam a bridge is thrown over the pool ; above the bridge the canal divides. The east branch winds around the foot of the Sharp mountain and strikes the river some distance above Port Carbon ; the west branch is about 200 yards in length before it enters the river. From this dam the "Mount Carbon rail road" proceeds.

That road was projected as an outlet for the rich coal formations of the Norwegian creek valleys. The east and west branches of this stream rise at the foot of Mine hill, which is itself a vast body of coal, about a mile and a half apart, running parallel to it for a short distance. Thence they have a southerly course at right angles with the general bearings of the coal veins, and cutting through their successive hills wind round to their confluence at the head of Pottsville ; from that point the joint streams have a southerly course to the river at Mount Carbon. The distance in a direct line from Mine hill to Sharp mountain is about $3\frac{1}{2}$ miles, the intervening space being filled up by coal hills, which, with their respective vallies, may be compared to the waves of the sea, suddenly arrested in their course. Each of these hills contain one or more seams of coal, averaging eight feet in thickness, every cubic yard yielding a ton weight.

The rail road was commenced in October, 1829, by an incorporated company, and finished in September, 1831. It has 18 feet surface width, occupied by two tracks from the head of both branches to the main line, and thence to the landings at MountCarbon, where a third track is added to facilitate the turning off to the respective places of shipment. Each track is 4 feet $8\frac{1}{2}$ inches wide, with a horseway in the centre, strewed with broken stone. At every 8 feet, a drain 18 inches in depth, filled with broken stone, crosses to the side ditches ; the stone forming a bed on which the sleepers or tyes rest. On the sleepers, which are of oak, cheek blocks or cradles of the same material are treenailed, in which the rails rest, and are securely wedged, being thereby elevated above the part of the sleeper which crosses the horseway. In some places however the cheeks and sleepers form one piece. The rails are also of oak, and on the main line, on both tracks, are 6 inches by 10, and are also of that size on the heavy track on the branches ; but on the light or ascending track of the latter, the rails are 6 inches by 8. The rails are shod with iron bars 2 inches wide by three eighths in thickness, bevelled on the edge and having the nail holes counter sunk. Near the termination of the road at Mount Carbon it is supported on stone piers, above the landings. At this point there are on the left, the mines of Messrs. Morris ; and on the opposite side of the river, on the "Lippencott and Richards" tract, the mines wrought by Mr. Baraclough. The road here leaves the Schuylkill at its junction with the Norwegian creek; streching up the valley of the latter and crossing its stream several times, it runs parallel with the Greenwood improvements, directly through Pottsville to the forks, a distance of 6,208 feet from the piers. Below the forks are the mines of Mr. McKechney,and several openings on land belonging to D. I. Rhoads, Esq.

On the east branch, which is 14,200 feet in length, the first lateral above the forks belongs to the North American company,and leads to their Centreville collieries,where they have twelve openings upon the celebrated Lewis and Spohn veins. The coal obtained here is in high estimation, and has greatly aided in establishing the reputation of the Schuylkill anthracite in the eastern markets. Beyond this point, the road passes through Benjamin Potts' lands and again strikes the Spohn vein at the east mines of the North American company. The Hillsborough tract is next on the right, on which are several openings; thence the road diverges to the left, through the celebrated "Peach mountain tract" belonging to Mr. John White, and passes five openings made by him. Thence it continues by the "Rose hill tract" of Mr. L. Ellmaker, on which are several mines leased by Messrs. Warners, Wade and others, near the hamlet of Wadesville, a thriving little place laid out by Mr. Ellmaker. Above this town the lateral road from Capt. Wade's mine comes down. The main east branch terminates on the "Flowery field tract" of Messrs. Bonsall, Wetherill and Cummings, which has been extensively worked by several individuals.

The west branch commences at Marysville on the "*Oak hill tract*," and is 16,400 feet in length. On this estate are the mines leased by Messrs. Smith, Hart, Maxwell, Wade, Hall, Dennis, Gallagher and Martin; among which are the celebrated Diamond and Oak hill veins. Here is a commodious and pleasantly situated hotel, kept by Mr. Gallagher, at a sufficient distance from Pottsville for a pleasant excursion. Below Oak hill are the Green park and Clinton tracts, the former belonging to Mr. John White, and the latter to Mrs. Spohn. At Green park, there is one opening, under the direction of Mr. James Dill. Adjoining this is the Belmont estate also of Mr. White; and next the *Thouron tract*, a portion of which has been purchased by Mr. B. Potts,—the Spohn vein passes through it. Contiguous are the Spohn, Lewis, and Duncan estates. The rail road here passes Mr. B. Potts saw mill and extends in a perfectly straight line, a mile in length, nearly to the junction with the main road. This road is constructed in a very substantial manner, at an expense of $11,000 the mile. (*See Schuylkill co., Norwegian t-ship.*)

The prosperity of Pottsville has been dependent in a great measure on the coal trade, the increase of which has been very extraordinary, and is yet progressing, as will appear by the following table of coal shipped to Philadelphia, since the year 1825, viz.

In 1825,	5,000
1826,	16,767
1827,	31,360
1828,	47,284
1829,	79,973
1830,	87,192
1831,	81,854
1832, to June 30,	60,000

Yet as the great proportion of the mining population will be provided for at or near the mines, and most probably through their employers, the increase of the town may not be greatly promoted by the increase of the coal trade. But the citizens have another source of prosperity in view. The Schuylkill navigation, commencing here, forms an important link in the communication between the Delaware and Susquehannah, at Sunbury and Danville, arresting there the descending trade of the north and west branches of the latter river, and forming the channel for the return supplies of the immense country watered by them. A rail road after actual survey, has been deemed practicable, at the cost of $11,400 per mile, and the distance is about 45 miles. An act of assembly was passed in 1826, amended by another of 1828, authorizing the incorporation of a company, for constructing such road, which in point of distance, geographical facilities, ease of construction and convenience for trade, promises advantages said not to be enjoyed by any other route. The distance saved between Sunbury and Philadelphia, by way of Columbia, being 16 miles, and by the Union canal 50 ms. Between Danville by the Columbia rail road 34 miles, and by the Union canal 66 miles. A company for making this road has been formed, and the whole stock is subscribed, and the road is under contract. Pottsville must become the entrepot between the Susquehannah and the Delaware, and its commercial advantages may be greater than its most speculative inhabitants have calculated. Two lines of stages run between Pottsville and Philadelphia daily. A line to Sunbury and Danville, and another by Port Carbon to Tamaqua and Mauch Chunk. Pottsville is eight miles by the road N. W. from Orwigsburg, 175 N. from W. C., and 67 N. E. from Harrisburg.

Powell's creek and valley, Hallifax t-ship, Dauphin co., between Peter's and the Short mtn. They have a S. W. course of about 21 ms. The former enters the Susquehannah r. about 2 ms. N. of its confluence with the Juniata r.

Presq'isle, (*See Erie.*)

Preston, t-ship, Wayne co., situated 30 miles N. E. of Bethany; contains by the census of 1830, 290 inhabitants, and in 1828, 50 taxables; 8 frame houses, 39 log ones, 1 tavern, 1 grist mill, 1 store, 6 saw mills, 14 looms, and 1 school. The t-ship is hilly; soil, gravel and loam, well timbered with white and yellow pine, hemlock, and chestnut. Taxable property in 1829, seated lands, $23,137; unseated, 69,372; personal estate, including occupations, &c., $2853; rate, 4 mills on the dollar.

Pricetown, Ruscomb Manor t-ship, Berks co., 9 miles N. E. of Reading, containing about 25 dwellings, 1 store, 2 taverns and a tannery.

Prospect hill, a lofty eminence of Lower Providence t-ship, Montgomery co., over which the Perkiomen t-pike passes. From its apex, a delightful view is had of the surrounding country, including the Skippack and Perkiomen hills. It is 5 ms. N. W. of Norristown.

Prospect hill, a mountain filling the N. W. angle of Chestnut Hill t-ship, Northampton co.

Prospectville, small village of Muddy Creek t-ship, Butler co., contains 6 or 8 dwellings, 1 tavern and 1 store.

Providence, t-ship, Bedford co., bounded N. by Hopewell t-ship, E. by Bethel and Belfast, S. by Southampton, and W. by Coleraine t-ships. Centrally distant from the town of Bedford, 11 ms; greatest length 13, breadth 12 miles. Area, 80,000 acres; surface, mountainous; soil, gravel. Pop. in 1830, 2209; taxables, 413. The Raystown branch of the Juniata runs E. to the middle of the t-ship, whence it takes a N. W. course. It is traversed by the t-pike road from McConnelstown to Bedford, on which, near the W. boundary, and on the river, is the p-town of Bloody run. The river receives from the t-ship Brush creek, Shaver's creek, and Clear creek.

Providence, t-ship, Luzerne co., bounded N. by Abington and Greene, N. E. by Blakeley, S. E. by Covington, S. W. and S. by Pittston, W. by Exeter, and N. W. by Falls t-ships.

Anthracite coal is found here in abundance, and easily mined. The Lackawannock and the Roaring brook furnish mill power to an indefinite extent, which is already applied to several mills and 1 forge, in the t-ship. And Abbott's and Capous creeks may be applied to like purposes. The Capous range and Moosic mountains form the sides of the valley. The former rising to the height of 1125 ft. The Philadelphia and Great Bend t-pike passes through its northern division, and the Luzerne and Wayne county t-pike has its commencement here. A village called Centreville has been recently laid out upon the r., and is fast improving. It is situated about 17 ms. N. E. from Wilkesbarre, has a p-o.; distant, 238 ms. N. W. from W. C., and 130 from Harrisburg, and contained in 1830, 976 inhabitants. The t-ship has a very irregular shape. Its greatest length E. and W. exceeds 10 ms., and greatest breadth N. and S. is about 6 miles; area, 35,840 acres.

Providence, Upper, t-ship, Montgomery co., bounded on the N. E. by Perkiomen, S. E. by Lower Providence, S. W. by the Schuylkill river, and N. W. by Limerick t-ship. Greatest length N. W. and S. E. 8½ ms., greatest breadth 6 ms.; area, 13,048 acres. The Perkiomen creek separates this t-ship from Lower Providence, and Mingo creek, a small stream, flows near the western boundary. The county poor house is situated in this t-ship, on the bank of the Schuylkill r. The Reading t-pike road runs parallel with, and within a mile of the N. E. line, upon which is a fine stone bridge of several arches, across the Perkiomen creek, at which is a p-o., called Perkiomen Bridge, 150 miles from W. C., 82 from Harrisburg, and 7 from Norristown. The "Trap," a p-t. and small village, lies on the same road, 9 ms. N. W. from Norristown, and 26 from Philadelphia. Surface of the country is hilly; soil, red shale, gravelly loam. Pop. in 1830, 1682; taxables in 1828, 326.

Providence, Lower, t-ship, Montgomery co., bounded N. E. by Perkiomen and Worcester t-ships, S. E. by Norriton t-ship, S. by the r. Schuylkill, and W. by the Perkiomen creek. Greatest length N. and S. 8 miles, breadth 5½ ms. The Perkiomen cr. divides this t-ship from Upper Providence, and the Skippack creek passes through its northern angle to its confluence with the former. The Norristown and Reading t-pike, and the Germantown and Perkiomen t-pike roads unite here, about a mile E. of the Perkiomen creek. There is a lead mine on the E. bank of the Perkiomen creek, from which considerable ore of rich quality has been taken. It is now the property of the Messrs. Wetherill, of Philadelphia. Evansburg, a p-town and small village, lies on the Germantown t-pike, and on the N. E. boundary of the t-ship, 7 ms. N. E. of Norristown, and 24 from Philadelphia. The surface of the t-ship is hilly; the soil red shale, well cultivated and productive. Pop. in 1830, 1193; taxables in 1828, 237.

Providence, Upper, t-ship, Delaware co., bounded N. by Newtown, N. E. by Marple, S. by Nether Providence, W. by Middletown, and N. W. by Edgemont. Centrally distant W. from Philadelphia 13 miles; from Chester 6 ms. north; length 4 ms., breadth 2½; surface, rolling; soil, loam; area in acres, 3840. Pop. in 1830, 748; taxables in 1828, 160. Crum creek forms the eastern, and Ridley creek the western boundary.

Providence, Nether, Delaware co., bounded N. by U. Providence, E. by Springfield, S. E. by Ridley, S. W. by Chester, and W. by Middleton. Centrally distant from Philadelphia 12 ms. W., from Chester 3½ miles N. Length 4, breadth 2 ms.; surface, level; soil, clay, well cultivated and abundantly productive. Pop. in 1830, 747; taxables in 1828, 158. Ridley creek follows the W., and Crum creek the E. boundary, uniting on the S., and thence flowing to the Delaware. There is a p-o. in the t-ship, 124 ms. from W. C., and 92 from Harrisburg.

Pugh town, p-t. and village, Coventry t-ship, Chester co., in the extreme S. W. angle of the t-ship, on French creek, 35 ms. N. W. from Philadelphia, and 12 ms. N. of West Chester, 137 N. E. from W. C., 70 S. E. from Harrisburg.

Punxatawny, p-t. of Young t-ship, Jefferson co., in a fork of the Mahoning creek, from 16 to 20 ms. S. E. of Brookville, 216 ms. N. W. from W. C., and 160 from Harrisburg; contains 15 dwellings, 2 taverns, and a store.

Pusey's creek, a tributary of the Octarara creek, which rises in West Fallowfield t-ship, Chester co., and flows S. W. to its recipient.

Pymatuning, t-ship, Mercer county, bounded N. by N. Salem, E. by Delaware, and S. by Shenango t-ships, and W. by the state of Ohio. Centrally distant N. W. from the boro' of Mercer, 12 ms.; greatest length 8, breadth 6 ms.; area, 30,720 acres; surface, level; soil, clay and loam. Pop. in 1830, 1297; taxables, 203;

taxable property in 1829, real estate, $74,571; personal, 8235; rate, 5 mills to the dollar. The Shenango creek enters the t-ship below the middle of the E. boundary, and crosses it to the S. W. angle, receiving near the centre of the t-ship, the Pymatuning creek, which enters the N. W. angle from the state of Ohio. On the W. side of the Shenango, and on the line separating this from Shenango t-ship, lies the p-town of Sharon.

Quakake creek, Northampton co., rises near the head of Little Schuylkill in Schuylkill co., and running eastwardly through Lausanne t-ship, falls into the Lehigh river at the foot of the Broad mtn., upon the W. side. It is a mountain torrent, on which several mills are built, but it is unnavigable throughout its course.

Quakake valley, Lausanne t-ship, Northampton co., lies between the Broad mtn. and the Spring mtn., and is named from the creek which passes through it.

Quakertown, p-t. and village of Richland t-ship, Bucks co., on the t-pike road from Philadelphia to Bethlehem, 37 ms. N. N. W. from the former, and 15 ms. south from the latter, and 17 ms. N. W. of Doylestown, 172 ms. N. E. of W. C., 86 E. of Harrisburg. It is a small neat town of a single street, containing about 40 dwellings, 2 stores, 3 taverns, and a Quaker meeting house, situated in a rich and thriving settlement.

Quaker hills, a congregation of lofty hills in Perry co., N. of Sherman's cr. in Tyrone and Rye t-ships.

Quaker lake and creek, Silver Lake t-ship, Susquehannah co. The lake is centrally situated in the t-ship, and near the Bridgewater turnpike. It discharges its waters by the creek into Silver creek, whence they flow into Snake creek, a tributary of the Susquehannah r.

Quemahoning creek, Somerset co., rises by two branches, the N. and E. forks in Somerset t-ship, and flows N. E. through, and along Jenner t-ship, into Stoney creek.

Quemahoning, t-ship, Somerset co., bounded N. and E. by Shade and Stoney Creek t-ships, S. by Somerset, and W. by Jenner t-ships. Centrally distant N. E. from Somerset borough, 11 ms.; greatest length 8, breadth 5 ms.; area, 15,360 acres; surface, hilly; soil, light gravel. Pop. in 1830, 1102; taxables, 190; taxable property in 1829, real estate, $480 92; personal, including occupations, 6180; rate of tax, 5 mills on the dollar. Stoney creek bounds it on the E., and McConaughey run, and Quemahoning creek on the W. The t-pike road to Greensburg runs N. W. through the t-ship, on which lies the p-t. of Stoystown near Stoney creek; Higgin's creek, and Well's creek, are tributaries of Stoney creek, which rise in Somerset t-ship, and flow through this t-ship to Stoney creek.

Quigleys's mills, p-o., Centre co., 207 ms. N. W. from W. C., and 100 from Harrisburg.

Quincy, p-o., Franklin co., 83 ms. N. W of Washington, and 58 S. W. of Harrisburg.

Quitapahilla creek, Lebanon co., rises about 2 ms. E. of the borough of Lebanon, and flows a W. and N. W. course of about 14 ms. to the Swatara creek, receiving in its way Furnace creek, Meadow run, and Killinger's run. It forms the connecting link on the Union canal, between the Swatara and the Tulpehocken.

Rabersburg, p-t., Miles t-ship, Centre co., in Brush valley, 16 ms. E. of Bellefonte, 201 N. W. from W. C., and 93 from Harrisburg, contains some 15 or 20 dwellings, store and tavern. The valley possesses a rich limestone soil.

Raccoon creek, East Hanover t-ship, Lebanon co., a small tributary of the Swatara, into which it falls near the western boundary of the co.

Raccoon cr. and valley, and Raccoon ridge, Perry co., rises on the E. border of Saville t-ship, and flows through Raccoon valley N. of Raccoon ridge, and S. of the Tucarora mtn. to the r. Juniata, opposite to Millerstown. The length of the creek, valley and ridge, is about 12 miles.

Raccoon creek, rises in Smith t-ship, Washington co., and flows N. through Hopewell and Moon t-ships, Beaver co., into the r. Ohio.

Raccoon, p-o. Smith t-ship, Washington co., 241 ms. N. W. from W. C. and 219 from Harrisburg.

Radnor, t-ship, Delaware co., bounded N. E. by Montgomery co., S. E. by Haverford and Marple t-ships, S. W. by Newtown t-ship, and N. W. by Chester co. Central distance from Phil., 13 ms N. W.; from Chester, 12 ms. N.; length $3\frac{1}{2}$, breadth $3\frac{1}{4}$ ms.; area, 7680 acres; surface, hilly; soil, loam. Pop. 1830, 1097; taxables in 1828, 257. Darby creek crosses the S. W. angle of the t-ship, and receives from it several considerable tributaries. The Phil. and Lancaster turnpike road traverses it diagonally. There are three houses for public worship, one of which is Radnor church. There is a p-o. at the Spread eagle tavern, on the Lancaster turnpike road.

Ragged mountain, Southampton t-ship, Bedford co.

Rainesburg, p-t., Bedford co., 105 ms. N. W. from W. C. and 113 W. from Harrisburg; contains 20 dwellings, 2 stores and 2 taverns.

Ramy's kill, a mill stream of Upper Smithfield t-ship, Pike co., which flows into the r. Del. about 2 miles above the southern boundary of the t-ship.

Randolph, village of Hempfield t-ship, Westmoreland co., on the turnpike road from Bedford to Greensburg; 3 ms. E. of the latter; contains 12 dwellings, a tavern and store.

Randolph, t-ship, Crawford co., centrally distant about 12 miles E. of Meadville. Pop. in 1830, 561. There is a p-o. here called after the t-ship, 309 miles N. W. of W. C., and 248 from Harrisburg.

Raphoe, t-ship, Lancaster co., bounded N. by Lebanon co., E. by Warwick t-ship, S. by Hempfield and Lampeter, and W. by West Donegal t-ship; centrally distant from Lancaster, 12 ms. N. W. Greatest length, 11; greatest breadth, $6\frac{6}{4}$ ms.; area, 26,367 acres; surface, rolling; soil, limestone, gravel and sand. Pop. 1831, 3430; taxables, 690. The Great and Little Chiques embrace this t-ship on all sides except the N.; the former flowing on the E. and S. E. and the latter on the W., uniting at the S. W. angle. The p-t. of Manheim, lies on the Great Chiques about 10 ms. N. W. of the city of Lancaster. The Lancaster and Harrisburg turnpike road crosses the southern part of the t-ship. There are in the t-ship, one furnace called Mt. Hope, at the head of Big Chiques creek; 23 grist-mills; 6 fulling mills; 8 saw mills; 2 hemp mills, and 6 carding machines.

Rattling creek, Brunswick t-ship, Schuylkill co., flows from the N. side of the Blue mtns. into the Little Schuylkill creek, near the confluence of the latter with the main Schuylkill r.

Rattling gap, p-o., Lycoming co., 218 ms. N. W. of W. C., and 109 from Harrisburg.

Raub's ferry and p-o., Northampton co., Williams t-ship, 6 ms. below Easton, on the road from Easton to Bristol, and on the Delaware r. There is here a dwelling, store and tavern. It is 196 ms. from W. C. and 109 from Harrisburg.

Rawlinsville, p-t. Lancaster co., 95 ms. from W. C., and 51 from Harrisburg.

Rays hill, Bedford co., a mtn. range, running N. E. from the S. boundary of the state to Harbour mtn. in Providence t-ship, a distance of about 22 ms. It forms the boundary between Southampton and Bethel t-ships.

Reading, borough, post and county town, Berks co., situated on the E. bank of the r. Schuylkill, one mile below the mouth of Tulpehocken creek, 54 ms. N. W. of Philadelphia, about the same distance E. of Harrisburg, and 143 N. E. from W. C. Pop. in 1820, 4278; 1830, 5631. The town was laid out in 1748, by Thomas and Richard Penn, proprietaries and governors in chief of the province, and private owners of the ground plot. The plan adopted was that of Lancaster, with some improvements suggested by experience. The streets are spacious, running in straight lines and intersecting each other at right angles. There are five streets running E. and W., and nine running N. and S. The court house stands upon a square in the centre, 200 by 220 feet. There are two semi-annual fairs, beginning the 4th of June and 27th October, and lasting two days; held under a grant by deed of the proprietaries, July 30th, 1766. They are continued to this time under the German appellation of Jahr-Markts, *yearly markets*, though at present they are resorted to only by the country youth of either sex for the purpose of hilarity. The two weekly market days, Wednesday and Saturday, though recognized and re-established by the act of assembly of 1813, have their origin in a grant contained in the deed of the proprietaries above mentioned. The town was erected into a borough by act of assembly, passed in 1783; altered and repealed by an act of 1813, under which it elects a legislative town council and burgesses, whose duty it is to carry the ordinances into effect. Reading contains between seven and eight hundred houses, including a court house, public offices, and jail, and two market houses. There are ten churches or houses of public worship; those of the Lutherans, German Reformed, Episcopalians, Presbyterians, Universalists, Baptists, Quakers, Catholicks and Methodists, and one belonging to the people of color. The town is well provided with houses of public entertainment, most of them spacious and comfortable, and one upon an elegant and extensive scale. The river which is here about six hundred feet wide, is crossed by two substantial covered bridges, of frame work, supported on stone piers and abutments, erected at county expense. The Schuylkill canal, extending from Phil. to Pottsville, passes through the town. The Union canal, connecting the waters of the Schuylkill with the invaluable internal improvements of the state, mingles with that river at Reading, where a dam across the river forms a fine sheet of water, and a convenient harbor for boats. Seated in the heart of a fertile limestone country, on a great turnpike road leading from Philadelphia to the western counties, and enjoying the advantages of two extensive and important canals, both in successful operation, Reading bids fair to become one of the most considerable inland towns in the state. Its present condition is prosperous, and flourishing in a high degree; all its tenements being occupied, and a large annual addition of houses having been found necessary to accommodate its increasing population. It is surrounded by streams affording abundance of water power, and has long enjoyed an extensive trade in flour and grain. Here are two banks and twenty large stores, besides many smaller ones, all which appear to be doing profitable business. The place is celebrated for its manufactures of wool hats, by which a large portion of its industrious inhabitants are maintained, and many considerable fortunes have been realized. It is supposed that from twenty to thirty thousand dozens of hats are made here annually, which go to supply the southern and western markets to a great extent. Among other trades and manufactures are coach makers, cabinet makers, rope makers, shoe makers, brick makers, printers, saddlers, several breweries, two distilleries, black and white smiths, lime burners, a large manufactory of stoneware recently established, and such other handicrafts as the necessities and comforts of a populous town require. Four newspapers are issued weekly in the borough, two in the English and two in the German language. One of the latter, the "Readinger Adler," has been published without intermission for thirty-five years, and is believed to enjoy the largest circulation of any country paper in the state. There are two daily mails between Phil. and Reading, and several daily lines of stages pass through it from Phil. to Harrisburg or Pottsville. Several individuals in and about Reading have applied themselves seccessfully to the cultivation of foreign grapes, and the town is furnished with that agreeable fruit in moderate quantities, from vineyards within its own limits or in its vicinity. Wine also has been made to a considerable amount, and a species of rough claret, known by the name of "Reading red," is not without its admirers in the good town. No town in the Union perhaps surpasses Reading in salubrity and beauty of situation. Standing upon a plateau formed by the depression of magnificent hills towards the river, the town plot is sufficiently level for the purposes of convenience, and elevated enough to prevent the stagnation of water on its surface, forming a just medium between too hilly and too flat. The hills around afford a rich variety of prospects for the lovers of the picturesque. The Blue mountains on the north, at the distance of 17 miles, are distinctly visible, and corresponding hills on the E. and W. form a beautiful amphitheatre, of which the parterre exhibits a succession of well cultivated farms blooming in luxuriant vegetation. On the rise of the mtn. behind the borough is Hampden spring, a copious source of pure water, which has been conducted into the town in iron pipes, at a comparatively small expense, and distributes an abundant supply amongst the inhabitants by means of ordinary hydrants. The pop. of Reading as well as that of the county, consists principally of Germans, well known for habits of economy and persevering industry. The English language, however, is generally spoken, and is taught in nearly all the schools, amounting to about 20 in number. There is besides an academy, in which the Greek and Latin languages are taught, together with mathematics and general literature, a large and handsome edifice, erected with funds granted by the state legislature, and endowed with several thousand acres of unseated land derived from the same source.

Reading, t-ship, Adams co., bounded N. by Latimore t-ship, E. by York co., S. by Hamilton t-ship, and W. by Mount Pleasant, Strabane and Tyrone t-ships. Centrally distant N. E. from Gettysburg 13 ms.; greatest length 8, breadth 6 miles; area, 15,360 acres; surface, level; soil, red shale and slate. Pop. in 1830, 1001; taxables, 159. It is drained on the N. E. by Muddy run, a tributary of the Bermudian creek, and on the W. and S. by the Conewago creek. The t-pike road from Carlisle to Hanover runs S. through the western part of the t-ship. The p-t. of Berlin lies on the S. side of the Conewago creek, near the S. E. angle of the t-ship.

Reamstown, p-t. and village, Cocalico t-ship, Lancaster co., on the road from Lancaster to Reading, 15 ms. from each, 123 from W. C., and 42 from Harrisburg; contains about 40 dwellings, stores and taverns.

Rebersburg. (*See Rabersburg.*)

Reeds run, E. Hanover t-ship, Lebanon co., a small tributary of the Swatara creek.

Reesville, p-o., Upper Merion t-ship, Montgomery county. (*See Merion, Upper.*)

Red Stone creek, Fayette co., rises with many branches in Union t-ship, and flows N. W. between Manallen and Franklin, Red Stone and Washington t-ships, to the Monongahela r. having a course of near twenty ms.

Red Bank creek, Armstrong co., is formed by the union of the Big and Little Sandy Lick creeks, near the E. line of the co., and flows by a W. course of about 12 ms., (in a direct line) through Red Bank and Toby t-ships into the Allegheny r. It is a rapid stream, and has two considerable falls.

Red Bank, t-ship, Armstrong co.,

named from the above mentioned cr., is bounded N. by Clarion t-ship, E. by Jefferson co., S. by Mahoning cr., which divides it from Kittanning and Wayne t-ships, and W. by Toby t-ship. Centrally distant from Kittanning borough N. E. 15 ms. The p-o., bearing the name of the t-ship, is 235 ms. from W. C., and 188 from Harrisburg. It is drained by Red Bank, Mahoning and Beaver creeks, the last a tributary of the Mahoning. Alum is found in the S. W. angle of the t-ship, upon the N. bank of that stream. Greatest length 15, breadth 12 miles; area, 81,920 acres; surface, partly hilly, partly rolling; soil, loam. Pop. in 1830, 1660; valuation in 1829, of seated lands, $57,116; of unseated lands, $26,180; of personal estate, 12,054 dollars.

Red mountain, a high and long hill which crosses from Brunswick t-ship, into West Penn t-ship, Schuylkill co.

Red Clay creek, rises in E. Marlborough t-ship, Chester co., and flows S. E. through Kennet into the state of Delaware. It turns several mills in its course through Pennsylvania.

Red run, Swatara t-ship, Lebanon co., a tributary of the Swatara cr.

Red Run, p-o., Lycoming co., 222 ms. N. W. from W. C., and 113 from Harrisburg.

Red Stone, t-ship, Fayette co., bounded N. by Washington, E. by Franklin and Manallen, S. by German, and W. by Luzerne. Centrally distant from Union Town, about 8 ms. Greatest length 7, breadth 6 ms.; area, 16,400 acres; surface, rolling; soil, limestone and gravel. Pop. in 1830, 1209; taxables, 241. It is drained by Red Stone and Dunlap's creeks, the one on the N. E., and the other on the S. W., flowing N. W. into the Monongahela r. Their mouths are scarce more than a mile asunder, and between them and on the latter, is the p-t. of Brownsville. The national road runs through the t-ship, & through the town.

Rehrersburg, Lower Tulpehocken t-ship, Berks co., p-t., on the road from Reading to Sunbury, about 22 ms. from the former; containing between 40 and 50 houses, 3 taverns, 3 stores, 1 church, Presbyterian and Lutheran. It is distant 148 miles from W. C., and 38 from Harrisburg.

Richboro', p-t. of Bucks co., distant from W. C. 158 ms., and from Harrisburg 126.

Richfield, p-o., Mifflin co., 168 ms. N. W. from W. C., and 61 from Harrisburg.

Rich Valley creek, a branch of Swamp creek, Upper Salford t-ship, Montgomery co.

Rich hill, a noted elevation in the E. part of Warrington t-ship, York county.

Rich hill, t-ship, Green co., bounded N. by Washington co., E. by Morris and Centre t-ships, S. by Aleppo t-ship, and W. by the state of Virginia. Centrally distant from Waynesburg 14 ms.; greatest length 8½, breadth 8 miles; area, 35,840 acres; surface, hilly; soil, loam. Pop. in 1830, 1875; taxables, 329. The t-ship is drained W. by the N. and S. forks of Wheeling creek, and E. by Gray's Fork of Ten Mile creek.

Richland, t-ship, Bucks co., bounded N. by Springfield, E. by Haycock, S. E. & S. by Rockhill, and W. by Milford. Central distance N. W. from Philadelphia 37 ms., from Doylestown 15 ms.; greatest length 5½ ms., breadth 4; area, 14,476 acres; surface, level; soil, clay. Pop. in 1830, 1719; taxables in 1828, 344. It is drained by the Tohickon creek, which has many ramifications in the t-ship. The t-pike road from Philadelphia to Bethlehem passes through the S. W. angle, upon which is situated Quakertown, a village of 40 dwellings, having a p-o., and a Quaker meeting.

Richland, Lancaster co., a small village on the t-pike road from Lancaster to Harrisburg, partly in the t-ship of Donegal and partly in the t-ship of Mountjoy, the road dividing the t ships; 18 ms. N. W. of the city of Lancaster.

Richland, t-ship, Venango co., bounded N. by Rockland, S. by the Clarion r., E. by Beaver Creek t-ship, and W. by the Allegheny r. Centrally distant S. E. from Franklin borough 15 ms.; greatest length 10 miles, breadth 5½ ms.; area, 22,400 acres; surface, hilly; soil, limestone. Pop. in 1830, 692; taxables, 130. The p-t. of Foxburg lies in the extreme southern point of the t-ship, at the confluence of the Clarion and Allegheny rivers, 203 ms. N. W. of Harrisburg.

Richmond, t-ship, Tioga co.; surface, hilly; soil, gravelly. Pop. in 1830, 583; taxables in 1828, 100.

Richmond, small village on the E. bank of the Delaware r., Northern Liberties t-ship, Philadelphia county, about 2 ms. above the city. There are about 20 dwellings here, 2 taverns, and a small store.

Richmond, a p-town in Lower Mt. Bethel t-ship, Northampton co., situated at the head of a small stream to which it gives name, about 2 miles west of the Delaware r. It is on the main road from Easton to the Delaware Water gap, and about 13 ms. from the former place, 203 N. E. from W. C., and 116 from Harrisburg. It contains 20 dwellings, 2 stores, 2 taverns, and 2 tanneries.

Richmond, t-ship, Berks co., bounded N. by Greenwich, S. by Ruscomb-manor, E. by Maxatawny, S. E. by Rockland, S. W. by Maiden creek, N. W. by Windsor t-ships. Its greatest length is 5, and greatest breadth 4 ms.; area, 12,480 acres. Pop. in 1810, 971; in 1820, 1135; in 1830, 1550; taxables in 1828, 268; surface, level; gravel and limestone soil, of good quality, well cultivated; value, from 40 to 60 dollars an acre. Contains 2 churches common to the Lutherans and Presbyterians. Iron ore is found near the border of Maiden Creek t-ship. Hunter's grist mill, furnace and forge, is on Moselem creek, in this t-ship. Coxtown is partly in this t-ship, and partly in Ruscomb-manor.

Richmond, t-ship, Crawford county. Pop. in 1830, 252.

Ridley, t-ship, Delaware co., bounded N. by Upper Darby, E. by Darby, S. by the r. Delaware, W. by Chester and Providence, and N. W. by Springfield. Central distance from Philadelphia, 10 ms.; length 4 miles, breadth 3¼; area, 6400 acres; surface, level; soil, clay. Pop. in 1830, 1058; taxables, 279. Darby creek runs along the S. E. boundary, and Crum creek and Ridley creek form the western line. The Little Crum creek crosses the t-ship from N. to S. centrally. On these streams are large quarries of stone, adapted to building and curbing, and large quantities are annually sent thence to Philadelphia.

Ridley creek rises in E. Goshen t-ship, Chester co., and flows by a S. easterly course of about 18 ms. thro' Delaware co., into the river Delaware.

Ridgebury, p-t-ship, Bradford co., bounded N. by the state of N. Y., E. by Athens t-ship, S. by Springfield, and W. by Wells t-ships. Centrally distant N. W. from Towanda 18 ms.; greatest length 6¼, breadth 6 ms.; area, 23,040 acres; surface, hilly; soil, gravelly loam. Pop. in 1830, 560; taxables, 102. The Susquehannah and Tioga t-pike road runs centrally N. and S. through the t-ship, which is drained by Bently and South creeks, both flowing northwardly into the Tioga river, in the state of N. Y. The p-o. is 261 ms. N. W. from W. C., and 150 from Harrisburg.

Ridgeville, p-t., Greenwood t-ship, Mifflin co., on the S. side of W. Mahantango creek, embosomed by mtns., and on the road from Calhounsville to Selin's grove, about 25 ms. N. E. of Lewistown.

Ridgeway, (named after Jacob Ridgeway, of Philadelphia, who is the owner of large tracts of land here), t-ship of Jefferson co., bounded N. and E. by McKean co., S. E. by Clearfield co., S. by Young t-ship, and W. by Rose t-ship; length 23, breadth 17 ms.; area, 262,040 acres; surface, rolling; timber, oak, and heavy. The t-ship is drained by Toby's creek and

Clarion river, and Kersey's creek, and their tributaries. Ridgeway and Montmorency are p-offices of the t-ship. The former is on Clarion river, distant 25 or 30 ms. N. E. from Brookeville, the county town, 236 from W. C., and 165 from Harrisburg. The latter lies about 6 ms. further from these places.

Ring creek, a mill stream, and tributary of Pickering creek, rises in Vincent t-ship, Chester co., and flows into its recipient in Pikeland t-ship.

Rittersville, p-o., Lehigh co., 181 ms. from W. C., and 88 from Harrisburg.

Rising Sun, village, Philadelphia co. (*See Sunville.*)

Rix's gap, a passage through the Moosic mountain in Canaan t-ship, Wayne co., along which the Milford and Owego t-pike road runs.

Roaring brook or Gulley creek, a tributary of the Lackawannock river, rises in Sterling t-ship, Wayne co., and flows N. W. through Covington and Providence t-ships, by a sinuous course of about 20 ms., cutting the Moosic mtn. in its way. It is a good mill stream, and drives several mills and a forge.

Roaring creek, Big, has 2 branches, one on the N., the other on the S. of Little, Columbia co.

Roaring creek, Little, a small stream which rises in the Shamokin hills, and flows N. through Rush t-ship, Northumberland co., into the Susquehannah about 2 ms. below Big Roaring creek.

Roaring creek, p-o., Roaring creek valley, Catawissa t-ship, Columbia co., 187 ms. from W. C., and 77 from Harrisburg.

Robinson, t-ship, Washington co., bounded N. E. by Allegheny co., S. E. and S. by Cecil t-ship, S. W. and W. by Smith t-ship, and N. W. by Hanover t-ship; centrally distant from Washington bor. N. 16 ms. Greatest length 10, breadth, 3 ms.; area, 14,080 acres; surface hilly, rather rolling; soil, loam. Pop. 1830, 944; taxables, 188. It is drained on the N. by Raccoon creek, on the E. by branches of Chartier's creek and Montour's run. The p-r. from Pittsburg to Steubenville, runs W. through the t-ship.

Robison, t-ship, Allegheny co., bounded N. by the Ohio r., E. by St. Clair t-ship, S. by Fayette and W. by Moon t-ships; centrally distant from Petersburg, 6 ms. N. W. Greatest length, 6½ ms.; breadth, 6 ms.; area, 16,640 acres; surface, hilly; soil, loam. Pop. 1830, 1371; taxables, 233. Chartier's creek is on the S. E. and Montour's run on the W. boundary. The turnpike road from Pittsburg to Steubenville, runs westward through the t-ship.

Robstown, p-t. of South Huntingdon t-ship, Westmoreland co., on the turnpike road from Somerset to Washington, and on the E. bank of the Youghiogheny r. 13 ms. S. W. from Greensburg, 206 from W. C., and 184 from Harrisburg; contains from 60 to 70 dwellings, 3 taverns and 4 stores.

Robinson's run, a large branch of Chartier's creek, flowing centrally and eastwardly through Fayette t-ship, Allegheny co.

Robeson, t-ship, Berks co., bounded N.E. by the Schuylkill r., E. by Union t-ship, and by Chester co., S. by Caernarvon t-ship, W. by Breeknock and N. W. by Cumru t-ship. The Allegheny creek and Hay creek run N. E. through the t-ship into the Schuylkill r. Greatest length, 6¼ ms.; breadth, 5; area, 21,000 acres; surface, hilly; soil, gravelly and sterile. Pop. 1810, 1807; 1820, 2065; 1830, 1970; taxables, 1828, 371. There is a forge on Allegheny creek, and another on Hay creek; and two churches, one pertaining to the Lutherans and the other to the Presbyterians; both centrally situated in the t-ship.

Rock run, on the line of E. Nantmeal and Coventry t-ships, Chester co.; a mill stream and tributary of French creek.

Rock creek, Adams co., divides Cumberland t-ship from Strabane and Mountjoy t-ships, and flows S. into the state of Md.

Rockland, t-ship, Berks co., bounded N. by Maxatawny, N. E. by Long Swamp, S. E. by District and Pike t-ships, S. by Oley, W. by Ruscombmanor, and N. W. by Richmond townships; greatest length, 5 ms.; breadth, 4; area, 12,000 acres. Pop. 1810, 1026; 1820, 1131; 1830, 1342; taxables, 1828, 257. The surface is very hilly; soil, gravel, poor and indifferently cultivated; value from 15 to 20 dolls. per acre. There is one church common to the German Lutherans and Presbyterians. The township contains one furnace and two forges.

Rockhill, t-ship, Bucks co., bounded N. by Richland and Haycock, E. by Bedminster, S. E. by Hilltown, t-ships, S. W. by Montgomery co., and W. by Milford t-ship. Central distance from Phil. N. N. W. 33 ms., from Doylestown 12 ms.; greatest length, 7½ ms.; greatest breadth, 5 ms.; area, 19,618 acres; surface, hilly; soil, gravelly. Pop. 1830, 2012; taxables, 1828, 424. It is drained by a small branch of the Tohickon creek, and by the N. E. branch of the Perkiomen. Sellersville is the p-t., the office is known as "Rockhill" p-o. It is 171 ms. from W. C.; 92 from Harrisburg.

Rockland, township, Venango co., bounded N. by Cranberry t-ship, E. by Elk Creek t-ship, S. by Richland t-ship, and S. W. and W. by the Allegheny r. Centrally distant from Franklin bor., 9 ms.; greatest length, 11½ miles; breadth, 8 ms.; area, 38,400 acres; surface, hilly; soil, rich loam. Pop. 1830, 768; taxables, 126. It is drained N. W. by Six Mile run, S W. by Schull's run.

Rocky ridge, a mountain link in Henderson t-ship, Huntingdon co., rising on the N. bank of the Juniata river, and running N. W. about 11 ms., forming in this t-ship the E. boundary of Kishcoquillas valley.

Rocksville, hamlet of Northampton t-ship, Bucks co., on the road from Smithfield to Newtown, 13 ms. S. E. from Doylestown, contains 3 or 4 dwellings.

Rockdale, t-ship, Crawford co., one of the northern t-ships of the county. Pop. 1830, 225; surface, hilly; soil, loam, well adapted to grass. Is drained by French creek and its tributaries. P-o. is distant 305 ms. from W. C. and 244 from Harrisburg.

Rohrsburg, post-office, Columbia co.

Rome, t-ship, Crawford co. Pop. 1830, 365.

Roseburg, marked as a town in Clarion t-ship, Armstrong co.; there are however not more than two dwellings in it.

Rose, t-ship, a very large t-ship including almost one half of the county of Jefferson; bounded N. by Warren co., E. by Pine Creek and Ridgeway t-ships, S. by Perry t-ship, and W. by Armstrong and Venango counties; length 39, breadth 12 ms.; area, 289,520 acres; surface, hilly; soil, gravelly loam; timber, oak. Pop. 1830, between 6 and 700. It is drained by Toby's creek and Sandy Lick creek, and their branches.

Rose, p-o. Potter co., near Rose lake, so called from the P. M. James Rose; is 298 ms. distant N. W. from W. C. and 192 from Harrisburg.

Roseland, p-o. Cambria co., 182 ms. from W. C. and 124 from Harrisburg.

Ross, township, Northampton co., bounded N. by Chestnut Hill, S. by Moore, Bushkill, and Plainfield, E. by Hamilton, and W. by Towamensing t-ships; greatest length, 9½ ms.; greatest breadth, 6 ms.; surface, on the S. mountainous, on the N. pretty level; soil, limestone and gravel. Pop. 1830, 838; taxables, 1828, 140. It is drained chiefly by the head waters of the Aquanshicola creek, which traverse it in a southwesterly course. The break in the Blue mtn., known as the Wind gap, is in the S. E. angle of the t-ship, through which passes the northern turnpike road from Easton.

Ross town, p-t., Warrington t-ship, York co., about 12 ms. N. W. from York borough, 100 ms. from W. C. and 17 from Harrisburg.

Rosscommon, a p-t., Ross t-ship, Northampton co., 14 ms. from Easton, on the road from that town to Wilkesbarre.

Ross, t-ship, Allegheny co., bounded N. by Pine t-ship, E. by Indiana, S. E. by the Allegheny r., S. W. by the Ohio r., and W. by Ohio t-ship. Centrally distant N. from Pittsburg 4 ms.; greatest length, 7, breadth, 6 ms; area, 23,040 acres; surface, hilly; soil, loam. Pop. 1830, 2196; taxables, 725. The t-ship is drained by Pine creek and its branches, Cirties run, Wood, Spruce and Hawser's runs. The flourishing borough of Allegheny lies in the N. point of the confluence of the Allegheny with the Monongahela river, united to Pittsburg by a bridge, (see Allegheny borough). The p-t. of Perrysville is near the northern line of the t-ship, distant from Pittsburg about 8 miles. The turnpike road from Pittsburg to Butler, runs N. through the t-ship.

Rost Raver, t-ship, Westmoreland co., bounded N. by Allegheny co., E. by the Youghiogheny river, which separates it from S. Huntingdon t-ship, S. by Fayette co., and W. by the Monongahela r., which separates it from Washington co. Centrally distant S. W. from Greensburg, 17 ms.; greatest length, 8, breadth, 7½ ms.; area, 23,680 acres; surface, hilly; soil, limestone. Pop. in 1830, 1721; taxables, 342. The p-office, called after the t-ship, is distant 212 ms. from W. C. and 190 from Harrisburg.

Roulet, t-ship, Potter co., occupying the north west part of the co., contains in length 20 miles N. and S., and 5 miles in breadth E. and W., having an area of 64,000 acres. It is named after Mr. Roulet, an extensive land owner of the county. It has a post office; distance 292 miles N. W. from W. C., and 183 from Harrisburg.

Round top, a noted hill of Warrington t-ship, York co., S. of Stephenson's mountain.

Roush's creek, Berks co., rises in Alsace and flows through Exeter t-ship, in a south easterly course of about 9 miles to the Schuylkill, and turns several mills by its waters.

Roxbury, post town, Lurgan t-ship, Franklin co., on the Conedogwinit creek, on the east side of the Blue mountain, 12 miles N. of Chambersburg and 28 S. W. of Carlisle, 43 from Harrisburg, and 97 from Washington city.

Roxbury, Henderson t-ship, Huntingdon county, contains 6 or 7 dwellings, a church and school, and a smith's shop.

Roxborough, t-ship, Philadelphia co., bounded N.E. by Germantown t-ship, S. E. by Penn t-ship, S. W. and N. W. by Montgomery co. Centrally distant from Philadelphia N. W. 7½ miles; length 5 miles; breadth 2 ms.; area, 5,760 acres; surface, hilly and rocky; soil, clay and loam. Pop. in 1830, 3,334; taxables, 642. The Wissahickon creek enters the t-ship on the N. E. and winds through a valley remarkable for its rugged and picturesque scenery. The Wissahickon or Ridge road turnpike runs N. through the t-ship. There are several mechanics, two or three stores, and several taverns, at one of which 7 ms. from the city, is the post office of the t-ship, called after it. The village of Manyunk, also 7 miles from the city, lies on the river Schuylkill, and the canal which connects the pool of Fair Mount with that of Flat rock. The dam presents a beautiful cascade forming a prominent feature of a very picturesque scene. Below it is a fine bridge over the river. In the N. W. angle of the t-ship near the river is a valuable quarry of soap stone (a variety of the steatite.)

Ruffs creek, Morgan t-ship, Greene co., a tributary of Ten Mile creek, the chief drain of the t-ship.

Rumfield creek, Wysox t-ship, Bradford co., rises in Orwell, but has its chief source in the former t-ship, upon the S. E. line of which it enters the Susquehannah.

Rural valley, post office, Armstrong co., 224 miles from W. C., and 190 from Harrisburg.

Ruscombmanor, t-ship, Berks county, bounded N. and N. W. bv Maiden creek and Richmond t-ships, east by Rockland, S. E. by Oley, S.W. by Alsace. Its greatest length is 4 ms. by 4 in breadth; area, 10,000 acres. Pop. in 1810, 932; in 1820, 1056; in 1830, 1243; taxables in 1828, 250. The surface of the country is very hilly; soil gravelly, poor and indifferently cultivated; value from 15 to 25 dollars per acre; towns Pricetown and Cox'stown.

Rush, t-ship, Schuylkill co., bound. N. E. by Luzerne co., E. by Northampton co., S. by West Penn t-ship, W. and N. W. by Schuylkill t-ship. Its greatest length in a direct line N. W. and S. E. is 15 ms.; mean breadth 7½ miles. Area by estimate, about 62,080 acres. It is mostly covered with mountains and high hills, scarce explored except in its southern section, which has of late acquired much interest, from the anthracite coal mines which it contains. This valuable mineral most probably extends throughout the t-ship, into the Mahanoy and the ridges which form that chain. There are several country roads traversing the t-ship, and the Little Schuylkill rail road penetrates its southern coal fields. There is a salt spring on the west side of the river above the mouth of Panther creek. The villages of Tuscarora, Tamaqua and Home, are coal creations. Pop. in 1830, 359; taxables 72.

Rush, t-ship, Susquehannah county, bounded N. by Middleton t-ship, E. by Silver lake and Bridgewater t-ships, S. by Springville and W. by Bradford co. Greatest length, 9 ms., breadth 6 miles; area, 34,560 acres. It is drained by the Wyalusing creek, the north and middle branch from the north, and Lake creek and Deer Lick creek from the south. It has a post office called Rushville. The Wyalusing mountains extend across its western boundary. The surface is hilly; soil gravelly loam. Pop. in 1830, 643; taxables 1828, 102.

Rushville, post town, Rush t-ship, Susquehannah county; distant 265 miles from W. C., and 154 from Harrisburg.

Rush creek, Lower Mahantango t-ship, Schuylkill co., a tributary of Long Pine creek.

Russellville, post town, Chester co., 99 miles N. of W. C., and 62 S. E. from Harrisburg.

Russellville, small town of Pine Grove t-ship, Warren co., on the right bank of the Conewango creek, and eight miles N. of Warren borough.

Rush, t-ship, Northumberland co., bounded north by Point t-ship and by Columbia co., east by Columbia co., S. by Shamokin t-ship and W. by Augusta. Centrally distant N. from Sunbury 9 miles; greatest length 6½ ms., breadth 5 miles; area, 14,720 acres; surface, hilly and vales; soil, alluvial and gravel. Pop. in 1830, 1078; taxables, 245. Little roaring creek divides it from Columbia co., and Gravel run separates it from Augusta. The Pottsville and Danville rail road passes in a north west direction through the t-ship.

Rush, t-ship, Centre county, bounded W. and N. by Clearfield county, N. E. by Patton t-ship, S. E. by the main Allegheny ridge, which separates it from Half Moon t-ship, and S. by Huntingdon co. Centrally distant S. W. from Bellefonte 24 miles; greatest length 19, breadth eight miles; area, 56,960 acres; surface very mountainous; soil, limestone in the valleys. Pop. in 1830, 410; taxables 81. The t-ship is drained chiefly by Mushanon creek, which forms the boundary between it and Clearfield co. Coal and iron are abundant here, and iron works are erected at Phillipsburg on Cold Stream creek, a tributary of the Mushanon. A turnpike road leads from Phillipsburg to Bellefonte, distant 25 miles.

Rush, t-ship, Dauphin co., bounded N. by Jackson t-ship, E. by Schuylkill co., S. partly by Lebanon co., partly by Hanover t-ship, and W. by Middle Paxton. Centrally distant from Harrisburg N. E. 20 ms. Greatest length 22, breadth 5 miles; area,

64,400 acres. This is a very mountainous and sterile district. Its population in 1830, did not exceed 58 souls, and 8 taxables.

Rutland, t-ship, Tioga county, surface hilly; soil gravelly. Pop. in 1830, 687; taxables in 1828, 98. The post office of the t-ship, bearing the same name, is distant from W. C. 254 ms., and from Harrisburg 148.

Rye, t-ship, Perry co., bounded N. by Juniata t-ship, E. by Juniata and Susquehannah rivers, S. by Cumberland co., and W. by Tyrone t-ship. Centrally distant from Bloomfield 6 miles. Greatest length 13, breadth 10 miles; area, 58,880 acres; surface mountainous; soil, gravel and limestone. Pop. in 1830, 842; taxables, 162. Little Juniata creek, Sherman's creek and Fishing creek are the most considerable streams. The post town of Petersburg lies on the Susquehannah river, a short distance below the mouth of the Juniata. The Pennsylvania canal crosses the river above the town by the pool at Duncan's island, and divides into two branches, ascending the Susquehannah and Juniata rivers respectively. At the mouth of Sherman's creek, a forge has lately been erected by Messrs. Stephen Duncan and John D. Mahon, who have also the privilege of a toll bridge over the creek.

Ryerson's station, post office, Greene co., 249 miles N. W. from W. C. and 242 S. W. from Harrisburg.

Rynd's post office, Venango county, called after the post master, Abm. Rynd, 288 miles from W. C., and 221 from Harrisburg.

Sadsbury, t-ship, Chester co., bounded N. by West Caln, E. by East Caln, S. by East and West Fallowfield, and W. by Lancaster co. Central distance from Philadelphia 37 ms. N. W. and from West Chester 15 ms. W. Length 8¾, breadth 3¼ ms.; area 16,620 acres; surface hilly; soil gravelly. Pop. in 1830, 1875; taxables in 1828, 347. It is drained by the Octarara creek on the W., and by Buck run and the West Branch of the Brandywine river on the E. The Philadelphia turnpike road and the Columbia rail road pass through it from E. to W.; on the former is the village of Sadsbury, and the Black Horse, at each of which is a post office. The Wilmington and Lancaster turnpike road crosses the S. W. angle.

Sadsburyville, p-t. and v., Sadsbury t-ship, Chester co. 43 ms. by the turnpike road W. from Philadelphia and 15 ms. from West Chester, 131 ms. N. W. from W. C., and 57 S. E. from Harrisburg, contains some half dozen dwellings, store and tavern.

Sadsbury, t-ship, Crawford co. Pop. 1830, 902.

Sadsbury, t-ship, Lancaster county, bounded N. by Salisbury t-ship, E. by Chester co., S. by Colerain t-ship, and W. by Bart. Centrally distant S. W. from the city of Lancaster, 16 ms. Greatest length 5½, greatest breadth 5 ms.; area 12,111 acres; surface hilly and rolling; soil limestone and clay. Pop. in 1830, 1230; taxables 235. The Octarara creek rises near and flows along the eastern boundary, and gives motion to three forges within the t-ship, and one immediately below its southern line. Mine ridge runs along the N. boundary, at the foot of which on the Wilmington and Lancaster turnpike road is a post office called the "Gap," established at the "*Gap tavern.*" There are in the t-ship 3 forges, 1 distillery, 1 tanyard, 8 grist mills and 3 saw mills.

St. Clairsville, t. of St. Clair t-ship, Bedford co. on the road leading to Hollidaysburg, about 10 ms. N. of Bedford borough; contains about 20 dwellings, 1 store and 2 taverns.

St. Clair, t-ship, Bedford co., bounded N. by Greene t-ship, E. by Woodberry and Bedford t-ships, S. by Napier t-ship, and W. by Somerset co. Centrally distant from Bedford borough N. E. 12 ms. Greatest length 14, breadth 10½ ms.; area 44,800 acres; surface hills and valleys; soil clay and loam. Pop. in 1830, 2134; taxables 336.

St. Clair, t-ship, Allegheny county,

bounded N. by the Ohio and Monongahela rivers, E. by Mifflin t-ship, S. by Washington co. and W. by Fayette and Robinson t-ships. Centrally distant S. W. from Pittsburg 6 ms. Greatest length 12, breadth 8 ms. It is drained by Chartier's creek and Sawmill run. Coal abounds on the bank of the river. The p-t. of Birmingham lies on the Allegheny, opposite to and about a mile below Pittsburg. Area of the t-ship 39,040 acres; surface hilly; soil loam. Pop. in 1830, 4614; taxables 965.

St. Thomas, t-ship, Franklin co., bounded N. E. by Letterkenny t-ship, E. by Hamilton, S. by Antrim, S. W. by Peters and N. W. by Metal t-ships. Centrally distant from Chambersburg 7 ms. Greatest length 11½, breadth 7 ms.; area 25,600 acres; surface rolling; soil, slate, with veins of limestone. Pop. in 1830, 1778; taxables 328. The t-ship is drained by Back creek and its tributaries. The turnpike road from Chambersburg to McConnellstown, crosses the t-ship, and centrally upon it lies the p-t. of St. Thomas, 7 ms. W. from Chambersburg, 97 N. W. from W. C. and 57 S. W. from Harrisburg. The town contains about 90 dwellings, 2 churches common to several denominations of Christians, 3 stores and 4 taverns. The surrounding country is well cultivated and productive.

St. Mary's, p-o., Chester co., 139 ms. N. W. from W. C. and 64 S. E. of Harrisburg.

Salem Corners, a p-t. Wayne co. Salem t-ship, 20 ms. S. W. from Bethany, containing 10 or 12 dwellings, 2 taverns, and two stores.

Salem, t-ship, Luzerne co. bounded N. E. and S. E. by the Susquehannah r., S. W. by the co. of Columbia, and N. W. by Huntington and Union tps. The North Branch canal passes thro' the t-ship. Anthracite coal has been found in its hills, but its extent has not been ascertained. A p-o. is established at Beach Grove; and the town of Berwick extends into its S. W. angle; a church is erected about 2 ms. from the p-o. It contains 620 inhabitants; and by the returns of 1828, 158 taxables. The t-ship has a very irregular form. Its greatest length E. and W. is about 7 miles, and greatest breadth N. and S. about 6 miles. Area, 1,920 acres.

Salem, t-ship, Wayne co. bounded N. by Canaan, E. by Palmyra, S. by Sterling t-ship, and Pike co. and W. by Luzerne co. Its greatest length is about 9 miles, and greatest breadth about 8 ms. It is watered by Waullenpaupack creek, and the western branch, and other tributaries of that stream. The Easton and Belmont and the Luzerne and Wayne turnpike roads cross each other, where there is a post town called "Salem Corners." Surface, hilly; soil, gravel and loam; well timbered. Pop. in 1830, 593; taxables, in 1828, 117; taxable property in 1829, seated lands, $32,784; unseated, 74,105; personal, including occupations, 6,635. The t-ship contains about 90 dwellings, 3 stores, 3 taverns, 2 grist mills, 4 saw mills, 1 fulling mill, 1 carding machine, 37 looms, and 4 schools.

Salem, t-ship, Westmoreland co., bounded N. by Washington t-ship, E. by Loyalhanna r. S. by Hempfield and Unity t-ships, and W. by Franklin t-ship. Centrally distant N. from Greensburg, 9 ms.; greatest length, 11½, breadth, 10½ miles; area, 49,920 acres; surface hilly; soil, loam and gravel. Pop. in 1830, 2,294. Taxables, 440. It is drained N. by Beaver Dam run, and E. by Crabtree creek. The turnpike road from Ebensburg to Pittsburg crosses the t-ship diagonally, from S. E. to N. W., and on it in the W. part of the t-ship, is the post town of New Salem, distant N. 8 ms. from Greensburg, 200 from W. C., and 178 from Harrisburg, contains 20 dwellings, 4 taverns, and 2 stores.

Salem, New. (See preceding article.)

Salem, t-ship, Mercer co., bounded N. by Crawford co., E. by Sandy cr. t-ship, S. by Delaware t-ship; and west by West Salem t-ship; centrally distant N. W. of Mercer borough 14 ms.; greatest length, 8.

breadth, 6 ms.; area, 30,720 acres; surface, level; soil, clay and loam. Pop. 1830, 1,117; taxables, 194; taxable property in 1829, real estate, $85,438; personal $10,246; rate, 4 mills on the dollar. It is watered by the little Shenango and Crooked crs. which unite in the W. part of the t-ship, and flow W. to the Big Shenango.

Salem, W. t-ship, Mercer co. bounded N. by Crawford co., E. by Salem t-ship, S. by Pymatuning t-ship, and W. by the state of Ohio; centrally distant N. W. from Mercer borough, 17 ms.; greatest length, 8, breadth 6 ms. area, 30,720 acres; surface, level; soil, clay and loam. Pop. 1830, 1,850; taxables, 340; taxable property in 1829, real estate, $173,729; personal, 20,480. It is drained by the Shenango creek, which enters it on the N. and flows near the E. line, issuing from the t-ship by the S. E. corner; in a fork of the creek lies the p-t. of Greenville.

Salford, Lower, t-ship, Montgomery county, bounded on the N. E. by Franconia, S. E. by Towamensing, S. by Perkiomen, W. and N. W. by Upper Salford. Greatest length 5½ miles, greatest breadth 5 miles; area about 16,000 acres. The north east branch of the Perkiomen creek runs along the western boundary, and two branches of the Skippack creek pass through the t-ship. Central distance from Philadelphia about 25 miles, from Norristown 10 miles. Pop. in 1830, 830; taxables in 1828, 167; surface rolling; soil, red shale and loam.

Salford, Upper, t-ship, Montgomery country, bounded N. by Marlborough, on the N. E. by Bucks co., on the S. E. by Franconia and Lower Salford, S. by Perkiomen, S. W. by Frederick t-ships. Greatest length 8 miles, greatest breadth 5 miles. Perkiomen creek and Rich Valley creek run along the west and north west boundary and the N. E. branch of the Perkiomen along the S. W. boundary. Sumanytown, a post town, is on the line separating this and Marlborough t-ship; surface, level; soil, red shale and loam. Pop. in 1830, 1108; taxables in 1828, 250. Centrally distant from Norristown 10 miles N. N. W.

Salsberg, t-ship, Lehigh co., bounded north by Northampton t-ship and the Lehigh river, E. by Lower Saucon t-ship, Northampton co., S. E. by Upper Saucon, S. W. by Upper Milford and Macungy, and N. W. by Whitehall t-ships. It is drained by the Little Lehigh creek and one of its tributaries, and is intersected by many country roads. The South mountain runs along its S. E. boundary, at the foot of which is a small village, distant about two miles from Allentown S.E., called Smiths, and another about five miles S. S. W. from Northampton, called Emaus, a Moravian village. The surface of the country is rolling, soil limestone, of excellent quality and carefully cultivated. Iron ore is found in the mountain. Pop. in 1830. 1342; taxables in 1828, 331. Taxable property 1829, real estate $321,897; personal 11,650; rate of levy 13 cts. in the $100. Assessed value of lands 35, 25, 18 dollars per acre, according to quality.

Saltzburg, post town, Conemaugh t-ship, Indiana co., on the E. bank of the Conemaugh river, 10 miles N.W. of Blairsville, and 17 miles S. W. of the borough of Indiana, 206 miles from W. C., and 175 from Harrisburg; contains 20 dwellings, 2 stores, 2 taverns, 1 Presbyterian church. It has its name from the many salt works in the vicinity.

Salisbury, post town, Union t-ship, Huntingdon co., upon the road leading from Fort Littleton to Huntingdon, 15 miles south east from the latter; contains about 20 dwellings, 2 stores, 2 taverns, 1 smith shop, 1 tanyard and 1 church.

Salisbury, t-ship, Lancaster county, bounded N. by Caernarvon, E. by Chester co., S. by Sadsbury t-ship, and W. by Strasburg, Leacock and Earl t-ships. Centrally distant E. from Lancaster about 16 miles; greatest length 8, greatest breadth 6 miles; area, 26,624 acres; surface rolling; soil, limestone. Pop. in 1830, 3205;

taxables, 604. It is drained by the Pecquea creek, upon the branches of which are several mills and one forge. The Welsh mountain runs along the north, and Mine ridge upon its south boundary. Upon the eastern line, about two and a half miles south of the north line, is the small village of Cambridge. The Philadelphia and Lancaster turnpike road, and the state rail road cross the southern part of the t-ship ; on the former within two miles of the western boundary is the "Salisbury" post office, at a small village of 6 or 8 houses of the same name, 123 miles from W. C., and 49 from Harrisburg. Slaymaker's, a noted tavern and post house, is on the same road about half way between the east and west boundaries.

Salisbury, p-town, Elk Lick t-ship, Somerset co., near the Little Youghiogheny river, distant 17 miles S. of Somerset borough, contains 30 dwellings, 2 taverns, 2 stores, 1 German Reformed church.

Salmon run., a tributary of the Conewago creek, which rises and has its whole course in Dover t-ship, York co.

Salt Lick creek, Great Bend t-ship, Susquehannah co., rises in New Milford t-ship, and flows northerly into the Susquehannah river, at the Great Bend. It is a rapid stream, affording good mill seats, for which purpose it is used. It has its name from the salt licks found upon it. It is too small for navigation.

Salt Lick, t-ship, Fayette county, bounded N. and N. E. by Westmoreland co., S. E. by Somerset co., S. W. by Wharton t-ship, and N. W. by Connellsville and Bullskin t-ships. Centrally distant from the town of Union 18 miles N. E.; greatest length 20 miles, breadth 14 miles ; area 81, 280 acres ; surface hilly, mountainous ; soil gravelly loam. Pop. in 1830, 1,499 ; taxables 262. Laurel hill is on the east, and Chestnut ridge on the west boundary. The Youghiogheny river is on the south, in the bend of which are some vestiges of ancient fortifications. The r. receives from the t-ship Indian creek and some smaller streams. On the former are some iron works, consisting of two furnaces.

Sambo creek, rises in Pike co., and flowing south westerly through the N. W. corner of Smithfield t-ship, Northampton county, falls into Broadhead's creek in Stroud t-ship. It is not navigable, but turns several mills.

Sandy creeks, Big and Little, Fayette co., rise in Wharton t-ship, and flow S. uniting in the state of Maryland and running into Cheat river. Salt and iron are found on these streams.

Sandy creek, rises in the south part of Crawford co., and flowing south east, enters Mercer co., in Sandy Creek t-ship, and thence into Sandy Lake t-ship, where it receives the waters from Sandy lake, thence by an E. course it runs into the Allegheny river. Its whole course is more than 30 miles, and it is navigable for boats about 14 miles from its mouth to Sandy lake.

Sandy Creek, t-ship, Mercer county, bounded north by Crawford co., E. by French Creek t-ship, S. by Coolspring t-ship, and W. by Salem. Centrally distant north from Mercer about 13 miles. Greatest length 8, breadth 6 miles ; area, 30,720 acres ; surface, level ; soil, gravelly loam. Pop. in 1830, 1048 ; taxables, 165. Taxable property in 1829, real estate $75,017. Personal, 12,386 ; rate of tax, 4 mills on the dollar. It is drained E. by Sandy creek and west by the Little Shenango. The turnpike road from Mercer to Meadville runs north and centrally through the t-ship, on which and on a small branch of Sandy creek, is the post town of Georgetown.

Sandy creek, Northampton county, otherwise called Spring creek, rises near the head of the Nescopeck, in Luzerne county, and running eastwardly, falls into the Lehigh near the line of Luzerne. It flows entirely through a wilderness, and although it has a number of fine mill seats, no mills are yet erected on it. Sandy creek has a large branch coming from the north, called "Terrapin pond creek."

Sandy Hill, Lower Dublin t-ship, Philadelphia co., on the Bustleton and Smithfield turnpike road, about 2 ms. south west of Bustleton and 4 ms. from Frankford, is a pleasant village of about a dozen houses. In the vicinity of this place, Ralph Sandiford, the celebrated opposer of slavery and advocate of civil liberty, formerly resided. His grave is by the road side on his own farm; the spot was formerly designated by a stone, on which we were told he was the son of John Sandiford of Liverpool, that he had borne a faithful testimony against slavery, and died at about the age of 40 years, A. D. 1733. Hard by the grave of Sandiford is an old house, with a high roof, marked on a stone in the front "I. A. 1696." This is probably the most ancient building in the t-ship.

Sandy Lake, t-ship, Mercer county, bounded N. by French Creek t-ship, E. by Venango co., S. by Wolf Creek t-ship, and west by Coolspring t-ship. Centrally distant N. E. from Mercer borough 10 miles. Greatest length 8, breadth 6 miles; area, 30,720 acres. It is drained E. by Sandy creek, into which flow the waters of Sandy lake, a pool in the N. W. angle of the t-ship. Surface level; soil, clay and loam; pop. in 1830, 741; taxables, 143; taxable property 1829, real estate $45,045; personal 6,188; rate 4 mills in the dollar.

Sandy Creek, t-ship, Venango co., bounded N. by French Creek t-ship, N. E. by Sandy creek, E. by Allegheny river, and S. by Scrub Grass t-ship and Irwin t-ship. Centrally distant south west from the borough of Franklin 7 miles. Greatest length 9, breadth 6 miles; area, 26,240 acres; surface hilly; soil, gravel, loam. It is thinly populated and is attached to French Creek t-ship. Little Sandy creek crosses the t-ship from south west to north east, upon which there is a forge.

Sandy furnace, post office of Sandy Creek t-ship, Venango county, 283 miles north west from W. C., and 216 from Harrisburg.

Sarah Manor, (See Whip's cove.)

Saratoga, t-ship, Venango county, bounded N. by Bear t-ship, E. by Jefferson county, south by Toby's creek and Farmington t-ships, and west by Teonista t-ship. Centrally distant N. E. from Franklin t-ship 30 miles. Greatest length 6, breadth $5\frac{1}{2}$ miles; area, 21,120 acres; surface hilly; soil, gravelly loam. It is scantily populated, and is annexed to Teonista t-ship. The t-ship is drained by the Teonista creek, which crosses the N. W. angle, and by its tributaries, Coon's, John's, and Raccoon creeks.

Saucon creek, rises in Upper Milford t-ship, Lehigh county, and running north easterly falls into the Lehigh river, on the south side, about four ms. below Bethlehem, in Northampton co. It gives its name to two t-ships, one of Lehigh co., and the other of Northampton co., and has a number of fine mills upon it, but is not navigable.

Saucon, Lower, t-ship, Northampton co., bounded N. by the river Lehigh, E. by Williams t-ship, S. E. by Bucks co., S. W. by Upper Saucon, Lehigh co., and W. by Salsberg in the latter county. Greatest length $6\frac{1}{2}$, width $4\frac{1}{2}$ miles; surface hilly; soil, gravel and limestone. Pop. in 1830, 2,308; taxables in 1828, 446. Chief town is Hellerstown. It is watered by Saucon creek and its tributaries, and the Lehigh. Two bridges cross the Lehigh from this t-ship, Jarret's bridge, and one from Bethlehem. There is a post office named after the t-ship, distant 187 miles from W. C. and 97 from Harrisburg.

Saucon, Upper, t-ship, Lehigh co., bounded N. E. by Lower Saucon, S. E. by Bucks co., S. W. by Upper Milford and N. W. by Salsberg townships. Its greatest length is $5\frac{1}{2}$ miles, and greatest width about 5 ms.; area, 15,360 acres. It is drained by the Saucon creek, which runs through it in a north east direction towards the Lehigh river. The Springhouse and Bethlehem turnpike road runs north and south through the t-ship. Frysburg, a small village and post town, lies on this road near the south east boundary, at which there is a church. There is also another place of worship on the same road, within a mile of the N. E. line, and yet another in the t-ship. The surface is diversified; the South mountain occupies its northern part, and its spurs reach to the southern boundary. Iron ore is found in the mountain. The valleys are of limestone, and the whole under cultivation. Pop. in 1830, 1905; taxables in 1828, 388. Value of taxable property in 1829, real estate $410,381; personal estate $24,640; rate of tax 13 cts. on the $100; assessed value of lands 1st quality, 35; 2d quality 25; 3d quality 18 dollars per acre. There are in the t-ship 6 grist mills, 4 saw mills, 3 oil mills, one clover mill, 9 stores, 6 taverns, 5 schools. The centre of the t-ship is about 6 miles distant from Allentown or Northampton, the county town.

Saw kill, mill stream, Upper Smithfield t-ship, Pike co., rises in some ponds, and has its whole course within the t-ship, and flows into the Delaware near Milford. It turns several mills.

Saville, t-ship, Perry co., bounded N. by the Tuscarora mountain, which separates it from Mifflin co., S. by Tyrone t-ship, E. by Juniata t-ship, and W. by Toboyne t-ship. Centrally distant N. W. from Bloomfield 9 ms.; greatest length 8½, breadth 7½ miles; area, 38,400 acres; surface, mountainous; soil, limestone in the valleys, gravel and slate on the hills. Pop. in 1830, 1319; taxables, 287. It is drained by the Great Buffalo creek, in the forks of one of whose tributaries, in the N. E. angle of the t-ship, lies the village of Ickesburg, about 9 ms. N. W. of Bloomfield.

Schall's Store, p-t., Berks co., 157 ms. N. E. of W. C., and 66 from Harrisburg.

Schmicksburg, p-t. of Mahoning t-ship, Indiana co., on the Little Mahoning creek, about 20 ms. N. of Indiana borough, 212 from W. C., and 181 from Harrisburg; contains 6 or 8 dwellings, and a store.

Schuylkill, co., was separated from the counties of Berks and Northampton, by act of assembly passed 1st March, 1811, and embraces the t-ships of Brunswick, Schuylkill, Manheim, Norwegian, Upr. Mahantango, Lower Mahantango, formerly in Berks co., and the t-ships of W. Penn and Rush, formerly in Northampton. It is bounded N. by Luzerne, N. E. by Northampton, S. E. by Lehigh, S. by Berks, S. W. by Dauphin, and N. W. by Northumberland and Columbia counties; length 37, breadth 13 ms.; area, 475 ms. Its surface is generally hilly, nay mountainous, and the soil, except near the streams, and some rare and favored spots, is rough, rocky, and sterile. It is drained principally by the Mahanoy, Mahantango, and Swatara creeks, which flow into the Susquehannah, and the several head branches of the Schuylkill r. Central lat. 40° 40′ N., long. 47′ E. from W. C. The whole co. is of transition formation, and abounds with anthracite coal; but no iron ore has yet been discovered of a quality sufficiently good for smelting. The county is covered in its whole extent by several ridges of mtns., which are distinguished in places by various names. The Blue or Kittatinny mtn., separates it from Lehigh and Berks counties. The Second mtn. is next in range, the Sharp mtn. the third, the Broad mtn. the fourth, the Mahantango the fifth, and the Mahanoy, the sixth; which, passing through Schuylkill co. from Luzerne, divides it from Columbia and Northumberland on the N. W, Some other hills, known as the Green mtn., the Long Sugar Loaf mtn., encumber its northern section.

This county is drained by streams which run in various directions. On the east, the Nesquihoning, Mauch Chunk, Mahoning and Lizard creeks have their sources, and by courses almost due east, seek the Lehigh. On the S., the Schuylkill is the principal drain. On the S. W., the Swatara, rising in the Blue mtn., flows along its northern base, into Lebanon co. On the W., Long Pine, Deep Creek, Mahantango and Mahanoy creeks, flow into Northumberland co., and thence to the Susquehannah; whilst on the N. W., the head waters of Catawissa creek intersect the hills in several directions. The Schuylkill r. which gives the name to the co., has its sources almost entirely within it. There are two principal branches which unite in a gorge of the Blue mtn., at a spot now called Port Clinton, at which a small village is erected. From this place we follow the main branch of the river for about 11 ms., in a meandering, but almost northerly course to Schuylkill Haven, another village of late growth, containing above 40 houses; here the stream again forks into the E. and W. branches; the E. branch has a N. E. direction for 4 ms. to Pottsville, thence by an E. course of 14 ms. through the Schuylkill valley, we approach its head, in Rush t-ship, between the Tuscarora and Locust mtns. Two ms. above Pottsville, the volume of the r. is swelled by Mill creek. The W. branch is formed by the junction of several small streams, among which is the W. West branch, which rise in the Broad mtn., and unite at the foot of the Sharp mtn., whence it flows, to meet the E. branch at Schuylkill Haven, receiving in its course several small creeks; and below this village the river is further augmented by several considerable tributaries. The Little Schuylkill or Tamaqua r., rises in Northampton co., and flowing S. westerly, it receives from the Broad mountain, Neyforts, Hosasock, and Codorus creeks, thence by a S. course it passes between the Tuscarora and the Mauch Chunk mtns., thence resuming a S. W. course, it runs, winding round the bases of several mtns., to meet the main r. at Port Clinton, being augmented at almost every mile by a mtn. torrent, which pours into it on either hand.

The improvements of the Schuylkill navigation company extend along the bank of the main r., 110 ms., and through this co. to Port Carbon, 2 ms. above Pottsville. In this distance the ascent is overcome by 129 locks. The Union canal company have constructed a basin or reservoir, with an area of upwards of 700 acres, in a gorge of the Blue mtns., through which the Swatara passes, from which a supply of water is taken by a canal along the Swatara to the Union canal. A rail road has been graded and prepared by the same company, 5 ms. in length, which connects the canal with the coal region.

The roads of the county, considering the wildness of its surface and the sparseness of its population, are numerous, and they wind in most cases, through the valleys and gorges of the mtns. in all directions; in some instances they boldly cross the hills, or run along their summits. A turnpike road, made under an act of assembly passed 25th March, 1805, from Reading to Sunbury, 75 ms., passes with a N. W. inclination through this county, communicating with Port Clinton, Orwigsburg, Pottsville and Newcastle. This road has been made of stone and natural earth, at an expense of $142,000; of which sum the state subscribed $80,000.

Among the very many important improvements which have been consequent to the improved navigation of the Schuylkill and the development of the coal region of this county, the rail roads are not the least considerable. The Schuylkill valley rail road, commences at Port Carbon, at the head of the canal, and confluence of Mill creek with the Schuylkill, and terminates at Tuscarora, distant 10 ms. There are 15 lateral rail roads, communicating with the several mines, whose aggregate length may amount also to ten ms. The cost of the main road was $60,000, and of the laterals 20,000. Mill creek rail road commences at Port Carbon, and extends up Mill creek 4 ms. It cost about $14,000. Three ms. of lateral rail-roads intersect this, and were made at an expense of about $2000 per mile. The West Branch rail road commences at Schuylkill Haven, and terminates at the foot of the Broad mtn. Its length, including W. West branch is 15 ms.; estimated cost $150,000. There are about 5 ms. of lateral road, connected with it, estimated to have cost $2000 per mile. The Mount Carbon rail road commences at Mount Carbon, and extends up the 2 branches of the Norwegian creek, a distance of 9 ms. Estimated cost about $100,000. It is intersected by many lateral roads. Of the Pine Grove rail road, made by the Union canal company, we have already spoken; its estimated cost is $30,000. The Little Schuylkill rail road commences at Port Clinton, and extends up that stream to the mines, a distance of about 23 ms. A most important rail road from Pottsville to Danville is now being constructed, connecting the Schuylkill navigation at this point, with the Susquehannah at Sunbury and Danville. A company was incorporated in 1831, under an act of assembly, passed 8th April, 1826, with a capital of $500,000, and the road is in progress.

Upon Mine hill, near the gap, is one of those singular curiosities, a rocking stone. It is a flat rock, about 18 ft. long and 3 ft. thick, so nicely poised on another, that an infant's touch can make it move like the scales of a balance.

Orwigsburg is the county town. The other notable villages owe their existence to the working of the collieries, and are Mount Carbon, Pottsville, Port Carbon, Tuscarora, Middleport, Patterson, New Philadelphia, St. Clairsville, Newcastle, Schuylkill Haven, Port Clinton, Minersville, Carbondale, &c. &c.

The pop. of the county was in 1820, 11,339; by the census of 1830, is 20,783, of which 11,665 were white males; 9,072 white females; 116 free colored males; 90 free colored females; 1145 aliens; 5 blind; 14 deaf and dumb. Schuylkill forms a part of the Lancaster district of the supreme court; and together with Lebanon and Dauphin, constitutes the 12th judicial district of the county courts. President Judge, Calvin Blythe. The courts are holden at Orwigsburg, on the last Mondays of March, July, October, and Dec.

Election districts.—Schuylkill, with Berks and Lehigh, forms the 7th congressional district; represented in the 22d congress by Henry A. Muhlenberg and Henry King. With Berks it forms the 6th senatorial district, which sends two members to the senate of the state. Schuylkill sends one member to the house of representatives. The public buildings are, a large and convenient brick court house, and county offices; a stone jail. An academy at Orwigsburg was incorporated by act 29th March, 1813, and a donation of $2000 granted by the legislature, with condition that poor children, not exceeding four in number, shall be taught therein gratis, annually. The trustees have erected in the town a convenient building for a school. The greater portion of this county is too mountainous and broken for profitable agricultural pursuits, and but for its mineral wealth, it would have remained for years a wooded and undisturbed desert. The abundance of excellent anthracite coal which the mountains contain, and for which the improvement of the river has provided a market, has raised the whole country in value. 81,000 tons of coal were sent from the mines during the past year, which at an average price of 6 dolls. per ton has returned $486,000. It has been asserted, but we think with exaggeration, that $40,000,000 have been invested here in the coal business. But coal is not the only source of wealth in this county: the manufacture of iron is carried on to a considerable extent. The iron works now in operation are Greenwood furnace and forge, and the Schuylkill, Brunswick, Pine Grove, Mahanoy and Swatara forges, which manufacture from 5 to 6 hundred tons annually. The ore for the Greenwood furnace has hitherto been chiefly obtained from Potts Grove and Reading, by the Canal. These works belong to and are conducted by Messrs. John & Benjamin Pott. Messrs. Jones, Keim & Co. have also an establishment, called Windsor foundry, the castings of which are excellent in workmanship as in metal.

By the assessment of 1829, the taxable property of the county amounted, real estate, to $1,815,263, and personal estate, at $85,188, and the rate of tax was 27 mills in the dollar.

Schuylkill county paid into the state treasury in 1831, for

Tax on offices,	$734 62
Tax on writs,	865 15
Tavern licenses,	261 36
Duties on dealers in foreign merchandize,	772 32
Tin and clock pedlars' licenses,	57
Hawkers' and pedlars' licenses,	15 20
	$2696 63

STATISTICAL TABLE OF SCHUYLKILL COUNTY.

Townships &c.	Greatest Lth.	Greatest Bth.	Population. 1820.	Population. 1830.	taxables.
Barry,	10	6		443	73
Brunswick,	14	9	1,974	2,298	371
Lower Mahantango,	11 1-2	11½	937	1,234	225
Manheim,	9	8½	2,164	2,160	315
Norwegian,	10	5	615	3,869	417
Orwigsburg bo.			600	773	139
Pine Grove,	13	9	1,868	1,609	217
Rush,	15	9	253	359	72
Schuylkill,	16	8	546	1,200	93
Union,			367	477	93
Upper Mahantango,	16 1-2	3½	853	1,150	191
West Penn,	10	7	1,152	1,379	262
Wayne,				1,436	247
Pottsville bor.				2,474	784
			11,339	20,783	2,715

Schuylkill valley and rail road, Schuylkill co. This valley is narrow and lies between the Sharp mtn. and Mine hill, and commencing near Pottsville, runs eastwardly about 12 miles. Both sides of the valley abound with excellent anthracite coal. The river Schuylkill, which is here but a creek, has its course from its primal fountain through this valley; and the valuable mines are approached by the rail road that follows the banks, which are nearly parallel with the direction of the coal strata. Deep ravines extend from from the road northward to Mine hill, through which, commonly, a small stream of water runs, cutting the veins transversely, so that they can be advantageously worked above the water level. Thus about two miles above Port Carbon, at the mouth of Zachariah's r. are the "*Five Point mines*" which are very extensive, and produce first rate coal. Along the run, a lateral rail road may be made communicating with many valuable coal beds. One mile above Bollen and Curry's mines, is the "*Bopp tract*" owned by Messrs. Hubley. Indian run divides this tract, along which a lateral road may be also made to mines of approved quality. The next, upon the river is the "Barlow and Evans" tract, near the mouth of Silver creek, four miles above Port Carbon. This stream passes through Mine hill, and gives access to the large and valuable tracts of Messrs. Burd, Patterson, Geissonheimer, and others. On the Glentworth and valley furnace tracts, is another lateral road, a mile above which is another stream, running through the valley furnace property, up which a lateral road has also been made to some fine mines. Above this lies Middleport, a new p-t. at the confluence of the Kaskawilian creek with the Schuylkill. Up this stream, laterals have been made to Mine hill, by the proprietors of the land known as the '*Jacob Stahl*,' '*Olioger*' & '*Bushey tracts*,' on each of which, openings have been made into beds of good quality. The next lateral road is up Laurel creek to the De Long collieries, owned by Mr. Lawton, and Blight, Wallace, & Co. One mile above this is the town of Patterson, owned by Messrs Patterson, Swift, and Porter. Big creek, which penetrates the Mine hill, and divides the coal strata advantageously, passes through this place. The river, the road, and the Mine hill, are much nearer to each other, than below, having gradually converged from a mile above Port Carbon. As the road follows the course of the river, at many of the bends it intersects the veins transversely, for they range invariably 17° N. of E. This circumstance is worthy of notice, as it shows that the coal is by no means confined to the N. side of the river; and there are on the S. several fine tracts, as at Middleport, the valuable property of Messrs. Robb & Winebrenner, known as the "Jacob Ladig," and part of that owned by Messrs. Porter, Emerick & Kom, called the 'Heister tract.' Next above Patterson, lies the "Peter Ladig tract" of Mr. Biddle, and the "Reber tract," owned by the same gentleman, and Mr. Edwin Swift. These are rich in coal, and advantageously situated. Pebble run divides the strata finely for mining operations, about a mile and a half above Big cr. It passes over the "Reber tract," and divides Mine hill, here called Locust mtn. Next to the "Reber tract," is the "Tuscarora tract" of Mr. Wm. Lawton, and Blight, Wallace, & Co. a large tract containing the following veins, viz;—

A 20 ft.	vein	opened by	Davidson & Turner.
10	do	do	Greer & Ellet.
8	do	do	Wm Littell.
9	do	do	Stack & Clard.
7	do	do	do
11	do	do	do
16	do	do	Rees.
43	do	do	do
124 feet.			

The next tract above this is also a large one, belonging to Mr. Joseph Lyons and Jacob Alter. The river rises from the springs of this tract, which divide the ground advantageously for mining. The veins which we have just noticed, are said to have 400 feet breast above the water level.

The cost of the main rail-way was about $55,000, and that of the laterals about 20,000. The main railway is now a stage and post road, forming the most direct and pleasant communication between Pottsville and Mauch Chunk.

The town of Tuscarora is at the head of the valley and rail-road. It contains about a dozen houses, a store and two taverns. One of them, a new and very large hotel, competent for the entertainment of many guests. But we believe that the hospitable fire has never yet been lighted in it.

Schuylkill river, so called by the first Dutch settlers, but known by the aborigines by the names of Nittabaconck, or Mai-nai-unk, rises by three principal branches, in Schuylkill co. all of them having their sources N. of of the Sharp mtn. The middle or main branch rises on the N. side of the Tuscarora mtn., and runs S. W. about 14 miles, to Pottsville, through a narrow valley, called Schuylkill valley, formed by Mine hill or Locust mtn. and the Sharp mtn.; from Pottsville it assumes a south course of about 5 ms. to Schuylkill Haven, where it receives the West branch, composed of the main West branch, and the W. West branch; thence by a S. E. course, following the meanders of the stream about 14 miles, to Port Clinton, on the N. side of the Blue mtn. where the third branch or Little Schuylkill unites with it. This last branch also rises in the Locust mtn. and its sources interlock with those of the main branch. It has a course almost due S. of 30 ms. The river having thus collected its strength, breaks its way through a deep and narrow ravine, and enters upon a champagne country at the village of Hamburg, near the N. line of Berks co., thence preserving a southwardly course of about 80 miles, passing the towns of Reading, Pottsville, Norristown, Manyunk, and the city of Philadelphia, it empties into the Delaware about 7 ms. below the city. The Schuylkill receives, in its course, many tributaries, the most important of which are the Tulpehocken from the W., and the Perkiomen from the E. In its natural state, it was ordinarily navigable for boats to Reading, and in seasons of high water, some 30 miles further; vessels of 300 to 400 tons ascend to the western wharves of the city; where on a range with Vine street it is 1264, and on a range with Cedar street it is 2040 ft. in width; the average depth at common tides, is from 13 to 14 feet.

There have been expended on the improvement of this river, the sum of $3,000,000, and a still further sum is necessary to render it adequate to the transit of the products of the country upon it. A connexion between the Delaware and Susquehannah, by means of the Schuylkill, is said to have been suggested by Wm. Penn, so early as the year 1690.

Schuylkill, t-ship, Schuylkill county, bounded N. E. by Northampton, E. by Rush t-ship, S. by Brunswick, W. by Norwegian and Barry, and N. W. by Columbia co. The t-ship has somewhat the shape of a boot, with the foot pointing N. eastward. Its greatest length is about 16 ms., and greatest breadth about 8 ms.; area, 65,920 acres. It comprehends one of the richest sections of the coal country, having within it the Sharp mtn., Mine hill or Locust mtn., the Broad mtn. and the Mahanoy mtn., in all of which anthracite abounds. It embraces also the greater portion of Schuylkill valley and rail road, along which many mines have been opened, for a particular description of which, (*see Schuylkill valley.*) The Catawissa creek crosses the northern section of the t-ship, where it is navigable for canoes; and the Great and Little Mahanoy creeks cross it S. westwardly. And S. of the sharp mtn., Tumbling creek flows in the same direction towards the Schuylkill, below mt. Carbon. It contains the villages of Middleport, a p-t., Greenfield, Louisburg, and, we believe, Patterson. The roads from McKeansburg to Catawissa and Sunbury pass through the t-ship. The surface of the country is mountainous; the soil chiefly of white gravel, alternating with red shale, and generally sterile. Pop. in 1830, 1200; taxables, 200; in 1828, 93.

Schuylkill, t-ship, Chester co., on the r. Schuylkill, taken from Charleston and Pikeland t-ships. Greatest length $4\frac{1}{2}$, breadth $2\frac{1}{4}$ ms.; surface, level; soil, sandy loam. It is watered by French creek and Stoney creek. Pop. in 1830, 1434; taxables, 332; assessed value, $315,757; real estate, personal and occupations, $9112. Schuylkill p-o. is 134 ms. from W. C., and 80 from Harrisburg. There are 3 villages in the t-ship, viz., Phœnixville, Chester co. landings, and Perrysville.

Schuylkill Haven, p-t. in Manheim t-ship, Schuylkill co., a town laid out in 1829, by Mr. Daniel I. Rhodes and others, immediately below the confluence of the West branch of the Schuylkill r. with the main stream. The West Branch rail road commences here, and extends up to the confluence of the branches of the river, whence radiations follow the direction of the two streams to the foot of the Broad mtn., making a distance together of 15 ms. A large body of excellent limestone is said to have been discovered here. A lock for weighing canal boats and their freights has been erected here by the Schuylkill navigation company. The town consists of about 40 dwellings, a grist and saw mill, several stores and hotels. As the shipping port of a very extensive portion of the Schuylkill county coal region, it will probably become a place of considerable business. It is about 5 miles W. of Orwigsburg, 171 N. of W. C., and 55 N. E. of Harrisburg.

Schwaben creek, Upper Mahanoy t-ship, Northumberland co., rises in that t-ship, and flows through a broad valley into Lower Mahanoy t-ship, where it unites with the Mahanoy creek.

Scollop hill, so called from its shape, is situated in Brunswick t-ship, Schuylkill co., near to the banks of the Schuylkill r. It is remarkable for the tunnel of the canal which passes thro' it. Its northern point is about 3 ms. S. of Orwigsburg.

Scotch valley, Morris t-ship, Huntingdon co., lies between the Canoe and Brush mtns. It is drained S. by Canoe creek, which flows into the Frankstown branch of the Juniata.

Scott township, Wayne co., bounded N. by the state of N. Y., N. E. by the Delaware r., E. by Buckingham t-ship, S. by Mt. Pleasant t-ship, and W. by Susquehannah co. Greatest length 12 ms., greatest breadth 10½ ms. It is drained by the tributaries of the Starucca creek, which empties into the Susquehannah river, and by Shrawder's and Shohokin creeks, which flow to the Delaware; surface, hilly; well timbered with beech and maple; soil, gravel and loam. Pop. in 1830, 216; taxables in 1828, 44; taxable property in 1829, lands seated, $15,338; unseated, $63,226; personal estate, including occupations, 3232.

Scott, p-o., Scott t-ship, Wayne co., 30 ms. N. of Bethany, 283 from W. C., and 184 from Harrisburg.

Scott's creek, Falls t-ship, Bucks co., a short and inconsiderable stream of Pennsbury manor.

Scottsville, p-o., Luzerne co., 263 ms. N. of W. C., and 154 from Harrisburg.

Scrub ridge, a mtn. range of Air t-ship, Bedford co., extending N. E. and S. W. about 15 ms.

Scrub Grass creek, rises in Irwin t-ship, Venango co., and runs through Scrub Grass t-ship N. E., into the Allegheny river, having a semi-circular course of about 10 ms.

Scrub Grass, t-ship, Venango co., bounded N. by Sandy Creek t-ship, N. E. and E. by the Allegheny river, S. by Butler co., and W. by Irwin t-ship. Centrally distant S. from Franklin borough 11 ms.; greatest length 8, breadth 7 ms.; area, 23,680 acres; surface, rolling; soil, limestone, coal abundant. Pop. in 1830, 812; taxables, 210. The t-ship is watered by Scrub Grass and Little Scrub Grass creeks, which flow N. E. into the river.

Second mountain. This name is given to a ridge in the N. boundary of Brunswick t-ship, Schuylkill co., S. of the Sharp mtn. It is also given to the ridge in various places, which runs across the country, next N. to the Blue mtn.

Second Fork, p-t., Clearfield co., 254 ms. N. W. of W. C., and 154 from Harrisburg.

Seelen's Grove, p-t. and borough, Penn t-ship, Union co., upon the Susquehannah r., at the confluence of Penn's creek with that stream, 10 ms. S. E. of New Berlin, and 159 N. W. of W. C., and 50 from Harrisburg; contains 70 to 100 dwellings, 6 stores, 4 taverns, and 1 church, and between 6 and 700 inhabitants. The great public road along the Susquehannah, runs through the town; it is the great thoroughfare, not only between the southern and northern counties, but between the southern and the northern states and Canada.

Segarsville, p-t., Heidelberg t-ship, Lehigh co., on the road to Northampton, near the W. line of the t-ship, distant 18 ms. N. W. from Northampton. The only church of the t-ship is within two ms. of the village, which lies on the Jordan creek, and contains about 20 dwellings, a store and tavern. It is distant from W. C. 185 ms., and from Harrisburg 85 ms.

Sellersville, p-t. of Rockhill t-ship, Bucks co., on the t-pike road from Philadelphia to Bethlehem, 11 ms. N. of Doylestown, 166 from W. C., and 91 E. from Harrisburg; contains 6 or 7 dwellings, a mill, tavern, and store.

Sergeant, t-ship, McKean co., bounded N. by Keating, E. by Walker, S. by Cooper, and W. by Ogden t-ship. Centrally distant from Smethport S. 8 ms.; length 13, breadth 9½ ms.; area, 57,200 acres; surface, high levels; soil, gravel, loam, and slate. Pop. in 1830, 230. The t-ship is drained N. by Potatoe and Stanton creeks, tributaries of the Allegheny r., the former flowing near the E., and the latter near the W. boundary; and S. by Cooper and Rich Valley creeks. On Potatoe cr. is a p-o. at a settlement called Norwich, where there are several dwellings, distant about 8 ms. S.

E. of Smethport, 281 N. W. from W. C., and 202 from Harrisburg.

Setzler's Store, p-o., Chester co., 138 ms. N. of W. C., and 72 from Harrisburg.

Seventy-six, p-o., Beaver co., 256 ms. from W. C., and 234 from Harrisburg.

Sewickly creeks, Big and Little, of Ohio t-ship, Allegheny co. The first is a considerable stream, and receives a branch from Beaver co.; the second has a course of five or six ms. only.

Sewickly creeks, Big and Little, Westmoreland co.; the former rises in Unity and Hempfield t-ships, and flows by a comparative course W. about 20 ms., to the Youghiogheny r., receiving the latter, which rises also in Hempfield t-ship, about 2 ms. above its mouth.

Sewickly, North, t-ship, Beaver co., bounded N. by Shenango t-ship, E. by Butler co., S. by New Sewickly t-ship, and W. by Beaver r. Centrally distant N. E. from Beaver borough 10 ms.; greatest length 9½, breadth 8½ ms. Slippery Rock creek enters the t-ship from the N. E., and the Conequenessing from the S. E., and uniting N. of the centre of the t-ship, flow S. W. into Beaver river; area, 47,360 acres; surface, rolling; soil, loam and limestone. Pop. in 1830, 2475; taxables, 412. The p-o. of the t-ship is distant 263 ms. N. W. from W. C., and 238 W. from Harrisburg.

Sewickly, New, t-ship, Beaver co., bounded N. by North Sewickly t-ship, E. by Butler and Allegheny counties, S. by Allegheny co. and Big Sewickley creek, and W. by the Ohio river. Centrally distant E. from Beaver borough 5 ms.; surface, hilly; soil, loam. Pop. in 1830, 1902; taxables, 412. The falls of the Big Beaver are in this t-ship, and near them, is the p-t. of Brighton.

Sewickly Bottom, p-o., Ohio t-ship, Allegheny co., 237 ms. N. W. from W. C., and 215 W. of Harrisburg.

Shade's creeks, Big and Little, two small streams which rise in Covington t-ship, Luzerne co., and flow through the great Swamp into the Lehigh r., between Pumpion rock falls, and Stoddartsville.

Shade, t-ship, Somerset co., bounded N. by Cambria co., E. by Bedford co., S. by Allegheny and Stoney cr. t-ships, and W. by Quemahoning, Jenner and Conemaugh t-ships. Centrally distant N. E. from Somerset borough 18 ms.; greatest length 12, breadth 11 ms.; area, 85,400 acres; surface, level; soil, wet and adapted to grazing. Pop. in 1830, 1135; tax. 222; taxable property in 1829, real estate, $45,248; personal, 6328. The Allegheny mtn. is on the E. boundary, Stoney creek on the west. Shade creek rises in the S. E. part of the co., and flows N. W. to Stoney cr. and its tributaries penetrate every part of the t-ship. Shade furnace lies on the creek near the centre of the t-ship, near which is *Shade Works* p-o. The town of *Germany*, a town on paper merely, lies on Conevers fork, about 5 ms. W. of the mountain. The t-pike road from Bedford to Greensburg, is on the S. boundary.

Shade creek, a tributary of the Great Aughwich creek, rises in Dublin t-ship, Huntingdon co., and flows N. W. about 10 ms. through Shade mtn. to its recipient.

Shade mountain, a ridge of the Allegheny chain, which rises in Bedford co., and runs N. E. through Huntingdon into Mifflin co. In length above 40 ms.

Shade gap, in Shade mtn., through which Shade creek flows, gives name to a p-o. 117 ms. N. of W. C., and 67 from Harrisburg.

Shade, p-o., Shade t-ship, Somerset co., near Shade furnace.

Shaffers, p-o., Northampton co., 210 ms. N. E. from W. C., and 111 from Harrisburg.

Shaefferstown, p-t. of Heidelberg t-ship, Lebanon co., 8 ms. S. E. of the boro' of Lebanon, 129 N. from W. C., and 32 E. from Harisburg; contains about 100 dwellings, 4 stores, 4 taverns, 1 Lutheran and 1 Presbyterian church.

Shamokin, t-ship, Northumberland co., bounded N. by Rush, E. by Columbia co., S. E. by Schuylkill co., S. W. by Little Mahanoy t-ship, and W. by Augusta township. Centrally distant from Sunbury about 13 miles. Greatest length 16 miles, breadth 10 miles ; area, 56,960 acres ; surface hilly, valleys ; soil, alluvial, red shale and gravel. Pop. in 1830, 1909. Big Roaring creek flows N. W. along its eastern boundary and the Shamokin creek through the t-ship from S. E. to N. W. Snyder's town is on the latter about two miles from the W. line. The Sunbury and Danbury turnpike roads cross the t-ship. It has four churches, with a circle of 4 miles in diameter. A post office is established on the Sunbury road about the middle of the t-ship, called after the t-ship, and distant 174 miles N. from W. C. and 64 from Harrisburg. There are about a dozen dwellings, store and tavern here, and the name "Shamokin," of Indian derivation, is given to the town.

Shamokin creeks, Great and Little, the former rises in the S. E. angle of Shamokin t-ship, Northumberland co., and flows a N. W. course by Snyder's town in that t-ship, and thence across Augusta t-ship, to within two miles of Sunbury, and thence turning S. W. it empties into the Susquehannah river about the same distance below that town. It receives the Little Shamokin nearly opposite to Sunbury. The course of the main stream is about 30 miles, and of its tributary which rises in Augusta t-ship on the north side of the Mahanoy mountain and flows N. W. about 9 miles.

Shamokin hills, Northumberland co. run E. and W. across the county, N. of the Shamokin creek, and form the boundary between Rush and Shamokin t-ships.

Shamokin island, Northumberland co., in the north branch of the Susquehannah river, above its junction with the west branch, between the towns of Northumberland and Sunbury.

Shanksville, village of Stoney Creek t-ship, Somerset co., 9 miles E. of Somerset borough, contains 10 or 12 dwellings, one store, a grist mill, saw mill, and fulling mill.

Sharp mountain. This name is given to the third range north of the Kittatinny mountains through the greater part of its extent in Schuylkill county. It may be said to commence at Cold Spring in Lebanon co., and to run N. E. about 75 miles, to near the head of the east branch of the Schuylkill river, and thence under the names of Tuscarora and Mauch Chunk mountain, 16 miles to the river Lehigh. The range in fact extends from Cold Spring run westward, 15 or 16 miles to within 3 miles of the Susquehannah, under the name of the "*Third mountain*," having altogether a length of about 70 miles. During the whole of this distance it is characterized by its sharp ascent and narrow apex. It is remarkable as forming in all that course the south boundary of the anthracite coal region of Pennsylvania.

Sharp's mills, post office, Indiana co., 197 miles N. W. from W. C. and 165 from Harrisburg.

Sharon, village, Brighton township, Beaver co. (See Bridgewater.)

Sharon, post town of Pymatuning t-ship, Mercer co., on the line dividing that t-ship from Shenango, and on the west bank of Shenango creek, about 14 miles west of the borough of Mercer, 281 N. W. of W. C., and 249 from Harrisburg ; contains some 20 dwellings, stores and taverns.

Shartlesville, post town, Berks co. 156 miles from W. C. and 48 from Harrisburg.

Shaver's creek, Providence t-ship, Bedford co., a tributary of the Raystown branch of the Juniata. Its course is from south to north.

Shaver's Creek, post office, West t-ship, Huntingdon co., 152 miles N. W. from W. C, and 88 S. W. from Harrisburg, at the town of Petersburg.

Shaw's Meadows, post office, Northampton co., 226 miles N. E. of W. C. and 125 from Harrisburg.

Shawney Town, Plymouth t-ship, Luzerne county, on the northern bank of the Susquehannah river, about 5 miles S. W. of Wilkesbarre. This place and the rich alluvial flats around it formed the favorite seat of the Shawanese after their expulsion from the forks of the Delaware.

Sheimer'sville, a village in Lower Saucon t-ship, Northampton co., on the road from Phil. to the Wind gap, containing four dwellings, one tavern, 1 store, 1 grist mill, 1 oil mill.

Shellsburg, a p-t. of Napier t-ship, Bedford co., on the turnpike road leading from the town of Bedford to Greensburg; 8 ms. N. W. of the latter; 135 ms. from W. C.; 113 from Harrisburg. Contains about 50 dwellings, 4 stores and 3 taverns.

Shenango, town-ship, Beaver co., bounded N. by Mercer co., E. by Butler co., S. by North Sewickly t-ship, and W. by Beaver r. Centrally distant N. from Beaver, 18 ms.; greatest length 12½, breadth 6 ms.; area, 37,120 acres; surface rolling; soil, loam and limestone. Pop. 1830, 1907; taxables, 308. The Shenango creek flows into Beaver r. across the N. W. angle of the t-ship, and Slippery Rock creek crosses the t-ship near the E. boundary.

Sherman's creek, Perry co., rises on the W. border of the county, and flows by a course generally E. more than 40 ms. to the Susquehannah at the town of Petersburg, draining the greater portion of the county.

Shenango, township, Mercer co., bounded N. by Pymatuning t-ship, E. by Lackawanock, S. by Mahoning, and W. by Ohio state. Centrally distant S. W. of Mercer borough, 11 ms.; greatest length 8, breadth 6 ms.; area, 30,720 acres; surface, level; soil, clay and loam. Pop. 1830, 656; taxables, 294; taxable property in 1829, real estate, $76,481; personal, 21,871; rate of tax, 4 mills on the dollar. The Shenango creek, from which the t-ship has its name, flows from N. W. to S. E. through it. P-o., 261 ms. N. W. from W. C. and 230 from Harrisburg.

Shenango creek, or Small river, rises in the N. W. angle of Crawford co., in Beaver t-ship, and flows S. E. into Delaware t-ship, Mercer co., where, making what is termed the Big Bend, it runs W. and S. W. into Shenango t-ship, whence turning S. E. it runs through that and Mahoning t-ships, into the Mahoning r. Shenango t-ship, Beaver co., and with its recipient forms Big Beaver river.

Shenango, North, t-ship of Crawford co., pop. 1830, 952.

Shenango, South, t-ship, Crawford co., pop. 1830, 662.

Sheshequin, t-ship, Bradford co., bounded N. by Athens t-ship, E. and S. by Wysox, and W. by the Susquehannah river. Centrally distant N. from Towanda, 7 ms.; greatest length 6, breadth 3¼ ms.; area, 9520 acres; surface, hilly; soil, gravelly loam. Pop. 1830, 720; taxables in 1828, 124. It is drained by several small creeks which flow into the Susquehannah r. The p-o. called after the t-ship, is 247 ms. N. W. of W. C. and 136 from Harrisburg.

Shepperdstown, p-t., Cumberland co., 102 ms. N. of W. C. and 8 W. from Harrisburg.

Shickshinny mountain, Luzerne co., extends across Huntingdon, Salem, and Union t-ships, and along the bank of the Susquehannah, whose course it breaks, and deflects at right angles. A ferry is established across the r. at the extremity of the angle.

Shickshinny creek, Luzerne co., is formed by three considerable streams which flow from various parts of the Shickshinny mtn. into the Susquehannah r., where its course is arrested and turned by the mtn. The main branch of the creek flows S. through Union t-ship; the second rises in Huntingdon and the third in Salem t-ship; all are rapid and good mill streams

Shickshinny, p-o., Union t-ship, Luzerne co., 211 ms. from W. C. and 101 from Harrisburg.

Shinersville, p-t., of Cherry t-ship, Lycoming co., upon the Berwick turnpike road, about 35 ms. N. E. of Williamsport; 225 from W. C., and 114 from Harrisburg. Contains some half dozen dwellings, store and tavern.

Shippen, t-ship, McKean co., bounded N. by Walker, E. by Potter and Lycoming counties, S. by Clearfield co., and W. by Cooper and Burlington t-ships. Centrally distant S. E. from Smethport, 25 ms.; greatest length 15, breadth 9 ms.; area, 85,760 acres; surface, rough and mountainous; soil, barren, slate on the hills, rich alluvion in the valleys. It is drained by the Driftwood and another branch of the Sinnemahoning creek. Upon the former there are some salt springs and salt works at a settlement of two or three families, called Emporium, where is also the p-o. of the t-ship, called "Shippen." The whole pop. was in 1830, 110 souls.

Shippensburg, t-ship, Cumberland co., bounded N. and E. by Newtown t-ship, S. by Southampton, W. by Franklin county, and N. W. by Hopewell t-ship. Centrally distant from the borough of Carlisle, W. 20 ms.; greatest length, about 6 ms.; breadth, 5; area, 12,800 acres; surface, level; soil, limestone. Pop. in 1830, 1800; taxables, 1828, 333; value of real estate, $199,448.

Shippen, t-ship, Tioga co., surface hilly; soil, gravel and loam. Pop. 1830, 122; taxables, 1828, 69.

Shippensburg, p-t. and borough, on the W. boundary of Cumberland co., 21 ms. S. W. of Carlisle, 37 from Harrisburg, 136 W. of Phil., and 11 N. E. of Chambersburg. The town is situated in the heart of a fertile country, and contains about 300 dwellings and 1808 inhabitants. Its pop. in 1810 was 1159, in 1820, 1410. Means run, a mill stream and branch of the Conedogwinit creek, passes through it and turns some mills in the town. There are here about 270 dwellings, 1 Presbyterian, 1 Seceder, 1 Methodist and 1 Lutheran church. The town was incorporated by an act of assembly, 21st January, 1819.

Shippensville, p-t. Venango co., on the turnpike road from Brookville to Franklin, 17 ms. S. E. of the latter; 256 from W. C., and 189 from Harrisburg; contains 16 or 20 dwellings, store and 2 taverns, and a number of tradesmen.

Shiremanstown, p-t. of Cumberland co., 106 ms. from W. C. and 4 from Harrisburg.

Shirley, t-ship, Huntingdon co., bounded N. by the Juniata r., N. E. by Mifflin co., E. by Tell t-ship, S. by Springfield, and W. by Union t-ships. Centrally distant from Huntingdon borough, 10 ms.; greatest length 10, breadth 10 ms.; area, 62,080 acres; surface, hilly; soil, clay. Pop. 1830, about 1500; taxables, 292. Iron is found abundantly in the t-ship, and some iron works are erected. The p-t. of Shirleysburg, is near the E. border of Aughwick creek, 16 ms. S. of Huntingdon borough. In 1828 there were in the t-ship, 4 grist mills, 7 distilleries, 2 tan yards, 1 carding machine, and 1 powder mill.

Shirleysburg, p-t., Shirley t-ship, Huntingdon co., near the Aughwick creek, 16 ms. S. of Huntingdon borough; contains 30 dwellings, 3 taverns, 3 stores, 1 distillery, 2 physicians. It is 128 ms. N. W. from W. C. and 78 S. W. from Harrisburg.

Shrewsbury, p-t-ship, York county, bounded N. by York t-ship, E. by Hopewell, S. by the state of Maryland, and W. by Codorus t-ship. Centrally distant S. from the borough of York 10 ms. Greatest length 11¾, breadth 9 ms.; area 44,800 acres; surface undulating; soil gravelly and poor. Pop. in 1830, 2571; taxables 394. Taxable property in 1829, real estate $343,197; personal 17,711; occupations 29,975; total 390,883; rate 25 cts in the $100. The S. branch of Codorus creek bounds it W., and the E. branch on the N. and E. The turnpike road from York to Baltimore, runs S. through the t-ship, upon which in the S. part, lies the town of Strasburg, at which is a p-o. called after the t-ship 72 ms. from W. C. and 38 from Harrisburg.

Shoemaker-town, a small hamlet on the Willow Grove turnpike, Cheltenham t-ship, Montgomery co. There are here a very fine grist mill, a store and 4 or 5 good dwellings. It is about 8 miles from Philadelphia.

Shohokin creek, a small tributary of the Delaware river, rises in and has its whole course through Scott t-ship, Wayne co., and joins the river about a mile above the south east corner of the t-ship. It is a mill stream, but not navigable.

Shoholo creek, has its source in Lackawanna and Upper Smithfield townships, Pike co., and running a N. E. course forms the boundary between these t-ships, and empties into the Delaware 4 or 5 ms. below the Lackawaxen creek, turning several mills in its course.

Shrawder's creek, mill stream, Scott t-ship, Wayne county, rises about the centre of the t-ship, and flows N. E. into the Delaware.

Shrewsbury, t-ship, Lycoming co., bounded N. by Tioga co., E. by Cherry t-ship, S. by Penn t-ship, and W. by Elkland t-ship. Centrally distant from Williamsport N. E. 25 miles. Greatest length 21 ms.; breadth 8 miles; area 64,000 acres; surface mountainous; soil various. Pop. in 1830, about 400; taxables 71. Value of taxable property 1829, seated lands, &c. $18,745, ; unseated lands, &c. 20,122 ; personal estate 3157 ; rate of levy ¾ of 1 per cent. It is drained W. by the Loyalsock, Little Loyalsock and Muncy creeks. There are several small lakes in the t-ship, and abundance of coal and iron. The p-o. is at Mount Lewis.

Siddons Town, post town, Monohan t-ship, York co., on the road leading to Harrisburg, 20 N. W. of the boro' of York.

Sideling hill, a noted chain of the Allegheny mountain, running N. E. from the Maryland line through Bedford and Huntingdon counties to the Juniata river, a distance of more than 50 miles. It is penetrated only by two streams, the Conoloway creek on the south, and a branch of the Aughwick creek on the border of Bedford and Huntingdon counties.

Sidney's knob, a noted hill and spur of the Tuscarora mountain, in the E. border of Dublin township, Bedford county.

Silver creek, Silver Lake t-ship, Susquehannah co., flows from Silver lake S. E. into Snake creek. It is a fine mill stream, with several mills upon it, but is not navigable.

Silver creek, Schuylkill township, Schuylkill co. a small stream which falls into the Schuylkill river about 4 miles east of Port Carbon. It is important only as affording access and drainage to the coal mines.

Silver Spring, t-ship, Cumberland co., is bounded N. by Perry co., E. by Pennsborough t-ship, S. by Monroe t-ship, and W. by N. Middleton t-ship. Centrally distant N. E. from Carlisle 7 miles ; greatest length 7, breadth 5 miles ; area, 22,400 acres ; surface hilly with fine valleys ; soil, lime and slate. Pop. in 1830, 1792 ; taxables in 1828, 477 ; valuation of real estate $839,318. The Conedogwinit creek runs centrally through the t-ship from E. to W., receiving two small tributaries from it. The turnpike road from Harrisburg to Carlisle passes westerly through it, upon which 6 miles from Carlisle, is the small town of Kingstown.

Silver Lake, t-ship, Susquehannah co., bounded N. by New York, E. by Lawsville, S. by Bridgewater and W. by Choconut and Middletown t-ships. It is drained from the W. by branches of the Choconut creek, and from the E. by the tributaries of Snake creek, among which, the most noted is Silver creek, flowing from the lake which gives name to the t-ship. Silver lake received its name from Dr. Robert H. Rose, who has a handsome seat upon its bank. It is a beautiful sheet of water, three-fourths of a mile in length and half a mile in breadth. There are other small lakes in the t-ship. Quaker lake, about 2 miles N. E. of Silver lake, is somewhat larger than the latter, and an intermediate one somewhat smaller. The township is small, of an oblong form. Greatest length N. and S. about 9 ms. breadth E. and W. 5 miles; area, 28, 800 acres; surface hilly; soil, loam, clay and gravel; pop. in 1830, 516; taxables in 1828, 81. The Bridgewater and Wilkesbarre turnpike road is continued through this t-ship to the New York line. There is a post office on the bank of Silver lake, at the seat of Dr. Rose; distant 280 miles from W. C., 172 from Harrisburg.

Sinking run, rises in Macungy t-ship and flows easterly in S. Whitehall t-ship, Lehigh co., where it sinks into the ground about 5 miles W. of Northampton borough. It is supposed to have a subterraneous course of more than a mile southward, and to rise at the fountain of Cedar creek in Macungy, where it has sufficient force to turn a large grist mill at about six perches from the fountain.

Sinking Valley mills, post office, Sinking Valley, Huntingdon co., 170 miles from W. C., 113 from Harrisburg.

Sinking run, Sinking valley, Tyrone t-ship, Huntingdon co., is a considerable stream, which gives name to the valley through which it runs. This stream rises in the south boundary of the t-ship, and flows north a few miles to sink into the earth, as do also some smaller streams of the same valley. During the revolutionary war this valley became remarkable on account of the lead mines which were wrought here, under the auspices of the state. The following description of this valley, and of the mining operations once carried on in it, we are assured merits full credit. In the prosecution of the mining scheme, some miners from Europe were employed; a large log fort was erected for their protection, and considerable quantities of valuable ore were obtained. Several regular shafts were sunk to a considerable depth. Lead enough was made to give a favorable idea of the value of the mines. The work, however, was abandoned on account of the dangers from Indian incursions, and the disqualification of European nature for a forest life. Iron ore is also found in the valley of every species, and in the greatest abundance. The surrounding hills abound with white flint, and from their abrupt forms and thick covering of pines, have a very sombre appearance.

Among the *swallows* which absorb several of the largest streams of the valley, and after conveying them for several miles under ground, return them to the surface, that called the Arch spring is the most remarkable. It is a deep hollow in the limestone rock, about 30 feet in width, with a rude arch of stone hanging over it, forming a passage for the water, which gushes forth with some violence and in such quantity as to form a fine stream, which after a short course buries itself again in the bosom of the earth. Many pits nearly 300 feet deep open into this subterraneous river, at the bottom of which the water appears of the color of ink, though as pure as that which sparkles from the rocky fountain.

The stream again emerges to day and runs along the surface for a few rods among rocky hills, when it enters the mouth of a large cave, whose aperture is sufficient to admit a sloop with her sails full spread. Within, the cave is about 20 feet high, declining somewhat as it proceeds, along which runs a ledge of loose rocks, affording a tolerable safe passage. In the middle of the cave the bodies and branches of trees are seen lodged quite up to the roof, whence it may be inferred that the water swells to the very top during freshets, when the surrounding mountains pour into this channel the clouds which break upon their sides, and marks on the external sides of the cave show that the waters escape thence into the lower country. Having continued about 400 yards into the hill, the cave widens at a sudden turn, which prevents discovery until you are within it, into a spacious saloon, at the bottom of which is a precipitous fall, and a vortex of amazing force, by which large pieces of timber are immediately absorbed, and carried out of sight. The water boils up with great violence when such substances are thrown into it, but it soon after subsides. The stream is supposed to continue its subterraneous course for several miles beneath the Brush and Canoe mountains, and to reappear by two branches in Canoe valley, and to fall into the Frankstown branch of the Susquehannah at the point where it breaks through Tussey's mountain.

Sinnemahoning river, rises by Bennet's branch in Fox t-ship, Clearfield co., and flowing N. E. between 30 and 40 miles, receives the Driftwood branch, which has its source near the centre of McKean co., thence running west about 5 miles, it receives the east branch, which rises in Potter co., and thence by a S. E. course of about 11 miles, it unites with the W. branch of the Susquehannah river, having a comparative course of more than 50 ms.

Sinnemahoning, post office, Lycoming co., Chapman t-ship.

Skinner's Eddy, post office, Luzerne co., 267 miles from W. C., and 157 from Harrisburg.

Skippack creek, Montgomery co., rises by several branches in Franconia, Hatfield, Gwynnedd and Worcester t-ships, and flows S. W. through Lower Salford, Towamensing, Perkiomen and Skippack t-ships, and unites with Perkiomen creek about the middle of the line which divides Upper and Lower Providence t-ships, and 4 miles from the mouth of that stream.

Skippack, post office, Perkiomen and Skippack t-ships, Montgomery co., about 5 miles above Norristown, 160 N. E. from W. C. and 99 from Harrisburg. (See Perkiomen.)

Slate creek, post office, Armstrong county.

Slate lick, post office, Lycoming county.

Slippery Rock creek, tributary of Beaver river, rises by many branches in Butler, Mercer and Venango t-ships, which unite in the N. E. angle of Beaver co., and receiving the Conequenessing from the S. E., fall into the river 12 miles N. of the borough of Beaver.

Slippery Rock, t-ship, Butler county, bounded N. by Mercer t-ship, E. by Parker, S. by Centre and Muddy Creek t-ships, and W. by Mercer co. Centrally distant N. W. from Butler borough 15 miles. Greatest length 13½, breadth 6 miles; area, 43,200 acres; surface hilly; soil, loam. Pop. in 1830, 1541; taxables, 312. It is drained by Slippery Rock creek, and Wolf creek, its tributary. The turnpike road from Butler to Mercer runs through the W. part of the t-ship, and on it is a post office and the small town of Centreville. The post office has the name of the t-ship, and is 254 miles from W.C., and 214 from Harrisburg.

Slippery Rock, t-ship, Mercer co., bounded N. by Springfield t-ship, N. E. by Wolf Creek t-ship, S. E. by Butler co., S. by Beaver co., and W. by Neshannock t-ship. Centrally distant S. E. of Mercer borough 11 ms. Greatest length 9½, breadth 8; area, 32,200 acres; surface level; soil, clay and loam. Pop. in 1830, 1523; taxables 258. Slippery Rock creek crosses the S. E. angle of the t-ship, and on it lies the p-t. of Hacklandsburg. Taxable property in the t-ship 1829, real estate $61,976; personal 9,264; rate of tax 5½ mills on the dollar.

Slut's run, a small stream in Plumstead t-ship, Bucks co., which falls into the Delaware river opposite Black's Eddy.

Smethport, post town and st. jus. of McKean co., in Keating t-ship, at the confluence of Stanton with Potatoe creek, 273 miles N. W. from W. C., and 209 from Harrisburg. Contains about 40 dwellings, a grist mill, saw mill and fulling mill, 2 stores, 2 taverns of brick and frame—a court house and county offices, spacious and commodious also of brick—a stone prison, &c. &c. There is a newspaper printed here. An academy endowed with considerable estate, by John Keating, Esq. and others, and with 2000 dollars by the act of assembly 19th Jan., 1829, by which the institution was incorporated.

Smith's gap, an opening in the Blue mountain, in Moore t-ship, Northampton co., through which a road passes to Bethlehem.

Smith, t-ship, Washington county, bounded N. and W. by Hanover township, E. by Robinson, S. E. by Mount Pleasant, and S. W. by Cross Creek t-ships. Centrally situated N. W. from Washington borough 16 miles. Greatest length 10, breadth 6 miles; area, 26,040 acres; surface pretty level; soil, loam. Pop. in 1830, 2089; taxables 398. It is drained N. W. by Raccoon creek and its branches. Burgettstown, a post town, is centrally situated in the t-ship, on Burgett's branch of Raccoon creek.

Smith's mills, post town, Clearfield co., 188 miles N. W. of W. C., and 120 from Harrisburg.

Smithfield creek, Northampton co., is formed by the union of the Pokono, Broadhead's and McMichael's creeks, near the village of Stroudsburg. It is navigable a very short distance above the river Delaware, into which it enters.

Smithfield, t-ship, Northampton co, bounded N. by Pike co., S. E. by the river Delaware, which separates it from New Jersey, S. by Upper Mount Bethel, and W. by Stroud t-ship. The t-ship forms a triangle with a curved base. Its greatest length is 8½ ms.; and greatest breadth 7¾ ms; surface, hilly; soil, gravel. Pop. 1830, 1080; taxables, 1828, 194. It is watered by the Delaware river, Mill, Marshall's, Smithfield and Cherry creeks. Dutotsburg is the only village. This t-ship is remarkable for the Delaware Water gap, an opening supposed to have been forced by the river through the Blue mountain; forming one of the most picturesque scenes in the state.

Smithfield, Middle, t-ship, Pike co., bounded northward by Palmyra and Delaware t-ships, S. by Northampton co., E. by the Delaware r., and W. by the Lehigh r. It is watered on the W. by the latter river and its tributaries, Trout creek and the Great and Little Tobyhanna; and on the west by the Delaware and its confluents, Broadhead's, Marshall's, Mill and Bushkill creeks. The Belmont and Easton turnpike passes through the t-ship and connects with another turnpike. The surface of the township is broken and hilly; the soil is gravelly loam; the timber, pine, hemlock, beech, maple and oak. It is little cultivated and thinly inhabited. Pop. 1830, about 1300; taxables in 1828, 249. Its greatest length is 30, and its average width, 5½ ms.

Smithfield, Upper, t-ship, Pike co., bounded N. and E. by the Delaware river, S. by Delaware, and W. by Lackawanna t-ships. Shohola creek runs a N. E. course, along almost the whole of its western boundary, and Big Pond, Glass, Saw, and Ramy's creeks, all have their sources and courses within the t-ship, and empty into the Delaware river. The Milford and Owego turnpike crosses the t-ship centrally, in a N. W. direction. Milford, the county town, is located in it, and lies upon the Delaware, 55 ms. above Easton. The greatest length of the t-ship, E. and W. is 14½ ms.; greatest width N. and S. 12½ ms.; surface, hilly; soil, generally loam. Pop. in 1830, about 1300.

Smithfield, post township, Bradford co., bounded N. by Athens t-ship, E. by Ulster, S. by Burlington t-ships, and W. by Springfield. Centrally distant from Towanda, 9 ms.; greatest length, 7½ ms.; breadth, 6½ ms.; area, 24,320 acres; surface, hilly; soil, gravelly loam. Pop. 1830, 1126; taxables, 197. The t-ship is drained chiefly by Tom Jack's and Brown's creeks. East Smithfield p-o. is 249 ms. N. W. from W. C., and 138 from Harrisburg; and North Smithfield

253 from the former and 142 from the latter.

Smithfield, p-t. George, t-ship, Fayette co., between the N. fork of George creek and York's run; 8 ms. S. W. of Union town; 171 miles N. W. from W. C. and 170 S. W. from Harrisburg; contains about 60 dwellings, 1 church, 1 school, 3 stores and 2 taverns.

Smithfield, p-t, Porter t-ship, Huntingdon co., on the W. side of the Frankstown branch of the Juniata, opposite to the borough of Huntingdon. A turnpike road runs from this town to Ebensburg, in Columbia co.

Smithfield, village, p-t. of Moreland t-ship, Philadelphia co., 14 ms. from Philadelphia by the Frankford, Bustleton and Smithfield turnpike road; contains between 30 and 40 dwellings, 2 stores and 2 taverns.

Smythfield, village, Somerset co., contains 30 dwellings, 3 taverns, 4 stores and a Methodist church.

Snake creek, Susquehannah co., a fine mill stream but not navigable, which empties into the Susquehannah r. in the state of New York, but near to the N. E. angle of Lawsville t-ship, Penn.

Snake Spring valley, Coleraine t-ship, Bedford co., bounded E. by Tussey's mtn., and W. by Dunning's mtn. and S. by the Raystown branch of the Juniata r.

Snyder's tavern, or Snydersville, p-t. of Northampton co., on the north and south turnpike road, 24 miles from Easton; contains 2 dwellings, a store, saw mill and grist mill; distant 212 ms. N. E. of W. C. and 112 from Harrisburg.

Snyderstown, village of Shamokin t-ship, Northumberland co., on the Shamokin creek; 8 ms. S. E. of Sunbury; contains about 50 dwellings, 1 store, 1 tavern, and 1 church common to the German Reformed and Baptists.

Snyderstown, a hamlet of Turbut t-ship, Northumberland co.; centrally situated about 6 ms. N. E. from Milton borough.

Sodom, a hamlet of Chilisquaque t-ship, Northumberland co., on the Chilisquaque creek; 7 ms. N. of Sunbury; contains 8 or 10 dwellings, 2 taverns and 2 stores. Chilisquaque p-o. is in the town, distant 172 miles from W. C. and 62 from Harrisburg.

Solomon's creek, Luzerne co., rises in Wilkesbarre and Hanover t-ships, and flows N. W. into the Susquehannah river. Upon this stream there is a cascade about 3 ms. from Wilkesbarre, where it passes down the Wyoming mtn. It consists of 2 pitches, between rocky cliffs on each side, which confine the creek in a very narrow channel. The whole perpendicular fall may be about 30 ft.

Solebury, t-ship, Bucks co., bounded N. and E. by the r. Delaware, S. by Upper Makefield, W. by Buckingham, and N. W. by Plumstead. Centrally distant from Philadelphia 30 ms; greatest length 7¾ ms., breadth 4½; area, 17,312 acres; surface, rolling; soil, clay and sandy loam. Pop. in 1830, 2961; taxables, 563; by a census of 1827, the t-ship contained 166 dwellings, 150 out houses, 928 white inhabitants, and no blacks. Beside the Delaware, the only streams of the t-ship are a small creek on the N. W., and Pidcocks creek on the S. E. boundaries, and that flowing from Ingham's, or the Great spring. This copious and extraordinary fountain, called by the aborigines, Aquetong, rises from a hollow near the road side, of which the stone on the S. E. side is red shale, whilst that on the N. W. is limestone. The water is remarkably clear and cold in the summer, and does not freeze in the winter. The volume is sufficient, with 18 or 20 ft. fall, to drive 2 pair of stones throughout the year. There are 5 good mill seats upon it, from its source to the confluence of the Delaware at New Hope, a distance of 3 ms. The villages of this t-ship are New Hope, Centre, Lumberville and Milton. New Hope and Lumberville are p-towns. There are two fine bridges across the Delaware, one at New Hope, and the other at Centre. A daily line of stages runs by New Hope to Easton.

Smoketown, a small hamlet of W. Pennsborough t-ship, Cumberland co., 6 miles west of the borough of Carlisle.

Somerhill, t-ship, Cambria co., bounded N. by Cambria and Allegheny t-ships, E. by the Allegheny mtn., S. by Conemaugh t-ship, and W. by Indiana co. Centrally distant from Ebensburg S. 8 ms.; greatest length 21 ms., breadth 9 ms.; surface, hilly; soil, limestone and clay, coal abundant. Pop. in 1830, 852; taxables, 158; valuation of taxable property in 1829, seated lands, &c., $23,741; unseated lands, $17,543; personal, 5016; rate of levy 8½ mills on the dollar.

Somerhill, t-ship, Crawford co. Pop. in 1830, 845.

Somerfield, p-o., Somerset co., 195 ms. N. W. from W. C., and 173 W. from Harrisburg

Somerset, t-ship, Washington co., bounded N. and W. by Strabane and Nottingham, E. by Fallowfield, S. E. by Pike run, S. W. by W. Bethlehem. Centrally distant S. E. from Washington borough 12 ms.; greatest length 8½, breadth 7½ ms.; area, 30,080 acres; surface, hilly; soil, loam. Pop. in 1830, 1573; taxables, 259. It is drained by the N. and S. forks of Pigeon creek on the E., and by branches of Little Chartier's creek on the W. The t-pike road from Greensburg to Washington borough, runs along the N. boundary. The p-t. of Bentleysville lies on the S. fork of Pigeon creek, 15 miles S. E. from Washington.

Somerset, county, was separated from Bedford by act of 17th April, 1795, and is now bounded N. by Cambria, E. by Bedford, S. by Allegheny co., in the state of Maryland, W. by Fayette co., Pennsylvania, and N. W. by Westmoreland co.; greatest length 38 ms., mean width 28; area, 1066 sq. ms. Central lat. 40° N., and long. from W. C. 2° 22′ E.

The great portion of the county lies W. of the main ridge of the Allegheny, and the whole is embraced by that ridge and the Little Allegheny mtn. on the E., and the Laurel hill on the W.; and is therefore within the great secondary formation of the state. Salt, coal and iron, are found in various parts of the co. The first is most abundant in the eastern and northern sections; the others may be obtained in every t-ship. Beside the mtns. we have named, there is a considerable elevation running in from Maryland, through nearly half the county, which is called Negro mtn., and forms a dividing ridge for the waters. Yet, the county cannot be termed very hilly; part is rolling, and part level; the soil, generally of loam, is well adapted to grain, and the clayey portions peculiarly fitted for meadow grasses.

Few counties in the state are better watered. In Somerset and Stoney Creek t-ships, the streams are divided, and form the elevated land which separates them they flow N. and S. Towards the north runs Stoney creek, a chief constituent of the Conemaugh r., which unites at Johnstown with the Little Conemaugh. Stoney creek receives from the co. on the left, the Quemahoning creek, which has two considerable forks, and several smaller tributaries, and from the right, Shade creek, which has also numerous ramifications. In the S. eastern part of the county, Castleman's r. rises in Greenville t-ship, near the state line, and flowing N. W. through a gap of the main Allegheny, receives in Mifflin t-ship Cox's creek, which runs southward by the town of Somerset to meet it; thence deflecting S. W., the river flows to the western boundary, and unites with the Youghiogheny. Laurel creek rises in Somerset t-ship, and running southward parallel with the Laurel mtn., also pours its waters into the Youghiogheny r., within a mile below the mouth of Castleman's r.

Three t-pike roads pass through the co.; one through Somerset borough, to the town of Washington, in Washington co.; another from Bedford, by

Steystown to Greensburg, and thence to Pittsburg; and the Cumberland or National road, which traverses by the town of Petersburg, the S. W. angle of the co. Upon these, and on the principal country roads, good bridges, generally of stone, are erected.

The towns of the county, are Somerset borough, Milford, Lexington, Petersburg, Smithfield, Salisbury, Steystown, Jennerville, Shanksville, Berlin, &c.

The population of the county, composed chiefly of German descendants, was in 1810, 11,284; in 1820, 13,890; and in 1830, 17,741; of whom 9075 were white males, 8583 white females, 41 free colored males, 41 free colored females, 1 slave; of these there were 70 aliens, 10 blind, 9 deaf and dumb; the taxables in 1828, 3340.

This population is divided into the following religious sects, viz., the Lutheran, having 17 churches; German Reformed 12, Methodists 8, Menonists 5, Baptists 4, Omish 4, English Presbyterians 2, and Roman Catholic 1. A county Bible society has been established, and Sunday schools and tract societies in every district. An academy at the borough of Somerset was incorporated in 1810, and received from the state a donation of $2000. *Country schools* are supported by the inhabitants in every t-ship, which are well attended in the winter season.

Large quantities of wheat, and rye, and oats are raised, the latter of which is uncommonly heavy. But the chief rural business is grazing. The breed of cattle is somewhat peculiar, being very small horned, and is much esteemed. The butter is of excellent quality, and is exported in large quantities. Much attention is also given to the breeding of sheep. The chief manufactures are of flour, iron, and whiskey. There are in the county, 65 grist mills, 90 saw mills, 12 fulling mills, and 25 carding engines for wool, 3 furnaces, and 3 forges, and 20 distilleries. The cultivation of the grape has been successfully attempted; of which there is a notable plantation near Steystown, established about 5 years since.

Somerset, Bedford, and Cambria counties form the 13th judicial district; sending one member to congress; Somerset and Bedford alone constitute the 22nd senatorial district, sending one member to the senate of the state; and the county sends two members to the house of representatives.

By the assessment of 1829, the taxable property of the county was valued, viz., seated lands, $1,086,864; unseated, $43,444; personal property, including occupations, 108,064. The market price of good lands will vary from 6 to 30 dols. the acre, according to situation and improvement.

This co. paid into the state treasury in 1831, for tax on writs,	183 00
Tavern licenses,	451 21
Duties on dealers in foreign merchandise,	190 10
Tin and clock pedlars' licenses,	85 50
	$909,81

STATISTICAL TABLE OF SOMERSET CO.

Townships &c.	Greatest lth.	Greatest bth.	Area in acres.	Population 1820.	Population 1830.	Taxables
Addison,	10	6	35,000	861	1,185	234
Allegheny,	14	6	55,200	372	506	95
Brothers Valley,	11	8	55,500	1,683	1,875	378
Conemaugh,	9	4	16,360	378	767	130
Elk Lick,	10	8	52,080	1,197	1,531	241
Greenville,	7	6	19,200	394	545	107
Jenner,	10	8	48,800	1,129	1,167	208
Milford,	16	7	59,600	1,394	1,749	340
Quemahoning,	8	5	15,360	796	1,102	190
Stoney Creek,	10	7	46,840	754	1,025	175
Somerset	16	10	86,800	1,954	2,515	475
Somerset boro',			188	442	649	426
Southampton,	9	8	45,960	540	710	126
Shade,	12	11	85,400	948	1,135	222
Turkeyfoot,	13	9	70,560	1,138	1,281	199
			692,548	13,890	17,741	3,340

Somerset, t-ship, Somerset county, bounded N. by Jenner and Quemahoning t-ships, E. by Stoney Creek and Brothers Valley t-ships, S. by Milford t-ship, and W. by Westmoreland co. Greatest length 16, breadth 10 miles; area, 86,800 acres; surface rolling; soil, yellow clay. Pop. in 1830, 2,515; taxables, 475. Taxable property in 1829, $181,784, real estate ; personal 15,528 ; rate 5 mills on the dollar. Laurel hill is on the W. boundary. The t-ship is drained southward by Laurel Hill creek, Middle creek, and Cox's creek, and N. by Wells' creek and the N. and E. forks of the Quemahoning. The turnpike road from Bedford to Pittsburg crosses the t-ship, and through the borough of Bedford.

Somerset, post town and borough, Somerset t-ship, Somerset co., lying on Cox's creek and on the turnpike road leading from Bedford to Pittsburg 37 miles W. of Bedford, and 237 W. of Philadelphia, 165 from W. C., and 143 from Harrisburg. It was incorporated by act of assembly 5th March, 1804, enlarged and explained by act 7th April, 1807. It contains about 150 dwellings, 7 stores, 6 taverns, a court house, and prison of stone, and county offices of brick, an academy, to which the legislature granted $2000 in 1810, 1 German Reformed, 1 Lutheran, 1 Methodist churches, two school houses.

Somerton, post office, Philadelphia co., Moreland t-ship, 151 miles from W. C., and 113 from Harrisburg, and about 14 from Philadelphia.

Somerville, small village of Lower Makefield t-ship, Bucks co., on the road from Attleborough to Yardleyville, 17 miles S. E. from Doylestown; contains 5 or 6 dwellings.

Sougart, a small hamlet of Willistown t-ship, Chester co., 18 miles N. W. of Philadelphia, and 5½ miles N.E. of West Chester.

Soudersburg, a small village of Lampeter t-ship, Lancaster co., on the turnpike road from Lancaster to Philadelphia ; distant E. from the former about 8 miles.

South creek, Bradford co., rises in Springfield t-ship, and flows northerly through Wells and Ridgebury t-ships, into the Tioga r., in the state of N. Y., having a course of about 10 ms.

Southampton, t-ship, Bucks county, bounded N. E. by Northampton, S. E. by Bensalem, S. W. by Philadelphia co. and Montgomery co., and N. W. by Warminster t-ship. Centrally distant from Philadelphia 17 ms., and 12 ms. S. E. of Doylestown ; length 4¾, breadth 2½ ms. ; area, 8254 acres ; surface, rolling ; soil, sandy loam. Pop. in 1830, 1228 ; taxables, 234. The Poquessing creek flows through the S. E. angle, and a branch of the Pennypack crosses the S. W. Southampton Quaker meeting is in the N. W. angle.

Southampton, t-ship, Cumberland co., bounded N. E. by Newtown t-ship, S. E. by Manallen t-ship, Adams co., S. W. by Southampton t-ship, Franklin co., and N. W. by Shippensburg t-ship. Centrally distant S. W. from Carlisle 18 ms. ; greatest length 6, breadth 5 ms. ; area, 17,040 acres ; surface, hilly ; soil, limestone. Pop. in 1830, 1484 ; taxables, 256 ; taxable property in 1829, $501,424. A considerable portion of the t-ship is covered by the S. mtn. ; but this ridge here, as in many other places, is susceptible of cultivation. A small stream rising in the hills, flows N. W. 3 or 4 ms., and is then lost in a limestone sink.

Southampton, t-ship, Somerset co., bounded N. by Allegheny t-ship, E. by Bedford co., S. by the state of Maryland, and W. by Greenville and Brothers' Valley t-ships. Centrally distant S. E. from the borough of Somerset 20 ms. ; greatest length 9, breadth 8 ms. ; area, 45,960 acres ; surface, very hilly; soil, red gravel. Pop. in 1830, 710; taxables, 222; taxable property in 1829, real estate, $21,869 ; personal, including occupations, 4200 ; rate of tax, 5 mills on the dollar. The t-ship is drained by Wills creek and its tributaries, Scaffold Camp run, Laurel run, and Savage run. The falls of Wills creek are near the N. boundary ; upon this creek, near the centre of the t-ship, are salt springs, at which salt works were formerly in operation. The p-o. is named after the t-ship.

South creek, p-o., Wells t-ship, Bradford co., about 260 ms. from W. C., and 148 from Harrisburg.

Southampton, t-ship, Franklin co., bounded on the N. E. by Cumberland co., S. E. by Adams co., S. W. by Letterkenny and Green t-ships, and N. W. by Fannet t-ship. Centrally distant N. E. from Chambersburg 13 ms.; greatest length 20¾, breadth 5 ms.; area, 21,760 acres; surface, level; soil, chiefly limestone. Pop. in 1830, 1655; taxables, 266. The Conedogwinit creek runs along the N. W. line, and Mean's run, its tributary, on the S. E. The borough of Shippensburg, belonging to Cumberland, has been taken in part from this t-ship; a t-pike road runs from it to Chambersburg.

Southampton, t-ship, Bedford co., bounded N. by Coleraine and Providence, E. by Bethel t-ship, S. by the state of Maryland, and W. by Cumberland Valley t-ship. Centrally distant S. from Bedford borough 12 ms.; greatest length 14, breadth 12½ ms.; area, 93,440 acres; surface, mountainous; soil, slate. Pop. in 1830, 1322; taxables, 270.

Southwark, district of, a suburb of the city of Philadelphia. This district was separated from the county of Philadelphia for certain local purposes, by act of assembly 26th March, 1762, which gave to it the following limits, viz.: "Beginning at South-st. in the city, and running thence along the several courses of the road commonly called the Passyunk road, including the same, 296 perches to a corner; thence S. 45° E. to a road called the Moyamensing road; thence along a lane known by the name of Keeler's lane to Greenwich road; thence E. to the r. Delaware; thence up the several courses of the said r. to South-st.; and thence along the south side of the said street to the place of beginning. These limits were confirmed by the act of 18th April, 1794, which incorporated the district, and authorized its government by 15 commissioners, five of whom are elected annually to serve for the term of three years. The greatest length of the district is 1¼ ms., by a breadth of like measure. It contains 760 acres of level alluvial ground; covered in 1830, by about 4000 dwellings, and a pop. of 20,746 souls. There are many very handsome and commodious buildings within this suburb, but there are also a great proportion of two story frame dwellings; and generally, the habitations are inferior in style and extent to those of the city and Northern Liberties. The streets are commonly paved, watched, lighted, and regulated as in the city, and the district is supplied with Schuylkill water from the city water works. The navy yard, and several valuable ship and boat yards, and a marine rail way are on the river Delaware. A brick tower for the manufacture of shot, rises to a great height and is visible from all parts of the district. The district improves rapidly, but most of the houses lately erected, are of brick, two stories, and adapted to the comfortable habitation of persons who depend upon their labor for their subsistence. (*See Philadelphia.*)

Sparta, p-o., Morris t-ship, Washington co., 10 ms. S. of Washington borough; 239 ms. N. W. from W. C. and 212 from Harrisburg.

Sparta, t-ship, Crawford co., pop. in 1830, 304.

Spread Eagle, or Litersville, p-t., of Radnor t-ship, Delaware co., on the Philadelphia and Lancaster turnpike road, 14 ms. from the former; 136 ms. from W. C., and 83 S. E. from Harrisburg; contains 8 or 10 dwellings, a tavern and store.

South West, unorganized t-ship, Warren co., bounded N. by Spring Creek t-ship, E. by Deerfield, S. by Venango co., and W. by Crawford co., centrally distant S. W. 20 ms. It is drained by the branches of Oil creek, has an undulating surface, and contains much good arable land, but few inhabitants.

Spitzberg hill, a distinguished eminence in Linn t-ship, Lehigh co., lying between branches of the Maiden creek.

Spring mills, p-t., Centre co., Ferguson t-ship, 187 ms. from W. C. and 80 from Harrisburg.

Spring, t-ship, Centre co., bounded N. E. by Walker t-ship, S. E. by Potter t-ship, S. W. by Ferguson and Patton t-ships, and N. W. by Boggs t-ship. Greatest length 10, breadth 7 ms.; area, 34,480 acres.; surface, mountainous on the N. E. and S. W. level in the interval. The t-ship is drained by Spring and Logan creeks, which unite at Bellefonte, and passing thence through the Bald Eagle ridge, on the N. W. line, empty into the Bald Eagle creek above Milesboro'; and by Buffalo run which courses the east foot of Bald Eagle mtn. for about 9 ms., & also unites with Spring creek, which is navigable for boats to Bellefonte, about 2 ms. from its mouth. Iron is abundant in the t-ship; many iron works are erected here. (*See Bellefonte.*) The turnpike roads from Lewistown and Phllipsburg cross the t-ship and unite at Bellefonte. Soil in the valleys, limestone. Pop., exclusive of the borough of Bellefonte, in 1830, 1307; taxables, 284.

Spring creek, Centre co., rises in Ferguson t-ship, and flowing through its N. angle, runs diagonally N. W. through Spring t-ship, into Bald Eagle creek; receiving in its course of 20 miles, many tributaries. It gives motion to many mills and iron works.

Spring Dale, p-o., Allegheny co., 235 ms. N. W. of W. C. and 207 from Harrisburg.

Spring creek, Northampton county. (*See Sandy creek.*)

Spring Grove, p-t., Lancaster co., 99 ms. from W. C. and 56 from Harrisburg, in Earl t-ship, at Spring Grove forge.

Spring mountain, Lausanne t-ship, Northampton co. It is noted as forming the southern boundary of the Beaver Meadow coal formation.

Spring mountain, Little, is a continuation of the Mahanoy mtn.; it runs nearly parallel with the Spring mtn and along the N. W. line of Lausanne t-ship, Northampton co., and is the north boundary of the Beaver Meadow coal field.

Spring creek, Londonderry t-ship, Dauphin co., a tributary to the Swatara; it is a short stream, but has several mills and a forge upon it.

Spring creek, or Terrapin pond creek, Sugarloaf t-ship, Luzerne co., flows along the southern side of Hell Kitchen mtn., where it joins the Lehigh below Rock Eddy falls.

Spring House, a noted tavern and p-o., in Gwynnedd t-ship, Montgomery co., the point of departure of the Spring House and Bethlehem turnpike road; 9 ms. N. E. from Norristown; 155 from W. C., and 98 from Harrisburg.

Springfield, t-ship, Montgomery co., bounded N. and N. E. by Upper Dublin, E. by Cheltenham t-ship, S. and S. W. by Philadelphia co., W. and N. W. by Whitemarsh t-ship. Central distance from Philadelphia 10 ms. N. W., from Norristown, 7 miles N. E. Its form is very irregular; greatest length, 6 miles; greatest breadth, 2 ms.; area, 4163 acres. It is drained by a branch of the Wissahickon creek. The Chestnut Hill and Spring House turnpike road crosses it, on which is a small village called Flour town, within a mile of which is Springfield meeting house. Surface, rolling; soil, limestone. Pop. 1830, 668; taxables, 1828, 166.

Springfield, t-ship, Bucks county, bounded N. E. by Durham t-ship, S. E. by Nockamixon, S. by Haycock, S. W. by Richland and Milford, and N. W. by Lehigh co. Central distance from Philadelphia, 40 ms. N.; from Doylestown, 15 miles N. W.; greatest length $10\frac{1}{2}$, greatest breadth 4 ms.; area, 18,312 acres. Durham creek flows in a meandering course N. E. nearly through the t-ship, and branches of the Tohickon creek drain it on the S. W. The former has many mills upon it; and Springtown, at which there is a p-o., lies in the forks of one of its confluents and on the road to Easton. Springfield church is centrally situated. Bursenton, another small village, 2 miles S. E. of Springtown, lies on the road to Ottsville. Surface, rolling; soil, sandy loam. Pop. 1830, 2078; taxables, 1828, 429.

Springfield, Lancaster co., a small village on the turnpike road from Lancaster to Harrisburg, distant from the former about 18 ms. N. W. It lies partly in E. Donegal and partly in Mount Joy t-ships.

Springfield, t-ship, Delaware co., bounded N. by Marple, E. by Upper Darby, S. E. and S. by Ridley, and W. by Nether Providence. Central distance from Philadelphia, 12 miles W.; from Chester 4 ms. N.; length, $3\frac{1}{4}$, breadth $2\frac{1}{4}$ ms. Pop. 1830, 700; taxables, 1828, 144. Crum creek runs along the western boundary. Springfield church is in the angle formed by the intersection of the roads from Darby and Chester.

Springville, t-ship, Susquehannah co., bounded N. by Bridgewater, E. by Brooklyn t-ship, S. by Luzerne co., and W. by Auburn and Rush t-ships. Its greatest length N. and S. is 8 miles; mean breadth 7 miles; area, 35,840 acres. The middle and main branches of Meshoppen creek flow S. W. through the t-ship, and the Wilkesbarre and Bridgewater turnpike road crosses it in a N. E. direction. There is a p-o. called Springville near the south boundary of the t-ship. The surface is hilly; the soil, loam, clay and gravel. Pop. 1830, 1514; taxables, 1828, 213. There is also a p-o. in the t-ship, on the turnpike road leading to Montrose, and a small village called after the t-ship, Springville 4 corners; containing about 25 houses, an Episcopal church, 2 taverns, and 2 or 3 stores; distant 265 ms. from W. C. and 157 from Harrisburg.

Springfield, p-t., W. Pennsborough t-ship, Cumberland co., on the west border, near the Chambersburg turnpike road. It has its name from a large spring, which at its source, gives motion to several mills. The town is 14 ms. S. W. of Carlisle, and contains about 50 dwellings, one store and one tavern.

Springfield, post t-ship, Bradford co., bounded N. by Ridgebury, E. by Smithfield, S. by Troy and Burlington, and W. by Columbia t-ships. Centrally distant N. W. from Towanda, 15 ms.; greatest length $7\frac{1}{2}$, breadth $6\frac{1}{2}$ ms.; area, 30,720 acres; surface, hilly; soil, gravelly loam. Pop. 1830, 765; taxables, 160. The Susquehannah and Tioga turnpike runs northerly through the t-ship, which is drained by Bentley's creek on the N., and by branches of Sugar creek on the south. There is a p-o. in the S. W. angle of the t-ship, on the line which divides it from Troy. P-o. is 255 ms. N. W. from W. C. and 143 from Harrisburg.

Spring Garden, t-ship, York co., bounded N. E. by Hallam, S. E. by Windsor and York, W. by West Manchester, and N. W. by East Manchester. Greatest length $8\frac{1}{2}$, breadth $4\frac{1}{2}$ ms. The Codorus creek runs along the W. and N. W. boundary. The borough of York lies chiefly in this t-ship, to which Freystown, about 2 miles E. may be considered a suburb. The county poor house and house of employment is in this t-ship, near the borough. Area of the township, 14,728 acres; surface, level; soil, limestone and loam. Pop. 1830, 1603; taxables, 276; taxable property in 1829, real estate, $422,733; personal, 13,925; occupations, 24,400; total, 461,058; rate, 25 cents in the $100.

Springhill, t-ship, Fayette, county, bounded N. by German, E. by George t-ships, S. by the state of Md., and W. by Cheat and Monongahela rivers. Centrally distant S. W. from Uniontown, 12 ms.; greatest length, $8\frac{1}{2}$, breadth $6\frac{1}{2}$ ms.; area, 23,680 acres; surface, level; soil, limestone. Pop. 1830, 1934; taxables, 457. It is drained by George creek, at the confluence of which with the Monongahela, lies the p-t. of New Geneva, distant 12 ms. S. W. of Uniontown. Iron is found in several places on the banks of George creek. There is also a p-o. called by the name of the t-ship, 221 ms. N. W. from W. C., and 203 S. E. from Harrisburg. There is a furnace and forge near the S. boundary, for which the ore is obtained from the t-ship.

Spring, t-ship, Crawford co., pop. 1830, 690.

Spring Creek, t-ship, Warren co., bounded N. by Columbus t-ship, E. by Broken Straw t-ship, W. by Crawford and Erie t-ships, and S. by Deerfield and South West t-ships Centrally distant from the borough of Warren, 18 ms.; length 8, breadth 7 ms.; area, 35,840 acres; surface, broken and rocky; soil, gravel, stony and scarce arable. Pop. 1830, 214; taxables, 1828, 57. The Broken Straw creek divides the t-ship into two nearly equal parts, crossing it diagonally from N. W. to S. E. There is a p.o. in the t-ship called by its name, distant 335 ms. N. W. of W. C., and 271 from Harrisburg.

Springfield, t-ship, Mercer county, bounded N. by Cool Spring t-ship, E. by Wolf Creek t-ship, S. by Slippery Rock t-ship, and W. by Lackawannock t-ship. Greatest length 8, breadth 6 ms.; area, 30,720 acres; surface, level; soil, clay and loam. Taxables, 1828, 180; taxable property in the t-ship in 1829, real estate, $82,307; personal, 9222; rate of tax 4 mills on the dollar. The t-ship is drained by the Neshannock creek, which runs S. W. through it. Upon the creek and in the N. W. angle of the t-ship is the borough of Mercer, the county town.

Springfield, t-ship, Huntingdon co., bounded N. by Shirley and Union t-ships, E. by Tell and Dublin t-ships, S. by Bedford co., and W. by Union t-ship. Centrally distant from Huntingdon borough S. 21 ms.; greatest length 11, breadth 10 ms.; area, 52,480 acres; surface, hilly; soil, limestone in the valleys Pop. 1830, 656; taxables, 231. It is drained by the Great Aughwick creek and its branches, which flow N. to the Juniata r. Iron ore abounds in the t-ship, and and there are some iron works on Aughwick creek, called Springfield furnace, at which there is a p-o., and another at Three Springs. There are also in the t-ship, 2 grist mills, 5 saw mills, 1 distillery and 1 tan yard.

Springfield, t-ship, Erie co. bounded N. by Lake Erie, E. by Fairfield and Elk Creek t-ships, S. by Conneaut t-ship, and W. by the state of Ohio. Length 8, breadth 6 miles; area, 24,320 acres. It is drained by Crooked creek, Elk creek and Raccoon creek. There is a p-o., at Springfield cross roads. Surface, hilly; soil, loam. Pop. 1830, 1520; taxables, 281.

Springfield cross roads, Springfield t-ship, Erie co., 24 ms. S. W. of Erie; 330 N. W. from W. C.; 269 from Harrisburg; contains 25 or 30 dwellings, several stores and taverns.

Springtown, p-t. of Springfield t-ship, Bucks co., 179 ms. N. from W. C.; 93 N. E. from Harrisburg; contains 6 or 8 dwellings, a tavern and store.

Spring Garden, district of Phil. co., was taken from Penn t-ship, and incorporated by an act of assembly of 22d March, 1813, by which act and its supplement of 22d March, 1827, it received the following boundary, viz.: Beginning at the middle of Sixth-st. in Vine-st., and running northwardly along the middle of Sixth-st. to a point 200 ft. north of the north side of Poplar lane; thence N. westerly, parallel with, and at the distance of 200 ft. from the said north side of Poplar lane to the middle of Broad-st.; thence parallel with Vine-st. to the r. Schuylkill; thence by the several courses of the said r. to Vine-st., and thence along the north side of Vine-st. to the middle of Sixth-st. aforesaid, the place of beginning. By the foregoing acts the government of this district is vested in fifteen commissioners, five of whom are elected annually, to serve for three years. The district includes many of the objects of interest appurtenant to the city, viz.. Fairmount water works, the eastern penitentiary, the house of refuge, the city hospital, the extensive floor cloth manufactory of Mr. McCauley, Lemon hill, at which are the gardens, much celebrated, of Mr. Pratt, the state rail road, the great single arched bridge over the Schuylkill, and many manufactories for cotton, woollen, sawing marble by steam, &c. &c. The district grows rapidly, and a large city in all probability will in a few years cover its surface. In this t-ship, also, lies the thriving village of Francisville, at which is a manufactory of glass. (*See Phil.*)

Stahler's, p-o., Lehigh co., 188 ms. from W. C., and 92 from Harrisburg.

Standing Stone, p-o., Bradford co., 245 ms. N. W. from W. C., and 143 from Harrisburg.

Stanhope, p-o., Northampton co., 196 ms. from W. C., and 109 from Harrisburg.

Starrets creek, Brunswick t-ship, Schuylkill co., flows into Pine creek about 4 ms. S. E. from Orwigsburg, near the Lutheran church.

Starucca creek, rises in Scott t-ship, Wayne co., where it is fed by three small lakes, and running N. W. it falls into the river Susquehannah in Harmony t-ship, Susquehannah co., about 4 ms. below the state line. It is a rapid stream, affording fine mill seats the whole of its course, but is not navigable either for rafts or boats.

Starrucca, p-o., Wayne co., 284 ms. from W. C., and 186 from Harrisburg.

State Line, p-o., Franklin co., 73 ms. N. W. from W. C., and 64 S. W. from Harrisburg.

Stuckertown, p-town, Forks t-ship, Northampton co., on the road from Easton to the Wind gap, 6 ms. from the former, contains 5 dwellings, a store and a tavern.

Stumptown, p-t. of Bethel t-ship, Lebanon co., about 9 ms. N. E. of Lebanon borough, 139 ms. from W. C., and 29 from Harrisburg, contains 25 or 30 dwellings, a store and tavern.

Sterling, t-ship, Wayne co., bounded N. by the west branch of Waullenpaupack creek, which separates it from Salem t-ship, E. by the south branch of the same creek, which divides it from Lehigh co., S. by Lehigh co., and W. by Luzerne co. Its form is irregular; its greatest length is 10 ms., greatest breadth 7 ms. It is drained on the N. and E. by the Waullenpaupack creek and its tributaries, and on the W. by the Lehigh r. which has its source in this t-ship. The Easton and Belmont turnpike road passes centrally through it. There is a p-o. called "Sterling," 26 ms. S. of Bethany; 237 from W. C. and 146 from Harrisburg. The t-ship contains between 60 and 70 houses, 2 or 3 stores, as many taverns, 2 grist mills, 6 saw mills, 1 carding machine, 24 looms, and 3 schools. Surface, hilly; soil, gravel and loam. Pop. 1830, 495; taxables, 1828, 84; taxable property in 1829, seated, $38,426; unseated, $53,650; personal, including occupations, 6145; rate 4 mills to the dollar.

Sterling ford, on the Tohickon creek, near the point of junction of the t-ships of Haycock, Nockamixon and Tinicum, in Bucks co.

Stephenson's mountain, a prominent hill in the S. E. angle of Monohan t-ship, York co.

Sterrel's gap in the Blue mountain, Middletown t-ship, Cumberland co.; 111 ms. from W. C., and 25 from Harrisburg.

Stewartsville, p-t., North Huntingdon t-ship, Westmoreland co., on the turnpike road from Greensburg to Pittsburg, 12 ms. N. W. of the former, 204 from W. C. and 181 from Harrisburg; contains 12 dwellings, 1 tavern and 2 stores.

Stockport, p-t., on the Delaware r., Buckingham t-ship, Wayne co.; 150 ms. N. of Phil., and 33 from Bethany; 291 N. from W. C., and 188 from Harrisburg. By act of 18th March, 1816, authority was given to incorporate a company for building a bridge across the river here, but the work has never been executed.

Stockertown, p-o., Northampton co., 196 ms. from W. C. and 109 from Harrisburg.

Stoddartsville, p-t. of Covington t-ship, Luzerne co., on the right bank of the Lehigh r., 18 ms. N. E. of Wilkesbarre; 239 from W. C. and 131 from Harrisburg; contains 4 or 5 houses, tavern, store and mill. Some years since it was considered a thriving place, but it is now in a ruinous condition.

Stoney Creek, t-ship, Somerset co., bounded N. by Shade t-ship, E. by Allegheny t-ship, S. by Brothers Valley t-ship, and W. by Somerset and Quemahoning t-ships. Centrally distant N. E. from the borough of Somerset, 12 ms.; greatest length 10, breadth 7 ms.; area, 46,840 acres; surface, level; soil, clay. Pop. 1830, 1025; taxables, 175; taxable property in 1829, real estate, $57,587; personal property, 7408; rate of tax, 5 mills on the dollar. The Allegheny mtn. is on the E. line. The t-ship is drained chiefly by Stoney creek, which receives from it Rhoads and Callender's creeks, & some smaller streams. The turnpike road from Bedford to Stoystown passes along the N. boundary, near which, on the Allegheny mountain, lies Millar's breast work. Iron ore is found in abundance on Stoney creek, in the N. W. angle of the t-ship.

Stoney creek, Northampton co., a small stream rising between the Pohopoko mountain and the Tobyhanna creek, and flowing through the Pine swamp, after a course of six or eight miles falls into the Lehigh upon the east side. It is a rapid water, drives several mills and affords convenient sites for others.

Stoney creek, Dauphin co., rises in Rush t-ship, and flows S. W. between the Second and Third mtn. through Middle Paxton t-ship to the Susquehannah r. It has a course of more than 20 miles, and turns several mills near its mouth. Port Lyon or Dauphin, a small village, lies in the fork formed by its confluence with the r.

Stoney run, Monohan t-ship, York co., runs N. through the t-ship, about 4 miles, to the Yellow Breeches creek.

Stoney creek, the south branch of Conemaugh river, rises in Brothers Valley t-ship, Somerset co., and flows N. W. into Conemaugh t-ship, Cambria co., where it unites with the Little Conemaugh at Johnstown, having a comparative course of about 36 miles, and receiving many considerable streams. It is navigable for boats for about 5 miles from its mouth.

Stout's p-o., so called after the P. M., Isaac Stout; 191 ms. N. E. from W. C. and 103 from Harrisburg.

Stoner'stown, a village of Hopewell t-ship, Bedford co., on the Raystown branch of the Juniata r., 19 miles N. W. of Bedford borough.

Stoystown, post town and borough of Quemahoning t-ship, Somerset co., on Stoney creek, and on the road from Bedford to Greensburg, 29 miles W. from the former, and 10 miles N. E. from the borough of Somerset, 155 N. W. from W. C., and 133 from Harrisburg, contains 40 dwellings, 4 taverns 4 stores and one German Reformed church. The town was erected into a borough by act 29th March, 1819.

Stoughstown, a small village of Newton t-ship, Cumberland co., on the turnpike road leading from Carlisle to Chambersburg, near the east boundary of the t-ship, distant W. from the former about 14 miles, 107 from W. C., 31 W. from Harrisburg; contains 10 or 12 houses, a store and tavern.

Strabane, t-ship, Adams co., bounded N. by Manallen and Tyrone t-ships, E. by Mount Pleasant, S. by Mount Joy, and W. by Cumberland t-ships; greatest length $9\frac{3}{4}$, breadth $7\frac{1}{4}$ ms; area 20,480 acres; surface level; soil, slate. Pop. in 1830, 1308; taxables 265. It is drained on the N. by the Conewago creek, which receives from the t-ship Beaver Dam run and Swift run; on the S. E. by Plumb run, and on the W. by Rock creek which separates it from Cumberland. On this stream Gettysburg, the county town, lies. Hunterstown, a post town, is centrally situated in the t-ship, and New Chester is in the N. E. angle on the Conewago creek. The first is about 6, and the second 9 miles N. E. of Gettysburg.

Strabane, t-ship, Washington co., bounded N. by Cecil, N. E. by Peters, E. by Nottingham and Somerset, S. by Amwell, W. by Canton, and N.W. by Chartier's t-ships. Greatest length 11, breadth 9½ miles ; area, 35,840 acres; surface hilly ; soil loam. Pop. in 1830, 2599 ; taxables 461. The town is drained by Chartier's and Little Chartier's creeks, which unite on the N. W. boundary. The turnpike road from Greensburg runs centrally through it, and the national road, forming part of the S. boundary, crosses the S. W. angle. The borough of Washington is partly in this t-ship.

Strasburg, t-ship, Lancaster co., bounded N. by Leacock, E. by Salisbury, S. E. by Bart, S. W. by Martic and N. W. by Lampeter t-ships. Centrally distant from the city of Lancaster about 9 miles. Greatest length 11½ miles, greatest breadth 6 miles ; area, 25,000 acres ; surface partly hilly, partly rolling ; soil, limestone. Pop. in 1830, 4,036 ; taxables 843. Pecquea creek runs on the N. and W. boundary, Beaver creek on the S. W., and Little Beaver creek flows centrally through the t-ship. On the first there is a forge near the E. boundary. Mine ridge divides it on the S. E. from Bart. The post town and pleasant village of Strasburg is on the "New Lancaster road," and the post town and village of Paradise on the Philadelphia and Lancaster turnpike. The t-ship contains 9 distilleries, 1 tannery, 1 fulling mill, 12 grist mills, 12 saw mills, 1 oil mill, and 1 pottery.

Strasburg, post town and village, Strasburg t-ship, Lancaster co., on the "New Lancaster road," 8 miles E. of the city of Lancaster, and 55 W. of Philadelphia, 116 miles from W. C., and 48 from Harrisburg ; it contains about 140 dwellings, 1 church, 6 stores and 6 taverns. An academy here was incorporated by act 13th Feb. 1823.

Strasburg, Shrewsbury t-ship, York co., on the turnpike road leading from the borough of York to Baltimore, 13 miles S. of the borough.

Strasburg, Upper, post town, Letterkenny t-ship, Franklin co., in a fork of Herren's branch of Conedogwinit creek, 10 miles N. W. of Chambersburg, 13 W. of Shippensburg and 53 E. of Bedford, 43 south east of Harrisburg, and 99 N. W. from W.C.

Strattonville, post town of Clarion t-ship, Armstrong co., on the Mercer and Roseburg turnpike road, about 25 miles N. E. of Kittanning, 249 from W. C., and 180 from Harrisburg ; contains 12 or 15 dwellings, 1 tavern and 1 store.

Strawhntown, a post town and village of Haycock t-ship, Bucks co., on the road from Montgomery square to Hellerstown, about 15 miles N. W. of Doylestown, 175 miles from W. C., 100 from Harrisburg. It contains 12 or 14 dwellings, a store and tavern.

Strickersville, post town, Chester co. 99 miles N. of W. C., and 74 S. E. from Harrisburg.

Strimestown, a small hamlet of Conewago t-ship, York co., near the north line of the t-ship, about 9 miles north of the borough of York, on the road to Newbury.

Strongtown, Wheatly t-ship, Indiana co., on the turnpike road from Indiana borough to Kittanning, 15 miles N. W. from the former, contains 6 dwellings, 2 taverns and a store.

Stroudsburg, a post town and borough, in Northampton county, Stroud t-ship, on the north bank of Smithfield creek, which is formed by the junction near the town of Broadhead's cr. with the Pokono and McMichael's creeks. It is built upon one street, and is the fourth in size in the county. An academy was established here in 1814. The town is three miles N. W. from the Delaware Water gap, 219 from W. C., 118 from Harrisburg, and 30 from Easton. It contains about 80 houses, 2 taverns, 4 stores, 1 grist mill, a tannery, and two places of public worship, one for the Methodists and the other for the Quakers. The town and t-ship may be considered as a Quaker settlement. On the N. of the town runs Broadhead's creek, down which great quantities of lumber are annually sent to market. On the south, the Pokono, a stream sufficiently large for any kind of hydraulic power, is seen occasionally dashing over the bluffs of rocks into the vortex below, and hurrying away as if impatient to mingle with the former. On the east are gentle eminences, well cultivated, and which give agreeable notions of plenty and comfort. The landscape is picturesqe, and the country healthy, and the place will repay the labor of a visit, whether made for pleasure or health. There is an academy in the town, which was incorporated by act of assembly, 28th day of March, 1814, and the town was incorporated by act of 6th February, 1815.

Stroud, t-ship, Northampton county, bounded N. by Pike co., N. W. by Pokono t-ship, S. W. by Hamilton, S. by Upper and Lower Mount Bethel and E. by Smithfield t-ships. Greatest length 8 miles, greatest width 5½ miles; surface partly hilly and partly level; soil, gravel and limestone. Pop. in 1830, 1631; taxables, 275. The t-ship is abundantly watered by the Smithfield creek and its tributaries, Sambo, Broadhead, Sullivan, Pokono and McMichael's creeks, and by Cherry creek.

Sudon's creek, has its chief source in a small lake in Northmoreland t-ship, Luzerne co., and flows easterly in a very serpentine course through Exeter t-ship, into the Susquehannah river. It is a mill stream, but not navigable.

Sugar Grove, t-ship, Warren co., bounded N. by the state of N. York, E. by Pine Grove t-ship, S. by Broken Straw and Spring Creek t-ships, and W. by Columbus t-ship. Centrally distant N. W. from Warren boro' 13 miles. Length 9, breadth 6½ ms.; area, 32,640 acres; surface undulating; soil, fertile loam. Pop. in 1830, 745; taxables in 1828, 133. It is drained by Couwnyanda creek, in a bend of which lies the post town of Sugar Grove, south by Little Broken Straw creek, Young's and Jackson's runs.

Sugar Creek, t-ship, Venango co., bounded N.E. and E. by Sugar creek, S. and S. W. by French creek and N. W. by Crawford co. Centrally distant N. W. from Franklin 8 miles. Greatest length 9, breadth 5 ms.; area 20,480 acres; surface level; soil, rich loam, coal abundant. Pop. in 1830, 1058; taxables, 134. The turnpike road from Franklin, passes N.W. thro' the t-ship.

Sugar creek, Venango co., rises in Crawford co., and flows S. through Plumb t-ship, and between Oil Creek and Sugar Creek t-ships, in Venango co. into French creek, about 4 miles above the borough of Franklin.

Sugar Grove, Warren co., is situated in the t-ship of that name, on the Stillwater creek, one and a half miles south of the New York state line. It contains about 16 dwelling houses, 1 store, 2 taverns, sundry mechanics, a saw and grist mill. It is pleasantly situated and surrounded with groves of sugar maple, hence the name. There is a post office here 15 miles N. W. from Warren borough, 327 from W. C., and 254 from Harrisburg.

Sugar Loaf, t-ship, Luzerne co., (so named from a mountain which at a distance appears shaped like the sugar loaf,) bounded N. E. by Hanover, S. E. by Northampton co., S. by Schuylkill county, S. W. by Columbia co., and N.W. by Nescopeck and Newport t-ships. It is very mountainous. The valleys of the Nescopeck and Black creeks contain some excellent land, which is pretty generally settled and well cultivated. Its streams afford excellent mill sites. The Berwick and Easton turnpike and great stage road passes through it, and a canal is in contemplation across the Nescopeck summit, to unite the waters of the Lehigh and Susquehannah.—(*See Nescopeck creek.*) Its population is German. Exports, the various kinds of grain. Conyngham, in this t-ship, is a thriving and prosperous village, where there is a post office. Sugar Loaf contains 1486 inhabitants, and by the returns of 1828, 287 taxables. Its greatest length is about 23 miles, greatest breadth 8 ms.; area, 85,760 acres. The north boundary runs its whole length along the Nescopeck mountain, and Bucks mountain, a broken range, traverses the t-ship E. and W. parallel to, and about five ms. S. thereof. Yager's mountain is part of the Nescopeck range. Hell Kitchen mountain commences at the head of Nescopeck valley, and extends to the Lehigh river. Pismire hill lies south of Bucks mountain. There are two mountains here that have the name of Sugar Loaf, one in the centre of Nescopeck valley, and the other on the S. W. boundary of the t-ship. The chief tributaries to the Nescopeck creek are, the Little Nescppeck, Oley and Black creeks. Green Mountain run, Spring or Terrapin Pond creek, Sandy creek, and Laurel run flow to the Lehigh.

Sugar Loaf mountain. There are two hills of this name in Sugar Loaf t-ship, Luzerne co., the one a high conical pyramid rising from the centre of Nescopeck valley; it is isolated and has a singular form, whence it derives its name,—the other is called the Long Sugar Loaf mountain, and crosses the S. W. boundary of the township from Schuylkill t-ship.

Sugar Loaf, t-ship, Columbia county, bounded N. by Lycoming co., E. by Luzerne co., S. by Fishing Creek t-ship, and W. by Greenwood. Centrally distant from Danville N. E. 22 miles. Greatest length 9½ miles, breadth 8 miles; area, 36,480 acres; surface diversified; soil, sand and gravel. Pop. in 1830, 678; taxables 127. Bald mountain and North mountain, portions of the Allegheny, cover the northern part. Fishing creek flows south through it, receiving in its course many tributaries from right and left. Sugar Loaf post office is 201 miles N. of W. C., and 91 from Harrisburg.

Sugar creek, Little, Asylum t-ship, Bradford co., rises centrally within the t-ship, whence it receives several tributaries and flows north east into the Susquehannah river, turning several mills in its course.

Sugar creek, Bradford co., rises in Tioga co., on the extreme east boundary, and flows easterly through the the t-ships of Troy, Burlington, and Towanda, into the Susquehannah r. receiving in its course of 25 ms. many considerable streams.

Sugar Creek, t-ship, Armstrong co. bounded N. by Perry t-ship, N. E., E and S. E. by the Allegheny river, S. by Buffalo t-ship, and W. by Butler co. Centrally distant N. W. from Kittanning borough 10 miles. Greatest length 12, breadth 11½ ms.; area, 57,600 acres; surface hilly; soil, loam. Pop. in 1830, 1870; taxables 344. The t-ship is drained by Sugar creek, a small stream, by Denniston's run, Limestone and Buffalo creeks.

Sugar valley, Huntingdon and Mifflin counties, in Shirley t-ship of the one and Lack t-ship of the other, is bounded S. W. by Log mountain and N. W. by the Blue ridge.

Sugar valley, Centre co., Logan t-ship, between 2 ridges of the Nittany mountains. It is about 13 miles long and is drained by Big Fishing creek, which after running more than 10 ms. S. W. is lost in the fissures of the limestone rock. The post office here is 210 miles N. W. from W. C. and 102 from Harrisburg.

Sugar lake, Wayne t-ship, Crawford co. a handsome sheet of water over a mile in diameter, whence proceeds a branch of Sugar creek running S. E. into Sugar Creek t-ship, Venango co. It gives name to a post office near it, which is 307 ms. N. W. of W. C., and 240 from Harrisburg.

Sugar Creek, post office, Wayne

t-ship, Crawford co., 291 miles N. W. of W. C., and 224 from Harrisburg.

Sullivan's creek, Northampton co., rises in Tobyhanna t-ship, and flowing an eastern and southern course, falls into Smithfield creek near Stroudsburg.

Sullivan, t-ship, Tioga co., bounded N. by Jackson t-ship, E. by Bradford co., S. and S. E. by Lycoming co., and W. by Covington t-ship. Centrally distant S. E. of Wellsborough 20 miles. It is drained by the head waters of Tioga river. Its surface is hilly; soil gravelly, but well timbered. The E. and W. state road runs thro' it, upon which is the post town bearing the name of the t-ship. Distant from W. C. 248 miles, from Harrisburg 142.

Summer hill, West Penn township, Schuylkill co., a spur of the Second mountain, called here the Tamaqua mountain.

Sumneytown, post town, on the line dividing Upper Salford from Marlborough t-ship, Montgomery co.; about 20 miles N. E. of Norristown, 166 from W. C., and 98 from Harrisburg, contains 12 dwellings, 1 tavern, 2 stores. There are three powder mills in the neighborhood.

Summit hill, a lofty eminence of Salem t-ship, Luzerne co., crossing the t-ship centrally from E. to W. and abutting on the Susquehannah river, where a ferry is established. It sends forth several small streams which seek the river in various directions.

Sunbury, post town, borough and seat of justice of Northumberland co., in Augusta t-ship, on the east side of the Susquehannah river, 2 miles below the town of Northumberland and 56 N. of Harrisburg, and 164 N. W. of Philadelphia. The town is beautifully situated on the river bank below the Shamokin dam. The town contains about 250 dwellings, 15 stores, 10 taverns, 3 churches belonging to the Presbyterians, German Reformed and Methodists respectively,—a court house, and county offices of brick, a prison of stone. The centre turnpike road runs E. to Pottsville, and a connection will probably be made at no distant day with the Danville and Pottsville rail road, should that be completed. But it would seem most desirable to make the road immediately and primarily to Sunbury, since that town may command the commerce of the west as well as the north branch of the Susquehannah river. A bridge about a mile above the town connects it with Northumberland. This structure was made by a joint stock company in 1814. It is in two parts, separated by Shamokin island, and cost $90,000, of which the state subscribed $50,000. Its length is 1825 feet, width 32, height above the ordinary level of the water 41 feet, resting on 8 stone piers. The arches are of wood, protected by a roof from the weather.

Sunbury, small village of Centre t-ship, Butler co., lately laid out, and contains only a few buildings of wood. It is situated on the state road from Butler to Franklin, 10 miles from the former.

Sunville, post town, Philadelphia co., partly in Penn t-ship and partly in the t-ship of the Northern Liberties, on the Germantown road, 3 miles from Philadelphia, at the fork formed by the Willow Grove turnpike. It contains about 60 dwellings, 4 stores, 4 taverns, three at least of which bear the figure of the "rising sun," by which name the village is commonly known. It is a pleasant spot, through which several stages pass daily to and from the city.

Surgeon's Hall, post office, Allegheny co., 226 miles N. W. of W. C., and 204 W. of Harrisburg.

Susquehannah county was provisionally erected from Luzerne county by the act of 21st Feb. 1810, which gave it the following boundaries: "beginning at the 40th mile stone standing on the N. line of the state, and running south along the east line of Ontario (now Bradford co.) to a point due east of the head of Wyalusing falls in the r. Susquehannah ; thence due east to the western line of Wayne county ; thence northerly along the said W. line to the aforesaid N. line of the state,and thence W. along the said line to the 40th mile stone. It was fully organized for judicial and other purposes by act 24th March, 1812. Its name was given from the circumstance that through this county the Susquehannah river first enters the state. The form of the county is rhomboidal. It is 34 miles long and 24 broad and contains 816 square ms., or 522,240 acres. Central lat. 41° 50′, long. W. from W. C. 1° 10′ E.

Lying principally N. W. of the broken and depressed chains of the Allegheny mountains, the county belongs to the great secondary formation of the W., except the S. E. angle, which pertains to the transition. But neither bituminous coal nor iron, abundant in the middle and southern counties of the secondary, have to our knowledge been discovered here. Anthracite we are told has been discovered in the transition, on the head waters of the Lackawannock, in Clifford t-ship. The surface of the country generally, is formed into gradual and easy hills, lying chiefly in ridges, conforming to the water courses, and these hills may commonly be cultivated to the tops, and are the best adapted to grain. But there are some elevations which have the name of mountains. The Oquago mountain lies N. of the Susquehannah river near the northern boundary, and extends parallel with the line ten miles. The Moosic mountain is low and has a very gradual ascent. It lies on the head of Lackawannock creek, and extends N. and S. about 16 miles. Its soil is excellent. Mount Ararat is a spur of the Moosic mountain in the N. E. section of the county. Its soil is also excellent and its summit easy of access. The Elk mountain is the extreme knob of Tunkhannock mountain, on the N. E., and forms the eastern termination of the main Allegheny mtn. in Pennsylvania. It is in the eastern part of the county, in Clifford township.

The Susquehannah river enters the N. E. angle of the county, in Harmony t-ship, and flowing round the east and south base of the Oquago mountain for about 16 miles, making the "Great Bend," returns to the state of New York ; and thence after an immense sweep through Broome and Tioga counties, N. Y. and Bradford co., Pennsylvania, it again reaches in the N.W.angle of Luzerne,within less than 5 miles of the S. W. angle of Susquehannah. As all the other streams of the county are tributary to this, they flow N. W. and S. as from the centre to the circumference of a circle. Thus proceeding parallel with the northern boundary from the east to the west, we cross the Starucca, the Conewanta, Mitchell's, Salt Lick, Snake, Chochonut and Apollacan creeks, all which flow northward ; following the western boundary we traverse several branches of the Wyalusing creek ; and along the southern line we have four branches of the Meshoppen, and several tributaries of the Tunkhannock creek. On Snake creek about five miles from the river, is a salt spring, situated so low, however, as to be overflowed by the waters of a small neighboring stream, and rendered unfit for the manufacture of salt ; yet some excellent salt has at times been made from it. Near the spring is a slate quarry which appears to be extensive, and may in time become valuable. The spring and quarry are in the t-ship of Lawsville. There are several small lakes in Bridgewater, Silver Lake, and other t-ships, the principal of which are the lake near the t. of Montrose, Silver lake and Quaker lake. Upon the bank of Silver lake, Dr. Robert H. Rose, an early settler and very large land holder of the county, has his beautiful and magnificent seat, surrounded by one of the largest farms in Pennsylvania, in the cultivation of which, in the sale of his lands, and in the enjoyments of an extensive and well selected library, he finds ample and delightful employment. There is a cataract on the Starucca creek with a fall of between 40 and 50 feet.

The agricultural productions are the ordinary kinds of grain of the more southern counties. But there is much variety in the adaptation of the soil to them. Wheat, rye and barley have been cultivated with success, although neither the soil nor climate are very congenial with either. Rye and oats produce abundant and excellent crops, the latter frequently weighing from 35 to 40 lbs. the bushel—and buckwheat grows uncommonly well. The summers are too short and cold for the most successful culture of Indian corn. The greatest obstacle to the culture of grain is the luxuriance of the natural grasses. The *red top* or herds-grass and white clover grow spontaneously and abundantly, in the richest land; and large tracts that have never been ploughed, will yield a heavy swath of these grasses. The winter grain is sown usually in October. Oats about the first of May. Barley from the 15th of that month to the 1st of June, and Indian corn also about the 1st of June. Grass is commonly cut during the month of July; wheat about the 1st of August; oats and barley a month later.

The spring here is much later than in the southern counties. Rigorous winter continues until the last of April. About the first of May vegetation springs into life and advances with singular rapidity. From tables kept in the higher parts of the county the mercury ranges about 10° of Fahrenheit lower than in the country around Philadelphia. This is doubtless caused by the greater altitude of the country, which in many instances is from 1500 to 2000 feet above the tide; and this circumstance probably contributes to the remarkable healthiness of the inhabitants; no epidemics are known here, and autumnal fevers are eradicated by a summer residence.

There are several turnpike roads in the county; the Belmont and Oquago road crosses N. W. through Jackson and Harmony t-ships; the Coshocton and Great Bend through Gibson, Jackson, New Milford, and Great Bend t-ships; the Milford and Owego running from Milford on the Delaware to Owego on the Susquehannah, crosses the county diagonally and centrally by Montrose; the Bridgewater and Wilkesbarre; the Clifford and Wilkesbarre; the New Milford and Montrose; the Philadelphia and Great Bend; and the Abington and Waterford, are, we believe, already made; and the Milford and Owego, and the Dundaff and Honesdale roads are authorized by the legislature to be constructed.

The towns are Montrose, the st. jus. Dundaff, Friendsville, Great Bend, Harmony, Springville, Fairdale, New Milford, &c.

The population of the county is composed chiefly of emigrants from the New England states and their descendants, and amounted in 1820 to 9,960, and in 1830 16,785, of whom 8,429 were white males, 8,283 white females, 34 free black males, 39 free black females. Of these, 221 were aliens, 6 were deaf and dumb, and 6 blind. The exports of the county consist of live stock, lumber, wheat, rye, oats and Indian corn.

The public buildings consist of the court house, public offices, and prison at Montrose, a banking house at that town and another at Dundaff, (the banks, however, are extinct,) and 12 or 15 churches belonging to Episcopalians, Presbyterians, Methodists and Baptists.

There is an academy at Montrose, incorporated in 1816, to which the legislature gave a donation of $2000, and a boarding school for females at the Great Bend village. Private schools at which the rudiments of an English education are taught, are established in every neighborhood. There is a public library at Montrose, and two weekly newspapers are published there, viz. the Susquehannah Register, and Independent Volunteer; and 1 at Dundaff, called the Dundaff Republican.

By the assessment of 1829, the taxable real property of the co. was valued at $903,375, viz. seated lands at $646,299 ; unseated lands at $257, 076 ; personal property, including occupations,$91,090 ; improved lands of good quality sell at 12 dollars the acre, unimproved at 3 dollars.

This county paid into the state treasury in 1831,

For tax on writs,	262 50
Tavern licenses,	232 01
Duties on dealers in foreign mdz.	301 18
Tin and clock pedlars' licenses,	57
	$852 69

At Dundaff is an extensive glass manufactory, where during the week ending 14 Nov. 1831,there were made 15,550 feet or 380 boxes of window glass, 8 by 10.

STATISTPICAL TABLE OF SUSQUEHANNAH COUNTY.

Townships, &c.	Greatest lth.	Greatest bth.	Area in acs.	Population. 1820.	Population. 1830.	Taxables
Auburn,	8	6	30,720	218	516	65
Bridgewater,	10	8 1-2	47,360	1,994	2,450	381
Brooklyn,	11	5	26,880	880	1,350	187
Clifford,	8	5	25,600	681	866	167
Choconut,	8	6	30,720	508	780	130
Dundaff,					298	
Gibson,	6	3 1-2	19,560	914	1,081	196
Great Bend,	6	6	23,040	527	797	114
Harford,	6 1-2	5 1-2	22,880	642	999	173
Herrick,	6	3 1-2	19,560		468	88
Harmony,	8	6	30,720	173	341	53
Jackson,	8	6 1-2	32,000	265	641	101
Lawsville,	8	6	30,720	473	873	129
Lennox,	8	6	30,720	214	546	74
Middleton,	9	6	34,560	547	683	114
Milford, New,	7 1-2	6 1-2	30,240	614	1,000	152
Montrose bor.					415	84
Rush,	9	6	34,560	242	643	102
Silver Lake,	9	5	28,800	456	516	81
Springville,	8	7	35,840	702	1,514	213
Waterford,				790		
Total,				9,960	16,777	2,594

Susquehannah, t-ship, Dauphin co., bounded N. by Middle Paxton, S. by Swatara, E. by Lower Paxton t-ships, and W. by the Susquehannah r. Greatest length 7, breadth 6 miles ; area, 12,800 acres ; surface, gentle declivities ; soil, alluvion and gravel. Pop. 1830, 1451 ; taxables, 232, exclusive of the borough of Harrisburg. The Blue mtn. crosses the north part of the t-ship, and the ancient r. bank has a notable elevation above the present shore. Paxton creek enters the t-ship near about the middle of the E. line, and flows S. through it, nearly parallel with the r. Harrisburg lies partly within the precincts of the t-ship.

Susquehannah, t-ship, Cambria co., lately taken from Alleheny t-ship, is bounded N. by Clearfield co., E. by Clearfield and Allegheny t-ships, S. by Cambria t-ship, and W. by Indiana co. Surface, rolling ; soil, clay and loam. Pop. 1830, 722 ; taxables, 118 ; value of taxable property in 1829, seated lands, $23,741 ; unseated lands, $24,733 ; personal est., $4070 ; rate of levy, $8\frac{1}{2}$ mills.

Susquehannah river, is emphatically the river of Pennsylvania. Two of its main branches, the West and the Juniata, rise and have their whole courses within her territory, and the third or N. E. branch, with the great stem, reach 250 ms. in length through the state. And it is the primitive and imperative duty of the commonwealth, to *gain* and to *preserve* for her exclusive use, the commerce of the country washed by this r., exceeding 22,000 square ms. in extent ; abounding in mineral and agricultural wealth, and destined to become the home of millions of intelligent beings. The north eastern or greatest branch of this r., rises in the northern ridge of the Catsbergs, from the Otsego lake, in the angle between the heads of the Coquago branch of the Delaware & Chenango rivers, and opposite to the Mohawk r., and reaching within 10 ms. of the great canal of N. Y. It flows thence a southwesterly course of some 45 ms., receiving the Unadilla and other accessions in its way into Pa., in Susquehannah co., and Harmony t-ship ; thence by the E. and S. sides of the Oquago mtn. it returns to the state of N. Y., and at the village of Binghampton, receives the Chenango r., about 12 ms. by the r. below the Pa. line. The Chenango r. has its extreme northern sources in Madison co., and in the S. E. angle of Oneida co., within 16 ms. of the Oneida lake, and 15 from the angle of the great canal, and in the angle between the sources of the Mohawk and Seneca rivers; from Binghampton the r. pursues a course a little S. of W. for about 25 ms. to Owego, where it receives the Owego r.; thence by a S. W. course of 8 miles, it re-enters Pa. in Athens t-ship, Bradford co.; and about 7 ms. below the state line, unites with the Chemung, as it is called in N. York, or the Tioga r., as it is commonly termed in Pa.

The two great northern constituents of the Susquehannah enclose the long and navigable lakes, Seneca and Cayuga; the former of which stretches in almost a direct line from the great canal to the mouth of Newtown creek, about 20 ms. by comparative courses from Tioga point; and the latter stretches also from the line of the great canal to within 30 ms. of the Susquehannah at the mouth of the Owego. These lakes have respectively a length of more than 40 miles, and form the most admirable and direct channels for connecting the basin of the Susquehannah with lake Ontario.

The Susquehannah and its tributaries, even N. of the Penn. state, are highly important in a commercial point of view, for the transportation to market, of the lumber, plaster, salt, wheat, pork, whiskey, and other agricultural products of the southwestern part of New York, a district now containing near 250,000 inhabitants. From an estimate of the delegates to a convention held in January, 1831, to consider the grievances said to result from the dams made in the lower part of the r., by the Pennsylvania canal commissioners, it appears that 73,000 bushels of wheat, 15,000,000 feet of lumber, besides a large amount of other products, have descended the Chemung from Elmira and the adjacent towns annually. That upon the Susquehannah, the village of Owego alone sends 10,000 barrels of salt, 4000 tons of plaster, 10,000 bushels of wheat, &c.; and that more than 600 arks and rafts descend the r. from the village of Binghampton and the towns above Unadilla, Bainbridge, Guilford, Greene, &c.

Ithaca is 29 ms. from Owego, and between these places a rail road is contemplated, for which a company has been incorporated. The Chemung canal terminates at Newtown or Elmira, and the Chemung river will connect this canal with that proposed by Pennsylvania. On the Seneca lake a steamboat plies between the village of Havana at the south end, and that of Geneva, in Ontario co., at the north. This lake is about 45 miles long, studded on both sides with villages. The country between it and Seneca lake is not surpassed by any in the state of N. Y. It is represented as a perfect garden, whose rich and abundant produce would reach Philadelphia by the Chemung canal. From Geneva, the Seneca canal, 20 miles long, sets forth and intersects the Cayuga lake and Erie canal, at Montezuma.

From Tioga point, four miles south of the line of the state, the Susquehannah flows by comparative courses 60 miles to the mouth of the Lackawannock creek in the centre of Luzerne co., at the head of the Wyoming valley, having crossed nearly at right angles, several ridges, including the main one of the Apalachian chain. Turning now at right angles, the magnificent stream flows down the Wyoming valley, which it leaves at the Nanticoke falls, where the highest dam of the canal navigation has been erected. A few miles below this point the Nescopeck creek enters the river, by which it is proposed to connect, with a canal, the waters of the Susquehannah with the Lehigh and Delaware rivers. From the Nanticoke dam to Northumberland, the distance is somewhat less than 60 ms., and the North Branch canal, which follows the right bank of the r. is 55½ ms. in length. Immediately below Northumberland the west branch of the Susquehannah unites with the N.

eastern branch, and a dam has been thrown across the r. here 9½ feet high, and 2783 feet long, with a chute for the passage of rafts and arks 62 feet wide and 650 feet long.

The west branch of the Susquehannah rises in Cambria co., within the Appalachian valley and in the secondary formation. It pursues a N. E. course through Clearfield co., receiving Clearfield creek, and Mushanon creek from the south, and the Sinnemahoning and Kettle creeks, and some less streams from the north. Having penetrated deep into Lycoming county it turns to the S. E. and E., and receiving from the N. Pine, Lycoming, Loyalsock and Muncy creeks, and from Centre co. on the south, the Bald Eagle creek, all large streams, it bends south through the main ridge of the Allegheny, and continues that course to its union with the N. E. branch at Northumberland, having a comparative course of about 175 ms. A canal ascends the W. branch from Northumberland to the Muncy dam at the Muncy hills, 24½ miles, and thence 14 ms. to the Big Island, opposite to the mouth of the Bald Eagle creek; thus affording improved means of transportation for the coal and iron of Lycoming, and the iron of Centre counties.

From the mouth of the W. branch, the united streams pursue a general direction a little W. of S. about 40 ms.; and the canal keeps the western bank to Duncan's island, where it crosses the r. by a dam and towing bridge into Dauphin co.

The Juniata r. (for a particular description of which see that article,) is a mountain stream which has its whole course upon the central transition formation, nearly from W. to E. crossing the Appalachian ridges in several places. The canal communicating by means of a rail road portage over the back bone of the Allegheny mtns. with the Allegheny r., pursues the valley of the Juniata.

Below the mouth of the Juniata, the Susquehannah pursues a S. E. direction for 80 ms., by comparative courses, and being precipitated from the primitive on to the sea sand formation, loses its name and river character in the Chesapeake bay. In this distance it passes through three mtn. ranges, the Kittatinny above, the South mtn. below Harrisburg, and what Mr. Darby calls the South East mtn. below the mouth of the Conestoga creek. The canal pursues the eastern bank 24 ms. to Middletown, at the mouth of the Swatara creek, and thence to the borough of Columbia, 18 ms. From this borough the rail road to Phil. distant 81 ms. is now being made.

Considered geographically, the waters of the Susquehannnah form links which connect the river with those of the great lakes and the St. Lawrence, and with those of the Ohio and Mississippi, and by itself it affords an outlet to the ocean for the products of a very extensive and varied region. Considered geologically, we find in its basin all the formations of the earth, from the highest class of primitive rocks to the most recent alluvion, upon the most extensive scale. And it is remarkable that the courses and fitness for navigation appear to be altogether independent of the rock formation; and that the mountains, though causing some sinuosities in the streams, have no influence upon their general course; that the rivers break through the hills and the rocks, almost at right angles on their way to the ocean.

The course of the north and west branches of the Susquehannah from their sources to their point of union, present scarce any difficulty in descending navigation; when the waters are high, there being few and inconsiderable falls or rapids. Below Northumberland, however, McKees half falls, Foster's falls, Hunter's falls and Brushy rock; and below Middletown the Swatara falls, the Great Conewago falls, Halderman's ripples and the Spinning Wheel; below Columbia for 20 ms., a succession of rapids and rocky obstructions render the navigation extremely perilous.

A view of the actual state of the r., for commercial purposes, before the commencement of the Pennsylvania system of internal improvements, and of the extent and value of the productions of the Susquehannah valley, may serve to justify the policy of the state to those who, feeling the pressure of a light but new weight in taxation, and seeing only the error resulting from the inexperience and incompetence of the agents employed, are disposed inconsiderately to reprobate the enterprise. For much of the matter of this exposition, we are indebted to an article written in 1827, by David Scott, Esq., president judge of the 11th judicial district, and late president of the board of canal commissioners. He remarks,

"To the territory drained by this noble river, within the states of Penn. and N. Y., containing above 20,000 square miles, and a population of more than half a million, nature has pointed out the valley of the Susquehannah as the great high way to market."

"The Susquehannah is regarded as a navigable river. It is so in a limited sense. Viewed in its whole extent, in connection with its great branches, its ascending navigation is extremely limited and difficult. Its descending navigation is uncertain and of short duration, and both are at all times hazardous. A voyage across the Atlantic does not involve so much danger to life and property, as the navigation of the river from Newtown, in the state of N. Y., to the head of tide. It is believed that the difficulties, delays, dangers, and losses which at present attend the navigation of this river, are little known and less understood, except by those interested in the river trade."

"Since the opening of the Erie canal and the construction of turnpike roads from the Susquehannah to the valley of the Delaware, the Hudson and the lakes, boats on the Susquehannah, for the transportation of the ascending trade, have gradually disappeared, until not a single one is found plying on the river above Northumberland. Merchandize can be transported, by wagons, from the city of Phila. the city of N. York, and the heads of the Seneca and Cayuga lakes, with more expedition, at less expense and less hazard, than by the river."

"The descending navigation of the Susquehannah is uncertain, of short duration, and at all times dangerous. Property can only be floated down in the time of high floods, which seldom occur except at the breaking up of the ice and the melting of the snow in the spring season. During these floods the river is not navigated with any degree of safety or success, if at all, for more than a week or ten days. The consequence is, that the whole trade of the Susquehannah descends at nearly the same time; the markets, which are at all times very uncertain, in the towns and villages along the river, are overstocked; the owners have incurred expenses which they cannot meet without sales, and they are frequently obliged to sell at a ruinous sacrifice."

"It sometimes happens that there is no spring flood, sufficient for the descending trade. When this is the case, great losses are sustained by the owners, not only in consequence of the embarrassments incident to disappointments and failure of market, but also on account of the deterioration, if not the entire destruction, of many articles by the keeping. A summer flood after the failure of the spring flood generally proves ruinous. Being disappointed, and having property on hand, the owners embark it upon the summer flood. The water evaporates, the river falls, and with it all their hopes, before they reach a market. Indeed, very little property ever reached its intended destination by a summer flood."

"Round and square timber, scantling boards and plank, are floated down in rafts. All other articles are floated down in arks, which, although they carry from 40 to 50 tons each, are very frail vessels, and are liable to many destructive accidents."

"The loss occasioned by accidents incident to river navigation, exposure to the weather, &c. is estimated at 5 per cent upon the gross amount of exports."

"The whole amount of property which descended the river last year, was estimated at four millions and a half. The tonnage required for the transportation of those articles which could not be floated in rafts, must have amounted to more than 100,000 tons. 1500 arks arrived at Port Deposit, and it is known that there were many, and it is fair to presume that at least 500, found a market for their lading at the towns and villages along the r. above that place."

"Estimating the loss incident to river navigation at 5 per cent, which is certainly very low, and the amount of exports at four and a half millions, the gross amount of loss annually sustained would be 225,000 dollars. Besides this there is, (and must always continue to be, whatever improvements may be made in the descending navigation,) an enormous sacrifice in the item of arks. An ark of sufficient capacity to carry 40 or 50 tons, will cost at least 65 dollars. It can never re-ascend the river, and consequently must be sold for any price which can be obtained for it. The average price of an ark at the place of destination is 15 dollars. The loss then upon 2000 arks, the estimated number which descended the river last year, and which is annually increasing, will amount to 100,000 dollars, which, added to the estimated loss by accidents, &c. make the enormous sum of 325,000 dollars —a sum, it is believed, equal to the interest on the capital necessary for canalling the Susquehannah from the New York to the Maryland line. The whole of this sum, and other items of considerable magnitude, would be saved to the individuals interested, and consequently serve to increase the aggregate wealth of the state by a canal navigation. The expenses of navigating an ark of the common capacity, (40 or 50 tons,) from the Wyoming valley to the head of tide, amount to 120 dollars. Tne transportation of the same tonnage by canal boats, it is believed, would greatly diminish this item of expenditure."

"The country above the Wyoming valley is supplied with merchandize from the city of New York. The surplus products are floated down the river, sold, and the proceeds taken in cash by the merchants to New York, and there laid out in goods, which are transported by water to some point on the Hudson; or by the Erie canal to the head of the Seneca or Cayuga lake; and thence by wagons to the valley of the Susquehannah. Indeed a considerable portion of the merchandize at this time vended in Luzerne co. is purchased in New York, and thence transported in wagons—the difference in the distance between Wilkesbarre and Phil. and Wilkesbarre and N. Y. being very trifling. When a canal shall have been constructed along the valley of the Susquehannah from the northern boundary of the state to intersect the Pennsylvania canal, the whole country above that point will be supplied with merchandize from the city of Philadelphia and most of the produce of the country will find its way there to market. Until this is done Philadelphia can never enjoy the trade of the Susquehannah. Hence to the interest of the state in general and of Philadelphia in particular, the necessity and importance of this great improvement."

"Of the 2 thousand arks which descended the Susquehannah last year, at least 1500 must have received their lading above Harrisburg. The lumber which annually descends the river is estimated at 175 millions of feet, the whole or nearly the whole of which comes also from the country above Harrisburg. As before stated, the whole of this property nearly, in ordinary seasons, and in the present state of the river navigation, must arrive in the course of a week or ten days; and when arrived at this point the principal part of the expenses will have been incurred; and the flood having borne it thus far, will quickly bear it further and with trifling additional expense. Under these circumstances it never can be expected that the trade of the Susquehannah will stop at any point where the Pennsylvania canal shall intersect that river; that the owners will unload, store and reload, and incur all the expense, vexation and delay, incident to a transhipment to Philadelphia by the Union or any other canal connecting the Susquehannah and the Schuylkill or Delaware rivers."

"If there was a safe and easy ascending and descending navigation by canal along the valley of the Susquehannah, the products of the country would not be hurried to market in the course of a few days, in time of a high flood, in craft of unwieldy size and frail structure; but the season would be occupied in their transportation in boats which would pass through the Pennsylvania canal to Philadelphia; losses by accident or exposure would seldom or never occur; an immense saving would be made in the item of arks; the trade would annually and rapidly increase; the extensive forest of wild lands upon our northern border would be immediately settled and improved; towns, villages and manufactories would spring up along the line; an impulse would be given to industry and enterprize, the market would soon assume a fixed character; and it is believed that the whole country drained by the Susquehannah and its tributaries, above its intersection with the Pennsylvania canal, would be supplied with merchandize from Philadelphia."

"In the present state of the river, and after every thing shall have been done, which can be done to improve the descending navigation, by the natural channel, the immense and increasing trade of the Susquehannah will continue to be, as it has hitherto been, divided between New York and Baltimore. Nothing can save it, nor the other advantages before enumerated, to the state, or direct it to Philadelphia, but a canal from the northern boundary of the state to the Pennsylvania canal, along the valley of the Susquehannah. It is certainly worth contending for, and if not secured it will not be on account of deficiency in facilities and means. Of the first, nature has been liberal in her gifts; of the last the state can furnish abundance."

Mr. Scott makes a statement to prove, that the tolls upon such a canal would pay a full interest upon the capital employed in its construction; but as the state has concured with him, that the trade of the Susquehannah is worth contending for, and has already made the canal along its banks 126½ miles from Columbia to the Wyoming valley, and will in due season extend it to the state line, it is not necessary to exhibit here the elements of his calculation. But we may properly state his views of the practicability of the whole route, as it forms an interesting feature of this highly interesting valley.

"From the survey of Mr. Bennet, it is ascertained, that the total distance from the northern line of the state upon the Tioga or Chemung river to Northumberland is 161 miles 18 chains; total fall 343,413 feet; from the state line on the Susquehannah to Northumberland is 161 miles 18 chains; fall 337,093 feet."

"From the surveys already made and from the geological structure of Pennsylvania, it is doubted whether there can be found within her limits, so great a distance in so direct a line, requiring so little lockage. The average fall per mile in the whole distance is but a fraction more than two feet, and from the head of the Wyoming valley to Northumberland, a distance of seventy one miles, including the two principal falls upon this branch of the river, the Nanticoke and Nescopeck, the average fall per mile is a fraction less than one foot nine ins."

"The Susquehannah and its tributaries afford abundant supplies of water, and it is believed they may be used at every desirable point, as feeders to a canal."

"From the report of Mr. Bennet it appears also, that the proportion of rock excavation will be unusually small, when compared with the distance, on either side of the river; and that the soil throughout the whole explored route is principally alluvial, composed of clay and sand; and some mixture of ground, in which clay predominates, is of firm texture, and of easy excavation."

"It is also believed that few, if any of the narrow passes, where the bases of the mountains or hills composed of rock, form the banks of the river, present greater difficulties in the construction of a canal, than are to be met with at Peters, Short and the Kittatinny mountains; and that no point upon the whole line presents impediments so formidable, as are found at Butler's falls upon the Delaware, where the canal of the Hudson and Delaware canal company is now in successful progress."

We shall conclude the description of this noble river which we repeat, we trust, is to be kept, ***Pennsylvania's own***, because the most certain means of her increase in wealth and happiness, by a notice of the width of the river in various places and of the great bay into which it pours its waters. At the great bend far above the point of union of the Tioga with the main stream, the river is 600 feet wide. At Wilkesbarre it is 700 ft., at Nescopeck and Berwick 1256 feet; at Lewisburg 1120 feet; at Northumberland 1825 feet; at Harrisburg 2876; at Columbia 5690; but at McCall's ferry the river is contracted to 600 feet, by high and rocky margins, and its channel marred by many and lofty rocks. At all the places we have mentioned bridges have been thrown over the river, and other have been erected at Duncan's island and at Danville. The Chesapeake bay, into which the river empties, is the most extensive and peculiar in the United States. Its length from N. to S. is 175 miles; through its western bank flow many large tributary streams, the chief of which are James and York rivers, Rappahanock, Potomac, Patuxent and Patapsco.

Port Deposit is on the left bank of the Susquehannah in Cecil county, Maryland, at the head of tide water and about a mile below the lowest bridge over the river. Here the produce not sold above is accumulated, and was formerly transferred to sloops and wholly sent to Baltimore. Since the completion of the Delaware and Chesapeake canal, however, a considerable portion of the Susquehannah produce is brought to its legitimate market; and some hundred sloops laden with it are borne by the canal and the river Delaware to the city of Philadelphia. When by sound policy and vigorous exertion of her abundant strength, Philadelphia shall have gained the whole of this trade, then, but not till then, she will obtain the full return for her already heavy expenditure.

Susquehannah according to Mr. Chapman and Mr. Heckewelder, is derived from the Indian word ***Saosquehaanunk***, meaning long, crooked river.

Swamp Churches, post town, New Hanover t-ship, Montgomery county, 16 miles north of Norristown; contains a Lutheran church and a German Reformed church, a post office, a tanyard, 2 taverns, 2 stores, and 8 dwellings.

Swamp creek, rises in Pike t-ship, Berks co., and flows S. E. through Douglass, New Hanover and Frederick t-ships into the Perkiomen creek. It is a mill stream, has many mills upon it, but is not navigable.

Swamp creek, another tributary of the Perkiomen creek, rises in Milford t-ship, Bucks co., and flows S. into Marlborough t-ship, Montgomery co., where it unites with its recipient.

Swamp creek, a mill stream and tributary of the Cocalico creek, rises and has its whole course in Cocalico t-ship.

Swan tavern, post office, Lancaster co. Hempfield t-ship, on the turnpike road from Lancaster to Harrisburg, about 6 miles from the former.

Swatara creek, or river, for it claims that rank, rises in Schuylkill co., on the S. side of the Broad mountain, about 15 miles S. W. of Orwigsburg, and cutting its way through the Sharp and Second mountains, flows by Pine Grove village, and enters Lebanon co. on the N. E. angle, through which it flows by a very devious course, receiving near the western boundary of the county, the Quitapahilla creek; thence it flows S.W. through Dauphin co., to the Susquehannah river, near Middletown, having an entire comparative course of about 50 miles. The valley of this stream, as far as the Quitapahilla, forms the channel of the Union canal; from that point a navigable feeder has been constructed to the Great dam in the gorge of the Blue mountain. (See Union Canal in the first part of this work.)

Swatara creek, Little, rises at the foot of the Blue mountain in Upper Tulpehocken t-ship, Berks co., and flowing S. W. forms the boundary between Bethel and Tulpehocken t-ships in the same co.; thence it crosses Bethel and Swatara t-ships, Lebanon co. and falls into the Great Swatara about a mile below Jones'town. It turns, in its course of about 20 miles, many mills.

Swatara hill, Pine Grove township, Schuylkill co., a lofty hill which rises between the Blue and Second mountains, and extends eastwardly through the t-ship.

Swatara, t-ship, Lebanon co., bounded N. by Dauphin co., E. by Bethel t-ship, S. by Lebanon, and W. by Annville and East Hanover. Centrally distant from the borough of Lebanon 9 ms.; greatest length 12 ms., breadth $3\frac{1}{2}$ miles; area, 15,360 acres; surface N. and S. hilly, centre level; soil gravelly. Pop. in 1830, 1510; taxables, 281. Swatara creek crosses the t-ship between the Blue and the Second mountain, and flows along the whole western boundary, receiving from the t-ship Hole creek, Oil creek, Red run, the Little Swatara and some minor streams. Jones'town, the post town, lies on the Little Swatara near its confluence with the Great Swatara, on the south of which, Bunker hill is a distinguished eminence.

Swatara, Lower, t-ship, Dauphin co. bounded N. by Susquehannah and Lower Paxton t-ships, E. by Swatara creek, which divides it from Derry and Londerry t-ships, W. and S. W. by the Susquehannah river; centrally distant from Harrisburg S. E. 5 miles; greatest length 9, breadth 5 miles; area, 15,800 acres; surface hilly; soil limestone and slate. Pop. in 1830, 1822; taxables in 1828, 323; taxable property in 1832, $401,029. Besides the streams on its boundaries, Spring creek and two other small streams flow into the Susquehannah. The Union canal follows the west bank of the Swatara creek to Middletown, and communicates with the Susquehannah by an outlet lock, and with the state canal, which pursues the E. bank of the Susquehannah river. The Lancaster and Harrisburg turnpike road passes through Middletown, and a small village called High Spire in the t-ship, and the Harrisburg and Reading turnpike road E. and W. through it. Upon this road is the poor house of the county. Part of the town of Harrisburg is in this township.

Sweden, post t-ship, Potter co., contains something more than 100 inhabitants and 29 taxables. The country has scarcely been explored, and, with very little exception, remains in its native wild state.

Swift run, Mount Pleasant t-ship, Adams co., a tributary of the Conewago creek.

Swope town, Earl t-ship, Lancaster co., on the road from Waynesburg to Harrisburg, 13 miles N. E. from the city of Lancaster, a small village.

Sylvania, post office, Bradford co., 263 miles from W. C., and 147 from Harrisburg.

Tafton, post office, Pike co., named after Royal Taft, the post master, 271 miles N. E. of W. C., and 173 from Harrisburg.

Tallmansville, post office, Wayne co., called after the post master, Elihu Tallman, 278 miles from W. C., 179 from Harrisburg.

Taconey creek, Big, rises in Abington t-ship, Montgomery co., above Shoemaker town, and flows thence S. E. through Cheltenham t-ship, into Philadelphia co., and thence, forming the division between Bristol and Northern Liberty t-ships and Oxford, into the river Delaware, at the village of Bridesburg, and below the U.S. arsenal, the precincts of which it laves. It is a very excellent mill stream, and turns many mills and manufactories. It receives the Little Tacony cr. from Oxford t-ship, below the borough of Frankford.

Tamaqua, or Little Schuylkill river. The eastern branch of the Schuylkill r. rises in Rush t-ship, Schuylkill co., and near the boundary of Northampton co., and at the foot of the Spring mountain, and by a devious but southward course joins the main stream at Port Clinton, on the north side of the Kittatinny or Blue mountain, receiving many small tributaries in its route. Along the valley of this stream a rail road has been constructed, 23 miles in length, from Port Clinton by Tamaqua village into the coal region.

Tamaqua, a post town and village of Rush t-ship, Schuylkill co., on the Tamaqua or Little Schuylkill river, at the head of the rail road, communicating with Port Clinton. It was commenced in 1829, and now contains about 30 dwellings, 2 hotels, 3 stores. It is situated in a wild mountainous and barren country, and its prosperity depends upon the operations in the coal mines which surround it. Anthracite coal here is abundant and of excellent quality, and found in large veins. It is about 14 miles N. E. of Orwigsburg, 191 from W. C., and 83 from Harrisburg.

Tamaqua mountain, West Penn t-ship, Schuylkill co., is a western continuation of the Mahoning hill, and crosses the township near its centre.

Tarentum, post town of Deer t-ship, Allegheny co., on the right bank of the Allegheny river, and on the state canal, 18 or 20 miles above Pittsburg, 231 from W. C., and 203 from Harrisburg; was laid out by Judge Breckenridge of Florida, and contains between 30 and 40 houses, and is a thriving village.

Taylor'sville, post town of Upper Makefield t-ship, Bucks co., on the bank of the Delaware river, 14 miles S. E. from Doylestown, 169 N. E. from W. C., and 123 E. from Harrisburg and 37 from Philadelphia; contains 8 or 10 dwellings, a store and tavern. There is a ferry across the river, but a bridge is about to be erected under an act of assembly, passed in 1831.

Taylor'stown, Buffalo t-ship, Washington co., on the Buffalo creek, 8 ms. W. of Washington borough; contains 30 or 40 dwellings, several stores and taverns.

Taylor's ferry, over the Delaware river, in Upper Makefield t-ship, Bucks co., about 27 miles from Philadelphia N. E., and 14 miles E. of Doylestown. (See Taylor'sville.)

Taylor's stand, post office, Crawford co., 316 miles N. W. of W. C., and 257 from Harrisburg.

Tell, t-ship, Huntingdon co., bounded north by Mifflin co., E. by Franklin co., S. by Dublin t-ship, and W. by Springfield and Shirley t-ships. Centrally distant from Huntingdon boro' 22 miles; greatest length 11½, breadth 5 miles; area, 28,800 acres; surface mountainous; soil, limestone in the valleys. Pop. in 1830, 824; taxables 171. The Tuscarora mountain is on the E. and the Shade mountain on the W. boundary; between them lies the Tuscarora valley, through which runs the Tuscarora cr. In 1828 the t-ship contained 1 grist mill, 1 saw mill and 2 distilleries.

Teonista, t-ship, Warren co., bounded N. by the Allegheny river, E. by Kenjua t-ship, S. by Jefferson and Venango counties, and W. by Limestone t-ship. The t-ship is not organized, or has lately been organized. Its surface is somewhat hilly. The soil generally pretty good, especially the river and creek bottoms. It is drained by the main and several branches of the Teonista creek.

Ten Mile creek, a considerable tributary of the Monongahela river, formed by two great branches, one,the S. branch, rising in Rich Hill t-ship, Green co., flows E. through the whole county to Clarkesville. The N. branch rises in Morris t-ship, Washington co., and flows S. E. also to Clarkesville, whence the united streams run about 3 ms. to the river. Both forks have many branches which are valuable mill streams.

Teonista, t-ship, Venango county, bounded N. by Hickory t-ship, E. by Saratoga t-ship, S. by Pine Grove and Farmington t-ships, and W. by the Allegheny river, which separates it from Allegheny t-ship. Centrally distant 22 miles N. E. from Franklin borough; greatest length 12, breadth $5\frac{1}{2}$ miles; area, 28,800 acres; surface hilly; soil gravelly. Pop. in 1830, 480; taxables 134. There is a post office here called after the t-ship.

Teonista creek, or river, rises near the S. boundary of Warren co., and flows N. E. about 12 miles; then turning to the S. it runs about 10 ms. to the N. boundary of Venango co., thence by a course varying W., S.W. and W. it passes through Bear, Saratoga and Teonista t-ships into the Allegheny river, about 28 miles above the borough of Franklin. It is a large stream formed by many tributaries.

Terrapin Pond creek, Northampton co., a branch of Sandy creek.

Terrace mountain, Union township, Huntingdon co. rises near Stonerstown on the Raystown branch of the Juniata river, and runs N. E. about 22 ms. to the main branch of that river, forming the W. boundary of Union t-ship.

Terrytown, post town, Bradford co., 253 miles N. W. from W. C., and 142 from Harrisburg, a small village.

Thompson's run, Allegheny co., rises in Plumb t-ship, and flows S. W. about 7 ms. to Turtle creek, forming in part the boundary between Wilkins and Plumb t-ships.

Thompsonstown, p-t., Fermanagh t-ship, Mifflin co., on the Juniata r. and state canal, and on the turnpike road leading from Lewistown eastward, and about 25 ms. from that town; 141 ms. from W. C., and 34 from Harrisburg; contain between 40 and 50 dwellings, 3 taverns and 2 or 3 stores.

Thornbury, t-ship, Chester county, bounded on the E. and S. by Thornbury t-ship, Delaware co., on the W. by Birmingham t-ship, and on the N. by West town t-ship. Centrally distant from Phil. 20 ms. N. E.; from West Chester about 4 ms. S.; length $4\frac{1}{4}$, breadth $1\frac{1}{4}$ ms.; area, 2240 acres; surface, level; soil, sandy loam. Pop. 1830, 183; taxables, 42. Chester creek flows through it eastwardly, and a small tributary of the Brandywine r. westerly.

Thornbury, t-ship, Delaware co., bounded N. E. by Edgemont, S. E. by Middletown, S. by Concord, S. W. by Birmingham, and N. W. by Chester co. Central distance from Phil. about 20 ms. W.; from Chester, 10 ms. N. W.; surface, hilly; soil, sandy loam. Pop. 1830, 610; taxables, 124. Chester creek crosses the t-ship S. eastwardly. A small village centrally situated in the t-ship, is called Thornton. There is a p-o. here, distant 119 ms. from W. C. and 87 from Harrisburg.

Three forges, p-o. of Woodbury t-ship, Bedford co., 140 ms. N. W. of W. C. and 118 W. of Harrisburg.

Three springs, p-o., Huntingdon co., 125 ms. N. W. of W. C. and 73 S. W. from Harrisburg.

Tinicum, t-ship, Bucks co., bounded N. and E. by the r. Delaware, S. by Plumstead t-ship, W. by Bedminster, and N. W. by Nockamixon townships. Central distance N. from Phil. 37 ms., and 12 ms. N. E. from Doylestown; greatest length $8\frac{3}{4}$, greatest breadth 7 ms.; area, 18,497 acres; surface, partly rolling, partly level;

soil, sandy loam. Pop. 1830, 2078; taxables, 429. The Tohickon creek runs along its S. boundary; Tinicum creek traverses the t-ship centrally, and empties into the Delaware opposite to an island which bears the name of Tinicum island. There are two churches in the t-ship, a p-o. at Ottsville on the N. W. boundary, and another at Erwin on the Del. The Delaware canal follows the bank of the r. through the t-ship.

Tinicum creek, and island, (see the preceding article.)

Tinicum, t-ship, Delaware county, bounded by Darby t-ship on the N., by Phil. co. on the E., the r. Del. on the S., and Ridley t-ship on the W. and N. W. Central distance from Phil., about 9 ms. S. W.; length $3\frac{1}{2}$, by $1\frac{1}{4}$. This t-ship is an island formed by the Delaware r., Darby creek, and Bow creek. Its soil is rich alluvion or marsh, and occupied chiefly for grazing farms, upon which vast numbers of cattle are fatted for the Phil. market. A lazaretto is established here, at which there is a spacious hospital, and also excellent dwellings for the resident physician and other officers. Pop. 1830, 182; taxables, 1828, 30.

Tinicum island, lies opposite the t-ship, above described, in the r. Del., and is included in the t-ship. Hog island is above Tinicum, and also in the county of Delaware.

Tinkertown, a small village on the line dividing Northampton and Warwick t-ships, Bucks co., 20 ms. N. of Phil., 7 ms. S. W. of Doylestown.

Tioga county, was taken from Lycoming by act 26th March, 1804. By the act of 21st March, 1806, the seat of justice was established at Wellsborough. In 1808, the county was so far organized as to elect county commissioners, and in 1812, was fully organized for judicial purposes. The county is bounded on the N. by the state of New York, E. by Bradford co., S. by Lycoming, and W. by Potter. It is 35 ms. long by 33 wide. It comprehends 1100 square ms., or about 704,000 acres. Central lat. 41° 46′ N., long. 20° W. from Washington city.

The county lies altogether in the great western secondary formation, and abounds in salt, iron and coal. The following geographical and mineralogical sketch of the county, is from a report of Lieut. G. W. Hughes, to a committee appointed by the citizens of Newtown, N. Y., to cause a more thorough investigation of the coal beds, and other minerals on the Tioga, or S. branch of the Chemung river.

Canal port, Peters camp, is situated in lat. 41° 50′ N., near the head waters of the Tioga r., in Tioga co., and at a distance of 20 ms. in a right line direction from the southern boundary of N. Y. The distance from thence to the mouth of the feeder of the contemplated Chemung canal, is 12 miles. The Tioga is navigable at certain seasons of the year, within 5 ms. of the canal port,and may be made so at a very little expense to that place. No river offers greater facilities for slack water navigation, than the Tioga. Its waters are generally smooth, but occasionally interrupted by small ripples, which may, however, be easily obviated or removed; the bed has few obstructions, and those not of a formidable nature: and by narrowing the channel an abundance of water may be obtained at any season of the year. The country through which the Tioga flows, is in general smooth and unbroken, with a gradual descent towards the summit level of the Chemung canal; the soil is highly productive and thickly settled. The country at Canal port is rough and mountainous at a short distance from the r., and in these mountains coal is found, and occurs most abundantly in the eastern range. In a ravine on the N. side of the mtn. a number of excavations have been made. The first indication perceived, is a dark blackish clay, with occasionally small fragments of bituminous coal; by penetrating a short distance, a stratum of shale is found, strongly impregnated with bitumen, and continuing the excavation for about six feet, a bed of coal, generally not more than a few inches in thickness when first discovered, but becomes 2 or 3 and even 4 feet thick, penetrating to the distance of 20 feet; and in some cases the stratum of clay and minerals, which alternates with the coal, terminates, and the layers of coal unite, forming a single bed. The strata of coal and the alternating strata of minerals seem to be of the wedge like form, the smaller end of the former, and the larger end of the latter, being on the exterior surface of the mtn.; this renders it demonstrable that the strata of minerals continually decreasing must soon terminate; the strata of coal continually increasing must soon unite and form the mass of the mtn. This supposition is strengthened by the fact, that wherever excavations are made, coal is invariably found, and that indications of it are seen on the very summit, at an elevation of 200 feet above the lowest beds. On the north side of the mtn. sulphuret of iron (pyrites) occurs in the strata of coal in regular layers, and when thrown together in heaps, exposed to the action of the atmosphere, is converted into copperas; large quantities of which might be manufactured annually, at little or no expense. The argillaceous oxide of iron is found disseminated through it, in what the miners call kidneys; a name which they have applied to those small regular masses, on account of their peculiar shape. On the S. side the sulphuret is not found, neither are the kidneys as abundant as on the N. The magnetic oxide of iron occurs in large thick beds, which alternate with the coal; a single mass of this ore, which has rolled down into the ravine, would have weighed half a ton. Iron ore is found in this place in inexhaustible quantities, and consists of the magnetic, red, brown and argillaceous oxides, with the most of their varieties, such as yellow, red, and brown ochre, nodular and granular oxides; and they are said to be of a quality equal to any in the world.

It is not in this range alone that the coal is found; but it occurs in inexhaustible quantities on the western side of the river, where it is also accompanied by an abundance of iron ore. This coal appears to be of the first, or independent formation of Werner, and is associated with the following minerals, to wit: micaceous and ferruginous sand stone, composed of quartz, with mica and feldspar; the ores of iron above enumerated: shale or argillaceous slate, which is micaceous, and bituminous; pudding stone, composed of rolled pebbles, cemented by a ferruginous sand or clay. Strata of shale are, in a great number of cases, contiguous to the upper and lower surfaces of these beds of coal, constituting the roof and floor of the bed. That which covers the bed is bituminous; while that which is below has imbibed little or no bitumen. Any of the rocks, however, of this formation, may form the roof or floor of a bed of coal.

The coal at Canal port is principally of the variety called slaty; but passes by insensible changes into the other varieties. Its color is either pure black or with a slight tinge of brown or grey. It frequently presents an irised or pavonine tarnish. Its structure is foliated or slaty, and its layers usually divide into rhomboidal prisms. It is sometimes composed of distinct lamular concretions. Its cross fracture is even or slightly conchoidal, and frequently uneven: its lustre is resinous, more or less shining and sometimes splendent. It is easily broken, and its specific gravity varies from 1.3 to 1.45. It burns easily, with a whitish flame, yielding a black smoke, and a feeble but not unpleasant bituminous odor. The products of combustion are chiefly carbonic acid and water, and a small quantity of sulphurous acid. The remainder, which is never less than three per cent., but frequently much greater, is generally composed of scoria mixed with ashes. It yields, by distillation, ammonia, carburetted hydrogen and empyreumatic oil. This coal is essentially constituted of carbon and bitumen, the proportions of which are variable; carbon is the predominating ingredient, and frequently constitutes nearly three fourths of the whole. Small portions of earth and oxide of iron are discovered by chemical analysis. The co. of Tioga appears to be very rich in a mineralogical point of view, but has never been properly explored. Bismuth has lately been found in the vicinity of the coal beds, but the exact location of it has been concealed, for interested motives, by the discoverer. From the specimens examined and all the circumstances of the case, there can be no doubt that the discovery has actually been made; and when the situation is rendered public, it will become very valuable as an article of commerce. It is the native metal, and only requires refining; which operation is simple and easy, consisting in dissolving it in nitric acid, decomposing the nitrate by water, edulcorating the oxide, and reducing it to a metallic state by heating in a covered crucible with black flux. It is said to occur in an extensive bed, at least 2 feet thick. Bismuth, in its metallic state, is employed in the composition of pewter, soft solder, printers' types, &c., and is added to lead to increase its hardness. Its oxide renders glass more fusible, and if added in large quantities gives it a yellowish tinge. The subnitrate is used in medicines as an anti-spasmodic, &c.

Nearly all the bismuth of commerce is imported from Saxony, and it has rarely if ever been found before in the United States. Other minerals are found near Pine creek, near the coal bed (and an ore of lead,) which were represented as occurring in vast abundance. Ores of gold and silver have also been discovered there, but not in sufficient quantities to render them a valuable consideration.

The Tioga river is the main stream of the county, rising in Sullivan t-ship upon the eastern line of the co., and making a semicircular course of about 15 ms., it runs N. through the county about 27 ms. to the state of N. Y. It receives from the east several small streams, of which Mill creek is the principal; from the S. W. Crooked creek, and from the W. near and parallel with the state line, Cowanesque creek, both of which are important streams. The Tioga is navigable for 30 ms. above the state line. The S. W. part of the co. is drained by Pine creek, which enters the co. by a westerly course, and preserves it to the centre of Delmar t-ship, where at the Big meadow, it turns southward, and flows through this and Lycoming co. into the W. branch of the Susquehannah. Pine creek is navigable throughout all its course in this county, and has a volume not inferior to that of the Tioga r., with whose waters some of its tributaries interlock. The extreme S. E. boundary is formed by the Lycoming creek. A canal is projected along the valley of the Tioga r., from the coal mines to the Chemung canal; its practicability is said to have been ascertained, and a survey of the route completed, and a company, called the Tioga navigation company, has been incorporated. The quantity and quality of the bituminous coal near Blossburg or Canal port, would seem fully to warrant this enterprize. The Cowanesque is navigable for 30 ms. from its mouth.

The principal timber is beech, maple, oak, elm, hemlock, hickory and bass or linn. The uplands in the vicinity of the larger streams, are well covered with white pines of a superior quality. Sugar maple abounds in many places, and large quantities of sugar are made from this valuable tree.

The settlement of this county was commenced in 1797–8, chiefly by emigrants from Connecticut, claiming under the unfortunate title, which has caused so much trouble and litigation to Northern Pennsylvania; but which, being compromised and fully settled, the titles here are unexceptionable. In 1810 the pop. was 1687; in 1820, 4021, and by the census of 1830, 9062, of whom 4770 were white males, 4245 white females; 22 free black males, 25 free black females: of whom there were 21 aliens, one blind, and one deaf and dumb. The pop., therefore, has been more than doubled in each decennial period.

The chief business of the county is in lumber, though some iron works have been erected upon the Tioga r., at Blossburg, within the last 3 years. From Pine creek, the principal scene of the lumber trade, more than 5,000,000 of feet of sawed lumber were sent to market in the spring of 1832. A very small portion of the lumber of this region has yet found its way to the Philadelphia market; the entrance to the Union canal at Middletown being so blocked up in the busy season, that the raft men have preferred their old market. This will, probably, not be the case, when the canal shall have been completed on the branches of the Susquehannah, and a facility of getting to market without the aid of freshets, shall prevent the vast accumulations of lumber which have hitherto occurred at the opening of the spring trade. Still the greatest quantity of lumber will probably descend in rafts, unless the dams on the river compel the descending trade to abandon it.

Wellsborough, situated in the territorial centre of the county, is the seat of justice. It lies on the E. and W. state road, leading through all the northern counties, and the N. and south state road from Newbury to the 109 mile stone. Besides which Covington 4 corners, Blossburg, Lawrenceville, Knoxville, &c. are villages of the county.

At Wellsborough an academy was incorporated by act of assembly of 1817, which gave it a donation of $2000. In this institution the usual branches of an academical education are taught successfully; besides which there is a primary school in the town, and like schools in such thickly settled neighborhoods as can maintain them.

Tioga co. belongs to the 9th congressional district, composed of Union, Northumberland, Columbia, Lycoming, Luzerne, Susquehannah, Tioga, Bradford, Potter and McKean, sending 3 members to congress: and to the 11th senatorial district, formed of Bradford, Susquehannah and Tioga, and united with Bradford, it sends 2 members to the house of representatives. These counties also form the 11th judicial district, to which the counties of Potter and McKean are also attached.

Tioga county paid into the state treasury in 1831, for

Tax on writs,	$170
Tavern licenses,	108 68
Duties on dealers in foreign merchandize,	46 75
State maps,	4 75
	$330 18

Tioga Point, Athens t-ship, Bradford co., a peninsula formed by the Susquehannah and Tioga rivers. (See Athens.)

Tioga, or Chemung river, rises in Tioga co., near its eastern boundary, and running about 15 miles in a semicircular course it assumes a northern direction, which it preserves for about 27 miles into Steuben co., state of N. York, where it receives the Canisteo and Conhocton rivers; thence deflecting E. and S. E. it passes the town of Painted Post and Newtown, and re-enters Pennsylvania in the N. W. angle of Athens t-ship, Bradford co., through which it passes to unite with the Susquehannah river, having a total comparative length of about 80 miles. This river and its principal tributaries are navigable for arks and boats.

Tioga, t-ship, Tioga co., bounded N. by Lawrence t-ship, E. by Jackson, S. by Covington, and W. by Elkland t-ships. Centrally distant N. E. from Wellsborough 13 ms. It forms a quadrangular figure of 6½ by 6 miles; area 17,940 acres; surface hilly; soil, gravel and clay and alluvion. Pop. in 1830, 408 ; taxables in 1828, 100. The Tioga river runs N. through the t-ship and receives from it on the right, Mill creek, and on the left Crooked creek, at the confluence of which with the river is the post office, called after the t-ship, distant N. W. 254 miles from W. C., and 148 from Harrisburg.

Toboyne, westernmost t-ship of Perry co., bounded N. by Mifflin co., E. by Saville and Tyrone t-ships, S. by Cumberland co., and W. by Franklin co. Centrally distant W. from Bloomfield 20 miles; greatest length 16½, breadth 10½ miles ; area, 84,480 acres ; surface mountainous ; soil, limestone, slate and gravel. Population in 1830, 2310 ; taxables 557. It is drained by Sherman's creek. Of the many ranges of hills which cover the t-ship, the following have names given to them, Blue mtn., Bower's mtn., Conecocheague hill, and the Tuscarora mtn., which lie in the above order proceeding from the south. There is a post office at Morelands, and a small hamlet centrally situated at Limestone spring.

Toby's creek, a small tributary of the Susquehannah river, which rises in Dallas t-ship, Luzerne co., and flows a S. E. course through Plymouth and Kingston t-ships, and passing about, insulates the town of Wyoming, and thence by a S. W. course enters the r.

Toby's creek, an important tributary of the Allegheny river. (See Clarion river.)

Toby's creek, Little, rises in Toby's Creek t-ship, Venango co., and flows S. W. by a course of about 14 miles, into Clarion river or Great Toby's creek, at the S. W. angle of Paint Creek t-ship.

Toby, t-ship, Armstrong co., bounded north by Clarion river, east by Red Bank and Clarion townships, S. and S. W. by the Allegheny river, and N. W. by Perry t-ship. Centrally distant N. from Kittanning 15 ms.; greatest length 17, breadth 8½ miles ; area, 46,080 acres ; surface partly hilly and partly rolling ; soil, loam. Pop. in 1830, 1362 ; taxables 263. Besides the streams above mentioned, the t-ship has Licking creek, Cherry run, Catfish and Red Bank creeks. Salt is found in the N. part of the township, and copperas near Red Bank creek. The post office is 236 miles N. W. from W. C., and 190 from Harrisburg.

Toby's Creek, t-ship, Venango co., bounded N. by Saratoga t-ship, E. by Jefferson co., S. by Clarion river or Toby's creek, W. by Paint Creek and Farmington t-ships. It is drained by Little Toby's creek on the S. W. and Raccoon creek on the N. W. Centrally distant E. from Franklin boro' 30 miles ; greatest length 10, breadth 5 miles ; area 2340 acres ; surface rolling ; soil, gravel and loam. Pop. very scanty. The t-ship is not organized, but is attached to Pine Creek township.

Tobyhanna creek, Northampton co., rises in Pike co., and running a south westerly course receives the waters of Big and Little Tunkhanna creeks, and falls into the Lehigh about two miles below Stoddartsville. The Tobyhanna flows thro' a swampy country for several miles, and is not so much broken, but that it would serve the purposes of raft navigation for some miles, if rafts could descend the Upper Lehigh. The country along its banks is a wilderness, and no mills are yet erected on it, although there are several good seats.

Tobyhanna, t-ship, Northampton co. bounded N. E. by Pike co., and N. W. by Luzerne co., S. E. by Pokono t-ship, S. by Chesnut Hill t-ship, and W. by Towamensing t-ship. Its greatest length E. and W. is 16 ms., greatest breadth N. and S. 13 miles. Its surface is hilly ; soil, gravel and barren. The country is a desert, and contains only 279 inhabitants and 50 taxables. It is watered by the Tobyhanna creek and its tributaries.

Tobyhanna, post office, on the Tobyhanna creek, Pike co., and on the road from Easton to the Big Bend of the Susquehannah, 230 miles from W. C., and 138 from Harrisburg.

Tohickon creek, Bucks co., rises in Springfield t-ship, and by a very devious course of 25 miles, but mainly S. E., falls into the Delaware two ms. above Lumberville. It is a mill stream with several mills upon it.

Tom Jack's creek, Burlington t-ship, Bradford co., rises in Smithfield t-ship, whence it receives several branches and flows south to Sugar creek.

Tom's creek, Lower Chanceford t-ship, York co., a tributary of Muddy creek.

Towamensing, t-ship, Northampton co., bounded N. and W. by Luzerne co., N. E. by Tobyhanna t-ship, E. by Chesnut Hill and Ross t-ships, S. by Lehigh t-ship, S. W. by Penn t-ship, W. by the Lehigh river which divides it from Mauch Chunk and Lausanne t-ships. Greatest length on the eastern line is 24 miles. Its width is very irregular. Opposite Mauch Chunk, the widest part, it is about 10 miles wide. It is a mass of mountains, and three fourths of it a desert; containing in its great extent not more than 1171 inhabitants, and 238 taxables, and a single place of public worship, for Lutherans, near its southwest boundary. The great swamp or "Shades of Death" commences in its northern part and a succession of mountains extends to its southern boundary, terminating with the Blue Ridge. The soil of the t-ship, like that of the other mountainous parts of the country is gravel,—and in many places is very well timbered. The post office, called after the t-ship, is situated on the road from the Lehigh Water gap to Mauch Chunk at the mouth of Big creek, 194 miles from W. C., and 87 from Harrisburg.

Towamensing, t-ship, Montgomery co., bounded N. E. by Hatfield, S.E. by Gwynedd, S. by Worcester, W. by Lower Salford, and N. W. by Franconia. Greatest length 3½ ms., greatest breadth 3 miles; area, 5,400 acres. It is drained by the Skippack and Towamensing creeks. Has a church, centrally situated. Distant from Philadelphia 20 miles, from Norristown 9 miles. Surface level; soil, red shale; pop. in 1830, 669; taxables in 1828, 163.

Towanda, t-ship, Bradford county, bounded N. by Ulster, E. by the Susquehannah river, S. and S. E. by Monroe t-ship, and W. by Burlington t-ship. Greatest length 7½, breadth 5 miles; area, 16,640 acres; surface hilly; soil, gravelly loam. Pop. in 1830, 978; taxables 157. It is drained chiefly by Sugar creek, which empties into the Susquehannah about 2 miles N. of the town of Towanda. Bituminous coal is said to abound in the valleys of this t-ship.

Towanda, post town and seat of justice of Bradford co., situated in Towanda t-ship, on the W. bank of the Susquehannah river, 128 ms. N. from Harrisburg, and 139 from W. C. The t. was incorporated 5th March, 1828.

Trap, post town and small village of Upper Providence t-ship, Montgomery co., on the Reading turnpike road, 9 miles from Norristown, and 26 from Philadelphia, 152 from W. C., and 80 from Harrisburg. It contains 15 dwellings, 2 stores and 4 taverns, a church common to the Lutheran and German Reformed societies, and a school house.

Traumbarsville, p-t. of Milford t-ship, Bucks co., about 16 ms. N. of Doylestown, 160 from W. C., and 85 E. of Harrisburg.

Travis creeks, Big and Little, Hanover t-ship, Beaver co., rise in the township and flow S. E. into Raccoon creek.

Trexlertown, p-t. of Macungy t-ship, Lehigh co., situated at the junction of the Northampton and Millerstown roads, distant about 8 ms. from Northampton, 170 N. from W. C., and 75 E. from Harrisburg; contains some half a dozen dwellings, store and tavern. There is a Lutheran church near it.

Tredypin, t-ship, Chester county, bounded N. by Charleston t-ship, and by Montgomery co., E. by Montgomery county, S. by Delaware co. and by Easton t-ship, W. by Willistown and East Whiteland t-ships. Centrally distant about 17 miles N. W. from Philadelphia, and 10 ms. N. E. from West Chester. Length $4\frac{1}{4}$ ms., breadth $4\frac{1}{4}$ miles ; area, 8,950 acres ; surface gentle declivity ; soil, limestone. Pop. in 1830, 1,582 ; taxables 319. The Valley creek runs through the N. W. angle of the t-ship, and the Philadelphia and Lancaster turnpike road crosses the S. W. angle, in which is situated the noted tavern, the sign of General Paoli, at which there is a post office, about 18 ms. W. of Philadelphia. On the road running through the t-ship to Norristown there are two churches, one in the E. the other in the W. part of the t-ship.

Triangle pond, a small lake and tributary of the Little Wapwallopen creek, in Newport t-ship Luzerne co. near the eastern boundary of the t-ship.

Tripoli, New, a village of Linn t-ship, Lehigh co., situate on a branch of Maiden creek, about fifteen miles N. W. from Northampton and 3 ms. S. W. of Segarsville.

Trough creek and valley, Union t-ship, Huntingdon co. The creek is formed by two branches which approach each other from S. and N. and unite about the middle of the t-ship, and forcing their way through Terrace mountain unite with the Raystown branch of the Juniata river. The creek gives name to a post office, distant 133 miles from W. C. and 81 from Harrisburg.

Trout creek, Lehigh county, rises at the foot of the Blue mountain in Heidelburg township, and running eastwardly falls into the Lehigh river about two miles below the Water gap. It turns several mills but does not admit of navigation.

Trout creek, rising in Pike county, Middle Smithfield t-ship, flows S. W. through the N. E. angle of Tobyhanna t-ship, Northampton co. and falls into the Lehigh river near the junction of Lehigh, Northampton and Luzerne counties.

Trout creek, Lancaster co. rises at the foot of the Conewago hills and flows S. E. into the Cocalico creek, forming the dividing line between Elizabeth and Cocalico t-ships.

Trout Run, post office, Jackson t-ship, Lycoming county, 210 miles N. W. of W. C. and 101 from Harrisburg.

Troy, New, a post town and village of Kingston township, Luzerne co. situated near the junction of Abraham's creek and the Susquehannah r., upon Abraham's plain distinguished as the fatal battle ground, on which the United States troops were defeated and massacred by the Indians and Tories under Brandt and Butler on the 3d July, 1778. The town contains about 40 dwellings, stores, taverns and a mill. Population, about 250. Anthracite coal is found in its immediate vicinity.

Troy, post township, Bradford co. bounded N. by Columbia and Springfield t-ship, E. by Burlington t-ship, S. by Franklin and Canton t-ships, and W. by Tioga co. Distance 192 miles E. of N. from Harrisburg and 18 miles W. of Towanda. Greatest length $9\frac{3}{4}$ miles, breadth $4\frac{1}{2}$ miles, area 24,960 acres; surface hilly ; soil gravelly loam ; pop. in 1830, 874 ; taxables 173. It is drained by the branches of Sugar creek which flow through it eastwardly to the Susquehannah.

Troy, t-ship, Crawford co. pop. in 1830, 146.

Trucksville, post office, Luzerne co. 228 miles N. from W. city, and 120 from Harrisburg.

Tucquan creek, Martick t-ship, Lancaster co. rises in the Martick hills and flows a S. W. course about 5 miles into the Susquehannah above McCall's ferry.

Tullytown, post town, Falls t-ship, Bucks co. on the turnpike road leading from Bristol to Trenton, 4 miles from the former, contains some half dozen dwellings, store and tavern and several mechanic shops.

Tulpehocken, Upper, t-ship, Berks co. bounded N. by the Blue mountain, which separates it from Schuylkill county, S. by Heidelberg township, S. and W. by Lebanon co. and E. by the township of Upper Bern. Its greatest length is eleven and greatest breadth 7 miles; area 48,000 acres. Its surface is diversified; soil, limestone and gravel, very productive; pop. in 1830, 1456; taxables 268. It is drained by the Northkill, which separates it from Upper Bern t-ship, on the E. and little Northkill, tributaries of the Tulpehocken. The Union canal follows the latter stream along the greater portion of the southern boundary. A church of brick appertaining to the Presbyterians and Lutherans, is near the little Northkill, on the road from Rehrersburg to Hamburg.

Tulpehocken, Lower, Berks co. was separated from Upper Tulpehocken. It is bounded N. by the Little Swatara creek, S. by the Tulpehocken creek, E. by Lebanon co. and W. by Upper Tulpehocken t-ship; length 8, breadth 6 ms. Besides the streams on its upper and nether boundary, it is watered by the source of Mill creek. Rehrersburg, Wohleberstown and Stouchtown, are villages of the t-ship. The first on the road to Sunbury, 21 miles from Reading; the second, on the road to Jonestown, and the third on the turnpike road from Harrisburg to Reading, about 15 miles from the latter. The soil is limestone and gravel, generally well cultivated in grain, and productive. There are two churches near Stouchtown, and one called Hosters church, near Mill creek, all of which are common to the German Presbyterians and Lutherans.

Tulpehocken creek, rises in Lebanon co. Lebanon t-ship. and flows E. and S. E. above 30 miles through Lehigh and Berks co. into the Scuylkill, near and above the town of Reading. It is a fine constant stream, and is studded with mills along its whole course. The Union canal ascends the valley of this stream to near its source, and thence crosses to the valley of the Quitapahilla creek, distant from that of the Tulpehocken, about five miles.

Tumbling creek rises in Schuylkill t-ship, Schuylkill co. south of the Sharp mountain along whose base it flows into the Schuylkill below mount Carbon.

Tunkhanna creek, Tobyhanna t-ship, Northampton co. a tributary of the Tobyhanna creek. It divides itself into two branches the smaller of which is called the little Tunkhanna. Both have their sources in Pike co.

Tunkhannock, t-ship, Luzerne co. bounded N. by Susquehannah co.; E. by Nicholson and Abington; S. E. by Falls; S. W. by the Susquehannah river which separates it from Eaton and Windham, and N. W. by Braintrim t-ships. The soil along the Susquehannah and the valley of the Tunkhannock creek is productive, and the highlands, a considerable portion of which may be cultivated, are covered with valuable timber, consisting of white pine, oak, chestnut, &c. A village, advantageously situated near the mouth of the Tunkhannock, contains a post office, several stores and mechanics' shops, and, from its local position, promises to be a place of considerable importance. The t-ship produces large quantities of lumber, and some of the products of agriculture, for market. It is situated about 28 miles N. of Wilkesbarre, and contains 1039 inhabitants by the census of 1830, and 183 taxables by the return of 1828. The Meshoppen creek, and the Tunkhannock creek and its tributaries flow through the township into the Susquehannah river. Tunkhannock mountain crosses it diagonally, sending forth spurs upon every side. Triangle hill, one of the spurs of this township, near the southern boundary, has an elevation of 640 ft. above the river. The Wilkesbarre and Montrose turnpike road runs northerly through the t-ship. The form of the t-ship is irregular; its greatest length E. and W. is about 11 miles, greatest breadth N. and S. about 9 miles. Area, 51,200 acres.

Tunkhannock creek, a long and large stream, rises in Jackson t-ship. Susquehannah co. at the foot of mount Ararat, and flows S. W. through Luzerne co. into the Susquehannah river, upon the N. side of Tunkhannock mountain, receiving many considerable tributaries from either hand in its course, among which the South branch is the most important.

Tunkhannock valley, Luzerne and Susquehannah cos. extending along the Tunkhannock creek, is very crooked and irregular, about a mile wide, lessening in some places to a half mile, and is about 35 ms. long. It is mostly cultivated, and generally thickly settled.

Tunkhannock post town and village, of Tunkhannock t-ship. Luzerne co. situated on the N. side of the Tunkhannock creek at its confluence with the Susquehannah river.

Turbett, t-ship, formerly of Mifflin co. now of Juniata, bounded N. by Milford t-ship, N. E. by the Juniata r. E. by Greenwood t-ship, S. by the Tuscarora mtn. Centrally distant from Lewistown S. E. 11 miles; greatest length 19, breadth 3 miles; area, 29,560 acres; surface, hills and valleys; soil, limestone, slate and gravel. Pop. in 1830, 1134; taxables 242. The Tuscarora creek bounds the t-ship on the N. running through the Tuscarora valley into the Juniata r. The Tuscarora valley p-o. is on the creek, in the S. W. part of the t-ship.

Tunnelview, p-t. Indiana co. 199 ms. from W. C. and 171 from Harrisburg.

Turbut, t-ship, Northumberland co. bounded N. by Lycoming co. E. by Columbia co. S. by Chilisquaque t-ship, and W. by the west branch of the Susquehannah r. Centrally distant from Sunbury about 14 miles north; greatest length 11, greatest breadth 9 miles; area 46,720 acres; surface level; soil, alluvial and limestone. Pop. in 1830, 3388; taxables, 636. It is drained by Delaware run, Warrior, Muddy and Limestone runs, all of which flow westerly to the Susquehannah river. Watsonburg, Snyderstown and Milton are villages of this t-ship; the first and last are p-towns. Limestone ridge crosses the t-ship on the S. boundary.

Turbutville, p-o. of Turbut t-ship, Northumberland co.

Turkey ridge and valley. The former forms part of the boundary line between Mifflin and Perry cos. extending from the r. Juniata N. E. to the Susquehannah r. about 15 ms. The valley is on the N. side of the ridge, and is bounded E. by the latter river and W. by Cocalimus creek.

Turkeyfoot, township, Somerset co. bounded N. by Milford t-ship, E. by Elk Lick, S. by Addison t-ship, and W. by Fayette co. Centrally distant S. W. from Bedford 15 ms.; greatest length 13, breadth 9 ms.; area 70,560 acres; surface hilly; soil, fertile loam. Pop. in 1830, 1281; taxables 199. Taxable property in 1829, real estate $68,197; personal 7408; rate 5 mills in the dollar. The Laurel mtn. is on the W. and the Negro mtn. on the E. boundary. Hog Back ridge lies between Castleman's r. and the Youghiogheny. Castleman's r. and Laurel Hill creek divide the t-ship in nearly three equal parts, flowing through from N. to S. to the Youghiogheny r. Salt is found near the N. boundary on Laurel Hill creek. Turkeyfoot p-o. is near the S. boundary, W. of Castleman's r. The p-o. named after the t-ship, is 185 miles N. W. from W. C. and 163 from Harrisburg.

Turtle creek, rises in Salem t-ship, Westmoreland co. and flows W. about 17 ms. into the Monongahela river, 12 ms. above Pittsburg, forming the S. E. and S. boundary of Plumb t-ship, and dividing Wilkins and Versailles t-ships in Allegheny co. It is navigable for canoes about 10 ms.

Tuscarora mtn. Schuylkill co. on the dividing line between Rush and West Penn t-ships. It is the western continuation of the Mauch Chunk mtn. and, like it, abounds in anthracite coal, many veins of which have lately been opened. To reach these mines the Schuylkill valley rail road, extending 12 ms. from Port Carbon, has been constructed, and also another railroad on Little Schuylkill river. (See Tamaqua.)

Tuscarora, village, Rush township, Schuylkill co. on the N. side of Tuscarora mtn. at the head of the main Schuylkill r. and of the Schuylkill valley rail road. It is one of the Alladin lamp creations of the coal trade, and consists of about a dozen dwellings, much scattered, two hotels, one a large and commodious frame building. It is inhabited chiefly by miners, and is located in a wild and barren country. Its existence and prosperity will depend upon the progress of mining the anthracite coal. It is about 16 ms. N. E. of Orwigsburg, 183 from W. C. and 78 from Harrisburg.

Tuscarora creek and valley, Huntingdon and Juniata cos., between Tuscarora and Shade mountains. The creek and valley commence in Tell t-ship, Huntingdon co., and run N. E. between 30 and 35 ms. to the Juniata river; passing through Lack and Turbett t-ships, of Juniata co. There is a p-o. here, named after the valley, 140 miles from W. C. and 53 from Harrisburg.

Tuscarora mountain, a noted ridge, of the Appalachian system, which may be considered as commencing at the Potomac river in Maryland, and running N. E. near 70 miles, forms the E. boundary of Bedford, Huntingdon and Mifflin counties.

Tuscarora, t-ship, Mifflin co., formerly a part of Lack t-ship; surface mountainous; soil, in the valleys, limestone; pop. in 1830, 827; taxables in 1828, 195. (See Lack t-ship, in the description of which, the above is included.)

Tuscarora creek, rises in a small lake in Auburn t-ship, Susquehannah co., and flows S. W. through that t-ship, into Bedford co. where it receives some considerable tributaries, and thence by a south course unites with the Susquehannah river in Braintrim t-ship, Luzerne county.

Tyburn, small village of Falls t-ship, Bucks co., on the turnpike road leading from Bristol to Trenton, 7 miles from the former, and 3 from the latter. Contains some half dozen dwellings, store and tavern.

Tyrone, t-ship, Adams co., bounded N. by Cumberland co. E. by Huntingdon township, S. by Reading and Strabane t-ships, and W. by Manallen. Centrally distant N. E. from Gettysburg 10 miles; greatest length, 10, breadth, 4 miles; area, 15,360 acres; surface, level; soil, red shale and gravel; pop. in 1830, 817; taxables, 159. Bermudian creek forms part of the eastern boundary, and the Conewago cr. the southern. Heidelburg, a town of the t-ship, is distant 9 miles N. E. from Gettysburg.

Tyrone, t-ship Perry co., bounded N. by Limestone ridge which separates it from Saville t-ship, S. by the Blue mountain, E. by Rye t-ship, and W. by Toboyne t-ship, and by Cumberland co. Centrally distant S. W. from Bloomfield 7 miles; greatest length 9, breadth 8 miles; area 42,880 acres; surface, mountainous; soil limestone in the valleys, gravel and slate on the hills; pop. in 1830, 2758, taxables, 384. It is drained by Sherman's creek, which receives many considerable streams from the t-ship. Pisgah Hill is south of that stream, and Quaker Hills on the north. Between them and on the N. margin of the stream is a noted spring called the Warm spring. The post town of Landisburg, centrally situated in the t-ship, is on this stream about 8 miles S. W. of Bloomfield. The poor house of the co. is situated about a mile N. of the village. Montour's run rises in the Limestone ridge and flows S. by Landisburg into Shermans' creek.

Tyrone, t-ship, Fayette co. bounded N. by Jacob's creek, which divides it from Westmoreland co., E. by Bullskin t-ship, S. E. by Connellsville t-ship, S. and W. by the Youghiogheny r. which separates it from Dunbar, Franklin, and Washington t-ships. Iron is found on both sides of Jacob's creek. The t-ship is centrally situated 13 miles N. of Union town; greatest length 12 miles, breadth 4 miles, area 21,760 acres; surface, hilly; soil, limestone; pop. in 1830, 1139; taxables, 235.

Tyrone, t-ship, Huntingdon county.

Ulster, t-ship Bradford co., bounded N. by Athens t-ship, E. by the Susquehannah river, S. by Towanda and W. by Smithfield t-ships. Centrally distant from the town of Towanda N. W. 7 miles. Greatest length $7\frac{1}{4}$, breadth $2\frac{1}{4}$ miles; area, 7,040 acres; surface hilly; soil, gravelly loam. Pop. in 1830, 405; taxables 7. Post office, called after the t-ship, dist. from W. C. 246 miles, and from Harrisburg 135.

Union county, formerly a part of Northumberland, was separated from it by the act of 22d March, 1813, and includes all that part of the latter co. which lay on the west side of the river Susquehannah and the west branch of the same. By the commissioners appointed pursuant to this act, the seat of justice was located at New Berlin, upon Penn's creek, about 10 miles above its junction with the Susquehannah. The county is bounded N. by Lycoming, E. by the Susquehannah river and the west branch, S. by Mifflin co. and west by Centre. Greatest length 26 miles, mean breadth 21, area 551 square miles. Central lat. 40° 50′ N., long. from W. C., 0° 8′ west.

This county, which, although mountainous, is not rugged, lies in the range of the Alleghenies, and in the central transition formation. The branches of the mountains traverse it in a direction about east, north east. The chief ridges are the White Deer, Nittany, Buffalo, Jack's and Shade mtns.; of which Jack's mtn. is most lofty, being considered the highest ground in the co.

For some years the attention of the public has been directed to the discovery of iron ore. The external indications of this useful mineral present themselves in many places, but as yet no considerable body has been found. In Buffalo valley, in White Deer, in Hartley t-ship, and many other places there is iron ore of a good quality, in rolled masses, and geodes on the surface of the ground. Mines have been opened, but in no instance has the quantity been sufficient to encourage the miner to prosecute his labors. Of bog iron, a large body lies in the flat extending from the Sunbury ferry to the neighborhood of Selin's Grove; its quality is said to be good. It is cellular and of light brown color. Another bed of bog iron ore was discovered on Philip Herrold's farm, ten miles below Selin's Grove. This also is cellular, of a darker color, and much harder and heavier than the first mentioned. It was accidentally discovered in digging a drain connected with the canal.

Lead ore has been discovered, of a rich quality, and indications of this metal are found in the long narrows in Hartley t-ship.

A body of iron pyrites was some years since accidentally discovered in digging a mill race on Jacob Kehr's land, on Penn's creek, about 4 miles above New Berlin; a spring issues from the rock, the water of which immediately blackens any tin or iron vessel into which it is put. Mineral coal has of late been eagerly sought for, and lands supposed to contain it have risen greatly in price. Black slate and bituminous shale, which are considered indications of coal, have been found in places.

The valleys of this county are generally fertile, but some of them are exuberantly so. Buffalo valley includes the greater part of five t-ships, viz., White Deer, Kelly, Buffalo, W. Buffalo, and Hartley. Its soil is the most productive limestone, and its surface, with some trifling exceptions, admirably adapted to agriculture. On Buffalo creek, which drains it, there are 5 or 6 valuable grist mills and other water works. On the White Deer creek also, there are many mills, among which, those of Mr. Daniel Caldwell merit particular attention, consisting of a 3 story stone grist mill, a saw mill, fulling mill, carding machine, and a distillery. Penn's creek divides the county nearly in the middle. The country on the S. is more broken, and the soil inferior to that of the N.; still it is fertile, particularly along the valley of Middle creek. Traversing the county from N. to S., we cross the following streams, viz., White Deer creek, which, rising in Lycoming co., flows E. in the valley between White Deer mtn., and the Nittany mtn.; Buffalo creek, which rises W. of the Buffalo mountains in Centre co., by two branches, and runs E. through Buffalo valley; Penn's creek, which has its source in the W. side of the Path Valley mtn., in the southern part of Centre co., breaks through the mtn. and runs E. through Union co., draining the valley N. of Jack's mtn. Little Mahoniely or Middle creek, formed by 2 branches, 1 from Jack's mountain, the other from Black Oak ridge, flows E. through, and drains the fine and rich valley, bounded N. by Jack's, and S. by Shade mtn. South of the Shade mtn. is the W. Mahantango creek, which forms part of the boundary between Mifflin and Union counties. The 2 first of the streams we have named flow into the W. branch of the Susquehannah r.; the remainder incorporates with the main stream. The Pennsylvania canal ascends the west bank of the main r. through this co., opposite to Northumberland, where, crossing the W. branch by a pool, it follows the eastern bank of that stream through Northumberland co.

The only t-pike road in the county, we believe, is that which proceeds from Lewisburg on the Susquehannah, to Bellefonte, a distance of 19 ms.

The chief towns of the co., are New Berlin, New Columbia, Selin's Grove, Freeburg, Adamsburg, Beaver, Middleburg, Centreville, Hartleyton, and Mifflinsburg.

Union co. is inhabited chiefly by the descendants of Germans, whose fathers were the first settlers. The population is, as is usual in Pennsylvania, divided into several religious sects, which rank in numerical strength in the following order: Lutherans, German Reformed, Presbyterians, Methodists and Baptists; there are probably others, but they are not numerous. There are altogether about 21 churches in the co., and several religious and moral institutions, such as a county Bible society, Sunday school and temperance societies, &c. The pop. in 1820, was 18,619, and in 1830, 20,656, of whom 10,485 were white males, 10,116 white females, 26 free colored males, 27 free colored females, 2 slaves; of these, there were 11 deaf and dumb, 9 blind, and 27 aliens; taxables in 1828, 3772.

The business of the inhabitants is principally confined to agriculture, and the arts which minister unto it. There are in the county 42 grist mills, 61 saw mills, 13 fulling mills, 6 oil mills, 16 distilleries, at which more than 50,000 bushels of grain are distilled. There is a furnace and forge in Hartley t-ship, a forge in Penn t-ship, and an iron foundry in W. Buffalo t-ship.

The provision for education here is not remarkable; primary schools are established in every vicinage, and an academy was incorporated in 1827 at Mifflinsburg, and received from the state treasury the sum of $2000. There are, however, five instruments of instruction in the form of weekly journals, published in the co., viz., the Lewisburg Journal, the Union Times, the Union Telegraph, the Jackson Herald, and the Anti-Masonic Advocate (German.)

The taxable value of the lands of the county was, in 1829, rated at $2,891,851. Their marketable value may be stated, first rate at from $40 to 60; second rate at from $30 to 40; third rate at from 5 to $15 the acre.

This county belongs to the 9th congressional district, composed of Union, Northumberland, Columbia, Luzerne, Susquehannah, Bradford, Lycoming, Potter and McKean, and Tioga, sending three members to congress. Northumberland and Union form the 9th senatorial district, sending one member to the state senate; and Union alone sends 2 members to the house of representatives. Columbia, Northumberland, and Union form the 8th judicial district, over which Seth Chapman, Esq., presides. The courts are holden at New Berlin, on the second Monday after the commencement of the courts in Lycoming. The co. is attached to the middle district of the supreme court, which holds a session annually at Sunbury in the month of June.

This county paid into the state treasury in 1831, for tax on writs,	205	32
Tavern licenses,	692	17
Duties on dealers in foreign merchandize,	446	28
State maps,	9	50
Tax on collateral inheritances,	10	92
Tax for pamphlet laws,	1	93
" for hawkers and pedlar's licenses,	15	20
	$1381	32

STATISTICAL TABLE OF UNION CO.

Townships &c.	Greatest lth.	bth.	Area in acres.	Population. 1820.	1830.	Taxables
Beaver,	10	8	51,840	2,036	2,280	359
Buffalo, E.	8	7	19,200	2,376	2,130	548
Buffalo, W.	15	6	50,560	1,183	1,404	415
Chapman,	10½	4	17,920		1,094	221
Centre,	8	8	30,080	2,094	1,952	350
Hartley,	18	10	38,000	1,314	1,730	329
Kelly,	6	4	12,160		739	129
Penn,	7	7	24,320		2,304	429
Union,	10	5	21,760	1,754	2,085	361
Perry,	15	7	32,000	1,330	1,050	200
Washington,	8	5	17,040	1,427	1,097	210
White Deer,	6½	4	17,280	1,677	1,295	221
Mifflinsburg,				620	663	
Lewisburg Bo.				579	924	
				18,619	20,749	3,772

Union, p-t. and borough and seat of justice of Fayette co., in Union t-ship, in a fork of Redstone creek, about 4 ms. W. of Laurel hill, 186 from Harrisburg, 276 W. from Phil., and 12 S. E. from Brownsville; lat. 39° 54′ N., long. 2° 45′ W. of W. C. The Cumberland or national turnpike road passes through it. It contains about 280 dwellings. Madison college, under the care of the Pittsburg conference of the Methodist Episcopal church, was established here in the year 1825, and incorporated by act of assembly, 7th March, 1827. It has about 60 students. There was also an academy here, incorporated by act 4th Feb., 1808, by which a donation of $2000 was given to it; but this institution was merged in the college. There are here 4 churches, 5 schools, 15 stores, 8 taverns, and a grist and saw mill, driven by water.

Union, t-ship, Fayette co., bounded N. by Franklin and Dunbar, E. by Wharton, S. W. by George and W. by Manallen t-ships. Greatest length 9, breadth 8½ ms.; area, 33,920 acres; surface, level; soil, limestone. Pop. 1830, 2475. It is drained by Redstone creek, which rises and has many branches in the t-ship. On a south branch, iron is abundant, and a furnace in operation. On a S. E. branch, near Monroe village, salt water is found. There is a sulphur spring upon an eastern branch. Uniontown, the seat of justice of the co. is centrally situated (*See Uniontown*) on the national road, S. E. of which about 3 ms. lies the t. of Monroe.

Union, t-ship, Mifflin co., bounded N. W. by Stone ridge, which separates it from Huntingdon co., N. by Path Valley mtn. dividing it from Centre co., E. by Armagh t-ship, S. E. by Derry and Wayne t-ships, and S. W. by Huntingdon co. Centrally distant W. from Lewistown, 8 miles; greatest length 13 ms., breadth 6; area, 28,800 acres; surface, mountainous; soil in the valleys, limestone. Pop. 1830, 1757; taxables, 343. The Kishcoquillas valley runs through the t-ship N. W. and S. E., bounded E. by Jack's mtn., and W. by Stone mtn. In the S. part of the valley lies Horreltown, near which is a sinking spring; on the N. part, lies the p-t. of Belleville.

Union, t-ship, Berks co., bounded N. E. by the r. Schuylkill and the canal, S. by Chester co., W. and N. W. by Robeson. It is drained by Mill creek and the head waters of French creek. Its greatest length is 5¼ ms.; greatest breadth 4 ms.; area, 14,000 acres. Unionville, a small village on the r. is the p-t. Pop. 1810, 706; 1820, 921; 1830, 1046; taxables, 1828, 191. Surface, very hilly; soil, gravel, very poor; value when improved, from 15 to $20 per acre.

Hopewell furnace is on a branch of French creek, and a forge on Sixpence creek.

Unionville, a p-t. and small village of about a dozen houses, in Union t-ship, Schuylkill co.

Union, t-ship, Luzerne co., bounded N. E. by Lehman and Plymouth, S. E. by the Susquehannah r. which separates it from Newport and Nescopeck, S. W. by Salem and Huntingdon t-ships, and N. W. by Lycoming co. Surface, very uneven; much of it may be cultivated. Hemlock, Shickshinny and Huntingdon creeks head in, or flow through this t-ship, which afford sufficient mill power. The North Branch canal passes through it. Its agricultural products are pork, grain and whiskey. It contains 1075 inhabitants, and by the return of 1828, 151 taxables. The t-ship is of an oblong form, but cut diagonally by the line of Lycoming co. Its length on the longest side N. W. and S. E. is about 19 ms., and width 8 ms.; area, 80,000 acres. Bowman's range of the Allegheny mtns. passes through the northern part of the t-ship, and the Shickshinny to the south, along the r. The p-o., having the name of the t-ship, is 208 miles from W. C. and 88 ms. from Harrisburg.

Union, t-ship, Schuylkill co., new t-ship, taken from Pine Grove and Manheim t-ships; surface, mountainous; soil, red shale, valleys fertile. Pop. 1830, 477; taxables, 1828, 93.

Unison, p-o., Luzerne co., 218 ms. from W. C. and 98 from Harrisburg.

Unity, t-ship, Westmoreland co., bounded N. E. by Loyalhanna r., S. E. by Ligonier and Donegal t-ships, S. by Mount Pleasant t-ship, W. by Hempfield and N. W. by Salem t-ships. Centrally distant E. from Greensburg, 7 ms.; greatest length 13, breadth 12 ms.; area, 39,680 acres; surface, hilly; soil, limestone, gravel, loam. Pop. 1830, 2990; taxables, 548. The t-ship is drained on the N. W. by Crabtree creek, on the S. by Big Sewickly creek, and on the S. E. by Nine Mile run. The t-pike road from Bedford to Greensburg runs W. through the t-ship; on it lies the p-t. of Youngstown, 9 ms. E. of Greensburg. The p-t. of Pleasant Unity is in the S. part of the t-ship, on the S. side of Big Sewickly creek, about 8 ms. S. E. of Greensburg.

Union furnace, p-o., Huntingdon co., 160 ms. N. W. from W. C. and 102 S. W. from Harrisburg.

Union, t-ship, Huntingdon county, bounded N. by the Juniata r., which separates it from Henderson t-ship, E. by Shirley and Springfield t-ships, S. by Bedford co., and W. by Hopewell t-ship. Centrally distant from Huntingdon S. 15 ms.; greatest length 18 ms., breadth 9 ms.; area, 86,400 acres; surface, mountainous; soil, gravel. Pop. in 1830, 1370; taxables, 266. Jack's mtn. lies on the E. boundary, thence westward is Hares valley, Sideling hill, Trough creek and valley, bounded by Terrace mtn. on the W. Broad Top mtn. lies in the S. part of the t-ship, N. of which is Plank Cabin valley. The t-ship, in 1828, contained 4 grist mills, 4 saw mills, 3 distilleries, 1 fulling mill, 1 tan yard, 1 carding machine.

Union, t-ship, Union co., bounded N. by Buffalo t-ship, E. by the river Susquehannah and by the W. branch of that r., S. by Blue ridge and Penn creek, and W. by West Buffalo t-ship. Greatest length 10, breadth 5 ms.; area, 21,760 acres; surface, mountainous; soil, limestone. Pop. 1830, 2085; taxables, 361. New Berlin, the county town, is on the left bank of Penn's creek.

Union, t-ship, Erie co., bounded N. by Amity t-ship, E. by Wayne, S. by Crawford co., and W. by Le Boeuf t-ship. Centrally distant from Erie S. E. 22 ms.; greatest length 7, breadth 5 ms.; area, 22,400 acres. Pop. 1830, 238; taxables, 1828, 44; surface, hilly; soil, gravelly loam, well adapted to grazing. Drained by the S. branch of French creek, which runs centrally E. and W. through it. P-o. at Union mills, 319 ms. N. W. of W. C. and 252 from Harrisburg.

Uniontown, village of Mifflin t-ship, Dauphin co., on the waters of the Mahantango creek, near the line between Mifflin and Lyken's t-ships, on the road from Gratztown to Sunbury, 34 ms. N. of Harrisburg; contains 20 dwellings, 1 store and 1 tavern.

Unionville, p-t., E. Marlborough t-ship, Chester co., about 9 ms. S. W. from West Chester, 107 N. from W. C., and 70 S. E. from Harrisburg; contains about 20 dwellings, 1 tavern, 2 stores and a malt house.

Unionville, small village of Butler co., on the turnpike road from Butler to Mercer, five miles from the former, contains 8 or 10 log houses, two taverns and a store.

Uwchlan, t-ship, Chester co., bounded N. E. by Vincent and Pikeland t-ships, S. E. by West Whiteland, S. by E. Caln, W. by Brandywine and W. Nantmeal, and N. by E. Nantmeal t-ships. Centrally distant from Philadelphia about 30 ms.; length 7 ms., breadth 3¾ ms.; area, 1300 acres; surface, gentle declivity; soil, sandy loam. Pop. in 1830, 1423; taxables, 273. The E. branch of the Brandywine flows along the S. W. boundary, on which is situated Mary Anne forge. Uwchlan ch. is near the middle of the t-ship. There is a p-o. in the t-ship bearing its name, distant from W. C. 128 ms., and 70 S. E. from Harrisburg.

Valley creek. This name is given to two streams which rise in the great valley of Chester co., near the line which divides the t-ships of East and West Whiteland; the one flows easterly along the base of the Northern hills to the r. Schuylkill, near which it forms the boundary between Montgomery and Chester counties, and gives motion to the mills at Valley Forge. The other flows S. W. into the E. branch of the Brandywine r., and is also a valuable mill stream, which turns many wheels in its course.

Valley Forge, p-t. of Schuylkill t-ship, Chester co., at the confluence of the valley creek with the r. Schuylkill, about 12 ms. N. E. from West Chester, 20 ms. N. W. from Philadelphia, 142 N. from W. C., and 84 S. E. of Harrisburg; contains about 30 houses, a cotton manufactory, having 2000 spindles, a rolling mill, a gun manufactory extensively carried on, a merchant grist mill, and 1 tavern, and 2 stores. The place derives its name from a forge which formerly stood here. The tavern, gun factory, and about 10 dwellings are in Chester co.; the creek being the line.

Valley, (the), p-o. of Miffln co., 171 ms. from W. C., and 64 from Harrisburg.

Valley Hill, p-o. of Chester co.

Venango co., was formed from Allegheny and Lycoming counties, by virtue of the act of 12th March, 1800, and was organized for judicial purposes by the act of 1st April, 1805. By act 28th March, 1806, the state granted $1500 to aid in the erection of the public buildings, and the site for the seat of justice was fixed in the town of Franklin by act 26th March, 1808. The co. is bounded on the N. by Crawford and Warren counties, E. by Jefferson co., S. E. by Armstrong co., S. W. by Butler co., and W. by Mercer; greatest length 38, width 29 ms.; area, 1114 sq. ms. Central lat. 41° 24′ N., long. 2° 40′ W. from W. city.

This co. lies wholly within the great secondary formation, and the minerals common to it are usually found here. Iron ore is very abundant; salt and nitre are found in various parts of the county, and coal in many places. On Oil creek are several springs of the species of bitumen, known as seneca oil.

The face of the country is hilly and somewhat broken, being deeply furrowed by the many streams which spread over it in every direction. Along these streams are some extensive and rich alluvial flats; the soil generally may be considered of good quality. The Allegheny r. enters the county from Warren, on the line between Allegheny and Hickory t-ships, and meanders through it by a S. W., S. and S. E. course, and quits it on the boundary line between Scrub Grass and Richland t-ships, having through all its windings a length of 70 ms. within the county. It receives from the co. on the E., Teonista cr., Hemlock cr., Six Mile run, and on the southern boundary Toby's creek or Clarion r., which is also the recipient of a number of streams which flow from the county southwardly. On the W. the Allegheny r. receives from the co., Oil creek, Sugar creek, French creek, Sandy creek, Scrub Grass creek, and some smaller streams. The Allegheny is navigable for steam boats four or five months in the year, into Warren co., and the Pennsylvania canal, stretching to lake Erie, follows the bank of French creek from the r., 43 ms. To the mouth of this cr. steam boats of 2 or 3 hundred tons have ascended. The t-pike road leading to Erie, crosses the co. by Franklin N. W., and diagonally.

The co. was settled chiefly by emigrants from other parts of Pennsylvania; and in 1810, contained 3060 inhabitants, in 1820, 4915, and in 1830, 9128, of whom 4759 were white males, 4339 white females, 1 male, 1 female slave, 12 free colored males, 16 females. Among these, 16 aliens, 2 blind, and 7 deaf and dumb; taxables in 1828, 1930. The prevailing religious sects are Presbyterian, Methodist, Episcopalian, Baptist and Lutheran, who have established several valuable religious and moral institutions, viz., a county Bible society, temperance societies, Sunday schools, &c.

The only manufacture in the co. worthy of particular attention is that of iron, for which there is a furnace at the mouth of Oil creek, one on Sandy creek, and another on Scrub Grass creek; a bloomery in Teonista t-ship, a furnace on Little Toby's cr., and two forges on French cr.

The exports of the co. are wheat, corn, iron, hay, lumber, and sand stone for the manufacture of glass, vast quantities of which are sent to the glass houses at Pittsburg.

The towns of the county are few and far between, viz., Franklin, the county t., Cooperstown, Hickory t., Shippensville, and Foxburg, &c.

The Venango academy, incorporated in the year 1812, is located in the town of Franklin, and has received from the state a donation of $2000. In thickly settled neighborhoods, primary schools are established, and tolerably well supported. The public buildings in the county town consist of a court house and offices of brick, a jail of stone, and a brick Episcopal, and a frame Presbyterian church.

By the assessment of 1829, the value of taxable property was, real estate $635,000; personal, including occupations, $95,000. The marketable value of improved lands is stated at from 6 to 8 dols. the acre; of unimproved, at 2 dols. the acre.

Erie, Crawford, Mercer, Warren and Venango, form the 18th congressional district, sending one member to the senate. Warren, Armstrong, Indiana, Jefferson and Venango make the 24th senatorial district of the state, sending one member to the senate, and Venango and Warren elect one member to the house of representatives. Venango, Mercer, Crawford and Erie, compose the 6th judicial district, of which Henry Shippen is president. The courts are holden at Franklin, on the 1st Mondays in November, February, May and August. The county belongs to the western district of the supreme court, which holds an annual session at Pittsburgh on the first Monday in September.

Venango county paid into the state treasury in 1832, for tax on writs,	63 25
Tavern licenses,	108 64
Duties on dealers in foreign merchandize,	73 04
State maps,	28 50
	$283,43

Van Winkles creek, Susquehannah co., rises in Jackson t-ship, and flows southward through Harford, into Lenox, where it unites with the Tunkhannock creek. It turns some mills in its course but is too small to be navigable.

Venango, t-ship, Erie co., bounded N. by N. E. t-ship, E. by the state of N. Y., S. by Union t-ship, and W. by Beaver Dam t-ship. Centrally distant S. E. from Erie 12 ms.; greatest length 6 by 5½ ms.; area, 211,230 acres; surface, hilly; soil, loam and gravel. Pop. in 1830, 683: taxables, 108. It is drained by the N. Branch of the French creek, which flows S. through the t-ship. Lake Pleasant lies in the S. W. angle of the t-ship, and discharges its waters by a short stream into French creek.

Venango, t-ship, Crawford co. Pop. in 1830, 886.

Venango Furnace, p-o., 275 miles from W. C., and 225 from Harrisburg.

Venango, t-ship, Butler co., bounded N. by Venango co., E. by Armstrong co., S. by Parker t-ship, and W. by Mercer t-ship; it is the remote N. E. t-ship of the county. Length 10, breadth 5 ms.; area, 32,000 acres; surface, hilly; soil, loam, gravel, slate. Coal and iron are abundant, and of excellent quality. Pop. in 1830, 499; taxables in 1828, 102. It is drained westwardly by the head waters of Slippery Rock creek, and E. by several small runs, which flow into the Allegheny river.

Vernon, t-ship, Crawford co. Pop. in 1830, 797.

Versailles, t-ship, Allegheny co., bounded N. by Wilkins and Plumb t-ships, E. by Westmoreland co., S. by Youghiogheny r., which separates it from Elizabeth t-ship, and W. by the Monongahela r. Beside the rivers it is drained by Turtle creek, which separates it from Wilkins and Plumb t-ships, and by Long run. It is centrally distant from Pittsburg S. E. 12 miles; greatest length 6, breadth 5 ms.; area, 10,240 acres; surface, hilly; soil, loam. Pop. in 1830, 911; taxables, 233. The t-pike road from Greensburg to Pittsburg passes thro' the N. E. angle of the t-ship. The p-t. of McKeesport lies at the confluence of the Youghiogheny with the Allegheny r., and the p-t. of Perritsport, at the junction of Turtle creek with the latter r.

Village Green, a post town of Aston t-ship, Delaware co., on the road from Chester to Chads ford, distant 4 ms. from the former, 126 miles from W. C., and 87 S. E. from Harrisburg; contains 6 dwellings, one tavern, blacksmith shop, school house and Methodist meeting.

Vineyard creek, Porter t-ship, Huntingdon co, a tributary of Juniata river, which flows S. around the Warrior ridge, by McConnelsburg into the river, opposite to and below Huntingdon borough.

Vincent, t-ship, Chester co., bounded N. E. by the r. Schuylkill, which divides it from Montgomery county, S. E. by Pikeland, S. W. by Uwchlan and N. W. by East Nantmeal and Coventry t-ships. Centrally distant from Philadelphia N.W. about 30 ms., from West Chester 12 miles north. Length 9½, breadth 5 miles; area 23,500 acres; surface hilly; soil, sandy loam. Pop. in 1830, 2,147; taxables 411. The turnpike road to Morgantown crosses the S. W. part of the t-ship. Stoney creek, French creek and Ring creek flow through it. There is a post office in the t-ship, called Vincent, 142 miles N. of W. C. and 75 ms. S. E. from Harrisburg.

Wagontown, post town, Chester co., 130 miles N. of W. C., and 70 miles S. E. of Harrisburg.

Walker, t-ship, Huntingdon co., bounded N. by Porter t-ship, N. E. by Henderson t-ship, S. E. by Union, S. W. by Hopewell and W. by Woodberry t-ships. Greatest length 7, breadth 6 miles; area, 22,400 acres; surface hilly; soil in the valleys limestone. The Raystown branch of the Juniata girds it on the S. and E., and Vineyard creek crosses it to the river, opposite the town of Huntingdon. McConnellsburg is a village of the township.

Walker, t-ship, McKean co., bounded N. by Keating t-ship, E. by Potter co., S. by Shippen t-ship, and W. by Sergeant t-ship. Centrally distant from Smethport S. E. 13 miles; length 9½, breadth 9 miles; area, 54,720 acres; surface hilly and broken; soil gravelly loam, heavily timbered. It is drained N. by a tributary of the Allegheny river.

Walker, t-ship, Mifflin co.; surface mountainous, with fine valleys, in which is a productive limestone soil. Pop. in 1830, 1379; taxables in 1828, 401.

Walker, t-ship, Centre co., bounded N. E. by Lamar t-ship, S. E. by Miles t-ship, S. W. by Spring t-ship, and N. W. by Howard t-ship. Centrally distant N. E. from Bellefonte 8 miles; greatest length 10, breadth 5½ miles; area, 28,160 acres; surface diversified; soil, in the valleys limestone. Pop. in 1830, 1076; taxables, 224. The t-ship consists chiefly of the southern half of the Nittany valley, enclosed on the N. W. by the Muncy mountain and on the S. E. by the Nittany mountain. It is drained by Little Fishing creek. Post office 200 miles from W. C., 93 from Harrisburg.

Walkersville, post town of Half Moon t-ship, Centre co., on the E. side of Bald Eagle ridge, 14 miles S. W. of Bellefonte.

Wallsville, post office, Luzerne co., 248 miles from W. C., and 140 from Harrisburg.

Wallace's town, Warrior Mark t-ship Huntingdon co., near the N. boundary of the t-ship, about 20 miles N. W. of the borough of Huntingdon, a small hamlet.

Walnut creek, Erie co., rises in Beaver Dam t-ship, and flows by a westerly course of about 14 ms. thro' Mill Creek, McKean and Fairview t-ships into Lake Erie.

Wappessening creek, rises in Choconut t-ship, Susquehannah co., and flows N. W. through Bradford co., into the state of New York, and thence into the Suspuehannah r., a few ms. above Smithborough. It is a large stream and affords fine mill seats.

Wapwallopen creeks, Great and Little, both rise in Hanover t-ship, Luzerne co., and flow westerly through Newport and Nescopeck t-ships into the r. Susquehannah. They are separated in their course of about 15 ms. by the mountain of the same name. Both are navigable for canoes a short distance from the river. Barnet's cr. contributes to the volume of the former and Loon lake and Triangle pond to that of the latter. Upon the Great Wapwallopen are some noted falls, about half a mile distant from the Susquehannah river. The water falls perpendicularly over a rock thirty feet. Here are some fine mills. The cascade is known also by the name of Wapehawley falls.

Wapwallopen hill, a mountainous ridge of Luzerne co., which rises on the Susquehannah r. in Luzerne co. and runs eastwardly through the t-ships of Nescopeck, Newport and Hanover. It separates two streams, each of which bears its name.

Wapwallopen Valley, Luzerne co., formed by the Wapwallopen mountain on the N., and the Nescopeck on the south. The Great Wapwallopen cr. flows through it. The Berwick turnpike road passes thro' it for about 7 ms.

Warminster, t-ship, Bucks county, bounded N. E. by Warwick and Northampton t-ships, S. E. by Southampton, S. W. by Montgomery co., and N. W. by Warrington township. Central distance from Philadelphia 17 miles N.; from Doylestown 8 ms. S. E.; length 4½, breadth 2½ ms.; area, 5,397 acres; surface hilly; soil, gravel and sandy loam. Pop. in 1830, 709; taxables in 1828, 155. The W. branch of the Neshaminy creek passes through the N. E. angle, and several small tributaries of the Pennypack flow southwardly from the t-ship into that stream. Hartsville is the post office of the t-ship, which is known as Warminster post office.

Warringdon, t-ship, Bucks county, bounded N. E. by Doylestown and Warwick t-ships, S. E. by Warminster, S. W. by Mongomery co., N.W. by New Britain t-ship. Centrally distant 20 miles N. of Philadelphia, and 6 miles S. of Doylestown; surface rolling; soil, loam. Pop. in 1830, 512; taxables in 1828, 113; greatest length 4, breadth 2½ miles; area, 5,397 acres. The west branch of the Neshaminy creek crosses the S. eastern angle. Newville, a post town, lies on the line dividing the t-ship from Warwick. The W. branch of the Neshaminy crosses the S. E. angle of the township.

Warner's creek, Manheim t-ship, Schuylkill co., a tributary of the river Schuylkill, which flows easterly into that stream opposite Scollop hill, and near the tunnel of the canal.

Warrington, t-ship, York co., bounded N. by Monohan and Fairview townships, E. by Newberry, S. E. by Dover, S. W. by Washington townships. Centrally distant from the borough of York 13 miles; greatest length 8¾, breadth 7¼ ms; area, 23,040 acres; surface hilly; soil, red shale, poor; pop. in 1830, 1230; taxables, 263. Taxable property, 1829, real estate $147,300; personal 12,515; occupations 16,735; total 176,550; rate 25 cts. in the $100. The Conewago creek follows the south east boundary, and receives Beaver creek from the t-ship. Rosstown lies 2 miles N. W. of Conewago creek and about 12 miles from York borough. Rich Hill is a noted prominence on the E., and Round Top on the N. of the t-ship. Rossville is the post town.

Warrington, small village of Buffalo t-ship, Armstrong co., on the turnpike road leading from Kittanning to Butler, about 6 miles W. from the former; contains some half a dozen dwellings and tavern.

Warren county, was formed from Allegheny and Lycoming counties, by act 12th March, 1800. By the act 1st April, 1805, the county was annexed to Venango for judicial purposes. By an act of 18th April, 1795, the town of "Warren" was directed to be laid out at the confluence of the Conewango creek with the Allegheny r., to contain 300 acres; to be divided into town lots, with seven hundred acres of land adjoining thereto, for out lots; the town lots to contain not more than one third of an acre, and the out lots not more than 5 acres. By act 16th March, 1819, the county was fully organized for judicial purposes, and the seat of justice located at the town of Warren. The county is bounded N. by the state of N. Y., E. by McKean co., S. by Jefferson and Venango counties, and W. by Erie and Crawford counties. Its form is oblong, having on the longest lines E. and W. 32 ms., and on the shorter N. and S. 26 ms.; area, 832 square ms. or 532,480 acres; central lat. 41° 50′ N.; long. from Washington city, 2° 22′ W.

Although this county is in the great secondary formation, which, in Penn. commonly abounds with coal, salt and iron, we are not aware that either of these articles have yet been discovered here. It is probable, however, that they lie here much deeper than in the more southern counties. The face of the county is much diversified. The t-ships on the north border, are of good quality second rate land, and would sustain a dense pop. The surface is moderately undulating, but not hilly; and in a scope of 150,000 acres, there are scarce an hundred that will not make a tolerable farm. The timber is principally sugar maple and beech, interspersed with oak, chestnut, linn, cucumber, cherry, white wood, and occasionally extensive groves of pine, on or near the banks of the streams. The second tier of t-ships, south of the first, and north of the Allegheny r., has a more varied character. That part which lies between the Conewango and Broken Straw creeks, is similar in surface to that we have described, except so much as is within two or three ms. of the r., which is timbered with oak, chestnut, and pine, and is esteemed better for wheat, than the beech and maple lands. The land between the Broken Straw creeks is stony, indeed, and in the language of an eastern land speculator, will probably never be *settled*, unless by an earthquake. W. and S. of this is a large body of good arable land. The soil of the r. bottoms is deemed first rate; of which, including the *second bottom*, there are from 40 to 50,000 acres in the county, besides the creek bottoms, which are little inferior in quality. This soil when properly cultivated, commonly produces 50 bushels of corn to the acre; and 60, nay 70 bushels have frequently been obtained, and other grain, except wheat, in proportion. Wheat upon these rich soils grows too rankly and perishes in its luxuriance. Thirty bushels of corn and 20 of wheat is an average crop on the uplands. The country on the S. E. of the Allegheny was until lately little known and scarce explored, and was supposed uninhabitable. It has been principally sold for taxes, and purchased by the county commissioners, who (the period for redemption having expired) have within a few years made extensive sales. Some of the purchasers have removed to the land, and find it of better quality than they expected. It is heavily timbered with the various species of forest trees common to the other parts of the county.

Few countries of similar extent are so well supplied with streams of excellent water, adapted to hydraulic purposes. The Allegheny enters the county by its N. E. angle and crossing it diagonally, flows from it, in the S. W., having a course of more than 50 ms. within the co., and an average width of 25 rods. It presents extensive sheets of slack water, alternating with short ripples, with falls of about 2 feet, over which in dry seasons the stream is not more than 18 inches deep, whilst in the pools it is from 6 to 12 feet. Ten double saw mills are driven by the main stream between Warren town and the state line. The Conewango creek enters the county 12 ms. N. of, and empties into, the Allegheny at Warren. This is a large and navigable stream; from Russell's mills (5 miles) to the N. Y. line, it is deep and sluggish, and will admit of steamboat navigation during the whole year, when not frozen, and it preserves this character for 30 miles above the mills. From the mills to Warren (7 ms.) it is more rapid; the fall in this distance being 60 feet; but loaded keel boats ascend in a full state of the water without difficulty. There are 4 double and 2 single saw mills on these rapids. The Broken Straw creek is next in size and importance. It rises in the state of N. Y. and enters Penn. near the W. corner of the county, runs a S. course about 25 ms. and empties into the Allegheny 7 ms. below Warren. Nine ms. from its mouth, it receives the Little Broken Straw, another excellent mill stream. The lumber business is very extensively carried on by these creeks, there being more than 30 saw mills upon them. The Teonista creek is another important stream, rising S. of the Allegheny, in this and McKean counties, and running E. and S. W. and uniting with the Allegheny 30 ms. below Warren. It is the most serpentine stream in the county, little interrupted by ripples, is remarkably smooth and gentle, and is navigable for canoes of 3 tons, 40 ms. from its mouth. There are several saw mills upon it. There are several other mill streams, the Kenjua, Stillwater, Tidiouto, Coffee, and Fair Bank creeks; Jackson's, Ashley's, Valentine's and Morrison's runs, all which have mills upon them.

There are four considerable villages in the county, Warren, Youngsville, Sugar Grove and Pine Grove; and two others lately laid out, viz: Lottsville, on the Little Broken Straw, in Sugar Grove t-ship, and Fayette on a branch of the Big Broken Straw, in Columbus t-ship; both having a valuable water power, are rapidly increasing.

The public buildings consist of small neat court house, of brick, with a cupola and bells, the county offices of stone, and a prison also of stone, so small and insecure, however, that it has more than once, it is said, been mistaken for a *turkey pen*. There is also an academy at the town of Warren, incorporated in 1822, which has received a donation of 500 acres of land from the state. There is a newspaper published in the town of Warren, called "The Warren Gazette."

The means of reaching market, of obtaining supplies, and of conducting generally the commercial business of this county, have been much increased, by the adaptation of steamboats to the waters of the Allegheny river. Boats on the Blanchard construction may now ascend the river to Warren, during a greater part of the year ; and by damming the river at the greater ripples, a sufficient depth of water will be obtained at all times.

This county, with Erie, Crawford, Mercer and Venango, forms the 18th congressional district, sending one member to congress ; with Venango, Armstrong, Indiana, and Jefferson, it constitutes the 24th senatorial district, sending one member to the senate ; united with Venango, it sends one member to the house of representatives. Warren pertains to the 6th judicial district, to which also belong Venango, Mercer, and Crawford counties. President, Henry Shippen, Esq. The courts are holden on the first Mondays after those of Venango co. The county belongs to the western district of the supreme court, which holds a session at Pittsburg on the first Monday of September, annually.

Warren county paid into the state treasury, in 1831,

For tax on writs,	$165 38
Tavern licenses,	142 50
Duties on dealers in foreign merchandize,	324 20
	$632 08

The population of the county was, in 1830, 4706, of whom 2507 were white males, 2185 white females, 10 free colored males, 4 females. In this number were included 65 aliens, 2 blind and 2 deaf and dumb.

The value of taxable property in the county, by the assessment of 1829, was $466,472.

Warren, p-t. and seat of Justice of Warren co. is situated on a level plain of about 300 acres, on the N. bank of the Allegheny river, and W. of the Conewango creek, at the junction of these streams, 313 miles N. W. from W. C., and 240 from Harrisburg. The town is principally built on the river. The bank is about forty feet high, and commands a fine view of the stream above and below the town. It is acknowledged on all hands to be one of the most eligible and handsome situations for a town on the river. It was laid out by the authority of the state, and the lots sold by a commissioner appointed for that purpose.—The town plot consists of 500 lots, one third of an acre each, laid out into blocks of sixteen lots each. The streets run on every side of these blocks and cross at right angles. The principal streets are one hundred feet wide, the others, sixty. Near the centre of the plot and at the crossing of two 100 feet streets, four lots of an acre each, are left for the public buildings. This is called the diamond. The only public buildings here, are a brick court house, and public offices of stone, fire proof. The court house is not large, but neat and convenient, substantially built and well finished, with a well toned bell in it, weighing with a yoke 362 lbs. A jail also, although it has once or twice been mistaken for a turkey pen. The village contains sixty dwelling houses, mostly frame, two stories high, finished and painted white, and tenanted. Five stores well filled, three taverns, two tanneries, two blacksmith shops, five shoemakers, one saddler and harness maker, two chair makers, and a wheelwright, one cabinet maker, two carpenters and joiners, one hatter, one wagon maker, six lawyers, two doctors, one baker, two masons, six free masons, two saw mills, and a grist mill. An academy, incorporated by act of assembly 2d April, 1822, by which 500 acres of land were given to it.

Warren, small town of Kiskiminitas, t-ship, Armstrong co. upon the Kiskiminitas river, about 20 ms. S. of Kittanning, contains 20 houses, 3 stores, and 2 taverns.

Warren tavern, p-o. of E. Whiteland t-ship, Chester co., 18 miles W. of Philadelphia, on the turnpike road leading to Lancaster, 131 ms. N. of W. C., and 77 S. E. from Harrisburg.

Warrensburg, a post town and small hamlet of Berks co., on the turnpike road from Philadelphia to Reading, distant 12 miles from the latter, containing about a dozen dwellings, a tavern, a church, pertaining to the English Presbyterians.

Warren, post t-ship, Bradford co. bounded N. by the state of N.York, E. by Susquehannah co., S. by Pike and Orwell t-ships, and W. by Windham t-ship. Centrally distant from Towanda N. E. 17 ms. Greatest length 6 ms., breadth 6 ms. area 21,760 acres. Surface hilly, soil gravelly loam. Population, in 1830, 756, taxables, 133. It is drained by Wepasening creek, (and its branches) which flows N. W. into the Susquehannah river. South Warren post office is 270 miles N. W. from W. C. 159 from Harrisburg.—Warrenham is also a post office of the t-ship.

Warren t-ship, Franklin co. bounded N. by Peters, E. by Montgomery t-ship, S. by Maryland, and W. by Bedford co. Centrally distant from Chambersburg 21 ms., greatest length 11, breadth 5 ms., area 49,920 acres. Surface, mountainous ; soil, lime and slate. Population in 1830, 572. This is a very mountainous t-ship. The Great and Little Cove mountain bound it W. and E., and in the intervening valley, Little Cove creek flows S. to Licking creek.

Warrior run, Turbut t-ship, Northampton co., a small tributary of the Susquehannah, which flows into that r. below the village of Watsonsburg.

Warrior ridge, Bedford co., a mountain range, which extends from the south boundary of the state, N. E. through Southampton and Providence t-ships to the Raystown branch of the Juniata river.

Warrior ridge, Huntingdon co. Porter t-ship, running N. about 8 ms. from McConnellsburg, to the Frankstown branch of the Juniata river, and thence N. E. into Barre t-ship.

Warrior's Mark, t-ship, Huntingdon co., bounded N. by Centre co., S. E. by Franklin, S. W. by Tyrone and Antes t-ships. Centrally distant N.W. from Huntingdon borough, 18 miles ; greatest length, 13, breadth, 6 miles ; area, 20,480 acres; surface, mountainous ; soil in valley, limestone.—Taxables in 1828, 284. The western part of the t-ship is covered by the Allegheny mountain, and Bald Eagle ridge. Through the last of which the Juniata river finds its way, and courses the S. W. boundary. Little Bald Eagle creek and several other small streams. E. of the ridge, salt and iron are found, near Tyrone iron works. The p-town of Birmingham lies on the river, and Warrior's Mark town near the N. line. The latter, also a p-town, containing 20 dwellings, 2 stores, 1 tavern, &c. The t-ship contained in 1828, 5 grist mills, 4 saw mills, 2 distilleries, 1 fulling mill, 1 slitting and rolling mill, 1 mill for cleaning clover seed, 1 paper mill and 1 furnace.

Warwick, t-ship, Bucks co., bounded N. and N. W. by Doylestown, E. by Buckingham and Wrightstown t-ships, S. E. by Northampton, S. W. by Warminster and Warringdon. Centrally distant from Phil. 21 ms. N., and 5 miles S. E. from Doylestown ; greatest length $5\frac{1}{4}$ ms., greatest width $3\frac{1}{4}$ ms. ; area, 10,678 acres ; surface, hilly ; soil, sandy loam and gravel. Pop. 1830, 1132 ; taxables, 1828, 216. The main and W. branches of the Neshaminy creek flow S. E. through the t-ship. The poor house of the co. is located on a farm in the N. W. angle, and Warwick meeting house in the

S. W. angle. Hartsville and Newville, post towns, lie on the S. E. boundary, Bridge point on the N. W. line, Tinkertown on the S. E. and Jamieson's cross roads in the centre of the t-ship.

Warwick, t-ship, Lancaster county, bounded N. by Lebanon co., E. by Elizabeth, Cocalico and Earl t-ships, S. by Manheim and Hempfield t-ships, and W. by Raphoe t-ship. Centrally distant N. from the city of Lancaster, about 9 ms.; greatest length, E. and W. 10½, greatest breadth, N. and S. 9 ms.; area, 37,012 acres; surface, rolling; soil, limestone, clay and gravel. Pop. 1830, 3848; taxables, 735. Great Chiques creek runs on the W. boundary; Hanmer and Cocalico creeks on the E., and Moravia creek rises near Litiz and flows S. E. into the last. The p-t. of Litiz is 2 miles N. of the S. boundary, and 8 ms. N. of Lancaster, and one mile N. of it is the small village of Warwick. The t-ship contains 14 distilleries, 3 tanyards, 1 fulling mill, 13 grist mills 7 saw mills, 1 brewery, 2 hemp mills, 1 oil mill, 1 carding machine, 1 snuff mill.

Warwick, a small village of Warwick t-ship, Lancaster co., 9 ms. due N. of the city of Lancaster.

Washington county, was taken from Westmoreland by the act of 28th March, 1781, and is now bounded N. by Beaver, N. E. by Allegheny, E. by Westmoreland and Fayette, and S. by Greene counties, and W. by the state of Virginia. Greatest length 32, mean width 28 ms.; area, 888 square ms.; central lat. 40° 14′ N., long. from W. C. 3° 12′ W.

Lying in the great western secondary formation, the co. possesses the minerals usually found in that formation, coal, iron and salt. But salt licks are not numerous, nor is there any iron made in the co. Like the greater portion of Western Pa., this county, surveyed from an elevation and from a distance, has the appearance of one vast plain; but it is in reality deeply indented by many streams, which have formed valleys of greater or lesser width and depth, and the surface has, therefore, a rolling character, and in some places may be termed hilly.

The Monongahela r. flows N. full 25 ms. along the eastern border, receiving in its course Ten Mile creek, which forms the southern border of the county, Pike run, Pigeon creek and several small streams. Peter's creek, Chartier's creek and Raccoon creek are also tributaries of that river from this co., but their *embouchures* are in Allegheny co., into which they flow northerly. Herman's creek, Cross creek, Buffalo creek, Wheeling creek, Fish creek and their several branches are tributaries of the Ohio r. into which they flow westward.

The seat of justice was established at the present borough of Washington, by commissioners appointed in the act of 1781; besides this town, there are now in the co. 21 towns and villages, viz.: Centreville, Bealesville, Hillsboro', Williamsburg, Martinsburg, Buffalo, Claysville, West Alexandria Taylor'stown, West Middletown, Mount Pleasant, Burgettstown, Canonsburg, Williamsport, Columbia, Greenfield, Briceland's cross roads, Frederickstown, Amity, Bentley'sville and Findleyville, for a description of which see their respective titles.

This co. was first settled by emigrants from the north of Ireland, by others from New Jersey, by Germans from Europe, and from other parts of this state, and is now inhabited by their descendants. In 1790 the pop. was 23,866; in 1800, 28,293; in 1810, 36,289; 1820, 40,038; and in 1830, 42,869; of whom 21,254 were white males; 20,640, females; 422 free black males; 443 females, 1 slave. There were aliens 192, blind 19, 24 deaf and dumb. The prevailing religious sects are Presbyterian, Seceder, Methodist and Baptist; but there are others, among which are some Catholics, who have a chapel near W. Alexandria, and Episcopalians, who have one, perhaps more churches in the co. There may be in the co. from 15 to 20 churches belonging to various denominations. There are here a county Bible society, an auxiliary missionary society, and tract and Sunday school associations. Much attention has been given by the citizens to the means of education; primary schools have been established in almost every neighborhood, and there are two colleges in the co., Washington college in Washington borough, and Jefferson college at Canonsburg. For an account of these institutions see " Washington bor." and Canonsburg. At the colleges there are respectable libraries, and a public library is established in Mercer t-ship.

The chief business of the county is agriculture, breeding and grazing cattle. There are some small manufactories of wool, one at Washington, 1 in Cross Creek t-ship and a third in Buckingham t-ship; and at Williamsport on the Monongahela r. is an extensive manufactory of window glass. The market for grain in the county having been overstocked, the inhabitants have devoted their attention for some years past to the breeding of horses, cattle and sheep, in which they have been eminently successful. Many fine horses are annually sold for the eastern and southern markets, and large quantities of stock cattle are exported on the hoof; whilst the sheep have increased in the ratio of 20 per cent. per annum, until they amount to 200,000, and occupy a fourth of the cultivated lands of the county, producing annually 600,000 pounds of wool, at an average price of 60 cts. per lb. The cleared land is estimated at about 250,000 acres, and is capable on an average of maintaining 2 sheep to the acre, without rendering the population dependent on others for the agricultural products they need, and now procure from their own farms. On this data it is estimated that the co. can maintain a half million of sheep, yielding annually 1,500,000 lbs. of washed wool, about one third of which is requisite to supply the home consumption.

No country in the world is better adapted to the growing of wool than the western parts of Penn. and the adjoining parts of Ohio and Va., and for this purpose no portion surpasses Washington county. The wool from such flocks as have been judiciously managed, has been found to improve in quality and increase in quantity, and much of it will bear comparison with the best Saxon wool. About one half the number of sheep are full blood and mixed merinos. There are, however, notwithstanding this attention to sheep, considerable quantities of wheat, rye and whiskey exported.

The taxable valuation of the real estate of the co., by the assessment of 1829, was, $4,146,422; of personal estate, including occupations, $553,781; rate of tax 2 $\frac{12}{100}$ mills in the dollar. The average market price of improved lands, is $10 the acre, and woodland brings as much as arable.

There are three turnpike roads in the co. The road from Somerset to Washington borough; the road from Washington to Pittsburg, and the national road, which crosses the Monongahela from Brownsville, Fayette co. and runs N. W. to the borough of Washington, and thence westerly to Wheeling.

Washington co. forms the 20th senatorial district of the state, sending one member to the senate. It also constitutes the 15th congressional district, represented by one member in congress. It elects three members to the house of representatives of the state legislature. Connected with Fayette and Greene, it forms the 14th judicial district, over which Thomas H. Baird, Esq. presides. The courts are holden at Washington on the Mondays following those of Greene, which sit on the third Mondays of March, June, September and December. It pertains to the western district of the supreme court, which holds a session at Pittsburg, on the third Monday of September, annually.

This co. paid into the state treasury in 1831,

For tax on writs, -	$415 89
Tavern licenses, - -	683 55
Duties on dealers in foreign merchandize, -	763 33
State maps, - -	33 25
Tax on collateral inheritances,	108 85
Pamphlet laws, - -	3 33
Tin and clock pedlars' licenses, - -	57
	$265 20

STATISTICAL TABLE OF WASHINGTON COUNTY.

Townships, &c.	Greatest Lt.	Greatest Bth.	Population. 1820,	Population. 1830,	Taxables.
Amwell,	11	9 1-2	1825	1733	359
Bethlehem, E.	9	7	2239	2606	535
Bethlehem, W.	12	7	2187	2048	389
Buffalo,	7	6 1-2	1430	1516	340
Borough of Washington,			1687	1816	325
Cross Creek,	9	8	1908	2147	438
Canton,	10	5	1276	1218	241
Cecil,	9	4 1-2	1154	1107	240
Chartiers,	7 1-2	7	1330	1575	399
Donegal,	8	6 1-2	1879	2093	470
Fallowfield,	7	7	2020	2142	383
Findlhy, E.	8 1-2	5	1967	1219	406
Hopewell,	10	7	2186	1897	431
Hanover,	8 1-2	7 1-2	1329	1573	247
Mount Pleasant,	7	4 1-2	1254	1327	278
Morris,	9	7	1713	2048	383
Nottingham,	9	5 1-2	2098	2118	348
Peters,	9	4	1265	1196	259
Pike Run,	10	4 1-2	1967	2081	357
Robinson,	10	3	925	944	188
Somerset,	8 1-2	7 1-2	1540	1573	259
Smith,	10	6	1848	2089	398
Strabane,	11	9 1-2	2571	2599	461
West Findlay,	9 1-2	6		1218	
Borough of Canonsburg,				792	
Borough of Middletown,				297	
			40038	42680	8134

Washington, t-ship, Franklin co., bounded N. by Guilford, E. by Adams co., S. by the state of Maryland, and W. by Antrim t-ship. Centrally distant from Chambersburg, S. W., 11 ms.; greatest length 10½, breadth 8½ ms.; area, 49,920 acres; surface, rolling; soil, chiefly slate. Pop. in 1830, 5184; taxables, 751. The t-ship is drained by two branches of the Antictam creek, which flows S. into Maryland. The S. mountain covers a great portion of the E. boundary. A turnpike road leads from Maryland to Waynesburg, and thence through Green castle westward.

Washington, t-ship, Fayette county, bounded N. by Westmoreland co., E. by the Youghiogheny river, which separates it from Tyrone and Franklin t-ships, S. by Redstone t-ship, and W. by the Monongahela river, which divides it from Washington co.; centrally distant from Uniontown, 12 ms. Greatest length 8, breadth 7 miles; area, 32,000 acres; surface, rolling; soil, limestone and loam. Population in 1830, 2926; taxables, 551. Red stone creek is on the S. boundary, and at its confluence with the Monongahela, are established the Washington glass works. The Little Red stone creek rises in the t-ship by two branches, and flows N. W. to the Monongahela. Cook's run flows S. W. to the same river; and at its confluence on the south side, is the p-town of Cookstown, near which iron ore is found.—The p-town of Perryopolis lies on the Youghiogheny, N. of Washington run. The p-town of Belle Vernon is on the Monongahela, in the extreme N. W. angle of the t-ship.

Washington, borough, and seat of justice of Washington co., partly in Canton and partly in Strabane t-ships, 26 miles S. W. of Pittsburg. This is a large and flourishing town, containing about 300 dwellings, generally of brick, many of which are three stories high; several stores and taverns, a woollen factory, driven by steam, and 4 churches, 1 Presbyterian, 1 Baptist, 1 Methodist and 1 Unionist, and a college. An academy was founded here so early as 1787, when the state granted the institution 5000 acres of the unappropriated lands of the commonwealth; and in 1797, the sum of $3000, to assist in the completion of the buildings. In 1806, the academy was converted into a college, in which all the property of the former was vested. A further donation of $5000 was granted to the institution in 1821.

The college buildings are 120 feet in length, and 40 in breadth, and will accommodate with lodging 36 students, and from 150 to 200 with rooms for recitation. The central building is of stone, the wings of brick. The institution possesses a pneumatic and an electrical apparatus, maps, globes, an orrery, a college library of 400 vols. and a student's library of about 600. Attached to the college are two literary societies, instituted for promoting emulation among the students. There are three professors, including the principal. The branches of learning taught, are such as are usual in the department of arts in the university. The expense incident to education and maintenance of a student here, does not exceed $125 per annum. The following was the state of the college in 1828. 135 alumni, of whom, 125 were then living; 26 of whom were ministers of the gospel; 24 then alive. Eleven graduated in 1827, 39 under graduates, viz: 8 seniors, 11 juniors, 8 sophomores, 12 freshmen. 9 students professing religion. The act of 1797 above cited, provided for the admission into the institution, of any number of students, not exceeding 10, who may be offered, in order to be taught reading, writing, and arithmetic, *gratis*, none to continue longer than two years. There were 3 pupils under this provision, in 1828. The average number of students, since its foundation, is 60.

Washington, t-ship, Indiana county, bounded N. by Mahoning t-ship, E. by Greene t-ship, S. by Centre and Armstrong t-ships, and W. by Armstrong county. Greatest length, 11, breadth, 10 miles; area, 48,000 acres; surface, hilly; soil, clay. Pop. in 1830, 957; taxables, 265. The t-ship is drained S. by Crooked creek and its branches, and W. by Plumb creek. The borough of Indiana is on the S. boundary, near the E. line.

Washington, t-ship, Union county, bounded N. by Middle creek, which divides it from Penn t-ship; E. by Chapman t-ship; S. by Perry, and W. by Centre t-ship. Centrally distant S. E. from New Berlin, 8 ms. Greatest length, 8 ms.; breadth, 5; area, 17,040 acres; surface, diversified; soil, limestone and gravel. Pop. in 1830, 2,085; taxables, 210. The p-town of Freeburg is centrally situated in the t-ship, on a branch of Middle creek. The taxable property of the t-ship in 1829, was, real estate $175, 536; pers. property, yielding $16 69; occupations, yielding $47 44. The rate of levy was 15 cts. in the $100.

Washington, t-ship, Westmoreland co. bounded N. E. by the Kiskiminitas river, which separates it from Armstrong and Indiana counties, S. E. by Salem t-ship, S. W. by Franklin t-ship and N. W. by Allegheny t-ship. Centrally distant from Greensburg N. 16 miles. Greatest length 9, breadth 8 miles; area, 32,640 acres; surface hilly; soil loam and gravel. Pop. in 1830, 2,153; taxables 354. It is drained chiefly by Beaver Dam run, which flows N. W. through the middle of the t-ship. The post town of N. Washington is centrally situated in the township.

Washington, North, post town of Washington t-ship, Westmoreland co. near Beaver Dam run, 18 or 20 miles N. W. from Greensburg, 215 from W. C., and 193 from Harrisburg; contains 10 dwellings, 2 taverns and one store.

Washington, post town and borough, Manor t-ship, Lancaster co., on the E. bank of the Susquehannah river, about 9 miles west by south from Lancaster city. Pop. in 1830, 607; contains about 100 dwellings. It was incorporated by act 13th April, 1827, and includes the village of Charleston, which is separated from it by Steman's run.

Washington, post town, Derry t-ship Columbia co., on the Chilisquaque creek, 7 ms. N. W. from Danville.

Washington, t-ship, York county, bounded N. E. by Warrington t-ship, S. E. by Conewago and Paradise t-ships, W. by Adams co., N. W. by Franklin t-ship. Centrally distant from the borough of York N. W. 13 miles. Greatest length 9, breadth 3½ miles; area, 15,360 acres; surface level; soil, red shale, of good quality. Pop. in 1830, 1037; taxables 247; taxable property, 1829, real estate $234,913; personal 12,735; occupations 20,847—total $268,495. Bermudian creek flows S. W. through the t-ship to the Conewago creek, receiving from it several tributaries.

Washington, t-ship, Lycoming co., bounded N. by Clinton t-ship, E. by that t-ship and the Susquehannah river, S. by Union co., W. by Nippenose t-ship. Centrally distant S. E. from Williamsport 6 miles. Greatest length 10, breadth 10 miles; area, 55,200 acres; surface mtnous; soil, various, chiefly limestone and clay. Pop. in 1830, about 1200; taxables 240; value of taxable property in 1829, seated lands, &c. $62,251; unseated $3000; personal estate $10,154; rate of levy ¾ of one per cent. It is drained by White Deer Hole creek, Black Hole creek, Hagerman's run, and several smaller streams. The valley between the Bald Eagle mountain on the N., and the White Deer mtn. on the S., is very fertile and thickly populated.

Washingtonville, post office and village, Derry t-ship, Columbia co., 7 miles S. W. of Danville, 182 N. from W. C., and 72 from Harrisburg; contains 30 dwellings, two taverns and 2 stores.

Watsonburg, Turbett t-ship, Northumberland co., on the Susquehannah river, about 15 miles N. of Sunbury, 180 from W. C., and 71 from Harrisburg; contains 20 dwellings, 1 store and 2 tåverns, and some mills south of the town.

Waterford, t-ship, Erie co., bounded N. by Beaver Dam and Venango t-ships, E. by Amity, S. by Le Boeuf t-ship, and W. by Conneaut and Mc Kean t-ships. Centrally distant S. E. from the borough of Erie 13 miles. Greatest length 7, breadth 5 miles; area, 22,400 acres; surface hilly; soil, gravelly loam. Pop. in 1830, 1006; taxables 186. Le Boeuf cr. enters the t-ship in the N. W. angle, and flowing in a semi-circular course around the town of Waterford, empties nto Le Boeuf lake in the S. W. angle of the t-ship. From the lake a copious stream issues southward to French creek. The post town of Waterford lies E. of the lake, 15 miles S. from Erie by the turnpike road and 23 miles N. E. from Meadville, also by turnpike road. At high water the Le Boeuf creek is navigable to the town. The town formerly bore the name of Le Boeuf. There is an academy here, incorporated by act of 2d April, 1811, and 500 acres of land with certain lots were appropriated to its use. The town contains about 50 dwellings, 3 or 4 stores, 4 taverns. There is also a post office, distant 319 miles N. W. of W. C., and 252 from Harrisburg.

Waterford, post town of Lack t-ship, Juniata co., in the Tuscarora valley, on the Tuscarora creek, about 18 ms. S. W. of Lewistown, 131 from W. C. and 62 from Harrisburg.

Waterloo, post town of Lack t-ship, Juniata co., in the Tuscarora valley, on the Tuscarora creek, 22 miles S. W. of Lewistown, 123 from W. C., and 70 from Harrisburg.

Waterstreet, post town of Morris t-ship, Huntingdon co., on the turnpike road and Juniata river, a short distance above Alexandria, distant N.W. from W. C. 157 miles, and S. W. from Harrisburg 99 miles; contains some half a dozen dwellings.

Waullenpaupack creek, a large tributary of the Lackawaxen creek, forms a considerable portion of the boundary between Wayne and Pike counties, runs a north easterly and a very crooked course of more than 20 miles. It has many tributbries from east and west, on most of which mills are erected. It has a broad, alluvial flat, extending the whole of its length; and a high cataract, over which it is precipitated with great violence into the Lackawaxen. It is navigable about 15 or 20 miles to the great falls; for the greater portion of this distance it flows with scarce perceptible motion. At the head of the falls the bed is suddenly sunk, and forms a chasm, into which the water pours, down a depth of 70 feet, and then rushing furiously through a deep and rocky channel, dashes over three successive cataracts within a distance of a mile and a half of the mouth of the creek : producing a total fall in that distance of 150 feet. The width of the creek above the falls is 70 feet. At the upper fall there are two saw and one grist mills. A short distance above which a wooden bridge crosses and connects the route of the Milford and Oswego turnpike.

Wayne county,* was erected from a part of Northampton, by an act of assembly 21st March, 1798, and was therein described as "all that part of Northampton co., lying to the northward of a line to be drawn, and beginning at the west end of George Michael's farm on the river Delaware, in Middle Smithfield township, and from thence a straight line to the mouth of Trout creek on the Lehigh, adjoining Luzerne co. But the creation of Pike county, in 1814, has changed this line, and Wayne county is now bounded on the north by the state line between Pennsylvania and New York, in lat. 42° north, extending along this line 6 miles, north eastwardly by the western shore of the Delaware r., which separates it from New York, to the Big Eddy, a distance of 30 miles in a direct line, but of 45 by the meanderings of the r.; south east and south by Pike co., and west by Luzerne and Susquehannah counties. The area is 436,429 acres. Central lat. 41° 40′ N., long. from W. C. 1° 42′ E. Pop. principally German, was in 1830, 7,663, of whom 4,083 were white males ; 3,549 white females ; 15 colored males ; 16 colored females, all free ; 1 person blind and three deaf and dumb. In 1800 the population was 2,562 ; in 1810, 4,125, and in 1820, 4,127. Pike co. was taken from Wayne in 1814.

The surface of this county is very unequal, comprizing much of the variety pertaining to mountainous regions. Its principal features are a continuous upland which occupies the largest portion, indented by long narrow valleys, and a few lofty eminences, to which only the name of mountains should be applied. The general elevation of this table land is estimated at thirteen hundred feet above the level of tide water.

Moosic mountain rises above the upland about 600 feet, having a total elevation of 1910 feet above the tide. Its southern extremity is in Luzerne co. whence it extends in a direction east of north, crossing the west line of Wayne co. in Canaan t-ship, and subsiding in Mount Pleasant township, forming for some distance a barrier between this and the adjacent counties on the west. Beyond the northern extremity of the Moosic rises Mount Ararat, which reaches a short distance into Preston t-ship, and is about as high as the former. The summits of these mountains overlook the country, the former to the east, the latter to the west, as far as the eye can reach. Still further north, and between the head waters of the Lackawanna creek is the Sugar Loaf mountain, comparatively a small eminence. Besides these, are some hills of minor note, a few only of which are designated by particular names.

The highlands are much broken by the ramifications of the valleys and the subsidence of their bases. These inequalities, however, offer no insuperable obstacles to cultivation, the slopes being, commonly, gentle.

The valleys are the peculiar drains of the country ; each having its proper channel, into which the springs and rivulets flow. Lakes are formed in every t-ship, except Sterling. These elegant little sheets of water, clear as crystal, comprise from 50 to 300 acres, and contribute much to the beauty of the landscapes. Their outlets form some of the capital streams of the co. At first, the course of the waters is generally rapid, and this circumstance with the favorable slopes of the banks, affords innumerable situations for mills.

* For much of this article, we are indebted to an able sketch of this county, by Jacob S. Davis, Esq.

From the northern part of the county the Susquehannah receives a portion of her waters by the *Starucca* and *Lackawanna* creeks, which have their sources within a few rods of each other, in Preston t-ship, but taking opposite directions, they discharge themselves into the Susquehannah, upwards of a hundred miles apart. The heads of the Great Equinunk, which flows into the Delaware on the north eastern side of the county, and of the west branch of Lackawaxen, running southward, are also in the same vicinity. In wet seasons, the most proximate of these heads unite, and thus form a complete inosculation of the Delaware and Susquehannah waters. The Moosic mountain, rising like a wall along a great part of the western line of the county, determines the waters from its eastern foot to the Lackawaxen river; but beyond its southern extremity the waters again diverge from a small space. The Lackawanna creek again receives a branch from this co., rising in a laurel swamp, where are also the sources of the Lehigh river, the Tobyhanna and Waullenpaupack creeks; all running in different directions towards the Susquehannah, the Lehigh and the Lackawaxen.

Delaware river receives from this county, Shrawder's, Shohokin, Great Equinunk, Little Equinunk, Holester's, Cashes', Corkins' creeks, and Lackawaxen river. The Great Equinunk is a stream of some magnitude. There is much alluvial flat along the Delaware. The upland declivity is lofty, bold, and sometimes precipitous. The greater part of the shore in Manchester t-ship, from the mouth of the Great Equinunk downward, is bounded by lofty rocks, almost perpendicular, from the water's edge, which effectually interrupt a direct land communication along the river for that distance.

Lackawaxen r. flows through the middle of the co., in a deep valley, which no where exceeds a half mile in width, and its margins are alluvial, fertile flats. It unites the waters of the greatest part of the co.; the principal tributaries are, the Dyberry, flowing through a valley similar to that of the Laxawaxen; the west branch, which drains a like valley, is deemed the main stream, and which, uniting with the Dyberry, forms the true Lackawaxen. Middle creek enters this r. near the south eastern line of the co., and the Waullenpaupack on the county line; both are of considerable magnitude. The channel of the former is rocky, and its course rapid. The latter has a broad alluvial flat extending its whole length, and a high cataract, over which it is precipitated with great violence into the Lackawaxen.

From the head of the Waullenpaupack flats, the creek, after a previous rapid course, flows in a sinuous channel, for a distance of 15 ms. with scarcely any perceptible motion. At the head of the falls the bed is suddenly sunk and forms a chasm, into which the water pours down a depth of 70 feet, and thence rushing furiously through a deep and rocky channel, it dashes over three successive cataracts within a distance of a mile and a half of the mouth of the creek; producing a total fall in that distance of 150 feet. The width of the creek above the falls is 70 feet. At the upper fall there are two saw and 1 grist mills; a short distance above which a wooden bridge crosses and connects the route of the Milford and Owego turnpike. The remains of Wilsonville, the ancient seat of justice of Wayne co. are near this place, but local policy has transferred the scene of public business elsewhere, and the creek is now the common boundary of Wayne and Pike counties.

The Lackawaxen canal, constructed by the Delaware and Hudson canal company, extends from Honesdale down by the eastern and northern side of the Lackawaxen r. to its mouth. (*See description of canal.*)

Six turnpike roads, completed and in good condition, run through this co. ***The Coshocton and Great Bend*** turnpike commences at the village of Damascus on the Del. r. at the termination of the turnpike from Newburg to Coshocton. At this place there is a substantial bridge across the r., 550 feet in length; thence the road passes through the t-ships of Damascus, Lebanon and Mount Pleasant, and extends to the great bend of the Susquehannah. The company for its formation was incorporated 29th March, 1804.

The Milford and Owego turnpike road commences at Milford, in Pike co., and enters Wayne at Wilsonville, whence it passes through the t-ships of Palmyra, Dyberry and Canaan, by Clarkesville to Rix's gap, and by Montrose, in Susquehannah co., to Owego in the state of N. Y. Company incorporated June 26, 1807. State subscription $31,000, half the capital.

The Bethany and Dingman's choice turnpike road commences at Centreville in Mount Pleasant t-ship, and extends through the borough of Bethany, and the t-ships of Dyberry and Palmyra, to its intersection with the Milford and Owego turnpike in Pike co. Company incorporated April 2, 1811; state subscription, $8000.

The Belmont and Easton turnpike road commences at Belmont, in Mount Pleasant t-ship, and passes through the t-ships of Canaan, and Salem and Sterling to the south line of Wayne co., and thence to the Easton and Wilkesbarre t-pike in Northampton co. Company incorporated March 13, 1812; state subscription, $17,500.

The Belmont and Oghquaga turnpike road commences at Belmont, and extends in a notherly direction, crossing the W. line of the co., in Preston t-ship, and thence continues in a direction to Oghquaga in the state of N. Y. Company incorporated Feb. 26, 1817; state subscription. $5000.

The Luzerne and Wayne co. turnpike road commences in the former co. and enters the latter near Salem corners, whence passing through Salem and Palmyra t-ships, it continues to its intersection with the Milford and Owego turnpike in Pike co. Company incorporated Feb. 24, 1820. Authority has been given by act of 31st March, 1823, for making the Ararat turnpike road in Wayne and Susquehannah counties; Jan. 24, 1824, the Mount Pleasant road in Wayne; 17th Jan., 1828, the Lackawaxen road in Wayne; 3d April, 1829, the Wilsonville and Lackawaxen road in Wayne; 2d April, 1830, the Honesdale and Clarkesville; 17th Jan., 1831, the Honesdale and Germanville; 30th March, of the same year, the Honesdale and Big Eddy roads, also in Wayne; 2d March, 1831, the Cherry ridge and Lackawanna, in Luzerne and Wayne; 14th March, the Dundaff and Honesdale, in Susquehannah and Wayne, and 25th March, the Bethany and Honesdale roads in Wayne co. Many of these owe their inception to the improvements of the Delaware and Hudson company, and are made with a view to obtain the advantages of their canal.

From Honesdale a rail road extends up the valley of the W. branch of the Lackawaxen, and crossing the river near the mouth of Vanorba brook, continues in a western direction through Canaan t-ship, and across the Moosic mtn., at Rix's gap, to Carbondale; being 16 ms. in length; overcoming an elevation of 1812 feet, by 8 inclined planes; one of which is near the mouth of Vanorba; two on the eastern and five on the western side of the mtn. At the head of each inclined plane, is erected a stationary steam engine, for the purpose of assisting the wagons in their ascent and descent.

The chief towns are Bethany, the seat of justice for the co., Honesdale, Centreville, Damascus, Clarkesville, Salem Corners, &c.

Anthracite coal is found on the sources of the Lackawanna in this co., but it has been most fully developed on the W. of the Moosic mtn. Clay iron ore has also been discovered, near Belmont, in nodules and amorphous masses. Some of those nodules exhibit only a shell filled with a dark blueish liquid, of the consistence of paint, or with a compact substance of the same color, of different degrees of hardness, but always capable of being cut with a knife. A specimen of this ore yielded 33 per cent. of metallic iron.

The public buildings of this sparse-settled co., are a court house and fire proof offices of brick; an academy established and incorporated under an act of assembly, 4th March, 1813, to which the commonwealth made a donation of $1000. All of which are in the county town of Bethany.

Wayne, with Northampton, Lehigh and Pike counties, forms the 12th senatorial district; and, joined with Northampton and Pike, sends four members to the house of representatives. Bucks, Northampton, Wayne and Pike, form the 8th congressional district of the state. Luzerne, Pike and Wayne, compose the 11th judicial district. Courts are held at Bethany on the 4th Mondays of Jan., April, August and Nov. President, David Scott, Esq.

By the assessment of 1829, the taxable property of the co. was valued at, real estate, including seated and unseated lands, $1,200,894; personal estate, including occupations, $99,069.

STATISTICAL TABLE OF WAYNE CO.

Townships, &c.	Greatest Lth.	Greatest Bth.	Population in 1820,	Population in 1830,	Taxables
Buckingham,	11 1-2	11 1-2	385	179	40
Bethany borough,			193	327	59
Canaan,	12	8	526	1134	187
Damascus,	12	10	366	613	128
Dyberry,			733	1078	232
Honesdale village,				433	
Lebanon,	6 1-2	6	145	285	58
Mount Pleasant,	12	6 1-2	874	1258	227
Palmyra,			215	404	76
Salem,	9	8	306	593	117
Sterling,	10	7	384	495	84
Preston,				290	50
Scott,	12	10 1-2		216	44
Manchester,				183	42
Berlin,				175	37
			4127	7663	1381

The county paid into the state treasury in 1831, for

Tax on writs,	$174 42
Tavern licenses,	39 80
Duties on dealers in foreign merchandize,	180 89
Tin and clock pedlars' licenses,	114
Hawkers' and pedlars' licenses,	7 60
	$516 71

Wayne, t-ship, Greene co., bounded N. by Aleppo, Centre and Franklin t-ships, E. by Whitely t-ship, S. by the state of Virginia, and W. by Aleppo. Centrally distant from Waynesburg S. W. 15 ms.; greatest length 11, breadth 10 ms.; area, 34,560 acres; surface, hilly; soil, loam. Pop. in 1830, 1130; taxables, 187. The t-ship is drained by Dunkard's creek, which flows along its S. boundary, and by several small tributaries of that stream.

Wayne, t-ship, Armstrong county, bounded N. by Mahoning creek, which divides it from Red Bank t-ship, E. by Indiana co., S. by Plumb Creek t-ship, and W. by Kittanning t-ship. Centrally distant N. E. from Kittanning borough 11 ms.; greatest length 11, breadth 7½ ms.; area, 40,000 acres; surface, undulating; soil, loam. Pop. in 1830, 878; taxables, 153. Cowanshannock and Pine creeks flow W. through the t-ship, and Plumb cr. crosses the S. E. boundary.

Wayne, t-ship, Mifflin co., bounded N. E. by Derry and Milford t-ships, S. E. by Lack t-ship, and by the Juniata r., which also bounds it on the S. and S. W., separating it from Huntingdon co., N. W. by Jack's mtn. which divides it from that co. and from Union t-ship. Part of the S. E. boundary runs through Sugar Valley. The Juniata r. running N. W., divides the t-ship into two unequal parts. On the E. side, nearly parallel with the r., runs Blue ridge. On the W., between the r. and Limestone ridge, is the Juniata valley, and between Limestone ridge and Jack's mtn. are Long Hollow, and Ferguson's valley. The t-pike road from Lewistown to Huntingdon runs S. W. through the t-ship.

On the road, and on the W. bank of the river, and on the state canal, lies the p-t. of Waynesburg. Hamiltonville lies in the south part of the t-ship.

Wayne, t-ship, Lycoming co., bounded N. W. and N. by the W. branch of the Susquehannah r., E. by Nippenose t-ship, S. by Centre co., and S. W. by Bald Eagle t-ship. Centrally distant S. W. from Williamsport 17 ms.; greatest length 11 miles, breadth 8½ ms.; area, 39,680 acres; surface, mountainous; soil, limestone. Pop. in 1830, about 350; taxables, 63; value of taxable property in 1829, seated lands, &c., $9971; unseated lands, $11,401; rate of levy, ¾ of one per cent. Nippenose, or Oval Limestone valley lies partly in this t-ship, in which many streams rise but lose themselves in the fissures of the limestone rock.

Wayne, t-ship, Erie co., bounded N. by Concord t-ship, E. by Warren co., S. by Crawford co., and W. by Union; it is the extreme S. E. t-ship of the co. Centrally distant from Erie, 25 miles; greatest length 7, breadth 5 ms.; area, 22,500 acres; surface, hilly; soil, gravelly loam. Pop. in 1830, 197; taxables, 44. Drained W. by the S. branch of French creek, S. E. by a tributary of Frampton's branch of Broken Straw creek.

Wayne, t-ship, Crawford co., in the S. E. angle of the co. The t-pike road from Franklin to Meadville runs diagonally N. W. across it. Sugar lake, a small sheet of water about a mile in circumference, lies in it, and is the source of a branch of Sugar cr. Sugar Creek and Sugar Lake are the names of p-offices in the t-ship. Pop. in 1830, 250.

Waynesburg, p-t., borough, and seat of justice of Greene co., in Franklin t-ship, within 1 mile of the centre of the co., situated in a beautiful valley near the N. bank of Ten Mile creek, about 12 ms. from its mouth. It is surrounded by a rich soil, abundance of timber, excellent stone for building, and great quantities of mineral coal. The town was incorporated by act of assembly, 29th January, 1816. It contains about 80 dwellings, many of them of brick and dressed stone. Three houses for public worship, one of brick, another of stone, and a third of wood. The court house is a handsome brick structure, the gaol is of stone. There are 1 brewery, 4 tanneries, 9 stores, and 3 taverns; and an excellent school, in which the classics and mathematics are taught.

Waynesburg, p-t. and village of Honeybrooke t-ship, Chester co., on the Downingstown and Harrisburg t-pike road, 38 ms. N. W. of Philadelphia, and 16 from West Chester, 13 W. of Downingstown, contains 32 dwelling houses, 4 of which are brick, a Methodist meeting house, 2 taverns, 2 stores, 1 physician, and 200 inhabitants. The p-o. here is called Honeybrooke, and is 131 ms. from W. C., and 56 from Harrisburg. This town is the birth place of Gen. Anthony Wayne.

Waynesburg, p-t. and borough of Washington t-ship, Franklin co., on the t-pike road leading to Green Castle and Mercersburg, 15 ms. S. E. from Chambersburg, 79 N. W. from W. C., and 56 S. W. from Harrisburg; contains from 140 to 150 dwellings, chiefly of stone, 2 churches, 1 pertaining to the Presbyterians and Lutherans, the other to the German Reformed. There are about 850 inhabitants. The surrounding country is limestone, well cultivated and productive; the town was incorporated 21st December, 1818.

Waynesburg, t., Wayne t-ship, Mifflin co., on the W. bank of the Juniata r., on the state canal, and on the t-pike road leading from Lewistown to Huntingdon, in the Juniata valley, and 11 ms. S. W. of Lewistown; contains 25 or 30 dwellings, 1 Presbyterian church, 5 stores, 5 taverns, and 1 grist mill.

Weaverstown, of Berks co., on the road from Reading to Manatawny cr., about 9 ms. from the former; contains about 20 dwellings, store and tavern;

and near it is a church, common to the German Lutherans, and Presbyterians.

Weaversburg, Allen t-ship, Northampton co., 16 ms. from Easton, on the road from Allentown to Bath, contains about 6 dwellings, 1 mill, 1 tannery and 1 store.

Webster's store, p-o., Lancaster co., 86 ms. N. W. from W. C., and 54 S. W. from Harrisburg.

Weigelstown, Dover t-ship, York co., on the road from York borough to Ross town, about 5 ms. N. W. of the former.

Weisport, a small village, Northampton co., on the Lehigh canal, and in Lehigh t-ship, near the site of old fort Allen.

Weissenburg, t-ship, Lehigh county, bounded on the N. E. by Lowhill, on the S. E. by Macungy, on the S. W. by Berks co., and N. W. by Linn. Greatest length about 6½ ms., greatest width about 5½ ms.; area, about 21,120 acres. It is watered by Jordan creek and its tributaries, Willow run and Linn run, and intersected by many roads. The centre of the t-ship is about 12 ms. from Northampton; a church is located in the forks of Willow run, and there is another in the t-ship. The surface is hilly and broken, and the soil gravelly. Pop. in 1830, 1285; taxables in 1828, 260; value of taxable property in 1829, real estate, $174,728; personal, $10,804; rate of levy, 13 cts. on the $100; assessed value of land per acre, $18, 12, 7, according to quality. There are here 6 grist mills, 3 saw mills, 2 stores, 3 taverns, 6 school-houses, and a p-o., called after the t-ship, distant 180 ms. from W. C., and 72 from Harrisburg.

Wells, t-ship, Bradford co., bounded N. by the state of N. Y., E. by Ridgebury t-ship, S. by Columbia t-ship, and W. by Tioga co. Centrally distant from Towanda N. W. 24 ms.; greatest length 7, breadth 7 ms.; area, 30,720 acres; surface, hilly; soil, gravelly loam. Pop. 1830, 752; taxables, 130. The t-ship is drained by South creek and its tributaries, and by a branch of Seely creek, all of which flow northerly into the Tioga r. in the state of N. Y.

Wells valley, Hopewell t-ship, Bedford co., between Harbor mtn. and Broad mtn. It is drained by Wells creek, which flows W. to the Raystown branch of the Juniata.

Wellsborough, p-t., borough and seat of justice of Tioga co., is located in the territorial centre of the co., on Crooked creek, 3 ms. from the navigable waters of Pine creek, and at the intersection of the E. and W. state road leading through all the counties in the northern range, and the N. and S. state road leading from Newberry to the 109 mile stone on the state line; about 50 ms. a little W. of N. from Williamsport, 253 from W. C., and 147 from Harrisburg. The village contains about 50 indifferent dwelling houses, a court house and jail of no very respectable appearance, 4 stores, 2 taverns, 2 smith shops, 2 tanyards, 1 printing office, from which is issued a weekly paper, 2 shoemaker shops, and, fortunately, but one distillery. An academy, endowed by the legislature in 1817, with $2000, and a school for small children, both of which are respectably supported. In the former, the usual branches of an academical course are successfully taught, and pupils from a distance may obtain boarding in respectable private families at very moderate rates. This t. has not increased so rapidly, as from its favorable situation, in the heart of a first rate beech and maple country, might have been expected, owing, chiefly, to an unfortunate dispute respecting the location of the seat of justice. But this question being now considered settled, those interested in its welfare look forward to early and valuable improvements. The town was incorporated by the act of 16th March, 1830.

Welsh mountain, a considerable eminence which rises in Lancaster co. and extends along the northern boundary of Chester, being in length about 12 ms. It lies about 16 ms. N. W. of West Chester, and about 13 ms. S. of Reading.

Welsh run, a tributary of the west branch of the Conecocheague creek, Montgomery t-ship, Franklin co. It gives name to a p-o. of that t-ship, distant 82 ms. N. W. from W. C., and 64 S. E. from Harrisburg.

Wepassening creek, Bradford co., rises in Choconut t-ship, Susquehannah co., and flows S. W. through Warren t-ship, Bradford co., thence bending N. W. it runs through Windham t-ship, to unite with the Susquehannah r., in the state of N. Y., receiving in its course of 15 ms. through those t-ships, several considerable streams.

Werefordsburg, Bethel t-ship, Bedford co., on the Great Conoloway creek, within 2 ms. of the S. line of the state, and 23 ms. S. W. from the borough of Bedford, contains a dozen dwellings, 1 store and 1 tavern.

Wesleyville, small village of Mill Creek t-ship, Erie co., about 3 ms. N. E. of the borough of Erie.

West Chester, p-t. and seat of justice of Chester co., is situated on the dividing ridge between the waters of Chester creek and the Brandywine, 2 ms. E. of the latter stream, 5 ms. S. of the Great Limestone valley, and Lancaster and Phil. turnpike road, and 23 from Phil., 115 N. from W. C., and 75 S. E. from Harrisburg. The Strasburg road passes through it westward, intersected by one from the Great Valley to Wilmington. The place was formerly called the Turk's head, from the sign of the only tavern here. The town owes its existence to the removal of the seat of justice to the site, from *Old* Chester, by virtue of an act passed 22d March, 1784, obtained principally by the exertions of Col. Hannum, an active member of the assembly of that period, who dwelt here. It was erected into a borough in the year 1799, whose boundaries embrace an area of one mile and a quarter square, taken wholly from the t-ship of Goshen, having the t-ship of East Bradford for its western limit. In the year 1800, the inhabitants amounted to 374; in 1810, to 471; in 1820, to 552; in 1830, to 1252, and in December, 1831, the pop. was about 1500; voters, about 250. The original plan of the town consisted of 4 contiguous squares, with 2 principal sts. crossing in the centre. In 1829, several streets were opened, and new squares formed on the S. W. side of the primitive squares, by William Everhart, Esq. There are 234 dwelling houses within the borough limits, of which 200 are in the village, and the residue on the adjacent farms. The assessed value of the borough in 1831, was, LANDS, including 11 small farms with town lots, $167,618; buildings, subject to taxation, $167,974; horses, 118 in number, $4970; cows and working oxen, 124 in number, $1860; occupations and professions, taxed, $59,800; stocks, bonds, mortgages, &c. yielding dividends or interest, $530,287; total, $932,509. The number of taxable inhabitants is, males, 293; females, 32; total, 325; of the male taxables 7 are *blacks*, being housekeepers. The public buildings in the borough are, the court house and prison, finished in 1786; the county offices, built in 1791; market houses, *old* one built in 1802, new one, 100 ft. long, built in 1831; an academy, built and incorporated in 1812; Roman Catholic chapel, built in 1793; Methodist Episcopal church, built in 1816; 2 Quaker meeting houses, 1 built in 1812, the other in 1830. The institutions of a public character are the p-o. established in 1802; bank of Chester co., with a capital paid in of $90,000, chartered in 1814; library founded in 1814; cabinet of natural science, founded in 1826, incorporated 1831; atheneum, founded and incorporated 1827; female boarding school, established in 1830; six day schools of various grades and dates; 2 fire companies, 1 established in the year 1800, the other in 1818; one volunteer corps of infantry, formed 1830. Four weekly newspapers, viz.: the American Republican, commenced at Downingstown, 1808, transferred to West Chester, 1822; Village Record, commenced 1809; National Republican Advocate, commenced 1828; Anti-Masonic Register and Examiner, commenced 1829. The literary institutions of this town are highly creditable to its inhabitants, and form exemplars for other county towns of the state, which, we are pleased to see, have been in part copied by Norristown and Doylestown. Among the occupations and establishments in the borough may be enumerated the following, viz.: 5 male teachers, 8 female do., 2 clergymen, 1 president judge, 20 attorneys at law, 1 conveyancer, 2 notaries, 5 justices of the peace, 4 physicians, 2 apothecaries, 4 confectioners, 1 brewery, 2 bakers, 2 butchers, 15 stores of dry goods, groceries and hardware, 8 taverns and a splendid new hotel, 2 oyster and beer houses, 1 tobacconist, 1 pottery, 1 tannery, 2 curriers' shops, 4 printing offices, 8 tailors, 6 boot and shoemakers, 2 hatters, 3 saddlers, 2 coach makers, 2 wheel wrights, 4 black smiths, 2 copper do. and tin plate workers, 1 silver plater, 1 gun smith, 1 lock smith, 3 cabinet makers, 2 chair makers, 2 cedar coopers, 5 masons and bricklayers, 2 plasterers, 7 carpenters, 3 painters, glaziers and paper hangers, 3 watch makers, 2 weavers, 3 brick kilns, 2 lumber and coal yards. The side walks of the streets were first paved with bricks in the year 1823. The two principal streets were macadamized in the years 1829 and 1830.

One daily line of mail stages passes through the borough, between Phil. and Lancaster; one tri-weekly mail stage runs the same way between Phil. and Baltimore, and two daily lines of stages run between West Chester and Phil. The mail is also carried on horseback daily, between West Chester and Downingstown, and weekly between West Chester and Wilmington, Elkton, Chester and Norristown. The improvements in the borough and surrounding country, have been such, that the enterprizing citizens of the county have constructed a rail way from the town to intersect the state rail road between Phil. and Columbia at the Warren tavern.

The zealous and enlightened editor of the Village Record exclaims, "What is to prevent the town from growing to four times its present size? In a high and healthy situation, surrounded by the richest and best cultivated lands—an extensive market for cattle—the county town of one of the most wealthy and populous counties in the state—provisions plenty and cheap,—why should it not become a place for manufacturing—especially for all those manufactures that do not demand water power to drive them. Besides, from the liberal and praiseworthy enterprize of Wm. Everhart, Esq., town lots beautifully and eligibly situated, may now be obtained on moderate terms. Where can capitalists invest their money more advantageously than by purchasing lots and building here?"

West town, t-ship, Chester county, bounded N. by E. and W. Goshen, E. by Willistown t-ships, S. by Thornbury t-ship of Del., and Thornbury of Chester counties, and W. by E. Bradford. Central distance N. W. from Phil., about 20 ms.; from West Chester, about 3 ms. S. E.; length $5\frac{3}{4}$, breadth $1\frac{1}{2}$ ms.; area, 5550 acres; surface level; soil, sandy loam. Pop. 1830, 741; taxables, 1828, 136. It is drained by Chester creek. The noted boarding schools pertaining to the society of Friends, for males and females, are established here. There are 2 places of public worship in the t-ship.

West Grove, p-o., Chester co., 96 ms. N. of W. C., and 71 S. E. from Harrisburg.

West Philadelphia, p-t., Phil. co., immediately W. of the Schuylkill r., opposite to the city and extending chiefly along the Lancaster turnpike road. There are some 30 or 40 buildings here, and several stores and taverns.

West, t-ship, Huntingdon county, bounded N. by Tussey's mountain, E. by Barre t-ship, S. E. by Mifflin co., S. by Henderson t-ship, and W. by Porter t-ship. Centrally distant N. from the borough of Huntingdon 8 ms. Greatest length 12, breadth 6 miles; area, 32,000 acres; surface mountainous; soil, limestone in valleys. Pop. in 1830, 1,650; taxables 328. Warrior ridge crosses the t-ship about the middle, and Stone mtn. is on the S.E. boundary. Standing Stone creek runs through the t-ship S. W. and east of Warrior's ridge, near which on the S. boundary is a warm spring. The post t. of Petersburg is on the N. side of the Frankstown branch of the Juniata river at the confluence of Shaver's creek with that stream. The post office is called "*Shaver's Creek*," distant 152 miles from W. C., and 88 from Harrisburg. There were in the t-ship in 1828, 5 grist mills, 10 saw-mills, 7 distilleries, 2 forges, and one tanyard.

Westfield, t-ship, Tioga co., bounded N. by New York, E. by Deerfield t-ship, S. by what is now or was formerly Delmar t-ship, and W. by Potter co. It is the extreme N. W. t-ship of the co. centrally distant from Wellsborough 20 miles. It is an oblong of 11 by 6½ miles; area, 49,280 acres; surface hilly; soil, gravel and clay. Pop. in 1830, 494; taxables in 1828, 65. It is drained E. by Cowanesque creek, which flows into the Tioga river. The post office, named after the t-ship, is 286 miles N. W. from W. C. and 189 from Harrisburg.

Westmoreland county, was formed from part of Bedford by act of assembly, twenty-sixth February, 1773, and is now bounded N. by Armstrong and Indiana counties, S. by Somerset, E. by Bedford, W. by Washington and N. W. by Allegheny counties. Length 37, width 29 miles; area, 1004 square miles. Central lat. 40° 18′ N., long. from W. C. 2° 32′ W.

This county, lying W. of the main ridge of the Allegheny, is in the great secondary formation, and abounds with the minerals common to that formation. Iron ore is found in Donegal, Ligonier, Fairfield, Derry, Unity, and Mount Pleasant t-ships. Salt works are numerous; there being in operation four on the Sewickly creek, 3 on the Allegheny river and 17 on the Conemaugh and the Kiskiminitas rivers. Bituminous coal of the best quality may be obtained from all the hills. The Laurel mountain forms the eastern boundary; parallel to, and 12 miles west thereof, runs the Chesnut ridge, from whose summit the western surface of the county has the appearance of a vast plain of verdure. It is, however, broken into hills by the streams and water courses, whose valleys have commonly a depth and breadth proportionate to the magnitude of the volumes of water which flow in them.

The county is abundantly watered, the Conemaugh or Kiskiminitas river coursing the whole of the northern boundary, and pouring its waters into the Allegheny r. which bounds it for the distance of 12 miles on the N. W. The Conemaugh receives from the co. Roaring run, Tub Mill creek, Mc Gee's run, and the Loyalhanna river; from the point of confluence of the last stream the Conemaugh bears the name of Kiskiminitas, and receives in addition, Beaver Dam run, before its junction with the Allegheny. The Loyalhanna rises at the western base of the Laurel hill, and runs a N. W. course, breaking through the Chesnut ridge, for more than 40 ms. to its recipient. The Youghiogheny enters the county from the S. E. between Rostraver and S. Huntingdon t-ships, and flows N. W. thro' it for about 10 ms. and thence along the W. boundary, about 5 miles further. It is augmented from the county by Jacob's creek, which follows the south boundary for about 25 miles by the course of the stream; by the Big Sewickly, which flowing from the vicinity of Greensburg south and west, unites with the Youghiogheny opposite to the N. E. point of Rostraver t-ship, having received the Little Sewickly about two miles above its mouth. Into all these larger streams many lesser ones flow. The state canal follows the valley of the Conemaugh, along the northern bank of the river, parallel with the northern line of the co.

Three turnpike roads cross the co., one leading from Ebensburg to Pittsburg; another passing from Bedford through Greensburg to Pittsburg, and the third from Somerset, passes thro' the south part of the county by Mount Pleasant and Robstown to the borough of Washington in Washington county.

The towns of the co. are Greensburg, the county town, Mount Pleasant, Robstown, Port Royal, Mansfield, Laughlintown, Ligonier, Fairfield, Lockport, Bolivar, Bridstone, N. Derry, Youngstown, Pleasant Unity, Huckleberry, Randolph, N. Alexandria, New Salem, Murraysville, Nolandsville, North Washington, Grapeville, Adamsburg, Jeffersonville and Stewartsville. (For a description of which see those titles respectively.)

Westmoreland co. was originally settled by German and Irish emigrants, and is now inhabited by their descendants. The population amounted in 1790 to 16,018; in 1800 to 22,726; in 1810 to 26,492; in 1820 to 30,540; in 1830 to 38,500; of whom 19,591 were white males, 18,531 females; 182 free black males, 195 females; 1 slave. There were in this number 237 aliens, 14 blind, 30 deaf and dumb.

The principal religious sects of the county are Presbyterians, who have 15 churches; German Reformed, and Lutherans who have in common 18 churches; Baptists who have three; Episcopalian 1; Methodist 8; Seceders 5; making together 50 churches, all of which are generally supplied with pastors, and are opened for divine worship every Sabbath.

Country schools are established in every vicinity, in number adequate to the instruction of the rising generation in the rudiments of an English education; and are well attended during the whole year. An academy was incorporated at Greensburg in 1810, to which the state made a donation of $2,000. In this institution the languages and mathematics are taught to 25 pupils.

The chief business of the inhabitants is agriculture, breeding cattle and sheep, the manufacture of salt and some iron. Their exports are wheat, rye, corn, and live stock. There are 24 salt works in the county in operation, which are competent to produce 2000 barrels of salt each per annum, or 48,000 barrels, worth at $\$2\frac{12}{100}$ the barrel, $96,000. There is one furnace and one forge in the county; the first, belonging to Col. Matthias, is in Fairfield t-ship, the latter, the property of Mr. Alexander Johnston, is on the Loyalhanna creek, in Unity township. There is a small manufactory of woollens at Murraysville. The chief market for the surplus produce of the county is at present Pittsburg; but when the Pennsylvania canal shall have been completed, the eastern part of the state, including Philadelphia, will prove the best market.

The value of taxable property in the co. by the assessment of 1829 was, real estate $3,185,801; personal estate, including occupations $290,203. The market value of improved lands is from 10 to 15 dollars the acre; of lands unimproved from 2 to $4. Much of the soil of the county is of the best quality.

Westmoreland, Indiana and Jefferson counties constitute the 17th congressional district of the state, sending one member to congress. Alone, Westmoreland forms the 18th senatorial district of the state, sending one member to the senate, and has three members in the house of representatives.

Westmoreland, Cambria, Indiana and Armstrong make the 10th judicial district, over which John Young, Esq. presides. The courts are holden at Greensburg, on the last Mondays of February, May, August and Nov. The county belongs to the western district of the supreme court.

Westmoreland paid into the state treasury in 1831, for

Tax on writs,	$472 87
Tavern licenses,	761 16
Duties on dealers in foreign mdz.	630 33
State maps,	23 75
Tin and clock pedlars' licenses,	57
Hawkers' and pedlars' licenses,	22 80
	$1967 91

STATISTICAL TABLE OF WESTMORELAND COUNTY.

Townships, &c.	Area in acres.	Population. 1810.	1820.	1830.	Taxables.
Allegheny,	43,520		1388	2058	291
Derry,	74,880	2380	2301	3890	613
Donegal,	60,160	2147	2564	2052	337
E. Huntingdon,	23,640	1267	1383	1516	299
Fairfield,	55,680	1973	2685	2422	288
Franklin,	32,000	1542	1757	2168	405
Greensburg bor.		685	770	810	144
Hempfield,	56,320	3444	3885	4565	701
Ligonier,	51,200			1916	372
Mount Pleasant,	19,200	1780	2060	2381	433
N. Huntingdon,	40,320	2345	2217	3170	564
Rostraver,	23,680	1786	1679	1721	342
Salem,	49,920	1518	1965	2294	440
S. Huntingdon,	23,680	1656	2004	2294	385
Unity,	39,680	2174	2436	2990	548
Washington,	32,640	1695	1478	2153	354
		26392	30540	38500	6516

Wexford, post office, Allegheny co. 237 miles from W. C., and 215, from Harrisburg.

Wharton, t-ship, Fayette co., bounded N. E. by Salt Lick t-ship, E. by Henry Clay t-ship, S. by the state of Maryland, and W. by George and Union t-ships. Centrally distant from Uniontown, S. E. 11 ms.; greatest length 21, breadth 9 ms.; area, 76,800 acres; surface, mountainous; soil, gravel. Pop. in 1830. 809. The Youghiogheny river flows along its E. and N. boundary, and receives from the t-ship, many small streams. Big and Little Sandy creeks drain it on the S. The national road crosses it, diagonally, from S. E. to N.W. on which, is a p-office, near Braddock's grave. Iron ore, sulphur, and salt springs are found in various parts of the t-ship. The Laurel hill chain is broken by the Youghiogheny river, on the E. boundary, but is continued S., by Sugar Loaf hill and other mountains.

Wheatfield, t-ship, Perry co.; surface, hilly; soil, slate and gravel.—Pop. in 1830, 1,485; taxables, 384.

Wheatfield, t-ship, Indiana co., bounded N. by Greene t-ship, E. by Cambria co., S. by the Conemaugh river, which divides it from Westmoreland co., and W. by Black Lick and Centre t-ships. Centrally distant from Indiana borough, S. W. 13 miles; greatest length 13, breadth 10½ ms.; area, 78,720 acres; surface, hilly; soil, clay; pop. in 1830, 2961; taxables, 551. It is drained by the South branch of Yellow creek, by Black Lick creek and the river, and by several smaller streams. The state canal follows the S. boundary. The turnpike road from Ebensburg to Blairsville runs W. through the t-ship, and on it lies the post town, Armagh, 13 ms. E. of Blairsville; Strongstown is also on the turnpike road from Ebensburg to Kittanning, 14 ms. E. of the latter.

Wheeling creek, of Virginia and Pennsylvania, flows into the Ohio, at the town of Wheeling. It receives from Greene and Washington counties, Pennsylvania, many tributaries.

Whip's cove, or Sarah's manor, a valley of Bethel t-ship, Bedford co., lying between Raystown and Sideling hills, which encompass it on the W., N. and E.

White Clay creek, rises in Londonderry t-ship, Chester co., and flows S. E. through London Grove t-ship, from which it receives several tributaries, and thence through New London and London Britain t-ships, into the state of Delaware. There are several mills on the main stream and branches.

White Deer mountain, a chain of the Allegheny, which, running E. and W. divides Union and Centre cos. from Lycoming co. The W. branch of the Susquehannah river washes its eastern base.

White Deer, post office, Lycoming co., 183 miles from W. C., and 74, from Harrisburg.

White Deer, t-ship, Union county, bounded N. by White Deer mountain, E. by the W. branch of the river Susquehannah, S. by Buffalo and Kelly t-ships, and W. by W. Buffalo. Centrally distant from New Berlin, 12 ms. Greatest length 6½, breadth, 4 miles; area, 17,280 acres; surface, mountainous; soil, limestone, gravel and alluvion. Pop. in 1830, 1295; taxables, 221. Between White Deer mountain and Nittany mountain, there is a narrow valley, through which White Deer creek flows into the Susquehannah river. The post town of New Columbia, lies in the S. E angle of the t-ship, upon the river. There is a post office in the t-ship, called "Whitely."

Whitehall, p-town, Madeira t-ship, Columbia co., 4 ms. N. W. of Jersey town, and 10 miles of Danville; 201 from W. C., and 91 from Harrisburg. Contains 4 or 5 dwellings, a tavern and store.

White Hall, small village of Ferguson t-ship, Centre co., about 3 ms. W. of Pattenville, and 14 miles S. of Bellefonte.

Whitehall, North, t-ship, Lehigh co. bounded N. and E. by the Lehigh river, which separates it from Northampton co., S. by S. Whitehall t-ship, W. by Lowhill t-ship, and N. W. by Heidelberg t-ship. Greatest length, N. E. and S. W. 8 miles; greatest breadth N. and S. 7 ms.; area 26,120 acres. Its figure is very irregular. It is drained on the S., by the Jordan and Coply creeks, and on the N., by several small tributaries of the Lehigh river. Is intersected by numerous roads, which centre in one, leading to Northampton borough, from which it is centrally distant about 8 miles. Its surface is level; soil, limestone, rich and well cultivated. There are two churches in the t-ship, one near the N. W. boundary, and the other, on the S., near Coply creek. Pop. in 1830, 2008; taxables, 1828, 375; taxable property in 1829, real estate, $362.636; personal, 26,775; rate of tax, 13 cents on the $100; assessed value of lands, 35, 25, 18 dollars, according to quality. There is a post office, called after the t-ship, distant 186 ms. from W. C., and ninety three from Harrisburg.

Whitehall, South, t-ship, Lehigh co., bounded N. by North Whitehall, E. by the Lehigh river, which separates it from Hanover t-ship, and by Northampton t-ship; S. E. by Salsberg t-ship; S. W. by Macungy t-ship. Its greatest length is about 7 miles, and greatest width about 6 miles; area, 18,560 acres; surface, level; soil, limestone, carefully cultivated, and abundantly productive. It is watered by the Jordan and Cedar creeks. Sinking run, a small stream, flows into it from Macungy, and is lost in a limestone sink, about 5 miles a little S. of West Allentown. Cavern spring rises near the mouth of a limestone cavern, within two miles of the borough; on the Northwest, is a large fountain, and pours its waters into the Jordan creek. This cavern has an entrance of 10 or 12 feet high, and has been penetrated about an hundred feet, into the hill, to a stream of water. There is a Lutheran church about 4 ms. W. of the borough. Pop. in 1830, 1952; taxables in 1828, 331; value of taxable property in 1829, real estate, $492,105; personal estate, $34,980; assessed value of lands, 35, 25, 18 dollars per acre, according to quality; rate of levy, 13 cents in the $100. The post office, called after the t-ship, is 179 ms. from W. C. and 85 from Harrisburg.

White Horse, post office, Somerset co., 149 miles from W. C., and 127, from Harrisburg.

Whiteland, East, t-ship, Chester co. bounded N. by Charleston t-ship, E. by Tredypin, S. by Willistown and E. Goshen, and W. by W. Whiteland. Central distance from Philadelphia, N. W. 20 miles; from West Chester, N. E. 6 ms.; length 4, breadth, 2½ ms.; area, 6530 acres; surface, level; soil limestone, excellently cultivated, and highly productive. Pop. in 1830, 994; taxables in 1828, 197. This t-ship lies in the great valley. The Philadelphia and Lancaster turnpike, and the turnpike to Morgantown, pass through it. On the former, at the foot of the southern bound of the valley, is the "Warren tavern," at which there is a post office. On the same road is Chester co. academy, incorporated, to which the state has given 2000 dollars.

Whiteland, West, t-ship, Chester co. bounded N. by Pikeland, and Charleston t-ships, E. by E. Whiteland, S. by E. and W. Goshen, W. by E. Caln, and N. W. by Uwchlan. Centrally distant from Philadelphia N.W. about 27 miles, and from W. Chester 4 miles N.; length 4 miles; breadth, 3½ miles; area, 8100 acres; surface, level; soil, limestone. Pop. in 1830, 850; taxables, 150. This t-ship lies in the great valley. The Philadelphia and Lancaster turnpike, and Columbia rail road, passes through it. The Southern valley creek crosses it diagonally from E. to W. turning several mills in its course. The post office of the t-ship is 127 ms. N. of W. C., and 73 S. E. from Harrisburg.

Whitely, t-ship. Greene co., bounded N. E. by Cumberland and Greene t-ships, E. by Dunkard t.ship, S. by the state of Virginia, W. by Wayne and N. W. by Franklin t-ships. Centrally distant S. E. from Waynesburg 8 ms. Greatest length 10, breadth, 7 miles; area, 38,400 acres; surface, rolling; soil, loam. Pop. in 1830, 1875; taxables, 329. Whitely creek rises on the W. boundary, and flows E. through Greene and Monongahela t-ships into the Monongahela r., having a course of about 15 ms. Dunkard's creek receives several small tributaries from the S. part of the t-ship.

White Marsh, t-ship, Montgomery co., bounded N. E. by Upper Dublin, S. E. by Springfield t-ship and Philadelphia co., S. W. by the Schuylkill r., and W. by Plymouth t-ship, and N. W. by Gwynnedd. Mean length 6 ms., width 2 ms.; area, 7680 acres. The Wissahickon passes diagonally through the t-ship. Centrally situated about 11 ms. N. W. from Philadelphia, and 5 ms. E. of Norristown; surface, level; soil, red shale and loam. Pop. in 1830, 1924; taxables in 1828, 379. The Ridge and the Germantown t-pike roads cross the t-ship in a N. W. direction, and approximate within a quarter of a mile of each other, near Barren hill church which lies between them. The p-o. called after the t-ship, is 14 ms. from W. C., and 110 from Harrisburg.

White Marsh, p-v. of White Marsh t-ship, Montgomery co., on the Spring House t-pike road, 14 ms. from Philadelphia, and 8 ms. S. E. from Norristown, and on the Wissahickon creek, contains a tavern, a store, a large grist and merchant mill, several dwellings, and an Episcopal church. There are several lime kilns in the neighborhood.

Whitpaine, t-ship, Montgomery co., bounded N. E. by Gwynnedd, S. E. by Whitemarsh, S. by Norriton and Plymouth, W. and N. W. by Worcester. Greatest length 4½ ms., greatest breadth 3 ms.; area, 8640 acres. Centrally distant from Philadelphia 15 ms. N. W., and from Norristown 4 ms. N. E. It may be remarked for its rarity, that there is no considerable stream of water in this t-ship. Surface, level; soil, red shale and loam. Pop. in 1830, 1137; taxables in 1828, 249.

White run, a tributary of Rock cr., which rises in Mount Pleasant t-ship, Adams co.

Whitestown, p-o., Butler co., 244 ms. from W. C., and 212 from Harrisburg.

Wiconisco creek, rises in Schuylkill co., E. of Peter's mtn., and flows by a devious course in Williams valley, & N. of Berry's mtn. thro' the t-ships of Lykens, Mifflin and Upper Paxton, Dauphin co., into the Susquehannah r., about 20 ms. above Harrisburg, receiving the Little Wiconisco creek and other streams, and turning many mills in its way. The Little Wiconisco rises in Mifflin t-ship, and runs S. W., joining the greater at Millersburg, a short distance above its confluence with the r.

Wilalloways creek, rises in Mount Pleasant t-ship, Adams co., and flows S. W. into the state of Maryland, forming the boundary between Mount Joy and Germany t-ships.

Wild Cat mountain, W. Penn t-ship, Schuylkill co., a spur of the Sharp mountain.

Wilkesbarre, t-ship, Luzerne co., is bounded N. E. by Pittston, E. by Bear creek, which separates it from Covington, S. W. by Hanover, and N. W. by the Susquehannah r., which divides it from Plymouth and Kingston t-ships. It has its name from the borough, which is the chief town of the t-ship and the co. Its greatest length S. E. and N. W. is about 14 ms., and its greatest width 6 ms.; area, 35,200 acres. The Wyoming mtn. crosses the t-ship centrally, in a N. E. direction, and the surface of the country between the river and the mtn. is level, and the soil rich alluvion. S. E. of the mtn the country is hilly and comparatively sterile. This t-ship is in the midst of the anthracite formation, and contains an inexhaustible quantity of this mineral. No portion of the Wyoming valley affords greater facilities for the transportation of coal, or offers greater inducements to prosecute that trade. The coal field extends from the river to near the top of the mountain, a distance of about 2 ms. The strata are from 6 to 24 ft. in thickness, and are every where exposed, where intersected by the streams and rivulets from the mtn. The coal has a brilliancy and richness rarely equalled, and no where surpassed. The Easton and Wilkesbarre t-pike road is located longitudinally through the t-ship, and country roads radiate from the borough in various directions. Mill creek, Laurel run and Solomon's creek flow from the mountains into the river, and Bear cr. and its tributaries carry the waters from the S. E. to the Lehigh. The pop. of the t-ship was in 1830, 2233; taxables by the return of 1828, 355.

Wilkesbarre, borough, p-t. and co. t., Wilkesbarre t-ship, Luzerne co., was laid out about the year 1773, on ground adjacent to the then Wyoming fort, by Col. Durkee, a resident, under the title of the Susquehannah company of Connecticut, from whom it received its name, in compliment to Wilkes and Barre, two celebrated members of the British parliament, friendly to the American cause during the revolution. The t. lies on the E. side of the Susquehannah r.; the streets are laid out at right angles, having a square of about 4 acres in the centre of the plot, the sides of which form an angle of 45° with the street, so that the four principal streets enter the square at its corners. In this are the public buildings, consisting of a court house, county offices and jail. It contains an academy, a meeting house, an Episcopal church, 8 or 10 stores, as many taverns, a number of mechanic shops, and about 100 dwelling houses. The Wyoming bank of Wilkesbarre, was established here by act of assembly in 1829. The academy has much reputation in the country, and has from 25 to 50 students of both sexes. The Latin and Greek languages, mathematics, and the various branches of an English ducation are taught here, and many young men have been prepared for college in this institution. The Wyoming seminary for the education of young ladies, recently established in the borough, under the care of Mrs. Chapman, is justly acquiring public favor. There is not, perhaps, in Pennsylvania, a more desirable place of residence than Wilkesbarre; situated in a rich and healthy valley, surrounded by mtns., on the bank of one of the noblest rivers of N. America; it combines the means of comfort, and the charms of the most delightful and picturesque scenery, with the prospect of active and lucrative trade. Lat. 41° 16′ N.; distant 222 ms. from W. C., and 114 from Harrisburg. Pop. in 1830, between 7 and 8 hundred. The borough is now in a very thriving condition;

many new buildings are being erected, and business of every kind rapidly increasing, and the coal trade, and that growing from agricultural products, which will find a ready and certain way to market by the N. Branch canal, will soon become of great importance.

The following is a statement in relation to the mtn. around the borough:

	Yards.
Distance to the top of the mtn. S. E.,	4685
Perpendicular height of the same,	305
Distance to the top of the mountain N. W., ...	5,583
Perpendicular height of the same,	227
Distance from the top of one mtn. to the other, ...	10,103
Width of the river from the top of one bank to the other, . . .	298
Elevation of the eastern bank above low water mark, . . .	9
Average height of the mountains above low water mark, . .	275

Wilkins, t-ship, Allegheny co., bounded N. E. and E. by Plumb t-ship, S. by Turtle creek which separates it from Versailles t-ship, S. W. by the Monongahela r., W. by Pitt t-ship, and N. W. by the Allegheny river. Centrally distant E. from Pittsburg about 10 ms.; greatest length 8½, breadth 6 ms.; area, 22,640 acrs.; surface, hilly or undulating; soil, loam and alluvial. Pop. in 1830, 1917; taxables, 395. Plumb creek is on the N. E., Thomson's run on the S. E. lines. The t-pike road from Greensburg to Pittsburg crosses the S. part of the t-ship diagonally; and on it, near the E. boundary, is the town of Howardsville, a mere name; and on the W. boundary, in a fork of Nine Mile run, is the town of Wilkinsburg, the former 10, and the latter 7 miles S. E. of Pittsburgh. Wilkinsburg contains about 50 dwellings, 3 stores, and 3 taverns.

Wilkinsburg, (*see preceding article*).

Williamsburg, small town of Strabane t-ship, Washington co., on the National road, 3 ms. S. E. of Washington borough; contains 1 tavern, & 8 or 10 dwellings.

Williamsburg, p-t. and borough of Woodberry t-ship, Huntingdon co., on the right bank of the Juniata r., 12 ms. N.W. of Huntington borough, 155 ms. from W. C., and 102 from Harrisburg; contains about 100 dwellings, 8 or 10 of which are brick, the remainder frame and log; 4 houses for public worship, 2 schools, 13 stores, 10 or 12 taverns, 4 blacksmiths' shops, 2 tan yards, 1 brewery, 2 distilleries, 1 apothecary, 1 sadler, 2 chair makers, 2 wagon makers. The state canal runs by the town. The town was incorporated 19th Feb., 1828.

Williamstown, p-t. of Lancaster co., 121 ms. from W. C., 47 from Harrisburg.

Williams, t-ship, Northampton co., bounded N. by the Lehigh r., E. by the Delaware r., S. by Bucks and Lehigh counties, and W. by Lower Saucon t-ship. Greatest length 6 ms., greatest width 3 ms. The whole surface is nearly covered by the S. mtn., or Lehigh hills, which abound in iron ore of various kinds, and of the best quality. The t. of Williamsport lies in the forks of the river; and a town plot, called S. Easton, has been laid out lately by the Lehigh coal and canal company, on the pool at the mouth of the Lehigh r., where some good buildings have already been erected, and where great inducements are offered for the establishment of manufactures. (*See Easton, South*). The soil of the t-ship is gravel and limestone; it is rich, well cultivated, and productive of wheat, corn and grass. Pop. in 1830, 2707; taxables in 1828, 339. The t-ship is drained principally by Fray's run, which by its tributaries receives the waters from N. and S.

Williamsburg, p-t., Northampton co., on the main road from Easton to the Delaware Water gap, about 16 ms. from Easton, and about 3 ms. W. from the Delaware r. in Upper Mt. Bethel t-ship. It contains 10 dwellings, 2 stores, 1 tavern, and 80 inhabitants.

Williamsburg, village, Bloom t-ship, Columbia co., on Fishing creek, 3 ms. above Bloomsburg, and 13 N. E. from Danville; contains 1 store, 1 tavern, 8 or 10 dwellings, and a Methodist church.

Williamsport, a small village in Williams t-ship, Northampton co., at the S. fork of the Lehigh and Delaware rivers, opposite to Easton, containing 12 dwellings, and 1 tavern. The Delaware canal passes between the town and the river.

Williamsport, formerly Parkinson's ferry, Fallowfield t-ship, Washington co., at the confluence of Pigeon creek with the Monongahela r., 18 ms. E. of Washington borough, 214 from W. C., and 192 from Harrisburg; contains from 80 to 100 dwellings, 5 or 6 stores, 4 taverns, and a manufactory of window glass.

Williamsport, p-t. borough and seat of justice of Lycoming co., in Loyalsock t-ship, on the N. side of the W. Branch of the Susquehannah r., 87 ms. N. W. of Harrisburg, 65 miles S. of Tioga, 36 N. by W. from Northumberland, and 160 N. W. from Philadelphia. The state canal is designed to run through this town. Value of taxable property in 1829, real estate, $26,034; personal, 14,744. An academy here, incorporated by act 2d April, 1811, by which $2000 was granted to the institution, on condition that a number of poor children, not exceeding 5, should be taught therein annually, gratis. There are in the t. about 150 dwellings, 1 German Lutheran, and 1 Methodist church, a spacious and neat court house and county offices of brick, 8 stores and 8 taverns.

Willistown, t-ship, Chester county, bounded N. by Tredypin, E. by Easton and by Delaware co., S. by Del. co., and W. by West town and East Goshen t-ships. Centrally distant from Phil., 20 ms. N. W.; from West Chester, about 6 ms. N. E.; length 5½ ms., breadth 3¼; area, 11,800 acres; surface, gentle declivity; soil, gravelly. Pop. 1830, 1411; taxables, 317. Ridley creek passes through the S. W., and Crum creek through the N. W. parts of the t-ship. Sougart is a small hamlet on the West Chester road. In this t-ship a monument has been erected to the memory of the martyrs of American liberty, who were slaughtered near the Paoli tavern, by the British forces under the command of Gen. Grey, on the night of the 19-20th of Sept., 1777.

Willowgrove, p-t. and village, Moreland t-ship, Montgomery co., 12 ms. N. of Phil., and 16 ms. N. E. from Norristown, 150 from W. C., and 112 from Harrisburg, on the turnpike road which terminates here. It is pleasantly situated in a vale, and contains about a dozen stone dwellings, 2 stores, and 3 taverns. The place has many attractions, and is much frequented in the summer season by the citizens of Phil.

Willoughby run, a tributary of Marsh creek, Cumberland t-ship, Adams co.

Wills' mountain, rises in the state of Md., on the N. side of Wills' creek, and runs N. E. into Bedford co., a short distance N. of the town of Bedford, having a length of near 30 ms.

Wills' creek, rises in Southampton t-ship, Somerset co., and flows by a devious, but generally N. E. course, through the Little Allegheny mtn. into Londonderry t-ship, Bedford co., whence, after receiving a branch from the N., it runs S. into Md., and to the Potomac at the town of Cumberland.

Wilson's creek, Brunswick t-ship, Schuylkill co., flows westwardly into the Little Schuylkill r., about 9 or 10 ms. from its confluence with the Great Schuylkill.

Wilsonville, Palmyra t-ship, Pike co., formerly the seat of justice of Wayne co., situated near the Waullenpaupack creek, and the Milford and Owego turnpike road, and near the great falls of that creek. The prosperity of this t. was checked by the removal of the seat of justice; it may possibly revive, by the general improvements of the country, consequent on the facilities of transportation produced by the Delaware and Hudson canal and rail road.

Wind gap, an opening in the Blue mtn., very abrupt, and extending from the top nearly to the bottom of the mtn. No stream now passes through it, but it is conjectured that it was formed by the Delaware r., which at some remote period is supposed to have filled a lake behind this barrier; and having been impeded here by ice, to have forced its present way through the Water gap, distant about 15 ms. from the Wind gap. The road from Easton to Wilkesbarre passes through this breach. There is a p-o. here, distant 12 ms. N. N. W. from Easton, and 63 ms. a little W. of N. from Phil., 202 from W. C., and 107 from Harrisburg.

Windham, t-ship, Luzerne county, bounded N. E. by the Susquehannah r., which separates it from Braintrim and Tunkhannock, S. E. by Eaton and Northmoreland, S. W. by Lehman t-ships, and N. W. by the co. of Bradford. Its surface is mountainous, yet it contains some excellent land; most of its soil will admit of cultivation. The Mahoopeny, the Big and Little Mahoopeny mtns. are distinguished hills, and the t-ship is drained by the Mahoopeny creek, the W. branch of the Mahoopeny, and by the Little Mahoopeny. The Big and Little Mahoopeny are strong and never failing mill streams, and its forest contains the finest of timber. It produces large quantities of lumber for market; and within a few years, considerable attention has been paid to grazing, and several dairies have produced excellent cheese. It is centrally situated about 25 ms. N. W. from Wilkesbarre, contains a p-o. and 1094 inhabitants, and by the return of 1828, 182 taxables. Its shape is made very irregular by the windings of the Susquehannah: its greatest length is 13 ms., and breadth 11 ms.

Windham, post t-ship, Bradford co., bounded N. by the state of N. Y., E. by Warren t-ship, S. by Orwell, and W. by Athens t-ships. Centrally distant from Towanda, N. E. 14 miles; greatest length 6, breadth 5½ miles; area, 19,200 acres; surface, hilly; soil, gravel. Pop. 1830, 655; taxables, 121. It is drained by the Wepassening creek, which flows N. W. through it into the Susquehannah r., in the state of N. Y. P-o. is 264 ms. N. W. of W. C., and 153 from Harrisburg.

Wingohocking creek, Philadelphia co., rises in Germantown t-ship, near Mount Airy, and flows about 7 miles through that and Bristol t-ship, into Tacony creek. It has a considerable branch which rises near the N. W. line of Bristol t-ship. There are on the main stream several mills and factories, and on the branch a grist mill, with a singular natural dam.

Windsor, t-ship, Berks co., is bounded on the N. E. by Albany t-ship, E. by Greenwich and Richmond, S. by Maiden creek, W. by Upper Bern t-ships, and N. W. by Schuylkill co. Its greatest length is 8 ms.; greatest breadth 5¼ ms.; area, 24,450 acres. The Schuylkill river and canal run along the western boundary, and Maiden creek forms the eastern boundary. The Blue mtn. fills the N. W. corner. The village and p-t. of Hamburg lies on the turnpike road to Northumberland and near the river, below the Water gap, and about 15 ms. N. of Reading. A church, used by the Lutherans and Presbyterians, is centrally situated in the t-ship, and another near to Hamburg. There is also a furnace belonging to the Messrs. Kerns, at the foot of the Blue mtn., at the head of a tributary of Maiden creek. The surface of the t-ship is hilly, and its soil gravelly, and generally sterile. Pop. 1830, 2298; taxables, 1828, 368; value of lands from 5 to 30 dolls. per acre.

Windsor, post t-ship, York county, bounded N. by Spring Garden and Hallam t-ships, E. by the Susquehannah r., S. E. by Upper Chanceford, S. W. by Hopewell, and W. by York t-ships. Centrally distant from the borough of York, 8 ms.; greatest length 9, breadth 9 ms.; area, 33,200 acres; surface, hilly; soil, gravelly loam. Pop. 1830, 2760; taxables, 481; taxable property in 1829, real estate, $310,252; personal, $19,955;

occupations, $41,835; total, 372,042; rate, 25 cts. in the $100. It is drained by a branch of Grist creek on the N., and by Cabin Branch run, Fishing creek and Beaver run on the E. There is a p-o. at Margaretta furnace, on Fishing creek, and another named after the t-ship, 98 ms. from W. C., and 36 from Harrisburg.

Wissahickon creek, rises in Montgomery t-ship, Montgomery co., and flows S. E. through Gwynnedd, Upper Dublin, and White Marsh t-ships into Philadelphia co.; thence through Germantown and Roxbury t-ships into the r. Schuylkill, about a mile above the falls, and 5 from the city. This is a very rapid stream, upon which there are several valuable grist mills, cotton and other factories. It winds through a very romantic valley.

Windrock, t-ship, Venango county, bounded N. by E. Branch, E. by Allegheny t-ship, S. by the Allegheny r., and W. by Oil creek. Centrally distant N. E. from Franklin borough 11 ms.; greatest length 8, breadth 5½ ms.; area, 19,200 acres; surface, hilly; soil, gravel and loam. It is drained S. by Pitthole creek. There are very few inhabitants in the t-ship, which is not organized but is annexed to Allegheny t-ship.

Wohleberstown, Tulpehocken t-ship, Berks co., village, containg 10 or 12 dwellings, 2 taverns, smith shop, &c.

Wolf run, a small tributary of Black creek, which rises in Catawissa valley and runs N. E. into the creek, in Sugar Loaf t-ship, Luzerne co., at its entrance into the Buck mtn.

Wolf creek, Mercer co., rises in Sandy Lake t-ship, and flows south through Wolf Creek t-ship into Slippery Rock creek, in Butler co., having a course of about 20 miles.

Wolf Creek, t-ship, Mercer county, bounded N. by Sandy Lake t-ship, E. by Venango co., S. E. by Butler co., S. W. by Slippery Rock t-ship, W. by Springfield t-ship. Centrally distant from the borough of Mercer S.E. 10 ms.; greatest length 10½, breadth 6 miles; area, 35,000 acres; surface level; soil, clay and loam. Pop. in 1830, 1244; taxables 229; taxable property in 1829, real estate $83,650; personal 11,966; rate of tax 4 mills on the dollar. It is drained by Wolf creek, which flows S. and centrally through the t-ship.

Womelsdorff, post town and flourishing village of Berks co., situated on the turnpike road from Reading to Harrisburg, about 14 miles W. from the former, 88 E. from the latter, and 148 miles N. from W. C.; contains from 75 to 100 dwellings, a church common to the Presbyterians and Lutherans, 5 taverns, 3 stores, a pottery, several saddlers, a brewery, &c. &c., inhabited chiefly by Germans. The country about it is limestone, rich and well cultivated. Average value of first rate land from 50 to 60 dollars per acre.

Worcester, t-ship, Montgomery co. bounded N. by Towamensing, E by Gwynnedd and Whitpaine, S. by Norriton and Lower Providence, W. by Perkiomen and N. W. by Lower Salford t-ships. Its form is somewhat in shape of an L. Greatest length 4¾ ms., breadth 4½ miles; area, 8,640 acres. It is drained by a branch of the Skippack creek, which crosses it diagonally, upon which there are several mills. Worcester church is centrally situated in the t-ship, distant about 19 miles N. W. from Philadelphia, and 5 miles from Norristown. Surface level; soil red shale. Pop. in 1830, 1185; taxables in 1828, 249. The post office, called after the t-ship, is distant 157 miles N. E. of W. C., and 102 from Harrisburg.

Wormleysburg, E. Pennsbury t-ship, Cumberland co., on the Susquehannah river opposite to Harrisburg, and 16 miles east of the borough of Carlisle; contains from 20 to 25 dwellings, a store and tavern.

Woodberry, t-ship, Huntingdon co., bounded N. E. by Porter t-ship, S. E. by Hopewell, S. W. by Bedford co., W. by Frankstown t-ship, and N. W. by Morris t-ship. Centrally distant S. W. from Huntingdon 14 ms.; greatest length 21, breadth 10 miles; area, 55,680 acres; surface mountainous; soil, limestone. Pop. in 1830, 1765; taxables 495. Tussey's mountain lies on the E. boundary, west of which flows Clover creek. Dock mountain is on the west, and along its east foot runs Piney creek. Both creeks flow N. into the Raystown branch of the Juniata river, about 4 miles apart; between them on the river lies the post town of Williamsport. There were in the t-ship in 1828, 5 grist mills, 13 saw mills, 6 distilleries, 2 fulling mills, 2 furnaces, 1 forge, 1 oil mill, 1 brewery, and 4 tan yards.

Woodberry, t-ship, Bedford county, bounded N. by Huntingdon co., E. by Hopewell t-ship, S. by Coleraine and Bedford t-ships, and W. by St. Clair and Greenfield t-ships. Centrally distant N. E. from the town of Bedford 16 ms. Greatest length 18½, breadth 8½ miles; area, 60,800 acres; surface mountains and valleys; soil, limestone, slate and gravel. Pop. in 1830, 3375; taxables 582. Tussey's mtn. is on the east, and Dunning's mountain on the west. The t-ship is drained S. by Yellow creek and its several branches, and N. by a tributary of the Frankstown branch of the Juniata river. Woodberry and Martinsburg are post towns of the t-ship. There is also a post office between the Three Spring branch and the Middle branch of Yellow creek. Iron is found in several parts of the t-ship.

Woodberry, post town, Woodberry t-ship, Bedford county, on the Middle branch of Yellow creek, 15 miles N. of the borough of Bedford, 136 miles from W. C. and 114 from Harrisburg; contains 20 dwellings, 3 stores, 2 taverns, belonging to Messrs. Stoeneberger and Kean.

Woodbridge, village of George t-ship, Fayette co., on the S. fork of George creek, 9 miles S. W. of Union t-ship, contains about 30 dwellings, 1 church 1 school, 1 store and 1 tavern.

Wooden Bridge creek, Dublin t-ship, Bedford co., a tributary of the Great Aughwick creek.

Woodville, post town, Middlesex t-ship, Butler co., on the turnpike road from Pittsburg to Butler borough and on a branch of Glade run, 9 miles S. W. of Butler borough.

Woodcock, t-ship, Crawford county, drained by Woodcock creek. The post office of the t-ship, called "Woodcock," is 305 miles N. W. of W. C., and 244 from Harrisburg. Pop. in 1830, 1130.

Woodcock valley, Hopewell t-ship, Huntingdon co., bounded E. by Allegripus, and W. by Tussey's mountain, a rich limestone valley. There is a post office here called after the valley.

Wrightstown, t-ship, Bucks county, bounded N. E. by Upper Makefield, S. E. by Newtown, S. by Northampton, S. W. by Warwick and N. W. by Buckingham t-ships. Centrally distant from Philadelphia 24 miles N., and 7 miles S. E. of Doylestown; length 3½, breadth 3 ms.; area, 5082 acres; surface level; soil clay; pop. in 1830, 660; taxables in 1828, 148. The Neshaminy creek forms its southern boundary, and two tributaries of that stream traverse it. Pennsville, a small village and post town on the road to New Hope, is the post town. Wrightstown church is near the S. E. boundary, at which there is a collection of 4 or 5 houses.

Wrightsville, post town and village on the west side of the Susquehannah, opposite the borough of Columbia, with which it communicates by a covered bridge of 5690 feet in length. A turnpike road runs S. W. from this town through the borough of York, from which Wrightsville is distant 11 miles. This is a thriving village, containing more than fifty dwellings.

Wrays hill, a noted mountain extending from Hopewell t-ship, Bedford co. into Union township, Huntingdon county.

Wrangletown, a small hamlet of Middleton t-ship, Delaware co., six miles W. of Chester; contains 4 or 5 dwellings, store and tavern.

Wyalusing creek, rises in Bridgewater t-ship, Susquehannah co., and by a south west and devious course of more than 30 miles, runs into the Susquehannah river in Bradford co. It receives from the N. the middle and north branches, and from the south Beard's Mill creek, Lake creek, Deer Lick creek and several less considerable streams; all of which afford fine seats for mills, and many are erected on them. It passes into Bradford co., about 2 miles below its main forks. It is a public highway, and navigable for rafts about 13 miles from the mouth. There are several mills on the creek in that distance, but their dams have slopes constructed to admit the passage of rafts. Boats cannot ascend.

Wyalusing, t-ship, Bradford co., bounded N. by Orwell and Pike t-ships, E. by Susquehannah co., S. by Luzerne co., and by Asylum township, Bradford co., and west by the last t-ship. Centrally distant from Towanda S. W. 12 ms.; greatest length 10½, breadth 10½ miles; area, 50,040 acres; surface hilly; soil, gravelly loam. Pop. in 1830, 753; taxables 174. It is drained by the Wyalusing creek, which crosses it centrally and diagonally to the Susquehannah river, receiving several tributaries from the t-ship in its course. The are two post offices in the township, Wyalusing and Wyalusing Centre. The former 254 miles from W. C., and 143 from Harrisburg, and the latter 260 miles from Washington City, and 149 from Harrisburg.

Wyoming valley, a name with which are connected many interesting circumstances, equally cherished by the poet, the novelist and the historian, and it is still

——— The loveliest land of all
That see the Atlantic wave their morn restore.

The Susquehannah river, which enters the Appalachian system of mountains at Towanda in Bradford co., by breaking the western chain, rolls the great volume of its waters over a rocky bed, through several ridges in rapid succession, and enters the Wyoming valley, by a marked mountain pass, above the mouth of the Lackawannock creek, called the "Lackawannock gap;" thence flows in a serpentine course about twenty miles, leaves the valley through another opening of the same mountain, termed the "Nanticoke gap." These passages, which have width only sufficient to admit the river, are partly faced with perpendicular rocks, covered by a thick growth of pine and laurel trees, which have a fine appearance, when viewed from the river, or from the road which winds along the bases of the bluffs. The river is in most places about two hundred yards wide, from 4 to 20 feet deep, and moves with a very gentle current, except at the rapids, or when swelled with rain, or melted snows. Near the centre of the valley, it has a rapid called the "Wyoming falls," and another, at the lower gap, designated as the "Nanticoke falls." Several tributary streams fall into it, upon each side, after passing through rocky passes, in the mountains, forming beautiful cascades as they descend to the plain. From the N. W., are Toby's creek, Moses' creek and Island run; from the S. E., Mill creek, Laurel run, Solomon's creek, and Nanticoke creek, all affording excellent mill sites, and abounding with fish, among which the "speckled trout" is the most remarkable.

The particular valley of Wyoming is a continuation of that of the Lackawannock, and taken together, has an extent of 32 ms. in length, by a mean breadth of 2½ miles.

The Nanticoke gap is supposed to have been first formed, and to have been gradually lowered by abrasion. Above and below Wilkesbarre, extensive alluvial flats, of different elevations, extend, with every appearance of having once formed the bottom of standing water. Wilkesbarre is built on one of these plains, 18 or 20 ft. above the ordinary level of the adjacent streams. The plains here, as every where else along the upper Susquehannah, though differing in elevation, are generally in two stages. The lower and more recent is still exposed to occasional submersion, and is composed of soil but little mixed with rounded pebbles. The second stage is elevated above any rise that can now take place, of the waters of the river, and is formed of a congeries of rounded and amorphous stones and sand.

From these plains the mountains rise abruptly, though seldom precipitately, and are generally clothed with timber to their summits. Bold peaks and precipices do, however, sometimes present themselves, and give variety to this truely picturesque region. Dr. Silliman speaks of the beautiful valley in the following terms. "Its form is that of a very long oval or ellipsis. It is bounded by grand mountain barriers, and watered by a noble river and its tributaries. The first glance of a stranger entering it at either end, or crossing the mountain ridges which divide it, (like the happy valley of Abyssinia) from the rest of the world, fills him with peculiar pleasure, produced by a fine landscape, containing richness, beauty and grandeur. From Prospect hill, on the rocky summit of the eastern barrier, and from Ross hill on the west, the valley of Wyoming is seen in one view, as a charming whole, and its lofty and well defined boundaries exclude more distant objects from mingling in the scene. Few landscapes that I have beheld can vie with the valley of Wyoming." But,

——— Not even the poets song,
Or pencils skill, can sketch thy waters wide;
Blue Susquehannah! as thou sweep'st a ,ng
Through these wild woods that wave upon thy side;
Here dashing o'er the rocks in crested pride;
There stealing silently the shades among;
Here hiding they bright ripples 'midst the trees;
There flashing to the sun, and foaming to the breeze!

The mineral wealth of this mountain valley is as remarkable as its natural attractions. Iron and mineral coal abound. Large quantities of argillaceous or clay iron ore are connected with the coal strata of this valley; and bog ores also abound here. And when the difficulties hitherto experienced in the case of the anthracite, in the smelting of iron shall be overcome, (and overcome they will be) the means for an extensive manufacture of iron will be here at hand; the products of which may be transported, by the canal which has already entered the valley, to every part of the country.

The whole region is one anthracite coalfield. The coal lies in beds of every thickness, from one to twenty seven feet. None are regarded by the proprietors, that have not three or four feet of thickness; few are wrought that are less than six; many are found from six to twelve; a considerable number from twelve to twenty, and several mines are from twenty to twenty five feet or more, of solid coal. (See "coal formation," in the introduction.)

That a more *precise* idea may be formed of the coal region, we give a description of one mine, from many, situated in Plymouth township, about four miles below Wilkesbarre.— The tract contains about seventy five acres. The stratum of coal at present worked, is 27 feet thick, and evidently extends over the whole tract; of a quality which is not surpassed. The tract presents a front of many perches, along a ravine down which a small rivulet and the road from the mine to the river pass. The coal stratum, which is at the side and elevated above the rivulet, rises regularly, so that the miners are never troubled by the accumulation of water. There are at present three tunnels into the mine, and more may be advantageously made. The roof is composed of solid rock, of grind stone grit, covered with gravel,clay, and apparently with another stratum of coal. It is supported by pillars of coal, left standing at regular distances. It is found as the mine penetrates the mountain, that the thickness of the stratum increases, and the quality of the coal improves. The mine has been partially worked, for twenty years; during the last seven, five thousand tons have been taken from it, annually; yet not *an acre of the stratum of coal* has been excavated. Agreeably to the standard rule of calculating coal in mines, allowing one cubic yard to the ton, there are five millions of tons in this single bed; and if fifty thousand tons were taken from it per annum, it would require one hundred years to exhaust it.

In story, Wyoming is not less rich, than in natural beauty, and mineral treasure. This lonely valley was not only the favorite resort of the aborigines of America, known to our forefathers, but was beloved by a race, who possessed it, ages before the Lenni Lenape trod the soil, and who deemed it worth defending by arts and arms. Remains of ancient fortifications have been discovered, which were constructed by a race of people, very different in their habits from those who occupied the place when first visited by the whites. Most of these ruins have been much obliterated by the plough, and their forms cannot now be distinctly traced. That which is most entire was examined by Mr. Chapman, the historian of Wyoming, during the summer of 1817. It is situated in Kingston t-ship, upon a level plain, on the north side of Toby's creek, about 150 feet from its bank, and about a half a mile from its confluence with the Susquehannah. It is of an elliptical form, having its longest diameter from the N. W. to the S. E., at right angles to the creek, 337 feet; and its shortest diameter from N. E. to S. W. 270 feet. On the S. W. side, appears to have been a gate way about 12 feet wide, opening to the great eddy of the river, into which the creek falls. From present appearances the wall consisted, probably, of only one mound, or rampart, which, in height and thickness, seems to have been the same on all sides, and was constructed of earth; the plain on which it stands not abounding in stone. On the outside of the rampart is an unwalled trench, made apparently by the removal of the earth of which the former is composed.—The creek is bounded by a high and steep bank on the side of the fortress, and at ordinary times has sufficient depth to admit the ascent of canoes to this point, from the river. When the Europeans first came to Wyoming, this plain was covered with a primitive forest, consisting principally of oak and yellow pine; and the trees on the rampart and in the trench, were as large as those in any other part of the valley; one great oak particularly, upon being cut down, was ascertained to have flourished seven hundred years. The Indians had no tradition concerning these fortifications, nor any knowledge of the purposes for which they were erected. They were perhaps constructed about the same time with those on the waters of the Ohio, and probably by a similar people and for similar purposes.

An additional evidence of the residence here of a race more intelligent and skillful, than the Lenape, is found in a vase of earthenware, discovered in Braintree t-ship, in 1807, by the washing away of a part of the bank of the river, by an extraordinary freshet. The pot was found entwined by the roots of a tree which had grown around it, six feet below the surface of the earth. The tree which grew over it was more than 2 feet in diameter, and it must therefore have lain here for ages. The vase, which was in the possession of the editor of the Wyoming paper in 1828, holds about two quarts, is thus described by him.—"The bottom is round; it swells gradually to the middle and then decreases in size to the top; the lower half is like the bottom of a gourd, and the upper part like the top of an urn. It is very thin and light, perfectly smooth inside, but on the outside beautifully and regularly figured." Such relics should be carefully preserved and more minutely described by their fortunate possessors; as they may enable us to trace some affinity between yet existing races, and that which was driven out or extirpated by the Lenape.

According to the traditions of the Delawares, their ancestors, the Lenni Lenape, soon after their inroad from beyond the Mississippi, occupied this valley. It subsequently became the seat of the Shawnese and the Nanticokes, and the Delawares again inhabited it, being exiled thither by their imperious conquerors, the Six Nations. The Shawnese abandoned it in 1773, in consequence of their defeat in battle with the Delawares and the Nanticokes in 1755. The Delawares, who clung with great tenacity to this favorite possession, refused to part with it until 1668, when by treaty at Fort Stanwix, they released to the proprietaries of Pennsylvania, all their territory within the chartered bounds of the colony. Our space does not permit us to trace here the history of the wars between the Indians and the whites, nor the long, protracted contest between the Pennsylvanian and Connecticut settlers, connected with this valley. But we refer to our introduction for a concise notice of them. These contentions have long been quieted, and the New England emigrants and the Pennsylvania grantees, and their descendants, are alike obedient, industrious and valuable citizens, and Wyoming enjoys the repose and prosperity, justly due to its unrivalled beauty and ample resources.

Wysox, post t-ship, Bradford co., bounded N. by Athens t-ship, E. by Orwell and Wyalusing t-ships, S. W. by the Susquehannah r., and W. by Sheshequin t-ship. Greatest length 12, breadth 12 ms.; area, 30,000 acres; surface, hilly; soil, gravelly loam. Pop. 1830, 1351; taxables, 205. The t-ship is drained chiefly by Rumfield and Wysox creeks. The latter rises in Windham t-ship and flows S. W. into the Susquehannah r., about 5 ms. below the town of Towanda. The p-o. of the t-ship is 241 ms. N. W. of W. C., and 130 from Harrisburg.

Wysox creek, (see the preceding article.)

Yager's mountain, Sugar Loaf t-ship, Luzerne co., a spur of the Nescopeck mtn. lying in the forks of the Nescopeck and Oley creeks.

Yardleyville, p-t., on the right bank of Delaware r., Makefield t-ship, Bucks co., pleasantly situated, chiefly on the upper bank of the river, 18 ms. S. E. from Doylestown, 4 ms. above Trenton and Morrisville, 165 from W. C., and 112 from Harrisburg; contains about 20 dwellings, 2 stores, 2 taverns, one of which is a "temperance house," a grist mill and saw mill. There is a ferry here across the Del.

Yellow creek, Bedford co., rises in Woodberry t-ship, with many branches, and flows S. E. and E. into the Raystown branch of the Juniata r.

Yellow spring, a mineral spring in Canoe valley, Morris t-ship, Huntingdon co., near the turnpike road leading to Huntingdon. There is a p-o. here, distant 163 ms. N. W. from W. C., and 105 W. from Harrisburg.

Yellow springs, Pikeland township, Chester co., p-o., and a noted and beautiful watering place, having the advantage of mineral springs, and baths, a fine picturesque and healthy country, 2 excellent public houses, with the accommodations and enjoyments usual at such places. It is on the Morgantown turnpike road, 9 ms. N. of W. Chester, 25 N. W. from Phil., 16 ms. W. from Norristown, 128 from W. C. and 74 from Harrisburg.

York county, was erected by act of assembly, 9th Aug., 1749, and lies along the southern border of the state, and is bounded on the S. by the Md. line, extending due E. and W. 43 ms., on the E. by Lancaster and Dauphin counties, along the western shore of the Susquehannah river, in length 51 ms., on the N. by Cumberland co., in length 18 ms., and on the

W. by Adams co., in length about 28 ms.; covering an area of 900 square ms. or 576,000 acres.

The county is divided between the three geological formations. The primitive occupies nearly the eastern half of the county; the secondary, the central portion, and contains a strip of limestone about 5 ms. in breadth, in which is marble of an excellent quality. The transition, or old red sand stone formation, claims the remainder. The chain of hills known as the Conewago hills, cross the S. E. angle, and the South mtn. bounds the co. on the N. W. In Windsor t-ship, on the Susquehannah, there is abundance of iron ore, well adapted for casting, and, though formerly not prized for forging, has latterly been used successfully for that purpose. Slate of excellent quality for roofing is found in Peach Bottom t-ship, and bituminous coal has been discovered within 2 ms. of the borough of York, but from late examinations, the quantity is supposed to be inconsiderable.

The co. is finely watered, the noble Susquehannah flowing along its greatest length; the several branches and smaller streams discharging themselves into the Great Codorus, the Conewago and the Yellow Breeches, which, together with Muddy creek, Fishing creek, Beaver creek, Creutz creek, Cabbin branch, Canadochly and Otter creeks, with others, flow eastwardly into the r. The Codorus is a very fine stream, running through the town of York, and has lately been rendered navigable by artificial means, through the enterprize and liberality of the citizens of that borough. The Yellow Breeches flows along the N. W. boundary of the co. A canal of about 1 mile in length has been cut around the Conewago falls, by which the descending trade of the r. may avoid the dangers of that rapid.

The southern turnpike road from Pittsburg, enters the co. at Wrightsville, opposite Columbia, and passes through it in a S. W. direction by the borough of York. A turnpike road running N. 10 ms., connects the borough with York Haven on the Susquehannah r., and enables it to participate fully in the trade of the r. From the borough, another turnpike road runs southward about 20 ms. into Md., and thence to Baltimore. A fourth turnpike crosses the S. W. angle of the co., from Hanover into Md., uniting with the turnpike road from Carlisle, and another from the town of Berlin, in Adams co. From Berlin, the road is continued northward to Dillstown, in Carroll t-ship, York co. From York Haven, a turnpike road follows the bank of the r. to the W. end of the bridge at Harrisburg.

The co. is divided into 25 t-ships, and contains a number of flourishing towns and villages, among which are York, Frystown, Butztown, Hanover, Shrewsbury, Wrightsville, Liverpool, New Holland, Strinestown, York Haven, Newburg, New Market, Lewisburg, Dillstown, Dover, Mechanicsburg, Jefferson, Franklin, Rosstown and Weiglestown, and others of less note.

It is now about a century since the first settlements were made in this co., by Germans and emigrants from the North of Ireland. In the year 1722, Sir William Keith, by a warrant dated at Conestogo, 18th June, directed the location and survey of a manor of about 70,000 acres of land, in the name and for the use of Springet Penn, to be called "Springetsbury Manor;" but the boundaries were afterward changed and fixed by another survey. Prior to 1728, unauthorized settlers seated themselves on lands in this county, but were removed at the close of that year, by proprietary authority, at the request of the Indians. In May, 1729, James and John Hendricks and others, with the approbation of the government, established themselves on and near the Codorus creek, not far distant from the present borough of York. In the year 1731, Thomas Cressap and his coadjutors, established themselves upon the lands from which the above mentioned intruders had been removed, and under pretence of title from Md., occasioned long and angry contentions, attended frequently with bloodshed, which were terminated only by the capture of Cressap, on the 24th Sept., 1736, and the interference of the king and council for determining the vexed question of the boundary. At this period there were probably between 3 and 400 inhabitants within the present limits of the co. Washington, Warrenton, and Newbury t-ships were chiefly settled by Quakers.

The pop. of York co. in 1790, was 37,747; and in 1800, after the subtraction of Adams co. from it, 25,643; in 1810, 31,938; in 1820, 38,759, and in 1830, 42,658; of whom, 20,704 were white males; 20,950 white females; 482 free black males; 497 free black females; 6 male and 19 female slaves. There were included in this number 350 aliens; 25 blind, and 23 deaf and dumb.

The chief religious sects of the co. are Lutherans, German Reformed, Presbyterians, Methodists, Episcopalians, Quakers, Catholics, and Moravians, who have altogether in the co. about 30 churches. There is a county Bible society, and Sunday school associations are formed pretty generally throughout the county. At York, the Dorcas society, composed of charitable females, has alleviated much distress among the poor, by providing them with necessary clothing during the winter, made up by the members at their weekly meetings.

The business of the co. is chiefly in agriculture, or in manufactures immediately connected with it, and there is perhaps no county in the state that may boast of greater success in the cultivation of the earth. The skill of the farmers has been much improved by the instructions, and their emulation excited by the example of Mr. Charles A. Barnitz of York. He has introduced and rendered common the finest breeds of neat cattle, sheep and swine, and has originated several new subjects of culture. Among the latter, the grape and the sunflower; both of these will yearly obtain greater consideration. The cultivation of the vine has been carried on in the co. with great and growing success, and the *vignerons* improve in the preparation of its juice. As the culture of the sun flower, *helianthus annuus*, is a novel matter among us, we shall probably render our farmers a service by a few remarks on the mode of cultivation, and on the uses to which this plant is applicable.

"The sun flower," says Mr. Barnitz, "is cultivated like Indian corn, planted in *rows* three ft. apart, and the *stocks* 18 inches. Any land which produces corn, will yield from 50 to 60 bushels the acre, and it is worth 75 cts. the bushel. The single headed kind is preferable, and as soon as ripe, which is known by its shattering—the heads are taken off, carted to the barn floor, & immediately threshed out with the flail; it should be cleaned with the fan, and then spread out, and occasionally turned or stirred to become dry; if left in a large heap it may mould. By an improved mode of extracting the oil, a bushel of seed yields a gal. of oil, 3 qts. cold pressed, and one qt. by heating. The cake when ground, is very nutritive as cattle feed, and will pay the expense of the miller. A bushel of seed will plant about 10 acres. I can furnish any gentleman disposed to cultivate it, with the best seed. I expect to raise about 500 bushels this season, (1830) and have engaged others in raising probably as much more."

The produce obtained by Mr. Barnitz is large, but has been equalled by others; yet 30 bushels the acre would be a safe calculation for the farmer.

The oil is applicable to the uses of the clothier, and is preferable to the rancid olive oil, commonly used for preparing the wool for the card and loom; it is highly esteemed in the manufacture of printers ink, for burning in lamps where purity and brilliancy, as in parlors, are required. It is a good salad oil, taken medicinally, as effective as the castor oil, without the nausea of the latter; it is a palatable and nutricious food for all kinds of cattle, but should be ground before given to them; and the cake left after the expression of the oil, is more desirable than that of flax seed. The strong fibrous, and some other parts of the plant, may be made into pack thread, instead of hemp, and the white shining silvery fibrous substance, which it contains in large proportions, into paper; and the large roots, naked stems, and other waste parts may be used as fuel.

The following is an imperfect sketch of the annual exports of York co., viz.:

125,000 barrels of flour, valued at	$625,000
2,704,000 galls. of whiskey,	611,200
500,000 bushels of grain, wheat, rye, corn, oats, &c.,	375,000
1000 bushels clover seed at 5,	5,000
100,000 barrels pork,	50,000
700 tons iron castings,	38,500
	$1,704,700

There are 2 furnaces and 4 forges in the co. Margaretta furnace, 11 ms. E. from the town of York, and 3 ms. W. of the Susquehannah r., in the valley of Canodockly in Windsor t-ship, on the Cabbin Branch, has the ore bank immediately at the works, and the coaling convenient, and is capable of making 2000 tons of pigs and other castings annually. It is the property of Henry Y. Slaymaker & Co. There is a forge here also, belonging to the same firm. A steam furnace, belonging to Mr. Israel Gardner, is situated in the t. of York, where all kinds of castings are made.

Codorus forge on the Codorus cr., near the Susquehannah r., pertaining to the heirs of Henry B. Grubb, makes about 400 tons of bar iron annually. Spring forge, also on the Codorus creek, makes about 350 tons annually; it belongs to Thomas B. Coleman. The same proprietor owns Castle Finn forge, 28 ms. S. E. of York borough, in Lower Chauceford t-ship, on Muddy creek, 3 ms. from the r., which makes about 400 tons annually. There are three tilt mills in the co., several steam mills, and a small woollen and cotton manufactory.

The best lands in the co., with comfortable improvements, are worth from 70 to 100 dols. the acre, according to quantity, quality and situation. Very inferior lands may be bought at 5, and the average value may be $20 thro'-out the co. The assessed value in 1829, of lands, was $7,051,458; personal property, $351,117; occupations, $740,768.

York co. alone forms the 10th congressional district, sending 1 member to congress; connected with Adams, it constitutes the 14th senatorial district, sending 2 members to the senate; alone, it sends 3 members to the house of representatives. York and Lancaster counties, compose the 2nd judicial district of the state, over which Walter Franklin, Esq., presides. The courts are holden in York on the 1st Mondays in January, April, August and November, and the co. belongs to the Lancaster district of the Supreme court, which holds a session in Lancaster on the 3d Monday in May, annually.

STATISTICAL TABLE OF YORK COUNTY.

Townships, &c.	Greatest Lth.	Greatest Bth.	Population 1820.	Population 1830.	Taxables.
Cadorus,	13	6 1-2	2183	2331	505
Conewago,	7 1-2	6	945	1094	221
Dover,	8 1-2	7	1816	1874	400
E. Manchester,	8 1-2	5	1914	2212	505
Fairview,	9	7	1764	1885	369
Fawn,	6	6	803	785	174
Franklin,	5	4	973	1003	224
Hallam,	5 1-2		2062	1876	348
Hanover borough,		5	946	1006	185
Heidleburg,	6 1-2	6	1313	1523	286
Hopewell,	10	8 1-2	1630	1941	370
L. Chauceford,	9 1-2	8	965	1051	216
Manheim,	10 1-2	6 3-4	1306	1278	302
Monaghan,	7 1-2	4	1158	1219	148
Newberry,	10 1-2	7	1794	1833	385
Paradise,	8	8	1837	1805	406
Peach Bottom,	9	5	928	898	204
Shrewsbury,	11 3-4	9	1983	2571	394
U. Chauceford,	9	9	1248	1177	270
Washington,	9	3 1-2	1061	1037	247
Warrington,	8 3-4	7 1-4	1274	1230	263
W. Manchester,	7	6 1-4	1973	1369	255
Windsor,	9	9	2096	7260	481
York,	10	6	2007	1181	239
York Borough,			3545	4316	843
Spring Garden,	8 1-2			1603	276
Caroll t-ship, lately erected.					
			62,658	12,658	8.526

This county paid into the state treasury for dividends on t-pike stock, $1325 00
Tax on writs, 139 20
Tavern licenses, (1830), 1573 10
Duties on dealers in foreign merchandize, 668 94
Tax on collateral inheritances, 18 01

$3,724 16

York sulphur springs, Latimore t-ship, Adams co., on the Bermudian creek near its intersection of the Carlisle and Hanover turnpike road, distant from Carlisle S. 15 miles; from York W. 20 miles; from Harrisburg S. W. 22 miles, and from Gettysburg N. E. 12 miles. A visiter writes of these springs: "they undoubtedly possess sanative qualities, and are situated on a spot so elevated, that every breeze must have 'healing on its wings.' The buildings are extensive and comfortable, and the creature comforts provided by the obliging Mr. McCash are unexceptionable, unless cause of exception there be in provocation to excess, which a well supplied table and good cheer presents. This is a favorite resort of the fashionable Baltimoreans. Board 8 dollars per week."

York Haven, post and thriving town of Newberry t-ship, York co., on the Susquehannah river, west side, below Conewago falls, opposite to Portsmouth. A turnpike road leads from this town to the borough of York, 10 miles distant. It is 97 miles from W. C. and 14 from Harrisburg. Much of the descending trade of Susquehannah r. is arrested here, the market being sustained by the Baltimoreans.

York, t-ship, York county, bounded N. W. by Spring Garden t-ship, N. E. and E. by Windsor, S. by Hopewell and Newberry t-ships, and W. by Codorus t-ship. Centrally distant S. W. from the borough of York 5 ms. Greatest length 10, breadth 6 miles; area, 17,280 acres; surface undulating; soil, gravel and not very rich. Pop. in 1830, 1181; taxables 239; taxable property in 1829, real estate $149,481; personal 9,838; occupation 13,723; total 173,042.

York, post town, borough and seat of justice of York co. lies on the Codorus creek, partly in Spring Garden and partly in West Manchester t-ships, about 83 miles west from Philadelphia, 21 from Lancaster, and 11 from Columbia, and about 25 S. of Harrisburg. Lat. 39° 57′ N. long. W. C. 0° 17′ W. It is built on a plain, with streets at right angles with each other, and contains about 700 dwellings and many stores and taverns. The public buildings consist of a court house and county offices, of brick. The court house was occupied by congress when driven from Philadelphia during the revolutionary war. It is now too small for the business of the county. An academy, also of brick, to which the state has given $2,000—a county prison of stone—a poor house a short distance from the town. There are 9 churches in the town, viz—Lutheran, German Reformed, Moravian, Episcopal, Roman Catholic, Presbyterian, Methodist, Quaker and African Methodist, all substantial brick buildings except the last, which is of frame. A Bible society, Sunday school union, and a female charitable association called "Dorcas." In the cemetery of the German Reformed church is the grave and a monument erected to the memory of Philip Livingston, a member of congress, who died during the session of that body in York, in 1777. The monument consists of a pyramidal shaft of white marble, surmounted with an urn. A slackwater navigation has lately been made along the Codorus creek, from the borough to the Susquehannah, a distance of 11 miles, of which 8 consists of artificial pools and 3 of canal, with 9 locks, said to be executed in a very superior manner. This is a rich and thriving town, as is apparent by its increase of population. It contained in 1820, 3,545 inhabitants; and in 1830, 4,216 and 843 taxables. The value of real estate by the triennial assessment of

1829, was $550,623; of personal estate subject to taxation, $10,155; of occupations, $118,305; total, $679,083.

In the vicinity the grape has been very successfully and extensively cultivated, and considerable quantities of wine of good quality are produced here. The town is supplied by a company incorporated in 1806, with wholesome spring water.

Youghiogheny river, rises in the extreme S. W. angle of Maryland and flows a N. E. course of thirty miles comparative length to the Pennsylvania line. It enters the state aross the S. boundary on the line dividing Fayette and Somerset counties, and receives from the latter some 3 ms. below the Horse Shoe bend, Castleman's river, its northern branch; thence turning N. W. it breaks thro' the Laurel hill N. of the Sugar Loaf mountain, and the Chesnut ridge, 5 miles S. E. of Connellsville, and preserves the same course to its union with the Monongahela at McKeesport, 18 miles above Pittsburg. Its comparative length in the state is about 70 miles through the counties of Fayette and Westmoreland. This river heads with the Cheat branch of the Monongahela r., with the N. branch of the Potomac, and by Castleman's river with the Juniata and Kiskiminitas. It is navigable to Ohiopile falls, in Fayette county, 60 miles above its junction with the Monongahela. This is a fine mountain stream, possessing in all seasons except those of long drought, sufficient water for the supply of the most spacious canal, and is the contemplated chain for connecting the waters of the Potomac with the Ohio.

Youngstown, post town and boro' of Unity t-ship, Westmoreland co., on the turnpike road from Bedford to Greensburg, S. of the Loyalhanna river, and 9 miles E. of the latter town, 182 from W. C. and 160 from Harrisburg; contains about 40 dwellings, 4 stores, 2 taverns and 1 German church. It was incorporated by act of assembly 2d April, 1831.

Youngsville, post town, Warren co. is situated on each side of the Big Broken Straw creek, 3 miles from its mouth, 10 miles W. of Warren borough, 313 N. W. from W. C., and 357 from Harrisburg. It contains about twenty dwelling houses, 3 stores, 2 taverns, and the necessary mechanics in a country village, and a commodious Methodist meeting house. Some of the largest and best cultivated farms in the county, lie in the neighborhood of this village.

Young, t-ship, Indiana co., bounded N. by Armstrong, E. by Blacklick, S. by Conemaugh t-ships, and W. by Armstrong co. Centrally distant S. W. from Indiana 12 miles. Greatest length 8, breadth 5 ms.; area, 18,560 acres; surface hilly; soil, rich loam. It is drained by Black Legs creek, which flows S. W. to the Conemaugh river. The t-ship was taken from Conemaugh since 1830.

Youngwoman'stown, post office of Chapman t-ship, Lycoming co., 245 miles from W. C., and 138 from Harrisburg.

Young, t-ship, Jefferson co., bounded N. by Pine Creek township, E. by Clearfield co., S. by Indiana co., and W. by Perry township. Length and breadth 9 miles; area, 51,840 acres; surface rolling; soil, gravelly loam, timber, oak, &c. Pop. in 1830, about 400. It is drained principally by the Mahoning, and by Canoe creek, its tributary. Punxatawny, situated in a fork of the former, is the post town; it is a village of 15 houses, tavern and store.

Zachariah run, a small tributary of the Schuylkill river, in Schuylkill township, Schuylkill co., which falls into the river about 2 miles above Port Carbon.

Zelienople, a small village adjacent to the town of Harmony, in Conequenessing t-ship, Butler co., on the south side of the Conequenessing creek, 15 ms. S. W. by W. from Butler boro', contains from 35 to 40 dwellings, 2 stores, 2 taverns, and some mills.

A TABLE

OF ALL THE POST OFFICES IN PENNSYLVANIA,

Their distances from Washington and Harrisburg, the counties in which situated, and the names of the post masters; taken from the most recent documents of the post office department.

ADAMS COUNTY.

Offices.	Post Masters.	Ms. from W.	Ms. from H.
Abbottstown,	Jacob Fahnestock,	86	32
East Berlin,	Christian Picking,	90	24
Fairfield,	W. Johnston,	84	42
Fountaindale,	Joseph Bauger,	71	46
Gettysburg,	Wm. W. Bell,	76	34
Hampton,	Charles Blish,	90	28
Heidlersburg,	Abel Pittendurf,	81	24
Keener's Mills,	Wm. B. Willson,	85	35
New Oxford,	Francis Hildt,	87	36
Petersburg,	Francis Leas,	77	20
York Sulphur Springs	Harman Wireman,	85	20

ALLEGHENY COUNTY.

Offices.	Post Masters.	Ms. from W.	Ms. from H.
Bakerstown,	James Jones,	239	217
Clinton,	John Pollock,	246	224
Elizabeth,	Samuel Walker,	240	216
Gambles,	John Gamble,	210	188
Herriottville,	Jas. Herriot,	233	211
McKeesport,	Hugh Rowland,	212	189
Noblestown,	Hanson S. Chadwick,	234	212
Perryville,	Conrad Reel,	230	208
Pittsburg,	Wm. Eichbaum, Jun.	223	201
Sewickly Bottom,	David Shields,	237	215
Spring Dale,	John Keen,	235	207
Surgeons Hall,	Joseph Curry,	226	204
Tarentum,	John F. Metlin,	231	203
Wexford,	Martin Byrne.	237	215

ARMSTRONG COUNTY.

Offices.	Post Masters.	Ms. from W.	Ms. from H.
Apollo,	John Wort,	219	188
Callensburg,	Sidle Lobough,	251	191
Clarion,	Philip Corbet,	247	174
Elderton,	Wm. D. Barclay,	202	170
Freeport,	Henry S. Weaver,	225	197
Glade Run,	Elisha D. Barrett,	214	181
Hulingsburgh,	Samuel Wilson,	242	185
Kiskiminitas,	Andrew Boggs,	210	188
Kittaning,	Alexander Reynolds,	215	183
Lawrenceburgh,	Michael McCullough,	241	201
Leechburgh,	David Leech,	227	196
Limestone,	James Sloan,	241	182
Maple Grove,	Matthew Hosey,	231	199
Red Bank,	John Money,	235	188
Rural Valley,	John Patterson,	224	190
Slatelick,	Joseph Ralston,		
Strattansville,	Robert Barber,	249	180
Toby,	David Stoner,	236	190

BEAVER COUNTY.

Offices.	Post Masters.	Ms. from W.	Ms. from H.
Beaver,	James Alexander,	251	229
Chenango,	Wm. Cairns, Jun.	261	230
Economy,	Wm. Smith,	241	219
Fallston,	Hall Wilson,		
Frankfort,	James Dungan,	254	231
Georgetown,	Thos. Foster,	263	241
Griersburg,	Stephen Todd,	263	241
Hookestown,	Joseph McFarren,	258	241
Mount Jackson,	Wm. Henry,	275	243
North Sewickly,	Ab. S. Severns,	263	238
Ohioville,	John Clark,	262	240
Seventy Six,	Wm. McAllister,	256	234

BEDFORD COUNTY.

Offices.	Post Masters.	Ms. from W.	Ms. from H.
Alum Bank,	Thomas Vickroy,	136	114
Bedford,	John H. Hofius,	126	105
Bloody Run,	David Man, Jun.	118	96
Burnt Cabins,	Nathaniel Kelly,	109	59
Hopewell,	Isaiah Davis,	127	105
Licking Creek,	John Duffield,	99	76
Martinsburgh,	John Bingham,	134	112
McConnelsburgh,	Wm. Duffield,	93	70
Morris Cove,	Martin Lay, Jun.	132	110
Rainsburgh,	John Folck, Jun.	135	113
Schellsburg,	Peter Levy,	135	113
Stonerstown,	Geo. Roads,	124	102
Three Forges,	John G. McKee,	140	118
Woodbury,	John McKieran,	136	114
Fort Littleton,	Jacob Trout,	103	64

BERKS COUNTY.

Offices.	Post Masters.	Ms. from W.	Ms. from H.
Adamsville,	Isaac Adams,	152	61
Bethel,	Abraham K. Clark,	144	34
Boyerstown,	Daniel Boyer,	159	68
Brower,	Wm. George,	147	66
Brumfieldville,	Henry Auman,	153	62
Colebrookdale,	Christop. K. Shultz,	163	72
Cootstown,	Joseph Heist,	160	69
Dale,	David Schall,	164	71
Douglassville,	Abraham Hesser,	147	64
Geiger's Mills,	Joseph M. K. Potts,	138	63
Grimville,	Daniel B. Grim,	156	67
Hamburgh,	John Shenk,	156	56
Hereford,	Jacob Hillegass,		
Joanna Furnace,	A. H. Richards,	135	60
Klinesville,	Peter Kline, Jun.	152	63
Long Swamp,	Reuben Trexler,	162	71
Maiden Creek,	Samuel Beard,	151	60
Maxatawny,	Jonas Rodrock,	165	74
Morgantown,	David Morgan, Jun.	133	58
Mount Airy,	John Evans,	152	61
New Jerusalem,	Andrew Shiffert,	156	65
Oley Furnace,	Jacob W. Snyder,	153	62
Reading,	Samuel Ritter,	143	52
Rehrersburgh,	George Harner,	148	38
Schall's Store,	Wm. Schall,	157	66
Shartlesville,	Solomon Albright,	156	48
Union Iron Works,	Penrose Wiley,	157	66
Womelsdorf,	Lewis W. Richards,	148	38

BRADFORD COUNTY.

Offices.	Post Masters.	Ms. from W.	Ms. from H.
Alba,	Irad Wilson,	241	129
Asylum,	Simson Stevens,	248	137
Athens,	Ebenezer Backus,	252	143
Burlington,	Addison McDowell,	249	138
Canton,	James Parsons,	246	137
Columbia Cross Rds.	Elisha S. Goodrich,	254	148
East Smithfield,	Seth Salisbury,	249	138
Edsallville,	Samuel Edsall,	262	150
Franklindale,	John Knapp,	248	137
French's Mills,	Wm. H. French,	268	162
Le Raysville,	Josiah Benham,	257	146
Litchfield,	Daniel Bush,		
Milltown,	Wm. W. Rice,	256	146
Monroetown,	Abner C. Rockwell,	237	126

BRADFORD COUNTY, (Continued.)

Offices.	Post Masters.	Ms. from W.	Ms. from H.
New Albany,	Charles W. Ladd,	227	116
North Branch,	Sylvester Taylor,		
North Smithfield,	James C. Pierce,	253	142
Orwell,	Chauncey Frisbie,	252	141
Pike,	Jesse Ross,	260	149
Ridgebury,	James Covell,	261	150
Sheshequin,	Joseph Kingsbury,	247	136
South Creek,	George Hyde,	260	148
South Warren,	Benjamin Buffington,	270	159
Springfield,	William Evans,	255	143
Standing Stone,	Jonathan Stevens, Jr.	245	134
Sylvania,	Reuben Nash, Jun.	263	147
Terrytown,	George F. Horton,	253	142
Towanda,	Nathaniel N. Betts,	239	128
Troy,	George Kress,	259	148
Ulster,	Abraham Goodwin,	246	135
Warrenham,	Andrew Coburn,		
Windham,	William Russell,	264	153
Wyalusing,	John Taylor,	254	143
Wyalusing Centre,	Raphael Stone,	260	149
Wysox,	J. M. Piollet,	241	130

BUCKS COUNTY.

Offices.	Post Masters.	Ms. from W.	Ms. from H.
Andalusia,	Michael Jacoby,	157	119
Attleboro,	James Flowers,	163	125
Aurora,	Charles Hillegass,	173	87
Bristol,	John Bessonett,	156	118
Brownsburgh,	Stacey Brown,	174	123
Buckingham,	Alexander J. Case,	164	112
Bucksville,	Nicholas Buck,	177	106
Bursonville,	William Burson,	185	99
Danboro',	Joseph Kaisinger,	165	112
Davisville,	John Davis,	169	118
Dolington,	Oliver Hough,	171	133
Doylestown,	Manassah H. Snyder,	160	107
Dublin,	Newton Rowland,	166	97
Durham,	Thomas Long,	182	111
Erwinna,	Hugh Erwin,	186	122
Hartsville,	William Bready,	156	113
Hilltown,	Elisha Lunn,	168	97
Hulmesville,	William Hulme,	161	123
Line Lexington,	Jacob C. Nyce,	168	96
Lumberville,	William L. Hoppock,	175	124
Mattsville,	John Matts,	175	89
Mechanicksville,	Peter Lester,	165	112
Monroe,	John H. Johnson,	195	113
Morrisville,	George Laning,	165	127
New Britain,	Isaac W. James,	164	104
New Hope,	Joseph D. Murray,	170	119
Newton,	Asa Cary,	167	129
Ottsville,	John Emery,	174	109
Pennsville,	James Gaine,	162	116
Pleasant Valley,	Lewis Ott,	179	93
Point Pleasant,	John F. Youngken,	177	126
Quakertown,	Jacob Dudson,	172	86
Richboro',	Richard L. Thomas,	158	126
Rock Hill,	John Sellers,	171	92
Seller's Tavern,	Thomas Sellers,	166	91
Spinnerstown,	Henry Haring,	171	99
Springtown,	Christopher H. Witte,	179	93
Strawntown,	William Stokes,	175	100
Taylorsville,	John B. Taylor,	169	123
Trumbaursville,	John P. Ball,	160	85
Tullytown,	Joseph Hutchinson,	161	117
Upper Black Eddy,	David Weirman,	191	118
Yardleyville,	Mahlon Dungan,	165	112

BUTLER COUNTY.

Offices.	Post Masters.	Ms. from W.	Ms. from H.
Baldwin,	Peter Beighly,	249	209
Butler,	John Gilchrist,	236	204
Coylesville,	Henry Coyle,	226	194
Cranberry,	James Frazier,	244	213
Harmony,	John Fleming,	249	218
Harrisville,	James Owens,	261	221
Murrinsville,	Hugh Murrin, Jun.	251	211
Portersville,	Robert Craig,	252	220
Slippery Rock,	Isaac S. Pearson,	254	214
Whitestown,	Edward White,	244	212

CAMBRIA COUNTY.

Offices.	Post Masters.	Ms. from W.	Ms. from H.
Ebensburgh,	John Lloyd,	178	131
Johnstown,	Shipley Triestly,	160	138
Loretto,	Peter Christy,	184	137
Munster,	Matthew Buckanan,	183	130
Roseland,	Edward Shoemaker,	182	124

CENTRE COUNTY.

Offices.	Post Masters.	Ms. from W.	Ms. from H.
Aaronsburg,	Adam Gentsel,	196	88
Bellefonte,	Hamilton Humes,	192	85
Boalsburg,	Charles Rainey,	183	82
Cedar Spring,	Samuel H. Wilson,	208	101
Halfmoon,	John Blair,	178	101
Howard,	Hezekiah B. Packer,	202	95
Logan,	John Zimmerman,	199	92
Milesburgh,	Joseph Green, Jun.	194	87
Milheim,	Daniel Keen,	193	86
Mill Hall,	Nathan Harvey,	215	108
Nittany,	H. F. W. Schultze,	208	101
Old Fort,	George Youngman,	182	75
Philipsburg,	John Plumb, Jun.	186	114
Pine Grove Mills,	Daniel O. Bryan,	177	88
Potter's Mills,	James Potter,	178	71
Quigle's Mills,	Michael Quigle,	207	100
Rebersburgh,	Philip Reitzell,	201	93
Spring Mills,	David Duncan,	187	80
Sugar Valley,	Anthony Kleckner,	210	102
Walker,	James Hutchison,	200	93

CHESTER COUNTY.

Offices.	Post Masters.	Ms. from W.	Ms. from H.
Avon Dale,	John Malin,	99	70
Blackhorse,	Samuel Jackson,	129	55
Brandywine Manor,	Joseph F. Grier,	129	63
Chatham,	Joseph Wood,	100	66
Chester Springs,	Henry Olwine,	127	69
Clingans,	William Baker,	105	62
Coatesville,	Benjamin J. Miller,	114	60
Cochronsville,	Stephen H. Cochran,	102	59
Dilworthtown,	William Speakman,	118	79
Doe Run,	Hayes Clark,	107	64
Downingtown,	Isaac Downing,	122	68
East Nantmeal,	Samuel R. Kirk,	140	65
Embreeville,	William Embree,	106	73
Fountain Inn,	Nathan Frame,		
Frazer,	Henry Souders,	128	74
Goshenville,	A. L. Williamson,	119	79
Guthriesville,	James B. Guthrie,	126	66
Hamarton,	Abraham Hamor,	107	75
Honey Brook,	John Lewis,	131	56
Hopewell Cotton W's.	Samuel J. Dickey,	94	68
Humphreysville,	John Tilson,	108	65
Israel's Mills,	Isaac G. Israel,		
Jennersville,	L. D. Ankrim,	96	65
Kennett's Square,	Caleb Heald,	103	71
Kimberton,	Samuel Shearer,	130	76
Kimblesville,	George Kimble,	97	72
Lionville,	Mordecai Lee,	126	72
Loag,	S. E. Williamson,	136	63
London Grove,	David Walton,	97	68
Marsh,	Water Dewees,	136	61
Marshallton,	George Andress,	117	74
McWilliamstown,	J. P. McWilliams,	112	63
Mount Vernon,	Samuel Ross,	104	64
New Garden,	Jacob Taylor,	99	73
N. London Cross Rds.	S. A. Cunningham,	93	68
Oxford,	Timothy Kirk,	92	66
Paoli,	S. Davis,	133	79
Parkersville,	John Parker, Jun.	109	81
Phenixville,	Joseph C. King,	132	77
Pughtown,	Garrett Hooper,	137	70
Russellville,	Charles Wallace,	99	62
Sadsburyville,	John Kendig,	131	57
Saint Marys,	Abraham Dehaven,	139	64
Schuylkill,	Abel Fitzwater,	134	80
Setzler's Store,	Frederick Setzler,	138	72
Strickersville,	Evan Garrett,	99	74
Thornbury,	Thomas W. Stevens,	119	79
Unionville,	Charles Buffington,	107	70
Uwchland,	Isaac Evans,	128	70
Valley Forge,	John Rogers,	142	84
Valley Hill,	Samuel Guss,		

CHESTER COUNTY, (Continued.)

Offices.	Post Masters.	Ms. from W.	Ms. from H.
Vincent,	William Rogers,	142	75
Wagontown,	Joseph Hughes,	130	70
Warren Tavern,	Charles Fahnestock,	131	77
West Chester,	John Newlin,	115	75
West Grove,	James Kelton,	96	71
West Nantmeal,	James Bones,	132	66
West Whiteland,	Levi Evans,	127	73

CLEARFIELD COUNTY.

Offices.	Post Masters.	Ms. from W.	Ms. from H.
Bennett's Branch,	Erasmus Morey,	236	136
Brockville,	Isaac Webb,	222	149
Clearfield,	Thomas Hemphill,	201	129
Clearfield Ridge,	Benjamin Spackman,	197	125
Curwinsville,	William Irwin,	198	132
Fox,	Vine S. Brockway,	227	144
Fruit Hill,	Thomas McNeil,	188	130
Hellen,	Philetus Clark,	221	149
Karthaus,	Ferdinand Hurnthal,	219	112
Kerseys,	James Green,	236	154
Kylersville,	John Kyler,	194	122
Luthersburg,	George Hoover,	212	146
Pine Street,	William M. Mason,	202	162
Second Fork,	William Shepard,	254	154
Smith's Mills,	Amasa Smith,	178	120

COLUMBIA COUNTY.

Offices.	Post Masters.	Ms. from W.	Ms. from H.
Berwick,	Robert McCurdy,	196	86
Bloomsburgh,	John Barton,	185	75
Buckhorn,	Hugh Allen,	189	79
Catawissa,	Michael Fornwald,	182	72
Danville,	James Loughead,	175	65
Derry,	John Heslet,	187	77
Espy,	Samuel Worman,	188	78
Fishing Creek,	John M. Buckalew,	199	89
Greenwood,	Joseph Heacock,	205	96
Jerseytown,	James Barrett,	198	89
McDowell's Mills,	Mathew McDowell,	188	78
Mifflinville,	Benjamin Seidle,	190	80
Millville,	David Eves,	202	93
Mooresburg,	Hugh McElrath,	181	71
Orangeville,	Jacob Bittenbender,	191	81
Roaring Creek,	Azima Vallerchamp,	187	77
Rohrsburg,	Elijah G. Ricketts,		
Sugar Loaf,	Joseph Jackson,	201	91
Washingtonville,	George Smith,	182	72
Whitehall,	Isaac Hendershot,	201	91

CRAWFORD COUNTY.

Offices.	Post Masters.	Ms. from W.	Ms. from H.
Bloomfield,	Stephen Bloomfield,	313	246
Centreville,	David Winton,	307	240
Conneautville,	William Power,	313	252
East Bloomfield,	George White,	323	262
Evansburgh,	Robert Stewart,	305	244
Guy's Mills,	Samuel Harroun,	307	246
Harmonsburgh,	William Alderman,	305	244
Hart's Cross Roads,	Joseph Linn,	305	250
Kingsley's,	Ransom Kingsley,	313	247
Line Mills,	Amos Line,	311	250
Meadville,	Daniel Andrews,	297	236
Oil Creek,	Joseph L. Chase,	297	230
Penn Line,	Jabez Holcomb,	318	257
Randolph,	John Brown,	309	248
Rockdale,	Joseph Gray,	305	244
Sugar Creek,	John Greer, Jun.	291	224
Sugar Lake,	Archibald Stewart,	307	240
Taylor's Stand,	Silas Taylor,	316	257
Woodcock,	Peter Faulkner,	305	244

CUMBERLAND COUNTY.

Offices.	Post Masters.	Ms. from W.	Ms. from H.
Allen,	Samuel Hyor,	107	16
Carlisle,	Robert Lamberton,	104	18
Dickinson,	William Gillelan,	108	36
Hogestown,	Jacob Hoyer,	113	9
Lisburn,	William Lloyd,	110	13
Mechanicsburg,	John Mason,	105	11
Newburgh,	Joseph Barr,	109	37
New Cumberland,	Asa White,	113	3
Newville,	William Barr,	115	29

CUMBERLAND COUNTY, (Continued.)

Offices.	Post Masters.	Ms. from W.	Ms. from H.
Papertown,	W. Barbour, Jun.		
Sheperdstown,	David Sheffer,	102	8
Shippensburgh,	David McClure,	100	38
Shiremantown,	Jacob Rupp,	106	4
Sterrett's Gap,	George Bower,	111	25
Stoughstown,	John Stough,	107	31

DAUPHIN COUNTY.

Offices.	Post Masters.	Ms. from W.	Ms. from H.
Dauphin,	Peter Miller,	119	9
Gratz,	Peter Orndoff,	151	38
Halifax,	Henry Sheaffer,	131	17
Harrisburg,	James Peacock,	110	
High Spire,	Jeremiah Kirk,	105	6
Hummelstown,	George Fox,	119	9
Linglestown,	David Umberger,	118	8
Middletown,	William Lauman,	102	9
Millersburgh,	Isaac Gerhart,	137	23
Peter's Mountain	Cornelius Baskins,	125	15
West Hanover,	Simon Lingle,	126	16

DELAWARE COUNTY.

Offices.	Post Masters.	Ms. from W.	Ms. from H.
Buck Tavern,	Jonathan Miller,	143	88
Chester,	M. Deshong,	121	95
Cheyney's Shops,	William Cheyney,	121	81
Concord M. House,	Samuel Hewes,	122	83
Darby,	George Serrill,	129	103
Edgemont,	William Sell,	123	83
Gibbon's Tavern,	Joseph Gibbons,	126	94
Hamor's Store,	Caleb D. West,	129	93
Haverford,	Lewis Bennett,	135	98
Ivy Mills,	Garrett Lewis,	122	83
Leiperville,	Jonathan Roberts,	123	97
Marcus Hook,	John Marshall,	116	95
Nether Providence,	John Wells,	124	92
Newtown Square,	Davis Beaumont,	131	94
Painter's Cross roads,	William Painter,	116	84
Pleasant Hill,	William Smith,	125	86
Spread Eagle,	Edward Siter,	136	83
Thornton,	John King,	119	80
Village Green,	Samuel F. Hewes,	126	87

ERIE COUNTY.

Offices.	Post Masters.	Ms. from W.	Ms. from H.
Beaver Dam,	Samuel Smith,	325	258
Elk Creek,	Joseph Wells,	336	275
Erie,	James Hughs,	333	272
Fairview,	Walter W. Warner,	340	279
Gray's Settlement,	Amos Graves, Jun.	327	266
Greenfield,	Elijah J. Woodruff,	348	287
Harbor Creek,	Daniel Goodwin,	339	278
Lexington,	David Sawdy,	326	265
Northeast,	James Smedly,	348	287
Northville,	Orrin Wyllys,	352	291
Phillipsville,	James Phillips,	345	284
Springfield Cross Rds.	R. P. Woodworth,	330	269
Union Mills,	William Miles,	319	252
Waterford,	Joseph Derickson,	319	258
Wattsburgh,	Levi Wilcox,	329	268
Wesleyville,	Almond Fuller,	367	248

FAYETTE COUNTY.

Offices.	Post Masters.	Ms. from W.	Ms. from H.
Belvernon,	Solomon Speers,	217	194
Brownsville,	Martin Tierman, Jun.	205	198
Bryants,	Henry Van Pelt,	179	178
Connellsville,	Joseph Herbert,	196	173
Cookstown,	George M. Kendall,	214	191
East Liberty,	John W. Burney,	201	178
Masontown,	Elisha Longhead,	222	204
McClellandtown,	Frederick Struble,	209	200
Merritstown,	Josephus Lindsley,	209	194
New Geneva,	James W. Nicholson,	217	199
New Salem,	C. Balsinger,	207	179
Perryopolis,	William Symmes,	209	186
Searight,	Thomas Grier,	199	190
Smithfield,	Samuel Sackett, Jun.	171	170
Spring Hill,	Absalom Morris,	221	203
Uniontown,	John Campbell,	193	184
Upper Middletown,	John Morrison,	206	183

FRANKLIN COUNTY.

Offices.	Post Masters.	Ms. from W.	Ms. from H.
Amberson's Valley,	David Kilgore,	116	61
Chambersburg,	John Findlay, Sen.	90	48
Concord,	James Wilson,	120	54
Dry Run,	William Campbell,	113	63
Fannetsburgh,	Chambers Anderson,	105	55
Fayetteville,	Frederick Ashbaugh,	94	52
Green Castle,	John Watson,	77	59
Green Village,	James McNulty,	95	43
Jackson Hall,	Frederick Roemer,	90	54
London,	Benjamin Stinger,	102	63
Mercersburgh,	Elliot T. Lane,	83	71
Quincy,	Jacob Byer,	83	58
Roxbury,	Thomas Pumroy,	103	43
Saint Thomas,	James Edwards,	97	57
State Line,	D. Brumbaugh, Jun.	73	64
Upper Strasburg,	Wm. McClellan,	99	47
Waynesboro',	Joseph Deardoff,	79	56
Welsh Run,	John Eldon,	82	64

GREENE COUNTY.

Offices.	Post Masters.	Ms. from W.	Ms. from H.
Carmichaels,	Myers Seaton,	221	210
Clarksville,	Goodwin B. Goodrich	217	210
Greensboro',	Charles A. Black,	217	199
Harvey's,	William S. Harvey,	241	234
Jefferson,	Thomas Fletcher,	215	214
Mount Morris,	Boas Boydston,	225	239
Newtown,	James Stevens,	233	231
Ryerson's Station,	Samuel Vanata,	249	242
Waynesburg,	Andrew Buchanan,	229	222
Whiteley,	Jonathan Morris,	225	207

HUNTINGDON COUNTY.

Offices.	Post Masters.	Ms. from W.	Ms. from H.
Alexandria,	John Porter,	155	97
Antestown,	John Bell,	177	119
Birmingham,	James Clarke,	163	105
Blairs Gap,	John Walker,	158	120
Canoe Creek,	Henry Leamer,	168	110
Coffee Run,	Evan Davis,	141	89
Colerain Forge,	Joseph Barnett,	163	102
Collinsville,	Robert McNamara,	184	126
Ennisville,	Jeremiah C. Betts,	170	93
Frankstown,	Thomas Johnston,	172	114
Graysville,	David Campfield,	169	96
Hollidaysburgh,	Peter Hewit,	174	116
Huntingdon,	Isaac Dorland,	148	90
Jacks,	Alexander Rogers,	137	79
Manor Hill,	John Love,	163	105
Newry,	Robert McNamara,	156	122
Shade Gap,	Brice Blair,	117	67
Shaver's Creek,	Valentine Wingert,	152	88
Shirleysburgh,	John Long,	128	78
Sinking Valley Mills,	David Beyer,	170	112
Springfield Furnace,	Samuel Royer,	150	107
Three Springs,	George Hudson,	125	73
Trough Creek,	Robert Speer,	133	81
Union Furnace,	Michael Wallace,	160	102
Warrior's Mark,	S. W. Stonebraker,	168	110
Water Street,	Lewis Mytinger,	157	99
Williamsburgh,	Adolphus Patterson,	155	102
Woodcock Valley,	Andrew Freaker,		
Yellow Springs,	Maxwell Kinkaid,	163	105

INDIANA COUNTY.

Offices.	Post Masters.	Ms. from W.	Ms. from H.
Armagh,	Thomas Stewart,	175	141
Blacklegs,	John H. Morrison,	202	170
Blairsville,	George Mulhollan, Jr.	189	161
Great Saltworks,	William L. Lafferty,	207	175
Indiana,	Jonathan Ayers, Jun.	189	157
Mahoning,	John Ewing,	206	174
Saltsburgh,	Philip Meckling,	206	175
Sharp's Mills,	Jonathan Peacock,	197	165
Schmicksburgh,	John Kerr,	212	181

JEFFERSON COUNTY.

Offices.	Post Masters.	Ms. from W.	Ms. from H.
Brockwayville,	Alonzo Brockway,	226	154
Brookville,	Jared B. Evans,	238	165
Montmorency,	James L. Gillis,	242	171
Punxatawney,	John W. Jenks,	216	160
Ridgeway,	Reuben A. Aylworth,	236	165

LANCASTER COUNTY.

Offices.	Post Masters.	Ms. from W.	Ms. from H.
Adamstown,	Henry Flickinger,	133	46
Arbela,	Christian Sherts, Jr.	120	46
Bainbridge,	George Blattenberger,	103	18
Bart,	James M. Quigg,	110	54
Brickersville,	Samuel S. Rex,	122	45
Buck,	John Dance,	92	54
Cains,	John Cain,	128	64
Chestnut Level,	Philip Housekeeper,	89	51
Churchtown,	Edward Davis,	129	54
Colerain,	Hugh Andrews,	104	61
Columbia,	William P. Beatty,	99	28
Conestoga,	Enoch Megrady,	107	43
Earl,	Amos S. Kinzer,	123	49
East Hempfield,	Jacob Myers,	115	33
Elizabethtown,	John Maglauchlin,	110	17
Ephrata,	John Gross,	125	38
Fairmont,	Samuel Kinzer,	117	43
Falmouth,	John C. Klein,	98	15
Gap,	James G. Henderson,	125	51
(The) Hat,	William Lightner,	122	48
Hinkleton,	Isaac Winters,	128	43
Intercourse,	Benjamin Fraim,	120	46
Kirk's Mills,	Jacob Kirk,	85	63
Lampeter,	Henry Miller, Jun.	114	40
Lancaster,	M. Dickson,	109	35
Leacock,	John Gillgore,	116	42
Leesburgh,	James K. Menough,	118	44
Litiz,	Frederick A. Zitsman	117	43
Little Britain,	Isaac J. Hutton,	81	58
Manheim,	John Bartruff,	119	39
Manor,	George G. Brush,	102	31
Marietta,	James A. Sterrit,	102	25
Martickville,	Jacob Holl,	100	46
Maytown,	James B. Ferree,	104	23
Millersville,	John Evans,	109	38
Mount Joy,	Okey Hendrickson,	117	24
Mount Hope,	Edward B. Grubb,	124	34
Mountville,	Ira Woodworth,	103	32
Neffsville,	William Farney,	113	39
New Holland,	Henry Roland,	121	47
New Providence,	Benjn. B. Eshleman,	129	63
Paradise,	David Witner, Jun.	118	44
Piquea,	Adam Barr,	126	62
Rawlinsville,	Morgan Rawlins,	95	51
Reamstown,	Frederick Ziegler,	129	42
Salisbury,	Wm. D. Slaymaker,	123	49
Spring Grove,	John Ramsay,	99	56
Strasburg,	William Russel,	116	48
Swan,	James Dickinson,		
Webster's Store,	Jeremiah Brown, Jr.	86	54
Williamstown,	Christian Hess,	121	47

LEBANON COUNTY.

Offices.	Post Masters.	Ms. from W.	Ms. from H.
Annville,	John Killinger,	129	19
Campbelltown,	John Wolfersberger,	125	15
East Hanover,	John Harper, Jun.	131	21
Jonestown,	Martin Meily,	136	26
Lebanon,	Jacob Karch,	134	24
Meadowville,	Baltzer Orth,	131	21
Myerstown,	William Stoever,	141	31
Palmyra,	Adam Kittering,	124	14
Shaefferstown,	Frederick Oberli,	129	32
Stumptown,	Amos Shannon,	139	29

LEHIGH COUNTY.

Offices.	Post Masters.	Ms. from W.	Ms. from H.
Allentown,	Henry Weaver,	178	85
Emaus,	John J. Giering,	183	90
Fogelsville,	Solomon Fogel,	176	76
Fryburgh,	Daniel Cooper,	178	92
Jacksonville,	John Oswald,	183	75
Lowhill,	Jacob Zimmerman,	182	82
Lowhill Port,	John Shefferstine,	179	76
Lynnville,	Sohn Seiberling,	186	81
Macungy,	Charles Sarber,	185	87
New Tripoli,	Samuel Camp,	187	79
North Whitehall,	Benjamin S. Levan,	186	93
Rittersville,	Michael Ritter,	181	88
Saegersville,	Joseph Saeger,	185	85
South Whitehall,	John Billig,	179	85
Stahler's.	Henry Dillinger,	188	92

LEHIGH COUNTY, (Continued.)

Offices.	Post Masters.	Ms. from W.	Ms. from H.
Trexlertown,	David Schall,	170	75
Wisenburgh,	Michael Richert,	180	72

LUZERNE COUNTY.

Offices.	Post Masters.	Ms. from W.	Ms. from H.
Abington,	Andrew Bedford,	245	137
Beech Grove,	Nathan Beach,	203	95
Braintrem,	Daniel Sterling,	264	154
Carbondale,	James W. Goff,	247	139
Centre Moreland,	David Westover,	214	94
Columbus,	John Koons,	202	92
Conyngham,	William Drum,	206	96
Dallas,	James Mott,	214	104
Eaton,	Asa Lee,	251	143
Exeter,	Lewis Jones, Jun.	237	129
Factoryville,	John Wilson,	250	142
Falls,	Henry Roberts,	242	134
Greenville,	Charles Berry,	251	141
Harveyville,	Benjamin Harvey,	204	94
Huntsville,	Truman Atherton,	220	110
Kingston,	William C. Reynolds,	223	115
Nanticoke,	David Thomson,	215	107
Nescopeck,	George Penrose,	196	86
New Covington,	David Dale,	241	144
New Troy,	William Swetland,	228	120
Nicholson,	Nathan Bacon,	254	146
North Moreland,	Asa Keeler,	242	134
Pittston,	Thomas Smith,	232	124
Pittston Ferry,	John Allment,	231	123
Plainsville,	Samuel Saylor,	227	119
Plymouth,	John Turner,	219	109
Providence,	John Vaughn,	238	130
Scottsville,	John Fassett,	263	154
Shickshinny,	Steven Vaughn,	211	101
Skinner's Eddy,	John Sturdevant,	267	157
Stoddartsville,	Arnold Colt,	239	131
Trucksville,	Jacob Rice,	228	120
Tunkhannock,	Henry Stark,	250	142
Union,	Zerah Marvin,	208	88
Unison,	Conrad Kunkle,	218	98
Wallsville,	Ezra Wall,	248	140
Wilkesbarre,	Andrew Beaumont,	222	114

LYCOMING COUNTY.

Offices.	Post Masters.	Ms. from W.	Ms. from H.
Bald Eagle,	Alexander Mahen,	214	107
Brown,	Williams McMeen,		
Carpenter's Mills,	Samuel Stull,	204	95
Cherry,	Freeman Fairchild,	221	110
Dunnsburgh,	Jared P. Huling,	219	112
Eldridville,	Edward A. Eldred,	223	112
Emporium,	Philip Banks,		
Hill's Grove,	John C. Hill,	211	100
Hughesville,	Theodore Wells,	196	85
Jersey Shore,	Samuel Humes,	211	102
Lairdsville,	John Laird,	203	92
Lycoming Creek,	William McKinney,	201	92
Mount Lewis,	Charles Howlett,	212	101
Muncy,	William A. Petrikin,	190	80
Newbury,	Samuel Caldwell,	198	89
Nippenose,	Daniel Antes,	213	104
Ratling Gap,	William Clark,	218	109
Shinersville,	Henry W. Cooper,	225	114
Sinnamahoning,	Buckman Claflin,		
Slate Creek,	Jacob Tomb,		
Trout Run,	Samuel Hepburne,	210	101
White Deer,	Hugh Donley,	183	74
Williamsport,	Henry Hughes,	196	87
Youngwomanstown,	John Quigley,	245	138

McKEAN COUNTY.

Offices.	Post Masters.	Ms. from W.	Ms. from H.
Allegheny Bridge,	Nathaniel Dennis,	288	215
Cerestown,	Robert Clendenon,	307	198
Clermontville,	Samuel Gillis,	272	201
Keating,	Horace Coleman,	285	188
Norwich,	Jonathan Colegrove,	281	202
Shippen,	Elihu Chadwick,	293	186
Smithport,	Orlo J. Hamlin,	273	200

MERCER COUNTY.

Offices.	Post Masters.	Ms. from W.	Ms. from H.
Culbertson's,	Joseph Culbertson,	283	265
Harlensburgh,	John Boyd,	260	228

MERCER COUNTY, (Continued.)

Offices.	Post Masters.	Ms. from W.	Ms. from H.
Henderson,	Robert Henderson,	280	223
Hillville,	David Stevens,	279	247
Mercer,	Thomas Coffey,	267	235
New Bedford,	John McCready,	279	237
New Castle,	Joseph T. Boyd,	264	232
New Wilmington,	Joseph Cowden,	274	242
Sharon,	Thomas J. Porter,	281	249
West Greenville,	James R. Wick,	281	244

MIFFLIN COUNTY.

Offices.	Post Masters.	Ms. from W.	Ms. from H.
Allensville,	Christopher Horrel,	163	84
Belleville,	Francis McCoy,	169	77
Brown's Mills,	John Norris,	167	60
East Waterford,	Enoch L. Anderson,	131	62
Lewistown,	M. J. Walters,	162	55
McAllesterville,	Hugh Wilson,	158	51
McVeytown,	Richard Miles,	150	66
Mexico,	James Thompson,	147	40
Mifflintown,	David Crawford,	150	43
Newtown Hamilton,	Samuel Thompson,	148	41
Oakland Mills,	David McClure,		
Richfield,	John Wallis,	168	61
Thompsontown,	John McGary,	141	34
Tuscarora Valley,	James Milliken,	140	53
(The) Valley,	William Thompson,	171	64
Waterloo,	William H. Patterson,	123	70

MONTGOMERY COUNTY.

Offices.	Post Masters.	Ms. from W.	Ms. from H.
Barren Hill,	John Dager,	148	93
Centre Square,	James Bush,	153	106
Franconia,	Samuel Wambold,	171	76
Gulf Mills,	Joseph King,	146	90
Gwynned,	David Acuff,	157	96
Hatboro',	Joseph B. Yerkes,	152	114
Hillegass,	George Hillegass,	170	77
Horsham,	Charles Jarrett,	153	114
Jeffersonville,	Edward L. Bean,	145	87
Jenkinton,	Jacob L. Grant,	146	108
Kulpsville,	Charles C. Kulp,	162	91
Limerick,	Dieter Bucher,	150	75
Lower Merion,	John W. Dubbs,	150	93
Montgomery,	Henry Slight,	160	100
New Hanover,	Isaac Feather,	150	75
Norristown,	James Wells,	143	88
Perkiomen Bridge,	Edward Evans,	150	82
Pleasantville,	Frederick W. Hoover,	158	103
Pottstown,	Thomas Child,	143	68
Skippack,	Abraham Everhart,	160	99
Springhouse,	John W. Murray,	155	98
Sumneytown,	George Shaid,	166	83
Trapp,	John Todd,	152	80
Union Square,	Thomas J. White,	161	94
Upper Dublin,	Isaac Thomas,	153	107
Upper Hanover,	Tobias Sellers,	173	84
Upper Merion,	Charles Lyle,	139	87
White Marsh,	William Burk,	148	110
Willow Grove,	Isaac Morris,	150	112
Worcester,	Abraham Warner,	157	102

NORTHAMPTON COUNTY.

Offices.	Post Masters.	Ms. from W.	Ms. from H.
Bath,	B. D. Barnes,	200	107
Beaver Meadows,	William H. Wilson,	211	106
Bethlehem,	Owen Rice,	184	91
Butztown,	Andrew Oberly,	187	94
Cherryville,	Wm. S. Ammerman,	190	97
Craig's Meadow,	John Lander,	223	128
Dill's Ferry,	Jacob Utt,	210	123
Dutotsburgh,	Luke Broadhead,	215	128
Easton,	Abraham Horn,	190	101
East Penn,	John Lentz,	191	91
Experiment Mills,	John T. Bell,	216	128
Freemansburgh,	Levi D. Bodder,	187	97
Hecktown,	Jacob Schweitzer,	191	98
Hellertown,	Daniel C. Freytag,	183	93
Jacobsburgh,	David Gausler,	197	104
Kernesville,	Jonas Snyder,	195	102
Kreidersville,	George Weber,	194	101
Lausanne,	Samuel Wolf,	208	108
Lehighton,	John Davis,	192	85
Lehigh Gap.	Thomas Craig, Jun.	195	92

NORTHAMPTON COUNTY, (Contin'd.)

Offices.	Post Masters.	Ms. from W.	Ms. from H.
Lower Saucon,	Samuel Leidy,	187	97
Martin's Creek,	William McIlhaney,	198	111
Mauch Chunk,	Josiah White,	196	89
Mount Bethel,	Jacob Weiss,	208	121
Mount Pocono,	A. Levering, Jun.	221	122
Nazareth,	John Beitol,	194	101
Raubsville,	George Raub,	196	109
Richmond,	Charles Weaver,	203	116
Shafers,	Charles Broadhead,	210	111
Shaw's Meadows,	Simon Heller,	226	125
Snydersville,	Peter Snyder,	212	112
Stanhope,	Simon Gruber,	222	130
Stockertown,	Joseph Levers,	196	109
Stone Church,	Benjamin Depue,	205	118
Stouts,	Isaac Stout,	191	103
Stroudsburgh,	Michael H. Dreher,	219	118
Towamensing,	Peter Stem,	194	87
Wind Gap,	John Weaver,	202	109

NORTHUMBERLAND COUNTY.

Offices.	Post Masters.	Ms. from W.	Ms. from H.
Augusta,	Samuel Bloom, Jun.	163	57
Chilisquaque,	Christian Shroyer,	172	62
Dalmatia,	Martin A. Stock,	146	36
Liberty Pole,	Jacob Snyder,	172	62
Mahanoy,	Jonathan Reitzell,	155	45
McEwensville,	Alexander McEwen,	180	70
Milton,	William Jodan,	176	66
Northumberland,	John Cowden,	164	54
Pottsgrove,	James Reed,	175	67
Shamokin,	Abbe C. Barret,	174	64
Sunbury,	John G. Martin,	162	52
Turbotville,	Jacob Maurer,		
Watsontown,	David Watson,	180	71

PERRY COUNTY.

Offices.	Post Masters.	Ms. from W.	Ms. from H.
Andersonburgh,	James R. Morrison,	127	40
Beelan's Ferry,	Francis Beelan,	129	43
Clark's Ferry,	Eleazer Owen,	137	43
Douglass Mills,	Anthony Black,	129	42
Elliotsburgh,	Henry C. Hackett,	121	34
Ickesburgh,	William Roberts,	126	39
Juniata,	John W. Bosserman,	131	44
Juniata Falls,	Alexander Watson,	130	20
Junction,	John B. Klein,	127	17
Landisburgh,	Francis Kelly,	117	30
Liverpool,	James Jackman,	139	29
Millerstown,	Edward Purcell,	136	29
Montgomery's Ferry,	Wm. Montgomery,	136	26
New Bloomfield,	Joseph Duncan,	122	36
New Buffalo,	John Livingston,	130	20
New Germantown,	James Ewing,	128	46
New Port,	Ephraim Bosserman,	127	41
Oak Grove Furnace,	John Hays,	114	28

PHILADELPHIA COUNTY.

Offices.	Post Masters.	Ms. from W.	Ms. from H.
Bustleton,	Enoch C. Edwards,	148	110
Byberry,	Benjamin R. Banes,	153	115
Chesnut Hill,	Jacob Guyer,	146	107
Falls of Schuylkill,	John Wood,	141	101
Frankford,	Edmund McVaugh,	141	103
Germantown,	Geo. Hergesheimer,	142	104
Holmesburgh,	Jacob Waterman,	145	107
Kensington,	John Simon, Jun.	137	99
Kingsessing,	Isaac Leech,	132	102
Manayunk,	John Stott,	143	98
Milestown,	William T. Wilson,	142	104
Penn Township,	Jeremiah Hukill,	137	99
Philadelphia,	Thomas Sergeant,	136	98
Rising Sun,	Jacob Billger,	139	101
Roxboro',	Robert F. Levering,	144	97
Somerton,	Grover Roberts,	151	113
West Philadelphia,	Jacob Lentner, Jun.	134	100

PIKE COUNTY.

Offices.	Post Masters.	Ms. from W.	Ms. from H.
Bushkill,	Henry Peters,	232	137
Darlingsville,	Samuel Darling,	261	169
Delaware,	William Brodhead,	239	144
Dingman's Ferry,	Levi Vanelten,	244	149
Hornbeck's,	Jacob Hornbeck,	242	147

PIKE COUNTY, (Continued.)

Offices.	Post Masters.	Ms. from W.	Ms. from H.
Milford,	Benjamin A. Bidlack,	249	157
Tafton,	Royal Taft,	271	173
Tobyhanna,	George L. Nagle,	230	138

POTTER COUNTY.

Offices.	Post Masters.	Ms. from W.	Ms. from H.
Cowdersport,	Timothy Ives,	283	174
Dolbee's,	Benjamin D. Dolbee,	299	190
Harrison Valley,	Ansel Purple,	294	188
Rose's,	James Rose,	298	192
Roulette,	Samuel Streeter,	292	183
Sweeden,	Samuel Taggart,	290	180

SCHUYLKILL COUNTY.

Offices.	Post Masters.	Ms. from W.	Ms. from H.
Broad Mountain,	Charles Isard,	179	71
Freedensburgh,	Jacob Mennig,	161	51
McKeansburgh,	John Yost,	167	
Middleport,	Jacob Huntzinger,	182	74
Minersville,	James Macpherson,	179	71
Orwigsburgh,	Henry Raush,	167	59
Pine Grove,	John Barr,	151	41
Port Carbon,	Elisha S. Warne,	177	69
Port Clinton,	Moncure Robinson,	160	60
Pottsville,	Enos Chichester,	175	67
Schuylkill Haven,	Isaac Dengler,	171	55
Tamaqua,	Abraham Rex,	191	83
Tuscarora,	Joseph A. Davidson,	183	78
West Penn,	Gideon Oswald,	179	76
West Tamaqua,	H. Brown Ward,	186	81

SOMERSET COUNTY.

Offices.	Post Masters.	Ms. from W.	Ms. from H.
Berlin,	John Fletcher,	157	135
Elk Lick,	Peter Shirer,		
Gebhart's,	John Webster,	154	132
Laurel Hill,	Elijah Denison,	162	140
Meyer's Mills,	Peter Meyer,		
Shade,	William H. Gahagen,		
Somerfield,	William Frey,	195	173
Somerset,	John Webster,	165	143
Southampton,	Peter Boyer,		
Stoyestown,	Jonathan Statler,	155	133
Turkey Foot,	David King,	185	163
White Horse,	Orson Case,	149	127

SUSQUEHANNAH COUNTY.

Offices.	Post Masters.	Ms. from W.	Ms. from H.
Birchardsville,	Jabez A. Birchard,	280	172
Brooklyn,	Thomas Garland,	267	159
Choconut,	Lewis Chamberlin,	285	177
Dimocksville,	Orry Burns,	274	175
Dundaff,	Horace G. Phelps,	256	148
Ellerslie,	S. Milligan,	287	179
Fairdale,	Asa Olmstead,	273	162
Friendsville,	Thomas Christian,	283	175
Gibson,	George Stiles,	263	184
Great Bend,	Jason Wilson,	285	177
Harewood,	Joseph Macomber,	282	174
Harford,	Saxa Seymour,	264	156
Jackson,	Jonas Blanding,	282	185
Lanesboro',	Charles Hatch,	295	187
Lawsville,	Allen Upson,	279	171
Lawsville Centre,	Reuben Ives,		
Lenox,	Oakley Reynerson,	258	150
Montrose,	William L. Post,	271	163
New Milford,	John Badger,	290	183
Rushville,	Daniel Ross,	265	154
Silver Lake,	Robert H. Rose,	280	172
Springville,	Spencer Hickcox,	261	153
Springville 4 Corners,	Perrin Ross,	265	157

TIOGA COUNTY.

Offices.	Post Masters.	Ms. from W.	Ms. from H.
Blossburgh,	John H. Knapp,	235	126
Brookfield,	Isaac H. Metcalf,	291	185
Covington,	Ephraim B. Gerrauld,	241	135
Crooked Creek,	Thomas Keeney,	262	156
Daggett's Mills,	Seth Daggett,	277	159
Dartmouth,	Justus Dartt,	254	148
Elk Land,	Joel Parkhurst,	273	167
Ingham,	Ezra Wood,	269	156
Knoxville,	Cotton Knox,	282	176
Lawrenceville,	Hiram Beebe,	261	155

TIOGA COUNTY, (Continued.)

Offices.	Post Masters.	Ms. from W.	Ms. from H.
Liberty,	Jacob Lovegood,	225	116
Mainsburgh,	John Main,	250	144
Mansfield,	Asa Mann,	246	140
Nelson,	Samuel Snow,	268	162
Pine Creek,	Daniel Fuller,	265	159
Rutland,	Bethuel Bentley,	254	148
Sullivan,	Henry Rew,	248	142
Tioga,	James Goodrich,	254	148
Wellsboro',	William Bache,	253	147
Westfield,	H. B. Trowbridge,	286	180

UNION COUNTY.

Offices.	Post Masters.	Ms. from W.	Ms. from H.
Beavertown,	Daniel Beckley,	169	59
Freeburgh,	John Hilbish,	157	47
Hartleton,	John F. Wilson,	179	71
Lewisburgh,	Alexander Graham,	172	63
McKee's Half Falls,	B. L. McCarty,	148	38
Middleburgh,	Frederick Stees, Jun.	162	52
Mifflinburgh,	Jacob Maize,	173	65
Mount Pleasant Mills,	Philip Schnee,	152	42
New Berlin,	Charles Baum,	168	60
New Columbia,	Henry R. Waggoner,	177	68
Selin's Grove,	P. Frederick Dering,	159	50

VENANGO COUNTY.

Offices.	Post Masters.	Ms. from W.	Ms. from H.
Agnew's Mills,	John Agnew,	248	203
Cherry Tree,	Samuel Irwin,	293	226
Cooperstown,	Salmon S. Bates,	287	220
Foxburgh,	Samuel Marshall,	243	203
Franklin,	John Evans,	279	212
Holland,	Austin Merrick,	302	235
Myers,	Henry Myers, Jun.	256	197
Perry,	William Neill,	301	234
Rynds,	Ambrose Rynd,	288	221
Sandy Furnace,	Samuel F. Plumer,	283	216
Shippensville,	Richard Shippen,	256	189
Tionesta,	James L. Chase,		
Venango Furnace,	John Anderson,	275	225

WARREN COUNTY.

Offices.	Post Masters.	Ms. from W.	Ms. from H.
Coffee Creek,	David Curtis,	336	266
Conewango,	Nathaniel A. Lowry,	320	247
Deerfield,	Samuel Parshall,	309	242
Green Valley,	Harry Abbott,	331	258
Irvine,	William A. Irvine,	322	247
Kinzua,	Andrew Marsh,	327	230
Lottsville,	Hewlet Lott,	332	259
Spring Creek,	George Yager,	335	271
Sugar Grove,	Andalotia Pier,	327	254
Warren,	Josiah Hall,	313	240
Youngsville,	Alfred Vanarnam,	330	257

WASHINGTON COUNTY.

Offices.	Post Masters.	Ms. from W.	Ms. from H.
Amity,	Zachariah Sharp,	241	228
Beallsville,	Joseph Buffington,	218	206
Bentleyville,	George Passmore,	222	202
Briceland's Cross Rds.	A. W. Semple,	248	228
Buffalo,	Abraham Wotring,	244	225
Burgettstown,	Stephen Smith,	246	223
Cannonsburgh,	Andrew Munroe,	236	219
Claysville,	Green Vansickle,	239	222
Cross Creek Village,	Joseph Cook,	245	227
East Bethlehem,	John Rogers,	210	203
Eldersville,	George Elliott,	250	227
Finleyville,	Robert Finley,	220	199
Fredericktown,	Israel Dalbey,	213	206
Hickory,	William Walker,	239	222
Hillsboro',	Samuel Standley,	217	210
Independence,	Richard Carter,	248	231
Millsboro',	George Cromlow,	214	207
Paris,	Richard Ward,	253	233
Parkinson's Ferry,	Jesse Martin,	214	192
Patterson's Mills,	James Patterson,	249	231

WASHINGTON COUNTY, (Continued.)

Offices.	Post Masters.	Ms. from W.	Ms. from H.
Rackoon,	Joseph Crafford,	241	219
Sparta,	John Lindley,	239	222
Washington,	Thomas Morgan,	229	212
West Alexandria,	James Stephenson,	245	228
West Buckingham,	John Buckingham,		
West Middletown,	David Craig,	243	225
West Finley,	William Burns,	249	242

WAYNE COUNTY.

Offices.	Post Masters.	Ms. from W.	Ms. from H.
Bethany,	Ephraim H. Hamlin,	265	162
Cherry Ridge,	Thomas Lindsey,	264	165
Clarkstown,	Thomas Clark,	257	158
Coolbaughs,	Moses W. Coolbaugh,	228	133
Damascus,	Walter S. Vail,	290	191
Hamlinton,	Oliver Hamlin,	241	150
Honesdale,	Charles Forbes,	268	165
Mount Republic,	Alva W. Norton,	263	164
Pleasant Mount,	Henry W. Stone,	269	170
Scott,	Gershom Williams,	283	184
South Canaan,	John H. Bulen,	248	157
Starucca,	David Spoor,	284	186
Sterling,	William T. Noble,	237	146
Stockport,	Samuel Preston,	291	188
Tallmansville,	Elihu Tallman,	278	179

WESTMORELAND COUNTY.

Offices.	Post Masters.	Ms. from W.	Ms. from H.
Adamsburgh,	William Black,	198	176
Bolivar,	James Dicky,	189	166
Donegal,	Christian Fetter,	183	161
Greensburgh,	Simon Drum, Jun.	192	170
Laughlintown,	George Lehmer,	170	148
Ligonier,	Noah Mendell,	174	151
Livermore,	Charles McLaughlin,	196	168
Madison,	Henry G. Spayth,	200	178
McKean's Old Stand,	Henry Null,	199	177
Mount Pleasant,	John Smith,	194	172
Murraysville,	James Murray,	214	186
New Alexandria,	Samuel Galbreth,	199	171
New Derry,	John Rhey,	188	166
North Washington,	Daniel F. Carpenter,	215	193
Pleasant Unity,	Henry Graff,	189	167
Robbstown,	William Brookens,	206	184
Rosstraver,	David Rankin,	212	190
Salem Cross Roads,	Adam Sylvis,	200	178
Stewartsville,	Samuel H. Daily,	204	181
West Fairfield,	Irwin Elliott,	184	161
Youngstown,	Judah Case,	182	160

YORK COUNTY.

Offices.	Post Masters.	Ms. from W.	Ms. from H.
Bermudian,	Gideon Griest,	96	18
Chanceford,	James S. Clarkson,	94	40
Codorus,	Martin Shearer,	89	38
Dillsburgh,	G. L. Shearer,	98	12
Dover,	Englebart Melchinger	94	23
Fawn Grove,	John F. McJilton,	81	52
Franklintown,	Martin Carl,	100	14
Guilford,	Anthony Stewart,	78	44
Hanover,	Peter Muller,	80	27
Hetricks,	John Hershner,	83	44
Lewisberry,	Hiram Starr,	107	10
Loganville,	Robert Wilson,	79	31
Lower Chanceford,	Robert Cowen,	90	49
Manchester,	John T. Ubil,	93	18
Margaretta Furnace,	Henry Y. Slaymaker,	97	35
Newberrytown,	T. Wickersham,	102	14
Peachbottom,	James McConkey,	80	60
Pigeon Hill,	Peter Klinefelter,	90	32
Rossville,	Michael Wallet,	100	17
Shrewsbury,	Philip Folckemmer,	72	38
Sidonsburgh,	Peter Sidle,		
Windsor,	Francis Grove,	98	36
Wrightsville,	James Kerr,	99	29
York,	Daniel Small,	87	24
York Haven,	Charles M. Poor,	97	14

www.ingramcontent.com/pod-product-compliance
Lightning Source LLC
Chambersburg PA
CBHW070619270326
41926CB00011B/1743

* 9 7 8 0 7 8 8 4 2 8 8 8 3 *